1 2 e

Managerial Economics

Mark Hirschey

University of Kansas

SOUTH-WESTERN
CENGAGE Learning

Australia • Brazil • Japan • Korea • Mexico • Singapore • Spain • United Kingdom • United States

SOUTH-WESTERN
CENGAGE Learning

Managerial Economics, 12th Edition

Mark Hirschey

VP/Editorial Director: Jack W. Calhoun

Acquisitions Editor: Mike Roche

Developmental Editor: Amy Ray

Editorial Assistant: Laura Cothran

Marketing Manager: Brian Joyner

Content Project Manager: Lysa Oeters

Sr. Manufacturing Coordinator: Sandee Milewski

Production Service: Integra

Sr. Art Director: Michelle Kunkler

Cover and Internal Designer: Diane Gliebe/Design Matters

Cover Image: © iStockphoto.com

For product information and technology assistance, contact us at **Cengage Learning Academic Resource Center, 1-800-423-0563**

For permission to use material from this text or product, submit all requests online at **www.cengage.com/permissions** Further permissions questions can be emailed to **permissionrequest@cengage.com**

Library of Congress Control Number: 2007941977

Student Edition
ISBN 13: 978-0-324-58886-6
ISBN 10: 0-324-58886-0

Student Edition with PAC
ISBN 13: 978-0-324-58484-4
ISBN 10: 0-324-58484-9

South-Western Cengage Learning
5191 Natorp Boulevard
Mason, OH 45040
USA

Cengage Learning products are represented in Canada by Nelson Education, Ltd.

For your course and learning solutions, visit **academic.cengage.com**
Purchase any of our products at your local college store or at our preferred online store **www.ichapters.com**

Printed in the United States of America
1 2 3 4 5 6 7 12 11 10 09 08

Dedication

For Christine—I still do.

About the Author

Mark Hirschey, Ph.D. (University of Wisconsin-Madison), is the Anderson W. Chandler Professor of Business at the University of Kansas, where he teaches undergraduate and graduate courses in managerial economics and finance. Professor Hirschey is president of the Association of Financial Economists and member of several professional organizations. He has published articles in the *American Economic Review, Review of Economics and Statistics, Journal of Business, Journal of Business and Economic Statistics, Journal of Finance, Journal of Financial Economics, Journal of Industrial Economics,* and other leading academic journals. He is editor of *Advances in Financial Economics,* and past editor of *Managerial and Decision Economics.* Professor Hirschey is also author of *Fundamentals of Managerial Economics* and *Investments: Analysis & Behavior.*

Brief Contents

Contents

Part 2: Demand Analysis and Estimation **111**

Part 3: Production and Competitive Markets   243

Part 4: Imperfect Competition   455

Part 5: Long-Term Investment Decisions   629

Preface

Billy Beane, general manager of Major League Baseball's Oakland A's had a problem: How can a small-market club with a tight budget consistently win in the Major Leagues? He decided on a simple, but uncommon approach. Beane focused on signing the most effective baseball players based on their proven ability to help teams win, not on basis of their unrealized potential. In baseball, conventional wisdom says to sign big, strong, and fast hitters; and pitchers able to throw the baseball 95 mph. Beane defied tradition by fielding a team comprised of hitters with high on-base percentage, and pitchers who throw strikes and get lots of ground outs. Read Michael Lewis's *Moneyball* to get the blow-by-blow account on how Beane built winning teams of young affordable players and inexpensive castoff veterans.

You might wonder why Warren Buffett and Charlie Munger, chairman and vice-chairman Berkshire Hathaway, Inc., enthusiastically recommend *Moneyball* to their friends and stockholders. Why would two of the most successful business managers and investors of all time actively promote a book about baseball? The answer is simple: Beane's management of the Oakland A's shows how successful one can become simply by being rational and focusing on the most useful data available. That's just common sense, but in baseball common sense is rarely employed. Common sense is sometimes uncommon in business too.

Economic concepts show how to apply common sense to understand business and solve managerial problems. Economic intuition is really useful. It helps managers decide on which products to produce, costs to consider, and prices to charge. It also helps them decide on the best hiring policy and the most effective style of organization. Students and future managers need to learn these things. The topics covered in managerial economics are powerful tools that can be used to make them more effective and their careers more satisfying. By studying managerial economics, those seeking to further their business careers learn how to more effectively collect, organize and analyze information.

A key feature of this book is its depiction of the firm as a cohesive organization. Effective management involves an integration of the accounting, finance, marketing, personnel, and production functions. This integrative approach demonstrates that important managerial decisions are *interdisciplinary* in the truest sense of the word. Over the years, I have come to appreciate that students find understanding of the business firm as a unified whole, rather than a series of unrelated parts, as one of the most valuable lessons of managerial economics.

Although both microeconomic and macroeconomic relations have implications for managerial decision making, this book concentrates on microeconomic topics. Following development of the economic model of the firm, the vital role of profits is examined. Because economic decision making often requires an elementary understanding of optimization techniques and statistical relations, those basic concepts are described early in the text. Because demand for a firm's products plays a crucial role in determining its profitability and ongoing success, demand analysis and estimation is an essential area of study. An important part of this study is an investigation of the basic forces of demand and supply. This naturally leads to discussion of economic forecasting and methods for assessing forecast reliability. Production theory and cost analysis are then explored as means for understanding the economics of resource allocation and employment.

Once the internal workings of a successful firm are understood, attention can turn toward consideration of the firm's external economic environment. Market structure analysis provides the foundation for studying the external economic environment and for defining an effective competitive strategy. The role of government in the market economy, including the constraints it imposes on business, requires a careful examination of regulation and antitrust law. Risk analysis and capital budgeting are also shown as methods for introducing marginal analysis into the long-range strategic planning and control process. Finally, given government's increasing role in managing demand and supply for basic services, such as education and health care, the use of economic principles to understand and improve public management is also considered.

Managerial Economics, 12th Edition, takes a practical problem-solving approach. The focus is on the economics—not the mathematics—of the managerial decision process. Quantitative tools are sometimes employed, but the emphasis is on economic intuition.

CHANGES IN THE 12TH EDITION

Managerial Economics and *Fundamentals of Managerial Economics* defined the field, and continue to play an important role in shaping the teaching of managerial economics. Both are published to help students use basic economic concepts to understand and improve the managerial decision-making process. Despite sharing a common objective, *Managerial Economics* and *Fundamentals of Managerial Economics* use slightly different methods. *Managerial Economics* features an intuitive *calculus-based* treatment of economic theory and analysis; *Fundamental of Managerial Economics* uses an intuitive *noncalculus-based* approach.

Students and instructors will find that *Managerial Economics*, 12th Edition provides an efficient calculus-based introduction and guide to the optimization process. Chapter 2, *Economic Optimization,* illustrates how the concept of a derivative can be used as a practical tool to understand and apply marginal analysis. *Multivariate Optimization and the Lagrangian Technique,* Appendix 2B, examines the optimization process for equations with three or more variables. Such techniques are especially helpful when managers face constrained optimization problems, or decision situations with limited alternatives. Throughout the text, a wide variety of problems describing real-world decisions can be solved using such techniques.

Like *Fundamentals of Managerial Economics*, students and instructors will find that *Managerial Economics,* 12th Edition provides an intuitive guide to marginal analysis and basic economic relations. Although differential calculus is an obviously helpful tool for understanding the process of economic optimization, it is important that students not let mathematical manipulation get in the way of their basic grasp of economic concepts. The concept of a marginal can also be described graphically in an intuitive noncalculus-based approach. Once students learn to grasp the importance of marginal revenue and marginal cost concepts, the process of economic optimization becomes intuitively obvious.

Although those using a non-calculus based approach can safely skip parts of Chapter 2 and Appendix 2B, all other material is fully and completely assessable. With practice using a wide variety of problems and examples throughout the text, all students are able to gain a simple, practical understanding of how economics can be used to understand and improve managerial decisions. I've used both calculus-based and noncalculus-based approaches in my own MBA classes. Both work.

Of course, the environment in which managerial decisions are made is constantly changing. To maintain its value as an educational resource, a textbook must be enhanced and updated. This revision of *Managerial Economics* contains a number of important additions and improvements. Every chapter has been thoroughly revised and refined in response to valuable suggestions provided by students and their instructors. The following section highlights some of most important changes.

Content

- Chapter 2 has been completely rewritten to clarify key economic concepts and the intuition of marginal analysis. A new Appendix 2A, *Math Analysis for Managers,* has also been added to help students that might benefit from a quick review of basic math concepts.
- Chapter 4, *Demand Analysis,* gives expanded coverage of economic principles used to understand the underpinnings of demand at the individual and market levels. This material gives an essential theoretical backdrop for subsequent analysis of demand estimation and pricing practices.
- Chapter 7, *Production Analysis and Compensation Policy,* now delves more deeply into important labor market issues that confront both employers and their employees. This material provided the background for expanded class discussion of a variety of related issues, such as minimum wage policy, imperfectly competitive labor markets, and internal labor markets.
- Chapter 9, *Linear Programming,* is new. Linear programming is an especially useful tool for addressing problems encountered in a number of business, engineering, financial, and scientific applications. This chapter illustrates how linear programming can be used to quickly and easily solve real-world decision problems.
- Chapter 14, *Game Theory and Competitive Strategy,* has been extensively revised to make clear essential game theory concepts and show how firms use these ideas to improve decision making when payoffs depend on actions taken by others.
- Chapter 15, *Pricing Practices,* has been expanded to include discussion of two-part pricing practices that are often featured in markets for distinctive goods and services. Transfer pricing practices for competitive and imperfectly competitive markets has been added in a new appendix to the chapter.

Learning Aids

- Each chapter incorporates a wide variety of simple numerical examples and detailed practical illustrations of chapter concepts. These features portray the valuable use and real-world implications of covered material.
- Each chapter includes *four* short Managerial Applications boxes to show current examples of how the concepts introduced in managerial economics apply to real-world situations. New Managerial Applications based on articles from the

Internet or *Barron's, Business Week, Forbes, Fortune,* and *The Wall Street Journal* are provided. This feature stimulates student interest and offers a popular basis for classroom discussion.

- The book incorporates several new regression-based illustrations of chapter concepts using actual company data, or hypothetical data adapted from real-world situations. Like all aspects of the text, this material is self-contained and intuitive.

- Effective managers must be sensitive to the special challenges posed by an increasingly global marketplace. To increase student awareness of such issues, a number of examples, Managerial Applications, and case studies that relate to global business topics are featured.

- Each chapter is accompanied by a case study that provides in-depth treatment of chapter concepts. To meet the needs of all instructors and their students, these case studies are written to allow, but do not require, a computer-based approach. These case studies are fully self-contained and especially helpful to instructors who wish to more fully incorporate the use of basic spreadsheet and statistical software in their courses.

- 370 new end-of-chapter questions and problems are provided, after having been subject to necessary revision and class testing. Questions are designed to give students the opportunity to grasp basic concepts on an intuitive level and express their understanding in a nonquantitative fashion. Problems cover a wide variety of decision situations and illustrate the role of economic analysis from within a simple numerical framework.

- Each chapter includes *two* self-test problems with detailed solutions to show students how economic tools and techniques can be used to solve practical business problems. These self-test problems are a proven study aid that greatly enhances the learning value of end-of-chapter questions and problems.

Ancillary Package

Managerial Economics, 12th Edition, is supported by the most comprehensive ancillary package available in managerial economics to make teaching and learning the material both easy and enjoyable.

Instructor's Manual The *Instructor's Manual* offers learning suggestions, plus detailed answers and solutions for all chapter questions and problems. Case study data are also provided to adopters with the *Instructor's Manual.*

Aplia It is a proven fact that students will do better in their course work if they come to class prepared. We have teamed up with Aplia, an online interactive tool that will help them experiment and learn economics. Aplia's activities are engaging and are based on discovery learning, letting them take an active part in the learning process. By completing these assignments online, they come to class better prepared to participate in discussions and relate to economic theories in managerial economics. Please contact your Cengage representative for more information about Aplia.

Test Bank A comprehensive *Test Bank* is also provided that offers a variety of multiple-choice questions, one-step, and multistep problems for every chapter. Full solutions are included, of course. With nearly 1,000 questions and problems, the *Test Bank* is a valuable tool for exam preparation.

Acknowledgments

A number of people have aided in the preparation of *Managerial Economics,* 12th Edition. Helpful suggestions and constructive comments have been received from a great number of instructors and students who have used previous editions. Numerous reviewers have also provided insights and assistance in clarifying difficult material. Among those who have been especially helpful in the development of this edition are: Barry Keating, University of Notre Dame; Stephen Conroy, University of San Diego; Xu Wang, Texas A&M University; Michael Brandl, University of Texas—Austin; Neil Garston, California State University—Los Angeles; Albert Okunade, University of Memphis; David Carr, University of South Dakota; Steven Rock, Western Illinois University; Mel Borland, Western Kentucky University; Tom Staley, San Francisco State University.

I am also indebted to the South-Western staff and would like to give special thanks to Mike Roche for 20 years of editorial and marketing contributions. Amy Ray for her help on this edition and the many editions of the book she has worked on through the years. Michelle Kunkler for conceptualizing the new look and feel. Betty Jung and Brian Joyner for working to promote the new edition to professors, students, and the Cengage Learning sales force. And to Lysa Oeters and her team at Integra for making the 12th edition a reality. Christine Hauschel read the entire manuscript, gave numerous helpful suggestions, and helped make the revision process lots of fun. Chris deserves a special word of thanks (Thanks!).

Every effort has been made to minimize errors in the book. However, errors do occasionally slip through despite diligent efforts to provide an error-free package of text and ancillary materials. Readers are invited to correspond with me directly concerning any corrections or other suggestions.

Finally, more than ever before, it is obvious that economic efficiency is an essential ingredient in the successful management of both business and public-sector organizations. Like any dynamic area of study, the field of managerial economics continues to undergo profound change in response to the challenges imposed by a rapidly evolving environment. It is exciting to participate in these developments. I sincerely hope that *Managerial Economics,* 12th Edition, contributes to a better understanding of the usefulness of economic theory.

For students, I hope it makes $ense.

Mark Hirschey
mhirschey@ku.edu
March 2008

Overview of Managerial Economics

PART 1

Nature and Scope of Managerial Economics

Warren E. Buffett, celebrated chairman of Omaha, Nebraska-based Berkshire Hathaway, Inc., started an investment partnership with $100 in 1956 and went on to accumulate a personal net worth in excess of $50 billion.

Buffett is famous for his razor-sharp focus on the competitive advantages of Berkshire's wide assortment of operating companies, including Benjamin Moore (paints), Borsheim's (jewelry), Clayton Homes, Dairy Queen, Fruit of the Loom, GEICO (insurance), General Re Corporation (reinsurance), MidAmerican Energy, the Nebraska Furniture Mart, See's Candies, and Shaw's Industries (carpet and floor coverings). Berkshire subsidiaries commonly earn more than 30 percent per year on invested capital, compared with the 10 percent to 12 percent rate of return earned by other well-managed companies. Additional contributors to Berkshire's outstanding performance are substantial common stock holdings in American Express, Coca-Cola, Procter & Gamble, and Wells Fargo, among others. As both a skilled manager and an insightful investor, Buffett likes wonderful businesses with high rates of return on investment, lofty profit margins, and consistent earnings growth. Complicated businesses that face fierce competition and require large capital investment are shunned.[1]

Buffett's success is powerful testimony to the practical usefulness of managerial economics. Managerial economics answers fundamental questions. When is the market for a product so attractive that entry or expansion becomes appealing? When is exit preferable to continued operation? Why do some professions pay well, while others offer only meager pay? Successful managers make good decisions, and one of their most useful tools is the methodology of managerial economics.

HOW IS MANAGERIAL ECONOMICS USEFUL?

Economic theory and methodology lay down rules for improving business and public policy decisions.

Evaluating Choice Alternatives

Managerial Economics
Applies economic tools and techniques to business and administrative decision making.

Managerial economics helps managers recognize how economic forces affect organizations and describes the economic consequences of managerial behavior. It also links economic concepts and quantitative methods to develop vital tools for managerial decision making. This process is illustrated in Figure 1.1.

---

1   Information about Warren Buffett's investment philosophy and Berkshire Hathaway, Inc., can be found on the Internet, http://www.berkshirehathaway.com.

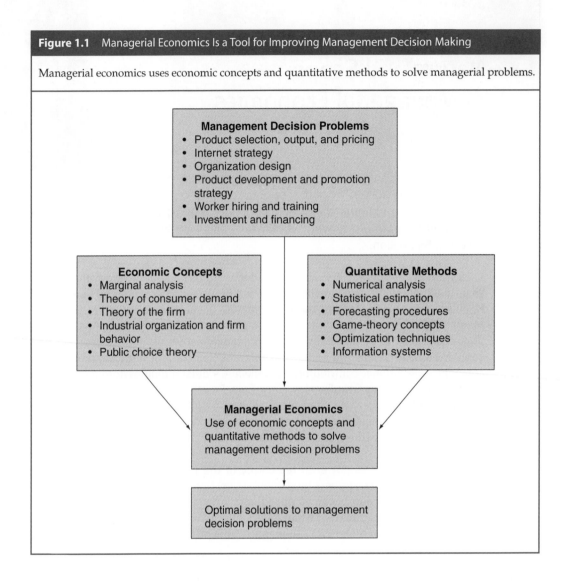

Figure 1.1   Managerial Economics Is a Tool for Improving Management Decision Making

Managerial economics uses economic concepts and quantitative methods to solve managerial problems.

Managerial economics identifies ways to achieve goals efficiently. For example, suppose a small business seeks rapid growth to reach a size that permits efficient use of national media advertising, managerial economics can be used to identify pricing and production strategies to help meet this short-run objective quickly and effectively. Similarly, managerial economics provides production and marketing rules that permit the company to maximize net profits once it has achieved growth or market share objectives.

Managerial economics has applications in both profit and not-for-profit sectors. For example, an administrator of a nonprofit hospital strives to provide the best medical care possible given limited medical staff, equipment, and related resources. Using the tools and concepts of managerial economics, the administrator can determine the optimal allocation of these limited resources. In short, managerial economics helps managers arrive at a set of operating rules that aid in the efficient use of scarce human and capital resources. By following these rules, businesses, nonprofit organizations, and government agencies are able to meet objectives efficiently.

Making the Best Decision

To establish appropriate decision rules, managers must understand the economic environment in which they operate. For example, a grocery retailer may offer consumers a highly price-sensitive product, such as milk, at an extremely low markup over cost—say, 1 percent to 2 percent—while offering less price-sensitive products, such as nonprescription drugs, at markups of as high as 40 percent over cost. Managerial economics describes the logic of this pricing practice with respect to the goal of profit maximization. Similarly, managerial economics reveals that auto import quotas reduce the availability of substitutes for domestically produced cars, raise auto prices, and create the possibility of monopoly profits for domestic manufacturers. It does not explain whether imposing quotas is good public policy; that is a decision involving broader political considerations. Managerial economics only describes the predictable economic consequences of such actions.

Managerial economics offers a comprehensive application of economic theory and methodology to management decision making. It is as relevant to the management of government agencies, cooperatives, schools, hospitals, museums, and similar not-for-profit institutions as it is to the management of profit-oriented businesses. Although this text focuses primarily on business applications, it also includes examples and problems from the government and nonprofit sectors to illustrate the broad relevance of managerial economics.

Managerial Application 1.1

Business Ethics

In *The Wall Street Journal* and the popular press, you can sometimes find evidence of unscrupulous business behavior. However, unethical conduct is inconsistent with value maximization and contrary to the enlightened self-interest of management and other employees. If honesty didn't pervade corporate America, the ability to conduct business would collapse. Eventually, the truth always comes out, and when it does the unscrupulous lose out. For better or worse, we are known by the standards we adopt.

To become successful in business, everyone must adopt a set of principles. Ethical rules to keep in mind when conducting business include:

- Above all else, keep your word. Say what you mean, and mean what you say.
- Do the right thing. A handshake with an honorable person is worth more than a ton of legal documents from a corrupt individual.
- Accept responsibility for your mistakes, and fix them. Be quick to share credit for success.
- Leave something on the table. Profit *with* your customer, not *off* your customer.

- Stick by your principles. Principles are not for sale at any price.

Does the "high road" lead to corporate success? Consider the experience of one of America's most famous winners—Omaha billionaire Warren E. Buffett, chairman of Berkshire Hathaway, Inc. Buffett and Charlie Munger, the number-two man at Berkshire, are famous for doing multimillion-dollar deals on the basis of a simple handshake. At Berkshire, management relies upon the character of the people that they are dealing with rather than expensive accounting audits, detailed legal opinions, or liability insurance coverage. Buffett says that after some early mistakes he learned to go into business only with people whom he likes, trusts, and admires. While, a company won't necessarily prosper because its managers display admirable qualities, Buffett says he has never made a good deal with a bad person.

Doing the right thing not only makes sense from an ethical perspective, it makes business sense too!

See: Peter Berkowitz, "Ethics 101," *The Wall Street Journal Online*, October 8, 2007, http://online.wsj.com.

THEORY OF THE FIRM

Firms are useful for producing and distributing goods and services.

Expected Value Maximization

At its simplest level, a business enterprise represents a series of contractual relationships that specify the rights and responsibilities of various parties (see Figure 1.2). People directly involved include customers, stockholders, management, employees, and suppliers. Society is also involved because businesses use scarce resources, pay taxes, provide employment opportunities, and produce much of society's material and services output. The model of business is called the **theory of the firm.** In its simplest version, the firm is thought to have profit maximization as its primary goal. The firm's owner-manager is assumed to be working to maximize the firm's short-run profits. Today, the emphasis on profits has been broadened to encompass uncertainty and the time value of money. In this more complete model, the primary goal of the firm is long-term **expected value maximization.**

The **value of the firm** is the present value of the firm's expected future net cash flows. If cash flows are equated to profits for simplicity, the value of the firm today, or its **present value,** is the value of expected profits, discounted back to the present at an appropriate interest rate.[2]

This model can be expressed as follows:

$$\text{Value of the Firm} = \text{Present Value of Expected Future Profits}$$

$$= \frac{\pi_1}{(1+i)^1} + \frac{\pi_2}{(1+i)^2} + \cdots + \frac{\pi_n}{(1+i)^n} \qquad \textbf{1.1}$$

$$= \sum_{t=1}^{n} \frac{\pi_t}{(1+i)^t}$$

Theory of the Firm
Basic model of business.

Expected Value Maximization
Optimization of profits in light of uncertainty and the time value of money.

Value of the Firm
Present value of the firm's expected future net cash flows.

Present Value
Worth in current dollars.

Here, π_1, π_2, ..., π_n represent expected profits in each year, t, and i is the appropriate interest, or discount, rate. The final form for Equation (1.1) is simply a shorthand expression in which sigma (Σ) stands for "sum up" or "add together." The term

$$\sum_{t=1}^{n}$$

means, "Add together as t goes from 1 to n the values of the term on the right." For Equation (1.1), the process is as follows: Let $t = 1$ and find the value of the term $\pi_1/(1+i)^1$, the present value of year 1 profit; then let $t = 2$ and calculate $\pi_2/(1+i)^2$, the present value of year 2 profit; continue until $t = n$, the last year included in the analysis; then add up these present-value equivalents of yearly profits to find the current or present value of the firm.

Because profits (π) are equal to total revenues (TR) minus total costs (TC), Equation (1.1) can be rewritten as

$$\text{Value} = \sum_{t=1}^{n} \frac{TR_t - TC_t}{(1+i)^t} \qquad \textbf{1.2}$$

---

2   Discounting is required because profits obtained in the future are less valuable than profits earned presently. One dollar today is worth more than $1 to be received a year from now because $1 today can be invested and, with interest, grow to a larger amount by the end of the year. One dollar invested at 10 percent interest would grow to $1.10 in one year. Thus, $1 is defined as the present value of $1.10 due in 1 year when the appropriate interest rate is 10 percent.

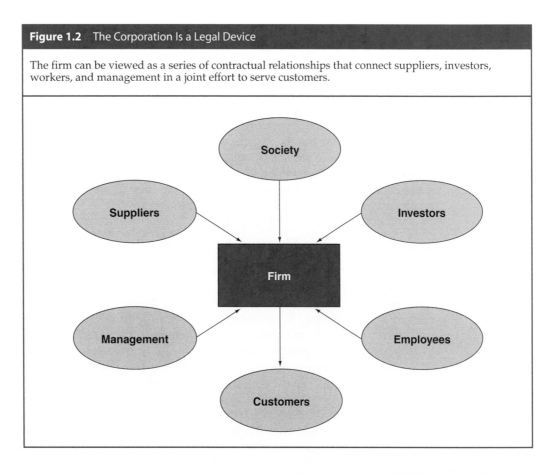

Figure 1.2 The Corporation Is a Legal Device

The firm can be viewed as a series of contractual relationships that connect suppliers, investors, workers, and management in a joint effort to serve customers.

This expanded equation can be used to examine how the expected value maximization model relates to a firm's various functional departments. The marketing department often has primary responsibility for promotion and sales (TR); the production department has primary responsibility for development costs (TC); and the finance department has primary responsibility for acquiring capital and, hence, for the discount factor (i) in the denominator. Important overlaps exist among these functional areas. The marketing department can help reduce costs for a given level of output by influencing customer order size and timing. The production department can stimulate sales by improving quality. Other departments, for example, accounting, human resources, transportation, and engineering, provide information and services vital to sales growth and cost control. The determination of TR and TC is a difficult and complex task. All managerial decisions should be analyzed in terms of their effects on value, as expressed in Equations (1.1) and (1.2).

Constraints and the Theory of the Firm

Organizations frequently face limited availability of essential inputs, such as skilled labor, raw materials, energy, specialized machinery, and warehouse space. Managers often face limitations on the amount of investment funds available for a particular project or activity. Decisions can also be constrained by contractual requirements. For example, labor contracts limit flexibility in worker scheduling and job assignments. Contracts sometimes require that a minimum level of output be produced to meet delivery requirements. In most instances, output must also meet quality requirements. Some common examples of output quality constraints are nutritional requirements for feed mixtures, audience exposure requirements for marketing promotions, reliability requirements for electronic products, and customer service requirements for minimum satisfaction levels.

Legal restrictions, which affect both production and marketing activities, can also play an important role in managerial decisions. Laws that define minimum wages, health and safety standards, pollution emission standards, fuel efficiency requirements, and fair pricing and marketing practices all limit managerial flexibility.

The role that constraints play in managerial decisions makes the topic of constrained optimization a basic element of managerial economics. Later chapters consider important economic implications of self-imposed and social constraints. This analysis is important because value maximization and allocative efficiency in society depend on the efficient use of scarce economic resources.

Limitations of the Theory of the Firm

Optimize
Seek the best solution.

Satisfice
Seek satisfactory rather than optimal results.

In practice, do managers try to **optimize** (seek the best result) or merely **satisfice** (seek satisfactory rather than optimal results)? Do managers seek the sharpest needle in a haystack (optimize), or do they stop after finding one sharp enough for sewing (satisfice)? How can one tell whether company support of the United Way, for example, leads to long-run value maximization? Are generous salaries and stock options necessary to attract and retain managers who can keep the firm ahead of the competition? When a risky venture is turned down, is this inefficient risk avoidance? Or does it reflect an appropriate decision from the standpoint of value maximization?

It is impossible to give definitive answers to questions like these, and this dilemma has led to the development of alternative theories of firm behavior. Some of the more prominent alternatives are models in which size or growth maximization is the assumed primary objective of management, models that argue that managers are most concerned with their own personal utility or welfare maximization, and models that treat the firm as a collection of individuals with widely divergent goals rather than as a single, identifiable unit. These alternative theories, or models, of managerial behavior have added to our understanding of the firm. Still, none can supplant the basic value maximization concept as a foundation for analyzing managerial decisions. Examining why provides additional insight into the value of studying managerial economics.

Research shows that vigorous competition typically forces managers to seek value maximization in their operating decisions. Competition in the capital markets forces managers to seek value maximization in their financing decisions as well. Stockholders are, of course, interested in value maximization because it affects their rates of return on common stock investments. Managers who pursue their own interests instead of stockholders' interests run the risk of losing their job. Unfriendly takeovers are especially hostile to inefficient management that is replaced. Moreover, recent studies show a strong correlation between firm profits and managerial compensation. Management has strong economic incentives to pursue value maximization through their decisions.

It is sometimes overlooked that managers must consider all relevant costs and benefits before they can make reasoned decisions. It is unwise to seek the best technical solution to a problem if the costs of finding such a solution greatly exceed resulting benefits. As a result, what often appears to be satisficing on the part of management can be interpreted as value-maximizing behavior once the costs of information gathering and analysis are considered. Similarly, short-run growth maximization strategies are often consistent with long-run value maximization when the production, distribution, and promotional advantages of large firm size are better understood.

Finally, the value maximization model also offers insight into a firm's voluntary "socially responsible" behavior. The criticism that the traditional theory of the firm emphasizes profits and value maximization while ignoring the issue of social responsibility is important and will be discussed later in the chapter. For now, it will prove useful to examine the concept of profits, which is central to the theory of the firm.

PROFIT MEASUREMENT

Free enterprise depends upon profits and the profit motive. Both play a role in the efficient allocation of economic resources worldwide.

Business Versus Economic Profit

Business Profit
Residual of sales revenue minus the explicit accounting costs of doing business.

Profit is usually defined as the residual of sales revenue minus the explicit costs of doing business. It is the amount available to fund equity capital after payment for all other resources used by the firm. This definition of profit is accounting profit, or **business profit.**

The economist also defines profit as the excess of revenues over costs. However, inputs provided by owners, including entrepreneurial effort and capital, are resources that must be compensated. The economist includes a normal rate of return on equity capital plus an opportunity cost for the effort of the owner-entrepreneur as costs of doing business, just as the interest paid on debt and the wages are costs in calculating

Managerial Application 1.2

The World Is Turning to Capitalism *and* Democracy

Capitalism and democracy are mutually reinforcing. Some philosophers have gone so far as to say that capitalism and democracy are intertwined. Without capitalism, democracy may be impossible. Without democracy, capitalism may fail. At a minimum, freely competitive markets give consumers broad choices, and reinforce the individual freedoms protected in a democratic society. In democracy, government does not grant individual freedom. Instead, the political power of government emanates from the people. Similarly, the flow of economic resources originates with the individual customer in a capitalistic system. It is not centrally directed by government.

Capitalism is socially desirable because of its decentralized and customer-oriented nature. The menu of products to be produced is derived from market price and output signals originating in competitive markets, not from the output schedules of a centralized planning agency. Resources and products are also allocated through market forces. They are not earmarked on the basis of favoritism or social status. Through their purchase decisions, customers dictate the quantity and quality of products brought to market.

Competition is a fundamentally attractive feature of the capitalistic system because it keeps costs and prices low. By operating efficiently, firms are able to produce the maximum quantity and quality of goods and services. Mass production is, by definition, production for the masses. Competition also limits concentration of economic and political power. Similarly, the democratic form of government is inconsistent with consolidated economic influence and decision making.

Totalitarian forms of government are in retreat. China has experienced violent upheaval as the country embarks on much-needed economic and political reforms. In the former Soviet Union, Eastern Europe, India, and Latin America, years of economic failure forced governments to dismantle entrenched bureaucracy and install economic incentives. Rising living standards and political freedom have made life in the West the envy of the world. Against this backdrop, the future is bright for capitalism *and* democracy!

See: "EU, China Agree to Monitor Clothing Exports to Europe," *The Wall Street Journal Online,* October 9, 2007, http://online.wsj.com.

Normal Rate of Return
Average profit necessary to attract and retain investment.

Economic Profit
Business profit minus the implicit costs of capital and any other owner-provided inputs.

business profit. The risk-adjusted **normal rate of return** on capital is the minimum return necessary to attract and retain investment. Similarly, the opportunity cost of owner effort is determined by the value that could be received in alternative employment. In economic terms, profit is business profit minus the implicit (noncash) costs of capital and other owner-provided inputs used by the firm. This profit concept is called **economic profit.**

The concepts of business profit and economic profit can be used to explain the role of profits in a free-enterprise economy. A normal rate of return is necessary to induce individuals to invest funds rather than spend them for current consumption. Normal profit is simply a cost for capital; it is no different from the cost of other resources, such as labor, materials, and energy. A similar price exists for the entrepreneurial effort of a firm's owner-manager and for other resources that owners bring to the firm. Opportunity costs for owner-provided inputs are often a big part of business profits, especially among small businesses.

Variability of Business Profits

Profit Margin
Accounting net income divided by sales.

Return on Stockholders' Equity
Accounting net income divided by the book value of total assets minus total liabilities.

In practice, reported profits fluctuate widely. Table 1.1 shows business profits for a sample of 30 well-known industrial giants: companies that comprise the Dow Jones Industrial Average. Business profit is often measured in dollar terms or as a percentage of sales revenue, called **profit margin,** as in Table 1.1. The economist's concept of a normal rate of profit is typically assessed in terms of the realized rate of **return on stockholders' equity** (ROE). Return on stockholders' equity is defined as accounting net income divided by the book value of the firm. As seen in Table 1.1, the average ROE for industrial giants found in the Dow Jones Industrial Average falls in a broad range around 15 percent to 25 percent per year. Although an average annual ROE of roughly 10 percent can be regarded as a typical or normal rate of return in the United States and Canada, this standard is routinely exceeded by companies such as Coca-Cola, which has consistently earned a ROE in excess of 35 percent per year. It is a standard seldom met by Alcoa, Inc., a company that sometimes suffers massive losses as it cuts costs and increases product quality in the face of tough environmental regulations and foreign competition.

Some of the variation in ROE depicted in Table 1.1 represents the influence of differential risk premiums. In the pharmaceuticals industry, for example, hoped-for discoveries of effective therapies for important diseases are often a long shot at best. Thus, profit rates reported by Merck, Pfizer, and other leading pharmaceutical companies overstate the relative profitability of the drug industry; it could be cut by one-half with proper risk adjustment. Similarly, reported profit rates can overstate differences in economic profits if accounting error or bias causes investments with long-term benefits to be omitted from the balance sheet. For example, current accounting practice often fails to consider advertising or research and development expenditures as intangible investments with long-term benefits. Because advertising and research and development expenditures are immediately expensed rather than capitalized and written off over their useful lives, intangible assets can be grossly understated for certain companies. The balance sheet of Coca-Cola does not reflect the hundreds of millions of dollars spent to establish and maintain the brand-name recognition of Coca-Cola, just as Pfizer's balance sheet fails to reflect research dollars spent to develop important product names like cholesterol-lowering Lipitor (the world's best-selling drug), Inspra (for the treatment of congestive heart failure), and Viagra (for the treatment of male impotence). As a result, business profit rates for both Coca-Cola and Pfizer overstate each company's true economic performance.

Table 1.1   Profitability of Corporate Giants Included in the Dow Jones Industrial Average

Company Name	Industry Name	Sales Revenue ($ million)	Net Income ($ million)	Net Worth ($ millions)	Return on Sales (MGN, %)	Return on Equity (ROE, %)
American International Group (AIG)	Property & Casualty Insurance	113,194	14,014	101,521	12.4	13.8
Alcoa Inc.	Aluminum	30,379	2,159	14,580	7.1	14.8
Altria Group	Cigarettes	101,407	12,022	39,627	11.9	30.3
American Express Company	Credit Services	27,136	3,729	10,454	13.7	35.7
AT&T Inc.	Telecom Services—Domestic	63,055	7,356	115,849	11.7	6.3
Caterpillar Inc.	Farm & Construction Machinery	41,517	3,537	6,863	8.5	51.5
Citigroup Inc.	Money Center Banks	96,431	21,185	118,856	22.0	17.8
Du Pont de Nemours	Chemicals—Major Diversified	28,982	3,148	9,212	10.9	34.2
Exxon Mobil Corporation	Major Integrated Oil & Gas	377,635	39,500	113,105	10.5	34.9
General Electric	Conglomerates	163,391	20,666	112,394	12.6	18.4
General Motors	Auto Manufacturers—Major	206,708	−9,579	11,165	−4.6	−85.8
Hewlett-Packard Company	Diversified Computer Systems	94,081	6,518	38,006	6.9	17.1
Honeywell International Inc.	Conglomerates	31,367	2,078	9,712	6.6	21.4
Intel Corporation	Semiconductor—Broad Line	35,382	5,044	36,717	14.3	13.7
International Business Machines Corp.	Diversified Computer Systems	91,423	9,415	28,486	10.3	33.1
Johnson & Johnson	Drug Manufacturers—Major	53,324	11,053	39,352	20.7	28.1
JPMorgan Chase & Co.	Money Center Banks	59,107	13,645	116,143	23.1	11.7
McDonald's Corporation	Restaurants	21,586	2,873	15,446	13.3	18.6
Merck & Co.	Drug Manufacturers—Major	22,636	4,434	17,540	19.6	25.3
Microsoft Corporation	Application Software	46,057	11,909	36,708	25.9	32.4
3M Company	Conglomerates	22,923	3,851	9,953	16.8	38.7
Pfizer Inc.	Drug Manufacturers—Major	48,371	11,016	70,897	22.8	15.5
Procter & Gamble	Cleaning Products	73,602	9,554	63,889	13.0	15.0
The Boeing Company	Aerospace/Defense—Major Diversified	61,530	2,206	4,741	3.6	46.5
The Coca-Cola Company	Beverages—Soft Drinks	24,088	5,080	16,892	21.1	30.1
The Home Depot, Inc.	Home Improvement Stores	90,837	5,761	25,054	6.3	23.0
The Walt Disney Company	Entertainment—Diversified	35,156	4,341	32,746	12.3	13.3
United Technologies Corporation	Conglomerates	47,829	3,732	17,292	7.8	21.6
Verizon Communications Inc.	Telecom Services—Domestic	88,144	5,480	48,432	6.2	11.3
Wal-Mart Stores, Inc.	Discount, Variety Stores	348,650	12,179	61,573	3.5	19.8
Average		84,864	8,264	44,773	12.4	20.3
Median		56,216	5,620	34,727	12.1	20.6

Data source: *MSN/Money*, March 10, 2007, http://moneycentral.msn.com/investor/finder/customstocks.asp.

WHY DO PROFITS VARY AMONG FIRMS?

Many firms earn significant economic profits or experience meaningful losses.

Disequilibrium Profit Theories

Frictional Profit Theory
Abnormal profits observed following unanticipated changes in demand or cost conditions.

One explanation of economic profits or losses is **frictional profit theory.** It states that markets are sometimes in disequilibrium because of unanticipated changes in demand or cost conditions. Unanticipated shocks produce positive or negative economic profits for some firms.

For example, automated teller machines (ATMs) make it possible for customers of financial institutions to easily obtain cash, enter deposits, and make loan payments. Though ATMs render obsolete many of the functions that used to be carried out at branch offices, they foster ongoing consolidation in the industry. Similarly, new user-friendly software increases demand for high-powered personal computers (PCs) and boosts returns for efficient PC manufacturers and software vendors. A rise in the use of plastics and aluminum in automobiles drives down the profits of steel manufacturers. Over time, barring impassable barriers to entry and exit, resources flow into or out of financial institutions, computer manufacturers, and steel manufacturers, thus driving rates of return back to normal levels. During interim periods, profits might be above or below normal because of frictional factors that prevent instantaneous adjustment to new market conditions.

Monopoly Profit Theory
Above-normal profits caused by barriers to entry that limit competition.

A further explanation of above-normal profits is the **monopoly profit theory,** an extension of frictional profit theory. Some firms earn above-normal profits because they are sheltered from competition by high barriers to entry. Economies of scale, high capital requirements, patents, or import protection enable some firms to build monopoly positions that allow above-normal profits for extended periods. Monopoly profits can also arise because of luck (being in the right industry at the right time) or from anticompetitive behavior. Unlike other potential sources of above-normal profits, monopoly profits are often seen as unwarranted and subject to heavy taxes or otherwise regulated.

Compensatory Profit Theories

Innovation Profit Theory
Above-normal profits that follow successful invention or modernization.

Innovation profit theory describes above-normal profits that arise following successful invention or modernization. For example, innovation profit theory suggests that Microsoft Corporation has earned superior rates of return because it successfully introduced and marketed the graphical user interface, a superior image-based rather than command-based approach to computer software instructions. Microsoft has continued to earn above-normal returns as other firms scramble to offer a wide variety of "user friendly" software for personal and business applications. Only after competitors have introduced and successfully saturated the market for user-friendly software will Microsoft profits be driven down to normal levels. Similarly, Apple Corporation has earned above-normal rates of return as an early innovator with its iPod line of portable digital music and video players. With increased competition from Microsoft's line of Zune devices, among others, it remains to be seen if Apple can maintain its position in the portable digital device market, or will instead see its market dominance and above-normal returns decline. As in the case of frictional or disequilibrium profits, profits that are due to innovation are susceptible to the onslaught of competition from new and established competitors.

Compensatory Profit Theory
Above-normal rates of return that reward efficiency.

In general, **compensatory profit theory** describes above-normal rates of return that reward firms for extraordinary success in meeting customer needs and maintaining efficient operations. If firms that operate at the industry's average level of efficiency receive normal rates of return, it is reasonable to expect firms operating at above-average levels of efficiency to earn above-normal rates of return. Inefficient firms earn below-normal rates of return.

Compensatory profit theory also recognizes economic profit as an important reward to the entrepreneurial function of owners and managers. Every product starts as an idea for serving better some established or perceived need of existing or potential customers. This need remains unmet until someone designs, plans, and implements a solution. The opportunity for economic profits is an important motivation for such entrepreneurial activity.

Role of Profits in the Economy

Each of the preceding theories describes economic profits obtained for different reasons. In some cases, several theories may apply. An efficient manufacturer like Boeing may earn an above-normal rate of return in accordance with compensatory theory, but, during a strike by competitor Airbus employees, these above-average profits may be augmented by frictional profits. Microsoft's profit position can be partly explained by all four theories: The company has earned high frictional profits while Google, IBM, and Oracle, among a host of others, scramble to offer new computer software, games, and services; Microsoft has earned monopoly profits because it has some copyright and patent protection; it has certainly benefitted from successful innovation; and it is well managed and thus has earned compensatory profits.

Economic profits play an important role in any market-based economy. Above-normal profits serve as a valuable signal that firm or industry output should be increased. Expansion by established firms or entry by new competitors occurs quickly during high-profit periods. Just as above-normal profits signal the need for expansion and entry, below-normal profits signal the need for contraction and exit. Economic profits are

Managerial Application 1.3

Google on Social Responsibility

Form S-1 registration statements are filed with the Securities and Exchange Commission by companies that want to sell shares to the investing public. Usually written by lawyers and filled with legalese, Google cofounder Larry Page shattered Wall Street tradition when he used the company's S-1 statement to lay out Google's philosophy on the social responsibility of business.

"Don't be evil," Page wrote. "We believe strongly that in the long term, we will be better served—as shareholders and in all other ways—by a company that does good things for the world even if we forgo some short-term gains. This is an important aspect of our culture and is broadly shared within the company."

"We aspire to make Google an institution that makes the world a better place. With our products, Google connects people and information all around the world for free. We are adding other powerful services such as Gmail that provides an efficient 1-gigabyte Gmail account for free. By releasing services for free, we hope to help bridge the digital divide. AdWords connects users and advertisers efficiently, helping both. AdSense helps fund a huge variety of online web sites and enables authors who could not otherwise publish." In 2003, the company created Google Grants to fund programs in which hundreds of nonprofits address issues, including the environment, poverty, and human rights, and receive free advertising to further their mission. In 2004, the company committed part of the proceeds from its initial public offering and 1 percent of ongoing profits to fund the Google Foundation, an organization intended to ambitiously apply innovation and resources toward the solution of world problems.

Google is committed to optimize for the long term, and will support high-risk, high-reward projects and manage them as a portfolio. The company will be run collaboratively in an effort to attract creative, committed new employees. It will be interesting to track their progress.

See: http://www.sec.gov/Archives/edgar/data/1288776/000119312504073639/ds1.htm.

one of the most important factors affecting the allocation of scarce economic resources. Above-normal profits also reward innovation and efficiency, just as below-normal profits penalize stagnation and inefficiency. Profits play a vital role in providing incentives for innovation and productive efficiency and in allocating scarce resources.

ROLE OF BUSINESS IN SOCIETY

Business makes a big contribution to economic betterment in the United States and around the globe.

Why Firms Exist

Firms exist because they are useful. They survive by public consent to serve social needs. If social welfare could be precisely measured, business firms might be expected to operate in a manner that maximizes some index of social well-being. Maximization of social welfare requires answering the following important questions: What combination of goods and services (including negative by-products, such as pollution) should be produced? How should goods and services be provided? How should goods and services be distributed? These are the most vital questions faced in a free-enterprise system, and they are key social issues.

Although the process of market-determined production and allocation of goods and services is highly efficient, problems sometimes arise in an unconstrained market economy. Society has developed methods for alleviating these problems through the political system. To illustrate, the economics of producing and distributing electric power are such that only one firm can efficiently serve a given community. Furthermore, there is no good substitute for electric lighting. As a result, electric companies are in a position to exploit consumers; they could charge high prices and earn excessive profits. To avoid potential exploitation, prices charged by electric companies and other utilities are held to levels thought to be just sufficient to provide a fair rate of return on investment. In theory, the regulatory process is simple. In practice, it is costly, and difficult to implement. It can be arbitrary and a poor, but sometimes necessary, substitute for competition.

Problems can also occur when, because of economies of scale or other barriers to entry, a limited number of firms serve a given market. If firms compete fairly with each other, no difficulty arises. However, if they conspire with one another in setting prices, they may be able to restrict output, obtain excessive profits, and reduce social welfare. Antitrust laws are designed to prevent such collusion. Like direct regulation, antitrust laws contain arbitrary elements and are costly to administer, but they too are necessary if social justice is to be served.

The market economy sometimes faces difficulty when firms impose costs on others by dumping wastes into the air or water. If a factory pollutes the air, causing nearby residents to suffer lung ailments, a meaningful cost is imposed on those people and society in general. Failure to shift these costs back onto the firm and, ultimately, to the consumers of its products, means that the firm and its customers benefit unfairly by not having to pay the full costs of production. Pollution and other externalities may result in an inefficient and inequitable allocation of resources. In both government and business, considerable attention is directed at the problem of internalizing these costs. Some of the practices used to internalize social costs include setting health and safety standards for products and work conditions, establishing emissions limits on manufacturing, and imposing fines or closing firms that do not meet established standards.

Social Responsibility of Business

What does all this mean with respect to the social responsibility of business? Is the value maximization theory of the firm adequate for examining issues of social responsibility and for developing rules that reflect the role of business in society?

As seen in Figure 1.3, firms are primarily economic entities and can be expected to analyze social responsibility from within the context of the economic model of the firm. This is an important consideration when examining inducements used to channel the efforts of business in directions that society desires. Similar considerations should also be taken into account before applying political pressure or regulations to constrain firm operations. For example, from the consumer's standpoint it is desirable to pay low rates for gas, electricity, and telecom services. If public pressures drive rates down too

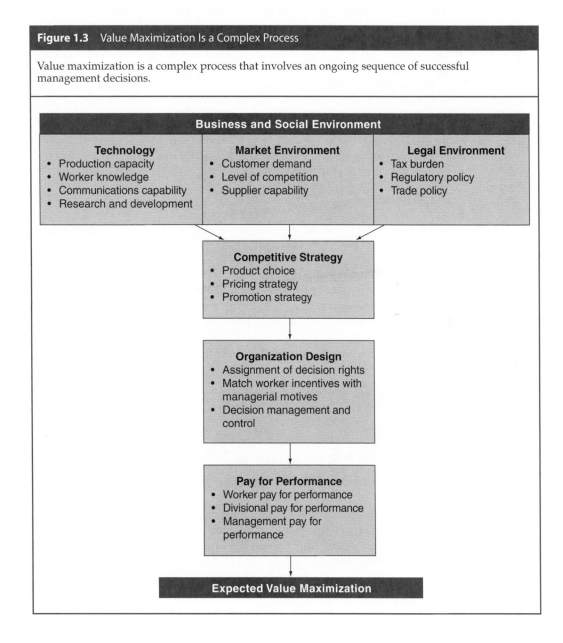

Figure 1.3 Value Maximization Is a Complex Process

Value maximization is a complex process that involves an ongoing sequence of successful management decisions.

Business and Social Environment

Technology
- Production capacity
- Worker knowledge
- Communications capability
- Research and development

Market Environment
- Customer demand
- Level of competition
- Supplier capability

Legal Environment
- Tax burden
- Regulatory policy
- Trade policy

Competitive Strategy
- Product choice
- Pricing strategy
- Promotion strategy

Organization Design
- Assignment of decision rights
- Match worker incentives with managerial motives
- Decision management and control

Pay for Performance
- Worker pay for performance
- Divisional pay for performance
- Management pay for performance

Expected Value Maximization

Managerial Application 1.4

The Internet Revolution

In the fifteenth century, the printing press made widespread dissemination of written information easy and inexpensive. The printing press sends information from the printer to the general public. It is a one-way method of communication. In the new millennium, we have the Internet. Not only is transmitting information via the Internet cheaper and faster than in the printed form, but it is also a two-way method of communication. The Internet is a revolutionary communications tool because it has the potential for feedback from one consumer to another, or from one company to another.

For the first time, the Internet gives firms and their customers in New York City, in Jackson Hole, Wyoming, and in the wilds of Africa the same timely access to widely publicized economic news and information. With the Internet, up-to-the-minute global news and analysis are just mouse clicks away. The Internet also gives global consumers and businesses the opportunity to communicate with one another and thereby *creates* fresh news and information. Over the Internet, customers can communicate about pricing or product quality concerns.

Businesses can communicate about the threat posed by potential competitors. The Internet makes the production of economic news and information democratic by reducing the information-gathering advantages of very large corporations and the traditional print and broadcast media.

With the Internet, the ability to communicate economic news and information around the globe is just a mouse click away. With the Internet, companies are able to keep in touch with suppliers on a continuous basis. Internet technology makes "just in time" production possible, if not mandatory. It also puts companies in touch with their customers 24 hours a day, 7 days a week. 24/7 is more than a way of doing business; it has become the battle cry of the customer-focused organization.

Internet technology is a blessing for efficient companies with products customers crave. It is a curse for the inefficient and slow to adapt.

See: "Dictators and the Internet," *The Wall Street Journal Online*, October 9, 2007, http://online.wsj.com.

---

low, however, utility profits could fall below the level necessary to provide an adequate return to investors. In that event, capital would flow out of regulated industries, innovation would cease, and service would deteriorate. When such issues are considered, the economic model of the firm provides useful insight. This model emphasizes the close relation between the firm and society, and indicates the importance of business participation in the development and achievement of social objectives.

STRUCTURE OF THIS TEXT

Objectives

This text should help you accomplish the following objectives:

- Develop a clear understanding of the economic method in managerial decision making.
- Acquire a framework for understanding the nature of the firm as an integrated whole as opposed to a loosely connected set of functional departments.
- Recognize the relation between the firm and society and the role of business as a tool for social betterment.

Throughout the text, the emphasis is on the *practical* application of economic analysis to managerial decision problems.

Development of Topics

The value maximization framework is useful for characterizing actual managerial decisions and for developing rules that can be used to improve those decisions. The basic test of the value maximization model, or any model, is its ability to explain real-world behavior. This text highlights the complementary relation between theory and practice. Theory is used to improve managerial decision making, and practical experience leads to the development of better theory.

Chapter 2, "Economic Optimization," begins by examining the important role that marginal analysis plays in the optimization process. The balancing of marginal revenues and marginal costs to determine the profit-maximizing output level is explored, as are other fundamental economic relations that help organizations employ scarce resources efficiently. All of these economic relations are considered based on the simplifying assumption that cost and revenue relations are known with certainty. Later in the book, this assumption is relaxed, and the more realistic circumstance of decision making with uncertainty is examined. This material shows how optimization concepts can be effectively employed in situations when managers have extensive information about the chance or probability of certain outcomes, but the end result of managerial decisions cannot be forecast precisely.

The concepts of demand and supply are basic to understanding the effective use of economic resources. The general overview of "Demand and Supply" in Chapter 3 provides a framework for the more detailed inquiry that follows. Chapter 4, "Demand Analysis," emphasizes that the successful management of any organization requires a complete understanding of the demand for its products. The demand function relates the sales of a product to such important factors as the price of the product itself, prices of other goods, income, advertising, and even weather. The role of demand elasticities, which measure the strength of relations expressed in the demand function, is also emphasized. Given the challenges posed by a rapidly changing global environment, a careful statistical analysis of demand relations is often conducted to provide the information necessary for effective decision making. Tools used by managers in the statistical analysis of demand relations are the subject of Chapter 5, "Demand Estimation." Issues addressed in Chapter 6, "Forecasting," provide a useful framework for the estimation of demand and cost relations.

Chapters 7 and 8 examine production and cost concepts. The economics of resource employment in the manufacture and distribution of goods and services is the focus of this material. These chapters present economic analysis as a context for understanding the logic of managerial decisions and as a means for developing improved practices. Chapter 7, "Production Analysis and Compensation Policy," develops rules for optimal employment and demonstrates how labor and other resources can be used in a profit-maximizing manner. Chapter 8, "Cost Analysis and Estimation," focuses on the identification of cost–output relations so that appropriate decisions regarding product pricing, plant size and location, and so on can be made. Chapter 9, "Linear Programming," introduces a tool from the decision sciences that can be used to solve a variety of optimization problems. This technique offers managers input for short-run operating decisions and information helpful in the long-run planning process.

The remainder of the book builds on the foundation provided in Chapters 1 through 9 to examine a variety of topics in the theory and practice of managerial economics. Chapter 10, "Competitive Markets," offers perspective on the nature of competition in vigorously competitive markets; Chapter 11, "Performance and Strategy in Competitive Markets," shows how firms succeed in competitive markets by being cheaper, faster, or better than the competition. Chapter 12, "Monopoly and Monopsony," illustrates how product differentiation, barriers to entry, and the availability of information interact to determine the vigor of competition in markets dominated by a single seller (monopoly) or a single buyer (monopsony). Chapter 13, "Monopolistic Competition and Oligopoly," considers industries in which interactions among competitors are normal. In Chapter 14, "Game Theory and Competitive Strategy," competition among the few is described with an eye toward understanding and improving business strategy. Chapter 15, "Pricing Practices," shows how the forces of supply and demand interact in settings where market power is prevalent. Importantly, this chapter analyzes pricing practices commonly observed in business and shows how they reflect the predictions of economic theory.

Chapter 16, "Risk Analysis," illustrates how the predictions of economic theory can be applied in the real-world setting of uncertainty; and Chapter 17, "Capital Budgeting," examines key elements of an effective long-term planning framework. Chapter 18, "Organization Design and Corporate Governance," offers insight concerning the value-maximizing design of the firm and documents the importance of business ethics. Finally, Chapter 19, "Government in the Market Economy," studies the role of government and how the tools and techniques of managerial economics can be used to analyze and improve public sector decisions.

SUMMARY

Managerial economics focuses on the application of economic theory and methodology to the solution of practical business problems.

- **Managerial economics** applies economic theory and methods to business and administrative decision making.

- The basic model of the business enterprise is called the **theory of the firm.**

- The primary goal is seen as long-term **expected value maximization.**

- The **value of the firm** is the present value of the firm's expected future net cash flows, where **present value** is the value of expected cash flows discounted back to the present at an appropriate interest rate.

- Valid questions are sometimes raised about whether managers really **optimize** (seek the best solution) or merely **satisfice** (seek satisfactory rather than optimal results). Most often, especially when information costs are considered, managers can be seen as optimizing.

- **Business profit,** or accounting profit, is the residual of sales revenue minus the explicit accounting costs of doing business.

- Business profit often incorporates a **normal rate of return** on capital, or the minimum return necessary to attract and retain investment for a particular use.

- **Economic profit** is business profit minus the implicit costs of equity and other owner-provided inputs used by the firm.

- **Profit margin,** or net income divided by sales, and the **return on stockholders' equity,** or accounting net income divided by the book value of total assets minus total liabilities, are practical indicators of firm performance.

- **Frictional profit theory** describes abnormal profits observed following unanticipated changes in product demand or cost conditions.

- **Monopoly profit theory** asserts that above-normal profits are sometimes caused by barriers to entry that limit competition.

- **Innovation profit theory** describes above-normal profits that arise as a result of successful invention or modernization.

- **Compensatory profit theory** holds that above-normal rates of return can sometimes be seen as a reward to firms that are extraordinarily successful in meeting customer needs, maintaining efficient operations, and so forth.

The use of economic methodology to analyze and improve the managerial decision-making process combines the study of theory and practice. The primary virtue of managerial economics lies in its usefulness. It works!

QUESTIONS

Q1.1 Is it appropriate to view firms primarily as economic entities?

Q1.2 Explain how the valuation model given in Equation (1.2) could be used to describe the integrated nature of managerial decision making across the functional areas of business.

Q1.3 Describe the effects of each of the following managerial decisions or economic influences on the value of the firm:

A. The firm is required to install new equipment to reduce air pollution.

B. Through heavy expenditures on advertising, the firm's marketing department increases sales substantially.

C. The production department purchases new equipment that lowers manufacturing costs.

D. The firm raises prices. Quantity demanded in the short run is unaffected, but in the longer run, unit sales are expected to decline.

E. The Federal Reserve System takes actions that lower interest rates dramatically.

F. An expected increase in inflation causes generally higher interest rates, and, hence, the discount rate increases.

Q1.4 In the wake of corporate scandals at Enron, Tyco, and WorldCom, some argue that managers of large, publicly owned firms sometimes make decisions to maximize their own welfare as opposed to that of stockholders. Does such behavior create problems in using value maximization as a basis for examining managerial decision making?

Q1.5 How is the popular notion of business profit different from the economic profit concept? What role does the idea of normal profits play in this difference?

Q1.6 Which concept—the business profit concept or the economic profit concept—provides the more appropriate basis for evaluating business operations? Why?

Q1.7 Some argue that prescription drug manufacturers, like Pfizer, gouge consumers with high prices and make excessive profits. Others contend that high profits are necessary to give leading pharmaceutical companies the incentive to conduct risky research and development. What factors should be considered in examining the adequacy of profits for a firm or industry?

Q1.8 Why is the concept of enlightened self-interest important in economics?

Q1.9 "In the long run, a profit-maximizing firm would never knowingly market unsafe products. However, in the short run, unsafe products can do a lot of damage." Discuss this statement.

Q1.10 Is it reasonable to expect firms to take actions that are in the public interest but are detrimental to stockholders? Is regulation always necessary and appropriate to induce firms to act in the public interest?

CASE *Study* Is Coca-Cola the "Perfect" Business?[3]

What does a perfect business look like? For Warren Buffett and his partner Charlie Munger, vice chairman of Berkshire Hathaway, Inc., it looks a lot like Coca-Cola. To see why, imagine going back in time to 1885, to Atlanta, Georgia, and trying to invent from scratch a nonalcoholic beverage that would make you, your family, and all of your friends rich.

Your beverage would be nonalcoholic to ensure widespread appeal among both young and old alike. It would be cold rather than hot so as to provide relief from climatic effects. It must be ordered by name—a trademarked name. Nobody gets rich selling easy-to-imitate generic products. It must generate a lot of repeat business through what psychologists call conditioned reflexes. To get the desired positive conditioned reflex, you will want to make it sweet, rather than bitter, with no after-taste. Without any after-taste, consumers will be able to drink as much of

---

3   See Charles T. Munger, "How Do You Get Worldly Wisdom?" *Outstanding Investor Digest,* December 29, 1997, 24–31.

continued

your product as they like. By adding sugar to make your beverage sweet, it gains food value in addition to a positive stimulant. To get extra-powerful combinatorial effects, you may want to add caffeine as an additional stimulant. Both sugar and caffeine work; by combining them, you get more than a double effect, you get what Munger calls a "lollapalooza" effect. Additional combinatorial effects could be realized if you design the product to appear exotic. Coffee is another popular product, so making your beverage dark in color seems like a safe bet. By adding carbonation, a little fizz can be added to your beverage's appearance and its appeal.

To keep the lollapalooza effects coming, you will want to advertise. If people associate your beverage with happy times, they will tend to reach for it whenever they are happy, or want to be happy. (Isn't that always, as in "Always Coca-Cola"?) Make it available at sporting events, concerts, the beach, and at theme parks—wherever and whenever people have fun. Enclose your product in bright, upbeat colors that customers tend to associate with festive occasions (another combinatorial effect). Red and white packaging would be a good choice. Also make sure that customers associate your beverage with festive occasions. Well-timed advertising and price promotions can help in this regard—annual price promotions tied to the Fourth of July holiday, for example, would be a good idea.

To ensure enormous profits, profit margins and the rate of return on invested capital must both be high. To ensure a high rate of return on sales, the price charged must be substantially above unit costs. Because consumers tend to be least price sensitive for moderately priced items, you would like to have a modest "price point", say roughly $1 to $2 per serving. This is a big problem for most beverages because water is a key ingredient, and water is very expensive to ship long distances. To get around this cost-of-delivery difficulty, you will not want to sell the beverage itself, but a key ingredient, like syrup, to local bottlers. By selling syrup to independent bottlers, your company

can also better safeguard its "secret ingredients." This also avoids the problem of having to invest a substantial amount in bottling plants, machinery, delivery trucks, and so on. This minimizes capital requirements and boosts the rate of return on invested capital. Moreover, if you correctly price the key syrup ingredient, you can ensure that the enormous profits generated by carefully developed lollapalooza effects accrue to your company, and not to the bottlers. Of course, you want to offer independent bottlers the potential for highly satisfactory profits in order to provide the necessary incentive for them to push your product. You not only want to "leave something on the table" for the bottlers in terms of the bottlers' profit potential, but they in turn must also be encouraged to "leave something on the table" for restaurant and other customers. This means that you must demand that bottlers deliver a consistently high-quality product at carefully specified prices if they are to maintain their valuable franchise to sell your beverage in the local area.

If you had indeed gone back to 1885, to Atlanta, Georgia, and followed all of these suggestions, you would have created what you and I know as The Coca-Cola Company. To be sure, there would have been surprises along the way. Take widespread refrigeration, for example. Early on, Coca-Cola management saw the fountain business as the primary driver in cold carbonated beverage sales. They did not foretell that widespread refrigeration would make grocery store sales and in-home consumption popular. Still, much of Coca-Cola's success has been achieved because its management had, and still has, a good grasp of both the economics and the psychology of the beverage business. By getting into rapidly growing foreign markets with a winning formula, they hope to create local brand-name recognition, scale economies in distribution, and achieve other "first mover" advantages like the ones they have nurtured in the United States for more than 100 years.

As shown in Figure 1.4, in a world where the typical company earns 10 percent rates of

continued

Figure 1.4 Coca-Cola Is a Wonderful Business

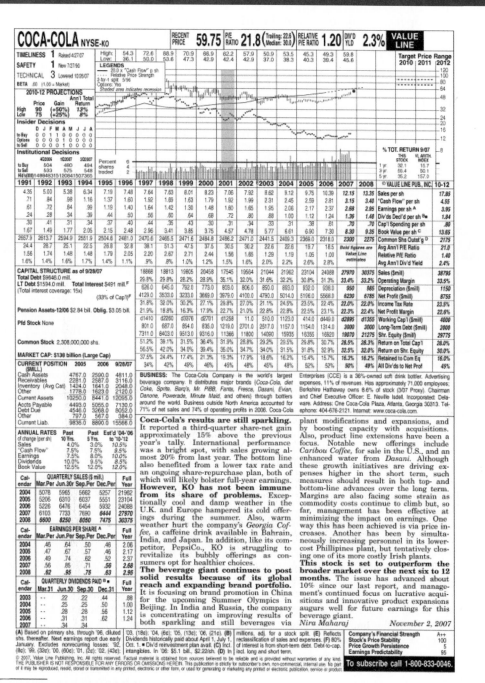

continued

return on invested capital, Coca-Cola earns three and four times as much. Typical profit rates, let alone operating losses, are unheard of at Coca-Cola. It enjoys large and growing profits, and requires practically no tangible capital investment. Almost its entire value is derived from brand equity derived from generations of advertising and carefully nurtured positive lollapalooza effects. On an overall basis, it is easy to see why Buffett and Munger regard Coca-Cola as a "perfect" business.

A. One of the most important skills to learn in managerial economics is the ability to identify a good business. Discuss at least four characteristics of a good business.

B. Identify and talk about at least four companies that you regard as having the characteristics listed here.

C. Suppose you bought common stock in each of the four companies identified here. Three years from now, how would you know if your analysis was correct? What would convince you that your analysis was wrong?

SELECTED REFERENCES

Adams, Renee B. and Daniel Ferreira. "A Theory of Friendly Boards." *Journal of Finance* 62, no. 1 (February, 2007): 217–250.

Bernheim, B. Douglas and Antonio Rangel. "Toward Choice-Theoretic Foundations for Behavioral Welfare Economics." *American Economic Review* 97, no. 2 (May, 2007): 464–470.

Bloch, Francis, Garance Genicot, and Debraj Ray. "Reciprocity in Groups and the Limits to Social Capital." *American Economic Review* 97, no. 2 (May, 2007): 65–69.

Bloom, Nick. "Uncertainty and the Dynamics of R&D." *American Economic Review* 97, no. 2 (May, 2007): 250–255.

Boone, Audra L., Laura Casares Field, Jonathan M. Karpoff, and Charu G. Raheja. "The Determinants of Corporate Board Size and Composition: An Empirical Analysis." *Journal of Financial Economics* 85, no. 1 (July, 2007): 66–101.

Bourguignon, Francois and Mark Sundberg. "Aid Effectiveness—Opening the Black Box." *American Economic Review* 97, no. 2 (May, 2007): 316–321.

Cremer, Jacques, Luis Garicano, and Andrea Prat. "Language and the Theory of the Firm." *Quarterly Journal of Economics* 122, no. 1 (February, 2007): 373–407.

Cukrowski, Jacek and Manfred M. Fischer. "Efficient Organization of Information Processing." *Managerial and Decision Economics* 28, no. 1 (January, 2007): 13–26.

Glimcher, Paul William, Joseph Kable, and Kenway Louie. "Neuroeconomic Studies of Impulsivity: Now Or just as Soon as Possible?" *American Economic Review* 97, no. 2 (May, 2007): 142–147.

Goos, Maarten and Alan Manning. "Lousy and Lovely Jobs: The Rising Polarization of Work in Britain." *Review of Economics and Statistics* 89, no. 1 (February, 2007): 118–133.

Harford, Jarrad and Kai Li. "Decoupling CEO Wealth and Firm Performance: The Case of Acquiring CEOs." *Journal of Finance* 62, no. 2 (April, 2007): 917–949.

Hart, Oliver and John Moore. "Incomplete Contracts and Ownership: Some New Thoughts." *American Economic Review* 97, no. 2 (May, 2007): 182–186.

Heron, Randall A. and Erik Lie. "Does Backdating Explain the Stock Price Pattern Around Executive Stock Option Grants?" *Journal of Financial Economics* 83, no. 2 (February, 2007): 271–295.

Hochberg, Yael V., Alexander Ljungqvist, and Yang Lu. "Whom You Know Matters: Venture Capital Networks and Investment Performance." *Journal of Finance* 62, no. 1 (February, 2007): 251–301.

Levy, Gilat. "Decision Making in Committees: Transparency, Reputation, and Voting Rules." *American Economic Review* 97, no. 1 (March, 2007): 150–168.

MacLeod W. Bentley. "Can Contract Theory Explain Social Preferences?" *American Economic Review* 97, no. 2 (May, 2007): 187–192.

Nonaka, Ikujiro. "The Knowledge-Creating Company." *Harvard Business Review* 85, no. 7, 8 (July 1, 2007): 162–171.

Rayo, Luis and Gary S. Becker. "Evolutionary Efficiency and Happiness." *Journal of Political Economy* 115, no. 2 (April, 2007): 302–337.

Robson, Arthur J. and Larry Samuelson. "The Evolution of Intertemporal Preferences." *American Economic Review* 97, no. 2 (May, 2007): 496–500.

Weinberger, David. "If You Love Your Information, Set It Free." *Harvard Business Review* 85, no. 6 (June 1, 2007): 20–21.

Economic Optimization

Managers make tough choices that involve benefits and costs. Until recently, however, it was simply impractical to compare the relative pluses and minuses of a large number of managerial decisions under a wide variety of operating conditions. For many large and small organizations, economic optimization remained an elusive goal. It is easy to understand why early users of personal computers were delighted when they learned how easy it was to enter and manipulate operating information in spreadsheets. Spreadsheets were a pivotal innovation because they put the tools for insightful demand, cost, and profit analysis at the finger tips of decision makers. Today's low-cost but powerful PCs and user-friendly software make it possible to efficiently analyze company-specific data and broader information from the Internet. It has never been easier or more vital to consider the implications of managerial decisions under an assortment of operating scenarios.

Effective managers must collect, organize, and process relevant operating information. However, efficient information processing requires more than electronic computing capability; it requires a fundamental understanding of basic economic relations. Within such a framework, powerful PCs and a wealth of operating and market information become an awesome aid to effective managerial decision making.

This chapter introduces fundamental principles of economic analysis. These ideas form the basis for describing all demand, cost, and profit relations. Once basic economic relations are understood, optimization techniques can be applied to find the best course of action.[1]

ECONOMIC OPTIMIZATION PROCESS

Effective managerial decision making is the process of arriving at the best solution to a problem.

Optimal Decisions

Should the quality of inputs be enhanced to better meet low-cost import competition? Is a necessary reduction in labor costs efficiently achieved through an across-the-board decrease in staffing, or is it better to make targeted cutbacks? Following an increase in

---

1 See Dianah Wisenberg Brin, "UnitedHealth Net Rises on Efficiency," *The Wall Street Journal Online*, October 18, 2007, http://online.wsj.com.

product demand, is it preferable to increase managerial staff, line personnel, or both? These are the types of questions facing managers on a regular basis that require a careful consideration of basic economic relations. Answers to these questions depend on the objectives and preferences of management. Just as there is no single "best" purchase decision for all customers at all times, there is no single "best" investment decision for all managers at all times. When alternative courses of action are available, the decision that produces a result most consistent with managerial objectives is the **optimal decision.**

Optimal Decision
Choice alternative
that produces
a result most
consistent with
managerial
objectives.

A challenge that must be met in the decision-making process is characterizing the desirability of decision alternatives in terms of the objectives of the organization. Decision makers must recognize all available choices and portray them in terms of appropriate costs and benefits. The description of decision alternatives is greatly enhanced through application of the principles of managerial economics. Managerial economics also provides tools for analyzing and evaluating decision alternatives. Economic concepts and methodology are used to select the optimal course of action in light of available options and objectives.

Principles of economic analysis form the basis for describing demand, cost, and profit relations. Once basic economic relations are understood, the tools and techniques of optimization can be applied to find the best course of action. Most important, the theory and process of optimization gives practical insight concerning the value maximization theory of the firm. Optimization techniques are helpful because they offer a realistic means for dealing with the complexities of goal-oriented managerial activities.

Maximizing the Value of the Firm

In managerial economics, the primary objective of management is assumed to be maximization of the value of the firm. This *value maximization* objective was introduced in Chapter 1 and is again expressed in Equation (2.1):

$$\text{Value} = \sum_{t=1}^{n} \frac{\text{Profit}_t}{(1+i)^t} = \sum_{t=1}^{n} \frac{\text{Total Revenue}_t - \text{Total Cost}_t}{(1+i)^t} \qquad \textbf{2.1}$$

Maximizing Equation (2.1) is a complex task that involves consideration of future revenues, costs, and discount rates. Total revenues are directly determined by the quantity sold and the prices obtained. Factors that affect prices and the quantity sold include the choice of products made available for sale, marketing strategies, pricing and distribution policies, competition, and the general state of the economy. Cost analysis includes a detailed examination of the prices and availability of various input factors, alternative production schedules, production methods, and so on. Finally, the relation between an appropriate discount rate and the company's mix of products and both operating and financial leverage must be determined. All these factors affect the value of the firm as described in Equation (2.1).

To determine the optimal course of action, marketing, production, and financial decisions must be integrated within a decision analysis framework. Similarly, decisions related to personnel retention and development, organization structure, and long-term business strategy must be combined into a single integrated system that shows how managerial initiatives affect all parts of the firm. The value maximization model provides an attractive basis for such integration. Using the principles of economic analysis, it is also possible to analyze and compare the higher costs or lower benefits of alternative, suboptimal courses of action.

REVENUE RELATIONS

Effective production and pricing decisions depend upon a careful understanding of revenue relations.

Price and Total Revenue

Spreadsheet
Table of electronically stored data.

Equation
Analytical expression of functional relationships.

Total Revenue
It is a function of output.

Tables are the simplest and most direct form for presenting economic data. When these data are displayed electronically in the format of an accounting income statement or balance sheet, the tables are referred to as **spreadsheets.** When the underlying relation between economic data is simple, tables and spreadsheets may be sufficient for analytical purposes. In such instances, a simple graph or visual representation of the data can provide valuable insight. Complex economic relations require more sophisticated methods of expression. An **equation** is an expression of the functional relationship or connection among economic variables.

The easiest way to examine basic economic concepts is to consider the functional relations incorporated in the basic valuation model. Consider the relation between output, Q, and **total revenue,** TR. Using functional notation, total revenue is

$$TR = f(Q) \qquad\qquad \textbf{2.2}$$

Equation (2.2) is read as, "Total revenue is a function of output." The value of the dependent variable (total revenue) is determined by the independent variable (output).

Managerial Application 2.1

The Ethics of Greed Versus Self-Interest

Capitalism is based on voluntary exchange between self-interested parties. Market-based exchange is voluntary; both parties must perceive benefits, or profit, for market transactions to take place. If only one party were to benefit from a given transaction, there would be no incentive for the other party to cooperate and no voluntary exchange would take place. A self-interested capitalist must also have in mind the interest of others. In contrast, a truly selfish individual is only concerned with himself or herself, without regard for the well-being of others. Self-interested behavior leads to profits and success under capitalism; selfish behavior does not.

Management guru Peter Drucker has written that the purpose of business is to create a customer—someone who will want to do business with you and your company on a regular basis. In a business deal, *both* parties must benefit. If not, there will be no ongoing business relationship.

The only way this can be done is to make sure that you continually take the customer's perspective. Can customer demand be met better, cheaper, or faster? Don't wait for customers to complain or seek alternate suppliers, seek out ways of helping before they become obvious. When customers benefit, so do you and your company. Take the customer's perspective, always. Similarly, it's best to see every business transaction from the standpoint of the person on the other side of the table.

In dealing with employees, it's best to be honest and forthright. If you make a mistake, admit it and go on. When management accepts responsibility for its failures, they gain the trust of employees and their help in finding solutions for the inevitable problems that always arise. In a job interview, for example, strive to see how you can create value for a potential employer. It's natural to see things from one's own viewpoint; it is typically much more beneficial to see things from the perspective of the person sitting on the other side of the table.

See: Peter Berkowitz, "Ethics 101," *The Wall Street Journal Online*, October 8, 2007, http://online.wsj.com.

The variable to the left of the equal sign is called the **dependent variable.** Its value depends on the size of the variable or variables to the right of the equal sign. Variables on the right-hand side of the equal sign are called **independent variables.** Their values are determined independently of the functional relation expressed by the equation.

Equation (2.2) does not indicate the specific relation between output and total revenue; it merely states that some relation exists. Equation (2.3) provides a more precise expression of this functional relation:

$$TR = P \times Q \qquad\qquad \textbf{2.3}$$

where P represents the price at which each unit of Q is sold. Total revenue is equal to price times the quantity sold. If price is constant at, say, $3.50 regardless of the quantity sold, the relation between quantity sold and total revenue is

$$TR = \$3.50 \times Q$$

In agricultural commodity markets, small producers are able to sell as much output as they can produce at the going price. If the going price of corn is indeed $3.50 per bushel, the total revenue derived by an individual farmer from corn sales would simply be $TR = \$3.5Q$, where Q is the number of bushels of corn produced and sold. In most instances, however, firms face a downward-sloping demand curve. This means that prices must be cut to increase the quantity sold. The following illustration shows how linear demand curves can be easily estimated, and how companies can profitably use such information.

Suppose that the quantity sold rises as price is reduced, as shown in Table 2.1. Notice that 4 units of output (in 000) are sold at a price of $18, and the quantity sold rises to 7 units per month when price is reduced to $13.50. This is enough information to allow the firm to estimate a linear demand curve for its product. When a linear demand curve is written as

$$P = a + bQ \qquad\qquad \textbf{2.4}$$

Table 2.1 Revenue and Price Relations

Quantity Sold (000 per month)	Price ($)	Total Revenue $TR = P \times Q$	Marginal Revenue $MR = \partial TR / \partial Q$
0	24.00	$0.00	—
1	22.50	22.50	22.50
2	21.00	42.00	19.50
3	19.50	58.50	16.50
4	18.00	72.00	13.50
5	16.50	82.50	10.50
6	15.00	90.00	7.50
7	13.50	94.50	−4.50
8	12.00	96.00	−1.50
9	10.50	94.50	−1.50
10	9.00	90.00	−4.50

a is the intercept and *b* is the slope coefficient. Because 4 units were sold at a price of $18, and 7 units were sold at the price of $13.50, two points on the firm's linear demand curve are identified. It is possible to identify the firm's linear demand curve by solving for the two unknowns, *a* and *b:*

$$18 = a + b(4)$$
$$\text{minus } \underline{13.5 = a + b(7)}$$
$$4.5 = -3b$$
$$b = -1.5$$

By substitution, if $b = -1.5$, then:

$$18 = a + b(4)$$
$$18 = a - 1.5(4)$$
$$18 = a - 6$$
$$a = 24$$

In this case, the firm's demand curve can be written:

$$P = \$24 - \$1.5Q$$

This functional relation between price and output, shown in Figure 2.1, implies the following relation between total revenue and the quantity sold:

$$TR = P \times Q$$
$$= (\$24 - 1.5\,Q) \times Q$$
$$= \$24Q - \$1.5Q^2$$

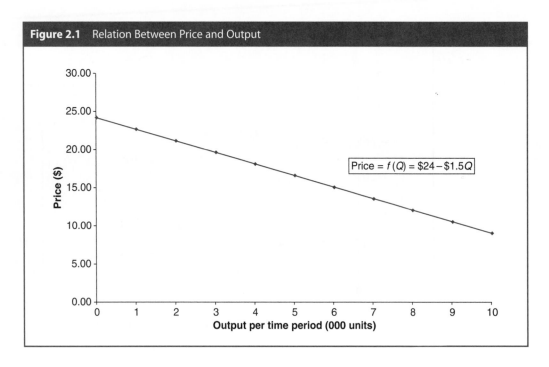

Figure 2.1   Relation Between Price and Output

Price = f(Q) = $24 − $1.5Q

Price ($)

Output per time period (000 units)

To be sure, such relations are only useful approximations within the range of price-output combinations used to derive them. For example, the firm could use such a demand curve to estimate quantity demanded during a given period for prices ranging from $24 to $9 per unit. It should not be used to estimate the number of units that might be sold at exceptionally low prices like $5, or at exceedingly high prices, like $30. The firm has no market experience at such extreme prices, and the estimated linear demand curve should not be presumed outside its range of experience.

Marginal Revenue

Precise information about the effect of a change in output on total revenue is given by the marginal relation between revenue and output. Total, average, and marginal relations are very useful in optimization analysis. Whereas the definitions of totals and averages are well known, the meaning of marginal relations needs some explanation. A marginal relation is the change in the dependent variable caused by a 1-unit change in an independent variable. **Marginal revenue** (*MR*) is the change in total revenue associated with a 1-unit change in output:

Marginal Revenue
Change in total revenue associated with a 1-unit change in output.

$$MR = \partial TR/\partial Q \qquad \qquad \textbf{2.5}$$

where the large Greek letter delta is used to express the word "change." Thus, the expression $MR = \partial TR/\partial Q$ is read as follows: "Marginal revenue is the change in total revenue caused by a 1-unit change in the number of units sold (*Q*)."

As shown in Table 2.1 and Figure 2.2, total revenue rises from $72 to $82.50 when units sold rises from 4 to 5 units. This means that marginal revenue is $10.50 over the range from 4 to 5 units. Similarly, marginal revenue is $7.50 over the range from 5 to 6 units. Notice that marginal revenue is positive so long as total revenue is increasing,

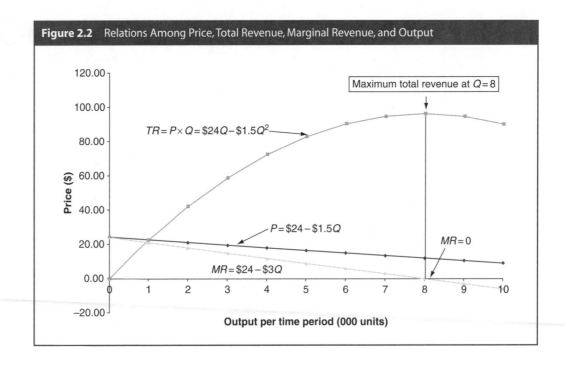

Figure 2.2   Relations Among Price, Total Revenue, Marginal Revenue, and Output

as is true over the range from 1 to 8 units sold. Notice also that total revenue begins to decrease beyond 8 units sold, where marginal revenue turns negative. In general, marginal revenue is positive when total revenue is increasing, but marginal revenue becomes negative when total revenue is decreasing.

When a linear relation exists between price and the number of units sold, a linear relation also exists between marginal revenue and units sold. In such instances, both price and marginal revenue relations begin at the same point, but marginal revenue falls twice as fast as price with respect to output. In the present example,

$$P = \$24 - \$1.5Q$$
$$TR = \$24Q - \$1.5Q^2$$
$$MR = \partial TR / \partial Q = \$24 - \$3Q$$

As shown in Table 2.1, marginal revenue is 1.50 when the number of units sold rises over the range from 7 to 8. When the number of units sold continues to rise over the range from 8 to 9, marginal revenue becomes negative, or -1.50. In general, marginal revenue shows the rate of change in total revenue that occurs with change in the number of units sold.

Revenue Maximization Example

Revenue Maximization
Activity level that generates the highest revenue, $MR = 0$.

At every output level, the marginal revenue relation can be used to precisely identify the change in total revenue that occurs with a 1-unit change in the number of units sold. **Revenue maximization** occurs at the point of greatest total revenues. For example, to find the revenue-maximizing output level, set $MR = 0$, and solve for Q:

$$MR = 0$$
$$\$24 - \$3Q = 0$$
$$3Q = 24$$
$$Q = 8$$

From this marginal revenue relation, $MR = 0$ when $Q = 8$ because $MR = \$24 - \$3(8) = 0$. When $Q = 8$, total revenue is maximized at $96 because

$$TR = \$24Q - \$1.5Q^2$$
$$= \$24(8) - \$1.5(8^2)$$
$$= \$96$$

As shown in Figure 2.2, if fewer than 8 units are sold, total revenue can be increased with an expansion in output. If more than 8 units were sold, total revenue would decline from $96 and could be increased with a reduction in volume. Only at $Q = 8$ is total revenue maximized.

In some instances, savvy firms employ a short-run revenue-maximizing strategy as part of their long-term profit maximization. Enhanced product awareness among consumers, increased customer loyalty, potential economies of scale in marketing and promotion, and possible limitations in competitor entry and growth are all potential advantages of short-term revenue maximization. To be consistent with long-run profit maximization, such advantages of short-run revenue maximization must be at least sufficient to compensate for the corresponding loss in short-run profitability.

Managerial Application 2.2

Do Firms Really Optimize?

Have you ever been at a sporting event when a particular athlete's play became the center of attention, and wondered: "Where did that woman study physics?" or "Wow, who taught that guy physiology?" Nobody asks those questions. Discussion usually centers on the players' skill, finesse, or tenacity. Natural talent must be developed through long hours of dedicated training and intense competition before one can become an accomplished athlete. But if you think about it, successful athletes must also know a great deal about angles, speed, and acceleration.

While success in sports requires that one understand the basic principles of physics and physiology, most athletes develop their "feel" for their sports on the tennis court, golf course, baseball diamond, or gridiron. Similarly, some very successful businesses are run by people with little or no formal training in accounting, finance, management, or marketing. These executives' successes testify to their ability to develop a feel for business in much the same way that the successful athlete develops a feel for his or her sport.

Although the term optimization may be foreign to such individuals, the methodology of optimization is familiar to each of them in terms of their everyday business practice. Adjusting prices to avoid stock-out situations, increasing product quality to "meet the competition," and raising salaries to retain valued employees all involve a practical understanding of optimization concepts.

The behavior of both the successful athlete and the successful executive can be described as consistent with a process of optimization. The fact that some practitioners learn managerial economics through hands-on experience rather than in the classroom doesn't diminish the value of the formal educational experience. Useful theory describes and predicts actual business decisions. The old saw, "That may be okay in theory, but it doesn't work in practice," is plainly incorrect. Economic theory is useful for one simple reason—it works.

See: Phred Dvorak, "Eureka: Inventor Finds Bottom Line Seals the Deal," *The Wall Street Journal Online*, August 20, 2007, http://online.wsj.com.

COST RELATIONS

Meeting customer demand efficiently depends upon a careful understanding of cost relations.

Cost Functions
Relations between cost and output.

Short-run Cost Functions
Cost relations when fixed costs are present; used for day-to-day operating decisions.

Long-run Cost Functions
Cost relation when all costs are variable; used for long-term planning.

Short Run
Operating period during which the availability of at least one input is fixed.

Total Cost

Proper use of relevant cost concepts requires an understanding of various relations between costs and output, or **cost functions.** Two basic cost functions are used in managerial decision making: **short-run cost functions,** used for day-to-day operating decisions, and **long-run cost functions,** used for long-term planning. In economic analysis, the **short run** is the operating period during which the availability of at least one input is fixed. In the **long run,** the firm has complete flexibility with respect to input use.

Total costs are comprised of fixed and variable expenses. **Fixed costs** do not vary with output. These costs include interest expenses, rent on leased plant and equipment, depreciation charges associated with the passage of time, property taxes, and salaries for employees not laid off during periods of reduced activity. Because all costs are variable in the long run, long-run fixed costs always equal zero. In economic analysis, the **short run** is the operating period during which the availability of at least one input is fixed. In the **long run,** the firm has complete flexibility with respect to input use. In the short run, operating decisions are typically constrained by prior capital expenditures. In the long run, no such restrictions exist. For example, a management consulting firm

Long Run
Period of complete
flexibility with
respect to input use.

Total Costs
Fixed and variable
expenses.

Fixed Costs
Expenses that
do not vary with
output.

Variable Costs
Expenses that
fluctuate with
output.

operating out of rented office space might have a short-run period as brief as a few weeks, the time remaining on the office lease. A firm in the hazardous waste disposal business has significant long-lived assets and may face a 20- to 30-year period of operating constraints. **Variable costs** fluctuate with output. Expenses for raw materials, depreciation associated with the use of equipment, the variable portion of utility charges, some labor costs, and sales commissions are all examples of variable expenses. In the short run, both variable and fixed costs are often incurred. In the long run, all costs are variable.

A sharp distinction between fixed and variable costs is neither always possible nor realistic. For example, CEO and staff salaries may be largely fixed, but during severe business downturns, even CEOs take a pay cut. Similarly, salaries for line managers and supervisors are fixed only within certain output ranges. Below a lower limit, supervisors and managers get laid off. Above an upper limit, additional supervisors and managers get hired. The longer the duration of abnormal demand, the greater the likelihood that some fixed costs will actually vary.

In equation form, total cost can be expressed as the sum of fixed and variable costs:

$$TC = FC + VC \qquad\qquad\qquad\qquad \textbf{2.6}$$

As shown in Table 2.2, total cost is the simple sum of the variable cost and fixed cost categories. With respect to the cost figures shown in Table 2.2, the fixed and variable cost categories can be expressed in equation form as

$$FC = \$8$$
$$VC = \$4Q + \$0.5Q^2$$

Notice that fixed costs are constant at $8 and do not depend upon the level of output, whereas variable costs rise with the amount of production. In this example, variable costs rise faster than output because the variable cost function is quadratic in nature; it

Table 2.2 Cost Output Relations

Quantity Sold (000 per month)	Fixed Cost ($)	Variable Cost ($)	Total Cost ($)	Marginal Cost $MC = \partial TC/\partial Q$	Average Cost $AC = TC/Q$
0	8.00	0.00	8.00	—	—
1	8.00	4.50	12.50	4.50	12.50
2	8.00	10.00	18.00	5.50	9.00
3	8.00	16.50	24.50	6.50	8.17
4	8.00	24.00	32.00	7.50	8.00
5	8.00	32.50	40.50	8.50	8.10
6	8.00	42.00	50.00	9.50	8.33
7	8.00	52.50	60.50	10.50	8.64
8	8.00	64.00	72.00	11.50	9.00
9	8.00	76.50	84.50	12.50	9.39
10	8.00	90.00	98.00	13.50	9.80

involves output squared, or Q^2, because total cost equals fixed cost plus variable cost, the total cost function can be expressed in equation form as:

$$TC = \$8 + \$4Q + \$0.5Q^2$$

Because total cost is the sum of fixed plus variable costs, and variable costs rise with output, total costs rise with the amount produced.

Marginal and Average Cost

Marginal Cost
Change in total cost associated with a 1-unit change in output.

Marginal cost is the change in total cost associated with a 1-unit change in output.

$$MC = \partial TC / \partial Q \qquad \textbf{2.7}$$

where the large Greek letter delta is again used to express the word "change." Thus, the expression $MC = \partial TC / \partial Q$ is read as follows: "Marginal cost is the change in total cost caused by a 1-unit change in the number of units produced (Q)."

As shown in Table 2.2 and Figure 2.3, total cost rises from $24.50 to $32.00 when the number of units produced rises from 3 to 4 units. This means that marginal cost is $7.50 when output rises over the range from 3 to 4 units. Similarly, marginal cost is $8.50 over the range from 4 to 5 units. Notice that marginal cost is positive and increasing over the range from 1 to 10 units produced. Marginal cost is almost always positive because almost all goods and services entail at least some labor and/or materials. It is also common for marginal costs to rise as output expands, but this in not universally true.

Average Cost
Total cost divided by the number of units produced.

Average cost (AC) is simply total cost divided by the number of units produced:

$$AC = TC / Q \qquad \textbf{2.8}$$

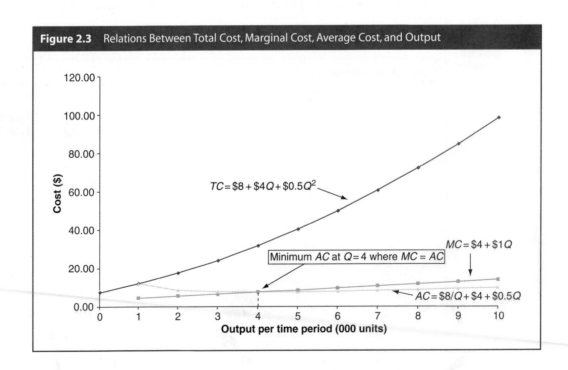

Figure 2.3 Relations Between Total Cost, Marginal Cost, Average Cost, and Output

$TC = \$8 + \$4Q + \$0.5Q^2$

Minimum AC at $Q = 4$ where $MC = AC$

$MC = \$4 + \$1Q$

$AC = \$8/Q + \$4 + \$0.5Q$

Cost ($)

Output per time period (000 units)

In Table 2.2, notice that average cost is falling when $MC < AC$. Also notice that average cost is rising when $MC > AC$. This is always true. Whenever the marginal is less than the average, the average will fall. Whenever the marginal is greater than the average, the average will rise. If the marginal is equal to the average, the average is at either a minimum or a maximum. Distinguishing maximums from minimums is easy with a simple numerical example. If $MC = AC$, and average cost falls with an expansion in output, then AC is at a maximum. If $MC = AC$, and average cost rises with an expansion in output, then AC is at a minimum.

Average Cost Minimization Example

At every output level, the relationship between marginal cost and output indicates the change in total cost that will occur with a 1-unit change in the number of units produced. Similarly, the relationship between marginal cost and average cost can be studied to determine the change in average cost that will occur with a 1-unit change in the number of units produced. For example, the total cost and marginal cost relations described by the data in Table 2.2 can be written as[2]

$$TC = \$8 + \$4Q + \$0.5Q^2$$
$$MC = \partial TC/\partial Q = \$4 + \$1Q$$

Because average cost is total cost divided by the number of units produced, the average cost relation is

$$AC = TC/Q$$
$$= (\$8 + \$4Q + \$0.5Q^2)/Q$$
$$= \$8/Q + \$4 + \$0.5Q$$

Average Cost Minimization
Activity level that generates the lowest average cost, $MC = AC$.

With **average cost minimization,** the lowest possible average cost is achieved. To find the average-cost minimizing output level, set $MC = AC$, and solve for Q:

$$MC = AC$$
$$\$4 + \$1Q = \$8/Q + \$4 + \$0.5Q$$
$$0.5Q = \frac{8}{Q}$$
$$Q^2 = \frac{8}{0.5}$$
$$Q = \sqrt{16}$$
$$= 4$$

Notice that when $Q = 4$, $MC = AC = \$8$. Moreover, from Table 2.2 and Figure 2.3 it is obvious that average cost is rising when $Q > 4$, so $Q = 4$ indicates a point of minimum (rather than maximum) average cost.

---

2   Both marginal and total cost relations can be expressed as a function of output, or inferred by inspection of underlying data, such as that contained in Table 2.2. As appropriate, both marginal and total relations will be explicitly expressed throughout this text to make easier the process of necessary manipulation. Some instructors and their students take advantage of elementary calculus to help find optimal solutions for economic problems. The appendices to this chapter illustrate how calculus concepts can be used to clarify relations among marginals, averages, and totals and the importance of these relations in the optimization process.

From a strategic point of view, the point of minimum average cost is important because it shows the level of output necessary to achieve maximum productive efficiency. In some cases, small firms find that in order to be competitive, they need to "get big, or get out" of a particular market. At the same time, it is important to recognize that average-cost minimization involves consideration of cost relations only; no revenue relations are considered in the process of minimizing average costs. To determine the profit-maximizing activity level, both revenue and cost relations must be considered.

PROFIT RELATIONS

Profit maximization involves a careful comparison of revenue and cost relations.

Total and Marginal Profit

Total Profit
Difference between total revenue and total cost.

Total profit is simply the difference between total revenue and total cost. Because the letter "P" is used to describe price, economists often use the lower case Greek letter π (read pi) to signify profit. Therefore,

$$\pi = TR - TC$$ **2.9**

Managerial Application 2.3

Market-Based Management

A native of Wichita, Kansas, Charles G. Koch received a bachelor's degree in general engineering and masters degrees in nuclear and chemical engineering from the Massachusetts Institute of Technology. Since 1967, Koch has been the chairman of the board and CEO of Koch Industries, Inc., a diverse group of companies engaged in refining and chemicals, process equipment and technologies, fibers and polymers, minerals, commodity and financial trading, and forest and consumer products. Familiar Koch brands include Dixie® cups, Georgia-Pacific®, LYCRA® spandex, Quilted Northern® tissue, and STAINMASTER® carpet. Based upon 2006 sales of over $90 billion, *Forbes* magazine calls Koch Industries the largest privately held company in the world. With enviable profit margins, Koch Industries is also one of the most successful business organizations, public or private.

The amazing success of Koch Industries can be traced to the company's development and implementation of Market-Based Management (MBM), a business philosophy that fosters principled, entrepreneurial behavior among its employees. MBM is organized and interpreted through five dimensions:

- *Vision:* Determining where and how the organization can create the greatest long-term value based upon competitive advantages.

- *Virtue and Talents:* Helping ensure that people with the right values, skills, and capabilities are hired, retained, and developed.
- *Knowledge Processes:* Creating, sharing, and applying relevant knowledge to discover how employees and practices can become more profitable.
- *Decision Rights:* Ensuring the right people are in the right roles with the right authority to make decisions and holding them accountable. Focus on comparative advantage and proven ability to create long-term value.
- *Incentives:* Rewarding people according to the value created for the organization.

In 2007, Charles Koch and his brother David ranked #9 and #10, respectively, on *Forbes* annual list of the 400 richest Americans. Sandwiched between Dell founder Michael Dell (#8) and Microsoft cofounder Paul Allen (#11), the Koch brothers are each worth an estimated $17 billion. Their business success is powerful testimony to the value of applying basic economic principles in business.

See: The Market Based Management Institute Web site is at http://mbminstitute.org/index.cfm.

Marginal Profit
Change in total profit due to a 1-unit change in output.
$M\pi = MR - MC$.

Marginal profit is the change in total profit due to a 1-unit change in output:

$$M\pi = \partial\pi/\partial Q \qquad\qquad \textbf{2.10}$$

Once again, the large Greek letter delta is used to express the word "change." Thus, the expression $M\pi = \partial\pi/\partial Q$ is read: "Marginal profit is the change in total profit caused by a 1-unit change in the number of units sold (Q)." Equivalently, marginal profit can be thought of as the difference between marginal revenue and marginal cost:

$$M\pi = MR - MC \qquad\qquad \textbf{2.11}$$

Table 2.3 combines the revenue and cost data described in Tables 2.1 and 2.2 to show how total and marginal profits vary with output (the number of units sold). When $Q = 0$, total revenue is zero, and fixed costs represent the money loss for the firm. When $Q = 0, \pi = -\$8$. Given that $M\pi > 0$, total profit rises as output expands over the range from $Q = 1$ to $Q = 5$. However, beyond $Q = 5$, the increase in total cost associated with an expansion in output exceeds the increase in total revenue, and total profit begins to decline.

Profit Maximization Rule
Profit is maximized when $M\pi = MR - MC = 0$ or $MR = MC$, assuming profit declines with further expansion in Q.

In general, total profit will rise if $M\pi > 0$. Total profit will fall whenever $M\pi < 0$. Similarly, total profit will rise so long as $MR > MC$ because that means $M\pi > 0$. Total profit will fall if $MR < MC$ because that means $M\pi < 0$. The **profit maximization rule** states that total profit will be maximized when marginal profit equals zero, provided that profit declines with a further expansion in output. In functional form, profit is maximized only if

$$M\pi = 0 \qquad\qquad \textbf{2.12}$$

and profit falls with a further increase in output. Because $M\pi = MR - MC = 0$ at the profit-maximizing activity level,

$$MR = MC \qquad\qquad \textbf{2.13}$$

Once again, profit maximization requires that profit falls with any further increase in output.

Profit Maximization Example

Table 2.3 and Figure 2.4 show the profit and marginal profit implications of the revenue relations described in Table 2.1, and the cost relations depicted in Table 2.2. In Table 2.3, notice that profit is rising over the range from $Q = 1$ to $Q = 5$ where marginal profit is positive. Profit is falling over the range from $Q = 6$ to $Q = 10$ where marginal profit is negative. Zero profits are achieved at the lower and upper **breakeven points**. In equation form, the relevant profit relation can be expressed as

Breakeven Points
Output levels with zero profit.

$$\pi = TR - TC$$
$$= \$24Q - \$1.5Q^2 - (\$8 + \$4Q + \$0.5Q^2)$$
$$= -\$8 + \$20Q - \$2Q^2$$

Table 2.3 Quantity, Revenue, Cost, and Profit Relations

Quantity Sold (000 per month)	Fixed Cost	Variable Cost ($)	Price P = $24 − $1.5Q ($)	Total Revenue TR = P × Q ($)	Marginal Revenue MR = ∂TR/∂Q	Total Cost TC = $8 + $4Q + $0.5Q² ($)	Marginal Cost MC = ∂TC/∂Q	Average Cost AC = TC/Q	Total Profit π = TR − TC ($)	Marginal Profit Mπ = MR − MC
0	8	16.00	24.00	0.00	—	8.00	—	—	−8.00	—
1	8	14.50	22.50	22.50	22.50	12.50	4.50	12.50	10.0	18.00
2	8	13.00	21.00	42.00	19.50	18.00	5.50	9.00	24.0	14.00
3	8	11.50	19.50	58.50	16.50	24.50	6.50	8.17	34.0	10.00
4	8	10.00	18.00	72.00	13.50	32.00	7.50	8.00	40.0	6.00
5	8	8.50	16.50	82.50	10.50	40.50	8.50	8.10	42.0	2.00
6	8	7.00	15.00	90.00	7.50	50.00	9.50	8.33	40.0	−2.00
7	8	5.50	13.50	94.50	−4.50	60.50	10.50	8.64	34.0	−6.00
8	8	4.00	12.00	96.00	−1.50	72.00	11.50	9.00	24.0	−10.00
9	8	2.50	10.50	94.50	−1.50	84.50	12.50	9.39	10.0	−14.00
10	8	1.00	9.00	90.00	−4.50	98.00	13.50	9.80	−8.0	−18.00

Figure 2.4 Relations Between Total Profit, Marginal Profit, and Output

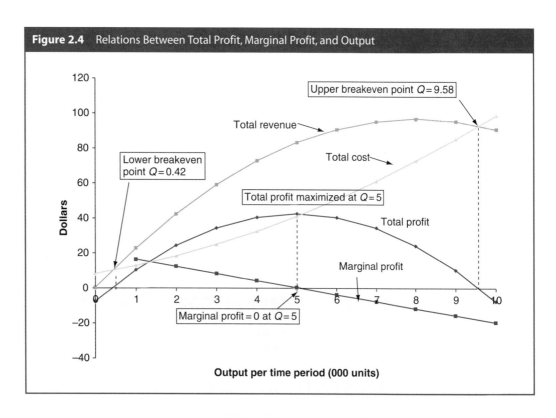

Similarly, the relevant marginal profit relation can be expressed as

$$M\pi = MR - MC$$
$$= \$24 - \$3Q - (\$4 + \$1Q)$$
$$= \$20 - \$4Q$$

At every output level, the marginal profit relation can be used to precisely identify the change in total profit that occurs with a 1-unit change in the number of units sold. To find the profit-maximizing output level, set $M\pi = 0$, and solve for Q:

$$M\pi = 0$$
$$\$20 - \$4Q = 0$$
$$4Q = 20$$
$$Q = 5$$

From this marginal profit relation, $M\pi = 0$ when $Q = 5$. Also observe that $MR = MC$ at this point bec-ause $MR = \$24 - \$3(5) = \$9$ and $MC = \$4 + \$1(5) = \$9$ when $Q = 5$. As shown in Figure 2.4, when $Q = 5$, total profit is maximized at \$42 because

$$\pi = -\$8 + \$20Q - \$2Q^2$$
$$= -\$8 + \$20(5) - \$2(5^2)$$
$$= \$42$$

If fewer than 5 units were sold, total profit could be increased with an expansion in output. If more than 5 units were sold, total profit would decline from \$42 and could be increased with a reduction in volume. Only at $Q = 5$ is total profit maximized.

At the profit-maximizing activity level, $MR = MC$ and the added amount of revenue brought in by the last unit produced (marginal revenue) is just sufficient to offset added cost (marginal cost), and profit would fall with an expansion in production. Because almost all goods and services entail the use of at least some labor and raw materials, $MC > 0$ in all but the most unusual circumstances. This fact has important implications for profit versus revenue maximization. With a downward-sloping demand curve, both price and marginal revenue decline following an increase in the number of units sold, and $MR = MC$ will occur at a lower level of activity than where $MR = 0$. The amount produced and sold at the profit-maximizing activity level will be the same as the amount produced and sold at the revenue-maximizing activity level only in the unlikely event that $MR = MC = 0$. The profit-maximizing activity level will also tend to differ from the average-cost–minimizing activity level where $MC = AC$. Recall that finding the point of lowest average costs involves a consideration of marginal cost and average cost relations only, no revenue implications are considered. The point of profit maximization can be less than, equal to, or greater than the point of average cost minimization.

INCREMENTAL CONCEPT IN ECONOMIC ANALYSIS

When economic decisions have a lumpy rather than continuous impact on output, use of the incremental concept is appropriate.

Marginal Versus Incremental Concept

It is important to recognize that marginal relations measure the effect associated with *unitary changes* in output. Many managerial decisions involve a consideration of changes that are broader in scope. For example, a manager might be interested in analyzing the potential effects on revenues, costs, and profits of a 25 percent increase in the firm's production level. Alternatively, a manager might want to analyze the profit impact of introducing an entirely new product line, or assess the cost impact of changing an entire production system. In all managerial decisions, the study of *differences* or *changes* is the key element in the selection of an optimal course of action. The marginal concept, although correct for analyzing unitary changes in output, is too narrow to provide a general methodology for evaluating all alternative courses of action.

The incremental concept is the economist's generalization of the marginal concept. Incremental analysis involves examining the impact of alternative managerial decisions or courses of action on revenues, costs, and profit. It focuses on changes or differences among available alternatives. The **incremental change** is the change resulting from a given managerial decision. For example, the incremental revenue of a new item in a firm's product line is measured as the difference between the firm's total revenue before and after the new product is introduced.

Incremental Change
Change resulting from a given managerial decision.

Incremental Profits

Incremental profit is the profit gain or loss associated with a given managerial decision. Total profit increases so long as incremental profit is positive. When incremental profit is negative, total profit declines. Similarly, incremental profit is positive (and total profit increases) if the incremental revenue associated with a decision exceeds the incremental cost. The incremental concept is so intuitively obvious that it is easy to overlook both its

Incremental Profit
Gain or loss associated with a given managerial decision.

Managerial Application 2.4

Behavioral Economics

Economic theory is built on the premise that men and women are capable of conducting the sometimes complex calculations necessary to productively seek wealth and avoid unnecessary labor. As a result, material and financial transactions among individuals and organizations reflect rational, self-interested human behavior. During the late nineteenth century, respected and highly influential economists built sophisticated mathematical models to describe "economic man," a person who acted rationally out of self-interest with complete knowledge and the desire for wealth. While the economic man concept was originally intended as a necessary abstraction from economic and human realities, the study of economics evolved during the twentieth century toward the view that actual human behavior closely parallels that of homo economicus (economic man).

Recently, a new and exciting branch of economics, called "behavioral economics," has emerged to question the descriptive and predictive capability of the economic man concept. Critics argue that utility maximization requires a complex understanding of human emotions and economic phenomena that is far beyond the cognitive ability of most economic agents. Economic decisions are thought to reflect widespread uncertainty, rather than the precise calculations of fully informed and dispassionate decision makers.

Behavioral economists argue that perfect knowledge never exists, and that all economic activity involves uncertainty and risk.

Behavioral economics differs from more traditional approaches by arguing that

- People tend to make decisions based on approximate rules of thumb (using "bounded rationality"), not fully informed rational analyses.
- The way problems are presented ("framed") affects economic decisions.
- Observed market outcomes often vary from rational expectations and market efficiency.

Some traditional economists are skeptical of the experimental and survey-based methods used by behavioral economists, and stress the importance of preferences revealed through market transactions (revealed preferences) rather than simply declared in surveys or experimental settings (stated preferences). Proponents of behavioral economics note that neoclassical models sometimes fail to predict real-world outcomes and that behavioral insight can be used to improve upon traditional approaches.

See: Ann Davis and Neil King, "Bears Smell Oil Bubble as Price Soars," *The Wall Street Journal Online*, October 19, 2007, http://online.wsj.com.

significance in managerial decision making and the potential for difficulty in correctly applying it.

For this reason, the incremental concept is sometimes violated in practice. For example, a firm may refuse to sublet excess warehouse space for $5,000 per month because it figures its cost as $7,500 per month—a price paid for a long-term lease on the facility. However, if the warehouse space represents excess capacity with no current value to the company, its historical cost of $7,500 per month is irrelevant and should be disregarded. The firm would forego $5,000 in profits by turning down the offer to sublet the excess warehouse space. Similarly, any firm that adds a standard allocated charge for fixed costs and overhead to the true incremental cost of production runs the risk of turning down profitable business.

Care must also be exercised to ensure against incorrectly assigning overly low incremental costs to a decision. Incremental decisions involve a time dimension that cannot be ignored. Not only must all current revenues and costs be considered, but any likely future revenues and costs also must be incorporated in the analysis. For example, assume that the excess warehouse space described earlier came about following a downturn in the overall economy. Also, assume that the excess warehouse space was sublet for 1 year at a price of $5,000 per month, or a total of $60,000. An incremental loss might be experienced if the firm later had to lease additional, more costly space to accommodate an unexpected increase in production. If $75,000 had to be spent to replace the sublet warehouse facility, the decision to sublet would involve an incremental loss of $15,000. To be sure, making accurate projections concerning the future pattern of revenues and costs is risky and subject to error. Nevertheless, expectations about the future cannot be ignored in incremental analysis.

Another example of the incremental concept involves measurement of the incremental revenue resulting from a new product line. Incremental revenue includes not only the revenue received from sale of a new product, but also any change in the revenues generated over the remainder of the firm's product line. Incremental revenues rise when revenues jump for related products. Similarly, if a new item takes sales away from another of the firm's products, this loss in revenue must be accounted for in measuring the incremental revenue of the new product.

Incremental Concept Example

To further illustrate the incremental concept, consider the financing decision typically associated with business plant and equipment financing. Suppose a buyer has its $100,000 purchase offer accepted by the seller of a small retail facility. The buyer must obtain financing to complete the transaction. The best rates are at a local financial institution that offers a renewable 5-year mortgage at 9 percent interest with a down payment of 20 percent, or 9.5 percent interest on a loan with only 10 percent down. In the first case, the buyer is able to finance 80 percent of the purchase price; in the second case, the buyer is able to finance 90 percent. For simplicity, assume that both loans require interest payments only during the first 5 years. After 5 years, either note could be renewable at then-current interest rates and would be restructured with monthly payments designed to amortize the loan over 20 years. An important question facing the buyer is: What is the incremental cost of additional funds borrowed when 90 percent versus 80 percent of the purchase price is financed?

Because no principal payments are required, the annual financing cost under each loan alternative can be calculated easily. The 80 percent loan requires a 20 percent down payment and has annual financing costs in dollar terms of

$$80\% \text{ Loan Financing Cost} = \text{Interest Rate} \times \text{Loan Percentage} \times \text{Purchase Price}$$
$$= 0.09 \times 0.8 \times \$100,000$$
$$= \$7,200$$

The corresponding annual financing cost for the 90 percent loan involving a 10 percent down payment is

$$90\% \text{ Loan Financing Cost} = \text{Interest Rate} \times \text{Loan Percentage} \times \text{Purchase Price}$$
$$= 0.095 \times 0.9 \times \$100,000$$
$$= \$8,550$$

To calculate the incremental cost of added funds borrowed under the 90 percent financing alternative, the borrower must compare the amount of incremental financing costs incurred with the incremental amount of funds borrowed. In dollar terms, the incremental financing cost per year is

$$\text{Incremental Financing Cost} = 90\% \text{ Loan Financing Cost} - 80\% \text{ Loan Financing Cost}$$
$$= \$8,550 - \$7,200$$
$$= \$1,350$$

These incremental financing costs must be compared to the incremental amount borrowed, where

$$\text{Incremental Amount Borrowed} = 90\% \text{ Loan Amount} - 80\% \text{ Loan Amount}$$
$$= \$90,000 - \$80,000$$
$$= \$10,000$$

In percentage terms, the incremental cost of the additional funds borrowed under the 90 percent financing alternative is

$$\text{Incremental Financing Cost Percentage} = \frac{\text{Incremental Financing Cost}}{\text{Incremental Amount Borrowed}}$$
$$= \frac{\$1,350}{\$10,000}$$
$$= 0.135 \text{ or } 13.5\%$$

The incremental cost of funds for the last $10,000 borrowed under the 90 percent financing alternative is 13.5 percent, not the 9.5 percent interest rate quoted for the entire loan. Although the high incremental cost of funds for loans that reflect relatively little down payments may be surprising to some borrowers, it is not unusual. Lenders demand high rates of interest for loans that involve substantial risk, and the chance of default is much higher when 90 percent, as opposed to 80 percent, of the purchase price is financed. When it comes to low down payment mortgages, both borrowers and lenders need to beware!

The incremental concept is important for managerial decisions because it focuses attention on relevant differences among available alternatives. Revenues and costs unaffected by a given choice are irrelevant to that decision and should be ignored in the analysis.

SUMMARY

Effective managerial decision making is the process of finding the best solution to a given problem. Both the methodology and tools of managerial economics play an important role in this process.

- The decision alternative that produces a result most consistent with managerial objectives is the **optimal decision.**

- Tables are the simplest and most direct form for presenting economic data. When these data are displayed electronically in the format of an accounting income statement or balance sheet, the tables are referred to as **spreadsheets.**

- An **equation** is an expression of the functional relationship or connection among economic variables. For example, **total revenue** (sales) is a function of output. The value of the **dependent variable** (total revenue) is determined by the independent variable (output). The variable to the left of the equal sign is called the dependent variable. Its value depends on the size of the variable or variables to the right of the equal sign. Variables on the right-hand side of the equal sign are called **independent variables.** Their values are determined independently of the functional relation expressed by the equation.

- **Marginal revenue** is the change in total revenue associated with a 1-unit change in output. **Revenue maximization** occurs at the output level that generates the greatest total revenue. To find the revenue-maximizing output level, set $MR = 0$, and solve for Q.

- Proper use of relevant cost concepts requires an understanding of various relations between costs and output, or **cost functions.** Two basic cost functions are used in managerial decision making: **short-run cost functions,** used for day-to-day operating decisions, and **long-run cost functions,** used for long-term planning. In economic analysis, the **short run** is the operating period during which the availability of at least one input is fixed. In the **long run,** the firm has complete flexibility with respect to input use.

- **Total costs** are comprised of fixed and variable expenses. **Fixed costs** do not vary with output. **Variable costs** fluctuate with output. In the short run, both variable and fixed costs are often incurred. In the long run, all costs are variable.

- **Marginal cost** is the change in total cost associated with a 1-unit change in output. **Average cost** is simply total cost divided by the number of units

produced. The lowest possible average cost is achieved at the point of **average cost minimization.** To find the average-cost–minimizing output level, set $MC = AC$, and solve for Q.

- **Total profit** is simply the difference between total revenue and total cost. **Marginal profit** is the change in total profit due to a 1-unit change in output. Equivalently, marginal profit can be thought of as the difference between marginal revenue and marginal cost, $M\pi = MR - MC$. Total profit will rise if $M\pi > 0$. Total profit will fall whenever $M\pi < 0$. The **profit maximization rule** states that total profit will be maximized when $M\pi = 0$. Because $M\pi = MR - MC = 0$ at the profit-maximizing activity level, $MR = MC$. Zero profits are achieved at the lower and upper **breakeven points.**

- When economic decisions have a lumpy rather than continuous impact on output, use of the incremental concept is appropriate. The **incremental change** is the change resulting from a given managerial decision. **Incremental profit** is the profit gain or loss associated with a given managerial decision. The incremental concept focuses attention on relevant differences among available alternatives. Revenues and costs unaffected by a given choice are irrelevant to that decision and should be ignored.

Each of these concepts is fruitfully applied in the practical analysis of managerial decision problems. As seen in later chapters, economic analysis provides the underlying framework for the study of all profit, revenue, and cost relations.

QUESTIONS

Q2.1 In 2007, Chrysler Group said it would cut 13,000 jobs, close a major assembly plant, and reduce production at other plants as part of a restructuring effort designed to restore profitability at the auto maker by 2008. Its German parent, DaimlerChrysler, said it is looking into further strategic options with partners to optimize and accelerate the plan as it seeks the best solutions for its struggling U.S. unit. Does this decision reflect an application of the global or partial optimization concept? Explain.

Q2.2 "The personal computer is a calculating device and a communicating device. Spreadsheets incorporate

the best of both characteristics by allowing managers to determine and communicate the optimal course of action." Discuss this statement and explain why computer spreadsheets are a popular means for expressing and analyzing economic relations.

Q2.3 For those 50 or older, membership in AARP, formerly known as the American Association of Retired Persons, brings numerous discounts for health insurance, hotels, auto rentals, shopping, travel planning, and so on. Use the marginal profit concept to explain why vendors seek out bargain-priced business with AARP members.

Q2.4 If a baseball player hits .285 during a given season, the player's lifetime batting average of .278 will rise. Use this observation to explain why the marginal cost curve always intersects the related average cost curve at either a maximum or a minimum point.

Q2.5 Southwest Airlines is known for offering cut-rate promotional fares to build customer awareness, increase market share, and boost revenues in new markets. Would you expect total revenue to be maximized at an output level that is typically greater than or less than the short-run profit-maximizing output level? Is such an approach incompatible with long-run profit maximization?

Q2.6 Intel Corp. designs, develops, manufactures, and sells integrated circuit solutions for wireless data and personal computer (PC) applications. The company is expanding rapidly to achieve hoped-for reductions in average costs as output expands. Does the point of minimum long-run average costs always represent the optimal activity level?

Q2.7 McDonald's restaurants do the bulk of their business at lunchtime, but have found that promotionally priced meals at breakfast and dinner make a significant profit contribution. Does the success of McDonald's restaurants in this regard reflect an effective application of the marginal profit concept or the incremental profit concept? Explain.

Q2.8 Economists have long argued that if you want to tax away excess profits without affecting allocative efficiency, you should use a lump-sum tax instead of an excise or sales tax. Use the concepts developed in the chapter to support this position.

Q2.9 "It is often impossible to obtain precise information about the pattern of future revenues, costs, and interest rates. Therefore, the process of economic optimization is futile." Discuss this statement.

Q2.10 In estimating regulatory benefits, the Environmental Protection Agency (EPA) and other government agencies typically assign a value of approximately $6 million to each life saved. What factors might the EPA consider in arriving at such a valuation? How would you respond to criticism directed at the EPA that life is precious and cannot be valued in dollar terms?

SELF-TEST PROBLEMS AND SOLUTIONS

ST2.1 Profit versus Revenue Maximization. Presto Products, Inc., recently introduced an innovative new frozen dessert maker with the following revenue and cost relations:

$$P = \$60 - \$0.005Q \qquad\qquad TC = \$88,000 + \$5Q + \$0.0005Q^2$$
$$MR = \partial TR/\partial Q = \$60 - \$0.01Q \qquad\qquad MC = \partial TC/\partial Q = \$5 + \$0.001Q$$

A. Set up a spreadsheet for output (Q), price (P), total revenue (TR), marginal revenue (MR), total cost (TC), marginal cost (MC), total profit (π), and marginal profit ($M\pi$). Establish a range for Q from 0 to 10,000 in increments of 1,000 (i.e., 0, 1,000, 2,000, …, 10,000).

B. Use the spreadsheet to create a graph with TR, TC, and π as dependent variables, and units of output (Q) as the independent variable. At what price–output combination is total profit maximized? At what price–output combination is total revenue maximized?

C. Determine these profit-maximizing and revenue-maximizing price–output combinations analytically. In other words, use the profit and revenue equations to confirm your answers to part B.

D. Compare the profit-maximizing and revenue-maximizing price–output combinations, and discuss any differences. When will short-run revenue maximization lead to long-run profit maximization?

ST2.1 SOLUTION

A. A table or spreadsheet for Presto output (Q), price (P), total revenue (TR), marginal revenue (MR), total cost (TC), marginal cost (MC), total profit (π), and marginal profit ($M\pi$) appears as follows:

| | | | | **Presto Products** | | | |
Units of Output ($)	Price ($)	Total Revenue ($)	Marginal Revenue ($)	Total Cost ($)	Marginal Cost ($)	Total Profit ($)	Marginal Profit ($)
0	60	0	60	88,000	5	−88,000	55
1,000	55	55,000	50	93,500	6	−38,500	44
2,000	50	100,000	40	100,000	7	0	33
3,000	45	135,000	30	107,500	8	27,500	22
4,000	40	160,000	20	116,000	9	44,000	11
5,000	35	175,000	10	125,500	10	49,500	0
6,000	30	180,000	0	136,000	11	44,000	−11
7,000	25	175,000	−10	147,500	12	27,500	−22
8,000	20	160,000	−20	160,000	13	0	−33
9,000	15	135,000	−30	173,500	14	−38,500	−44
10,000	10	100,000	−40	188,000	15	−88,000	−55

B. The price–output combination at which total profit is maximized is $P = \$35$ and $Q = 5,000$ units. At that point, $MR = MC$ and total profit is maximized at \$49,500. The price–output combination at which total revenue is maximized is $P = \$30$ and $Q = 6,000$ units. At that point, $MR = 0$ and total revenue is maximized at \$180,000. Using the Presto table or spreadsheet, a graph with TR, TC, and π as dependent variables, and units of output (Q) as the independent variable appears as follows:

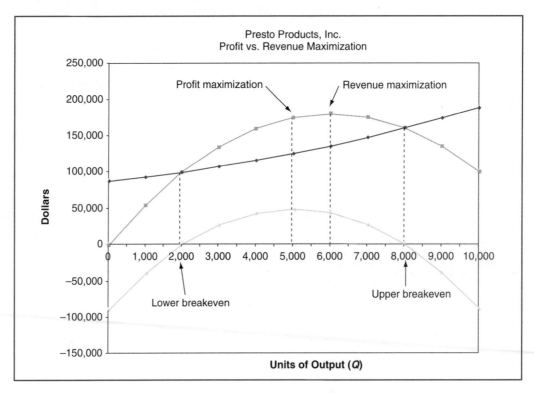

C. To find the profit-maximizing output level analytically, set $M\pi = MR - MC = 0$ or $MR = MC$, and solve for Q. Because

$$MR = MC$$
$$\$60 - \$0.01Q = \$5 + \$0.001Q$$
$$0.011Q = 55$$
$$Q = 5,000$$

At $Q = 5,000$,

$$P = \$60 - \$0.005(5,000)$$
$$= \$35$$
$$\pi = -\$188,000 + \$55(5,000) - \$0.0055(5,000^2)$$
$$= \$49,500$$

This is a profit maximum because total profit is falling for $Q > 5,000$. To find the revenue-maximizing output level, set $MR = 0$, and solve for Q. Thus,

$$MR = \$60 - \$0.01Q = 0$$
$$0.01Q = 60$$
$$Q = 6,000$$

At $Q = 6,000$,

$$P = \$60 - \$0.005(6,000)$$
$$= \$30$$
$$\pi = TR - TC$$
$$= (\$60 - \$0.005Q)Q - \$88,000 - \$5Q - \$0.0005Q^2$$
$$= -\$88,000 + \$55Q - \$0.0055Q^2$$
$$= -\$88,000 + \$55(6,000) - \$0.0055(6,000^2)$$
$$= \$44,000$$

This is a revenue maximum because total revenue is decreasing for output beyond $Q > 6,000$.

D. Given downward-sloping demand and marginal revenue curves and positive marginal costs, the profit-maximizing price–output combination is *always* at a higher price and lower production level than the revenue-maximizing price-output combination. This stems from the fact that profit is maximized when $MR = MC$, whereas revenue is maximized when $MR = 0$. It follows that profits and revenue are only maximized at the same price–output combination in the unlikely event that $MC = 0$.

In pursuing a short-run revenue rather than profit-maximizing strategy, Presto can expect to gain a number of important advantages, including enhanced product awareness among consumers, increased customer loyalty, potential economies of scale in marketing and promotion, and possible limitations in competitor entry and growth. To be consistent with long-run profit maximization, these advantages of short-run revenue maximization must be at least worth Presto's short-run sacrifice of $5,500 ($= \$49,500 - \$44,000$) in monthly profits.

ST2.2 Average-Cost Minimization. Pharmed Caplets is an antibiotic product with monthly revenues and costs of

$$TR = \$900Q - \$0.1Q^2 \qquad\qquad TC = \$36,000 + \$200Q + \$0.4Q^2$$
$$MR = \partial TR / \partial Q = \$900 - \$0.2Q \qquad MC = \partial TC / \partial Q = \$200 + \$0.8Q$$

A. Set up a spreadsheet for output (Q), price (P), total revenue (TR), marginal revenue (MR), total cost (TC), marginal cost (MC), average cost (AC), total profit (π), and marginal profit ($M\pi$). Establish a range for Q from 0 to 1,000 in increments of 100 (i.e., 0, 100, 200, ..., 1,000).

B. Using the spreadsheet, create a graph with MR, MC, and AC as dependent variables and units of output (Q) as the independent variable. At what price–output combination is total profit maximized? Why? At what price–output combination is average cost minimized? Why?

C. Determine these profit-maximizing and average-cost–minimizing price–output combinations analytically. In other words, use revenue and cost equations to confirm your answers to part B.

D. Compare the profit-maximizing and average-cost–minimizing price–output combinations, and discuss any differences. When will average-cost minimization lead to long-run profit maximization?

ST2.2 SOLUTION

A. A table or spreadsheet for output (Q), price (P), total revenue (TR), marginal revenue (MR), total cost (TC), marginal cost (MC), average cost (AC), total profit (π), and marginal profit ($M\pi$) appears as follows:

Units of Output	Price ($)	Total Revenue ($)	Marginal Revenue ($)	Total Cost ($)	Marginal Cost ($)	Average Cost	Total Profit ($)	Marginal Profit ($)
0	900	0	900	36,000	200	—	$36,000	700
100	890	89,000	880	60,000	280	600.00	29,000	600
200	880	176,000	860	92,000	360	460.00	84,000	500
300	870	261,000	840	132,000	440	440.00	129,000	400
400	860	344,000	820	180,000	520	450.00	164,000	300
500	850	425,000	800	236,000	600	472.00	189,000	200
600	840	504,000	780	300,000	680	500.00	204,000	100
700	830	581,000	760	372,000	760	531.43	209,000	0
800	820	656,000	740	452,000	840	565.00	204,000	−100
900	810	729,000	720	540,000	920	600.00	189,000	−200
1,000	800	800,000	700	636,000	1,000	636.00	164,000	−300

B. The price–output combination at which total profit is maximized is $P = \$830$ and $Q = 700$ units. At that point, $MR = MC$ and total profit is maximized at $209,000. The price–output combination at which average cost is minimized is $P = \$870$ and $Q = 300$ units. At that point, $MC = AC = \$440$. Using the spreadsheet, a graph with AC and MC as dependent variables and units of output (Q) as the independent variable appears as follows:

C. To find the profit-maximizing output level analytically, set $M\pi = MR - MC = 0$ or $MR = MC$, and solve for Q:

$$MR = MC$$
$$\$900 - \$0.2 = \$200 + \$0.8Q$$
$$Q = 700$$

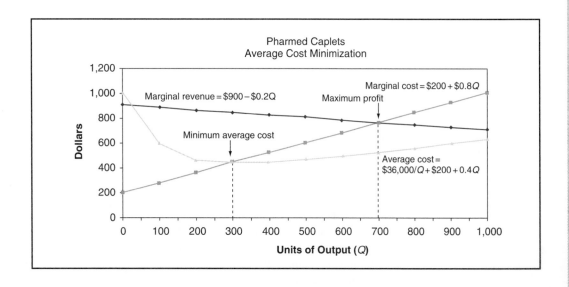

At $Q = 700$,

$$P = TR/Q$$
$$= (\$900Q - \$0.1Q^2)/Q$$
$$= \$900 - \$0.1(700)$$
$$= \$830$$
$$\pi = TR - TC$$
$$= \$900Q - \$0.1Q^2 - \$36,000 - \$200Q - \$0.4Q^2$$
$$= -\$36,000 + \$700(700) - \$0.5(700^2)$$
$$= \$209,000$$

This is a profit maximum because profits are falling for $Q > 700$.

To find the average-cost–minimizing output level, set $MC = AC$, and solve for Q:

$$AC = TC/Q$$
$$= (\$36,000 + \$200Q + \$0.4Q^2)/Q$$
$$= \$36,000Q^{-1} + \$200 + \$0.4Q$$

It follows that:

$$MC = AC$$
$$\$200 + \$0.8Q = \$36,000Q^{-1} + \$200 + \$0.4Q$$
$$0.4Q = 36,000Q^{-1}$$
$$0.4Q^2 = 36,000$$
$$Q^2 = 36,000/0.4$$
$$Q^2 = 90,000$$
$$Q = 300$$

At $Q = 300$,

$$P = \$900 - \$0.1(300)$$
$$= \$870$$
$$\pi = -\$36,000 + \$700(300) - \$0.5(300^2)$$
$$= \$129,000$$

This is an average-cost minimum because average cost is rising for $Q > 300$.

D. Given downward-sloping demand and marginal revenue curves and a U-shaped (or quadratic) AC function, the profit-maximizing price–output combination will *often* be at a different price and production level than the average-cost–minimizing price-output combination. This stems from the fact that profit is maximized when $MR = MC$, whereas average cost is minimized when $MC = AC$. Profits are maximized at the same price–output combination as where average costs are minimized in the unlikely event that $MR = MC$ and $MC = AC$ and, therefore, $MR = MC = AC$.

It is often true that the profit-maximizing output level differs from the average cost-minimizing activity level. In this instance, expansion beyond $Q = 300$, the average-cost–minimizing activity level, can be justified because the added gain in revenue more than compensates for the added costs. Note that total costs rise by \$240,000, from \$132,000 to \$372,000 as output expands from $Q = 300$ to $Q = 700$, as average cost rises from \$440 to \$531.43. Nevertheless, profits rise by \$80,000, from \$129,000 to \$209,000, because total revenue rises by \$320,000, from \$261,000 to \$581,000. The profit-maximizing activity level can be less than, greater than, or equal to the average-cost–minimizing activity level depending on the shape of relevant demand and cost relations.

PROBLEMS

P2.1 Graphic Analysis

A. Given the output (Q) and price (P) data in the following table, calculate total revenue (TR) and marginal revenue (MR):

Q	P	$TR = P \times Q$	$MR = \partial TR / \partial Q$
0	\$10		
1	9		
2	8		
3	7		
4	6		
5	5		
6	4		
7	3		
8	2		
9	1		
10	0		

B. Graph these data using "dollars" on the vertical axis and "quantity" on the horizontal axis. At what output level is revenue maximized?

C. Why is marginal revenue less than average revenue at each price level?

P2.2

A. Fill in the missing data for price (*P*), total revenue (*TR*), marginal revenue (*MR*), total cost (*TC*), marginal cost (*MC*), profit (π), and marginal profit (*M*π) in the following table:

Q	P ($)	TR = P × Q ($)	MR = ∂TR/ ∂Q ($)	TC ($)	MC = ∂TC/ ∂Q ($)	π ($)	Mπ = ∂π/ ∂Q ($)
0	160	0	—	0	0	0	—
1	150	150	150	25	25	125	125
2	140			55	30		100
3		390			35	300	75
4			90	130		350	
5	110	550		175			
6		600	50		55	370	
7		630		290	60		−30
8	80	640		355		285	
9					75		−85
10		600		525			

B. At what output level is profit maximized?

C. At what output level is revenue maximized?

D. Discuss any differences in your answers to parts B and C.

P2.3 Marginal Analysis. Characterize each of the following statements as true or false, and explain your answer.

A. If marginal revenue is less than average revenue, the demand curve will be downward sloping.

B. Profits will be maximized when total revenue equals total cost.

C. Given a downward-sloping demand curve and positive marginal costs, profit-maximizing firms will always sell less output at higher prices than will revenue-maximizing firms.

D. Marginal cost must be falling for average cost to decline as output expands.

E. Marginal profit is the difference between marginal revenue and marginal cost and will always equal zero at the profit-maximizing activity level.

P2.4 Marginal Analysis: Tables. Meredith Grey is a regional sales representative for Dental Laboratories, Inc., a company that sells alloys created from gold, silver, platinum, and other precious metals to several dental laboratories in Washington, Oregon, and Idaho. Grey's goal is

to maximize total monthly commission income, which is figured at 8 percent of gross sales. In reviewing monthly experience over the past year, Grey found the following relations between days spent in each state and monthly sales generated:

Washington		Oregon		Idaho	
Days	Gross Sales ($)	Days	Gross Sales ($)	Days	Gross Sales ($)
0	$10,000	0	$0	0	$6,250
1	25,000	1	8,750	1	12,500
2	37,500	2	16,250	2	17,500
3	47,500	3	22,500	3	21,250
4	55,000	4	26,250	4	23,750
5	60,000	5	28,750	5	25,000
6	62,500	6	30,000	6	25,000
7	62,500	7	31,250	7	25,000

A. Construct a table showing Grey's marginal sales per day in each state.

B. If administrative duties limit Grey to only 10 selling days per month, how should they be spent to maximize commission income?

C. Calculate Grey's maximum monthly commission income.

P2.5 Marginal Analysis: Tables. Climate Control Devices, Inc., estimates that sales of defective thermostats cost the firm $50 each for replacement or repair. Boone Carlyle, an independent engineering consultant, has recommended hiring quality control inspectors so that defective thermostats can be identified and corrected before shipping. The following schedule shows the expected relation between the number of quality control inspectors and the thermostat failure rate, defined in terms of the percentage of total shipments that prove to be defective.

Number of Quality Control Inspectors	Thermostat Failure Rate (%)
0	5.0
1	4.0
2	3.2
3	2.6
4	2.2
5	2.0

The firm expects to ship 250,000 thermostats during the coming year, and quality control inspectors each command a salary of $60,000 per year.

A. Construct a table showing the marginal failure reduction (in units) and the dollar value of these reductions for each inspector hired.

B. How many inspectors should the firm hire?

C. How many inspectors should be hired if additional indirect costs (lost customer goodwill and so on) were to average 30 percent of direct replacement or repair costs?

P2.6 Price and Total Revenue. The Portland Sea Dogs, the AA affiliate of the Boston Red Sox major league baseball team, have enjoyed a surge in popularity. During a recent home stand, suppose the club offered $5 off the $12 regular price of reserved seats, and sales spurted from 3,200 to 5,200 tickets per game.

A. Derive the function that describes the price–output relation with price expressed as a function of quantity (tickets sold). Also express tickets sold as a function of price.

B. Use the information derived in part A to calculate total revenues at prices in $1 increments from $5 to $15 per ticket. What is the revenue-maximizing ticket price? If variable costs are negligible, is this amount also the profit-maximizing ticket price?

P2.7 Profit Maximization: Equations. 21st Century Insurance offers mail-order automobile insurance to preferred-risk drivers in the Los Angeles area. The company is the low-cost provider of insurance in this market but doesn't believe its annual premium of $1,500 can be raised for competitive reasons. Rates are expected to remain stable during coming periods; hence, $P = MR =$ $1,500. Total and marginal cost relations for the company are as follows:

$$TC = \$41,000,000 + \$500Q + \$0.005Q^2$$
$$MC = \partial TC/\partial Q = \$500 + \$0.01Q$$

A. Calculate the profit-maximizing activity level.

B. Calculate the company's optimal profit, and optimal profit as a percentage of sales revenue (profit margin).

P2.8 Not-for-Profit Analysis. The Denver Athlete's Club (DAC) is a private, not-for-profit athletic club located in Denver, Colorado. DAC currently has 3,500 members but is planning on a membership drive to increase this number significantly. An important issue facing John Blutarsky, DAC's administrative director, is the determination of an appropriate membership level. In order to efficiently employ scarce DAC resources, the board of directors has instructed Blutarsky to maximize DAC's operating surplus, defined as revenues minus operating costs. They have also asked Blutarsky to determine the effects of a proposed agreement between DAC and a neighboring club with outdoor recreation and swimming pool facilities. Plan A involves paying the neighboring club $100 per DAC member. Plan B involves payment of a fixed fee of $400,000 per year. Finally, the board has determined that the basic membership fee for the coming year will remain constant at $2,500 per member irrespective of the number of new members added and whether plan A or plan B is adopted.

In the calculations for determining an optimal membership level, Blutarsky regards price as fixed; therefore, $P = MR =$ $2,500. Before considering the effects of any agreement with the neighboring club, Blutarsky projects total and marginal cost relations during the coming year to be as follows:

$$TC = \$3,500,000 + \$500Q + \$0.25Q^2$$
$$MC = \partial TC/\partial Q = \$500 + \$0.5Q$$

where Q is the number of DAC members.

A. Before considering the effects of the proposed agreement with the neighboring club, calculate DAC's optimal membership and operating surplus levels.

B. Calculate these levels under plan A.

C. Calculate these levels under plan B.

P2.9 Average Cost Minimization.   Giant Screen TV, Inc., is a Miami-based importer and distributor of 60-inch screen HDTVs for residential and commercial customers. Revenue and cost relations are as follows:

$$TR = \$1,800Q - \$0.006Q^2$$
$$MR = \partial TF/\partial Q = \$1,800 - \$0.012Q$$
$$TC = \$12,100,000 + \$800Q + \$0.004Q^2$$
$$MC = \partial TC/\partial Q = \$800 + \$0.008Q$$

A. Calculate output, marginal cost, average cost, price, and profit at the average cost-minimizing activity level.

B. Calculate these values at the profit-maximizing activity level.

C. Compare and discuss your answers to parts A and B.

P2.10 Incremental Analysis.   Founded in 1985, Starbucks Corporation offers brewed coffees, espresso beverages, cold blended beverages, various complementary food items, and related products at over 12,000 retail outlets in the United States Canada, the United Kingdom, Thailand, Australia, Germany, China, Singapore, Puerto Rico, Chile, and Ireland. Over 100 outlets are featured in the Greater Chicago Land area alone. For a new unit in Chicago's O'Hare Airport, suppose beverage customers spend an average $4 on beverages with an 80 percent gross margin, and food customers spend an average $5 on sandwiches and salads with a 50 percent gross margin. In both cases, gross margin is simply price minus input cost and does not reflect variable labor and related expenses. Customer traffic throughout the day is as follows:

Hour of Day	Beverage Customers	Food Customers	Profit Contribution ($)
06:00	150	50	605.00
07:00	250	100	1,050.00
08:00	200	75	827.50
09:00	175	50	685.00
10:00	100	25	382.50
11:00	200	75	827.50
12:00	200	175	1,077.50
13:00	125	150	775.00
14:00	75	75	427.50
15:00	50	50	285.00
16:00	100	25	382.50
17:00	75	50	365.00
18:00	50	75	347.50
19:00	50	25	222.50
20:00	25	25	142.50
21:00	25	10	105.00
22:00	25	10	105.00
Total	1,875	1,045	8,612.50

A. Assume labor, electricity, and other incremental costs are $175 per hour of operation; calculate the profit-maximizing hours of operation per day.

B. Assume the store is open 365 days per year, and that incremental rental costs are $2 million per year. Calculate optimal incremental profits. Should Starbucks close this site?

CASE *Study*

Spreadsheet Analysis of the EOQ at the Neighborhood Pharmacy, Inc.

A spreadsheet is a table of data organized in a logical framework similar to an accounting income statement or balance sheet. At first, this marriage of computers and accounting information might seem like a minor innovation. However, it is not. For example, with computerized spreadsheets it becomes possible to easily reflect the effects on revenue, cost, and profit of a slight change in demand conditions. Similarly, the effects on the profit-maximizing or breakeven activity levels can be easily determined. Various "what if?" scenarios can also be tested to determine the optimal or profit-maximizing activity level under a wide variety of operating conditions. Thus, it becomes easy to quantify in dollar terms the pluses and minuses (revenues and costs) of alternate decisions. Each operating and planning decision can be easily evaluated in light of available alternatives. Through the use of spreadsheet formulas and so-called "macros," managers are able to locate maximum or minimum values for any objective function, based on the relevant marginal relations. Therefore, spreadsheets are a very useful tool that can be employed to analyze a variety of typical optimization problems.

To illustrate the use of spreadsheets in economic analysis, consider the hypothetical case of The Neighborhood Pharmacy, Inc. (NPI), a small but rapidly growing operator of a number of large-scale discount pharmacies in the greater Boston, Massachusetts, metropolitan area. A key contributor to the overall success of the company is a system of tight controls over inventory acquisition and carrying costs. The company's total annual costs for acquisition and inventory of pharmaceutical items are composed of the purchase cost of individual products supplied by wholesalers (purchase costs); the clerical, transportation, and other costs associated with placing each individual order (order costs); and the interest, insurance, and other expenses involved with carrying inventory (carrying costs). The company's total inventory-related costs are given by the expression

$$TC = P \times X + \Theta \times X/Q + C \times Q/2$$

where TC is inventory-related total costs during the planning period, P is the purchase price of the inventory item, X is the total quantity of the inventory item that is to be ordered (used) during the planning period (use requirement), Θ is the cost of placing an individual order for the inventory item (order cost), C is inventory carrying costs expressed on a per unit of inventory basis (carrying cost), and Q is the quantity of inventory ordered at any one point in time (order quantity). Here Q is NPI's decision variable, whereas every other variable contained in the total cost function is beyond control of the firm (exogenous). In analyzing this total cost relation, NPI is concerned with picking the order quantity that will minimize total inventory-related costs. The optimal- or total-cost–minimizing order quantity is typically referred to as the "economic order quantity."

During the relevant planning period, the per unit purchase cost for an important prescribed (ethical) drug is $P = \$4$, the total estimated use for the planning period is $X = 5{,}000$, the cost of placing an order is $\Theta = \$50$, and the per unit carrying cost is $C = \$0.50$, calculated as the current interest rate of 12.5 percent multiplied by the per unit purchase cost of the item.

continued

A. Set up a table or spreadsheet for NPI's order quantity (Q), inventory-related total cost (TC), purchase price (P), use requirement (X), order cost (Θ), and carrying cost (C). Establish a range for Q from 0 to 2,000 in increments of 100 (i.e., 0, 100, 200, …, 2,000).

B. Based on the NPI table or spreadsheet, determine the order quantity that will minimize the company's inventory-related total costs during the planning period.

C. Placing inventory-related total costs, TC, on the vertical or Y-axis and the order quantity, Q, on the horizontal or X-axis, plot the relation between inventory-related total costs and the order quantity.

SELECTED REFERENCES

Bandiera, Oriana, Iwan Barankay, and Imran Rasul. "Incentives for Managers and Inequality Among Workers: Evidence from a Firm-Level Experiment." *Quarterly Journal of Economics* 122, no. 2 (May, 2007): 729–773.

Brunnermeier, Markus K., Christian Gollier, and Jonathan A. Parker. "Optimal Beliefs, Asset Prices, and the Preference for Skewed Returns." *American Economic Review* 97, no. 2 (May, 2007): 159–165.

Butler, David J. and Graham C. Loomes. "Imprecision as an Account of the Preference Reversal Phenomenon." *American Economic Review* 97, no. 1 (March, 2007): 277–297.

Caplin, Andrew and Mark Dean. "The Neuroeconomic Theory of Learning." *American Economic Review* 97, no. 2 (May, 2007): 148–152.

Desai, Mihir A., Alexander Dyck, and Luigi Zingales. "Theft and Taxes." *Journal of Financial Economics* 84, no. 3 (June, 2007): 591–623.

Dynan, Karen E. and Enrichetta Ravina. "Increasing Income Inequality, External Habits, and Self-Reported Happiness." *American Economic Review* 97, no. 2 (May, 2007): 226–231.

Easterly, William. "Was Development Assistance a Mistake?" *American Economic Review* 97, no. 2 (May, 2007): 328–332.

Fehr, Ernst and Lorenz Goette. "Do Workers Work More if Wages Are High? Evidence from a Randomized Field Experiment." *American Economic Review* 97, no. 1 (March, 2007): 298–317.

Fehr, Ernst and Klaus M. Schmidt. "Adding a Stick to the Carrot? The Interaction of Bonuses and Fines." *American Economic Review* 97, no. 2 (May, 2007): 177–181.

Ferreira, Miguel A. and Paul A. Laux. "Corporate Governance, Idiosyncratic Risk, and Information Flow." *Journal of Finance* 62, no. 2 (April, 2007): 951–989.

Geweke, John. "Bayesian Model Comparison and Validation." *American Economic Review* 97, no. 2 (May, 2007): 60–64.

Golosov, Mikhail and Aleh Tsyvinski. "Optimal Taxation with Endogenous Insurance Markets." *Quarterly Journal of Economics* 122, no. 2 (May, 2007): 487–534.

Gomes, Orlando. "Investment in Organizational Capital." *Managerial and Decision Economics* 28, no. 2 (March, 2007): 107–113.

Mintzberg, Henry. "Productivity Is Killing American Enterprise." *Harvard Business Review* 85, no. 7, 8 (July 1, 2007): 25.

Slone, Ruben E., John T. Mentzer, J. Paul Dittmann. "Are You the Weakest Link in Your Company's Supply Chain?" *Harvard Business Review* 85, no. 9 (September 1, 2007): 116–127.

Appendix 2A

Math Analysis for Managers

This appendix provides a brief and selective discussion of mathematical terms and methods commonly used in managerial economics. The first section covers basic properties of real numbers that help us understand how to solve equations. It is followed by an explanation of the use of exponents and radicals. The next section describes the fundamentals of equations, their different forms, and the operations used to manipulate them. The following section explains the use of logarithms. The final section covers some basic rules of calculus.

PROPERTIES OF REAL NUMBERS

This section reviews some important properties of real numbers. These properties are basic to our understanding of how to manipulate numerical values.

Transitive Property

If X, Y, and Z are real numbers, then

$$\text{if } X = Y \text{ and } Y = Z, X = Z$$

This means that if two numbers are both equal to a third number, they are equal to each other. For example, if $X = Y$ and $Y = 5$, then $X = 5$.

Commutative Properties

If X and Y are real numbers, then

$$X + Y = Y + X \text{ and } XY = YX$$

This means that you can add or multiply numbers in any order. For example, $2 + 3 = 3 + 2 = 5$ and $2(3) = 3(2) = 6$.

Associative Properties

If X, Y, and Z are real numbers, then

$$X + (Y + Z) = (X + Y) + Z \text{ and } X(YZ) = (XY)Z$$

This means that for purposes of addition or multiplication, numbers can be grouped in any convenient manner. For example, $3 + (4 + 5) = (3 + 4) + 5 = 12$ and $3(4 \times 5) = (3 \times 4)5 = 60$.

Distributive Properties

If X, Y, and Z are real numbers, then

$$X(Y + Z) = XY + XZ \text{ and } (X - Y)Z = XZ + YZ$$

This means that within the context of an equation, the order of addition or multiplication is immaterial; that is, it is possible to first multiply and then add, or vice versa. For example, $3(4 + 5) = 3(4) + 3(5) = 27$ and $3(4 + 5) = 3(9) = 27$.

Inverse Properties

For each real number X, there is a number $-X$, called the *additive inverse* or *negative* of X, where

$$X + (-X) = 0$$

For example, because $5 + (-5) = 0$, the additive inverse of 5 is -5. Similarly, the additive inverse of -5 is 5. For each real number X, there also is a unique number, X^{-1}, called the *multiplicative inverse* or *reciprocal* of X, where

$$X \times \frac{1}{X} = \frac{X}{X} = 1$$

The expression $1/X$ can be written X^{-1}, *so* $X(1/X) = X \times X^{-1} = X/X = 1$. For example, $4(1/4) = 4 \times 4^{-1} = 4/4 = 1$. This property holds for all real numbers except 0, for which the reciprocal is undefined.

Exponents and Radicals

Exponents and radicals can be thought of as abbreviations in the language of mathematics. For example, the product

$$X \times X \times X = X^3$$

In general, for a positive integer n, X^n is an abbreviation for the product of n X's. In X^n, the letter X is called the *base* and the letter n the *exponent* (or *power*). If $Y = X^n$, X is called the nth root of Y. For example, $2 \times 2 \times 2 = 2^3 = 8$ and 2 is the third root of 8. Any number raised to the first power equals itself, $X^1 = X$ (e.g., $7^1 = 7$), and any number raised to the zero power equals one—that is, $X^0 = 1$ for $X \neq 0$ (0^0 is not defined). Some numbers do not have an nth root that is a real number. For example, because the second power, or square, of any real number is nonnegative, there is no real number that is the second, or square, root of -9.

It is also common to write

$$\frac{1}{X \times X \times X \times \cdots \times X} = \frac{1}{X^n} = X^{-n}$$

This implies that $1/X^{-n} = X^n$. In general, whenever we move a number raised to a power from the numerator (top) to the denominator (bottom) of an expression, the sign of the exponent, or power, is multiplied by -1, and vice-versa. For example, $1/(2 \times 2 \times 2) = 1/2^3 = 2^{-3} = 0.125$.

The symbol $\sqrt[n]{X}$ is called a *radical*. Here n is the *index*, $\sqrt{}$ is the *radical sign*, and X is the *radicand*. For convenience, the index is usually omitted in the case of principal square roots, so $\sqrt{X}$ is written instead of $\sqrt[2]{X}$. Therefore, $\sqrt{16} = \sqrt[2]{16} = 4$. If X is positive and m and n are integers where n is also positive, then

$$\sqrt[n]{X^m} = X^{m/n}$$

For example, $\sqrt{2^4} = 2^{4/2} = 2^2 = 4$. Similarly, $\sqrt{9} = 9^{1/2} = 3$.

The basic rule for multiplication is $X^m \times X^n = X^{m+n}$ and for division is $X^m/X^n = X^{m-n}$. For example, $3^3 \cong 3^2 = 3^{3+2} = 3^5 = 243$, and $3^3/3^2 = 3^{3-2} = 3^1 = 3$.

EQUATIONS

A statement that has two algebraic expressions which are related is called an *equation*. The two expressions that make up an equation are called its *members* or *sides*. They are often separated by the symbol $=$, which is called an *equality* or *equals sign*. In solving an equation or finding its roots, we often manipulate the original equation in order to generate another equation that will be somewhat easier to solve.

Equivalent Operations

There are three operations that can be performed on equations without changing their solution values; hence, the original and subsequent equations are called *equivalent*. These operations are

Addition (Subtraction) Operation. Equivalence is maintained when adding (subtracting) the same variable to (from) both sides of an equation, where the variable is the same as that occurring in the original equation. For example, if $6X = 20 + 2X$, subtracting $2X$ from both sides gives the equivalent equation $4X = 20$.

Multiplication (Division) Operation. Equivalence is maintained when multiplying (dividing) both sides of an equation by the same nonzero constant. For example, if $4X = 20$, dividing both sides by 4 gives the equivalent equation $X = 5$.

Replacement Operation. Equivalence is maintained when replacing either side of an equation by an equivalent expression. For example, if $X(X - 4) = 3$, replacing the left side by the equivalent expression $X^2 - 4X$ gives an equivalent equation $X^2 - 4X = 3$.

It is worth emphasizing that each of these operations can be applied to any equation with the effect that the resulting equation will be mathematically identical to the original.

Equations may take a wide variety of functional forms. Three of the more frequently encountered are described next.

Linear Equations

An equation *linear* in the variable X can be written as

$$aX + b = 0$$

where a and b are constants and a is called the slope *coefficient* and b the *intercept*.

A linear equation is sometimes referred to as a *first-degree equation* or *equation of degree one*. To solve the linear equation $2X + 6 = 14$, we apply the subtraction and division operations to find $2X = 8$ and $X = 4$.

Quadratic Equations

An equation *quadratic* in the variable X can be written as

$$aX^2 + bX + c = 0$$

where a, b, and c are constants and $a \neq 0$. Here a and b are slope coefficients and c is the intercept.

A quadratic equation is sometimes referred to as a *second-degree equation* or *equation of degree two*. Whereas linear equations have only one root, quadratic equations sometimes have two different roots. The solutions to quadratic equations are easily found through application of the *quadratic* formula. If $aX^2 + bX + c = 0$ and a, b, and c are constants where $a \neq 0$, then

$$X = \frac{-b \pm \sqrt{b^2 - 4ac}}{2a}$$

The solutions for the values of X are called the *roots* of the quadratic equation. For example, if $2X^2 - 15X + 18 = 0$, then $X = +15 \pm \left(\sqrt{225 - 4(2)(18)} \right) / 2(2) = (15 \pm 9)/4 = 6$ and 1.5. In many instances, one or both of the solved values for a quadratic equation will be negative. If the quadratic equation is a profit function and X is output, for example, any root $X < 0$, implying negative output, will be mathematically correct but meaningless from an economic standpoint. Therefore, when applying the quadratic formula to problems in managerial economics, one must use judgment to identify those solution values that are both mathematically correct and economically relevant.

Multiplicative Equations

An equation *multiplicative* in the variables X and Z can be written as

$$Y = aX^{b_1}Z^{b_2}$$

where a is the constant and b_1 and b_2 are exponents.

For example, $Y = 5X^2Z^3$ where $X = 3$ and $Z = 4$ has the solution $Y = 5(3^2)(4^3) = 5(9)(64) = 2,880$. Multiplicative equations are often employed in managerial economics, particularly in demand, production, and cost analyses.

Exponential Functions

Certain multiplicative functions are referred to as *exponential functions*. The function $Y = b^x$, where $b > 0$, $b \neq 1$, and X is any real number, is referred to as an *exponential function to the base b*. Exponential functions often are constructed using e, the Naperian Constant

($=2.71828 \cdots$) as a base. Thus, for example, the equation $Y = e^2$ means $Y = (2.71828 \cdots)^2$. Although e may seem a curious number to adopt as the base in an exponential function, it is usefully employed in economic studies of compound growth or decline.

Logarithmic Functions

For the purposes of economic analysis, multiplicative or exponential relations often are transformed into a linear *logarithmic form*, where

$$Y = \log_b X \text{ if and only if } X = b^Y$$

Here Y is a *logarithmic function to the base b*. $Y = \log_b X$ is the logarithmic form of the exponential $X = b^Y$. For example, $\log_{10} 1{,}000 = 3$ is the logarithmic equivalent of the exponential $10^3 = 1{,}000$. For much of the work in managerial economics, logarithms are written using either the base 10, called *common logarithms,* or the base e (=Naperian Constant $= 2.71828 \cdots$), called *natural logarithms*. Natural logarithms typically are denoted by the notation "ln" rather than "log e."

Some important basic properties of logarithms are

Product Property. The logarithm of a product is the sum of logarithms:

$$\ln XY = \ln X + \ln Y$$

For example, $\ln 6 = \ln(3 \times 2) = \ln 3 + \ln 2 = 1.099 + 0.693 = 1.792$. It is important to note that the logarithm of a sum is *not* the sum of logarithms.

Quotient Property. The logarithm of a quotient is the difference of logarithms:

$$\ln \frac{X}{Y} = \ln X - \ln Y$$

For example, $\ln 1.5 = \ln 3/2 = \ln 3 - \ln 2 = 1.099 - 0.693 = 0.406$. Here, note that the logarithm of a quotient is *not* the quotient of logarithms.

Power Property. The logarithm of a number X raised to the exponent n, X^n, is the exponent times the logarithm of X:

$$\ln X^n = n \ln X$$

For example, $\ln 9 = \ln 3^2 = 2 \ln 3 = 2(1.099) = 2.198$.

Using the properties of logarithms, we see that there is a simple logarithmic transformation for any multiplicative or exponential function. For example, the logarithmic transformation of the multiplicative equation $Y = 5X^2Z^3$ can be written as $\ln Y = \ln 5 + 2 \ln X + 3 \ln Z$. Here we have used the natural logarithm of X, although the transformation would be the same using common logs or logs to any other base.

It is important to recognize the symmetry between the logarithmic and exponential functions. It is an important property of each that

$$\ln e^X = X \text{ and } e^{\ln X} = X$$

In words, the logarithm to the base e of the number e raised to the power X equals X. Similarly, the number e raised to the power $\ln X$ equals X. For example, $\ln e^1 = 1$ and $e^{\ln 1} = 1$. This means that any number or equation transformed into logarithmic form through use of logarithms can be converted back into original form through exponential transformation. For example, recall from earlier discussion that the multiplicative equation $Y = 5X^2Z^3$ has the logarithmic equivalent $\ln Y = \ln 5 + 2 \ln X + 3 \ln Z$. It follows that if $X = 3$ and $Z = 4$, then $Y = 5(3^2)(4^3) = 5(9)(64) = 2{,}880$ and $\ln Y = \ln 5 + 2 \ln 3 + 3 \ln 4 = 1.609 + 2.197 + 4.159 = 7.965$. Equivalence requires that $\ln 2{,}880 = 7.965$ and $e^{7.965} = 2{,}880$, which is indeed the case.

The practical relevance of this symmetry between logarithms and exponential functions is that, for example, a multiplicative demand relation can be analyzed in linear logarithmic form using widely available computer-software regression packages and converted back into original form through exponential transformation for purposes of numerical evaluation.

CONCEPT OF A MARGINAL

In Chapter 2, a *marginal* is defined as the change in the value of the dependent variable associated with a 1-unit change in an independent variable. This relationship can be more precisely specified by examining the nature of a change in a function. Consider the unspecified function $Y = f(X)$, which is read "Y is a function of X." Using Δ (delta) to denote change, the change in the value of the independent variable, X, is given by the notation ΔX and the change in the dependent variable, Y, is given by ΔY.

The ratio $\Delta Y / \Delta X$ provides a very general specification of the marginal concept:

$$\text{Marginal } Y = \frac{\Delta Y}{\Delta X}$$

The change in Y, ΔY, divided by the change in X, ΔX, indicates the change in the dependent variable associated with a 1-unit change in the value of X.

Figure 2A.1, which graphs a function relating Y to X, illustrates this relation. For values of X close to the origin, a relatively small change in X creates a large change

---

Figure 2A.1   Changing $\Delta Y / \Delta X$ over the Range of a Curve

The ratio $\Delta Y / \Delta X$ changes continuously along a curved line.

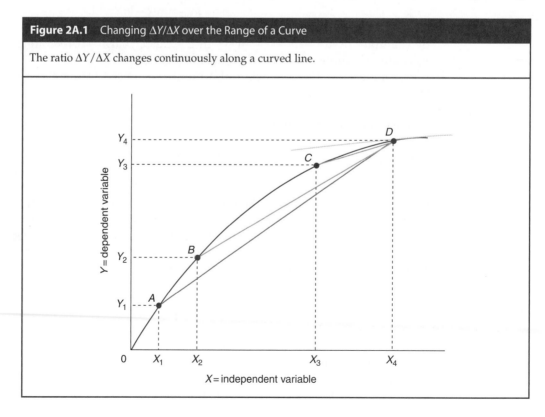

in Y. Thus, the value of $\Delta Y/\Delta X$—for example, $(Y_2 - Y_1)/(X_2 - X_1)$—is relatively large, showing that a small increase in X induces a large increase in Y. The situation is reversed the farther out one moves along the X axis. A large increase in X—say, from X_3 to X_4—produces only a small increase in Y, from Y_3 to Y_4; thus $\Delta Y/\Delta X$ is small.

Figure 2A.1 shows the marginal relation between X and Y changes at different points along the curve. When the curve is relatively steep, the dependent variable, Y, is highly responsive to changes in the independent variable, X; but when the curve is relatively flat, Y responds less significantly to changes in X. Notice, however, that the general expression of the marginal relation in Equation (2A.1) does not necessarily capture this changing marginal relation. For example, using that equation one could estimate the marginal relation as

$$\frac{\Delta Y}{\Delta X} = \frac{Y_4 - Y_1}{X_4 - X_1}$$

This measure of the marginal is shown in Figure 2A.1 as the slope of the line connecting points A and D. We can see that this measure of the marginal is considerably smaller than the estimate one would obtain looking at the change $(Y_2 - Y_1)/(X_2 - X_1)$, the slope of a straight line connecting points A and B, and larger than the marginal found for the change $(Y_4 - Y_3)/(X_4 - X_3)$, the slope of a straight line connecting points C and D.

The problem is that $(Y_4 - Y_1)/(X_4 - X_1)$ measures the average change in Y for a 1-unit change in X between points A and D. Since this "average" marginal value may differ significantly from the actual marginal at a point such as D, it has limited value for decision making and could, in fact, lead to incorrect decisions.

If a decision maker wanted to know how Y varies for changes in X around point D, the relevant marginal would be found as $\Delta Y/\Delta X$ for a very small change in X around X_4. The mathematical concept for measuring the nature of such very small changes is called a *derivative*. A derivative, then, is simply a precise specification of the marginal value at a particular point on a function. The mathematical notation for a derivative is

$$\frac{dY}{dX} = \lim_{\Delta X \to 0} \frac{\Delta Y}{\Delta X}$$

which is read, "The derivative of Y with respect to X equals the limit of the ratio $\Delta Y/\Delta X$, as ΔX approaches zero."[3]

This concept of the derivative as the limit of a ratio is precisely equivalent to the slope of a curve at a point. Figure 2A.1 also presents this idea. Notice that the *average* slope of the curve between points A and D is measured as:

$$\frac{\Delta Y}{\Delta X} = \frac{Y_4 - Y_1}{X_4 - X_1}$$

and is shown as the slope of the line connecting the two points. Similarly, the average slope of the curve can be measured over smaller and smaller intervals of X and shown by other chords, such as those connecting points B and C with D. At the limit, as ΔX approaches zero around point D, the ratio $\Delta Y/\Delta X$ is equal to the slope of a line drawn tangent to the curve at point D. The slope of this tangent is defined as the derivative,

---

3   If the value of a function $Y = f(X)$ approaches a constant Y^* as the value of the independent variable, X, approaches X^*, Y^* is called the *limit* of the function $f(X)$ as X approaches X^*. This would be written as $\lim_{X \to X^*} f(X) = Y^*$. For example, if $Y = X - 4$, the limit of this function as X approaches 5 is 1; that is $\lim_{X \to 5}(X - 4) = 1$. This says that the value of X approaches but does not quite reach 5; the value of the function $Y = X - 4$ comes closer and closer to 1. This concept of a limit is examined in detail in any introductory calculus textbook.

dY/dX, of the function at point D; it measures the marginal change in Y associated with a very small change in X at that point.

To illustrate the relation between the mathematical concept of a derivative and the economic concept of a marginal, the dependent variable, Y, might be total revenue and the independent variable, X, might be output. The derivative dY/dX then shows precisely how revenue and output are related at a specific output level. Because the change in revenue associated with a change in output is defined as the marginal revenue, the derivative of the total revenue provides a precise measure of marginal revenue at any specific output level. A similar situation exists for total cost: The derivative of the total cost function at any output level indicates the marginal cost at that output.

Derivatives provide much useful information in managerial economics. Therefore, it is important to examine the rules for finding the derivatives of certain frequently encountered functions.

RULES FOR DIFFERENTIATING A FUNCTION

Determining the derivative of a function is not a particularly difficult task; it simply involves applying a basic formula to the function. This section presents the basic formulas or rules for differentiation. Proofs are omitted here, but can be found in any introductory calculus textbook.

Constants

The derivative of a constant is always zero; that is, if Y is a constant:

$$\frac{dY}{dX} = 0$$

This situation is graphed in Figure 2A.2 for the example $Y = 2$. Because Y is defined as a constant, its value does not vary as X changes and, hence, dY/dX must be zero.

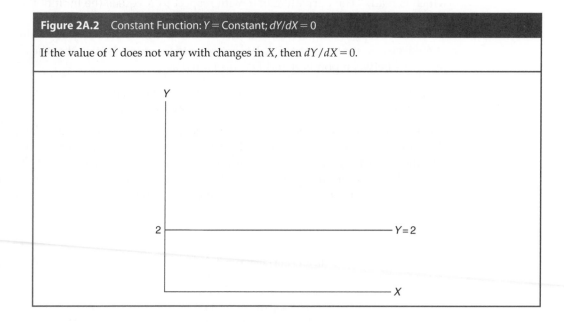

Figure 2A.2   Constant Function: $Y =$ Constant; $dY/dX = 0$

If the value of Y does not vary with changes in X, then $dY/dX = 0$.

Powers

The derivative of a power function such as $Y = aX^b$, where a and b are constants, is equal to the exponent b multiplied by the coefficient a times the variable X raised to the $b - 1$ power:

$$Y = aX^b$$

$$\frac{dY}{dX} = b \times a \times X^{(b-1)}$$

For example, given the function

$$Y = 2X^3$$

then

$$\frac{dY}{dX} = 3 \times 2 \times X^{(3-1)} = 6X^2$$

Two further examples of power functions should clarify this rule. The derivative of the function $Y = X^3$ is given as

$$\frac{dY}{dX} = 3 \times X^2$$

The exponent, 3, is multiplied by the implicit coefficient, 1, and in turn by the variable, X, raised to the second power.

Finally, the derivative of the function $Y = 0.5X$ is:

$$\frac{dY}{dX} = 1 \times 0.5 \times X^0 = 0.5$$

The implicit exponent, 1, is multiplied by the coefficient, 0.5, times the variable, X, raised to the zero power. Because any number raised to the zero power equals 1, the result is 0.5.

Again a graph may help clarify the power function concept. In Figure 2A.3, the last two power functions given above, $Y = X^3$ and $Y = 0.5X$, are graphed. Consider first $Y = 0.5X$. The derivative of this function, $dY/dX = 0.5$, is a constant, indicating that the slope of the function is a constant. This can be readily seen from the graph. The derivative measures the *rate of change*. If the rate of change is constant, as it must be if the basic function is linear, the derivative of the function must be constant. The second function, $Y = X^3$, rises at an increasing rate as X increases. The derivative of the function, $dY/dX = 3X^2$, also increases as X becomes larger, indicating that the slope of the function is increasing or that the rate of change is increasing.

Sums and Differences

The following notation is used throughout the remainder of this section to express a number of other important rules of differentiation:

$$U = g(X): U \text{ is an unspecified function, } g, \text{ of } X$$

$$V = h(X): V \text{ is an unspecified function, } h, \text{ of } X$$

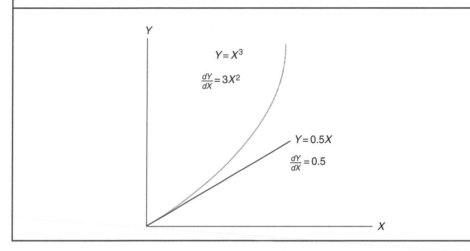

Figure 2A.3 Power Functions

The derivative of the linear function $Y = 0.5X$ is constant. The derivative of the nonlinear function $Y = X^3$ rises as X increases.

The derivative of a sum (difference) is equal to the sum (difference) of the derivatives of the individual terms. Thus, if $Y = U + V$, then:

$$\frac{dY}{dX} = \frac{dU}{dX} + \frac{dV}{dX}$$

For example, if $U = g(X) = 2X^2$, $V = h(X) = -X^3$, and $Y = U + V = 2X^2 - X^3$, then:

$$\frac{dY}{dX} = 4X - 3X^2$$

Here the derivative of the first term, $2X^2$, is found to be $4X$ by the power rule; the derivative of the second term, $-X^3$, is found to be $-3X^2$ also by that rule; and the derivative of the total function is the sum of the derivatives of the parts.

Consider a second example of this rule. If $Y = 300 + 5X + 2X^2$, then

$$\frac{dY}{dX} = 0 + 5 + 4X$$

The derivative of 300 is 0 by the constant rule; the derivative of $5X$ is 5 by the power rule; and the derivative of $2X^2$ is $4X$ by the power rule.

Products

The derivative of the product of two expressions is equal to the sum of the first term multiplied by the derivative of the second *plus* the second term times the derivative of the first. Thus, if $Y = U \times V$, then

$$\frac{dY}{dX} = U \times \frac{dV}{dX} + V \times \frac{dU}{dX}$$

For example, if $Y = 3X^2(3 - X)$, then, letting $U = 3X^2$ and $V = (3 - X)$, we get

$$\frac{dY}{dX} = 3X^2\left(\frac{dY}{dX}\right) + (3 - X)\left(\frac{dY}{dX}\right)$$

$$= 3X^2(-1) + (3 - X)(6X)$$
$$= -3X^2 + 18X - 6X^2$$
$$= 18X - 9X^2$$

The first factor, $3X^2$, is multiplied by the derivative of the second, -1, and added to the second factor, $3 - X$, times the derivative of the first, $6X$. Simplifying results in the preceding final expression.

Quotients

The derivative of the quotient of two expressions is equal to the denominator multiplied by the derivative of the numerator *minus* the numerator times the derivative of the denominator, all divided by the square of the denominator. Thus, if $Y = U/V$, then

$$\frac{dY}{dX} = \frac{V \times \frac{dU}{dX} - U \times \frac{dV}{dX}}{V^2}$$

For example, if $U = 2X - 3$ and $V = 6X^2$, then

$$Y = \frac{2X - 3}{6X^2}$$

and

$$\frac{dY}{dX} = \frac{(6X^2)2 - (2X - 3)12X}{36X^4}$$
$$= \frac{12X^2 - 24X^2 + 36X}{36X^4}$$
$$= \frac{36X - 12X^2}{36X^4}$$
$$= \frac{3 - X}{3X^3}$$

The denominator, $6X^2$, is multiplied by the derivative of the numerator, 2. Subtracted from this is the numerator, $2X - 3$, times the derivative of the denominator, $12X$. The result is then divided by the square of the denominator, $36X^4$. Algebraic reduction results in the final expression of the derivative.

Logarithmic Functions

The derivative of a logarithmic function $Y = \ln X$ is given by the expression

$$\frac{dY}{dX} = \frac{d \ln X}{dX} = \frac{1}{X}$$

This also implies that if $Y = \ln X$, then $dY = (1/X)dX = dX/X$. Because dX is the change in X by definition, dX/X is the percentage change in X. Derivatives of logarithmic functions have great practical relevance in managerial economics given the prevalence of multiplicative (and hence linear in the logarithms) equations used to describe demand, production, and cost relations. For example, the expression $Y = aX^b$ has an equivalent logarithmic function $\ln Y = \ln a + b \ln X$, where $d \ln Y/d \ln X = (dY/Y)/(dX/X) = b$. Here b is called the *elasticity* of Y with respect to X, because it reflects the percentage effect on Y of a 1 percent change in X. The concept of elasticity is introduced and extensively examined in Chapter 4 and discussed throughout the remaining chapters.

Function of a Function (Chain Rule)

The derivative of a function of a function is found as follows: If $Y = f(U)$, where $U = g(X)$, then

$$\frac{dY}{dX} = \frac{dY}{dU} \times \frac{dU}{dX}$$

For example, if $Y = 2U - U^2$ and $U = 2X^3$, then dY/dX is found as follows:
Step 1:

$$\frac{dY}{dU} = 2 - 2U$$

Substituting for U, creates the expression:

$$\frac{dY}{dU} = 2 - 2(2X^3)$$

$$= 2 - 4X^3$$

Step 2:

$$\frac{dY}{dX} = 6X^2$$

Step 3:

$$\frac{dY}{dX} = \frac{dY}{dU} \times \frac{dU}{dX}$$

$$= (2 - 4X^3)6X^2$$

$$= 12X^2 - 24X^5$$

Further examples of this rule should indicate its usefulness in obtaining derivatives of many functions.
Example 1:

$$Y = \sqrt{X^2 - 1}$$

Let $U = X^2 - 1$. Then $Y = \sqrt{U} = U^{1/2}$.

$$\frac{dY}{dU} = \frac{1}{2}U^{-1/2}$$

$$= \frac{1}{2U^{1/2}}$$

Substituting $X^2 - 1$ for U in the derivative results in

$$\frac{dY}{dU} = \frac{1}{2(X^2 - 1)^{1/2}}$$

Because $U = X^2 - 1$,

$$\frac{dY}{dU} = 2X$$

Using the function of a function rule, $dY/dX = dY/dU \cong dU/dX$, so

$$\frac{dY}{dX} = \frac{1}{2(X^2-1)^{1/2}} \times 2X$$

$$= \frac{X}{\sqrt{X^2-1}}$$

Example 2:

$$Y = \frac{1}{X^2-2}$$

Let $U = X^2 - 2$. Then $Y = 1/U$, and the quotient rule yields

$$\frac{dY}{dU} = \frac{U \times 0 - 1 \times 1}{U^2}$$

$$= -\frac{1}{U^2}$$

Substituting $(X^2 - 2)$ for U obtains

$$\frac{dY}{dU} = -\frac{1}{(X^2-2)^2}$$

Because $U = X^2 - 2$,

$$\frac{dU}{dX} = 2X$$

Therefore,

$$\frac{dY}{dX} = \frac{dY}{dU} \times \frac{dU}{dX} = -\frac{1}{(X^2-2)^2} \times 2X$$

$$= -\frac{2X}{(X^2-2)^2}$$

Example 3:

$$Y = (2X+3)^2$$

Let $U = 2X + 3$. Then $Y = U^2$ and

$$\frac{dY}{dU} = 2U$$

Because $U = 2X + 3$,

$$\frac{dY}{dU} = 2(2X+3)$$

$$= 4X + 6$$

and

$$\frac{dU}{dX} = 2$$

Thus,

$$\frac{dY}{dX} = \frac{dY}{dU} \times \frac{dU}{dX} = (4X+6)2$$

$$= 8X + 12$$

Appendix 2B

Multivariate Optimization and the Lagrangian Technique

Multivariate Optimization
Process of optimization for equations with three or more variables.

Because many economic relations involve more than two variables, it is useful to examine the concept of **multivariate optimization,** the process of optimization for equations with three or more variables. Demand is often a function of the product's own price, the price of other goods, advertising, income, and other factors. Similarly, cost is determined by output, input prices, the nature of technology, and so on. As a result, multivariate optimization is often used in the process of optimization.

Partial Derivative Concept

Consider the demand function for a product where the quantity demanded, Q, is determined by the price charged, P, and the level of advertising, A:

$$Q = f(P, A) \qquad \textbf{2B.1}$$

When analyzing multivariate relations, such as Equation (2B.1), one is interested in the marginal effect of each independent variable on the dependent variable. Optimization requires an analysis of how change in each independent variable affects the dependent variable, *holding constant the effect of all other independent variables.* The partial derivative is the concept used for this type of marginal analysis.

Based on the demand function of Equation (2B.1), it is possible to examine two partial derivatives:[4]

1. The partial of Q with respect to price is $\partial Q / \partial P$.
2. The partial of Q with respect to advertising expenditure is $\partial Q / \partial A$.

Rules for determining partial derivatives are essentially the same as those for simple derivatives. The concept of a partial derivative involves an assumption that all variables except the one with respect to which the derivative is being taken remain unchanged.

---

4 The symbol ∂, the Greek letter *delta*, is used to denote a partial derivative. In oral and written expression, the word *derivative* is frequently omitted. Reference is typically made to the *partial* of Q rather than the *partial derivative* of Q.

Other variables are treated as constants. For example, consider the demand function facing MacGyver, Inc.:

$$Q = 5,000 - 10P + 40A + PA - 0.8A^2 - 0.5P^2 \qquad \textbf{2B.2}$$

where Q is quantity, P is price (in dollars), and A is advertising expenditures (in hundreds of dollars).

In this function there are two independent variables, P and A, so two partial derivatives can be evaluated. Because A is treated as a constant, the partial derivative of Q with respect to P is

$$\frac{\partial Q}{\partial P} = 0 - 10 + 0 + A - 0 - P$$

$$= -10 + A - P$$

In determining the partial of Q with respect to A, P is treated as a constant. The partial with respect to A is

$$\frac{\partial Q}{\partial A} = 0 - 0 + 40 + P - 1.6A - 0$$

$$= 40 + P - 1.6A$$

Maximizing Multivariate Functions

The maximization or minimization of multivariate functions is similar to that for single variable functions. All first-order partial derivatives must equal zero.[5] Thus, maximization of the function $Q = f(P, A)$ requires

$$\frac{\partial Q}{\partial P} = 0$$

and

$$\frac{\partial Q}{\partial A} = 0$$

To illustrate this procedure, reconsider the MacGyver demand function, Equation (2B.2), given previously:

$$Q = 5,000 - 10P + 40A + PA - 0.8A^2 - 0.5P^2$$

To maximize the value of this function, each partial must equal zero:

$$\frac{\partial Q}{\partial P} = -10 + A - P = 0$$

and

$$\frac{\partial Q}{\partial A} = 40 + P - 1.6A = 0$$

---

5   Second-order requirements for determining maxima and minima are complex and are not necessary for the types of managerial problems considered in this text. A full discussion of these requirements can be found in any elementary calculus text.

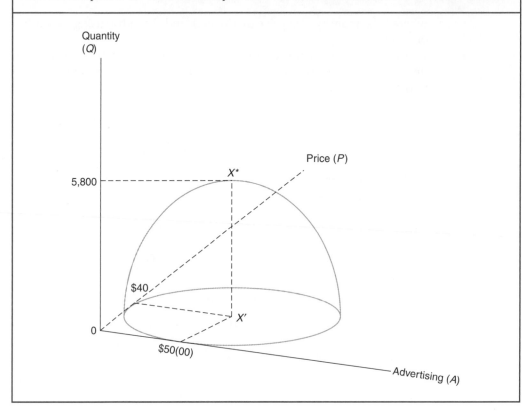

Figure 2B.1 Finding the Maximum of a Function of Two Variables: $Q = 5{,}000 - 10P + 40A + PA - 0.8A^2 - 0.5P^2$

All first-order partial derivatives are set equal to zero to find the maximum of a multivariate function.

Solving these two equations simultaneously yields the values $P = \$40$ and $A = \$5{,}000$.[6] Inserting these numbers for P and A into Equation (2B.2) results in a value for Q of 5,800. Therefore, the maximum value of Q is 5,800.

This process can be visualized by referring to Figure 2B.1, a 3-dimensional graph of Equation (2B.2). For positive values of P and A, Equation (2B.2) maps out a surface with a peak at point X^*. At the peak, the surface of the figure is level. Alternatively stated, a plane that is tangent to the surface at point X^* is parallel to the PA plane. This means that the slope of the figure with respect to either P or A is zero, as is required for locating the maximum of a multivariate function.

CONSTRAINED OPTIMIZATION

In many decision problems faced by managers, there are constraints that limit options available to the decision maker. For example, a production manager may be charged with minimizing total cost, subject to the requirement that specified quantities of each of the

---

6   Because $-10 + A - P = 0$, $P = A - 10$. Substituting this value for P into $40 + P - 1.6A = 0$ gives $40 + (A - 10)$ $-1.6A = 0$, which implies that $0.6A = 30$ and $A = 50$(in 00s), or \$5,000. Given this value, $P = A - 10 = 50 - 10 = \$40$.

firm's products be produced. At other times, the production manager may be concerned with maximizing output, subject to limitations on the quantities of various resources (labor, materials, or equipment) available for use.

Role of Constraints

Constrained Optimization
Decision situations that involve limited choice alternatives.

Managers frequently face **constrained optimization** problems, decision situations with limited alternatives. Marketing managers are often charged with the task of maximizing sales, subject to the constraint that they not exceed a fixed advertising budget. Financial officers typically work within constraints imposed by financing requirements and creditor restrictions.

Constrained optimization problems can be solved in several ways. Where the constraint equation is not overly complex, it can be solved in terms of one decision variable, and then that variable can be substituted for in the objective function that the firm wishes to maximize or minimize.[7] This approach converts the problem to one of unconstrained maximization or minimization, which can be solved using methods outlined previously.

This procedure can be clarified by examining its use in a constrained minimization problem. Suppose a firm produces its product on two assembly lines and operates with the following total cost function:

$$TC = \$3X^2 + \$6Y^2 - \$1XY$$

where X represents the output produced on one assembly line and Y the production from the second. Management seeks to determine the least-cost combination of X and Y, subject to the constraint that total output of the product is 20 units. The constrained optimization problem is
Minimize

$$TC = \$3X^2 + \$6Y^2 - \$1XY$$

subject to

$$X + Y = 20$$

Solving the constraint for X and substituting this value into the objective function results in

$$X = 20 - Y$$

and

$$TC = \$3(20 - Y)^2 + \$6Y^2 - \$1(20 - Y)Y$$
$$= \$3(400 - 40Y + Y^2) + \$6Y^2 - \$1(20Y - Y^2)$$

---

7   This section examines techniques for solving constrained optimization problems in which the constraints can be expressed as equations. Some constraints impose only upper or lower limits on the decision maker and, therefore, may not be "binding" at the optimal solution. Constraints of this second, more general, type are properly expressed as inequality relations. In such instances another optimizing technique, linear programming, is used to analyze the problem.

$$= \$1{,}200 - \$120Y + \$3Y^2 + \$6Y^2 - \$20Y + \$Y^2$$
$$= \$1{,}200 - \$140Y + \$10Y^2 \qquad\qquad \textbf{2B.3}$$

Now it is possible to treat Equation (2B.3) as an unconstrained minimization problem. Solving it requires taking the derivative of the total cost function, setting that derivative equal to zero, and solving for the value of Y:

$$\frac{dTC}{dY} = -\$140 + \$20Y = 0$$
$$20Y = 140$$
$$Y = 7$$

A check of the sign of the second derivative evaluated at that point insures that a minimum has been located:

$$\frac{dTC}{dY} = -\$140 + \$20Y$$
$$\frac{d^2TC}{dY^2} = \$20$$

Because the second derivative is positive, $Y = 7$ is indeed a minimum.

Substituting 7 for Y in the constraint equation allows one to determine the optimal quantity to be produced on assembly line X:

$$X + 7 = 20$$
$$X = 13$$

Thus, production of 13 units of output on assembly line X and 7 units on line Y is the least-cost combination for manufacturing a total of 20 units of the firm's product. The total cost of producing that combination is

$$TC = \$3(13^2) + \$6(7^2) - \$1(13 \times 7)$$
$$= \$507 + \$294 - \$91$$
$$= \$710$$

Lagrangian Multipliers

Unfortunately, the substitution technique used in the preceding section is not always feasible. Constraint conditions are sometimes too numerous or complex for substitution to be used. In these cases, the technique of *Lagrangian multipliers* can be used.

Lagrangian Technique
Method for solving constrained optimization problems.

The **Lagrangian technique** for solving constrained optimization problems is a method that calls for optimizing a function that incorporates the original objective function and the constraint conditions. This combined equation, called the Lagrangian function, is created in such a way that when it is maximized or minimized the original objective function is also maximized or minimized, and all constraints are satisfied.

A reexamination of the constrained minimization problem shown previously illustrates this technique. Recall that the firm sought to minimize the function $TC = \$3X^2 + \$6Y^2 - \$1XY$, subject to the constraint that $X + Y = 20$. Rearrange the constraint to bring all terms to the right of the equal sign:

$$0 = 20 - X - Y$$

This is always the first step in forming a Lagrangian expression.

Multiplying this form of the constraint by the unknown factor λ and adding the result to the original objective function creates the Lagrangian expression:[8]

$$L_{TC} = \$3X^2 + \$6Y^2 - \$1XY + \lambda(20 - X - Y) \qquad \textbf{2B.4}$$

L_{TC} is defined as the Lagrangian function for the constrained optimization problem under consideration.

Because it incorporates the constraint into the objective function, the Lagrangian function can be treated as an unconstrained optimization problem. The solution to the unconstrained Lagrangian problem is *always* identical to the solution of the original constrained optimization problem. To illustrate, consider the problem of minimizing the Lagrangian function constructed in Equation (2B.4). At a minimum point on a multivariate function, all partial derivatives must equal zero. The partials of Equation (2B.4) can be taken with respect to the three unknown variables, X, Y, and λ, as follows:

$$\frac{\partial L_{TC}}{\partial X} = 6X - Y - \lambda$$

$$\frac{\partial L_{TC}}{\partial Y} = 12Y - X - \lambda$$

and

$$\frac{\partial L_{TC}}{\partial \lambda} = 20 - X - Y$$

Setting these three partials equal to zero results in a system of three equations and three unknowns:

$$6X - Y - \lambda = 0 \qquad \textbf{2B.5}$$
$$-X + 12Y - \lambda = 0 \qquad \textbf{2B.6}$$

and

$$20 - X - Y = 0 \qquad \textbf{2B.7}$$

Notice that Equation (2B.7), the partial of the Lagrangian function with respect to λ, is the constraint condition imposed on the original optimization problem. The Lagrangian function is constructed so that the derivative of the function taken with respect to the Lagrangian multiplier, λ, always gives the original constraint. So long as this derivative is zero, as it must be at a local extreme (maximum or minimum), the constraint conditions imposed on the original problem is met. Further, because the last term in the Lagrangian expression must equal zero ($0 = 20 - X - Y$), the Lagrangian function reduces to the original objective function, and the solution to the unconstrained Lagrangian problem is always the solution to the original constrained optimization problem.

---

8   The Greek letter *lambda*, λ, is typically used in formulating Lagrangian expressions.

Completing the analysis for the example illuminates these relations. To begin, it is necessary to solve the system of equations to obtain optimal values of X and Y. Subtracting Equation (2B.6) from Equation (2B.5) gives

$$7X - 13Y = 0 \qquad\qquad \textbf{2B.8}$$

Multiplying Equation (2B.7) by 7 and adding Equation (2B.8) to this product gives the solution for Y:

$$140 - 7X - 7Y = 0$$
$$7X - 13Y = 0$$
$$140 - 20Y = 0$$
$$140 = 20Y$$
$$Y = 7$$

Substituting 7 for Y in Equation (2B.7) yields $X = 13$, the value of X at the point where the Lagrangian function is minimized.

Because the solution of the Lagrangian function is also the solution to the firm's constrained optimization problem, 13 units from assembly line X and 7 units from line Y is the least-cost combination of output that can be produced subject to the constraint that total output must be 20 units. This is the same answer obtained previously, using the substitution method.

The Lagrangian technique is a more powerful technique for solving constrained optimization problems than the substitution method; it is easier to apply with multiple constraints, and it provides valuable supplementary information. This is because the Lagrangian multiplier itself has an important economic interpretation. Substituting the values of X and Y into Equation (2B.5) gives the value of λ:

$$6 \times 13 - 7 - \lambda = 0$$
$$\lambda = \$71$$

Here, λ is interpreted as the marginal cost of production at 20 units of output. It means that if the firm were allowed to produce only 19 instead of 20 units of output, total costs would fall by approximately \$71. If the output requirement were 21 instead of 20 units, costs would increase by roughly that amount.[9]

Because $\lambda = \$71$ can be interpreted as the marginal cost of production, an offer to purchase another unit of output for \$100 is acceptable because it results in a \$29 marginal profit. Conversely, an offer to purchase an additional unit for \$50 would be rejected because a marginal loss of \$21 would be incurred. Lambda (or λ) can be thought of as a planning variable, because it provides valuable information concerning the effects of altering current activity levels.

Another example provides additional perspective on the Lagrangian method. The profit function

$$\pi = -\$10{,}000 + \$400Q - \$2Q^2$$

---

9   Technically, λ indicates the marginal change in the objective function solution associated with an infinitesimally small change in the constraint. It only approximates the change in total cost that would take place if one more (or less) unit of output were produced.

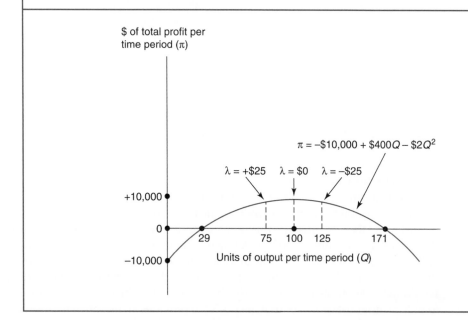

Figure 2B.2 The Role of Constraints in Profit Maximization

When profit is maximized, $\lambda = \$0$.

$ of total profit per time period (π)

$\pi = -\$10,000 + \$400Q - \$2Q^2$

$\lambda = +\$25$ $\lambda = \$0$ $\lambda = -\$25$

+10,000

0

29   75 100 125   171

−10,000

Units of output per time period (Q)

where π is total profit and Q is output in units, is maximized at $Q = 100$ with $\pi = \$10,000$ because $\partial\pi/\partial Q = \$400 - \$4Q = 0$ if $Q = 100$. The impact of constraints in the production process, and the value of the Lagrangian method, can be portrayed by considering the situation in which each unit of output requires 4 hours of unskilled labor, and a total of only 300 hours of unskilled labor is currently available to the firm. In this instance, the firm seeks to maximize the function $\pi = -\$10,000 + \$400Q - \$2Q^2$, subject to the constraint $4Q = 300$ (because $L = 4Q$). Rearrange the constraint to bring all terms to the right of the equal sign:

$$0 = 300 - 4Q$$

Multiplying this form of the constraint by λ and adding the result to the original objective function creates the Lagrangian expression:

$$L\pi = -\$10,000 + \$400Q - \$2Q^2 + \lambda(300 - 4Q) \qquad \textbf{2B.9}$$

with the following partials:

$$\frac{\partial L\pi}{\partial Q} = 400 - 4Q - 4\lambda$$

and

$$\frac{\partial L\pi}{\partial \lambda} = 300 - 4Q$$

Setting these two partials equal to zero results in a system of two equations and two unknowns. Solving provides the values $Q = 75$, $\lambda = \$25$, and, from the objective function, $\pi = \$8,750$. The constraint on unskilled labor has reduced output from 100 to 75 units and has reduced total profits from $10,000 to $8,750. The value $\lambda = \$25$ indicates that should a 1-unit expansion in output become possible, total profits would rise by $25. This information indicates that the maximum value of additional unskilled labor is $6.25 per hour, because each unit of output requires 4 hours of labor. Assuming there are no other costs involved, $6.25 per hour is the most the firm would pay to expand employment.

The effects of relaxing the constraint as progressively more unskilled labor becomes available are illustrated in Figure 2B.2. If an additional 100 hours of unskilled labor, or 400 hours in total, is available, the output constraint would become $0 = 400 - 4Q$, and solved values $Q = 100$, $\lambda = \$0$, and $\pi = \$10,000$ would result. The value $\lambda = \$0$ indicates that unskilled labor no longer constrains profits when 400 hours are available. Profits are maximized at $Q = 100$, which is the same result obtained in the earlier unconstrained solution to this profit maximization problem.

In this instance, the output constraint becomes *nonbinding* because it does not limit the profit-making ability of the firm. Indeed, the firm is not willing to employ more than 400 hours of unskilled labor. To illustrate this point, consider the use of 500 hours of unskilled labor and the resulting constraint $0 = 500 - 4Q$. Solved values are $Q = 125$, $\lambda = -\$25$, and $\pi = \$8,750$. The value $\lambda = -\$25$ indicates that 1 additional unit of output, and the expansion in employment that results, would *reduce* profits by $25. Conversely, a 1-unit reduction in the level of output would increase profits by $25. Clearly, the situation in which $\lambda < 0$ gives the firm an incentive to reduce input usage and output, just as $\lambda > 0$ provides an incentive for growth.

Lagrangian Multiplier, λ
Marginal effect on the objective function of decreasing or increasing the constraint requirement by one unit

To generalize, a **Lagrangian multiplier, λ,** indicates the marginal effect on the objective function of decreasing or increasing the constraint requirement by one unit. Often, as in the previous examples, the marginal relation described by the Lagrangian multiplier provides economic data that help managers evaluate the potential benefits or costs of relaxing constraints.

PROBLEM

2B.1 Lagrangian Multipliers. Amos Jones and Andrew Brown own and operate Amos & Andy, Inc., a Minneapolis-based installer of conversion packages for vans manufactured by the major auto companies. Amos & Andy has fixed capital and labor expenses of $1.2 million per year, and variable materials expenses average $2,000 per van conversion. Recent operating experience suggests the following annual demand relation for Amos & Andy products:

$$Q = 1,000 - 0.1P$$

where Q is the number of van conversions (output) and P is price.

A. Calculate Amos & Andy's profit-maximizing output, price, and profit levels.

B. Using the Lagrangian multiplier method, calculate profit-maximizing output, price, and profit levels in light of a parts shortage that limits Amos & Andy's output to 300 conversions during the coming year.

C. Calculate and interpret λ, the Lagrangian multiplier.

D. Calculate the value to Amos & Andy of having the parts shortage eliminated.

Demand and Supply

Gasoline demand in the United States grows by roughly 2 percent to 3 percent per year, primarily as a result of rising economic activity. Also contributing to this trend is the U.S. consumers' strong preference for less–fuel-efficient vehicles, like minivans, SUVs, and light-duty trucks. Supply–demand imbalances can become acute when gasoline consumption rises by nearly 10 percent during the "summer driving season." Recent increases in gas prices have been blamed on the growing demand from emerging economies like China and India, and on fears of oil supply restrictions tied to political instability in Iran, Nigeria, and Venezuela. High pump prices are directly tied to the escalating cost of crude. For every $1 increase in the cost of a barrel of oil, there is an average increase of about 2.5 cents per gallon in the price of gasoline.

In addition to restrictions tied to political instability and bad weather, gasoline supplies in the United States have tightened because of scarce refining capacity. Nobody wants a new oil refinery built in their own backyard. If a refinery capacity bottleneck occurs in California, for example, consumers must rely on tankers to ship gasoline from the half-dozen refineries around the world that can produce the state's clean-burning gasoline. Even the closest refinery, in the state of Washington, is 7 to 10 days away. In the meantime, even temporary supply disruptions lead to skyrocketing gasoline prices.

In short, don't merely blame Exxon for high gas prices. Blame worsening demand and supply conditions.[1]

BASIS FOR DEMAND

Goods and services have ready markets if they directly satisfy consumer wants, or help firms produce products that satisfy consumer wants.

Direct Demand

Demand
Total quantity customers are willing and able to purchase under various market conditions.

Demand is the quantity of a good or service that customers are willing and able to purchase during a specified period under a given set of economic conditions. The time frame might be an hour, a day, a month, or a year. Conditions to be considered include the price of the good in question, prices and availability of related goods, expectations of price changes, consumer incomes, consumer tastes and preferences, advertising

---

1   See Guy-Chazan, "Oil-Stock Drawdown Fuels Price Rise," *The Wall Street Journal Online*, October 20, 2007, http://online.wsj.com.

expenditures, and so on. The amount of the product that consumers are prepared to purchase, its demand, depends on all these factors.

For managerial decision making, a prime focus is on market demand. Market demand is the aggregate of individual, or personal, demand. Insight into market demand relations requires an understanding of the nature of individual demand. Individual demand is determined by the value associated with acquiring and using any good or service and the ability to acquire it. Both are necessary for effective individual demand. Desire without purchasing power may lead to want, but not to demand. There are two basic models of individual demand. One, known as the *theory of consumer behavior*, relates to the **direct demand** for personal consumption products. This model is appropriate for analyzing individual demand for goods and services that directly satisfy consumer desires. The value or worth of a good or service, its **utility**, is the prime determinant of direct demand. Individuals are viewed as attempting to maximize the total utility or satisfaction provided by the goods and services they acquire and consume. This optimization process requires that consumers focus on the marginal utility (gain in satisfaction) of acquiring additional units of a given product. Product characteristics, individual preferences (tastes), and the ability to pay are all important determinants of direct demand.

Direct Demand
Demand for consumption products.

Utility
Value.

Derived Demand

Goods and services are sometimes acquired because they are important inputs in the manufacture and distribution of other products. The outputs of engineers, production workers, sales staff, managers, lawyers, consultants, office business machines, production facilities and equipment, natural resources, and commercial airplanes are all examples of goods and services demanded not for direct consumption but rather for their use in providing other goods and services. Their demand is derived from the demand for the products they are used to provide. Input demand is called **derived demand**.

Derived Demand
Demand for inputs used in production.

The demand for mortgage money is an example. The quantity of mortgage credit demanded is not determined directly; it is derived from the more fundamental demand for housing. The demand for air transportation to resort areas is not a direct demand but is derived from the demand for recreation. Similarly, the demand for producers' goods and services used to manufacture products for final consumption is derived. Aggregate demand for consumption goods and services determines demand for the capital equipment, materials, labor, and energy used to manufacture them. For example, the demands for steel, aluminum, and plastics are all derived demands, as are the demands for machine tools and labor. None of these producers' goods are demanded because of their direct value to consumers but because of the role they play in production.

Demand for producers' goods and services are closely related to final products demand. An examination of final product demand is an important part of demand analysis for intermediate, or producers', goods. For products whose demand is derived rather than direct, demand stems from their value in the manufacture and sale of other products. They have value because their employment has the potential to generate profits. Key components in the determination of derived demand are the marginal benefits and marginal costs associated with using a given input or factor of production. The amount of any good or service used rises when its marginal benefit, measured in terms of the value of resulting output, is greater than the marginal costs of using the input, measured in terms of wages, interest, raw material costs, or related expenses. Conversely, the amount of any input used in production falls when resulting marginal benefits are less than the marginal cost of employment. In short, derived demand is related to the profitability of using a good or service.

Managerial Application 3.1

How the Internet Affects Demand and Supply

From an economic perspective, the Internet is the enemy of high prices and high profit margins. By greatly expanding the scope of the market, the Internet effectively eliminates geographic boundaries, especially for easily transported goods and services. This greatly increases the elasticity of demand and supply.

For example, in the pre-Internet era, anyone looking for a good deal on a high-quality vacuum cleaner might have gone to the local Wal-Mart, Target, or a specialty shop to look for the best bargain available. With the Internet, consumers can log onto Google.com, or your favorite Internet search engine, do a search on vacuum cleaners, and get data on hundreds of high-quality vacuums at extremely attractive prices. For example, with $15–$20 for shipping via Federal Express or UPS, it's possible to have vacuums delivered in Lawrence, Kansas, from http://www.vacdepot.com/ in Houston, Texas, at prices far below those offered by the local vacuum cleaner shop.

Successful Internet retailers offer bargain prices, a broad assortment of attractive products, and speedy delivery. They also effectively handle returns and basic customer service. Of course, traditional retailers cannot stand idly by as Internet-based retailers drive them out of business. They must fight back with competitive prices, high-quality products and an enticing in-store shopping experience. Borders is a good example of a bookseller that has effectively distinguished itself from Amazon.com and other Internet retailers by offering an appealing in-store shopping experience.

When considering the economic potential of Internet-based commerce, it's important to keep in mind that successful firms use Internet technology to maintain significant competitive advantages. The Internet, by itself, seldom confers long-lasting competitive advantages. The Internet is a marvelous communications device that greatly improves access to information about product quality, prices, and performance. The Internet broadens the market, and makes demand and supply much more sensitive to changing economic conditions.

See: Michael Connolly, "Internet Change Seeks to Avoid Splintering the Web," *The Wall Street Journal Online*, October 11, 2007, http://online.wsj.com.

Regardless of whether a good or service is demanded by individuals for final consumption (direct demand) or as an input used in providing other goods and services (derived demand), the fundamentals of economic analysis offer a basis for investigating demand characteristics. For final consumption products, utility maximization as described by the theory of consumer behavior explains the basis for direct demand. For inputs used in the production of other products, profit maximization provides the underlying rationale for derived demand. Because both demand models are based on the optimization concept, fundamental direct demand and derived demand relations are essentially the same.

MARKET DEMAND FUNCTION

Demand Function
Relation between quantity sold and factors influencing its level.

The market **demand function** for a product is a statement of the relation between the aggregate quantity demanded and all factors that affect this quantity.

Determinants of Demand

In functional form, a demand function may be expressed as

$$\text{Quantity of Product } Y \text{ Demanded} = f(\text{Price of } Y, \text{ Prices of Related Products } (X),$$
$$\text{Income, Advertising, and so on.)}$$

3.1

The generalized demand function expressed in Equation (3.1) lists variables that commonly influence demand. For use in managerial decision making, the relation between quantity and each demand-determining variable must be specified. To illustrate, assume that the demand function for the automobile industry is

$$Q = a_1P + a_2P_X + a_3I + a_4Pop + a_5i + a_6A \qquad \textbf{3.2}$$

This equation states that the quantity of new domestic automobiles demanded during a given year (in millions), Q, is a linear function of the average price of new domestic cars (in \$), P; the average price for new import luxury cars, a prime substitute (in \$), P_X; disposable income per household (in \$), I; population, (in millions), Pop; average interest rate on car loans (in percent), i; and industry advertising expenditures (in \$ millions), A. The terms $a_1, a_2, ..., a_6$ are called the parameters of the demand function. Assume that the parameters of this demand function are known with certainty as shown in the following equation:

$$Q = -500P + 250P_X + 125I + 20{,}000Pop - 1{,}000{,}000i + 600A \qquad \textbf{3.3}$$

Equation (3.3) states that automobile demand falls by 500 for each \$1 increase in the average price charged by domestic manufacturers; it rises by 250 with every \$1 increase in the average price of new import luxury cars (P_X); it increases by 125 for each \$1 increase in disposable income per household (I); it increases by 20,000 with each additional million persons in the population (Pop); it decreases by 1 million for every 1 percent rise in interest rates (i); and it increases by 600 with each unit (\$1 million) spent on advertising (A).

To derive an estimate of industry demand in any given year, each parameter in Equation (3.3) is multiplied by the value of the related variable and then summed. Table 3.1 illustrates this process, showing that the estimated annual demand for new domestic automobiles is 8 million cars, assuming the stated values of each independent variable.

Industry Demand Versus Firm Demand

Market demand functions can be specified for an entire industry or for an individual firm, though somewhat different variables would typically be used in each case.

Table 3.1 Estimating Industry Demand for New Automobiles

Independent Variable (1)	Parameter Estimate (2)	Estimated Value for Independent Variable During the Coming Year (3)	Estimated Demand (4) = (2) × (3)
Average price for new cars (P) (\$)	−500	30,000	−15,000,000
Average price for new import luxury cars (P_X) (\$)	250	60,000	15,000,000
Disposable income, per household (I) (\$)	125	56,000	7,000,000
Population (pop) (millions)	20,000	300	6,000,000
Average interest rate (i) (%)	−1,000,000	8	−8,000,000
Industry advertising expenditures (A) (\$ million)	600	5,000	3,000,000
Total demand (cars)			8,000,000

Variables representing competitors' actions would be stressed in firm demand functions. For example, a firm's demand function would typically include competitors' prices and advertising expenditures. The quantity demanded for the firm's product line is negatively related to its own prices, but demand is positively related to the prices charged by competing firms. Demand would typically increase with the firm's own advertising expenditures, but it could increase or decrease with additional advertising by other firms.

The parameters for specific variables ordinarily differ in industry versus firm demand functions. Consider the positive influence of population growth on the demand for Toyota automobiles as opposed to automobiles in general. Although the effect is positive in each instance, the parameter value in the Toyota demand function would be much smaller than that in the industry demand function. Only if Toyota had 100 percent of the market—that is, if Toyota were the industry—would the parameters for firm and industry demand be identical.

Because firm and industry demand functions differ, different models or equations must be estimated for analyzing these two levels of demand. However, demand concepts developed in this chapter apply to both firm and industry demand functions.

DEMAND CURVE

Demand Curve
Relation between price and the quantity demanded, holding all else constant.

The **demand curve** expresses the relation between the price charged for a product and the quantity demanded, holding constant the effects of all other variables.

Demand Curve Determination

A demand curve is shown in the form of a graph, and all variables in the demand function except the price and quantity of the product itself are held fixed. In the automobile demand function given in Equation (3.3), for example, one must hold income, population, interest rates, and advertising expenditures constant to identify the demand curve relation between new domestic automobile prices and quantity demanded.

To illustrate, consider the relation depicted in Equation (3.3) and Table 3.1. Assuming that import luxury car prices, income, population, interest rates, and advertising expenditures are all held constant at their Table 3.1 values, the relation between the quantity demanded of new domestic cars and price is expressed as[2]

$$Q = -500P + 250(\$60,000) + 125(\$56,000) + 20,000(300)$$
$$-1,000,000(8) + 600(\$5,000) \qquad \textbf{3.4}$$
$$= 23,000,000 - 500P$$

Alternatively, when price is expressed as a function of output, the industry demand curve [Equation (3.4)] can be written

$$P = \$46,000 - \$0.002Q \qquad \textbf{3.5}$$

---

2   An 8 percent interest rate assumption might seem high by today's standards when 2.9 percent financing or \$2,500 rebates are sometimes offered to boost new car sales during slow periods. However, so-called "teaser" rates of 2.9 percent are subsidized by the manufacturer. That's why promotions feature 2.9 percent financing *or* \$2,500 rebates. In such instances, the alternative \$2,500 rebate is a good estimate of the amount of interest rate subsidy offered by the manufacturer.

Equations (3.4) and (3.5) both represent the demand curve for automobiles given specified values for all other variables in the demand function. Equation (3.5) is shown graphically in Figure 3.1 because it is common to show price as a function of quantity in demand analysis. As is typical, a reduction in price increases the quantity demanded; an increase in price decreases the quantity demanded. The -500 slope coefficient for the price variable in Equation (3.4) means that a $1 increase in the average price of new domestic automobiles would reduce the quantity demanded by 500 cars. Similarly, a $1 decrease in the average price of new domestic automobiles would increase quantity demanded by 500 cars. When price is expressed as a function of quantity, as in Equation (3.5), a 1-unit increase in Q would lead to a $0.002 reduction in the average price of new domestic cars. A 1-million car decrease in Q would lead to a $2,000 increase in average prices.

Relation Between the Demand Curve and Demand Function

The relation between the demand curve and the demand function is important and worth considering in somewhat greater detail. Figure 3.2 shows three demand curves for automobiles. Each curve is constructed in the same manner as that depicted in Equations (3.4) and (3.5) and then portrayed in Figure 3.1. In fact, $D_{8\%}$ is the same automobile demand curve characterized by Equation (3.5) and Figure 3.1. If $D_{8\%}$ is the appropriate demand curve, then 8 million new domestic automobiles can be sold at an average price of $30,000, whereas 10 million automobiles could be sold at an average price of $26,000, but only 6 million automobiles can be sold at an average price of $34,000. This variation is

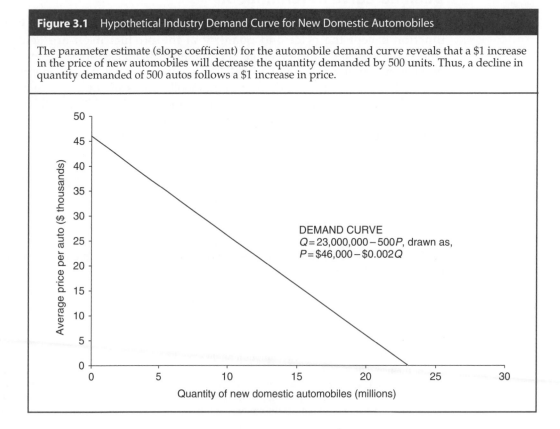

Figure 3.1   Hypothetical Industry Demand Curve for New Domestic Automobiles

The parameter estimate (slope coefficient) for the automobile demand curve reveals that a $1 increase in the price of new automobiles will decrease the quantity demanded by 500 units. Thus, a decline in quantity demanded of 500 autos follows a $1 increase in price.

DEMAND CURVE
$Q = 23,000,000 - 500P$, drawn as,
$P = \$46,000 - \$0.002Q$

Average price per auto ($ thousands)

Quantity of new domestic automobiles (millions)

Change in the Quantity Demanded
Movement along a given demand curve reflecting a change in price.

Shift in Demand
Switch from one demand curve to another following a change in a nonprice determinant of demand.

described as a **change in the quantity demanded**, defined as a movement along a single demand curve. As average price drops from \$34,000 to \$30,000 to \$26,000 along $D_{8\%}$, the quantity demanded rises from 6 million to 8 million to 10 million automobiles. A change in the quantity demanded refers to the effect on sales of a change in price, holding constant the effects of all other demand-determining factors.

A **shift in demand**, or switch from one demand curve to another demand curve, reflects a change in one or more nonprice variables in the product demand function. In the automobile demand function example, a decrease in interest rates causes an increase in automobile demand, because the interest rate parameter of -1 million indicates that demand and interest rates are inversely related—that is, they change in opposite directions. When demand is inversely related to a factor such as interest rates, a reduction in the factor leads to rising demand and an increase in the factor leads to falling demand.

$D_{6\%}$ is another automobile demand curve. The sole difference between $D_{8\%}$ and $D_{6\%}$ is that $D_{8\%}$ assumes an interest rate of 8 percent rather than the 6 percent interest rate used to construct $D_{6\%}$. Because the interest rate parameter is negative, a decrease in interest rates causes an increase in automobile demand. Holding all else equal, a 2 percent reduction in interest rates leads to a 2 million-unit [$=-1$ million $\times (-2)$] increase in automobile demand. A 2 percent decrease in average interest rates leads to an upward or rightward shift in the original demand curve $D_{8\%}$ to the new demand curve $D_{6\%}$. This also means that a 2 percent interest rate reduction will increase automobile demand

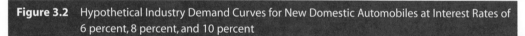

Figure 3.2   Hypothetical Industry Demand Curves for New Domestic Automobiles at Interest Rates of 6 percent, 8 percent, and 10 percent

An upward or rightward shift in the original demand curve from $D_{8\%}$ to $D_{6\%}$ follows a 2 percent fall in interest rates from 8 percent to 6 percent; a downward or leftward shift from $D_{8\%}$ to $D_{10\%}$ reflects a 2 percent rise in interest rates from 8 percent to 10 percent.

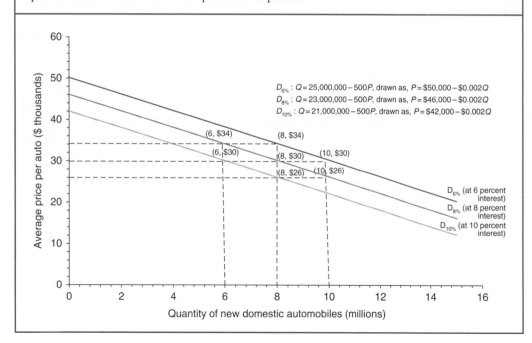

by 2 million units at each price level. At an average price of $30,000, for example, a 2 percent reduction in interest rates increases automobile demand from 8 million to 10 million units per year, as shown on $D_{6\%}$. Also as shown on $D_{6\%}$, after a 2 percent decrease in interest rates, the original quantity of 8 million automobiles could be sold at a higher average price of $34,000. Notice that demand curve $D_{8\%}$ indicates that only 8 million units could be sold at an average industry price of $30,000, when interest rates average 8 percent per year.

A 2 percent increase in interest rates, from 8 percent to 10 percent, causes an inward or leftward shift in the original demand curve $D_{8\%}$ to the new demand curve $D_{10\%}$. A 2 percent increase in interest rates reduces automobile demand by 2 million cars at each price level. At a price of $30,000, a 2 percent increase in interest rates reduces demand for new domestic cars from 8 million cars, the $D_{8\%}$ level, to only 6 million units, the $D_{6\%}$ level. With interest rates at 10 percent, demand for 8 million cars would only arise at the lower average price of $26,000, the $D_{10\%}$ level, again holding all other demand-determining factors constant.

From the advertising parameter of 600, it is possible to infer that demand and advertising are positively related. Rising demand follows increases in advertising, and falling demand follows reductions in advertising. The shift from $D_{8\%}$ to $D_{6\%}$ in Figure 3.2, for example, could also have resulted from a $3.33 billion increase in industry advertising rather than a 2 percent reduction in interest rates, or it could be the result of a $1.67 billion increase in industry advertising coupled with a 1 percent reduction in interest rates. In each case, the resulting demand curve is given by the equation $Q = 25,000,000 - 500P$, or $P = \$50,000 - \$0.002Q$. Similarly, the downward shift from $D_{8\%}$ to $D_{10\%}$ in Figure 3.2 could

Managerial Application 3.2

ISP Customers Learn About Demand and Supply

In 1996, America Online, Inc., the leader in the burgeoning Internet Service Provider (ISP) industry, succumbed to pressure from competitors and cut its price for unlimited access to the Internet to $19.95 per month. Usage skyrocketed. Since flat-rate pricing doesn't penalize unlimited usage, many subscribers simply decided to leave their connection running all day and night. Because of surging popularity among novice users, long-time subscribers found themselves locked out of the AOL system. Dedicated users became especially irate when AOL kept running TV commercials and offering promotional rates to new subscribers when it was clearly unable to handle the traffic such promotions generated. Subscriber frustration turned to litigation, and AOL was hit with lawsuits charging the company with negligence and consumer fraud.

Overloaded, facing lawsuits and the potential of massive defections from dissatisfied customers, AOL made a radical decision. AOL slashed marketing efforts aimed at recruiting new subscribers and stepped up investment in network capacity. Continuing growth in the popularity of the Internet

has allowed AOL to boost spending on infrastructure, and even raise its fixed-rate monthly charge for unlimited access. Still, AOL suffers from having to employ a fixed-rate pricing structure that is incapable of balancing demand and supply. Like all ISPs, AOL suffers from a business plan featuring fixed-rate pricing that encourages unlimited demand and time-dependent supply costs that are variable with usage. Unlike local phone service, where fixed costs predominate and marginal usage costs are near zero, ISPs closely resemble long-distance telephone service providers. ISP costs are closely tied to time of usage, and efficient pricing must be on a per unit basis.

With time-based pricing, ISP demand will be curtailed during peak hours and the practice of novice users logging on for days at a time will end. In the meantime, frustrated ISP customers will suffer from demand–supply imbalances created by the industry's fixed-rate pricing model.

See: Bobby White, "Its Creators Call Internet Outdated, Offer Remedies," *The Wall Street Journal Online*, October 2007, http://online.wsj.com.

have resulted from a $3.33 billion decrease in industry advertising rather than a 2 percent increase in interest rates, or it could be the result of a $1.67 billion decrease in industry advertising coupled with a 1 percent increase in interest rates. In each case, the resulting demand curve is given by the equation $Q = 21,000,000 - 500P$, or $P = \$42,000 - \$0.002Q$.

The distinction between changes in the quantity demanded, which reflect movements along a given demand curve, and changes in demand, which reflect shifts from one demand curve to another, is extremely important. Failure to understand the causes of changes in demand for a company's products can lead to costly, even disastrous, mistakes in managerial decision making. The task of demand analysis is made especially difficult by the fact that under normal circumstances, not only prices but also prices of other goods, income, population, interest rates, advertising, and most other demand-related factors vary from period to period. Sorting out the impact of each factor makes demand analysis one of the most challenging aspects of managerial economics.

BASIS FOR SUPPLY

The profit motive determines the quantity of a good or service that producers are willing and able to sell during a given period.

How Output Prices Affect Supply

Supply
Total quantity offered for sale under various market conditions.

The **supply** of a product in the market is the aggregate amount supplied by individual firms. The supply of products arises from their ability to enhance the firm's value maximization objective. The amount of any good or service supplied will rise when the marginal benefit to producers, measured in terms of the value of output, is greater than the marginal cost of production. The amount of any good or service supplied will fall when the marginal benefit to producers is less than the marginal costs of production. Thus, individual firms will expand or reduce the quantity supplied based on the expected impact on profits.

Among the factors influencing the quantity supplied of a product, the price of the product itself is often the most important. Higher prices increase the quantity of output producers want to bring to market. When marginal revenue exceeds marginal cost, firms increase the quantity supplied to earn the greater profits associated with expanded output. Higher prices allow firms to pay the higher production costs that are sometimes associated with expansions in output. Conversely, lower prices typically cause producers to reduce the quantity supplied. At the margin, lower prices can have the effect of making previous levels of production unprofitable.

The prices of related goods and services can also play an important role in determining supply of a product. If a firm uses resources that can be used to produce several different products, it may switch production from one product to another, depending on market conditions. For example, the supply of gasoline typically declines in autumn when the price of heating oil rises. Gasoline supply typically increases during the spring and summer months with the seasonal decline in heating oil prices. Whereas the substitution of one output for another can cause an inverse relation between the supply of one product and the price of a second product, complementary production relationships result in a positive relation between supply and the price of a related product. For example, ore deposits containing lead often also contain silver. An increase in the price of lead can therefore lead to an expansion in both lead and silver production.

Other Factors That Influence Supply

Technology is another key determinant of product supply. The current state of technology refers to the manner in which inputs are transformed into output. An improvement in the state of technology, including any product invention or process innovation that reduces production costs, increases the quantity and/or quality of products offered for sale at a given price.

Changes in input prices also affect supply in that an increase in input prices will raise costs and reduce the quantity that can be supplied profitably at a given market price. Alternatively, a decrease in input prices increases profitability and the quantity supplied at a given price.

For some products, especially agricultural products, weather can play an important role in determining supply. Temperature, rainfall, and wind all influence the quantity that can be supplied. Heavy rainfall in early spring, for example, can delay or prevent the planting of crops, significantly limiting supply. Abundant rain during the growing season can greatly increase the available supply at harvest time. An early freeze that prevents full maturation or heavy snow that limits harvesting activity can reduce the supply of agricultural products.

Managerial decision making requires understanding both individual firm supply and market supply conditions. Market supply is the aggregate of individual firm supply, so it is ultimately determined by factors affecting firm supply. Firm supply is examined in greater detail in Chapters 7 and 8. For now, meaningful insight can be gained by understanding the nature of market supply.

MARKET SUPPLY FUNCTION

Supply Function
Relation between supply and all factors influencing its level.

The market **supply function** for a product is the relation between the quantity supplied and all factors affecting that amount.

Determinants of Supply

In functional form, a supply function can be expressed as

Quantity of Product Y Supplied $= f$(Price of Y, Prices of Related Products (X), Current State of Technology, Input Prices, Weather, and so on.) **3.6**

The generalized supply function expressed in Equation (3.6) lists variables that influence supply. As is true with the demand function, the supply function must be made explicit to be useful for managerial decision making.

To illustrate, consider the automobile industry example discussed previously and assume that the supply function has been specified as follows:

$$Q = b_1 P + b_2 P_{SUV} + b_3 W + b_4 S + b_5 E + b_6 i$$ **3.7**

This equation states that the number of new domestic automobiles supplied during a given period (in millions), Q, is a linear function of the average price of new domestic cars (in \$), P; average price of new sport utility vehicles (SUVs) (in \$), P_{SUV}; average hourly price of labor (wages in \$ per hour), W; average cost of steel (\$ per ton), S; average cost of energy (\$ per mcf natural gas), E; and average interest rate (cost of capital in percent), i. The terms b_1, b_2, ... , b_6 are the parameters of the supply function. Note that no explicit term describes technology, or the method by which inputs are combined to produce output. The current state of technology is an underlying, or implicit, factor in the industry supply function.

Substituting a set of assumed parameter values into Equation (3.7) gives the following supply function for the automobile industry:

$$Q = 2{,}000P - 500P_{SUV} - 100{,}000W - 15{,}000S - 125{,}000E - 1{,}000{,}000i \qquad \textbf{3.8}$$

Equation (3.8) indicates that the quantity of automobiles supplied increases by 2,000 units for each $1 increase in the average price charged; it decreases by 500 units for each $1 increase in the average price of new SUVs; it decreases by 100,000 units for each $1 increase in wage rates, including fringes; it decreases by 15,000 units with each $1 increase in the average cost of steel; it decreases by 125,000 units with each $1 increase in the average cost of energy; and it decreases by 1 million units if interest rates rise 1 percent. Thus, each parameter indicates the effect of the related factor on supply from domestic manufacturers.

To estimate the supply of automobiles during the coming period, each parameter in Equation (3.8) is multiplied by the value of its respective variable and these products are then summed. Table 3.2 illustrates this process, showing that the supply of autos, assuming the stated values of the independent variables, is 8 million units.

Industry Supply Versus Firm Supply

Just as in the case of demand, supply functions can be specified for an entire industry or an individual firm. Even though factors affecting supply are often similar in industry supply versus firm supply functions, the relative importance of such influences can differ dramatically. At one extreme, if all firms used identical production methods and identical equipment, had salaried and hourly employees who were equally capable and identically paid, and had equally skilled management, then individual firm supply and industry supply functions would be closely related. Each

Table 3.2 Estimating Industry Supply for New Automobiles

Independent Variable (1)	Parameter Estimated (2)	Estimated Value for Independent Variable During the Coming Year (3)	Estimate Supply (4)=(2) × (3)
Average price for new cars (P) ($)	2,000	30,000	60,000,000
Average price for sport utility vehicles (P_{SUV}) ($)	−500	42,500	−21,250,000
Average hourly wage rate, including fringe benefits (W) ($)	−100,000	100	−10,000,000
Average cost of steel, per ton (S) ($)	−15,000	800	−12,000,000
Average cost of energy input, per mcf natural gas (E) ($)	−125,000	6	−750,000
Average interest rate (i) (in %)	−1,000,000	8	−8,000,000
Total supply (cars)			8,000,000

firm would be similarly affected by changes in supply conditions. Each parameter in the individual firm supply functions would be smaller than in the industry supply function, however, and would reflect each firm's relative share of the market.

More typically, firms within a given industry adopt somewhat different production methods, use equipment of different vintage, and employ labor of varying skill and compensation levels. In such cases, individual firm supply levels can be affected quite differently by various factors. Chinese automakers, for example, may be able to offer subcompacts in the United States profitably at average industry prices as low as, say, $15,000 per automobile. On the other hand, U.S. auto manufacturers, who have historically operated with a labor cost disadvantage, may only be able to offer supply of subcompacts at average industry prices in excess of, say, $26,000. This means that at relatively high average prices for the industry above $26,000 per unit, both foreign and domestic auto manufacturers would be actively engaged in car production. At relatively low average prices below $26,000, only foreign producers would offer cars. This would be reflected by different parameters describing the relation between price and quantity supplied in the individual firm supply functions for Chinese and U.S. automobile manufacturers.

Individual firms supply output only when doing so is profitable. When industry prices are high enough to cover the marginal costs of increased production, individual firms expand output, thereby increasing total profits, and the value of the firm. To the extent that the economic capabilities of industry participants vary, so too does the scale of output supplied by individual firms at various prices.

Similarly, supply is affected by production technology. Firms operating with highly automated facilities incur large fixed costs and relatively small variable costs.

Managerial Application 3.3

The Import Supply Battle in the U.S. Auto Industry

The "Big Three" U.S. manufacturers typically account for 60 percent to 65 percent of the U.S. market. Japanese name plates account for roughly 25 percent; European makes are responsible for the remainder. Despite a continuing erosion in market share during the 1980s and 1990s, General Motors (GM) remains by far the largest company in the U.S. auto market. GM's current market share is in the 30 percent to 35 percent range, followed by the Ford Motor Company with roughly 25 percent, DaimlerChrysler and Toyota with 10 percent to 15 percent each, Honda roughly 6 percent, and Nissan roughly 4 percent; other companies, like Hyundai (Kia), Mazda, Mitsubishi, Subaru, and Volkswagen, account for the rest.

As companies fight for market share, many new products are aimed at market niches. Chrysler, for example, returned from the brink of bankruptcy in the 1980s to record profits in the 1990s on the basis of its astonishing success with minivans. At the same time, Ford took aim at Chrysler's lucrative Jeep franchise with the Ford Explorer and outran both Jeep and Chevrolet to take first place in the sport utility vehicle (SUV) segment. Meanwhile, Mercedes has made significant inroads in the luxury segment of the SUV market, while Honda has successfully launched "economy" SUVs.

To gain entry into important market niches, everyone seems to be merging or working together. During recent years, GM bought Saab; Ford bought Jaguar, Land Rover, and Volvo; and Chrysler hooked up with Mercedes. The three largest U.S. manufacturers all enjoy important links with foreign producers, thus blurring the distinction between foreign and domestic vehicles. From a consumer's standpoint, import competition has been a beneficial spur to innovation and quality improvement, as it keeps the lid on auto industry prices and profits. The active interplay of demand and supply through stiff global competition seems to be the industry's—and the consumer's—best bet for an efficiently functioning auto market.

See: Michael Connolly, "Demand for Small Cars Tests Auto Makers' Financial Ingenuity," *The Wall Street Journal Online*, October 22, 2007, http://online.wsj.com.

The supply of product from such firms is likely to be relatively insensitive to price changes when compared to less automated firms, for which variable production costs are higher and thus more closely affected by production levels. Relatively low-cost producers can and do supply output at relatively low market prices. Of course, both relatively low-cost and high-cost producers are able to supply output profitably when market prices are high.

SUPPLY CURVE

Supply Curve
Relation between price and the quantity supplied, holding all else constant.

The **supply curve** expresses the relation between the price charged and the quantity supplied, holding constant the effects of all other variables.

Supply Curve Determination

As is true with demand curves, supply curves are often shown graphically, and all independent variables in the supply function except the price of the product itself are fixed at specified levels. In the automobile supply function given in Equation (3.8), for example, it is important to hold constant the price of SUVs and the prices of labor, steel, energy, and other inputs to examine the relation between automobile price and the quantity supplied.

To illustrate the supply determination process, consider the relation depicted in Equation (3.8). Assuming that the price of trucks, the prices of labor, steel, energy, and interest rates are all held constant at their Table 3.2 values, the relation between the quantity supplied and price is

$$Q = 2{,}000P - 500(\$42{,}500) - 100{,}000(\$100) - 15{,}000(\$800)$$
$$-125{,}000(\$6) - 1{,}000{,}000(8) \qquad \textbf{3.9}$$
$$-52{,}000{,}000 + 2{,}000P$$

Alternatively, when price is expressed as a function of output, the industry supply curve [Equation (3.9)] can be written

$$P = \$26{,}000 + \$0.0005Q \qquad \textbf{3.10}$$

Equations (3.9) and (3.10), which represent the supply curve for domestically produced automobiles given the specified values of all other variables in the supply function, are shown graphically in Figure 3.3. When the supply function is pictured with price as a function of quantity, or as $P = \$26{,}000 + \$0.0005Q$, industry supply will rise by 4 million new domestic cars if average price rises by \$2,000, or $1/0.0005$. Industry supply increases by 2,000 units with each \$1 increase in average price above the \$26,000 level. The \$26,000 intercept in this supply equation implies that the domestic car industry would not supply any new cars at all if the industry average price fell below \$26,000. At average prices below that level, low-cost imports would supply the entire industry demand.

Relation Between Supply Curve and Supply Function

Like the relation between the demand curve and the demand function, the relation between the supply curve and the supply function is very important in managerial decision making. Figure 3.4 shows three supply curves for automobiles: $S_{6\%}$, $S_{8\%}$, and $S_{10\%}$.

Figure 3.3   Hypothetical Industry Supply Curve for New Domestic Automobiles

For industry prices above $26,000, the supply curve parameter estimate (slope coefficient) shows that a $1 increase in the average price of new automobiles will increase the quantity supplied by 2,000 units.

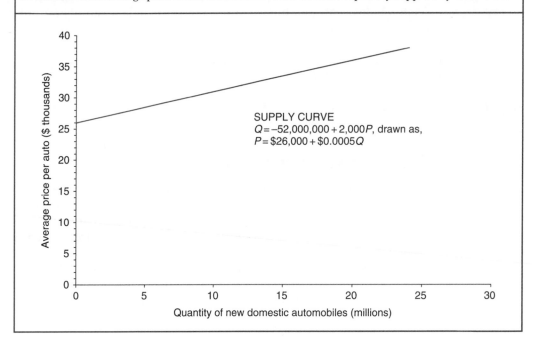

$S_{8\%}$ is the same automobile supply curve determined by Equations (3.9) and (3.10) and shown in Figure 3.3. If $S_{8\%}$ is the appropriate supply curve, then 8 million automobiles would be offered for sale at an industry average price of $30,000. Only 4 million automobiles would be offered for sale at an average price of $28,000; but industry supply would total 12 million automobiles at an average price of $32,000. Such movements along a given supply curve reflect a **change in the quantity supplied**. As average price rises from $28,000 to $30,000 to $32,000 along $S_{8\%}$, the quantity supplied increases from 4 million to 8 million to 12 million automobiles.

Change in the Quantity Supplied Movement along a given supply curve reflecting a change in price.

Supply curves $S_{6\%}$ and $S_{10\%}$ are similar to $S_{8\%}$. The differences are that $S_{6\%}$ is based on a 6 percent interest rate, whereas $S_{10\%}$ assumes a 10 percent interest rate. Recall that $S_{8\%}$ is based on an interest rate assumption of 8 percent. Because the supply function interest rate parameter is $-1,000,000$, a 2 percent fall in interest rates leads to a 2 million-unit increase in automobile supply at each automobile price level. This increase is described as a downward or rightward shift in the original supply curve, $S_{8\%}$, to the new supply curve $S_{6\%}$. Conversely, a 2 percent rise in interest rates leads to a 2 million-unit decrease in automobile supply at each automobile price level. This reduction is described as an upward or leftward shift in the original supply curve $S_{8\%}$ to the new supply curve $S_{10\%}$.

To avoid confusion, remember that $S_{10\%}$ lies *above* $S_{8\%}$ in Figure 3.4, whereas $D_{10\%}$ lies *below* $D_{8\%}$ in Figure 3.2. Similarly, it is important to keep in mind that $S_{6\%}$ lies *below* $S_{8\%}$ in Figure 3.4, but $D_{6\%}$ lies *above* $D_{8\%}$ in Figure 3.2. These differences stem from the fact that a rise in demand involves an *upward* shift in the demand curve, whereas a fall in demand involves a *downward* shift in the demand curve. Conversely, a rise in supply involves a *downward* shift in the supply curve; a fall in supply involves an *upward* shift in the supply curve.

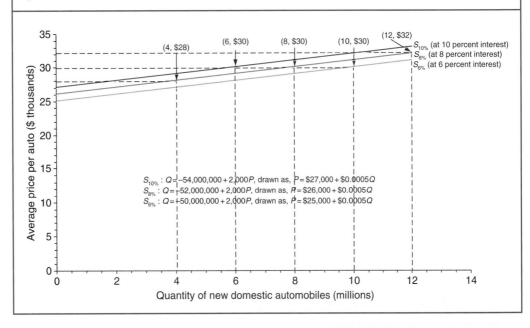

Figure 3.4 Hypothetical Industry Supply Curves for New Domestic Automobiles at Interest Rates of 6 percent, 8 percent, and 10 percent

An upward or leftward shift from $S_{8\%}$ to $S_{10\%}$ reflects a 2 percent rise in interest rates from 8 percent to 10 percent; a downward or rightward shift in the original supply curve from $S_{8\%}$ to $S_{6\%}$ follows a 2 percent fall in interest rates from 8 percent to 6 percent.

At a price of $30,000, for example, a 2 percent rise in interest rates reduces automobile supply from 8 million units, the $S_{8\%}$ level, to 6 million units, the $S_{10\%}$ level. This reduction in supply reflects the fact that previously profitable production no longer generates a profit because of the increase in capital costs. At a price of $30,000, a 2 percent reduction in interest rates increases automobile supply from 8 million units, the $S_{8\%}$ level, to 10 million units, the $S_{6\%}$ level. Supply rises following this decline in interest rates because, given a decline in capital costs, producers find that they can profitably expand output at the $30,000 price level from 8 million to 10 million units.

Shift in Supply
Movement from one supply curve to another following a change in a nonprice determinant of supply.

A **shift in supply**, or a switch from one supply curve to another, indicates a change in one or more of the nonprice variables in the product supply function. In the automobile supply function example, an increase in truck prices leads to a decrease in automobile supply, because the SUV price parameter of −400 indicates that automobile supply and truck prices are inversely related. This reflects the fact that as SUV prices rise, holding all else constant, auto manufacturers have an incentive to shift from automobile to SUV production. When automobile supply is inversely related to a factor such as SUV prices, rising SUV prices lead to falling automobile supply, and falling SUV prices lead to rising automobile supply. From the negative parameters for the price of labor, steel, energy, and interest rates, it is also possible to infer that automobile supply is inversely related to each of these factors.

A change in interest rates is not the only factor that might be responsible for a change in the supply curve from $S_{8\%}$ to $S_{6\%}$ or $S_{10\%}$. From the steel cost parameter of −15,000, it is possible to infer that supply and steel costs are inversely related. Falling supply follows an increase in steel costs, and rising supply follows a decrease in steel costs. The shift from

$S_{8\%}$ to $S_{10\%}$ in Figure 3.4, which reflects a decrease in supply, could have resulted from a $133.33 per ton increase in steel costs rather than a 2 percent increase in interest rates. Alternatively, this change could result from a $66.66 per ton increase in steel costs plus a 1 percent increase in interest rates. In each case, the resulting supply curve is given by the equation $Q = -54,000,000 + 2,000P$, or $P = \$27,000 + \$0.0005Q$. Similarly, the shift from $S_{8\%}$ to $S_{6\%}$ in Figure 3.4, which reflects an increase in supply, could have resulted from a $133.33 per ton decrease in steel costs rather than a 2 percent decrease in interest rates from 8 percent to 6 percent. This change could also result from a $66.66 per ton decrease in steel costs plus a 1 percent decrease in interest rates. In each case, the resulting supply curve is given by the equation $Q = -50,000,000 + \$2,000P$, or $P = \$25,000 + \$0.0005Q$.

For some products, a positive relation between supply and other factors such as weather is often evident. This is especially true for agricultural products. If supply were positively related to weather, perhaps measured in terms of average temperature, then rising supply would follow rising average temperature and falling supply would accompany falling average temperature. Weather is not included in the automobile supply function because there is no close relation between automobile supply and weather.

The distinction between changes in the quantity supplied, which reflect movements along a given supply curve, and a shift in supply, which reflects movement from one supply curve to another, is important, as was the distinction between changes in the quantity demanded and a shift in demand. Because the prices of related products, input prices, taxes, weather, and other factors affecting supply can be expected to vary from one period to the next, assessing the individual importance of each factor becomes a challenging aspect of managerial economics.

Managerial Application 3.4

MBA Demand and Supply

The Master of Business Administration (MBA) degree is typically granted after 1 to 2 years of intensive graduate school study in the theory and practice of business management. Once earned, the MBA degree certifies that the recipient has general competency in the major functional areas of business: accounting, finance, management, and marketing. Important subspecialties include economics, organizational behavior, strategy, operations management, international business, information systems, supply chain management, and public policy. What makes the MBA degree extraordinarily useful is that it gives recipients a firm-wide perspective on important managerial decisions. MBAs coordinate efforts across functional areas to ensure that the firm is operating efficiently and maximizing profit opportunities.

Full-time MBA programs normally last 2 years, and appeal to students with a variety of undergraduate degrees and a reasonable amount of work experience. Accelerated MBA programs last 18 months or less and involve a heavier course load. Part-time MBA programs hold classes on weekday evenings and are popular with working professionals who take a relatively light course load for 3 or more years until graduation. Executive MBA programs, developed for high-level managers, often meet on weekends and allow top executives to earn an MBA in 2 years or less while working full time.

The number of MBA degrees conferred has seen explosive growth in the United States, jumping from less than 5,000 MBAs per year in the 1960s to more than 100,000 MBAs per year today. MBAs typically enjoy an increase in salary of $15,000 to $40,000 per year, but that varies widely depending upon work experience, graduate school reputation, job type, industry, and regional job market conditions. Costs can be substantial. Tuition and fees range from as low as $15,000 per year at high-quality regional schools, to $50,000 per year and more at elite private schools. Just considering out-of-pocket costs, the return on investment (ROI) for full-time MBA programs routinely exceeds 50 percent per year. Part-time MBA programs avoid the opportunity costs of full-time programs and generate even higher ROIs.

No wonder the MBA is a popular degree!

See: http://www.businessweek.com/bschools/.

MARKET EQUILIBRIUM

Equilibrium
Perfect balance in
demand and supply.

When quantity demanded and quantity supplied are in perfect balance at a given price, the product market is said to be in **equilibrium**.

Surplus and Shortage

Surplus
Excess supply.

Shortage
Excess demand.

A **surplus** is created when producers supply more of a product at a given price than buyers demand. Surplus describes a condition of excess supply. Conversely, a **shortage** is created when buyers demand more of a product at a given price than producers are willing to supply. Shortage describes a condition of excess demand. Neither surplus nor shortage will occur when a market is in equilibrium, because equilibrium is defined as a condition in which the quantities demanded and supplied are exactly in balance at the current market price. Surplus and shortage describe situations of market disequilibrium because either will result in powerful market forces being exerted to change the prices and quantities offered in the market.

To illustrate the concepts of surplus and shortage consider the demand and supply curves for the automobile industry example depicted in Figure 3.5. Note that the demand curve is the same hypothetical demand curve shown in Figure 3.1, and it is also $D_{8\%}$ in Figure 3.2. The supply curve shown is the same one illustrated in Figure 3.3, and shown as $S_{8\%}$ in Figure 3.4. To clarify the concepts of surplus, shortage, and market equilibrium,

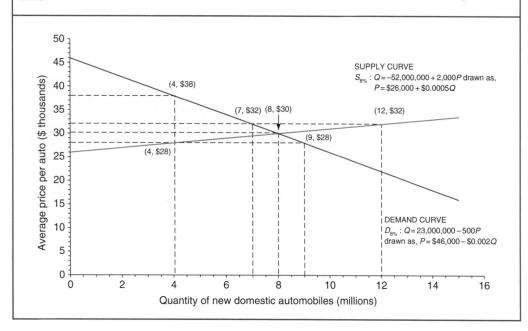

Figure 3.5 Surplus, Shortage, and Market Equilibrium

At an industry average price of $32,000, excess supply creates a surplus of 5 million units exerting downward pressure on both price and output levels. Similarly, excess demand at a price of $28,000 creates a shortage of 5 million units and upward pressure on both prices and output. Market equilibrium is achieved when demand equals supply at a price of $30,000 and quantity of 8 million units.

SUPPLY CURVE
$S_{8\%} : Q = -52,000,000 + 2,000P$ drawn as,
$P = \$26,000 + \$0.0005Q$

DEMAND CURVE
$D_{8\%} : Q = 23,000,000 - 500P$
drawn as, $P = \$46,000 - \$0.002Q$

it becomes useful to focus on the relation of the quantity supplied and the quantity demanded at each of three different hypothetical market prices.

At a market price of $32,000, the quantity demanded is 7 million units. This is easily derived from Equation (3.4), the market demand curve; $Q_D = 23,000,000 - 500(\$32,000) = 7$ million cars. The quantity supplied at an industry average price of $32,000 is derived from the market supply curve, Equation (3.9), which indicates that $Q_S = -52,000,000 + 2,000(\$32,000) = 12$ million cars. At an average automobile price of $32,000, the quantity supplied greatly exceeds the quantity demanded. This difference of 5 million cars per year ($=12-7$) constitutes a surplus.

An automobile surplus results in a near-term buildup in inventories and downward pressure on market prices and production. This is typical for a market with a surplus of product. Prices tend to decline as firms recognize that consumers are unwilling to purchase the quantity of product available at prevailing prices. Similarly, producers cut back on production as inventories build up and prices soften, reducing the quantity of product supplied in future periods. The automobile industry uses rebate programs and dealer-subsidized low–interest rate financing on new cars to effectively combat the problem of periodic surplus automobile production.

A different type of market imbalance is also illustrated in Figure 3.5. At an average price for new domestic cars of $28,000, the quantity demanded rises to 9 million cars, $Q_D = 23,000,000 - 500(\$28,000) = 9$ million. At the same time, the quantity supplied falls to 4 million units, $Q_S = -52,000,000 + 2,000(\$28,000) = 4$ million. This difference of 5 million cars per year ($=9-4$) constitutes a shortage. Shortage, or excess demand, reflects the fact that, given the current productive capability of the industry (including technology, input prices, and so on), producers cannot profitably supply more than 4 million units of output per year at an average price of $28,000, despite buyer demand for more output.

Shortages exert a powerful upward force on both market prices and output levels. In this example, the demand curve indicates that with only 4 million automobiles supplied, buyers would be willing to pay an industry average price of $38,000 [$=\$46,000 - \$0.002(4,000,000)$]. Consumers would bid against one another for the limited supply of automobiles and cause prices to rise. The resulting increase in price would motivate manufacturers to increase production while reducing the number of buyers willing and able to purchase cars. The resulting increase in the quantity supplied and reduction in quantity demanded work together to eventually eliminate the shortage.

The market situation at a price of $30,000 and a quantity of 8 million automobiles per year is displayed graphically as a balance between the quantity demanded and the quantity supplied. This is a condition of market equilibrium. There is no tendency for change in either price or quantity at a price of $30,000 and a quantity of 8 million units. The graph shows that any price above $30,000 results in surplus production. Prices in this range create excess supply, a buildup in inventories, and pressure for an eventual decline in prices to the $30,000 equilibrium level. At prices below $30,000, shortage occurs, which creates pressure for price increases. With prices moving up, producers are willing to supply more product and the quantity demanded declines, thus reducing the shortage.

Market Equilibrium Price
Market clearing price.

Only a market price of $30,000 brings the quantity demanded and the quantity supplied into perfect balance. This price is referred to as the **market equilibrium price**, or the market clearing price, because it just clears the market of all supplied product. Table 3.3 shows the surplus of quantity supplied at prices above the market equilibrium price and the shortage that results at prices below the market equilibrium price.

In short, surplus describes an excess in the quantity supplied over the quantity demanded at a given market price. A surplus results in downward pressure on both

Table 3.3	Surplus, Shortage, and Market Equilibrium in the New Car Market with 8 percent Interest Rates			
	Average Price for Domestic Automobiles ($) (1)	Supply ($S_8\%$) (2)	Demand ($D_8\%$) (3)	Surplus (+) or Shortage (−) (4)=(2) − (3)
	50,000	48,000,000	0	48,000,000
	47,500	43,000,000	0	43,000,000
	45,000	38,000,000	500,000	37,500,000
	42,500	33,000,000	1,750,000	31,250,000
	40,000	28,000,000	3,000,000	25,000,000
	37,500	23,000,000	4,250,000	18,750,000
	35,000	18,000,000	5,500,000	12,500,000
	32,500	13,000,000	6,750,000	6,250,000
	30,000	8,000,000	8,000,000	0
	27,500	3,000,000	9,250,000	−6,250,000
	25,000	0	10,500,000	−10,500,000
	22,500	0	11,750,000	−11,750,000
	20,000	0	13,000,000	−13,000,000
	17,500	0	14,250,000	−14,250,000
	15,000	0	15,500,000	−15,500,000
	12,500	0	16,750,000	−16,750,000
	10,000	0	18,000,000	−18,000,000
	7,500	0	19,250,000	−19,250,000
	5,000	0	20,500,000	−20,500,000
	2,500	0	21,750,000	−21,750,000
	0	0	23,000,000	−23,000,000

market prices and Industry output. Shortage describes an excess in the quantity demanded over the quantity supplied at a given market price. A shortage results in upward pressure on both market prices and industry output. Market equilibrium describes a condition of perfect balance in the quantity demanded and the quantity supplied at a given price. In equilibrium, there is no tendency for change in either price or quantity.

Comparative Statics: Changing Demand

Managers typically control a number of the factors that affect product demand or supply. To make appropriate decisions concerning those variables, it is often useful to know how altering those decisions affect market conditions. Similarly, the direction and magnitude of changes in demand and supply that are due to uncontrollable external factors, such as income or interest rate changes, need to be understood so that managers can develop strategies and make decisions that are consistent with market conditions.

Comparative Statics Analysis
Study of changing demand and supply conditions.

One relatively simple but useful analytical technique is to examine the effects on market equilibrium of changes in economic factors underlying product demand and supply. This is called **comparative statics analysis**. In comparative statics analysis, the role of factors influencing demand is often analyzed while holding supply conditions constant.

Similarly, the role of factors influencing supply can be analyzed by studying changes in supply while holding demand conditions constant. Comparing market equilibrium price and output levels before and after various hypothetical changes in demand and supply conditions has the potential to yield useful predictions of expected changes.

Figures 3.6 and 3.7 illustrate the comparative statics of changing demand and supply conditions. Figure 3.6(a) combines the three automobile demand curves shown in Figure 3.2 with the automobile supply curve $S_{8\%}$ of Figure 3.4. The demand-related effects of changes in interest rates on the market price and quantity of automobiles are illustrated. Given the supply curve S, *and assuming for the moment that supply does not change in response to changes in interest rates*, the intersections of the three demand curves with the supply curve indicate the market price and quantity combinations expected at different interest rates.

At the intersection of $D_{6\%}$, which corresponds to a 6 percent interest rate, and the supply curve $S_{8\%}$ supply and demand are equal at a price of $30,800 and quantity of 9.6 million units. This result is obtained by simultaneously solving the equations for $D_{6\%}$ and $S_{8\%}$ to find the single price and quantity that satisfies both:

$$D_{6\%}: Q_D = 25,000,000 - 500P$$
$$S_{8\%}: Q_S = -52,000,000 + 2,000P$$

Demand and supply are equal at a price of $30,800 because

$$Q_D = Q_S$$
$$25,000,000 - 500P = -52,000,000 + 2,000P$$
$$2,500P = 77,000,000$$
$$P = \$30,800$$

Figure 3.6 (a)   Comparative Statics of (A) Changing Demand, or (B) Changing Supply

(a) Holding supply conditions constant, demand will vary with changing interest rates. Demand increases with a fall in interest rates; demand falls as interest rates rise.

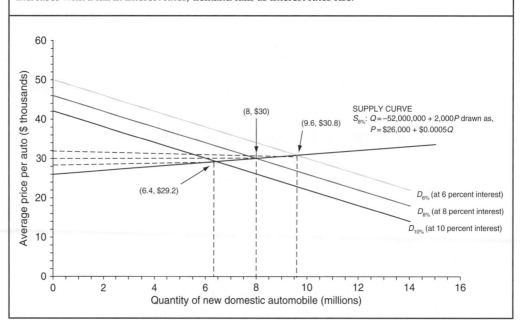

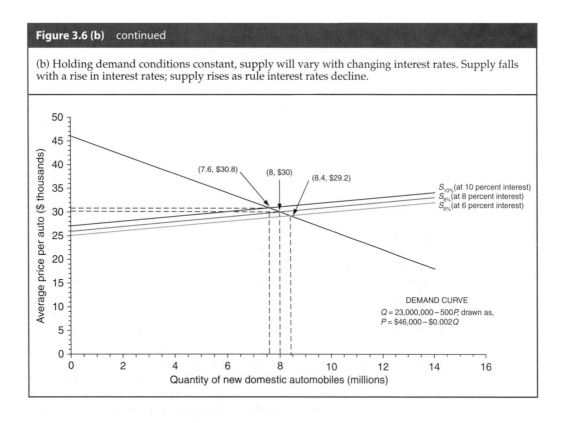

Figure 3.6 (b)   continued

(b) Holding demand conditions constant, supply will vary with changing interest rates. Supply falls with a rise in interest rates; supply rises as rule interest rates decline.

The related quantity is found by substituting this $30,800 price into either the demand curve $D_{6\%}$ or the supply curve $S_{8\%}$:

$$D_{6\%}: Q_D = 25{,}000{,}000 - 500(\$30{,}800)$$
$$= 9.6 \text{ million}$$
$$S_{8\%}: Q_S = -52{,}000{,}000 + 2{,}000(\$30{,}800)$$
$$= 9.6 \text{ million}$$

Using the same procedure to find the market clearing price–quantity combination for the intersection of $D_{8\%}$ (the demand curve for a 8 percent interest rate), with $S_{8\%}$ an equilibrium price of $30,000 and quantity of 8 million units is found. With interest rates at 10 percent (curve $D_{10\%}$), the market clearing price and quantity is $29,200 and 6.4 million units. Clearly, the level of interest rates plays an important role in the buyer's purchase decision. With higher interest rates, car buyers purchase fewer automobiles and only at progressively lower prices. In part, this reflects the fact that most car purchases are financed, and at higher interest rates, the total cost of buying an automobile is greater.

Comparative Statics: Changing Supply

Figure 3.6(b) combines the three automobile supply curves shown in Figure 3.4 with the automobile demand curve $D_{8\%}$ of Figure 3.2. The market equilibrium price and quantity effects of changing interest rates are illustrated, holding demand conditions constant *and, in particular, assuming that demand does not change in response to changes in interest rates.* Given the market demand curve $D_{8\%}$, a 2 percent fall in interest rates from 10 percent to 8 percent causes the equilibrium quantity supplied to rise from 7.6 million units on $S_{10\%}$ to 8 million units on $S_{8\%}$; a further 2 percent drop in interest rates from 8 percent to 6 percent causes the equilibrium quantity supplied to rise from 8 million units on $S_{8\%}$ to 8.4 million units on $S_{6\%}$. Similarly, in light of the market demand curve $D_{8\%}$, a 2 percent fall in interest rates from 10 percent to 8 percent causes the equilibrium price to fall from $30,800 to $30,000; a further 2 percent drop in interest rates from 8 percent to 6 percent causes the equilibrium price to fall from $30,000 to $29,200. As interest rates fall, producers find that they can profitably supply more output, even as average price falls, given the capital cost savings that would accompany lower interest rates. The effects of lower interest rates on supply are dramatic and reflect the highly capital-intensive nature of the automobile industry.

Comparative Statics: Changing Demand *and* Supply

From this analysis of hypothetical automobile demand and supply relations, it is clear that interest rates are an important factor influencing demand *and* supply. Factors related to overall economic activity often have important influences on both demand and supply. Figure 3.7 illustrates the comparative statics of changing demand *and* changing supply conditions by showing the net effects of changing interest rates. Here $S_{6\%}$ and $D_{6\%}$, both of which assume a 6 percent interest rate, yield an equilibrium price–output combination of $30,000 and 10 million cars; $S_{8\%}$ and $D_{8\%}$, which assume an 8 percent interest rate, yield an equilibrium price–output combination of $30,000 and 8 million units; $S_{10\%}$ and $D_{10\%}$, which assume a 10 percent interest rate, result in a price–output equilibrium of $30,000 and 6 million units. These price–output combinations reflect the combined effects of changing interest rates on demand and supply. The comparative statics of changes in any of the other factors that influence demand and supply can be analyzed in a similar fashion.

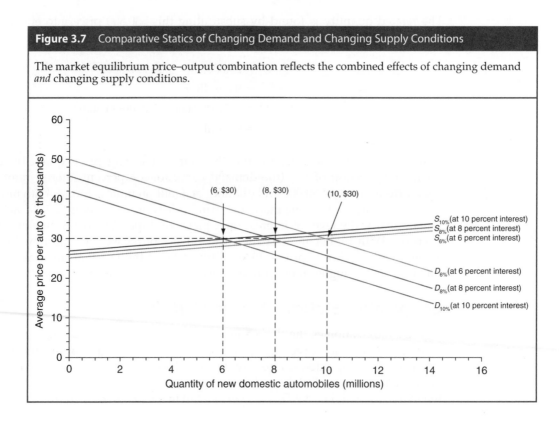

Figure 3.7   Comparative Statics of Changing Demand and Changing Supply Conditions

The market equilibrium price–output combination reflects the combined effects of changing demand *and* changing supply conditions.

SUMMARY

This chapter illustrates how the forces of supply and demand establish the prices and quantities observed in the markets for all goods and services.

- **Demand** is the quantity of a good or service that customers are willing and able to purchase under a given set of economic conditions. **Direct demand** is the demand for products that directly satisfy consumer desires. The value or worth of a good or service, its **utility**, is the prime determinant of direct demand. The demand for all inputs is **derived demand** and determined by the profitability of using various inputs to produce output.

- The market **demand function** for a product is a statement of the relation between the aggregate quantity demanded and all factors that affect this quantity. The **demand curve** expresses the relation between the price charged for a product and the quantity demanded, holding constant the effects of all other variables.

- A **change in the quantity demanded** is a movement along a single demand curve. A **shift in demand**, or shift from one demand curve to another, reflects a change in one or more of the nonprice variables in the product demand function.

- The term **supply** refers to the quantity of a good or service that producers are willing and able to sell under a given set of conditions. The market **supply** function for a product is a statement of the relation between the quantity supplied and all factors affecting that quantity. A **supply curve** expresses the relation between the price charged and the quantity supplied, holding constant the effects of all other variables.

- Movements along a supply curve reflect **change in the quantity supplied**. A **shift in supply**, or a switch from one supply curve to another, indicates a change in one or more of the nonprice variables in the product supply function.

- A market is in **equilibrium** when the quantity demanded and the quantity supplied is in perfect balance at a given price. **Surplus** describes a condition of excess supply. **Shortage** is created when buyers demand more of a product at a given price than producers are willing to supply. The **market equilibrium price** just clears the market of all supplied product.

- In **comparative statics analysis**, the role of factors influencing demand or supply is analyzed while holding all else equal.

A fundamental understanding of demand and supply concepts is essential to the successful operation of any economic organization. The concepts introduced in this chapter provide the structure for the more detailed analysis of demand and supply in subsequent chapters.

QUESTIONS

Q3.1 What key ingredients are necessary for the creation of economic demand?

Q3.2 Memory chip maker Micron Technology, Inc., enjoys strong demand for its products from manufacturers of computers and intelligent electronics. Describe the difference between direct demand and derived demand.

Q3.3 The Ford Escape Hybrid is the first gas-electric hybrid SUV produced and sold in North America. How would Ford estimate the demand influence of growing environmental awareness by consumers?

Q3.4 The Energy Department estimates that domestic demand for natural gas will grow by more than 40 percent between now and 2025. Distinguish between a demand function and a demand curve. What is the difference between a change in the quantity demanded and a shift in the demand curve?

Q3.5 What key ingredients are necessary for the creation of economic supply?

Q3.6 The United States is a big exporter of animal feeds, corn, meat, fruits, vegetables, and other agricultural commodities. Explain how foreign trade affects the domestic supply of such products.

Q3.7 Distinguish between a supply function and a supply curve. What is the difference between a change in the quantity supplied and a shift in the supply curve?

Q3.8 "Dynamic rather than static demand and supply conditions are typically observed in real-world markets. Therefore, comparative statics analysis has only limited value." Discuss this statement.

Q3.9 Contrast the supply and demand conditions for new Ph.D.s in economics and accounting. Why do such large differences in starting salaries seem to persist over time?

Q3.10 Suppose the personal income tax was replaced with a national sales tax. How would this affect aggregate supply, aggregate demand, and interest rates?

SELF-TEST PROBLEMS AND SOLUTIONS

ST3.1 Demand and Supply Curves. The following relations describe demand and supply conditions in the lumber–forest products industry:

$$Q_D = 80{,}000 - 20{,}000P \qquad \text{(Demand)}$$
$$Q_S = -20{,}000 + 20{,}000P \qquad \text{(Supply)}$$

where Q is quantity measured in thousands of board feet (1 square foot of lumber, 1 inch thick) and P is price in dollars.

A. Set up a spreadsheet to illustrate the effect of price (P), on the quantity supplied (Q_S), quantity demanded (Q_D), and the resulting surplus (+) or shortage (−) as represented by the difference between the quantity supplied and the quantity demanded at various price levels. Calculate the value for each respective variable based on a range for P from $1.00 to $3.50 in increments of 10¢ (i.e., $1.00, $1.10, $1.20, . . . , $3.50).

B. Using price (P) on the vertical or Y-axis and quantity (Q) on the horizontal or X-axis, plot the demand and supply curves for the lumber–forest products industry over the range of prices indicated previously.

ST3.1 SOLUTION

A. A table or spreadsheet that illustrates the effect of price (P), on the quantity supplied (Q_S), quantity demanded (Q_D), and the resulting surplus (+) or shortage (−) as represented by the difference between the quantity supplied and the quantity demanded at various price levels is as follows:

Lumber and Forest Industry Supply and Demand Relationships			
Price	Quantity Demanded	Quantity Supplied	Surplus (+) or Shortage (−)
$1.00	60,000	0	−60,000
1.10	58,000	2,000	−56,000
1.20	56,000	4,000	−52,000
1.30	54,000	6,000	−48,000
1.40	52,000	8,000	−44,000

1.50	50,000	10,000	−40,000
1.60	48,000	12,000	−36,000
1.70	46,000	14,000	−32,000
1.80	44,000	16,000	−28,000
1.90	42,000	18,000	−24,000
2.00	40,000	20,000	−20,000
2.10	38,000	22,000	−16,000
2.20	36,000	24,000	−12,000
2.30	34,000	26,000	−8,000
2.40	32,000	28,000	−4,000
2.50	30,000	30,000	0
2.60	28,000	32,000	4,000
2.70	26,000	34,000	8,000
2.80	24,000	36,000	12,000
2.90	22,000	38,000	16,000
3.00	20,000	40,000	20,000
3.10	18,000	42,000	24,000
3.20	16,000	44,000	28,000
3.30	14,000	46,000	32,000
3.40	12,000	48,000	36,000
3.50	10,000	50,000	40,000

B. Using price (P) on the vertical Y-axis and quantity (Q) on the horizontal X-axis, a plot of the demand and supply curves for the lumber–forest products industry is as follows:

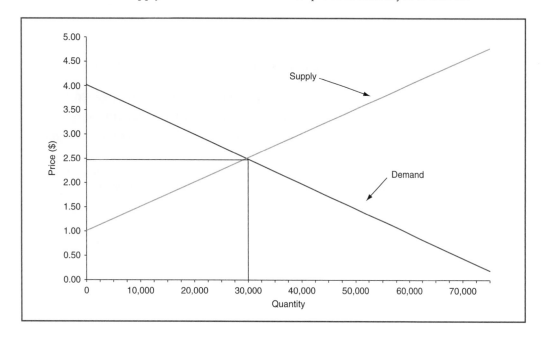

ST3.2 Supply Curve Determination. Information Technology, Inc., is a supplier of math coprocessors (computer chips) used to speed the processing of data for analysis on personal computers. Based on an analysis of monthly cost and output data, the company has estimated the following relation between the marginal cost of production and monthly output:

$$MC = \$100 + \$0.004Q$$

A. Calculate the marginal cost of production at 2,500, 5,000, and 7,500 units of output.

B. Express output as a function of marginal cost. Calculate the level of output when $MC = \$100$, 125, and 150.

C. Calculate the profit-maximizing level of output if wholesale prices are stable in the industry at $150 per chip and, therefore, $P = MR = \$150$.

D. Derive the company's supply curve for chips assuming $P = i$. Express price as a function of quantity and quantity as a function of price.

ST3.2 SOLUTION

A. Marginal production costs at each level of output are

$$Q = 2,500: MC = \$100 + \$0.004(2,500) = \$110$$
$$Q = 5,000: MC = \$100 + \$0.004(5,000) = \$120$$
$$Q = 7,500: MC = \$100 + \$0.004(7,500) = \$130$$

B. When output is expressed as a function of marginal cost

$$MC = \$100 + \$0.004Q$$
$$0.004Q = -100 + MC$$
$$Q = -25,000 + 250MC$$

The level of output at each respective level of marginal cost is

$$MC = \$100: Q = -25,000 + 250(\$100) = 0$$
$$MC = \$125: Q = -25,000 + 250(\$125) = 6,250$$
$$MC = \$150: Q = -25,000 + 250(\$150) = 12,500$$

C. Note from part B that $MC = \$150$ when $Q = 12,500$. Therefore, when $MR = \$150$, $Q = 12,500$ will be the profit-maximizing level of output. More formally

$$MR = MC$$
$$\$150 = \$100 + \$0.004Q$$
$$0.004Q = 50$$
$$Q = 12,500$$

D. Because prices are stable in the industry, $P = MR$, this means that the company will supply chips at the level of output where

$$MR = MC$$

and, therefore, that

$$P = \$100 + \$0.004Q$$

This is the supply curve for math chips, where price is expressed as a function of quantity. When quantity is expressed as a function of price

$$P = \$100 + \$0.004Q$$
$$0.004Q = -100 + P$$
$$Q = -25{,}000 + 250P$$

PROBLEMS

P3.1 Demand and Supply Curves. The following relations describe monthly demand and supply conditions in the metropolitan area for recyclable aluminum:

$$Q_D = 317{,}500 - 10{,}000P \qquad \text{(Demand)}$$
$$Q_S = 2{,}500 + 7{,}500P \qquad \text{(Supply)}$$

Where Q is quanity measured in pounds of scrap aluminum and P is price in cents. Complete the following

Price (1)	Quantity Supplied (2)	Quantity Demanded (3)	Surplus (+) or Shortage (−) (4) = (2) − (3)
15¢			
16			
17			
18			
19			
20			

P3.2 Demand and Supply Curves. The following relations describe monthly demand and supply relations for dry cleaning services in the metropolitan area:

$$Q_D = 500{,}000 - 50{,}000P \qquad \text{(Demand)}$$
$$Q_S = -100{,}000 + 100{,}000P \qquad \text{(Supply)}$$

where Q is quantity measured by the number of items dry cleaned per month and P is average price in dollars.

A. At what average price level would demand equal zero?

B. At what average price level would supply equal zero?

C. Calculate the equilibrium price–output combination.

P3.3 Demand Analysis. The demand for housing is often described as being highly cyclical and very sensitive to housing prices and interest rates. Given these characteristics, describe the effect of each of the following in terms of whether it would increase or decrease the quantity demanded or the demand for housing. Moreover, when price is expressed as a function of quantity, indicate whether the effect of each of the following is an upward or downward movement along a given demand curve or involves an outward or inward shift in the relevant demand curve for housing. Explain your answers.

A. An increase in housing prices

B. A fall in interest rates

C. A rise in interest rates

D. A severe economic recession

E. A robust economic expansion

P3.4 Demand and Supply Curves. Demand and supply conditions in the market for unskilled labor are important concerns to business and government decision makers. Consider the case of a federally mandated minimum wage set above the equilibrium, or market clearing, wage level. Some of the following factors have the potential to influence the demand or quantity demanded of unskilled labor. Influences on the supply or quantity supplied may also result. Holding all else equal, describe these influences as increasing or decreasing, and indicate the direction of the resulting movement along or shift in the relevant curve(s).

A. An increase in the quality of secondary education

B. A rise in welfare benefits

C. An increase in the popularity of self-service gas stations, car washes, and so on

D. A fall in interest rates

E. An increase in the minimum wage

P3.5 Demand Function. The Creative Publishing Company (CPC) is a coupon book publisher with markets in several southeastern states. CPC coupon books are sold directly to the public, sold through religious and other charitable organizations, or given away as promotional items. Operating experience during the past year suggests the following demand function for CPC's coupon books:

$$Q = 5,000 - 4,000P + 0.02Pop + 0.25I + 1.5A$$

where Q is quantity, P is price ($), Pop is population, I is disposable income per household ($), and A is advertising expenditures ($).

A. Determine the demand faced by CPC in a typical market in which $P = \$10$, $Pop = 1,000,000$ persons, $I = \$60,000$, and $A = \$10,000$.

B. Calculate the level of demand if CPC increases annual advertising expenditures from $10,000 to $15,000.

C. Calculate the demand curves faced by CPC in parts A and B.

P3.6 Demand Curves. The Eastern Shuttle, Inc., is a regional airline providing shuttle service between New York and Washington, DC. An analysis of the monthly demand for service has revealed the following demand relation:

$$Q = 26,000 - 500P - 250P_{OG} + 200I_B - 5,000S$$

where Q is quantity measured by the number of passengers per month, P is price ($), P_{OG} is a regional price index for other consumer goods (1967 = 1.00), I_B is an index of business activity, and S, a binary or dummy variable, equals 1 in summer months and 0 otherwise.

A. Determine the demand curve facing the airline during the winter month of January if $P_{OG} = 4$ and $I_B = 250$.

B. Determine the demand curve facing the airline, quantity demanded, and total revenues during the summer month of July if $P = \$100$ and all other price-related and business activity variables are as specified previously.

P3.7 Supply Function. A review of industry-wide data for the jelly and jam manufacturing industry suggests the following industry supply function:

$$Q = -59,000,000 + 500,000P - 125,000P_L$$
$$- 500,000P_K + 2,000,000W$$

where Q is cases supplied per year, P is the wholesale price per case ($), P_L is the average price paid for unskilled labor ($), P_K is the average price of capital (in percent), and W is weather measured by the average seasonal rainfall in growing areas (in inches).

A. Determine the industry supply curve for a recent year when $P_L = \$8$, $P_K = 10$ percent, and $W = 20$ inches of rainfall. Show the industry supply curve with quantity expressed as a function of price and price expressed as a function of quantity.

B. Calculate the quantity supplied by the industry at prices of $50, $60, and $70 per case.

C. Calculate the prices necessary to generate a supply of 4 million, 6 million, and 8 million cases.

P3.8 Supply Curve Determination. Olympia Natural Resources, Inc., and Yakima Lumber, Ltd., supply cut logs (raw lumber) to lumber and paper mills located in the Cascades Mountain region in the state of Washington. Each company has a different marginal cost of production, depending on its own cost of landowner access, labor and other cutting costs, the distance cut logs must be shipped, and so on. The marginal cost of producing 1 unit of output, measured as 1,000 board feet of lumber (where 1 board foot is 1 square foot of lumber, 1 inch thick), is

$$MC_O = \$350 + \$0.00005Q_O \qquad \text{(Olympia)}$$
$$MC_Y = \$150 + \$0.0002Q_Y \qquad \text{(Yakima)}$$

The wholesale market for cut logs is vigorously price competitive, and neither firm is able to charge a premium for its products. Thus, $P = MR$ in this market.

A. Determine the supply curve for each firm. Express price as a function of quantity and quantity as a function of price. (Hint: Set $P = MR = MC$ to find each firm's supply curve.)

B. Calculate the quantity supplied by each firm at prices of $325, $350, and $375. What is the minimum price necessary for each individual firm to supply output?

C. Assuming these two firms make up the entire industry in the local area, determine the industry supply curve when $P < \$350$.

D. Determine the industry supply curve when $P > \$350$. To check your answer, calculate quantity at an industry price of $375 and compare your result with part B.

P3.9 Supply Curve Determination. Cornell Pharmaceutical, Inc., and Penn Medical, Ltd., supply generic drugs to treat a wide variety of illnesses. A major product for each company is a generic equivalent of an antibiotic used to treat postoperative infections. Proprietary cost and output information for each company reveal the following relations between marginal cost and output:

$$MC_C = \$10 + \$0.004Q_C \qquad \text{(Cornell)}$$
$$MC_P = \$8 + \$0.008Q_P \qquad \text{(Penn)}$$

The wholesale market for generic drugs is vigorously price competitive, and neither firm is able to charge a premium for its products. Thus, $P = MR$ in this market.

A. Determine the supply curve for each firm. Express price as a function of quantity and quantity as a function of price. (Hint: Set $P = MR = MC$ to find each firm's supply curve.)

B. Calculate the quantity supplied by each firm at prices of $8, $10, and $12. What is the minimum price necessary for each individual firm to supply output?

C. Assuming these two firms make up the entire industry, determine the industry supply curve when $P < \$10$.

D. Determine the industry supply curve when $P > \$10$. To check your answer, calculate quantity at an industry price of $12 and compare your answer with part B.

P3.10 Market Equilibrium. Eye-de-ho Potatoes is a product of the Coeur d'Alene Growers' Association. Producers in the area are able to switch back and forth between potato and wheat production, depending on market conditions. Similarly, consumers tend to regard potatoes and wheat (bread and bakery products) as substitutes. As a result, the demand and supply of Eye-de-ho Potatoes are highly sensitive to changes in both potato and wheat prices.

Demand and supply functions for Eye-de-ho Potatoes are as follows:

$$Q_D = -1,450 - 25P + 12.5P_W + 0.1Y \qquad \text{(Demand)}$$
$$Q_S = -100 + 75P - 25P_W - 12.5P_L + 10R \qquad \text{(Supply)}$$

where P is the average wholesale price of Eye-de-ho Potatoes ($ per bushel), P_W is the average wholesale price of wheat ($ per bushel), Y is income (GDP in $ billions), P_L is the average price of unskilled labor ($ per hour), and R is the average annual rainfall (in inches). Both Q_D and Q_S are in millions of bushels of potatoes.

A. When quantity is expressed as a function of price, what are the Eye-de-ho Potatoes demand and supply curves if $P_W = \$4$, $Y = \$15{,}000$ billion, $P_L = \$8$, and $R = 20$ inches?

B. Calculate the surplus or shortage of Eye-de-ho Potatoes when $P = \$1.50$, $\$2$, and $\$2.50$.

C. Calculate the market equilibrium price–output combination.

| CASE *Study* | Spreadsheet Analysis of Demand and Supply for Sunbest Orange Juice |

Spreadsheet analysis is an appropriate means for studying the demand and supply effects of possible changes in various exogenous and endogenous variables. Endogenous variables include all important demand- and supply-related factors that are within the control of the firm. Examples include product pricing, advertising, product design, and so on. Exogenous variables consist of all significant demand- and supply-related influences that are beyond the control of the firm. Examples include competitor pricing, competitor advertising, weather, general economic conditions, and related factors.

In comparative statics analysis, the marginal influence on demand and supply of a change in any one factor can be isolated and studied in depth. The advantage of this approach is that causal relationships can be identified and responded to, if appropriate. The disadvantage of this marginal approach is that it becomes rather tedious to investigate the marginal effects of a wide range of demand and supply influences. It is here that spreadsheet analysis of demand and supply conditions becomes useful. Using spreadsheet analysis, it is possible to learn the demand and supply implications of an almost limitless range of operating scenarios. Rather than calculating the effects of only a few possibilities, it is feasible to consider even rather unlikely outcomes. A complete picture of the firm's operating environment as well as strategies for responding to a host of operating conditions can be drawn up.

To illustrate this process, consider the hypothetical case of Sunbest Orange Juice, a product of California's Orange County Growers' Association. Both demand and supply of the product are highly sensitive to changes in the weather. During hot summer months, demand for Sunbest and other beverages grows rapidly. On the other hand, hot, dry weather has an adverse effect on supply by reducing the size of the orange crop.

Demand and supply functions for Sunbest are as follows:

$$Q_D = 1{,}000{,}000 - 25{,}000{,}000P + 10{,}000{,}000P_S \\ + 1{,}600Y + 50{,}000T \qquad \text{(Demand)}$$

$$Q_S = 8{,}000{,}000P - 100{,}000P_L - 120{,}000P_K \\ - 150{,}000T \qquad \text{(Supply)}$$

where P is the average wholesale price of Sunbest ($ per case), P_S is the average wholesale price of canned soda ($ per case), Y is disposable income per household ($), T is the average daily high temperature (degrees), P_L is the average price of unskilled labor ($ per hour), and P_K is the risk-adjusted cost of capital (in percent).

continued

During the coming planning period, a wide variety of operating conditions are possible. To gauge the sensitivity of demand and supply to changes in these operating conditions, a number of scenarios that employ a range from optimistic to relatively pessimistic assumptions have been drawn up in Table 3.4.

Demand and supply functions for Sunbest orange juice can be combined with data on the operating environment to construct estimates of demand, supply, and the amount of surplus or shortage under each operating scenario.

A. Set up a spreadsheet to illustrate the effects of changing economic assumptions on the demand for Sunbest orange juice. Use the demand function to calculate demand based on three different underlying assumptions concerning changes in the operating environment. First, assume that all demand factors change in unison from levels indicated in the Optimistic Scenario #1 to the levels indicated in Pessimistic Scenario #10. Second, fix all demand factors except the price of Sunbest at Scenario #6 levels, and

Table 3.4 Sunbest Demand and Supply Conditions

Operating Environment for Demand	Price of Sunbest (P)	Price of Soda (P_s)	Disposable Income (Y)	Temperature (T)
Optimistic Scenario 1	$6.00	$5.00	$67,500	81.25
2	5.80	4.90	66,500	81.00
3	5.60	4.80	65,500	80.75
4	5.40	4.70	64,500	80.50
5	5.20	4.60	63,500	80.25
6	5.00	4.50	62,500	80.00
7	4.80	4.40	61,500	79.75
8	4.60	4.30	60,500	79.50
9	4.40	4.20	59,500	79.25
Pessimistic Scenario 10	4.20	4.10	58,500	79.00

Operating Environment for Supply	Price of Sunbest (P)	Price of Labor (P_L)	Cost of Capital (P_K)	Temperature (T)
Optimistic Scenario 1	$6.00	$16.75	7.50	81.25
2	5.80	17.00	8.00	81.00
3	5.60	17.25	8.50	80.75
4	5.40	17.50	9.00	80.50
5	5.20	17.75	9.50	80.25
6	5.00	18.00	10.00	80.00
7	4.80	18.25	10.50	79.75
8	4.60	18.50	11.00	79.50
9	4.40	18.75	11.50	79.25
Pessimistic Scenario 10	4.20	19.00	12.00	79.00

continued

then calculate the quantity demanded at each scenario price level. Finally, fix all demand factors except temperature at Scenario #6 levels, and then calculate demand at each scenario temperature level.

B. Set up a spreadsheet to illustrate the effects of changing economic assumptions on the supply of Sunbest orange juice. Use the supply function to calculate supply based on three different underlying assumptions concerning changes in the operating environment. First, assume that all supply factors change in unison from levels indicated in the Optimistic Scenario #1 to the levels indicated in Pessimistic Scenario #10. Second, fix all supply factors except the price of Sunbest at Scenario #6 levels, and then calculate the quantity supplied at each scenario price level. Finally, fix all supply factors except temperature at Scenario #6 levels, and then calculate supply at each scenario temperature level.

C. Set up a spreadsheet to illustrate the effect of changing economic assumptions on the surplus or shortage of Sunbest orange juice that results from each scenario detailed in part A and part B. Which operating scenario results in market equilibrium?

SELECTED REFERENCES

Berrada, Tony, Julien Hugonnier, and Marcel Rindisbacher. "Heterogeneous Preferences and Equilibrium Trading Volume." *Journal of Financial Economics* 83, no. 3 (March, 2007): 719–750.

Gali, Jordi, Mark Gertler, and J. David Lopez Salido. "Markups, Gaps, and the Welfare Costs of Business Fluctuations." *Review of Economics and Statistics* 89, no. 1 (February, 2007): 44–59.

Gamba, Andrea and Alberto Micalizzi. "Product Development and Market Expansion: A Real Options Model." *Financial Management* 36, no. 1 (Spring, 2007): 91–112.

Golosov, Mikhail and Robert E. Lucas Jr. "Menu Costs and Phillips Curves." *Journal of Political Economy* 115, no. 2 (April, 2007): 171–199.

Horowitz, Ira. "If You Play Well They Will Come—and Vice Versa: Bidirectional Causality in Major-League Baseball." *Managerial and Decision Economics* 28, no. 2 (March, 2007): 93–105.

Livshits, Igor, James MacGee, and Michele Tertilt. "Consumer Bankruptcy: A Fresh Start." *American Economic Review* 97, no. 1 (March, 2007): 402–418.

Lochner, Lance. "Individual Perceptions of the Criminal Justice System." *American Economic Review* 97, no. 1 (March, 2007): 444–460.

Louis, Henock and Hal White. "Do Managers Intentionally use Repurchase Tender Offers to Signal Private Information? Evidence from Firm Financial Reporting Behavior." *Journal of Financial Economics* 85, no. 1 (July, 2007): 205–233.

Love, Inessa, Lorenzo A. Preve, and Virginia Sarria Allende. "Trade Credit and Bank Credit: Evidence from Recent Financial Crises." *Journal of Financial Economics* 83, no. 2 (February, 2007): 453–469.

Lowry, Michelle and Kevin J. Murphy. "Executive Stock Options and IPO Underpricing." *Journal of Financial Economics* 85, no. 1 (July, 2007): 39–65.

Ludwig, Jens and Douglas L. Miller. "Does Head Start Improve Children's Life Chances? Evidence from a Regression Discontinuity Design." *Quarterly Journal of Economics* 122, no. 1 (February, 2007): 159–208.

Lundblad, Christian. "The Risk Return Tradeoff in the Long Run: 1836–2003." *Journal of Financial Economics* 85, no. 1 (July, 2007): 123–150.

Macho Stadler, Ines, David Perez Castrillo, and Reinhilde Veugelers. "Licensing of University Inventions: The Role of a Technology Transfer Office." *International Journal of Industrial Organization* 25, no. 3 (June, 2007): 483–510.

Nimalendran, M., Jay R. Ritter, and Donghang Zhang. "Do Today's Trades Affect Tomorrow's IPO Allocations?" *Journal of Financial Economics* 84, no. 1 (April, 2007): 87–109.

Pabilonia, Sabrina Wulff and Jennifer Ward Batts. "The Effect of Child Gender on Parents' Labor Supply: An Examination of Natives, Immigrants, and Their Children." *American Economic Review* 97, no. 2 (May, 2007): 402–406.

Demand Analysis and Estimation

2

PART

Demand Analysis

Managerial economics provides a useful framework for understanding how consumers make trade-offs. Time is scarce, so entertainment companies must understand the factors that college students consider when trying to decide whether to play a video game or go to a movie. Money is scarce, so those same entertainment companies also strive to understand how much customers are willing to pay for the newest video graphics, or Internet access to the latest videos games. Every consumer decision involves trade-offs between price, quantity, quality, timeliness, and a host of related factors. The consideration of such trade-offs, and the methods used by consumers to make consumption decisions, is called the study of consumer behavior. How do consumers make economic decisions?

The study of consumer behavior is of obvious practical relevance when considering the pricing and production decisions made by businesses. It is also of practical relevance when considering public policy decisions that directly or indirectly affect consumers. How will national park attendance be affected when usage fees are applied? How will gasoline usage and the amount imported from foreign suppliers be affected when federal gasoline taxes are raised by 10¢ per gallon? At the state level, will an increase in the income tax or an increase in the sales tax raise more revenue? Answering such questions requires a careful understanding of the theory of consumer behavior. Consumer behavior theory is useful for both describing and predicting consumer decisions.[1]

UTILITY THEORY

The ability of goods and services to satisfy consumer wants is the basis for consumer demand.

Basic Assumptions

Utility
Satisfaction tied to consumption.

Nonsatiation Principle
More is better.

Consumer behavior theory rests upon three basic assumptions regarding the **utility** tied to consumption. First, *more is better*. Consumers always prefer more to less of any good or service. Economists refer to this as the **nonsatiation principle**. Of course, at any specific place and time, consumers do become sated. The nonsatiation principle is best considered within the context of money income where more money brings additional satisfaction or well-being.

---

1   See Rebecca Smith, "Electricity Demand is Far Outpacing New-Supply Sources," *The Wall Street Journal Online,* October 17, 2007, http://online.wsj.com.

Second, *preferences are complete.* When preferences are complete, consumers are able to compare and rank the benefits tied to consumption. If preferences are complete, consumers know they prefer spicy chicken wraps to shredded beef wraps, or *vice versa.* If both provide the same amount of satisfaction or utility, the consumer is said to display **indifference** between the two. Indifference implies equivalence in the eyes of the consumer. A consumer can be indifferent between goods and services that are distinct in a physical sense. What's important in the case of consumer indifference is that two products yield the same amount of satisfaction or well-being to the consumer.

> **Indifference**
> Two goods provide the same amount of satisfaction or utility.

Third, *preferences are transitive.* When preferences are transitive, consumers are able to rank order the desirability of various goods and services. If a consumer prefers spicy chicken wraps to shredded beef wraps, and prefers shredded beef wraps to vegetarian wraps, then that consumer also prefers spicy chicken wraps to vegetarian wraps. Consumer understanding of **ordinal utility** makes possible a rank ordering of preferred goods and services. If consumers had understanding of **cardinal utility,** they would know how much spicy chicken wraps are preferred, say 2:1 or 3:1, over vegetarian wraps. However, nobody has to know how much more desirable spicy chicken wraps are compared to vegetarian wraps in order to make a simple choice between the two. All that's necessary is to know that one product is preferred to another product.

> **Ordinal Utility**
> Rank ordering of preferences, for example, *A* is better than *B*.

> **Cardinal Utility**
> Understanding of the intensity of preference, for example, *A* = 2*B*.

With these basic assumptions, the foundation exists for a more detailed examination of the benefits tied to consumption.

Utility Functions

> **Utility Function**
> Descriptive statement that relates well-being to the consumption of goods and services.

A **utility function** is a descriptive statement that relates satisfaction or well-being to the consumption of goods and services and can be written in the general form:

$$\text{Utility} = f(\text{Goods, Services}) \qquad \textbf{4.1}$$

> **Utils**
> Unit of utility or well-being.

Table 4.1 shows a 2-product utility function. Each element in the table shows the amount of utility derived from the consumption of each respective combination of goods (*Y*) and services (*X*). For example, consumption of 3 units of *X* and 3 units of *Y* provides 68 **utils** (units of satisfaction), consumption of one of *X* and ten of *Y* provides 80 utils, and so on. Each product is measured in terms of the *number* of dresses, *hours* of financial planning

Table 4.1 Utility Derived from Consumption of Various Combinations of Goods and Services

Goods (Y)	Services (X)									
	1	2	3	4	5	6	7	8	9	10
1	25	36	46	55	63	70	76	81	85	88
2	37	48	58	67	75	82	88	93	97	100
3	47	58	68	77	85	92	98	103	107	110
4	55	66	76	85	93	100	106	111	115	118
5	62	73	83	92	100	107	113	118	122	125
6	68	79	89	98	106	113	119	124	128	131
7	73	84	94	103	111	118	124	129	133	136
8	77	88	98	107	115	122	128	133	137	140
9	79	90	100	109	117	124	130	135	139	142
10	80	91	101	110	118	125	131	136	140	143

services, *days* of vacation, and so on. Bundles of items desired by consumers are called **market baskets** because they reflect combinations of goods and services available in the marketplace.

Market Baskets
Bundles of items desired by consumers.

The utility derived from consumption is intangible. However, consumers reveal their preferences through purchase decisions and thereby provide tangible evidence of utility. The utility function depicted in Table 4.1 is displayed graphically in Figure 4.1. The height of the bar associated with each combination of goods and services indicates the level of utility provided through the consumption of those items.

Marginal Utility

Marginal Utility
Added satisfaction derived from a 1-unit increase in consumption.

Whereas total utility measures the consumer's overall level of satisfaction derived from consumption activities, **marginal utility** measures the added satisfaction derived from a 1-unit increase in consumption of a particular good or service, holding consumption of

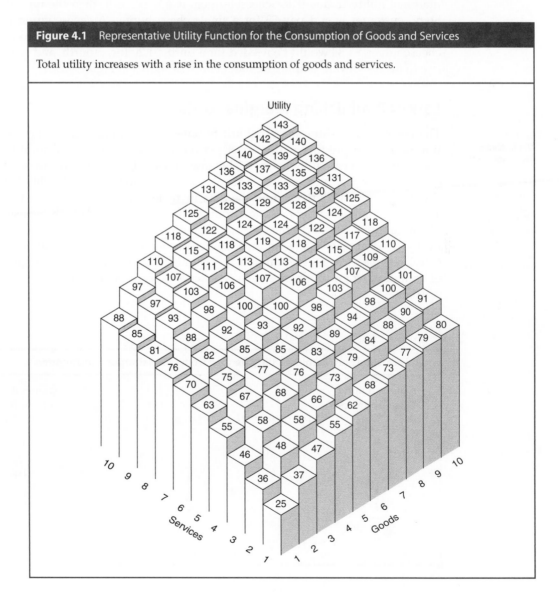

Figure 4.1 Representative Utility Function for the Consumption of Goods and Services

Total utility increases with a rise in the consumption of goods and services.

other goods and services constant. Marginal utility tends to diminish as consumption increases within a given time interval.

Suppose Table 4.2 illustrates the utility derived by a typical customer of the Hamburger Stand from consumption of a one-quarter pound cheeseburger during a single meal. According to the table, the marginal utility from consuming an initial cheeseburger is 5 units ($MU_{H=1} = 5$). Marginal utility is 4 units for a second cheeseburger, 3 units for a third, and so on.

If each cheeseburger costs $3, the cost per unit (util) of satisfaction derived from consuming the first cheeseburger is 60¢ (=$3/5 utils). A second cheeseburger costing $2.40 produces 4 utils of additional satisfaction at a cost of 60¢ per util. Diminishing marginal utility increases the cost of each marginal unit of satisfaction. If the typical Hamburger Stand customer had alternative consumption opportunities providing one additional unit of utility for 60¢ each, customers would be willing to increase the quantity of cheeseburgers purchased only if cheeseburger prices fell. If the required price/marginal utility trade-off for cheeseburgers is 60¢ per util, then the typical Hamburger Stand customer would pay $3 for a single cheeseburger. A cheeseburger price of $2.40 (=60¢ × 4 utils) would be necessary to induce the typical customer to buy a second cheeseburger, $1.80 would be needed for a third, $1.20 for a fourth, and so on. This gives rise to the downward-sloping demand curve as shown in Figure 4.2.

Law of Diminishing Marginal Utility

Law of Diminishing Marginal Utility
As an individual increases consumption of a given product within a set period of time, the marginal utility gained from consumption eventually declines.

The **law of diminishing marginal utility** states that as an individual increases consumption of a given product within a set period of time, the marginal utility gained from consumption eventually declines. This law gives rise to a downward-sloping demand curve for all goods and services. The law of diminishing marginal utility is illustrated in Table 4.3, which is derived from the data in Table 4.1. When service is held constant at 4 units, the marginal utility derived from consuming goods falls with each successive unit of consumption. Similarly, the consumption of services is subject to diminishing marginal utility. Holding goods consumption constant at 1 unit, the marginal utility derived from consuming services falls continuously. The added benefit derived through consumption of each product grows progressively smaller as consumption increases, holding the other constant.

Table 4.2 Total and Marginal Utility Derived from Cheeseburger Consumption

Quarter-Pound Cheeseburgers Per Meal, Q	Total Utility, U	Marginal Utility, MU	Maximum Acceptable Cheeseburger Price at 60 ¢ Per Util
0	0	—	3.60
1	5	5	3.00
2	9	4	2.40
3	12	3	1.80
4	14	2	1.20
5	15	1	0.60
6	15	0	—

Figure 4.2 Downward-sloping Demand Curve for Cheeseburgers

Downward-sloping demand curves stem from the principle of diminishing marginal utility of consumption.

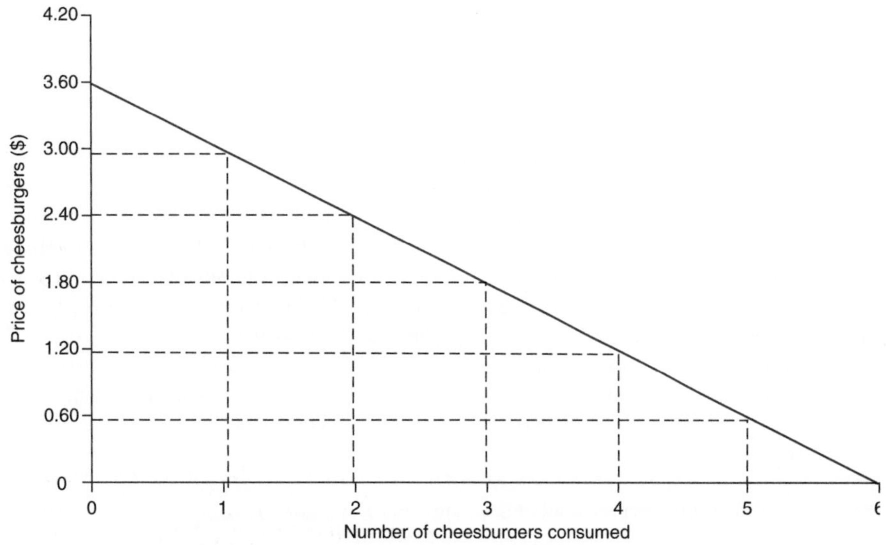

To a greater or lesser degree, goods and services can be substituted for one another. For example, a consumer may own many suits and dry clean each suit only occasionally. A consumer may own only a few suits but dry clean each one frequently. In the first instance, the consumer has bought a market basket with a high proportion of total expenditures devoted to suits (goods) and relatively little devoted to dry cleaning services. The latter market basket is weighted less toward goods and more toward services.

Table 4.3 Total and Marginal Utility of Goods and Services

Quantity	Goods (Y) Total Utility	Goods (Y) Marginal Utility ($MU_Y \mid X = 4$)	Services (X) Total Utility	Services (X) Marginal Utility ($MU_X \mid Y = 1$)
1	55	—	25	—
2	67	12	36	11
3	77	10	46	10
4	85	8	55	9
5	92	7	63	8
6	98	6	70	7
7	103	5	76	6
8	107	4	81	5
9	109	2	85	4
10	110	1	88	3

Managerial Application 4.1

Odd-number Pricing Riddle

To consumers, a 99¢ price typically "feels" a lot cheaper than $1. As a result, the 99¢ price is much more common than $1. Odd-number pricing is most common for goods and services offered in price-competitive environments. For example, most states require retail gasoline prices to be prominently displayed so that drivers can easily evaluate prices from curbside as they drive down the street. This makes the retail gasoline market viciously price competitive. Just think of the times you have gone out of your way to save 2¢ or 3¢ per gallon, or less than 50¢ on a tank of gas. Gasoline customers are notoriously price sensitive, and gasoline retailers know this. Perhaps that is why gasoline retailers use odd-numbered pricing to such an extreme that gas prices are typically expressed in terms of 9/10 of a cent. Can you think of another consumer product where the price charged is expressed in terms of 9/10 of a cent?

While everyone can observe the popularity of odd-number pricing, economists don't know *why* buyers are

lured by a 99¢ price and turned off by a $1 price. Is there some failure in the computational ability of buyers? Does it have something to do with the way the brain processes information? One innovative explanation for the popularity of odd-number pricing is that readers of Latin-based languages like English process written material from left to right. As you read this page, you are processing information from left to right. The first digit processed when a consumer notes a price of $6.99 is the number six, not the higher number seven, as would be the case with a price of $7. In the English-speaking world, a price of $6.99 seems "significantly" less than $7.

Interestingly, in the Arab world, where information is processed from right to left, odd-numbered pricing is uncommon.

See: Andrew Edwards and Kevin Kingsbury, "Prices for 3M's Optical Films Will Fall for Some Customers," *The Wall Street Journal Online,* October 20, 2007, http://online.wsj.com.

INDIFFERENCE CURVES

A large number of market baskets can be created that provide the same level of utility.

Basic Characteristics

Indifference Curves
Representation of all market baskets that provide a given consumer the same amount of utility or satisfaction.

Indifference curves represent all market baskets that provide a given consumer the same amount of utility or satisfaction.

Indifference curves have four essential properties.

First, *higher indifference curves are better.* Consumers prefer more to less, so they prefer higher indifference curves that represent greater combinations of goods and services to lower indifference curves that represent smaller combinations of goods and services. As illustrated in Figure 4.3, indifference curves that are found upward and to the right are preferred to lower indifference curves found downward and to the left.

Second, *indifference curves do not intersect.* Holding goods constant, an indifference curve involving a greater amount of services must give greater satisfaction. Holding services constant, an indifference curve involving a greater amount of goods must give greater satisfaction. This stems from the fact that goods and services both provide consumer benefits, and reflect the "more is better" principle. If indifference curves crossed, this principle would be violated.

Third, *indifference curves slope downward.* The slope of an indifference curve shows the trade-off involved between goods and services. Because consumers like both goods and services, if the quantity of one is reduced, the quantity of the other must increase to maintain the same degree of utility. As a result, indifference curves have negative slopes.

Figure 4.3   Representative Indifference Curves Based on Table 4.1 Data

Indifference curves show market baskets of goods and services that provide the same utility.

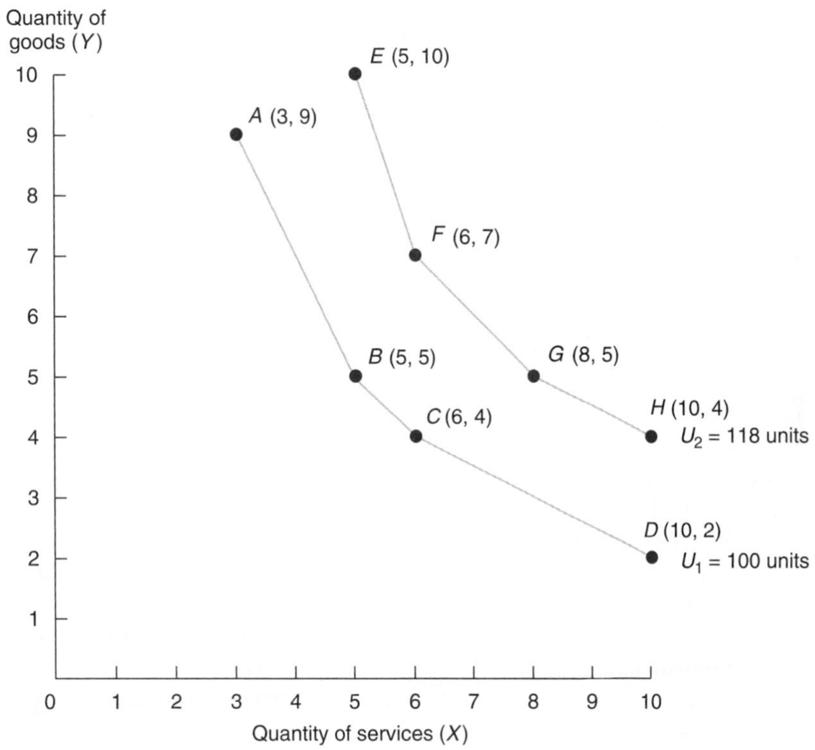

And fourth, *indifference curves bend inward (are convex to the origin)*. The slope of an indifference curve shows the rate at which consumers are willing to trade-off goods and services. When goods are relatively scarce, the law of diminishing marginal utility means that the added value of another unit of goods will be large in relation to the added value of another unit of services. Conversely, when goods are relatively abundant, the added value of another unit of goods will be small in relation to the added value of another unit of services. This gives indifference curves a bowed inward, or concave to the origin, appearance.

Consumer preferences can be illustrated graphically using indifference curves. To illustrate, Figure 4.3 shows two indifference curves based on the data contained in Table 4.1. Note that 100 units of satisfaction can be derived from the consumption of three X and nine Y (point A), five X and five Y (point B), six X and four Y (point C), and ten X and two Y (point D). Therefore, each of these points lies on the $U_1 = 100$ indifference curve. Similarly, 118 units of satisfaction are derived from consumption of five X and ten Y (point E), six X and seven Y (point F), eight X and five Y (point G), and ten X and four Y (point H). Therefore, all these points lie on the $U_2 = 118$ indifference curve.

An indifference curve is constructed by connecting all the points representing market baskets that provide the same utility. This construction assumes that consumption can be split between market baskets. For example, the line segment between points A and B on the $U_1 = 100$ indifference curve represents a combination of market baskets A and B. The midpoint of this line segment represents consumption of one-half of market basket A plus one-half of market basket B. Similarly, the midpoint of the GH line segment represents a 50/50 combination of the G and H market baskets.

Perfect Substitutes and Perfect Complements

Substitutes
Products that serve the same purpose.

Complements
Products that are best consumed together.

Perfect Substitutes
Goods and services that satisfy the same need or desire.

Perfect Complements
Goods and services consumed together in the same combination.

Substitutes are goods and services that can be used to fulfill a similar need or desire. Goods and services that become more desirable when consumed together are called **complements.** Going to the movies and renting a DVD are close substitutes. At the same time, many consumers like to consume buttered popcorn and soda at the movie theater. Movies, buttered popcorn, and soda are often complements.

Insight concerning the indifference curve concept can be gained by considering what indifference curves look like for the logical extremes of **perfect substitutes** and **perfect complements.** Perfect substitutes are goods and services that satisfy the same need or desire. Perfect complements are goods and services consumed together in the same combination.

Because almost all goods and services have at least some small degree of uniqueness or individual appeal, it's difficult to find good examples of perfect substitutes. Take Pepsi and Coca-Cola, for example. Many consumers drink both. That's why competition is so fierce for shelf space at the grocery store. A summertime pricing promotion featuring 12-packs of Diet Coke can cause sales of Diet Coke to skyrocket, and make sales of Diet Pepsi plummet. Still, many devoted Pepsi drinkers will turn down even promotionally priced Coke in favor of Pepsi. Coke and Pepsi are close substitutes, but they are not perfect substitutes. Good example of near-perfect substitutes are provided by Visa debit cards and Visa credit cards, generic and branded drugs, drive-through and dine-in service at your favorite fast-food restaurant, and DVD movie rentals versus purchases [see Figure 4.4(a)].

There are lots of simple examples of perfect complements. Casual shoes and sandals are good substitutes, but a right shoe and a left shoe are perfect complements. They are always worn together in a 1:1 ratio. Similarly, most homes have a single clothes washer and clothes dryer (1:1 ratio), cars have four tires (4:1 ratio), and so on. As shown in Figure 4.4(b), bicycle tires and bicycle frames are "consumed" in a 2:1 ratio. No matter how many frames you have, you can't have more than one bicycle if you have only two tires. You cannot have more than two bicycles if you have no more than two bicycle frames.

When goods and service can be freely but imperfectly substituted, indifference curves have the U-shape depicted in Figure 4.4(c). Understanding the trade-offs involved in consumption helps greatly in understanding consumer behavior. To fully understand consumer decisions, the benefits tied to consumption must be weighed against cost considerations.

BUDGET CONSTRAINTS

Consumer choice involves a trade-off between the satisfaction gained from consumption and cost considerations.

Characteristics of Budget Constraints

Budget Constraint
Combinations of products that can be purchased for a fixed amount.

A **budget constraint** represents all combinations of products that can be purchased for a fixed amount. To derive a budget constraint, add up the amount of spending on goods and services that is feasible with a given budget. The amount of spending on goods is equal to the product of P_Y, the price of goods, times Y, the quantity purchased. Similarly,

Figure 4.4 Perfect Substitutes and Perfect Complements

(a) Perfect substitutes are reflected in straight-line indifference curves.

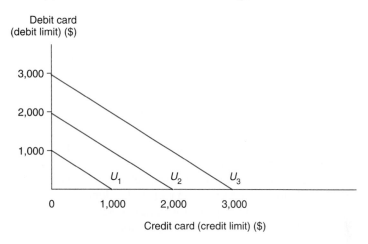

(b) Perfect complements are reflected in L-shaped indifference curves.

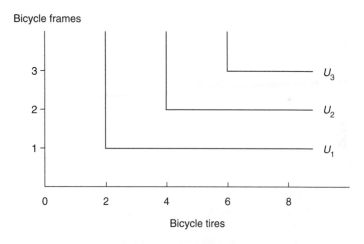

(c) Imperfect substitutes are reflected in U-shaped indifference curves.

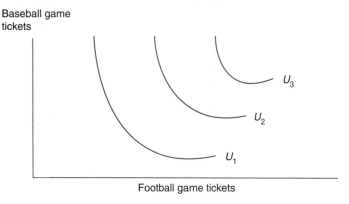

total spending on services is $P_X \times X$. When these amounts are added together, the budget constraint is

$$\text{Total Budget} = \text{Spending on Goods} + \text{Spending on Services}$$
$$B = P_Y Y + P_X X$$

Solving this expression for Y so that it can be graphed as in Figure 4.5(a) results in

$$Y = B/P_Y + (P_X/P_Y)X \qquad \qquad \textbf{4.2}$$

The first term in Equation (4.2) is the Y-axis intercept of the budget constraint. This Y-axis intercept indicates the quantity of product Y that can be purchased with a given budget, *assuming that zero units of product X are purchased.* The slope of the budget constraint is equal to $-P_X/P_Y$ and measures the relative prices of the products being purchased. A change in the budget amount B leads to a parallel shift in the budget constraint; change in the relative prices of items being purchased causes the slope of the budget constraint to rotate.

For example, if the price for goods is \$250 per unit and \$100 per unit for services, the relevant budget constraint can be written:

$$B = \$250Y + \$100X$$

or

$$Y = B/\$250 - (\$100/\$250)X$$

Table 4.4 The Consumer's Budget Constraint

The budget constraint shows various bundles of goods and services that can be bought with a given level of spending.

Quantity of Goods	Price of Goods ($)	Spending on Goods ($)	Quantity of Services ($)	Price of Services ($)	Spending on Services ($)	Total Spending ($)
4.00	250	1,000.0	0.000	100	0.00	1,000
3.75	250	937.50	0.625	100	62.50	1,000
3.50	250	875.00	1.250	100	125.00	1,000
3.25	250	812.50	1.875	100	187.50	1,000
3.00	250	750.00	2.500	100	250.00	1,000
2.75	250	687.50	3.125	100	312.50	1,000
2.50	250	625.00	3.750	100	375.00	1,000
2.25	250	562.50	4.375	100	437.50	1,000
2.00	250	500.00	5.000	100	500.00	1,000
1.75	250	437.50	5.625	100	562.50	1,000
1.50	250	375.00	6.250	100	625.00	1,000
1.25	250	312.50	6.875	100	687.50	1,000
1.00	250	250.00	7.500	100	750.00	1,000
0.75	250	187.50	8.125	100	812.50	1,000
0.50	250	125.00	8.750	100	875.00	1,000
0.25	250	62.50	9.375	100	937.50	1,000
0.00	250	0.00	10.000	100	1,000.00	1,000

As shown in Table 4.4, a maximum of 4 units of goods ($Y = \$1,000/\$250$) could be purchased with a $1,000 budget. This assumes, of course, that the entire $1,000 is spent on goods and not on services. If all $1,000 is devoted to the purchase of services, a maximum of 10 units of services ($X = \$1,000/\$100$) could be purchased. These market baskets ($0X, 4Y$ and $10X, 0Y$) represent the endpoints of the $B_1 = \$1,000$ budget constraint shown in Figure 4.5(a). This budget constraint identifies all combinations of goods and services that can be purchased for $1,000. Notice that $1,000 is insufficient to purchase any market basket lying on the $U_1 = 100$ or $U_2 = 118$ indifference curves. A minimum expenditure of $1,500 is necessary before point D ($10X$ and $2Y$) on the $U_1 = 100$ level of satisfaction can be achieved, and a minimum of $2,000 is necessary before point H ($10X$ and $4Y$) on the $U = 118$ level can be reached.

Effects of Changing Income and Changing Prices

The effect of a budget increase is to shift a budget constraint outward and to the right. The effect of a budget decrease is to shift a budget constraint inward and to the left. So long as the relative prices of goods and services remain constant, budget constraints remain parallel, as shown in Figure 4.5(a). This follows because so long as relative prices remain constant, the slope of the budget constraint also remains constant.

Figure 4.5 Consumption Effects of Changes in Budget and Relative Prices

(a) An increase in budget results in a parallel outward shift in the budget constraint. (b) A price cut allows purchase of a greater quantity with a given budget.

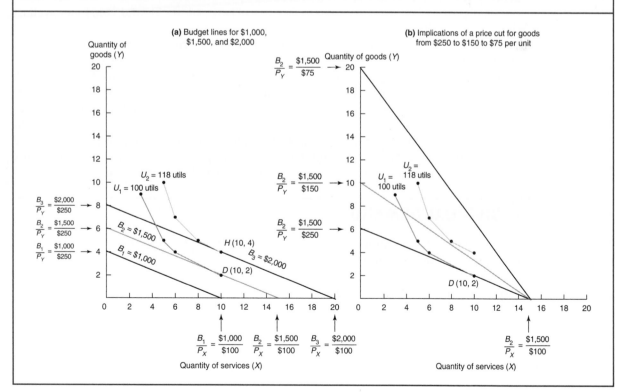

The effect of a change in relative prices is shown in Figure 4.5(b). Here the budget of $1,500 and the $100-per-unit price of services remain constant, whereas the price of goods falls progressively from $250, to $150, to $75 per unit. As the price of goods falls, a given budget will purchase more goods. Thus, a maximum of 6 units of goods can be purchased at a price of $250 per unit, 10 units can be purchased at a price of $150, and 20 units at a price of $75.

A fall in the price of goods or services permits an increase in consumption and consumer welfare. If both prices fall by a given percentage, a parallel rightward shift in the budget constraint occurs that is identical to the effect of an increase in budget. For example, the increase in consumption made possible by an increase in budget from $B_2 = \$1,500$ to $B_3 = \$2,000$ as shown in Figure 4.5(a) could also be realized following a decrease in the price of goods from $250 to $187.50 and of services from $100 to $75.

Income and Substitution Effects

Income Effect

Increase in overall consumption made possible by a price cut, or decrease in overall consumption that follows a price increase.

Substitution Effect

Change in relative consumption that occurs as consumers substitute cheaper products for more expensive products.

The **income effect** of a price change is the increase in overall consumption made possible by a price cut, or decrease in overall consumption that follows a price increase. The income effect shifts buyers to a higher indifference curve following a price cut or shifts them to a lower indifference curve following a price increase. The **substitution effect** of a price change describes the change in relative consumption that occurs as consumers substitute cheaper products for more expensive products. The substitution effect results in an upward or downward movement along a given indifference curve. The total effect of a price change on consumption is the sum of income and substitution effects.

Using the previous example, the total effect of a change in the price of goods is shown in Figure 4.6(a). When $P_Y = \$250$ and $P_X = \$100$, $U_1 = 100$ is the highest level of satisfaction that can be achieved with a $1,500 budget. This involves consumption of 10 units of service and 2 units of goods, or point D (where $X = 10$ and $Y = 2$). Following a cut in the price of goods from $P_{Y1} = \$250$ to $P_{Y2} = \$140$, consumption of the $X = 8$ and $Y = 5$ market basket becomes possible at a total cost of $1,500 ($= \$100 \times 8 + \$140 \times 5$), and consumer welfare rises from $U = 100$ to $U = 118$. This change in consumption involves two components. The leftward movement along the $U_1 = 100$ indifference curve to point C (where $X = 6$ and $Y = 4$), a tangency with the dashed hypothetical budget constraint representing the new relative prices for goods and services but *no income gain*, is the substitution effect. It reflects the substitution of lower-priced goods for the relatively more expensive services. Notice that given the new lower price for goods, consumption at point C costs only $1,160 ($= \$100 \times 6 + \$140 \times 4$). In this case, the cut in price from $P_{Y1} = \$250$ to $P_{Y2} = \$140$ saves the consumer $340 ($= \$1,500 - \$1,160$). This is equivalent to an increase in income. The upward shift from point C on the $U_1 = 100$ indifference curve to point G on the $U_2 = 118$ indifference curve is made possible by the income effect of the price reduction for goods.

INDIVIDUAL DEMAND

The demand curve for an individual consumer depends upon the size of the consumer's budget consumption preferences.

Price–consumption Curve

Market baskets that maximize utility at different prices for a given item.

Price–consumption Curve

If income and the prices of other goods and services are held constant, a reduction in the price of a given item causes consumers to choose different market baskets. Various market baskets that maximize utility at different prices for a given item trace out the consumer's **price–consumption curve,** as shown in Figure 4.7.

Figure 4.6   Income and Substitution Effects Following a Reduction in the Price of Goods

(a) A price change will result in both income and substitution effects.

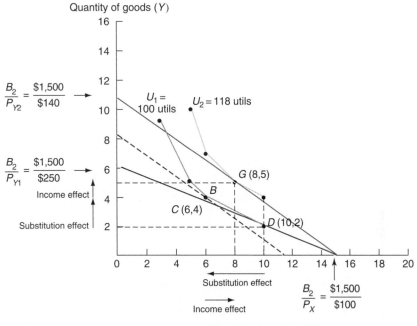

(b) Income and substitution effects give rise to a downward-sloping demand curve.

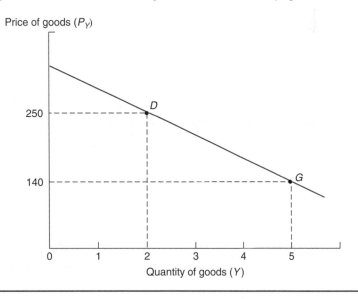

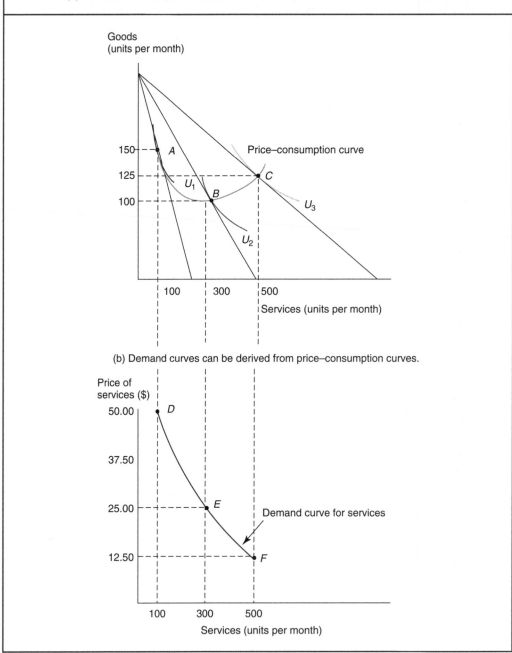

Figure 4.7   Price–consumption Curves Show How Charging Prices Affect Optimal Consumption

(a) Market baskets that maximize utility for various service prices trace cut the price – consumption curve. Part (b) Illustrates the individual dmand curve for services.

When income and the price of goods are held constant, Figure 4.7(a) shows how a reduction in the price of services causes an individual consumer to choose different market baskets. Notice how the utility derived from consumption rises from U_1 (point A), to U_2 (point B), to U_3 (point C) with a rise in the consumption of services and a decline in goods consumption. In this case, falling service prices cause increases in the quantity demanded of services, and a reduction in demand for goods. Note how the demand for goods fluctuates from 150 units per month (point *A*), to 100 (point *B*), to 125 (point *C*) as the quantity of services demanded rises from 100, to 300, to 500 units per month. In Figure 4.7(b), also notice how this rise in the quantity demanded of services is caused by falling service prices. As shown in Figure 4.7(b), reductions in the price of services from $50, to $25, to $12.50 cause increases in the quantity demanded from 100 units per month (point *D*), to 300 units per month (point *E*), to 500 units per month (point *F*).

The price–consumption curve shown in Figure 4.7(a) depicts how the optimal consumption of both goods and services are affected by changing prices for services. A similar price–consumption curve could be used to illustrate how the optimal consumption of both goods and services are affected by changing prices for goods. The curve illustrated in Figure 4.7(b) is the demand curve for services. It shows how the quantity demanded of services rises in a response to a fall in the price for services. A similar individual demand curve could be used to illustrate how the quantity demanded of goods rises in a response to a fall in goods prices.

Income–Consumption Curve

Income–Consumption Curve
Utility-maximizing combinations of goods and services at every income level.

The **income–consumption curve** portrays the utility-maximizing combinations of goods and services at every income level. As shown in Figure 4.8, the income–consumption curve slopes upward because the consumption of both goods and services can rise with growing income. Whereas an individual demand curve shows the relation between price and quantity demanded, or movement along the demand curve, the income–consumption curve shows shifts in demand from one demand curve to another as income changes.

Assuming that the prices of goods and services remain constant, the income–consumption curve as illustrated in Figure 4.8(a) shows how rising income creates growing satisfaction by allowing consumption of market baskets with more goods and services. Notice how the utility derived from consumption rises from U_1 (point *G*), to U_2 (point *H*), to U_3 (point *I*) with a rise in the budget constraint from $B_1 = \$250$, to $B_2 = \$500$, to $B_3 = \$750$. As described in Chapter 2, growing income results in a rightward shift of the demand curve. As income rises from B_1, to B_2, to B_3, in Figure 4.8(a), the demand for services shifts rightward from D_1, to D_2, to D_3 in Figure 4.8(b).

It is worth emphasizing that price–consumption curves and income–consumption curves focus on different aspects of demand. Price–consumption curves show how optimal consumption is affected by changing prices, or movements along the demand curve. Income–consumption curves illustrate the effects of shifts in demand due to changing income.

Engle Curve
A plot of the relationship between income and the quantity consumed of a good or service.

Engle Curves

A plot of the relationship between income and the quantity consumed of a good or service is called an **Engle curve,** named after economist Ernst Engle. Engle curves are closely related to income–consumption curves.

Normal Goods
Goods and services with rising consumption at higher levels of income.

The income–consumption curve shown in Figure 4.8(a) portrays the optimal consumption of goods and services at every income level, where the effects of changing income are illustrated with goods on the *Y*-axis and services on the *X*-axis. In Figure 4.8(a), the income–consumption curve has a positive slope, meaning that consumption of both types of products rises with income. If consumers have a tendency to buy more of a product as their income rises, such products are called **normal goods.** This is true for most goods and services. If consumers tend to buy less of a product following an increase in income, such products are called **inferior goods.** The term inferior good does not necessarily reflect

Inferior Goods
Goods and services with falling consumption at higher levels of income.

Figure 4.8   Income–Consumption Curves Show How Changing Income Affects Optimal Consumption

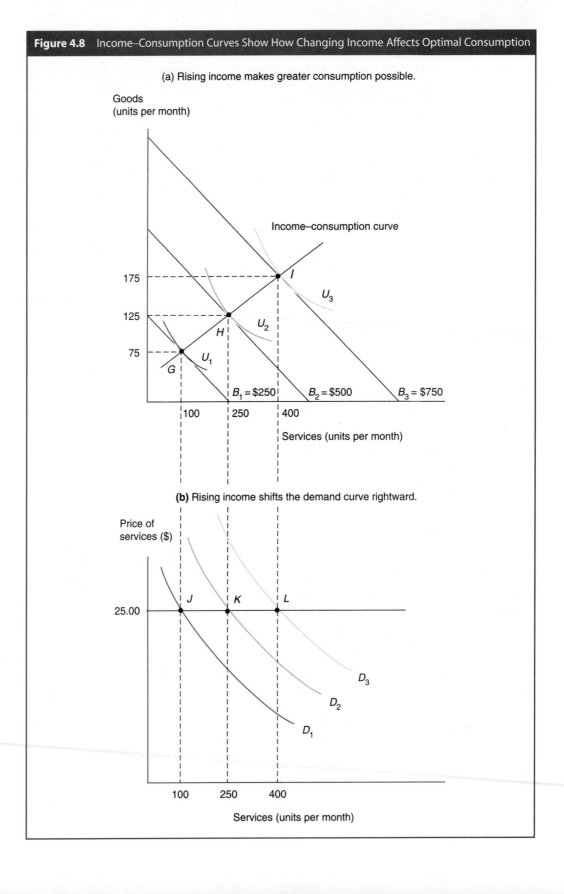

(a) Rising income makes greater consumption possible.

Goods
(units per month)

Income–consumption curve

U_3

U_2

U_1

175

125

75

H

G

$B_1 = \$250$ $B_2 = \$500$ $B_3 = \$750$

100   250   400

Services (units per month)

(b) Rising income shifts the demand curve rightward.

Price of
services ($)

J K L

25.00

D_3

D_2

D_1

100   250   400

Services (units per month)

substandard quality. It simply refers to the fact that consumption and income tend to be inversely related for certain products, such as bus rides and hamburgers.

Engle curves plot the effects of changing income on consumption using a graph with income on the vertical Y-axis and consumption on the horizontal X-axis. Because most products are normal goods that display a positive relationship between income and consumption, income–consumption curves and Engle curves tend to have a positive slope. In the case of inferior goods, income–consumption curves and Engle curves have a negative slope.

Figure 4.9(a) depicts an Engle curve for a normal good with rising consumption as income grows. This upward-sloping Engle curve is derived directly from Figure 4.8(a). In both graphs, the consumption of services rises from 100 when B_1 is \$250, to 250 when

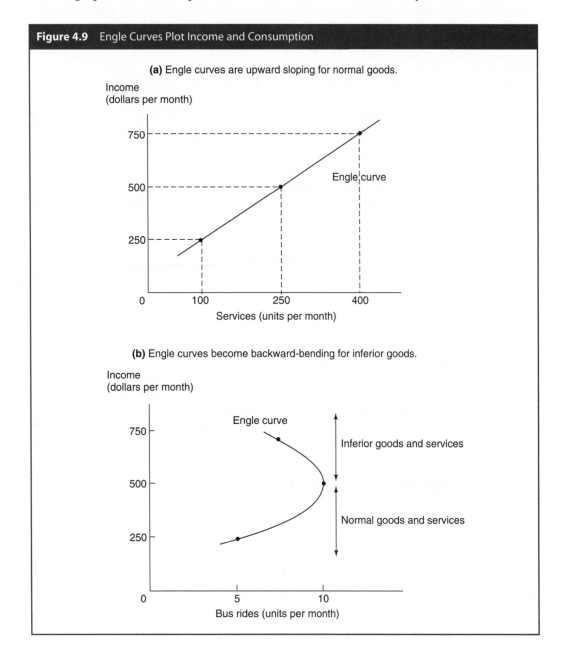

Figure 4.9 Engle Curves Plot Income and Consumption

(a) Engle curves are upward sloping for normal goods.

(b) Engle curves become backward-bending for inferior goods.

Managerial Application 4.2

Relationship Marketing

Saturn prides itself on the notion that it manufactures a superior automotive product, and provides superior service. Part of this superior service involves listening better to its customers and responding to their suggestions. During early summer, for example, thousands of Saturn owners typically respond to the company's invitation to attend a 3-day picnic at company headquarters in Spring Hill, Tennessee. Not only is it a way to thank owners for their business, but it is a proven means of building customer loyalty. Mail-order merchants Cabela's, L.L. Bean, and Lands' End, among others, deploy impressive computer capabilities to track and anticipate customer needs better. At Cabela's, for example, customers that order camping equipment and hiking boots are good candidates for the company's camping and outdoor gear catalog. Lands' End customers who order chinos and other casual attire also receive specialized catalogs. At L.L. Bean, the company's unconditional 100 percent satisfaction guarantee keeps valued customers coming back. At FedEx, highly profitable customers get special attention.

Car companies, mail-order merchants, airlines (with frequent flyer programs), and hotels with repeat business customers are obvious candidates for effective relationship marketing. The untapped potential for relationship marketing lies in new and innovative applications. For example, if a company wants to sell detergent, it might obtain a database of large families and offer them a bargain price. While a typical product promotion effort would stop there, relationship marketing goes further. Relationship marketing would suggest that the firm offer such families a free washer or dryer if they remained a loyal customer for, say, 5 years. Because the markup on detergent is substantial, such a long-term promotion could be highly beneficial for both the customer and the company.

The logic behind relationship marketing is simple. It costs much more to get a new customer than it does to keep a current one, so the retention of valued customers is key to long-term success.

See: Ronald Alsop, "Students and Nonprofits: Mutually Beneficial Relationships," *The Wall Street Journal Online*, May 8, 2007, http://online.wsj.com.

B_2 is \$500, and 400 when B_3 is \$750. Notice also that the consumption of goods rises in Figure 4.8(a) from 75 when B_1 is \$250, to 125 when B_2 is \$500, and 175 when B_3 is \$750. As a result, the Engle curve for goods would also be upward sloping as is true for all normal goods and services.

Engle curves slope upward for all normal goods and services, but are backward-bending in the case of inferior goods and services. As shown in Figure 4.9(b), the consumption of some goods and services, like bus rides and hamburgers, can actually begin to fall as income rises. The wealthy tend to choose automobile transportation rather than bus rides, and prefer steak to hamburger. In Figure 4.9(b), the number of bus rides taken per month rises up to an income level of \$500 per month, after which point the number of bus rides taken begins to fall as income rises. When income exceeds \$500 per month, an inverse relation exists between bus rides and income. Over this range, bus rides are an inferior good.

OPTIMAL CONSUMPTION

Given consumer preferences and budget constraint information, it is possible to determine optimal consumption.

Optimal Market Basket
Best feasible combination of goods and services.

Marginal Utility and Consumer Choice

The best allocation of a budget is the allocation that maximizes the utility, or satisfaction, derived from consumption. The resulting **optimal market basket** of goods and services must satisfy two important conditions.

First, *the optimal market basket lies on the budget line.* Remember, the budget line represents all combinations of goods and services that can be purchased for a fixed amount. Market basket combinations that lie above and to the right of the budget lines drawn in Figures 4.5 and 4.6, for example, are too expensive to purchase with the given limited funds. Purchase of market baskets that lie below and to the left of these budget lines would leave funds unspent, and reduce consumption of valuable goods and services. The best feasible market basket combination lies on the budget line.

And second, *the optimal market basket reflects consideration of marginal benefits and marginal costs.* Marginal analysis involves a comparison between added costs and added benefits. In terms of consumption decisions, consumers must weigh the relative marginal benefits and relative marginal costs derived from consumption. At the margin, if consumers derive twice as much satisfaction from the consumption of goods as from the consumption of services, then consumers would be willing to pay twice the marginal cost (price) for goods as opposed to services.

For example, suppose you had just finished a vigorous late-afternoon workout at a local health club. Only after quenching a burning thirst would it seem reasonable to order dinner or some snacks. Such behavior is a common reflection of the type of marginal analysis that everyone conducts when making consumption decisions. If a given consumer consistently chooses a given market basket over another less expensive market basket, then the consumer has a **revealed preference** for the chosen market basket. A revealed preference is a documented desire for a given good or service over some other less expensive good or service.

Revealed Preference
Declared choice.

Marginal Rate of Substitution

The discrete utility-function data used to derive the indifference curves shown in Figure 4.3 (see Table 4.1 and Figure 4.1) can be generalized by assuming that the consumption of goods and services can be varied continuously rather than incrementally. In the resulting utility function, indifference curves have the smooth shapes shown in Figure 4.4(c). The slope at each point along such indifference curves measures the consumer's rate of substitution among products.

In Figure 4.10, the slope of each indifference curve equals the change in goods (∂Y) divided by the change in services (∂X). This relation, called the **marginal rate of substitution,** is simply the change in consumption of Y (goods) necessary to offset a given change in the consumption of X (services) if the consumer's overall level of utility is to remain constant. This can be stated as

Marginal Rate of Substitution
Change in consumption of Y (goods) necessary to offset a given change in the consumption of X (services) if the consumer's overall level of utility is to remain constant.

$$MRS = \partial Y / \partial X = \text{Slope of an Indifference Curve} \qquad \textbf{4.3}$$

The marginal rate of substitution (MRS) diminishes as the amount of substitution increases. For example, in Figure 4.10, as more goods are substituted for services, the amount of services necessary to compensate for a given loss of goods will continue to fall. As more services are substituted for goods, the amount of goods necessary to compensate for a given loss of services will continue to fall. This pattern means that the negative slope of each indifference curve tends to approach zero as one moves from left to right.

The slope of an indifference curve is directly related to the concept of diminishing marginal utility. The marginal rate of substitution is equal to −1 times the ratio of the marginal utility derived from the consumption of each product [$MRS = -1(MU_X/MU_Y)$].

Figure 4.10 Optimal Market Baskets for Consumption

The optimal path for consumption is found when $P_X/P_Y = MU_X/MU_Y$.

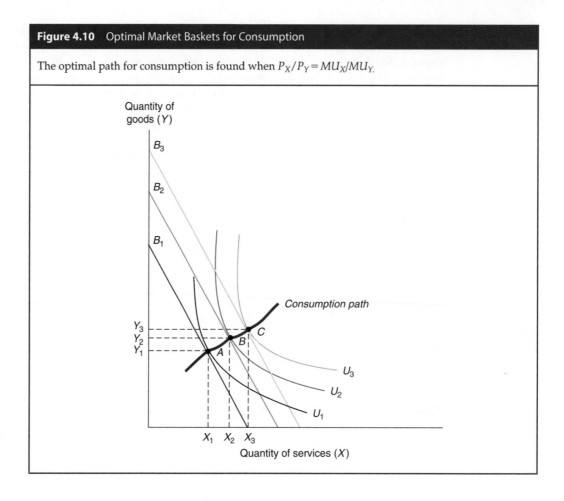

Remember that the loss in utility associated with a small reduction in Y is equal to the marginal utility of Y, MU_Y, multiplied by the change in Y, ∂Y. Algebraically, this is shown as follows:

$$\partial U = MU_Y \times \partial Y \qquad \textbf{4.4}$$

Similarly, the change in utility associated with a change in the consumption of X is

$$\partial U = MU_X \times \partial X \qquad \textbf{4.5}$$

Along an indifference curve, the absolute value of ∂U must be equal for a given substitution of Y for X. In other words, because utility is held constant along an indifference curve, the loss in utility following a reduction in Y must be fully offset by the gain in utility associated with an increase in X. Thus, ∂U in both Equations (4.4) and (4.5) must be equal in size and have an opposite sign from a given ∂Y and ∂X. Therefore, along an indifference curve,

$$-(MU_X \times \partial X) = MU_Y \times \partial Y \qquad \textbf{4.6}$$

Transposing the variables in Equation (4.6) produces

$$-MU_X/MU_Y = \partial Y/\partial X$$
$$MRS_{XY} = \text{Slope of an Indifference curve} \qquad \textbf{4.7}$$

Thus, the slope of an indifference curve [shown in Equation (4.3) to be equal to $\partial Y/\partial X$] is determined by the ratio of marginal utilities derived from each product. As one moves from left to right in Figure 4.10, the slope of each indifference curve goes from a large negative number toward zero. As seen in Equation (4.7), this implies that MU_X decreases relative to MU_Y as the relative consumption of X progressively increases.

Utility Maximization

To allocate expenditures efficiently among various products, one must consider both the marginal utility derived from consumption and the prices for each product. Utility is maximized when the marginal utility derived from each individual product is proportional to the price paid. This is illustrated graphically in Figure 4.10 which shows that optimal market baskets of goods and services are indicated by points of tangency between respective indifference curves and budget constraints.

If an individual has the funds indicated by budget constraint B_1, the optimal consumption combination occurs at point A, the point of tangency between the budget constraint and indifference curve U_1. The combination (X_1, Y_1) is the lowest-cost market basket that provides the U_1 level of utility. All other (X, Y) combinations on the U_1 indifference curve lie on higher budget constraints. Similarly, (X_2, Y_2) is the lowest-cost combination of goods and services that provides utility at the U_2 level, (X_3, Y_3) is the lowest-cost market basket that provides a U_3 level of utility, and so on.

The fact that optimal consumption occurs at points of tangency between budget constraints and indifference curves reflects an important economic principle. Recall that the slope of a budget constraint is -1 times the ratio of the product prices, or $-P_X/P_Y$. Recall also that the slope of an indifference curve equals to the marginal rate of substitution, shown in Equation (4.7) as -1 times the ratio of the marginal utilities for each product, or $-MU_X/MU_Y$. Therefore, optimal consumption combinations exist when the price ratios for goods and services equal the ratios of their marginal utilities:

$$\text{Slope of an Indifference Curve} = \text{Slope of a Budget Constraint}$$
$$-MU_X/MU_Y = -P_X/P_Y \qquad \textbf{4.8}$$

Alternatively,

$$-MU_X/P_X = -MU_Y/P_Y \qquad \textbf{4.8a}$$

Utility is maximized when products are purchased at relative prices that equal the relative marginal utility derived from consumption. As given by Equation (4.8(a)), with optimal consumption proportions, an additional dollar spent on a given consumption item adds as much to total utility as would a dollar spent on any other item.

Consumption Path
Optimal combinations of products as consumption increases.

In Figure 4.10 point A represents an optimal allocation, because X_1 and Y_1 provide the highest possible utility for the B_1 expenditure level. Similarly, points B and C represent efficient allocations for the B_2 and B_3 expenditure levels. By connecting all points of tangency between indifference curves and budget constraints (such as points A, B, and C), a **consumption path** depicts optimal market baskets as the budget level grows.

DEMAND SENSITIVITY ANALYSIS: ELASTICITY

Demand analysis focuses on measuring the sensitivity of demand to changes in a range of important factors.

Elasticity Concept

Elasticity
The percentage change in a dependant variable, Y, resulting from a 1 percent change in the value of an independent variable, X.

A measure of responsiveness used in demand analysis is **elasticity**, defined as the percentage change in a dependent variable, Y, resulting from a percentage change in the value of an independent variable, X. The equation for calculating elasticity is

$$\text{Elasticity} = \frac{\text{Percentage Change in } Y}{\text{Percentage Change in } X} \qquad \textbf{4.9}$$

The concept of elasticity simply involves the percentage change in one variable associated with a given percentage change in another variable. Elasticities are often used in demand analysis to measure the effects of changes in demand-determining variables. The elasticity concept is also used in production and cost analysis to evaluate the effect of changes in input on output, and the effect of output changes on costs. In finance, elasticity is used to measure operating leverage.

Endogenous Variables
Factors such as price and advertising that are within the control of the firm.

Factors such as price, product quality, and advertising that are within the control of the firm are **endogenous variables.** Factors outside the control of the firm, such as consumer incomes, competitor prices, and the weather, are **exogenous variables.** Both types of influences are important. For example, a firm must understand the effects of changes in both prices and consumer incomes to determine the price cut necessary to offset the decline in sales caused by a business recession. Similarly, the sensitivity of demand to changes in advertising must be quantified if the firm is to respond appropriately to an increase in competitor advertising.

Exogenous Variables
Factors outside the control of the firm, such as consumer incomes, competitor prices, and the weather.

Point Elasticity

Point Elasticity
It measures elasticity at a given point on a function.

Point elasticity measures elasticity at a given point on a function. The point elasticity concept is used to measure the effect on a dependent variable, Y, of a very small or marginal (say, 0 percent to 5 percent) change in an independent variable, X. Using the lowercase Greek letter epsilon, ε, as the symbol for point elasticity, point elasticity is

$$\text{Point Elasticity} = \varepsilon_X = \frac{\text{Percentage Change in } Y}{\text{Small Percentage Change in } X}$$

$$= \frac{\partial Y/Y}{\partial X/X}$$

$$= \partial Y/\partial X \times X/Y \qquad \textbf{4.10}$$

The $\partial Y/\partial X$ term in the point elasticity formula is the marginal relation between Y and X, and shows the effect on Y of a 1-unit change in X. Point elasticity is determined by multiplying this marginal relation by the relative size of X to Y, or the X/Y ratio at the point being analyzed. Therefore, point elasticity measures the percentage effect on Y of a percentage change in X at a given point on a function. If $\varepsilon_X = 5$, a 1 percent increase in X will lead to a 5 percent increase in Y, and a 1 percent decrease in X will lead to a

5 percent decrease in Y. When $\varepsilon_X > 0$, Y changes in the same positive or negative direction as X. Conversely, when $\varepsilon_X < 0$, Y changes in the opposite direction of changes in X. For example, if $\varepsilon_X = -3$, a 1 percent increase in X will lead to a 3 percent decrease in Y, and a 1 percent decrease in X will lead to a 3 percent increase in Y.

Arc Elasticity

Arc Elasticity
Average elasticity over a given range of a function.

Although the point elasticity concept can give accurate estimates of the effect on Y of small changes in X, it is not used to measure the effect on Y of large-scale (more than 5 percent) changes in X. Because elasticity typically varies at different points along a function, the **arc elasticity** formula was developed to calculate an average elasticity over a given range. Using the uppercase Roman letter E as the symbol for arc elasticity, arc elasticity is

$$
\begin{aligned}
\text{Arc Elasticity} = E_X &= \frac{\text{Percentage Change in } Y}{\text{Large Percentage Change in } X} \\[6pt]
&= \frac{\dfrac{\text{Change in } Y}{\text{Average } Y}}{\dfrac{\text{Large Change in } X}{\text{Average } X}} \\[6pt]
&= \frac{\dfrac{(Y_2 - Y_1)}{(Y_2 + Y_1)/2}}{\dfrac{(X_2 - X_1)}{(X_2 + X_1)/2}} \\[6pt]
&= \frac{\Delta Y/(Y_2 + Y_1)}{\Delta X/(X_2 + X_1)} \\[6pt]
&= \Delta Y/\Delta X \times (X_2 + X_1)/(Y_2 + Y_1) \qquad \textbf{4.11}
\end{aligned}
$$

Like point elasticity, arc elasticity measures the percentage change in Y caused by a percentage change in X. The sole difference is that point elasticity measures the effects on Y of small changes in X while arc elasticity measures the effects on Y of large-scale changes in X. The arc elasticity formula eliminates the problem of deciding which end of a given range to use as a base, and measures the relation between two variables over a *range* of data.

PRICE ELASTICITY OF DEMAND

Price Elasticity of Demand
Responsiveness of quantity demanded to changes in the price of the product itself, holding constant the values of all other variables in the demand function.

Demand elasticity analysis starts with the study of how quantity demanded is related to price changes.

Price Elasticity Formula

The **price elasticity of demand** measures the responsiveness of quantity demanded to changes in the price of the product itself, holding constant the values of all other variables in the demand function.

Using the formula for point elasticity, price elasticity is

$$\text{Point Price Elasticity} = \varepsilon_P = \frac{\text{Percentage Change in Quantity}(Q)}{\text{Small Percentage Change in Price }(P)}$$

$$= \frac{\partial Q/Q}{\partial P/P}$$

$$= \partial Q/\partial P \times P/Q \qquad\qquad \textbf{4.12}$$

where $\partial Q/\partial P$ is the marginal change in quantity following a 1-unit change in price, and P and Q are price and quantity, respectively, at a given point on the demand curve.

An example can be used to illustrate the calculation and use of the price elasticity formula. Assume that the management of a movie theater is interested in analyzing movie ticket demand. Also assume that monthly data for the past year suggests the following demand function:

$$Q = 7{,}000 - 5{,}000P + 6{,}000P_{DVD} + 150I + 1{,}000A$$

where Q is the quantity of movie tickets, P is average ticket price (in dollars), P_{DVD} is the 3-day new-release movie rental price at DVD outlets in the area (in dollars), I is average disposable income per household (in thousands of dollars), and A is monthly advertising expenditures (in thousands of dollars). Numbers that appear before each variable in such a function are called coefficients or parameter estimates. They indicate the expected change in movie ticket sales associated with a 1-unit change in each independent variable. For example, the number $-5{,}000$ indicates that the quantity of movie tickets demanded falls by 5,000 units with every \$1 increase in the price of movie tickets, or $\partial Q/\partial P = -5{,}000$. Similarly, a \$1 increase in the price of DVD rentals causes a 6,000-unit increase in movie ticket demand, or $\partial Q/\partial P_{DVD} = 6{,}000$. A \$1,000 (1-unit) increase in disposable income per household leads to a 150-unit increase in demand, or $\partial Q/\partial I = 150$, and a \$1,000 (1-unit) increase in advertising leads to a 1,000-unit increase in demand, or $\partial Q/\partial A = 1{,}000$.

For a typical theater, suppose that $P_{DVD} = \$4$, and income and advertising are \$60,000 and \$20,000, respectively. At these typical values, the movie ticket demand curve is

$$Q = 7{,}000 - 5{,}000P + 6{,}000(4) + 150(60) + 1{,}000(20)$$
$$= 60{,}000 - 5{,}000P$$

This demand curve can be used to calculate the point price elasticity of demand at any price. For example, when $P = \$8$, $Q = 60{,}000 - 5{,}000(8) = 20{,}000$; if $P = \$10$, $Q = 60{,}000 - 5{,}000(10) = 10{,}000$. Therefore,

$$\text{At } P = \$8,\ \varepsilon_P = \partial Q/\partial P \times P/Q = -5{,}000 \times 8/20{,}000 = -2$$
$$\text{At } P = \$10,\ \varepsilon_P = \partial Q/\partial P \times P/Q = -5{,}000 \times 10/10{,}000 = -5$$

When $P = \$8$, $\varepsilon_P = -2$ means that a 1 percent increase in movie ticket prices will result in a 2 percent decrease in quantity demanded. Conversely, a 1 percent decrease in movie ticket prices will result in a 2 percent increase in quantity demanded. Because the quantity demanded moves in the opposite direction from price changes, point price elasticities of demand are uniformly negative. Notice that the point price elasticity of demand varies depending upon the price (P) charged and the number of units sold (Q). The price elasticity of demand becomes more negative (a larger negative number) at higher prices because the price sensitivity of consumers tends to grow as prices increase.

The arc price elasticity of demand is used to analyze the sensitivity of quantity demanded to price changes over an extended range of prices. Using E_P as the symbol for arc elasticity, the arc price elasticity is

$$\text{Arc Price Elasticity} = E_P = \frac{\text{Percentage Change in } Q}{\text{Large Percentage Change in } P}$$

$$= \frac{\Delta Q/(Q_2 + Q_1)}{\Delta P/(P_2 + P_1)}$$

$$= \Delta Q/\Delta P \times (P_2 + P_1)/(Q_2 + Q_1) \qquad \textbf{4.13}$$

In the present example, the arc price elasticity of demand for movie tickets over the price range from \$8 to \$10 is

$$\text{Between \$8 and \$10, } E_P = \Delta Q/\Delta P \times (P_2 + P_1)/(Q_2 + Q_1)$$

$$= (10,000 - 20,000)/(\$10 - \$8) \times$$

$$(\$10 + \$8/(10,000 + 20,000))$$

$$= -3$$

This means that, on average, a 1 percent change in price leads to a 3 percent change in quantity demanded when movie ticket prices lie within the range from \$8 to \$10 per ticket.

Price Elasticity and Total Revenue

Depending on the degree of price elasticity, a reduction in price can increase, decrease, or leave unchanged the total revenue. A good estimate of price elasticity makes it possible to accurately estimate the effect of price changes on total revenue. For decision-making purposes, three specific ranges of price elasticity have been identified. Using $|\varepsilon_P|$ to denote the absolute value of the price elasticity, three ranges for price elasticity are

1. $|\varepsilon_P| > 1.0$, defined as elastic demand.
   Example: $\varepsilon_P = -3.2$ and $|\varepsilon_P| = 3.2$.

2. $|\varepsilon_P| = 1.0$, defined as unitary elasticity.
   Example: $\varepsilon_P = -1.0$ and $|\varepsilon_P| = 1.0$.

3. $|\varepsilon_P| < 1.0$, defined as inelastic demand.
   Example: $\varepsilon_P = -0.5$ and $|\varepsilon_P| = 0.5$.

Elastic Demand
Situation in which a price change leads to a more than proportionate change in quantity demanded.

Unitary Elasticity
Situation in which price and quantity changes exactly offset each other.

Inelastic Demand
Situation in which a price change leads to a less than proportionate change in quantity demanded.

With **elastic demand,** $|\varepsilon_P| > 1$ and the relative change in quantity is larger than the relative change in price. A given percentage increase in price causes quantity to decrease by a larger percentage. If demand is elastic, a price increase lowers total revenue and a decrease in price raises total revenue. **Unitary elasticity** is a situation in which the percentage change in quantity divided by the percentage change in price equals -1. Because price and quantity are inversely related, a price elasticity of -1 means that the effect of a price change is *exactly* offset by the effect of a change in quantity demanded. The result is that total revenue, the product of price times quantity, remains constant. With **inelastic demand,** a price increase produces a less than proportionate decline in the quantity demanded, so total revenues rise. Conversely, when demand is inelastic, a price decrease generates a less than proportionate increase in quantity demanded, so total revenues fall. These relations are summarized in Table 4.5.

Table 4.5 Relationship Between Price Elasticity and Total Revenue

Elasticity	Implies	Following a Price Increase:	Following a Price Decrease:
Elastic demand, $\lvert\varepsilon_p\rvert > 1$	$\partial Q/Q > \partial P/P$	Revenue decreases	Revenue increases
Unitary elasticity, $\lvert\varepsilon_p\rvert = 1$	$\partial Q/Q = \partial P/P$	Revenue uncharged	Revenue unchanged
Inelastic demand, $\lvert\varepsilon_p\rvert < 1$	$\partial Q/Q < \partial P/P$	Revenue increases	Revenue decreases

Price elasticity can range from completely inelastic, where $\varepsilon_p = 0$, to perfectly elastic, where $\varepsilon_p = -\infty$. To illustrate, consider an extreme case in which the quantity demanded is independent of price so that some fixed amount, Q^*, is demanded regardless of price. When the quantity demanded of a product is completely insensitive to price, $\partial Q/\partial P = 0$, the price elasticity will equal zero, irrespective of the value of P/Q. The demand curve for such a good or service is perfectly vertical, as shown in Figure 4.11.

The other limiting case, that of infinite price elasticity, describes a product that is completely sensitive to price. The demand curve for such a good or service is perfectly horizontal, as shown in Figure 4.12. Here the ratio $\partial Q/\partial P = -\infty$ and $\varepsilon_p = -\infty$, regardless of the value of P/Q.

The economic properties of these limiting cases should be understood. A firm faced with a vertical or perfectly inelastic demand curve could charge any price and still sell Q^* units. Theoretically, such a firm could appropriate all of its customers' income or wealth. Conversely, a firm facing a horizontal or perfectly elastic demand curve could sell an unlimited quantity of output at the price P^*, but it would lose all sales if it raised prices by even a small amount. Such extreme cases are rare, but monopolies that sell necessities

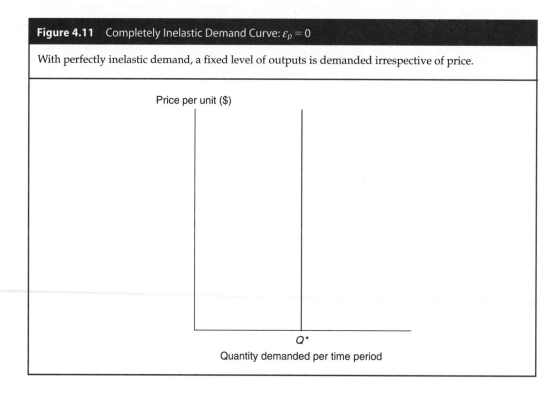

Figure 4.11   Completely Inelastic Demand Curve: $\varepsilon_p = 0$

With perfectly inelastic demand, a fixed level of outputs is demanded irrespective of price.

Price per unit ($)

Q^*

Quantity demanded per time period

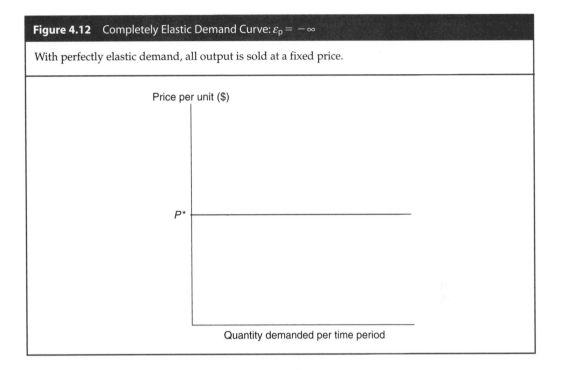

Figure 4.12 Completely Elastic Demand Curve: $\varepsilon_p = -\infty$

With perfectly elastic demand, all output is sold at a fixed price.

such as pharmaceuticals enjoy relatively inelastic demand. Firms in highly competitive industries, like grocery retailing, face highly elastic demand.

PRICE ELASTICITY AND MARGINAL REVENUE

There are direct relations between price elasticity, marginal revenue, and total revenue.

Elasticity Varies Along a Linear Demand Curve

All linear demand curves, except perfectly elastic or perfectly inelastic ones, are subject to varying elasticity at different points on the curve. Any linear demand curve is price elastic at some output levels but inelastic at others. To see this, recall again the definition of point price elasticity expressed in Equation (4.12):

$$\varepsilon_P = \partial Q/\partial P \times P/Q$$

The slope of a linear demand curve, $\partial Q/\partial P$, is constant. So too is its reciprocal, $1/(\partial Q/\partial P) = \partial P/\partial Q$. However, notice that the ratio P/Q varies from 0 at the point where the demand curve intersects the horizontal axis and price equals zero, to $+\infty$ at the vertical price axis intercept where quantity equals zero. Because the price elasticity formula for a linear curve involves multiplying a negative constant by a ratio that varies between zero and $+\infty$, the price elasticity of a linear curve must range from zero to $-\infty$.

Figure 4.13 illustrates this relation. As one moves along the demand curve towards the vertical axis, the ratio P/Q approaches infinity and ε_p approaches negative infinity. As one moves along the demand curve towards the horizontal axis, the ratio P/Q approaches

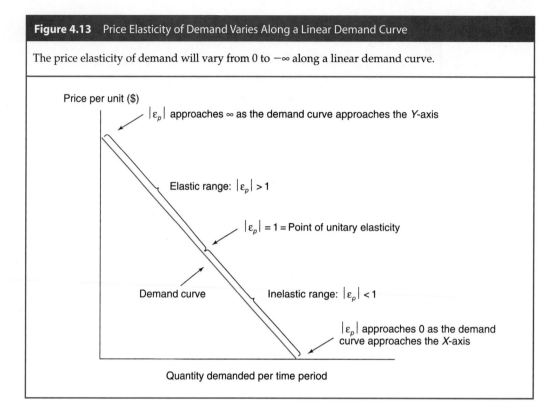

Figure 4.13 Price Elasticity of Demand Varies Along a Linear Demand Curve

The price elasticity of demand will vary from 0 to $-\infty$ along a linear demand curve.

Price per unit ($)

$|\varepsilon_p|$ approaches ∞ as the demand curve approaches the Y-axis

Elastic range: $|\varepsilon_p| > 1$

$|\varepsilon_p| = 1 =$ Point of unitary elasticity

Demand curve

Inelastic range: $|\varepsilon_p| < 1$

$|\varepsilon_p|$ approaches 0 as the demand curve approaches the X-axis

Quantity demanded per time period

zero, causing ε_p also to approach zero. At the midpoint of the demand curve $\partial Q/\partial P \times P/Q = -1$. This is the point of unitary elasticity.

Price Elasticity and Price Changes

The relation between price elasticity and total revenue can be clarified by examining Figure 4.14 and Table 4.6. Figure 4.14(a) reproduces the demand curve shown in Figure 4.13 along with the associated marginal revenue curve. The demand curve shown in Figure 4.14(a) is of the general linear form

$$P = a - bQ$$

where a is the intercept and b is the slope coefficient. It follows that total revenue (TR) can be expressed as

$$
\begin{aligned}
TR &= P \times Q \\
&= (a - bQ) \times Q \\
&= aQ - bQ^2
\end{aligned}
$$

By definition, marginal revenue (MR) is the change in revenue following a 1-unit expansion in output, $\partial TR/\partial Q$, and can be written

$$MR = \partial TR/\partial Q = a - 2bQ$$

Figure 4.14   Relations Among Price Elasticity and Marginal, Average, and Total Revenue:
(a) Demand (Average Revenue) and Marginal Revenue Curves; (b) Total Revenue

In the range in which demand is elastic with respect to price, marginal revenue is positive and total revenue increases with a reduction in price. In the inelastic range, marginal revenue is negative and total revenue decreases with price reductions.

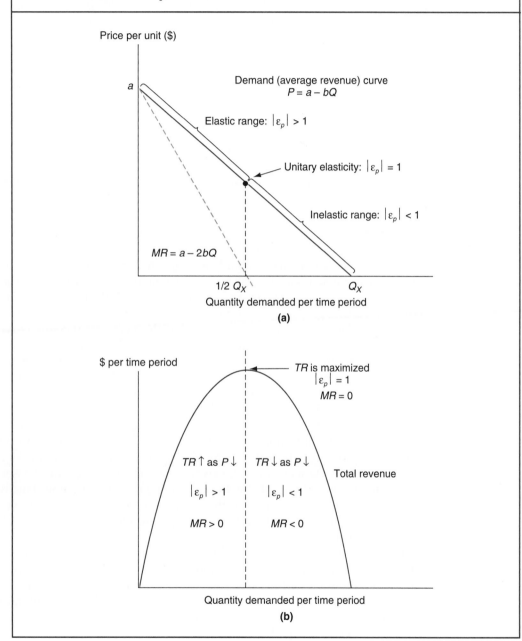

Table 4.6 Price Elasticity and Revenue Relations: A Numerical Example

Price P ($)	Quantity Q	Total Revenue $TR = P \times Q$ ($)	Marginal Revenue $MR = \Delta TR$ ($)	Arc Elasticity[a] E_P
100	1	100	—	—
90	2	180	80	−6.33
80	3	240	60	−3.40
70	4	280	40	−2.14
60	5	300	20	−1.44
50	6	300	0	−1.00
40	7	280	−20	−0.69
30	8	240	−40	−0.47
20	9	180	−60	−0.29
10	10	100	−80	−0.16

[a] Because the price and quantity data in the table are discrete numbers, the price elasticities have been calculated by using the arc elasticity equation

$$E_P = \frac{\Delta Q}{\Delta P} \times \frac{P_2 + P_1}{Q_2 + Q_1}$$

The relation between the demand (average revenue) and marginal revenue curves becomes clear when one compares a linear demand curve with its associated marginal revenue curve. Each curve has the same intercept a. Both curves begin at the same point along the vertical price axis. However, the marginal revenue curve has twice the negative slope of the demand curve. This means that the marginal revenue curve intersects the horizontal axis at $1/2\ Q_X$, given that the demand curve intersects at Q_X. Figure 4.14(a) shows that marginal revenue is positive in the range where demand is price elastic, zero where $\varepsilon_P = -1$, and negative in the inelastic range. Thus, there is an obvious relation between price elasticity and both average and marginal revenue.

As shown in Figure 4.14(b), price elasticity is also closely related to total revenue. Total revenue increases with price reductions in the elastic range (where $MR > 0$) because the increase in quantity demanded at the new lower price more than offsets the lower revenue per unit received at that reduced price. Total revenue peaks at the point of unitary elasticity (where $MR = 0$), because the increase in quantity associated with the price reduction exactly offsets the lower revenue received per unit. Finally, total revenue declines when price is reduced in the inelastic range (where $MR < 0$) where the relative increase in quantity is less than the percentage decrease in price, and not large enough to offset the reduction in revenue per unit sold.

The numerical example in Table 4.6 illustrates these relations. It shows that from 1 to 5 units of output, demand is elastic, $|\varepsilon_P| > 1$, and a reduction in price increases total revenue. For example, decreasing price from $80 to $70 increases output from 3 to 4 units. Marginal revenue is positive over this range of output, and total revenue increases from $240 to $280. For output greater than 6 units and prices less than $50, demand is inelastic, $|\varepsilon_P| < 1$. Here price reductions result in lower total revenue because the increase in quantity demanded is not large enough to offset the lower price per unit. With total revenue decreasing as output expands, marginal revenue must be negative. For example, reducing price from $30 to $20 results in revenue declining from $240 to $180 even though output increases from 8 to 9 units; marginal revenue in this case is −$60.

Managerial Application 4.3

Haggling in the Car Business

The car business lives and dies on the basis of rebates, special dealer incentives, intensive consumer advertising, and haggling. Traditionally, car dealers buy from the manufacturers at an invoice price less special seasonal discounts designed to push slow-moving stock out the door and keep the factories humming. Car dealers also receive "give-backs" from manufacturers, depending upon the total amount of business that they've done during the course of the year. Give-backs might average 3 percent for the first $1 million of invoices for cars and trucks sold during the year, and rise in increments as the total amount of dealer volume rises. This makes it possible for manufacturers to reward their highest volume dealers, and give all dealers a big incentive to "move iron", as they say in the auto business.

Price haggling is also an intrinsic part of car buying. The most price-conscious consumers consult car prices, invoice amounts, and rebate opportunities on the Internet. They also travel from dealer to dealer seeking the best price or financing package. Price haggling works, especially toward the end of each calendar month when dealer incentives are at stake, or when sales personnel are eligible for incentive bonus payments. No dealer wants to see a potential customer walk out the door, and walking works. Less price-conscious customers focus more on style, color, option packages, or the timeliness of delivery, and pay more for their vehicles. Because a trade-in of a used vehicle is typically involved, car buyers and sellers actually haggle over the net price after trade-in allowances rather than the price of a new or used car. Even if everyday low pricing becomes popular in the car business, there can never be the same degree of price certainty possible in a true "one price" environment. So long as trade-ins are involved, price haggling is always going to be part of the new or used car buying experience.

See: Gordon Fairclough, "China's Car-Price Wars Dent Profits," *The Wall Street Journal Online*, September 19, 2007, http://online.wsj.com.

PRICE ELASTICITY AND OPTIMAL PRICING POLICY

Price elasticity of demand data along with detailed cost information gives firms the tools necessary for setting optimal prices.

Optimal Price Formula

Because demand curves slope downward, two effects on revenue follow a price reduction: (1) By selling an additional unit, total revenue goes up by P; (2) However, by charging a lower price, some revenue is lost on units sold previously at the higher price. This effect is captured by $Q \times \partial P / \partial Q$. Therefore, when price is a function of output, the change in total revenue following a change in output (marginal revenue) is given by the expression

$$MR = \partial TR/Q = \partial(P \times Q)/\partial Q$$
$$= P + Q \times \partial P/\partial Q$$

When the above expression is multiplied by P/P, a simple relationship between marginal revenue and the point price elasticity of demand is identified

$$MR = P + Q \times \partial P/\partial Q$$
$$= P + P(Q/P \times \partial P/\partial Q)$$
$$= P + P(1/\varepsilon_P)$$
$$= P[1 + (1/\varepsilon_P)]$$

Because $\varepsilon_P < 0$, the expression $1 + (1/\varepsilon_P)$ is always less than one, and $MR < P$. The gap between MR and P will fall as the price elasticity of demand increases (in absolute value terms). When price elasticity is relatively low, the profit-maximizing price is much greater than marginal revenue. When the quantity demanded is highly elastic with respect to price, the profit-maximizing price is close to marginal revenue. Because $MR = P[1 + (1/\varepsilon_P)]$, and $MR = MC$ at the profit-maximizing activity level, the relation between the profit-maximizing price and the point price elasticity of demand, called the **optimal price formula,** is

Optimal Price Formula

For any downward-sloping demand curve, maximum profits result when $P = MC/[1 + (1/\varepsilon_P)]$.

$$P^* = MC/[1 + (1/\varepsilon_P)] \qquad\qquad \textbf{4.14}$$

In practice, the profit-maximizing price P^* can be easily calculated when given point price elasticity of demand and marginal cost information.

Optimal Pricing Policy Example

Suppose that manager George Stevens notes a 2 percent increase in weekly sales following a 1 percent price discount on The Kingfish fishing reels. The point price elasticity of demand for The Kingfish fishing reels is

$$\varepsilon_P = \frac{\text{Percentage Change in Quantity } (Q)}{\text{Small Percentage Change in Price } (P)}$$
$$= 2/(-1)$$
$$= -2$$

If relevant marginal costs are $25 per unit, and given $\varepsilon_p = -2$, from Equation (4.14), the profit-maximizing price is

$$P^* = \$25/[1 + (1/(-2))]$$
$$= \$50$$

Therefore, the optimal retail price for The Kingfish fishing reels is $50.

To see how the optimal price formula can be used for planning purposes, suppose Stevens can order reels through a different distributor and reduce marginal costs by $1 to $24 per unit. Under these circumstances, the new optimal retail price is

$$P^* = \$24/[1 + (1/(-2))]$$
$$= \$48$$

Thus, the optimal retail price would fall by $2 following a $1 reduction in The Kingfish's relevant marginal costs. Therefore, the optimal price formula can serve as the basis for calculating profit-maximizing prices under current cost and market-demand conditions, as well as under a variety of potential circumstances. Table 4.7 shows how profit-maximizing prices vary for a product with a $25 marginal cost as the point price elasticity of demand varies. The less elastic is demand, the greater is the difference between price and marginal cost. Conversely, as the absolute value of the price elasticity of demand increases (i.e., as demand becomes more price elastic), the profit-maximizing price gets closer and closer to marginal cost.

Table 4.7 Price Elasticity and Optimal Pricing Policy

Point Price Elasticity	Marginal Cost ($)	Profit-Maximizing Price ($)
−1.25	25	25.00
−1.50	25	75.00
−2.50	25	41.67
−5.00	25	31.25
−10.00	25	27.78
−25.00	25	26.04

In practice, there are three major influences on price elasticities: (1) the extent to which a good is considered a necessity; (2) the availability of substitute goods; and (3) the proportion of income spent on the product. A relatively constant quantity of electricity for residential lighting will be purchased almost irrespective of price, at least in the short run. There is no close substitute for electric service. However, goods such as men's and women's clothing face considerably more competition, and the quantity demanded depends more on price. The quantity demanded of "big ticket" items such as automobiles, homes, and vacation travel accounts for a large share of consumer income and is relatively sensitive to price. The quantity demanded for less expensive products, such as soft drinks, candy, and cigarettes, can be relatively insensitive to price. Given the low percentage of income spent on "small ticket" items, consumers often find that searching for the best deal available is not worth the time and effort.

CROSS-PRICE ELASTICITY OF DEMAND

Demand for most products is also influenced by changes in the prices of other products.

Cross-Price Elasticity Formula

Cross-Price Elasticity
Responsiveness of demand for one product to changes in the price of another.

The concept of **cross-price elasticity** is used to examine the responsiveness of demand for one product to changes in the price of another. Point cross-price elasticity is given as

$$\text{Point Cross-Price Elasticity} = \varepsilon_{PX} = \frac{\text{Percentage Change in Quantity of } Y\ (Q_Y)}{\text{Small Percentage Change in Price of } X\ (P_X)}$$

$$= \frac{\partial Q_Y/Q_Y}{\partial P_X/P_X}$$

$$= \partial Q_Y/\partial P_X \times P_X/Q_Y \qquad \textbf{4.15}$$

where Y and X are two different products. Similarly, arc cross-price elasticity is given as

$$\text{Arc Cross-Price Elasticity} = E_{PX} = \frac{\text{Percentage Change in Quantity of } Y\ (Q_Y)}{\text{Large Percentage Change in Price of } X\ (P_X)}$$

$$= \frac{\Delta Q_Y/(Q_{Y2} + Q_{Y1})}{\Delta P_X/(P_{X2} + P_{X1})}$$

$$= \Delta Q_Y/\Delta P_X \times (P_{X2} + P_{X1})/(Q_{Y2} + Q_{Y1}) \qquad \textbf{4.16}$$

Cross-price elasticity information is an important tool in demand analysis.

Substitutes and Complements

Substitutes
Products that serve
the same purpose.

Demand for beef is related to the price of chicken. As the price of chicken increases, so does the demand for beef; as consumers substitute beef for the now relatively more expensive chicken. On the other hand, a price decrease for chicken leads to a decrease in the demand for beef as consumers substitute chicken for the now relatively more expensive beef. In general, a direct relation between the price of one product and the demand for a second product holds for all **substitutes.** A price increase for a given product will increase demand for substitutes; a price decrease for a given product will decrease demand for substitutes.

Complements
Products that are
best consumed
together.

Some goods and services—for example, cameras and film—exhibit a completely different relation. For them, a price increase in one product typically leads to a reduction in demand for the other. Goods that are inversely related in this manner are known as **complements;** they are used together rather than in place of each other. Finally, cross-price elasticity is zero, or nearly zero, for unrelated goods.

To illustrate, suppose a study identifies how demand for in-home health care services (Q_Y) is related to price changes for prescription drugs (D), hospital services (H), and vacation travel (T). If

$$\varepsilon_{PD} = \partial Q_Y / \partial P_D \times P_D / Q_Y = -3$$
$$\varepsilon_{PD} < 0, \text{meaning that } Q_Y \text{ and prescription drugs are complements.}$$

$$\varepsilon_{PH} = \partial Q_Y / \partial P_H \times P_H / Q_Y = 4.5$$
$$\varepsilon_{PH} > 0, \text{meaning that } Q_Y \text{ and hospital services are substitutes.}$$

$$\varepsilon_{PT} = \partial Q_Y / \partial P_T \times P_T / Q_Y = 0$$
$$\varepsilon_{PT} = 0, \text{meaning that demand for } Q_Y \text{ and travel are independent.}$$

Cross-price elasticity information is especially important for firms with a wide variety of products because meaningful substitute or complementary relations can exist within the firm's own product line. Cross-price elasticity information also allows firms to measure the degree of competition in the marketplace. If the cross-price elasticity between a firm's output and products produced in related industries is large and positive, the firm may face the imminent threat of competitor encroachment.

INCOME ELASTICITY OF DEMAND

For many goods, income is an important determinant of demand.

Income Elasticity Formula

Income Elasticity
Responsiveness of
demand to changes
in income, holding
constant the
effect of all other
variables.

The **income elasticity** of demand measures the responsiveness of demand to changes in income, holding constant the effect of all other variables that influence demand. Letting I represent income, point income elasticity is defined as

$$\text{Point Income Elasticity} = \varepsilon_I = \frac{\text{Percentage Change in Quantity } (Q)}{\text{Small Percentage Change in Income } (I)}$$

$$= \frac{\partial Q/Q}{\partial I/I}$$

$$= \partial Q/\partial I + I/Q \qquad \textbf{4.17}$$

Similarly, arc income elasticity is defined as

$$\text{Arc Income Elasticity} = E_I = \frac{\text{Percentage Change in Quantity } (Q)}{\text{Large Percentage Change in Income } (I)}$$

$$= \frac{\Delta Q/(Q_2 + Q_1)}{\Delta I/(I_2 + I_1)}$$

$$= \Delta Q_Y/\Delta I \times (I_2 + I_1)/(Q_2 + Q_1) \qquad \textbf{4.18}$$

Demand analysis typically includes consideration of effects tied to changing income.

Normal Versus Inferior Goods

For normal goods, individual and aggregate demand is positively related to income. Income and the quantity purchased typically move in the same direction; that is, income and sales are directly rather than inversely related. Hence, $\varepsilon_I > 0$ for normal goods. Such a positive relation between demand and income does not hold for inferior goods. Individual consumer demand for such products as beans and potatoes, for example, tends to fall as incomes rise because consumers replace them with more desirable alternatives. For inferior goods, $\varepsilon_I < 0$. In the case of inferior goods, individual demand actually rises during an economic downturn. As workers get laid off from their jobs, for example, they might tend to substitute potatoes for meat, hamburgers for steak, bus rides for automobile trips, and so on. As a result, demand for potatoes, hamburgers, bus rides, and other inferior goods may rise during recessions. Their demand is **countercyclical.**

Countercyclical
Falls with rising income, and rises with falling income.

For most products, income elasticity is positive, indicating that demand rises as the economy expands and national income increases. Products for which $0 < \varepsilon_I < 1$ are referred to as **noncyclical normal goods,** because demand is relatively unaffected by changing income. Sales of most convenience goods, such as toothpaste, candy, soda, and movie tickets, account for only a small share of the consumer's overall budget, and spending on such items tends to be relatively unaffected by changing economic conditions. For goods having $\varepsilon_I > 1$, referred to as **cyclical normal goods,** demand is strongly affected by changing economic conditions. Purchase of "big ticket" items such as homes, automobiles, boats, and recreational vehicles can be postponed and tend to be put off by consumers during economic downturns. Housing demand, for example, can collapse during recessions and skyrocket during economic expansions. Relations between income and product demand are summarized in Table 4.8.

Noncyclical Normal Goods
Products for which demand is relatively unaffected by changing income.

Cyclical Normal Goods
Products for which demand is strongly affected by changing income.

Table 4.8 Relationship Between Income and Product Demand		
Inferior goods (countercyclical)	$\varepsilon_I < 0$	Basic foodstuffs, generic products, bus rides
Noncyclical normal goods	$0 < \varepsilon_I < 1$	Toiletries, movies, liquor, cigarettes
Cyclical normal goods	$\varepsilon_I > 1$	Automobiles, housing, vacation travel, capital equipment

Managerial Application 4.4

What's in a Name?

When it comes to financial information, privately held Mars Incorporated, in MacLean, Virginia, is secretive. With annual sales of $15 billion in pet foods, candies, and other food products, the company is also immensely profitable. According to *Forbes*' annual survey, Forrest Edward Mars, Sr., Edward Mars, Jr., Jacqueline Mars Vogel, John Mars, and the rest of the clan are worth more than *$16 billion*—one of the richest families in the world. How does Mars do it? That's simple: brand-name advertising.

Like top rivals Hershey's, Nestle, and Ralston Purina, Mars advertises like mad to create durable brand names. Since 1954, M&M's Peanut and M&M's Chocolate Candies have been known by the slogan "Melts in your mouth—not in your hand." With constant reminders, the message hasn't been lost on consumers who also flock to other Mars candies like Royals Mint Chocolate, Kudos Granola Bars, Skittles Fruit Chews, Snickers Candy & Ice Cream Bars, and Starburst Fruit Chews. Brand-name advertising is also a cornerstone of Mars marketing of Kal-Kan petfoods, Expert,

a superpremium dog- and cat-food line, and Sheba and Whiskas cat foods.

Mars is like many top-tier consumer products companies; their good name is their most valuable asset. For example, while Coca-Cola enjoys undeniable economies of scale in distribution, nothing is more valuable than its telltale moniker in white-on-red background. For Philip Morris, the Marlboro brand is the source of a large and growing river of cash flow. In the United States, more than one-half of all cigarettes are sold on the basis of a red-and-white box and the rugged image of a weather-beaten and sun-dried cowboy. Owners of trademarks such as *Astroturf*, *Coke*, *Frisbee*, *Kleenex*, *Kitty Litter*, *Styrofoam*, *Walkman*, and *Xerox* employ a veritable army of lawyers in an endless struggle against "generic" treatment. They know that well-established brand-name products enjoy enormous profits.

See: Susanne Craig, "Wall Street's Case of ... Sifma: Sound Like a Disease? Securities Trade Group Debates Its Acronym," *The Wall Street Journal Online*, June 18, 2007, http://online.wsj.com.

SUMMARY

- Consumer behavior theory rests upon three basic assumptions regarding the **utility** (or satisfaction) tied to consumption. First, the **nonsatiation principle** states more is better. Second, preferences are complete. If two goods provide the same utility, the consumer is **indifferent** between the two. Third, consumer understanding of **ordinal utility** makes possible a rank ordering of preferred goods and services. If consumers had understanding of **cardinal utility,** they would know how much one product is preferred over another.

- A **utility function** is a descriptive statement that relates well-being to the consumption of goods and services. Bundles of items desired by consumers are called **market baskets.** Whereas total utility measures the consumer's overall level of satisfaction derived from consumption activities, **marginal utility** measures the added satisfaction derived from a 1-unit increase in consumption, holding consumption of other goods and services constant. The **law of diminishing marginal utility**

states the marginal utility gained from consumption eventually declines.

- **Indifference curves** represent all market baskets that provide the same amount of utility. Market baskets are comprised of **substitutes,** products that serve the same purpose, and **complements,** products that are best consumed together. **Perfect substitutes** are products that satisfy the same need or desire. **Perfect complements** are products consumed together in the same combination. A **budget constraint** shows all combinations of products that can be purchased for a fixed amount.

- The **income effect** of a price change is the increase in overall consumption made possible by a price cut, or decrease in overall consumption that follows a price increase. The **substitution effect** of a price change describes the change in relative consumption that occurs as consumers substitute cheaper products for more expensive products.

- Market baskets that maximize utility at different prices for a given item trace out the consumer's **price–consumption curve.** The **income–consumption curve** portrays the utility-maximizing combinations of goods and services at every income level. A plot of the relationship between income and the quantity consumed is called an **Engle curve.** If consumers buy more of a product as income rises, such products are called **normal goods.** If consumers buy less of a product following an increase in income, such products are called **inferior goods.**

- The **optimal market basket** is the best market basket combination on the budget line. If a consumer consistently chooses a market basket that is more expensive than another market basket, the consumer has a **revealed preference** for the chosen market basket. The **marginal rate of substitution** is the change in consumption of Y (goods) necessary to offset a given change in the consumption of X (services) if the consumer's overall level of utility is to remain constant. Utility is maximized when products are purchased at relative prices that equal the relative marginal utility derived from consumption. The **consumption path** depicts optimal market baskets as the budget level grows.

- Factors within the control of the firm are **endogenous variables;** factors outside the control of the firm are **exogenous variables. Elasticity** is the percentage change in a dependent variable, Y, resulting from a 1 percent change in the value of an independent variable, X. **Point elasticity** measures elasticity at a point on a function. **Arc elasticity** measures the average elasticity over a given range of a function.

- The **price elasticity of demand** measures the responsiveness of quantity demanded to changes in the price of the product itself. With **elastic demand,** a price increase will lower total revenue and a decrease in price will raise total revenue. With **unitary elasticity** the effect of a price change is *exactly* offset by the effect of a change in quantity demanded, and total revenue is constant. With **inelastic demand** a price increase causes a less than proportionate decline in quantity demanded, so total revenues rise. Conversely a price decrease produces a less than proportionate increase in quantity demanded, so total revenue falls. The **optimal price formula** is $P^* = MC/[1 + (1/\varepsilon_P)]$. Given point price elasticity information, and data on marginal costs, profit-maximizing prices can be easily calculated.

- A direct positive relation between the price of one product and the demand for another holds for all **substitutes.** Products that are inversely related in terms of price and quantity are known as **complements;** they are used together rather than in place of each other. **Cross-price elasticity** is used to examine the responsiveness of demand for one product to changes in the price of another product.

- **Income elasticity** measures the responsiveness of demand to changes in income. For normal goods, income and demand move in the same direction. For inferior goods, demand falls as incomes rise because consumers replace them with more desirable alternatives. Demand for such products is **countercyclical,** actually rising during recessions and falling during economic booms. For **noncyclical normal goods,** $0 < \varepsilon_I < 1$ and demand is moderately affected by changing income. For **cyclical normal goods,** $\varepsilon_I > 1$ and demand is strongly affected by changing economic conditions.

This chapter provides a valuable, albeit brief, introduction to several key concepts that are useful in the practical analysis of demand.

QUESTIONS

Q4.1 "The utility derived from consumption is intangible and unobservable. Therefore, the utility concept has no practical value." Discuss this statement.

Q4.2 Is an increase in total utility or satisfaction following an increase in income consistent with the law of diminishing marginal utility?

Q4.3 Prospective car buyers are sometimes confronted by sales representatives who argue that they can offer a vehicle that is "just as good as a BMW, but at one-half the price." Use the indifference concept to explain why the claims of the sales representative are not credible.

Q4.4 Following a price change for Diet Coke, explain how retailers use sales information to learn if Doritos snack chips represent a complement or substitute for Diet Coke.

Q4.5 During the past 40 years the average price of a new single-family home has risen by a factor of ten, making the cost of housing prohibitive for many Americans. Over the same time frame, however, the number of units sold per year has more than doubled. Are these data inconsistent with the idea of a downward-sloping demand curve for new housing?

Q4.6 What would an upward-sloping demand curve imply about the marginal utility derived from consumption? Why aren't upward sloping demand curves observed in the real world?

Q4.7 How is a price–consumption curve related to a demand curve?

Q4.8 An estimated 80 percent increase in the retail price of cigarettes is necessary to cause a 30 percent drop in the number of cigarettes sold. Would such a price increase help or hurt tobacco industry profits? What would be the likely effect on industry profits if this price boost was simply caused by a $1.50 per pack increase in cigarette excise taxes?

Q4.9 Individual consumer demand declines for inferior goods as personal income increases because consumers replace them with more desirable alternatives. Is an inverse relation between demand and national income likely for such products?

Q4.10 In the United States, high-wage workers shun public transit and drive cars to work. These same high-income individuals often support massive subsidies for public transit. Use the concept of revealed preference to explain the public demand for transportation. Can you explain this consumer behavior by high-income individuals?

SELF-TEST PROBLEMS AND SOLUTIONS

ST4.1 Individual Demand Curve. Alex P. Keaton is an ardent baseball fan. The following table shows the relation between the number of games he attends per month during the season and the total utility he derives from baseball game consumption:

Number of Baseball Games Per Month	Total Utility
0	0
1	50
2	90
3	120
4	140
5	150

A. Construct a table showing Keaton's marginal utility derived from baseball game consumption.

B. At an average ticket price of $25, Keaton can justify attending only one game per month. Calculate Keaton's cost per unit of marginal utility derived from baseball game consumption at this activity level.

C. If the cost/marginal utility trade-off found in part B represents the most Keaton is willing to pay for baseball game consumption, calculate the prices at which he would attend two, three, four, and five games per month.

D. Plot Keaton's baseball game demand curve.

ST4.1 SOLUTION

A.

Number of Baseball Games Per Month	Total Utility	Marginal Utility
0	0	—
1	50	50
2	90	40
3	120	30
4	140	20
5	150	10

B. At one baseball game per month, $MU = 50$. Thus, at a $25 price per baseball game, the cost per unit of marginal utility derived from baseball game consumption is $P/MU = \$25/50 = \$0.50$ or 50¢ per util.

C. At a maximum acceptable price of 50¢ per util, Keaton's maximum acceptable price for baseball game tickets varies according to the following schedule:

Number of Games Per Month	Total Utility	Marginal Utility $MU = \partial U/\partial G$	Maximum Acceptable price at 50¢ per MU
0	0	—	—
1	50	50	$25.00
2	90	40	20.00
3	120	30	15.00
4	140	20	10.00
5	150	10	5.00

D. Keaton's baseball ticket demand curve is

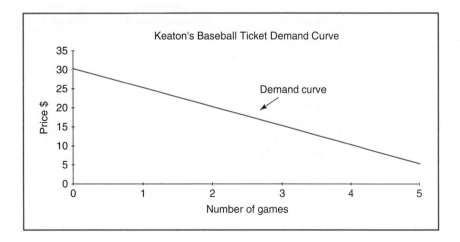

ST4.2 Elasticity Estimation.   Distinctive Designs, Inc., imports and distributes dress and sports watches. At the end of the company's fiscal year, brand manager Charlie Pace has asked you to evaluate sales of the sports watch line using the following data:

Month	Number of Sports Watches Sold	Sports Watch Advertising Expenditures	Sports Watch Price, P	Dress Watch Price, P_D
July	4,500	$10,000	26	50
August	5,500	10,000	24	50
September	4,500	9,200	24	50
October	3,500	9,200	24	46
November	5,000	9,750	25	50
December	15,000	9,750	20	50
January	5,000	8,350	25	50
February	4,000	7,850	25	50
March	5,500	9,500	25	55
April	6,000	8,500	24	51
May	4,000	8,500	26	51
June	5,000	8,500	26	57

In particular, Pace has asked you to estimate relevant demand elasticities. Remember that to estimate the required elasticities, you should consider only the months when the other important factors considered in the preceding table have not changed. Also note that by restricting your analysis to consecutive months, changes in any additional factors not explicitly included in the analysis are less likely to affect estimated elasticities. Finally, the average arc elasticity of demand for each factor is simply the average of monthly elasticities calculated during the past year.

A. Indicate whether there was or was not a change in each respective independent variable for each month pair during the past year.

Month-Pair	Sports Watch Advertising Expenditures, A	Sports Watch Price, P	Dress Watch Price, P_D
July–August	_____	_____	_____
August–September	_____	_____	_____
September–October	_____	_____	_____
October–November	_____	_____	_____
November– December	_____	_____	_____
December–January	_____	_____	_____
January–February	_____	_____	_____
February–March	_____	_____	_____
March–April	_____	_____	_____
April–May	_____	_____	_____
May–June	_____	_____	_____

B. Calculate and interpret the average advertising arc elasticity of demand for sports watches.

C. Calculate and interpret the average arc price elasticity of demand for sports watches.

D. Calculate and interpret the average arc cross-price elasticity of demand between sports and dress watches.

ST4.2 SOLUTION

A.

Month-Pair	Sports Watch Advertising Expenditures, A	Sports Watch Price, P	Dress Watch Price, P_D
July–August	No change	Change	No change
August–September	Change	No change	No change
September–October	No change	No change	Change
October–November	Change	Change	Change
November–December	No change	Change	No change
December–January	Change	Change	No change
January–February	Change	No change	No change
February–March	Change	No change	Change
March–April	Change	Change	Change
April–May	No change	Change	No change
May–June	No change	No change	Change

B. In calculating the arc advertising elasticity of demand, consider only consecutive months when there was a change in advertising but no change in the prices of sports and dress watches:

<u>August–September</u>

$$E_A = \frac{\Delta Q}{\Delta A} \times \frac{A_2 + A_1}{Q_2 + Q_1}$$

$$= \frac{4{,}500 - 5{,}500}{\$9{,}200 - \$10{,}000} \times \frac{\$9{,}200 + \$10{,}000}{4{,}500 + 5{,}500}$$

$$= 2.4$$

<u>January–February</u>

$$E_A = \frac{\Delta Q}{\Delta A} \times \frac{A_2 + A_1}{Q_2 + Q_1}$$

$$= \frac{4{,}000 - 5{,}000}{\$7{,}850 - \$8{,}350} \times \frac{\$7{,}850 + \$8{,}350}{4{,}000 + 5{,}000}$$

$$= 3.6$$

On average, $E_A = (2.4 + 3.6)/2 = 3$ and demand will rise 3 percent, with a 1 percent increase in advertising. Thus, demand appears quite sensitive to advertising.

C. In calculating the arc price elasticity of demand, consider only consecutive months when there was a change in the price of sports watches, but no change in advertising nor the price of dress watches:

July–August

$$E_P = \frac{\Delta Q}{\Delta P} \times \frac{P_2 + P_1}{Q_2 + Q_1}$$

$$= \frac{5,500 - 4,500}{\$24 - \$26} \times \frac{\$24 + \$26}{5,500 + 4,500}$$

$$= -2.5$$

November–December

$$E_P = \frac{\Delta Q}{\Delta P} \times \frac{P_2 + P_1}{Q_2 + Q_1}$$

$$= \frac{15,000 - 5,000}{\$20 - \$25} \times \frac{\$20 + \$25}{15,000 + 5,000}$$

$$= -4.5$$

April–May

$$E_P = \frac{\Delta Q}{\Delta P} \times \frac{P_2 + P_1}{Q_2 + Q_1}$$

$$= \frac{4,000 - 6,000}{\$26 - \$24} \times \frac{\$26 + \$24}{4,000 + 6,000}$$

$$= -5$$

On average, $E_P = [(-2.5) + (-4.5) + (-5)]/3 = -4$. A 1 percent increase (decrease) in price will lead to a 4 percent decrease (increase) in the quantity demanded. The demand for sports watches is, therefore, elastic with respect to price.

D. In calculating the arc cross-price elasticity of demand, we consider only consecutive months when there was a change in the price of dress watches, but no change in advertising nor the price of sports watches:

September–October

$$E_{PX} = \frac{\Delta Q}{\Delta P_X} \times \frac{P_{X2} + P_{X1}}{Q_2 + Q_1}$$

$$= \frac{3,500 - 4,500}{\$46 - \$50} \times \frac{\$46 - \$50}{3,500 + 4,500}$$

$$= 3$$

May–June

$$E_{PX} = \frac{\Delta Q}{\Delta P_X} \times \frac{P_{X2} + P_{X1}}{Q_2 + Q_1}$$

$$= \frac{5,000 - 4,000}{\$57 - \$51} \times \frac{\$57 + \$51}{5,000 + 4,000}$$

$$= 2$$

On average, $E_{PX} = (3 + 2)/2 = 2.5$. Since $E_{PX} > 0$, sports and dress watches are substitutes.

PROBLEMS

P4.1   Utility Theory.   Determine whether each of the following statements is true or false. Explain why.

A. According to the theory of consumer behavior, more is always better.

B. Consumers must understand how much one product is preferred over another in order to rank order consumption alternatives.

C. A market basket is a descriptive statement that relates satisfaction or well-being to the consumption of goods and services.

D. The nonsatiation principle abstracts from time and place considerations.

E. Marginal utility measures the consumer's overall level of satisfaction derived from consumption activities.

P4.2   Law of Diminishing Marginal Utility.   Indicate whether each of the following statements is true or false. Explain why.

A. The law of diminishing marginal utility states that as an individual increases consumption of a given product within a set period of time, the utility gained from consumption eventually declines.

B. When prices are held constant, a diminishing marginal utility for consumption decreases the cost of each marginal unit of satisfaction.

C. Marginal utility measures the added satisfaction derived from a 1-unit increase in consumption, holding consumption of other goods and services constant.

D. When goods are relatively scarce, the law of diminishing marginal utility means that the added value of another unit of goods will be small in relation to the added value of another unit of services.

E. The law of diminishing marginal utility gives rise to a downward-sloping demand curve for all goods and services.

P4.3   Indifference Curves.   Suggest briefly whether each of the following statements about indifference curves that show preferences between goods and services is true or false and defend your answer.

A. Consumers prefer higher indifference curves that represent greater combinations of goods and services to lower indifference curves that represent smaller combinations of goods and services.

B. Indifference curves slope downward because if the quantity of one consumer product is reduced, the quantity of the other must also decrease to maintain the same degree of utility.

C. The slope of an indifference curve shows the rate at which consumers are willing to trade-off goods and services.

D. The fact that indifference curves do not intersect stems from the "more is better" principle.

E. In difference curves bend inward (are convex to the origin) because if goods are relatively abundant, the added value of another unit of goods will be small in relation to the added value of another unit of services.

P4.4 Budget Constraints. Holding all else equal, indicate how each of the following changes would affect a budget constraint that limits consumption of goods (Y) and services (X). Explain your answer.

A. Deflation that uniformly drops the price of all goods and services.

B. Inflation that consistently increases the price of all goods and services.

C. Technical change that reduces the price of goods, but leaves the price of services unchanged.

D. Economic growth that boosts the level of disposable income.

E. Government-mandated health care coverage for workers that boosts the price of goods by 3 percent and increases the price of services by 5 percent.

P4.5 Elasticity. The demand for personal computers can be characterized by the following point elasticities: price elasticity $= -5$, cross-price elasticity with software $= -4$, and income elasticity $= 2.5$. Indicate whether each of the following statements is true or false, and explain your answer.

A. A price reduction for personal computers will increase both the number of units demanded and the total revenue of sellers.

B. The cross-price elasticity indicates that a 5 percent reduction in the price of personal computers will cause a 20 percent increase in software demand.

C. Demand for personal computers is price elastic and computers are cyclical normal goods.

D. Falling software prices will increase revenues received by sellers of both computers and software.

E. A 2 percent price reduction would be necessary to overcome the effects of a 1 *percent decline in income.*

P4.6 Optimal Pricing. In an effort to reduce excess end-of-the-model-year inventory, Harrison Ford offered a 1 percent discount off the average price of 4WD Escape Gas-Electric Hybrid SUVs sold during the month of August. Customer response was wildly enthusiastic, with unit sales rising by 10 percent over the previous month's level.

A. Calculate the point price elasticity of demand for Harrison Ford 4WD Escape Gas-Electric Hybrid SUVs sold during the month of August.

B. Calculate the profit-maximizing price per unit if Harrison Ford has an average wholesale (invoice) cost of $23,500 and incurs marginal selling costs of $350 per unit.

P4.7 Cross-Price Elasticity.

The South Beach Cafe recently reduced appetizer prices from $12 to $10 for afternoon "early bird" customers and enjoyed a resulting increase in sales from 90 to 150 orders per day. Beverage sales also increased from 300 to 600 units per day.

A. Calculate the arc price elasticity of demand for appetizers.

B. Calculate the arc cross-price elasticity of demand between beverage sales and appetizer prices.

C. Holding all else equal, would you expect an additional appetizer price decrease to $8 to cause both appetizer and beverage revenues to rise? Explain.

P4.8 Income Elasticity.

Ironside Industries, Inc., is a leading manufacturer of tufted carpeting under the Ironside brand. Demand for Ironside's products is closely tied to the overall pace of building and remodeling activity and, therefore, is highly sensitive to changes in national income. The carpet manufacturing industry is highly competitive, so Ironside's demand is also very price-sensitive.

During the past year, Ironside sold 30 million square yards (units) of carpeting at an average wholesale price of $15.50 per unit. This year, household income is expected to surge from $55,500 to $58,500 per year in a booming economic recovery.

A. Without any price change, Ironside's marketing director expects current-year sales to soar to 50 million units because of rising income. Calculate the implied income arc elasticity of demand.

B. Given the projected rise in income, the marketing director believes that a volume of 30 million units could be maintained despite an increase in price of $1 per unit. On this basis, calculate the implied arc price elasticity of demand.

C. Holding all else equal, would a further increase in price result in higher or lower total revenue?

P4.9 Cross-Price Elasticity.

B. B. Lean is a catalog retailer of a wide variety of sporting goods and recreational products. Although the market response to the company's spring catalog was generally good, sales of B. B. Lean's $140 deluxe garment bag declined from 10,000 to 4,800 units. During this period, a competitor offered a whopping $52 off their regular $137 price on deluxe garment bags.

A. Calculate the arc cross-price elasticity of demand for B. B. Lean's deluxe garment bag.

B. B. B. Lean's deluxe garment bag sales recovered from 4,800 units to 6,000 units following a price reduction to $130 per unit. Calculate B. B. Lean's arc price elasticity of demand for this product.

C. Assuming the same arc price elasticity of demand calculated in part B, determine the further price reduction necessary for B. B. Lean to fully recover lost sales (i.e., regain a volume of 10,000 units).

P4.10 Advertising Elasticity. Enchantment Cosmetics, Inc., offers a line of cosmetic and perfume products marketed through leading department stores. Product manager Erica Kane recently raised the suggested retail price on a popular line of mascara products from $9 to $12 following increases in the costs of labor and materials. Unfortunately, sales dropped sharply from 16,200 to 9,000 units per month. In an effort to regain lost sales, Enchantment ran a coupon promotion featuring $5 off the new regular price. Coupon printing and distribution costs totaled $500 per month and represented a substantial increase over the typical advertising budget of $3,250 per month. Despite these added costs, the promotion was judged to be a success, as it proved to be highly popular with consumers. In the period prior to expiration, coupons were used on 40 percent of all purchases and monthly sales rose to 15,000 units.

A. Calculate the arc price elasticity implied by the initial response to the Enchantment price increase.

B. Calculate the effective price reduction resulting from the coupon promotion.

C. In light of the price reduction associated with the coupon promotion and assuming no change in the price elasticity of demand, calculate Enchantment's arc advertising elasticity.

D. Why might the true arc advertising elasticity differ from that calculated in part C?

CASE *Study*

Optimal Level of Advertising

The concept of multivariate optimization is important in managerial economics because many demand and supply relations involve more than two variables. In demand analysis, it is typical to consider the quantity sold as a function of the price of the product itself, the price of other goods, advertising, income, and other factors. In cost analysis, cost is determined by output, input prices, the nature of technology, and so on.

To explore the concepts of multivariate optimization and the optimal level of advertising, consider a hypothetical multivariate product demand function for CSI, Inc., where the demand for product Q is determined by the price charged, P, and the level of advertising, A:

$$Q = 5,000 - 10P + 40A + PA - 0.8A^2 - 0.5P^2$$

When analyzing multivariate relations such as these, one is interested in the marginal effect of each independent variable on the quantity sold, the dependent variable. Optimization requires an analysis of how a change in each independent variable affects the dependent variable, holding constant the effect of all other independent variables. The partial derivative concept is used in this type of marginal analysis.

In light of the fact that the CSI demand function includes two independent variables, the price of the product itself and advertising, it is possible to examine two partial derivatives: the partial of Q with respect to price, or $\partial Q/\partial P$, and the partial of Q with respect to advertising expenditures, or $\partial Q/\partial A$.

In determining partial derivatives, all variables except the one with respect to which the derivative is being taken remain unchanged. In this instance, A is treated as a constant when the partial derivative of Q with respect to P is analyzed; P is treated as a constant when the partial derivative

---

continued

of Q with respect to A is evaluated. Therefore, the partial derivative of Q with respect to P is

$$\partial Q/\partial P = 0 - 10 + 0 + A - 0 - P$$
$$= -10 + A - P$$

The partial with respect to A is

$$\partial Q/\partial A = 0 - 0 + 40 + P - 1.6A - 0$$
$$= 40 + P - 1.6A$$

Solving these two equations simultaneously yields the optimal price/output–advertising combination. Because $-10 + A - P = 0$, $P = A - 10$. Substituting this value for P into $40 + P - 1.6A = 0$, gives $40 + (A - 10) - 1.6A = 0$, which implies that $0.6A = 30$ and $A = 50(00)$ or \$5,000. Given this value, $P = A - 10 = 50 - 10 = \$40$. Inserting these numbers for P and A into the CSI demand function results in a value for Q of 5,800. Therefore, the maximum value of Q is 5,800 reflects an optimal price of \$40 and optimal advertising of \$5,000.

One attractive use of computer spreadsheets is to create simple numerical examples that can be used to conclusively show the change in sales, profits, and other variables that occur as one approaches and moves beyond the profit-maximizing activity level.

A. Set up a table or spreadsheet for CSI, that illustrates the relationships among quantity (Q), price (P), the optimal level of advertising (A), the advertising–sales ratio (A/S), and sales revenue (S). In this spreadsheet, use formula functions to set

$$Q = 5,000 - 10P + 40A + PA - 0.8A^2 - 0.5P^2$$
$$A = \$25 + \$0.625P$$
$$A/S = (100 \times A)/S$$
$$S = P \times Q$$

Establish a range for P from 0 to \$125 in increments of \$5 (i.e., \$0, \$5, \$10, ..., \$125). To test the sensitivity of all other variables to extreme bounds for the price variable, also set price equal to \$1,000, \$2,500, and \$10,000.

B. Based on the CSI table or spreadsheet, determine the price–advertising combination that will maximize the number of units sold.

C. Give an analytical explanation of the negative quantity and sales revenue levels observed at very high price–advertising combinations. Do these negative values have an economic interpretation as well?

SELECTED REFERENCES

Ameriks, John, Andrew Caplin, and John Leahy. "Retirement Consumption: Insights from a Survey." *Review of Economics and Statistics* 89, no. 2 (May, 2007): 265–274.

Battalio, Robert, Andrew Ellul, and Robert Jennings. "Reputation Effects in Trading on the New York Stock Exchange." *Journal of Finance* 62, no. 3 (June, 2007): 1243–1271.

Choi, Syngjoo, Raymond Fisman, Douglas M. Gale, and Shachar Kariv. "Revealing Preferences Graphically: An Old Method Gets a New Tool Kit." *American Economic Review* 97, no. 2 (May, 2007): 153–158.

Gul, Faruk and Wolfgang Pesendorfer. "Welfare Without Happiness." *American Economic Review* 97, no. 2 (May, 2007): 471–476.

Kawaguchi, Daiji. "A Market Test for Sex Discrimination: Evidence from Japanese Firm-Level Panel Data." *International Journal of Industrial Organization* 25, no. 3 (June, 2007): 441–460.

Ko, K. Jeremy and Zhijian (James) Huang. "Arrogance Can Be a Virtue: Overconfidence, Information Acquisition, and Market Efficiency." *Journal of Financial Economics* 84, no. 2 (May, 2007): 529–560.

Kosmopoulou, Georgia and Dakshina G. De Silva. "The Effect of Shill Bidding Upon Prices: Experimental Evidence." *International Journal of Industrial Organization* 25, no. 2 (April, 2007): 291–313.

Lodish, Leonard M. and Carl F. Mela. "If Brands Are Built over Years, Why Are They Managed Over Quarters?" *Harvard Business Review* 85, nos. 7, 8 (July, 2007): 104–112.

Minier, Jenny. "Nonlinearities and Robustness in Growth Regressions." *American Economic Review* 97, no. 2 (May, 2007): 388–392.

Mitchell, Mark, Lasse Heje Pedersen, and Todd Pulvino. "Slow Moving Capital." *American Economic Review* 97, no. 2 (May, 2007): 215–220.

Pachon, Julian, Murat Erkoc, and Eleftherios Iakovou. "Contract Optimization with Front-End Fare Discounts for Airline Corporate Deals." *Transportation Research: Part E: Logistics and Transportation Review* 43, no. 4 (July, 2007): 425–441.

Perrigne, Isabelle and Quang Vuong. "Identification and Estimation of Bidders' Risk Aversion in First-Price Auctions." *American Economic Review* 97, no. 2 (May, 2007): 444–448.

Porter, Philip K. "The Paradox of Inelastic Sports Pricing." *Managerial and Decision Economics* 28, no. 2 (March, 2007): 157–158.

Prince, Jeffrey T. "The Beginning of Online/Retail Competition and Its Origins: An Application to Personal Computers." *International Journal of Industrial Organization* 25, no. 1 (February, 2007): 139–156.

Puller, Steven L. "Pricing and Firm Conduct in California's Deregulated Electricity Market." *Review of Economics and Statistics* 89, no. 1 (February, 2007): 75–87.

Demand Estimation

Proctor & Gamble Co. (P&G) helps consumers clean up. Households around the world rely on "new and improved" Tide to clean their clothes, Ivory and Ariel detergents to wash dishes, and Pantene Pro-V to shampoo and condition hair. Other P&G products dominate a wide range of lucrative, but slow-growing, product lines, including: disposable diapers (Pampers), feminine hygiene (Always), and facial moisturizers (Oil of Olay). P&G's ongoing challenge is to figure out ways of continuing to grow aggressively outside the United States, while it cultivates the profitability of dominant consumer franchises at home in the United States. Tide, for example, has been "new and improved" almost continuously over its 70-year history. Ivory virtually introduced the concept of bar soap nearly 100 years ago; Jif peanut butter and Pampers disposable diapers are more than 40 years old.

How does P&G succeed in businesses where others routinely fail? Quite simply, P&G is a marketing juggernaut. Although P&G's vigilant cost cutting is legendary, its marketing expertise is without peer. Nobody does a better job at finding out what consumers want. At P&G, demand estimation is the lynchpin of its enormously successful "getting close to the customer" operating philosophy.[1]

This chapter considers consumer interviews, surveys, market experiments, and regression analysis as effective means for finding out what customers want. Inexpensive PCs and user-friendly software make accurate market demand estimation easier than ever before.

INTERVIEW AND EXPERIMENTAL METHODS

Successful companies know the answer to a simple question: What do customers want?

Consumer Interviews

Consumer Interview
Questioning customers to estimate demand relations.

The **consumer interview** (or survey) method requires questioning customers or potential customers to estimate the relation between demand and a variety of underlying factors. Unfortunately, consumers are often unable or unwilling to provide accurate answers to hypothetical questions. If an interviewer asked how you would react to a 1 percent, 2 percent, or 3 percent increase in the price of a specific brand of spaghetti

---

1 Anjali Cordeiro, "For Companies Like P&G, It's Not Easy Going 'Green'," *The Wall Street Journal Online*, October 10, 2007, http://online.wsj.com.

sauce, could you respond accurately? Could you accurately predict your reaction to shifting the emphasis of the firm's media advertising campaign from the product's natural ingredients to the fact that it is high in fiber or low in cholesterol? Because most consumers are unable to answer such questions—even for major expense categories such as apparel, food, and entertainment—it is difficult for survey techniques to accurately estimate demand relations.

This is not to imply that consumer surveys have little value. Using subtle inquiries, a trained interviewer can extract useful information from consumers. For example, an interviewer might ask questions about several competing goods and learn that most customers are unaware of existing price differentials. This is an indication that demand may not be highly sensitive to price changes, so a producer should not attempt to increase the quantity sold by reducing prices. Similar questions can be used to determine whether consumers are aware of advertising programs, what their reaction is to the ads, and so on. Such survey information can be used to make better managerial decisions.

Market Experiments

Market Experiments
Demand estimation in a controlled environment.

An alternative technique for obtaining useful product demand information involves **market experiments.** In a popular method, firms study one or more markets with specific prices, packaging, or advertising, and then vary controllable factors over time or between markets. For example, Del Monte Corporation may have determined that uncontrollable consumer characteristics are similar in Denver and Salt Lake City. Del Monte could raise the relative price of sliced pineapple in Salt Lake City, and then compare pineapple sales in the two markets. Alternatively, Del Monte could initiate a series of weekly price changes in one market, then determine how these changes affect sales. With several markets, the firm might also be able to use census or survey data to determine how demographic characteristics such as income, family size, educational level, and ethnic background affect demand.

Market experiments have several serious shortcomings, however. They are expensive and usually undertaken on a scale too small to allow high levels of confidence in the results. Market experiments are seldom run for sufficiently long periods to indicate the long-run effects of various pricing, advertising, or packaging strategies. Difficulties associated with uncontrolled parts of market experiments also hinder their use. Changing economic conditions during the experiment can invalidate the results, especially if the experiment includes several separate markets. A local strike, layoffs by a major employer, or a severe snowstorm can ruin a market experiment. Likewise, a change in a competing product's promotion, price, or packaging can distort the results. There is also the danger that the customers lost during the experiment as a result of price manipulations may not be regained when the experiment ends. Moreover, the high cost of such experiments necessarily limits the sample size, which can make inference, from the sample to the general population, tenuous.

SIMPLE DEMAND CURVE ESTIMATION

Simple linear demand curves can give useful insight for pricing and promotion decisions.

Simple Linear Demand Curves

Sophisticated demand estimation is accurate and cost effective. Nobody drives a jet to a grocery store located within easy walking distance. Similarly, nobody employs expensive, time-consuming, and complicated demand estimation techniques when inexpensive and simple methods work just fine. The following illustration shows how a linear demand curve can be easily estimated, and how companies can profitably use such information.

The Portland Sea Dogs are the AA affiliate of the Boston Red Sox major league baseball team. Suppose the club offered $2 off the $12 regular price of reserved seats, and sales spurted from 3,200 to 4,000 seats per game. This is enough information to estimate a simple linear demand curve written as

$$P = a + bQ \tag{5.1}$$

Here a is the intercept and b is the slope coefficient. Because 3,200 seats were sold at a regular price of $12 per game, and 4,000 seats were sold at the discount price of $10, two points on the firm's linear market demand curve are identified. Given this information, it is possible to identify the linear market demand curve by solving the system of two equations with two unknowns, a and b:

$$12 = a + b(3,200)$$
$$\text{minus } 10 = \underline{a + b(4,000)}$$
$$2 = -800b$$
$$b = -0.0025$$

By substitution, if $b = -0.0025$, then

$$12 = a + b(3,200)$$
$$12 = a - 0.0025(3,200)$$
$$12 = a - 8$$
$$a = 20$$

Therefore, the demand curve can be written

$$P = \$20 - \$0.0025Q$$

The Portland Sea Dogs could use this curve to estimate the quantity demanded for ticket prices in the range from $10 to $12 per ticket. It should not be used to estimate the number of tickets that might be sold at exceptionally low prices like $5, or at exceedingly high prices, like $20. The estimated linear market demand curve should not be presumed far outside the range of experience.

Using Simple Linear Demand Curves

Before considering ancillary revenues, the Portland Sea Dogs' ticket-revenue–maximizing price typically results in maximum profits because almost all of the costs associated with producing a single sporting event like a baseball game are fixed. To find the revenue-maximizing output level, set $MR = 0$, and solve for Q. Because

$$TR = P \times Q$$
$$= (\$20 - \$0.0025Q)Q$$
$$= \$20Q - \$0.0025Q^2$$
$$MR = \partial TR / \partial Q$$
$$MR = \$20 - \$0.005Q = 0$$
$$0.005Q = 20$$
$$Q = 4,000$$

At $Q = 4,000$,

$$P = \$20 - \$0.0025(4,000)$$
$$= \$10$$

Total revenue at a price of $10 is

$$TR = P \times Q$$
$$= \$10 \times 4,000$$
$$= \$40,000$$

This is a ticket-revenue–maximizing level of output because total ticket revenue is decreasing for output beyond $Q > 4,000$, or $\partial^2 TR / \partial Q^2 < 0$. If total costs are fixed, this revenue-maximizing price will also result in maximum profits. In the sports world, it is worth mentioning that even promotionally priced tickets can result in high profits if the added customers are big buyers of high profit margin parking services, and high-margin concessions like soda pop, beer, candy, and hot dogs. In such instances, revenue per unit must include direct and indirect receipts.

SIMPLE MARKET DEMAND CURVE ESTIMATION

Market demand is the firm's total demand from various customer groups.

Graphing the Market Demand Curve

Market Demand Curve
Price–quantity demanded relation for all customers.

The **market demand curve** shows the total amount customers are willing to buy at various prices under current market conditions. Many firms serve various customer groups like retail and wholesale, domestic and foreign, student and other customers. To calculate the total amount of demand, the market demand curve must be calculated as the sum of the demand curves from each customer group.

To illustrate, suppose the data shown in Table 5.1 illustrate domestic and foreign demand information for a product produced by Chicago-based USG Corp., a building products manufacturer. In equation form, relevant demand and cost relations are as follows:

$$P_D = \$100 - \$0.001Q_D \text{ (Domestic Demand)}$$
$$P_F = \$80 - \$0.004Q_F \text{ (Foreign Demand)}$$
$$TC = \$1,200,000 + \$24Q \text{ (Total Cost)}$$

Table 5.1 Market Demand Is Domestic Plus Foreign Demand

Price ($)	Domestic Demand	Foreign Demand	Market Demand	Total Revenue	Total Cost ($)	Total Profit ($)
100	—	—	—	—	1,200,000	−1,200,000
95	5,000	—	5,000	475,000	1,320,000	−845,000
90	10,000	—	10,000	900,000	1,440,000	−540,000
85	15,000	—	15,000	1,275,000	1,560,000	−285,000
80	20,000	—	20,000	1,600,000	1,680,000	−80,000
75	25,000	1,250	26,250	1,968,750	1,830,000	138,750
70	30,000	2,500	32,500	2,275,000	1,980,000	295,000
65	35,000	3,750	38,750	2,518,750	2,130,000	388,750
60	40,000	5,000	45,000	2,700,000	2,280,000	420,000
55	45,000	6,250	51,250	2,818,750	2,430,000	388,750
50	50,000	7,500	57,500	2,875,000	2,580,000	295,000
45	55,000	8,750	63,750	2,868,750	2,730,000	138,750
40	60,000	10,000	70,000	2,800,000	2,880,000	−80,000
35	65,000	11,250	76,250	2,668,750	3,030,000	−361,250
30	70,000	12,500	82,500	2,475,000	3,180,000	−705,000
25	75,000	13,750	88,750	2,218,750	3,330,000	−1,111,250

To find the market demand curve, it is necessary to express quantity as a function of price for both domestic and foreign (or export) customers. Then, add these quantities together to calculate the total quantity demanded at each price. For domestic customers,

$$P_D = \$100 - \$0.001Q_D$$
$$0.001Q_D = 100 - P_D$$
$$Q_D = 100{,}000 - 1{,}000P_D$$

For foreign customers,

$$P_F = \$80 - \$0.004Q_F$$
$$0.004Q_F = 80 - P_F$$
$$Q_F = 20{,}000 - 250P_F$$

For domestic plus foreign customers, the market demand curve can be expressed with quantity as a function of price as

$$Q = Q_D + Q_F$$
$$= 100{,}000 - 1{,}000P + 20{,}000 - 250P$$
$$= 120{,}000 - 1{,}250P$$

For graphic purposes, demand curves are typically expressed with price as the dependent variable on the vertical Y-axis. Quantity is shown as the independent variable on the horizontal X-axis. Therefore, to graph the market demand curve, price must be expressed as a function of quantity:

$$Q = 120{,}000 - 1{,}250P$$
$$1{,}250P = 120{,}000 - Q$$
$$P = \$96 - \$0.0008Q$$

Figure 5.1 illustrates the company's customer demand curves for each of the domestic and foreign customer groups when price is expressed as a function of quantity. Figure 5.1 also illustrates how the market demand curve for domestic plus foreign customers can be graphed with price as a function of quantity.

Evaluating Market Demand

From Table 5.1, market demand can be seen as the sum of the quantity demanded by each customer group at each specific market price. Notice from the domestic demand curve that the highest price domestic customers are willing to pay is $100. For prices below $100, the quantity demanded by domestic customers grows with falling prices. In contrast, the highest price foreign customers are willing to pay is $80. For prices above $80, only domestic customers are buyers, foreign demand is zero. Thus, for prices above $80, the demand curve for domestic customers is the market demand curve. For prices below $80, market demand will originate from both domestic and foreign customers, and market demand is simply the sum of the quantity demanded by both customer groups.

The advantage gained from selling in both domestic and foreign markets is that firms are able to serve customers more profitably. From Table 5.1, the profit-maximizing output level can be seen as 45,000 units, where 40,000 units are sold to domestic customers and 5,000 units are sold to foreign customers. The profit-maximizing price is $60 per unit. This profit-maximizing

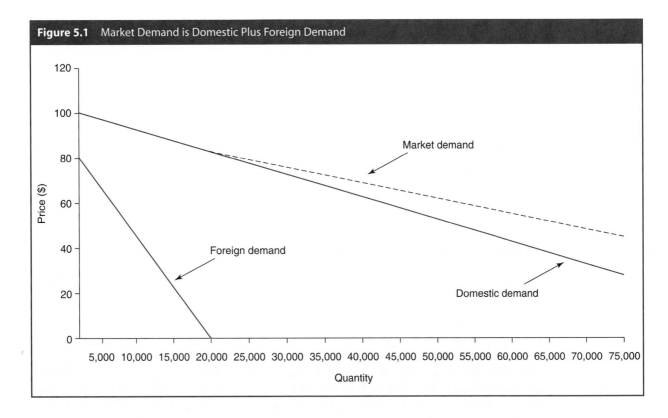

Figure 5.1 Market Demand is Domestic Plus Foreign Demand

price–output combination is found by setting $MR = MC$ and solving for quantity and price. This is equivalent to setting $M\pi = MR - MC = 0$ and solving for quantity and price.

Total revenue from domestic plus foreign customers is

$$TR = P \times Q$$
$$= (\$96 - \$0.0008Q) \times Q$$
$$= \$96Q - \$0.0008Q^2$$
$$MR = \partial TR/\partial Q = \$96 - \$0.0016Q$$
$$TC = \$1,200,000 + \$24Q$$
$$MC = \partial TC/\partial Q = \$24$$

The profit-maximizing activity level occurs where $MR = MC$. This is also where $M\pi = 0$.

$$MR = MC$$
$$\$96 - \$0.0016Q = \$24$$
$$0.0016Q = \$72$$
$$Q = 45,000$$

At $Q = 45,000$,

$$P = \$96 - \$0.0008(45,000)$$
$$= \$60$$
$$\pi = TR - TC$$

$$= \$96Q - \$0.0008Q^2 - (\$1,200,000 + \$24Q)$$
$$= -\$0.0008Q^2 + \$72Q - \$1,200,000$$
$$= -\$0.0008(45,000)^2 + \$72(45,000) - \$1,200,000$$
$$= \$420,000$$

This is a profit maximum since profit is decreasing for $Q > 50,000$. (Note: $\partial^2\pi/\partial Q^2 < 0$.)

IDENTIFICATION PROBLEM

Firms sometimes face problems in estimating demand relations because of the interplay between demand and supply conditions.

Changing Nature of Demand Relations

Demand curve estimation is sometimes relatively simple, especially in the case of stable short-run demand relations. If a manufacturer has a substantial backlog of purchase orders, the pace of future sales can sometimes be estimated precisely. For example, aerospace manufacturer Boeing sells options for the future delivery of airplanes to major airlines such as United, American, and Delta. This allows Boeing to accurately predict the pace of future sales and adjust production schedules accordingly. Still, demand estimation involves error, even when a large and growing backlog of customer orders is evident. During the aftermath of terrorist attacks on New York City and Washington, DC, in 2001, for example, airlines canceled orders for hundreds of millions of dollars of aircraft following an unexpected downturn in passenger and freight traffic. Delivery options were canceled at a cost of millions of dollars; production schedules had to be reworked at great expense.

The dynamic nature of demand relations makes it tough to accurately estimate demand, and even tougher to determine the effect on demand of modest changes in prices, advertising, credit terms, prices of competing products, and so on. The unpredictable nature of the overall economy is another factor that makes demand estimation difficult. When the income elasticity of demand is high, demand tends to vary more than the corresponding changes in economic activity. This is especially true for cyclical goods such as household appliances, machine tools, and raw materials. Demand for many goods and services also tends to be sensitive to changes in competitor prices, competitor advertising, interest rates, and the weather.

Interplay of Demand and Supply

It is sometimes difficult to obtain accurate estimates of demand relations because linkages exist among most economic variables. Consider the difficulty of estimating the demand curve for a given product X. If data are available on the price charged and the quantity purchased at several points in time, a logical first step is to plot this information as in Figure 5.2. Can the line AB be interpreted as a demand curve? The curve connecting points 1, 2, and 3 is negatively sloped, indicating the typical inverse relation between the price charged for a product and the quantity demanded. Moreover, each data point represents the quantity of X purchased at a particular price. Nevertheless, these data offer an insufficient basis to draw the conclusion that AB is in fact the demand curve for X.

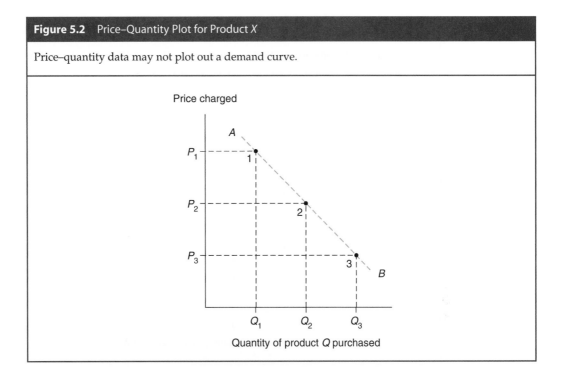

Figure 5.2 Price–Quantity Plot for Product *X*

Price–quantity data may not plot out a demand curve.

A demand curve shows the relation between the price charged and the quantity demanded, holding constant the effects of all other variables in the demand function. To plot a demand curve, it is necessary to obtain data on the price–quantity relation, while keeping fixed all other factors in the demand function. The price–quantity data used to construct Figure 5.2 are insufficient to produce a demand curve because the effects of all other demand-related variables may or may not have changed. Consider Figure 5.3, in which price–quantity data are plotted along with hypothetical supply and demand curves for product *X*. These data points indicate the simultaneous solution of supply and demand relations at three points in time. The intersection of the supply curve and the demand curve at each point in time results in the plotted price–quantity points, but the line *AB* is *not* a demand curve. In Figure 5.3, nonprice variables in the supply and demand functions have changed between each data point.

Shifts in Demand and Supply

Suppose, for example, that new and more efficient facilities for producing *X* are completed between observation dates. This would cause a shift of the supply curve from S_1 to S_2 to S_3. Similarly, the price of a complementary product may have fallen or consumer incomes may have risen, so at any given price, larger quantities of *X* are demanded in later periods. Such influences result in a shift of the demand curve from D_1 to D_2 to D_3. When supply and/or demand curves shift over time, as is typical, the accurate estimation of demand–supply relations at any one point in time is difficult.

In the present example, both the supply and demand curves shift over time. This results in a declining price as the quantity purchased grows. The three intersection points

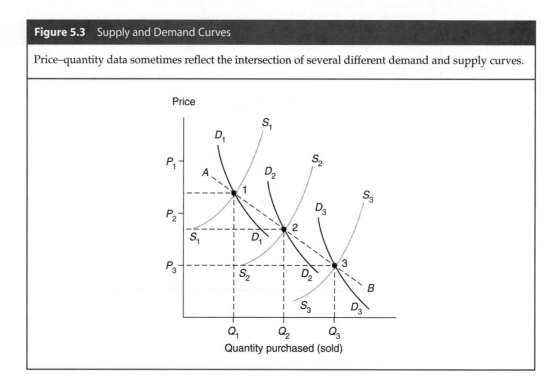

Figure 5.3   Supply and Demand Curves

Price–quantity data sometimes reflect the intersection of several different demand and supply curves.

of supply curves and demand curves shown in Figure 5.3—points 1, 2, and 3—are the same points plotted in Figure 5.2. But these are not three points on a single demand curve for Product X. Each point is on a *distinct* product demand curve that reflects different economic conditions. The relevant demand curve is shifting over time, so connecting each data point does not trace out a single demand curve for X.

Incorrectly interpreting the line AB (which connects points 1, 2, and 3) as a demand curve can lead to incorrect managerial decisions. If a firm makes this mistake, it might infer a high price elasticity for the product and assume that a reduction in price from P_1 to P_2 would increase quantity demanded from Q_1 to Q_2. An expansion of this magnitude might well justify such a price reduction. However, such a price cut would actually result in a much smaller increase in the quantity demanded because the true demand curve, D_1, is much less elastic than the line AB. Thus, a price reduction is in fact much less desirable than implied by the line AB.

Given the close link between demand and supply curves, data on prices and quantities must be used carefully in demand curve estimation. If the demand curve has not shifted but the supply curve *has* shifted, price–quantity data can be used to estimate demand relations. If sufficient information exists to determine how each curve has shifted between data observations, demand curve estimation is also possible. For example, if a technical breakthrough occurs in the manufacture of a product so that industry costs fall while demand conditions are stable, the situation depicted in Figure 5.4 may arise. The demand curve, which initially was unknown, is assumed to be stable. The supply curve shifts from S_1 to S_2 to S_3. Each price–quantity point represents the intersection of the supply curves and the demand curves. Because demand-determining factors other than price are assumed to be stable, points 1, 2, and 3 all lie on the same demand curve. The demand curve DD is estimated by connecting the three data points. Such a situation can occur with computers and electronics. Rapid innovation often allows prices for watches, calculators, personal computers, and related products to fall markedly within a very short period of time.

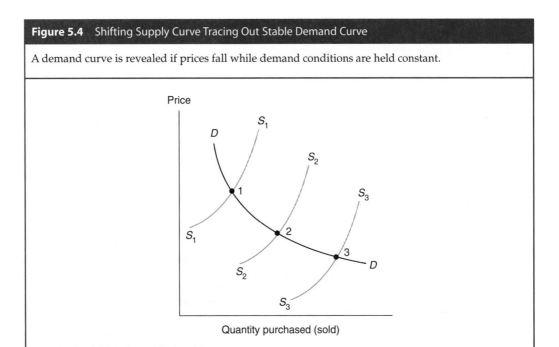

Figure 5.4 Shifting Supply Curve Tracing Out Stable Demand Curve

A demand curve is revealed if prices fall while demand conditions are held constant.

Simultaneous Relations

Simultaneous Relation
Concurrent association.

Identification Problem
Difficulty of estimating an economic relation in the presence of simultaneous relations.

Because the market price–output equilibrium at any point in time is determined by the forces of demand and supply, a **simultaneous relation,** or concurrent association, exists between demand and supply. Shifts in demand and supply curves must be distinguished from movements along individual supply and demand curves. The problem of estimating any given economic relation in the presence of important simultaneous relations is known as the **identification problem.** To separate shifts in demand or supply from changes or movements along a single curve, information about changes in demand and supply conditions is necessary to identify and estimate demand and supply relations. Sometimes, this information is hard to find. In such instances, standard statistical techniques, such as ordinary least squares regression analysis, do not provide reliable estimates of demand or supply functions. More advanced statistical techniques, such as two-stage least squares or seemingly unrelated regression analysis, are necessary. Fortunately, the identification problem is usually not so severe as to preclude the use of widely familiar regression techniques. Even when the identification problem is quite severe, consumer interviews and market experiments can sometimes be used to obtain relevant information.

Regression Analysis
Statistical technique that describes relations among dependent and independent variables.

REGRESSION ANALYSIS

Regression analysis is a powerful statistical technique used to describe the ways in which important economic variables are related.

Deterministic Relation
Association that is known with certainty.

What Is a Statistical Relation?

A **deterministic relation** is an association between variables that is known with certainty. For example, total revenue equals price times quantity, or $TR = P \times Q$. Once the levels

Managerial Application 5.2

Market Experiments on the Web

In pre-Internet days, companies spent huge amounts of time and money simply trying to measure perceptions about how well customer needs have been met by the firm's products. Now, companies can instantaneously review customer orders and see how well the company is actually satisfying customer needs. Early adopters of Internet-based customer delivery systems have learned (or relearned) a number of fundamental marketing concepts:

- Successful companies define value in terms of product attributes desired by the customer. In old-fashioned terminology, customers are always right.
- Customer value depends upon both physical and situational characteristics of products. What, how, and when are often equally important to the customer.
- Customer value perceptions are dynamic and can change rapidly over time.

The Internet is spawning a revolution in the way things are made and services are delivered. Companies as diverse as BMW, Dell Computer, Levi Strauss, Mattel, McGraw-Hill, and Wells Fargo are all embracing Internet technology as a means for learning and delivering precisely what consumers want. In fact, these and a growing list of companies are building customized products designed by millions of customers. Dell led the way by allowing customers to order computers assembled to exact specifications. Now, manufacturers are allowing customers to order computer-fitted apparel, like Levi's cut to fit your body. Men can stop worrying about why 37 inch pant waist sizes aren't offered; women can stop trying to figure out what the size "petite large" means. Just use the Internet to tell Eddie Bauer, Lands' End, or Levi's how to cut your own perfect fit. Using Internet technology, customers can also buy customized blends of vitamins, music compilations on CDs, and mortgage payment terms. Professors can also assign "textbooks" whose chapters are compiled from diverse material written by a variety of authors. This Internet-spawned revolution is just another step along the path of serving customer needs quicker, better, and cheaper.

See: "Ban on Internet Tax Advances in House," *The Wall Street Journal Online*, October 11, 2007, http://online.wsj.com.

of price and output are known with certainty, total revenue can be exactly determined. Total revenue is an example of a deterministic relation. Similarly, if total cost equals, for example, $5 times quantity, then total cost can be exactly determined once the level of output is known. If all economic relations were deterministic, total revenues and total costs could be exactly determined at the start of every planning period. However, few economic relations are deterministic in nature. Economic variables are often related in ways that cannot be predicted with absolute accuracy.

Statistical Relation
Imprecise link between two variables.

A **statistical relation** exists between two economic variables if the average of one is related to another, but it is impossible to predict with certainty the value of one based on the value of another. If $TR = \$5Q$ on average, then a 1-unit increase in quantity would result in an average $5 increase in total revenue. Sometimes the actual increase in total revenue would be more than $5, sometimes it would be less.

Time Series
Daily, weekly, monthly, or annual sequence of economic data.

Cross Section
Sample of firm, market, or product data taken at a given point in time.

When a statistical relation exists, the exact relation between two economic variables is not known with certainty and must be estimated. The most common means for doing so is to gather and analyze historical data. A **time series** of data is a daily, weekly, monthly, or annual sequence of data on an economic variable such as price, income, cost, or revenue. To judge the trend in profitability over time, a firm would analyze the time series of profit numbers. A **cross section** of data is a group of observations on an important economic variable at any given point in time. If a firm were interested in learning the relative importance of market share versus advertising as determinants of profitability, it might analyze a cross section of profit, advertising, and market share data for a variety of regional or local markets.

Scatter Diagram
Plot of *XY* data.

The simplest and most common means for analyzing a sample of historical information is to plot and visually study the data. A **scatter diagram** is a plot of data where the dependent variable is plotted on the vertical axis (*Y*-axis), and the independent variable is plotted on the horizontal axis (*X*-axis). Figure 5.5 shows scatter diagrams that plot the relation between the quantity sold and six different factors that have the potential to influence demand. Figure 5.5(a) depicts an inverse relation between the quantity sold and price, the independent *X* variable. An increase in price leads to a decrease in the quantity demanded; a reduction in price leads to an increase in the quantity demanded. In Figure 5.5(b), a direct relation is illustrated between the amount of advertising and demand. This means that an increase in advertising causes an increase in the level of product demand; conversely, a decrease in advertising causes a decrease in demand. No relation is evident between demand and the price of product *X*, an independent good, as shown in Figure 5.5(c). In Figure 5.5(d), a positive nonlinear relation between demand and income is illustrated. This implies that product *Y* is a cyclical normal good.

Scatter plot diagrams can give an instinctive "feel" for the data. However, the choice of which variable to call "dependent" or "independent" is often haphazard. Scatter diagrams illustrate correlation between variables; they do not establish causality. To warrant the inference of cause and effect, the correlation between two series of data must be interpreted in the light of experience or economic theory.

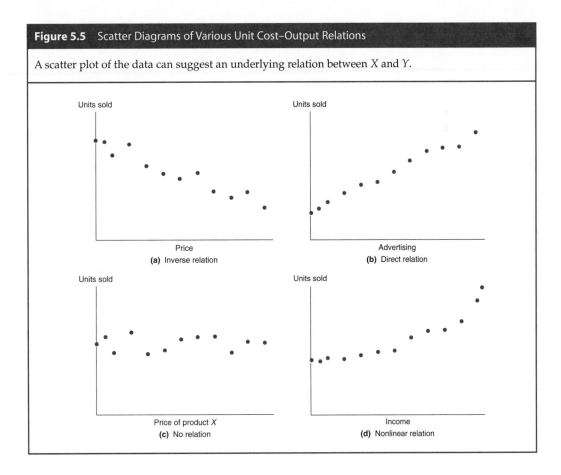

Figure 5.5 Scatter Diagrams of Various Unit Cost–Output Relations

A scatter plot of the data can suggest an underlying relation between *X* and *Y*.

Specifying the Regression Model

The first step in regression analysis is to specify the variables to be included in the regression model. Product demand, measured in physical units, is the dependent variable when specifying a demand function. Independent variables that influence demand always include the price of the product and generally include the prices of complementary and competitive products, advertising expenditures, and income. Demand functions for expensive durable goods, such as automobiles and houses, also include interest rates and other credit terms; those for ski equipment, beverages, or air conditioners include weather conditions. Determinants of demand for capital goods, such as industrial machinery, include profit rates, capacity utilization ratios, interest rates, trends in wages, and so on.

The second step is to obtain reliable data. Data must be gathered on total output or demand, price, credit terms, capacity utilization ratios, wage rates, and the like. Obtaining accurate data is not always easy, especially if the study involves time-series data over a number of years. Some key variables, such as consumer sentiment, may have to be estimated.

Once variables have been specified and data have been gathered, the functional form of the regression equation must be determined. This form reflects the way in which independent variables are assumed to affect the dependent variable. The most common specification is a **linear model** such as

Linear Model
Straight-line
relation.

$$Q = b_0 + b_P P + b_A A + b_I I \qquad\qquad \textbf{5.2}$$

Q represents the unit demand for a particular product, P is the price charged, A represents advertising expenditures, and I is per capita disposable income. In a linear regression model, the marginal effect of each X variable on Y is constant. The broad appeal of linear functions stems from the fact that many demand and cost relations are approximately linear. Furthermore, the most popular regression technique, ordinary least squares, can be used to estimate the coefficients b_0, b_P, b_A, and b_I for linear equations.

**Multiplicative
model**
Nonlinear relation
that involves
X variable
interactions.

Another common regression model is the **multiplicative model:**

$$Q = b_0 P^{b_P} A^{b_A} I^{b_I} \qquad\qquad \textbf{5.3}$$

A multiplicative model is used when the marginal effect of each independent variable depends on the value of all independent variables in the regression equation. For example, the effect of a price increase on the quantity demanded often depends not just on the price level but also on the amount of advertising, competitor prices, and so on. Allowing for such changes in the marginal relation is sometimes more realistic than the implicit assumption of a constant marginal in the linear model.

The benefit of added realism for the multiplicative model has no offsetting cost in terms of added complexity in estimation. Equation (5.3) can be transformed into a linear relation by using logarithms as

$$\log Q = \log b_0 + b_P \log P + b_A \log A + b_I \log I \qquad\qquad \textbf{5.4}$$

When written in this form, the coefficients $\log b_0$, b_P, b_A, and b_I can be easily estimated using ordinary least squares. These coefficients can also be interpreted as estimates of the constant *elasticity* of Y with respect to X, or the percentage change in Y due to a 1 percent change in X. It is worth noting that multiplicative or log-linear models imply constant elasticity.

Least Squares Method

The method of least squares estimates, or fits, the regression line that minimizes the sum of squared deviations between the best-fitting line and the set of original data points. The technique is based on the minimization of squared deviations to avoid the problem of having positive and negative deviations cancel one another out. To illustrate, assume that Electronic Data Processing (EDP), Inc. is a small but rapidly growing firm that provides electronic data processing services. Table 5.2 shows EDP monthly data on unit sales (Q) and personal selling expenses (PSE) over the past year (12 observations). A **simple regression model** that relates unit sales and personal selling expenditures for EDP is written

Simple Regression Model
Relation between one dependent Y variable and one independent X variable.

$$\text{Unit Sales}_t = Y_t = b_0 + b_X X_t + u_t \qquad \textbf{5.5}$$

where unit sales in month t is the dependent Y variable and the level of personal selling expenditures in month t is the independent output, or X variable; u_t is a residual or disturbance term that reflects the influences of stochastic or random elements. When time-series data are examined, as they are in this example, the term t is used to signify a time-period-specific subscript. If cross section data were being examined—for example, unit sales in a number of regional markets during a given month—the various regional markets would be designated using the subscript i. This is called a simple regression model because it involves only one dependent Y variable and one independent X variable. A **multiple regression model** entails one Y variable but includes two or more X variables. Other possibilities for independent X variables include price, advertising, income, and so on.

Multiple Regression Model
Relation between one Y variable and two or more X variables.

Table 5.2 Units Sold and Personal Selling Expenditures for Electronic Data Processing, Inc.

Month	Units Sold	Personal Selling Expenditures ($)	Fitted Value for Units Sold	Unexplained Residuals
January	2.500	43,000	2,702.04	−202.04
February	2.250	39,000	2,330.47	−80.47
March	1,750	35,000	1,958.91	−208.91
April	1,500	34,000	1,866.01	−366.01
May	1,000	26,000	1,122.88	−122.88
June	2,500	41,000	2,516.26	−16.26
July	2,750	40,000	2,423.36	326.64
August	1,750	33,000	1,773.12	−23.12
September	1,250	26,000	1,122.88	127.12
October	3,000	45,000	2,887.82	112.18
November	2,000	32,000	1,680.23	319.77
December	2,000	34,000	1,866.01	133.99
Average	2,021	35,667	2,020.83	0.00

Figure 5.6 shows a plot of actual EDP unit sales and personal selling expense data from Table 5.2 along with a plot of the best-fitting line for the relevant simple regression model. The b_0 intercept marks the intersection of the regression line with the sales axis. The b_X coefficient is the slope of the regression line, and the u_t error term measures the vertical deviation of each tth data point from the fitted regression line. The least squares technique minimizes the total sum of squared u_t values by the choice of the b_0 and b_X coefficients. When b_0 and b_X coefficient estimates are combined with actual data on the independent X-variable (the level of personal selling expenditures) as shown in Equation (5.5), the estimated, or fitted, total unit sales values shown in Table 5.2 can be calculated. These fitted values are connected to form the fitted regression line drawn in Figure 5.6. Fitted values for the dependent Y variable indicate the expected unit sales level for a given level of personal selling expenditures, or X variable.

Figure 5.6 Regression Relation Between Units Sold and Personal Selling Expenditures for Electronic Data Processing (EDP), Inc.

The regression line minimizes the sum of squared deviations.

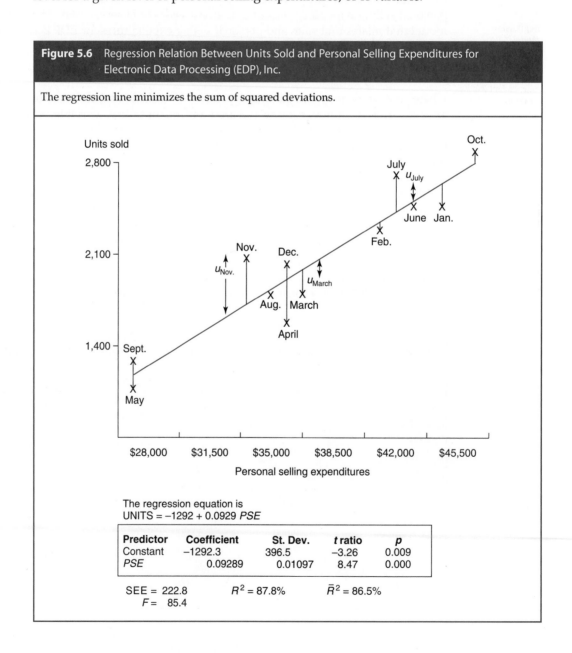

The regression equation is
UNITS = −1292 + 0.0929 *PSE*

Predictor	Coefficient	St. Dev.	t ratio	p
Constant	−1292.3	396.5	−3.26	0.009
PSE	0.09289	0.01097	8.47	0.000

SEE = 222.8 R^2 = 87.8% $\bar{R}^2$ = 86.5%
F = 85.4

Managerial Application 5.3

Lies, Damn Lies, and Government Statistics

Once a reliable source of timely and accurate statistics on the U.S. economy, the federal government's system for gathering and interpreting economic data has fallen on hard times. To illustrate, consider the tough question: How much have prices risen or fallen lately?

Think about how much more you are paying for monthly long-distance telephone service and you'll see what economists mean when they complain about adjusting for quality improvements. Chances are that your monthly long-distance bill is higher today than it was 5 years ago, but your higher bill is accounted for by more frequent and/or longer phone conversations, Internet service, and so on. The cost per minute for long-distance phone service has fallen precipitously for decades. How about the cost for a personal computer? While the price of a PC has fallen from roughly $3,000 to $1,000 during the last decade, desktop computers are more powerful and easier to use than a room full of computers as in the 1970s. Even when products change little, consumers adapt buying habits to moderate the effects of price increases. How do you account for the fact that

shoppers shift to apples when oranges jump from 79¢ to 89¢ per pound?

The problem is that admittedly imperfect government statistics involve errors and bias. Government statisticians are slow to recognize the effects of new technology and better products. The producer price index, which contains thousands of values for products such as bolts and valves, still has no accurate measure for semiconductors or for communications equipment, arguably the biggest category of producer durables.

What should be done? To better measure consumer prices, electronic scanning data must be utilized. Price and production indexes must also reflect quality adjustments for new products and technologies, and surveys of changes in employment must be refined. In some instances, government spending on data gathering and analysis needs to be increased. Americans and their government simply need to know what's *really* happening in the economy.

See: FedStats is the gateway to statistics from over 100 U.S. Federal agencies, http://www.fedstats.gov/.

MEASURES OF REGRESSION MODEL SIGNIFICANCE

Powerful desktop personal computers with sophisticated, user-friendly statistical software make the estimation of complex demand relations quick and easy.

Standard Error of the Estimate

Standard Error of the Estimate (SEE)
Standard deviation of the dependent Y variable after controlling for the influence of all X variables.

A useful measure for examining the accuracy of any regression model is the **standard error of the estimate** (SEE), or the standard deviation of the dependent Y variable after controlling for the influence of all X variables. The SEE increases with the amount of scatter about the sample regression line. If each data point were to lie exactly on the regression line, then the SEE would equal zero because each $\hat{Y}_t$ (or estimated value of Y_t) would exactly equal Y_t. If there is a great deal of scatter about the regression line, then $\hat{Y}_t$ differs greatly from Y_t, and the SEE will be large.

The SEE provides a helpful means for estimating confidence intervals around any particular $\hat{Y}_t$, *given* values for the independent X variables. Because the best estimate of the t th value for the dependent variable is $\hat{Y}_t$, the SEE is used to determine just how accurate a prediction $\hat{Y}_t$ is likely to be. If the u_t error terms are normally distributed about the regression equation, as would be true when large samples of more than 30 or so observations are analyzed, there is a 95 percent probability that the dependent variable will lie within the range $\hat{Y}_t \pm (1.96 \times \text{SEE})$, or within roughly 2 SEE. The probability is 99 percent that any given $\hat{Y}_t$ will lie within the range $\hat{Y}_t \pm (2.576 \times \text{SEE})$, or within roughly 3

SEE. When very small samples of data are analyzed, critical values slightly larger than 2 or 3 are multiplied by the SEE to obtain the 95 percent and 99 percent confidence intervals. Precise values can be obtained from a t table such as that found in Appendix C.

The SEE concept is portrayed in Figure 5.7. The least squares regression line is illustrated as a bold straight line; the upper and lower 95 percent confidence interval limits are shown as broken curved lines. On average, 95 percent of all actual data observations will lie within roughly 2 SEE. Given a value X_t, the interval between the upper and lower confidence bounds can be used to predict the corresponding Y_t value with a 95 percent probability that the actual outcome will lie within that confidence interval. Notice that this confidence interval widens for extreme values of sample observations. As a result, little confidence can be placed in the predictive value of a regression equation extended beyond the range of sample observations.

In the EDP demand estimation example, the SEE is 222.8. This means that the standard deviation of actual Y_t values about the regression line is 222.8 sales units because the SEE is always in the same units as the dependent Y variable. There is a 95 percent probability that any given observation Y_t will lie within roughly 2 standard errors of the relevant $\hat{Y}_t$ estimate. Unit sales during the month of July totals 2,750 units, for example, and the expected or fitted unit sales level is 2,423.36 [$= -1,292.3 + 0.09289$ (40,000)]. The corresponding confidence bounds for the 95 percent confidence interval are $2,423.36 \pm (2 \times 222.8)$. This means that there is roughly a 95 percent chance that actual

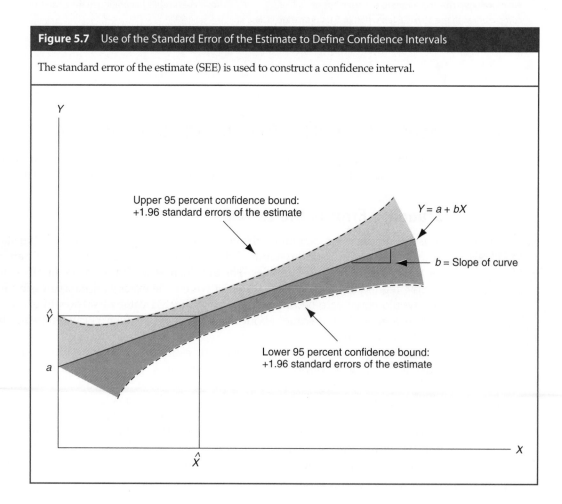

Figure 5.7   Use of the Standard Error of the Estimate to Define Confidence Intervals

The standard error of the estimate (SEE) is used to construct a confidence interval.

unit sales for a month in which $40,000 is spent on personal selling will fall in a range from 1,977.76 to 2,868.96. Similarly, there is a 99 percent probability that actual unit sales will fall within roughly 3 standard errors of the predicted value, or in the range from 1,754.66 to 3,092.06. The wider the confidence interval, the greater is the likelihood that actual values will be found within the predicted range.

Goodness of Fit

Correlation Coefficient
Goodness of fit measure for a simple regression model.

In a simple regression model with only one independent variable, the **correlation coefficient,** r, measures goodness of fit. The correlation coefficient falls in the range between 1 and -1. If $r = 1$, there is a perfect direct linear relation between the dependent Y variable and the independent X variable. If $r = -1$, there is a perfect inverse linear relation between Y and X. In both instances, all actual values for Y_t fall exactly on the regression line. The regression equation explains all of the underlying variation in the dependent Y variable in terms of variation in the independent X variable. If $r = 0$, zero correlation exists between the dependent and independent variables; they are autonomous. When $r = 0$, there is no relation at all between actual Y_t observations and fitted $\hat{Y}_t$ values.

Coefficient of Determination
Measure of the goodness of fit for a multiple regression model; the square of the coefficient of multiple correlations.

In multiple regression models in which more than one independent X variable is considered, the squared value of the coefficient of multiple correlation is used in a similar manner. The square of the coefficient of multiple correlation, called the **coefficient of determination,** or R^2, shows how well a multiple regression model explains changes in the value of the dependent Y variable. R^2 is the proportion of total variation in the dependent variable explained by the full set of independent variables. In equation form, R^2 is written

$$R^2 = \frac{\text{Variation Explained by Regression}}{\text{Total Variation in } Y} \qquad \textbf{5.6}$$

R^2 can take on values ranging from 0 percent, indicating that the model provides no explanation of the variation in the dependent variable, to 100 percent, indicating that all of the variation is explained by the independent variables. The coefficient of determination for the regression model illustrated in Figure 5.6 is 87.8 percent, meaning that 87.8 percent of the total variation in EDP unit sales can be explained by the underlying variation in personal selling expenditures. If R^2 is relatively high, deviations about the regression line are relatively small, as shown in Figure 5.8. In such instances, actual Y_t values are close to the regression line and values for u_t are small.

Degrees of Freedom
Number of observations beyond the minimum needed to calculate a given regression statistic.

Because R^2 always approaches 100 percent as the number of estimated coefficients approaches the sample size, statisticians have developed a method for adjusting R^2 to account for the number of **degrees of freedom.** Degrees of freedom is the number of observations beyond the absolute minimum needed to calculate a given regression statistic. The **corrected coefficient of determination,** denoted by the symbol overline $\overline{R}^2$, is calculated as

Corrected Coefficient of Determination
Downward adjustment to R^2 in light of the number of data points and estimated coefficients.

$$\overline{R}^2 = R^2 - \left(\frac{k-1}{n-k}\right)(1 - R^2) \qquad \textbf{5.7}$$

where n is the number of observations (data points) and k is the number of estimated coefficients (intercept plus the number of slope coefficients). The downward adjustment to R^2 is large when n, the sample size, is small relative to k, the number of coefficients being estimated. Note that $\overline{R}^2$ always involves a downward adjustment to R^2. This downward adjustment to R^2 is small when n is large relative to k.

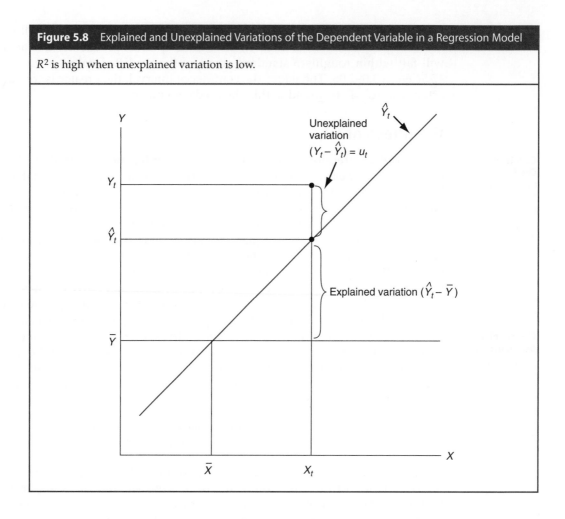

Figure 5.8 Explained and Unexplained Variations of the Dependent Variable in a Regression Model

R^2 is high when unexplained variation is low.

In the EDP example, $\overline{R}^2 = 86.5$ percent—a relatively modest downward adjustment from $R^2 = 87.8$ percent; it suggests that the high level of explanatory power achieved by the regression model cannot be attributed to a small sample size.

F Statistic

F Statistic
Measure of statistical significance for the share of dependent variable variation explained by the regression model.

Both R^2 and $\overline{R}^2$ give evidence on whether the proportion of explained variation is relatively high or low. The **F statistic** tells if the independent variables as a group explain a statistically significant share of variation in the dependent Y variable. The F statistic adjusted for degrees of freedom is defined

$$F_{k-1,\,n-k} = \frac{\text{Explained Variation}/(k-1)}{\text{Unexplained Variation}/(n-k)}$$

$$= \frac{R^2/(k-1)}{1 - R^2/(n-k)} \qquad\qquad \textbf{5.8}$$

Once again, n is the number of observations (data points) and k is the number of estimated coefficients (intercept plus the number of slope coefficients). The F statistic is used to indicate whether a significant share of variation in the dependent variable has been explained by the regression model. The hypothesis actually tested is that the dependent Y variable is statistically *unrelated* to all the independent X variables included in the model. If this hypothesis cannot be rejected, variation explained by the regression is small. At the extreme, if $R^2 = 0$, then $F = 0$ and the regression equation provides absolutely no explanation of variation in the dependent Y variable. As the F statistic increases from zero, the hypothesis that the dependent Y variable is not statistically related to one or more of the regression's independent X variables becomes easier to reject. At some point the F statistic becomes sufficiently large to reject the independence hypothesis and warrants the conclusion that at least some of the model's X variables explain variation in the dependent Y variable.

Critical F values depend on the number of degrees of freedom related to both the numerator and the denominator of Equation (5.8). In the numerator, degrees of freedom equals one less than the number of coefficients estimated in the regression equation $(k - 1)$. The degrees of freedom for the denominator of the F statistic equals the number of data observations minus the number of estimated coefficients $(n - k)$. The critical value for F is denoted as F_{f_1, f_2}, where f_1, the degrees of freedom for the numerator, equals $k - 1$, and f_2, the degrees of freedom for the denominator, equals $n - k$.

The F statistic for the EDP example involves $f_1 = k - 1 = 2 - 1 = 1$, and $f_2 = n - k = 12 - 2 = 10$ degrees of freedom. Also note that the calculated $F_{1,10} = 71.73 > 10.04$, the critical F value for the $\alpha = 0.01$ or 99 percent confidence level. This means there is less than a 1 percent chance of observing such a high F statistic when there is no link between the dependent Y variable and the entire group of X variables. Given the ability to reject the hypothesis of no relation at the 99 percent confidence level, it will always be possible to reject this hypothesis at the lower, 95 percent and 90 percent, confidence levels. Because the significance with which the no-relation hypothesis can be rejected is an important indicator of overall model fit, rejection should always take place at the highest possible confidence level.

As a rule of thumb, a calculated F statistic greater than 3 permits rejection of the hypothesis that there is no relation between the dependent Y variable and the X variables at the $\alpha = 0.05$ significance level (with 95 percent confidence). As seen in Figure 5.9, a calculated F statistic greater than 5 typically permits rejection of the hypothesis that there is no relation between the dependent Y variable and the X variables at the $\alpha = 0.01$ significance level (with 99 percent confidence). Critical F values are adjusted upward when sample size is small in relation to the number of coefficients included in the regression model. In such instances, precise critical F values must be obtained from Appendix C.

JUDGING VARIABLE SIGNIFICANCE

Coefficient estimates and their standard deviations (or standard errors) are used to measure the precision of the relation between the dependent Y variable and a given X variable.

Two-Tail t Tests

t statistic
Approximately normal test statistic with a mean of zero and a standard deviation of 1.

When the standard deviation of a given estimated coefficient is small, a strong relation is suggested between X and Y. When the standard deviation of a coefficient estimate is relatively large, the underlying relation between X and Y is typically weak. A variety of statistical tests can be conducted based on the size of an estimated coefficient and its standard deviation. These tests are based on alternate versions of the **t statistic,** or test statistic. The t statistic has an approximately normal distribution with a mean of zero

Figure 5.9 *F* Distribution with 4 and 30 Degrees of Freedom (for a regression model with an intercept plus four *X* variables tested over 35 observations)

The *F* distribution is skewed to the right but tends toward normality as degrees of freedom become very large.

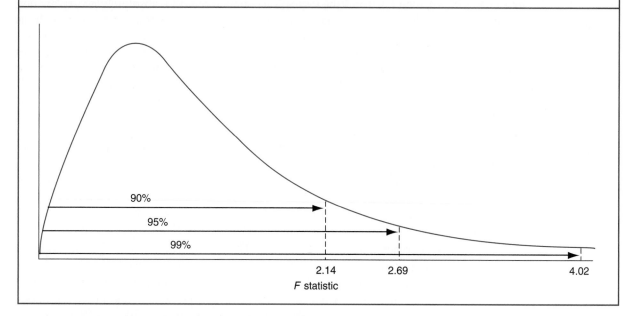

90%

95%

99%

2.14   2.69   4.02
F statistic

Managerial Application 5.4

Spreadsheet and Statistical Software for the PC

The personal computer revolution in business really got underway in the 1980s following the publication of powerful and easy-to-use spreadsheet software. Microsoft's *Excel* has blown away the original standard, *Lotus* 1–2–3, to make income statement and balance sheet analysis quick and easy. Recent versions incorporate a broad range of tools for analysis, including: net present value, internal rate of return, linear programming, and regression. Such software also allows managers to analyze and display operating data, using a wide variety of charting and graphing techniques. For basic statistical analysis, *Excel* features easy-to-use statistical capabilities like regression and correlation analysis.

For more detailed analysis, thousands of successful companies worldwide, including GE, 3M, and Ford Motor Company, use *MINITAB* statistical software. The latest version, *MINITAB Release 15*, is a complete stat package that makes statistical analysis easy and fast. For example, the *Stat Guide* is extremely helpful for interpreting statistical graphs and analysis. *MINITAB Student* software is a streamlined and economical version of *Professional MINITAB*, designed specially for

introductory general and business statistics courses. The latest release of *MINITAB Student* features an intuitive and easy-to-use interface, clear manuals and online help. *MINITAB* is a powerful programming language with sufficient documentation to help even novice users analyze data and interpret results.

For advanced statistical processing software, *SPSS*® 11.0 *for Windows*® embodies powerful statistical tools for in-depth analysis and modeling of business and economic data. *SPSS*® 11.0 *for Windows*® helps managers access data easily, quickly prepare data for analysis, analyze data thoroughly, and present results clearly. *SPSS*® 12.0 *for Windows*® is packed with online tutorials and plenty of examples to guide users, while interactive charts and tables help users understand and present their results effectively.

More than simply changing historical methods of data manipulation and analysis, this user-friendly software for the PC is fundamentally changing the way managers visualize and run their businesses.

See: For MINITAB software, http://www.minitab.com; for SPSS, http://www.spss.com.

and a standard deviation of 1. Notice that the bulk of the region under the bell-shaped curve in Figure 5.10 lies in the area around zero, the mean value of the t statistic. Fully 95 percent of the region under the bell-shaped curve lies within the territory between -1.96 and $+1.96$, or roughly ± 2. Only 5 percent of the area under the bell-shaped curve lies in the "tails" of the distribution, or in the region below the value -1.96 or beyond the value $+1.96$. This area is referred to as the rejection region, because one can be 95 percent confident that such values are *not* typical of t statistics with a true mean of zero. Because 99 percent of the region under the bell-shaped curve lies within the territory between -2.576 and $+2.576$, or roughly ± 3, only 1 percent of the area under the bell-shaped curve lies in the lower tail below -2.576, or in the upper tail beyond $+2.576$.

In regression analysis, a t test is performed to learn if an individual slope coefficient estimate is zero, or $b_X = 0$. This is known as the null hypothesis. If X and Y are indeed unrelated, then the b slope coefficient for a given X variable equals zero. If the $b_X = 0$ hypothesis can be rejected, then it is possible to infer that $b \neq 0$ and that a relation between Y and X does in fact exist. The t statistic with $n - k$ degrees of freedom used to test the $b_X = 0$ hypothesis is given by the expression

$$t_{n-k} = \frac{\hat{b}_X}{\text{Standard Deviation of } \hat{b}_X}$$

5.9

Once again, n is the number of observations (data points) and k is the number of estimated coefficients (intercept plus the number of slope coefficients). Notice that the t statistic

Figure 5.10 t Distribution

For large samples, the t statistic is normally distributed with a mean of zero and a standard deviation of 1.

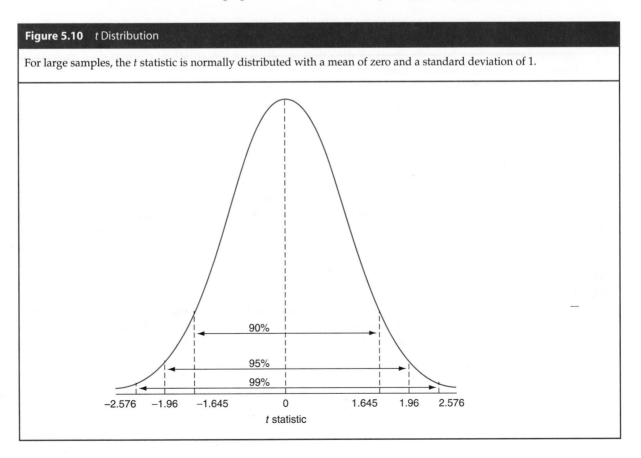

measures the size of an individual coefficient estimate relative to the size of its underlying standard deviation. Both the size of b_X and its underlying stability are important in determining if, on average, $b_X \neq 0$. When $n - k > 30$, a calculated t statistic greater than 2 usually permits rejection of the hypothesis that there is no relation between the dependent Y variable and a given X variable at the $\alpha = 0.05$ significance level (with 95 percent confidence). A calculated t statistic greater than 3 typically permits rejection of the hypothesis that there is no relation between the dependent Y variable and a given X variable at the $\alpha = 0.01$ significance level (with 99 percent confidence). Critical t values are adjusted upward when sample size is small in relation to the number of estimated coefficients. When $n - k < 30$, precise critical t values can be obtained from the t table in Appendix C.

Two-tail t Tests
Tests of the $b = 0$ hypothesis.

Tests of the hypothesis $b_X = 0$ are referred to as **two-tail t tests** because either very small negative t values or very large positive t values can lead to rejection. Hypothesis tests that simply relate to matters of effect or influence are called two-tail t tests. Returning to the EDP example, the estimated coefficient for the personal selling expenditures X variable is 0.09289. Given a standard deviation of only 0.01097, the calculated t statistic $= 8.47 > 3.169$, the critical t value for a two-tail test with $n - k = 10$ degrees of freedom at the $\alpha = 0.01$ significance level. With 99 percent confidence, the hypothesis of no effect can be rejected. The probability of encountering such a large t statistic is less than 1 percent [hence the probability (p) value of 0.000 in Figure 5.6] when there is in fact no relation between the total units Y variable and the personal selling expenditures X variable.

One-Tail t Tests

It is sometimes interesting to determine whether a given variable, X, has a positive or a negative effect on Y or whether the effect of variable X_1 is greater or smaller than the effect of variable X_2. Tests of direction (positive or negative) or comparative magnitude are called **one-tail t tests.**

One-tail t Tests
Tests of direction or comparative magnitude.

To understand the difference between one-tail and two-tail t tests, it is necessary to appreciate the nature of the t distribution. As shown in Figure 5.10, 90 percent of the area under the bell-shaped curve is between $t = -1.645$ and $t = +1.645$, 95 percent is between $t = -1.96$ and $t = +1.96$, and 99 percent is between $t = -2.576$ and $t = +2.576$. At these values, both tails of the t statistic distribution contain 10 percent, 5 percent, and 1 percent of the total area, respectively. For example, if there is in fact no relation between Y and a given X variable, the probability of a calculated t value that falls outside the bounds ± 1.645 is only 10 percent. Under these circumstances, the chance of a calculated t value that is less than -1.645 is only 5 percent; the chance of a calculated t value greater than $+1.645$ is 5 percent. If $t = 1.645$, it is possible to reject the $b_X = 0$ hypothesis with 90 percent confidence; it is possible to reject the $b_X < 0$ hypothesis with 95 percent confidence. In a two-tail t test, rejection of the null hypothesis occurs with a finding that the t statistic is not in the *region around zero*. In one-tail t tests, rejection of the null hypothesis occurs when the t statistic is in one specific tail of the distribution.

In the EDP example, the estimated coefficient for the personal selling expenditures X variable is 0.09289 with a standard deviation of 0.01097. The calculated t statistic $= 8.47 > 2.764$, the critical t value for a one-tail t test with $n - k = 10$ degrees of freedom at the $\alpha = 0.01$ significance level. With 99 percent confidence, the negative effect hypothesis can be rejected. The probability of encountering such a large positive t statistic is less than 1 percent [hence the probability (p) value of 0.000 in Figure 5.6] when there is in fact a negative relation between the total units Y variable and the personal selling expenditures X variable.

SUMMARY

This chapter introduces methods for characterizing and estimating demand relations.

- The **consumer interview,** or survey, method involves questioning customers or potential customers to estimate demand relations. An alternative technique for obtaining useful information about product demand involves **market experiments.**

- The **market demand curve** shows the total amount customers are willing to buy at various prices under present market conditions. The best technique for estimating the market demand curve is the method that provides necessary accuracy at minimum cost.

- Because the market price–output equilibrium at any point in time is determined by the forces of demand and supply, a **simultaneous relation,** or concurrent association, exists between demand and supply. The problem of estimating an economic relation in the presence of such simultaneity is the **identification problem.**

- **Regression analysis** is a powerful statistical technique that describes the way in which a dependent Y variable is related to one or more independent X variables. A **deterministic relation** is known with certainty. A **statistical relation** exists if the average of one variable is related to another, but it is impossible to predict with certainty the value of one based on the value of another. A **time series** is a daily, a weekly, a monthly, or an annual sequence of data on an economic variable such as price, income, cost, or revenue. A **cross section** of data is a group of observations on an important economic variable at any given point in time.

- The simplest means for analyzing a sample is to plot and visually study the data. A **scatter diagram** is a data illustration in which the dependent variable is plotted on the vertical axis, and the independent variable is shown on the horizontal axis. The most common regression model specification is a **linear model** or straight-line relation. Another common regression model form is a **multiplicative model,** which involves interactions among all the X variables. A **simple regression model** involves one dependent Y variable and one independent X variable. A **multiple regression model** entails one Y variable but includes two or more X variables.

- A useful measure for examining the overall accuracy of regression models is the **standard error of the estimate** (SEE), or the standard deviation of the dependent Y variable after controlling for the influence of all X variables. In a simple regression model with only one independent variable, the **correlation coefficient,** r, measures goodness of fit. The square of the coefficient of multiple correlation, called the **coefficient of determination,** or R^2, shows how well a multiple regression model explains changes in the value of the dependent Y variable. In statistical studies, the sample analyzed must be large enough to provide 30 or more **degrees of freedom,** or observations beyond the minimum needed to calculate a given regression statistic. The **corrected coefficient of determination,** denoted by the symbol $\overline{R}^2$, is a downward adjustment in R^2 in light of the number of data points and estimated coefficients. The **F statistic** offers evidence on the statistical significance of the proportion of dependent variable variation that has been explained.

- The **t statistic** is a test statistic that has an approximately normal distribution with a mean of zero and a standard deviation of 1. Hypothesis tests that relate to matters of effect or influence of the independent variables are called **two-tail t tests.** Tests of direction (positive or negative) or comparative magnitude are called **one-tail t tests.**

Methods examined in this chapter are commonly used by large and small organizations in their statistical analysis of demand relations.

QUESTIONS

Q5.1 Describe some of the limitations of market experiments.

Q5.2 "When I go to the grocery store, I find cents-off coupons totally annoying. Why can't they just cut the price and do away with the clutter?" Discuss this statement and explain why coupon promotions are an effective means of promotion for grocery retailers, and popular with many consumers.

Q5.3 Explain how shifting demand and supply curves makes market demand estimation difficult.

Q5.4 "Rapid innovation in the development, assembly, and delivery of personal computers has led to a sharply downward-sloping market demand curve for Dell, Inc." Discuss this statement.

Q5.5 "Demand for higher education is highest among the wealthy. This has led to an upward-sloping demand curve for college education. The higher the tuition charged, the greater is demand." Discuss this statement.

Q5.6 How do linear and log-linear models differ in terms of their assumptions about the nature of demand elasticities?

Q5.7 If a regression model estimate of total profit is $50,000 with a standard error of the estimate of $25,000, what is the chance of an actual loss?

Q5.8 A simple regression $TR = a + bQ$ is not able to explain 19 percent of the variation in total revenue. What is the coefficient of correlation between TR and Q?

Q5.9 In a regression-based estimate of a demand function, the beta coefficient for advertising equals 3.75 with a standard deviation of 1.25 units. What is the range within which there can be 99 percent confidence that the actual parameter for advertising can be found?

Q5.10 Managers often study the profit margin–sales relation over the life cycle of individual products, rather than the more direct profit–sales relation. In addition to the economic reasons for doing so, are there statistical advantages as well? (Note: Profit margin equals profit divided by sales.)

SELF-TEST PROBLEMS AND SOLUTIONS

ST5.1 Linear Demand Curve Estimation. To ensure a big fan turnout for a traditional rival, suppose the Arizona State Sun Devils offer one-half off the $16 regular price of reserved seats for a women's basketball game, and sales jumped from 1,750 to 2,750 tickets.

A. Calculate ticket revenues at each price level. Did the pricing promotion increase or decrease ticket revenues?

B. Estimate the reserved seat demand curve, assuming that it is linear.

C. How should ticket prices be set to maximize total ticket revenue? Contrast this answer with your answer to part A.

ST5.1 Solution

A. The total revenue function for the Arizona State Sun Devils is

$$TR = P \times Q$$

Then, total revenue at a price of $16 is

$$TR = P \times Q$$
$$= \$16 \times 1,750$$
$$= \$28,000$$

Total revenue at a price of $8 is

$$TR = P \times Q$$
$$= \$8 \times 2{,}750$$
$$= \$22{,}000$$

The pricing promotion caused a decrease in ticket revenues.

B. When a linear demand curve is written as

$$P = a + bQ$$

a is the intercept and b is the slope coefficient. From the data given previously, two points on this linear demand curve are identified. Given this information, it is possible to exactly identify the linear demand curve by solving the system of two equations with two unknowns, a and b:

$$16 = a + b(1{,}750)$$
$$\text{minus } 8 = a + b(2{,}250)$$
$$8 = -1{,}000b$$
$$b = -0.008$$

By substitution, if $b = -0.008$, then

$$16 = a + b(1{,}750)$$
$$16 = a - 0.008(1{,}750)$$
$$16 = a - 14$$
$$a = 30$$

Therefore, the reserved seat demand curve can be written

$$P = \$30 - \$0.008Q$$

C. To find the revenue-maximizing output level, set $MR = 0$, and solve for Q. Because

$$TR = P \times Q$$
$$= (\$30 - \$0.008Q)Q$$
$$= \$30Q - \$0.008Q^2$$
$$MR = \partial TR/\partial Q$$
$$MR = \$30 - \$0.016Q = 0$$
$$0.016Q = 30$$
$$Q = 1{,}875$$

At $Q = 1{,}875$,

$$P = \$30 - \$0.008(1{,}875)$$
$$= \$15$$

Total revenue at a price of $15 is

$$TR = P \times Q$$
$$= \$15 \times 1{,}875$$
$$= \$28{,}125$$

(Note: $\partial^2 TR / \partial Q^2 < 0$. This is a ticket-revenue–maximizing output level because total ticket revenue is decreasing for output beyond $Q > 1{,}875$.)

ST5.2 Regression Analysis.

The use of regression analysis for demand estimation can be further illustrated by expanding the Electronic Data Processing (EDP), Inc., example described in the chapter. Assume that the link between units sold and personal selling expenditures described in the chapter gives only a partial view of the impact of important independent variables. Potential influences of other important independent variables can be studied in a multiple regression analysis of EDP data on contract sales (Q), personal selling expenses (PSE), advertising expenditures (AD), and average contract price (P). Because of a stagnant national economy, industry-wide growth was halted during the year, and the usually positive effect of income growth on demand was missing. Thus, the trend in national income was not relevant during this period. For simplicity, assume that relevant factors influencing EDP's monthly sales are as follows:

Month	Units Sold	Price ($)	Advertising Expenditures ($)	Personal Selling Expenditures ($)
January	2,500	3,800	26,800	43,000
February	2,250	3,700	23,500	39,000
March	1,750	3,600	17,400	35,000
April	1,500	3,500	15,300	34,000
May	1,000	3,200	10,400	26,000
June	2,500	3,200	18,400	41,000
July	2,750	3,200	28,200	40,000
August	1,750	3,000	17,400	33,000
September	1,250	2,900	12,300	26,000
October	3,000	2,700	29,800	45,000
November	2,000	2,700	20,300	32,000
December	2,000	2,600	19,800	34,000
Average	2,021	3,175	19,967	35,667

Units Sold, Price, Advertising and Personal Selling Expenditures for Electronic Data Processing, Inc.

If a linear relation between unit sales, contract price, advertising, and personal selling expenditures is hypothesized, the EDP regression equation takes the following form:

$$Sales = Y_t = b_0 + b_P P_t + b_{AD} AD_t + b_{PSE} PSE_t + u_t$$

where Y is the number of contracts sold, P is the average contract price per month, AD is advertising expenditures, PSE is personal selling expenses, and u is a random disturbance term— all measured on a monthly basis over the past year.

When this linear regression model is estimated over the EDP data, the following regression equation is estimated (t statistics in parentheses):

$$Units_t = -117.513 - 0.296\,P_t + 0.036\,AD_t + 0.066\,PSE_t$$
$$\quad\quad (-0.35) \quad (-2.91) \quad\quad (2.56) \quad\quad (4.61)$$

where P_t is price, AD_t is advertising, PSE_t is selling expense, and t statistics are indicated within parentheses. The standard error of the estimate or SEE is 123.9 units, the coefficient of determination or $R^2 = 97.0$ percent, the adjusted coefficient of determination is $\overline{R}^2 = 95.8$ percent, and the relevant F statistic is 85.4.

A. What is the economic meaning of the $b_0 = -117.513$ intercept term? How would you interpret the value for each independent variable's coefficient estimate?

B. How is the standard error of the estimate (SEE) employed in demand estimation?

C. Describe the meaning of the coefficient of determination, R^2, and the adjusted coefficient of determination, $\overline{R}^2$.

D. Use the EDP regression model to estimate fitted values for units sold and unexplained residuals for each month during the year.

ST5.2 SOLUTION

A. The intercept term $b_0 = -117.513$ has no clear economic meaning. Caution must always be exercised when interpreting points outside the range of observed data and this intercept, like most, lies far from typical values. This intercept cannot be interpreted as the expected level of unit sales at a zero price, assuming both advertising and personal selling expenses are completely eliminated. Similarly, it would be hazardous to use this regression model to predict sales at prices, selling expenses, or advertising levels well in excess of sample norms.

Slope coefficients provide estimates of the change in sales that might be expected following a 1-unit increase in price, advertising, or personal selling expenditures. In this example, sales are measured in units, and each independent variable is measured in dollars. Therefore, a $1 increase in price can be expected to lead to a 0.296-unit reduction in sales volume per month. Similarly, a $1 increase in advertising can be expected to lead to a 0.036-unit increase in sales; a $1 increase in personal selling expenditures can be expected to lead to a 0.066-unit increase in units sold. In each instance, the effect of independent X variables appears quite consistent over the entire sample. The t statistics for price and advertising exceed the value of 2, meaning that there can be 95 percent confidence that price and advertising have an effect on sales. The chance of observing such high t statistics for these two variables when in fact price and advertising have no effect on sales is less than 5 percent. The t statistic for the personal selling expense variable exceeds the value of 3, the critical t value for the $\alpha = 0.01$ (99 percent confidence level). The probability of observing such a high t statistic when in fact no relation exists between sales and personal selling expenditures is less than 1 percent.[2] Again, caution

---

2   The t statistic for personal selling expenses exceeds 3.355, the precise critical t value for the $\alpha = 0.01$ level and $n - k = 12 - 4 = 8$ degrees of freedom. The t statistic for price and advertising exceeds 2.306, the critical t value for the $\alpha = 0.05$ level and 8 degrees of freedom, meaning that there can be 95 percent confidence that price and advertising affect sales. Note also that $F_{3,8} = 85.40 > 7.58$, the precise critical F value for the $\alpha = 0.01$ significance level.

must be used when interpreting these individual regression coefficients. It is important not to extend the analysis beyond the range of data used to estimate the regression coefficients.

B. The standard error of the estimate, or SEE, of 123.9 units can be used to construct a confidence interval within which actual values are likely to be found based on the size of individual regression coefficients and various values for the X variables. For example, given this regression model and the values $P_t = \$3,800$, $AD_t = \$26,800$, and $PSE_t = \$43,000$ for each respective independent X variable during the month of January; the fitted value $\hat{Y}_t = 2,566.88$ can be calculated (see part D). Given these values for the independent X variables, 95 percent of the time actual observations for the month of January will lie within roughly 2 standard errors of the estimate; 99 percent of the time actual observations will lie within roughly 3 standard errors of the estimate. Thus, approximate bounds for the 95 percent confidence interval are given by the expression $2,566.88 \pm (2 \times 123.9)$, or from 2,319.08 to 2,814.68 sales units. Approximate bounds for the 99 percent confidence interval are given by the expression $2,566.88 \pm (3 \times 123.9)$, or from 2,195.18 to 2,938.58 sales units.

C. The coefficient of determination is $R^2 = 97.0$ percent; it indicates that 97 percent of the variation in EDP demand is explained by the regression model. Only 3 percent is left unexplained. Moreover, the adjusted coefficient of determination is $\overline{R}^2 = 95.8$ percent; this reflects only a modest downward adjustment to R^2 based upon the size of the sample analyzed relative to the number of estimated coefficients. This suggests that the regression model explains a significant share of demand variation—a suggestion that is supported by the F statistic. $F_{3,8} = 85.4$ and is far greater than 5, meaning that the hypothesis of no relation between sales and this group of independent X variables can be rejected with 99 percent confidence. There is less than a 1 percent chance of encountering such a large F statistic when in fact there is no relation between sales and these X variables as a group.

D. Fitted values and unexplained residuals per month are as follows:

Demand Function Regression Analysis for Electronic Data Processing, Inc.

Month	Units Sold	Price ($)	Advertising Expenditures ($)	Personal Selling Expenditures ($)	Fitted Value for Units Sold	Unexplained Residuals
January	2,500	3,800	26,800	43,000	2,566.88	−66.88
February	2,250	3,700	23,500	39,000	2,212.98	37.02
March	1,750	3,600	17,400	35,000	1,758.35	−8.35
April	1,500	3,500	15,300	34,000	1,646.24	−146.24
May	1,000	3,200	10,400	26,000	1,029.26	−29.26
June	2,500	3,200	18,400	41,000	2,310.16	189.84
July	2,750	3,200	28,200	40,000	2,596.51	153.49
August	1,750	3,000	17,400	33,000	1,803.83	−53.83
September	1,250	2,900	12,300	26,000	1,186.56	63.44
October	3,000	2,700	29,800	45,000	3,133.35	−133.35
November	2,000	2,700	20,300	32,000	1,930.90	69.10
December	2,000	2,600	19,800	34,000	2,074.97	−74.97
Average	2,021	3,175	19,967	35,667	202.83	0.00

PROBLEMS

P5.1   Demand Estimation Concepts.   Identify each of the following statements as true or false and explain why.

A. The effect of a $1 change in price is constant, but the elasticity of demand will vary along a linear demand curve.

B. In practice, price and quantity tend to be individually rather than simultaneously determined.

C. A demand curve is revealed if prices fall while supply conditions are held constant.

D. The effect of a $1 change in price will vary, but the elasticity of demand is constant along a log-linear demand curve.

E. Consumer interviews are a useful means for incorporating subjective information into demand estimation.

P5.2   Regression Analysis.   Identify each of the following statements as true or false and explain why:

A. A parameter is a population characteristic that is estimated by a coefficient derived from a sample of data.

B. A one-tail t test is used to indicate whether the independent variables as a group explain a significant share of demand variation.

C. Given values for independent variables, the estimated demand relation can be used to derive a predicted value for demand.

D. A two-tail t test is an appropriate means for testing direction (positive or negative) of the influences of independent variables.

E. The coefficient of determination shows the share of total variation in demand that cannot be explained by the regression model.

P5.3   Revenue Versus Profit Maximization.   The Best Buy Company, Inc., is a leading specialty retailer of consumer electronics, personal computers, entertainment software, and appliances. The company operates retail stores and commercial Web sites, the best known of which is bestbuy.com. Recently, this site offered a home theater unit with a 5-disc DVD player, MP3 playback, and digital AM/FM. At a price of $1,100, weekly sales totaled 2,500 units. After a $100 online rebate was offered, weekly sales jumped to 5,000 units.

Using these two price–output combinations, the relevant linear demand and marginal revenue curves can be estimated as

$$P = \$1,200 - \$0.04Q \quad \text{and} \quad MR = \$1,200 - \$0.08Q$$

A. Calculate the revenue-maximizing price–output combination and revenue level. If Best Buy's marginal cost per unit is $800, calculate profits at this activity level assuming $TC = MC \times Q$.

B. Calculate the profit-maximizing price–output combination. Also calculate revenues and profits at the profit-maximizing activity level.

P5.4 Revenue Versus Profit Maximization.
On weekends during summer months, Eric Cartman rents jet skis at the beach on an hourly basis. Last week, Cartman rented jet skis for 20 hours per day at a rate of $50 per hour. This week, rentals fell to 15 hours per day when Cartman raised the price to $55 per hour.

Using these two price–output combinations, the relevant linear demand and marginal revenue curves can be estimated as

$$P = \$70 - \$1Q \quad \text{and} \quad MR = \$70 - \$2Q$$

A. Calculate the revenue-maximizing price–output combination. How much are these maximum revenues? If marginal cost is $30 per hour, calculate profits at this activity level, assuming $TC = MC \times Q$.

B. Calculate the profit-maximizing price–output combination along with revenues and profits at this activity level.

P5.5 Linear Demand Curve Estimation.
Xerox Corporation develops, manufactures, and services document equipment and software solutions worldwide. Assume the company offered $75 off the $1,475 regular price on the Phaser 6360, a durable high-speed color copier, and Internet sales jumped from 700 units to 800 units per week (see http://www.office.xerox.com).

A. Estimate the color copier demand curve, assuming that it is linear.

B. If marginal costs per unit are $650, calculate the profit-maximizing price–output combination. [Remember: The marginal revenue curve has the same intercept as the demand curve, but has twice its negative slope (falls twice as fast).]

P5.6 Linear Demand Curve Estimation.
Kenny McCormick manages a 100-unit apartment building and knows from experience that all units will be occupied if rent is $900 per month. McCormick also knows that, on average, one additional unit will go unoccupied for each $10 increase in the monthly rental rate.

A. Estimate the apartment rental demand curve assuming that it is linear and that price is expressed as a function of output.

B. Calculate the revenue-maximizing apartment rental rate. How much are these maximum revenues?

C. If all costs are fixed, what is the profit-maximizing number of vacant apartments? Explain your answer.

P5.7 Market Demand.
Gregory House, a Philadelphia-based management consultant, has been asked to calculate and analyze market demand for a new video game that is to be marketed to retail (*R*) and wholesale (*W*) customers over the Internet.

The client estimates fixed costs of $750,000 per year for the product, and that licensing fees and other marginal costs will be $20 per unit. The client has also provided the following annual demand information:

$$P_R = \$62.50 - \$0.0005Q_R$$
$$P_W = \$50 - \$0.002Q_W$$

A. Express quantity as a function of price for both retail and wholesale customers. Add these quantities together to calculate the market demand curve. Graph the retail, wholesale, and market demand curves for prices ranging from $65 to $35 per unit.

B. Fill in the following table:

		Market Demand is Retail Plus Wholesale Demand				
Price ($)	Retail Demand	Wholesale Demand	Market Demand	Total Revenue	Total Cost	Total Profit
65						
60						
55						
50						
45						
40						
35						

C. Calculate the profit-maximizing price–output combination and total profit?

P5.8 Identification Problem. Business is booming for Consulting Services, Inc. (CSI), a local supplier of computer set-up consulting services. The company can profitably employ technicians as quickly as they can be trained. The average hourly rate billed by CSI for trained technician services and the number of billable hours (output) per quarter over the past six quarters are as follows:

	Q–1	Q–2	Q–3	Q–4	Q–5	Q–6
Hourly rate ($)	20	25	30	35	40	45
Billable hours	2,000	3,000	4,000	5,000	6,000	7,000

Quarterly demand and supply curves for CSI services are

$$Q_D = 4,000 - 200P + 2,000T \qquad \text{(Demand)}$$
$$Q_S = -2,000 + 200P \qquad \text{(Supply)}$$

where Q is output, P is price, T is a trend factor, and $T = 1$ during Q–1 and increases by 1 unit per quarter.

A. Express each demand and supply curve in terms of price as a function of output.

B. Plot the quarterly demand curves for the last six quarterly periods. (Hint: Let $T = 1$ to find the Y intercept for Q–1, $T = 2$ for Q–2, and so on.)

C. Plot the CSI supply curve on the same graph.

D. What is this problem's relation to the identification problem?

P5.9 Multiple Regression. Colorful Tile, Inc., is a rapidly growing chain of ceramic tile outlets that caters to the do-it-yourself home remodeling market. In 2007, 33 stores were operated in small to medium-size metropolitan markets. An in-house study of sales by these outlets revealed the following (standard errors in parentheses):

$$Q = 4 - 5P + 2A + 0.2I + 0.25HF$$
$$(3) \quad (1.8) \quad (0.7) \quad (0.1) \quad (0.1)$$
$$R^2 = 93\%, \text{Standard Error of the Estimate} = 6$$

Here, Q is tile sales (in thousands of cases), P is tile price (per case), A is advertising expenditures (in thousands of dollars), I is disposable income per household (in thousands of dollars), and HF is household formation (in hundreds).

A. Fully evaluate and interpret these empirical results on an overall basis using R^2, $\overline{R}^2$, F statistic and SEE information.

B. Is quantity demanded sensitive to "own" price?

C. Austin, Texas, was a typical market covered by this analysis. During 2007 in the Austin market, price was $5, advertising was $30,000, income was an average $55,000 per household, and the number of household formations was 4,000. Calculate and interpret the relevant advertising point elasticity.

D. Assume that the preceding model and data are relevant for the coming period. Estimate the probability that the Austin store will make a profit during 2008 if total costs are projected to be $300,000.

P5.10 Multiplicative Demand Functions. Getaway Tours, Inc., has estimated the following multiplicative demand function for packaged holiday tours in the East Lansing, Michigan, market, using quarterly data covering the past 4 years (16 observations):

$$Q_y = 10 P_y^{-1.10} P_x^{0.5} A_y^{3.8} A_x^{2.5} I^{1.85}$$
$$R^2 = 80\%, \text{Standard Error of the Estimate} = 20$$

Here, Q_y is the quantity of tours sold, P_y is average tour price, P_x is average price for some other good, A_y is tour advertising, A_x is advertising of some other good, and I is per capita disposable income. The standard errors of the exponents in the preceding multiplicative demand function are

$$b_{P_y} = 0.04, b_{P_x} = 0.35, b_{A_y} = 0.5, b_{A_x} = 0.9, \quad \text{and} \quad b_I = 0.45$$

A. Is tour demand elastic with respect to price?

B. Are tours a normal good?

C. Is X a complement good or substitute good?

D. Given your answer to part C, can you explain why the demand effects of A_y and A_x are both positive?

CASE *Study*   Demand Estimation for Mrs. Smyth's Pies

Demand estimation for brand-name consumer products is made difficult by the fact that managers must rely on proprietary data. There simply is not any publicly available data which can be used to estimate demand elasticities for brand-name orange juice, frozen entrees, pies, and the like—and with good reason. Competitors would be delighted to know profit margins across a broad array of competing products so that advertising, pricing policy, and product development strategy could all be targeted for maximum benefit. Product demand information is valuable and jealously guarded.

To see the process that might be undertaken to develop a better understanding of product demand conditions, consider the hypothetical example of Mrs. Smyth's, Inc., a Chicago-based food company. In early 2008, Mrs. Smyth's initiated an empirical estimation of demand for its gourmet frozen fruit pies. The firm is formulating pricing and promotional plans for the coming year, and management is interested in learning how pricing and promotional decisions might affect sales. Mrs. Smyth's has been marketing frozen fruit pies for several years, and its market research department has collected quarterly data over 2 years for six important marketing areas, including sales quantity, the retail price charged for the pies, local advertising and promotional expenditures, and the price charged by a major competing brand of frozen pies. Statistical data published by the U.S. Census Bureau (http://www.census.gov) on population and disposable income in each of the six Metropolitan Statistical Areas were also available for analysis. It was therefore possible to include a wide range of hypothesized demand determinants in an empirical estimation of fruit pie demand. These data appear in Table 5.3.

Table 5.3 Mrs. Smyth's Gourmet Frozen Fruit Pie Regional Market Demand Data, 2006–1 to 2007–4

Year–Quarter	Unit Sales (Q)	Price ($)	Advertising Expenditures ($)	Competitors' Price ($)	Income ($)	Population	Time Variable
Atlanta–Sandy Springs–Marietta, GA							
2006–1	193,334	6.90	15,827	7.40	48,421	5,055,856	1
2006–2	170,041	7.79	20,819	5.18	49,038	5,091,361	2
2006–3	247,709	6.21	14,062	5.65	49,663	5,127,115	3
2006–4	183,259	7.29	16,973	6.60	50,296	5,163,120	4
2007–1	282,118	6.87	18,815	6.81	50,938	5,199,378	5
2007–2	203,396	6.46	14,176	5.22	51,587	5,235,891	6
2007–3	167,447	7.17	17,030	5.59	52,245	5,272,660	7
2007–4	361,677	5.72	14,456	6.21	52,911	5,309,688	8
Chicago–Naperville–Joliet, IL–IN–WI							
2006–1	401,805	6.57	27,183	5.34	50,456	9,509,448	1
2006–2	412,312	6.62	27,572	6.56	51,100	9,526,087	2
2006–3	321,972	7.82	34,367	6.23	51,751	9,542,755	3
2006–4	445,236	6.57	26,895	6.47	52,411	9,559,452	4
2007–1	479,713	6.91	30,539	5.75	53,079	9,576,178	5
2007–2	459,379	6.48	26,679	5.20	53,756	9,592,933	6
2007–3	444,040	6.44	26,607	5.66	54,441	9,609,718	7
2007–4	376,046	7.79	32,760	5.23	55,136	9,626,532	8

continued

Table 5.3 Mrs. Smyth's Gourmet Frozen Fruit Pie Regional Market Demand Data, 2006–1 to 2007–4

Year–Quarter	Unit Sales (Q)	Price ($)	Advertising Expenditures ($)	Competitors' Price ($)	Income ($)	Population	Time Variable
Dallas–Fort Worth–Arlington, TX							
2006–1	255,203	7.07	19,880	7.46	44,249	5,952,784	1
2006–2	270,881	6.60	19,151	6.69	44,813	5,986,874	2
2006–3	330,271	6.07	15,743	6.45	45,385	6,021,160	3
2006–4	313,485	6.54	17,512	5.44	45,963	6,055,642	4
2007–1	311,500	6.30	16,984	5.66	46,549	6,090,322	5
2007–2	370,780	5.81	15,698	6.62	47,143	6,125,200	6
2007–3	152,338	8.00	22,057	7.43	47,744	6,160,278	7
2007–4	320,804	6.69	17,460	6.83	48,353	6,195,557	8
Los Angeles–Long Beach–Santa Ana, CA							
2006–1	738,760	6.21	42,925	5.93	53,929	13,030,242	1
2006–2	707,015	7.14	50,299	7.20	54,617	13,057,136	2
2006–3	699,051	5.43	37,364	5.39	55,313	13,084,085	3
2006–4	628,838	7.30	50,602	4.93	56,018	13,111,090	4
2007–1	631,934	7.60	53,562	6.26	56,732	13,138,151	5
2007–2	651,162	7.24	48,911	6.02	57,456	13,165,267	6
2007–3	765,124	7.06	49,422	7.43	58,188	13,192,440	7
2007–4	741,364	6.19	44,061	6.82	58,930	13,219,669	8
Minneapolis–St. Paul–Bloomington, MN–WI							
2006–1	291,773	5.78	13,896	6.18	58,959	3,176,146	1
2006–2	153,018	6.84	27,429	5.06	59,711	3,184,576	2
2006–3	574,486	6.42	31,631	7.17	60,472	3,193,029	3
2006–4	75,396	7.56	39,176	4.90	61,243	3,201,504	4
2007–1	590,190	5.61	33,538	5.53	62,024	3,210,002	5
2007–2	288,112	7.58	53,643	5.51	62,815	3,218,522	6
2007–3	276,619	7.58	60,284	5.84	63,616	3,227,065	7
2007–4	522,446	5.65	53,595	6.48	64,427	3,235,630	8
Washington–Arlington–Alexandria, DC–VA–MD–WV							
2006–1	395,314	6.26	22,626	7.02	48,717	5,297,098	1
2006–2	436,103	5.75	22,697	6.83	49,338	5,318,031	2
2006–3	336,338	6.86	25,475	4.85	49,967	5,339,048	3
2006–4	451,321	6.43	25,734	6.75	50,604	5,360,147	4
2007–1	352,181	6.49	23,777	6.68	51,249	5,381,330	5
2007–2	317,322	7.58	27,544	5.20	51,903	5,402,596	6
2007–3	422,455	6.17	23,852	5.20	52,565	5,423,947	7
2007–4	290,963	7.95	30,487	5.69	53,235	5,445,382	8
Average	391,917	6.74	29,204	6.09	53,114	7,087,461	

continued

The following regression equation was fit to these data:

$$Q_{it} = b_0 + b_1 P_{it} + b_2 A_{it} + b_3 PX_{it} + b_4 Y_{it} + b_5 Pop_{it} + b_6 T_{it} + u_{it}$$

Q is the quantity of pies sold during the tth quarter; P is the retail price in dollars of Mrs. Smyth's frozen pies; A represents the dollars spent for advertising; PX is the price, measured in dollars, charged for competing premium-quality frozen fruit pies; Y is the median dollars of disposable income per household; Pop is the population of the market area; T is the trend factor (2006–1 = 1,..., 2007–4 = 8); and u_{it} is a residual (or disturbance) term. The subscript i indicates the regional market from which the observation was taken, whereas the subscript t represents the quarter during which the observation occurred. Least squares estimation of the regression equation on the basis of the 48 data observations (eight quarters of data for each of six areas) resulted in the estimated regression coefficients and other statistics given in Table 5.4.

A. Describe the economic meaning and statistical significance of each individual independent variable included in the Mrs. Smyth's frozen fruit pie demand equation.

B. Interpret the coefficient of determination (R^2) for the Mrs. Smyth's frozen fruit pie demand equation.

C. Use the regression model and 2007–4 data to estimate 2008–1 unit sales in the Washington-Arlington-Alexandria market.

D. To illustrate use of the standard error of the estimate statistic, derive the 95 percent and 99 percent confidence intervals for 2008–1 unit sales in the Washington-Arlington-Alexandria market.

Table 5.4 Estimated Demand Function for Mrs. Smyth's Gourmet Frozen Fruit Pies

Variable (1)	Coefficient (2)	Standard Error of Coefficient (3)	t Statistic (4) = (2)/(3)
Intercept	529,774	271,331	1.95
Price (P)	−122,607	16,422	−7.47
Advertising (A)	5.838	1.65	3.54
Competitor Price (PX)	29,867	13,449	2.22
Income (Y)	2.043	3.762	0.54
Population (Pop)	0.030	0.004	7.50
Time (T)	2,815	4,539	0.62

Coefficient of determination = R^2 = 87.1%
Corrected coefficient of determination = $\bar{R}^2$ = 85.2%
F statistic = 45.16
Standard error of the estimate = SEE = 67,584

SELECTED REFERENCES

Autor, David H. and Mark G. Duggan. "Distinguishing Income from Substitution Effects in Disability Insurance." *American Economic Review* 97, no. 2 (May, 2007): 119–124.

Bajari, Patrick, Jeremy T. Fox, and Stephen P. Ryan. "Linear Regression Estimation of Discrete Choice Models with Nonparametric Distributions of Random Coefficients." *American Economic Review* 97, no. 2 (May, 2007): 459–463.

Clark, Ximena, Timothy J. Hatton, and Jeffrey G. Williamson. "Explaining U.S. Immigration, 1971–1998." *Review of Economics and Statistics* 89, no. 2 (May, 2007): 359–373.

Clarke, Jonathan, Ajay Khorana, Ajay Patel, and P. Raghavendra Rau. "The Impact of All-Star Analyst Job Changes on Their Coverage Choices and Investment Banking Deal Flow." *Journal of Financial Economics* 84, no. 3 (June, 2007): 713–737.

Coibion, Olivier, Liran Einav, and Juan Carlos Hallak. "Equilibrium Demand Elasticities Across Quality Segments." *International Journal of Industrial Organization* 25, no. 1 (February, 2007): 13–30.

Cyree, Ken B., James T. Lindley, and Drew B. Winters. "The Effect of Substitute Assets on Yields in Financial Markets." *Financial Management* 36, no. 1 (Spring, 2007): 27–47.

Das, Sanjiv R., Darrell Duffie, Nikunj Kapadia, and Leandro Saita. "Common Failings: How Corporate Defaults Are Correlated." *Journal of Finance* 62, no. 1 (February, 2007): 93–117.

Edelman, Benjamin, Michael Ostrovsky, and Michael Schwarz. "Internet Advertising and the Generalized Second-Price Auction: Selling Billions of Dollars Worth of Keywords." *American Economic Review* 97, no. 1 (March, 2007): 242–259.

Edwards, Amy K., Lawrence E. Harris, and Michael S. Piwowar. "Corporate Bond Market Transaction Costs and Transparency." *Journal of Finance* 62, no. 3 (June, 2007): 1421–1451.

Eisensee, Thomas and David Stromberg. "News Droughts, News Floods, and U.S. Disaster Relief." *Quarterly Journal of Economics* 122, no. 2 (May, 2007): 693–728.

Eliaz, Kfir and Andrew Schotter. "Experimental Testing of Intrinsic Preferences for NonInstrumental Information." *American Economic Review* 97, no. 2 (May, 2007): 166–169.

Hotchkiss, Julie L. and M. Melinda Pitts. "The Role of Labor Market Intermittency in Explaining Gender Wage Differentials." *American Economic Review* 97, no. 2 (May, 2007): 417–421.

Kroszner, Randall S., Luc Laeven, and Daniela Klingebiel. "Banking Crises, Financial Dependence, and Growth." *Journal of Financial Economics* 84, no. 1 (April, 2007): 187–228.

McAdams, David and Michael Schwarz. "Credible Sales Mechanisms and Intermediaries." *American Economic Review* 97, no. 1 (March, 2007): 260–276.

Vagstad, Steinar. "Should Auctioneers Supply Early Information for Prospective Bidders?" *International Journal of Industrial Organization* 25, no. 3 (June, 2007): 597–614.

Forecasting

A famous economist once remarked, "We have two classes of forecasters: Those who don't know—and those who don't know that they don't know." Experienced economists know that economic forecasting is fraught with uncertainty. To see why, consider the interrelated nature of economic forecasts. One might ask an economist, will the pace of real economic growth in the United States average an anemic 2 percent, a healthy 3 percent, or a robust 3.5 percent? What will be the rate of inflation? How will investors respond to a proposed change in the tax law, if and when such a change is passed by both houses of Congress and signed into law by the president? Most important, how is the rate of growth in the overall economy related to inflation, and how are both apt to be affected by an important change in tax law that, at this point, is only at the proposal stage?

Predicting trends in macroeconomic conditions and their impact on costs or demand for company goods and services is one of the most difficult responsibilities facing management. Predicting the effects of changes in the competitive microeconomic environment can also be daunting. However, forecasting is a necessary task because, for better or worse, all decisions are made on the basis of future expectations.[1] This chapter illustrates a number of forecasting techniques that have proven successful in forming accurate expectations in a wide variety of real-world applications.

FORECASTING APPLICATIONS

Managers must make informed forecasts when it comes to deciding on new product introductions, pricing products, or making hiring decisions.

Macroeconomic Applications

Macroeconomic Forecasting
Prediction of aggregate economic activity.

Macroeconomic forecasting involves predicting aggregate measures of economic activity at the international, national, regional, or state levels. Predictions of gross domestic product (GDP), unemployment, and interest rates by "blue chip" business economists capture the attention of national media, business, government, and the general public on a daily basis. GDP is the value at final point of sale of all goods and services produced in the domestic economy during a given period by both domestic and foreign-owned enterprises. Gross national product (GNP) is the value at final point of sale of all goods

---

1   See Elizabeth Landau, "Crude Falls on Stronger Dollar, Economic Worries," *The Wall Street Journal Online*, October 23, 2007, http://online.wsj.com.

and services produced by *domestic* firms. GNP does not reflect domestic production by foreign-owned firms (e.g., Toyota Camrys produced in Kentucky); GDP does.

Macroeconomic forecasts commonly reported in the press include predictions of consumer spending, business investment, home building, exports, imports, federal purchases, state and local government spending, and so on. Macroeconomic predictions are important because they are used by businesses and individuals to make day-to-day operating decisions and long-term planning decisions. If interest rates are projected to rise, homeowners may rush to refinance fixed-rate mortgages, although businesses float new bond and stock offerings to refinance existing debt or take advantage of investment opportunities. When such predictions are accurate, significant cost savings or revenue gains become possible.

The accuracy of any forecast is subject to the influence of controllable and uncontrollable factors. In the case of macroeconomic forecasting, uncontrollable factors loom large. Take interest rate forecasting, for example. The demand for credit and short-term interest rates rise if businesses seek to build inventories or expand plant and equipment, or if consumers wish to increase installment credit. The supply of credit rises and short-term interest rates fall if the Federal Reserve System acts to increase the money supply, or if consumers cut back on spending to increase savings. Interest rate forecasting is made difficult by the fact that business decisions to build inventories, for example, are largely based on the expected pace of overall economic activity—which itself depends on interest-rate expectations. The macroeconomic environment is interrelated in ways that are unstable and cannot be easily predicted.

Microeconomic Applications

Microeconomic Forecasting
Prediction of partial economic data.

Microeconomic forecasting involves the prediction of economic data at the industry, firm, plant, or product levels. Unlike predictions of GDP growth, which are widely followed in the press, the general public often ignores microeconomic forecasts of scrap prices for aluminum, the demand for new cars, or production costs for Crest toothpaste. It is unlikely that the *CBS Evening News* will ever be interrupted to discuss an upward trend in used-car prices, even though these data are an excellent predictor of new-car demand. When used-car prices surge, new-car demand often grows rapidly; when used-car prices sag, new-car demand typically drops. The fact that used-car prices and new-car demand are closely related is not surprising given the strong substitute-good relation that exists between used cars and new cars.

Trained and experienced analysts often find it easier to accurately forecast microeconomic trends, such as the demand for new cars, than macroeconomic trends, such as GDP growth. This is because microeconomic forecasts abstract from the multitude of interrelationships that together determine the macro economy. With specialized knowledge about changes in new-car prices, car import tariffs, car loan rates, and used-cars prices, among other factors, it is possible to focus on the fairly narrow range of important factors that influence new-car demand. In contrast, a similarly precise model of aggregate demand in the macro economy might involve thousands of economic variables and hundreds of functional relationships.

Forecast Techniques

Accurate forecasts require pertinent data that are current, complete, and free from error and bias. One of the most vexing data quality problems encountered in forecasting is the obstacle presented by government-supplied data that are often tardy and inaccurate. For example, the Commerce Department's Bureau of Economic Analysis "advanced" estimate of GDP for the fourth quarter of the year is typically published in late January of the following year. A "preliminary" revision to this estimate is then released by the Bureau of Economic Analysis on March 1; an official final revision is not made available until March 31, or until 90 days after the fact. Such delays induce uncertainty for those seeking to make projections about future trends in economic activity. Worse still, preliminary and final revisions to official GDP estimates are often large and unpredictable.

To overcome forecasting problems caused by error and bias, a variety of forecast methods can be employed. Some forecast techniques are basically quantitative; others are largely qualitative. The most commonly applied forecasting techniques can be divided into the following broad categories:

- Qualitative analyses
- Trend analysis and projection
- Exponential smoothing
- Econometric methods

The best forecast method for any particular task depends on the nature of the forecasting problem. It is always worth considering the distance into the future that one must forecast, the lead time available for making decisions, the level of accuracy required, the quality of data available for analysis, the stochastic or deterministic nature of forecast relations, and the cost and benefits associated with the forecasting problem. Trend analysis, market experiments, consumer surveys, and the leading indicator approach to forecasting are well suited for short-term projections. Forecasting with complex

Managerial Application 6.1

Economic Forecasting: The Art and the Science

Many do not understand why disagreement among forecasting economists is common and why this disagreement can produce divergent economic forecasts. These concerns reflect too little appreciation of the difficulty of economic forecasting. In the real world, "all else held equal" doesn't hold very often, if ever. To forecast GDP, for example, one must be able to accurately predict the future pattern of government spending, tax and monetary policy, consumer and business spending, dollar strength against foreign currencies, weather, and so on. Although typical patterns can be inferred on the basis of past trends, an unexpected drought, winter storm, or labor strike can disrupt economic activity, and upset the accuracy of economic forecasts.

In light of the uncertainties involved, it seems reasonable that different forecasting economists would accord differing importance to a wide variety of economic influences. Forecasters' judgment is reflected not only in the interpretation they give to the data generated by complex computer models but also in the models themselves.

Computers may generate economic forecasts, but they do so on the basis of programs written by economists. Computer-generated economic forecasts are only as sophisticated as the data employed, model analyzed, and the subsequent analysis.

Given the criticism often aimed at forecasters, it is ironic to note that the success of economic forecasting is responsible, at least in part, for some of its failures. Users have come to expect a nearly unattainable level of forecast accuracy. At the same time, users forget that forecasts can, by themselves, have important economic consequences. When consumers and businesses cut back on spending in reaction to the forecast of an impending mild recession, for example, they change the basis for the forecasters' initial prediction. By their behavior, they may also cause a steeper recession. This is the forecaster's dilemma: The future as we know it doesn't exist. In fact, it can't.

See: Phil Izo, "Economists' Outlook Grows a Bit Rosier," *The Wall Street Journal Online*, October 12, 2007, http://online.wsj.com.

econometric models and systems of simultaneous equations has proven somewhat more useful for long-run forecasting. Typically, the greater the level of sophistication, the greater is the cost. If the required level of accuracy is low, less sophisticated methods can provide adequate results at minimal cost. The acid test is simple: Can useful forecasts be generated?

QUALITATIVE ANALYSIS

Qualitative
Analysis
An intuitive
judgmental
approach to
forecasting based
on opinion.

Qualitative analysis is an intuitive approach to forecasting that can be useful if it allows for the systematic collection of data from unbiased and informed opinion.

Expert Opinion

Personal Insight
Forecast method
based on personal
or organizational
experience.

The most basic form of qualitative analysis forecasting is **personal insight,** in which an informed individual uses personal or company experience as a basis for developing future expectations. Although this approach is subjective, the reasoned judgment of informed individuals often provides valuable insight. When the informed opinion of several individuals is relied on, the approach is called forecasting through **panel consensus.** The panel consensus method assumes that several experts can arrive at forecasts that are superior to those that individuals generate. Direct interaction among experts can help insure that resulting forecasts embody all available objective and subjective information.

Panel Consensus
Forecast method
based on the
informed opinion
of several
individuals.

Delphi Method
Method that
uses forecasts
derived from
an independent
analysis of
expert opinion.

Although the panel consensus method often results in forecasts that embody the collective wisdom of consulted experts, it can be unfavorably affected by the forceful personality of one or a few key individuals. A related approach, the **Delphi method,** has been developed to counter this disadvantage. In the Delphi method, members of a panel of experts individually receive a series of questions relating to the underlying forecasting problem. Responses are analyzed by an independent party, who then tries to elicit a consensus opinion by providing feedback to panel members in a manner that prevents direct identification of individual positions. This method helps limit the steamroller or bandwagon problems of the basic panel consensus approach.

Survey Techniques

Survey
Techniques
Interview
or mailed
questionnaire
approach to
forecasting.

Survey techniques generally use interviews or mailed questionnaires that ask firms, government agencies, and individuals about their future plans. Businesses plan and budget virtually all their expenditures in advance of actual purchase or production decisions. Surveys asking about capital budgets, sales budgets, and operating budgets can thus provide useful forecast information. Government departments that prepare formal budgets also provide a wealth of information to the forecaster. Finally, because individual consumers routinely plan expenditures for such major items as automobiles, furniture, housing, vacations, and education, surveys of consumer intentions often accurately predict future spending on consumer goods.

Survey information may be all that is available in certain forecasting situations, as, for example, when a firm is attempting to project new product demand. Although surveys sometimes serve as an alternative to quantitative forecasting techniques, they frequently supplement rather than replace quantitative analysis. Their value stems from two influences. First, a hard-to-quantify psychological element is inherent in most economic behavior; surveys and other qualitative methods are especially well suited to picking up this phenomenon. Second, quantitative models generally assume stable consumer tastes. If tastes are actually changing, survey data can suggest the nature and direction of such changes.

TREND ANALYSIS AND PROJECTION

Trend Analysis
Forecasting the future path of economic variables based on historical patterns.

Trend analysis is based on the premise that future economic performance follows an established historical pattern.

Trends in Economic Data

Trend projection is predication on the assumption that historical relationships will continue into the future. All such methods use time-series data. Weekly, monthly, or annual series of data on sales and costs, personal income, population, labor force participation rates, and GDP are all examples of economic time series. A **secular trend** is the long-run pattern of increase or decrease in a series of economic data. **Cyclical fluctuation** describes the rhythmic variation in economic series that is due to a pattern of expansion or contraction in the overall economy. Seasonal variation, or **seasonality,** is a rhythmic annual pattern in sales or profits caused by weather, habit, or social custom. **Irregular or random influences** are unpredictable shocks to the economic system and the pace of economic activity caused by wars, strikes, natural catastrophes, and so on.

These four patterns are illustrated in Figure 6.1. Figure 6.1(a) shows secular and cyclical trends in sales of women's clothing. Figure 6.1(b) shows a seasonal pattern superimposed over the long-run trend (which, in this case, is a composite of the secular and cyclical trends), and random fluctuations around the seasonal curve.

Time-series analysis can be as simple as projecting or extrapolating an unadjusted trend. When one applies either simple graphic analysis or least squares regression techniques, historical data can be used to determine the average increase or decrease in the series during each period and then projected into the future. Time-series analysis can also be sophisticated, allowing examination of seasonal and cyclical patterns in addition to the basic trend.

Because extrapolation techniques assume that a variable will follow an established path, the problem is to determine the appropriate trend curve. In theory, one could fit any mathematical function to historical data and extrapolate to estimate future values. In practice, linear, simple power, or exponential curves are typically used for economic forecasting.

Secular Trend
Long-run pattern of increase or decrease.

Cyclical Fluctuation
Rhythmic fluctuation in an economic series due to expansion or contraction in the overall economy.

Seasonality
Rhythmic annual patterns in sales or profits.

Irregular or Random Influences
Unpredictable shocks to the economic system.

Linear Trend Analysis

Linear Trend Analysis
Assumes constant *unit* change over time.

Linear trend analysis assumes a constant period-by-period *unit* change in an important economic variable over time. Such a trend is illustrated in Figure 6.2, which displays the 20 years of sales data for Microsoft Corp. given in Table 6.1, along with a curve representing a linear relation between sales and time over the 1985–2004 period.

A linear relation between firm sales and time, such as that illustrated in Figure 6.2, can be written as

$$S_t = a + b \times t$$

6.1

Figure 6.1 Time-Series Characteristics: (A) Secular Trend and Cyclical Variation in Women's Clothing Sales; (B) Seasonal Pattern and Random Fluctuations

(a) The cyclical pattern in sales varies significantly from the normal secular trend. (b) Seasonal patterns, random fluctuations, and other influences cause deviations around the cyclical patterns of sales.

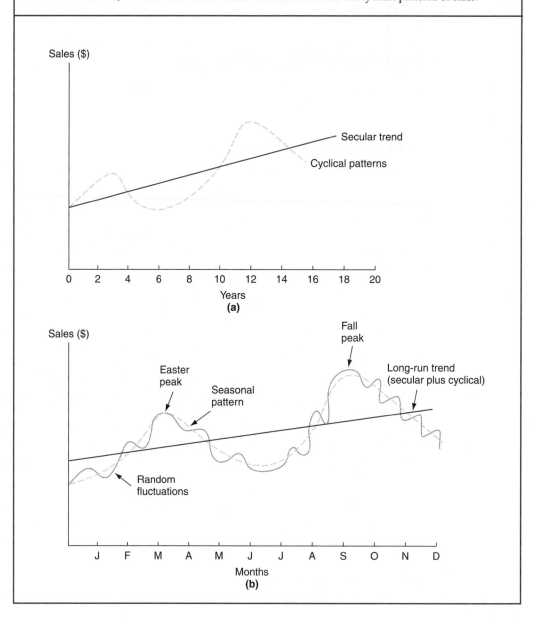

The coefficients of this equation can be estimated by using Microsoft sales data for the 1985–2004 period and the least squares regression method as follows (*t* statistics in parentheses)

$$S_t = -\$8,937.7 + \$1,908.5t \qquad R^2 = 87.2\% \qquad \textbf{6.2}$$
$$(-4.33) \quad (11.06)$$

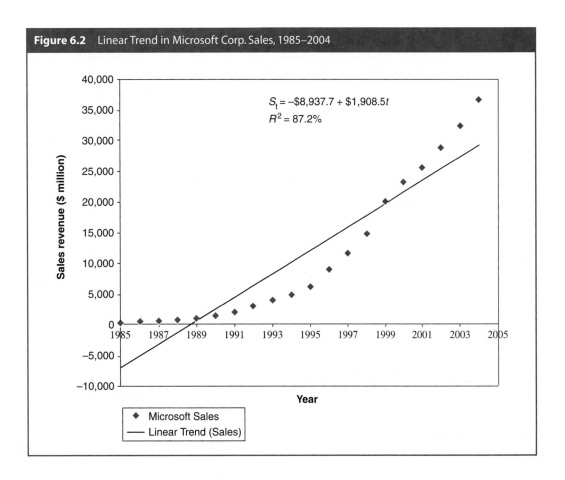

Figure 6.2   Linear Trend in Microsoft Corp. Sales, 1985–2004

$S_t = -\$8,937.7 + \$1,908.5t$

$R^2 = 87.2\%$

Although a linear trend projection for firm sales is relatively naive, an important trend element is obvious in Microsoft sales data. Using the linear trend equation estimated over the 1985–2004 period, it is possible to forecast firm sales for future periods. To do so, it is important to realize that in this model, $t = 1$ for 1985, $t = 2$ for 1986, and so on. This means that $t = 0$ in the 1984 base period. To forecast sales in any future period, simply subtract 1984 from the year in question to determine a relevant value for t.

For example, a sales forecast for the year 2010 using Equation (6.2) is

$$t = 2010 - 1984 = 26$$
$$S_{2010} = -\$8,937.7 + \$1,908.5(26)$$
$$= \$40,683 \text{ million}$$

Similarly, a sales forecast for Microsoft in the year 2015 is

$$t = 2015 - 1984 = 31$$
$$S_{2015} = -\$8,937.7 + \$1,908.5(31)$$
$$= \$50,226 \text{ million}$$

Note that these sales projections are based on a linear trend line, which implies that sales increase by a constant dollar amount each year. In this example, Microsoft sales are

Table 6.1 Sales Revenue for Microsoft Corp., 1985–2004

Year	Sales Revenue ($ millions)	Natural Logarithm of Sales Revenue (Base e)	Common Logarithm of Sales Revenue (Base 10)	Time Period	Fitted Sales (Linear)
1985	139.5	4.938	2.145	1	−7,029.2
1986	202.1	5.309	2.306	2	−5,120.6
1987	345.9	5.846	2.539	3	−3,212.1
1988	590.8	6.381	2.771	4	−1,303.6
1989	803.5	6.689	2.905	5	605.0
1990	1,183.4	7.076	3.073	6	2,513.5
1991	1,843.4	7.519	3.266	7	4,422.1
1992	2,758.7	7.923	3.441	8	6,330.6
1993	3,753.0	8.230	3.574	9	8,239.2
1994	4,649.0	8.444	3.667	10	10,147.7
1995	5,937.0	8.689	3.774	11	12,056.3
1996	8,671.0	9.068	3.938	12	13,964.8
1997	11,358.0	9.338	4.055	13	15,873.4
1998	14,484.0	9.581	4.161	14	17,781.9
1999	19,747.0	9.891	4.296	15	19,690.5
2000	22,956.0	10.041	4.361	16	21,599.0
2001	25,296.0	10.138	4.403	17	23,507.6
2002	28,635.0	10.262	4.457	18	25,416.1
2003	32,187.0	10.379	4.508	19	27,324.7
2004	36,500.0	10.505	4.562	20	29,233.2

Note: 2004 data are preliminary.

Data source: Company annual reports (various years).

projected to grow by $1,908.5 million per year. However, there are important reasons for believing that the true trend for Microsoft sales is nonlinear and that the forecasts generated by this constant change model will be relatively poor estimates of actual values. To see why a linear trend relation may be inaccurate, consider the relation between actual sales data and the linear trend shown in Figure 6.2. Remember that the least squares regression line minimizes the sum of squared residuals between actual and fitted values over the sample data. As is typical, actual data points lie above and below the fitted regression line. Note, however, that the pattern of differences between actual and fitted values varies dramatically over the sample period. Differences between actual and fitted values are generally positive in both early (1985–1990) and later (1999–2004) periods, whereas they are generally negative in the intervening 1991–1998 period. These differences suggest that the slope of the sales–time relation may not be constant but rather may be generally increasing over the 1985–1998 period. Under these circumstances, it may be more appropriate to assume that sales are changing at a constant annual *rate* rather than a constant annual *amount*.

Growth Trend Analysis
Assumes constant *percentage* change over time.

Growth Trend Analysis

Growth trend analysis assumes a constant period-by-period *percentage* change in an important economic variable over time. Such a forecast model has the potential to better capture the increasing annual sales pattern described by the 1985–2004 Microsoft sales data. This model is appropriate for forecasting when sales appear to change over time by a constant proportional amount rather than by the constant absolute amount assumption implicit in a simple linear model. The constant annual rate of growth model, assuming *annual* compounding, is described as follows:

$$\text{Sales in } t \text{ Years} = \text{Current Sales} \times (1 + \text{Growth Rate})^t$$
$$S_t = S_0(1 + g)^t \qquad \textbf{6.3}$$

In words, Equation (6.3) means that sales in t years in the future are equal to current-period sales, S_0, compounded at a constant annual growth rate, g, for a period of t years. Use of the constant annual rate of growth model involves determining the average historical rate of growth in sales and then using that rate of growth in a forecast equation such as Equation (6.3) to project future values.

Just as it is possible to estimate the constant rate of unit change in an economic time series by fitting historical data to a linear regression model of the form $Y = a + bt$, a constant annual rate of growth can also be estimated using that technique. The relevant growth rate is estimated using a linear regression model that is fit to a logarithmic transformation of the historical data. Taking common logarithms (to the base 10) of both sides of Equation (6.3) results in the expression

$$\log S_t = \log S_0 + \log (1 + g) \times t \qquad \textbf{6.4}$$

Notice that Equation (6.4) is an expression of the form

$$Y_t = a + bt$$

where $Y_t = \log S_t$, $a = \log S_0$, $b = \log (1 + g)$, and t is an independent, or X, variable. The coefficients $\log S_0$ and $\log (1 + g)$ can be estimated using the least squares regression technique.

Applying this technique to the Microsoft sales data for the 1985–2004 period results in the linear constant annual rate of growth regression model (t statistics in parentheses)

$$\log S_t = 2.2607 + 0.1285t \qquad R^2 = 96.6\% \qquad \textbf{6.5}$$
$$(33.30) \quad (22.67)$$

Sales revenue forecasts (in millions of dollars) can be determined by transforming this estimated equation back to its original form:

$$S_t = (\text{Antilog } 2.2607) \times (\text{Antilog } 0.1285)^t \qquad \textbf{6.6}$$

or

$$S_t = \$182.3(1.344)^t$$

In this model, \$182.3 million is the adjusted level of sales for $t = 0$, or 1984, because the first year of data used in the regression estimation, $t = 1$, was 1985. The number 1.344 equals 1 plus the average rate of growth using annual compounding, meaning that Microsoft sales increased at a 34.4 percent annual rate from 1984–2004.

To forecast sales in any future year by using this model, subtract 1984 from the year being forecast to determine t. Thus, a constant annual rate of growth model forecast for sales in 2010 is

$$S_{2010} = \$182.3(1.344^{26})$$
$$= \$397,345 \text{ million}$$

Similarly, a constant growth model forecast of Microsoft sales in the year 2015 is

$$S_{2015} = \$182.3(1.344^{31})$$
$$= \$1,742,465 \text{ million}$$

Another frequently used form of the constant growth model is based on an underlying assumption of *continuous*, as opposed to annual, compounding. The continuous growth model is expressed by the exponential equation

$$Y_t = Y_0 e^{gt} \qquad\qquad\qquad \textbf{6.7}$$

Taking the natural logarithm (to the base e) of Equation (6.7) gives

$$\ln Y_t = \ln Y_0 + gt$$

Under an exponential rate of growth assumption, the regression model estimate of the slope coefficient, g, is a direct estimate of the continuous rate of growth. For example, a continuous growth model estimate for Microsoft sales is (t statistics in parentheses)

$$\ln S_t = 5.2056 + 0.2959t \qquad R^2 = 96.6\% \qquad \textbf{6.8}$$
$$(33.30) \quad (22.68)$$

In this equation, the coefficient 0.2959 (= 29.59 percent) is a direct estimate of the continuous compounding growth rate for Microsoft sales. Notice that t statistics for the intercept and slope coefficients are identical to those derived for the constant annual rate of growth regression model [Equation (6.5)].

Again, sales revenue forecasts (in millions of dollars) can be derived by transforming this estimated equation back to its original form:

$$S_t = (\text{Exponentiate } 5.2056) \times (\text{Exponentiate } 0.2959)^t \qquad\qquad \textbf{6.9}$$

or

$$S_t = \$182.3(1.344)^t$$

Notice that Equations (6.6) and (6.9) are identical. Subject to rounding error, identical 2010 and 2015 sales forecasts result by using either the constant annual rate of growth or the continuous compounding assumption. Either method can be relied on with an equal degree of confidence as a useful basis for a constant growth model approach to forecasting.

Linear and Growth Trend Comparison

The importance of selecting the correct structural form for a trend model can be demonstrated by comparing the sales projections that result from the two basic approaches that have been considered. Recall that with the constant change model, Microsoft sales were projected to be $40.7 billion in 2010 and $50.2 billion in 2015. Compare these sales forecasts with projections of $397.3 billion in 2010 and $1,742.5 billion in 2015 for the constant growth rate model. Notice that the difference in the near-term forecasts (2010) is smaller than the difference between longer-term (2015) projections. This shows that if an economic time series is growing at a constant rate rather than increasing by a constant dollar amount, forecasts based on a linear trend model will tend to be less accurate the further one forecasts into the future.

Whether a firm is able to maintain a rapid pace of growth depends on a host of factors both within and beyond its own control. Successfully managing rapid growth over extended periods is extraordinarily difficult and rarely observed. While Microsoft has defied conventional wisdom by maintaining rapid growth for more than 30 years, its massive size will limit future growth at some point. When applying trend projection methods, it is important to establish the degree of similarity in growth opportunities between the historical and the forecast periods. An obvious problem is that the accuracy of trend projections depends upon a continuation of historical patterns for sales, costs, and profits. Serious forecasting errors resulted when this technique was employed in the periods just prior to unanticipated economic downturns in 1982, 1991, and 2001. Trend projections cannot predict cyclical turning points, and offer no help in describing *why* a particular series moves as it does. More sophisticated time-series forecasting methods, such as the Box–Jenkins technique, provide the means for analyzing trend, seasonal, cyclical, and random influences that often shape economic time series in complex business environments.

Managerial Application 6.2

Prediction Markets: The IEM

Prediction markets are speculative exchanges created for the purpose of making accurate forecasts. Tradable assets are created whose final cash value is tied to a particular political event, such as whether the next U.S. president be a Republican or a Democrat, or a specific economic event, such as a change in monetary policy by the Board of Governors of the Federal Reserve System.

Speculators who buy low and sell high are rewarded for improving the market prediction; those who buy high and sell low are punished for degrading the market prediction. Evidence suggests that prediction markets are often more accurate than the experts. Examples of prediction markets open to the public include the Hollywood Stock Exchange, the Iowa Electronic Markets (IEM), and TradeSports, among others. The Hollywood Stock Exchange (http://www.hsx.com) is the entertainment prediction market, and in 2006 correctly predicted 32 of 39 (82 percent) of the "big-category" Oscar nominees and 7 out of 8 (87.5 percent) top category winners. At tradesports.com, players predict who will be the next World Series Champion in baseball, Super Bowl winner in football, or NCAA champion in basketball.

One of the oldest and most famous prediction markets is the University of Iowa's IEM. The IEM is a group of real-money futures markets operated by the University of Iowa Tippie College of Business. Unlike normal futures markets, the IEM is not-for-profit. The IEM's low-stakes markets are run for educational and research purposes. The IEM allows traders to buy and sell contracts based on, among other things, election results and economic indicators. In the fall of 2007, for example, speculators paid 59.9¢ for a contract that would pay $1 if the Democratic candidate won the 2008 presidential election, and zero otherwise. This means that the market prediction was a 59.9 percent probability of a Democratic victory, versus a 40.1 percent probability of a Democratic defeat.

In late-2007, the Republicans had good reason to worry. The IEM's free-market approach has been highly accurate, especially when compared with traditional polling techniques.

See: The Iowa Electronic markets, http://www.biz.uiowa.edu/iem/.

BUSINESS CYCLE

Many important economic time series are regularly influenced by cyclical and seasonal variations.

What Is the Business Cycle?

The profit and sales performance of all companies depends to a greater or lesser extent on the vigor of the overall economy. As shown in Figure 6.3, business activity in the United States expands at a rate of roughly 7 percent per year when measured in terms of GDP. With inflation averaging about 4 percent per year, business activity has expanded at a rate of roughly 3 percent per year when measured in terms of inflation-adjusted, or real, dollars. During robust expansions, the pace of growth in real GDP can increase to an annual rate of 4 percent to 5 percent or more for brief periods. During especially severe economic downturns, real GDP can actually decline for an extended period. In the case of firms that use significant financial and operating leverage, a difference of a few percentage points in the pace of overall economic activity can make the difference between vigorous expansion and gut-wrenching contraction.

Business Cycle
Rhythmic pattern of contraction and expansion in the overall economy.

One of the most important economy-wide considerations for managers is the **business cycle,** or rhythmic pattern of contraction and expansion observed in the overall economy. Table 6.2 shows the pattern of business cycle expansion and contraction that has been experienced in the United States. During the post-World War II period, between 1945 and 2007, there have been ten complete business cycles. The average duration of each cyclical contraction is 10 months, when duration is measured from the previous cyclical peak to the low point or trough of the subsequent business contraction. The average duration of each cyclical expansion is 57 months, as measured by the amount of time from the previous cyclical trough to the peak of the following business expansion. Clearly, periods of economic expansion predominate, which indicates a healthy and growing economy.

Figure 6.3   Gross Domestic Product, 1950–present

Annual GDP growth has averaged 7.07% since 1950; real GDP growth and economic betterment has risen 3.39 per year.

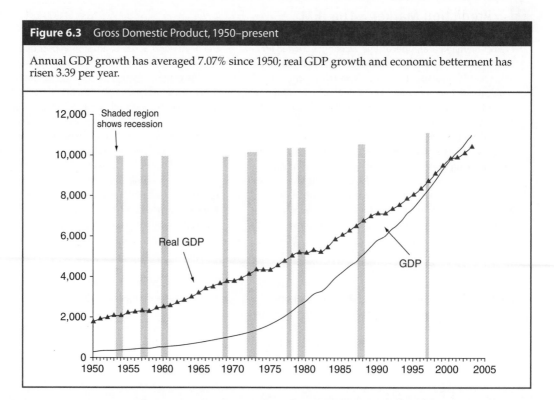

Table 6.2 U.S. Business Cycle Expansions and Contractions

Figures printed in **bold italic** are the wartime expansions (Civil War, World Wars I and II, Korean War, and Vietnam War); the wartime contractions; and the full cycles that include the wartime expansions.

Business Cycle Dates		Duration in Months			
Peak	**Trough**	Contraction	Expansion	Cycle	
(Quarterly dates are in parentheses)		(Peak to trough)	(Previous trough to this peak)	(Trough from previous trough)	(Peak from previous peak)
	December 1854 (IV)	—	—	—	—
June 1857 (II)	December 1858 (IV)	18	30	48	—
October 1860 (III)	June 1861 (III)	8	22	30	40
April 1865 (I)	December 1867 (I)	*32*	*46*	*78*	*54*
June 1869 (II)	December 1870 (IV)	18	18	36	50
October 1873 (III)	March 1879 (I)	65	34	99	52
March 1882 (I)	May 1885 (II)	38	36	74	101
March 1887 (II)	April 1888 (I)	13	22	35	60
July 1890 (III)	May 1891 (II)	10	27	37	40
January 1893 (I)	June 1894 (II)	17	20	37	30
December 1895 (IV)	June 1897 (II)	18	18	36	35
June 1899 (III)	December 1900 (IV)	18	24	42	42
September 1902 (IV)	August 1904 (III)	23	21	44	39
May 1907 (II)	June 1908 (II)	13	33	46	56
January 1910 (I)	January 1912 (IV)	24	19	43	32
January 1913 (I)	December 1914 (IV)	23	12	35	36
August 1918 (III)	March 1919 (I)	*7*	*44*	*51*	*67*
January 1920 (I)	July 1921 (III)	18	10	28	17
May 1923 (II)	July 1924 (III)	14	22	36	40
October 1926 (III)	November 1927 (IV)	13	27	40	41
August 1929 (III)	March 1933 (I)	43	21	64	34
May 1937 (II)	June 1938 (II)	13	50	63	93
February 1945 (I)	October 1945 (IV)	*8*	*80*	*88*	*93*
November 1948 (IV)	October 1949 (IV)	11	37	48	45
July 1953 (II)	May 1954 (II)	*10*	*45*	*55*	*56*
August 1957 (III)	April 1958 (II)	8	39	47	49
April 1960 (II)	February 1961 (I)	10	24	34	32
December 1969 (IV)	November 1970 (IV)	*11*	*106*	*117*	*116*
November 1973 (IV)	March 1975 (I)	16	36	52	47
January 1980 (I)	July 1980 (III)	6	58	64	74
July 1981 (III)	November 1982 (IV)	16	12	28	· 18
July 1990 (III)	March 1991 (I)	8	92	100	108
March 2001 (I)	November 2001 (IV)	8	120	128	128
Average, all cycles:					
1854–2001 (32 cycles)		17	38	55	56[a]
1854–1919 (16 cycles)		22	27	48	49[b]
1919–1945 (6 cycles)		18	35	53	53
1945–2001 (10 cycles)		10	57	67	67
Average, peacetime cycles:					
1854–2001 (27 cycles)		18	33	51	52[c]
1854–1919 (14 cycles)		22	24	46	47[d]
1919–1945 (5 cycles)		20	26	46	45
1945–2001 (8 cycles)		10	52	63	63

[a]31 cycles   [b]15 cycles   [c]26 cycles   [d]13 cycles

Data source: http://www.nber.org/cycles.html.

Economic Indicators

Economic Indicators
Data that describe projected, current, or past economic activity.

Composite Index
Weighted average of leading, coincident, or lagging economic indicators.

The Conference Board is a private research group that provides extensive data on a wide variety of **economic indicators** that describe projected, current, or past economic activity. Table 6.3 lists ten leading, four roughly coincident, and seven lagging economic indicators of business cycle peaks that are broadly relied upon in business cycle forecasting. A **composite index** is a weighted average of leading, coincident, or lagging economic indicators. Keep in mind that the weights (standardization factors) used in the construction of these composite indices vary over time. Combining individual data into a composite index creates a forecasting series with less random fluctuation, or noise. These composite series are smoother than the underlying individual data series and less frequently produce false signals of change in economic conditions. The

---

Table 6.3 Leading, Coincident and Lagging Economic Indicators

The Conference Board's Index of Leading Economic Indicators (LEI) is designed to signal peaks and troughs in the business cycle The LEI is derived from 10 leading indicators, four coincident indicators and seven lagging indicators The LEI is a useful barometer of economic activity over 3 to 6 months

Ten Leading Indicators

Average workweek of production workers in manufacturing
Average initial weekly claims for state unemployment insurance
New orders for consumer goods and materials, adjusted for inflation
Vendor performance (companies receiving slower deliveries from suppliers)
New orders for non-military capital goods, adjusted for inflation
New building permits issued
Index of stock prices
Money supply: M_2 adjusted for inflation
Spread between rates on 10-year Treasury bonds and Federal funds
Index of consumer expectations

Four Coincident Indicators

Manufacturing and trade sales
Employees on non-agricultural payrolls
Industrial production
Personal income minus transfer payments

Seven Lagging Indicators

Average duration of unemployment
Inventories to sales ratio, manufacturing and trade
Change in labor cost per unit of output, manufacturing
Average prime rate
Commercial and industrial loans
Consumer installment credit to personal income ratio
Change in consumer price index for services

Data source: The Conference Board, http://www.conference-board.org/economics/indicators/leading htm.

composite index of leading indicators usually turns down just prior to the start of a recessionary period. Similarly, this data series usually bottoms out and then starts to rise just prior to the start of each subsequent economic expansion. Just as leading indicators seem to earn that description based on their performance, coincident and lagging indicators perform as expected.

The basis for some of these leads and lags is obvious. For example, building permits precede housing starts, and orders for plant and equipment lead production in durable goods industries. Each of these indicators directly reflects plans or commitments for the activity that follows. Other barometers are not directly related to the economic variables they forecast. Common stock prices are a good leading indicator of general business activity. Although the causal linkage may not be readily apparent, stock prices reflect aggregate profit expectations by investors and thus give a consensus view of the likely course of future business conditions. At any point in time, stock prices both reflect and anticipate changes in aggregate economic conditions.

Economic Recessions

Economic Recession
Period of declining economic activity.

An **economic recession** is defined by the National Bureau of Economic Research (NBER), a private nonprofit research organization, as a significant decline in activity spread across the economy that lasts more than a few months. Recessions are visible in terms of falling industrial production, declining real income, shrinking wholesale–retail trade, and rising unemployment. Although many economic recessions consist of two or more quarters of declining real GDP, it is most accurate to describe recession as a period of *diminishing* economic activity rather than a period of *diminished* economic activity. A recession begins just after the economy reaches a peak of output and employment and ends as the economy reaches its trough. The period between a month of peak economic activity and the subsequent economic low point defines the length of a recession. During recessions, economic growth is falling or the economy is actually contracting. As shown in Figure 6.3, recessions in the United States are rare and tend to be brief.

Economic Expansion
Period of rising economic activity.

The period following recession is called **economic expansion.** In many cases, economic activity is below normal during both recessions and through the early part of the subsequent economic expansion. Some refer to periods of less than typical economic growth as slumps, but there is no official recognition or characterization of economic slumps. In any event, expansion is the normal state of the U.S. economy.

Recessions can be caused by any serious unanticipated economic or political event. For example, recessionary fears increased considerably following the tragic events of September 11, 2001. The terrorist attacks on New York City and Washington, DC, took an enormous human and economic toll. The U.S. economy is roughly 25 percent of global GDP. New York City alone contributes more than 4 percent to U.S. personal income, and accounts for almost 3 percent of U.S. nonfarm employment. This awful event was a serious shock for the U.S. and global economy.

In trying to assess economic consequences from the September 11, 2001, tragedies, it is important to understand economic conditions at the time of the crisis and how the economy has responded to adverse shocks in the past. Prior to the terrorist attacks, aggressive monetary policy in the United States pointed to recovery. Various leading economic indicators were starting to improve, but remained below the highest values reached during January, 2000. The Coincident Index of The Conference Board's Business Cycle Indicators clearly reflected tensions present in the U.S. economy when the tragedy took place. At that time, declines in U.S. industrial production and sales were almost exactly offset by rising personal income and employment. Outside the United States, only Australia displayed continuing strength in economic growth. Five important global economies—Japan, South Korea, France, Germany, and the United Kingdom—all showed economic weakness, thus placing the U.S. economy in a precarious position at a time of great national sorrow.

Table 6.4 highlights several unanticipated economic and political events that rocked the United States since 1960. These 17 events had the potential to adversely impact the U.S. economy, but occurred during times of economic prosperity. They also differed in terms of political implications. For example, in the attempted assassination of President Ronald Reagan (March 1981) and the bombing of the Alfred P. Murrah Federal Building in Oklahoma City (April 1995), those responsible were quickly apprehended and no subsequent political events followed. The Iraqi invasion of Kuwait (August 1990), on the other hand, precipitated the Gulf War.

Notice how underlying economic conditions at the time of each crisis were important to their eventual economic impact. Although the tragic events of September 11, 2001, are unprecedented, it is worth noting that economic conditions on September 11, 2001, were similar to those in existence at the time of the Oklahoma City bombing (April 1995) and the Iraqi invasion of Kuwait (August 1990). In each instance, the U.S. economy was decelerating. In the case of the Oklahoma City bombing, the slowdown ended within

Table 6.4 Selected Critical Economic and Political Events (1960–present)

Event	Date	Economic Growth
Cuban Missile Crisis	October 1, 1962	Decelerating
President John F. Kennedy Assassination	November 11, 1963	Decelerating
Reverend Martin Luther King Jr. Assassination	April 4, 1968	Accelerating
Robert F. Kennedy Assassination	June 5, 1968	Accelerating
Israeli Athletes Killed at Munich Olympics	September 5, 1972	Accelerating
OPEC Oil Embargo	October 25, 1973	Accelerating (followed by recession Nov. 1973)
President Ronald Reagan Assassination Attempt	March 30, 1981	Accelerating (sandwiched between recessions)
U.S. Marine Barracks Bombing in Lebanon	October 23, 1983	Accelerating
U.S. Stock Market Crash	October 27, 1987	Accelerating
Iraqi Invasion of Kuwait	Augest 2, 1990	Decelerating (beginning of recession July 1990)
Hurricane Andrew	August 16, 1992	Accelerating
World Trade Center Bombing	Februry 26, 1993	Accelerating
Oklahoma City Bombing	April 19, 1995	Decelerating
U.S. Embassy Bombings in Africa	August 7, 1998	Accelerating
Terrorist Attack on WTC and Pentagon	September 11, 2001	Decelerating
U.S. launches Operation Iraqi Freedom	March 19, 2003	Accelerating
Hurricane Katrina	August 23, 2005	Accelerating

Data source: The Conference Board.

8 months. We now know that the U.S. economy had entered a recession (July 1990–March 1991) prior to the Iraqi invasion, so it's fair to say that neither of these comparable events caused the U.S. economy to dip into recession. Based on the information shown in Table 6.4, it is fair to say that economic trends underway before unprecedented economic and political events greatly influence their economic consequences. The ultimate economic fallout from the terrorist attacks on New York City and Washington, DC, wasn't known until July 17, 2003, when NBER announced that the economy had reached the end of a brief recession in November 2001, and begun a slow upturn.

Significant time lags are often encountered between changes in the macro economy and their official recognition. Table 6.5 shows that NBER's Business Cycle Dating Committee usually waits 6 months to a year before officially recognizing that a major turning point in the economy has passed. This means that by the time a downturn in the economy is officially recognized the subsequent upturn has already begun! Slow reporting, hard to decipher leads and lags in the overall economy, and unpredictable ties between economic and political events combine to make accurate macroeconomic forecasting one of the toughest challenges faced in managerial economics.

Sources of Forecast Information

The National Bureau of Economic Research, Inc. (NBER), founded in 1920, is a private, nonprofit, nonpartisan research organization dedicated to promoting a greater understanding of how the economy works. Their research is conducted by more than 600 university professors around the country, the leading scholars in their fields. The NBER Web site (http://www.nber.org) is a treasure trove of forecast information and insight, and offers a host of links to valuable data resources. Consumer survey information included are the Consumer Expenditure Survey Extracts; Current Population Survey; Early Indicators of Later Work Levels, Disease, and Death; and vital statistics for births, deaths, marriage, and divorce. Links to macro data from government sources include: Federal Reserve Economic Data (FRED); official business cycle dates; experimental coincident, leading, and lagging

---

Table 6.5 Long Time Lags Are Experienced Before Turning Points in the Economy Are Documented

Official documentation of turning in the economy is the responsibility of the Business Cycle Dating Committee of the National Bureau of Economic Research.

Recent Announcement dates:

November 2001 trough announced July 17, 2003.
March 2001 peak announced November 26, 2001.
March 1991 trough announced December 22, 1992.
July 1990 peak announced April 25, 1991.
November 1982 trough announced July 8, 1983.
July 1981 peak announced January 6, 1982.
July 1980 trough announced July 8, 1981.
January 1980 peak announced June 3, 1980.

Data source: National Bureau of Economic Research, http://www.nber.org/cycles.html.

indexes; and savings and investment information for 13 countries. Industry data include the Manufacturing Industry Productivity Database, patent data, imports and exports by Standard Industrial Classification (SIC) category, and IRS information.

Resources for Economists (RFE) on the Internet is another extremely valuable Web site maintained by the American Economic Association and Professor Bill Goffe of the Department of Economics at the State University of New York (SUNY), Oswego campus (http://www.oswego.edu/~economic/econweb.htm). The table of contents for RFE lists hundreds of resources available on the Internet that are of interest to academic and practicing economists, and those interested in economics. RFE is a particularly good place to look for a broad array of business and economic forecasting resources on the Web. For example, under economic forecasting and consulting resources the reader will find the Conference Board's Leading Economic Indicators and various other nongovernmental data; economic commentary from Bank of America Economics and Financial Reports; macro, regional, and electrical forecasts from Foster Associates; microeconomic analysis from Glassman-Oliver Economic Consultants, Inc.; global financial market and foreign exchange analysis from *Wells Fargo Economic Reports,* and so on.

Information about economic trends is also found in leading business publications, like *Fortune, Business Week, The Wall Street Journal,* and *Barron's. Barron's* survey of economic indicators depicts the rate of change in the overall level of economic activity as indicated by GDP, durable and nondurable manufacturing, factory utilization, and other statistics. Also provided are specific data on the level of production in a wide range of basic industries such as autos, electric power, paper, petroleum, and steel. Data published weekly in

Managerial Application 6.3

The Stock Market and the Business Cycle

Many stock market prognosticators advise long-term investors to lighten up in advance of deteriorating economic conditions. Why buy and hold when the economic environment is worsening? Shouldn't smart investors hold cash until the economic experts know that recovery has begun? Then, business news reporters can issue the "all clear" sign, and savvy investors can re-establish long-term positions. If only life were that simple. Unfortunately, it's not.

Economic recessions are notoriously hard to identify. Typically, the National Bureau of Economic Research (NBER) is able to identify the start of an economic recession only months after the recession has begun. By the time economic recessions are identified, the economy is often already well on its way to recovery. In addition, the stock market usually starts to sag well in advance of economic downturns and rally in advance of economic recoveries. Near-term fluctuations in the stock market also give many false signals concerning economic conditions. As a famous economist once remarked, "the stock market has correctly forecast 10 of the last 6 recessions."

Look at how stock market prices change between important economic turning points and when such turns in the economy are officially recognized:

- November 2001 trough (S&P 500 = 1,034.51) announced July 17, 2003 (S&P 500 = 981.73)
- The March 2001 peak (S&P 500 = 1,160.33) announced November 26, 2001 (S&P 500 = 1,157.42)
- The March 1991 trough (S&P 500 = 375.22) announced December 22, 1992 (S&P 500 = 440.31)
- The July 1990 peak (S&P 500 = 356.15) announced April 25, 1991 (S&P 500 = 379.25)
- The November 1982 trough (S&P 500 = 138.93) announced July 8, 1983 (S&P 500 = 167.08)
- The July 1981 peak (S&P 500 = 130.92) announced January 6, 1982 (S&P 500 = 119.18)
- The July 1980 trough (S&P 500 = 121.67) announced July 8, 1981 (S&P 500 = 132.24)
- The January 1980 peak (S&P 500 = 114.16) announced June 3, 1980 (S&P 500 = 110.51)

Upshot: Trading stocks based upon NBER announcements is not a sophisticated way of market timing.

See: Mickey D. Levy, "No Recession in Sight," *The Wall Street Journal Online,* October 9, 2007, http://online.wsj.com.

Barron's include not only the level of production (what is made), but also distribution (what is sold), inventories (what is on hand), new orders received, unfilled orders, purchasing power, employment, and construction activity. *Forbes* magazine publishes its own biweekly index of economic activity using government data on consumer prices, manufacturers' new orders and inventories, industrial production, new housing starts, personal income, new unemployment claims, retail sales, and consumer installment credit.

EXPONENTIAL SMOOTHING

A variety of averaging techniques can be used to predict unit sales growth, revenue, costs, and profit performance.

Exponential Smoothing Concept

Exponential Smoothing
Averaging method for forecasting time series of data.

Exponential smoothing is a method for forecasting trends in unit sales, unit costs, wage expenses, and so on. The technique identifies historical patterns of trend or seasonality in the data and then extrapolates these patterns forward into the forecast period. Its accuracy depends on the degree to which established patterns of change are apparent and constant over time. The more regular the pattern of change in any given data series, the easier it is to forecast. Exponential smoothing (or "averaging") techniques are among the most widely used forecasting methods in business.

All leading methods of exponential smoothing involve the same essential process of data averaging. The data series to be forecast is assumed to be modeled by one, two, or three essential components. Key components represent the level, trend, or seasonality of the data being forecast. The level of the time series to be forecast is the average about which it fluctuates. This level may be constant or slowly changing. Trend is any systematic change in the level of the time series of data. If a given forecast model includes a trend, then that trend is either projected as a straight line into the future or as a gradually diminishing amount that eventually dies out. The seasonality of a time series is a pattern of change tied to weather, custom, or tradition. Retail sales typically exhibit a strong seasonal trend over the course of the year. Many stores book 30 percent or more of annual sales during the busy Christmas selling season. Seasonal components can be additive, meaning that seasonal patterns remain constant over time, or multiplicative, meaning that seasonal patterns grow with the average level of the series.

Figure 6.4 shows nine common profiles of data that can be forecast by using popular exponential smoothing techniques. They range in complexity from the constant level of data shown in Figure 6.4(a), to the more complex dampened trend with a multiplicative seasonal influence shown in Figure 6.4(i). To ensure that the correct exponential smoothing technique is chosen, a method with sufficient flexibility to conform to the underlying data must be used. A good first step in the exponential smoothing process is to graph the data series to be forecast and then choose the exponential smoothing method that best resembles the data.

One-Parameter (Simple) Exponential Smoothing

One-Parameter (Simple) Exponential Smoothing
Method for forecasting slowly changing levels.

In **one-parameter (simple) exponential smoothing,** the sole regular component is the level of the forecast data series. It is implicitly assumed that the data consist of irregular fluctuations around a constant or very slowly changing level. Simple exponential smoothing is appropriate for forecasting sales in mature markets with stable activity; it is inappropriate for forecasting in markets that are growing rapidly or are seasonal.

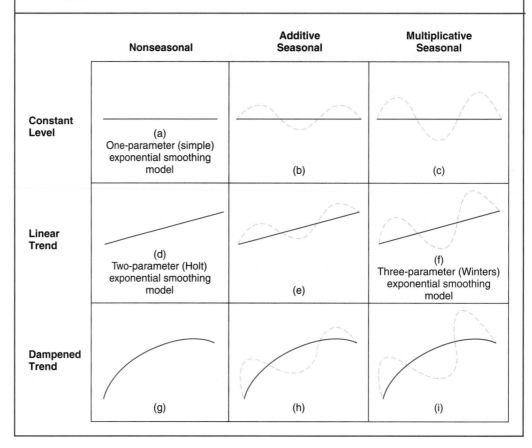

Figure 6.4   Nine Common Trends in Economic Time Series Can Be Forecast by Using Exponential Smoothing Methods

Forecasting economic time series often involves a consideration of changes in the level, trend, and/or seasonality of the data.

In the simple exponential smoothing model, each smoothed estimate of a given level is computed as a weighted average of the current observation and past data. Each weight decreases in an exponential pattern. The rate of decrease in the influence of past levels depends on the size of the smoothing parameter that controls the model's relative sensitivity to newer versus older data. The larger the value of the smoothing parameter, the more is the emphasis placed on recent versus distant observations. However, if the smoothing parameter is very small, then a large number of data points receive nearly equal weights. In this case, the forecast model displays a long "memory" of past values.

Two-Parameter (Holt) Exponential Smoothing

Two-Parameter (Holt) Exponential Smoothing
Method for forecasting stable growth.

Simple exponential smoothing is not appropriate for forecasting data that exhibit extended trends. In **two-parameter (Holt) exponential smoothing,** the data are assumed to consist of fluctuations about a level that is changing with some constant or slowly drifting linear trend. Two-parameter exponential smoothing is often called the Holt method, after its originator C. C. Holt.[2] Two-parameter exponential smoothing is appropriate for forecasting sales in established markets with stable growth; it is inappropriate in either stable or rapidly growing markets.

Holt's exponential smoothing model uses a smoothed estimate of the trend component as well as the level component to produce forecasts. In the two-parameter exponential smoothing forecast equation, the current smoothed level is added to a linear trend to forecast future values. The updated value of the smoothed level is computed as the weighted average of new data and the best estimate of the new level based on old data. The Holt method combines old and new estimates of the one-period change of the smoothed level, thus defining the current linear or local trend.

Three-Parameter (Winters) Exponential Smoothing

Three-Parameter (Winters) Exponential Smoothing
Method for forecasting seasonally adjusted growth.

The **three-parameter (Winters) exponential smoothing** method extends the two-parameter technique by including a smoothed multiplicative index to account for the seasonal behavior of the forecast series. The three-parameter exponential smoothing technique is often called the Winters method, after its originator P. R. Winters.[3] Because much economic data involve both growth trend and seasonal considerations, three-parameter exponential smoothing is one of the most commonly used forecasting methods. It is best suited for forecasting problems that involve rapid and/or changing rates of growth combined with seasonal influences. Three-parameter exponential smoothing is suitable for forecasting sales in both rapidly growing markets and in rapidly decaying markets with seasonal influences.

Winters' three-parameter exponential smoothing model assumes that each observation is the product of a deseasonalized value and a seasonal index for that particular month or quarter. The deseasonalized values are assumed to be described by the Holt model. The Winters model involves three smoothing parameters to be used in level, trend, and seasonal index smoothing equations. The Winters model forecast is computed similarly to the Holt model forecast and then multiplied by the seasonal index for the current period. Smoothing in the Winters model is similar to the Holt model, except that in the Winters model the measurement of level is deseasonalized through dividing by the seasonal index calculated 1 year before. The trend smoothing equations of the two models are identical. The seasonal index is estimated as the ratio of the current observation to the current smoothed level, averaged with the previous value for that particular period.

Practical Use of Exponential Smoothing

The important point to remember about exponential smoothing, or any forecast method, is that the choice of an appropriate forecasting technique depends on the pattern data that is to be forecast.

As a case in point, Figure 6.5 shows a typical pattern of sales for the life cycle of a product. Product life cycles often progress from the introduction point, to rapid growth and market penetration, to a mature phase of sales stability, to periods of declining market share and abandonment. Over this life cycle, different methods of sales forecasting may be appropriate.

---

2   C. C. Holt, *Forecasting Seasonals and Trends by Exponentially Weighted Moving Averages* (Pittsburgh, PA: Carnegie Institute of Technology, 1957).

3   P. R. Winters, "Forecasting Sales by Exponentially Weighted Moving Averages," *Management Science* 6 (April 1960), 324–342.

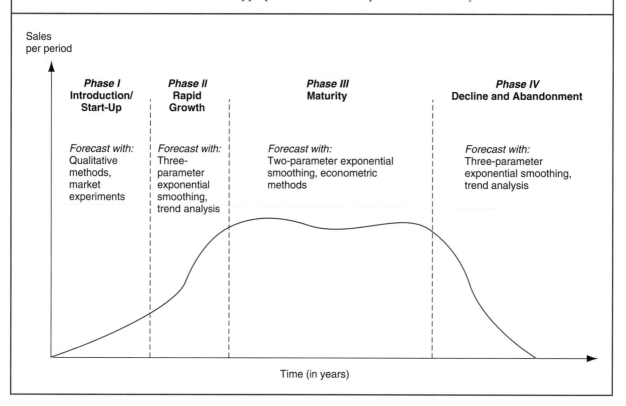

Figure 6.5   The Appropriate Forecast Technique Tends to Vary Over the Life Cycle of a Product

The life cycle of a product often involves an introduction or start-up period, followed by rapid growth, maturity, decline, and abandonment. The choice of an appropriate forecast technique varies over this cycle.

In the initial phase, and before the generation of significant market data, qualitative analyses and market experiments are highly appropriate. Once the product has been launched and is rapidly gaining market acceptance, in phase II, three-parameter exponential smoothing methods that involve level, trend, and seasonal components become relevant. In the mature phase of sales stability, phase III, two-parameter exponential smoothing models (or econometric models) that incorporate level and seasonal components are suitable. In the fourth and final phase of declining market share and abandonment, three-parameter exponential smoothing methods that involve level, trend, and seasonal components again become relevant.

ECONOMETRIC FORECASTING

Econometric Methods
Use of economic theory and statistical tools to forecast economic relations.

Econometric methods combine economic theory with statistical tools to predict economic relations.

Advantages of Econometric Methods

Econometric methods force the forecaster to make explicit assumptions about the linkages among the variables in the economic system being examined. In other words,

Managerial Application 6.4

How Good Is *Your* Forecasting Ability?

When making predictions of economic and social change, it is vitally important to be aware of broad trends in the overall economy. One valuable source of information on the U.S. economy is the *Statistical Abstract of the United States*. This annual publication of the U.S. Bureau of the Census offers a wealth of economic and demographic data that private and public sector analysts rely upon.

The following table offers insight concerning a number of important economic and social trends, and simple trend extrapolation estimates for the year 2010. Which forecasts will prove accurate? Which forecasts will be wide of the mark? How will these trends change over the *next* 20 years?

See: *Statistical Abstract of the United States*, http://www.census.gov/statab/www/.

Category	1990	2000[a]	Percent Change	2010 (est.)
ACT score, comp.	20.6	21.0	1.9%	21.4
Births (000)	4,158	3,942	−5.2%	3,737
Cable TV subscribers (mil.)	50.0	66.5	33.0%	88.4
Cash flow, corp. ($bil.)	$506	$943	86.4%	$1,757
Cellular telephone subscribers (mil.)	5.3	86.0	1522.6%	1,395.5
Corporate deaths (000)	546.5	512.4	−6.2%	480.4
Corporate startups (000)	541.1	597.8	10.5%	660.4
Corporations (000)	3,717	4,710	26.7%	5,968
Crude oil imports (mil. bbl)	2,151	3,187	48.2%	4,722
Crude oil production (mil. bbl)	2,685	2,147	−20.0%	1,717
Daily newspaper circulation (mil.)	62.3	56.0	−10.1%	50.3
Deaths (000)	2,148	2,338	8.8%	2,545
Divorces (000)	1,182	1,150	−2.7%	1,119
DJIA	2,810.20	11,357.50	304.2%	45,902
Employment (mil.)	118.8	135.2	13.8%	153.9
Farms (000)	2,146	2,172	1.2%	2,198
Federal govt. receipts ($bil.)	$1,032	$1,956	89.5%	$3,707
Federal govt. spending ($bil.)	$1,253	$1,790	42.9%	$2,557
GDP ($bil.)	$5,803	$9,963	71.7%	$17,105
GDP per capita	$26,834	$33,833	26.1%	$42,658
GDP, 1996 dollars ($bil.)	$6,708	$9,319	38.9%	$12,946
Golfers	27,800	26,427	−4.9%	25.122
Health care spending ($bil.)	$696	$1,211	74.0%	$2,107
Health care spending, Medicare ($bil.)	$110	$214	94.5%	$416
High school dropouts (000)	3,800	3,829	0.8%	3,858
High school grads (000)	8,370	6,999	−16.4%	5,853
Housing units (mil.)	94.2	105.7	12.2%	118.6
Housing units, owner-occupied (%)	63.9	67.4	5.5%	71.1
Induced abortions (000)	1,609	1,366	−15.1%	1,160
Interest rate, mortgage (%)	10.08	7.5	−26.1%	5.51
Interest rate, prime (%)	10.01	9.2	−7.8%	8.51
Marriages (000)	2,443	2,334	−4.5%	2,230
MLB attn. (000)	55,512	71,129	28.1%	91,139
MLB player salary ($000)	$598	$1,399	133.9%	$3,273
Motion picture receipts ($mil.)	$39,982	$66,229	65.6%	$109,706

Category	1990	2000[a]	Percent Change	2010 (est.)
Murders	23,400	15,500	−33.8%	10,267
NCAA basketball attn. (000)	28,741	28,032	−2.5%	27,340
NCAA football attn. (000)	35,330	37,491	6.1%	39.784
Partnerships (000)	1,554	1,759	13.2%	1,991
Patents	99,200	163,100	64.4%	268,161
Pay, Annual average	$23,600	$33,300	41.1%	$46,987
PhDs granted	36,068	42,063	16.6%	49.054
Population, African American (mil.)	30.0	34.7	15.7%	40.1
Population, Total (mil.)	247.8	281.4	13.6%	319.6
Profit margin (mfg., %)	3.9	6.3	61.5%	10
Profit, ROE (mfg., %)	10.6	16.7	57.5%	26
Profits, corp. ($bil.)	$402	$849	111.2%	$1,793
Profits, corp. (after tax, $bil.)	$261	$589	125.7%	$1,329
R&D ($mil.)	$152,039	$257,000	69.0%	$434,421
Retail store sales ($bil.)	$1,845	$3,232	75.2%	$5,662
SAT score, math	501	511	2.0%	521
SAT score, verbal	502	505	0.6%	508
Scientists and engineers (000)	758.5	974.6	28.5%	1,252.3
Scouts, boy (000)	4,293	4,956	15.4%	5,721
Scouts, girl (000)	2,480	2,749	10.8%	3,047
Trade exports ($bil.)	$394	$782	98.5%	$1,552
Trade imports ($bil.)	$495	$1,217	145.9%	$2,992
Travelers (Foreign to U.S.) (000)	39,363	46,395	17.9%	54,683
Travelers (U.S. to foreign) (000)	44,623	56,287	26.1%	71,000
Unemployment (mil.)	7.0	5.7	−18.6%	4.6

[a] 2000 figure or latest number available.

the forecaster must deal with causal relations. This produces logical consistency in the forecast model and increases reliability.

Another advantage of econometric methods is that the forecaster can compare forecasts with actual results and use insights gained to improve the forecast model. By feeding past forecasting errors back into the model, new parameter estimates can be generated to improve future forecasting results. The type of output provided by econometric forecasts is another major advantage. Because econometric models offer estimates of actual values for forecasted variables, these models indicate both the direction and magnitude of change. And finally, perhaps the most important advantage of econometric models relates to their ability to explain economic phenomena.

Single-Equation Models

Many managerial forecasting problems can be adequately addressed with single-equation econometric models. The first step in developing an econometric model is to express relevant economic relations in the form of an equation. When constructing a model for forecasting the regional demand for portable personal computers, one might hypothesize that computer demand (C) is determined by price (P), disposable income (I), population (Pop), interest rates (i), and advertising expenditures (A). A linear model expressing this relation is

$$C = a_0 + a_1P + a_2I + a_3Pop + a_4i + a_5A \qquad \textbf{6.10}$$

The next step in econometric modeling is to estimate the parameters of the system, or values of the coefficients, as in Equation (6.10). The most frequently used technique for parameter estimation is the application of least squares regression analysis with either time-series or cross-section data.

Once the model coefficients have been estimated, forecasting with a single-equation model consists of evaluating the equation with specific values for the independent variables. An econometric model used for forecasting purposes must contain independent or explanatory variables whose values for the forecast period can be readily obtained.

Multiple-Equation Systems

Although forecasting problems can often be analyzed with a single-equation model, complex relations among economic variables sometimes require use of multiple-equation systems. Variables whose values are determined within such a model are *endogenous*, meaning originating from within; those determined external to the system are referred to as *exogenous*. The values of endogenous variables are determined by the model; the values of exogenous variables are given externally. Endogenous variables are equivalent to the dependent variable in a single-equation system; exogenous and predetermined variables are equivalent to the independent variables.

Identities
Economic relations that are true by definition.

Multiple-equation econometric models are composed of two basic kinds of expressions: identities and behavioral equations. **Identities** express relations that are true by definition. The statement that profits (π) equal total revenue (TR) minus total cost (TC) is an example of an identity:

$$\pi = TR - TC \qquad \textbf{6.11}$$

Profits are defined by the relation expressed in Equation (6.11).

Behavioral Equations
Economic relations that are hypothesized to be true.

The second group of equations encountered in econometric models, **behavioral equations,** reflects hypotheses about how variables in a system interact with each other. Behavioral equations may indicate how individuals and institutions are expected to react to various stimuli.

Perhaps the easiest way to illustrate the use of multiple-equation systems is to examine a simple three-equation forecast model for equipment and related software sales for a personal computer retailer. As you recall, Equation (6.10) expressed a single-equation model that might be used to forecast regional demand for personal computers. Total revenues for a typical retailer usually include not only sales of personal computers but also sales of software programs (including computer games) and sales of peripheral equipment (e.g., monitors, printers, etc.). Although actual econometric models used to forecast total sales revenue from these items might include several equations and many variables, the simple system described in this section should suffice to provide insight into the multiple-equation approach without being overly complex. The three equations are

$$S_t = b_0 + b_1TR_t + u_1 \qquad \textbf{6.12}$$

$$P_t = c_0 + c_1C_{t-1} + u_2 \qquad \textbf{6.13}$$

$$TR_t = S_t + P_t + C_t \qquad \textbf{6.14}$$

where S is software sales, TR is total revenue, P is peripheral sales, C is personal computer sales, t is the current time period, $t-1$ is the previous time period, and u_1 and u_2 are error, or residual, terms.

Equations (6.12) and (6.13) are behavioral hypotheses. Equation (6.12) hypothesizes that current-period software sales are a function of the current level of total revenues; Equation (6.13) hypothesizes that peripheral sales depend on previous-period personal computer sales. The last equation in the system, Equation (6.14), is an identity. It defines total revenue as being the sum of software, peripheral equipment, and personal computer sales.

Stochastic disturbance terms in the behavioral equations, u_1 and u_2, are included because hypothesized relations are not exact. Other factors that can affect software and peripheral sales are not accounted for in the system. So long as these stochastic elements are random and their expected values are zero, they do not present a barrier to empirical estimation of system parameters. If error terms are not randomly distributed, parameter estimates will be biased and the reliability of model forecasts will be questionable. Large error terms, even if they are distributed randomly, reduce forecast accuracy.

To forecast next year's software and peripheral sales and total revenue as represented by this illustrative model, it is necessary to express S, P, and TR in terms of variables whose values are known or can be estimated at the moment the forecast is generated. In other words, each endogenous variable (S_t, P_t, and TR_t) must be expressed in terms of the exogenous and predetermined variables (C_{t-1} and C_t). Such relations are called reduced-form equations because they reduce complex simultaneous relations to their most basic and simple form. Consider the manipulations of equations in the system necessary to solve for TR via its reduced-form equation.

Substituting Equation (6.12) into (6.14)—that is, replacing S_t with Equation (6.12)—results in[4]

$$TR_t = b_0 + b_1 TR_t + P_t + C_t \qquad\qquad \textbf{6.15}$$

A similar substitution of Equation (6.13) for P_t produces

$$TR_t = b_0 + b_1 TR_t + c_0 + c_1 C_{t-1} + C_t \qquad\qquad \textbf{6.16}$$

Collecting terms and isolating TR in Equation (6.16) gives

$$(1 - b_1)TR_t = b_0 + c_0 + c_1 C_{t-1} + C_t$$

or, alternatively,

$$
\begin{aligned}
TR_t &= \frac{b_0 + c_0 + c_1 C_{t-1} + C_t}{(1 - b_1)} \\
&= \frac{(b_0 + c_0)}{(1 - b_1)} + \frac{c_1}{(1 - b_1)} C_{t-1} + \frac{1}{(1 - b_1)} C_t \qquad\qquad \textbf{6.17}
\end{aligned}
$$

Equation (6.17) now relates current total revenues to previous-period and current-period personal computer sales. Assuming that data on previous-period personal computer sales can be obtained and that current-period personal computer sales can be estimated by using Equation (6.10), Equation (6.17) provides a forecasting model that accounts for the

---

4   The stochastic disturbance terms (u_1 and u_2) have been dropped from the illustration because their expected values are zero. The final equation for TR, however, is stochastic in nature.

simultaneous relations expressed in this simplified multiple-equation system. In real-world situations, it is likely that personal computer sales depend on the price, quantity, and quality of available software and peripheral equipment. Then S, P, and C, along with other important factors, may all be endogenous, involving a number of relations in a complex multiple-equation system. Disentangling the important but often subtle relations involved makes forecasting with multiple-equation systems both intriguing and challenging.

JUDGING FORECAST RELIABILITY

Forecast Reliability
Predictive consistency.

Forecast reliability, or predictive consistency, must be adequately assessed prior to the implementation of any successful forecasting program.

Tests of Predictive Capability

To test predictive capability, a forecast model generated over one sample or period is used to forecast data for some alternative sample or period. The reliability of a model for predicting firm sales, such as that shown in Equation (6.2), can be tested by examining the relation between forecast and actual data for years beyond the period over which the forecast model was estimated. However, it is often desirable to test a forecast model without waiting for new data to become available. In such instances, one can divide available data into two subsamples, called a **test group** and a **forecast group.** The forecaster estimates a forecasting model using data from the test group and uses the resulting model to "forecast" the data of interest in the forecast group. A comparison of forecast and actual values can then be conducted to test the stability of the underlying cost or demand relation.

Forecast Reliability
Predictive consistency.

Forecast Group
Subsample of data used to test a forecast model.

Correlation Analysis

In analyzing a model's forecast capability, the correlation between forecast and actual values is of substantial interest. The formula for the simple correlation coefficient, r, for forecast and actual values, f and x, respectively, is

$$r = \frac{\sigma_{fx}}{\sigma_f \, \sigma_x}$$

6.18

where σ_{fx} is the covariance between the forecast and actual series, and σ_f and σ_x are the sample standard deviations of the forecast and actual series, respectively. Generally speaking, correlations between forecast and actual values in excess of 0.99 (99 percent) are highly desirable and indicate that the forecast model being considered constitutes an effective tool for analysis.

In cross-section analysis, in which the important trend element in most economic data is held constant, a correlation of 99 percent between forecast and actual values is rare. When unusually difficult forecasting problems are being addressed, correlations of 90 percent or 95 percent between forecast and actual data may prove satisfactory. In critical decision situations, forecast and actual data may have to exhibit correlation of 99.5 percent or 99.75 percent to generate a high level of confidence in forecast reliability.

Sample Mean Forecast Error
Estimate of average forecast error.

Sample Mean Forecast Error Analysis

Further evaluation of a model's predictive capability can be made through consideration of a measure called the **sample mean forecast error,** which provides a useful estimate of the average forecast error of the model. It is sometimes called the root mean squared forecast error and is denoted by the symbol U. The sample mean forecast error is calculated as

$$U = \sqrt{\frac{1}{n}\sum_{i=1}^{n}(f_i - x_i)^2}$$ **6.19**

where n is the number of sample observations, f_i is a forecast value, and x_i is the corresponding actual value. Deviations between forecast and actual values are squared in the calculation of the mean forecast error to prevent positive and negative deviations from canceling each other out. The smaller the sample mean forecast error, the greater the accuracy associated with the forecasting model.

CHOOSING THE BEST FORECAST TECHNIQUE

The best forecast technique is one that carefully balances marginal costs and Marginal benefits.

Data Requirements

The choice of an appropriate forecast technique often hinges on the amount of relevant historical data that is readily available and any obvious patterns in that data. For many important forecast problems, 10 years of monthly data (120 observations) are available and appropriate for forecasting future activity. In such cases, the full range of advanced forecast techniques can be considered. If only more restricted samples of data are available for analysis, then simpler forecast methods must be used.

If trend, cyclical, seasonal, or irregular patterns can be recognized, then forecast techniques that are capable of handling those patterns can be readily selected. For example, if the data are relatively stable, a simple exponential smoothing approach may be adequate. Other exponential smoothing models are appropriate for trending and seasonal data; the same model will not be applicable in all cases. As the forecast horizon increases, the cyclical pattern of economic data may also become significant. In these cases, the need to relate the forecast variable to economic, market, and competitive factors increases, because simple trend projections may no longer be appropriate.

Time Horizon Considerations

Experience shows that sophisticated time-series models can provide accurate short-term forecasts. In the short term, the momentum of existing consumer behavior often resists dramatic change. Over a 5-year period, however, customers can find new suppliers, and needs may change. For long-range forecasts, econometric models are often appropriate. In the long term, it is essential to relate the item being forecast to its "drivers," as explanatory factors are sometimes called.

The accuracy of econometric models depends on the precision with which explanatory factors can be predicted. Although these models can also be used in the short term, they are costlier and more complex than simple exponential smoothing methods. When economic conditions are stable, econometric models are seldom more accurate than more simple trend projections and exponential smoothing methods.

As shown in Table 6.6, simple trend, econometric models, and exponential smoothing methods are all used for problems involving 3-year to 5-year forecasts. Over this

Table 6.6 A Subjective Comparison of Alternative Forecast Techniques

	Qualitative Forecasting Methods				Quantitative Forecasting Methods						
					Statistical				Deterministic		
	Personal Insight	Delphi Method	Panel Consensus	Market Reasearch	Summary Statistics	Trend Projections	Exponential Smoothing	Econometric Models	Market Survey	Leading Indicator	Econometric Models
Patterns of data that can be recognized and handled easily.											
Trend	Not Applicable	Not Applicable	Not Applicable	✓	✓	✓	✓	✓	✓	✓	✓
Seasonal				✓	✓		✓	✓	✓		✓
Cyclical				✓	✓			✓	✓		✓
Minimum data requirements.	Not Applicable	Not Applicable		Low	Medium	Medium	High	Low	Medium	High	High
Time horizon for which method is appropriate.											
Short term (0–3 mos.)	✓	✓	✓	✓	✓	✓	✓	✓	✓	✓	✓
Medium term (12–24 mos.)	✓	✓	✓	✓	✓	✓	✓	✓	✓	✓	✓
Long term (2 years or more)			✓	✓	✓	✓		✓			✓
Accuracy											
Predicting patterns.	Medium	Medium	Medium	Medium	Low	Medium	Low	High	Low	Low	Low
Predicting turning points.	Low	Medium	Medium	Medium	NA	Low	Low	Medium	High	Medium	Medium
Applicability											
Time required to obtain forecast.	Medium	Medium	Medium	High	Low	Medium	Low	Medium	Medium	Medium	High
Ease of understanding and interpreting the results	High	High	High	High	High	High	Medium	High	High	High	Medium
Computer costs											
Development	Not Applicable	Not Applicable	Not Applicable	Medium	Medium	Medium	High	Medium	Low	High	High
Storage requirements				Low	Low	Medium	Low	Medium	NA	High	High
Running	High	High	High	Low	Low	Medium	Low	Medium	NA	NA	High

intermediate term, trend projection techniques are relatively inexpensive to apply, but may produce forecasts that are not as accurate as those resulting from econometric methods. When sufficient data exist and the need for accuracy is great, the use of exponential smoothing or econometric models is often recommended. Then, the generally superior short-term forecasting abilities of smoothing models emerge. Also evident over the intermediate term are the advantages of econometric models, which are superior in relating the data to be forecast to economic conditions, price changes, competitive activities, and other explanatory variables.

When both smoothing and econometric models yield similar forecasts, managers can be reasonably certain that the forecast is consistent with underlying assumptions and has a good chance of being accurate. When forecasts produced by two or more methods are significantly different, this is a warning to exercise extreme care.

Role of Judgment

To determine a suitable level of forecast accuracy, one must compare the costs and benefits of increased accuracy. When forecast accuracy is low, the probability of significant forecasting error is high, as is the chance of making suboptimal managerial decisions. Conversely, when forecast accuracy is high, the probability of substantial forecasting error is reduced and the chance of making erroneous managerial decisions is low. It is reasonable to require a relatively high level of forecast accuracy when the costs of forecast error are high. When only minor costs result from forecast error, inexpensive and less precise methods can be justified.

It is worth emphasizing that the objective of economic forecasting is to improve on the subjective judgments made by managers. All managers forecast; the goal is to make better forecasts. Nowhere in the forecasting process is the subjective judgment of managers relied on so heavily as it is in the selection of an appropriate forecast method. When it comes to the selection of the best forecast technique, there is no substitute for seasoned business judgment.

SUMMARY

This chapter examines several techniques for economic forecasting, including qualitative analysis, trend analysis and projection, econometric models, and input–output methods.

- **Qualitative analysis** is an intuitive approach to forecasting that is useful when based on unbiased, informed opinion. The **personal insight** method is one in which an informed individual uses personal or organizational experience as a basis for developing future expectations. The **panel consensus** method relies on the informed opinion of several individuals. In the **Delphi method,** responses from a panel of experts are analyzed by an independent party to elicit a consensus opinion. **Survey techniques** that use interviews or mailed questionnaires constitute another important forecasting tool, especially for short-term projections.

- **Trend analysis** involves characterizing the historical pattern of an economic variable and then projecting its future path based on experience. A **secular trend** is the long-run pattern of increase or decrease in economic data. **Cyclical fluctuation** describes the rhythmic variation in economic series that is due to a pattern of expansion or contraction in the overall economy. Seasonal variation, or **seasonality,** is a rhythmic annual pattern in sales or profits caused by weather, habit, or social custom. **Irregular or random influences** are unpredictable shocks to the economic system and the pace of economic activity caused by wars, strikes, natural catastrophes, and so on.

- A simple **linear trend analysis** assumes a constant period-by-period *unit* change in an important economic variable over time. **Growth trend analysis** assumes a constant period-by-period *percentage* change in an important economic variable over time.

- **Macroeconomic forecasting** involves predicting the pace of economic activity, employment, or interest rates at the international, national, or regional level. **Microeconomic forecasting** involves predicting economic performance at the industry, firm, or plant level.

- The **business cycle** is the rhythmic pattern of contraction and expansion observed in the overall economy. **Economic indicators** are series of data that successfully describe the pattern of projected, current, or past economic activity. A **composite index** is a weighted average of leading, coincident, or lagging economic indicators. An **economic recession** is a significant decline in activity spread across the economy that lasts more than a few months. Recessions are visible in terms of falling industrial production, declining real income, shrinking wholesale–retail transactions, and rising unemployment. An **economic expansion** exhibits rising economic activity.

- **Exponential smoothing** (or "averaging") techniques are among the most widely used forecasting methods. In **two-parameter (Holt) exponential smoothing,** the data are assumed to consist of fluctuations about a level that is changing with some constant or slowly drifting linear trend. The **three-parameter (Winters) exponential smoothing** method extends the two-parameter technique by including a smoothed multiplicative seasonal index to account for the seasonal behavior of the forecast series.

- **Econometric methods** use economic theory and mathematical and statistical tools to forecast economic relations. **Identities** are economic relations that are true by definition. **Behavioral equations** are hypothesized economic relations that are estimated by using econometric methods.

- **Forecast reliability,** or predictive consistency, must be accurately judged in order to assess the degree of confidence that should be placed in economic forecasts. A given forecast model is often estimated by using a **test group** of data and evaluated by using **forecast group** data. No forecasting assignment is complete until reliability has been quantified and evaluated. The **sample mean forecast error** is one useful measure of predictive capability.

The appropriate forecasting technique depends upon the distance into the future being forecast, the lead time available, the accuracy required, the quality of data available for analysis, and the nature of the economic relations involved in the forecasting problem.

QUESTIONS

Q6.1 Discuss some of the microeconomic and macroeconomic factors a firm must consider in its own sales and profit forecasting.

Q6.2 Forecasting the success of new product introductions is notoriously difficult. Describe some of the macroeconomic and microeconomic factors that a firm might consider in forecasting sales for a new teeth-whitening product.

Q6.3 Blue Chip Financial Forecasts gives the latest prevailing opinion about the future direction of the economy. Survey participants include 50 business economists from Deutsche Banc Alex. Brown, Banc of America Securities, Fannie Mae, and other prominent corporations. Each prediction is published along with the average or consensus forecast. Also published are averages of the ten highest and ten lowest forecasts; a median forecast; the number of forecasts raised, lowered, or left unchanged from a month ago; and a diffusion index that indicates shifts in sentiment that sometimes occur prior to changes in the consensus forecast. Explain how this approach helps limit the steamroller or bandwagon problems of the panel consensus method.

Q6.4 "Interest rates were expected to increase by 85 percent of all consumers in the May 2004 survey, more than ever before," said Richard Curtin, the director of the University of Michigan's Surveys of Consumers. "More consumers in the May 2004 survey cited the advantage of obtaining a mortgage in advance of any additional increases in interest rates than any other time in nearly 10 years," said Curtin. Discuss this statement and explain why consumer surveys are an imperfect guide to consumer expectations.

Q6.5 Explain why revenue and profit data reported by shippers such as FedEx Corp. and United Parcel Service, Inc., can provide useful information about trends in the overall economy.

Q6.6 In prepared remarks before Congress in mid-2007, Federal Reserve chairman Ben Bernanke testified: "The principal source of the slowdown in economic growth . . . has been the substantial correction in the housing market. [and] The near-term prospects for the housing market remain uncertain." What makes forecasting turning points difficult? What methods do economists use to forecast turning points in the overall economy?

Q6.7 Would a linear regression model of the advertising–sales relation be appropriate for forecasting the advertising levels at which threshold or saturation effects become prevalent? Explain.

Q6.8 Perhaps the most famous early econometric forecasting firm was Wharton Economic Forecasting

Associates (WEFA), founded by Nobel Prize winner Lawrence Klein. A spin-off of the Wharton School of the University of Pennsylvania, where Klein taught, WEFA was merged with Data Resources, Inc., in 2001 to form Global Insight. Describe the data requirements that must be met if econometric analysis is to provide a useful forecasting tool.

Q6.9 Cite some examples of forecasting problems that might be addressed using regression analysis of complex multiple-equation systems of economic relations.

Q6.10 What are the main characteristics of accurate forecasts?

SELF-TEST PROBLEMS AND SOLUTIONS

ST6.1 Gross Domestic Product (GDP) is a measure of overall activity in the economy. It is defined as the value at the final point of sale of all goods and services produced during a given period by both domestic and foreign-owned enterprises. GDP data for the 1950–2004 period shown in Figure 6.3 offer the basis to test the abilities of simple constant change and constant growth models to describe the trend in GDP over time. However, regression results generated over the entire 1950–2004 period cannot be used to forecast GDP over any subpart of that period. To do so would be to overstate the forecast capability of the regression model because, by definition, the regression line minimizes the sum of squared deviations over the estimation period. To test forecast reliability, it is necessary to test the predictive capability of a given regression model over data that was not used to generate that very model. In the absence of GDP data for future periods, say 2005–2010, the reliability of alternative forecast techniques can be illustrated by arbitrarily dividing historical GDP data into two subsamples: a 1950–1999 50-year test period, and a 2000–2004 5-year forecast period. Regression models estimated over the 1950–1999 test period can be used to "forecast" actual GDP over the 2000–2004 period. In other words, estimation results over the 1950–1999 subperiod provide a forecast model that can be used to evaluate the predictive reliability of the constant growth model over the 2000–2004 forecast period.

A. Use the regression model approach to estimate the simple linear relation between the natural logarithm of GDP and time (T) over the 1950–1999 subperiod, where

$$\ln GDP_t = b_0 + b_1 T_t + u_t$$

and $\ln GDP_t$ is the natural logarithm of GDP in year t, and T is a time trend variable (where $T_{1950} = 1$, $T_{1951} = 2$, $T_{1952} = 3$, . . ., and $T_{1999} = 50$); and u is a residual term. This is called a constant growth model because it is based on the assumption of a constant percentage growth in economic activity per year. How well does the constant growth model fit actual GDP data over this period?

B. Create a spreadsheet that shows constant growth model GDP forecasts over the 2000–2004 period alongside actual figures. Then, subtract forecast values from actual figures to obtain annual estimates of forecast error, and squared forecast error, for each year over the 2000–2004 period.

Finally, compute the correlation coefficient between actual and forecast values over the 2000–2004 period. Also compute the sample average (or root mean squared) forecast error. Based upon these findings, how well does the constant growth model generated over the 1950–1999 period forecast actual GDP data over the 2000–2004 period?

ST6.1 SOLUTION

A. The constant growth model estimated using the simple regression model technique illustrates the linear relation between the natural logarithm of GDP and time. A constant growth regression model estimated over the 1950–1999 50-year period (t statistic in parentheses), used to forecast GDP over the 2000–2004 5-year period, is

$$\ln GDP_t = 5.5026 + 0.0752t, \qquad R^2 = 99.2\%$$
$$(188.66) \quad (75.50)$$

The $R_2 = 99.2$ percent and a highly significant t statistic for the time trend variable indicate that the constant growth model closely describes the change in GDP over the 1950–1999 time frame. Nevertheless, even modest changes in the intercept term and slope coefficient over the 2000–2004 time frame can lead to large forecast errors.

B. Each constant growth GDP forecast is derived using the constant growth model coefficients estimated in part A, along with values for each respective time trend variable over the 2000–2004 period. Remember that $T_{2000} = 51$, $T_{2001} = 52$, ..., and $T_{2004} = 55$ and that the constant growth model provides predicted, or forecast, values for $\ln GDP_t$. To obtain forecast values for GDP_t, simply take the exponent (antilog) of each predicted $\ln GDP_t$ variable.

The following spreadsheet shows actual and constant growth model GDP forecasts for the 2000–2004 forecast period:

Year	GDP($)	ln GDP	Forecast ln GDP	Forecast GDP ($)	Forecast Error (GDP – Forecast GDP) ($)	Squared Forecast Error (GDP – Forecast GDP)² ($)	Time Period
2000	9,268.4	9.1344	9.3357	9,441.6	−173.2	29,994.1	51
2001	9,817.0	9.1919	9.4109	10,248.9	−431.9	186,561.8	52
2002	10,100.8	9.2204	9.4860	11,125.3	−1,024.5	1,049,657.6	53
2003	10,480.8	9.2573	9.5612	12,076.5	−1,595.7	2,546,191.5	54
2004	10,987.9	9.3045	9.6364	13,109.2	−2,121.3	4,499,913.7	55
Average	10,131.0	9.2217	9.4860	11,200.3	−1,069.3	1,662,463.7	
		Correlation	99.50%		Mean squared error	1,289.4	

The correlation coefficient between actual and constant growth model forecast GDP is $r_{GDP, FGDP} = 99.50$ percent. The sample root mean squared forecast error is $1,298.4 billion ($= \sqrt{\$ 1,662,463.7}$), or 12.7 percent of average actual GDP over the 2000–2004 period. Thus, despite the fact that the correlation between actual and constant growth forecast model values is relatively high, forecast error is also very high. Unusually modest economic growth at the start of the new millennium leads to large forecast errors when GDP data from more rapidly growing periods, like the 1950–1999 period, are used to forecast economic growth.

ST6.2 Multiple Regression.

Branded Products, Inc., based in Oakland, California, is a leading producer and marketer of household laundry detergent and bleach products. About a year ago, Branded Products rolled out its new Super Detergent in 30 regional markets following its success in test markets. This isn't just a "me too" product in a commodity market. Branded Products' detergent contains Branded 2 bleach, a successful laundry product in its own right. At the time of the introduction, management wondered whether the company could successfully crack this market dominated by Procter & Gamble and other big players.

The following spreadsheet shows weekly demand data and regression model estimation results for Super Detergent in these 30 regional markets:

Branded Products Demand Forecasting Problem						
Regional Market	Demand in Cases, Q	Price Per Case, P ($)	Competitor Price, P_X ($)	Advertising, A ($)	Household Income, I ($)	Estimated Demand, Q
1	1,290	137	94	814	53,123	1,305
2	1,177	147	81	896	51,749	1,206
3	1,155	149	89	852	49,881	1,204
4	1,299	117	92	854	43,589	1,326
5	1,166	135	86	810	42,799	1,185
6	1,186	143	79	768	55,565	1,208
7	1,293	113	91	978	37,959	1,333
8	1,322	111	82	821	47,196	1,328
9	1,338	109	81	843	50,163	1,366
10	1,160	129	82	849	39,080	1,176
11	1,293	124	91	797	43,263	1,264
12	1,413	117	76	988	51,291	1,359
13	1,299	106	90	914	38,343	1,345
14	1,238	135	88	913	39,473	1,199
15	1,467	117	99	867	51,501	1,433
16	1,089	147	76	785	37,809	1,024
17	1,203	124	83	817	41,471	1,216
18	1,474	103	98	846	46,663	1,449
19	1,235	140	78	768	55,839	1,220
20	1,367	115	83	856	47,438	1,326
21	1,310	119	76	771	54,348	1,304
22	1,331	138	100	947	45,066	1,302
23	1,293	122	90	831	44,166	1,288
24	1,437	105	86	905	55,380	1,476
25	1,165	145	96	996	38,656	1,208
26	1,328	138	97	929	46,084	1,291
27	1,515	116	97	1,000	52,249	1,478
28	1,223	148	84	951	50,855	1,226
29	1,293	134	88	848	54,546	1,314
30	1,215	127	87	891	38,085	1,215
Average	1,286	127	87	870	46,788	1,286
Minimum	1,089	103	76	768	37,809	1,024
Maximum	1,515	149	100	1,000	55,839	1,478

Regression Statistics	
R Square	90.4%
Standard Error	34.97
Observations	30

	Coefficients	Standard Error	t Statistics	P Value
Intercept	807.938	137.846	5.86	4.09301E-06
Price, P	−5.034	0.457	−11.02	4.34134E-11
Competitor price, P_x	4.860	1.006	4.83	5.73825E-05
Advertising, A	0.328	0.104	3.14	0.004293208
Household income, I	0.009	0.001	7.99	2.38432E-08

A. Interpret the coefficient estimate for each respective independent variable.

B. Characterize the overall explanatory power of this multiple regression model in light of R^2 and the following plot of actual and estimated demand per week.

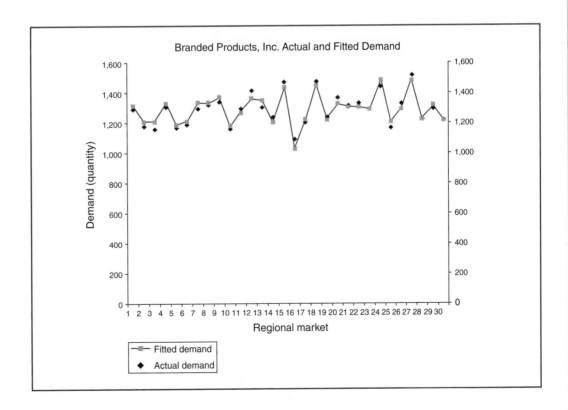

C. Use the regression model estimation results to forecast weekly demand in five new markets with the following characteristics:

Regional Forecast Market	Price Per Case, P	Competitor Price, P_X	Advertising, A	Household Income, I
A	115	90	790	41,234
B	122	101	812	39,845
C	116	87	905	47,543
D	140	82	778	53,560
E	133	79	996	39,870
Average	125	88	856	44,410

ST6.2 SOLUTION

A. Coefficient estimates for the P, P_X, A, and I independent X variables are statistically significant at the 99 percent confidence level. Price of the product itself (P) has the predictably negative influence on the quantity demanded, whereas the effects of competitor price (P_X), advertising (A) and household disposable income (I) are positive as expected. The chance of finding such large t statistics is less than 1 percent if, in fact, there were no relation between each variable and quantity.

B. The $R^2 = 90.4$ percent obtained by the model means that 90.4 percent of demand variation is explained by the underlying variation in all four independent variables. This is a relatively high level of explained variation and implies an attractive level of explanatory power. Moreover, as shown in the graph of actual and fitted (estimated) demand, the multiple regression model closely tracks week-by-week changes in demand with no worrisome divergences between actual and estimated demand over time. This means that this regression model can be used to forecast demand in similar markets under similar conditions.

C. Notice that each prospective market displays characteristics similar to those of markets used to estimate the regression model described above. Thus, the regression model estimated previously can be used to forecast demand in each regional market. Forecast results are as follows:

Regional Forecast Market	Price Per Case, P	Competitor Price, P_X	Advertising, A	Household Income, I	Forecast Demand, Q
A	115	90	790	41,234	1,285
B	122	101	812	39,845	1,298
C	116	87	905	47,543	1,358
D	140	82	778	53,560	1,223
E	133	79	996	39,870	1,196
Average	125	88	856	44,410	1,272

P6.1 Constant Growth Model. The U.S. Bureau of the Census publishes employment statistics and demand forecasts for various occupations.

Occupation	Employment (1,000)	
	1998	**2008**
Bill collectors	311	420
Computer engineers	299	622
Physicians' assistants	66	98
Respiratory therapists	86	123
Systems analysts	617	1,194

A. Using a spreadsheet or handheld calculator, calculate the 10-year growth rate forecast using the constant growth model with annual compounding, and the constant growth model with continuous compounding for each occupation.

B. Compare your answers and discuss any differences.

P6.2 Growth Rate Estimation. Almost 2 million persons per year visit wondrous Glacier National Park. Due to the weather, monthly park attendance figures varied widely during a recent year:

Month	Visitors	Percent Change
January	7,481	
February	9,686	29.5
March	13,316	37.5
April	24,166	81.5
May	89,166	269.0
June	255,237	186.2
July	540,488	111.8
August	528,716	−2.2
September	286,602	−45.8
October	57,164	−80.1
November	12,029	−79.0
December	6,913	−42.5
Average	152,580	42.4

A. Notice that park attendance is lower in December than in January, despite a 42.4 percent average rate of growth in monthly attendance. How is that possible?

B. Suppose the data described in the table measured park attendance over a number of years rather than during a single year. Explain how the arithmetic average annual rate of growth gives a misleading picture of the growth in park attendance.

P6.3 Sales Trend Analysis. Environmental Designs, Inc., produces and installs energy-efficient window systems in commercial buildings. During the past 10 years, sales revenue has increased from $25 million to $65 million.

A. Calculate the company's growth rate in sales using the constant growth model with annual compounding.

B. Derive a 5-year and a 10-year sales forecast.

P6.4 Cost Forecasting. Dorothy Gale, a quality control supervisor for Wizard Products, Inc., is concerned about unit labor cost increases for the assembly of electrical snap-action switches. Costs have increased from $80 to $100 per unit over the previous 3 years. Gale thinks that importing switches from foreign suppliers at a cost of $115.90 per unit may soon be desirable.

A. Calculate the company's unit labor cost growth rate using the constant rate of change model with continuous compounding.

B. Forecast when unit labor costs will equal the current cost of importing.

P6.5 Unit Sales Forecasting. Claire Littleton has discovered that the change in product A demand in any given week is inversely proportional to the change in sales of product B in the previous week. That is, if sales of B rose by X percent last week, sales of A can be expected to fall by X percent this week.

A. Write the equation for next week's sales of A, using the variables A = sales of product A, B = sales of product B, and t = time. Assume that there will be no shortages of either product.

B. Last week, 100 units of A and 90 units of B were sold. Two weeks ago, 75 units of B were sold. What would you predict the sales of A to be this week?

P6.6 Revenue Forecasting. Kate Austen must generate a sales forecast to convince the loan officer at a local bank of the viability of Marina Del Rey, a trendy west-coast restaurant. Austen assumes that next-period sales are a function of current income, advertising, and advertising by a competing restaurant.

A. Write an equation for predicting sales if Austen assumes that the percentage change in sales is twice as large as the percentage changes in income and advertising but that it is only one-half as large as, and the opposite sign of, the percentage change in competitor advertising. Use the variables S = sales, Y = income, A = advertising, and CA = competitor advertising.

B. During the current period, sales total $500,000, median income per capita in the local market is $71,400, advertising is $20,000, and competitor advertising is $66,000. Previous-period levels were $70,000 (income), $25,000 (advertising), and $60,000 (competitor advertising). Forecast next-period sales.

P6.7 Cost Forecasting. Dr. Izobel Stevens is supervising physician at the Westbury HMO, a New York City–based medical facility serving the poor and indigent. Stevens is evaluating the cost-effectiveness of a preventive maintenance program, and believes that monthly downtime on the packaging line caused by equipment breakdown is related to the hours spent each month on preventive maintenance.

A. Write an equation to predict next month's downtime using the variables D = downtime, M = preventive maintenance, t = time, a_0 = constant term, and a_1 = regression slope coefficient. Assume that downtime in the forecast (next) month decreases by the same percentage as preventive maintenance increased during the month preceding the current one.

B. If 40 hours were spent last month on preventive maintenance and this month's downtime was 500 hours, what should downtime be next month if preventive maintenance this month is 50 hours? Use the equation developed in part A.

P6.8 Sales Forecast Modeling.

Toys Unlimited Ltd., must forecast sales for a popular adult computer game to avoid stockouts or excessive inventory charges during the upcoming Christmas season. In percentage terms, the company estimates that game sales fall at double the rate of price increases and that they grow at triple the rate of customer traffic increases. Furthermore, these effects seem to be independent.

A. Write an equation for estimating the Christmas season sales, using the variables S = sales, P = price, T = traffic, and t = time.

B. Forecast this season's sales if Toys Unlimited sold 10,000 games last season at $15 each, this season's price is anticipated to be $16.50, and customer traffic is expected to rise by 15 percent over previous levels.

P6.9 Simultaneous Equations.

Mid-Atlantic Cinema, Inc., runs a chain of movie theaters in the east-central states and has enjoyed great success with a Tuesday Night at the Movies promotion. By offering half off its regular $9 admission price, average nightly attendance has risen from 500 to 1,500 persons. Popcorn and other concession revenues tied to attendance have also risen dramatically. Historically, Mid-Atlantic has found that 50 percent of all moviegoers buy a $5 cup of buttered popcorn. Eighty percent of these popcorn buyers, plus 40 percent of the moviegoers that do not buy popcorn, each spend an average of $4 on soda and other concessions.

A. Write an expression describing total revenue from tickets plus popcorn plus other concessions.

B. Forecast total revenues for both regular and special Tuesday night pricing.

C. Forecast the total profit contribution earned for the regular and special Tuesday night pricing strategies if the profit contribution is 30 percent on movie ticket revenues and 80 percent on popcorn and other concession revenues.

P6.10 Simultaneous Equations.

Supersonic Industries, based in Seattle, Washington, manufactures a wide range of parts for aircraft manufacturers. The company is currently evaluating the merits of building a new plant to fulfill a new contract with the federal government. The alternatives to expansion are to use additional overtime, to reduce other production, or both. The company will add new capacity only if the economy appears to be expanding. Therefore, forecasting the general pace of economic activity for the United States is an important input to the decision-making process. The firm has collected data and estimated the following relations for the U.S. economy:

Last year's total profits (all corporations) P_{t-1}	= $1,200 billion
This year's government expenditures G	= $2,500 billion
Annual consumption expenditures C	= $900 billion + 0.75$Y$
Annual investment expenditures I	= $920 billion + 0.9$P_{t-1}$
Annual tax receipts T	= 0.16GDP
Net exports X	= 0.03GDP
National income Y	= GDP − T
Gross domestic product (GDP)	= $C + I + G - X$

Forecast each of the preceding variables through the simultaneous relations expressed in the multiple-equation system. Assume that all random disturbances average out to zero.

CASE Study

Forecasting Global Performance for a Mickey Mouse Organization

The Walt Disney Company is a diversified worldwide entertainment company with operations in four business segments: media networks, parks and resorts, studio entertainment, and consumer products. The media networks segment consists of the company's television (ABC, ESPN, and Discovery) and radio networks, cable/satellite and international broadcast operations, production and distribution of television programming, and Internet operations. The studio entertainment segment produces live-action and animated motion pictures, television animation programs, musical recordings, and live stage plays. The consumer products segment licenses the company's characters and other intellectual property to manufacturers, retailers, show promoters, and publishers.

Disney parks and resorts are at the cornerstone of a carefully integrated entertainment marketing strategy. Through the parks and resorts segment, Walt Disney owns and operates four destination resorts in the United States, Japan, and France. In the United States, kids flock to Disneyland, California, and Walt Disney World, Florida—an immense entertainment center that includes the Animal Kingdom, Magic Kingdom, Epcot Center, and Disney-MGM Studios. During recent years, the company has extended its amusement park business to foreign soil with Tokyo Disneyland, Hong Kong Disneyland, and Euro Disneyland, located just outside of Paris, France. Disney's foreign operations provide an interesting example of the company's shrewd combination of marketing and financial skills. To conserve scarce capital resources, Disney was able to entice foreign investors to put up 100 percent of the financing required for both the Tokyo and

Paris facilities. In turn, Disney is responsible for the design and management of both operations, retains an important equity interest, and enjoys significant royalties on all gross revenues.

Disney is also a major force in the movie picture production business with Buena Vista, Touchstone, and Hollywood Pictures, in addition to the renowned Walt Disney Studios. The company is famous for recent hit movies such as *Finding Nemo, The Lion King, Pirates of the Caribbean: The Curse of the Black Pearl*, and *The Sixth Sense*, in addition to a film library including hundreds of movie classics like *Fantasia, Snow White*, and *Mary Poppins*, among others. Disney employs an aggressive and highly successful video marketing strategy for new films and re-releases from the company's extensive film library. The Disney Store, a chain of retail specialty shops, profits from the sale of movie tie-in merchandise, books, and recorded music. Also making a significant contribution to the bottom line are earnings from Disney's television operations which include ABC, The Disney Channel, the Discovery Channel, and sports juggernaut ESPN, the Entertainment and Sports Programming Network. The company's family entertainment marketing strategy is so broad in its reach that Disney characters such as Mickey Mouse, Donald Duck, and Goofy have become an integral part of the American culture. Given its ability to turn whimsy into outstanding operating performance, the Walt Disney Company is one firm that doesn't mind being called a "Mickey Mouse Organization."

Table 6.7 shows a variety of accounting operating statistics, including revenues, cash flow, capital spending, dividends, earnings, book value, and year-end share prices for the

continued

Table 6.7 Operating Statistics for The Walt Disney Company (all data in dollars per share)

Year	Revenues ($)	Cash Flow, ($)	Capital Spending ($)	Dividends, ($)	Earnings ($)	Book Value ($)	Year-End Stock Price[a] ($)
1980	0.59	0.11	0.10	0.02	0.09	0.69	1.07
1981	0.65	0.10	0.21	0.02	0.08	0.75	1.09
1982	0.64	0.09	0.38	0.03	0.06	0.80	1.32
1983	0.79	0.11	0.20	0.03	0.06	0.85	1.10
1984	1.02	0.13	0.12	0.03	0.06	0.71	1.25
1985	1.30	0.18	0.12	0.03	0.11	0.76	2.35
1986	1.58	0.24	0.11	0.03	0.15	0.90	3.59
1987	1.82	0.34	0.18	0.03	0.24	1.17	4.94
1988	2.15	0.42	0.37	0.03	0.32	1.48	5.48
1989	2.83	0.55	0.46	0.04	0.43	1.87	9.33
1990	3.70	0.65	0.45	0.05	0.50	2.21	8.46
1991	3.96	0.58	0.59	0.06	0.40	2.48	9.54
1992	4.77	0.72	0.35	0.07	0.51	2.99	14.33
1993	5.31	0.78	0.49	0.08	0.54	3.13	14.21
1994	6.40	0.97	0.65	0.10	0.68	3.50	15.33
1995	7.70	1.15	0.57	0.12	0.84	4.23	19.63
1996	10.50	1.32	0.86	0.14	0.74	7.96	23.25
1997	11.10	1.51	0.95	0.17	0.92	8.54	33.00
1998	11.21	1.52	1.13	0.20	0.90	9.46	30.00
1999	11.34	1.30	1.03	0.20	0.66	10.16	29.25
2000	12.09	1.98	1.02	0.21	0.90	11.65	28.44
2001	12.52	1.89	0.89	0.21	0.98	11.23	20.72
2002	12.40	1.06	0.53	0.21	0.55	11.48	16.31
2003	13.23	1.19	0.51	0.21	0.66	11.63	23.33
2007–2009[b]	18.10	2.25	0.45	0.21	1.65	17.55	

[a]Split-adjusted share prices.

[b]Value line estimates.

Data Sources: Company annual reports (various years), http://www.valueline.com, http://yahoo.com.

Walt Disney Company during the 1980–2003 period. All data are expressed in dollars per share to illustrate how individual shareholders have benefited from the company's growth. During this time frame, revenue per share grew at an annual rate of 14.5 percent per year, and earnings per share grew by 9.0 percent per year. These performance measures exceed industry and economy-wide norms. Disney employees, CEO Michael D. Eisner, and all stockholders profited greatly from the company's outstanding stock-price performance during the 1980s and 1990s, but have grown frustrated by stagnant results during recent years. Over the 1980–2003 period, Disney common stock exploded in price from $1.07 per share to $23.33, after adjusting for stock splits. This represents a 14.3 percent annual rate of return, and illustrates how Disney has

continued

been an above-average stock market performer. However, the stock price has grown stagnant since 1996, and stockholders are getting restless.

Given the many uncertainties faced by Disney and most major corporations, forecasts of operating performance are usually restricted to a fairly short time perspective. The Value Line Investment Survey, one of the most widely respected forecast services, focuses on a 3- to 5-year time horizon. For the 2007–2009 period, Value Line forecasts Disney revenues of $18.10, cash flow of $2.25, earnings of $1.65, dividends of $0.21, capital spending of $0.45, and book value per share of $17.55. Actual results will vary, but these assumptions offer a fruitful basis for measuring the relative growth potential of Disney.

The most interesting economic statistic for Disney stockholders is the stock price during some future period, say 2007–2009. In economic terms, stock prices represent the net present value of future cash flows, discounted at an appropriate risk-adjusted rate of return. To forecast Disney's stock price during the 2007–2009 period, one might use any or all of the data in Table 6.7. Historical numbers for a recent period, like 1980–2003, represent a useful context for projecting future stock prices. For example, Fidelity's legendary mutual fund investor Peter Lynch argues that stock prices are largely determined by future earnings per share. Stock prices rise following an increase in earnings per share and plunge when earnings per share plummet. Sir John Templeton, the father of global stock market investing, focuses on book value per share. Templeton contends that future earnings are closely related to the book value of the firm, or accounting net worth. "Bargains" can be found when stock can be purchased in companies that sell in the marketplace at a significant discount to book value, or when book value per share is expected to rise dramatically. Both Lynch and Templeton have built a large following among investors who have profited mightily using their stock market selection techniques.

As an experiment, it will prove interesting to employ the data provided in Table 6.7 to estimate regression models that can be used to forecast the average common stock price for The Walt Disney Company over the 2007–2009 period.

A. A simple regression model over the 1980–2003 period where the Y variable is the Disney year-end stock price and the X variable is Disney's earnings per share reads as follows (t statistics in parentheses):

$$P_t = -\$1.661 + \$31.388EPS_t, \quad R^2 = 86.8\%$$
$$(-1.13) \quad\quad (12.03)$$

Use this model to forecast Disney's average stock price for the 2007–2009 period using the Value Line estimate of Disney's average earnings per share for 2007–2009. Discuss this share price forecast.

B. A simple regression model over the 1980–2003 period where the Y variable is the Disney year-end stock price and the X variable is Disney's book value per share reads as follows (t statistics in parentheses):

$$P_t = \$3.161 + \$2.182BV_t, \quad R^2 = 76.9\%$$
$$(1.99) \quad\quad (8.57)$$

Use this model to forecast Disney's average stock price for the 2007–2009 period using the Value Line estimate of Disney's average book value per share for 2007–2009. Discuss this share price forecast.

C. A multiple regression model over the 1980–2003 period where the Y variable is the Disney year-end stock price and the X variables are Disney's earnings per share and book value per share reads as follows (t statistics in parentheses):

$$P_t = -\$1.112 + \$21.777EPS_t + \$0.869BV_t, \quad R^2 = 90.9\%$$
$$(-0.88) \quad\quad (5.66) \quad\quad (3.06)$$

continued

Use this model to forecast Disney's average stock price for the 2007–2009 period using the Value Line estimate of Disney's average earnings per share and book value per share for 2007–2009. Discuss this share price forecast.

D. A multiple regression model over the 1980–2003 period where the Y variable is the Disney year-end stock price and X variables include the accounting operating statistics shown in Table 6.7 reads as follows (t statistics in parentheses):

$$P_t = -\$2.453 + \$2.377REV_t + \$0.822CF_t +$$
$$\quad (-1.75) \quad (1.46) \quad (0.09)$$
$$\$13.603CAPX_t + \$17.706DIV_t + \$0.437EPS_t -$$
$$\quad (2.84) \quad (0.24) \quad (0.03)$$
$$\$1.665BV_t, \quad R^2 = 94.3\%$$
$$(-0.94)$$

Use this model and Value Line estimates to forecast Disney's average stock price for the 2007–2009 period. Check The Value Line Investment Survey at http://www.valueline.com. How did these regression-based forecasts perform?

SELECTED REFERENCES

Aguiar, Mark and Gita Gopinath. "Emerging Market Business Cycles: The Cycle Is the Trend." *Journal of Political Economy* 115, no. 1 (February, 2007): 69–102.

Akerlof, George A. "The Missing Motivation in Macroeconomics." *American Economic Review* 97, no. 1 (March, 2007): 5–36.

Burnside, Craig, Martin Eichenbaum, and Sergio Rebelo. "The Returns to Currency Speculation in Emerging Markets." *American Economic Review* 97, no. 2 (May, 2007): 333–338.

Hong, Harrison, Jeremy C. Stein, and Jialin Yu. "Simple Forecasts and Paradigm Shifts." *Journal of Finance* 62, no. 3 (June, 2007): 1207–1242.

Hong, Harrison, Walter Torous, and Rossen Valkanov. "Do Industries Lead Stock Markets?" *Journal of Financial Economics* 83, no. 2 (February, 2007): 367–396.

Murphy, Kevin M. and Robert H. Topel. "Social Value and the Speed of Innovation." *American Economic Review* 97, no. 2 (May, 2007): 433–437.

Moscarini, Giuseppe. "Competence Implies Credibility." *American Economic Review* 97, no. 1 (March, 2007): 37–63.

Nunn, Nathan. "Relationship-Specificity, Incomplete Contracts, and the Pattern of Trade." *Quarterly Journal of Economics* 122, no. 2 (May, 2007): 569–600.

Oberholzer Gee, Felix and Koleman Strumpf. "The Effect of File Sharing on Record Sales: An Empirical Analysis." *Journal of Political Economy* 115, no. 1 (February, 2007): 1–42.

Reyes, Jessica Wolpaw. "Reaching Equilibrium in the Market for Obstetricians and Gynecologists." *American Economic Review* 97, no. 2 (May, 2007): 407–411.

Rysman, Marc. "An Empirical Analysis of Payment Card Usage." *Journal of Industrial Economics* 55, no. 1 (March, 2007): 1–36.

Shanken, Jay and Guofu Zhou. "Estimating and Testing Beta Pricing Models: Alternative Methods and Their Performance in Simulations." *Journal of Financial Economics* 84, no. 1 (April, 2007): 40–86.

Shin, SeungJae, Martin B. Weiss, and Jack Tucci. "Rural Internet Access: Over-Subscription Strategies, Regulation and Equilibrium." *Managerial and Decision Economics* 28, no. 1 (January, 2007): 1–12.

Snowberg, Erik, Justin Wolfers, and Eric Zitzewitz. "Partisan Impacts on the Economy: Evidence from Prediction Markets and Close Elections." *Quarterly Journal of Economics* 122, no. 2 (May, 2007): 807–829.

Tetlock, Paul C. "Giving Content to Investor Sentiment: The Role of Media in the Stock Market." *Journal of Finance* 62, no. 3 (June, 2007): 1139–1168.

Production and Competitive Markets

3

PART

Production Analysis and Compensation Policy

During recent years, lower taxes on business investment have helped reduce the cost of capital, while skyrocketing health care costs have made employers think twice before adding more workers. Under these circumstances, some employers have clearly opted to expand plant and equipment to boost the productivity of current workers rather than add new employees. In the short run, this is good for business profits and tends to boost stock prices. In the long run, newer and better capital equipment can eliminate some of the high-wage jobs responsible for an increasing standard of living. A "jobless recovery" is the type of economic expansion that nobody cares to contemplate.

Reductions in the capital-gains tax rate and dividend tax rate have generated lots of controversy, but recent changes to depreciation rules may have a bigger influence on business hiring decisions. Business equipment used to be depreciated over its estimated economic life. Now, businesses are allowed to write off up to 50 percent of an asset's value in the first year. Some economists estimate that this has reduced the cost of capital by about 6 percent, and may explain why many businesses were reluctant to boost hiring as the economy began a slow economic recovery in 2002. Other economists note that business investment spurs economic growth which, in turn, tends to boost job opportunities. Tracking indirect effects is difficult, however, and makes tax policy controversial.

Firms rely upon economic theory to help them measure worker productivity and assess the productivity of all inputs.[1]

PRODUCTION FUNCTIONS

Productive efficiency is not simply about what or how to produce; it is about both.

Properties of Production Functions

Production Function
Maximum output that can be produced for a given amount of input.

A **production function** specifies the maximum output that can be produced for a given amount of input. Any improvement in technology, such as better equipment or a training program that enhances worker productivity, results in a new production function. Basic properties of production functions can be illustrated by examining a simple two-input, one-output system in which quantities of two inputs, X and Y, can be used to produce a

---

1 See Kelly Evans, "U.S. Economy Down, Not Out," *The Wall Street Journal Online*, October 6, 2007, http://online.wsj.com.

product, Q. Inputs X and Y might represent resources such as labor and capital or energy and raw materials. The product Q could be goods such as television sets, baseball gloves, or breakfast cereal; Q could also represent services such as medical care, education, or banking.

The production function for such a system can be written

$$Q = f(X, Y) \qquad \qquad \textbf{7.1}$$

Table 7.1 is a tabular representation of a two-input, single-output production system. Each element in the table shows the maximum quantity of Q that can be produced with a specific combination of X and Y. Table 7.1 shows, for example, that 2 units of X and 3 units of Y can be combined to produce 49 units of output; 5 units of X coupled with 5 units of Y results in 92 units of output; 4 units of X and 10 units of Y produce 101 units of Q, and so on. The units of input could represent hours of labor, dollars of capital, cubic feet of natural gas, tons of raw materials, and so on. Units of Q could be numbers of television sets or baseball gloves, cases of cereal, patient days of hospital care, customer transactions at an ATM banking facility, and so on.

Discrete Production Function
Production function with distinct input patterns.

The **discrete production function** described in Table 7.1 involves distinct, or "lumpy," patterns for input combinations illustrated in Figure 7.1. The height of the bars associated with each input combination indicates the output produced. The tops of the output bars map the production surface for the system.

Continuous Production Function
Production function where inputs can be varied in an unbroken marginal fashion.

The discrete production data shown in Table 7.1 and Figure 7.1 can be generalized by assuming that the underlying production function is continuous. A **continuous production function** is one in which inputs can be varied in an unbroken fashion rather than incrementally, as in the preceding example.

Returns to Scale and Returns to a Factor

Returns to Scale
Output effect of a proportional increase in all inputs.

The **returns to scale** characteristic of a production system is the relation between output and variation in all inputs taken together. Returns to scale affect the optimal size of a

---

Table 7.1 Representative Production Table

Units of Y Employed	Output Quantity									
10	52	71	87	101	113	122	127	129	130	131
9	56	74	89	102	111	120	125	127	128	129
8	59	75	91	99	108	117	122	124	125	126
7	61	77	87	96	104	112	117	120	121	122
6	62	72	82	91	99	107	111	114	116	117
5	55	66	75	84	92	99	104	107	109	110
4	47	58	68	77	85	91	97	100	102	103
3	35	49	59	68	76	83	89	91	90	89
2	15	31	48	59	68	72	73	72	70	67
1	5	12	35	48	56	55	53	50	46	40
	1	2	3	4	5	6	7	8	9	10
				Units of X employed						

Figure 7.1   Representative Production Surface

This discrete production function illustrates the output level resulting from each combination of inputs X and Y.

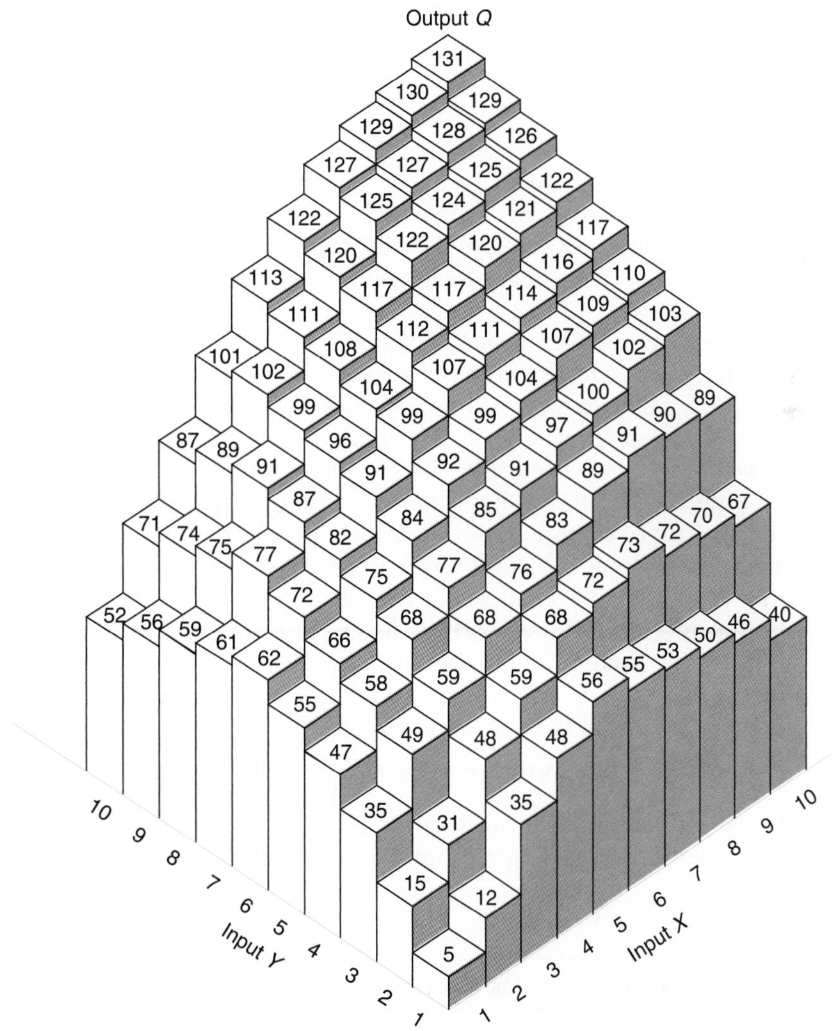

firm and its production facilities. They also affect the nature of competition and thus are important in determining the profitability of investment.

A second important relation in any production system is that between output and variation in only one of the inputs employed. **Returns to a factor** signals the relation between the quantity of an individual input (or factor of production) employed and the level of output produced. Factor productivity is the key to determining the optimal combination of inputs that should be used to manufacture a given product. Because an understanding of factor productivity aids in the study of returns to scale, it is worth considering factor productivity concepts first.

Returns to a Factor
Relation between output and variation in only one input.

TOTAL, MARGINAL, AND AVERAGE PRODUCT

The optimization process focuses upon marginal products for resources employed in a production system.

Total Product

Total Product
Whole output from a production system.

Total product is the amount of output created from a specific quantity of resource inputs. For example, suppose that Table 7.1 represents a production system in which Y is a capital resource and X represents labor input. If a firm is operating with a given level of capital (say, $Y = 2$), then the relevant production function for the firm in the short run is represented by the row in Table 7.1 corresponding to that level of fixed capital. Operating with 2 units of capital, output or total product depends on the quantity of labor (X) employed. This total product of X can be read from the $Y = 2$ row in Table 7.1. It is also shown in column 2 of Table 7.2 and is illustrated graphically in Figure 7.2.

The total product for a factor of production, such as labor, can be expressed as a function relating output to the quantity of the resource employed. For example, the equation $Q = f(X|Y = 2)$ relates Q (the total product of input X) to the quantity of X employed, fixing the quantity of input Y at 2 units. One would obtain other total product functions for X if the factor Y were fixed at levels other than 2 units.

Figure 7.3(a) shows how the amount of output produced rises with an increase in the amount of a single input, holding constant the amounts of other inputs employed. This figure depicts a continuous production function in which inputs can be varied in a marginal unbroken fashion, rather than discretely. Suppose the firm wishes to fix the amount of input Y at the level Y_1. The total product curve of input X, holding input Y constant at $Y = Y_1$, rises along the production surface as the use of input X is increased.

Marginal Product
Change in output associated with a 1-unit change in a single input.

Marginal and Average Product

Given the total product function for an input, both marginal and average products can be easily derived. The **marginal product** of a factor, MP_X, is the change in output associated

Table 7.2 Total Product, Marginal Product, and Average Product of Factor X Holding $Y = 2$			
Input Quantity (X)	Total Product of the Input (X)	Marginal Product of Input X ($MP_X = \partial Q/\partial X$)	Average Product of Input X ($AP_X = Q/X$)
1	15	+15	15.0
2	31	+16	15.5
3	48	+17	16.0
4	59	+11	14.8
5	68	+9	13.6
6	72	+4	12.0
7	73	+1	10.4
8	72	−1	9.0
9	70	−2	7.8
10	67	−3	6.7

Figure 7.2 Total, Average, and Marginal Product for Input X, Given $Y = 2$

(a) Holding Y at two units, total production first rises but then falls as the amount of X employed grows. (b) Total product rises as long as marginal product is positive.

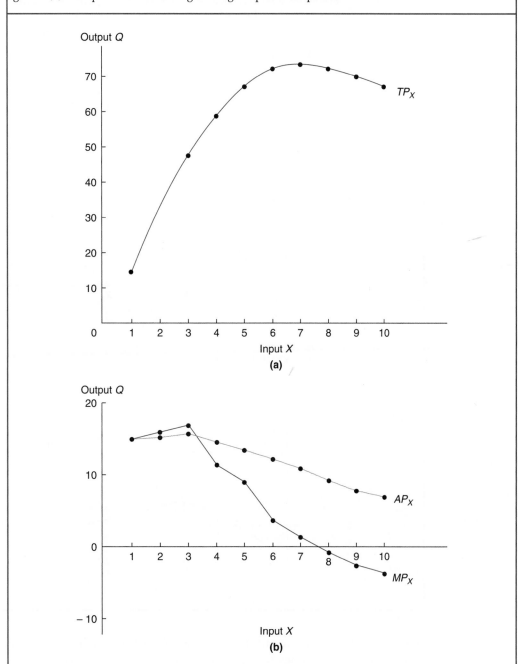

with a 1-unit change in the factor input, holding all other inputs constant. For a total product function such as that shown in Table 7.2 and Figure 7.2(a), marginal product is expressed as

$$MP_X = \frac{\partial Q}{\partial X}$$

7.2

Figure 7.3   Total, Marginal, and Average Product Curves: (a) Total Product Curve for X, Holding $Y = Y_1$; (b) Marginal Product Curve for X, Holding $Y = Y_1$

MP_X reaches a maximum at point A', where the slope of the TP_X curve is the greatest. AP_X is at a maximum where $MP_X = AP_X$. At point C, TP_X is at a maximum and $MP_X = 0$.

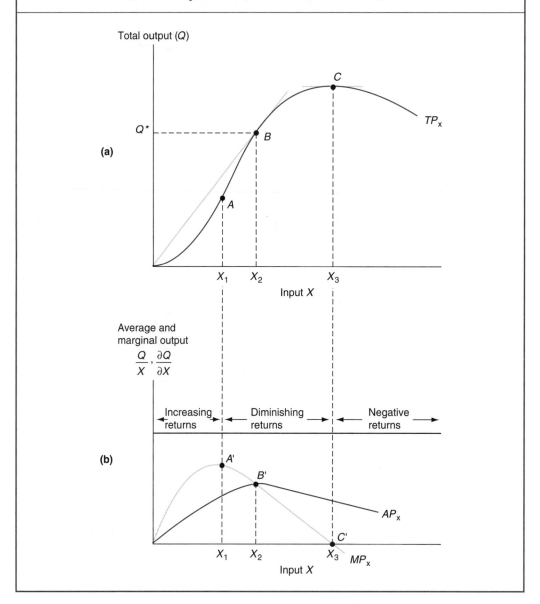

where ∂Q is the change in output resulting from a 1-unit change, ∂X, in the variable factor. This expression assumes that the quantity of the other input, Y, remains unchanged. Marginal product is shown in column 3 of Table 7.2 and in Figure 7.2(b).

Average product is total product divided by the number of units of input employed:

Average Product
Total product divided by units of input employed.

$$AP_X = \frac{Q}{X} \qquad\qquad \textbf{7.3}$$

The average product for X given $Y = 2$ units is shown in column 4 of Table 7.2 and in Figure 7.2(b). For a continuous total product function, as illustrated in Figure 7.3(a), marginal product equals the slope of the total product curve, whereas average product equals the slope of a line drawn from the origin to a point on the total product curve. Average and marginal product curves are shown in Figure 7.3(b).

Three points of interest, A, B, and C, can be identified on the total product curve in Figure 7.3(a). Each has a corresponding location on the average or marginal curves. Point A is the inflection point of the total product curve. The marginal product of X (the slope of the total product curve) increases until this point is reached, after which it begins to decrease. This can be seen in Figure 7.3(b) where MP_X reaches its highest level at A'.

The second point on the total product curve, B, indicates the output at which the average product and marginal product are equal. The slope of a line from the origin to any point on the total product curve measures the average product of X at that point, whereas the slope of the total product curve equals the marginal product. At point B, where X_2 units of input X are employed, a line from the origin is tangent to the total product curve, so $MP_X = AP_X$. The slopes of successive lines drawn from the origin to the total product curve increase until point B is reached, after which their slopes decline. The average product curve rises until it reaches B, then declines. This feature is also shown in Figure 7.3(b) as point B'. Here again, $MP_X = AP_X$ and AP_X is at a maximum.

The third point, C, indicates where the slope of the total product curve is zero and the curve is at a maximum. Beyond C the marginal product of X is negative, indicating that increased use of input X results in a *reduction* of total product. The corresponding point in Figure 7.3(b) is C', the point where the marginal product curve intersects the X-axis.

LAW OF DIMINISHING RETURNS TO A FACTOR

As the quantity of a variable input increases, with the quantities of all other factors being held constant, the resulting increase in output eventually diminishes.

Diminishing Returns to a Factor Concept

Law of Diminishing Returns
As the quantity of a variable input increases, the resulting rate of output increase eventually diminishes.

The **law of diminishing returns** states that the marginal product of a variable factor eventually declines as more of the variable factor is combined with other fixed resources. The law of diminishing returns is sometimes called the law of diminishing marginal returns to emphasize the fact that it deals with the diminishing marginal product of a variable input factor. The law of diminishing returns cannot be derived deductively. It is an empirical regularity of every known production system.

Consider an assembly line for the production of refrigerators. If only one employee is put to work, that individual must perform each of the activities necessary to assemble refrigerators. Output from such a combination of labor and capital is likely to be small. As additional units of labor are added to this production system—holding capital input constant—output is likely to expand rapidly. The improved use of capital resulting from an increase in labor could cause the marginal product per employee to increase over some range of additional labor. Such increasing marginal productivity reflects the benefits of worker specialization. An example in which the marginal product of an input increases over some range is presented in Table 7.2. The first unit of labor (input X) results in 15 units of production. With 2 units of labor, 31 units can be produced. The marginal

product of the second unit of labor $MP_{X=2} = 16$ exceeds that of the $MP_{X=1} = 15$. Similarly,
the addition of another unit of labor results in output increasing to 48 units, indicating a
marginal product of $MP_{X=3} = 17$ for the third unit of labor.

Eventually, sufficient labor is combined with the fixed capital input so that the benefits
of further labor additions begin to decline. Although the marginal product of labor is
positive and total output increases as more units of labor are employed, the marginal
product of labor will drop. The diminishing marginal productivity of labor is exhibited
by the fourth, fifth, sixth, and seventh units of input X in Table 7.2.

Conceivably, a point might be reached where the quantity of a variable input factor is so
large that total output actually begins to decline with additional employment of that factor.
This happens in Table 7.2 when more than 7 units of input X are combined with 2 units
of input Y. The eighth unit of X results in a 1-unit reduction in total output, $MP_{X=8} = -1$;
units 9 and 10 cause output to fall by 2 and 3 units, respectively. In Figure 7.3(b), regions
where the variable input factor X exhibits increasing, diminishing, and negative returns
have been labeled.

Illustration of Diminishing Returns to a Factor

Suppose Tax Advisors, Inc., has an office for processing tax returns in Scranton,
Pennsylvania. Table 7.3 shows that if the office employs one certified public accountant
(CPA), it can process 0.2 tax returns per hour. Adding a second CPA increases production
to 1 return per hour, and with a third, output jumps to 2.4 returns processed per hour.

Table 7.3 Production Function for Tax-Return Processing

Units of Labor Input Employed (CPAs)	Total Product of CPAs—Tax Returns Processed/Hour ($TP_{CPA} = Q$)	Marginal Product of CPAs ($MP_{CPA} = \partial Q$)	Average Product of CPAs ($AP_{CPA} = Q/X$)
1	0.2	0.2	0.20
2	1.0	0.8	0.50
3	2.4	1.4	0.80
4	2.8	0.4	0.70
5	3.0	0.2	0.60
6	2.7	−0.3	0.45

In this production system, the marginal product for the second CPA is 0.8 returns per hour as compared with 0.2 for the first CPA employed. The marginal product for the third CPA is 1.4 returns per hour. $MP_{CPA=2} = 0.8$ seems to indicate that the second CPA is four times as productive as the first, and $MP_{CPA=3} = 1.4$ says that the third CPA is more productive still. In production analysis, however, it is assumed that each unit of an input factor is like all other units of that same factor, meaning that each CPA is equally competent and efficient. If individual differences do not account for this increasing productivity, what does?

Typically, increased specialization and better utilization of other factors in the production process allow factor productivity to grow. As the number of CPAs increases, each can specialize. Also, additional CPAs may be better able to fully use computer, clerical, and other resources employed by the firm. Advantages from specialization and increased coordination cause output to rise at an increasing rate, from 0.2 to 1 return processed per hour as the second CPA is employed, and from 1 to 2.4 returns per hour as the third CPA is added.

In practice it is very rare to see input combinations that exhibit increasing returns for any factor. With increasing returns to a factor, an industry would come to be dominated by one very large producer—and that is seldom the case. Input combinations in the range of diminishing returns are commonly observed. If, for example, four CPAs could process 2.8 returns per hour, then the marginal product of the fourth CPA, $MP_{CPA=4} = 0.4$, would be less than the marginal product of the third CPA ($MP_{CPA=3} = 1.4$) and diminishing returns to the CPA labor input would be encountered.

The irrationality of employing inputs in the negative returns range, beyond X_3 in Figure 7.3, can be illustrated by noting that adding a sixth CPA would cause total output to fall from 3.0 to 2.7 returns per hour. The marginal product of the sixth CPA is −0.3 ($MP_{CPA=6} = -0.3$), perhaps because of problems with coordinating work among greater numbers of employees or limitations in other important inputs. No firm would pay an additional employee when employing that person reduces output. It is irrational to employ inputs in the range of negative returns.

INPUT COMBINATION CHOICE

Selection of an efficient input combination depends upon the relative productivity of each input.

Production Isoquants

Isoquant
Different input combinations used to efficiently produce a specified output.

Technical Efficiency
Least-cost production of a target level of output.

The term **isoquant**—derived from *iso*, meaning equal, and *quant*, from quantity—denotes a curve that represents the different combinations of inputs that can be efficiently used to produce a given level of output. Efficiency in this case refers to **technical efficiency**, meaning the least-cost production of a target level of output. If 2 units of X and 3 units of Y can be combined to produce 49 units of output, but they can also be combined less efficiently to produce only 45 units of output, the $X = 2$, $Y = 3$ input combination will lie only on the $Q = 49$ isoquant. The $X = 2$, $Y = 3$ combination resulting in $Q = 45$ is not technologically efficient because this same input combination can produce a larger output quantity. This combination would not appear in the production function nor on the $Q = 45$ isoquant. From Table 7.1 it is clear that 91 units of output can be produced efficiently by using the input combinations $X = 3$, $Y = 8$; $X = 4$, $Y = 6$; $X = 6$, $Y = 4$; or $X = 8$, $Y = 3$. These four input combinations all lie on the $Q = 91$ isoquant. Similarly, the combinations $X = 6$, $Y = 10$; $X = 7$, $Y = 8$; $X = 10$, $Y = 7$ all result in 122 units of production and, hence, lie on the $Q = 122$ isoquant.

These two isoquants are illustrated in Figure 7.4. Each point on the $Q = 91$ isoquant indicates a different combination of X and Y that can efficiently produce 91 units of output. For example, 91 units can be produced with 3 units of X and 8 units of Y, with 4 units of X and 6 units of Y, or with any other combination of X and Y on the isoquant $Q = 91$. A similar interpretation can be given for the isoquant $Q = 122$ units of output.

Every point on the Q_1 isoquant in Figure 7.5(c) represents input combinations that can be used to efficiently produce an equal quantity, or isoquant, of Q_1 units of output. The isoquant curve Q_2 maps out all input combinations that result in Q_2 units of production, and so on.

Figure 7.4   Representative Isoquants for Table 7.1

Each point on an isoquant represents a different combination of inputs X and Y that can be used to produce the same level of output.

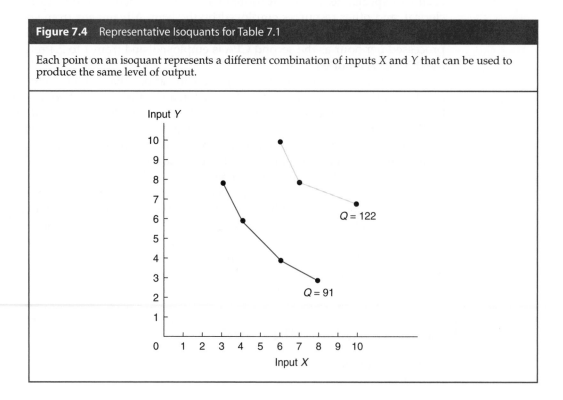

Input Factor Substitution

Input Substitution
Systematic replacement of productive factors.

In some production systems, **input substitution** is easily accomplished. In the production of electricity, for example, fuels used to power generators often represent readily substitutable inputs. Figure 7.5(a) shows isoquants for an electric power plant with boilers equipped to burn either oil or gas. Power can be produced by burning gas only, oil only, or varying amounts of each. In this instance, gas and oil are perfect substitutes,

Figure 7.5 Isoquants for Inputs with Varying Degrees of Substitutability: (a) Electric Power Generation; (b) Bicycle Production; (c) Dress Production

(a) Straight-line isoquants indicate perfect substitution. (b) A right-angle shape for isoquants reflects inputs that are perfect complements. (c) C-shaped isoquants indicate imperfect substitutability among inputs.

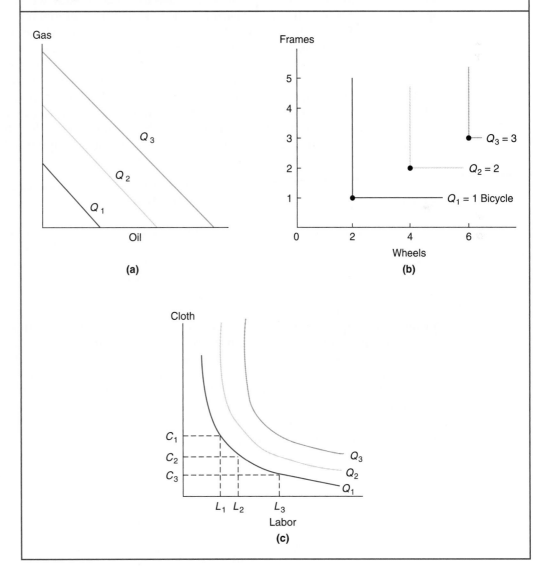

and the electricity isoquants are straight lines. Other examples of readily substitutable inputs include fish meal and soybeans to provide protein in a feed mix, energy and time in a drying process, and United Parcel Service and the U.S. Postal Service for package delivery. In each case, production isoquants are linear.

At the other extreme of substitutability lie production systems in which inputs are perfect complements; exact amounts of each input are required to produce a given quantity of output. Figure 7.5(b) illustrates isoquants for bicycles in which exactly two wheels and one frame are required to produce a bicycle. Wheels cannot be substituted for frames, nor vice versa. Pants and coats for men's suits, engines and bodies for trucks, and chemicals in specific compounds for prescription drugs are further examples of complementary inputs. Production isoquants for perfect complements take the shape of right angles, as indicated in Figure 7.5(b).

Figure 7.5(c) shows a production process in which inputs can be substituted for each other within limits. A dress can be made with a relatively small amount of labor (L_1) and a large amount of cloth (C_1). The same dress can also be made with less cloth (C_2) if more labor (L_2) is used because the dress maker can cut the material more carefully and reduce waste. Finally, the dress can be made with still less cloth (C_3), but workers must be so extremely painstaking that the labor input requirement increases to L_3. Although a relatively small addition of labor, from L_1 to L_2, reduces the input of cloth from C_1 to C_2, a very large increase in labor, from L_2 to L_3, is required to obtain a similar reduction in cloth from C_2 to C_3. The substitutability of labor for cloth diminishes from L_1 to L_2 to L_3. The substitutability of cloth for labor in the manufacture of dresses also diminishes, as can be seen by considering the quantity of cloth that must be added to replace each unit of reduced labor in moving from L_3 to L_1. Most labor–capital substitutions in production systems exhibit this diminishing substitutability.

Marginal Rate of Technical Substitution

Marginal Rate of Technical Substitution
Amount of one input that must be substituted for another to maintain constant output.

The **marginal rate of technical substitution (MRTS)** is the amount of one input factor that must be substituted for 1 unit of another input factor to maintain a constant level of output. The marginal rate of technical substitution usually diminishes as the amount of substitution increases. In Figure 7.5(c), as more and more labor is substituted for cloth, the increment of labor necessary to replace cloth increases.

The marginal rate of technical substitution is directly related to the slope of a production isoquant. To see this, note that the loss in output resulting from a small reduction in Y equals the marginal product of Y multiplied by the change in Y, $\partial Q = MP_Y \times \partial Y$. Similarly, the change in Q associated with the increased use of X is given by the expression $\partial Q = MP_X \times \partial X$. Along a given isoquant, the absolute value of ∂Q associated with offsetting changes in X and Y must be the same. The change in output associated with a reduction in input Y must be exactly offset by the change in output resulting from the increase in input X for output to remain constant—as it must along an isoquant. Therefore, along any isoquant,

$$-(MP_X \times \partial X) = (MP_Y \times \partial Y)$$

After rearranging terms, it is clear that the marginal rate of technical substitution equals isoquant slope

$$MRTS_{XY} = -\frac{MP_X}{MP_Y} = \frac{\partial Y}{\partial X} = \text{Slope of an Isoquant} \qquad \textbf{7.4}$$

In Figure 7.5(c), the isoquant Q_1 has a very steep negative slope at the point (L_1, C_1). When cloth is relatively abundant, the marginal product of labor is relatively high as compared with the marginal product of cloth. When labor is relatively abundant at, say, point (L_3, C_3), the marginal product of labor is low relative to the marginal product of cloth.

Rational Limits of Input Substitution

It is irrational for a firm to combine resources in such a way that the marginal product of any input is negative because this implies that output could be increased by using less of that resource.[2] For a production isoquant to be positively sloped, one of the input factors must have a negative marginal product. Input combinations lying along a positively sloped portion of a production isoquant are irrational and would be avoided by the firm.

In Figure 7.6, the rational limits of input substitution are where the isoquants become positively sloped. Limits to the range of substitutability of X for Y are indicated by the points of tangency between the isoquants and a set of lines drawn perpendicular to the Y-axis. Limits of economic substitutability of Y for X are shown by the tangents of lines perpendicular to the X-axis. Maximum and minimum proportions of Y and X that would be combined to produce each level of output are determined by points of tangency between these lines and the production isoquants.

Ridge Lines

Graphic bounds for positive marginal products.

It is irrational to use any input combination outside these tangents, or **ridge lines**. Such combinations are irrational because the marginal product of the relatively more abundant input is negative outside the ridge lines. Obviously, it would be irrational for a firm to buy and employ additional units that cause production to decrease.

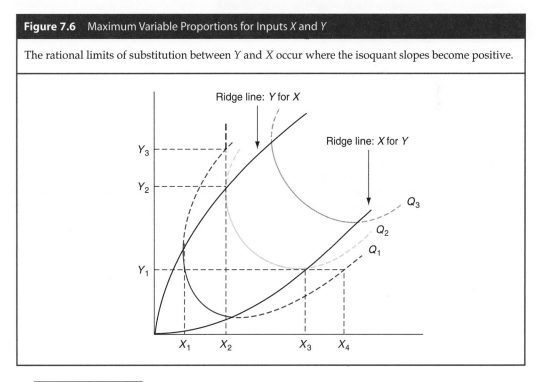

Figure 7.6 Maximum Variable Proportions for Inputs X and Y

The rational limits of substitution between Y and X occur where the isoquant slopes become positive.

---

2 This is technically correct only if the resource has a positive cost. A firm might employ additional workers even though the marginal product of labor was negative if it received an employment subsidy that more than offset the cost of the output reduction.

MARGINAL REVENUE PRODUCT AND OPTIMAL EMPLOYMENT

Selection of efficient input employment levels depends upon the ability of each input to produce profits.

Marginal Revenue Product

Marginal Revenue Product
Amount of revenue generated by employing the last input unit.

The economic productivity of an input is its **marginal revenue product**, or the additional net revenue generated by the last unit employed. In equation form, the marginal revenue product of input X, MRP_X, equals marginal product multiplied by the marginal revenue of output:

$$MRP_X = \frac{\partial TR}{\partial X}$$

$$= \frac{\partial Q}{\partial X} \times \frac{\partial TR}{\partial Q}$$

$$= MP_X \times MR_Q$$

7.5

Marginal revenue product is the economic value of a marginal unit of an input factor.[3]

Managerial Application 7.2

An Inconvenient Truth About Minimum Wages

The Fair Labor Standards Act (FLSA) of 1938 provides minimum standards for wages and overtime entitlement, and includes provisions related to child labor and equal pay. Early in the administration of the FLSA, it became apparent that uniform application of a Federal minimum wage was apt to produce an undesirable rise in unemployment among unskilled workers. In 1940, an amendment was enacted prescribing lower minimum wages in certain circumstances. On May 25, 2007, President Bush signed a bill that, among other things, increased the federal minimum wage in three steps: to $5.85 per hour effective July 24, 2007; to $6.55 per hour effective July 24, 2008; and to $7.25 per hour effective July 24, 2009.

Recent political discussion has focused on the benefits to be had from raising the Federal minimum wage. While everyone benefits from rising incomes among the working poor, it's important to consider hidden costs tied to raising minimum wages. Low-wage workers who keep their jobs obviously benefit from an increase in the Federal minimum wage. Low-wage workers who get laid off, or never hired

in the first place, because of minimum wage requirements suffer economic harm. Years ago, low-wage workers used to pump gas, carry out groceries, act as golf caddies, and perform a host of other services made uneconomic by high minimum wages. Self-serve labor provided by cost-conscious consumers has eliminated many low-wage employment opportunities. For example, consumers enjoy "free refills" on soda at fast-food restaurants while employers minimize labor costs by not having to fill drink orders. Similarly, restaurants have designed their businesses to minimize the need for waitresses, busboys, and dishwashers—all coveted jobs for low-wage workers. Those jobs are gone, and they are not coming back.

An inconvenient truth about increasing the Federal minimum wage is that doing so eliminates lots of low-wage jobs. That's bad for the working poor.

See: For detailed information, see the U.S. Department of Labor Employment Standards Administration Wage and Hour Division, http://www.dol.gov/esa/whd/flsa/.

---

3   The economic value of a marginal unit of an input factor is sometimes referred to as its value of marginal product (VMP), where $VMP_x = MP_x \times P_Q$. In a perfectly competitive market, $P_Q = MR_Q$ and $VMP_x = MRP_x$.

Table 7.4 illustrates marginal revenue product for a simple one-factor production system. The marginal revenue product values shown in column 4 assume that each unit of output can be sold for $25. The marginal revenue product of the first unit of X employed equals the 5 units of output produced times the $25 revenue received per unit, or $MRP_{X=1} = \$125$. The second unit of X adds 4 units of production, so $MRP_{X=2} = \$100$. Marginal revenue product for each additional unit of X is determined in this manner.

Optimal Level of a Single Input

To illustrate how the marginal revenue product concept is related to optimal input use, consider the following question: If the price of input X in the production system depicted in Table 7.4 is $60 per unit, how many units will the firm use? Clearly, the firm will employ 3 units of X because the value gained by adding the first 3 units exceeds marginal cost. When 3 units of X are employed, the third unit causes total revenues to rise by $75 while costing only $60. At the margin, employing the third unit of X increases total profit by $15 (= \$75 - \$60)$. A fourth unit of X would not be employed because the value of its marginal product ($50) is less than the cost of employment ($60); profit would decline by $10.

So long as marginal revenue exceeds marginal cost, profits must increase. In the context of production decisions, this means that profit will increase so long as the marginal revenue product of an input exceeds the marginal cost of employment. If marginal revenue product is less than the marginal cost of employment, marginal profit is negative, and the firm would reduce usage of that input.

The concept of optimal resource use can be clarified by examining a simple production system in which a single variable labor input, L, is used to produce a single product, Q. In general, profit maximization requires setting $M\pi = MR_Q - MC_Q = 0$. This occurs when $MR_Q = MC_Q$. If a single input L is employed, profit maximization requires setting the marginal cost of employment equal to the marginal revenue derived from employment. Because the marginal cost of employment is the price of L, optimal employment occurs when P_L is set equal to the marginal revenue product of L

$$MC_L = MR_L$$

$$\frac{\partial TC}{\partial L} = \frac{\partial TR_L}{\partial L}$$

7.6

$$P_L = MP_L \times MR_Q = MRP_L$$

Table 7.4 Marginal Revenue Product for a Single Input

Units of Input (X)	Total Product of X (Q)	Marginal Product of X ($MP_X = \partial Q/\partial X$)	Marginal Revenue Product of X ($MRP_X = MP_X \times \$25$)
1	5	5	$125
2	9	4	100
3	12	3	75
4	14	2	50
5	15	1	25

A profit-maximizing firm will always set marginal revenue product equal to price (marginal cost) for every input. If marginal revenue product exceeds the cost of an input, profits could be increased by employing additional units. If the marginal cost of an input factor is greater than its marginal revenue product, profit would increase by reducing employment. Only when $MRP = P$ is profit maximized. **Economic efficiency** is achieved in the overall economy if all firms employ resources so as to equate each input's marginal revenue product and marginal cost.

Economic Efficiency
Achieved when all firms equate input marginal revenue product and marginal cost (maximize profits).

Illustration of Optimal Employment

Determination of the optimal input level can be clarified by reconsidering the Tax Advisors, Inc., example, illustrated in Table 7.3. If three entry-level CPAs can process 2.4 returns per hour and employing a fourth CPA increases total output per hour to 2.8, then employing a fourth CPA reduces marginal product from $MP_{CPA=3} = 1.4$ to $MP_{CPA=4} = 0.4$. Employment is in a range of diminishing returns. Nevertheless, a fourth CPA should be hired if expanding employment will increase profits.

For simplicity, assume that CPA time is the only input required to process additional tax returns and that experienced CPAs earn $70 per hour, or roughly $140,000 per year including fringe benefits. If Tax Advisors, Inc., receives $200 in revenue for each tax return prepared by the fourth CPA, a comparison of the price of labor and marginal revenue product for the fourth CPA reveals

$$P_{CPA} < MRP_{CPA=4} = MR_Q \times MP_{CPA=4}$$

because

$$\$70 < \$80 = \$200 \times 0.4$$

If a fourth CPA is hired, total profits will rise by $10 per hour ($= \$80 - \$70$). Therefore, the additional CPA should be employed.

Because the marginal product for the fifth CPA equals 0.2, $MP_{CPA=5} = 0.2$, the marginal revenue product falls to only $40 per hour, or less than the $70-per-hour cost of hiring that person. The firm would incur a $30-per-hour loss by expanding hiring to that level and would, therefore, stop with employment of four CPAs.

This example assumes that CPA time is the only variable input involved in tax-return preparation. In reality, other inputs are apt to be necessary. Additional computer time, office supplies, and clerical support may also be required to increase output. If such were the case, determining the independent contribution or value of CPA input would be more complex. If *variable* overhead for CPA support staff and supplies equals 50 percent of sales revenue, then the **net marginal revenue**, or marginal revenue after all variable costs, for CPA time would be only $100 per unit ($= 0.5 \times MR_Q$). In this instance, Tax Advisors, Inc., would find that the $40 ($= 0.4 \times 0.5 \times \$200$) net marginal revenue product generated by the fourth CPA would not offset the necessary $70 per hour compensation expense. It would, therefore, employ no more than three CPAs, a level at which $MRP = 1.4 \times 0.5 \times \$200 = \$140 > \$70 = P_{CPA}$. The firm will employ additional CPAs only so long as their net marginal revenue product equals or exceeds their marginal cost (price of labor).

Net Marginal Revenue
Marginal revenue after all variable costs.

This explains why, for example, a law firm might hire new associates at annual salaries of $100,000 when it expects them to generate $250,000 per year in gross billings, or 1,250 billable hours at a rate of $200 per hour. If variable costs are $150,000 per associate, only $100,000 is available to cover associate salary expenses. When customers pay $200 per hour for legal services, they are paying for attorney time and expertise plus the support of legal secretaries, law clerks, office staff, supplies, facilities, and so on. By itself, new associate time is worth much less than $200 per hour. The net marginal revenue of new associate attorney time, or CPA time in the preceding Tax Advisors, Inc., example, is the *marginal* value created after allowing for the variable costs of all other inputs that must be increased to provide service.

OPTIMAL COMBINATION OF MULTIPLE INPUTS

Inputs are used in a cost-minimizing proportion when relative input prices equal relative marginal products.

Budget Lines

Isocost Curve (or Budget Line)
Line of constant costs.

Optimal input proportions can be found graphically for a two-input, single-output system by adding an **isocost curve** (or **budget line**) to the production isoquant diagram. Each point on an isocost curve represents a combination of inputs, say, X and Y, whose cost equals a constant expenditure. Budget lines illustrated in Figure 7.7 are constructed in the following manner: Let $P_X = \$500$ and $P_Y = \$250$, the prices of X and Y. For a given budget, say $B_1 = \$1,000$, the firm can purchase 4 units of Y ($= \$1,000/\$250$) and no units of X, or 2 units of X ($= \$1,000/\$500$) and none of Y. These two quantities represent the X and Y intercepts of a budget line, and a straight line connecting them identifies all combinations of X and Y that $\$1,000$ can purchase.

Figure 7.7 Isocost Curves

Each point on an isocost line represents a different combination of inputs that can be purchased at a given expenditure level.

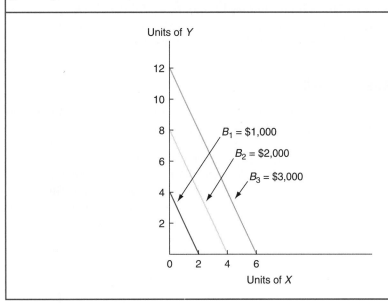

A budget line is merely a statement of the various combinations of inputs that can be purchased for a given dollar amount. The various combinations of X and Y that can be purchased for a fixed budget, B, are given by the expression

$$B = P_X \times X + P_Y \times Y$$

Solving this expression for Y so that it can be graphed, as in Figure 7.7, results in

$$Y = \frac{B}{P_Y} - \frac{P_X}{P_Y} X$$

The first term in this last equation is the Y-axis intercept of the isocost curve. It indicates the quantity of input Y that can be purchased with a given expenditure, assuming zero units of input X are bought. The slope of a budget line $\partial Y / \partial X = -P_X / P_Y$ and measures relative input prices. A change in the budget level, B, leads to a parallel shift in the budget line; changes in input prices alter the slope of the budget line.

These relations can be clarified by considering further the example illustrated in Figure 7.7. With a \$1,000 budget, the Y-axis intercept of the budget line has already been shown to be 4 units. Relative prices determine the slope of the budget line. Thus, in Figure 7.7 the slope of the isocost curves is given by the expression

$$\text{Slope} = \frac{-P_X}{P_Y} = \frac{-\$500}{\$250} = -2$$

Suppose that a firm has only \$1,000 to spend on inputs for the production of Q. Combining a set of production isoquants with the budget lines of Figure 7.7 to form Figure 7.8 indicates that the optimal input combination occurs at point A, the point of tangency between the budget line and a production isoquant. At that point, X and Y are combined in proportions that maximize the output attainable for an expenditure B_1. No other combination of X and Y that can be purchased for \$1,000 will produce as much output. All other (X, Y) combinations along the budget line through (X_1, Y_1) must intersect isoquants representing lower output quantities. The combination (X_1, Y_1) is the least-cost input combination that can produce output Q_1. All other (X, Y) combinations on the Q_1 isoquant lie on higher budget lines. Similarly, (X_2, Y_2) is the least-cost input combination for producing Q_2, and so on. All other possible combinations for producing Q_1, Q_2, and Q_3 are intersected by higher budget lines.

Expansion Path

Expansion Path
Optimal input combinations as the scale of production expands.

By connecting points of tangency between isoquants and budget lines (points A, B, and C), an **expansion path** is identified that depicts optimal input combinations as the scale of production expands.

At the point of optimal input combination, isocost and the isoquant curves are tangent and have equal slope. The slope of an isocost curve equals $-P_X / P_Y$. The slope of an isoquant curve equals the marginal rate of technical substitution of one input factor for another when the quantity of production is held constant. Therefore, for optimal input combinations, the ratio of input prices must equal the ratio of input marginal products:

$$\frac{P_X}{P_Y} = \frac{MP_X}{MP_Y} \qquad \qquad \textbf{7.7}$$

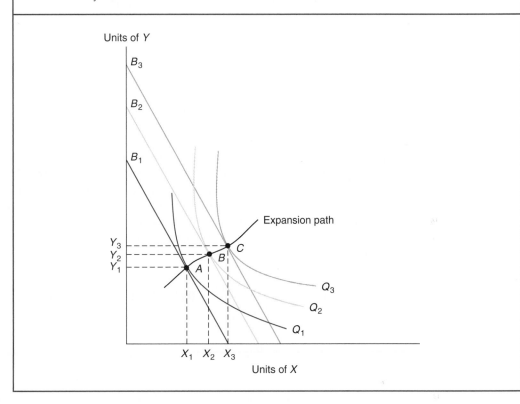

Figure 7.8   Optimal Input Combinations

The points of tangency between the isoquant and isocost curves depict optimal input combinations at different activity levels.

Alternatively, an optimal combination of inputs is achieved if the ratio of marginal product to price is the same for all inputs.

$$\frac{MP_X}{P_X} = \frac{MP_Y}{P_Y}$$

7.8

If the marginal product to price ratio is the same for all inputs, the marginal cost of output is the same across all inputs. Optimal input proportions are employed because an additional dollar spent on any input yields the same increase in output. Any input combination violating this rule is suboptimal because a change in input proportions could result in the same quantity of output at lower cost.

Illustration of Optimal Input Proportions

The Tax Advisors, Inc., example can further illustrate these relations. Assume that in addition to three CPAs, four bookkeepers are employed at a wage (including fringes) of $30 per hour and that $MP_{B=4} = 0.3$. This compares with a CPA compensation of $70 per hour and $MP_{CPA=3} = 1.4$. Based on these assumptions, the marginal product per dollar spent on each input is

$$\frac{MP_{B=4}}{P_B} = \frac{0.3}{\$30} = 0.01 \text{ Units Per Dollar (for bookkeepers)}$$

and

$$\frac{MP_{CPA=3}}{P_{CPA}} = \frac{1.4}{\$70} = 0.02 \text{ Units Per Dollar (for CPAs)}$$

Such an input combination violates the optimal proportions rule because the ratios of marginal products to input prices are not equal. The last dollar spent on bookkeeper input produces ("buys") 0.01 units of output (tax-return preparations), whereas the last dollar spent on CPA time produces twice as much, 0.02 units. By transferring $1 of cost from bookkeeper time to CPA time, the firm could increase total output by 0.01 tax-return preparations per hour without increasing total cost. Expenditures on the CPA input represent a better use of firm resources, and the company should reallocate resources to employ relatively more CPAs and relatively fewer bookkeepers.

The marginal product to price ratio indicates the marginal cost of output from a marginal unit of input X or Y. In this example, this implies that

$$MC_Q = \frac{P_B}{MP_{B=4}} = \frac{\$30}{0.3} = \$100 \text{ Per Unit (using bookkeepers)}$$

and

$$MC_Q = \frac{P_{CPA}}{MP_{CPA=3}} = \frac{\$70}{1.4} = \$50 \text{ Per Unit (using CPAs)}$$

Again, the superior economic productivity of CPAs is indicated; they are able to produce output at one-half the marginal cost of output produced by bookkeepers.

The determination of optimal input proportions is based upon only input prices and marginal product relations. Because the economic value of output is not considered, these data are insufficient to allow calculation of optimal employment *levels*. The next section introduces output value to determine the optimal level of resource employment.

OPTIMAL LEVELS OF MULTIPLE INPUTS

Profit maximization requires cost-minimizing input proportions at the best possible level of output.

Optimal Employment and Profit Maximization

If an optimal input combination is employed, the ratio of input prices will equal the ratio of marginal products, as shown in Equation (7.7). Similarly, an optimal combination of inputs is achieved if marginal product to price ratios are the same for all inputs [Equation (7.8)]. In both instances, the cost of a given level of output is minimized. However, cost minimization constitutes a necessary but insufficient condition for profit maximization. Profit maximization requires that a firm employ optimal input proportions and produce the most advantageous quantity of output.

Profits are maximized when inputs are employed so that price equals marginal revenue product for each input:

$$P_X = MP_X \times MR_Q = MRP_X \qquad \textbf{7.9}$$

and

$$P_Y = MP_Y \times MR_Q = MRP_Y \qquad \textbf{7.10}$$

The difference between cost minimization and profit maximization is simple. Cost minimization requires efficient resource use, as reflected by optimal input proportions. Profit maximization requires efficient resource use *and* production of an optimal level of output, as made possible by the most favorable employment of all inputs.

Illustration of Optimal Levels of Multiple Inputs

A final look at the Tax Advisors, Inc., example illustrates these relations. Recall that with three CPAs and four bookkeepers the marginal product to price ratios for each input indicates a need to employ more CPAs relative to the number of bookkeepers. Assume that hiring one more bookkeeper leaves unchanged their marginal product of 0.3 tax returns processed per hour ($MP_{B=5} = 0.3$). Also assume that with this increased

---

Managerial Application 7.3

What's Wrong with Manufacturing?

The share of gross domestic product (GDP) accounted for by manufacturing fell from 46.9 percent in 1959 to 31.3 percent in 2007. Over the same period, the share of the overall economy accounted for by services jumped from 40.7 percent to 57.9 percent; the share accounted for by construction (structures) has fallen modestly from 12.3 percent to 10.8 percent. Politicians, union leaders, and some business executives lament these trends and ask: What's wrong with manufacturing?

In fact, there is nothing wrong with U.S. manufacturing. Rapid productivity growth in manufacturing has lowered the relative price of manufactured goods, but demand has not grown proportionately. During recent decades, manufacturing productivity growth has exceeded productivity growth overall by about 1 percentage point per year. The disparity is even wider in recent years. An hour of work in manufacturing produces about four times as much today as it did 50 years ago; an hour of work in the nonfarm business sector produced about three times as much in 2000 as it did 50 years ago. This dramatic productivity differential has contributed to a decline in the price of manufactured goods relative to services.

The boost in real income from the relative price decline for manufactured goods has supported increased demand for goods and services; however, consumers increasingly want services. Per capita consumption of manufactured goods more than quadrupled in real dollars during the past 50 years, but the demand services grew even faster. For example, consumers often react to lower relative car prices by using their savings to buy more education or health care rather than to buy another car. It may be ironic that rapid productivity growth in the manufacturing sector has boosted demand for services even more than demand for manufactured goods, but a vibrant economy produces more of what consumers want as incomes rise.

Far from representing a "problem" for the U.S. economy, rapid productivity increases in manufacturing have been a large and continuing source of economic betterment.

See: Council of Economic Advisors, *Economic Report of the President* (United States Printing Office; Washington, DC, February 2007), Chapter 2, http://www.whitehouse.gov/cea/2007_erp.pdf.

employment of bookkeepers the marginal product of the fourth CPA increases from 0.4 to 0.7 tax returns processed per hour. The marginal productivity of an input factor (CPAs) is typically enhanced when used in conjunction with more of a complementary input, bookkeepers in this case. Now $MP_{B=5} = 0.3$ and $MP_{CPA=4} = 0.7$. With the costs of each input remaining constant at $P_B = \$30$ and $P_{CPA} = \$70$, the marginal product-to-price ratios are now equal:

$$\frac{MP_{B=5}}{P_B} = \frac{0.3}{\$30} = 0.01 \text{ Units Per Dollar (for bookkeepers)}$$

and

$$\frac{MP_{CPA=4}}{P_{CPA}} = \frac{0.7}{\$70} = 0.01 \text{ Units Per Dollar (for CPAs)}$$

The combination of four CPAs and five bookkeepers is now optimal from a cost-minimizing standpoint, and input *proportions* are optimal. However, it is unclear whether an optimal *level* of input has been employed. Does the resulting output level maximize profit? To answer this question, it becomes necessary to determine if marginal revenue product equals the marginal cost of each input. If net marginal revenue (*NMR*) per return remains at $\$100 = (\$200 \times 0.5)$, then

$$MRP_B = MP_B \times NMR_Q$$
$$= 0.3 \times \$100 = \$30$$
$$MRP_B = \$30 = P_B$$

and

$$MRP_{CPA} = MP_{CPA} \times NMR_Q$$
$$= 0.7 \times \$100 = \$70$$
$$MRP_{CPA} = \$70 = P_{CPA}$$

Marginal revenue product equals marginal cost for each input. The combination of four CPAs and five bookkeepers is an optimal level of employment because the resulting output quantity maximizes profit.

RETURNS TO SCALE

Increasing Returns to Scale
When the proportional increase in output is larger than an underlying proportional increase in input.

Constant Returns to Scale
When a given percentage increase in all inputs leads to an identical percentage increase in output.

Decreasing Returns to Scale
When output increases at a rate less than the proportionate increase in inputs.

Returns to scale describe how output responds to a proportionate increase in all inputs.

Output Elasticity and Returns to Scale

Increasing returns to scale are prevalent if the proportional increase in output is larger than the underlying proportional increase in inputs. **Constant returns to scale** exist when a given percentage increase in all inputs leads to that same percentage increase in output. If output increases at a rate less than the proportionate increase in inputs, **decreasing returns to scale** are present. Many production systems exhibit first increasing, then constant, then decreasing returns to scale. The region of increasing returns is attributable to specialization. As output increases, specialized labor can be used and efficient large-scale machinery can be used in the production process. Beyond some scale of operation, however, further gains from specialization are limited and coordination problems emerge. When coordination expenses more than offset additional benefits of specialization, decreasing returns to scale set in.

Returns to scale can be accurately determined for any production function through analysis of **output elasticity**. Output elasticity, ε_Q, is the percentage change in output associated with a 1 percent change in all inputs. Letting $\underline{X}$ represent all input factors,

Output Elasticity
Percentage change in output associated with a 1 percent change in all inputs.

$$\text{Point Output Elasticity} = \varepsilon_Q = \frac{\text{Percentage Change in Output } (Q)}{\text{Percentage Change in All Inputs } (\underline{X})} \qquad \textbf{7.11}$$

$$= \frac{\partial Q/Q}{\partial \underline{X}/\underline{X}} = \frac{\partial Q}{\partial \underline{X}} \times \frac{\underline{X}}{Q}$$

If $\underline{X}$ refers to capital, labor, energy, and so on, then the following relations hold.

If	Then	Returns to Scale Are
Percentage change in Q > Percentage change in $\underline{X}$	$\varepsilon_Q > 1$	Increasing
Percentage change in Q = Percentage change in $\underline{X}$	$\varepsilon_Q = 1$	Constant
Percentage change in Q < Percentage change in $\underline{X}$	$\varepsilon_Q < 1$	Diminishing

Thus, returns to scale can be analyzed by examining the relationship between the rate of increase in inputs and the quantity of output produced.

Returns to Scale Estimation

In most instances, returns to scale can be easily estimated. For example, assume that all inputs in the unspecified production function $Q = f(X, Y, Z)$ are increased by using the constant factor k, where $k = 1.01$ for a 1 percent increase, $k = 1.02$ for a 2 percent increase, and so on. Then, the production is

$$hQ = f(kX, kY, kZ)$$

where h is the proportional increase in Q resulting from a k-fold increase in each input factor. If $h > k$, then the percentage change in Q is greater than the percentage change in the inputs, $\varepsilon_Q > 1$, and the production function exhibits increasing returns to scale. If $h = k$, then the percentage change in Q equals the percentage change in the inputs, $\varepsilon_Q = 1$, and the production function exhibits constant returns to scale. If $h < k$, then the percentage change in Q is less than the percentage change in the inputs, $\varepsilon_Q < 1$, and the production function exhibits decreasing returns to scale.

For certain production functions, called homogeneous production functions, when each input factor is multiplied by a constant k, the constant can be completely factored out of the production function expression. Following a k-fold increase in all inputs, the production function takes the form $hQ = k^n f(X, Y, Z)$. The exponent n provides the key to returns-to-scale estimation. If $n = 1$, then $h = k$ and the function exhibits constant returns to scale. If $n > 1$, then $h > k$, indicating increasing returns to scale, whereas $n < 1$ indicates $h < k$ and decreasing returns to scale. In all other instances, the easiest means for determining the nature of returns to scale is through numerical example.

To illustrate, consider the production function $Q = 2X + 3Y + 1.5Z$. Returns to scale can be determined by learning how an arbitrary, say 2 percent, increase in all inputs affects output. If, initially, $X = 100$, $Y = 200$, and $Z = 200$, output is found to be

$$Q_1 = 2(100) + 3(200) + 1.5(200)$$
$$= 200 + 600 + 300 = 1{,}100 \text{ units}$$

Increasing all inputs by 2 percent (letting $k = 1.02$) leads to the input quantities $X = 102$, $Y = 204$, and $Z = 204$, and

$$Q_2 = 2(102) + 3(204) + 1.5(204)$$
$$= 204 + 612 + 306 = 1{,}122 \text{ units}$$

Because a 2 percent increase in all inputs has led to a 2 percent increase in output ($1.02 = 1{,}122/1{,}100$), this production system exhibits constant returns to scale.

From a theoretical standpoint, an appealing functional form for production function estimation is cubic, such as the equation

$$Q = a + bXY + cX^2Y + dXY^2 - eX^3Y - fXY^3$$

Such functions exhibit stages of first increasing and then decreasing returns to scale. In many instances, simple functional specifications can be used to estimate production functions. A **power production function** implies a simple multiplicative relation between output and input of the form

Power Production Function
Multiplicative relation between input and output.

$$Q = b_0 \, X^{b1} \, Y^{b2}$$

Power functions allow the marginal productivity of a given input to depend on the levels of *all* inputs, a realistic assumption in many production systems. Power functions are also easy to estimate in log-linear form using least squares regression analysis because a power production function is mathematically equivalent to

$$\log Q = \log b_0 + b_1 \log X + b_2 \log Y$$

Returns to scale are easily estimated by summing the exponents of power production functions or, equivalently, by summing log-linear model coefficient estimates. A sum greater than one indicates increasing returns. A sum equal to one indicates constant returns. If the sum is less than one, diminishing returns are indicated. Power functions have been successfully used in a large number of empirical production studies since Charles W. Cobb and Paul H. Douglas's pioneering work in the late 1920s. The impact of their work is so great that power production functions are frequently referred to as Cobb–Douglas production functions.

PRODUCTIVITY MEASUREMENT

Growing productivity improves economic welfare for the general population.

Managerial Application 7.4

CEO Compensation

Corporate boards of directors have been under the gun, and rightly so, to make sure that the CEO and other top management earn what they get paid. CEOs at the 500 largest U.S. corporations take home compensation in the form of salary, bonus, stock options, and stock appreciation that averages roughly $5 million per year, and which can run into hundreds of millions of dollars per year for the top-paid CEOs. Some CEOs really earn their pay. Top performers who run companies with rapidly growing revenues, profits, and stock prices can be worth tens of millions of dollars per year to their stockholders. The problem is that some highly paid CEOs preside over companies with diminishing business prospects and crumbling stock prices. In such instances it is difficult, if not impossible, to justify the amounts paid to poorly performing CEOs.

Almost all large corporations use heavy doses of performance-based pay to compensate their CEOs. Unfortunately, CEOs at many such companies have been involved in accounting shenanigans that temporarily boosted reported results and CEO compensation. Notorious examples include accounting scandals at AOL,

Adelphia, Enron, Global Crossing, ImClone Systems, Qwest Communications, Sunbeam, and Tyco International. The options backdating scandal that rocked executive suites at more the 150 large U.S. corporations also give egregious examples of CEO malfeasance and criminal behavior. CEOs and other top corporate officials were found guilty of secretly backdating option grants to coincide with low stock prices so that such options would be worth more money at the time of exercise. In so doing, CEOs exposed themselves and their companies to civil complaints issued by the Securities and Exchange Commission (SEC), and criminal sanctions instigated by U.S. Department of Justice and the Internal Revenue Service. Scores of top executives lost their jobs and had tens of million of dollars' worth of options grants reduced or eliminated. Companies were forced to restate tens of millions of dollars in revenues and profits.

For up-to-date information on compensation trends for CEOs of the largest U.S. corporations, check out the *Forbes* annual survey.

See: http://www.forbes.com/.

Economic Productivity

Productivity Growth
Rate of increase in output per unit of input.

The pace of economic betterment is measured by the rate of **productivity growth**, or rate of increase in output per unit of input.[4] For U.S. workers to earn higher wages than workers in other countries, U.S. labor productivity, or output per worker hour, must exceed that of lower-wage countries. The total amount of goods and services produced, as measured by GDP, can grow only if productivity or hours of work increase. As the baby boomers (those born between 1946 and 1964) reach retirement, growth in total hours of work across the U.S. economy will slow, and the United States will have to depend increasingly on productivity growth to drive increases in GDP. Since 1995, productivity growth has averaged over 2.5 percent per year, compared to an average growth rate of about 1.4 percent per year over the preceding 20 years. Most other major industrialized countries suffered a slowdown in productivity growth from 2000–2005, but in the United States, growth accelerated to 3.1 percent per year, the fastest productivity growth of any major industrialized country. If productivity continues to

---

4   This section summarizes information found in the Council of Economic Advisors, *Economic Report of the President* (United States Printing Office; Washington, DC, February 2007), Chapter 2, http://www.whitehouse.gov/cea/2007_erp.pdf.

grow at the 2000–2005 rate of 3.1 percent per year, the U.S. standard of living will double in about 23 years; at the slower 1973–1995 productivity growth rate of 1.4 percent per year, doubling the U.S. standard of living would take roughly 50 years.

Causes of Productivity Growth

Efficiency Gains
Improvements in how well labor and capital are used.

Capital Deepening
Growth in the amount of capital that workers have available for use.

Recent productivity growth in the United States has been driven by **efficiency gains**, measured in terms of how well labor and capital are used, and by **capital deepening**, or growth in the amount of capital that workers have available for use.

Businesses achieve efficiency gains when they devise better ways of organizing and using the equipment they own and the people they employ. Efficiency gains include both process innovations, which increase productivity by reducing the capital or labor needed to produce a unit of output, and product innovations, which increase productivity by increasing the value of output. For example, managers at a 3M tape manufacturing plant increased productivity by reorganizing part of their production process. By moving machines such as glue coaters and tape slitters closer to the packing equipment and robotic transporters, 3M substantially increased labor productivity at its plant. The reorganization reduced the need to move output

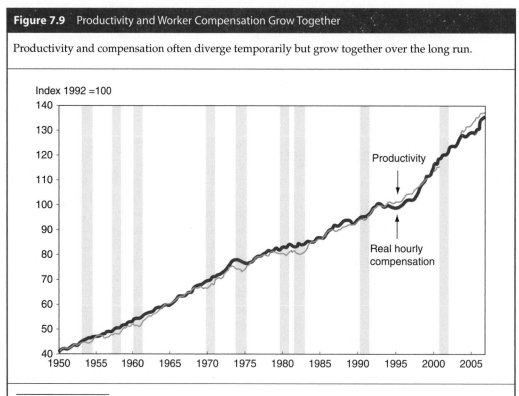

Figure 7.9 Productivity and Worker Compensation Grow Together

Productivity and compensation often diverge temporarily but grow together over the long run.

Note: These data cover all persons (including supervisory workers and proprietors) in the nonfarm business sector.

Real hourly compensation is hourly compensation deflated by the price deflator for nonfarm business output.

Shaded areas denote recessions.

Source: Department of Labor (Bureau of Labor Statistics).

See: Council of Economic Advisors, *Economic Report of the President* (United States Printing Office; Washington, DC, February 2007), p. 51, http://www.whitehouse.gov/cea/2007_erp.pdf.

around the plant, and cut the length of the production cycle. In addition, with all the packing supplies located in one place, managers could see when they had more than they needed and could cut costs by reducing excess inventories of supplies. This improvement is an efficiency gain because the plant produced more output without increasing capital or labor.

Capital deepening occurs when businesses invest in more or better machinery, equipment, and structures, all of which make it possible for their employees to produce more output. Examples of capital deepening include the purchase of more sophisticated machine tools for workers in the manufacturing sector, or a faster computer system for a hospital. Figure 7.9 illustrates how efficiency gains, capital deepening, and greater worker skill have contributed to U.S. productivity growth and rising worker earnings in recent years. The economic gains from productivity growth reach workers directly through growing worker compensation. Over long periods of time, productivity and compensation grow at about the same rate. When productivity grows faster than compensation, businesses' profits tend to rise because the value of the goods and services they sell rises faster than their payroll costs. As a result, profits tend to rise during periods of rapid productivity growth. As tight labor markets bid up employee compensation, the increase in labor costs cuts into profits, and profits return to normal levels. In this process, profits vary more dramatically than employee compensation, falling much more sharply during recessions and then growing much more quickly in the early parts of the recovery.

SUMMARY

This chapter introduces and analyzes the creative process of production. Several important properties of production systems are examined.

- A **production function** specifies the maximum output that can be produced for a given amount of inputs. A **discrete production function** involves distinct, or "lumpy," patterns for input combinations. In a **continuous production function**, inputs can be varied in an unbroken marginal fashion. **Returns to scale** describe the output effect of a proportional increase in all inputs. The relation between output and variation in only one of the inputs used is described as the **returns to a factor**.

- **Total product** is the total output from a production system. **Marginal product** is the change in output associated with a 1-unit change in an input, holding all other inputs constant. **Average product** is total product divided by the number of units of input employed. The **law of diminishing returns** states that as the quantity of a variable input increases, with the quantities of all other factors being held constant, the resulting rate of increase in output eventually diminishes.

- An **isoquant** represents the different combinations of inputs that can be used efficiently to produce a specified quantity of output. Efficiency in this case refers to **technical efficiency**, meaning the least-cost production of a target level of output.

- **Input substitution**, or the systematic replacement of productive factors, is an important consideration when judging the efficiency of any production system. The **marginal rate of technical substitution** measures the amount of one input that must be substituted for another to maintain a constant level of output. It is irrational for a firm to use any input combination outside **ridge lines** that indicate the bounds of positive marginal products.

- **Marginal revenue product** is the amount of revenue generated by employing the last unit of a given input. Profit maximization requires that marginal revenue product and price be set equal for each input. **Economic efficiency** is achieved when all firms employ resources so as to equate each input's marginal revenue product and marginal cost. It is important to focus upon the **net marginal revenue** of each input, after allowing for other variable costs. Similarly important is the firm's **isocost curve** (or **budget line**), or line of constant costs. An **expansion path** depicts optimal input combinations as the scale of production expands.

- **Increasing returns to scale** are prevalent if the proportional increase in output is larger than the underlying proportional increase in inputs. **Constant returns to scale** exist when a given percentage increase in all inputs leads to that same percentage increase in output. If output increases at a slower rate than inputs, **decreasing returns to scale** are present.

- **Output elasticity**, ε_Q, is the percentage change in output associated with a 1 percent change in all inputs. It is a practical means for returns-to-scale estimation. **Power production functions** indicate a multiplicative relation between input and output and are often used in production function estimation.

- The pace of economic betterment is measured by the rate of **productivity growth**, or rate of increase in output per unit of input. Recent productivity growth in the United States has been driven by **efficiency gains**, measured in terms of how well labor and capital are used, and by **capital deepening**, or growth in the amount of capital that workers have available for use.

The successful analysis and estimation of production relations is fundamental to the ongoing success of any organization. Concepts developed in this chapter can be used to understand, refine, and improve the policies of successful companies.

QUESTIONS

Q7.1 Is use of least-cost input combinations a necessary condition for profit maximization? Is it a sufficient condition? Explain.

Q7.2 "Output per worker is expected to increase by 10 percent during the next year. Therefore, wages can also increase by 10 percent with no harmful effects on employment, output prices, or employer profits." Discuss this statement.

Q7.3 Commission-based and piece-rate–based compensation plans are commonly employed by businesses. Use the concepts developed in the chapter to explain these phenomena.

Q7.4 "Hourly wage rates are an anachronism. Efficiency requires incentive-based pay tied to performance." Discuss this statement.

Q7.5 Explain why the MP/P relation is deficient as the sole mechanism for determining the optimal level of resource employment.

Q7.6 Clarify how profits are maximized and the optimal level of employment is achieved in a competitive labor market when the price of labor $P_L = MRP_L$.

Q7.7 "Oregon's minimum wage increased from \$4.75 in 1996 to \$5.50 in 1997, to \$6 in 1998, and to \$6.50 in 1999. According to a study by the Oregon Center for Public Policy, the minimum wage increases in Oregon did not harm welfare recipients' opportunities to find work. In fact, a larger percentage of welfare recipients in Oregon found jobs after the minimum wage increased than before the increases." Discuss how these facts could be consistent with a downward-sloping demand curve for unskilled labor.

Q7.8 Powerful unions like the AFL-CIO are staunch advocates for increasing the federal minimum wage despite the fact that highly trained and experienced AFL-CIO workers tend to earn far more than the minimum wage. Can you give an economic rationale for the AFL-CIO's position?

Q7.9 Cite some ways for increasing productivity growth in the United States.

Q7.10 Explain why company productivity is important to managers, employees, and investors. Is superior worker productivity a necessary and sufficient condition for above-average compensation?

SELF-TEST PROBLEMS AND SOLUTIONS

ST7.1 Optimal Input Usage. Medical Testing Labs, Inc., provides routine testing services for blood banks in the Los Angeles area. Tests are supervised by skilled technicians using equipment produced by two leading competitors in the medical equipment industry. Records for the current year show an average of 27 tests per hour being performed on the Testlogic-1 and 48 tests per hour on a new machine, the Accutest-3. The Testlogic-1 is leased for $18,000 per month, and the Accutest-3 is leased at $32,000 per month. On average, each machine is operated 25 eight-hour days per month.

A. Describe the logic of the rule used to determine an optimal mix of input usage.

B. Does Medical Testing Labs' usage reflect an optimal mix of testing equipment?

C. Describe the logic of the rule used to determine an optimal level of input usage.

D. If tests are conducted at a price of $6 each while labor and all other costs are fixed, should the company lease more machines?

ST7.1 SOLUTION

A.. The rule for an optimal combination of Testlogic-1 (T) and Accutest-3 (A) equipment is

$$\frac{MP_T}{P_T} = \frac{MP_A}{P_A}$$

This rule means that an identical amount of additional output would be produced with an additional dollar expenditure on each input. Alternatively, an equal marginal cost of output is incurred irrespective of which input is used to expand output. Of course, marginal products and equipment prices must both reflect the same relevant time frame, either hours or months.

B. On a per hour basis, the relevant question is

$$\frac{27}{\$18,000/(25 \times 8)} = \frac{48}{\$32,000/(25 \times 8)}$$
$$0.3 = 0.3$$

On a per month basis, the relevant question is

$$\frac{27 \times (25 \times 8)}{\$18,000} = \frac{48 \times (25 \times 8)}{\$32,000}$$
$$0.3 = 0.3$$

In both instances, the last dollar spent on each machine increased output by the same 0.3 units, indicating an *optimal mix* of testing machines.

C.. The rule for optimal input employment is

$$MRP = MP \times MR_Q = \text{Input Price}$$

This means that the level of input employment is optimal when the marginal sales revenue derived from added input usage is equal to input price, or the marginal cost of employment.

D. For each machine hour, the relevant question is

<u>Testlogic-1</u>
$$MRP_T = MP_T \times MR_Q = P_T$$
$$27 \times \$6 = \$18,000/(25 \times 8)$$
$$\$162 > \$90$$

<u>Accutest-3</u>
$$MRP_A = MP_A \times MR_Q = P_A$$
$$48 \times \$6 = \$32,000/(25 \times 8)$$
$$\$288 > \$160$$

Or, in per month terms

<u>Testlogic-1</u>
$$MRP_T = MP_T \times MR_Q = P_T$$
$$27 \times (25 \times 8) \times \$6 = \$18,000$$
$$\$32,400 > \$18,000$$

<u>Accutest-3</u>
$$MRP_A = MP_A 3 MR_Q = P_A$$
$$48 \times (25 \times 8) + \$6 = \$32,000$$
$$\$57,600 > \$32,000$$

In both cases, each machine returns more than its marginal cost (price) of employment, and expansion would be profitable.

ST7.2 Production Function Estimation.

Washington-Pacific, Inc., manufactures and sells lumber, plywood, veneer, particle board, medium-density fiberboard, and laminated beams. The company has estimated the following multiplicative production function for basic lumber products in the Pacific Northwest market using monthly production data over the past 2½ years (30 observations):

$$Q = b_0 L^{b_1} K^{b_2} E^{b_3}$$

where

Q = output
L = labor input in worker hours
K = capital input in machine hours
E = energy input in BTUs

Each of the parameters of this model was estimated by regression analysis using monthly data over a recent 3-year period. Coefficient estimation results were as follows:

$$\hat{b}_0 = 0.9; \hat{b}_1 = 0.4; \hat{b}_2 = 0.4; \quad \text{and} \quad \hat{b}_3 = 0.2$$

The standard error estimates for each coefficient are

$$\sigma_{\hat{b}_0} = 0.6; \sigma_{\hat{b}_1} = 0.1; \sigma_{\hat{b}_2} = 0.2; \sigma_{\hat{b}_3} = 0.1$$

A. Estimate the effect on output of a 1 percent decline in worker hours (holding K and E constant).

B. Estimate the effect on output of a 5 percent reduction in machine hours availability accompanied by a 5 percent decline in energy input (holding L constant).

C. Estimate the returns to scale for this production system.

ST7.2 SOLUTION

A. For Cobb–Douglas production functions, calculations of the elasticity of output with respect to individual inputs can be made by simply referring to the exponents of the production relation. Here a 1 percent decline in L, holding all else equal, will lead to a 0.4 percent decline in output. Notice that

$$\frac{\partial Q/Q}{\partial L/L} = \frac{\partial Q}{\partial L} \times \frac{L}{Q}$$

$$= \frac{(b_0 b_1 L^{b_1-1} K^{b_2} E^{b_3}) \times L}{Q}$$

$$= \frac{b_0 b_1 L^{b_1-1+1} K^{b_2} E^{b_3}}{b_0 L^{b_1} K^{b_2} E^{b_3}}$$

$$= b_1$$

And because $(\partial Q/Q)/(\partial L/L)$ is the percent change in Q due to a 1 percent change in L,

$$\frac{\partial Q/Q}{\partial L/L} = b_1$$

$$\partial Q/Q = b_1 \times \partial L/L$$

$$= 0.4(-0.01)$$

$$= -0.004 \text{ or } -0.4\%$$

B. From part A it is obvious that

$$\partial Q/Q = b_2(\partial K/K) + b_3(\partial E/E)$$

$$= 0.4(-0.05) + 0.2(-0.05)$$

$$= -0.03 \text{ or } -3\%$$

C. In the case of Cobb–Douglas production functions, returns to scale are determined by simply summing exponents because

$$Q = b_0 L^{b_1} K^{b_2} E^{b_3}$$

$$hQ = b_0(kL)^{b_1}(kK)^{b_2}(kE)^{b_3}$$

$$= k^{b_1+b_2+b_3} b_0 L^{b_1} K^{b_2} E^{b_3}$$

$$= k^{b_1+b_2+b_3} Q$$

Here $b_1 + b_2 + b_3 = 0.4 + 0.4 + 0.2 = 1$, indicating constant returns to scale. This means that a 1 percent increase in all inputs will lead to a 1 percent increase in output, and average costs will remain constant as output increases.

PROBLEMS

P7.1   Marginal Rate of Technical Substitution.   The following production table gives estimates of the maximum amounts of output possible with different combinations of two input factors, X and Y. (Assume that these are just illustrative points on a spectrum of continuous input combinations.)

Units of Y Used	Estimated Output Per Day				
5	210	305	360	421	470
4	188	272	324	376	421
3	162	234	282	324	360
2	130	188	234	272	305
1	94	130	162	188	210
	1	2	3	4	5
	Units of X used				

A. Do the two inputs exhibit the characteristics of constant, increasing, or decreasing marginal rates of technical substitution? How do you know?

B. Assuming that output sells for $3 per unit, complete the following tables:

X Fixed at 2 Units				
Units of Y Used	Total Product of Y	Marginal Product of Y	Average Product of Y	Marginal Revenue Product of Y
1				
2				
3				
4				
5				

Y Fixed at 3 Units				
Units of X Used	Total Product of X	Marginal Product of X	Average Product of X	Marginal Revenue Product of X
1				
2				
3				
4				
5				

C. Assume that the quantity of X is fixed at 2 units. If output sells for $3 and the cost of Y is $120 per day, how many units of Y will be employed?

D. Assume that the company is currently producing 162 units of output per day using 1 unit of X and 3 units of Y. The daily cost per unit of X is \$120 and that of Y is also \$120. Would you recommend a change in the present input combination? Why or why not?

E. What is the nature of the returns to scale for this production system if the optimal input combination requires that $X = Y$?

P7.2   Production Function Concepts.   Indicate whether each of the following statements is true or false. Explain your answers.

A. Decreasing returns to scale and increasing average costs are indicated when $\varepsilon_Q < 1$.

B. If the marginal product of capital falls as capital usage grows, the returns to capital are decreasing.

C. L-shaped isoquants describe production systems in which inputs are perfect substitutes.

D. Marginal revenue product measures the profit earned through expanding input usage.

E. The marginal rate of technical substitution will be affected by a given percentage increase in the marginal productivity of all inputs.

P7.3   Compensation Policy.   "Pay for performance" means that employee compensation closely reflects the amount of value derived from each employee's effort. In economic terms, the value derived from employee effort is measured by net marginal revenue product. It is the amount of profit generated by the employee, before accounting for employment costs. Holding all else equal, indicate whether each of the following factors would be responsible for increasing or decreasing the amount of money available for employee merit-based pay.

A. Government mandates for employer-provided health insurance

B. Rising productivity due to better worker training

C. Rising employer sales due to falling imports

D. Falling prices for industry output

E. Rising prevalence of uniform employee stock options.

P7.4   Returns to Scale.   Determine whether the following production functions exhibit constant, increasing, or decreasing returns to scale.

A. $Q = 0.5X + 2Y + 40Z$

B. $Q = 3L + 10K + 500$

C. $Q = 4A + 6B + 8AB$

D. $Q = 7L^2 + 5LK + 2K^2$

E. $Q = 10L^{0.5}K^{0.3}$

P7.5   Optimal Compensation Policy.   Café-Nervosa.com, based in Seattle, Washington, is a rapidly growing family business that offers a line of distinctive coffee products to local and regional coffee shops. Assume founder and president Frasier Crane is reviewing the company's sales force compensation plan. Currently, the company pays its three experienced sales staff members a salary based on years of service, past contributions to the company, and so on. Niles Crane, a new sales trainee and brother of Frasier Crane, is paid a more modest salary. Monthly sales and salary data for each employee are as follows:

Sales Staff	Average Monthly Sales ($)	Monthly Salary ($)
Roz Doyle	160,000	6,000
Daphne Moon	100,000	4,500
Martin Crane	90,000	3,600
Niles Crane	75,000	2,500

Niles Crane has shown great promise during the past year, and Frasier Crane believes that a substantial raise is clearly justified. At the same time, some adjustment to the compensation paid to other sales personnel also seems appropriate. Frasier Crane is considering changing from the current compensation plan to one based on a 5 percent commission. He sees such a plan as being fairer to the parties involved and believes it would also provide strong incentives for needed market expansion.

A. Calculate Café-Nervosa.com's salary expense for each employee expressed as a percentage of the monthly sales generated by that individual.

B. Calculate monthly income for each employee under a 5 percent of monthly sales commission–based system.

C. Will a commission-based plan result in efficient relative salaries, efficient salary levels, or both?

P7.6   Optimal Input Mix.   The First National Bank received 3,000 inquiries following the latest advertisement describing its 30-month IRA accounts in the *Boston World*, a local newspaper. The most recent ad in a similar advertising campaign in *Massachusetts Business*, a regional business magazine, generated 1,000 inquiries. Each newspaper ad costs $500, whereas each magazine ad costs $125.

A. Assuming that additional ads would generate similar response rates, is the bank running an optimal mix of newspaper and magazine ads? Why or why not?

B. Holding all else equal, how many inquiries must a newspaper ad attract for the current advertising mix to be optimal?

P7.7   Marginal Revenue Product of Labor.   To better serve customers interested in buying cars over the Internet, Smart Motors, Inc., hired Nora Jones to respond to customer inquiries, offer price quotes, and write orders for leads generated by the company's Web site. During the last year, Jones averaged 1.5 vehicle sales per week. On average, these vehicles sold for a retail price of $25,000 and brought the dealership a profit contribution of $1,000 each.

A. Estimate Jones' annual (50 workweek) marginal revenue product.

B. Jones earns a base salary of $60,000 per year, and Smart Motors pays an additional 28 percent of this base salary in taxes and various fringe benefits. Is Jones a profitable employee?

P7.8 Optimal Input Level. Ticket Services, Inc., offers ticket promotion and handling services for concerts and sporting events. The Sherman Oaks, California, branch office makes heavy use of spot radio advertising on WHAM-AM, with each 30-second ad costing $100. During the past year, the following relation between advertising and ticket sales per event has been observed:

$$\text{Sales (units)} = 5,000 + 100A - 0.5A^2$$
$$\partial \text{Sales (units)}/\partial \text{Advertising} = 100 - A$$

Here, A represents a 30-second radio spot ad, and sales are measured in numbers of tickets.

Rachel Green, manager for the Sherman Oaks office, has been asked to recommend an appropriate level of advertising. In thinking about this problem, Green noted its resemblance to the optimal resource employment problem studied in a managerial economics course. The advertising–sales relation could be thought of as a production function, with advertising as an input and sales as the output. The problem is to determine the profit-maximizing level of employment for the input, advertising, in this "production" system. Green recognized that a measure of output value was needed to solve the problem. After reflection, Green determined that the value of output is $2 per ticket, the net marginal revenue earned by Ticket Services (price minus all marginal costs except advertising).

A. Continuing with Green's production analogy, what is the marginal product of advertising?

B. What is the rule for determining the optimal amount of a resource to employ in a production system? Explain the logic underlying this rule.

C. Using the rule for optimal resource employment, determine the profit-maximizing number of radio ads.

P7.9 Net Marginal Revenue. Crane, Poole & Schmidt, LLC, is a successful Boston-based law firm. Worker productivity at the firm is measured in billable hours, which vary between partners and associates. Partner time is billed to clients at a rate of $250 per hour, whereas associate time is billed at a rate of $125 per hour. On average, each partner generates 25 billable hours per 40-hour workweek, with 15 hours spent on promotion, administrative, and supervisory responsibilities. Associates generate an average of 35 billable hours per 40-hour workweek and spend 5 hours per week in administrative and training meetings. Variable overhead costs average 50 percent of revenues generated by partners and 60 percent of revenues generated by associates.

A. Calculate the annual (50 workweek) net marginal revenue product of partners and associates.

B. If partners earn $175,000 and associates earn $70,000 per year, does the company have an optimal combination of partners and associates? If not, why not? Make your answer explicit and support any recommendations for change.

P7.10 Production Function Estimation. Consider the following Cobb–Douglas production function for bus service in a typical metropolitan area:

$$Q = b_0 L^{b_1} K^{b_2} F^{b_3}$$

where

Q = output in millions of passenger miles

L = labor input in worker hours

K = capital input in bus transit hours

F = fuel input in gallons

Each of the parameters of this model was estimated by regression analysis using monthly data over a recent 3-year period. Results obtained were as follows:

$$\hat{b}_0 = 1.2; \ \hat{b}_1 = 0.28; \ \hat{b}_2 = 0.63; \ \hat{b}_3 = 0.12$$

The standard error estimates for each coefficient are

$$\sigma_{\hat{b}_0} = 0.4; \ \sigma_{\hat{b}_1} = 0.15; \ \sigma_{\hat{b}_2} = 0.12; \ \sigma_{\hat{b}_3} = 0.07$$

A. Estimate the effect on output of a 4 percent decline in worker hours (holding K and F constant).

B. Estimate the effect on output of a 3 percent reduction in fuel availability accompanied by a 4 percent decline in bus transit hours (holding L constant).

C. Estimate the returns to scale for this production system.

CASE Study

Worker Productivity Among Giant U.S. Corporations

Traditional measures of firm productivity tend to focus on profit margins, the rate of return on stockholders' equity, or related measures like total asset turnover, inventory turnover, or receivables turnover. Profit margin is net income divided by sales and is a useful measure of a company's ability to manufacture and distribute distinctive products. When profit margins are high, it's a good sign that customer purchase decisions are being driven by unique product characteristics or product quality rather than by low prices. When profit margins are high, companies are also able to withstand periods of fluctuating costs or weak product demand without devastating consequences for net income. While high profit margins have the potential to attract new competitors, they also act as credible evidence that a firm offers a hard-to-imitate combination of attractive goods and services.

Return on equity (ROE), defined as net income divided by the accounting book value of stockholders' equity, is an attractive measure of firm performance because it reflects the effects of both operating and financial leverage. When ROE is high, the company is able to generate an attractive rate of return on the amount of money entrusted to the firm by shareholders in the form of common stock purchases and retained earnings. High profit

continued

margins give rise to high ROE, as do rapid turnover in inventory, receivables, and total assets. Rapid inventory turnover reduces the risk of profit-sapping product closeouts where slow-moving goods are marked down for quick sale. Rapid receivables turnover eases any concern that investors might have in terms of the firm's ability to collect money owed by customers. High total asset turnover, defined as sales divided by total assets, documents the firm's ability to generate a significant amount of business from its fixed plant and equipment.

Despite these obvious advantages, each of these traditional firm performance measures suffers certain shortcomings. Profit margins are strongly influenced by industry-related factors that might obscure superior firm productivity when firms from different industries are compared. For example, the automobile industry is huge and net profit margins for mediocre performers are commonly in the 2.5 percent to 3 percent range. Even standout performers, like Toyota, struggle to earn 6 percent on sales. Meanwhile, even mediocre banks commonly report profit margins in the 15 percent to 20 percent range. Similarly, and despite obvious advantages, ROE suffers as a performance measure because steep losses can greatly diminish retained earnings, decimate the book value of stockholders' equity, and cause ROE to soar. When companies buy back their shares in the open market at prices that greatly exceed accounting book values, the book value of shareholders' equity also falls, and can unfairly inflate the ROE measure. For these reasons, some analysts look to the growth in net income as a simple and less easily distorted measure of accounting profit performance.

However, the biggest problem with corporate performance measures based upon profit rates tied to sales, stockholders' equity, or assets has nothing to do with measurement problems tied to irregular profit and loss patterns or corporate restructuring. The biggest problem with traditional corporate profit measures is that they fail to reflect the firm's efficient use of human resources. In the services-based economy of the new millennium, the most telling indicator of a company's ability to compete is its ability to attract, train, and motivate a capable workforce. In economics, the term human capital is used to describe the investment made in workers and top management that make them more efficient and more profitable employees. Employee training and education are two of the most reliable tools that companies can use to keep an edge on the competition. However, determining an efficient amount of worker training and education is more tricky than it might seem at first.

In a competitive labor market, employees can expect to command a wage rate equal to the amount they could compel in their next-best employment opportunity. At least in part, this opportunity cost reflects employee productivity created by better worker training and education. Because dissatisfied workers can be quick to jump ship, employers must be careful to maintain a productive work environment that makes happy employees want to stay and contribute to the firm that paid for their education and training. Employers need capable and well-trained employees, but no employer wants to be guilty of training workers that end up working for the competition! All successful firms are efficient in terms of constantly improving employee productivity, and then motivating satisfied and capable employees to perform. In light of the importance placed upon capable and well-motivated employees, an attractive alternative means for measuring corporate productivity is in terms of profits and revenues per employee.

Table 7.5 gives interesting perspective on employee productivity by showing revenue per employee and profits per employee for the 30 giant corporations that together comprise the Dow Jones Industrial Average.

A. What firm-specific and industry-specific factors might be used to explain differences among giant corporations in the amount of revenue per employee and profit per employee?

continued

Table 7.5 Profits and Revenues Per Employee Among Giant U.S. Corporations

Company Name	Industry Name	Number of Employees	Income Per Employee	Industry Average Income Per Employee	Revenue Per Employee	Total Assets Per Employee
Alcoa Inc.	Aluminum	123,000	$21,675	$22,003	$253,463	$228,117
Altria Group	Cigarettes	175,000	49,514	45,423	390,714	351,643
American Express Company	Credit Services	65,400	59,908	331,246	434,985	86,997
American International Group (AIG)	Property & Casualty Insurance	106,000	142,925	185,552	1,067,868	106,787
AT&T Inc.	Telecom Services—Domestic	302,000	24,296	25,779	208,260	62,637
Boeing Company	Aerospace/Defense—Major Diversified	154,000	14,325	18,344	399,546	439,500
Caterpillar Inc.	Farm & Construction Machinery	95,334	36,262	29,738	445,512	353,628
Citigroup Inc.	Money Center Banks	327,000	68,812	78,587	286,310	5,762,440
Coca-Cola Company	Beverages—Soft Drinks	71,000	73,746	46,416	351,620	281,296
DuPont De Nemours	Chemicals—Major Diversified	59,000	53,085	46,249	491,220	442,098
Exxon Mobil Corporation	Major Integrated Oil & Gas	82,100	481,121	282,310	4,599,696	8,279,452
General Electric	Conglomerates	319,000	65,828	44,319	518,988	103,797
General Motors	Auto Manufacturers—Major	280,000	−7,031	23,958	740,532	444,319
Hewlett-Packard Company	Diversified Computer Systems	156,000	41,782	28,659	603,083	723,700
Home Depot, Inc.	Home Improvement Stores	364,000	15,827	16,982	249,552	474,149
Honeywell International Inc.	Conglomerates	118,000	18,415	44,319	272,602	272,602
Intel Corporation	Semiconductor—Broad Line	91,800	56,291	52,289	375,069	269,126
International Business Machines Corp.	Diversified Computer Systems	355,766	26,849	28,659	260,823	234,743
Johnson & Johnson	Drug Manufacturers—Major	122,200	84,460	80,265	453,102	362,481
JPMorgan Chase & Co.	Money Center Banks	176,314	79,535	78,587	358,004	7,665,415
McDonald's Corporation	Restaurants	465,000	6,585	9,875	47,606	33,324
Merch & Co.	Drug Manufacturers—Major	60,000	76,968	80,265	383,262	191,631
Microsoft Corporation	Application Software	71,000	167,732	113,910	648,690	454,083
3M Company	Conglomerates	75,333	51,799	44,319	304,301	334,718
Pfizer Inc.	Drug Manufacturers—Major	98,000	106,041	80,265	501,000	200,400

(continued)

continued

Procter & Gamble	Cleaning Products	138,000	70,065	66,173	533,348	266,674
United Technologies Corporation	Conglomerates	214,500	19,063	44,319	230,732	230,732
Verizon Communications Inc.	Telecom Services—Domestic	242,000	22,645	25,779	364,231	182,116
Wal-Mart Stores, Inc.	Discount, Variety Stores	1,900,000	6,634	7,503	183,500	440,400
Walt Disney Company	Entertainment—Diversified	133,000	33,932	52,236	264,331	158,598
Average		231,325	65,636	67,811	540,732	981,254

B. A multiple regression analysis based upon the data contained in Table 7.5 reveals the following (t statistics in parentheses):

Profit/Emp. = $1,269.016 + 0.220 Ind. Profit/Emp. +
   (0.17) (2.33)
   0.084 Rev./Emp. + 0.004 Ass./Emp.
   (8.22)   (1.20)

$R^2 = 89.7\%$, F statistic = 75.48

Interpret these results. Is profit per employee more sensitive to industry-specific or firm-specific factors for this sample of giant corporations?

SELECTED REFERENCES

Amiti, Mary and Lisa Cameron. "Economic Geography and Wages." *Review of Economics and Statistics* 89, no. 1 (February, 2007): 15–29.

Athey, Susan, Lawrence F. Katz, Alan B. Krueger, Steven Levitt, and James Poterba. "What Does Performance in Graduate School Predict? Graduate Economics Education and Student Outcomes." *American Economic Review* 97, no. 2 (May, 2007): 512–518.

Bergman, Nittai K. and Dirk Jenter. "Employee Sentiment and Stock Option Compensation." *Journal of Financial Economics* 84, no. 3 (June, 2007): 667–712.

Berk, Jonathan B. and Richard Stanton. "Managerial Ability, Compensation, and the Closed-End Fund Discount." *Journal of Finance* 62, no. 2 (April, 2007): 529–556.

Black, Sandra E., Paul J. Devereux, and Kjell G. Salvanes. "From the Cradle to the Labor Market? The Effect of Birth Weight on Adult Outcomes." *Quarterly Journal of Economics* 122, no. 1 (February, 2007): 409–439.

Caselli, Francesco and James Feyrer. "The Marginal Product of Capital." *Quarterly Journal of Economics* 122, no. 2 (May, 2007): 535–568.

Chandra, Amitabh and Douglas O. Staiger. "Productivity Spillovers in Health Care: Evidence from the Treatment of Heart Attacks." *Journal of Political Economy* 115, no. 1 (February, 2007): 103–140.

Compte, Olivier and Philippe Jehiel. "On Quitting Rights in Mechanism Design." *American Economic Review* 97, no. 2 (May, 2007): 137–141.

Cunha, Flavio and James Heckman. "The Technology of Skill Formation." *American Economic Review* 97, no. 2 (May, 2007): 31–47.

Dittmann, Ingolf and Ernst Maug. "Lower Salaries and no Options? on the Optimal Structure of Executive Pay." *Journal of Finance* 62, no. 1 (February, 2007): 303–343.

Feyrer, James. "Demographics and Productivity." *Review of Economics and Statistics* 89, no. 1 (February, 2007): 100–109.

Fisher, Jonas D. M. "Why Does Household Investment Lead Business Investment Over the Business Cycle?" *Journal of Political Economy* 115, no. 1 (February, 2007): 141–168.

Olken, Benjamin A. "Monitoring Corruption: Evidence from a Field Experiment in Indonesia." *Journal of Political Economy* 115, no. 2 (April, 2007): 200–249.

Visser, Bauke and Otto H. Swank. "On Committees of Experts." *Quarterly Journal of Economics* 122, no. 1 (February, 2007): 337–372.

Wulf, Julie. "Authority, Risk, and Performance Incentives: Evidence from Division Manager Positions Inside Firms." *Journal of Industrial Economics* 55, no. 1 (March, 2007): 169–196.

Appendix 7A

A Constrained Optimization Approach to Developing the Optimal Input Combination Relationships

The determination of optimal input proportions could be viewed either as a problem of maximizing output for a given expenditure level or, alternatively, as a problem of minimizing the cost of producing a specified level of output. This appendix shows how the Lagrangian technique for constrained optimization can be used to develop the optimal input proportion rule.

CONSTRAINED PRODUCTION MAXIMIZATION

Consider the problem of maximizing output from a production system described by the general equation

$$Q = f(X, Y) \qquad\qquad \textbf{7A.1}$$

subject to a budget constraint. The expenditure limitation can be expressed as

$$E^* = P_X \times X + P_Y \times Y \qquad\qquad \textbf{7A.2}$$

which states that the total expenditure on inputs, E^*, is equal to the price of input X, P_X, times the quantity of X employed, plus the price of Y, P_Y, times the quantity of that resource used in the production system. Equation (7A.2) can be written in the form of a Lagrangian constraint, as developed in Chapter 2, as

$$0 = E^* - P_X \times X - P_Y \times Y \qquad\qquad \textbf{7A.3}$$

The Lagrangian function for the maximization of the production function, Equation (7A.1), subject to the budget constraint expressed by Equation (7A.3), can then be written as

$$Max\ L_Q = f(X, Y) + \lambda(E^* - P_X \times X - P_Y \times Y) \qquad\qquad \textbf{7A.4}$$

Maximization of the constrained production function is accomplished by setting the partial derivatives of the Lagrangian expression taken with respect to X, Y, and ∂ equal to zero, and then solving the resultant system of equations. The partials of Equation (7A.4) are

$$\frac{\partial L_Q}{\partial X} = \frac{\partial f(X, Y)}{\partial X} - \partial P_X = 0 \qquad \textbf{7A.5}$$

$$\frac{\partial L_Q}{\partial \lambda} = \frac{\partial f(X, Y)}{\partial Y} - \partial P_Y = 0 \qquad \textbf{7A.6}$$

and

$$\frac{\partial L_Q}{\partial \lambda} = E^* - P_X \times X - P_Y \times Y = 0 \qquad \textbf{7A.7}$$

Setting these three partial derivatives to zero results in a set of conditions that must be met for output maximization subject to the budget constraint.

Note that the first terms in Equations (7A.5) and (7A.6) are the marginal products of X and Y, respectively. In other words, $\partial f(X, Y)/\partial X$ equals $\partial Q/\partial X$, which by definition is the marginal product of X. The same is true for $\partial f(X, Y)/\partial Y$. Thus, those two expressions can be rewritten as

$$MP_X - \lambda P_X = 0$$

and

$$MP_Y - \lambda P_Y = 0$$

or, alternatively, as

$$MP_X = \lambda P_X \qquad \textbf{7A.8}$$

and

$$MP_Y = \lambda P_Y \qquad \textbf{7A.9}$$

The conditions required for constrained output maximization, expressed by Equations (7A.8) and (7A.9), can also expressed by the ratio of equations. Thus

$$\frac{MP_X}{MP_Y} = \frac{\lambda P_X}{\lambda P_Y} \qquad \textbf{7A.10}$$

Canceling the lambdas in Equation (7A.10) results in the condition required for optimal input use developed in the chapter:

$$\frac{MP_X}{MP_Y} = \frac{P_X}{P_Y} \qquad \textbf{7A.11}$$

For maximum production, given a fixed expenditure level, the input factors must be combined in such a way that the ratio of their marginal products is equal to the ratio of their prices. Alternatively, transposing Equation (7A.11) derives the expression

$$\frac{MP_X}{P_X} = \frac{MP_Y}{P_Y}$$

Optimal input proportions require that the ratio of marginal product to price must be equal for all input factors.

CONSTRAINED COST MINIMIZATION

The relationship developed above can also be derived from the problem of minimizing the cost of producing a given quantity of output. In this case, the constraint states that some level of output, Q^*, must be produced from the production system described by the function $Q = f(X, Y)$. Written in the standard Lagrangian format, the constraint is $0 = Q^* - f(X, Y)$. The cost, or expenditure, function is given as $E = P_X + X + P_Y + Y$. The Lagrangian function for the constrained cost minimization problem, then, is

$$L_E = P_X \cdot X + P_Y \cdot Y + \lambda[Q^* - f(X, Y)] \qquad \textbf{7A.12}$$

As shown above, the conditions for constrained cost minimization are provided by the partial derivatives of Equation (7A.12):

$$\frac{\partial L_E}{\partial X} = P_X - \lambda \frac{\partial (f(X, Y))}{\partial X} = 0 \qquad \textbf{7A.13}$$

$$\frac{\partial L_E}{\partial Y} = P_Y - \lambda \frac{\partial (f(X, Y))}{\partial Y} = 0 \qquad \textbf{7A.14}$$

and

$$\frac{\partial L_E}{\partial \lambda} = Q^* - f(X, Y) = 0 \qquad \textbf{7A.15}$$

Notice that the terms on the left-hand side in Equations (7A.13) and (7A.14) are the marginal products of X and Y, respectively, so each of these expressions can be rewritten as

$$P_X - \lambda MP_X = 0$$

and

$$P_Y - \lambda MP_Y = 0$$

or, alternatively, as

$$P_X = \lambda MP_X \qquad \textbf{7A.16}$$

and

$$P_Y = \lambda MP_Y \qquad \textbf{7A.17}$$

Taking the ratio of Equation (7A.16) to Equation (7A.17) and canceling the lambdas again produces the basic input optimality relation:

$$\frac{P_X}{P_Y} = \frac{MP_X}{MP_Y}$$

PROBLEM

7A.1 Assume that a firm produces its product in a system described in the following production function and price data:

$$Q = 3X + 5Y + XY$$
$$P_X = \$3$$
$$P_Y = \$6$$

Here, X and Y are two variable input factors employed in the production of Q.

A. What are the optimal input proportions for X and Y in this production system? Is this combination rate constant regardless of the output level?

B. It is possible to express the cost function associated with the use of X and Y in the production of Q as $\text{Cost} = P_X X + P_Y Y$ or $\text{Cost} = \$3X + \$6Y$. Use the Lagrangian technique to determine the maximum output that the firm can produce operating under a $1,000 budget constraint for X and Y. Show that the inputs used to produce that level of output meet the optimality conditions derived in part A.

C. What is the additional output that could be obtained from a marginal increase in the budget?

D. Assume that the firm is interested in minimizing the cost of producing 14,777 units of output. Use the Lagrangian method to determine what optimal quantities of X and Y to employ. What will be the cost of producing that output level? How would you interpret λ, the Lagrangian multiplier, in this problem?

Cost Analysis and Estimation

Auto industry executives blamed a recent downturn in the auto business on higher interest rates, a slump in the housing market, mushrooming health care costs, and excessive government regulation. The truth is poor product quality, outdated design, lackluster marketing, and tough competition from foreign rivals have killed consumer interest in many of Detroit's recent offerings. Young people, and the young at heart, want energy-efficient cars that are cheap, fast, and fun to drive. To convince yourself of this, simply go downtown in almost any city or suburb in America on Friday or Saturday night. It won't be long before you get nearly blown off the sidewalk by some kid slouched behind the wheel of a "low-rider" with windows vibrating to the thump of ultra-amplified bass. In the 1970s or 1980s, that kid was in a Camaro or Firebird. Today, they probably drive a Honda Civic or Acura Integra. Both are relatively cheap, stylish, and easy to customize. If you're not into customizing, try a Toyota Celica GT-S 2133 Liftback 2D (6-Spd.). It's more than stylish, dependable, energy efficient, and bargain priced. It's fun to drive. A high-quality car is more than neat looking and dependable; it's a blast to get behind the wheel and take it out for a spin.

Cost estimation and control is part of the continual process of making products that exceed customer expectations. Quick fixes don't work. This chapter shows how making things faster, cheaper, and better requires a fundamental appreciation of cost concepts.[1]

ECONOMIC AND ACCOUNTING COSTS

Economic cost analysis goes beyond accounting information to measure both the obvious and hidden costs tied to managerial decisions.

Historical Versus Current Costs

Historical Cost
Actual cash outlay.

Current Cost
Amount paid under prevailing market conditions.

The link between economic and accounting values is sometimes tenuous. When costs are calculated for an income tax return, for example, use of **historical cost,** or the actual cash outlay is required. This is also generally true for annual 10-K reports to the Securities and Exchange Commission (SEC) and for reports to stockholders. Despite this usefulness, historical costs are not appropriate as the sole basis for many managerial decisions. Current costs are more relevant. **Current cost** is the amount that must be paid under prevailing market conditions. Current cost is influenced by the number of buyers and

---

1 See Joseph B. White, "Toyota Weighs New Versions Of Prius Hybrid," *The Wall Street Journal Online,* October 26, 2007, http://online.wsj.com.

sellers, technology, and inflation. For assets purchased recently, historical cost and current cost are typically the same. For assets purchased several years ago, historical cost and current cost can be quite different. With an inflation rate of 5 percent per year, prices double in less than 15 years and triple in roughly 22 years. Land purchased for $50,000 in 1980 often has a current cost in excess of $250,000. In California, Florida, Texas, and other rapidly growing areas, current costs run much higher. Just as no homeowner would sell his or her home for a lower price based on lower historical costs, no manager can afford to sell assets or products for less than current costs.

Current costs for tangible assets typically exceed historical costs because of inflation. In many high-tech industries, however, the rapid advance of technology has overcome the general rate of inflation. As a result, current costs are falling. Current costs for computers and electronic equipment are determined by what is referred to as **replacement cost,** or the cost of duplicating productive capability using existing technology.

Suppose a construction company has an inventory of 1 million board feet of lumber, purchased at a historical cost of $200,000, or $200 per 1,000 board feet (a board foot of lumber is 1 square foot of lumber, 1 inch thick). If lumber prices rise by 50 percent and the company is asked to bid on a new construction project, the replacement cost is the appropriate valuation of the lumber inventory because the company will have to pay $300,000 to replace the lumber it uses on the new construction project. In fact, the construction company could sell the lumber to others for the prevailing market price of $300,000. Under current market conditions, the lumber is worth $300,000. On the other hand, had lumbers prices fallen by 50 percent, the lower replacement cost of $100,000 would have been appropriate. For income tax purposes, however, the appropriate cost basis is still the $200,000 historical cost. Traditional accounting methods and the Internal Revenue Service (IRS) rely heavily on the historical cost concept because it can be applied consistently across firms and is easily verifiable. However, when historical and current costs differ markedly, reliance on historical costs sometimes leads to bad operating decisions with disastrous consequences.

Replacement Cost
The cost of duplicating productive capability using current technology.

Opportunity Costs

Opportunity cost is the foregone value associated with the current rather than next-best use of an asset. In other words, cost is determined by the highest-valued opportunity that must be turned down to allow current use. The cost of aluminum used in the manufacture of soft drink containers, for example, is determined by its value in alternative uses. Soft drink bottlers must pay an aluminum price equal to this value or the aluminum will be used in the production of alternative goods, such as airplanes, building materials, and cookware. Similarly, when speculation drove precious metals prices skyrocketing during the early 2000s, plastic and ceramic materials became a common substitute for dental gold and silver. Dental customers must be willing to pay a price for dental gold and silver that is competitive with the price paid by jewelry customers and industrial users. In the job market, your opportunity cost is defined by the income opportunity provided by your next-best employment opportunity. If another firm offers to double your salary, you may not be able to "afford" to turn them down. If so, the opportunity cost of staying with your current employer has become too high.

Opportunity Cost
Foregone value associated with current rather than next-best use of an asset.

Economic costs often involve out-of-pocket costs, or **explicit costs,** and opportunity costs, sometimes referred to as **implicit costs.** Wages, rent, utility expenses, payment for raw materials, and interest paid to the holders of the firm's bonds are examples of explicit expenses. Implicit costs associated with any decision are much more difficult

Explicit Cost
Out-of-pocket expenditures.

Implicit Cost
Noncash costs.

to compute. These costs do not involve cash expenditures and are therefore often overlooked in decision analysis. The rent that a shop owner could receive on buildings and equipment if they were not used in the business is an implicit cost of the owner's own retailing activity, as is the salary that an individual could receive by working for someone else instead of operating his or her own establishment.

For example, suppose that an established law practice, Crane, Poole & Schmidt, can be bought for $1 million. Attorney Denise Bauer has personal savings of $1 million to invest in such an enterprise; Brad Chase, another possible buyer, must borrow the entire $1 million at a cost of 15 percent, or $150,000 per year. Assume that operating costs are the same no matter who owns the practice and that Bauer and Chase are equally capable of completing the purchase. The $150,000 in annual interest expenses does not make Chase's economic costs greater than that of Bauer. Even though Chase has higher explicit interest costs, Bauer has implicit interest costs of a commensurate amount. If a 15 percent return can be earned by investing in other investments of equal risk, then Bauer's implicit investment opportunity cost is also $150,000 per year. In this case, Bauer and Chase each have financing cost of $150,000 per year. Chase's cost is implicit and Bauer's is explicit.

Will total operating costs be identical for both individuals? Not necessarily. Just as the implicit cost of capital must be included in the analysis, so too must implicit labor costs be included. If Bauer is an experienced litigator earning $250,000 a year and Chase is a junior tax specialist earning $150,000 annually, implicit labor costs will be different. Implicit labor costs are $250,000 for Bauer and $150,000 for Chase. On an annual basis, Bauer's capital plus labor costs are $400,000, all of which are implicit. Chase's capital plus labor costs are $300,000, including explicit capital costs of $150,000 plus implicit labor costs of $150,000.

ROLE OF TIME IN COST ANALYSIS

Relevant costs and benefits for any decision are limited to those that are affected by it.

Incremental Versus Sunk Cost

Incremental Cost
Change in cost caused by a given managerial decision.

Incremental cost is the change in cost caused by a given managerial decision. Whereas marginal cost is the change in cost following a 1-unit change in output, incremental costs typically involve multiple units of output. For example, incremental costs are the relevant consideration when an air carrier considers the cost of adding an additional departure from New York's La Guardia Airport to Boston's Logan Airport. When all current departures are full, it is impractical to consider adding a single passenger-mile unit of output. Similarly, the incremental cost concept comes into play when judging the costs of adding a new product line, advertising campaign, or production shift.

Profit Contribution
Profit before fixed charges.

Poor managerial decisions can result when the incremental concept is ignored or applied incorrectly. Suppose a retailer refuses to sublet excess office space for $2,500 per month because it figures cost as its mandatory lease payment of $5,000 per month. If the office space will indeed remain vacant, refusing to sublet the excess space will cause a $2,500 per month loss in **profit contribution,** or profit before fixed charges. Mandatory lease expenses will be incurred irrespective of whether the excess space is rented. By subletting, the retailer has the same interest and overhead expenses as before, plus $2,500 per month in revenues from the sublet.

Managerial Application 8.1

GE's "20-70-10" Plan

The General Electric Co. routinely identifies the top 20 percent, the middle 70 percent, and the bottom 10 percent of its 100,000 managerial and professional employees. According to Jack Welch, legendary former chairman of GE, the top 20 percent and middle 70 percent often trade places, but the bottom 10 percent tend to remain there. At GE, those employees found in the bottom 10 percent are given a chance to improve. However, if performance doesn't improve quickly, they had better find another job.

Among its managers and professionals, GE loses about 8,000 per year through turnover and attrition. Of those, about 60 percent, or 4,800, are forced out—both in good times and bad. Even among the highest-ranking 600 GE executives, about 60 leave each year. Fewer than 20 are due to retirement or opportunities elsewhere. There just isn't much empathy for under performance at GE. Welch was famous for arguing that underperforming managers and professionals will eventually be fired anyway, and delaying the inevitable is a form of "corporate cruelty."

Welch retired at the end of 2001, but GE has no plans to retire its 20-70-10 plan. Not only is the plan embraced by new CEO Jeffrey Immelt, other top corporations are seeking to emulate GE's success. While employee performance reviews have long been an important part of effective management, it's new for bosses to rank every employee in each department. Newer still is the practice of asking those at the bottom to leave. The rationale for tough performance reviews is that companies want to make way for promising new hires. Similarly, if downsizing becomes necessary, is it fair to throw out solid performers and keep weaker employees?

To be sure, GE's tough 20-70-10 plan has its detractors. Critics argue that top-to-bottom rankings are sometimes arbitrary. In some instances, discharged workers have filed lawsuits charging discrimination. Unfazed, GE and its imitators are going forward with their top-to-bottom rankings.

See: Rick Carew, "China Stock Run-Up Dooms GE Deal," *The Wall Street Journal Online*, October 24, 2007, http://online.wsj.com.

Care must be exercised to ensure against incorrectly assigning a lower than appropriate incremental cost. If excess capacity results from a temporary reduction in demand, this must be taken into account. Accepting the $2,500 per month renter is a mistake if doing so causes more profitable renters to be turned away. When excess capacity is caused by a temporary drop in demand, only short-term or month-to-month leases should be offered at the bargain price of $2,500 per month. In any event, all incremental costs, including those that might be incurred in the future, must be considered. Inherent in the incremental cost concept is the principle that any cost not affected by a decision is irrelevant to that decision. A cost that does not vary across decision alternatives is called a **sunk cost.** Sunk costs do not play a role in determining the optimal course of action.

Sunk Cost
Cost that does not vary across decision alternatives.

For example, suppose a firm has spent $5,000 on an option to purchase land for a new factory at a price of $500,000. Also assume that it is later offered an equally attractive site for $400,000. What should the firm do? The first thing to recognize is that the $5,000 spent on the purchase option is a sunk cost that must be ignored. If the firm purchases the first property, it must pay a price of $500,000. The newly offered property requires an expenditure of only $400,000 and results in a $100,000 savings. In retrospect, purchase of the $5,000 option was a mistake. The firm would compound their initial error and lose an additional $100,000 by following through with the purchase of the first property.

Cost Function
The cost–output relation.

How Is the Operating Period Defined?

Short-Run Cost Functions
Basis for day-to-day operating decisions.

Proper use of relevant cost concepts requires an understanding of the cost–output relation, or **cost function. Short-run cost functions** are used for day-to-day operating

Long-Run Cost Functions
Basis for long-range planning.

Short Run
Operating period during which at least one input is fixed.

Long Run
Planning period with complete input flexibility.

Planning Curves
Long-run cost relationship.

Operating Curves
Short-run cost relationship.

Fixed Cost
Expense that does not vary with output.

Variable Cost
Expense that fluctuates with output.

decisions; **long-run cost functions** are employed in the long-range planning process. The **short run** is the operating period during which the availability of at least one input is fixed. In the **long run,** the firm has complete flexibility. For example, a management consulting firm operating out of rented office space might have a short-run period as brief as a few weeks, the time remaining on the office lease. A firm in the hazardous waste disposal business has significant long-lived assets and may face a 20- to 30-year period of operating constraints.

The economic life of an asset and the degree of specialization affect the time length of operating period constraints. Consider a health maintenance organization's (HMO) automobile purchase for delivering home-based health care. If the car is a standard model without modification, it represents an unspecialized input factor with a resale value based on the used car market in general. If the car has been modified by adding refrigeration equipment for transporting perishable medicines, it becomes a more specialized input with full value only for those who need a vehicle with refrigeration equipment. In this case, the market price of the car might not equal its value in use to the HMO. To the extent that specialized input factors are employed, the short run is lengthened. When only unspecialized factors are used, the short run is condensed.

The amount of time required to order, receive, and install new equipment also influences the duration of the short run. Many manufacturers face delays of several months when ordering new plant and equipment. Air carriers must place their equipment orders 5 or more years in advance of delivery. Electric utilities frequently require 8 or more years to bring new generating plants on line. For such firms, the short-run operating period is an extended period of time.

Long-run cost curves are called **planning curves;** short-run cost curves are called **operating curves. Fixed costs** do not vary with output and are incurred only in the short run. **Variable costs** fluctuate with output in both the short and the long run. In the long run, plant and equipment are variable, so management can plan the most efficient physical plant, given an estimate of the firm's demand function. Once the optimal plant has been determined and the resulting investment in equipment has been made, short-run operating decisions are constrained by these prior decisions.

SHORT-RUN COST CURVES

Short-Run Cost Curve
Cost–output relation for a specific plant and operating environment

A **short-run cost curve** shows the minimum cost impact of output changes for a specific plant size and in a given operating environment.

Short-Run Cost Categories

Any change in the operating environment leads to a shift in short-run cost curves. For example, a general rise in wage rates leads to an upward shift; a fall in wage rates leads to a downward shift. Such changes must not be confused with movements along a given short-run cost curve caused by a change in production levels. For an existing plant, the short-run cost curve illustrates the minimum cost of production at various output levels under current operating conditions. Short-run cost curves are a useful guide to operating decisions.

Both fixed and variable costs affect short-run costs. Total cost at each output level is the sum of total fixed cost (a constant) and total variable cost. Using *TC* to represent total cost, *TFC* for total fixed cost, *TVC* for total variable cost, and *Q* for the quantity of output produced, various unit costs are calculated as follows:

$$\text{Total Cost} = TC = TFC + TVC \qquad \textbf{8.1}$$

$$\text{Average Fixed Cost} = AFC = \frac{TFC}{Q} \qquad \textbf{8.2}$$

$$\text{Average Variable Cost} = AVC = \frac{TVC}{Q} \qquad \textbf{8.3}$$

$$\text{Average Total Cost} = ATC = \frac{TC}{Q} = AFC + AVC \qquad \textbf{8.4}$$

$$\text{Marginal Cost} = MC = \frac{\partial TC}{\partial Q} \qquad \textbf{8.5}$$

These cost categories are portrayed in Table 8.1. Using these data, it is possible to identify the various cost relations as well as to examine cost behavior. Table 8.1 shows that *AFC* declines continuously with increases in output. *AC* and *AVC* also decline as long as they exceed *MC*, but increase when they are less than *MC*. So long as *MC* is less than *AC* and *AVC*, both average cost categories will decline. When *MC* is greater than *AC* and *AVC*, both average cost categories will rise. Marginal cost is the change in cost associated with a 1-unit change in output. Because fixed costs do not vary with output, they do not affect marginal costs. Only variable costs affect marginal costs. Therefore, marginal costs equal the change in total costs *or* the change in total variable costs following a 1-unit change in output. Also notice that *TFC* is invariant with increases in output and that *TVC* at each level of output equals the sum of *MC* up to that output.

Short-Run Cost Relations

Relations among short-run cost categories are shown in Figure 8.1. Figure 8.1(a) illustrates total cost and total variable cost curves. The shape of the total cost curve is

Table 8.1 Short-Run Cost Relations

Quantity Q	Total Cost $TC = TFC + TVC$ ($)	Marginal Cost $MC = \partial TC/\partial Q$	Total Fixed Cost TFC ($)	Total Variable Cost TVC ($)	Average Cost $AC = TC/Q$	Average Fixed Cost $AFC = TFC/Q$	Average Variable Cost $AVC = TVC/Q$
1	120	—	100	20		100.00	20.00
2	138	18	100	38	69.00	50.00	19.00
3	151	13	100	51	50.33	33.33	17.00
4	162	11	100	62	40.50	25.00	15.50
5	175	13	100	75	35.00	20.00	15.00
6	190	15	100	90	31.67	16.67	15.00
7	210	20	100	110	30.00	14.29	15.71
8	234	24	100	134	29.25	12.50	16.75
9	263	29	100	163	29.22	11.11	18.11
10	300	37	100	200	30.00	10.00	20.00

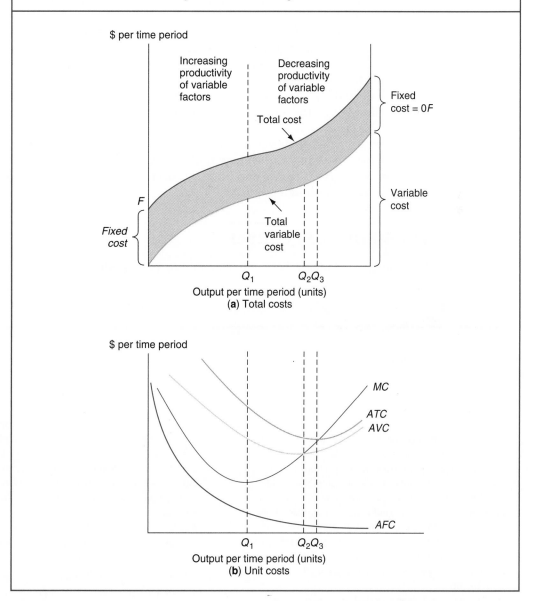

Figure 8.1   Short-Run Cost Curves

(a) The productivity of variable input factors determines the slope of both the total and variable cost curves. An increase (decrease) in fixed costs shifts the total cost curve upward (downward), but it has no effect on variable cost curves. (b) Marginal cost declines to Q_1. Both average total cost and average variable costs fall (rise) when marginal cost is lower (higher).

determined entirely by the total variable cost curve. The slope of the total cost curve at each output level is identical to the slope of the total variable cost curve. Fixed costs merely shift the total cost curve to a higher level. This means that marginal costs are independent of fixed cost.

The shapes of the total variable cost and total cost curves are determined by the productivity of variable input factors employed. The total variable cost curve in Figure 8.1

increases at a decreasing rate up to output level Q_1, then at an increasing rate. Assuming constant input prices, this implies that the marginal productivity of variable inputs first increases, then decreases. Variable input factors exhibit increasing returns in the range from 0 to Q_1 units and show diminishing returns thereafter. This is a typical finding. Fixed plant and equipment are usually designed to operate at a target production level. When operating below the target output level, some excess capacity results. In the below-target output range, production can be increased more than proportionately to increases in variable inputs. At above-target output levels, fixed factors are intensively used, and the law of diminishing returns takes over. There, a given percentage increase in variable inputs results in a smaller relative increase in output.

The relation between short-run costs and the productivity of variable input factors is also reflected by short-run unit cost curves, as shown in Figure 8.1(b). Marginal cost declines over the range of increasing productivity and rises thereafter. This imparts the familiar U-shape to average variable cost and average total cost curves. At first, marginal cost curves also typically decline rapidly in relation to the average variable cost curve and the average total cost curve. Near the target output level, the marginal cost curve turns up and intersects each of the AVC and AC short-run curves at their respective minimum points.

LONG-RUN COST CURVES

In the long run, the firm has complete input flexibility. All long-run costs are variable.

Managerial Application 8.2

Gaps in GAAP?

Generally Accepted Accounting Principles (GAAP) offer companies and their auditors a consistent set of rules to follow in their reporting of company income statement and balance sheet information. GAAP also offer a measure of "quality control" that assures investors that reported numbers have been consistently derived from a set of uniform principles applied to all companies. This makes it possible for investors to compare reported results over time, and across firms and industries. At least this is how GAAP works in theory. Sometimes, accounting practice falls far short of the ideal. In some instances, it seems as if companies and their auditors come up with the numbers the companies want, irrespective of actual economic performance.

Common accounting tricks that managers and investors must be on the lookout for include the following:

- **Misleading focus on pro forma results.** Some firms seek to minimize poor operating performance by encouraging investors to overlook standard accounting charges.

- **Excessive one-time R&D charges.** These one-time charges are taken at the time of an acquisition to cover expenses for research and development that is "in process" but not yet commercially viable. By separating these expenses from revenues that might be gained in the future, future earnings can be overstated.
- **Extravagant one-time "restructuring reserves."** When normal expenses are written off ahead of time, future earnings are overstated.
- **Aggressive revenue recognition.** When service contracts stretch out for years, booking revenue too early inflates sales and earnings.

The Securities and Exchange Commission has become concerned that the quality of financial reporting is eroding. It should be. If basic accounting practices ever lose credibility with investors and the general public, financial markets and economic performance would suffer greatly.

See: Chad Bray, "Nortel Settles with SEC Over Accounting," *The Wall Street Journal Online*, October 15, 2007, http://online.wsj.com.

Long-Run Total Costs

**Long-Run
Cost Curve**
Cost–output
relation for the
optimal plant in
the present
operating
environment.

The **long-run cost curve** shows the minimum cost for producing various levels of output assuming an ideal input combination. As in the case of short-run cost curves, wage rates, interest rates, plant configuration, and all other operating conditions are held constant. Any change in the operating environment leads to a shift in long-run cost curves. For example, product inventions and process improvements that occur over time cause a downward shift in long-run cost curves. Such changes must not be confused with movements along a given long-run cost curve caused by changes in the output level. Long-run cost curves reveal the nature of economies or diseconomies of scale and optimal plant sizes. They are a helpful guide to planning decisions.

If input prices are not affected by the amount purchased, a direct relation exists between long-run total cost and production functions. A production function that exhibits constant returns to scale is linear, and doubling inputs leads to doubled output. With constant input prices, doubling inputs doubles total cost and results in a linear total cost function. If increasing returns to scale are present, output doubles with less than a doubling of inputs and total cost. If production is subject to decreasing returns to scale, inputs and total cost must more than double to cause a twofold increase in output. A production function exhibiting first increasing and then decreasing returns to scale is illustrated, along with its implied cubic cost function, in Figure 8.2. Here, costs increase less than proportionately with output over the range in which returns to scale are increasing but at more than a proportionate rate after decreasing returns set in.

A direct relation between production and cost functions requires constant input prices. If input prices are a function of output, cost functions will reflect this relationship. Large-volume discounts can lower unit costs as output rises, just as costs can rise with the need to pay higher wages to attract additional workers at high output levels. The cost function for a firm facing constant returns to scale but rising input prices as output expands takes the shape shown in Figure 8.2. Quantity discounts produce a cost function that increases at a decreasing rate, as in the increasing returns section of Figure 8.2.

Economies of Scale

**Economies
of Scale**
Decreasing
long-run average
costs.

Economies of scale exist when long-run average costs decline as output expands. Labor specialization often gives rise to economies of scale. In small firms, workers generally do several jobs, and proficiency sometimes suffers from a lack of specialization. Labor productivity can be higher in large firms, where individuals are hired to perform specific tasks. This can reduce unit costs for large-scale operations.

Technical factors can also lead to economies of scale. Large-scale operation permits the use of highly specialized equipment, as opposed to the more versatile but less efficient machines used in smaller firms. Also, the productivity of equipment frequently increases with size much faster than its cost. A 500,000-kilowatt electricity generator costs considerably less than two 250,000-kilowatt generators, and it also requires less fuel and labor when operated at capacity. Quantity discounts give rise to money-related or pecuniary economies through large-scale purchasing of raw materials, supplies, and other inputs. These economies extend to the cost of capital when large firms have easy access to capital markets and can acquire funds at lower rates.

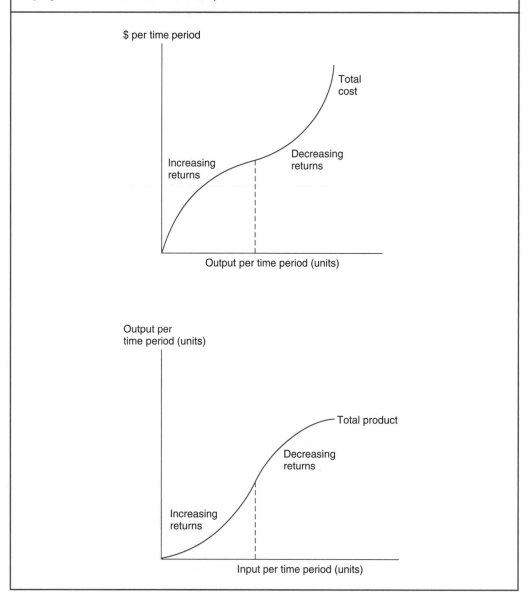

Figure 8.2 Total Cost Function for a Production System Exhibiting Increasing, Then Decreasing, Returns to Scale

With increasing returns to scale, total cost rises slower than total output. With decreasing returns to scale, total cost rises faster than total output. Total cost functions often display an S-shape, reflecting varying returns to scale at various activity levels.

At some output level, economies of scale are typically exhausted, average costs level out and begin to rise. Increasing average costs at high output levels are often attributed to limitations in the ability of management to coordinate large-scale organizations. Staff overhead also tends to grow more than proportionately with output, again raising unit costs. The current trend toward small to medium-sized businesses indicates that diseconomies limit firm sizes in many industries.

Cost Elasticities and Economies of Scale

Cost Elasticity
Percentage change in total cost associated with a 1 percent change in output.

It is often easy to calculate scale economies by considering cost elasticities. **Cost elasticity,** ε_C, measures the percentage change in total cost associated with a 1 percent change in output.

Using the point elasticity formula, the elasticity of cost with respect to output is

$$\varepsilon_C = \frac{\text{Percentage Change in Total Cost } (Tc)}{\text{Percentage Change in Output } (Q)} \qquad \textbf{8.6}$$

$$= \frac{\partial TC / TC}{\partial Q / Q}$$

$$= \frac{\partial TC}{\partial Q} \times \frac{Q}{TC}$$

Cost elasticity is related to economies of scale as follows:

If		Then	Which Implies
Percentage change in TC < Percentage change in Q,		$\varepsilon_c < 1$	Economies of scale (decreasing AC).
Percentage change in TC = Percentage change in Q,		$\varepsilon_c = 1$	No economies of scale (constant AC).
Percentage change in TC > Percentage change in Q,		$\varepsilon_c > 1$	Diseconomies of scale (increasing AC).

With a cost elasticity of less than one ($\varepsilon_C < 1$), costs increase at a slower rate than output. Given constant input prices, this implies higher output-to-input ratios and economies of scale. If $\varepsilon_C = 1$, output and costs increase proportionately, implying constant returns to scale. Finally, if $\varepsilon_C > 1$, costs increase faster than output, implying decreasing returns to scale. An *inverse* relation holds between cost elasticity and economies of scale, whereas a *direct* relation exists between output elasticity, ε_Q, and returns to scale. If $\varepsilon_C < 1$, average cost is falling and increasing returns to scale are observed. An output elasticity greater than one ($\varepsilon_Q > 1$) implies increasing returns to scale because output is increasing faster than input usage. If $\varepsilon_C > 1$, average cost is rising and decreasing returns to scale are observed. An output elasticity less than one ($\varepsilon_Q < 1$) implies decreasing returns to scale because output is increasing more slowly than input usage.

Long-Run Average Costs

Short-Run Cost Curve
Cost–output relation for a specific plant and operating environment.

Long-Run Cost Curve
Cost–output relation for the optimal plant in the present operating environment.

Short-run cost curves relate costs and output for a specific scale of plant. **Long-run cost curves** identify the optimal scale of plant for each production level. Long-run average cost (*LRAC*) curves can be thought of as an envelope of short-run average cost (*SRAC*) curves.

This concept is illustrated in Figure 8.3, which shows four short-run average cost curves representing four different scales of plant. Each of the four plants has a range of output over which it is most efficient. Plant A, for example, provides the least-cost production system for output in the range 0 to Q_1 units; plant B provides the least-cost system for output in the range Q_1 to Q_2; plant C is most efficient for output quantities Q_2 to Q_3; and plant D provides the least-cost production process for output above Q_3.

The solid portion of each curve in Figure 8.3 indicates the minimum long-run average cost for producing each level of output, assuming only four possible scales of plant. This can be generalized by assuming that plants of many sizes are possible, each only slightly larger than the preceding one. As shown in Figure 8.4, the long-run average cost curve is

Figure 8.3 Short-Run Cost Curves for Four Scales of Plant

Short-run cost curves represent the most efficient range of output for a given plant size. The solid portion of each *SRAC* curve indicates the minimum long-run average cost for each level of output.

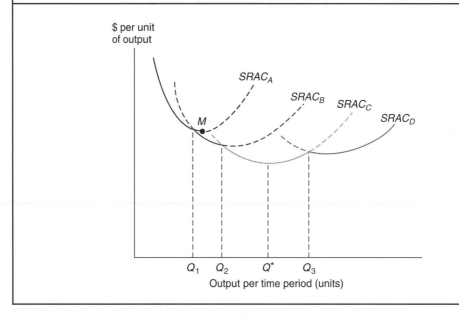

Figure 8.4 Long-Run Average Cost Curve as the Envelope of Short-Run Average Cost Curves

The long-run average cost curve is the envelope of short-run average cost curves. The optimal scale for a plant is found at the point of minimum long-run average costs.

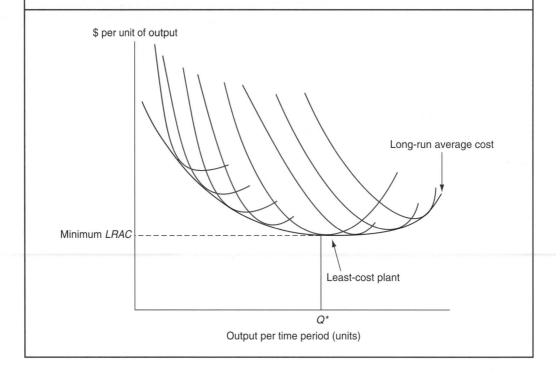

then constructed tangent to each short-run average cost curve. At each point of tangency, the related scale of plant is optimal; no other plant can produce that particular level of output at so low a total cost. Cost systems illustrated in Figures 8.3 and 8.4 display first economies of scale, then diseconomies of scale. Over the range of output produced by plants *A*, *B*, and *C* in Figure 8.3, average costs are declining; these declining costs mean that total costs are increasing less than proportionately with output. Because plant *D*'s minimum cost is greater than that for plant *C*, the system exhibits diseconomies of scale at this higher output level.

Production systems that reflect first increasing, then constant, then diminishing returns to scale result in U-shaped long-run average cost curves such as the one illustrated in Figure 8.4. With a U-shaped long-run average cost curve, the most efficient plant for each output level is typically not operating at the point where short-run average costs are minimized, as can be seen in Figure 8.3. Plant *A*'s short-run average cost curve is minimized at point *M*, but at that output level, plant *B* is more efficient; *B*'s short-run average costs are lower. In general, when economies of scale are present, the least-cost plant will operate at less than full capacity. Here, **capacity** refers not to a physical limitation on output but rather to the point at which short-run average costs are minimized. Only for that single output level at which long-run average cost is minimized (output *Q** in Figures 8.3 and 8.4) is the optimal plant operating at the minimum point on its short-run average cost curve.

Capacity
Output level at which short-run average costs are minimized.

Managerial Application 8.3

What'n Heck Is a FASB?

The Financial Accounting Standards Board (FASB) is a non-governmental body empowered by the Securities and Exchange Commission with responsibility for determining the nature and scope of accounting information. Started in 1973 as the logical successor to the accounting profession's Accounting Principles Board, the FASB develops new accounting standards in an elaborate process that reflects the views of accountants, business executives, security analysts, and the public. As a result, the FASB plays a key role in defining the specific information that must be incorporated in published corporate financial statements. FASB provides essential input concerning the framework for accounting balance sheets that define the current financial status of a company ("where it is"), and for accounting income statements that show changes in a company's financial performance ("where it is going"). By standardizing the content and format of such reports, FASB helps managers run their businesses better, and helps investors better monitor their investments.

The FASB is also instrumental in the resolution of a broad range of important and controversial accounting issues. For example, the FASB plays a key role in the debate over accounting policy issues, including the controversy on whether to require firms to use current market values rather than historical cost book values for accounts receivables, bonds, and intangible assets like brand names and patents. This is a highly controversial issue, because the market-value approach would lead to a much different picture of corporate assets and liabilities for many companies.

Given the wide range of important accounting issues being addressed, the role played by the FASB has grown steadily. At times, the public perception of the FASB has failed to match this pace. This is changing as the FASB's public visibility increases. FASB-inspired guidelines allow companies to report assets and incomes that are closer to real economic values. For investors, more detailed disclosure of income, assets, and liabilities are an important benefit of standardized accounting rules.

See: David Reilly, "FASB Won't Delay Market-Value Rule," *The Wall Street Journal Online*, October 17, 2007, http://online.wsj.com.

MINIMUM EFFICIENT SCALE

Minimum efficient scale (MES) is the output level at which long-run average costs are minimized.

Competitive Implications of Minimum Efficient Scale

MES is at the minimum point on a U-shaped long-run average cost curve (output Q^* in Figures 8.3 and 8.4) or at the corner of an L-shaped long-run average cost curve. The number of competitors and ease of entry are typically greater in industries with U-shaped long-run average cost curves than in those with L-shaped or downward-sloping long-run average cost curves. Competition is vigorous when MES is low relative to total industry demand. If MES is large relative to total industry output, barriers to entry can limit the number of potential competitors. However, when considering the competitive impact of MES, industry size must always be considered. Some industries are large enough to accommodate many effective competitors. Even though MES is large in an absolute sense, it can be relatively small and allow vigorous competition.

If the cost disadvantage to operating plants that are less than MES is modest, there will seldom be serious anticompetitive consequences. Somewhat higher production costs for small producers can be overcome by superior customer service and regional location to cut transport costs. Barrier-to-entry effects of MES require an MES that is large relative to industry demand and a steep slope for the long-run average cost curve at points below MES.

Transportation Costs and MES

Transportation costs include terminal, line-haul, and inventory charges associated with moving output from production facilities to customers. Terminal charges consist of handling expenses necessary for loading and unloading that do not vary with the distance shipped. They are as high for short hauls as for long hauls. Line-haul expenses include equipment, labor, and fuel costs associated with moving products a specified distance. Although line-haul expenses can be relatively constant on a per mile basis, they vary widely from one commodity to another. It costs more to ship a ton of fresh fruit 500 miles than to ship a ton of coal a similar distance. Fresh fruit comes in odd shapes and sizes and requires more container space per pound than a product like coal. Any product that is perishable, fragile, or particularly susceptible to theft (e.g., consumer electronics, cigarettes, liquor) has high line-haul expenses because of greater equipment, insurance, and handling costs. Finally, there is an inventory cost component to transportation costs related to the time element involved in shipping goods. The time required in transit is important because slower modes of transit delay delivery and the receipt of sale proceeds. Even though out-of-pocket expenses are greater, air cargo or motor carrier shipments speed delivery and can reduce the total economic costs of transporting valuable goods to market.

As more output is produced at a given plant, it becomes necessary to reach out to more distant customers. This can lead to increased transportation costs per unit sold. Figure 8.5 illustrates an L-shaped long-run average cost curve reflecting average production costs that first decline and then become nearly constant. Assuming relatively modest terminal and inventory costs, greater line-haul expenses cause transportation costs per unit to increase at a relatively constant rate. Before transportation costs, Q_A^* represents the MES plant size. Including transportation expenses, the MES plant size falls to Q_B^*. As transportation costs become increasingly important, MES will fall. When transportation

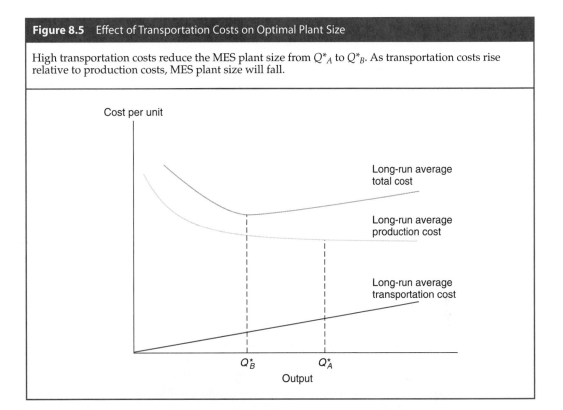

Figure 8.5 Effect of Transportation Costs on Optimal Plant Size

High transportation costs reduce the MES plant size from Q^*_A to Q^*_B. As transportation costs rise relative to production costs, MES plant size will fall.

costs are large in relation to production costs—as is the case with milk, bottled soft drinks, gravel, and cement—even small, relatively inefficient production facilities can be profitable when located near important markets. When transportation costs are relatively insignificant—as is the case of aluminum, electronic components, personal computers, and medical instruments—markets are national or international in scope, and significant economies of scale cause output to be produced at only a few large plants.

FIRM SIZE AND PLANT SIZE

Multiplant Economies of Scale
Cost advantages from operating multiple facilities in the same line of business or industry.

Multiplant Diseconomies of Scale
Cost disadvantages from managing multiple facilities in the same line of business or industry.

Optimal firm size depends upon the optimal size of production facilities, and the advantages or disadvantages of coordinating multiple plants.

Multiplant Economies and Diseconomies of Scale

Multiplant economies of scale are cost advantages that arise from operating multiple facilities in the same line of business or industry. **Multiplant diseconomies of scale** are cost disadvantages that arise from managing multiple facilities in the same line of business or industry.

To illustrate, assume a U-shaped long-run average cost curve for a given plant, as shown in Figure 8.4. If demand is sufficiently large, the firm will employ N plants, each of optimal size and producing Q^* units of output. In this case, what is the shape of the firm's long-run average cost curve? Figure 8.6 shows three possibilities. Each possible long-run average cost curve has important implications for the minimum efficient firm

Figure 8.6   Three Possible Long-Run Average Cost Curves for a Multiplant Firm

(a) Constant costs characterize a multiplant facility that has neither economies nor diseconomies of scale. (b) Average costs decline if a multiplant firm is more efficient than a single-plant firm. (c) The average costs of operating several plants can eventually rise when coordinating costs overcome mulitplant economies.

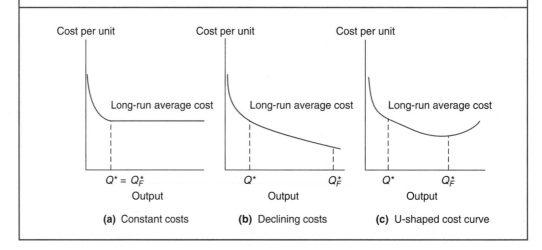

(a) Constant costs (b) Declining costs (c) U-shaped cost curve

size, Q_F^*. First, the long-run average cost curve can be L-shaped, as in Figure 8.6(a), if no economies or diseconomies result from combining plants. Second, costs could decline throughout the entire range of output, as in (b), if multiplant firms are more efficient than single-plant firms. When they exist, such cases are caused by economies of multiplant operation. For example, all plants may use a central billing service, a common purchasing or distribution network, centralized management, and so on. The third possibility, shown in (c), is that costs first decline beyond Q^*, the output of the most efficient plant, and then begin to rise. In this case, multiplant economies of scale dominate initially, but they are later overwhelmed by the higher costs of coordinating many operating units.

Because optimal plant and firm sizes are identical only when multiplant economies are negligible, the magnitude of both influences must be carefully considered in evaluating the effect of scale economies. Both intraplant and multiplant economies can have an important impact on minimum efficient firm size.

Economics of Multiplant Operation: An Example

An example can help clarify the relation between firm size and plant size. Consider Plainfield Electronics, a New Jersey-based company that manufactures industrial control panels. The firm's production is consolidated at a single Eastern Seaboard facility, but a multiplant alternative to centralized production is being considered. Estimated demand, marginal revenue, and single-plant production plus transportation cost curves for the firm are

$$P = \$940 - \$0.02Q$$

$$MR = \frac{\partial TR}{\partial Q} = \$940 - \$0.04Q$$

$$TC = \$250,000 + \$40Q + \$0.01Q^2$$

$$MC = \frac{\partial TC}{\partial Q} = \$40 + \$0.02Q$$

Plainfield's total profit function is

$$\pi = TR - TC$$
$$= P \times Q - TC$$
$$= (\$940 - \$0.02Q)Q - \$250,000 - \$40Q - \$0.01Q^2$$
$$= -\$0.03Q^2 + \$900Q - \$250,000$$

The profit-maximizing activity level with centralized production is the output level at which $M\pi = MR - MC = 0$ and, therefore, $MR = MC$. Setting marginal revenue equal to marginal cost and solving for the related output quantity gives

$$MR = MC$$
$$\$940 - \$0.04Q = \$40 + \$0.02Q$$
$$\$0.06Q = \$900$$
$$Q = 15,000$$

At $Q = 15,000$,

$$P = \$940 - \$0.02Q$$
$$= \$940 - \$0.02(15,000)$$
$$= \$640$$

and

$$\pi = -\$0.03(15,000^2) + \$900(15,000) - \$250,000$$
$$= \$6,500,000$$

Profits are maximized at the $Q = 15,000$ output level under the assumption of centralized production. At that activity level, $MC = MR = \$640$, and $M\pi = 0$.

To gain insight regarding the possible advantages of operating multiple smaller plants, the average cost function for a single plant must be examined. To simplify matters, assume that multiplant production is possible under the same cost conditions described previously. There are no multiplant economies or diseconomies of scale.

The activity level at which average cost is minimized is found by setting marginal cost equal to average cost and solving for Q:

$$AC = TC/Q$$
$$= (\$250,000 + \$40Q + \$0.01Q^2)/Q$$
$$= \$250,000Q^{-1} + \$40 + \$0.01Q$$

and

$$MC = AC$$
$$\$40 + \$0.02Q = \$250,000Q^{-1} + \$40 + \$0.01Q$$
$$250,000Q^{-1} = 0.01Q$$
$$Q^2 = \frac{250,000}{0.01}$$
$$Q = \sqrt{25,000,000}$$
$$= 5,000$$

Average cost is minimized at an output level of 5,000. This output level is the minimum efficient plant scale. Because the average cost-minimizing output level of 5,000 is far less than the single-plant profit-maximizing activity level of 15,000 units, the profit-maximizing level of total output occurs at a point of rising average costs. Assuming centralized production, Plainfield would maximize profits at an activity level of $Q = 15,000$ rather than $Q = 5,000$ because market-demand conditions are such that, despite the higher costs experienced at $Q = 15,000$, the firm can profitably supply output up to that level.

Because centralized production maximized profits at an activity level well beyond that at which average cost is minimized, Plainfield has an opportunity to reduce costs and increase profits by adopting the multiplant alternative. Although the single-plant $Q = 15,000$ profit-maximizing activity level and the $Q = 5,000$ average cost-minimizing activity level might suggest that multiplant production at three facilities is optimal, this is incorrect. Profits were maximized at $Q = 15,000$ under the assumption that both marginal revenue and marginal cost equal $640. However, with multiplant production and each plant operating at the $Q = 5,000$ activity level, marginal cost will be lowered and multiplant production will entail a new, higher profit-maximizing activity level. Notice that when $Q = 5,000$

$$MC = \$40 + \$0.02Q$$
$$= \$40 + \$0.02(5,000)$$
$$= \$140$$

With multiple plants all operating at 5,000 units per year, $MC = \$140$. It is profitable to expand production so long as the marginal revenue obtained exceeds this minimum $MC = \$140$. This assumes, of course, that each production facility is operating at the optimal activity level of $Q = 5,000$.

The optimal multiplant activity level for the firm, assuming optimal production levels of $Q = 5,000$ at multiple plants, can be calculated by equating MR to the multiplant $MC = \$140$

$$MR = \$140 = MC$$
$$\$940 - \$0.04Q = \$140$$
$$\$0.04Q = \$800$$
$$Q = 20,000$$

Given optimal multiplant production of 20,000 units and average cost-minimizing activity levels

$$\text{Optimal Number of Plants} = \frac{\text{Optimal Multiplant Activity Level}}{\text{Optimal Production Per Plant}}$$
$$= \frac{20,000}{5,000}$$
$$= 4 \qquad\qquad\qquad\qquad \textbf{8.7}$$

of 5,000 units for each plant, multiplant production at four facilities is suggested:
At $Q = 20,000$,

$$P = \$940 - \$0.02(20,000)$$
$$= \$540$$

and

$$\pi = TR - TC$$
$$= P \times Q - 4 \times TC \text{ Per Plant}$$
$$= \$540(20{,}000) - 4[\$250{,}000 + \$40(5{,}000) + \$0.01(5{,}000^2)]$$
$$= \$8{,}000{,}000$$

Multiplant production is preferable because it results in profits that are \$1.5 million greater than with the centralized production alternative. As shown in Figure 8.7, this follows from the firm's ability to concentrate production at the minimum point on the single-plant U-shaped average cost curve.

Finally, it is important to recognize that the optimal multiplant activity level of 20,000 units described in this example is based on the assumption that each production facility produces exactly 5,000 units of output and, therefore, $MC = \$140$. Marginal cost will only equal \$140 with production of $Q = 5{,}000$, or some round multiple thereof (e.g., $Q = 10{,}000$ from two plants, $Q = 15{,}000$ from three plants). The optimal multiplant activity-level calculation is more complicated when this assumption is not met. Plainfield could not produce $Q = 21{,}000$ at $MC = \$140$. For an output level in the 20,000

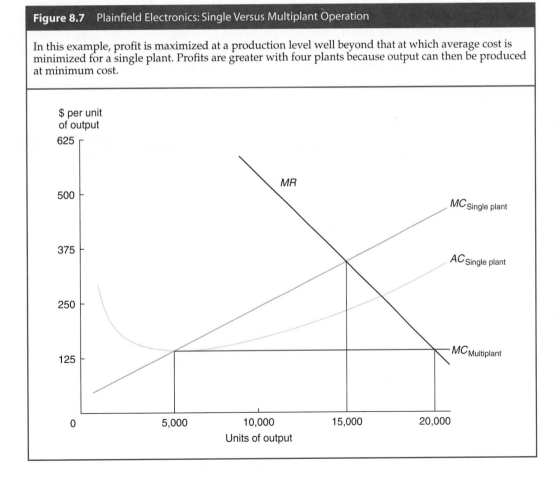

Figure 8.7   Plainfield Electronics: Single Versus Multiplant Operation

In this example, profit is maximized at a production level well beyond that at which average cost is minimized for a single plant. Profits are greater with four plants because output can then be produced at minimum cost.

to 25,000 range, it is necessary to equate marginal revenue with the marginal cost of each plant at its optimal activity level.

Plant Size and Flexibility

The plant that can produce an expected output level at the lowest possible cost is not always the optimal plant size. Consider the following situation. Demand for a product is uncertain, but is expected to be 5,000 units per year. Two possible probability distributions for this demand are given in Figure 8.8. Distribution *L* exhibits a low degree of variability in demand, and Distribution *H* indicates substantially higher variation in possible demand levels.

Now suppose that two plants can be employed to produce the required output. Plant *A* is geared to produce a specified output at a low cost per unit. If more or less than the specified output level is produced (in this case 5,000 units), unit production costs rise rapidly. Plant *B*, on the other hand, is more flexible. Output can be expanded or contracted without excessive cost penalties, but unit costs are not as low as those of plant *A* at the optimal output level. These two cases are shown in Figure 8.9.

Plant *A* is more efficient than plant *B* between 4,500 and 5,500 units of output; outside this range, *B* has lower costs. Which plant should be selected? The answer depends on the level and variability of expected average total costs. If the demand probability distribution with low variation, distribution *L*, is correct, the more specialized facility is optimal. If probability distribution *H* more correctly describes the demand situation, the lower minimum cost of more specialized facilities is more than offset by the possibility of very high costs of producing outside the 4,500- to 5,500-unit range. Plant *B* could then have lower expected costs or a more attractive combination of expected costs and potential variation.

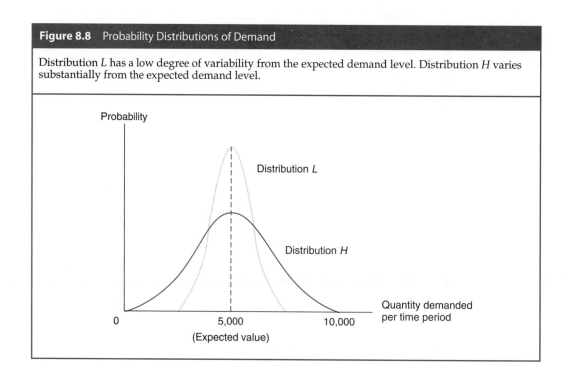

Figure 8.8 Probability Distributions of Demand

Distribution *L* has a low degree of variability from the expected demand level. Distribution *H* varies substantially from the expected demand level.

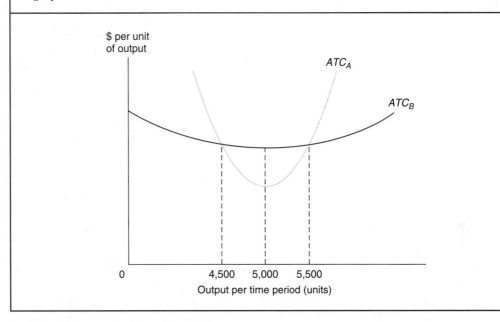

Figure 8.9 Alternative Plants for Production of Expected 5,000 Units of Output

Unit costs are lower for plant *A* than for plant *B* between 4,500 and 5,500 units of output. Outside this range, plant *B* has lowver unit costs.

LEARNING CURVES

Advantages to learning are present when average costs fall with greater production experience.

Learning Curve Concept

Learning Curve
Average cost reduction over time due to production experience.

When knowledge gained from manufacturing experience is used to improve production methods, the resulting decline in average costs is said to reflect the effects of the firm's **learning curve.** The learning curve, or experience curve, phenomenon affects average costs in a way similar to that for any technical advance that improves productive efficiency. Both involve a downward shift in the long-run average cost curve at all levels of output. Learning through experience permits the firm to produce output more efficiently at each and every output level.

To illustrate, consider Figure 8.10, which shows hypothetical long-run average cost curves for periods t and $t+1$. With increased knowledge about production methods gained through the experience of producing Q_t units in period t, long-run average costs have declined for every output level in period $t+1$, which means that Q_t units could be produced during period $t+1$ at an average cost of B rather than the earlier cost of C. The learning curve cost savings is BC. If output were expanded from Q_t to Q_{t+1} between these periods, average costs would fall from C to A. This decline in average costs reflects both the learning curve effect, BC, and the effect of economies of scale, AB.

To isolate the effect of learning or experience on average cost, it is necessary to identify the portion of average-cost changes over time that is due to other factors. One

Managerial Application 8.4

Bigger Isn't Always Better

When economies of scale are substantial, larger firms are able to achieve lower average costs of production or distribution than their smaller rivals. These cost advantages translate into higher and more stable profits, and a permanent competitive advantage for larger firms in some industries. When diseconomies of scale are operative, larger firms suffer a cost disadvantage when compared to their smaller rivals. Smaller firms are then able to translate the benefits of small size into a distinct competitive advantage.

In general, industries dominated by large firms tend to be those in which there are significant economies of scale, important advantages to vertical integration, and a prevalence of mass marketing. As a result, large organizations with sprawling plants emphasize large quantities of output at low production costs. Use of national media, especially TV advertising, is common. In contrast, industries in which "small is beautiful" tend to be those characterized by diseconomies of scale, considerable advantages to subcontracting for "just in time" assembly and manufacturing, and niche marketing that emphasizes the use of highly skilled individuals adept at personal selling. Small factories with

flexible production schedules are common. Rather than mass quantity, many smaller companies emphasize quality. Instead of the sometimes slow-to-respond hierarchical organizations of large companies, smaller companies feature "flat" organizations with decentralized decision making and authority.

Even though the concept of diseconomies of large size is well known, it is sometimes not appreciated how common the phenomenon is in actual practice. Many sectors of industrial manufacturing have found that the highly flexible and customer-sensitive nature of smaller companies can lead to distinct competitive advantages. The villain sometimes encountered by large-scale firms is not any diseconomy of scale in the production process itself, but rather the burden that size places on effective management. Big often means complex, and complexity results in inefficiencies and bureaucratic snarls that can strangle effective communication.

See: Susan Carey and Melanie Trottman, "Airlines Explore New Route," *The Wall Street Journal Online*, October 25, http://online.wsj.com.

of the most important of these changes is the effect of economies of scale. The change in average costs between periods t and $t+1$ can reflect the effects of both learning and economies of scale. The effects of important technical breakthroughs, causing a downward shift in $LRAC$ curves, and input-cost inflation, causing an upward shift in $LRAC$ curves, must also be constrained to quantify learning curve effects. Only when output scale, technology, and input prices are all held constant can the learning curve phenomenon be identified.

Figure 8.11 depicts the learning curve relation suggested by Figure 8.10. Note that learning results in dramatic average cost reductions at low total production levels, but generates increasingly modest savings at higher cumulative production levels. This reflects the fact many improvements in production methods become quickly obvious and are readily adopted. Later gains often come more slowly and are less substantial.

Learning Curve Example

The learning curve phenomenon is often characterized as a constant percentage decline in average costs as cumulative output increases. Suppose, for example, that average costs per unit for a new product were $100 during 2007 but fell to $90 during 2008. Also assume that average costs are in constant dollars, reflecting an accurate adjustment for input-price inflation, and the same basic technology is used in production. Given equal

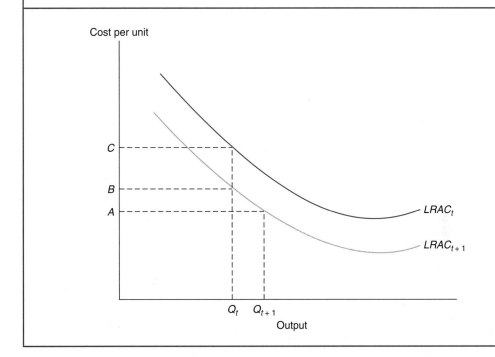

Figure 8.10   Long-Run Average Cost Curve Effects of Learning

Learning will cause a downward shift from $LRAC_t$ to $LRAC_{t+1}$. An average cost decline from C to A reflects the effects of both learning and economies of scale.

output in each period, the learning or experience rate, defined as the percentage by which average cost falls as output doubles, is the following:

$$\text{Learning Rate} = \left(1 - \frac{AC_2}{AC_1}\right) \times 100$$

$$= \left(1 - \frac{\$90}{\$100}\right) \times 100$$

$$= 10\% \qquad\qquad \textbf{8.8}$$

As cumulative total output doubles, average cost is expected to fall by 10 percent. If annual production remains constant, it will take 2 more years for cumulative output to double again. With the same learning rate, average costs will decline to $81 (90 percent of $90) in 2010. Because cumulative total output in 2010 will equal 4 years' production, at a constant annual rate, output will again double by 2014. At that time, the learning curve will have reduced average costs to $72.90 (90 percent of $81).

Because the learning curve concept is sometimes improperly described as a cause of economies of scale, it is worth emphasizing that the two are distinct concepts. Scale economies relate to cost differences associated with different output levels along a single *LRAC* curve. Learning curves relate cost differences to total cumulative output. They are measured by shifts in *LRAC* curves over time. These shifts result from improved production efficiencies stemming from knowledge gained through production experience. Care must be exercised to separate learning and scale effects in cost analysis. Learning or

Figure 8.11   Learning Curve on an Arithmetic Scale

The learning curve reflects the percentage decline in average cost as total cumulative output doubles from Q_t to $2Q_t$.

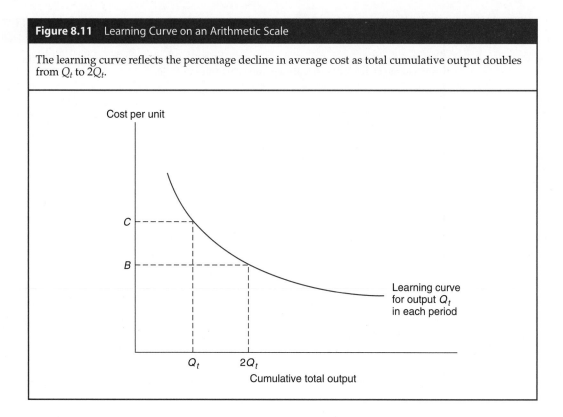

experience rates of 20 percent to 30 percent are sometimes reported. These high learning rates imply rapidly declining manufacturing costs as cumulative total output increases. It should be noted, however, that many learning curve studies fail to account adequately for the expansion of production. Reported learning or experience rates sometimes include the effects of both learning and economies of scale.

Strategic Implications of the Learning Curve Concept

A classic example illustrating the successful use of the learning curve concept is Dallas-based Texas Instruments (TI). TI's main business is producing semiconductor chips which are key components used to store information in computers and a wide array of electronic products. With growing applications for computers and "intelligent" electronics, the demand for semiconductors is expanding rapidly. Some years ago, TI was one of a number of leading semiconductor manufacturers. At this early stage in the development of the industry, TI made the decision to price its semiconductors well below then-current production costs, given expected learning curve advantages in the 20 percent range. TI's learning curve strategy proved spectacularly successful. With low prices, volume increased dramatically. Because TI was making so many chips, average costs were even lower than anticipated; it could price below the competition, and dozens of competitors were knocked out of the world market. Given a relative cost advantage and strict quality controls, TI rapidly achieved a position of dominant leadership in a market that became a source of large and rapidly growing profits.

To play an important role in competitive strategy, learning must be significant. Cost savings of 20 percent to 30 percent as cumulative output doubles must be possible. If only modest effects of learning are present, product quality or customer service often plays a greater role in determining firm success. Learning is also apt to be more important in industries with an abundance of new products or new production techniques rather than in mature industries with well-known production methods. Similarly, learning tends to be important in industries with standardized products and competition based on price rather than product variety or service. And finally, the beneficial effects of learning are realized only when management systems tightly control costs and monitor potential sources of increased efficiency. Continuous feedback of information between production and management personnel is essential.

ECONOMIES OF SCOPE

By virtue of their efficiency in the production of a given product, firms often enjoy cost advantages in the production of related products.

Economies of Scope Concept

Economies of Scope
Cost reduction from producing complementary products.

Economies of scope exist when the cost of joint production is less than the cost of producing multiple outputs separately. A firm will produce products that are complementary when producing them together is more efficient than producing them individually. Suppose that a regional airline offers regularly scheduled passenger service between midsize city pairs and that there is modest local demand for air parcel and small-package delivery service. Given current airplane sizes and configurations, it is often less costly for a single carrier to provide both passenger and cargo services in small regional markets than to specialize in one or the other. Regional air carriers often provide both services. Other examples of scope economies abound in the provision of goods and services. Indeed, the economies of scope concept explains why firms typically produce multiple products.

Economies of scope force management to consider direct and indirect benefits associated with individual lines of business. For example, some financial services firms regard checking accounts and money market mutual funds as "loss leaders." When one considers just the revenues and costs associated with marketing and offering checking services or running a money market mutual fund, they may just break even or yield only a marginal profit. However, successful firms like Dreyfus, Fidelity, and Merrill Lynch correctly see these funds as delivery vehicles for a vast array of financial services. By offering money market funds on an attractive basis, financial service companies establish a working relation with an ideal group of prospective customers for stocks, bonds, and other investments. When viewed as a marketing device, money market mutual funds may be one of the industry's most profitable financial products.

Exploiting Scope Economies

Economies of scope are important because they permit a firm to translate superior skill in a given product line into unique advantages in the production of complementary products. Effective competitive strategy often emphasizes product lines related to a firm's current stars, or areas of recognized strength.

For example, PepsiCo, Inc., has long been a leader in the soft drink market. Over time, the company has gradually broadened its product line to include various brands of regular and diet soft drinks, Gatorade, Tropicana, Fritos and Doritos chips, Grandma's Cookies, and other snack foods. PepsiCo can no longer be considered just a soft drink manufacturer.

It is a widely diversified beverages and snack food company for whom well over one-half of total current profits come from non-soft drink lines. PepsiCo's snack foods and sport drink product line extension strategy is effective because it capitalizes on the distribution network and marketing expertise developed in the firm's soft drink business. In the case of PepsiCo, soft drinks, snack foods, and sports beverages are a natural fit and a good example of how a firm has been able to take the skills gained in developing one star (soft drinks) and use them to develop others (snack foods, sport drinks).

The economies of scope concept offers a useful means for evaluating the potential of current and prospective lines of business. It naturally leads to definition of those areas in which the firm has a competitive advantage and its greatest profit potential.

COST-VOLUME-PROFIT ANALYSIS

Cost-Volume-Profit Analysis
Analytical technique used to study relations among costs, revenues, and profits.

Cost-volume-profit analysis, sometimes called breakeven analysis, is an important analytical technique used to study relations among costs, revenues, and profits.

Cost-Volume-Profit Charts

A basic cost-volume-profit chart is depicted in Figure 8.12. Output volume is measured on the horizontal axis; revenue and cost are shown on the vertical axis. Fixed costs are indicated by a horizontal line. Variable costs at each output level are measured by the distance between the total cost curve and the constant fixed costs. The total revenue

Figure 8.12   Linear Cost-Volume-Profit Chart

Output levels below the breakeven point produce losses. As output grows beyond the breakeven point, increasingly higher profits result.

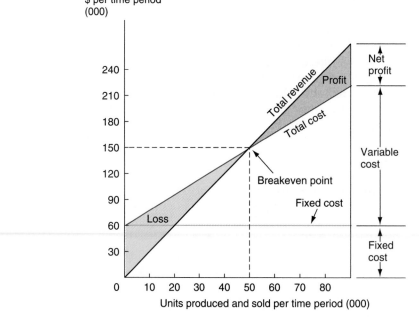

curve indicates the price–quantity relation; profits or losses at each output are shown by the distance between total revenue and total cost curves.

In Figure 8.12, fixed costs of $60,000 are represented by a horizontal line. Variable costs for labor and materials are $1.80 per unit, so total costs rise by that amount for each additional unit of output. Total revenue based on a price of $3 per unit is a straight line through the origin. The slope of the total revenue line is steeper than that of the total cost line. Below the breakeven point, found at the intersection of the total revenue and total cost lines, the firm suffers losses. Beyond the breakeven point, profits are earned. Figure 8.12 indicates a breakeven point for sales and costs at $150,000 at a production level of 50,000 units.

Cost-volume-profit charts usefully portray profit–output relations, but algebraic techniques are usually more efficient for analyzing decision problems. The algebra of cost-volume-profit analysis can be illustrated as follows. Let

$$P = \text{Price per unit sold}$$
$$Q = \text{Quantity produced and sold}$$
$$TFC = \text{Total fixed costs}$$
$$AVC = \text{Average variable cost}$$
$$\pi_C = \text{Profit contribution}$$

On a per unit basis, profit contribution equals price minus average variable cost ($\pi_C = P - AVC$). Profit contribution can be applied to cover fixed costs and then to provide profits. It is the foundation of cost-volume-profit analysis.

One useful application of cost-volume-profit analysis lies in the determination of breakeven activity levels. A **breakeven quantity** is a zero profit activity level. At breakeven quantity levels, total revenue ($TR = P \times Q$) equals total cost ($TC = TFC + AVC \times Q$):

Breakeven Quantity
A zero profit activity level.

$$\text{Total Revenue} = \text{Total Cost}$$
$$P \times Q = TFC + AVC \times Q$$
$$(P - AVC)Q = TFC$$

It follows that breakeven quantity levels occur where

$$Q_{BE} = \frac{TFC}{P - AVC}$$
$$= \frac{TFC}{\pi_C} \qquad \textbf{8.9}$$

Thus, breakeven quantity levels are found by dividing the per unit profit contribution into total fixed costs. In the example illustrated in Figure 8.12, $P = \$3$, $AVC = \$1.80$, and $TFC = \$60,000$. Profit contribution is $1.20 (= \$3.00 - \$1.80)$, and the breakeven quantity is $Q_{BE} = 50,000$ units.

Degree of Operating Leverage

Cost-volume-profit analysis is also a useful tool for analyzing the effects of operating leverage. The relation between operating leverage and profits is shown in Figure 8.13, which contrasts the experience of three firms, A, B, and C, with differing degrees of leverage. The fixed costs of firm B are typical. Firm A uses relatively less capital equipment and has lower fixed costs, but it has a steeper rate of increase in variable costs. Firm A breaks even at a lower activity level than does firm B. For example, at a production level of 40,000 units, B is losing $8,000, but A breaks even. Firm C is highly automated and has

Figure 8.13 Breakeven and Operating Leverage

The breakeven point for firm C occurs at the highest output level. Once this level is reached, profits rise at a faster rate than for firm A or B

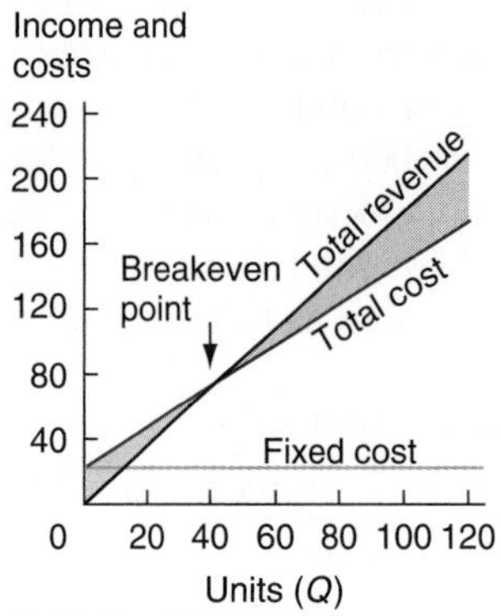

Income and costs

Firm A

Selling price = $2.00
Fixed cost = $20,000
Variable cost = $1.50Q

Units sold (Q)	Sales ($)	Cost ($)	Profit ($)
20,000	40,000	50,000	− 10,000
40,000	80,000	80,000	0
60,000	120,000	110,000	10,000
80,000	160,000	140,000	20,000
100,000	200,000	170,000	30,000
120,000	240,000	200,000	40,000

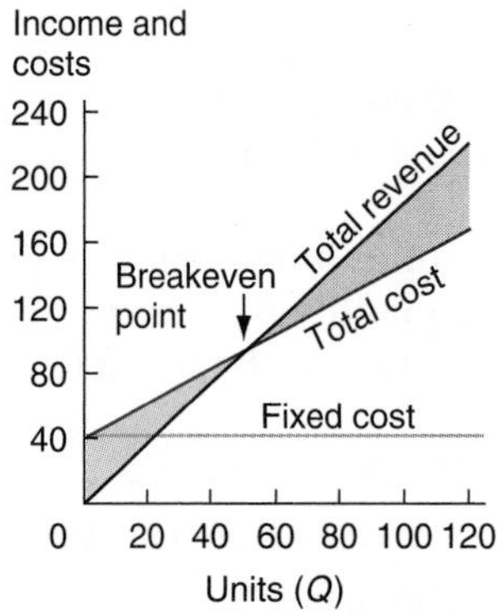

Income and costs

Firm B

Selling price = $2.00
Fixed cost = $40,000
Variable cost = $1.20Q

Units sold (Q)	Sales ($)	Cost ($)	Profit ($)
20,000	40,000	64,000	− 24,000
40,000	80,000	88,000	− 8,000
60,000	120,000	112,000	8,000
80,000	160,000	136,000	24,000
100,000	200,000	160,000	40,000
120,000	240,000	184,000	56,000

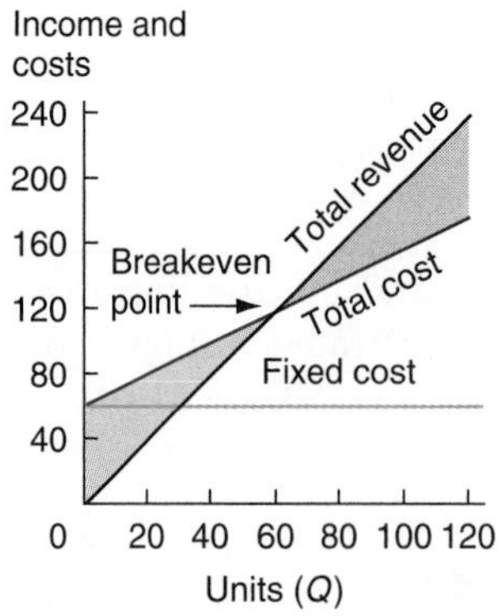

Income and costs

Firm C

Selling price = $2.00
Fixed cost = $60,000
Variable cost = $1.00Q

Units sold (Q)	Sales ($)	Cost ($)	Profit ($)
20,000	40,000	80,000	− 40,000
40,000	80,000	100,000	− 20,000
60,000	120,000	120,000	0
80,000	160,000	140,000	20,000
100,000	200,000	160,000	40,000
120,000	240,000	180,000	60,000

Degree of Operating Leverage

Percentage change in profit from a 1 percent change in output

the highest fixed costs, but its variable costs rise slowly. Firm C has a higher breakeven point than either A or B, but once C passes the breakeven point, profits rise faster than those of the other two firms.

The **degree of operating leverage** is the percentage change in profit that results from a 1 percent change in units sold:

$$\text{Degree of Operating Leverage} = \frac{\text{Percentage Change in Profit}}{\text{Percentage Change in Sales}}$$

$$= \frac{\partial\pi/\pi}{\partial Q/Q}$$

$$= \frac{\partial\pi}{\partial Q} \times \frac{Q}{\pi} \qquad\qquad \textbf{8.10}$$

The degree of operating leverage is the point elasticity of profits with respect to output. When based on linear cost and revenue curves, this elasticity will vary. The degree of operating leverage is always greatest close to the breakeven point.

For firm B in Figure 8.13, the degree of operating leverage at 100,000 units of output is 2.0, calculated as follows:[2]

$$DOL_B = \frac{\partial\pi/\pi}{\partial Q/Q}$$

$$= \frac{(\$41,600-\$40,000)/\$40,000}{(102,000-100,000)/100,000} = \frac{\$1,600/\$40,000}{2,000/100,000}$$

$$= \frac{4\%}{2\%} = 2$$

Here, π is profit and Q is the quantity of output in units.

The degree of operating leverage can be calculated at any level of output. The change in output is ∂Q. Fixed costs are constant, so the change in profit $\partial\pi = \partial Q(P-AVC)$, where P is price per unit and AVC is average variable cost. Any initial profit level $\pi = Q(P-AVC)-TFC$, so the percentage change in profit is

$$\frac{\partial\pi}{\pi} = \frac{\partial Q(P-AVC)}{Q(P-AVC)-TFC}$$

The percentage change in output is $\partial Q/Q$, so the ratio of the percentage change in profits to the percentage change in output, or profit elasticity, is

$$\frac{\partial\pi/\pi}{\partial Q/Q} = \frac{\partial Q(P-AVC)/[Q(P-AVC)-TFC]}{\partial Q/Q}$$

$$= \frac{\partial Q(P-AVC)}{Q(P-AVC)-TFC} \times \frac{Q}{\partial Q}$$

After simplifying, the degree of operating leverage formula at any given level of output is[3]

$$DOL \text{ at } Q \text{ units} = \frac{Q(P-AVC)}{Q(P-AVC)-TFC} \qquad\qquad \textbf{8.11}$$

---

2 This calculation arbitrarily assumes that $\partial Q = 2,000$. If $\partial Q = 1,000$ or $\partial Q = 4,000$, the degree of operating leverage still equals two, because these calculations are based on linear cost and revenue curves. However, if a base other than 100,000 units is chosen, the degree of operating leverage will vary.

3 Because $TFC = Q(AFC)$ and $AC = AVC + AFC$, where AFC is average fixed cost, Equation (8.11) can be reduced further to a form that is useful in some situations:

$$DOL = \frac{Q(P-AVC)}{Q(P-AVC)-Q(AFC)}$$

$$= \frac{P-AVC}{P-AC}$$

Using Equation (8.11), firm B's degree of operating leverage at 100,000 units of output is calculated as

$$DOL_B \text{ at } 100,000 \text{ units} = \frac{100,000(\$2.00 - \$1.20)}{100,000(\$2.00 - \$1.20) - \$40,000}$$

$$= \frac{\$80,000}{\$40,000} = 2$$

Equation (8.11) can also be applied to firms A and C. When this is done, firm A's degree of operating leverage at 100,000 units equals 1.67 and firm C's equals 2.5. With a 2 percent increase in volume, firm C, the firm with the most operating leverage, will experience a profit increase of 5 percent. For the same 2 percent gain in volume, the firm with the least leverage, firm A will have only a 3.3 percent profit gain. As seen in Figure 8.13, the profits of firm C are most sensitive to changes in sales volume, whereas firm A's profits are relatively insensitive to volume changes. Firm B, with an intermediate degree of leverage, lies between these two extremes.

Cost-volume-profit analysis helps explain relations among volume, prices, and costs. It is also useful for pricing, cost control, and other financial decisions. To study profit possibilities with different prices, a whole series of charts is necessary, with one chart for each price. With sophisticated spreadsheets, the creation of a wide variety of cost-volume-profit charts is relatively easy. If average costs change with output, such changes influence both the level and the slope of cost functions. Care must be exercised to ensure that cost-volume-profit analysis is not applied when underlying assumptions are violated.

SUMMARY

This chapter introduces a number of cost concepts, shows the relation between cost functions and production functions, and examines several cost analysis issues.

- For tax purposes, **historical cost,** or historical cash outlay, is the relevant cost. This is also generally true for annual 10-K reports to the Securities and Exchange Commission and for reports to stockholders. **Current cost,** the amount that must be paid under prevailing market conditions, is typically more relevant for decision-making purposes. Current costs are often determined by **replacement costs,** or the cost of duplicating productive capability using present technology. Another prime determinant of current cost is **opportunity cost,** or the foregone value associated with the current rather than the next-best use of a given asset. Economic costs typically involve out-of-pocket costs, or **explicit costs,** and noncash costs, called **implicit costs.**

- **Incremental cost** is the change in cost caused by a given managerial decision, and often involves multiple units of output. Incremental costs are a prime determinant of **profit contribution,** or profit before fixed charges. Neither is affected by **sunk costs,** which do not vary across decision alternatives.

- Proper use of relevant cost concepts requires an understanding of the cost–output relation, or **cost function. Short-run cost functions** are used for day-to-day operating decisions; **long-run cost functions** are employed in the long-range planning process. The **short run** is the operating period during which the availability of at least one input is fixed. In the **long run,** the firm has complete flexibility.

- Long-run cost curves are **planning curves;** short-run cost curves are **operating curves. Fixed costs** do not vary with output and are incurred only in the short run. **Variable costs** fluctuate with output in both the short and the long run. A **short-run cost curve** shows the minimum cost of output for a specific plant size and in a given operating environment. A **long-run cost curve** shows the minimum cost impact of output for the optimal plant size using current technology in the present operating environment.

- **Economies of scale** cause long-run average costs to decline. **Cost elasticity, ε_C,** measures the percentage change in total cost associated with a 1 percent change in output.

- **Capacity** refers to the output level at which short-run average costs are minimized. **Minimum efficient scale** (MES) is the output level at which long-run average costs are minimized.

- **Multiplant economies of scale** are cost advantages that arise from operating multiple facilities in the same line of business or industry. **Multiplant diseconomies of scale** are cost disadvantages that arise from managing multiple facilities in the same line of business or industry.

- When knowledge gained from manufacturing experience is used to improve production methods, the resulting decline in average cost reflects the firm's **learning curve. Economies of scope** exist when the cost of joint production is less than the cost of producing multiple outputs separately.

- **Cost-volume-profit analysis,** sometimes called breakeven analysis, is used to study relations among costs, revenues, and profits. A **breakeven quantity** is a zero profit activity level. The **degree of operating leverage** is the percentage change in profit that results from a 1 percent change in units sold; it can be understood as the elasticity of profits with respect to output.

Cost analysis poses a continuing challenge to management in all types of organizations. Using the concepts and tools discussed in this chapter, successful managers are able to manage costs effectively.

QUESTIONS

Q8.1 What advantages or disadvantages do you see in using current costs for tax and stockholder reporting purposes?

Q8.2 Assume that 2 years ago, you purchased a new Jeep Wrangler SE 4WD with a soft top for $16,500 using 5-year interest-free financing. Today, the remaining loan balance is $9,900 and your Jeep has a trade-in value of $9,500. What is your opportunity cost of continuing to drive the Jeep? Discuss the financing risk exposure of the lender.

Q8.3 Southwest Airlines offers four flights per weekday from Cleveland, Ohio, to Tucson, Arizona. If adding a fifth flight per weekday would cost $15,000 per flight, or $110 per available seat, calculate the incremental costs borne by Southwest following a decision to go ahead with a fifth flight per day for a minimal 60-flight trial period. What is the marginal cost? In this case, is incremental cost or marginal cost relevant for decision-making purposes?

Q8.4 Suppose the Big Enchilada restaurant has been offered a binding 1-year lease agreement on an attractive site for $5,200 per month. Before the lease agreement has been signed, what is the incremental cost per month of site rental? After the lease agreement has been signed, what is the incremental cost per month of site rental? Explain.

Q8.5 What is the relation between production functions and cost functions? Be sure to include in your discussion the effect of competitive conditions in input factor markets.

Q8.6 The definition of point output elasticity is $\varepsilon_Q = \partial Q/Q \div \partial \underline{X}/\underline{X}$ ($\underline{X}$ represents all inputs), whereas the definition of point cost elasticity is $\varepsilon_C = \partial C/C \div \partial Q/Q$. Explain why $\varepsilon_Q > 1$ indicates increasing returns to scale, whereas $\varepsilon_C < 1$ indicates economies of scale.

Q8.7 The president of a small firm has been complaining to the controller about rising labor and material costs. However, the controller notes that average costs have not increased during the past year. Is this possible?

Q8.8 With traditional medical insurance plans, workers pay a premium that is taken out of each paycheck and must meet an annual deduction of a few hundred dollars. After that, insurance picks up most of their health-care costs. Companies complain that this gives workers little incentive to help control medical insurance costs, and those costs are spinning out of control. Can you suggest ways of giving workers better incentives to control employer medical insurance costs?

Q8.9 Will firms in industries in which high levels of output are necessary for minimum efficient scale tend to have substantial degrees of operating leverage?

Q8.10 Do operating strategies of average cost minimization and profit maximization always lead to identical levels of output?

SELF-TEST PROBLEMS AND SOLUTIONS

ST8.1 Learning Curves. Suppose Modern Merchandise, Inc., makes and markets do-it-yourself hardware, housewares, and industrial products. The company's new Aperture Miniblind is winning customers by virtue of its high quality and quick order turnaround time. The product also benefits because its price point bridges the gap between ready-made vinyl blinds and their high-priced custom counterpart. In addition, the company's expanding product line is sure to benefit from cross-selling across different lines. Given the success of the Aperture Miniblind product, Modern Merchandise plans to open a new production facility near Beaufort, South Carolina. Based on information provided by its chief financial officer, the company estimates fixed costs for this product of $50,000 per year and average variable costs of

$$AVC = \$0.5 + \$0.0025Q$$

where AVC is average variable cost (in dollars) and Q is output.

A. Estimate total cost and average total cost for the projected first-year volume of 20,000 units.

B. An increase in worker productivity because of greater experience or learning during the course of the year resulted in a substantial cost saving for the company. Estimate the effect of learning on average total cost if actual second-year total cost was $848,000 at an actual volume of 20,000 units.

ST8.1 SOLUTION

A. The total variable cost function for the first year is

$$TVC = AVC \times Q$$
$$= (\$0.5 + \$0.0025Q)Q$$
$$= \$0.5Q + \$0.0025Q^2$$

At a volume of 20,000 units, estimated total cost is

$$TC = TFC + TVC$$
$$= \$50,000 + \$0.5Q + \$0.0025Q^2$$
$$= \$50,000 + \$0.5(20,000) + \$0.0025(20,000^2)$$
$$= \$1,060,000$$

Estimated average cost is

$$AC = TC/Q$$
$$= \$1,060,000/20,000$$
$$= \$53 \text{ per case}$$

B. If actual total costs were \$848,000 at a volume of 20,000 units, actual average total costs were

$$AC = TC/Q$$
$$= \$848,000/20,000$$
$$= \$42.40 \text{ per case}$$

Therefore, greater experience or learning has resulted in an average cost saving of \$10.60 per case since

$$\text{Learning effect} = \text{Actual } AC - \text{Estimated } AC$$
$$= \$42.40 - \$53$$
$$= -\$10.60 \text{ per case}$$

Alternatively,

$$\text{Learning rate} = \left(1 - \frac{AC_2}{AC_1}\right) \times 100$$
$$= \left(1 - \frac{\$42.40}{\$53}\right) \times 100$$
$$= 20\%$$

ST8.2 Minimum Efficient Scale Estimation.
Assume Kanata Corporation is a leading manufacturer of telecommunications equipment based in Ontario, Canada. Its main product is micro-processor controlled telephone switching equipment, called automatic private branch exchanges (PABXs), capable of handling 8 to 3,000 telephone extensions. Severe price-cutting throughout the PABX industry continues to put pressure on sales and margins. To better compete against increasingly aggressive rivals, the company is contemplating the construction of a new production facility capable of producing 1.5 million units per year. Kanata's in-house engineering estimate of the total cost function for the new facility is

$$TC = \$3,000 + \$1,000Q + \$0.003Q^2$$
$$MC = \partial TC/\partial Q = \$1,000 + \$0.006Q$$

where TC = Total Costs in thousands of dollars, Q = Output in thousands of units, and MC = Marginal Costs in thousands of dollars.

A. Estimate minimum efficient scale in this industry.

B. In light of current PABX demand of 30 million units per year, how would you evaluate the future potential for competition in the industry?

ST8.2 SOLUTION

A. Minimum efficient scale is reached when average costs are first minimized. This occurs at the point where $MC = AC$.

$$\text{Average Costs} = AC = TC/Q$$
$$= (\$3,000 + \$1,000Q + \$0.003Q^2)/Q$$
$$= \frac{\$3,000}{Q} + \$1,000 + \$0.003Q$$

Therefore,

$$MC = AC$$

$$\$1,000 + \$0.006Q = \frac{\$3,000}{Q} + \$1,000 + \$0.003Q$$

$$0.003Q = \frac{3,000}{Q}$$

$$\frac{3,000}{Q^2} = 0.003$$

$$Q^2 = 1,000,000$$

$$Q = 1,000$$

[Note: AC is rising for $Q > 1,000(000)$].

Alternatively, MES can be calculated using the point cost elasticity formula, since MES is reached when $\varepsilon_C = 1$.

$$\varepsilon_C = \frac{\partial TC}{\partial Q} \times \frac{Q}{TC}$$

$$\frac{(\$1,000 + \$0.006Q)Q}{(\$3,000 + \$1,000Q + \$0.003Q^2)} = 1$$

$$1,000Q + 0.006Q^2 = 3,000 + 1,000Q + 0.003Q^2$$

$$0.003Q^2 = 3,000$$

$$Q^2 = 1,000,000$$

$$Q_{MES} = 1,000$$

B. With a minimum efficient scale of 1 million units and total industry sales of 30 million units, up to 30 efficiently sized competitors are possible in Kanata's market.

$$\text{Potential Number of Efficient Competitors} = \frac{\text{Market Size}}{\text{MES Size}}$$

$$= 30,000,000/1,000,000$$

$$= 30$$

Thus, there is the potential for $n = 30$ efficiently sized competitors and, therefore, vigorous competition in Kanata's industry.

PROBLEMS

P8.1 **Cost Relations.** Determine whether each of the following is true or false. Explain why.

A. Average cost equals marginal cost at the minimum efficient scale of plant.

B. When total fixed cost and price are held constant, an increase in average variable cost will typically cause a reduction in the breakeven activity level.

C. If $\varepsilon_C > 1$, diseconomies of scale and increasing average costs are indicated.

D. When long-run average cost is decreasing, it can pay to operate larger plants with some excess capacity rather than smaller plants at their peak efficiency.

E. An increase in average variable cost always increases the degree of operating leverage for firms making a positive net profit.

P8.2   Cost Curves. Indicate whether each of the following involves an upward or downward shift in the long-run average cost curve or, instead, involves a leftward or rightward movement along a given curve. Also indicate whether each will have an increasing, decreasing, or uncertain effect on the level of average cost.

A. A rise in wage rates.

B. A decline in output.

C. An energy-saving technical change.

D. A fall in interest rates.

E. An increase in learning or experience.

P8.3   Incremental Cost. South Park Software, Inc. produces innovative interior decorating software that it sells to design studios, home furnishing stores, and so on. The yearly volume of output is 15,000 units. Selling price and costs per unit are as follows:

Selling Price		$250
Costs:		
Direct material	$40	
Direct labor	60	
Variable overhead	30	
Variable selling expenses	25	
Fixed selling expenses	20	−$175
Unit profit before tax		$75

Management is evaluating the possibility of using the Internet to sell its software directly to consumers at a price of $300 per unit. Although no added capital investment is required, additional shipping and handling costs are estimated as follows:

Direct labor	$30 per unit
Variable overhead	$5 per unit
Variable selling expenses	$2 per unit
Fixed selling expenses	$20,000 per year

Calculate the incremental profit that South Park would earn by customizing its instruments and marketing them directly to end users.

P8.4   Accounting and Economic Costs.   Three graduate business students are considering operating a fruit smoothie stand in the Harbor Springs, Michigan, resort area during their summer break. This is an alternative to summer employment with a local firm, where they would each earn $6,000 over the 3-month summer period. A fully equipped facility can be leased at a cost of $8,000 for the summer. Additional projected costs are $1,000 for insurance and $3.20 per unit for materials and supplies. Their fruit smoothies would be priced at $5 per unit.

A. What is the accounting cost function for this business?

B. What is the economic cost function for this business?

C. What is the economic breakeven number of units for this operation? (Assume a $5 price and ignore interest costs associated with the timing of lease payments.)

P8.5   Profit Contribution.   Angelica Pickles is manager of a Quick Copy franchise in White Plains, New York. Pickles projects that by reducing copy charges from 5¢ to 4¢ each, Quick Copy's $600-per-week profit contribution will increase by one-third.

A. If average variable costs are 2¢ per copy, calculate Quick Copy's projected increase in volume.

B. What is Pickles' estimate of the arc price elasticity of demand for copies?

P8.6   Cost-Volume-Profit Analysis.   Textbook publishers evaluate market size, the degree of competition, expected revenues, and costs for each prospective new title. With these data in mind, they estimate the probability that a given book will reach or exceed the breakeven point. If the publisher estimates that a book will not exceed the breakeven point based upon standard assumptions, they may consider cutting production costs by reducing the number of illustrations, doing only light copy editing, using a lower grade of paper, or negotiating with the author to reduce the royalty rate. To illustrate the process, consider the following data:

Cost Category	Dollar Amount
Fixed Costs	
Copyediting and other editorial costs	15,750
Illustrations	32,750
Typesetting	51,500
Total fixed costs	100,000
Variable Costs	
Printing, binding and paper	22.50
Bookstore discounts	25.00
Sales staff commissions	8.25
Author royalties	10.00
General and administrative costs	26.25
Total variable costs per copy	92.00
List price per copy	100.00

Fixed costs of $100,000 can be estimated quite accurately. Variable costs are linear and set by contract. List prices are variable, but competition keeps prices within a narrow range. Variable costs for the proposed book are $92 a copy, and the expected wholesale price is $100. This means that each copy sold provides the publisher with an $8 profit contribution.

A. Estimate the volume necessary to reach a breakeven level of output.

B. How many textbooks would have to be sold to generate a profit contribution of $20,000?

C. Calculate the economic profit contribution or loss resulting from the acceptance of a book club offer to buy 3,000 copies directly from the publisher at a price of $77 per copy. Should the offer be accepted?

P8.7 Cost Elasticity. Power Brokers, Inc. (PBI), a discount brokerage firm, is contemplating opening a new regional office in Providence, Rhode Island. An accounting cost analysis of monthly operating costs at a dozen of its regional outlets reveals average fixed costs of $4,500 per month and average variable costs of

$$AVC = \$59 - \$0.006Q$$

where AVC is average variable costs (in dollars) and Q is output measured by number of stock and bond trades.

A typical stock or bond trade results in $100 gross commission income, with PBI paying 35 percent of this amount to its sales representatives.

A. Estimate the trade volume necessary for PBI to reach a target return of $7,500 per month for a typical office.

B. Estimate and interpret the elasticity of cost with respect to output at the trade volume found in part A.

P8.8 Multiplant Operation. Appalachia Beverage Company, Inc. is considering alternative proposals for expansion into the Midwest. Alternative 1: Construct a single plant in Indianapolis, Indiana, with a monthly production capacity of 300,000 cases, a monthly fixed cost of $262,500, and a variable cost of $3.25 per case. Alternative 2: Construct three plants, one each in Muncie, Indiana; Normal, Illinois; and Dayton, Ohio, with capacities of 120,000, 100,000, and 80,000, respectively, and monthly fixed costs of $120,000, $110,000, and $95,000 each. Variable costs would be only $3 per case because of lower distribution costs. To achieve these cost savings, sales from each smaller plant would be limited to demand within its home state. The total estimated monthly sales volume of 200,000 cases in these three Midwestern states is distributed as follows: 80,000 cases in Indiana, 70,000 cases in Illinois, and 50,000 cases in Ohio.

A. Assuming a wholesale price of $5 per case, calculate the breakeven output quantities for each alternative.

B. At a wholesale price of $5 per case in all states, and assuming sales at the projected levels, which alternative expansion scheme provides Appalachia with the highest profit per month?

C. If sales increase to production capacities, which alternative would prove to be more profitable?

P8.9   Learning Curves. The St. Thomas Winery plans to open a new production facility in the Napa Valley of California. Based on information provided by the accounting department, the company estimates fixed costs of $250,000 per year and average variable costs of

$$AVC = \$10 + \$0.01Q$$

where AVC is average variable cost (in dollars) and Q is output measured in cases of output per year.

A. Estimate total cost and average total cost for the coming year at a projected volume of 4,000 cases.

B. An increase in worker productivity because of greater experience or learning during the course of the year resulted in a substantial cost saving for the company. Estimate the effect of learning on average total cost if actual total cost was $522,500 at an actual volume of 5,000 cases.

P8.10 Degree of Operating Leverage. Untouchable Package Service (UPS) offers overnight package delivery to Canadian business customers. UPS has recently decided to expand its facilities to better satisfy current and projected demand. Current volume totals 2 million packages per week at a price of $12 each, and average variable costs are constant at all output levels. Fixed costs are $3 million per week, and profit contribution averages one-third of revenues on each delivery. After completion of the expansion project, fixed costs will double, but variable costs will decline by 25 percent.

A. Calculate the change in UPS's weekly breakeven output level that is due to expansion.

B. Assuming that volume remains at 2 million packages per week, calculate the change in the degree of operating leverage that is due to expansion.

C. Again assuming that volume remains at 1 million packages per week, what is the effect of expansion on weekly profit?

CASE *Study*   **Estimating Hospitalization Costs for Regional Hospitals**

Cost estimation and cost containment are an important concern for a wide range of for-profit and not-for-profit organizations offering health-care services. For such organizations, the accurate measurement of costs per patient day (a measure of output) is necessary for effective management. Similarly, such cost estimates are of significant interest to public officials at the federal, state, and local government levels. For example, many state Medicaid reimbursement programs base their payment rates on historical accounting measures of average costs per unit of service. However, these historical average costs may or may not be relevant for hospital management decisions. During periods of substantial excess capacity, the overhead component of average costs may become irrelevant. When the facilities are fully used and facility expansion becomes necessary to increase services, then all costs, including overhead, are relevant. As a result, historical average costs provide a useful basis for planning purposes only if appropriate

continued

assumptions can be made about the relative length of periods of peak versus off-peak facility usage. From a public-policy perspective, a further potential problem arises when hospital expense reimbursement programs are based on average costs per day, because the care needs and nursing costs of various patient groups can vary widely. For example, if the care received by the average publicly supported Medicaid patient actually costs more than that received by non-Medicaid patients, Medicaid reimbursement based on average costs would be inequitable to providers and could create access barriers for Medicaid patients.

As an alternative to accounting cost estimation methods, one might consider using engineering techniques to estimate nursing costs. For example, the labor cost of each type of service could be estimated as the product of an approximation of the time required to perform each service and the estimated wage rate per unit of time. Multiplying this figure by an estimate of the frequency of service gives an engineering estimate of the cost of the service. A possible limitation to the accuracy of this engineering cost estimation method is that treatment of a variety of illnesses often requires a combination of nursing services. To the extent that multiple services can be provided simultaneously, the engineering technique will tend to overstate actual costs unless the effect of service "packaging" is allowed for.

Cost estimation is also possible by means of a carefully designed regression-based approach using variable cost and service data collected at the ward, unit, or facility level. Weekly labor costs for registered nurses (RNs), licensed practical nurses (LPNs), and nursing aides might be related to a variety of patient services performed during a given measurement period. With sufficient variability in cost and service levels over time, useful estimates of variable labor costs become possible for each type of service and for each patient category (Medicaid, non-Medicaid, etc.). An important advantage of

a regression-based approach is that it explicitly allows for the effect of service packaging on variable costs. For example, if shots and wound-dressing services are typically provided together, this will be reflected in the regression-based estimates of variable costs per unit.

Long-run costs per nursing facility can be estimated using either cross-section or time-series methods. By relating total facility costs to the service levels provided by a number of hospitals, nursing homes, or out-patient care facilities during a specific period, useful cross-section estimates of total service costs are possible. If case mixes were to vary dramatically according to type of facility, then the type of facility would have to be explicitly accounted for in the regression model analyzed. Similarly, if patient mix or service-provider efficiency is expected to depend, at least in part, on the for-profit or not-for-profit organization status of the care facility, the regression model must also recognize this factor. These factors plus price-level adjustments for inflation would be accounted for in a time-series approach to nursing cost estimation.

To illustrate a regression-based approach to nursing cost estimation, consider a hypothetical analysis of variable nursing costs conducted by the Southeast Association of Hospital Administrators (SAHA). Using confidential data provided by 40 regional hospitals, SAHA studied the relation between nursing costs per patient day and four typical categories of nursing services. These annual data appear in Table 8.2. The four categories of nursing services studied include shots, intravenous (IV) therapy, pulse taking and monitoring, and wound dressing. Each service is measured in terms of frequency per patient day. An output of 1.50 in the shots service category means that, on average, patients received one and one-half shots per day. Similarly, a value of 0.75 in the IV service category means that on average, patients received 0.75 units of IV therapy per day, and so on. In addition to four categories of nursing services, the not-for-profit or for-profit

continued

Table 8.2 Nursing Costs per Patient Day, Nursing Services, and Profit Status for 40 Hospitals in Southeastern States

Hospital	Nursing Care Costs Per Patient Day	Shots	IV Therapy	Pulse Taking	Wound Dressing	Profit Status (1 = For-profit, 0 = Not-for-profit)
1	300.92	0.29	0.51	3.49	0.27	0
2	283.65	0.15	0.59	3.32	0.62	0
3	329.65	0.26	0.85	3.05	0.29	1
4	343.71	0.23	0.67	2.26	0.57	0
5	389.03	0.47	0.79	2.43	0.68	0
6	299.01	0.41	0.86	2.48	0.66	1
7	437.97	0.42	0.90	3.81	0.49	0
8	284.74	0.25	0.63	2.96	0.34	0
9	404.65	0.50	0.93	2.27	0.60	0
10	293.70	0.27	0.67	2.51	0.61	0
11	264.58	0.38	0.62	2.93	0.39	0
12	299.71	0.14	0.76	2.17	0.37	0
13	323.81	0.16	0.91	2.07	0.47	0
14	434.45	0.27	0.98	3.17	0.68	0
15	374.17	0.48	0.87	3.45	0.33	0
16	304.61	0.43	0.61	2.96	0.30	0
17	354.46	0.09	0.82	3.17	0.54	0
18	340.21	0.12	0.71	3.96	0.41	0
19	348.13	0.04	0.76	3.39	0.70	0
20	353.52	0.41	0.84	2.61	0.41	0
21	309.01	0.22	0.83	2.62	0.47	1
22	406.12	0.32	0.56	4.00	0.59	0
23	309.04	0.40	0.84	3.46	0.50	1
24	406.94	0.29	0.72	3.85	0.65	0
25	317.12	0.14	0.91	2.74	0.29	0
26	369.23	0.15	0.80	3.73	0.72	1
27	300.31	0.31	0.75	3.12	0.26	0
28	402.08	0.37	0.72	2.76	0.73	0
29	434.40	0.40	0.96	2.72	0.72	0
30	272.48	0.35	0.62	2.31	0.37	0
31	316.30	0.08	0.68	3.80	0.33	0
32	351.71	0.34	0.63	3.58	0.53	0
33	359.90	0.46	0.89	3.44	0.46	0
34	331.36	0.39	0.54	3.40	0.56	0
35	335.54	0.17	0.84	2.58	0.43	1
36	402.26	0.48	0.91	3.75	0.36	0
37	373.28	0.25	0.81	3.49	0.53	0
38	440.67	0.16	0.86	3.34	0.68	0
39	262.83	0.43	0.51	3.05	0.43	1
40	333.86	0.45	0.82	3.59	0.33	1
Average	344.98	0.30	0.76	3.09	0.49	0.20

> **continued**

status of each hospital is also indicated. Using a "dummy" (or binary) variable approach, the profit status variable equals one for the eight for-profit hospitals included in the study and zero for the remaining 32 not-for-profit hospitals.

Cost estimation results for nursing costs per patient day derived using a regression-based approach are shown in Table 8.3.

A. Interpret the coefficient of determination (R_2) estimated for the nursing cost function.

B. Describe the economic and statistical significance of each estimated coefficient in the nursing cost function.

C. Average nursing costs for the 8 for-profit hospitals in the sample are only $318.52 per patient day, or $33.07 per patient day less than the $351.59 average cost experienced by the 32 not-for-profit hospitals. How can this fact be reconciled with the estimated coefficient of −39.156 for the for-profit status variable?

D. Would such an approach for nursing cost estimation have practical relevance for publicly funded nursing cost reimbursement systems?

Table 8.3 Nursing Cost Estimates Per Patient Day

Variable (1)	Coefficient (2)	Standard Error of the Coefficient (3)	t Statistic (4) = (2)/(3)
Intercept	−22.134	39.897	−0.55
Shots	72.765	32.251	2.26
IV	215.683	33.210	6.49
Pulse	36.242	7.736	4.68
Wound dressing	156.041	29.087	5.36
For-profit status	−39.156	10.426	−3.76

Coefficient of determination = R^2 = 76.81%
Standard error of estimate = SEE = $26.10

SELECTED REFERENCES

Alessandria, George and Horag Choi. "Do Sunk Costs of Exporting Matter for Net Export Dynamics?" *Quarterly Journal of Economics* 122, no. 1 (February, 2007): 289–336.

Chu, Leon Yang and David E. M. Sappington. "Simple Cost-Sharing Contracts." *American Economic Review* 97, no. 1 (March, 2007): 419–428.

Gordon, Elizabeth A., Elaine Henry, Timothy J. Louwers, Brad J. Reed. "Auditing Related Party Transactions: A Literature Overview and Research Synthesis." *Accounting Horizons* 21, no. 1 (March 1, 2007): 81–102.

Guvenen, Fatih. "Do Stockholders Share Risk More Effectively than Nonstockholders?" *Review of Economics and Statistics* 89, no. 2 (May, 2007): 275–288.

Han, Bing. "Stochastic Volatilities and Correlations of Bond Yields." *Journal of Finance* 62, no. 3 (June, 2007): 1491–1524.

Hansen, Lars Peter. "Beliefs, Doubts and Learning: Valuing Macroeconomic Risk." *American Economic Review* 97, no. 2 (May, 2007): 1–30.

Haushalter, David, Sandy Klasa, and William F. Maxwell. "The Influence of Product Market Dynamics on a Firm's

Cash Holdings and Hedging Behavior." *Journal of Financial Economics* 84, no. 3 (June, 2007): 797–825.

Helwege, Jean, Christo Pirinsky, and Rene M. Stulz. "Why Do Firms Become Widely Held? An Analysis of the Dynamics of Corporate Ownership." *Journal of Finance* 62, no. 3 (June, 2007): 995–1028.

Henderson, Daniel J. and Daniel L. Millimet. "Pollution Abatement Costs and Foreign Direct Investment Inflows to U.S. States: A Nonparametric Reassessment." *Review of Economics and Statistics* 89, no. 1 (February, 2007): 178–183.

Javidan, Mansour. "Forward-Thinking Cultures." *Harvard Business Review* 85, no. 7, 8 (July 1, 2007): 20.

Jo, Hoje and Yongtae Kim. "Disclosure Frequency and Earnings Management." *Journal of Financial Economics* 84, no. 2 (May, 2007): 561–590.

Kalay, Avner, Rajeev Singhal, and Elizabeth Tashjian. "Is Chapter 11 Costly?" *Journal of Financial Economics* 84, no. 3 (June, 2007): 772–796.

Klump, Rainer, Peter McAdam, and Alpo Willman. "Factor Substitution and Factor-Augmenting Technical Progress in the United States: A Normalized Supply-Side System Approach." *Review of Economics and Statistics* 89, no. 1 (February, 2007): 183–192.

Kohlbeck, Mark Terry D Warfield. "Unrecorded Intangible Assets: Abnormal Earnings and Valuation." *Accounting Horizons* 21, no. 1 (March 1, 2007): 23–41.

Mizik, Natalie and Robert Jacobson. "The Cost of Myopic Management." *Harvard Business Review* 85, nos. 7, 8 (July 1, 2007): 22, 24.

Linear Programming

Linear Programming, or so-called "Solver" PC software, is used to figure out the best answer to an assortment of managerial decision problems. It's a big improvement from the more basic "what if" approach to problem solving. In a traditional "what if" approach, one simply enters data in a computer spreadsheet and uses spreadsheet formulas and macros to calculate resulting solutions. The "what if" approach is that it allows managers to consider the cost, revenue, and profit implications of changes in a wide variety of operating conditions. An important limitation of the "what if" method is that it can become tedious searching for the best answer to planning and operating decisions.

Linear programming can be thought of as performing "what if in reverse." All you do is specify appropriate objectives and a series of constraint conditions, and the software will determine appropriate input values. When production goals are specified in light of operating constraints, linear programming can be used to identify the cost-minimizing operating plan. Alternatively, using linear programming techniques, a manager can find the profit-maximizing activity level by specifying production relationships and the amount of available resources.

Linear programming has proven to be an adept tool for solving problems encountered in a number of business, engineering, financial, and scientific applications. In a practical sense, typically encountered constrained optimization problems seldom have a simple rule-of-thumb solution. This chapter illustrates how linear programming can be used to quickly and easily solve real-world decision problems.[1]

BASIC ASSUMPTIONS

Linear Programming
A solution method for maximization or minimization decision problems subject to underlying constraints.

To know when **linear programming** techniques can be applied, it is necessary to understand basic underlying assumptions.

Inequality Constraints

Constraints often limit the resource employed to less than or equal to ($\leq$) some fixed amount available. In other instances, constraints specify that the quantity or quality of output must be greater than or equal to ($\geq$) some minimum requirement. Linear

---

1 See Michael Totty, "Making Sense of It All," *The Wall Street Journal Online,* September 24, 2007, http://online.wsj.com.

Optimal Solution
Best answer.

programming handles such constraint inequalities easily, making it useful for finding the **optimal solution** for many management decision problems.

A typical linear programming problem might be to maximize output subject to the constraint that no more than 40 hours of skilled labor per week be used. This labor constraint is expressed as an inequality where skilled labor is ≤40 hours per week. Such an operating constraint means that no more than 40 hours of skilled labor can be used, but some excess capacity is permissible, at least in the short run. If 36 hours of skilled labor were fruitfully employed during a given week, the 4 hours per week of unused labor is called excess capacity.

Linearity Assumption

As its name implies, linear programming can be applied only in situations in which the relevant objective function and constraint conditions are linear. Typical managerial decision problems that can be solved using the linear programming method involve revenue, cost, and profit functions. Each must be linear; as output increases, revenues, costs, and profits must increase in a linear fashion. For revenues to be a linear function of output, product prices must be constant. For costs to be a linear function of output, both returns to scale and input prices must be constant. Constant input prices, when combined with constant returns to scale, result in a linear total cost function. If both output prices and unit costs are constant, profits also rise in a linear fashion with output.

Product and input prices are relatively constant under conditions of pure competition. Linear programming methods are clearly applicable for firms in perfectly competitive industries with constant returns to scale. Linear programming is also applicable in many

Managerial Application 9.1

Karmarkar's LP Breakthrough

On a typical day, thousands of U.S. Air Force planes ferry cargo and military passengers around the globe. To keep those jets flying, the Military Airlift Command (MAC) must juggle schedules for pilots and other flight personnel. In addition, the MAC has to make literally millions of calculations to determine the most efficient flight route, cargo weight, fuel loading, and so on. After all of these details have been carefully accounted for, unexpected bad weather or emergency changes in priorities can force a complete recalculation of the entire flight plan.

Getting all of the pieces to fit together is a classic linear programming (LP) dilemma. If an LP computer program could help increase fuel efficiency by just 2 percent, it would be worth millions of dollars per year. Unfortunately, the complexity of the Air Force's transportation problem is so great that it once defied the capabilities of even the most sophisticated supercomputers. In 1984, that changed when Narendra K. Karmarkar, a young scientist at Bell Laboratories, discovered an algorithm, or mathematical

formula, that greatly speeds the process of solving even the most complex LP problems. In the traditional approach to solving LP problems, one corner of the feasible solution space is solved and compared to the solutions for adjacent points. If a better solution is found, the computer is instructed to move off in that direction. This iterative process continues until the program finds itself boxed in by inferior solutions. Karmarkar's algorithm employs a radically different approach. Working from within the interior of the feasible space, the Karmarkar method uses projective geometry to reconfigure the solution structure and determine optimal solutions.

Using Karmarkar's method, the LP approach is practical in a host of complicated applications, from assessing risk factors in stock and bond portfolios to setting up production schedules in industrial factories.

See: Scott Patterson and Anita Raghavan, "How Market Turmoil Waylaid the 'Quants,'" *The Wall Street Journal Online*, September 7, 2007, http://online.wsj.com.

other instances. Because linear programming is used for marginal analysis, it focuses on the effects of modest output, price, and input changes. For moderate changes in current operating conditions, a constant-returns-to-scale assumption is often valid. Similarly, input and output prices are typically unaffected by modest changes from current levels. As a result, revenue, cost, and profit functions are often linear when only moderate changes in operations are contemplated and use of linear programming methods is valid. Whenever the objective function and constraint conditions can be usefully approximated by linear relations, linear programming can also be fruitfully applied. Only when objective functions and constraint conditions are inherently nonlinear must more complicated *mathematical programming* techniques be applied. In most managerial applications, linear approximations seldom distort the analysis.

PRODUCTION PLANNING FOR A SINGLE PRODUCT

Linear programming has been widely used to solve production problems.

Production Processes

Assume that a firm produces a single product, Q, using two inputs, L and K, which might represent labor and capital. Instead of assuming continuous substitution between L and K, as in Chapter 7, assume that Q can be produced using only four input combinations. Four different production processes are available for making Q, each of which uses a different fixed combination of inputs L and K. The production processes might represent four different plants, each with its own fixed asset configuration and labor requirements. Alternatively, they could be four different assembly lines, each using a different combination of capital and labor.

The four production processes are illustrated as rays in Figure 9.1. Process A requires the combination of 15 units of L and 1 unit of K for each unit of Q produced. Process B uses 10 units of L and 2 units of K for each unit of output. Processes C and D use 7.5 units of L and 3 units of K, and 5 units of L with 5 units of K, respectively, for each unit of Q produced. Each point along the production ray for process A combines L and K in the ratio 15 to 1; process rays B, C, and D are developed in the same way. Each point along a single production ray combines the two inputs in a fixed ratio, with the ratios differing from one production process to another. If L and K represent labor and capital inputs, the four production processes might be different plants employing different production techniques. Process A is very labor intensive in comparison with the other production systems, whereas B, C, and D are based on increasingly capital-intensive technologies.

Point A_1 indicates the combination of L and K required to produce 1 unit of output using the A process. Doubling both L and K doubles the quantity of Q produced; this is indicated by the distance moved along ray A from A_1 to A_2. Line segment $0A_2$ is exactly twice the length of line segment $0A_1$ and thus represents twice as much output. Along production process ray A, the distance $0A_1 = A_1A_2 = A_2A_3 = A_3A_4 = A_4A_5$. Each of these line segments indicates the addition of 1 unit of output using increased quantities of L and K in the fixed ratio of 15 to 1. Output along a given ray increases proportionately with increases in each input factor. If each input is doubled, output is doubled. Each production process exhibits constant returns to scale.

Output is measured in the same way along the three other production process rays in Figure 9.1. Point C_1 indicates the combination of L and K required to produce 1 unit of Q using process C. The production of 2 units of Q using that process requires

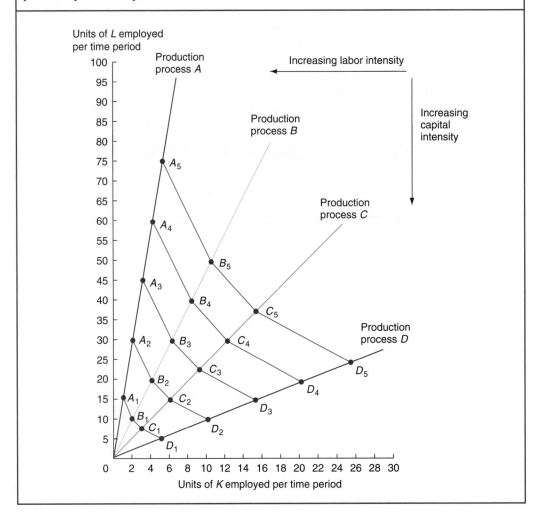

Figure 9.1   Production Process Rays in Linear Programming

Points along each process ray represent combinations of inputs L and K required for that production process to produce output.

the combination of L and K indicated at point C_2, and so on for points C_3, C_4, and C_5. Although production of additional units using process C is indicated by line segments of equal length, just as for process A, these line segments are of different lengths. Whereas each production process exhibits constant returns to scale, equal distances along *different* process rays do not ordinarily indicate equal output quantities.

Production Isoquants

Joining points of equal output on the four production process rays creates a set of isoquant curves. Figure 9.2 illustrates isoquants for $Q = 1, 2, 3, 4$, and 5. These isoquants have the same interpretation as those developed in production analysis. Each isoquant represents combinations of input factors L and K that can be used to produce a given

Figure 9.2   Production Isoquants in Linear Programming

Each point along an isoquant represents the output level resulting from a given combination of inputs. For example, point X depicts the production of four units of Q by using 25 units of L and 16 units of K.

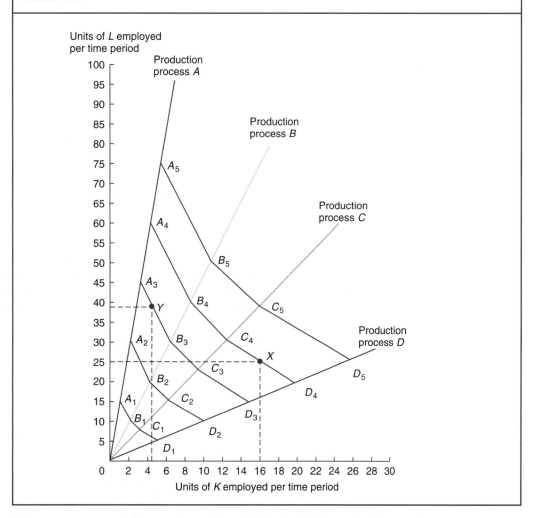

quantity of output. Production isoquants in linear programming are composed of linear segments connecting the various production process rays. Each of these isoquant segments is parallel to one another. For example, line segment A_1B_1 is parallel to segment A_2B_2; isoquant segment B_3C_3 is parallel to B_2C_2.

Points along each segment of an isoquant between two process rays represent a combination of output from each of the two adjoining production processes. Point X in Figure 9.2 represents production of 4 units of Q using 25 units of L and 16 units of K. None of the available production processes can manufacture Q using L and K in the ratio of 25 to 16, but that combination is possible by producing part of the output with process C and part with process D. In this case, 2 units of Q can be produced using process C and 2 units using process D. Production of 2 units of Q with process C uses 15 units of L and 6 units of K. For the production of 2 units of Q with process D, 10 units each of L and K are necessary.

Although no single production system is available that can produce 4 units of Q using 25 units of L and 16 units of K, processes C and D together can produce that combination.

All points lying along production isoquant segments can be interpreted in a similar manner. Each point represents a linear combination of output using the production process systems that bound the particular segment. Point Y in Figure 9.2 provides another illustration. At Y, 3 units of Q are produced, using a total of 38.5 units of L and 4.3 units of K.[2] This input–output combination is possible through a combination of processes A and B. This can be analyzed algebraically. To produce 1 unit of Q by process A requires 15 units of L and 1 unit of K. To produce 1.7 units of Q requires 25.5 (1.7×15) units of L and 1.7 (1.7×1) units of K. To produce a single unit of Q by process B requires 10 units of L and 2 units of K, so 1.3 units of Q requires 13 (10×1.3) units of L and 2.6 (2×1.3) units of K. Thus, point Y calls for the production of 3 units of Q in total, 1.7 units by process A and 1.3 units by process B, using a total of 38.5 units of L and 4.3 units of K.

Relative Distance Method
Graphic technique used to solve linear programming problems.

One method for determining the quantity to be produced by each production process at varying points along the isoquant is called the **relative distance method.** The relative distance method is based on the fact that the location of a point along an isoquant determines the relative shares of production for the adjacent processes. If point X in Figure 9.2 were on process ray C, all output would be produced using process C. Similarly, if X were on process ray D, all output would be produced using process D. Because point X lies between process rays C and D, both processes C and D will be used to produce this output. Process C will be used relatively more than process D if X is closer to process ray C than to process ray D. Similarly, process D will be used relatively more than process C if X is closer to process ray D than to process ray C. Because point X in Figure 9.2 lies at the midpoint of the $Q = 4$ isoquant segment between C_4 and D_4, it implies production using processes C and D in equal proportions. Thus, at point X, $Q = 4$, $Q_C = 2$, and $Q_D = 2$.

The relative proportions of process A and process B used to produce $Q = 3$ at point Y can be determined in a similar manner. Because Y lies closer to process ray A than to process ray B, point Y entails relatively more output from process A than from process B. The share of total output produced using process A is calculated by considering the distance B_3Y relative to B_3A_3. The share of total output produced using process B is calculated by considering the distance A_3Y relative to A_3B_3. Starting from point B_3, the segment B_3Y covers 56.6 percent of the total distance B_3A_3. This means that at point Y, about 56.6 percent of total output is produced using process A ($Q_A = 0.566 \times 3 = 1.7$) and 43.4 percent ($= 1.0 - 0.566$) using process B ($Q_B = 0.434 \times 3 = 1.3$). Alternatively, starting from point A_3, note that the segment A_3Y covers 43.4 percent of the total distance $A_3 B_3$. At point Y, 43.4 percent of total output is produced using process B and 56.6 percent using process A. Extreme accuracy would require painstaking graphic detail, but in many instances the relative distance method can readily approximate production intensities along isoquants.

Least-Cost Input Combinations

Adding isocost curves to a set of isoquants permits one to determine least-cost input combinations for the production of product Q. This is shown in Figure 9.3 under the

---

2   A common assumption in linear programming is that fractions are permissible. The solution value calling for $L = 38.5$ merely means that 38.5 hours of labor are required. If fractions are not permissible, a more complex technique called integer programming is required.

Figure 9.3 Determination of the Least-Cost Production Process

The tangency between the isoquant and isocost lines at point B_3 reveals the least-cost combination of inputs.

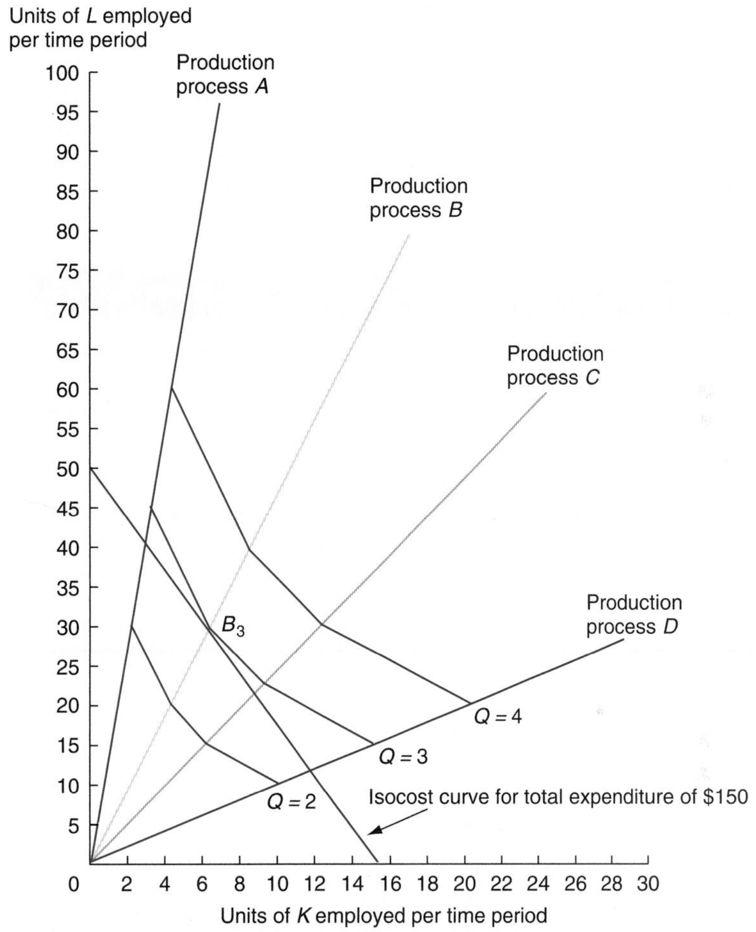

assumption that each unit of L costs \$3 and each unit of K costs \$10. The isocost curve illustrated indicates a total expenditure of \$150.

The tangency between the isocost curve and the isoquant curve for $Q=3$ at point B_3 indicates that process B, which combines inputs L and K in the ratio 5 to 1, is the least-cost method of producing Q. For any expenditure level, production is maximized by using process B. Alternatively, process B is the least-cost method for producing any quantity of Q, given the assumed prices for L and K.

Optimal Input Combinations with Limited Resources

Frequently, firms faced with limited inputs during a production period find it optimal to use inputs in proportions other than the least-cost combination. To illustrate, consider the effect of limits on the quantities of L and K available in the example. Assume that only 20 units of L and 11 units of K are available during the current production period and that the firm seeks to maximize output of Q. These constraints are shown in Figure 9.4. The horizontal line drawn at $L = 20$ indicates the upper limit on the quantity of L that can be employed during the production period; the vertical line at $K = 11$ indicates a similar limit on the quantity of K.

Feasible Space
Graphical region that is both technically and economically feasible and includes the optimal solution.

Production possibilities for this problem are determined by noting that, in addition to limitations on inputs L and K, the firm must operate within the area bounded by production process rays A and D. Combining production possibilities with input constraints restricts the firm to operate within the **feasible space** (shaded area) on $0PRS$ in Figure 9.4. Any point within this space combines L and K in a technically feasible ratio without exceeding availability limits on L and K. Because the firm is trying to maximize

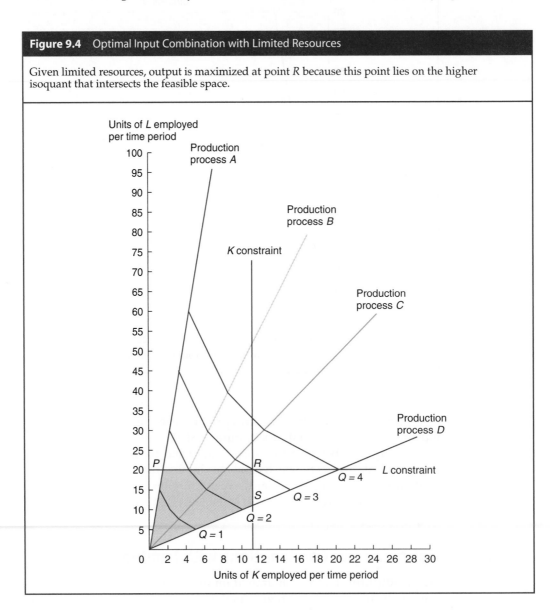

Figure 9.4   Optimal Input Combination with Limited Resources

Given limited resources, output is maximized at point R because this point lies on the higher isoquant that intersects the feasible space.

production of Q subject to constraints on the use of L and K, it should operate at the feasible space point that touches the highest possible isoquant. This is point R in Figure 9.4, where $Q = 3$.

Although it is possible to solve the foregoing problem by using carefully drawn graphs, it is typically easier to combine graphic analysis with analytical techniques to obtain accurate solutions efficiently. For example, consider Figure 9.4 again. Even if the isoquant for $Q = 3$ were not drawn, it would be apparent from the slopes of the isoquants for 2 or 4 units of output that the optimal solution to the problem must be at point R. It is obvious from the graph that maximum production is obtained by operating at the point where both inputs are fully employed. Because R lies between production processes C and D, the output-maximizing input combination uses only those two production processes. All 20 units of L and 11 units of K will be employed, because point R lies at the intersection of these two input constraints.

Using this information from the graph, it is possible to quickly and easily solve for the optimal quantities to be produced using processes C and D. Recall that each unit of output produced using process C requires 7.5 units of L. Thus, the total L required in process C equals $7.5 \times Q_C$. Similarly, each unit produced using process D requires 5 units of L, so the total L used in process D equals $5 \times Q_D$. At point R, 20 units of L are being used in processes C and D together, and the following must hold

$$7.5Q_C + 5Q_D = 20 \qquad\qquad \textbf{9.1}$$

A similar relation can be developed for the use of K. Each unit of output produced from process C requires 3 units of K, whereas process D uses 5 units of K to produce each unit of output. The total use of K in processes C and D equals 11 units at point R, so

$$3Q_C + 5Q_D = 11 \qquad\qquad \textbf{9.2}$$

Equations (9.1) and (9.2) both must hold at point R. Output quantities from processes C and D at that location are determined by solving these equations simultaneously. Subtracting Equation (9.2) from Equation (9.1) to eliminate the variable Q_D isolates the solution for Q_C:

$$7.5Q_C + 5Q_D = 20$$
$$\text{minus } 3.0Q_C + 5Q_D = 11$$
$$\overline{4.5Q_C = 9}$$
$$Q_C = 2$$

Substituting 2 for Q_C in Equation (9.2) determines output from process D:

$$3(2) + 5Q_D = 11$$
$$5Q_D = 5$$
$$Q_D = 1$$

Total output at point R is 3 units, composed of 2 units from process C and 1 unit from process D.

This combination of graphic and analytic techniques allows one to obtain precise linear programming solutions with relative ease.

Managerial Application 9.2

LP: More Than a Visual Approach

LP is often portrayed as a visual means of characterizing management problems. It is at least when a limited number of products or product dimensions are being analyzed. When the optimal level of production for two products is sought, for example, a simple graph of the appropriate LP problem gives managers a useful intuitive basis for considering the best means of meeting a variety of production criteria. When a multitude of products are offered, or when a large number of production characteristics must be considered, the typical LP problem becomes too complex to be visualized graphically. In such instances, computer-based solutions using spreadsheets offer a tractable alternative for analyzing and solving LP problems.

LP techniques are commonly used to solve problems in transportation routing, staff scheduling, and financial planning. Whenever a company needs to move a quantity of goods from and to multiple locations, such as plants, regional warehouses, or retail stores, it faces a practical LP problem. By minimizing route mileage, operating costs can also be minimized and outlays for capital investment can be kept at a minimum. Many companies routinely save thousands of dollars per year on shipping costs by solving LP problems of this type. Businesses and government agencies use LP methods to solve the problem of scheduling employees' working hours to meet customer service demands, which might vary by the hour or the day, in light of employee availability and preferences. Other examples of practical applications include models to help investors decide on the optimal allocation of a stock and bond portfolio.

Detailed user tips on successful LP applications, often with free follow-up from the author, can be found in an almost limitless number on the Internet. One of the best sites for getting started is sponsored by Lindo Systems, Inc. There you can find LP case studies for telecommunications network design, supply chain management, and so on. These examples provide the best reason to become familiar with the technique: LP works!

See: http://www.lindo.com.

PRODUCTION PLANNING FOR MULTIPLE PRODUCTS

The problem of finding an optimal output mix for multiproduct firms with input restrictions is readily solved with linear programming techniques.

Objective Function Specification

Suppose a firm produces products X and Y and uses inputs A, B, and C. To maximize profit before fixed expenses, the firm must determine optimal quantities of each product subject to constraints on input availability. Because the costs associated with constrained resources are fixed, maximizing the firm's profit contribution (or profit before fixed expenses) will result in the same production decisions as will profit maximization. Of course, fixed costs must ultimately be subtracted from profit contribution to determine net profits. Importantly, the output mix that maximizes profit contribution also maximizes net profit.

Objective Function
Equation that expresses the goal of a linear programming problem.

An equation that expresses the goal of a linear programming problem is called the **objective function.** Assume that the firm wishes to maximize total profits from two products, X and Y, during each period. If profit contribution per unit (the excess of price over average variable costs) is \$12 for product X and \$9 for product Y, the objective function is

$$\text{Maximize } \pi = \$12Q_X + \$9Q_Y \qquad \textbf{9.3}$$

Q_X and Q_Y represent the quantities of each product produced. The total profit contribution, π, earned by the firm equals the per unit profit contribution of X times Q_X produced and sold, plus the profit contribution of Y times Q_Y.

Constraint Equation Specification

Constraint equations specify the available quantities of each input and their usage in the production of X and Y. Table 9.1 shows that 32 units of input A are available in each period. Four units of A are required to produce each unit of X, whereas 2 units of A are necessary to produce 1 unit of Y. Because 4 units of A are required to produce a single unit of X, the total amount of A used to manufacture X can be written as $4Q_X$. Similarly, 2 units of A are required to produce each unit of Y, so $2Q_Y$ represents the total quantity of A used to produce product Y. Summing the quantities of A used to produce X and Y provides an expression for the total usage of A. Because this total cannot exceed the 32 units available, the constraint condition for input A is

$$4Q_X + 2Q_Y \leq 32 \qquad \textbf{9.4}$$

The constraint for input B is determined in a similar manner. One unit of input B is necessary to produce each unit of either X or Y, so the total amount of B employed is $1Q_X + 1Q_Y$. The maximum quantity of B available in each period is 10 units; thus, the constraint requirement associated with input B is

$$1Q_X + 1Q_Y \leq 10 \qquad \textbf{9.5}$$

Finally, the constraint relation for input C affects only the production of Y. Each unit of Y requires an input of 3 units of C, and 21 units of input C are available. Usage of C is given by the expression $3Q_Y$, and the relevant constraint equation is

$$3Q_Y \leq 21 \qquad \textbf{9.6}$$

Constraint equations play a major role in solving linear programming problems.

Nonnegativity Requirement

Because linear programming is merely a mathematical tool for solving constrained optimization problems, nothing in the technique itself ensures that an answer makes economic sense. In a production problem for a relatively unprofitable product, the mathematically optimal output level might be a *negative* quantity, clearly an impossible

Table 9.1 Inputs Available for Production of X and Y

Input	Quantity Available Per Time Period	Quantity Required Per Unit of Output	
		X	Y
A	32	4	2
B	10	1	1
C	21	0	3

solution. In a distribution problem, an optimal solution might indicate negative shipments from one point to another, which again is impossible.

To prevent economically meaningless results, a nonnegativity requirement must be introduced. This is merely a statement that all variables in the problem must be equal to or greater than zero. For the present production problem, the following expressions must be added:

$$Q_X \geq 0$$

and

$$Q_Y \geq 0$$

GRAPHIC SPECIFICATION AND SOLUTION

Having specified all the component parts of the firm's linear programming problem, the problem can be illustrated graphically and analyzed algebraically.

Analytic Expression

The decision problem is to maximize total profit contribution, π, subject to resource constraints. This is expressed as

$$\text{Maximize } \pi = \$12Q_X + \$9Q_Y \qquad\qquad \textbf{9.3}$$

subject to the following constraints:

Input A: $4Q_X + 2Q_Y \leq 32$ **9.4**

Input B: $1Q_X + 1Q_Y \leq 10$ **9.5**

Input C: $3Q_Y \leq 21$ **9.6**

where

$$Q_X \geq 0 \text{ and } Q_Y \geq 0$$

Each variable and coefficient is exactly as specified previously.

Graphing the Feasible Space

In Figure 9.5, the graph of the constraint equation for input A, $4Q_X + 2Q_Y = 32$ indicates the maximum quantities of X and Y that can be produced given the limitation on the availability of input A. A maximum of 16 units of Y can be produced if no X is manufactured; 8 units of X can be produced if the output of Y is zero. Any point along the line connecting these two outputs represents the maximum combination of X and Y that can be produced with no more than 32 units of A.

This constraint equation divides the XY plane into two half spaces. Every point lying on the line or to the left of the line satisfies the constraint expressed by the equation

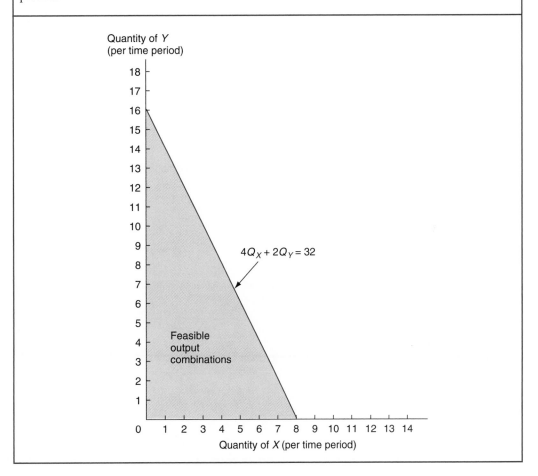

Figure 9.5 Constraint Imposed by Limitations on Input *A*

The constraint equation for input *A* represents the maximum combination of *X* and *Y* that can be produced with 32 units of *A*.

Quantity of *Y* (per time period)

$4Q_X + 2Q_Y = 32$

Feasible output combinations

Quantity of *X* (per time period)

$4Q_X + 2Q_Y = 32$; every point to the right of the line violates that expression. Only points on the constraint line or to the left of it are in the feasible space. The shaded area of Figure 9.5 represents the feasible area limited by the constraint on input *A*.

In Figure 9.6, the feasible space is limited further by adding constraints for inputs *B* and *C*. The constraint on input *B* is expressed as $Q_X + Q_Y = 10$. If no *Y* is produced, a maximum of 10 units of *X* can be produced; if output of *X* is zero, 10 units of *Y* can be manufactured. All combinations of *X* and *Y* lying on or to the left of the line connecting these two points are feasible with respect to utilization of input *B*.

The horizontal line at $Q_Y = 7$ in Figure 9.6 represents the constraint imposed by input *C*. Because *C* is used only in the production of *Y*, it does not constrain the production of *X*. Seven units are the maximum quantity of *Y* that can be produced with 21 units of *C* available.

These three input constraints, together with the nonnegativity requirement, completely define the feasible space shown as the shaded area of Figure 9.6. Only points within this area meet all constraints.

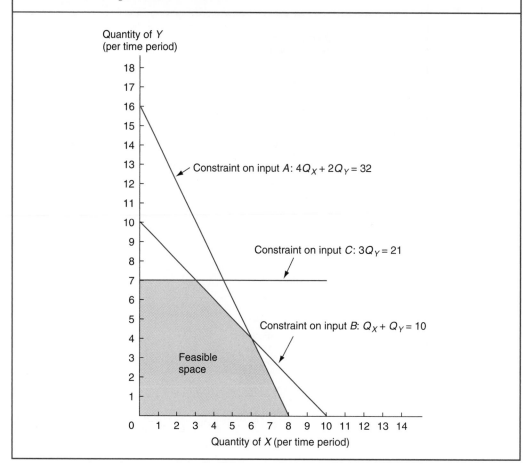

Figure 9.6 Feasible Space

The feasible space is reduced further by the addition of constraints on inputs B and C. Only points within the shaded region meet all constraints.

Graphing the Objective Function

The objective function, $\pi = \$12Q_X + \$9Q_Y$, can be graphed in Q_XQ_Y space as a series of isoprofit curves. This is illustrated in Figure 9.7, where isoprofit curves for \$36, \$72, \$108, and \$144 are shown. Each isoprofit curve illustrates all possible combinations of X and Y that result in a constant total profit contribution. For example, the isoprofit curve labeled $\pi = \$36$ identifies each combination of X and Y that results in a total profit contribution of \$36; all output combinations along the $\pi = \$72$ curve provide a total profit contribution of \$72; and so on. It is clear from Figure 9.7 that isoprofit curves are a series of parallel lines that take on higher values as one moves upward and to the right.

The general formula for isoprofit curves can be developed by considering the profit function $\pi = aQ_X + bQ_Y$, where a and b are the profit contributions of products X and Y, respectively. Solving the isoprofit function for Q_Y creates an equation of the following form:

$$Q_Y = \frac{\pi}{b} - \frac{a}{b} Q_X$$

Figure 9.7 Graphic Solution of the Linear Programming Problem

Points along the isoprofit line represent all possible combi nations of X and Y that result in the same profit level. Point M is on the highest isoprofit curve that intersects the feasible space. Thus, it represents the output combination that will maximize total profit given input constraints.

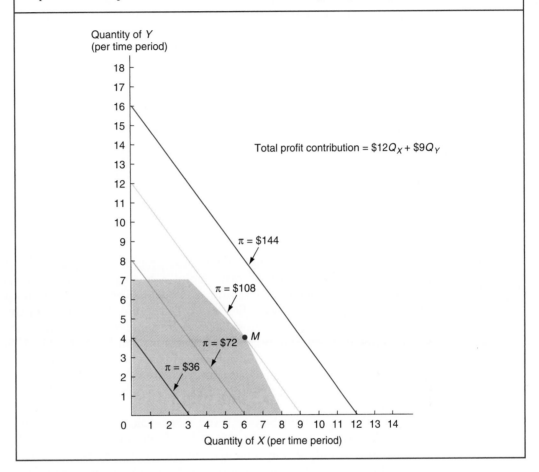

Given the individual profit contributions, a and b, the Q_Y intercept equals the profit level of the isoprofit curve divided by the profit per unit earned on Q_Y, π/b. Slope of the objective function is given by the relative profitability of the two products, $-a/b$. Because the relative profitability of the products is not affected by the output level, the isoprofit curves consist of a series of parallel lines. In this example, all isoprofit curves have a slope of $-12/9$, or -1.33.

Graphic Solution

Because the firm's objective is to maximize total profit, it should operate on the highest isoprofit curve obtainable. To see this point graphically, Figure 9.7 combines the feasible space limitations shown in Figure 9.6 with the family of isoprofit curves discussed above. Using this approach, point M in the figure is indicated as the optimal solution. At point M, the firm produces 6 units of X and 4 units of Y, and the total profit is $108 [=($12 × 6) + ($9 × 4)], which is the maximum available under the conditions stated in the problem. No other point within the feasible space touches so high an isoprofit curve.

Using the combined graphic and analytical method introduced in the preceding section, M can be identified as the point where $Q_X = 6$ and $Q_Y = 4$. At M, constraints on inputs A and B are binding. At M, 32 units of input A and 10 units of input B are being completely used to produce X and Y. Thus, Equations (9.4) and (9.5) can be written as equalities and solved simultaneously for Q_X and Q_Y. Subtracting two times Equation (9.5) from Equation (9.4) gives

$$4Q_X + 2Q_Y = 32$$
$$\text{minus } \underline{2Q_X + 2Q_Y = 20}$$
$$2Q_X = 12$$
$$Q_X = 6$$

Substituting 6 for Q_X in Equation (9.5) results in

$$6 + Q_Y = 10$$
$$Q_Y = 4$$

Corner Point

Spot in the feasible space where the X-axis, Y-axis, or constraint conditions intersect.

Notice that the optimal solution to the linear programming problem occurs at a **corner point** of the feasible space. A corner point is a spot in the feasible space where the X-axis, Y-axis, or constraint conditions intersect. The optimal solution to any linear programming problem always lies at a corner point. Because all of the relations in a linear programming problem must be linear by definition, every boundary of the feasible space is linear. Furthermore, the objective function is linear. Thus, the constrained optimization of the objective function takes place either at a corner of the feasible space or at one boundary face, as is illustrated by Figure 9.8.

In Figure 9.8, the linear programming example has been modified by assuming that each unit of either X or Y yields a profit of $5. In this case, the optimal solution to the problem includes any of the combinations of X and Y found along line LM. All of these combinations are feasible and result in a total profit of $50. If all points along line LM provide optimal combinations of output, the combinations found at corners L and M are also optimal. Because the firm is indifferent about producing at point L, or at point M, or at any point in between, any such location provides an optimal solution to the production problem.

The search for an optimal solution can be limited to just the corners of each linear programming problem's feasible space. This greatly reduces the number of necessary computations.

ALGEBRAIC SPECIFICATION AND SOLUTION

Algebraic techniques can be used to solve complex linear programming problems with user-friendly computer software.

Slack Variables

Factors that indicate the amount by which constraint conditions are exceeded.

Algebraic Specification

The concept of **slack variables** must be introduced to solve linear programming problems algebraically. In the case of less-than-or-equal-to constraints, slack variables *increase* the

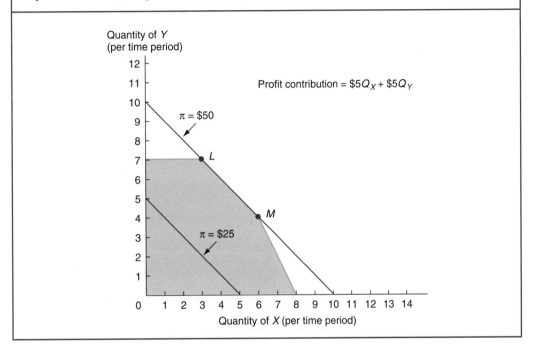

Figure 9.8 Graphic Solution of a Linear Programming Problem When the Objective Function Coincides with a Boundary of the Feasible Space

When the objective function coincides with the boundary of the feasible space, several different output combinations will produce maximum profits.

left side to equal the right side limits of each constraint condition. If the firm is faced with capacity constraints on input factors A, B, and C, the algebraic specification of the problem contains three slack variables: S_A, indicating the units of A that are not used in any given solution; S_B, representing unused units of B; and S_C, which measures the unused units of C.

With slack variables, each constraint equation converts to an equality rather than an inequality. After adding the relevant slack variable, the constraint on input A, $4Q_X + 2Q_Y \leq 32$, is

$$4Q_X + 2Q_Y + S_A = 32 \qquad \textbf{9.7}$$

where $S_A = 32 - 4Q_X - 2Q_Y$ is the amount of input A not used to produce X or Y. Similar equality constraints can be specified for inputs B and C. The equality form of the constraint on input B is

$$1Q_X + 1Q_Y + S_B = 10 \qquad \textbf{9.8}$$

The constraint equation for input C is

$$3Q_Y + S_C = 21 \qquad \textbf{9.9}$$

The introduction of slack variables not only simplifies algebraic analysis, but slack variable solution values also provide useful information. In a production problem, for example, slack variables with *zero* values at the optimal solution indicate inputs that are limiting factors and cause bottlenecks. Slack variables with *positive* values at the optimal solution indicate excess capacity in the related input factor. Slack variables cannot take on negative values, because this would imply that the amount of resource use exceeds available supply. The information provided by slack variable solution values is important in long-range planning and is a key benefit derived from algebraic solution methods.

The complete specification of the illustrative programming problem is as follows:

$$\text{Maximize } \pi = \$12Q_X + \$9Q_Y \qquad \qquad \textbf{9.3}$$

subject to these constraints

$$4Q_X + 2Q_Y + S_A = 32 \qquad \qquad \textbf{9.7}$$

$$1Q_X + 1Q_Y + S_B = 10 \qquad \qquad \textbf{9.8}$$

$$3Q_Y + S_C = 21 \qquad \qquad \textbf{9.9}$$

where

$$Q_X \geq 0, Q_Y \geq 0, S_A \geq 0, S_B \geq 0, S_C \geq 0$$

The problem is to find the set of values for variables Q_X, Q_Y, S_A, S_B, and S_C that maximizes Equation (9.3) and at the same time satisfies the constraints imposed by Equations (9.7), (9.8), and (9.9).

Algebraic Solution

A unique solution does not exist for this system of three constraint equations with five unknown variables; multiple solutions are possible. However, because the solution to any linear programming problem occurs at a corner of the feasible space, values can be determined for some of the unknown variables in Equations (9.7), (9.8), and (9.9). At each corner point, the number of known constraint conditions is exactly equal to the number of unknown variables. A single unique solution can be found for each variable at each corner point of the feasible space. The optimal solution is that corner point solution with the most desirable value for the objective function.[3]

Consider Figure 9.9, in which the feasible space for the illustrative problem has been graphed once again. At the origin, where neither X nor Y is produced, Q_X and Q_Y both equal zero. Slack variable exists in all inputs, however, so S_A, S_B, and S_C are all greater than zero. Now move up the vertical axis to point K. Here Q_X and S_C both equal zero, because no X is being produced and input C is being used to the fullest extent possible. However, Q_Y, S_A, and S_B all exceed zero. At point L, Q_X, Q_Y, and S_A are all positive, but S_B and S_C equal zero. The remaining corners, M and N, can be examined similarly. At each

---

3   In almost all linear programming problems, the number of nonzero-valued variables in all corner solutions exactly equals the number of constraints in the problem. Only under a particular condition known as *degeneracy*, when more than two constraints coincide at a single corner of the feasible space, are there fewer nonzerovalued variables.

Figure 9.9   Determination of Zero-Valued Variables at Corners of the Feasible Space

At all corner points of the feasible space, the number of nonzero-valued variables equals the number of constraint equations.

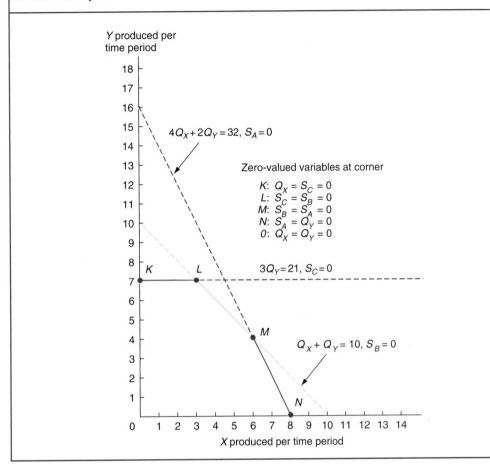

---

corner point, the constraints can be expressed as a system with three equations and three unknowns that can be solved algebraically.

Solving the constraint equations at each corner point provides values for Q_X and Q_Y, as well as for S_A, S_B, and S_C. The total profit contribution at each corner is determined by inserting relevant values for Q_X and Q_Y into the objective function [Equation (9.3)]. The corner solution that produces the maximum profit is the optimal solution to the linear programming problem. This iterative process is followed in the **simplex solution method.** Complex linear programming problems can be solved in only a few seconds when using the simplex method and desktop computers. They are long and tedious when done by hand, but the method can be illustrated for the current example.

For example, substituting zero values for Q_X and Q_Y into the constraint Equations (9.7), (9.8), and (9.9) results in a value for each slack variable that equals the total units available: $S_A = 32$, $S_B = 10$, and $S_C = 21$. At the origin, neither X nor Y is produced nor is any input used in production. Total profit contribution at the origin corner of the feasible

Simplex Solution Method
Iterative technique used to provide algebraic solutions for linear programming problems.

space is zero. Similarly, it is possible to examine the solution at a second corner point, N in Figure 9.9, where Q_Y and S_A equal zero. After making the appropriate substitution into constraint Equation (9.7), the value for Q_X is

$$4Q_X + 2Q_Y + S_A = 32 \qquad \qquad \textbf{9.7}$$
$$(4 \times Q_X) + (2 \times 0) + 0 = 32$$
$$4Q_X = 32$$
$$Q_X = 8$$

With the value of Q_X determined, it is possible to substitute into Equations (9.8) and (9.9) and determine values for S_B and S_C:

$$Q_X + Q_Y + S_B = 10 \qquad \qquad \textbf{9.8}$$
$$8 + 0 + S_B = 10$$
$$S_B = 2$$

and

$$3Q_Y + S_C = 21 \qquad \qquad \textbf{9.9}$$
$$(3 \times 0) + S_C = 21$$
$$S_C = 21$$

Total profit contribution at this point is

$$\pi = \$12Q_X + \$9Q_Y \qquad \qquad \textbf{9.3}$$
$$= (\$12 \times 8) + (\$9 \times 0)$$
$$= \$96$$

Next, assign zero values to S_B and S_A to reach solution values for point M. Substituting zero values for S_A and S_B in Equations (9.7) and (9.8) results in two equations with two unknowns:

$$4Q_X + 2Q_Y + 0 = 32 \qquad \qquad \textbf{9.7}$$

$$Q_X + Q_Y + 0 = 10 \qquad \qquad \textbf{9.8}$$

Multiplying Equation (9.8) by 2 and subtracting this result from Equation (9.7) provides the solution value for Q_X:

$$4Q_X + 2Q_Y = 32 \qquad \qquad \textbf{9.7}$$
$$\text{minus } \underline{2Q_X + 2Q_Y = 20}$$
$$2Q_X = 12$$
$$Q_X = 6$$

Then, substituting 6 for Q_X in Equation (9.8) finds $Q_Y = 4$. Total profit contribution in this case is $108 [= (\$12 \times 6) + (\$9 \times 4)]$. Similar algebraic analysis provides the solution for each remaining corner of the feasible space, as shown in Table 9.2. As illustrated in the earlier graphic analysis, the optimal solution occurs at point M, where 6 units of X and 4 units of Y are produced. Total profit is $108, which exceeds the profit at any other corner of the feasible space.

Table 9.2 Algebraic Solution to a Linear Programming Problem

Solution at Corner	Value of Variable					Total Profit Contribution ($)
	Q_Y	Q_Y	S_A	S_B	S_C	
O	0	0	32	10	21	0
N	8	0	0	2	21	96
M	6	4	0	0	9	108
L	3	7	6	0	0	99
K	0	7	18	3	0	63

At each corner point solution, values for each slack variable are also determined. For example, at the optimal solution (corner M) reached in the preceding section, S_A and S_B both equal zero, meaning that inputs A and B are used to the fullest extent possible. S_C is not equal to zero and must be solved for. To find the solution for S_C, $Q_Y = 4$ is substituted into constraint Equation (9.9):

$$3 \times Q_Y + S_C = 21$$
$$3 \times 4 + S_C = 21$$
$$S_C = 9$$

9.9

Managerial Application 9.3

LP on the PC!

Managers of small to medium-sized companies often plug hypothetical financial and operating data into spreadsheet software programs, and then recalculate profit figures to see how various changes might affect the bottom line. A major problem with this popular "What-if?" approach to decision analysis is the haphazard way in which various alternatives are considered. Dozens of time-consuming recalculations are often necessary before suggestions emerge that lead to a clear improvement in operating efficiency. Even then, managers have no assurance that more profitable or cost-efficient decision alternatives are not available.

The frustrations of "What-if?" analysis are sure to become a thing of the past with the increasing popularity of new *Solver* LP programs, included as a basic feature of spreadsheet software, like *Microsoft Excel. Solver* LP tools are capable of solving all but the toughest problems, and are extremely user-friendly for those with little LP training or computer experience. More powerful, but still easy to use, LP software is provided by Lindo Systems, Inc.

Lindo is the leading supplier of LP optimization software to business, government, and academia. Lindo software is used to provide critical answers to thousands of businesses, including over one-half of the *Fortune* 500. *What'sBest!* is an innovative LP program and a popular modeling tool for business problems. First released in 1985, *What'sBest!* soon became the industry leader specialized in tackling large-scale, real-world problems. Like more basic *Solver* LP programs, *What'sBest!* software is designed for the PC environment.

It is stunning to note how quickly inexpensive, powerful, and easy-to-use LP software for the PC has come forth. As new generations of user-friendly LP software emerge, appreciation of the value of the LP technique as a practical and powerful tool for decision analysis will continue to flourish as a practical and powerful tool for managerial decision making.

See: Home page information for *Lindo, Lingo,* and *What's Best!* software can be found on the Internet, http://www.lindo.com.

The optimal combination of X and Y completely exhausts available quantities of inputs A and B, but 9 units of input C remain unused. Because inputs A and B impose effective constraints on the firm's profits, more of each must be acquired to expand output. Input C is in excess supply, so the firm would certainly not want more capacity of C; it might even attempt to reduce its purchases of C during future periods. If C is a fixed facility, such as a machine tool, the firm might offer some of that excess capacity to other companies.

DUAL IN LINEAR PROGRAMMING

For every maximization problem, there exists a symmetrical minimization problem. For every minimization problem, there exists a symmetrical maximization problem.

Duality Concept

Primal
Original problem statement (symmetrical to dual).

Dual
Secondary problem statement (symmetrical to primal).

Pairs of related maximization and minimization problems are known as **primal** and **dual** linear programming problems. The concept of duality demonstrates the symmetry between the value of a firm's products and the value of resources used in production. Because of the symmetry between primal and dual problem specifications, either one can be constructed from the other and the solution to either problem can be used to solve both. This is helpful because it is sometimes easier to obtain the solution to the dual problem than to the original or primal problem.

Finally, the duality concept also allows one to evaluate the solution to a constrained decision problem in terms of the activity required for optimization and in terms of the economic impact of constraint conditions. Analysis of the constraint conditions and slack variable solutions frequently provides important information for long-range planning. In fact, the **primal solution** is often described as a tool for short-run operating decisions. The **dual solution** is often seen as a tool for long-range planning. The duality concept shows how operating decisions and long-range planning are related.

Primal Solution
Input for short-run operating decisions.

Dual Solution
Input for long-range planning.

Shadow Prices

Shadow prices
Implicit values.

To examine the duality concept, the idea of implicit values or **shadow prices** must be introduced. In the primal linear programming problem discussed previously, the values Q_X and Q_Y maximize the firm's profit subject to constraints imposed by limitations of input factors A, B, and C. Duality theory indicates that an identical operating decision would result if one had instead chosen to minimize the costs of resources employed in producing Q_X and Q_Y, subject to an output constraint.

The key to this duality is that relevant costs are not the acquisition costs of inputs but, rather, the economic costs of using them. For a resource that is available in a fixed amount, this cost is not acquisition cost but opportunity cost. Because the economic value of constrained resources is determined by their value in use rather than by historical acquisition costs, such amounts are called implicit values or shadow prices. The term *shadow price* is used because it represents the price that a manager would be willing to pay for additional units of a constrained resource. Comparing the shadow price of a resource with its acquisition price indicates whether the firm has an incentive to increase or decrease the amount acquired during future production periods. If shadow prices exceed acquisition prices, the resource's marginal value exceeds marginal cost and the firm has an incentive to expand employment. If acquisition cost exceeds the shadow price, there is an incentive to reduce employment.

DUAL SPECIFICATION

The duality concept can be demonstrated by developing and solving the dual program that relates to the primal program discussed previously.

Dual Objective Function[4]

In the original or primal problem statement, the goal is to maximize profits, and the (primal) objective function is

$$\text{Maximize } \pi = \$12Q_X + \$9Q_Y \qquad \textbf{9.3}$$

The dual problem goal is to minimize implicit values or shadow prices for the firm's resources. Defining V_A, V_B, and V_C as the shadow prices for inputs A, B, and C, respectively, and π^* as the total implicit value of the firm's fixed resources, the objective function (the dual) is

$$\text{Minimize } \pi^* = 32V_A + 10V_B + 21V_C \qquad \textbf{9.10}$$

Because the firm has 32 units of A, the total implicit value of input A is 32 times A's shadow price, or $32V_A$. If V_A, or input A's shadow price is found to be $1.50 when the dual equations are solved, the implicit value of A is $48 ($=32 \times \$1.50$). Inputs B and C are handled in the same way.

Dual Constraints

Primal problem constraints state that the total amount of each input used to produce X and Y must be equal to or less than the available quantity of input. In the dual, the constraints state that the total value of inputs used to produce 1 unit of X or 1 unit of Y must not be less than the profit contribution provided by a unit of these products. In other words, the shadow prices of A, B, and C times the amount of each of the inputs needed to produce a unit of X or Y must be equal to or greater than the unit profit contribution of X or of Y. Because resources have value only when used to produce output, they can never have an implicit value, or opportunity cost, that is less than the value of output.

In the example, unit profit is defined as the excess of price over variable cost, where price and variable cost are both constant, and profit per unit for X is $12 and for Y is $9. As shown in Table 9.1, each unit of X requires 4 units of A, 1 unit of B, and 0 units of C. The total implicit value of resources used to produce X is $4V_A + 1V_B$. The constraint requiring that the implicit cost of producing X be equal to or greater than the profit contribution of X is

$$4V_A + 1V_B \geq 12 \qquad \textbf{9.11}$$

---

4   Rules for constructing the dual linear programming problem from its related primal are provided in Appendix 9A at the end of this chapter.

Because 2 units of A, 1 unit of B, and 3 units of C are required to produce each unit of Y, the second dual constraint is

$$2V_A + 1V_B + 3V_C \geq 9 \qquad \textbf{9.12}$$

Because the firm produces only two products, the dual problem has only two constraint equations.

Dual Slack Variables

Dual slack variables can be incorporated into the problem, thus allowing the constraint conditions to be expressed as equalities. Letting L_X and L_Y represent the two slack variables, constraint Equations (9.11) and (9.12) become

$$4V_A + 1V_B - L_X = 12 \qquad \textbf{9.13}$$

and

$$2V_A + 1V_B + 3V_C - L_Y = 9 \qquad \textbf{9.14}$$

These slack variables are *subtracted* from the constraint equations, because greater-than-or-equal-to inequalities are involved. Using slack variables, the left-hand sides of the constraint conditions are thus *decreased* to equal the right-hand sides' profit contributions. Dual slack variables measure the *excess* of input value over output value for each product. Alternatively, dual slack variables measure the opportunity cost associated with producing X and Y. This can be seen by examining the two constraint equations. Solving constraint Equation (9.13) for L_X, for example, provides

$$L_X = 4V_A + 1V_B - 12$$

This expression states that L_X is equal to the implicit cost of producing 1 unit of X minus the profit contribution provided by that product. The dual slack variable L_X is a measure of the opportunity cost of producing product X. It compares the profit contribution of product X, \$12, with the value to the firm of the resources necessary to produce it.

A zero value for L_X indicates that the marginal value of resources required to produce 1 unit of X is exactly equal to the profit contribution received. This is similar to marginal cost being equal to marginal revenue at the profit-maximizing output level. A positive value for L_X indicates that the resources used to produce X are more valuable, in terms of the profit contribution they can generate, when used to produce the other product Y. A positive value for L_X measures the firm's opportunity cost (profit loss) associated with production of product X. The slack variable L_Y is the opportunity cost of producing product Y. It will have a value of zero if the implicit value of resources used to produce 1 unit of Y exactly equals the \$9 profit contribution provided by that product. A positive value for L_Y measures the opportunity loss in terms of the foregone profit contribution associated with product Y.

A firm would not choose to produce if the value of resources required were greater than the value of resulting output. It follows that a product with a positive slack variable (opportunity cost) is not included in the optimal production combination.

SOLVING THE DUAL PROBLEM

The dual programming problem can be solved with the same algebraic technique used to obtain the primal solution.

Dual Solution

In this case, the dual problem is

$$\text{Minimize } \pi^* = 32V_A + 10V_B + 21V_C \tag{9.10}$$

subject to constraints:

$$4V_A + 1V_B - L_X = 12 \tag{9.13}$$

and

$$2V_A + 1V_B + 3V_C - L_Y = 9 \tag{9.14}$$

where

$$V_A, V_B, V_C, L_X, \text{ and } L_Y \text{ all} \geq 0$$

Because there are only two constraints in this programming problem, the maximum number of nonzero-valued variables at any corner solution is two. One can proceed with the solution by setting three of the variables equal to zero and solving the constraint equations for the values of the remaining two. By comparing the value of the objective function at each feasible solution, the point at which the function is minimized can be determined. This is the dual solution.

To illustrate the process, first set $V_A = V_B = V_C = 0$, and solve for L_X and L_Y:

$$(4 \times 0) + (1 \times 0) - L_X = 12 \tag{9.13}$$
$$L_X = -12$$

$$(2 \times 0) + (1 \times 0) + 0 + (3 \times 0) - L_Y = 9 \tag{9.14}$$
$$L_Y = -9$$

Because L_X and L_Y cannot be negative, this solution is outside the feasible set.

The values just obtained are inserted into Table 9.3 as solution 1. All other solution values can be calculated in a similar manner and used to complete Table 9.3. It is apparent from the table that not all solutions lie within the feasible space. Solutions 5, 7, 9, and 10 meet the nonnegativity requirement while also providing a number of nonzero-valued variables that is exactly equal to the number of constraints. These four solutions coincide with the corners of the dual problem's feasible space. At solution 10, the total implicit value of inputs A, B, and C is minimized. Solution 10 is the optimum solution, where the total implicit value of employed resources exactly equals the $108 maximum profit primal solution. Thus, optimal solutions to primal and dual objective functions are identical.

Table 9.3 Solutions for the Dual Programming Problem

Solution Number	Value of Variable					Total Value Imputed to the Firm's Resources
	V_A	V_B	V_C	L_X	L_Y	
1	0	0	0	−12	−9	a
2	0	0	3	−12	0	a
3	0	0	b	0	b	a
4	0	9	0	−3	0	a
5	0	12	0	0	3	$120
6	0	12	−1	0	0	a
7	4.5	0	0	6	0	$144
8	3	0	0	0	−3	a
9	3	0	1	0	0	$117
10	1.5	6	0	0	0	$108

a Outside the feasible space.

b No solution.

At the optimal solution, the shadow price for input C is zero, $V_C = 0$. Because shadow price measures the marginal value of an input, a zero shadow price implies that the resource in question has a zero marginal value to the firm. Adding another unit of this input adds nothing to the firm's maximum obtainable profit. A zero shadow price for input C is consistent with the primal solution that input C is not a binding constraint. Excess capacity exists in C, so additional units of C would not increase production of either X or Y. The shadow price for input A of $1.50 implies that this fixed resource imposes a binding constraint. If an additional unit of A is added, the firm can increase total profit by $1.50. It would increase profits to buy additional units of input A at any price less than $1.50 per unit, at least up until the point at which A is no longer a binding constraint. This assumes that the cost of input A is currently fixed. If those costs are variable, the firm would be willing to pay $1.50 *above* the current price of input A to eliminate this constraint. Because availability of B also imposes an effective constraint, the firm can also afford to pay up to $6 for a marginal unit of B.

Finally, both dual slack variables equal zero at the optimal solution. This means that the implicit value of resources required to produce a single unit of X or Y is exactly equal to the profit contribution provided. The opportunity cost of producing X and Y is zero, meaning that the resources required for their production are not more valuable in some alternative use. This is consistent with the primal solution, because both X and Y are produced at the optimal solution.

Using the Dual Solution to Solve the Primal

The dual solution gives all the information necessary to determine the optimum output mix. The dual solution shows that input C does not impose a binding constraint on output of X and Y. Further, it demonstrates that $\pi = \pi^* = \$108$ at the optimum output of

X and Y. The dual solution also offers evidence on the value of primal constraint slack variables. To see this, recall the three constraints in the primal problem:

$$\text{Constraint on } A: \quad 4Q_X + 2Q_Y + S_A = 32$$
$$\text{Constraint on } B: \quad 1Q_X + 1Q_Y + S_B = 10$$
$$\text{Constraint on } C: \quad 3Q_Y + S_C = 21$$

The dual solution indicates that the constraints on A and B are binding, because both inputs have positive shadow prices, and only resources that are fully utilized have a nonzero marginal value. Accordingly, the slack variables S_A and S_B equal zero, and the binding primal constraints can be rewritten as

$$4Q_X + 2Q_Y = 32$$

and

$$1Q_X + 1Q_Y = 10$$

With two equations and only two unknowns, this system can be solved for Q_X and Q_Y. Multiplying the second constraint by 2 and subtracting from the first provides

$$4Q_X + 2Q_Y = 32$$
$$\text{minus } \underline{2Q_X + 2Q_Y = 20}$$
$$2Q_X = 12$$
$$Q_X = 6$$

and

$$6 + Q_Y = 10$$
$$Q_Y = 4$$

These values of Q_X and Q_Y, found after learning from the dual which constraints were binding, are identical to the values found by solving the primal problem directly. Having obtained the value for Q_Y, it is possible to substitute this value for Q_Y in constraint C and solve for the amount of slack in that resource:

$$3Q_Y + S_C = 21$$
$$S_C = 21 - 3 \times 4 = 9$$

These relations, which allow one to solve either the primal or the dual specification of a linear programming problem and then quickly obtain the solution to the other, can be generalized by the two following expressions:

$$\text{Primal Objective Variable}_i \times \text{Dual Slack Variable}_i / 0 \qquad \textbf{9.15}$$
$$\text{Primal Slack Variable}_j \times \text{Dual Objective Variable}_j / 0 \qquad \textbf{9.16}$$

Equation (9.15) states that if an ordinary variable in the primal problem takes on a nonzero value in the optimal solution to that problem, its related dual slack variable

Managerial Application 9.4

It's a RIOT on the Internet!

Here's an idea for you. How would you like access to a Remote Interactive Optimization Testbed (RIOT) on the Internet? It's an amazing Web site.

RIOT creates an interface between the World Wide Web and linear programming solver programs that allow anyone with access to the Web to submit a linear program and have it solved. There has been a proliferation of linear programming solver software since 1980, like *Cplex, Lingo, Minos,* and so on. However, each of these solver programs implement different algorithms, like the simplex method, and offer different solution options, like sensitivity analysis. Depending on the problem to be solved, some solvers can be more or less efficient than others in terms of speed, accuracy, number of iterations, and available options.

LP applications on RIOT range from the serious, like a Planar Robot Simulator with Obstacle Avoidance and Open-pit Mining problems, to the whimsical, like Major League Baseball and Basketball elimination problems. Over time, continuing improvements promise users the opportunity to find the optimal value (maximum or minimum) for any linear function of a certain number of variables given a

set of *m* linear constraints on these variables (equalities or inequalities).

Like everything on the Web, RIOT is still relatively new and bound to evolve rapidly over time. At this point, it is a free offering designed to achieve four main objectives:

- **Educational.** RIOT provides educational information via HTML and interactive problems presented through an easy-to-use interface.
- **Research.** RIOT showcases state-of-the-art algorithms developed locally by UC Berkeley Engineering faculty and others.
- **Comparative Research.** RIOT provides efficiency information for different algorithms that solve similar problems.
- **Showcase Applications.** RIOT provides a forum to showcase new and innovative applications of linear programming techniques.

RIOT is an enormously practical tool. It's on the Internet. It's free. What a RIOT!

See: RIOT's home page can be found on the Internet, http://riot.ieor.berkeley.edu/riot/index.html.

must be zero. Only if a particular Q_i is zero valued in the solution to the primal can its related dual slack variable, L_i, take on a nonzero value. A similar relation exists between the slack variables in the primal problem and their related ordinary variables in the dual, as indicated by Equation (9.16). If the primal slack variable is nonzero valued, then the related dual variable will be zero valued, and vice versa.

SUMMARY

Linear programming is a valuable technique for solving maximization or minimization problems, in which inequality constraints are imposed on the decision maker. This chapter introduces graphic and analytic approaches for setting up, solving, and interpreting the solutions to such problems.

- **Linear programming** is a proven tool used to isolate the best solution, or **optimal solution,** to decision problems. The technique is ideally suited to solving decision problems that involve an objective function to be maximized or minimized,

where the relevant objective function is subject to inequality constraints.

- Simple linear programming problems can be solved graphically using the **relative distance method.** The **feasible space** is the graphical region showing the linear programming problem solution space that is both technically and economically feasible.

- An equation that expresses the goal of a linear programming problem is called the **objective function.**

- The optimal solution to a linear programming problem occurs at the intersection of the objective function and a **corner point** of the feasible space. A corner point is a spot in the feasible space where the *X*-axis, *Y*-axis, or constraint conditions intersect.

- **Slack variables** indicate the amount by which constraint conditions are exceeded. In the case of less-than-or-equal-to constraints, slack variables are used to *increase* the left side to equal the right side limits of the constraint conditions. In the case of greater-than-or-equal-to constraints, slack variables are used to *decrease* the left side to equal the right side limits of the constraint conditions.

- The **simplex solution method** is an iterative method used to solve linear programming problems. In this procedure, computer programs find solution values for all variables at each corner point, then isolate that corner point with the optimal solution to the objective function.

- For every maximization problem in linear programming, there is a symmetrical minimization problem; for every minimization problem, there is a symmetrical maximization problem. These pairs of related maximization and minimization problems are known as the **primal** and **dual** linear programming problems.

- The **primal solution** is often described as a tool for short-run operating decisions, whereas the **dual solution** is often seen as a tool for long-range planning. Both provide management with valuable insight for the decision-making process.

- **Shadow prices** are implicit values or opportunity costs associated with linear-programming-problem decision variables. In the case of output, shadow prices indicate the marginal cost of a 1-unit increase in output. In the case of the constraints, shadow prices indicate the marginal cost of a 1-unit relaxation in the constraint condition.

During recent years, rapid advances in user-friendly computer software have allowed the widespread application of linear programming techniques to a wide array of problems in business, government, and the not-for-profit sector.

QUESTIONS

Q9.1 Give some illustrations of managerial decision situations in which you think the linear programming technique would be useful.

Q9.2 Why can't linear programming be used in each of the following circumstances?

A. Strong economies of scale exist.

B. As the firm expands output, the prices of variable factors of production increase.

C. As output increases, product prices decline.

Q9.3 Do equal distances along a given production process ray in a linear programming problem always represent an identical level of output?

Q9.4 Assume that output can be produced only using processes *A* and *B*. Process *A* requires inputs *L* and *K* to be combined in the fixed ratio $2L{:}4K$, and process *B* requires $4L{:}2K$. Is it possible to produce output efficiently using $3L$ and $3K$? Why or why not?

Q9.5 Describe the relative distance method used in graphic linear programming analysis.

Q9.6 Is the number of isocost, isorevenue, or isoprofit lines in a typical two-input bounded feasible space limited?

Q9.7 In linear programming, why is it so critical that the number of nonzero-valued variables exactly equal the number of constraints at corners of the feasible space?

Q9.8 Will maximizing a profit contribution objective function always result in also maximizing total net profits?

Q9.9 The primal problem calls for determining the set of outputs that will maximize profit, subject to input constraints.

A. What is the dual objective function?

B. What interpretation can be given to the dual variables called the shadow prices or implicit values?

C. What does it mean if a dual variable or shadow price equals zero?

Q9.10 How are the solution values for primal and dual linear programming problems actually employed in practice?

SELF-TEST PROBLEMS AND SOLUTIONS

ST9.1 Cost Minimization. Idaho Natural Resources (INR) has two mines with different production capabilities for producing the same type of ore. After mining and crushing, the ore is graded into three classes: high, medium, and low. The company has contracted to provide local smelters with 24 tons of high-grade ore, 16 tons of medium-grade ore, and 48 tons of low-grade ore each week. It costs INR $10,000 per day to operate mine A and $5,000 per day to run mine B. In a day's time, mine A produces 6 tons of high-grade ore, 2 tons of medium-grade ore, and 4 tons of low-grade ore. Mine B produces 2, 2, and 12 tons per day of each grade, respectively. Management's short-run problem is to determine how many days per week to operate each mine under current conditions. In the long run, management wishes to know how sensitive these decisions will be to changing economic conditions.

A report prepared for the company by an independent management consultant addressed the company's short-run operating concerns. The consultant claimed that the operating problem could be solved using linear programming techniques by which the firm would seek to minimize the total cost of meeting contractual requirements. Specifically, the consultant recommended that INR do the following:

$$\text{Minimize} \quad \text{Total Cost} = \$10{,}000A + \$5{,}000B$$

subject to

$6A + 2B \geq 24$	(high-grade ore constraint)
$2A + 2B \geq 16$	(medium-grade ore constraint)
$4A + 12B \geq 48$	(low-grade ore constraint)
$A \leq 7$	(mine A operating days in a week constraint)
$B \leq 7$	(mine B operating days in a week constraint)

or, in their equality form,

$$6A + 2B - S_H = 24$$
$$2A + 2B - S_M = 16$$
$$4A + 12B - S_L = 48$$
$$A + S_A = 7$$
$$B + S_B = 7$$

where

$$A, B, S_H, S_M, S_L, S_A, \text{ and } S_B \geq 0$$

Here, A and B represent the days of operation per week for each mine; S_H, S_M, and S_L represent excess production of high-, medium-, and low-grade ore, respectively; and S_A and S_B are days per week that each mine is not operated.

A graphic representation of the linear programming problem was also provided. The graph suggests an optimal solution at point X, where constraints 1 and 2 are binding. Thus, $S_H = S_M = 0$ and

$$6A + 2B - 0 = 24$$
$$\text{minus } \underline{2A + 2B - 0 = 16}$$
$$4A = 8$$
$$A = 2 \text{ days per week}$$

Substitute $A = 2$ into the high-grade ore constraint:

$$6(2) + 2B = 24$$
$$12 + 2B = 24$$
$$2B = 12$$
$$B = 6 \text{ days per week}$$

A minimum total operating cost per week of $50,000 is suggested, because

$$\text{Total Cost} = \$10,000A + \$5,000B$$
$$= \$10,000(2) + \$5,000(6)$$
$$= \$50,000$$

The consultant's report did not discuss a variety of important long-run planning issues. Specifically, INR wishes to know the following, holding all else equal:

A. How much, if any, excess production would result if the consultant's operating recommendation were followed?

B. What would be the cost effect of increasing low-grade ore sales by 50 percent?

C. What is INR's minimum acceptable price per ton if it is to renew a current contract to provide one of its customers with 6 tons of high-grade ore per week?

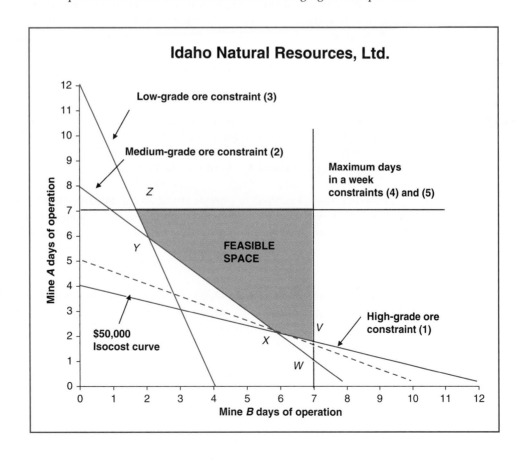

D. With current output requirements, how much would the cost of operating mine A have to rise before INR would change its operating decision?

E. What increase in the cost of operating mine B would cause INR to change its current operating decision?

ST9.1 SOLUTION

A. If the consultant's operating recommendation of $A = 2$ and $B = 6$ were followed, 32 tons of excess low-grade ore production would result. No excess production of high- or medium-grade ore would occur. This can be shown by solving for S_H, S_M and S_L at the recommended activity level.

From the constraint equations, we find the following:

$$(1) \quad 6(2) + 2(6) - S_H = 24$$
$$S_H = 0$$
$$(2) \quad 2(2) + 2(6) - S_M = 16$$
$$S_M = 0$$
$$(3) \quad 4(2) + 12(6) - S_L = 48$$
$$S_L = 32$$

B. There would be a *zero cost impact* of an increase in low-grade ore sales from 48 to 72 tons ($= 1.5 \times 48$). With $A = 2$ and $B = 6$, 80 tons of low-grade ore are produced. A 50 percent increase in low-grade ore sales would simply reduce excess production from $S_L = 32$ to $S_L = 8$, because

$$(3') \quad 4(2) + 12(6) - S_L = 72$$
$$S_L = 8$$

Graphically, the effect of a 50 percent increase in low-grade ore sales would be to cause a rightward shift in the low-grade ore constraint to a new constraint line with end points ($0B$, $18A$) and ($6B$, $0A$). While such a shift would reduce the feasible space, it would not affect the optimal operating decision of $A = 2$ and $B = 6$ (at Point X).

C. If INR didn't renew a contract to provide one of its current customers with 6 tons of high-grade ore per week, the high-grade ore constraint would fall from 24 to 18 tons per week. The new high-grade ore constraint, reflecting a parallel leftward shift, is written as

$$(1') \quad 6A + 2B - S_H = 18$$

and has end points ($0B$, $3A$) and ($9B$, $0A$). With such a reduction in required high-grade ore sales, the high-grade ore constraint would no longer be binding and the optimal production point would shift to point W, with $A = 1$ and $B = 7$ (because $S_M = S_B = 0$). At this point, high-grade ore production would equal 20 tons, or 2 tons more than the new high-grade ore requirement:

$$6(1) + 2(7) - S_H = 18$$
$$S_H = 2$$

with operating costs of

$$\begin{aligned} \text{Total Cost} &= \$10,000A + \$5,000B \\ &= \$10,000(1) + \$5,000(7) \\ &= \$45,000 \end{aligned}$$

Therefore, renewing a contract to provide one of its current customers with 6 tons of high-grade ore per week would result in our earlier operating decision with values of $A = 2$ and $B = 6$ and total costs of $50,000, rather than the $A = 1$ and $B = 7$ and total costs of $45,000 that would otherwise be possible. The marginal cost of renewing the 6-ton contract is $5,000, or $833 per ton.

$$\begin{aligned} \text{Marginal Cost} &= \frac{\text{Change in Operating Costs}}{\text{Number of Tons}} \\ &= \frac{\$50,000 - \$45,000}{6} \\ &= \$833 \text{ per ton} \end{aligned}$$

D. In general, the isocost relation for this problem is

$$C_0 = C_A A + C_B B$$

where C_0 is any weekly cost level, and C_A and C_B are the daily operating costs for mines A and B, respectively. In terms of the graph, A is on the vertical axis and B is on the horizontal axis. From the isocost formula we find the following:

$$A = C_0/C_A - (C_B/C_A)B$$

with an intercept of C_0/C_A and a slope equal to $-(C_B/C_A)$. The isocost line will become steeper as C_B increases relative to C_A. The isocost line will become flatter (slope will approach zero) as C_B falls relative to C_A.

If C_A increases to slightly more than $15,000, the optimal feasible point will shift from Point X (6B, 2A) to Point V (7B, 1.67A), because the isocost line slope will then be less than $-1/3$, the slope of the high-grade ore constraint ($A = 4 - (1/3)B$). Thus, an increase in C_A from $10,000 to at least $15,000, or an increase of *at least* $5,000, is necessary before the optimal operating decision will change.

E. An increase in C_B of *at least* $5,000 to slightly more than $10,000 will shift the optimal point from point X to point Y (2B, 6A), because the isocost line slope will then be steeper than -1, the slope of the medium-grade ore constraint ($A = 8 - B$).

An increase in C_B to slightly more than $30,000 will be necessary before point Z (1.67B, 7A) becomes optimal. With $C_B \geq \$30,000$ and $C_A = \$10,000$, the isocost line slope will be steeper than -3, the slope of the low-grade ore constraint, $A = 12 - 3B$.

As seems reasonable, the greater C_B is relative to C_A, the more mine A will tend to be employed. The greater C_A is relative to C_B, the more mine B will tend to be employed.

ST9.2 Profit Maximization.
Interstate Bakeries, Inc., is an Atlanta-based manufacturer and distributor of branded bread products. Two leading products, Low Calorie, Q_A, and High Fiber, Q_B, bread, are produced using the same baking facility and staff. Low Calorie bread requires 0.3 hours of worker time per case, whereas High Fiber bread requires 0.4 hours of worker time per case.

During any given week, a maximum of 15,000 worker hours are available for these two products. To meet grocery retailer demands for a full product line of branded bread products, Interstate must produce a minimum of 25,000 cases of Low Calorie bread and 7,500 cases of High Fiber bread per week. Given the popularity of low-calorie products in general, Interstate must also ensure that weekly production of Low Calorie bread be at least twice that of High Fiber bread.

Low Calorie bread is sold to groceries at a price of $42 per case; the price of High Fiber bread is $40 per case. Despite its lower price, the markup on High Fiber bread substantially exceeds that on Low Calorie bread. Variable costs are $30.50 per case for Low Calorie bread, but only $17 per case for High Fiber bread.

A. Set up the linear programming problem that the firm would use to determine the profit-maximizing output levels for Low Calorie and High Fiber bread. Show both the inequality and equality forms of the constraint conditions.

B. Completely solve the linear programming problem.

C. Interpret the solution values for the linear programming problem.

D. Holding all else equal, how much would variable costs per unit on High Fiber bread have to fall before the production level indicated in part B would change?

ST9.2 SOLUTION

A. First, the profit contribution for Low Calorie bread, Q_A, and High Fiber bread, Q_B, must be calculated.

$$\text{Profit Contribution Per Unit} = \text{Price} - \text{Variable Costs Per Unit}$$

Thus,

$$\pi_A = \$42 - \$30.50 = \$11.50 \text{ per case of } Q_A$$
$$\pi_B = \$40 - \$17 = \$23 \text{ per case of } Q_B$$

This problem requires maximization of profits, subject to limitations on the amount of each product produced, the acceptable ratio of production, and available worker hours. The linear programming problem is

$$
\begin{aligned}
\text{Maximize} \qquad & \pi = \$11.50Q_A + \$23Q_B \\
\text{subject to} \qquad & Q_A \geq 25,000 \\
& Q_B \geq 7,500 \\
& Q_A - 2Q_B \geq 0 \\
& 0.3Q_A + 0.4Q_B \leq 15,000
\end{aligned}
$$

In equality form, the constraint conditions are

(1)		$Q_A - S_A = 25,000$	(Low calorie constraint)
(2)		$Q_B - S_B = 7,500$	(High fiber constraint)
(3)		$Q_A - 2Q_B - S_R = 0$	(Acceptable ratio constraint)
(4)	$0.3Q_A + 0.4Q_B + S_W = 15,000$		(Worker hours constraint)

$$\text{where } Q_A, Q_B, S_A, S_B, S_R, S_W \geq 0$$

Here, Q_A and Q_B are cases of Low Calorie and High Fiber bread, respectively. S_A and S_B are variables representing excess production of Low Calorie and High Fiber bread, respectively. S_R is the amount by which the production of Low Calorie bread exceeds the minimally acceptable amount, given High Fiber production. S_W is excess worker capacity.

B. By graphing the constraints and the highest possible isoprofit line, the optimal Point X occurs where $S_R = S_W = 0$.

Thus,

$$\begin{aligned}
(1) && Q_A - S_A &= 25{,}000 \\
(2) && Q_B - S_B &= 0 \\
(3) && Q_A - 2Q_B - 0 &= 0 \\
(4) && 0.3Q_A + 0.4Q_B + 0 &= 15{,}000
\end{aligned}$$

From (3), $Q_A = 2Q_B$. Substituting this value into (4) yields

$$0.3(2Q_B) + 0.4Q_B = 15{,}000$$
$$Q_B = 15{,}000$$

From (3)

$$Q_A - 2(15{,}000) = 0$$
$$Q_A = 30{,}000$$

From (1)

$$30{,}000 - S_A = 25{,}000$$
$$S_A = 5{,}000$$

From (2)

$$15{,}000 - S_B = 7{,}500$$
$$S_B = 7{,}500$$

And the total profit contribution per week is

$$\pi = \$11.50(30{,}000) + \$23(15{,}000)$$
$$= \$690{,}000$$

C. Solution values can be interpreted as follows:

$Q_A = 30{,}000$	Optimal production of Low Calorie bread is 30,000 cases per week.
$Q_B = 15{,}000$	Optimal production of High Fiber bread is 15,000 cases per week.
$S_A = 5{,}000$	The production of Low Calorie bread exceeds the 25,000 case minimum by 5,000 units.

$S_B = 7,500$ The production of High Fiber bread exceeds the 7,500 case minimum by 7,500 units.

$S_R = 0$ The minimally acceptable 2:1 ratio of Low Calorie:High Fiber bread is produced.

$S_W = 0$ All worker hours are utilized; no excess worker capacity exists.

$\pi = \$690,000$ Maximum weekly profit contribution given constraints.

D. $7.67 per case. In the initial problem, there are two feasible solutions that are at the corners of the feasible space that is furthest away from the origin. The optimal solution point X entails production of $Q_A = 30,000$, $Q_B = 15,000$ and $\pi = \$690,000$. An inferior cornerpoint solution is at point Y where $Q_A = 40,000$, $Q_B = 7,500$ and $\pi = \$632,500$.

Analytically, point X is preferred to point Y because it emphasizes production of the higher- margin High Fiber bread. Graphically, point X is preferred to point Y because the slope of the isoprofit line ($= -2$) is "steeper" than the slope of the worker hours constraint (4) ($= -1.33$). If the slope of the isoprofit line became slightly less negative than the worker hours constraint, then the optimal production level would shift from point X to point Y.

In general, the isoprofit line formula is

$$\pi = \pi_A Q_A + \pi_B Q_B$$

or

$$Q_A = (\pi/\pi_A) - (\pi_B/\pi_A)Q_B$$

In this specific case, the isoprofit line is

$$Q_A = (\pi/\$11.50) - (\$23/\$11.50)Q_B$$

To intersect the feasible space at point Y rather than point X, the slope of this line would have to become slightly less negative than -1.33. To solve for the required level for π_B, note that if

$$\frac{\pi_B}{\$11.50} < 1.33$$

then

$$\pi_B < \$15.33$$

Given a price of High Fiber bread of $40 per unit, a profit contribution of $15.33 implies variable costs per unit of $24.67 because

$$\pi_B = \text{Price} - \text{Variable Costs Per Unit}$$
$$= \$40 - \$24.67$$
$$= \$15.33$$

Therefore, to change the optimal production point from point X to point Y, variable costs per unit on High Fiber bread would have to rise by *at least* $7.67 per unit:

$$\text{Change in Variable Costs} = \text{New Level} - \text{Initial Level}$$
$$= \$24.67 - \$17$$
$$= \$7.67$$

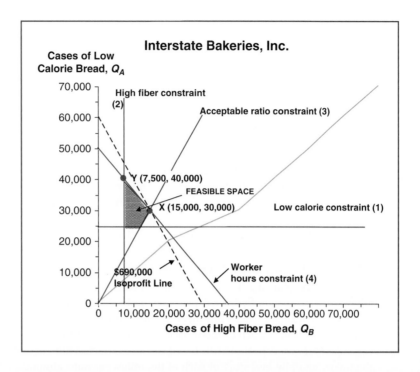

Interstate Bakeries, Inc.

PROBLEMS

P9.1 LP Basics. Indicate whether each of the following statements is true or false and explain why.

A. Constant returns to scale and constant input prices are the only requirements for a total cost function to be linear.

B. Changing input prices will always alter the slope of a given isocost line.

C. In profit-maximization linear programming problems, negative values for slack variables imply that the amount of an input resource employed exceeds the amount available.

D. Equal distances along a given process ray indicate equal output quantities.

E. Nonbinding constraints are constraints that intersect at the optimum solution.

P9.2 Fixed Input Combinations. Cherry Devices, Inc., assembles connectors and terminals for electronic products at a plant in New Haven, Connecticut. The plant uses labor (L) and capital (K) in an assembly line process to produce output (Q), where

$$Q = 0.025L^{0.5}K^{0.5}$$
$$MP_L = 0.0025(0.5)L^{-0.5}K^{0.5}$$
$$= \frac{0.0125K^{0.5}}{L^{0.5}}$$
$$MP_K = 0.025(0.5)L^{0.5}K^{-0.5}$$
$$= \frac{0.0125L^{0.5}}{K^{0.5}}$$

A. Calculate how many units of output can be produced with 4 units of labor and 400 units of capital and with 16 units of labor and 1,600 units of capital. Are returns to scale increasing, constant, or diminishing?

B. Calculate the change in the marginal product of labor as labor grows from 4 to 16 units, holding capital constant at 400 units. Similarly, calculate the change in the marginal product of capital as capital grows from 400 to 1,600 units, holding labor constant at 4 units. Are returns to each factor increasing, constant, or diminishing?

C. Assume now and throughout the remainder of the problem that labor and capital must be combined in the ratio 4L:400K. How much output could be produced if Cherry has a constraint of $L = 4,000$ and $K = 480,000$ during the coming production period?

D. What are the marginal products of each factor under the conditions described in part C?

P9.3   LP Setup and Interpretation.   The Syflansyd Nut Company has enjoyed booming sales following the success of its "Sometimes You Feel Like a Nut, Sometimes You Don't" advertising campaign. Syflansyd packages and sells four types of nuts in four different types of mixed-nut packages. These products include bulk (B), economy (E), fancy (F), and regular (R) mixed-nut packages. Each of these packages contains a different mixture of almonds (A), cashews (C), filberts (F), and peanuts (P). Based on its contracts with current suppliers, the company has the following daily inventory of each of the following nuts: almonds, 8,000 ounces; cashews, 7,000 ounces; filberts, 7,500 ounces; and peanuts, 10,000 ounces.

Given available inventory, it is management's goal to maximize profits by offering the optimum mix of the four package types. Profit earned per package type is as follows:

Bulk	$0.50
Economy	$0.25
Fancy	$1.25
Regular	$0.75

The composition of each of the four package types can be summarized as follows:

	Ounces Per Package			
	Bulk	**Economy**	**Fancy**	**Regular**
Almonds	35	2	3	2
Cashews	35	1	4	2
Filberts	35	1	3	2
Peanuts	35	8	2	6
Total	140	12	12	12

Solution values for the optimal number of packages to produce (decision variables) and excess capacity (slack variables) are the following:

$$B = 0$$

$$E = 0$$

$$F = 1,100$$
$$R = 1,300$$
$$S_A = 2,100$$
$$S_C = 0$$
$$S_F = 1,600$$
$$S_P = 0$$

A. Identify and interpret the appropriate Syflansyd objective function.

B. Using both inequality and equality forms, set up and interpret the resource constraints facing the Syflansyd Company.

C. Calculate optimal daily profit, and provide a complete interpretation of the full solution to this linear programming problem.

P9.4 Cost Minimization. Delmar Custom Homes (DCH) uses two types of crews on its Long Island, New York, home construction projects. Type A crews consist of master carpenters and skilled carpenters, whereas B crews include skilled carpenters and unskilled labor. Each home involves framing (F), roofing (R), and finish carpentry (FC). During recent months, A crews have demonstrated a capability of framing one home, roofing two, and doing finish carpentry for no more than four homes per month. Capabilities for B crews are framing three homes, roofing two, and completing finish carpentry for one during a month. DCH has agreed to build 10 homes during the month of July but has subcontracted 10 percent of framing and 20 percent of finish carpentry requirements. Labor costs are $60,000 per month for A crews and $45,000 per month for B crews.

A. Formulate the linear programming problem that DCH would use to minimize its total labor costs per month, showing both the inequality and equality forms of the constraint conditions.

B. Solve the linear programming problem and interpret your solution values.

C. Assuming that DCH can both buy and sell subcontracting services at prevailing prices of $8,000 per unit for framing and $14,000 per unit for finish carpentry, would you recommend that the company alter its subcontracting policy? If so, how much could the company save through such a change?

D. Calculate the minimum increase in A-crew costs necessary to cause DCH to change its optimal employment combination for July.

P9.5 Optimal Credit Policy. Kate Warner, a senior loan officer with Citybank in Cleveland, Ohio, has both corporate and personal lending customers. On average, the profit contribution margin or interest rate spread is 1.5 percent on corporate loans and 2 percent on personal loans. This return difference reflects the fact that personal loans tend to be riskier than corporate loans. Warner seeks to maximize the total dollar profit contribution earned, subject to a variety of restrictions on her lending practices. To limit default risk, Warner must restrict personal loans to no more than 50 percent of the total loans outstanding. Similarly, to ensure adequate diversification against business-cycle risk, corporate lending cannot exceed 75 percent of loaned funds. To maintain good customer relations by serving the basic needs of the local business community, Warner has decided to extend at least 25 percent of her total credit authorization to corporate customers on an ongoing basis. Finally, Warner cannot exceed her current total credit authorization of $100 million.

A. Using the inequality form of the constraint conditions, set up and interpret the linear programming problem that Warner would use to determine the optimal dollar amount of credit to extend to corporate (C) and personal (P) lending customers. Also formulate the LP problem using the equality form of the constraint conditions.

B. Use a graph to determine the optimal solution, and check your solution algebraically. Fully interpret solution values.

P9.6 Optimal Portfolio Decisions.

The James Bond Fund is a mutual fund (open-end investment company) with an objective of maximizing income from a widely diversified corporate bond portfolio. The fund has a policy of remaining invested largely in a diversified portfolio of investment-grade bonds. Investment-grade bonds have high investment quality and receive a rating of Baa or better by Moody's, a bond-rating service. The fund's investment policy states that investment-grade bonds are to be emphasized, representing at least three times the amount of junk bond holdings. Junk bonds pay high nominal returns but have low investment quality, and they receive a rating of less than Baa from Moody's. To maintain the potential for high investor income, at least 20 percent of the fund's total portfolio must be invested in junk bonds. Like many funds, the James Bond Fund cannot use leverage (or borrowing) to enhance investor returns. As a result, total bond investments cannot total more than 100 percent of the portfolio. Finally, the current expected return for investment-grade (I) bonds is 9 percent, and it is 12 percent for junk (J) bonds.

A. Using the inequality form of the constraint conditions, set up and interpret the linear programming problem that the James Bond Fund would use to determine the optimal portfolio percentage holdings of investment-grade (I) and junk (J) bonds. Also formulate the problem using the equality form of the constraint conditions. (Assume that the fund managers have decided to remain fully invested and therefore hold no cash at this time.)

B. Use a graph to determine the optimal solution, and check your solution algebraically. Fully interpret solution values.

C. Holding all else equal, how much would the expected return on junk bonds have to fall to alter the optimal investment policy determined in part B? Alternatively, how much would the return on investment-grade bonds have to rise before a change in investment policy would be warranted?

D. In anticipation of a rapid increase in interest rates and a subsequent economic downturn, the investment committee has decided to minimize the fund's exposure to bond price fluctuations. In adopting a defensive position, what is the maximum share of the portfolio that can be held in cash given the investment policies stated in the problem?

P9.7 Cost Minimization.

Carolina Power and Light (CP&L) is a small electric utility located in the Southeast. CP&L currently uses coal-fired capacity to satisfy its base load electricity demand, which is the minimum level of electricity demanded 24 hours per day, 365 days per year.

CP&L currently burns both high-sulfur eastern coal and low-sulfur western coal. Each type of coal has its advantages. Eastern coal is more expensive ($50 per ton) but has higher heat-generating capabilities. Although western coal doesn't generate as much heat as eastern coal, western coal is less expensive ($25 per ton) and doesn't cause as much sulfur dioxide pollution. CP&L's base load requirements are such that at least 2,400 million BTUs must be generated per hour. Each ton of eastern coal burned generates 40 million BTUs, and each ton of western coal burned generates 30 million BTUs. To limit sulfur dioxide emissions, the state's Environmental Protection Agency (EPA) requires CP&L to limit its total burning of sulfur to no more than 1.5 tons per hour. This affects

CP&L's coal usage, because eastern coal contains 2.5 percent sulfur and western coal contains 1.5 percent sulfur. The EPA also limits CP&L particulate emissions to no more than 900 pounds per hour. CP&L emits 10 pounds of particulates per ton of eastern coal burned and 15 pounds of particulates per ton of western coal burned.

A. Set up and interpret the linear program that CP&L would use to minimize hourly coal usage costs in light of its constraints.

B. Calculate and interpret all relevant solution values.

C. Holding all else equal, how much would the price of western coal have to rise before only eastern coal would be used? Explain.

P9.8 Profit Maximization. Creative Accountants, Ltd., is a small San Francisco-based accounting partnership specializing in the preparation of individual (I) and corporate (C) income tax returns. Prevailing prices in the local market are $125 for individual tax return preparation and $250 for corporate tax return preparation. Five accountants run the firm and are assisted by four bookkeepers and four secretaries, all of whom work a typical 40-hour workweek. The firm must decide how to target its promotional efforts to best use its resources during the coming tax preparation season. Based on previous experience, the firm expects that an average of 1 hour of accountant time will be required for each individual return prepared. Corporate return preparation will require an average of two accountant hours and two bookkeeper hours. One hour of secretarial time will also be required for typing each individual or corporate return. In addition, variable computer and other processing costs are expected to average $25 per individual return and $100 per corporate return.

A. Set up the linear programming problem that the firm would use to determine the profit-maximizing output levels for preparing individual and corporate returns. Show both the inequality and equality forms of the constraint conditions.

B. Completely solve and interpret the solution values for the linear programming problem.

C. Calculate maximum possible net profits per week for the firm, assuming that the accountants earn $1,500 per week, bookkeepers earn $500 per week, secretaries earn $10 per hour, and fixed overhead (including promotion and other expenses) averages $5,000 per week.

D. After considering the preceding data, one senior accountant recommended letting two bookkeepers go while retaining the rest of the current staff. Another accountant suggested that if any bookkeepers were let go, an increase in secretarial staff would be warranted. Which is the more profitable suggestion? Why?

E. Using the equality form of the constraint conditions, set up, solve, and interpret solution values for the dual linear programming problem.

F. Does the dual solution provide information useful for planning purposes? Explain.

P9.9 Revenue Maximization. Designed for Sales (DFS), Inc., an Evanston, Illinois-based designer of single-family and multifamily housing units for real estate developers, seeks to determine an optimal mix of output during the current planning period. DFS offers custom designs for single-family units, Q_1, for $3,000 and custom designs for multifamily units (duplexes, fourplexes, etc.), Q_2, for $2,000 each. Both types of output make use of scarce drafting, artwork, and architectural resources. Each custom design for single-family units requires 12 hours of drafting, 2 hours of artwork, and 6 hours of architectural input. Each custom design for multifamily units requires 4 hours of drafting, 5 hours of artwork, and 6 hours of architectural input. Currently, DFS has 72 hours of drafting, 30 hours of artwork, and 48 hours of architectural services available on a weekly basis.

A. Using the equality form of the constraint conditions, set up the primal linear program that Benes would use to determine the sales revenue-maximizing product mix. Also set up the dual.

B. Solve for and interpret all solution values.

C. Would DFS's optimal product mix be different with a profit-maximization goal rather than a sales revenue-maximization goal? Why or why not?

P9.10   Optimal Output.   Omaha Meat Products (OMP) produces and markets Cornhusker Plumpers, an extra-large frankfurter product being introduced on a test market basis into the St. Louis, Missouri, area. This product is similar to several others offered by OMP, and it can be produced with currently available equipment and personnel using any of three alternative production methods. Method A requires 1 hour of labor and 4 processing-facility hours to produce 100 packages of plumpers, 1 unit of Q_A. Method B requires 2 labor hours and 2 processing-facility hours for each unit of Q_B, and Method C requires 5 labor hours and 1 processing-facility hour for each unit of Q_C. Because of slack demand for other products, OMP currently has 14 labor hours and 6 processing-facility hours available per week for producing Cornhusker Plumpers. Cornhusker Plumpers are currently being marketed to grocery retailers at a wholesale price of $1.50 per package, and demand exceeds current supply.

A. Using the equality form of the constraint conditions, set up the primal and dual linear programs that OMP would use to maximize production of Cornhusker Plumpers given currently available resources.

B. Calculate and interpret all solution values.

C. Should OMP expand its processing-facility capacity if it can do so at a cost of $40 per hour?

D. Discuss the implications of a new union scale calling for a wage rate of $20 per hour.

CASE *Study*   A LP Pension Funding Model

Several companies have learned that a well-funded and comprehensive employee benefits package constitutes an important part of the compensation plan needed to attract and retain key personnel. An employee stock ownership plan, profit-sharing arrangements, and deferred compensation to fund employee retirement are all used to allow productive employees to share in the firm's growth and development. Among the fringe benefits offered under the cafeteria-style benefits plans is comprehensive medical and dental care furnished through local health maintenance organizations, on-site daycare centers for employee children, and

continued

"eldercare" support for the aging parents and other dependents of workers.

Many companies also provide their employees with so-called "defined benefit" pension plans. Under defined benefit plans, employers usually offer workers a fixed percentage of their final salary as a retirement annuity. In a typical arrangement, a company might offer employees a retirement annuity of 1.5 percent of their final salary for each year employed. A 10-year veteran would earn a retirement annuity of 15 percent of final salary, a 20-year veteran would earn a retirement annuity of 30 percent of final salary, and so on. Because each employee's retirement benefits are defined by the company, the company itself is obligated to pay for promised benefits.

Over time, numerous firms have found it increasingly difficult to forecast the future rate of return on invested assets, the future rate of inflation, and the morbidity (death rate) of young, healthy, active retirees. As a result, several organizations have discontinued traditional defined benefit pension plans and instead have begun to offer new "defined contribution" plans. A defined contribution plan features a matching of company plus employee retirement contributions, with no prescribed set of retirement income benefits defined beforehand. Each employee is typically eligible to contribute up to 10 percent of their pre-tax income into the plan, with the company matching the first 5 percent or so of such contributions. Both company and employee contributions compound on a tax-deferred basis until the point of retirement. At that time, employees can use their pension funds to purchase an annuity, or draw a pension income from earned interest, plus dividends and capital gains.

Defined contribution plans have some obvious advantages over traditional defined benefit pension plans. From the company's perspective, defined benefit pension plans became much less attractive when accounting rule changes during the late 1980s required them to record as a liability any earned but not funded pension obligations. Unfunded pension liabilities caused gigantic one-time charges against operating income during the early 1990s for AT&T, General Motors, IBM, and a host of other large corporations. Faced with enormous one-time charges during an initial catch-up phase, plus the prospect of massive and rapidly growing retirement expenses over time, many large and small firms have simply elected to discontinue their defined contribution plan altogether. From the employee's perspective, defined contribution plans are attractive because they are portable from one employer to another. Rather than face the prospect of losing pension benefits after changing from one employer to another, employees appreciate the advantage of being able to take their pension plans with them as they switch jobs. Defined contribution plans are also attractive because they allow employees to tailor retirement funding contributions to fit individual needs. Younger employees faced with the necessity of buying a home or paying for children's educational expenses can limit pension contributions to minimal levels; older workers with greater discretionary income and a more imminent retirement can provide the maximum pension contribution allowed by law. An added benefit of defined contribution compensation plans is that individual workers can allocate pension investments according to individual risk preferences. Older workers who are extremely risk averse can focus their investments on short-term government securities; younger and more venturesome employees can devote a larger share of their retirement investment portfolio to common stocks.

Workers appreciate companies that offer flexible defined contribution pension plans and closely related profit-sharing and deferred compensation arrangements. To maximize plan benefits, firms must make modest efforts to educate and inform employees about

continued

retirement income needs and objectives. Until recently, compensation consultants suggested that employees could retire comfortably on a retirement income that totaled 80 percent of their final salary. However, concerns about the underfunding of federal Social Security and Medicaid programs and apprehension about the rapid escalation of medical care costs make retirement with sufficient assets to fund a pension income equal to 100 percent of final salary a worthy goal. To fund such a nest egg requires substantial regular savings and an impressive rate of return on pension plan assets. Workers who save 10 percent of income for an extended period, say, 30 years, have historically been able to fund a retirement income equal to 100 percent of final salary. This assumes, of course, that the pension plan portfolio is able to earn significant returns over time. Investing in a broadly diversified portfolio of common stocks has historically provided the best returns. Since 1926, the real (after-inflation) rate of return on NYSE stocks is 6.4 percent per year; the real return on bonds is only 0.5 percent per year. Indeed, over every 30-year investment horizon during that time interval, stocks have beat short-term bonds (money market instruments) and long-term bonds. The added return from common stocks is the predictable reward for assuming the greater risks of stock-market investing. However, to be sure of earning the market risk premium on stocks, one must invest in several different companies (at least 30) for several years. For most pension plans, investments in no-load low-expense common stock index funds work best in the long run. However, bond market funds have a place in some pension portfolios, especially for those at or near the retirement age.

To illustrate the type of retirement income funding model that a company might make available to employees, consider the following scenario. Suppose that an individual employee has accumulated a pension portfolio worth $250,000 and hopes to receive initial post-retirement income of $500 per month, or $6,000 per year. To provide a total return from current income (yield) plus growth (capital gains) of at least 7 percent, a minimum of 25 percent of the portfolio should be invested in common stocks. To limit risk, stocks should total no more than 50 percent of the overall portfolio, and a minimum of 5 percent should be invested in long-term taxable bonds, 5 percent in medium-term tax-exempt bonds, and 5 percent in a short-term money market mutual fund. Moreover, not more than 75 percent of the overall portfolio should be invested in stocks plus long-term taxable bonds, and at least $30,000 should be available in money markets plus medium-term tax-exempt bonds to provide sufficient liquidity to fund emergencies. Assume that common stocks have a before-tax dividend yield of 3.5 percent, with expected growth from capital appreciation of 6.5 percent per year. Similar figures for long-term taxable bonds are 6 percent plus 1.5 percent, 4 percent plus 1 percent for medium-term tax-exempt bonds, and 4.5 percent plus 0 percent for money market instruments. Also assume that the effective marginal tax rate is 30 percent.

A. Set up the linear programming problem that a benefits officer might use to determine the total-return maximizing allocation of the employee's pension portfolio. Use the inequality forms of the constraint conditions.

B. Solve this linear programming problem and interpret all solution values. Also determine the employee's expected before-tax and after-tax income levels.

C. Calculate the amount of unrealized capital gain earned per year on this investment portfolio.

D. What is the total return opportunity cost of the $6,000 after-tax income constraint?

Rules for Forming the Dual Linear Programming Problem

Given the importance of duality, a list of simple rules that can be used to form the dual program to any given primal program would be useful. Four such rules exist. They are as follows:

1. Change a maximize objective to minimize, and vice versa.
2. Reverse primal constraint inequality signs in dual constraints (i.e., change $\geq$ to $\leq$, and $\leq$ to $\geq$).
3. Transpose primal constraint coefficients to get dual constraint coefficients.
4. Transpose objective function coefficients to get limits in dual constraints, and vice versa.

(The word *transpose* is a matrix algebra term that simply means that each row of coefficients is rearranged into columns so that Row 1 becomes Column 1, Row 2 becomes Column 2, and so on.)

To illustrate the rules for transformation from primal and dual, consider the following simple example.

PRIMAL PROBLEM

$$\text{Maximize} \quad \pi = \pi_1 Q_1 + \pi_2 Q_2 + \pi_3 Q_3$$
$$\text{subject to} \quad a_{11}Q_1 + a_{12}Q_2 + a_{13}Q_3 \leq r_1$$
$$a_{21}Q_1 + a_{22}Q_2 + a_{23}Q_3 \leq r_2$$
$$Q_1, Q_2, Q_3 \geq 0$$

where π is profits and Q is output. Thus, π_1, π_2 and π_3 are unit profits for Q_1, Q_2 and Q_3, respectively. The resource constraints are given by r_1 and r_2. The constants in the primal constraints reflect the input requirements for each type of output. For example, a_{11} is the amount of resource r_1 in one unit of output Q_1. Similarly, a_{12} is the amount of resource r_1 in one unit of output Q_2, and a_{13} is the amount of resource r_1 in one unit of output Q_3. Thus, $a_{11}Q_1 + a_{12}Q_2 + a_{13}Q_3$ is the total amount of resource r_1 used in production. The remaining input requirements, a_{21}, a_{22} and a_{23}, have a similar interpretation. For convenience, this primal problem statement can be rewritten in matrix notation as follows:

$$\text{Maximize} \quad \pi = \pi_1 Q_1 + \pi_2 Q_2 + \pi_3 Q_3$$

$$\text{subject to} \quad \begin{bmatrix} a_{11} \, a_{12} \, a_{13} \\ a_{21} \, a_{22} \, a_{23} \end{bmatrix} \times \begin{bmatrix} Q_1 \\ Q_2 \\ Q_3 \end{bmatrix} \leq \begin{bmatrix} r_1 \\ r_2 \end{bmatrix}$$

$$Q_1, Q_2, Q_3 \geq 0$$

Matrix notation is just a convenient means for writing large systems of equations. In going from matrix form back to equation form, one just multiplies each row element by each column element. For example, the left side of the first constraint equation is $a_{11} \times Q_1$ plus $a_{12} \times Q_2$ plus $a_{13} \times Q_3$, or $a_{11}Q_1 + a_{12}Q_2 + a_{13}Q_3$, and this sum must be less than or equal to r_1.

Given the expression of the primal program in matrix notation, the four rules for transformation given previously can be used to convert from the primal to the dual. Following these rules, the dual is written as follows:

DUAL PROBLEM

$$\text{Minimize} \quad \pi^* = r_1 V_1 + r_2 V_2$$

$$\text{subject to} \quad \begin{bmatrix} a_{11} \, a_{21} \\ a_{12} \, a_{22} \\ a_{13} \, a_{23} \end{bmatrix} \times \begin{bmatrix} V_1 \\ V_2 \end{bmatrix} \geq \begin{bmatrix} \pi_1 \\ \pi_2 \\ \pi_3 \end{bmatrix}$$

$$V_1, V_2 \geq 0$$

Then, converting from matrix back to equation form gives the following:

$$\text{Minimize} \quad \pi^* = r_1 V_1 + r_2 V_2$$
$$\text{subject to} \quad a_{11} V_1 + a_{21} V_2 \geq \pi_1$$
$$a_{12} V_1 + a_{22} V_2 \geq \pi_2$$
$$a_{13} V_1 + a_{23} V_2 \geq \pi_3$$
$$V_1, V_2 \geq 0$$

Here, V_1 and V_2 are the shadow prices for resources r_1 and r_2, respectively. Because r_1 and r_2 represent the quantities of the two resources available, the objective function measures the total implicit value of the resources available. Recalling the interpretation of a_{11} and a_{21} from the primal, it is obvious that $a_{11}V_1 + a_{21}V_2$ is the total value of inputs used to produce one unit of output Q_1. Similarly, $a_{12}V_1 + a_{22}V_2$ is the total value of inputs used in production of a unit of output Q_2, and $a_{13}V_1 + a_{23}V_2$ is the total value of inputs used in production of a unit of output Q_3.

Finally, the primal and dual linear programming problems can be fully specified through the introduction of slack variables. Remember that with less-than-or-equal-to constraints, the left side of the constraint equation must be brought up to equal the right side. Thus, slack variables must be added to the left side of such constraint equations. With greater-than-or-equal-to constraints, the left side of the constraint equation must be brought down to equal the right side. Thus, slack variables must be *subtracted from* the left side of such constraint equations. With this, the full specification of the preceding primal and dual linear programs can be written as follows:

Primal Problem	**Dual Problem**

Maximize $\quad \pi = \pi_1 Q_1 + \pi_2 Q_2 + \pi_3 Q_3$

subject to

$$a_{11}Q_1 + a_{12}Q_2 + a_{13}Q_3 + S_1 = r_1$$
$$a_{21}Q_1 + a_{22}Q_2 + a_{23}Q_3 + S_2 = r_2$$

$$Q_1, Q_2, Q_3, S_1, S_2 \geq 0$$

Minimize $\quad \pi^* = r_1 V_1 + r_2 V_2$

subject to

$$a_{11}V_1 + a_{21}V_2 - L_1 = \pi_1$$
$$a_{12}V_1 + a_{22}V_2 - L_2 = \pi_2$$
$$a_{13}V_1 + a_{23}V_2 - L_3 = \pi_3$$

$$V_1, V_2, L_1, L_2, L_3 \geq 0$$

where S_1 and S_2 are slack variables representing excess capacity of resources r_1 and r_2, respectively. L_1, L_2 and L_3 are also slack variables; they represent the amount by which the value of resources used in the production of Q_1, Q_2, and Q_3 exceeds the value of output as measured by π_1, π_2 and π_3, respectively. Thus, L_1, L_2 and L_3 measure the opportunity cost, or foregone profit, as a result of producing the last unit of Q_1, Q_2 and Q_3.

Understanding these basic rules simplifies construction of the dual, given a primal program, and facilitates understanding and interpretation of the constraints and coefficients found in both primal and dual linear programming problems.

SELECTED REFERENCES

Allison Oguru, E. A., M. S. Igben, and E. C. Chukwuigwe. "Revenue Maximizing Combination of Crop Enterprises in Bayelsa State of Nigeria: A Linear Programming Application." *Indian Journal of Agricultural Economics* 61, no. 4 (October–December, 2006): 667–676.

Amir, Rabah and Val E. Lambson. "Imperfect Competition, Integer Constraints and Industry Dynamics." *International Journal of Industrial Organization* 25, no. 2 (April, 2007): 261–274.

Bilgen, Bilge and Irem Ozkarahan. "A Mixed-Integer Linear Programming Model for Bulk Grain Blending and Shipping." *International Journal of Production Economics* 107, no. 2 (June, 2007): 555–571.

Bouras, David and Carole R. Engle. "Optimal Size of Fingerling to Understock in Catfish Grow-Out Ponds: An Application of a Multi-Period Integer Programming Model." *Aquaculture Economics and Management* 11, no. 2 (2007): 195–210.

Farmer, Adam, Jeffrey S. Smith, and Luke T. Miller. "Scheduling Umpire Crews for Professional Tennis Tournaments." *Interfaces* 37, no. 2 (March, 2007): 187–196, 205–206.

Horsley, Anthony and Andrew J. Wrobel. "Profit-Maximizing Operation and Valuation of Hydroelectric Plant: A New Solution to the Koopmans Problem." *Journal of Economic Dynamics and Control* 31, no. 3 (March, 2007): 938–970.

LeBlanc, Larry J. and Michael R Galbreth. "Implementing Large-Scale Optimization Models in Excel Using VBA." *Interfaces* 37, no. 4 (July, 2007): 370–382, 396.

Lev, Benjamin. "Branch-and-Bound Applications in Combinatorial Data Analysis." *Interfaces* 37, no. 1 (January, 2007): 83–85.

Lev, Benjamin. "Linear and Nonlinear Programming." *Interfaces* 37, no. 1 (January, 2007): 85–86.

Lev, Benjamin. "Introduction to Computational Optimization Models for Production Planning in a Supply Chain." *Interfaces* 37, no. 2 (March, 2007): 202–204.

Lia, Jai K., Jo Mina, Toshitsugu Otakeb, and Timothy Van Voorhisc. "Inventory and Investment in Setup and Quality Operations Under Return on Investment Maximization." *European Journal of Operations Research* 185, no. 2 (March 2008): 593–605.

Loveland, Jennifer L., Susan K. Monkman, and Douglas J. Morrice. "Dell Uses a New Production-Scheduling

Algorithm to Accommodate Increased Product Variety." *Interfaces* 37, no. 3 (May, 2007): 209–219, 305–306.

Osorio, Maria A., Nalan Gulpinar, and Berc Rustem. "A Mixed Integer Programming Model for Multistage Mean–Variance Post-Tax Optimization," *European Journal of Operations Research* 185, no. 2 (March 2008): 451–480.

Rathi, Sarika. "Optimization Model for Integrated Municipal Solid Waste Management in Mumbai, India." *Environment and Development Economics* 12, no. 1 (February, 2007): 105–121.

Zilinskas, A. "Linear Optimization Problems with Inexact Data." *Interfaces* 37, no. 3 (May, 2007): 301–302.

Competitive Markets

Grocery retailing is viciously competitive. Years ago, the neighborhood grocery store gave way to the large, modern supermarket with wide aisles, attractive displays, and a large selection of grocery and related items. Vigorous competition in the industry has kept prices down, and led to a continuing series of cost-reducing innovations. In the best of times, innovative and efficient grocery retailers have to struggle to maintain profit margins as low as 1 percent to 2 percent of sales.

One of the most significant competitive threats to the grocery retailing industry is posed by the growth of discount retailing juggernaut Wal-Mart Stores, Inc. Wal-Mart is taking an increasing share of the grocery retailing dollar in most major markets. Continued expansion threatens traditional grocery retailers across the United States. However, the growth of Wal-Mart is not the only reason for increasing competitive pressure on the traditional food operators. Warehouse clubs, dollar stores, and other non-traditional players, like both premium and lower-priced grocery chains, continue to divide the grocery retailing market long dominated by traditional supermarkets. Consumers want to save time and stretch their shopping dollar by concentrating their shopping activity on whole-line and specialty retailers that are able to provide a consistently satisfying shopping experience. In a sense, just as supermarkets made the neighborhood store obsolete, new-age retailers able to better satisfy customer needs are making the supermarket obsolete.[1]

This chapter documents the performance characteristics of competitive markets, and shows how the supply of goods and services is determined by competitive firms and industries.

COMPETITIVE ENVIRONMENT

Successful competitors understand and help shape the competitive atmosphere.

What Is Market Structure?

Market
Firms and individuals willing and able to buy or sell a given product.

Market Structure
The competitive environment.

A **market** consists of all firms and individuals willing and able to buy or sell a particular product at a given time and place. This includes individuals and firms currently engaged in buying and selling a particular product, as well as potential entrants. **Market structure** describes the competitive environment in the market for any good or service. Market structure is typically characterized on the basis of four important industry characteristics:

---

1   See Gary McWilliams and James Covert, "Wal-Mart's Strategy Spurs a Selloff," *The Wall Street Journal Online*, October 24, 2007, http://online.wsj.com.

the number and size distribution of active buyers and sellers and potential entrants, the degree to which products are similar or dissimilar, the amount and cost of information about product price and quality, and conditions of entry and exit.

Effects of market structure are measured in terms of the prices paid by consumers, availability and quality of output, employment and career advancement opportunities, and the pace of product innovation, among other factors. Generally speaking, the greater the number of market participants, the more vigorous is price and product quality competition. The more even the balance of power between sellers and buyers, the more likely it is that the competitive process will yield maximum benefits. However, a close link between the numbers of market participants and the vigor of price competition does not always hold true. For example, there are literally thousands of producers in most major milk markets. Price competition is nonexistent, however, given an industry cartel that is sustained by a federal program of milk price supports. Nevertheless, there are few barriers to entry, and individual milk producers struggle to earn a normal return. In contrast, price competition can be spirited in aircraft manufacturing, newspaper, Internet access, long-distance telephone service, and other markets with as few as two competitors. This is particularly true when market participants are constrained by the viable threat of potential entrants.

Vital Role of Potential Entrants

Potential Entrant
Person or firm posing a sufficiently credible threat of market entry to affect market price–output decisions.

A **potential entrant** is an individual or firm posing a sufficiently credible threat of market entry to affect the price–output decisions of incumbent firms. Potential entrants play extremely important roles in many industries. Some industries with only a few active participants might at first appear to hold the potential for substantial economic profits. However, a number of potential entrants can have a substantial effect on the price–output decisions of incumbent firms.

For example, Dell, HP-Compaq, Gateway, Apple, and other leading computer manufacturers are viable potential entrants into the computer component manufacturing industry. These companies use their threat of potential entry to obtain favorable prices from suppliers of microprocessors, monitors, and peripheral equipment. Despite having only a relative handful of active foreign and domestic participants, computer components manufacturing is both highly innovative and vigorously price competitive. In the same way, suppliers can also become effective potential entrants for the end user market. In the personal computer industry, Intel is a credible potential entrant. Few computer users would be reluctant to buy a personal computer bearing the Intel brand name. The mere threat of entry by potential entrants is sometimes enough to keep industry prices and profits in check and to maintain a high level of productive efficiency.

FACTORS THAT SHAPE THE COMPETITIVE ENVIRONMENT

The number and relative size of buyers and sellers is determined by the extent to which products are standardized, and by both entry and exit conditions.

Product Differentiation
Real or perceived differences in the quality of goods and services.

Product Differentiation

Real or perceived differences in the quality of goods and services offered to consumers lead to **product differentiation.** Sources of product differentiation include physical

Managerial Application 10.1

Benefits From Free Trade

Free trade is getting a bad rap. Critics contend that offshoring jobs and inexpensive imports are hurting low-skilled workers in the United States and Europe. In fact, the voluntary exchange of goods and services across national boundaries increases the well-being of everyone by promoting economic efficiency. Free trade gives firms and workers access to global markets, allowing them to increase output and lower average costs. Foreign competition forces domestic producers to lower prices, and imported goods and services provide consumers with greater choice. A liberal trade environment also provides a better climate for investment and innovation, thus raising the rate of economic growth.

The rapid recent increase in world trade is, in part, the result of the General Agreement on Tariffs and Trade (GATT), which was created after World War II to reduce import taxes and remove other barriers to international trade. Expanding opportunities for international trade have effects similar to those of technological improvements: For the same amount of input, more output will be produced. For several decades,

the United States has pursued trade liberalization through negotiations at the global, regional, and bilateral levels. The broadest and most important global forum for trade liberalization is the 148-member World Trade Organization (WTO). The WTO requires that the lowest tariffs offered to one WTO member must be offered to all members. This treatment, known as most-favored-nation (MFN) status, creates a level playing field of equal tariffs and trade concessions among member countries. While the WTO does not serve as a legislative body, it provides a valuable forum for trade negotiations as member countries pursue the goal of trade liberalization.

In addition to economic betterment, free trade promotes world peace. Notice how people from the United States and Canada enjoy a close friendship? They are also big trade partners.

See: Greg Hitt, "A Suggested Salve to Free-Trade Anxiety," *The Wall Street Journal Online*, October 15, 2007, http://online.wsj.com/.

differences, such as those due to superior research and development, plus any perceived differences due to effective advertising and promotion. Price competition tends to be most vigorous for homogenous products with few actual or perceived differences. The availability and cost of information about prices and output quality is another important determinant of the degree of competition. Competition is always most vigorous when buyers and sellers have easy access to detailed price–product performance information.

The availability of good substitutes increases the degree of competition. To illustrate, air passenger and cargo service between mid-size cities is often supplied by only a few airlines. Transportation service is available from several sources, however, and air carriers must compete effectively with autos, barges, bus lines, truck companies, and railroads. The substitutability of these modes of transportation for airline service increases the degree of competition in the transportation service market.

It is important to realize that market structures are not static. In the 1800s and early 1900s—before the introduction of trucks, buses, automobiles, and airplanes—railroads faced very little competition. Railroads could charge excessive prices and earn monopoly profits. Because of this exploitation, laws were passed giving public authorities permission to regulate railroad prices. Over the years, such regulation became superfluous given the rise of intermodal competition. Other firms were enticed by railroad profits to develop competing transportation service systems, which ultimately led to a much more **competitive market** structure. Today, few would argue that railroads retain significant monopoly power, and public regulation of the railroads has been greatly reduced.

Competitive Markets

Markets characterized by vigorous rivalry among competitors offering essentially the same product.

Production Methods

When minimum efficient scale is large in relation to overall industry output, only a few firms are able to attain the output size necessary for productive efficiency. In such instances, competitive pressures may allow only a few firms to survive. On the other hand, when minimum efficient scale is small in relation to overall industry output, many firms are able to attain the size necessary for efficient operation. Holding all else equal, competition tends to be most vigorous when many efficient competitors are present in the market. This is especially true when firms of smaller-than-minimum-efficient scale face considerably higher production costs, and when the construction of minimum-efficient-scale plants involves the commitment of substantial capital, skilled labor, and material resources. When construction of minimum-efficient-scale plants requires the commitment of only modest resources or when smaller firms face no important production cost disadvantages, economies of scale have little or no effect on the competitive potential of new or entrant firms.

Important physical characteristics of products can influence the degree of competition. A low ratio of distribution cost to total cost, for example, tends to increase competition by widening the geographic area over which any particular producer can compete. Rapidly perishable products have the opposite effect. In considering the level of competition for a product, the national, regional, or local nature of the market must be considered.

Entry and Exit Conditions

Barrier to Entry

Any factor or industry characteristic that creates an advantage for incumbents over new arrivals.

Barrier to Mobility

Any factor or industry characteristic that creates an advantage for large leading firms over smaller nonleading rivals.

Unwarranted above-normal profits can only exist in long-run equilibrium when substantial barriers to entry or exit are present. Similarly, customers will only tolerate persistently inefficient production methods when such barriers preclude more efficient competitors. A **barrier to entry** is any factor or industry characteristic that creates an advantage for incumbents over new arrivals. Legal rights such as patents and local, state, or federal licenses can present formidable barriers to entry in pharmaceuticals, cable television, television and radio broadcasting, and other industries. A **barrier to mobility** is any factor or industry characteristic that creates an advantage for large leading firms over smaller nonleading rivals. Factors that sometimes create barriers to entry and/or mobility include substantial economies of scale, scope economies, large capital or skilled-labor requirements, and ties of customer loyalty created through advertising and other means.

It is worth keeping in mind that barriers to entry and mobility can sometimes result in compensating advantages for consumers. Even though patents can lead to monopoly profits for inventing firms, they also spur valuable new product and process development. Although efficient and innovative leading firms make life difficult for smaller rivals, they can have the favorable effect of lowering prices and increasing product quality. Therefore, a complete evaluation of the economic effects of entry barriers involves a consideration of both costs and benefits realized by suppliers and customers.

Barrier to Exit

Any restriction on the ability of incumbents to redeploy assets from one industry or line of business to another.

Whereas barriers to entry can impede competition by making entry or nonleading firm growth difficult, competitive forces can also be diminished through barriers to exit. A **barrier to exit** is any restriction on the ability of incumbents to redeploy assets from one industry or line of business to another. During the late 1980s, for example, several state governments initiated legal proceedings to impede plant closures by large employers in the steel, glass, automobile, and other industries. By imposing large fines or severance taxes or requiring substantial expenditures for worker retraining, they created significant barriers to exit.

By impeding the asset redeployment that is typical of any vigorous competitive environment, barriers to exit can dramatically increase both the costs and risks of doing business. Even though one can certainly sympathize with the difficult adjustments faced by both workers and firms affected by plant closures, government actions that create barriers to exit can have the unintended effect of retarding industrial development.

COMPETITIVE MARKET CHARACTERISTICS

Special qualities of competitive markets illustrate why perfect competition is desirable from a social perspective.

Basic Features

Perfect Competition
Market characterized by a large number of buyers and sellers of a homogeneous product.

Perfect competition is a market structure characterized by a large number of buyers and sellers of essentially the same product. Each market participant is too small to influence market prices. Individual buyers and sellers are **price takers.** Customers and firms take market prices as given and devise their buying and selling strategies accordingly. Free and complete demand and supply information is available in a perfectly competitive market, and there are no meaningful barriers to entry and exit. As a result, vigorous price competition prevails. Only a normal rate of return on investment is possible in the long run. Economic profits are possible only during periods of short-run disequilibrium before rivals mount an effective competitive response.

Price Takers
Buyers and sellers that accept market prices as given and devise their buying and selling strategies accordingly.

Because perfect competition exists when individual producers have no influence on market prices, they are price takers as opposed to price makers. This lack of influence on price typically requires

- *Large numbers of buyers and sellers.* Each firm produces a small portion of industry output, and each customer buys only a small part of the total.
- *Product homogeneity.* The output of each firm is essentially the same as the output of any other firm in the industry.
- *Free entry and exit.* Firms are not restricted from entering or leaving the industry.
- *Perfect dissemination of information.* Cost, price, and product quality information is known by all buyers and all sellers.
- *Opportunity for normal profits in long-run equilibrium.* Ruthless price competition keeps $P = MC$ and $P = AR = AC$.

These basic conditions are too restrictive for perfect competition to be universal, but ready examples of perfectly competitive markets are available.

Examples of Competitive Markets

Many big agricultural product markets, the unskilled labor market, and much of retailing can be described as vigorously competitive, if not perfectly competitive. In the agricultural egg market, for example, each egg farmer produces eggs that are essentially identical to those offered by any other egg farmer. Similarly, each egg buyer purchases a small portion of aggregate production and there is no potential for buyers to receive a cut rate, or volume discount. Because both sellers and buyers are able to trade as many eggs as they want at the going price, both are price takers and the egg market is said to be perfectly competitive.

While there is a natural tendency to focus on consumer and business markets for final demand, it is important to remember that many prominent markets for intermediate goods and services are perfectly competitive. The unskilled labor market in many medium-sized to large cities fits this description because unskilled workers often have a ready market for their services at the going wage rate. Manufacturers also face vigorously competitive markets for many raw materials used in production, and for the energy used to heat buildings and power production facilities.

Many consumers enjoy shopping at discount retailers that offer a wide range of name-brand goods at razor-thin margins. As a result, manufacturers of distinctive products like Charmin, Tide, and Gillette may enjoy enviable profit margins, but retailers like Wal-Mart, Target, and Kohl's fight for market share with minuscule profit margins. Discount retailing is ruthlessly competitive. The restaurant business is also vigorously competitive. The restaurant business is one of the largest and most competitive businesses in the United States. According to industry statistics, the nation's 900,000 restaurants bring in roughly $450 billion in annual sales, an average of roughly $500,000 per year. There is a restaurant for every 300 people in the United States. With easy entry and exit, lots of buyers and sellers, good information, and standard food quality, it is next to impossible to make above-normal profits in many segments of the restaurant business.

Perhaps the stock market approaches the perfectly competitive ideal, but imperfections occur even there. For example, the acquisition or sale of large blocks of securities by institutional investors clearly affects prices, at least in the short run. Nevertheless,

Managerial Application 10.2

Is the Stock Market Perfectly Competitive?

The New York Stock Exchange (NYSE) is the largest organized U.S. securities market. Established in 1817, the NYSE is the primary marketplace for the common and preferred stocks of roughly 2,750 large and medium-size companies. The NYSE enjoys near-monopoly status by virtue of the fact that NYSE trading accounts for roughly 80 percent of the composite volume in listed company shares. The remainder is off-the-floor electronic trading by institutions and trading on eight smaller regional exchanges.

The National Association of Securities Dealers Automated Quotations service, or Nasdaq for short, is an electronic trading system for thousands of unlisted companies whose shares are traded on a negotiated basis among hundreds of brokers and dealers. Nasdaq's National Market System covers roughly 3,000 companies; Nasdaq Small Cap Issues include another 800 smaller companies. (More than 10,000 inactively traded stocks are listed in the "pink sheets.")

The Nasdaq multiple dealer market is designed to produce narrow bid-ask spreads through dealer competition. However, a lack of competition was suggested in a *Journal of Finance* article titled "Why Do Nasdaq Market Makers Avoid Odd Eighth Quotes?" by professors William G. Christie and Paul Schultz. They found that dealer bid-ask spreads for a large number of Nasdaq stocks were often at least 25¢, or twice the 1/8 (12.5¢) minimum, and raised the question of whether Nasdaq dealers implicitly colluded to maintain wide spreads. A federal lawsuit was brought alleging that 37 securities firms had indeed conspired to fix prices on the Nasdaq stock market by setting inside spreads. A settlement was reached in the Nasdaq price-fixing lawsuit, with Wall Street firms including Merrill Lynch & Co. and Citigroup's Salomon Smith Barney paying a record $1.03 billion settlement.

Artificially high trading costs are symptomatic of a less than perfectly competitive market. Therefore, even in the stock market, a market widely recognized as *almost* perfectly competitive, elements of inefficiency and monopoly pricing are sometimes present. *Caveat emptor!*

See: Luke Jeffs, "Swiss Exchange Reduces Costs as Trading Wanes," *The Wall Street Journal Online*, October 17, 2007, http://online.wsj.com/.

because up to 1,000 shares of any stock can be bought or sold at the current market price, the stock market approaches the ideal of a perfectly competitive market. Similarly, many firms make output decisions without any control over price, and examination of a perfectly competitive market structure provides insights into these operating decisions. A clear understanding of perfect competition also provides a reference point from which to analyze less vigorously competitive markets.

PROFIT MAXIMIZATION IN COMPETITIVE MARKETS

Cheaper, better, and faster is the mantra of the successful competitor.

Profit Maximization Imperative

In the dog-eat-dog world of competitive markets, resource-constrained competitors must skillfully produce the goods and services consumers want. Profit maximization and the efficiency it requires are necessary for long-term survival. Profit maximization always requires that a firm operate at the output level at which marginal revenue and marginal cost are equal. In competitive markets, firms are price takers. Their individual production decisions have no effect on market prices. At the present market price, they can sell as much output as they care to produce. With price constant, average revenue equals marginal revenue. Maximum profits result when market price is set equal to marginal cost for firms in a perfectly competitive industry.

Table 10.1 illustrates the process of profit maximization for CSI International, Ltd., an active competitor in a vigorously competitive industry. In this example, CSI is a price taker; the company's production decisions have no effect on the market price of $25. With stable prices, the market price is also equal to marginal revenue, $P = MR = \$25$. Fixed costs of $311,250 reflect financing costs, salaries, lease payments, and other overhead expenses incurred irrespective of the specific level of production. A **normal profit,** defined as the rate of return necessary to attract and retain capital investment, is included as part of the financing costs included in total costs. Therefore, the profit shown in Figure 10.1 is defined as **economic profit** and represents an above-normal rate of return. The firm incurs **economic losses** whenever it fails to earn a normal profit. In general, a firm might show a small accounting profit but be suffering economic losses because these profits are insufficient to provide an adequate return to the firm's stockholders. In such instances, firms are unable to replace plant and equipment and will exit the industry in the long run. Variable costs depend upon the amount produced, and total costs are simply fixed plus variable expenses. Average variable cost and average total cost are simply those cost categories divided by the total amount produced.

Notice that total profit is simply the difference between total revenues and total costs. To find the point of maximum profit, one need only scan down the profit column to find maximum total profits of $138,750 at 50,000 units of output.

Normal Profit
Rate of return necessary to attract and retain capital.

Economic Profit
An above-normal rate of return.

Economic Losses
Realized profits that are insufficient to attract and retain capital investment.

Role of Marginal Analysis

Marginal Analysis
Study of changes caused by economic decisions.

Discovering the point of optimal production is made easier with **marginal analysis.** Notice from Table 10.1 that total profit is maximized when the difference between marginal revenue and marginal cost, called marginal profit, equals zero. In general, profits are maximized when

Table 10.1 Competitive Firm Profits Are Maximized When Marginal Revenue Equals Marginal Cost

Units (1)	Price (2)	Total Revenue (3) = (1) × (2)	Fixed Cost (3)	Variable Costs (4)	Average Variable Cost (5) = (4)/(1)	Total Cost (6) = (3) + (4)	Average Total Cost (7) = (6)/(1)	Total Profit (TR − TC) (8) = (3) − (6)	Marginal Revenue (9) = $\partial TR/\partial Q$	Marginal Cost (10) = $\partial TC/\partial Q$	Marginal Profit (MR − MC) (11) = (9) − (10)
0	25	0	311,250	50,000		361,250		−361,250	25	5	20
5,000	25	125,000	311,250	80,000	16.00	391,250	78.25	−266,250	25	7	18
10,000	25	250,000	311,250	120,000	12.00	431,250	43.13	−181,250	25	9	16
15,000	25	375,000	311,250	170,000	11.33	481,250	32.08	−106,250	25	11	14
20,000	25	500,000	311,250	230,000	11.50	541,250	27.06	−41,250	25	13	12
25,000	25	625,000	311,250	300,000	12.00	611,250	24.45	13,750	25	15	10
30,000	25	750,000	311,250	380,000	12.67	691,250	23.04	58,750	25	17	8
35,000	25	875,000	311,250	470,000	13.43	781,250	22.32	93,750	25	19	6
40,000	25	1,000,000	311,250	570,000	14.25	881,250	22.03	118,750	25	21	4
45,000	25	1,125,000	311,250	680,000	15.11	991,250	22.03	133,750	25	23	2
50,000	25	1,250,000	311,250	800,000	16.00	1,111,250	22.23	138,750	25	25	0
55,000	25	1,375,000	311,250	930,000	16.91	1,241,250	22.57	133,750	25	27	−2
60,000	25	1,500,000	311,250	1,070,000	17.83	1,381,250	23.02	118,750	25	29	−4
65,000	25	1,625,000	311,250	1,220,000	18.77	1,531,250	23.56	93,750	25	31	−6
70,000	25	1,750,000	311,250	1,380,000	19.71	1,691,250	24.16	58,750	25	33	−8
75,000	25	1,875,000	311,250	1,550,000	20.67	1,861,250	24.82	13,750	25	35	−10
80,000	25	2,000,000	311,250	1,730,000	21.63	2,041,250	25.52	−41,250	25	37	−12

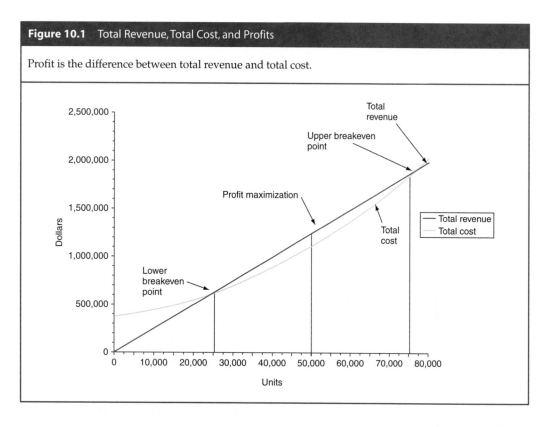

Figure 10.1 Total Revenue, Total Cost, and Profits

Profit is the difference between total revenue and total cost.

$$M\pi = MR - MC = 0 \qquad \textbf{10.1}$$

Because this point of profit maximization occurs where marginal revenue is set equal to marginal cost, an equivalent expression that must be met for profit maximization is that

$$MR = MC \qquad \textbf{10.2}$$

What is unique about the perfectly competitive market setting is that all firms are price takers. In this vigorously competitive market setting, profit maximization occurs when

$$P = MR = MC \qquad \textbf{10.3}$$

An added condition for profit maximization, sometimes referred to as a second-order condition, is that total profits must always be decreasing beyond the point where $MR = MC$.[2] Figure 10.2 illustrates this point. In the CSI example, $P = MR = MC = \$25$ at 50,000 units of output. From 0 to 50,000 units of output, marginal profit is positive because $MR > MC$, and total profit increases with additional production. For output levels in excess of 50,000 units, marginal profit is negative because $MR < MC$, and total profit falls with additional production. Profits are only maximized at 50,000 units of production where $M\pi = 0$ and $P = MR = MC$. As shown in Figure 10.2, at 50,000 units of output, $ATC = \$22.225$ and economic profit per unit is

---

2 Total profit is simply the difference between total revenue and total cost, or $\pi = TR - TC$. Using calculus notation, at the profit-maximizing point, marginal profit equals zero, or $\partial\pi/\partial Q = \partial TR/\partial Q - \partial TC/\partial Q = 0$. The first-order condition for profit maximization is simply that $\partial\pi/\partial Q = 0$. The second-order condition for profit maximization is that total profit be decreasing beyond this point, or $\partial^2\pi/\partial Q^2 < 0$.

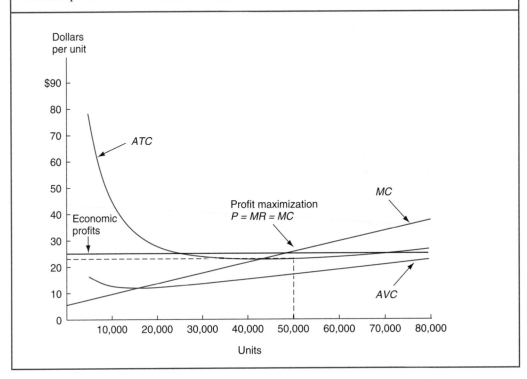

Figure 10.2   Competitive Firm Profits Are Maximized When Marginal Revenue Equals Marginal Cost

Profits are always maximized where $MR = MC$, In competitive markets, firms are price takers so maximum profits occur where $P = MR = MC$.

$2.775, where $\pi = (P - ATC) \times Q$. Total economic profits of $138,750 are earned at this activity level, $\pi = (\$25 - \$22.225) \times 50,000$. At 50,000 units of output, all profitable units are being produced and sold. No unprofitable production is offered.

Note that profits are always maximized where $M\pi = 0$ and $MR = MC$. What is unique about the competitive market setting is that, given competitive firms are price takers, the optimal production point occurs where $M\pi = 0$ and $P = MR = MC$.

The role of marginal analysis in competitive firm profit maximization can be further illustrated by considering the analytic solution to the CSI profit maximization problem. Assume that the firm's operating expenses are typical of 100 competitors in the relevant market and can be expressed by the following total and marginal cost functions:

$$TC = \$361,250 + \$5Q + \$0.0002Q^2$$
$$MC = \partial TC / \partial Q = \$5 + \$0.0004Q$$

where TC is total cost per year including capital costs, MC is marginal cost, and Q is the amount produced. Remember, in a competitive market firms are price takers and $P = MR = \$25$.

The optimal price–output combination can be determined by setting marginal revenue equal to marginal cost and solving for Q:

$$MR = MC$$
$$\$25 = \$5 + \$0.0004Q$$

$$\$0.0004Q = \$20$$
$$Q = 50,000$$

At this output level, maximum economic profits are

$$
\begin{aligned}
\pi &= TR - TC \\
&= \$25Q - \$361,250 - \$5Q - \$0.0002Q^2 \\
&= \$25(50,000) - \$361,250 - \$5(50,000) - \$0.0002(50,000^2) \\
&= \$138,750
\end{aligned}
$$

In the short run, the competitive firm will choose to produce $Q = 50,000$ units of output, and generate short-run economic profits of $138,750. The firm is able to obtain more than a normal or risk-adjusted rate of return on investment because capital costs are already included in the cost function. If there were 100 identical firms in the industry, industry output would total 5 million units per year.

In the long run, economic profits attract entry in competitive markets. Thus, the economic profits described in this short-run competitive market equilibrium will tend to dissipate over time. In long-run equilibrium, competitive markets are characterized by normal profits that neither entice new entrants nor cause bankruptcy and exit.

MARGINAL COST AND FIRM SUPPLY

Firms use marginal analysis to indicate the amount supplied under various market conditions.

Short-Run Firm Supply Curve

Competitive Firm Short-Run Supply Curve
The marginal cost curve, so long as $P > AVC$.

Firms use marginal analysis to determine the amount they wish to supply at various market prices. This output schedule is called the **competitive firm short-run supply curve.** Consider the cost curves in Figure 10.3. These cost curves have basic features common to most firms. The marginal cost curve (MC) is upward sloping, and the average total cost (ATC) curve is U-shaped. The ATC curve tends to fall as fixed costs are spread over increasing amounts of production, but then begin to rise due to rising marginal costs. Notice that ATC is falling so long as $MC < ATC$, and that ATC is rising where $MC > ATC$.

In Table 10.1, it is clear that the point of minimum ATC is reached in the output range between 40,000 and 45,000. The point of minimum ATC occurs where $Q = 42,500$ and $ATC = \$22$, and is found by setting $MC = ATC$ and solving for Q:

$$MC = ATC$$

$$\$5 + \$0.0004Q = \frac{\$361,250 + \$5Q + \$0.0002Q^2}{Q}$$

$$5 + 0.0004Q = \frac{361,250}{Q} + 5 + 0.0002Q$$

$$0.0002Q = \frac{361,250}{Q}$$

$$Q^2 = \frac{361,250}{0.0002}$$

$$Q = \sqrt{1,806,250,000}$$

$$Q = 42,500$$

Figure 10.3   Competitive Firm Supply Curve

(a) The Short-Run Firm Supply Curve Follows *MC* Curve if *MC* > *AVC* (b) The Long-Run Firm Supply Curve Follows *MC* Curve if *MC* > *ATC*.

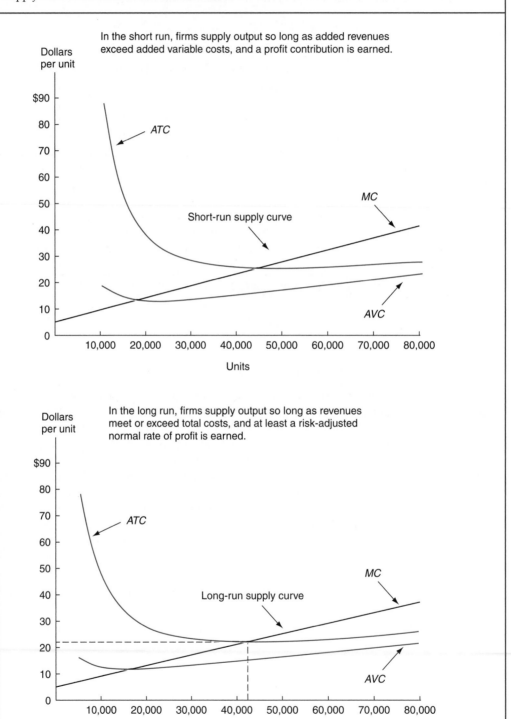

Similarly, in Table 10.1 it is clear that the point of minimum AVC is reached in the output range between 15,000 and 20,000, where $TVC = \$50{,}000 + \$5Q + \$0.0002Q^2$. The minimum point on the AVC occurs at $Q = 15{,}811$ and $AVC = \$11.32$, and is found by setting $MC = AVC$ and solving for Q:

$$MC = AVC$$

$$\$5 + \$0.0004Q = \frac{\$50{,}000 + \$5Q + \$0.0002Q^2}{Q}$$

$$5 + 0.0004Q = \frac{50{,}000}{Q} + 5 + 0.0002Q$$

$$0.0002Q = \frac{50{,}000}{Q}$$

$$Q^2 = 250{,}000{,}000$$

$$Q = 15{,}811$$

In Figure 10.2, the competitive market price (P) is shown as a horizontal line because competitive firms are price takers and, hence, $P = MR$. When the same price is charged to all customers, the market price is always equal to revenue per unit, or average revenue (AR). Thus, it is worth remembering that only in competitive markets is it true that $P = AR = MR = MC$ at the profit-maximizing activity level. For any given price, the competitive firm's profit-maximizing quantity of output is found by looking at the intersection of the horizontal demand curve with the upward sloping marginal cost curve. Because the firm's marginal cost curve shows the amount of output the firm would be willing to supply at any market price, *the marginal cost curve is the competitive firm's short-run supply curve so long as $P > AVC$* [see Figure 10.3(a)].

To understand the role of average variable costs in the firm's short-run decision to supply output, one must reflect on the firm's option to shut down and not produce anything at all. In the short run, the marginal cost curve is the competitive firm's supply curve so long as production at that level is more profitable, or causes lower operating losses, than ceasing production all together. If no output is produced, variable costs equal zero and only fixed costs are incurred. With no production, sales revenues equal zero and the firm experiences operating losses equal in amount to fixed costs. In fact, fixed costs represent the largest operating loss firms are willing to bear. If $P < AVC$, losses increase with the total amount produced and competitive firms would shut down and produce nothing rather than incur higher operating losses. If $P > AVC$, the firm's operating losses will decrease as output expands and firms will proceed to offer supply at the profit-maximizing, or loss-minimizing, point where $P = MR = MC$. This explains why the marginal cost curve is the competitive firm's short-run supply curve, but only so long as $P > AVC$.

Long-Run Firm Supply Curve

To ensure long-term viability, the competitive firm must cover all necessary costs of production and earn a profit sufficient to provide an adequate rate of return to the firm's stockholders. Without revenues sufficient to cover wages and other necessary costs of production, firms cannot continue to operate. This is plainly obvious. However, it is equally necessary that revenues be sufficient to provide stockholders with a normal profit. Without such normal profits, firms are unable to replace plant and equipment and will exit the industry in the long run.

In the short run, if $P > AVC$, the firm's operating losses will decrease as output expands and firms will proceed to offer supply at the profit-maximizing, or loss-minimizing, point where $P = MR = MC$. If $P < ATC$, revenues fail to cover necessary fixed costs, including a fair rate of return on investment. No firm can continue to operate indefinitely without paying necessary fixed costs and a normal profit. Eventually, machines and factories wear out and must be replaced. Leases expire and have to be renegotiated. In the long run, even cost categories that are traditionally regarded as fixed become variable. There are no fixed costs in the long run because firms can decide to exit the business.

Competitive Firm Long-Run Supply Curve
The marginal cost curve, so long as $P > ATC$.

Given the need to cover all fixed costs and earn a fair rate of return, *the marginal cost curve is the competitive firm's long-run supply curve so long as $P > ATC$* [see Figure 10.3(b)]. This is called the **competitive firm long-run supply curve.** So long as $P > ATC$, revenues are sufficient to cover all necessary fixed and variable costs of production, including a normal profit. When $P > ATC$, the long-run profit-maximizing activity level for competitive firms is found where $P = MR = MC$.

COMPETITIVE MARKET SUPPLY CURVE

Short-run market supply is the total amount offered by all competitors. In the long run, entry and exit cause supply to be perfectly elastic at the market price.

Managerial Application 10.3

Dot.com

With all the hoopla, it is tough to sort out what's real and what's Internet hype. For companies, building a publishing-only Web site is the first step to becoming an e-business. Most businesses have already done this. That's fine as far as it goes; it's an extremely cost-efficient way to distribute basic information. However, the payoff for business starts with "self-service" Web sites, where customers can do things like check the status of an account or trace a package online (like at FedEX). The real payoff begins with transaction-based Web sites that go beyond just buying and selling to create a dynamic and interactive flow of information.

An e-business is created when companies put their core processes online to improve service, cut costs or boost revenue. For example, IBM helped Charles Schwab Web enable their brokerage systems for online trading and customer service. Since opening, Schwab's Web service has generated over 1 million online accounts totaling over $50 billion in assets. E-business economics are compelling. According to management consultants, traditional bank transactions cost more than a dollar; the same transaction over the Web costs about 1¢. Issuing a paper airline ticket costs about $8; an e-ticket costs just $1. Customers love the convenience; management loves the lower costs.

While a number of companies use the Web to further exploit long-standing competitive advantages, it is not clear that companies can use the Web to *create* durable competitive advantages. Hoping to stand out from the crowd, some Internet merchants devote as much as 70 percent of total revenues to advertising. "Get ahead and stay ahead" is the mantra at Amazon.com, a company trying to create a durable online marketing presence in books, electronics, computers, toys and games, health and beauty aids, DVDs, and much more. To date, Amazon.com has proven adept at quickly growing online revenues. It's a widely recognized online leader. However, even for Amazon.com, building a distinctive presence on the Internet and online profits has proven elusive.

See: Mylene Mangalindan, "Amazon's Latest Thriller: Growth," *The Wall Street Journal Online*, October 24, 2007, http://online.wsj.com/.

Market Supply with a Fixed Number of Competitors

In the short run, the amount supplied in a competitive market is simply the sum of output produced by all established competitors. Consider a market comprised of 1,000 firms with costs identical to CSI, the firm described in Table 10.1. In that case, recall that the individual firm supply curve can be written

$$P = MC = \$5 + \$0.0004Q$$

The amount of firm supply at various market prices can be calculated when quantity is expressed as a function of price as

$$Q_F = -12{,}500 + 2{,}500P \qquad \text{(Firm supply)}$$

For any given market price, each firm will supply the amount of output necessary to equate marginal cost to the market price, as shown in Figure 10.4(a). So long as the market price exceeds average variable cost, each firm's marginal cost curve is its supply curve.

The market supply curve is derived by simply adding up the quantities supplied by all competitors. If the competitive market is comprised of 1,000 firms with identical marginal costs, market supply at every market price will total 1,000 times the quantity supplied by a single firm.

$$\begin{aligned} Q_M &= (-12{,}500 + 2{,}500P) \times 1{,}000 \\ &= -12{,}500{,}000 + 2{,}500{,}000P \qquad \text{(Market supply)} \end{aligned}$$

As shown in Figure 10.4(b), 1,000 identical competitors will supply 1,000 times the quantity supplied by a single firm.

Market Supply with Entry and Exit

In the long run, markets are dynamic rather than static. If established competitors earn above-average rates of return, new firms will have a strong incentive to enter the industry. Entry expands the number of firms in the industry, increases the quantity of goods and services supplied, shifts the supply curve rightward, and drives down prices and profits. On the other hand, if sluggish demand results in less than a normal profit for some competitors, plant and equipment will not be replaced as needed, and some firms will exit the industry. Exit reduces the number of firms in the industry, decreases the quantity of goods and services supplied, shifts the supply curve leftward, and allows prices and profits to rise for remaining competitors.

The ebb and flow of entry and exit continues until the resulting market price is just sufficient to provide enough revenues to cover necessary production costs and a normal profit. In the long run, the process of entry and exit continues until remaining competitors earn zero economic profit. Because average total costs include an allowance for normal profits, zero economic profits will only be earned when the market price equals average total cost.

Recall that because competitive firms are price takers, $P = AR = MR$ in competitive markets. At the same time, profit maximization requires that $MR = MC$. The zero economic profit condition requires that $AR = ATC$. This means that entry and exit in competitive markets will continue until such time that $P = AR = MR = MC = ATC$. As shown in

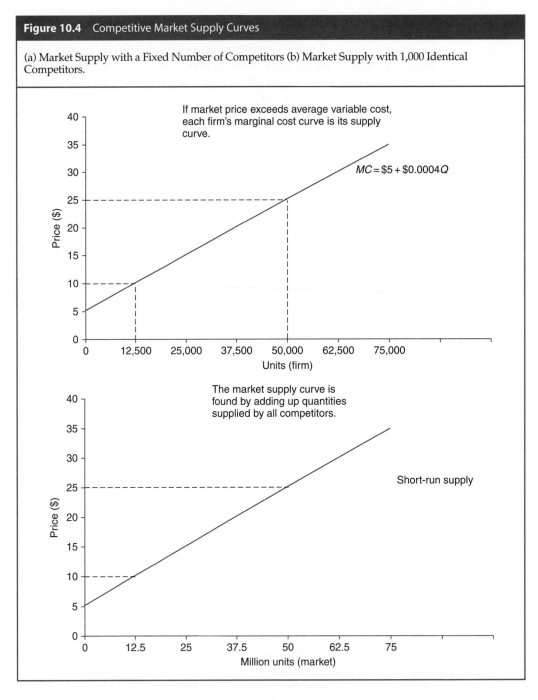

Figure 10.4 Competitive Market Supply Curves

(a) Market Supply with a Fixed Number of Competitors (b) Market Supply with 1,000 Identical Competitors.

Figure 10.5(a), the zero economic profit result from competitive market entry and exit causes the market price to equal the minimum point on each firm's *ATC* curve. The long-run competitive market supply curve is a horizontal line equal to the market price [see Figure 10.5(b)]. Any price above this point would generate profit, induce entry, and increase the total quantity supplied. Any price below this point would create losses, induce exit, and decrease the total quantity supplied. With entry and exit, the competitive market price adjusts so as to equal minimum *ATC*, and there are sufficient firms to satisfy market demand at this price.

Figure 10.5 Competitive Market Supply with Entry and Exit

(a) Competitive Firm's Supply Output at Minimum *ATC* (b) The Long-Run Competitive Market Supply Curve is a Horizontal Line.

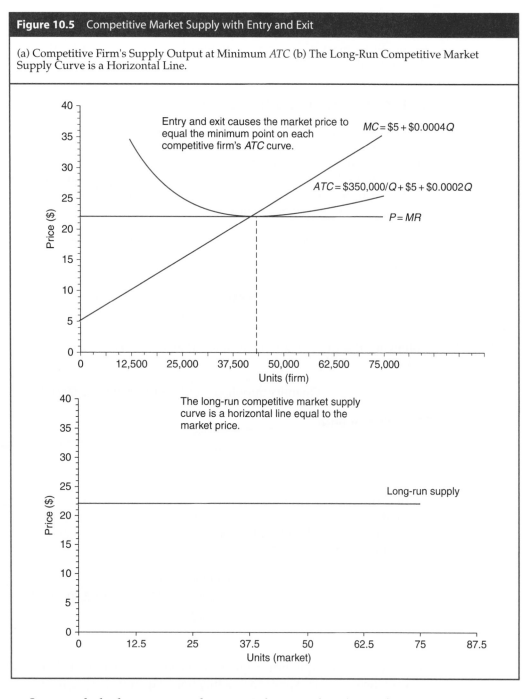

In general, the long-run supply curve is horizontal at the market price in competitive markets. However, in some competitive markets the long-run supply curve may slope upward and higher market prices may be necessary to bring forward additional supply. If the supply of needed inputs, like skilled labor, land, or raw materials is limited, higher costs can be associated with increased usage. If anything makes established competitors more cost-efficient than new entrants, then entry will only be observed at higher prices and the long-run supply curve will be upward sloping. Nevertheless, because firms can more easily enter or exit in the long run, long-run supply curves tend to be more elastic than short-run supply curves.

COMPETITIVE MARKET EQUILIBRIUM

Competitive market prices and quantities are determined by the interplay of market demand and market supply.

Balance of Supply and Demand

Market demand is the aggregation of quantities that customers seek to buy at each market price. Market supply reflects a summation of the quantities that individual firms are willing to supply at these same prices. The intersection of industry demand and supply curves determines both the equilibrium market price and quantity.

To illustrate, consider the market demand curve shown in Figure 10.6. This market demand curve is described by the equation

$$\text{Quantity Demanded} = Q_D = 53{,}500{,}000 - 500{,}000P \qquad \text{(Market demand)}$$

or, solving for price

$$\$500{,}000P = \$53{,}500{,}000 - Q_D$$
$$P = \$107 - \$0.000002Q_D$$

Following the prior example, assume that the market supply curve is given by the expression:

$$\text{Quantity Supplied} = Q_S = -12{,}500{,}000 + 2{,}500{,}000P \qquad \text{(Market supply)}$$

or, solving for price

$$\$2{,}500{,}000P = \$12{,}500{,}000 + Q_S$$
$$P = \$5 + \$0.0000004Q_S$$

To find the market equilibrium levels for price and quantity, simply set the market demand and market supply curves equal to one another so that $Q_D = Q_S$. For example, to find the market equilibrium price, equate the market demand and market supply curves where quantity is expressed as a function of price:

$$\text{Demand} = \text{Supply}$$
$$53{,}500{,}000 - 500{,}000P = -12{,}500{,}000 + 2{,}500{,}000P$$
$$3{,}000{,}000P = 66{,}000{,}000$$
$$P = \$22$$

To find the market equilibrium quantity, set equal the market demand and market supply curves where price is expressed as a function of quantity, and $Q_D = Q_S$:

$$\text{Demand} = \text{Supply}$$
$$\$107 - \$0.000002Q = \$5 + \$0.0000004Q$$
$$0.0000024Q = 102$$
$$Q = 42{,}500{,}000$$

Figure 10.6 illustrates the equilibrium price–output combination at a market price of $22 with an equilibrium output of 42.5 million units. This is a stable equilibrium at point A.

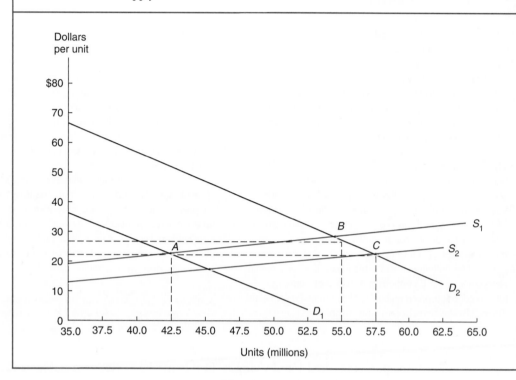

Figure 10.6   Competitive Market Equilibrium

The competitive market equilibrium price–output combination can be found by equating the market demand and market supply curves.

Given the tiny market share held by competitive firms, changes in firm output decisions are too small to affect market prices. In this example, market demand is given by the expression $P = \$107 - \$0.000002Q_D$. This means that a 1-unit increase in production would have an unnoticeable affect on price of $-\$0.000002$. An increase of 5,000 units is needed before even a 1 ¢ decrease in the market price would be observed! With market demand of 42.5 million units and 1,000 equal-sized competitors, each competitor produces and sells 42,500 units of output. For them, a 5,000-unit increase in production would be substantial. Because such a substantial increase in production would have no meaningful impact on the market price, the demand curve facing each individual firm is, for all practical purposes, horizontal or flat. Price can be assumed constant irrespective of the output level at which the firm chooses to operate.

Normal Profit Equilibrium

At the profit-maximizing output level of 42,500 units, $MR = MC$ and individual firm profits are maximized. At the profit-maximizing activity level, it is always true that $MR = MC$. This is true in competitive markets, and in every market setting. Given the horizontal market demand curve facing individual competitive firms, marginal revenue and price are also equal, $MR = P$. This is unique to the competitive market setting. In every other market setting, the firm faces a downward-sloping demand curve and, therefore, $P > MR$. In a competitive market, only normal profits are earned and the firm neither earns economic profits nor incurs economic losses. This means that in competitive market equilibrium $P = MR = MC = ATC$. When this condition holds for all firms, new firms are not encouraged to enter the market nor are existing

Managerial Application 10.4

The Enron Debacle

In November, 2001, Enron Corp. filed the largest voluntary Chapter 11 bankruptcy petition in U.S. history—a stunning collapse for a company worth more than $60 billion less than a year earlier. Historically, Enron's principal business was the transportation and marketing of natural gas and electricity to markets throughout the United States. More recently, the company built a large commodities trading, risk management, and financial services business that led to its eventual downfall.

Enron ran into trouble trading energy futures contracts—a hotly competitive market. A futures contract is a binding legal document that commits the buyer to take delivery, and the seller to make delivery, of an underlying asset in a specified quantity and quality at a specific delivery time and place. Because futures contracts involve *obligations* to buy and sell a specific commodity for a preset price, both buyers and sellers of futures contracts are exposed to the potential for unlimited losses in the event of adverse market conditions. Like stock options and stock index options, futures contracts on commodities like natural gas are called "financial derivatives" because their economic value is

derived from changes in the price of natural gas or some other underlying commodity.

To control risk and lend stability to futures markets, Congress enacted the Commodity Exchange Act in 1974 and established the Commodity Futures Trading Commission (CFTC), an independent federal regulatory agency with jurisdiction over futures trading. The CFTC strives to protect market participants against manipulation, abusive trade practices, and fraud. Critics contend that the Enron bankruptcy could have been averted had the company not won various regulatory exemptions in the Commodity Futures Modernization Act of 2000, a law that drastically reduced the power of government regulatory agencies overseeing futures markets. Without such exemptions, the CFTC might have regulated EnronOnline as an "organized exchange" and put controls in place to avoid financial disaster for Enron employees, investors, and trading partners.

See: David Reilly, "Risks Sparking Bailout were Still in Shadows by Post-Enron Rules," *The Wall Street Journal Online*, October 16, 2007, http://online.wsj.com/.

competitors pressured into leaving it. In this market, prices are stable at $22 per unit, and each firm is operating at the minimum point on its average cost curve. Accordingly, a stable equilibrium requires that firms operate with optimally sized plants.

Figure 10.6 also shows what happens when short-run market demand increases from D_1 to D_2. In the short run, the increase in market demand causes prices to rise from $22 (point A) to $27 (point B) per unit, and quantity rises in the market from 42.5 million to 55 million. Because price now exceeds ATC, established firms make economic profits and new firms are encouraged to enter the market. Entry shifts the short-run market supply curve rightward from S_1 to S_2. A new long-run equilibrium is established at point C. The equilibrium market price has returned to $22, but market supply has increased to 57.5 million units. To create this additional market supply, more optimally sized firms have entered the market. Again, in this new competitive market equilibrium, there are no economic profits. All firms earn a risk-adjusted, fair, or normal rate of return.

SUMMARY

Competition is said to be perfect when producers offer what buyers want at prices just sufficient to cover the marginal cost of production.

- **Market structure** describes the competitive environment in the market for any good or service.

A **market** consists of all firms and individuals willing and able to buy or sell a particular product. This includes firms and individuals currently engaged in buying and selling a particular product, as well as potential entrants. A **potential entrant** is an individual or firm posing a sufficiently credible threat of market entry to affect the price–output decisions of incumbent firms.

- Real or perceived differences in the quality of goods and services offered to consumers lead to **product differentiation**. Sources of product differentiation include actual physical differences, such as those due to superior research and development, plus any perceived differences due to effective advertising and promotion. Price competition tends to be most vigorous for homogenous products with few actual or perceived differences in hotly **competitive markets**.

- A **barrier to entry** is any factor or industry characteristic that creates an advantage for incumbents over new arrivals. Legal rights such as patents and local, state, or federal licenses can present formidable barriers to entry in pharmaceuticals, cable television, television and radio broadcasting, and other industries. A **barrier to mobility** is any factor or industry characteristic that creates an advantage for large leading firms over smaller nonleading rivals. A **barrier to exit** is any restriction on the ability of incumbents to redeploy assets from one industry or line of business to another.

- **Perfect competition** is a market structure characterized by a large number of buyers and sellers of essentially the same product. Each market participant is too small to influence market prices. Individual buyers and sellers are **price takers**. Firms take market prices as given and devise their production strategies accordingly.

- A **normal profit**, defined as the rate of return necessary to attract capital investment, is included as part of the financing costs included in total costs.

Therefore, the profit shown in Figure 10.1 is defined as **economic profit** and represents an above-normal rate of return. The firm incurs **economic losses** whenever it fails to earn a normal profit. In general, a firm might show a small accounting profit but be suffering economic losses because these profits are insufficient to provide an adequate return to the firm's stockholders.

- Discovering the point of optimal production is made easier with **marginal analysis**. Total profit is maximized when the difference between marginal revenue and marginal cost, called marginal profit, equals zero, $M\pi = MR - MC = 0$. Because this point of profit maximization occurs where marginal revenue is set equal to marginal cost, an equivalent expression that must be met for profit maximization is that $MR = MC$. What is unique about the perfectly competitive market setting is that all firms are price takers. In this vigorously competitive market setting, profit maximization occurs when $P = MR = MC$. An added condition for profit maximization, sometimes referred to as a second-order condition, is that total profits must always be decreasing beyond the point where $MR = MC$.

- The marginal cost curve is the **competitive firm short-run supply curve** so long as $P > AVC$. The sustainable level of output is given by the **competitive firm long-run supply curve**. Given the need to cover all fixed costs and earn a fair rate of return, the marginal cost curve is the competitive firm's long-run supply curve so long as $P > ATC$.

Many real-world markets do in fact closely approximate the perfectly competitive ideal. As a result, competitive market concepts provide a valuable guide to economic decision making.

QUESTIONS

Q10.1 Historically, the Regional Bell Operating Companies (RBOCs) had a monopoly on the provision of local voice phone service. Regulation has now been eased to permit competition from Competitive Local Exchange Carriers (CLECs), cable companies, satellite operators and wireless competitors. Is the local phone service market likely to become a vigorously competitive market?

Q10.2 One way of inferring competitive conditions in a market is to consider the lifestyle enjoyed by employees and owners. In vigorously competitive markets, employee compensation tends to be meager and profits are apt to be slim. Describe the perfectly competitive market structure and provide some examples.

Q10.3 Competitive firms are sometimes criticized for costly but superfluous product differentiation. Is there an easy means for determining if such efforts are in fact wasteful?

Q10.4 The Worker Adjustment and Retraining Notification Act (WARN) requires employers with 100 or more employees to provide notification 60 calendar days in advance of plant closings and mass layoffs. Advance notice gives workers and their families transition time to adjust to the prospective loss of employment, seek other jobs, or get necessary training. Some employers complain that WARN reduces necessary flexibility and makes them reluctant to open new production facilities. How are barriers to entry and exit similar? How are they different?

Q10.5 "A higher minimum wage means some low wage workers will get fired because there will be less money available for labor costs. An international minimum wage, scaled according to the working conditions and cost of living in a particular country, would allow local workers to benefit without significant trade disruption." Discuss this statement and explain why the demand curve is apt to be horizontal in the unskilled labor market.

Q10.6 "For smaller firms managed by their owners in competitive markets, profit considerations are apt to dominate almost all decisions. However, managers of giant corporations have little contact with stockholders, and often deviate from profit-maximizing behavior. Get real. Look at Tyco, for Pete's sake." Discuss this statement.

Q10.7 "If excess profits are rampant in the oil business, why aren't the stockholders of industry giants like Exxon Mobil, Chevron Texaco, and Royal Dutch Petroleum making huge stock-market profits?" Discuss this statement.

Q10.8 "Airline passenger service is a terrible high-fixed cost business featuring fierce price competition. With uniform safety, customers pick the lowest airfare with the most convenient departures. Except for pilots, nobody in the airline business makes any money." Use the competitive firm short-run supply curve concept to explain entry and exit in the airline passenger business. Why are pilots so well paid?

Q10.9 Suppose that a competitive firm long-run supply curve is given by the expression $Q_F = -500 + 10P$. Does this mean that the firm will supply -500 units of output at a zero price? If so, what does output of -500 units mean?

Q10.10 The long-run supply curve for a given competitive firm can be written as $Q_F = -250 + 8P$ or $P = \$31.25 + \$0.125Q_F$. Explain why the amount supplied by 50 such competitors is determined by multiplying the first expression by 50 rather than by multiplying the second expression by a similar amount.

SELF-TEST PROBLEMS AND SOLUTIONS

ST10.1 Market Supply. In some markets, cutthroat competition can exist even when the market is dominated by a small handful of competitors. This usually happens when fixed costs are high, products are standardized, price information is readily available, and excess capacity is present. Airline passenger service in large city-pair markets, and electronic components manufacturing are good examples of industries where price competition among the few can be vigorous. Consider three competitors producing a standardized product (Q) with the following marginal cost characteristics:

$$MC_1 = \$5 + \$0.0004Q_1 \qquad \text{(Firm 1)}$$
$$MC_2 = \$15 + \$0.002Q_2 \qquad \text{(Firm 2)}$$
$$MC_3 = \$1 + \$0.0002Q_3 \qquad \text{(Firm 3)}$$

A. Using each firm's marginal cost curve, calculate the profit-maximizing short-run supply from each firm at the competitive market prices indicated in the following table. For simplicity, assume price is greater than average variable cost in every instance.

Market Supply Is the Sum of Firm Supply Across all Competitors

Price ($)	Firm 1 Supply $P = MC_1 =$ $\$5 + \$0.0004Q_1$ and $Q_1 = -12,500 + 2,500P$	Firm 2 Supply $P = MC_2 =$ $\$15 + \$0.002Q_2$ and $Q_2 = -7,500 + 500P$	Firm 3 Supply $P = MC_3 =$ $\$1 + \$0.0002Q_3$ and $Q_3 = -5,000 + 5,000P$	Market Supply $P = \$3.125 +$ $\$0.000125P$ and $Q_S = -25,000 + 8,000P$ $(Q_S = Q_1 + Q_2 + Q_3)$
0				
5				
10				
15				
20				
25				
30				
35				
40				
45				
50				
55				
60				
65				
70				
75				
80				

B. Use these data to plot short-run supply curves for each firm. Also plot the market supply curve.

ST10.1   SOLUTION

A. The marginal cost curve constitutes the short-run supply curve for firms in perfectly competitive markets so long as price is greater than average variable cost.

Market Supply Is the Sum of Firm Supply Across all Competitors

Price ($)	Firm 1 Supply $P = MC_1 =$ $\$5 + \$0.0004Q_1$ and $Q_1 = -12,500 = 2,500P$	Firm 2 Supply $P = MC_2 =$ $\$15 + \$0.002Q_2$ and $Q_2 = -7,500 = 500P$	Firm 3 Supply $P = MC_3 =$ $\$1 + \$0.0002Q_3$ and $Q_3 = -5,000 + 5,000P$	Market Supply $P = \$3.125 +$ $\$0.000125P$ and $Q_I = -25,000 = 8,000P$ $(Q_I = Q_1 + Q_2 + Q_3)$
0	−12,500	−7,500	−5,000	−25,000
5	0	−5,000	20,000	15,000
10	12,500	−2,500	45,000	55,000
15	25,000	0	70,000	95,000

	Firm 1 Supply $P=MC_1=$ $5+0.0004Q_1$ and $Q_1=-12,500=2,500P$	Firm 2 Supply $P=MC_2=$ $15+0.002Q_2$ and $Q_2=-7,500=500P$	Firm 3 Supply $P=MC_3=$ $1+0.0002Q_3$ and $Q_3=-5,000+5,000P$	Market Supply $P=3.125+$ $0.000125P$ and $Q_I=-25,000=8,000P$ $(Q_I=Q_1+Q_2+Q_3)$
Market Supply Is the Sum of Firm Supply Across all Competitors (*continued*)				
Price ($)				
20	37,500	2,500	95,000	135,000
25	50,000	5,000	120,000	175,000
30	62,500	7,500	145,000	215,000
35	75,000	10,000	170,000	255,000
40	87,500	12,500	195,000	295,000
45	100,000	15,000	220,000	335,000
50	112,500	17,500	245,000	375,000
55	125,000	20,000	270,000	415,000
60	137,500	22,500	295,000	455,000
65	150,000	25,000	320,000	495,000
70	162,500	27,500	345,000	535,000
75	175,000	30,000	370,000	575,000
80	187,500	32,500	395,000	615,000

B.

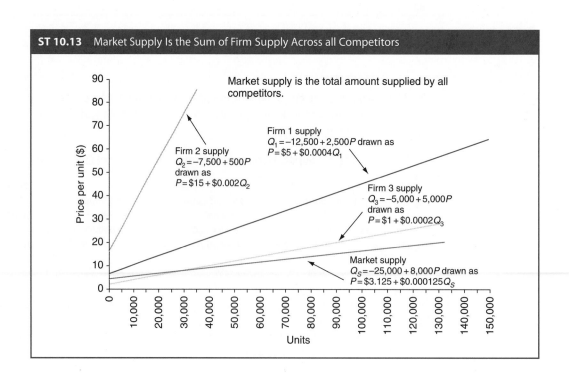

ST 10.13 Market Supply Is the Sum of Firm Supply Across all Competitors

ST10.2 Competitive Market Equilibrium.

Competitive market prices are determined by the interplay of aggregate supply and demand; individual firms have no control over price. Market demand reflects an aggregation of the quantities that customers will buy at each price. Market supply reflects a summation of the quantities that individual firms are willing to supply at different prices. The intersection of industry demand and supply curves determines the equilibrium market price. To illustrate this process, consider the following market demand curve where price is expressed as a function of output:

$$P = \$40 - \$0.0001Q_D \qquad \text{(Market demand)}$$

or equivalently, when output is expressed as a function of price

$$Q_D = 400{,}000 - 10{,}000P$$

Assume market supply is provided by five competitors producing a standardized product (Q). Firm supply schedules are as follows:

$$Q_1 = 18 + 2P \qquad \text{(Firm 1)}$$
$$Q_2 = 12 + 6P \qquad \text{(Firm 2)}$$
$$Q_3 = 40 + 12P \qquad \text{(Firm 3)}$$
$$Q_4 = 20 + 12P \qquad \text{(Firm 4)}$$
$$Q_5 = 10 + 8P \qquad \text{(Firm 5)}$$

A. Calculate the optimal quantity supplied by each firm at the competitive market prices indicated in the following table. Then, assume there are actually 1,000 firms just like each one illustrated in the table. Use this information to complete the Partial Market Supply and Total Market Supply columns.

Price ($)	Quantity Supplied by Firm (000) 1 + 2 + 3 + 4 + 5 = Partial Market Supply × 1,000 = Total Market Supply (000)
1	
2	
3	
4	
5	
6	
7	
8	

B. Sum the individual firm supply curves to derive the market supply curve. Plot the market demand and market supply curve with price as a function of output to illustrate the equilibrium price and level of output. Verify that this is indeed the market equilibrium price–output combination algebraically.

ST10.2 SOLUTION

A.

	Quantity Supplied by Firm (000)						
Price ($)	1	+ 2	+ 3	+ 4	+ 5	= Partial Market Supply × 1,000	= Total Market Supply (000)
1	20	18	52	32	18	140	140,000
2	22	24	64	44	26	180	180,000
3	24	30	76	56	34	220	220,000
4	26	36	88	68	42	260	260,000
5	28	42	100	80	50	300	300,000
6	30	48	112	92	58	340	340,000
7	32	54	124	104	66	380	380,000
8	34	60	136	116	74	420	420,000

The data in the table illustrate the process by which an industry supply curve is constructed. First, suppose that each of five firms in an industry is willing to supply varying quantities at different prices. Summing the individual supply quantities of these five firms at each price determines their combined supply schedule, shown in the Partial Market Supply column. For example, at a price of $2, the output supplied by the five firms are 22, 24, 64, 44, and 26 (thousand) units, respectively, resulting in a combined supply of 180(000) units at that price. With a competitive market price of $8, supply quantities would become 34, 60, 136, 116, and 74, for a total supply by the five firms of 420(000) units, and so on.

Now assume that there are 1,000 firms just like each one illustrated in the table. There are actually 5,000 firms in the industry, each with an individual supply schedule identical to one of the five firms illustrated in the table. In that event, the total quantity supplied at each price is 1,000 times that shown under the Partial Market Supply schedule. Because the numbers shown for each firm are in thousands of units, the total market supply column is in thousands of units. Therefore, the number 140,000 at a price of $1 indicates 140 million units; the number 180,000 at a price of $2 indicates 180 million units, and so on.

B. To find the market supply curve, simply sum each individual firm's supply curve, where quantity is expressed as a function of the market price:

$$Q_1 = Q_1 + Q_2 + Q_3 + Q_4 + Q_5$$
$$= 18 + 2P + 12 + 6P + 40 + 12P + 20 + 12P + 10 + 8P$$
$$= 100 + 40P \qquad \text{(Market Supply)}$$

Plotting the market demand curve and the market supply curve allows one to determine the equilibrium market price of $6 and the equilibrium market quantity of 340,000(000), or 340 million units.

To find the market equilibrium levels for price and quantity algebraically, simply set the market demand and market supply curves equal to one another so that $Q_D = Q_S$. To find the market equilibrium price, equate the market demand and market supply curves where quantity is expressed as a function of price:

$$\text{Demand} = \text{Supply}$$
$$400,000 - 10,000P = 100,000 + 40,000P$$
$$50,000P = 300,000$$
$$P = \$6$$

To find the market equilibrium quantity, set equal the market demand and market supply curves where price is expressed as a function of quantity, and $Q_D = Q_S$:

$$\text{Demand} = \text{Supply}$$
$$\$40 - \$0.0001Q = -\$2.5 + \$0.000025Q$$
$$0.000125Q = 42.5$$
$$Q = 340,000(000)$$

Therefore, the equilibrium price–output combination is a market price of $6 with an equilibrium output of 340,000(000), or 340 million units.

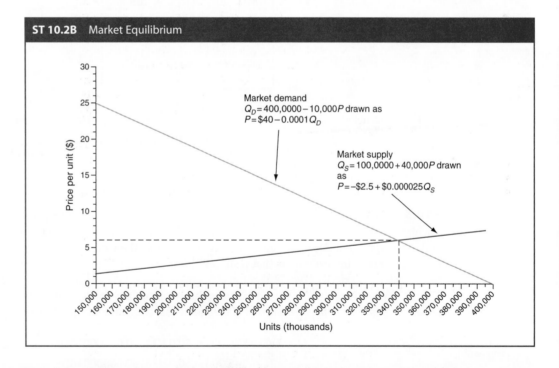

ST 10.2B Market Equilibrium

Market demand
$Q_D = 400,0000 - 10,000P$ drawn as
$P = \$40 - 0.0001Q_D$

Market supply
$Q_S = 100,0000 + 40,000P$ drawn as
$P = -\$2.5 + \$0.000025Q_S$

Price per unit ($)

Units (thousands)

PROBLEMS

P10.1 Competitive Markets Concepts. Indicate whether each of the following statements is true or false, and explain why.

A. In long-run equilibrium, every firm in a perfectly competitive industry earns zero profit.

B. Perfect competition exists in a market when all firms are price takers as opposed to price makers.

C. In competitive markets, $P > MC$ at the profit-maximizing output level.

D. Downward-sloping industry demand curves characterize perfectly competitive markets.

E. A firm might show accounting profits in a competitive market but be suffering economic losses.

P10.2 Short-Run Firm Supply. Mankato Paper, Inc., produces uncoated paper used in a wide variety of industrial applications. Newsprint, a major product, is sold in a perfectly competitive market. The following relation exists between the firm's newsprint output and total production costs:

Total Output (tons)	Total Cost ($)
0	25
1	75
2	135
3	205
4	285
5	375
6	475
7	600

A. Construct a table showing Mankato's marginal cost of newsprint production.

B. What is the minimum price necessary for Mankato to supply 1 ton of newsprint?

C. How much newsprint would Mankato supply at industry prices of $75 and $100 per ton?

P10.3 Short-Run Firm Supply. Florida is the biggest sugar-producing state, but Michigan and Minnesota are home to thousands of sugar beet growers. Sugar prices in the United States average about 20¢ per pound, or more than double the worldwide average of less than 10¢ per pound given import quotas that restrict imports to about 15 percent of the U.S. market. Still, the industry is perfectly competitive for U.S. growers who take the market price of 20¢ as fixed. Thus, $P = MR = 20$¢ in the U.S. sugar market. Assume that a typical sugar grower has fixed costs of $30,000 per year. Total variable cost (TVC), total cost (TC), and marginal cost (MC) relations are

$$TVC = \$15{,}000 + \$0.02Q + \$0.00000018Q^2$$
$$TC = \$45{,}000 + \$0.02Q + \$0.00000018Q^2$$
$$MC = \partial TC/\partial Q = \$0.02 + \$0.00000036Q$$

where Q is pounds of sugar, total costs include a normal profit.

A. Using the firm's marginal cost curve, calculate the profit-maximizing short-run supply curve for a typical grower.

B. Calculate the average variable cost curve for a typical grower, and verify that average variable costs are less than price at this optimal activity level.

P10.4 Long-Run Firm Supply. The retail market for unleaded gasoline is fiercely price competitive. Consider the situation faced by a typical gasoline retailer when the local market price for unleaded gasoline is $1.80 per gallon and total cost (*TC*) and marginal cost (*MC*) relations are

$$TC = \$40,000 + \$1.64Q + \$0.0000001Q^2$$
$$MC = \partial TC/\partial Q = \$1.64 + \$0.0000002Q$$

and Q is gallons of gasoline. Total costs include a normal profit.

A. Using the firm's marginal cost curve, calculate the profit-maximizing long-run supply curve for a typical retailer.

B. Calculate the average total cost curve for a typical gasoline retailer, and verify that average total costs are less than price at the optimal activity level.

P10.5 Short-Run Firm Supply. Farm Fresh, Inc., supplies sweet peas to canneries located throughout the Mississippi River Valley. Like many grain and commodity markets, the market for sweet peas is perfectly competitive. With $250,000 in fixed costs, the company's total and marginal costs per ton (*Q*) are

$$TC = \$250,000 + \$200Q + \$0.02Q^2$$
$$MC = \partial TC/\partial Q = \$200 + \$0.04Q$$

A. Calculate the industry prices necessary to induce short-run quantities supplied by the firm of 5,000, 10,000, and 15,000 tons of sweet peas. Assume that $MC > AVC$ at every point along the firm's marginal cost curve and that total costs include a normal profit.

B. Calculate short-run quantities supplied by the firm at industry prices of $200, $500, and $1,000 per ton.

P10.6 Short-Run Market Supply. New England Textiles, Inc., is a medium-sized manufacturer of blue denim that sells in a perfectly competitive market. Given $25,000 in fixed costs, the total cost function for this product is described by

$$TC = \$25,000 + \$1Q + \$0.000008Q^2$$
$$MC = \partial TC/\partial Q = \$1 + \$0.000016Q$$

where Q is square yards of blue denim produced per month. Assume that $MC > AVC$ at every point along the firm's marginal cost curve, and that total costs include a normal profit.

A. Derive the firm's supply curve, expressing quantity as a function of price.

B. Derive the market supply curve if New England Textiles is one of 500 competitors.

C. Calculate market supply per month at a market price of $2 per square yard.

P10.7 Long-Run Competitive Firm Supply. The Hair Stylist, Ltd., is a popular-priced hairstyling salon in College Park, Maryland. Given the large number of competitors, the fact that stylists routinely tailor services to meet customer needs, and the lack of entry barriers, it is reasonable to assume that the market is perfectly competitive and that the average $40 price equals marginal revenue, $P = MR = \$40$. Furthermore, assume that the firm's operating expenses are typical of the 100 firms in the local market and can be expressed by the following total and marginal cost functions

$$TC = \$5,625 + \$25Q + \$0.01Q^2$$
$$MC = \$25 + \$0.02Q$$

where TC is total cost per month including capital costs, MC is marginal cost, and Q is the number of hairstylings provided. Total costs include a normal profit.

A. Calculate the firm's profit-maximizing output level.

B. Calculate the firm's economic profits at this activity level. Is this activity level sustainable in the long run?

P10.8 Competitive Market Equilibrium. Dozens of Internet Web sites offer quality auto parts for the replacement market. Their appeal is obvious. Price-conscious shoppers can often obtain up to 80 percent discounts from the prices charged by original equipment manufacturers (OEMs) for such standard items as wiper blades, air filters, oil filters, and so on. With a large selection offered by dozens of online merchants, the market for standard replacement parts is vigorously competitive. Assume that market demand and supply conditions for windshield wiper blades can be described by the following relations

$$Q_D = 100 - 10P \qquad \text{(Market demand)}$$
$$Q_S = 15P \qquad \text{(Market supply)}$$

where Q is millions of replacement wiper blades and P is price per unit.

A. Graph the market demand and supply curves.

B. Determine the market equilibrium price–output combination both graphically and algebraically.

P10.9 Dynamic Competitive Equilibrium. Wal-Mart and other movie DVD retailers, including online vendors like Amazon.com, employ a two-step pricing policy. During the first 6 months following a theatrical release, movie DVD buyers are wiling to pay a premium for new releases. Total and marginal revenue relations for a typical newly released movie DVD are given by the following relations

$$TR = \$28Q - \$0.0045Q^2$$
$$MR = \partial TC/\partial Q = \$28 - \$0.009Q$$

Total cost (TC) and marginal costs (MC) for production and distribution are

$$TC = \$4,500 + \$3Q + \$0.0005Q^2$$
$$MC = \partial TC/\partial Q = \$3 + \$0.001Q$$

where Q is in thousands of units (DVDs). Because units are in thousands, both total revenues and total costs are in thousand of dollars. Total costs include a normal profit.

A. Use the marginal revenue and marginal cost relations given above to calculate DVD output, price, and economic profits at the profit-maximizing activity level for new releases.

B. After 6 months, price-sensitive DVD buyers appear willing to pay no more than $6 per DVD. Calculate the equilibrium price–output activity level in this situation. Is this a stable equilibrium?

P10.10 Stable Competitive Equilibrium. Bada Bing, Ltd., supplies standard 256 MB-RAM chips to the U.S. computer and electronics industry. Like the output of its competitors, Bada Bing's chips must meet strict size, shape, and speed specifications. As a result, the chip-supply industry can be regarded as perfectly competitive. The total cost and marginal cost functions for Bada Bing are

$$TC = \$1{,}000{,}000 + \$20Q + \$0.0001Q^2$$
$$MC = \partial TC/\partial Q = \$20 + \$0.0002Q$$

where Q is the number of chips produced. Total costs include a normal profit.

A. Calculate Bada Bing's optimal output and profits if chip prices are stable at $60 each.

B. Calculate Bada Bing's optimal output and profits if chip prices fall to $30 each.

C. If Bada Bing is typical of firms in the industry, calculate the firm's long-run equilibrium output, price, and economic profit levels.

CASE *Study*

Profitability Effects of Firm Size for DJIA Companies

Does large firm size, pure and simple, give rise to economic profits? This question has long been a source of great interest in both business and government, and the basis for lively debate over the years. Economic theory states that large relative firm size *within a given economic market* gives rise to the potential for above-normal profits. However, economic theory makes no prediction at all about a link between large firm size, pure and simple, and the potential for above-normal profits. By itself, it is not clear what economic advantages are gained from large firm size. Pecuniary or money-related economies of large size in the purchase of labor, raw materials, or other inputs are sometimes suggested. For example, some argue that large firms enjoy a comparative advantage in the acquisition of investment funds given their ready access to organized capital markets, like the New York Stock Exchange. Others contend that capital markets are themselves very efficient in the allocation of scarce capital resources and that all firms, both large and small, must offer investors a competitive rate of return in order to grow and prosper.

Still, without a doubt, the profitability effect of large firm size is a matter of significant business and public policy interest. Ranking

continued

among the largest corporations in the United States is a matter of significant corporate pride for employees, top executives, and stockholders. Sales and profit levels achieved by such firms are widely reported and commented upon in the business and popular press. At times, congressional leaders have called for legislation that would bar mergers among giant companies on the premise that such combinations create monolithic giants that impair competitive forces. Movements up and down lists of the largest corporations are chronicled, studied, and commented upon. It is perhaps a little known fact that, given the dynamic nature of change in the overall economy, few companies are able to maintain, let alone enhance, their relative position among the largest corporations over a 5- to 10-year period. With an annual attrition rate of 6 percent to 10 percent among the 500 largest corporations, it indeed appears to be "slippery" at the top.

To evaluate the link, if any, between profitability and firm size, it is interesting to consider the data contained in Table 1.1 on the corporate giants found within the Dow Jones Industrial Average (DJIA). These are profit and size data on 30 of the largest and most successful corporations in the world. Companies included in the DJIA are selected and reviewed by editors of *The Wall Street Journal*. For the sake of continuity, changes in the composition of the DJIA are rare. Changes occur twice a decade, and only after corporate acquisitions or other dramatic shifts in a component corporation's core business. When events necessitate a change in the DJIA, the entire index is reviewed and multiple component changes are often implemented simultaneously. There are no hard and fast rules for component selection. A major corporation is typically added to the DJIA only if it has an excellent reputation, demonstrates sustained growth, and is of interest to a large number of individual and institutional investors. Most importantly, the overall makeup of the DJIA is structured so as to be representative of the overall stock market. Despite its name, the DJIA is not limited to industrial stocks, at least as stocks are traditionally defined. The DJIA serves as a measure of the entire U.S. market, covering such diverse industries as financial services, technology, retail, entertainment, and consumer goods.

Table 1.1 shows profitability as measured by net income, and two standard measures of firm size. Sales revenue is perhaps the most common measure of firm size. From an economic perspective, sales is an attractive measure of firm size because it is not susceptible to accounting manipulation or bias, nor is it influenced by the relative capital or labor intensity of the enterprise. When size is measured by sales revenue, measurement problems tied to inflation, replacement cost errors, and so on are minimized. Another popular measure of firm size is net worth, or the book value of stockholders' equity, defined in accounting terms as total assets minus total liabilities. Stockholders' equity is a useful measure of the total funds committed to the enterprise by stockholders through paid-in capital plus retained earnings.

The simplest means for studying the link between profitability and firm size is to compare profits and firm size, when size is measured using sales and stockholders' equity. However, it is important to remember that a link between profits and firm size may mean nothing at all in terms of the effects of firm size on the rate of profitability. Big firms make big profits. There is no reason to fear large-firm exploitation in the economy just because big firms make lots of money. To consider if firm size might be a contributor to the pace of profitability, it is necessary to track the effects of firm size on the profit margin on sales (MGN) and the rate of return on stockholders' equity (ROE). A significant link between the rate of profitability and firm size is suggested to the extent that MGN and ROE tend to be highest among the very largest companies.

continued

The effects of firm size on profits and firm size on profit rates among the corporate giants found among the DJIA are shown in Table 10.2.

A. Based upon the findings reported in Table 10.2, discuss the relation between firm size and profitability, and the link, if any, between firm size and profit rates. In general, does large firm size increase profitability?

B. Using a spreadsheet, sort the DJIA according to profit rates and firm size. Use firm-specific information found on company Web sites or investment portals, like Yahoo! Finance or msn Money, to explain the superior profitability of these corporate giants.

C. What other important factors might be included in a more detailed study of the determinants of corporate profitability?

Table 10.2 Effects of Firm Size on Profitability (t statistics are in parentheses)

Dependent Variable	Size Measure	Intercept	Size Coefficient	R^2	F-Statistic
Profits	Sales	3624.531 (1.99)	0.055 (3.62)	31.8%	13.08
Profits	Net worth	895.853 (0.57)	0.165 (6.14)	57.4%	37.67
Profit margin (MGN)	Sales	0.149 (8.96)	−3.041E-07 (−2.20)	14.7%	4.83
Return on equity (ROE)	Net worth	0.228 (3.50)	−5.604E-07 (−0.51)	0.9%	0.26

SELECTED REFERENCES

Caves, Richard E. "In Praise of the Old I.O." *International Journal of Industrial Organization* 25, no. 1 (February, 2007): 1–12.

Davidson, Carl and Arijit Mukherjee. "Horizontal Mergers with Free Entry." *International Journal of Industrial Organization* 25, no. 1 (February, 2007): 157–172.

Deschenes, Olivier and Michael Greenstone. "The Economic Impacts of Climate Change: Evidence from Agricultural Output and Random Fluctuations in Weather." *American Economic Review* 97, no. 1 (March, 2007): 354–385.

Destefanis, Sergio and Vania Sena. "Patterns of Corporate Governance and Technical Efficiency in Italian Manufacturing." *Managerial and Decision Economics* 28, no. 1 (January, 2007): 27–40.

di Patti, Emilia Bonaccorsi and Giorgio Gobbi. "Winners Or Losers? The Effects of Banking Consolidation on Corporate Borrowers." *Journal of Finance* 62, no. 2 (April, 2007): 669–695.

Dichev, Ilia D. "What Are Stock Investors' Actual Historical Returns? Evidence from Dollar-Weighted Returns." *American Economic Review* 97, no. 1 (March, 2007): 386–401.

Djankov, Simeon, Caralee McLiesh, and Andrei Shleifer. "Private Credit in 129 Countries." *Journal of Financial Economics* 84, no. 2 (May, 2007): 299–329.

Downing, Chris and Stephen Oliner. "The Term Structure of Commercial Paper Rates." *Journal of Financial Economics* 83, no. 1 (January, 2007): 59–86.

Drehmann, Mathias, Jorg Oechssler, and Andreas Roider. "Herding with and Without Payoff Externalities—an Internet Experiment." *International Journal of Industrial Organization* 25, no. 2 (April, 2007): 391–415.

Duffie, Darrell and Gustavo Manso. "Information Percolation in Large Markets." *American Economic Review* 97, no. 2 (May, 2007): 203–209.

Gelan, Abera, Kaye Husbands Fealing, and James Peoples. "Inward Foreign Direct Investment and Racial Employment Patterns in US Manufacturing." *American Economic Review* 97, no. 2 (May, 2007): 378–382.

Moldovanu, Benny, Aner Sela, and Xianwen Shi. "Contests for Status." *Journal of Political Economy* 115, no. 2 (April, 2007): 338–363.

Prieger, James E. "Regulatory Delay and the Timing of Product Innovation." *International Journal of Industrial Organization* 25, no. 2 (April, 2007): 219–236.

Sutton, John. "Market Share Dynamics and the 'Persistence of Leadership' Debate." *American Economic Review* 97, no. 1 (March, 2007): 222–241.

Ziss, Steffen. "Hierarchies, Intra-Firm Competition and Mergers." *International Journal of Industrial Organization* 25, no. 2 (April, 2007): 237–260.

Performance and Strategy in Competitive Markets

To design effective policies for competitive markets, policy makers must decide when to intervene and when to adopt a hands-off strategy. This is tougher than it might seem. For example, consumer and business customers want cheap, reliable, and safe electric power, and no politician wants to be held responsible when the lights go out, or when electricity bills skyrocket. What makes energy market regulation especially difficult is the fact that the industry has distinctly different segments, including, exploration, production, transmission, and distribution. At the "front end" of the energy industry, exploration and production are vigorously competitive with thousands of active producers, strong incentives for cost-efficiency, and low profit margins. At the "back end" of the energy industry, transmission and distribution are dominated by large utilities with market power and the potential for cost inefficiency and excess profits.

The U.S. Federal Energy Regulatory Commission (FERC) must remain vigilant to ensure that local utilities do not gobble up independent power plants and then sell power to themselves rather than enter into arm's-length long-term supply contracts with independent power producers. FERC is concerned that such transactions might allow energy companies to develop pockets of market power, and the ability to set prices, in otherwise efficient markets. Such concern seems appropriate in light of recurring power crises in California and the collapse of former industry leader Enron Corp.[1]

This chapter shows how public policy decision makers assess performance, and how business leaders formulate effective competitive strategy in competitive markets.

COMPETITIVE MARKET EFFICIENCY

Competitive markets coordinate supply and demand and balance the economic interests of consumers and producers.

Why Is it Called Perfect Competition?

Welfare Economics
Study of how the allocation of economic resources affects the material well-being of consumers and producers.

Welfare economics is the study of how the allocation of economic resources affects the material well-being of consumers and producers. From a broad perspective, it is in society's best interest to have the benefits tied to consumption and production activity made as large as possible. Equilibrium prices and quantities that create an exact balance

---

1 See Guy Morgan, "Customers Are Best Served by Competitive Markets," *The Wall Street Journal Online*, April 3, 2007, http://online.wsj.com.

Social Welfare
Material well-being of society.

Consumer Surplus
Net benefit derived by consumers from consumption.

Producer Surplus
Net benefit derived by producers from production.

between supply and demand in perfectly competitive markets maximize the total **social welfare** derived from such activity.

Figure 11.1 shows **consumer surplus** in competitive market equilibrium. Consumer surplus is the amount that consumers are willing to pay for a given good or service minus the amount that they are required to pay. Consumer surplus describes the net benefit derived by consumers from consumption, where net benefit is measured in the eyes of the consumer. From the standpoint of society as a whole, consumer surplus is an attractive measure of the economic well-being of consumers.

Whereas consumer surplus is closely related to the demand curve for a product, **producer surplus** is closely related to the supply curve for a product. In a competitive market, the long-run market supply curve reflects the marginal cost of production so long as marginal costs are greater than average total cost. The market supply curve indicates the minimum price required by sellers as a group to bring forth production, and the height of the market supply curve measures minimum production cost at each activity level. Producer surplus is the amount paid to sellers above and beyond the required minimum. Producer surplus is the net benefit derived by producers from production. Just as consumer surplus is an appealing measure of consumer well-being, producer surplus is an attractive measure of the economic well-being of producers.

In competitive market equilibrium, social welfare is measured by the sum of net benefits derived by consumers and producers. As shown in Figure 11.1, social welfare is the sum of consumer surplus and producer surplus. When evaluating the amount of social welfare created through competitive market equilibrium, it is vital to remember two essential features of competitive markets. First, in competitive market equilibrium, goods and services are allocated to consumers who place the highest value upon

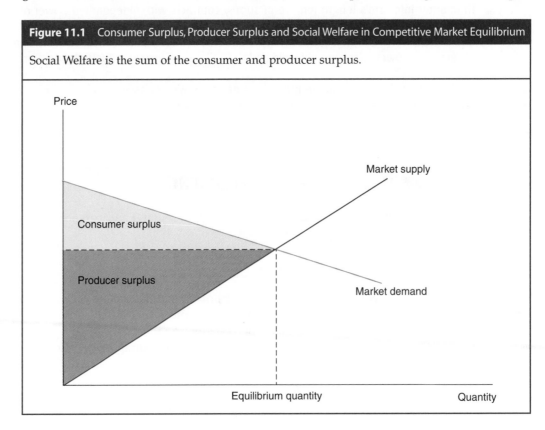

Figure 11.1 Consumer Surplus, Producer Surplus and Social Welfare in Competitive Market Equilibrium

Social Welfare is the sum of the consumer and producer surplus.

them. And second, production of goods and services is allocated among the most efficient producers. For both reasons, social welfare is maximized in competitive market equilibrium.

Deadweight Loss Problem

Any imperfection in competitive markets has the potential to harm economic efficiency. As shown in Figure 11.2, imagine that a restriction in market supply caused the amount produced to fall from Q_1 to Q_2, and provoked the rise in market price from P_1 to P_2. Important implications ensue for the amounts of consumer surplus and producer surplus. As a result of the price hike, the amount of consumer surplus is reduced by the area shown as P_1P_2AB. This area is the amount of additional revenue received by producers and represents a direct transfer of economic benefits from buyers to sellers. Following the price hike, producer surplus rises by that exact same amount, the area shown as P_1P_2AB. Price hikes cause a decrease in the economic well-being of consumers and increase the economic well-being of producers.

Deadweight Loss Problem
Decline in social welfare due to competitive market distortion.

Figure 11.2 also illustrates the **deadweight loss problem** associated with deviations from competitive market equilibrium. A deadweight loss is any economic loss suffered by consumers or producers that occurs as a result of market imperfections or government policies. Notice that the new market equilibrium reflects a reduction of consumer surplus in an amount equal to the area shown as ABD. This is in addition to the reduction in consumer surplus that is simply transferred to producers, shown as P_1P_2AB. The total loss in consumer surplus tied to the decline in quantity from Q_1 to Q_2 and price hike from P_1 to P_2 is represented by the area P_1P_2AD. The area P_1P_2AB depicts consumer surplus transferred to producer surplus; the area ABD shows consumer surplus that is not transferred to producers. It is simply lost following the change in market equilibrium.

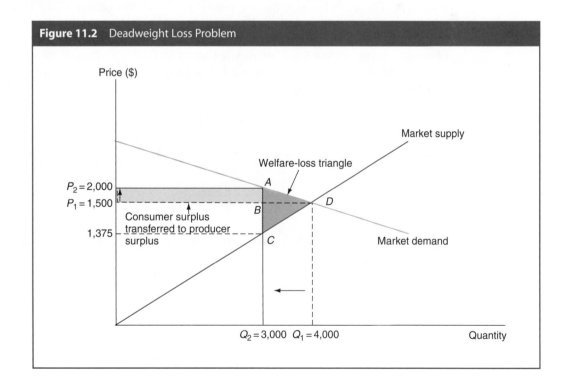

Figure 11.2 Deadweight Loss Problem

Also note that the change in market equilibrium causes two changes in the amount of producer surplus. In addition to the increase in producer surplus that is transferred from consumers, shown as the area P_1P_2AB, the amount of producer surplus is also reduced by the area BCD. The net change in producer surplus tied to the change in market equilibrium is represented by the area P_1P_2AB (transferred from consumers) minus the revenue represented by the area BCD. The area BCD shows producer surplus that is not transferred from consumers. This net benefit for producers tied to the amount produced is simply lost following the change in market equilibrium.

The deadweight loss problem stems from the fact that deviations from competitive market equilibrium result in lost net benefits derived from consumption and production. The total deadweight loss is the sum of deadweight losses suffered by consumers and producers. Because deadweight losses are often depicted as triangles when linear supply and demand curves are employed, deadweight losses are often described as the **welfare loss triangle.**

Welfare Loss Triangle
Graphic representation of deadweight loss when linear supply and demand curves are employed.

Deadweight Loss Illustration

To illustrate the deadweight loss problem and the welfare loss triangle concept, consider the fiercely competitive global aluminum industry. The largest aluminum producers are multinational companies with production, fabricating, and distribution facilities around the world. During recent years, world aluminum production totaled roughly 25 million metric tons per year. Leading producers are found in the United States, Russia, Canada, the European Union, China, Australia, and Brazil. The largest aluminum markets are in North America, Europe, and East Asia. The United States is both a major importer and exporter of aluminum. Approximately one-third of the U.S. supply of aluminum is imported from foreign producers in the form of primary ingot and scrap. U.S. producers export more than 10 percent of U.S. production in the form of ingot, scrap, and mill products. The aluminum industry operates about 500 plants in 40 U.S. states, and employs nearly 100,000 workers. The U.S. aluminum industry ranks first in the world in terms of annual primary aluminum production capacity, accounting for about 16 percent of world supply or over 4 million metric tons of metal.

Assume that the competitive market supply curve for aluminum is given by the equation

$$Q_S = -8,000 + 8P$$

or, solving for price,

$$8P = 8,000 + Q_S$$
$$P = \$1,000 + \$0.125Q_S$$

The competitive market demand curve for aluminum is given by the equation

$$Q_D = 7,000 - 2P$$

or, solving for price,

$$2P = 7,000 - Q_D$$
$$P = \$3,500 - \$0.5Q_D$$

To find the market equilibrium levels for price and quantity, simply set the market supply and market demand curves equal to one another so that $Q_S = Q_D$. For example, to find the market equilibrium price, equate the market demand and market supply curves where quantity is expressed as a function of price:

$$\text{Supply} = \text{Demand}$$
$$-8{,}000 + 8P = 7{,}000 - 2P$$
$$10P = 15{,}000$$
$$P = \$1{,}500 \text{ per ton}$$

To find the market equilibrium quantity, set equal the market supply and market demand curves where price is expressed as a function of quantity, and $Q_S = Q_D$:

$$\text{Supply} = \text{Demand}$$
$$\$1{,}000 + \$0.125Q = \$3{,}500 - \$0.5Q$$
$$0.625Q = 2{,}500$$
$$Q = 4{,}000 \text{ (000) tons}$$

As shown in Figure 11.2, the equilibrium price–output combination for aluminum is a market price of $1,500 with an equilibrium output of 4,000 (000) units.

Now, assume that an industry-wide strike has limited domestic supply to 3,000 tons of production. In this case, the amount supplied falls to 3,000 and the market price jumps to $2,000 per ton. The amount of deadweight loss suffered by consumers due to this supply restriction is given by the triangle bounded by *ABD* in Figure 11.2. Because the area of such a triangle is one-half the value of the base times the height, the value of lost consumer surplus equals

$$\text{Consumer Deadweight Loss} = \tfrac{1}{2}\,[(4{,}000 - 3{,}000) \times (\$2{,}000 - \$1{,}500)]$$
$$= \$250{,}000 \text{ (000)}$$

The amount of deadweight loss due to the supply restriction that is suffered by producers is given by the triangle bounded by *BCD*. Because the area of such a triangle is one-half the value of the base times the height, the value of lost producer surplus equals

$$\text{Producer Deadweight Loss} = \tfrac{1}{2}\,[(4{,}000 - 3{,}000) \times (\$1{,}500 - \$1{,}375)]$$
$$= \$62{,}500 \text{ (000)}$$

The total amount of deadweight loss due to the supply interruption suffered by consumers and producers is given by the triangle bounded by ACD. The area of such a triangle is simply the amount of consumer deadweight loss plus producer deadweight loss:

$$\text{Total Deadweight Loss} = \text{Consumer Loss} + \text{Producer Loss}$$
$$= \$250{,}000 \text{ (000)} + \$62{,}500 \text{ (000)}$$
$$= \$312{,}500 \text{ (000)}$$

Managerial Application 11.1

The Wal-Mart Phenomenon

In 1962, the first Wal-Mart store opened in Rogers, Arkansas. Five years later, Wal-Mart's 24 stores were bringing in $12.6 million in annual sales. Wal-Mart expanded outside Arkansas with stores in Sikeston, Missouri, and Claremore, Oklahoma, in 1968, and was incorporated as Wal-Mart Stores, Inc., in 1969. Today, with more than $325 billion in annual sales, the company that Sam Walton built has become the world's number one retailer.

Wal-Mart's focus on customer service and cheap prices has built a loyal following among consumers and made it a fierce competitor for other retailers. Wal-Mart is especially adept at generating lots of sales per square foot at its spartan retail outlets. With a net profit margin of only 3.5 percent, Wal-Mart generates sufficient volume to earn more than a 20 percent annual rate of return on stockholders' equity. This is phenomenal performance in the fiercely competitive discount retailing business, where industry profit rates average one-half as much as Wal-Mart makes, and long-term survival is a constant struggle. Domestic and international diversification into the grocery and membership warehouse club businesses promise dynamic future growth opportunities for Wal-Mart and its 1.5 million employees.

Wal-Mart's tremendous operating performance has been noticed on Wall Street. On October 1, 1970, Wal-Mart made an initial public offering of 300,000 shares of common stock at a price of $16.50 per share. Since then, Wal-Mart has had 11 two-for-one stock splits. If an investor bought 100 shares worth $1,650 in the initial public offering, that stake would have grown to a whopping 204,800 shares worth $50 per share by 2007. That's $10.2 million and represents a 26.6 percent annual rate of return over a 37-year period.

The Wal-Mart success story proves that tremendous wealth can be created in highly competitive markets by offering customers products that are cheaper, better, or faster than the competition.

See: Gary McWilliams, "Wal-Mart CEO Promises Improvements," *The Wall Street Journal Online*, October 24, 2007, http://online.wsj.com.

MARKET FAILURE

If market prices favor either buyers or sellers, or important costs or benefits tied to production and/or consumption are not reflected in prices, market efficiency suffers.

Structural Problems

Market Power
Ability to set prices and obtain above-normal profits for extended periods.

Market Failure
Situation when competitive market outcomes fail to efficiently allocate economic resources.

Failure by Market Structure
Situation when competitive markets malfunction because of market power.

In some markets, a small group of sellers is able to exert undue influence by unfairly increasing prices and restricting supply. In such instances, the prices paid by consumers exceed the marginal cost of production, and sellers are able to earn above-normal rates of return. Such above-normal profits are unwarranted in that they reflect the raw exercise of **market power**—they do not reflect superior efficiency or exceptional capability. In the case of sellers, market power is reflected in an ability to restrict output below competitive norms and the ability to obtain above-normal prices and profits for extended periods. In the case of buyers, undue market power is indicated when buyer influence results in less than competitive prices, output, and profits for sellers. In the labor market, employer power is reflected in lower than competitive wage rates. Generally speaking, **market failure** occurs when competitive market outcomes fail to sustain socially desirable activities or to eliminate undesirable ones.

A first cause of market failure is **failure by market structure.** For a competitive market to realize the beneficial effects of competition, it must have many sellers (producers) and buyers (customers), or at least the ready potential for many to enter. Some markets do not meet this condition. Consider, for example, water, power, and electric utility markets. If customer service can be most efficiently provided by a single firm, such providers would enjoy market power and could earn excess profits by limiting output and charging excessively high prices. As a result, utility prices and profits are typically placed under regulatory control with the goal of preserving the efficiency of large-scale production while preventing unwarranted high prices and excess profits. When the efficiency advantages of large size are not compelling, public policy often seeks to block the acquisition and exercise of market power by large firms.

Incentive Problems

Externalities
Uncompensated benefits or costs tied to production or consumption.

Differences between private and social costs or benefits are called **externalities.** A negative externality is a cost of producing, marketing, or consuming a product that is not borne by the product's producers or consumers. A positive externality is a benefit of production, marketing, or consumption that is not reflected in the product pricing structure and, hence, does not accrue to the product's producers or consumers. Environmental pollution is one well-known negative externality. Negative externalities also arise when employees are exposed to hazardous working conditions for which they are not fully compensated. Similarly, a firm that dams a river to produce energy and thereby limits the access of others to hydropower creates a negative externality.

Positive externalities can result if an increase in a firm's activity reduces costs for its suppliers, who pass these cost savings on to their other customers. For example, economies of scale in semiconductor production made possible by increased computer demand have lowered input costs for all users of semiconductors. As a result, prices have fallen for computers and a wide variety of "intelligent" electronics, video games, calculators, and so on. Positive externalities in production can result when a firm trains employees who later apply their knowledge in work for other firms. Positive externalities also arise when an improvement in production methods is transferred from one firm to another without compensation. The dam cited previously for its potential negative externalities might also provide positive externalities by offering flood control or recreational benefits.

Externalities lead to a difference between private and social costs and benefits. Firms that provide substantial positive externalities without compensation are unlikely to produce at the socially optimal level. Consumption activities that confer positive externalities may not reach the socially optimal level. In contrast, negative externalities can channel too many resources to a particular activity. Producers or consumers that generate negative externalities do not pay the full costs of production or consumption and tend to overutilize social resources. **Failure by incentive,** an important cause of market failure, is always a risk in markets where social values and social costs differ from private values.

Failure by Incentive
Situation when competitive markets malfunction because of externalities.

ROLE FOR GOVERNMENT

Government regulation of the market economy is a controversial topic because the power to tax or compel consumer and business behavior has economic consequences.

How Government Influences Competitive Markets

Government affects what and how firms produce, influences conditions of entry and exit, dictates marketing practices, prescribes hiring and personnel policies, and imposes a host of other requirements on private enterprise. For example, local telephone service monopolies are protected by a web of local and federal regulation that gives rise to above-normal rates of return while providing access to below-market financing. Franchises that confer the right to offer cellular telephone service in a major metropolitan area are literally worth millions of dollars and can be awarded in the United States only by the Federal Communications Commission (FCC). The federal government also spends hundreds of millions of dollars per year to maintain artificially high price supports for selected agricultural products such as milk and grain, but not chicken and pork. Careful study of the motivation and methods of such regulation is essential to the study of managerial economics because of regulation's key role in shaping the managerial decision-making process.

The pervasive and expanding influence of government in the market economy can be illustrated by considering the growing role played by the FCC, a once obscure agency known only for regulation of the broadcast industry and AT&T. The FCC currently holds the keys to success for a number of emerging communications technologies. The FCC determines the fate of digital audio broadcasting, which eliminates static on car radio channels; personal communication networks that make users accessible anywhere with a pocket phone; and interactive television, which lets customers order goods and communicate with others through a television set. The FCC has also taken on the controversial task of restricting indecent and obscene material on the Internet. As such, the FCC is the focus of debates over free speech and the government's role in shaping rapid advances in communications technology.

Although all sectors of the U.S. economy are regulated to some degree, the method and scope of regulation vary widely. Most companies escape price and profit restraint, except during periods of general wage–price control, but they are subject to operating regulations governing pollution emissions, product packaging and labeling, worker safety and health, and so on. Other firms, particularly in the financial and the public utility sectors, must comply with financial regulation in addition to such operating controls. Banks and savings and loan institutions, for example, are subject to state and federal regulation of interest rates, fees, lending policies, and capital requirements. Unlike firms in the electric power and telecommunications industries, banks and savings and loan institutions face no explicit limit on profitability.

Economic Efficiency
Least-cost production of desired goods and services.

Economic Regulation
Government control of production and/or consumption.

Social Equity
Fairness.

Consumer Sovereignty
Individual control over economic decisions.

Economic and social considerations enter into decisions of what and how to tax or regulate. From an **economic efficiency** standpoint, a given mode of tax or **economic regulation** is desirable to the extent that benefits exceed costs. In terms of efficiency, the question is whether market competition by itself is sufficient, or if it needs to be supplemented with government regulation. **Social equity,** or fairness, criteria are also weighed in the tax or regulatory decision-making process. If a given change in public policy provides significant benefits to the poor, society may willingly bear substantial costs in terms of lost efficiency.

Broad Social Considerations

Competition promotes efficiency by giving firms incentives to produce the types and quantities of products that consumers want. Preservation of consumer choice or **consumer sovereignty** is an important feature of competitive markets. By encouraging and rewarding individual initiative, competition greatly enhances personal freedom. Firms with market power can limit output and raise prices to earn economic profits, whereas firms in competitive markets refer to market prices to determine optimal output

Limit Concentration
Restrict economic and political power.

quantities. Public policy can be a valuable tool with which to control unfairly gained market power and restore control over price and quantity decisions to the public.

Another social purpose of taxation or regulatory intervention is to **limit concentration** of economic and political power. It has long been recognized that economic and social relations become intertwined and that concentrated economic power is generally inconsistent with the democratic process. The laws of incorporation, first passed during the 1850s, play an important role in the U.S. economic system. These laws have allowed owners of capital (stockholders) to pool economic resources without also pooling political influence, thereby allowing big business and democracy to coexist. Of course, the large scale of modern corporations has sometimes diminished the controlling influence of individual stockholders. In these instances, public policy has limited the growth of large firms to avoid undue concentration of political power.

Important social considerations often constitute compelling justification for government intervention in the marketplace. Deciding whether a public policy is warranted can become complicated because social considerations sometimes run counter to efficiency considerations.

SUBSIDY AND TAX POLICY

Subsidies give positive incentives for desirable performance; taxes confer penalties to limit undesirable performance.

Managerial Application 11.2

Corn Growers Discover Oil!

Firms in competitive markets can sometimes improve performance by finding new and innovative uses for their products. An example is provided by the use of sugar-rich kernels of corn to produce ethanol, a clean-burning fuel used in automobiles. Although the technology for ethanol production from corn has been available since the 1980s, recent strides have made the technology much more economical. Until recently, it took one bushel of corn to produce 2.6 gallons of ethanol. New refining methods now allow 2.8 gallons of ethanol to be produced from a single bushel of corn.

Most commercial ethanol operations are located in the Midwest near major corn-growing areas. In the future, the most attractive markets for expanding ethanol production may be near important population centers where air pollution is a major concern. Federal mandates require much of California, Long Island, New York City, and the lower Hudson Valley to reduce air pollution by using reformulated gas that contains a higher oxygen level. Although the natural gas derivative MTBE is a popular additive for reformulated

gasoline, MTBE is also a carcinogen found to be a serious contaminant in drinking water. The New York legislature and governor have approved a phase-out of MTBE in New York State. California has banned MTBE, and there are similar calls to do so nationally.

With MTBE on its way out, corn growers argue that ethanol is the next best available additive. Ethanol mixed with gasoline not only reduces air pollution by creating a cleaner burning mixture, but ethanol production also reduces our dependence on imported oil. Ethanol production creates a market for surplus farm products and thereby helps alleviate rural poverty. For example, an important by-product from ethanol production is dried distillers grain, an excellent livestock feed. For many, ethanol production is inherently attractive because creating automobile fuel from corn creates important social and environmental by-products. Paramount among these is a reduced reliance on foreign oil.

See: Kendall Wilson, "Ethanol Meets the Market," *The Wall Street Journal Online*, October 20 2007, http://online.wsj.com.

Subsidy Policy

Subsidy Policy
Government
support strategy.

Government sometimes responds to positive externalities by providing subsidies. **Subsidy policy** can be indirect, like government construction and highway maintenance grants that benefit the trucking industry. They can be direct payments, such as agricultural payment-in-kind (PIK) programs, special tax treatments, and government-provided low-cost financing. Tax credits on business investment and depletion allowances on natural resource extraction are examples of subsidies given in recognition of social benefits such as job creation and energy independence. Positive externalities associated with industrial parks induce government to provide local tax incremental financing or industrial revenue bond financing for such facilities. This low-cost financing is thought to provide compensation for the external benefits of economic development.

Tradable Emission Permits
Transferable
pollution licenses.

Tradable emission permits are pollution licenses granted by the government to firms and individuals. Rather than spend millions of dollars on new equipment, raw materials, or production methods to meet pollution abatement regulations, firms sometimes purchase tradable emission permits from other companies that are able to more easily reduce their own pollution. These tradable emission permits are a valuable commodity that can be worth millions of dollars. Opponents of this system argue that they infringe on the public's right to a clean and safe environment. Proponents contend that the costs of pollution abatement make trade-offs inevitable. Moreover, they argue that the tradable emission permits do not confer new licenses to pollute; they merely transfer licenses from one polluter to another. Nevertheless, by awarding tradable emission permits worth millions of dollars to the worst offenders of a clean environment, environmentally sensitive firms and consumers have been hurt, at least on a relative basis.

Deadweight Loss from Taxes

Local, state, or federal fines for exceeding specified weight limits on trucks, pollution taxes, and effluent charges are common examples of tax policies intended to limit negative externalities. Other per unit taxes are imposed as simple revenue-generating devices for local, state, and federal governments. The appropriate per unit tax is extremely difficult to determine because of problems associated with estimating the magnitude of negative externalities. For example, calculating some of the social costs of air pollution, such as more frequent house painting, is relatively straightforward. Calculating the costs of increased discomfort—even death—for emphysema patients is more difficult. Nevertheless, public policy makers must consider the full range of consequences of negative externalities to create appropriate and effective incentives for pollution control.

Figure 11.3 shows the price, output, and social welfare effects caused by a per unit tax on sellers of a good or service. A per unit tax on sellers has the effect of increasing buyer marginal costs at every output level. When a per unit tax of t is imposed on sellers, the market supply curve shifts inward to $MC + t$. The equilibrium level of output falls from Q_E to Q_t, and the market price for buyers rises from P_E to P_B. With the per unit tax, a difference is created between the price paid by buyers, P_B, and the price received by sellers, P_S. Also notice how imposition of a per unit tax has direct implications for the amounts of producer and consumer surplus. Prior to imposition of a per unit tax t, total revenues received by sellers were shown by the region $0P_EEQ_E$. Consumer surplus was equal to the area P_EAE; producer surplus was described by the region $0P_EE$. Following imposition of a per unit tax t, total revenues received by sellers fall to the area depicted by $0P_SDQ_t$. Consumer surplus declines to equal the area P_BAB; producer surplus declines to equal the area $0P_SD$. On the plus side, imposition of a per unit tax t generates new tax

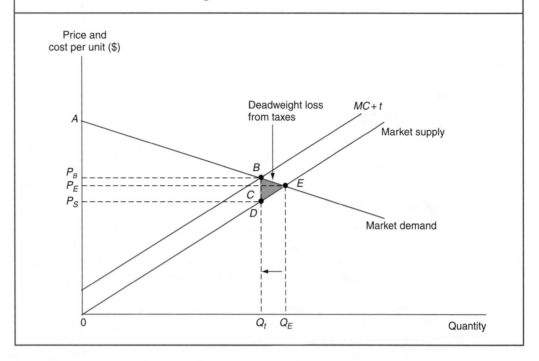

Figure 11.3 Taxes Create Deadweight Losses

A tax on sellers drives a wedge between the price paid by buyers and the amount received by sellers. Taxes also create a deadweight loss in social welfare.

Deadweight Loss of Taxation
Decline in social welfare due to decline in economic activity caused by taxes.

revenues equal to the area P_SP_BBD. However, these added tax revenues only partially compensate for the attendant losses in consumer surplus and producer surplus caused by the tax. Imposition of a per unit tax t creates a net loss in social welfare, or a **deadweight loss of taxation,** equal to the area BDE.

Per unit taxes cause deadweight losses because they reduce the amount of economic activity in competitive markets, and thereby prevent buyers and sellers from realizing some of the gains from trade. The loss in social welfare measured by the deadweight loss of taxation does not necessarily imply that per unit taxes are bad or should be avoided. However, it does suggest that the benefits derived from tax revenues are mitigated by social welfare losses tied to lost trade opportunities. From an economic perspective, imposition of a per unit tax is only advantageous if the benefits derived from added tax revenues are sufficient to overcome the economic costs tied to the deadweight loss in social welfare.

The example described in Figure 11.3 focuses upon the consumer surplus, producer surplus, and social welfare effects of a per unit tax on sellers. Similar effects result from a per unit tax on buyers. From an economic perspective, it does not matter whether unit taxes are levied on buyers or sellers of goods and services. When a per unit tax is levied on buyers, the market demand curve shifts downward by the amount of the tax. When a per unit tax is levied on sellers, as shown in Figure 11.3, the market supply curve shifts upward by that same amount. In both cases, imposition of a per unit tax increases the price paid by buyers and reduces the price received by sellers. Parallel losses in the amount of consumer surplus and producer surplus will occur. Per unit taxes on buyers and sellers both result in a deadweight loss of taxation that mitigates the net benefits derived from the spending of resulting tax revenues.

Although tax policy complements subsidy policy, an important distinction should not be overlooked. If society wants to limit the harmful consequences of air pollution, either subsidies for pollution reduction or taxes on pollution can provide effective incentives. Subsidies imply that firms have a right to pollute because society pays to reduce pollution. In contrast, a system of pollution tax penalties asserts society's right to a clean environment. Firms must reimburse society for the damage caused by their pollution. Some prefer tax policy as a method for pollution reduction on the grounds that it explicitly recognizes the public's right to a clean and safe environment.

TAX INCIDENCE AND BURDEN

Buyers and sellers typically share the economic hardship associated with taxation, regardless of how such taxes are levied.

Role of Elasticity

Tax Incidence
Point of tax collection.

Tax Burden
Economic hardship due to tax.

The question of who pays the economic cost of taxation can seldom be determined merely by identifying the taxed, fined, or otherwise regulated party. Although the point of tax collection, or the **tax incidence,** of pollution charges may be a given corporation, this **tax burden** may be passed on to customers or suppliers.

In general, who pays the economic burden of a tax or operating control regulation depends on the elasticities of supply and demand for the final products of affected firms. Figure 11.4 illustrates this issue by considering the polar extremes of perfectly elastic demand for final products [Figure 11.4(a)], and perfectly inelastic demand for final products [Figure 11.4(b)]. Identically upward-sloping MC curves (industry supply curves) are assumed in each instance. Here the effect of per unit tax is shown to increase marginal costs by a fixed amount per unit. This amount, t, can reflect pollution taxes per unit of output or regulation-induced cost increases.

Figure 11.4(a) shows that good substitutes for a firm's product and highly elastic demand prevent producers from passing taxes or regulation-induced cost increases on to customers. In this case, producers—including investors, employees, and suppliers—are forced to bear the economic burden of the tax or regulation. Falling rates of return on invested capital and high unemployment are symptomatic of such influences. Holding the elasticity of demand constant, the economic burden of taxation will tend to shift from customers toward producers (suppliers) as the elasticity of supply increases. Producers are prevented from passing taxes or regulation-induced cost increases on to customers as demand becomes highly elastic. When demand is perfectly elastic, producers bear the entire economic burden of a tax increase or regulation-induced cost increase.

Figure 11.4(b) shows the effect of tax increases or regulation-induced cost increases in the case of perfectly inelastic final-product demand. Without substitute products, producers can pass the burden of such a tax or regulation-induced cost increase on to customers. When demand is perfectly inelastic, the consumer pays all the costs of taxes or regulations. Holding the elasticity of demand constant, the economic burden of taxation will tend to shift from producers (suppliers) toward customers as the elasticity of supply decreases. When demand is perfectly inelastic, customers bear the entire economic burden of a tax increase or regulation-induced cost increase.

Elasticity also has implications for the amount of social welfare lost due to the deadweight loss of taxation. Holding the elasticity of demand constant, the deadweight

Figure 11.4 Tax Burden Allocation Under Elastic and Inelastic Demand

(a) Highly elastic product demand places the burden of regulation-induced cost increases on producers, who must cut production from Q_1 to Q_2. (b) Low elasticity of product demand allows producers to raise prices from P_1 to P_2, and consumers bear the burden of regulation-induced cost increases.

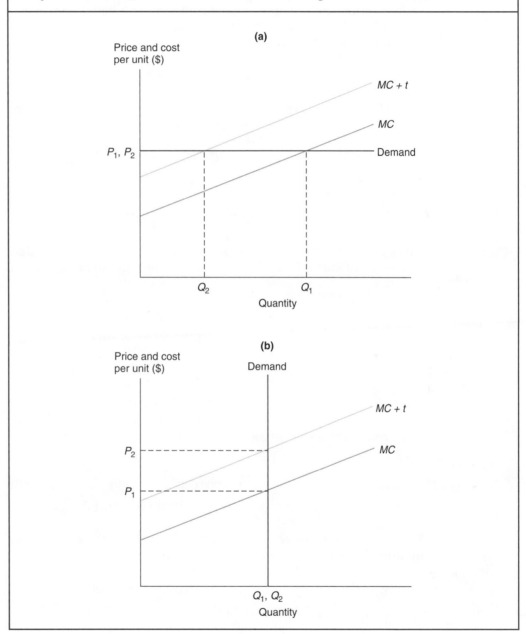

loss of a tax is small when supply is relatively inelastic. When supply is relatively elastic, the deadweight loss of a tax is large. Similarly, holding supply elasticity constant, the deadweight loss of a tax is small when demand is relatively inelastic. The deadweight loss of a tax is large when demand is relatively elastic.

Tax Cost–Sharing Example

To illustrate tax effects and the impact of regulation-induced cost increases, consider the effects of a new regulation prohibiting herbicide usage in corn production, perhaps because of fears about groundwater contamination. Assume that the industry is perfectly competitive, so the $3 market price of corn represents both average and marginal revenue per bushel ($P = MR = \$3$). The marginal cost relation for each farmer, before any new regulations are imposed, is

$$MC = \partial TC / \partial Q = \$0.6 + \$0.04Q$$

where Q is bushels of corn (in thousands). The optimal level of corn production per farm is calculated by setting $MR = MC$ and solving for Q:

$$MR = MC$$
$$\$3 = \$0.6 + \$0.04Q$$
$$\$0.04Q = \$2.4$$
$$Q = 60 \ (000) \text{ or } 60{,}000 \text{ bushels}$$

Given a perfectly competitive market, the supply curve for each producer is given by the marginal cost curve. From the marginal cost relation, the quantity of corn supplied by each farmer is

$$\text{Supply Price} = \text{Marginal Cost}$$
$$P = \$0.6 + \$0.04Q$$

or

$$Q = -15 + 25P$$

If the corn industry consists of 200,000 farmers with farms of equal size, total industry supply is

$$Q_S = 200{,}000(-15 + 25P)$$
$$= -3{,}000{,}000 + 5{,}000{,}000P \qquad \text{(Supply)}$$

To complete the industry profile prior to the new regulation on herbicides, assume that industry demand is given by the relation

$$Q_D = 15{,}000{,}000 - 1{,}000{,}000P \qquad \text{(Demand)}$$

In equilibrium,

$$Q_S = Q_D$$
$$-3{,}000{,}000 + 5{,}000{,}000P = 15{,}000{,}000 - 1{,}000{,}000P$$
$$6{,}000{,}000P = 18{,}000{,}000$$
$$P = \$3 \text{ per bushel}$$

and

$$Q_S = -3{,}000{,}000 + 5{,}000{,}000(3)$$
$$= 12{,}000{,}000 \ (000), \text{ or } 12 \text{ billion bushels}$$
$$Q_D = 15{,}000{,}000 - 1{,}000{,}000(3)$$
$$= 12{,}000{,}000 \ (000), \text{ or } 12 \text{ billion bushels}$$

Now assume that reducing herbicide usage increases the amount of tillage needed to keep weed growth under control and causes the yield per acre to drop, resulting in a 25 percent increase in the marginal costs of corn production. The economic effect of such a regulation is identical to that of a per unit tax that increases the marginal cost of production by 25 percent. For individual farmers, the effect on marginal costs is reflected as

$$MC' = 1.25(\$0.6 + \$0.04Q)$$
$$= \$0.75 + \$0.05Q$$

If only a few farmers in a narrow region of the country are subject to the new regulation, as would be true in the case of state or local pollution regulations, then market prices would remain stable at $3, and affected farmers would curtail production dramatically to 45,000 bushels each, because

$$MR = MC'$$
$$\$3 = \$0.75 + \$0.05Q$$
$$\$0.05Q = \$2.25$$
$$Q = 45 \ (000), \text{ or } 45{,}000 \text{ bushels}$$

Given a perfectly competitive industry and, therefore, a perfectly elastic demand for corn, local pollution regulations will force producers to bear the entire burden of regulation-induced cost increases.

A different situation arises when all producers are subject to the new herbicide regulation. In this instance, the revised individual-firm supply curve is

$$\text{Supply Price} = \text{Marginal Cost}$$
$$P = \$0.75 + \$0.05Q$$

or

$$Q = -15 + 20P$$

Total industry supply, assuming that all 200,000 farmers remain in business (something that may not happen if the resulting changes in profit levels are substantial), equals

$$Q_S' = 200{,}000(-15 + 20P)$$
$$= -3{,}000{,}000 + 4{,}000{,}000P \qquad \text{(New Supply)}$$

The equilibrium industry price/output combination is found where

$$Q_S' = Q_D$$
$$-3,000,000 + 4,000,000P = 15,000,000 - 1,000,000P$$
$$5,000,000P = 18,000,000$$
$$P = \$3.60 \text{ per bushel}$$

and

$$Q_S' = -3,000,000 + 4,000,000(3.60)$$
$$= 11,400,000 \text{ (000), or } 11.4 \text{ billion bushels}$$
$$Q_D = 15,000,000 - 1,000,000(3.60)$$
$$= 11,400,000 \text{ (000), or } 11.4 \text{ billion bushels}$$

At the new market price, each individual farm produces 57,000 bushels of corn:

$$Q = -15 + 20(3.60)$$
$$= 57 \text{ (000), or } 57,000 \text{ bushels}$$

Industry-wide regulation of herbicides has a smaller impact on producers because the effects of regulation are partially borne by consumers through the price increase from

Managerial Application 11.3

Measuring Economic Profits

Business managers, security analysts, and investors have long devoted careful attention to measuring the revenue and cash flow benefits of capital expenditures. Now, they are all sharpening their pencils to scrutinize the economic costs of corporate spending. Rather than just analyzing accounting numbers, focus has shifted to the market value-added, or economic value-added, from investment expenditures. Economic profits stemming from corporate expenditures can be thought of as the difference between economic benefits and economic costs:

Economic Profit = Adjusted Earnings − Capital Costs
= Adjusted Earnings − (Marginal Cost of Capital × Value of Capital employed)

Value maximization requires that the firm undertake all investment projects that generate positive economic profits; projects featuring economic losses should be rejected. For investment projects with positive economic profits, the greater those economic profits the more desirable the investment project.

When economic profits are calculated, cash flow numbers can be useful. Earnings before interest, taxes, depreciation and amortization (EBITDA) is one such measure. EBITDA avoids any errors in the application of accounting accrual methodology, but managers focused on EBITDA sometimes overlook the need to make necessary investments in plant and equipment. To ensure that funds for needed capital expenditures are available, prudent managers often focus on free cash flow, or EBITDA minus the cost of essential new plant and equipment.

Free cash flow retained in the organization must produce a return commensurate with that available on similar investment projects. Instead of adopting marginal investment projects that promise below-average returns, management typically uses free cash flow to buy back stock or repay borrowed funds. Focusing on economic profitability is helpful because it forces managers to explicitly consider the cost of capital in planning and operating decisions.

See: Timothy Aeppel, "Overseas Profits Provide Shelter For U.S. Firms," *The Wall Street Journal Online*, August 9, 2007, http://online.wsj.com.

$3 to $3.60 per bushel. This example illustrates why state and local authorities find it difficult to tax or regulate firms that operate in highly competitive national markets. Such taxes and regulations usually are initiated at the national level.

PRICE CONTROLS

Binding price floors or price ceiling distort economic performance and reduce social welfare.

Price Floors

Price Floor
Minimum price.

Perhaps the most famous price support program, or **price floor,** in the United States is administered by the U.S. Department of Agriculture (USDA) (see Figure 11.5). Currently, there are about 3 million people working on farms in the United States, comprising less than 2 percent of the labor force. This represents a sharp decline from

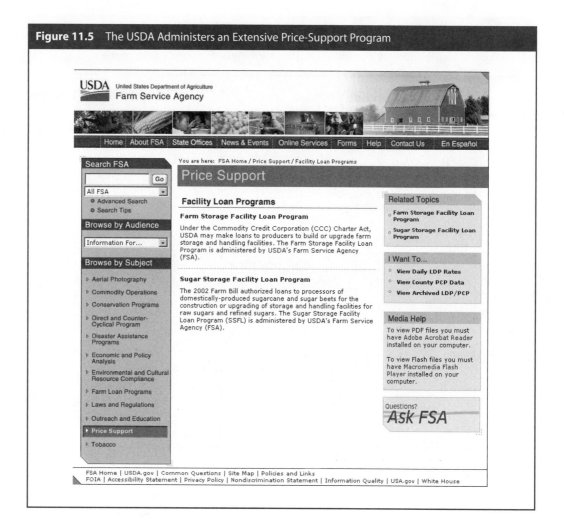

Figure 11.5 The USDA Administers an Extensive Price-Support Program

the 10 million or so who worked on farms 50 years ago, when farmers represented about 10 percent of the U.S. labor force. This decline in farm employment has been made possible by the enormous rate of productivity increase in agriculture. Today, less than one-third of the farmers produce more than twice the amount of agricultural output produced 50 years ago.

Sensitive to rural voters and powerful special-interest groups, politicians have embraced price floors as a means for increasing farmer incomes. A complex system of price floors, crop loans, production subsidies, and land set-aside programs has evolved to counteract the effects of rising agricultural productivity in the face of generally inelastic demand for foodstuffs. As shown in Figure 11.6(a), when price floors are set above the equilibrium market price, P_E, a modest surplus tends to result in the short run. Buyers react to higher than competitive prices by reducing the quantity demanded from Q_E to Q_D; producers react by increasing the quantity supplied from Q_E to Q_S. Excess production results in surplus, as measured by the difference between the quantity supplied and the quantity demanded, Surplus $= Q_S - Q_D$. In the long run, both demand and supply tend to be more elastic than in the short run [see Figure 11.6(b)]. This tends to accentuate

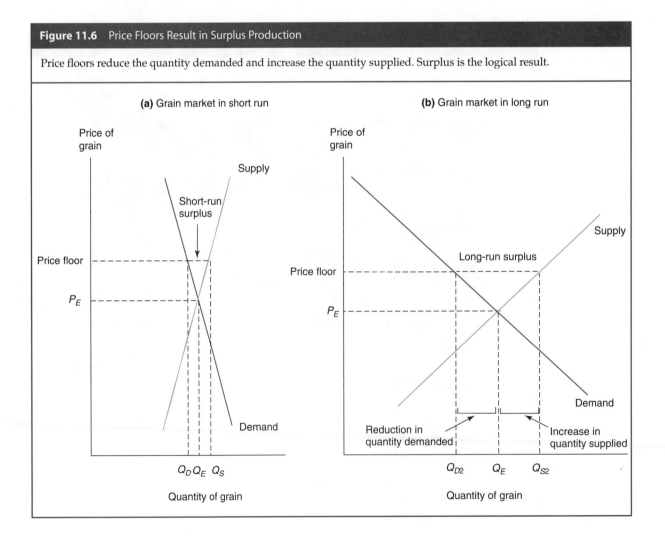

Figure 11.6   Price Floors Result in Surplus Production

Price floors reduce the quantity demanded and increase the quantity supplied. Surplus is the logical result.

(a) Grain market in short run

(b) Grain market in long run

the surplus situation as buyers continue to shift to other less costly alternatives, while producers scramble to increase supply.

Costly government-set price floors in agriculture products have persisted because politicians remain highly sensitive to rural voters and powerful special-interest groups. Other special-interest groups seeking to set artificially high price floors in vigorously competitive markets have been much less successful. The Organization of Petroleum Exporting Countries (OPEC) has repeatedly failed in its attempts to restrict supply and maintain artificially high prices in the oil market. In the short run, both supply and demand tend to be fairly inelastic in the oil market. In the long run, however, high oil prices bring sharp reductions in oil usage as consumers shift toward high-mileage cars, increased home insulation, and otherwise moderate energy use. At the same time, high oil prices attract exploration and rising supply. As a result, after adjusting for the rate of inflation, oil prices today are in line with those charged more than a generation ago.

The economic cost of surplus is not only measured by the amount of excess foodstuffs that become spoiled or are put to less than their best use, it is also measured by the amount of excess resources deployed in the production of unneeded agricultural products. Surplus represents a serious economic problem in that it signifies a significant loss in social welfare.

Price Ceiling
Maximum price.

Price Ceilings

A **price ceiling** is a costly mechanism for restraining excess demand. In the United States, price controls have sometimes been used during wartime to restrain "price gouging" by profiteers seeking to benefit from wartime shortages. In the 1970s, peacetime wage–price controls were instituted during the Nixon Administration to manage a perceived trade-off between wage increases and price inflation. Boards of citizens were appointed to judge the appropriateness of major wage and price increases. However, Nixon wage–price controls proved unworkable. Farmers stopped shipping cattle to market, while others drowned chickens in protest. Consumers emptied the shelves of supermarkets. Today, the failure of Nixon wage–price controls is cited as proof that wage–price controls are not an effective means for managing excess aggregate demand.

Despite convincing evidence that price ceilings are an ineffective means for restraining excess demand, some large cities continue to use price ceilings in an effort to make housing more affordable. Rent control in New York City is a prominent example. In New York City, landlords are restricted in terms of the rents they can charge tenants. Figure 11.7(a) shows the short-run effects of such rent control. In the short run, a price ceiling set below the equilibrium market price, P_E, results in a modest shortage situation. Renters react to lower than competitive rental rates by increasing the quantity demanded from Q_E to Q_D; landlords react by reducing the quantity supplied from Q_E to Q_S. Excess demand results in shortage, as measured by the difference between the quantity demanded and the quantity supplied: Shortage $= Q_D - Q_S$. Because demand and supply tend to be more elastic in the long run than in the short run [see Figure 11.7(b), shortages tend to grow over time as renters continue to expand their demand for low-cost housing, while landlords fail to keep up in terms of offering new supply.

Like surplus, shortage results in significant economic costs and represents a serious economic problem in that it signifies a significant loss in social welfare.

Figure 11.7   Price Ceilings Create a Supply Shortage

Price ceilings reduce the quantity supplied and increase the quantity demanded. Shortage is the logical result.

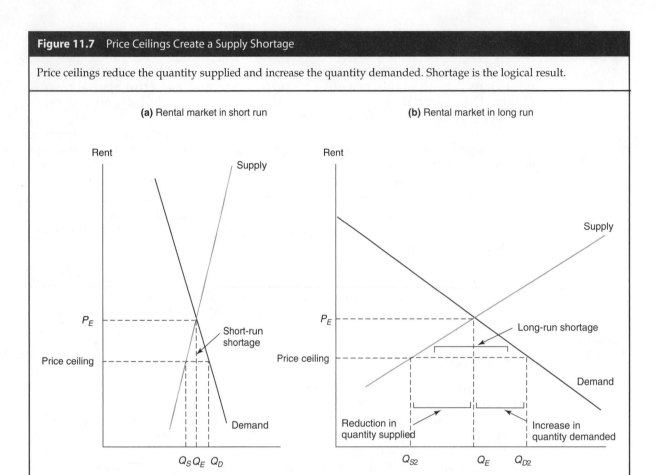

BUSINESS PROFIT RATES

In long-run equilibrium, profits in perfectly competitive markets provide a normal risk-adjusted rate of return.

Return on Stockholders' Equity

Return on Stockholders' Equity (ROE)
Net income divided by the book value of total assets minus total liabilities.

Business profit rates are best evaluated using the accounting rate of **return on stockholders' equity (ROE)**. ROE is net income divided by the book value of stockholders' equity, where stockholders' equity is total assets minus total liabilities. ROE can also be described as the product of three common accounting ratios. ROE equals the firm's profit margin multiplied by the total asset turnover ratio, all times the firm's leverage ratio:

$$\text{ROE} = \frac{\text{Net Income}}{\text{Equity}}$$

$$= \frac{\text{Net Income}}{\text{Sales}} \times \frac{\text{Sales}}{\text{Total Assets}} \times \frac{\text{Total Assets}}{\text{Equity}} \qquad \textbf{11.1}$$

$$= \text{Profit Margin} \times \frac{\text{Total Asset}}{\text{Turnover}} \times \text{Leverage}$$

Profit Margin

Net income expressed as a percentage of sales revenue.

Profit margin is the amount of profit earned per dollar of sales. When profit margins are high, robust demand or stringent cost controls, or both, allow the firm to earn a significant profit contribution. Holding capital requirements constant, profit margin is a useful indicator of managerial efficiency in responding to rapidly growing demand and/or effective measures of cost containment. However, rich profit margins do not necessarily guarantee a high rate of return on stockholders' equity. Despite high profit margins, firms in financial services and real estate operators often earn only modest rates of return because significant capital expenditures are required before meaningful sales revenues can be generated. It is important to consider the magnitude of capital requirements when interpreting the size of profit margins for a firm or an industry.

Total Asset Turnover

Sales revenue divided by the book value of total assets.

Total asset turnover is sales revenue divided by the book value of total assets. When total asset turnover is high, the firm makes its investments work hard in the sense of generating a large amount of sales revenue. A broad range of consumer service businesses enjoy high rates of total asset turnover that allow efficient firms to earn attractive rates of ROE despite modest profit margins. Despite modest profit margins and a conservative financial structure, retailing juggernaut Wal-Mart Stores, Inc., reports a sterling ROE by virtue of the fact that it accomplishes a total asset turnover rate that is well in excess of industry and corporate norms. Wal-Mart has learned that the wise use of assets is a key ingredient of success in the cutthroat discount retailing business.

Leverage

Ratio of total assets divided by stockholders' equity.

Leverage is often defined as the ratio of total assets divided by stockholders' equity. It reflects the extent to which debt is used in addition to common stock financing. Leverage amplifies firm profit rates over the business cycle. During economic booms, leverage can dramatically increase the firm's profit rate; during recessions and other economic contractions, leverage can just as dramatically decrease realized rates of return or lead to losses. Despite ordinary profit margins and modest rates of total asset turnover, ROE in the securities brokerage, hotel, and gaming industries can sometimes benefit through the use of risky financial leverage. It is worth remembering that a risky financial structure can lead to awe-inspiring profit rates during economic expansions, such as that experienced during the late 1990s, but it can also lead to huge losses during economic downturns, such as in 2001.

Typical Profit Rates

For the most successful large and small firms in the United States and Canada, ROE averages roughly 15 percent to 20 percent during a typical year, before deducting extraordinary items. After extraordinary items, ROE averages about 10 percent to 15 percent per year for such companies. After extraordinary charges, average ROE is comprised of a typical profit margin on sales revenue of approximately 5 percent to 10 percent, a standard total asset turnover ratio of roughly 1.0 times, and a common leverage ratio of about 2:1:

$$\text{Typical ROE} = \text{Profit Margin} \times \text{Total Asset Turnover} \times \text{Leverage}$$
$$= 5\% \text{ to } 10\% \times 1.0 \times 2.0$$
$$= 10\% \text{ to } 15\%$$

Managerial Application 11.4

Wonderful Businesses

After running a spectacularly successful private partnership, Warren Buffett gained control of textile manufacturer Berkshire Hathaway in 1965, at age 34. As chairman and CEO, Buffett built Berkshire into a $165 + billion holding company with an immense portfolio of publicly traded common stocks, including American Express, Coca-Cola, Procter & Gamble, and a host of diverse and enormously successful operating companies. The most important of Berkshire's operating subsidiaries are in the property and casualty insurance business. Included among these is GEICO, the fifth-largest auto insurer in the United States, General Re, one of the four largest reinsurers in the world, and the Berkshire Hathaway Reinsurance Group. Numerous business activities are also conducted through Berkshire's non-insurance subsidiaries, including Benjamin Moore (paint), Borsheim's (fine jewelry), Johns Manville (building products), International Dairy Queen (fast food), Mid-American Energy (pipelines), Nebraska Furniture Mart (furniture and appliances), and Shaw Industries (carpet).

During more than 40 years of Buffett's stewardship, Berkshire's net worth per share has compounded at more than 20 percent + per year. In an era when median *Fortune 500* companies count themselves lucky to earn half that much, Buffett's accomplishment is amazing—especially for a debt-free company. In addition to being uniquely capable as an investor and manager, Buffett has the uncommon ability to communicate his insights on management in a disarmingly modest and humorous fashion that is equally valuable for stock market investors and experienced business managers.

Among the most important lessons learned by Buffett is that "It is far better to buy a wonderful company at a fair price than a fair company at a wonderful price." In a difficult business, no sooner is one problem solved than another surfaces. Importantly, Buffett says "do not join with managers who lack admirable qualities, no matter how attractive the prospects of their business."

See: Shai Oster and Carolyn Cui, "Buffett's PetroChina Sale," *The Wall Street Journal Online*, October 12, 2007, http://online.wsj.com.

ROE is an attractive measure of firm performance because it shows the rate of profit earned on funds committed to the enterprise by its owners, the stockholders. When ROE is at or above 10 percent to 15 percent per year, the rate of profit is generally sufficient to compensate investors for the risk involved with a typical business enterprise. When ROE consistently falls far below 10 percent to 15 percent per year, profit rates are generally insufficient to compensate investors for the risks undertaken. Of course, when business risk is substantially higher than average, commensurately higher rate of return is required. When business risk is lower than average, somewhat lower than average profit rates provide an adequate return for investors.

How is it possible to know if business profit rates are sufficient to compensate investors for the risks undertaken? The answer is simple: just ask current and potential shareholders and bondholders. Shareholders and bondholders implicitly inform management of their risk/return assessment of the firm's performance on a daily basis. If performance is above the minimum required, the firm's bond and stock prices rise; if performance is below the minimum required, bond and stock prices fall. For privately held companies, the market's risk/return assessment comes when new financing is required. If performance is above the minimum required, financing is easy to obtain; if performance is below the minimum required, financing is difficult or impossible to procure. As a practical matter, firms must consistently earn a business profit rate or ROE of at least 10 percent to 15 percent per year in order to grow and prosper. If ROE consistently falls below this level, financing dries up and the firm withers and dies. If ROE consistently exceeds this level, new debt and equity financing are easy to obtain, and growth by new and established competitors is rapid.

MARKET STRUCTURE AND PROFIT RATES

High business profit rates are derived from some combination of high profit margins, quick total asset turnover, and high leverage.

Profit Rates in Competitive Markets

In perfectly competitive markets, profit margins are low. This stems from the fact that in a perfectly competitive market, theory suggests that $P = MC$ and $MC = AC$. As a result, when average cost includes a risk-adjusted normal rate of return on investment, $P = AC$. This means that when profit margin is measured as $(P - AC)/P$, profit margins will tend to be low and reflect only a normal rate of return in competitive markets.

Table 11.1 shows corporate profit rates for a variety of highly competitive industry groups. Although such industry groups correspond only loosely with economic markets, these data give a useful perspective on profit differences across a variety of important lines of business. As shown in Table 11.1, profit rates tend to be low across a broad range of industry groups producing standardized products in markets with low barriers to entry. Important capital-intensive business such as agriculture, mining, and retailing routinely earn subpar rates of return on invested capital. During periods of weak economic activity, such as during 2002–2003, many firms in competitive markets earn meager profits or suffer temporary losses.

Mean Reversion in Profit Rates

Over time, entry and nonleading firm growth in highly profitable competitive markets cause above-normal profits to regress toward the mean. Conversely, bankruptcy and exit allow the below-normal profits of depressed competitive markets to rise toward the mean. For example, good crop-growing weather often creates a windfall for farmers who enjoy a temporary surge in crop yields, or benefit from an unexpected decline in production costs. However, if such favorable conditions persist for an extended period, both new and established farmers would increase the amount planted, market supply would increase, and both prices and profits would fall and return to normal levels. Poor crop-growing weather has an opposite effect. Lower profits or losses are suffered by farmers who suffer from a temporary decline in crop yields, or who must withstand an unexpected surge in production costs. If such unfavorable conditions persist for an extended period, exit would occur and established farmers would decrease the amount planted. Market supply would decrease, and both prices and profits would eventually rise and return to normal levels.

Reversion to the Mean
Tendency of firm profit rates to converge over time toward long-term averages.

In competitive markets, the tendency of firm profit rates to converge over time toward long-term averages is called **reversion to the mean** (see Figure 11.8). Economic theory that predicts a mean reversion in business profits over time is accepted because of its simple and compelling logic and because it has predictive capability. High business profits often lead to booming capital expenditures and higher employment. Eventually, such expansion causes the marginal rate of return on investment to fall. Conversely, low business profits typically lead to falling capital expenditures, layoffs, and plant closings. Eventually, industry contraction leads to rising rates of return for survivors.

Table 11.1 Profit Rates in Highly Competitive Markets

Industry Group	Active Corporations	Profit Margin (% of sales)	Return on Equity (ROE)%
Retail trade			
Drug stores and proprietary stores	17,619	2.3	8.9
Furniture and home furnishings stores	48,678	1.6	9.5
Gasoline service stations	31,376	0.7	11.7
General merchandise stores	9,835	2.8	13.1
Hardware stores	10,677	0.6	4.1
Liquor stores	14,407	1.0	11.5
Retail stores	204,705	2.1	12.2
Wholesale trade			
Electrical goods	30,004	1.0	8.2
Farm-product raw materials	7,723	0.6	4.5
Generic drugs & drugstore sundries	5,997	0.8	5.4
Lumber and construction materials	16,413	1.8	17.0
Metals and minerals	6,377	1.6	9.0
Paper and paper products	11,362	1.4	5.5
Petroleum and petroleum products	13,828	1.1	7.8
Services			
Amusement & recreation services	102,948	4.7	9.4
Business services	407,400	4.8	16.8
Miscellaneous services	218,629	2.1	10.5
Motion picture theaters	1,711	2.5	5.7
Manufacturing			
Apparel and accessories	5,852	1.3	9.7
Fabricated textile products	5,154	2.3	11.0
Ferrous & primary metal products	2,189	2.5	8.2
Food and kindred products	4,218	3.2	10.1
Knitting mills	552	3.0	11.0
Leather and leather products	1,203	1.6	6.8
Logging, sawmills, and planing mills	11,694	1.1	2.9
Meat products	3,843	1.7	11.0
Metal cans and shipping containers	209	1.8	4.2
Millwork, plywood, and related products	4,318	2.2	5.4
Nonferrous metal industries	2,050	4.4	11.2
Nonmetallic mineral products	3,571	4.0	11.9
Pulp, paper, and board mills	293	1.9	3.2
Sugar and confectionery products	884	6.3	12.6
Textile mill products	3,048	3.6	13.7
Weaving mills and textile finishings	1,477	2.8	9.4
Transportation and public utilities			
Gas production and distribution	1,081	0.3	0.7
Transportation services	48,373	1.6	12.2
Water transportation	8,911	4.5	10.7
Finance, insurance & real estate			
Condominium management & housing associations	47,259	−3.2	−2.2
Real estate operators & building lessors	219,034	10.4	5.6
Real estate services	181,963	4.4	8.2
Sub-dividers & developers	64,645	3.1	4.5
Agriculture, forestry, and fishing			
Agricultural production	91,164	2.5	6.5
Agricultural services, forestry & fishing	71,950	2.4	14.7
Mining			
Coal mining	1,521	3.9	3.8
Copper, lead and zinc, gold and silver ores	1,159	−0.6	−0.3
Crude petroleum & natural gas	13,772	6.3	4.1
Crushed stone, sand & gravel	3,414	7.0	6.1
Metal mining	527	5.1	6.3
Nonmetallic minerals	396	2.6	4.0
Competitive markets	1,965,413	2.6	8.1
All corporations	4,619,858	8.1	15.4

Data source: U.S. corporate federal income tax data, May 8, 2007, http://www.bizstats.com/.

Figure 11.8 Profit Rates Display Mean Reversion over Time

Entry into high-profit industries drives down both prices and profits. Over time, entry causes above-normal profits to regress toward normal profit rate, whereas exit allows the below-normal profits of depressed industries to rise toward the mean.

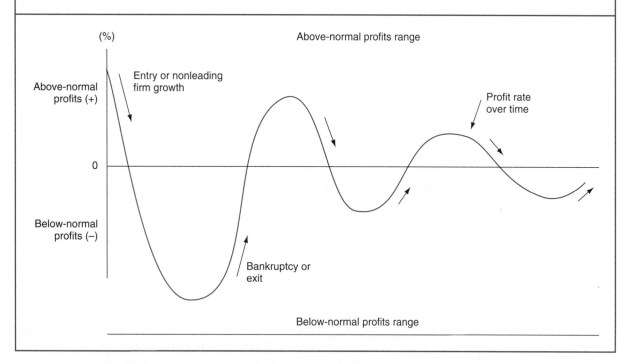

COMPETITIVE MARKET STRATEGY

In perfectly competitive markets, innovation and imitation by rivals makes ongoing survival a constant struggle.

Disequilibrium Profits
Short-term economic profits prior to long-term market adjustment.

Disequilibrium Losses
Below-normal returns suffered in the short run prior to long-term market adjustment.

Short-Run Firm Performance

In the short run, above-normal profits in perfectly competitive industries are sometimes simply **disequilibrium profits.** Disequilibrium profits are above-normal returns earned in the time interval that exists between when a favorable influence on industry demand or cost conditions first transpires and the time when competitor entry or growth finally develops. **Disequilibrium losses** are below-normal returns suffered in the time interval between when an unfavorable influence on industry demand or cost conditions first transpires and the time when exit or downsizing finally occurs.

When barriers to entry and exit are minimal, as they are in many competitive markets, competitor reactions tend to be quick and disequilibrium profits are fleeting. When barriers to entry and exit are significant, competitor reactions tend to be slow and disequilibrium profits can persist for extended periods. In the quintessential perfectly competitive industry, disequilibrium profits are immediately dissipated. In real-world markets, disequilibrium profits can persist over an entire business cycle even in the most competitive industries. In retailing, for example, labor and inventory costs have been cut dramatically following the introduction of computerized price scanners. Despite the vigorously price-competitive nature of the retailing business, early innovators who first adopted the bar code technology were able to earn above-normal profits for a number of years. Innovative grocery retailers have enjoyed dramatically lower costs with profit margins of 2 percent to 3.5 percent on sales, versus a more typical 1 percent, over a decade and more.

Economic Luck
Temporary good fortune due to some unexpected change in industry demand or cost conditions.

Within this context, firms in some competitive markets enjoy above-normal returns stemming from **economic luck,** or temporary good fortune due to some unexpected change in industry demand or cost conditions. For example, during 2007 many small to mid-size oil refineries and gasoline retailers benefited greatly when oil prices unexpectedly shot up following temporary oil shortages. At the same time, many other firms experienced economic losses following the unanticipated surge in energy costs. Both sets of companies experienced a reversal of fortune when energy prices plummeted. Grain farmers also benefit mightily when export demand for agricultural products skyrockets and suffer when export demand withers.

LONG-RUN FIRM PERFORMANCE

In long-run equilibrium, the typical firm in a perfectly competitive market has the potential for only a normal rate of return on investment. If many capable competitors offer identical products, vigorous price competition tends to eliminate disequilibrium profits. In the long run, good and bad fortune tends to average out. Luck cannot be relied upon as a source of durable above-average rates of return.

Competitive Strategy
Search for a durable advantage over competitors.

Economic Rents
Profits due to uniquely productive inputs.

Above-normal profits in perfectly competitive industries are usually transitory and typically reflect disequilibrium conditions. If above-normal returns persist for extended periods in a given industry or line of business, elements of uniqueness are probably at work. Superior efficiency leads to superior profitability, even in competitive markets. The search for an economic advantage or a favorable competitive position in an industry or line of business is called **competitive strategy.** If a competitive firm can offer products that are faster, better, or cheaper than the competition, then it will be able to earn **economic rents,** or profits due to uniquely productive inputs. For example, an exceptionally well-trained workforce, talented management, or superior land and raw materials can all generate economic rents in competitive markets and lead to above-normal profits. In parts of the country where school systems provide outstanding primary and secondary education, firms are able to hire a basic workforce with a high rate of literacy and strong basic skills. Businesses that are able to employ such workers at a typical wage are able to earn superior profits when compared with the average rate of return for all competitors. Local tax subsidies designed to attract investment and job opportunities can also lower the cost of capital and create economic rents for affected firms. In many parts of the country, such local government initiatives lead to economic rents for affected firms. On the other hand, if local taxes or government regulations prove to be especially onerous, economic losses can result for affected companies.

SUMMARY

Competitive markets represent an ideal form of market structure in the sense that equilibrium market price–output solutions maximize social welfare through a perfect balance of supply (cost) and demand (revenue) considerations.

- **Welfare economics** is the study of how the allocation of economic resources affects the material well-being of consumers and producers.

Equilibrium prices and quantities that create balance between supply and demand in perfectly competitive markets also maximize the total **social welfare** derived from such activity. The measurement of social welfare is closely related to **consumer surplus,** the net benefit derived by consumers from consumption, and **producer surplus,** the net benefit derived by producers from production.

- There is a **deadweight loss problem** associated with deviations from competitive market equilibrium. A deadweight loss is any loss suffered by consumers or producers that is not transferred, but is lost as a result of market imperfections or government policies. Because deadweight losses are often depicted as triangles when linear supply and demand curves are employed, deadweight losses are often described as the **welfare loss triangle.**

- **Market power** is reflected in the ability of sellers to restrict output below competitive norms and their ability to obtain above-normal prices and profits for extended periods. Undue market power is also indicated when buyer influence results in less than competitive prices, output, and profits for sellers. Generally speaking, **market failure** occurs when competitive market outcomes fail to sustain socially desirable activities or to eliminate undesirable ones. **Failure by market structure** is due to the absence of a sufficiently large number of buyers and sellers. Differences between private and social costs or benefits are called **externalities. Failure by incentive,** a second important type of market failure, is always a risk in markets where social values and social costs differ from the private costs and values of producers and consumers.

- From an **economic efficiency** standpoint, a given mode of tax or **economic regulation** is desirable to the extent that benefits exceed costs. **Social equity,** or fairness, criteria must also be carefully weighed when social considerations bear on the tax or regulatory decision-making process. Preservation of consumer choice or **consumer sovereignty** is an important feature of competitive markets. An important social purpose of taxation or regulatory intervention is to **limit concentration** of economic and political power.

- Government sometimes responds to positive externalities by providing subsidies. **Subsidy policy** can be indirect, like government construction and highway maintenance grants that benefit the trucking industry. **Tradable emission permits** are pollution licenses granted by the government to firms and individuals.

- Tax revenues only partially compensate for the attendant losses in consumer surplus and producer surplus caused by a tax. Imposition of a per unit tax creates a net loss in social welfare, or a **deadweight loss of taxation.** Although the point of tax collection, or the **tax incidence,** of pollution charges may be a given corporation, this **tax burden** may be passed on to customers or suppliers.

- Competitive markets are subject to the forces of supply and demand. In some instances, public policy sets a **price floor** in an effort to boost producer incomes. Price floors can result in surplus production and a significant loss in social welfare. In other instances, public policy sets a price ceiling. A **price ceiling** is a costly and seldom used mechanism for restraining excess demand. Price ceilings can result in excess demand, shortage, and a significant loss in social welfare.

- Business profit rates are best evaluated using the accounting rate of **return on stockholders' equity (ROE).** ROE is net income divided by the book value of stockholders' equity, and equals profit margin times total asset turnover times leverage. **Profit margin** is the amount of profit earned per dollar of sales. **Total asset turnover** is sales revenue divided by the book value of total assets. When total asset turnover is high, the firm makes its investments work hard in the sense of generating a large amount of sales volume. **Leverage** is often defined as the ratio of total assets divided by stockholders' equity. It reflects the extent to which debt and preferred stock are used in addition to common stock financing.

- In competitive markets, the tendency of firm profit rates to converge over time toward long-term averages is called **reversion to the mean.** In the short run, above-normal profits in perfectly competitive industries are sometimes simply **disequilibrium profits** that exist in the time interval between when a favorable influence on industry demand or cost conditions first transpires and the time when competitor entry or growth finally develops. **Disequilibrium losses** are below-normal returns suffered in the time interval between when an unfavorable influence on industry demand or cost conditions first transpires and the time when exit or downsizing finally occurs.

- Firms in some competitive markets enjoy above-normal returns stemming from **economic** luck, or temporary good fortune due to some unexpected change in industry demand or cost conditions. The search for an economic advantage or a favorable competitive position in an industry or line of business is called **competitive strategy.** If a competitive firm can offer products that are faster, better, or cheaper than the competition, then it will be able to earn **economic rents,** or profits due to uniquely productive inputs.

Competitive markets are sometimes burdened by imperfections that limit economic efficiency. As such, microeconomic concepts and methodology offer a valuable guide to both public policy and business decision making.

QUESTIONS

Q11.1 Your best income-earning opportunity appears to be an offer to work for a local developer during the month of June and earn $2,000. However, before taking the job, you accept a surprise offer from a competitor. If you actually earn $2,600 during the month, how much producer surplus have you earned? Explain.

Q11.2 Assume that you are willing to pay $1,100 for a new personal computer that has all the "bells and whistles." On the Internet, you buy one for the bargain price of $900. Unbeknownst to you, the Internet retailer's marginal cost was only $750. How much consumer surplus, producer surplus, and net addition to social welfare stems from your purchase? Explain.

Q11.3 After having declined during the 1970s and 1980s, the proportion of teenage smokers in the United States has risen sharply since the early 1990s. To reverse this trend, advertising programs have been launched to discourage teenage smoking, penalties for selling cigarettes to teenagers have been toughened, and the excise tax on cigarettes has been increased. Explain how each of these public policies affects demand for cigarettes by teenagers.

Q11.4 In 2004, OPEC reduced the quantity of oil it was willing to supply to world markets. Explain why the resulting price increase was much larger in the short run than in the long run.

Q11.5 The demand for basic foodstuffs, like feed grains, tends to be inelastic with respect to price. Use this fact to explain why highly fertile farmland will fetch a relatively high price at any point in time, but that rising farm productivity over time has a negative overall influence on farmland prices.

Q11.6 In 1990, Congress adopted a luxury tax to be paid by buyers of high-priced cars, yachts, private airplanes, and jewelry. Proponents saw the levy as an effective means of taxing the rich. Critics pointed out that those bearing the hardship of a tax may or may not be the same as those who pay the tax (the point of tax incidence). Explain how the elasticities of supply and demand in competitive markets can have direct implications for the ability of buyers and sellers to shift the burden of taxes imposed upon them. Also explain how elasticity information has implications for the amount of social welfare lost due to the deadweight loss of taxation.

Q11.7 Both employers and employees pay Social Security (FICA) on wage income. While the burden of this tax is designed to be borne equally by employers and employees, is a straight 50/50 sharing of the FICA tax burden likely? Explain.

Q11.8 The Fair Labor Standards Act establishes a federal minimum wage of $7.25 per hour effective July 24, 2009. Use your knowledge of market equilibrium and the elasticity of demand to explain how an increase in the minimum wage could have no effect on unskilled worker income. When will increasing the minimum wage have an income-increasing effect versus an income-decreasing effect. Which influence is more likely?

Q11.9 The New York City Rent Stabilization Law of 1969 established maximum rental rates for apartments in New York City. Explain how such controls can lead to shortages, especially in the long run, and other economic costs. Despite obvious disadvantages, why does rent control remain popular?

Q11.10 Wal-Mart founder Sam Walton amassed an enormous fortune in discount retailing, one of the most viciously competitive markets imaginable. How is this possible?

SELF-TEST PROBLEMS AND SOLUTIONS

ST11.1 Social Welfare. A number of domestic and foreign manufacturers produce replacement parts and components for personal computer systems. With exacting user specifications, products are standardized and price competition is brutal. To illustrate the net amount of social welfare generated in this hotly competitive market, assume that market supply and demand conditions for replacement tower cases can be described as

$$Q_S = -175 + 12.5P \qquad \text{(Market Supply)}$$
$$Q_D = 125 - 2.5P \qquad \text{(Market Demand)}$$

where Q is output in thousands of units and P is price per unit.

A. Graph and calculate the equilibrium price–output solution.

B. Use this graph to help you algebraically determine the amount of consumer surplus, producer surplus, and net social welfare generated in this market.

ST11.1 SOLUTION

A. The market supply curve is given by the equation

$$Q_S = -175 + 12.5P$$

or, solving for price,

$$12.5P = 175 + Q_S$$
$$P = \$14 + \$0.08Q_S$$

The market demand curve is given by the equation

$$Q_D = 125 - 2.5P$$

or, solving for price,

$$2.5P = 125 - Q_D$$
$$P = \$50 - \$0.4Q_D$$

Graphically, demand and supply curves appear as follows:

Algebraically, to find the market equilibrium levels for price and quantity, simply set the market supply and market demand curves equal to one another so that $Q_S = Q_D$. To find the market equilibrium price, equate the market demand and market supply curves where quantity is expressed as a function of price:

$$\text{Supply} = \text{Demand}$$
$$-175 + 12.5P = 125 - 2.5P$$
$$15P = 300$$
$$P = \$20$$

To find the market equilibrium quantity, set equal the market supply and market demand curves where price is expressed as a function of quantity, and $Q_S = Q_D$:

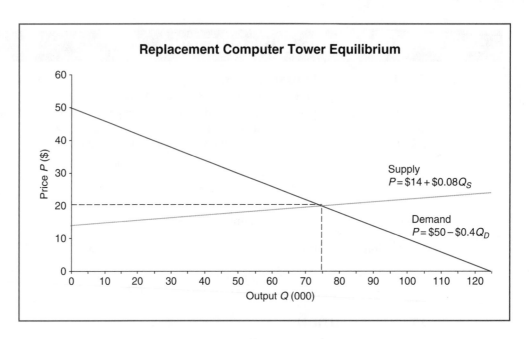

$$\text{Supply} = \text{Demand}$$
$$\$14 + \$0.08Q = \$50 - \$0.4Q$$
$$0.48Q = 36$$
$$Q = 75 \ (000)$$

The equilibrium price–output combination is a market price of $20 with an equilibrium output of 75 (000) units, as shown in the figure.

B. The value of consumer surplus is equal to the region under the market demand curve that lies above the market equilibrium price of $20. Because the area of such a triangle is one-half the value of the base times the height, the value of consumer surplus equals

$$\text{Consumer Surplus} = \frac{1}{2} \left[75 \times (\$50 - \$20) \right]$$
$$= \$1,125 \ (000)$$

In words, this means that at a unit price of $20, the quantity demanded is 75 (000) units, resulting in total revenues of $1,500 (000). The fact that consumer surplus equals $1,125 (000) means that customers as a group would have been willing to pay an additional $1,125 (000) for this level of market output. This is an amount above and beyond the $1,500 (000) paid. Customers received a real bargain.

The value of producer surplus is equal to the region above the market supply curve at the market equilibrium price of $20. Because the area of such a triangle is one-half the value of the base times the height, the value of producer surplus equals

$$\text{Producer Surplus} = \frac{1}{2} \left[75 \times (\$20 - \$14) \right]$$
$$= \$225 \ (000)$$

At a unit price of $20, producer surplus equals $225 (000). Producers as a group received $225 (000) more than the absolute minimum required for them to produce the market equilibrium output of 75 (000) units. Producers received a real bargain.

In competitive market equilibrium, social welfare is measured by the sum of net benefits derived by consumers and producers. Social welfare is the sum of consumer surplus and producer surplus:

$$\text{Social Welfare} = \text{Consumer Surplus} + \text{Producer Surplus}$$
$$= \$1,125 + \$225$$
$$= \$1,350\ (000)$$

ST11.2 Price Ceilings. The local government in a West Coast college town is concerned about a recent explosion in apartment rental rates for students and other low-income renters. To combat the problem, a proposal has been made to institute rent control that would place a $900 per month ceiling on apartment rental rates. Apartment supply and demand conditions in the local market are

$$Q_S = -400 + 2P \qquad\qquad \text{(Market Supply)}$$
$$Q_D = 5,600 - 4P \qquad\qquad \text{(Market Demand)}$$

where Q is the number of apartments and P is monthly rent.

A. Graph and calculate the equilibrium price–output solution. How much consumer surplus, producer surplus, and social welfare is produced at this activity level?

B. Use the graph to help you algebraically determine the quantity demanded, quantity supplied, and shortage with a $900 per month ceiling on apartment rental rates.

C. Use the graph to help you algebraically determine the amount of consumer and producer surplus with rent control.

D. Use the graph to help you algebraically determine the change in social welfare and deadweight loss in consumer surplus due to rent control.

ST11.2 SOLUTION
A. The competitive market supply curve is given by the equation

$$Q_S = -400 + 2P$$

or, solving for price,

$$2P = 400 + Q_S$$
$$P = \$200 + \$0.5Q_S$$

The competitive market demand curve is given by the equation

$$Q_D = 5,600 - 4P$$

or, solving for price,

$$4P = 5,600 - Q_D$$
$$P = \$1,400 - \$0.25Q_D$$

To find the competitive market equilibrium price, equate the market demand and market supply curves where quantity is expressed as a function of price:

$$Supply = Demand$$
$$-400 + 2P = 5,600 - 4P$$
$$6P = 6,000$$
$$P = \$1,000$$

To find the competitive market equilibrium quantity, set equal the market supply and market demand curves where price is expressed as a function of quantity, and $Q_S = Q_D$:

$$Supply = Demand$$
$$\$200 + \$0.5Q = \$1,400 - \$0.25Q$$
$$0.75Q = 1,200$$
$$Q = 1,600$$

Therefore, the competitive market equilibrium price–output combination is a market price of $1,000 with an equilibrium output of 1,600 units.

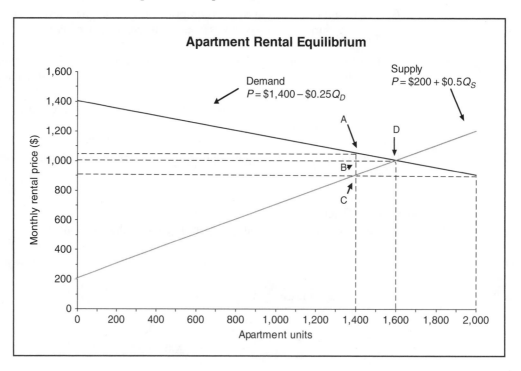

The value of consumer surplus is equal to the region under the market demand curve that lies above the market equilibrium price of $1,000. Because the area of such a triangle is one-half the value of the base times the height, the value of consumer surplus equals

$$Consumer\ Surplus = \tfrac{1}{2}\,[1,600 \times (\$1,400 - \$1,000)]$$
$$= \$320,000$$

In words, this means that at a unit price of $1,000, the quantity demanded is 1,600 units, resulting in total revenues of $1,600,000. The fact that consumer surplus equals $320,000 means that customers as a group would have been willing to pay an additional $320,000 for this level of market output. This is an amount above and beyond the $1,600,000 paid. Customers received a real bargain.

The value of producer surplus is equal to the region above the market supply curve at the market equilibrium price of $1,000. Because the area of such a triangle is one-half the value of the base times the height, the value of producer surplus equals

$$\text{Producer Surplus} = \tfrac{1}{2}\,[1{,}600 \times (\$1{,}000 - \$200)]$$
$$= \$640{,}000$$

At a rental price of $1,000 per month, producer surplus equals $640,000. Producers as a group received $640,000 more than the absolute minimum required for them to produce the market equilibrium output of 1,600 units. Producers received a real bargain.

In competitive market equilibrium, social welfare is measured by the sum of net benefits derived by consumers and producers. Social welfare is the sum of consumer surplus and producer surplus:

$$\text{Social Welfare} = \text{Consumer Surplus} + \text{Producer Surplus}$$
$$= \$320{,}000 + \$640{,}000$$
$$= \$960{,}000$$

B. The market demand at the $900 price ceiling is

$$Q_D = 5{,}600 - 4(900)$$
$$= 2{,}000 \text{ units}$$

The market supply at the $900 price ceiling is

$$Q_S = -400 + 2(900)$$
$$= 1{,}400 \text{ units}$$

The market shortage created by the $900 price ceiling is

$$\text{Shortage} = Q_D - Q_S$$
$$= 2{,}000 - 1{,}400$$
$$= 600 \text{ units}$$

C. Under rent control, the maximum amount of apartment supply that landlords are willing to offer at a rent of $900 per month is 1,400 units. From the market demand curve, it is clear that renters as a group are willing to pay as much as (or have a reservation price of) $1,050 per month to rent 1,400 apartments:

$$P = \$1{,}400 - \$0.25(1{,}400)$$
$$= \$1{,}050$$

Under rent control, the value of consumer surplus has two components. The first component of consumer surplus is equal to the region under the market demand curve that lies above the price of $1,050 per month. This amount corresponds to uncompensated value obtained by renters willing to pay above the market price all the way up to $1,400 per month. As in the case of an uncontrolled market, the area of such a triangle is one-half the value of the base times the height. The second component of consumer surplus under rent control is the uncompensated value obtained by renters willing to pay as much as $1,050 per month to rent 1,400 apartments, and who are delighted to rent for the controlled price of $900 per month. This amount corresponds to the amount of revenue represented by the rectangle defined by the prices of $1,050 and $900 and the quantity of 1,400 units. Notice that this second component of consumer surplus includes some value privately measured as producer surplus. Under rent control, the total amount of consumer surplus is

$$\text{Rent-Controlled Consumer Surplus} = \tfrac{1}{2}\,[1,400 \times (\$1,400 - \$1,050)]$$
$$+ [1,400 \times (\$1,050 - \$900)]$$
$$= \$245,000 + \$210,000$$
$$= \$455,000$$

In this case, consumer surplus rises from $320,000 to $455,000, a gain of $135,000 as a result of rent control.

The value of producer surplus is equal to the region above the market supply curve at the rent-controlled price of $900. Because the area of such a triangle is one-half the value of the base times the height, the value of producer surplus equals

$$\text{Producer Surplus} = \tfrac{1}{2}\,[1,400 \times (\$900 - \$200)]$$
$$= \$490,000$$

At a rent-controlled price of $900 per month, producer surplus falls from $640,000 to $490,000, a loss of $150,000.

D. The change in social welfare caused by rent control is measured by the change in net benefits derived by consumers and producers. The change in social welfare is the change in the sum of consumer surplus and producer surplus:

$$\text{Social Welfare Change} = \text{Consumer Surplus Change} + \text{Producer Surplus Change}$$
$$= \$135,000 - \$150,000$$
$$= -\$15,000 \text{ (a loss)}$$

This $15,000 deadweight loss in social welfare due to rent control has two components. First, there is a deadweight loss of consumer surplus from consumers unable to find a rent-controlled apartment but willing to pay upwards from the prior market equilibrium price of $1,000 per month up to $1,050 per month. This amount is equal to the area shown in the graph as ABD. Because the area of such a triangle is one-half the value of the base times the height, the first component of deadweight loss in consumer surplus equals

$$\text{Deadweight Loss in Consumer Surplus} = \tfrac{1}{2}\,[(1,600 - 1,400) \times (\$1,050 - \$1,000)]$$
$$= \$5,000$$

Second, there is a deadweight loss of producer surplus from landlords forced to rent at the rent-controlled price of $900 per month rather the market equilibrium price of $1,000 per month. This amount is equal to the area shown in the graph as BCD. Because the area of such a triangle is one-half the value of the base times the height, the second component of deadweight loss in consumer surplus equals

$$\text{Deadweight Loss in Producer Surplus} = \tfrac{1}{2}\,[(1,600 - 1,400) \times (\$1,000 - \$900)]$$
$$= \$10,000$$

PROBLEMS

P11.1 Social Welfare Concepts. Indicate whether each of the following statements is true or false, and explain why.

A. In competitive market equilibrium, social welfare is measured by the net benefits derived from consumption and production as measured by the difference between consumer surplus and producer surplus.

B. The market supply curve indicates the minimum price required by sellers as a group to bring forth production.

C. Consumer surplus is the amount that consumers are willing to pay for a given good or service minus the amount that they are required to pay.

D. Whereas consumer surplus is closely related to the supply curve for a product, producer surplus is closely related to the demand curve for a product.

E. Producer surplus is the net benefit derived by producers from production.

P11.2 Labor Policy. People of many different age groups and circumstances take advantage of part-time employment opportunities provided by the fast-food industry. Given the wide variety of different fast-food vendors, the industry is fiercely competitive, as is the unskilled labor market. In each of the following circumstances, indicate whether the proposed changes in government policy are likely to have an increasing, a decreasing, or an uncertain effect on employment in this industry.

A. Elimination of minimum wage law coverage for those working less than 20 hours per week.

B. An increase in spending for education that raises basic worker skills.

C. An increase in the employer portion of federally mandated FICA insurance costs.

D. A requirement that employers install expensive new worker-safety equipment.

E. A state requirement that employers pay 8 percent of wages to fund a new national health care program.

P11.3 Social Welfare. Natural gas is in high demand as a clean-burning energy source for home heating and air conditioning, especially in major metropolitan areas where air quality is a prime concern. The domestic supply of natural gas is also plentiful. Government reports predict that gas recoverable with current technology from domestic supply sources is sufficient to satisfy production needs for more than 50 years. Plentiful imports from Canada are also readily available to supplement domestic production. To illustrate the net amount of social welfare generated in this vigorously competitive market, assume that market supply and demand conditions are

$$Q_S = -2,000 + 800P \qquad \text{(Market Supply)}$$
$$Q_D = 4,500 - 500P \qquad \text{(Market Demand)}$$

where Q is output in Btus (in millions), and P is price per unit. A British thermal unit (Btu) is an English standard unit of energy. One Btu is the amount of thermal energy necessary to raise the temperature of one pound of pure liquid water by one degree Fahrenheit at the temperature at which water has its greatest density (39 degrees Fahrenheit).

A. Graph and calculate the equilibrium price–output solution.

B. Use this graph to help you algebraically determine the amount of consumer surplus, producer surplus, and net social welfare generated in this market.

P11.4 Deadweight Loss of Taxation.

To many upscale homeowners, no other flooring offers the warmth, beauty, and value of wood. New technology in stains and finishes calls for regular cleaning that takes little more than sweeping and/or vacuuming, with occasional use of a professional wood floor cleaning product. Wood floors are also ecologically friendly because wood is both renewable and recyclable. Buyers looking for traditional oak, rustic pine, trendy mahogany, or bamboo can choose from a wide assortment.

At the wholesale level, wood flooring is a commodity-like product sold with rigid product specifications. Price competition is ferocious among hundreds of domestic manufacturers and importers. Assume that market supply and demand conditions for mahogany wood flooring are

$$Q_S = -10 + 2P \qquad \text{(Market Supply)}$$
$$Q_D = 320 - 4P \qquad \text{(Market Demand)}$$

where Q is output in square yards of floor covering (000), and P is the market price per square yard.

A. Graph and calculate the equilibrium price–output solution before and after imposition of a $9 per unit tax.

B. Calculate the deadweight loss to taxation caused by imposition of the $9 per unit tax. How much of this deadweight loss was suffered by consumers versus producers? Explain.

P11.5 Lump Sum Taxes.

In 1998, California's newly deregulated power market began operation. The large power utilities in the state turned over control of their electric transmission facilities to the new Independent System Operator (ISO) to assure fair access to transmission by all generators. The new California Power Exchange (CalPX) opened to provide a competitive marketplace for the purchase and sale of electric generation. The deregulation required electric utilities to split their business into generation, transmission, and distribution businesses. The utilities continue to own all of the transmission and distribution facilities, but the ISO controls all of the transmission facilities. Utilities provide all distribution services, but customers are allowed to choose their energy supplier. The utilities were required to sell off 50 percent of their generating facilities. In addition, utilities have to sell all their electric generation to the Power Exchange and purchase all power for their customers through the Power Exchange. To illustrate the net amount of social welfare generated by a competitive power market, assume that market supply and demand conditions for electric energy in California are

$$Q_S = -87{,}500 + 1{,}250P \qquad \text{(Market Supply)}$$
$$Q_D = 250{,}000 - 1{,}000P \qquad \text{(Market Demand)}$$

where Q is output in megawatt hours per month (in thousands), and P is the market price per megawatt hour. A megawatt hour is 1 million watt-hours, where watt-hours is a common measurement of energy produced in a given amount of time, arrived at by multiplying voltage by amp hours. The typical California home uses 1 megawatt hour of electricity per month.

A. Graph and calculate the equilibrium price–output solution. Use this graph to help you algebraically determine the amount of producer surplus generated in this market.

B. Calculate the maximum lump-sum tax that could be imposed on producers without affecting the short-run supply of electricity. Is such a tax apt to affect the long-run supply of electricity? Explain.

P11.6 Demand Versus Supply Subsidy.

In Africa, the continent where the polio epidemic has been most difficult to control, international relief efforts aimed at disease eradication often work against a backdrop of civil unrest and war. In some countries, temporary cease-fire agreements must be negotiated to allow vaccination and prevent serious outbreaks from occurring. During peacetime and during war, low incomes make paying for the vaccine a real problem among the poor. To make the oral polio vaccine more affordable, either consumer purchases (demand) or production (supply) can be subsidized. Consider the following market demand and market supply curves for a generic oral polio vaccine:

$$Q_D = 24{,}000 - 1{,}600P \qquad \text{(Market Demand)}$$
$$Q_S = -2{,}000 + 1{,}000P \qquad \text{(Market Supply)}$$

where Q is output measured in doses of oral vaccine (in thousands), and P is the market price in dollars.

A. Vouchers have a demand-increasing effect. Graph and calculate the equilibrium price–output solution before and after the institution of a voucher system whereby consumers can use a $3.25 voucher to supplement cash payments.

B. Per-unit producer subsidies have a marginal cost-decreasing effect. Show and calculate the equilibrium price–output solution after the institution of a $3.25 per unit subsidy for providers of the oral polio vaccine. Discuss any differences between answers to parts A and B.

P11.7 Price Floors.

Each year, about 9 billion bushels of corn are harvested in the United States. The average market price of corn is a little over $2 per bushel, but costs farmers about $3 per bushel. Tax payers make up the difference. Under the 2002 $190 billion, 10-year farm bill, American taxpayers will pay farmers $4 billion a year to grow even more corn, despite the fact that every year the United States is faced with a corn surplus. Growing surplus corn also has unmeasured environmental costs. The production of corn requires more nitrogen fertilizer and pesticides than any other agricultural crop. Runoff from these chemicals seeps down into the groundwater supply, and into rivers and streams. Ag chemicals have been blamed for a 12,000-square-mile dead zone in the Gulf of Mexico. Overproduction of corn also increases U.S. reliance on foreign oil.

To illustrate some of the cost in social welfare from agricultural price supports, assume the following market supply and demand conditions for corn:

$$Q_S = -5{,}000 + 5{,}000P \qquad \text{(Market Supply)}$$
$$Q_D = 10{,}000 - 2{,}500P \qquad \text{(Market Demand)}$$

where Q is output in bushels of corn (in millions), and P is the market price per bushel.

A. Graph and calculate the equilibrium price–output solution. Use this graph to help you algebraically determine the amount of surplus production the government will be forced to buy if it imposes a support price of $2.50 per bushel.

B. Use this graph to help you algebraically determine the gain in producer surplus due to the support price program. Explain.

P11.8   Import Controls.   Critics argue that if Congress wants to make the tax code more equitable, a good place to start would be removing unfair tariffs and quotas. Today, there are more than 8,000 import tariffs, quotas, so-called voluntary import restraints, and other import restrictions. Tariffs and quotas cost consumers roughly $80 billion per year, or about $800 for every American family. Some of the tightest restrictions are reserved for food and clothing that make up a large share of low-income family budgets.

The domestic shoe market shows the effects of import controls on a large competitive market. Assume market supply and demand conditions for shoes are

$$Q_{US} = -50 + 2.5P \qquad \text{(Supply from U.S. Producers)}$$
$$Q_F = -25 + 2.5P \qquad \text{(Supply from Foreign Producers)}$$
$$Q_D = 375 - 2.5P \qquad \text{(Market Demand)}$$

where Q is output (in millions), and P is the market price per unit.

A. Graph and calculate the equilibrium price–output solution assuming there are no import restrictions, and under the assumption that foreign countries prohibit imports.

B. Use this graph to help you algebraically determine the amount of consumer surplus transferred to producer surplus and the deadweight loss in consumer surplus due to a ban on foreign imports. Explain.

P11.9   Protective Tariffs.   In the United States, steel production has remained constant since the 1970s at about 100 million tons per year. Large integrated companies, like U.S. Steel, remain important in the industry, but roughly 50 percent of domestic production is now produced by newer, nimble, and highly efficient mini-mill companies. Foreign imports account for roughly 30 percent of domestic steel use. In order to stem the tide of rising imports, President George W. Bush announced in 2002 that the United States would introduce up to 30 percent tariffs on most imported steel products. These measures were to remain in place for 3 years. To show how protective tariffs can help domestic producers, consider the following cost relations for a typical competitor in this vigorously competitive market:

$$TC = \$150,000 + \$100Q + \$0.15Q^2$$
$$MC = \partial TC/\partial Q = \$100 + \$0.3Q$$

where TC is total cost, MC is marginal cost, and Q is output measured by tons of hot-dipped galvanized steel. Cost figures and output are in thousands.

A. Assume prices are stable in the market, and $P = MR = \$400$. Calculate the profit-maximizing price–output combination and economic profits for a typical producer in competitive market equilibrium.

B. Calculate the profit-maximizing price–output combination and economic profits for a typical producer if domestic market prices rise by 30 percent following introduction of Bush's protective tariff.

P11.10 Generic Competition. The Federal Trade Commission seeks to ensure that the process of bringing new low-cost generic alternatives to the marketplace and into the hands of consumers is not impeded in ways that are anticompetitive. To illustrate the potential for economic profits from delaying generic drug competition for 1 year, consider cost and demand relationships for an important brand-name drug set to lose patent protection:

$$TR = \$10.25Q - \$0.01Q^2$$
$$MR = \partial TR/\partial Q = \$10.25 - \$0.02Q$$
$$TC = \$625 + \$0.25Q + \$0.0025Q^2$$
$$MC = \partial TC/\partial Q = \$0.25 + \$0.005Q$$

where TR is total revenue, Q is output, MR is marginal revenue, TC is total cost, including a risk-adjusted normal rate of return on investment, and MC is marginal cost. All figures are in thousands.

A. Set $MR = MC$ to determine the profit-maximizing price–output solution and economic profits prior to the expiration of patent protection.

B. Calculate the firm's competitive market equilibrium price–output solution and economic profits following the expiration of patent protection and onset of generic competition.

CASE *Study*   **The Most Profitable S&P 500 Companies**

While net income is an obviously useful indicator of a firm's profit-generating ability, it has equally obvious limitations. Net income will grow with a simple increase in the scale of the operation. A 2 percent savings account will display growing interest income over time, but would scarcely represent a good long-term investment. Similarly, a company that generates profit growth of only 2 percent per year would seldom turn out to be a good investment. In the same way, investors must be careful in their interpretation of earnings per share numbers. These numbers are artificially affected by the number of outstanding shares. Following a 2:1 stock split, for example, the number of shares outstanding will double, while share price and earnings per share will fall by one-half. However, such a stock split neither enhances nor detracts from the economic appeal of a company. Because the number of outstanding shares is wholly determined by vote of the company's stockholders, the specific earnings per share number for any given company at any point in time is somewhat arbitrary. Earnings per share numbers are only significant on a relative basis. At any point in time, the earnings per share number for a firm is relatively meaningless, but the rate of growth in earnings per share over time is a fundamentally important determinant of future share prices.

Because absolute measures, like net income, paint only an incomplete picture of corporate profitability, various relative measures of profitability are typically relied upon by investors. First among these is the accounting rate of return on stockholders' equity (ROE) measure. Simply referred to as ROE, the return on stockholders' equity measure is defined as net income divided by the book value of stockholders' equity, where stockholders' equity is the book value of total assets minus total liabilities. ROE tells how profitable a company is in terms of each dollar invested by shareholders and reflects the effects of both operating and financial leverage. A limitation of ROE is that it can sometimes be unduly influenced by share buybacks and other types of corporate restructuring. According to Generally Accepted Accounting Principals (GAAP), the

continued

book value of stockholders' equity is simply the amount of money committed to the enterprise by stockholders. It is calculated as the sum of paid-in capital and retained earnings, minus any amount paid for share repurchases. When "extraordinary" or "unusual" charges are significant, the book value of stockholders' equity is reduced, and ROE can become inflated. Similarly, when share repurchases are at market prices that exceed the book value per share, book value per share falls and ROE rises. Given the difficulty of interpreting ROE for companies that have undergone significant restructuring, and for highly leveraged companies, some investors focus on the return on assets, or net income divided by the book value of total assets. Like ROE, return on assets (ROA) captures the effects of managerial operating decisions. ROA also tends to be less affected than ROE by the amount of financial leverage employed. As such, ROE has some advantages over ROA as a fundamental measure of business profits. Irrespective of whether net income, profit margin, ROE, ROA, or some other measure of business profits is employed, consistency requires using a common basis for between-firm comparisons.

Table 11.2 shows ROE data for 30 of the most consistently profitable companies found within the Standard and Poor's 500 stock index. Beer titan Anheuser-Busch Companies, Inc.; personal products and drug manufacturer Johnson & Johnson, and consumer goods goliath Procter & Gamble Co. are enormously profitable when profits are measured using ROE. To get some useful perspective on the source of these enormous profits, it is worth considering the individual economic factors that contribute to high levels of ROE: profit margin, total asset turnover, and financial leverage. Among these three potential sources of high ROE, high profit margins are the most attractive contributing factor because high profit margins usually mean that high rates of ROE are sustainable for an extended period. Profit margins show the amount of profit earned per dollar of sales

revenue. On a per unit basis, profit margins can be expressed as $\pi/\text{Sales} = P - AC/P$. When profit margins are high, the company is operating at a high level of efficiency, competitive pressure is modest, or both. In a competitive market, $P = MC = AC$, so profit margins converge toward zero as competitive pressures increase. Conversely, $P > MC$ in monopoly markets, so profit margins can be expected to rise as competitive pressures decrease. High profit margins are clear evidence that the firm is selling distinctive products.

Considering the effects of profit margins on the market value of the firm is a simple means for getting some interesting perspective on the importance of profit margins as an indicator of the firm's ability to sustain superior profitability. The market value of the firm represents the stock market's assessment of the firm's future earnings power. If high profit margins suggest attractive profit rates in the future, then profit margins should have a statistically significant impact on the current market value of the firm. An attractive way to measure the stock market's assessment of profit margin data is to study the link between profit margins and the firm's P/E ratio. In the P/E ratio, "P" stands for the company's stock price, and "E" stands for company earnings, both measured on a per share basis. P/E ratios are high when investors see current profits as high, durable, and/or rapidly growing; P/E ratios are low when investors see current profits as insufficient, vulnerable, or shrinking.

The P/E ratio effects of ROE, profit margin, total asset turnover, and financial leverage for consistently profitable corporate giants found within the S&P 500 are shown in Table 11.3.

A. Describe some of the advantages and disadvantages of ROE as a measure of corporate profitability. What is a typical level of ROE, and how does one know if the ROE reported by a given company reflects an adequate return on investment?

continued

B. Define the profit margin, total asset turnover, and financial leverage components of ROE. Discuss the advantages and disadvantages of each of these potential sources of high ROE.

C. Based upon the findings reported in Table 11.3, discuss the relation between *P/E* ratios and profit margins, total asset turnover, and financial leverage. In general, which component of ROE is the most useful indicator of the firm's ability to sustain high profit rates in the future?

Table 11.2 High Profit Margins Indicate Competitive Advantages

Company Name	Industry	P/E Ratio (5-year avg.)	Return on Equity (%)	Profit Margin (Return on Sales, %)	Total Asset Turnover	Leverage Ratio Ratio
Altria Group	Cigarettes	14.0	33.5	12.7	0.9	3.1
American Standard Companies Inc.	General Building Materials	19.6	71.5	4.6	1.5	7.1
Anheuser-Busch Companies, Inc.	Beverages—Brewers	20.4	61.1	8.6	0.9	4.4
AutoZone, Inc.	Auto Parts Stores	15.5	115.7	9.7	1.3	8.5
Ball Corporation	Packaging & Containers	17.0	31.6	5.1	1.2	4.9
Black & Decker Corporation	Small Tools & Accessories	15.2	35.6	7.4	1.2	4.5
Caterpillar Inc.	Farm & Construction Machinery	21.0	30.6	8.1	0.8	7.0
Coach, Inc.	Textile—Apparel Footwear & Accessories	38.6	41.4	24.0	1.2	1.3
Coca-Cola Company	Beverages—Soft Drinks	24.1	32.0	21.0	0.8	1.9
Colgate Palmolive	Personal Products	23.7	187.0	12.1	1.4	6.6
Freeport-McMoRan	Copper	29.8	136.0	27.7	0.3	2.5
H&R Block, Inc.	Personal Services	15.7	32.3	8.5	0.5	6.1
Johnson & Johnson	Drug Manufacturers—Major	22.0	28.4	18.6	0.8	1.8
Kellogg Company	Food—Major Diversified	20.4	52.5	9.4	1.0	4.7
Lexmark International, Inc.	Computer Peripherals	21.0	28.4	6.8	1.7	2.7
3M Company	Conglomerates	23.3	33.3	18.8	1.1	2.3
McGraw-Hill Companies, Inc.	Publishing—Books	23.4	28.6	14.9	1.1	3.0
Oracle Corporation	Application Software	26.2	32.2	23.3	0.6	1.9
PepsiCo, Inc.	Beverages—Soft Drinks	24.5	33.2	16.2	1.2	1.9
Pitney Bowes Inc.	Business Equipment	21.6	44.1	10.2	0.6	12.7
Procter & Gamble	Cleaning Products	25.5	32.1	13.3	0.6	2.0
RadioShack Corporation	Electronics Stores	17.0	33.5	2.3	2.4	2.7
Rockwell Collins, Inc.	Aerospace/Defense Products & Services	22.5	33.0	13.2	1.2	2.5
Sara Lee Corp.	Food—Major Diversified	18.1	43.6	1.6	1.0	4.6
Sherwin-Williams Company	General Building Materials	16.0	29.3	7.4	1.6	2.6
Sunoco, Inc.	Oil & Gas Refining & Marketing	13.3	33.3	2.7	3.8	5.1
TJX Companies, Inc.	Discount, Variety Stores	19.2	38.8	4.5	3.0	2.7
Waters Corporation	Scientific & Technical Instruments	26.2	36.1	17.7	0.9	4.3
Wyeth	Drug Manufacturers—Major	25.1	32.0	20.7	0.6	2.5
Yum! Brands, Inc.	Restaurants	18.9	63.8	8.7	1.6	4.4
Average		21.3	48.8	12.0	1.2	4.1

Data source: MSN/Money, May 10, 2007, http://moneycentral.msn.com/investor/finder/customstocks.asp.

continued

Table 11.3 Profit Margins Can Be Good Indicators of Future Profits

Dependent Variable	Intercept	Return on Equity (ROE)	Profit Margin (MGN)	Total Asset Turnover (TAT)	Leverage (LVG)	R^2	F-Statistic
P/E ratio (5-year avg.)	20.4050 (12.42)	0.0182 (0.03)				1.6%	0.45
P/E ratio (5-year avg.)	14.2215 (11.69)		0.5896 (6.70)			61.6%	44.85
P/E ratio (5-year avg.)	24.8132 (14.16)			−2.8695 (−2.33)		16.3%	5.44
P/E ratio (5-year avg.)	24.4243 (13.78)				−0.7680 (−2.06)	13.1%	4.23
P/E ratio (5-year avg.)	13.5053 (3.80)		0.6124 (4.64)	0.4336 (0.38)	−0.0218 (−0.71)	61.8%	14.06

SELECTED REFERENCES

Bjork, Kaj Mikael and Christer Carlsson. "The Effect of Flexible Lead Times on a Paper Producer." *International Journal of Production Economics* 107, no. 1 (May, 2007): 139–150.

Delong, Gayle and Robert DeYoung. "Learning by Observing: Information Spillovers in the Execution and Valuation of Commercial Bank M&As." *Journal of Finance* 62, no. 1 (February, 2007): 181–216.

Desai, Mihir A., C. Fritz Foley, and James R. Hines Jr. "Dividend Policy Inside the Multinational Firm." *Financial Management* 36, no. 1 (Spring, 2007): 5–26.

Dinlersoz, Emin M. and Pedro Pereira. "On the Diffusion of Electronic Commerce." *International Journal of Industrial Organization* 25, no. 3 (June, 2007): 541–574.

Dittmar, Amy and Anjan Thakor. "Why Do Firms Issue Equity?" *Journal of Finance* 62, no. 1 (February, 2007): 1–54.

Fama, Eugene F. and Kenneth R. French. "Disagreement, Tastes, and Asset Prices." *Journal of Financial Economics* 83, no. 3 (March, 2007): 667–689.

Goldman, Dana and Tomas J. Philipson. "Integrated Insurance Design in the Presence of Multiple Medical Technologies." *American Economic Review* 97, no. 2 (May, 2007): 427–432.

Lagos, Ricardo and Guillaume Rocheteau. "Search in Asset Markets: Market Structure, Liquidity, and Welfare." *American Economic Review* 97, no. 2 (May, 2007): 198–202.

Lambrecht, Bart M. and Stewart C. Myers. "A Theory of Takeovers and Disinvestment." *Journal of Finance* 62, no. 2 (April, 2007): 809–845.

Lerner, Josh and Feng Zhu. "What Is the Impact of Software Patent Shifts? Evidence from Lotus v. Borland." *International Journal of Industrial Organization* 25, no. 3 (June, 2007): 511–529.

Lettau, Martin and Jessica A. Wachter. "Why Is Long-Horizon Equity Less Risky? A Duration-Based Explanation of the Value Premium." *Journal of Finance* 62, no. 1 (February, 2007): 55–92.

Liu, Qihong and Konstantinos Serfes. "Market Segmentation and Collusive Behavior." *International Journal of Industrial Organization* 25, no. 2 (April, 2007): 355–378.

Livingston, Miles and Glenn Williams. "Drexel Burnham Lambert's Bankruptcy and the Subsequent Decline in Underwriter Fees." *Journal of Financial Economics* 84, no. 2 (May, 2007): 472–501.

Officer, Micah S. "The Price of Corporate Liquidity: Acquisition Discounts for Unlisted Targets." *Journal of Financial Economics* 83, no. 3 (March, 2007): 571–598.

Sufi, Amir. "Information Asymmetry and Financing Arrangements: Evidence from Syndicated Loans." *Journal of Finance* 62, no. 2 (April, 2007): 629–668.

Imperfect Competition

4

PART

Monopoly and Monopsony

Important markets controlled by a single firm are often subject to government-mandated price and profit regulation. If water and sewer, garbage collection and removal, power and light, and local telecommunications services are provided by a single firm, such companies are typically subject to tight state and local regulation. In other instances, state and local governments sometimes provide services when there are obvious economic advantages of a sole provider.

The professional sports leagues are good examples of sole providers of highly differentiated products that are not regulated in the traditional sense. The National Football League, National Basketball Association, National Hockey League, and Major League Baseball are all unique providers of professional sports entertainment. All major professional sports restrict local franchises to a number that is substantially smaller than the number of cities or markets that can support a team. By maintaining artificial scarcity, the professional leagues exert enormous leverage when they force cities and regions to bid aggressively for the right to sponsor a team. It is now standard for cities and regions seeking a new professional sports franchise to promise team owners "relocation fees" and a new publicly funded stadium or arena with all revenue-generating rights and free rent. Such deals cause the value of professional sports franchises and local subsidy costs to soar.

This chapter shows how a single seller or a single buyer comes to dominate individual markets, and considers the appropriate role for economic regulation.[1]

MONOPOLY MARKET CHARACTERISTICS

Some big markets are controlled by a single seller. What is the nature of such markets?

Basic Features

Monopoly
A market structure characterized by a single seller of a highly differentiated product.

Price Makers
Buyers and sellers whose large transactions affect market prices.

Monopoly exists when a firm is the sole producer of a distinctive good or service that has no close substitutes. In other words, under monopoly the firm is the industry. Like competitive firms, the pricing discretion of monopoly firms is constrained by the customer's overall willingness to pay as reflected by downward-sloping market demand curves. Still, the absence of close substitutes gives monopoly firms a significant amount of discretion when it comes to setting prices. Monopoly firms are **price makers** as opposed

---

1 See Thomas M. Lenard and Paul H. Rubin, "Googling 'Monopoly'," *The Wall Street Journal Online*, August 21, 2007, http://interactive.wsj.com.

to firms in competitive markets who are price takers. This price-making ability stems from the fact that monopoly firms benefit from competitive advantages that constitute barriers to mobility for smaller nonleading competitors and barriers to entry for potential entrants. In perfectly competitive markets, free and complete demand and supply information is widely available. Monopoly firms enjoy informational advantages that create a competitive advantage. In contrast with the dog-eat-dog world of competitive markets, monopoly firms also enjoy the ability to earn above-normal profits in long-run equilibrium.

The capacity for monopoly firms to influence market prices stems from real competitive advantages. While the source of such competitive advantages can vary from one situation to another, all monopoly markets share the following common characteristics:

- *A single seller.* A single firm produces all industry output. The monopoly is the industry.
- *Unique product.* Monopoly output is perceived by customers to be distinctive and preferable to its imperfect substitutes.
- *Blockaded entry and/or exit.* Firms are heavily restricted from entering or leaving the industry.
- *Imperfect dissemination of information.* Cost, price, and product quality information is withheld from uninformed buyers.
- *Opportunity for economic profits in long-run equilibrium.* Distinctive products allow $P > MC$ and $P = AR > AC$ for efficient monopoly firms.

As in the case of perfect competition, these basic conditions are too restrictive for pure monopoly to be commonplace in actual markets. Few goods are produced by single producers, and fewer still are completely free from competition by close substitutes. Even regulated public utilities face some competition in most of their markets. Electricity providers approach pure monopoly in the residential lighting market, for example, but face strong competition from gas and oil suppliers in the heating market. In all industrial and commercial power markets, electric utilities face competition from gas- and oil-powered private generators. Even though unregulated monopoly rarely exists in mature markets, monopoly concepts can be very useful in examining the development of new markets and emergent technologies.

Examples of Monopoly

Classic examples of monopoly have been the public utilities, including electricity, gas, and sanitary services. Such examples remain commonplace, and price and profit regulation has long been administered in an effort to retain the cost advantages of single-firm production, but limit any excess or unwarranted monopoly profits. Until a few years ago, basic phone service was also provided by regulated monopolies, but technical innovations have undermined many traditional telecommunications monopolies and rendered much of the established regulation obsolete. Today all consumers have the opportunity to choose among a variety of long-distance providers, like AT&T, Qwest, Sprint, or Verizon, and most can choose to receive basic telephone service from the local phone company or cable TV providers. In most markets, cable TV providers also offer digital broadband service for fast Internet access and constitute effective competitors for the fast Digital Subscriber Line (DSL) service offered by traditional phone companies over the same (copper) wires used for regular phone service. This erosion of actual or perceived monopoly power in the telecommunications market is repeated in numerous other instances.

Economic historians note that the U.S. Postal Service has the longest history of monopoly power in the United States. It's even mentioned in the U.S. Constitution. The post office has used its monopoly power to maintain high prices and wages despite a reputation for poor service. However, aggressive new entrants and important technical innovations have combined to undermine even this well-established monopoly. Today, many consumers turn to UPS, FedEx or a host of competitors, when they seek fast, cost-effective, and sure delivery of valuable packages. At the same time, the telephonic transmission of scanned-in printed material using facsimile (FAX) machines, and then e-mail over the Internet have effectively eroded if not destroyed the postal service monopoly on the delivery of first-class mail.

Trade unions have also been criticized for the undue exercise of monopoly power in the labor market. For example, the International Longshore and Warehouse Union (ILWU) has approximately 42,000 members in over 60 local unions in the states of California, Washington, Oregon, Alaska, and Hawaii. A small group of members, about 10,000 dockworkers, control the flow of goods into and out of major seaports in California. Wielding the threat of a strike that could close ports and hobble the entire U.S. economy, the ILWU has successfully limited the introduction of productivity-enhancing technology and boosted member wages above $100,000 per year. Despite the obvious exercise of monopoly power, worker unions such as the ILWU are exempt from the country's antitrust laws. However, the monopoly power of unions such as the ILWU is undermined by the threat of government injunctions, growing competition from nonunion labor, and the ongoing decline in the importance of manufacturing in the overall economy. With the growing importance of value-added services, the unionized share of the workforce continues to decline. Today, less than one in seven of all workers belong to unions.

Among publicly traded corporations, Microsoft has recently successfully defended itself against "bundling" charges levied by the antitrust division of the U.S. Justice Department. In the Microsoft case, the U.S. Justice Department charged that the company illegally maintained and extended its domination of the software market by bundling Internet software with the Windows operating system. The company contended that it earned its dominant position in operating systems and applications software by providing low-priced, innovative products that consumers valued. For example, Microsoft Word now accounts for more than 90 percent of all word processing software sales; Excel's share of the spreadsheet market exceeds 95 percent. Microsoft's position seems to have been upheld by a court-approved settlement. Going forward, analysts agree that Microsoft has won the battle for desktop applications software, but caution that the battleground has shifted. Microsoft's most serious threat comes not from the U.S. Justice Department, but from insurgent competitors, like the Linux operating system, and from innovative "useware" employed to navigate and access Internet information.

On an international level, the Organization of the Petroleum Exporting Countries (OPEC) has long been criticized for its aggressive use of monopoly power to restrict output, create soaring oil prices, and wreak economic havoc. Starting in 1973, repeated examples of OPEC-inspired oil price shocks do in fact suggest the dangerous accumulation of monopoly power in oil production. At the same time, OPEC's share of world oil production is trending down from a bit more than one-third of world oil production, and overproduction by cheating members continues to undermine OPEC's position.

Managerial Application 12.1

The NCAA Cartel

With mass formations and gang tackling, the early game of football resulted in numerous injuries and deaths. In 1905, President Theodore Roosevelt summoned college leaders to the White House to encourage reform. At a subsequent meeting on December 28, 1905, the Intercollegiate Athletic Association of the United States (IAAUS) was formed. The IAAUS took its present name, the National Collegiate Athletic Association, in 1910.

For several years, the NCAA was a discussion group and rules-making body. In 1921, the first NCAA national championship was held: the National Collegiate Track and Field Championships. Gradually, more rules committees were formed and more championships were held. In 1951, Walter Byers, who previously had served as part-time executive assistant, was named executive director. A national headquarters was established in Kansas City, Missouri, in 1952. A program to control live television of football games and postseason bowl games was later approved. The association's membership was divided into three legislative and competitive divisions in 1973. Five years later, Division I members voted to create subdivisions I-A and I-AA in the sport of football. The NCAA began administering women's

athletics programs in 1980. Cedric W. Dempsey, the NCAA's executive director through 2002, was instrumental in the negotiation of a comprehensive championships rights agreement with CBS television worth $6 billion over 11 years. Today, the NCAA's national office staff of about 350 employees is based in Indianapolis, Indiana.

The NCAA views itself as a "bottom-up" organization in which the members rule the association. Critics contend it is a "top-down" organization that rules with an iron fist to suppress financial competition in college sports. NCAA limits on scholarships and other payments to athletes boost the profitability of college sports. Critics note that many college players come from poor families and are not sufficiently talented to make it to the professional ranks. Without NCAA controls, student-athletes might get paid for their college athletic prowess. With the NCAA in charge, student-athletes remain poor. College presidents, athletic directors, and coaches all get paid a lot. Only the student-athlete fails to share proportionately in the enormous wealth created by college athletics.

See: Jon Weinbach, "Inside College Sports' Biggest Money Machine," *The Wall Street Journal Online*, October 19, 2007, http://online.wsj.com.

PROFIT MAXIMIZATION UNDER MONOPOLY

Like any other firm, a monopoly maximizes profit by setting marginal revenue equal to marginal cost.

Price–Output Decisions

Under monopoly, the market demand curve is identical to the firm demand curve. Because market demand curves slope downward, monopolists also face downward-sloping demand curves. Profit maximization requires that firms operate at the output level at which marginal revenue and marginal cost are equal. However, in monopoly markets, firms are price makers. Their individual production decisions have the effect of setting market prices. Given a downward-sloping monopoly demand curve, price always exceeds marginal revenue under monopoly. This stems from the fact that price is average revenue, and a downward-sloping demand curve requires that marginal revenue is less than average revenue. In a competitive market, $P = MR = MC = AC$ in long-run equilibrium. In monopoly markets, profit maximization also requires $MR = MC$, but barriers to entry make above-normal profits possible and $P > AC$ in long-run equilibrium.

Table 12.1 illustrates the process of profit maximization for CSI International, Ltd., a monopoly firm operating subject to the market demand curve $P = \$50 - \$0.00025Q$.

Table 12.1 Monopoly Profits Are Maximized When Marginal Revenue Equals Marginal Cost

Units (1)	Price $P = \$50 -$ $\$0.00025Q$ (2)	Total Revenue (3) = (1) × (2)	Fixed Cost (4)	Variable Costs (5)	Average Variable Cost (6) = (5)/(1)	Total Cost (7) = (4) + (5)	Average Total Cost (8) = (7)/(1)	Total Profit (TR–TC) (9) = (3)–(7)	Marginal Revenue (10) = $\Delta TR/\Delta Q$	Marginal Cost (11) = $\Delta TC/\Delta Q$	Marginal Profit (12) = (MR – MC) (9) – (10)
0	50	0	311,250	50,000		361,250		−361,250	50	5	45
5,000	49	243,750	311,250	80,000	16.00	391,250	78.25	−147,500	48	7	41
10,000	48	475,000	311,250	120,000	12.00	431,250	43.13	43,750	45	9	36
15,000	46	693,750	311,250	170,000	11.33	481,250	32.08	212,500	43	11	32
20,000	45	900,000	311,250	230,000	11.50	541,250	27.06	358,750	40	13	27
25,000	44	1,093,750	311,250	300,000	12.00	611,250	24.45	482,500	38	15	23
30,000	43	1,275,000	311,250	380,000	12.67	691,250	23.04	583,750	35	17	18
35,000	41	1,443,750	311,250	470,000	13.43	781,250	22.32	662,500	33	19	14
40,000	40	1,600,000	311,250	570,000	14.25	881,250	22.03	718,750	30	21	9
45,000	39	1,743,750	311,250	680,000	15.11	991,250	22.03	752,500	28	23	5
50,000	38	1,875,000	311,250	800,000	16.00	1,111,250	22.23	763,750	25	25	0
55,000	36	1,993,750	311,250	930,000	16.91	1,241,250	22.57	752,500	23	27	−5
60,000	35	2,100,000	311,250	1,070,000	17.83	1,381,250	23.02	718,750	20	29	−9
65,000	34	2,193,750	311,250	1,220,000	18.77	1,531,250	23.56	662,500	18	31	−14
70,000	33	2,275,000	311,250	1,380,000	19.71	1,691,250	24.16	583,750	15	33	−18
75,000	31	2,343,750	311,250	1,550,000	20.67	1,861,250	24.82	482,500	13	35	−23
80,000	30	2,400,000	311,250	1,730,000	21.63	2,041,250	25.52	358,750	10	37	−27

In this example, CSI is a hypothetical price maker; the company's production decisions determine the market price. Because CSI's monopoly demand curve is downward sloping, the market price will exceed marginal revenue, $P > MR$, at each point along the demand curve. Fixed costs of $311,250 reflect financing costs, salaries, lease payments, and other overhead expenses incurred irrespective of the specific level of production. Notice that total profit is simply the difference between total revenue and total cost. To find the point of maximum profit, one need only scan down the profit column to find maximum total profits of $763,750 at 50,000 units of output. Because normal profit is included as part of the financing costs included in total costs, the profit shown in Figure 12.1 is economic profit and represents an above-normal rate of return. The firm incurs economic losses whenever it fails to earn a normal profit. Average variable cost and average total cost are simply those cost categories divided by the total amount produced.

In Figure 12.1, the monopoly demand curve is not horizontal, like in a competitive market. Marginal revenue is always less than price for output quantities greater than one because of the negatively sloped demand curve. Because the demand (average revenue) curve is negatively sloped and declining, the marginal revenue curve must lie below it. When a monopoly equates marginal revenue and marginal cost, it simultaneously determines the profit-maximizing output level and market price for its product. As illustrated in Figure 12.1, the monopoly produces 50,000 units of output at an average total cost of $22.23 per unit, and sells this output at a price of $37.50. Profits, which equal $763,750 [=($37.50 – $22.23) × 50,000], are at a maximum. Remember, 50,000 units is an optimal output level only because $MR = MC$ and average revenue, or price, is greater than average variable cost, as shown in Figure 12.1. If the market price is below average variable cost, losses could be minimized by shutting down.

Figure 12.1 Monopoly Profits Are Maximized When Marginal Revenue Equals Marginal Cost

Profits are always maximized where $MR = MC$. In monopoly markets, firms are price makers so maximum profits occur where $MR = MC$ but $P > MR$.

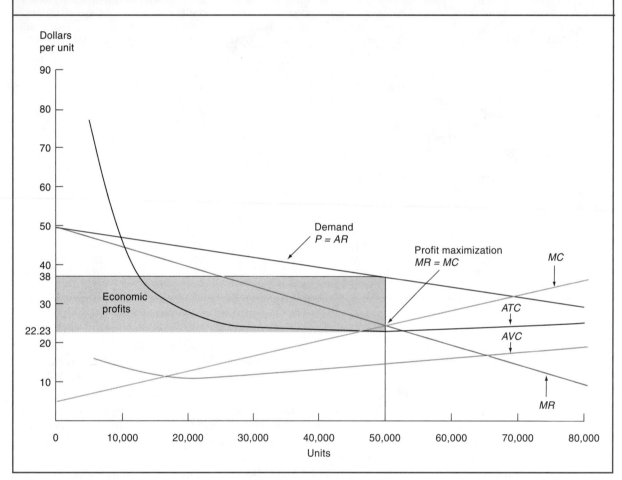

Role of Marginal Analysis

As in the case of competitive markets, discovering the point of optimal production for a monopoly firm is made easier with marginal analysis. Notice from Table 12.1 that total profit is maximized when the difference between marginal revenue and marginal cost, called marginal profit, equals zero. As in the case of competitive markets, monopoly profits are maximized when

$$M\pi = MR - MC = 0 \qquad \textbf{12.1}$$

Because this point of profit maximization occurs where marginal revenue is set equal to marginal cost, an equivalent expression that must be met for profit maximization in both competitive and monopoly markets is that

$$MR = MC \qquad \textbf{12.2}$$

As in the case of competitive market firms, an added condition for profit maximization by monopoly firms, sometimes referred to as a second-order condition, is that total profits must always be decreasing beyond the point where $MR = MC$.[2]

Two factors make profit maximization by monopoly firms unique. Like all markets, monopoly markets are characterized by downward-sloping demand curves. However, because the monopoly firm serves the entire market, the monopoly firm demand curve is downward sloping. This means that the monopoly demand curve is always above the marginal revenue curve in monopoly markets

$$P = AR > MR \qquad\qquad \textbf{12.3}$$

Because profit maximization requires $MR = MC$, price will always exceed marginal cost at the profit-maximizing point in monopoly markets.

The role of marginal analysis in monopoly firm profit maximization can be further illustrated by considering the analytic solution to the CSI profit maximization problem. Assume that the monopoly firm total revenue, marginal revenue, total cost, and marginal cost functions are

$$TR = \$50Q - \$0.00025Q^2$$
$$MR = \partial TR/\partial Q = \$50 - \$0.0005Q$$
$$TC = \$361,250 + \$5Q + \$0.0002Q^2,$$
$$MC = \partial TC/\partial Q = \$5 + \$0.0004Q$$

where TR is total revenue, MR is marginal revenue, TC is total cost per year including capital costs, MC is marginal cost, and Q is the amount produced.

The optimal price–output combination can be determined by setting marginal revenue equal to marginal cost and solving for Q:

$$MR = MC$$
$$\$50 - \$0.0005Q = \$5 + \$0.0004Q$$
$$\$0.0009Q = \$45$$
$$Q = 50,000$$

At this output level, maximum economic profits are

$$\pi = TR - TC$$
$$= \$50Q - \$0.00025Q^2 - \$361,250 - \$5Q - \$0.0002Q^2$$
$$= -\$361,250 + \$45Q - \$0.00045Q^2$$
$$= -\$361,250 + \$45(50,000) - \$0.00045(50,000)^2$$
$$= \$763,750$$

Under monopoly, the $Q = 50,000$ activity level results in maximum economic profits of $763,750. This means that the monopoly firm is able to obtain more than a normal, or

---

2   Total profit is simply the difference between total revenue and total cost, or $\pi = TR - TC$. Using calculus notation, at the profit-maximizing point, marginal profit equals zero, or $\partial \pi / \partial Q = \partial TR / \partial Q - \partial TC / \partial Q = 0$. The first-order condition for profit maximization is simply that $\partial \pi / \partial Q = 0$. The second-order condition for profit maximization is that total profit be decreasing beyond this point, or $\partial^2 \pi / \partial Q^2 < 0$.

risk-adjusted, rate of return on investment because capital costs are already included in the cost function. Because $MR = MC$, this is a short-run equilibrium. Because barriers to entry or other advantages of monopoly preclude effective competition, such economic profits can persist for monopolists in long-run equilibrium.

SOCIAL COSTS OF MONOPOLY

A loss in social welfare is caused by the fact that monopoly markets produce too little output at too high a price when compared with competitive markets.

Monopoly Underproduction

Any market characterized by monopoly sells less output at higher prices than would be the case if the same market were perfectly competitive. From the perspective of the firm and its stockholders, the benefits of monopoly are measured in terms of the economic profits that are possible when competition is reduced or eliminated. From a broader social perspective, these private benefits must be weighed against the costs borne by consumers in the forms of higher prices and reduced availability of desired products. Employees and suppliers also suffer from the reduced employment opportunities associated with lower production in monopoly input markets.

Monopoly Underproduction
Tendency for monopoly firms to restrict output to increase prices and earn economic profits.

From a social perspective, the most closely focused-upon source of inefficiency tied to monopoly stems from the fact that monopoly firms have incentives to restrict output so as to create scarcity and earn economic profits. **Monopoly underproduction** results when a monopoly curtails output to a level at which the marginal value of resources employed, as measured by the marginal cost of production, is less than the marginal social benefit derived. Marginal social benefit is measured by the price that customers are willing to pay for additional output. Under monopoly, marginal cost is less than the price charged at the profit-maximizing output level.

In addition to the underproduction problem, monopoly can result in social costs if monopolists fail to employ cost-effective production methods. Formidable entry barriers, particularly those that stem from government licenses or franchises, can shelter inefficient monopoly firms from the risk of losing market share to more efficient rivals. In competitive markets, vigorous cost control and productive efficiency is a way of life. On the other hand, the "easy life" sometimes afforded monopoly firms is an often-cited economic disadvantage when viewed from a broad social perspective. Productive inefficiency is not apt to be a problem in the case of newly created monopoly derived from the introduction of distinctive new goods and services. However, productive inefficiency is a common concern of public officials who oversee regulated public utilities.

Deadweight Loss from Monopoly

Deadweight Loss From
Decline in social welfare due to the drop in mutually

Monopoly Problem
beneficial trade activity caused by monopoly.

The tendency for monopoly firms to restrict output to increase prices and earn economic profits gives rise to a **deadweight loss from monopoly problem.** Like any restriction on supply, the reduced levels of economic activity typical of monopoly markets create a loss in social welfare due to the decline in mutually beneficial trade activity.

The deadweight loss from monopoly problem can be demonstrated by considering the loss in social welfare that would occur if an important competitive market was converted into a monopoly market. In the case of the U.S. telecommunications services market, this would represent a "back to the future" type of transformation because, for most of the twentieth century, this market was dominated by the American Telephone and Telegraph Company (AT&T), a powerful regulated monopoly. In 1984, the Bell System was broken into eight companies by agreement between AT&T and the U.S. Department of Justice. In place of the old Bell System was a new AT&T and seven regional Bell operating companies (RBOCs). An important benefit of the change was that long-distance telephone service became an intensely competitive business. Today, a host of long-distance carriers and the RBOCs face competition from Voice over Internet Protocol (VoIP) service offered by cable operators and the ongoing substitution of wireless and Internet (instant messaging) communications for traditional wireline service.

Assume that the competitive market supply curve for unlimited monthly long-distance telephone service (in millions of customers) is given by the equation

$$Q_S = -40 + 4P$$

or, solving for price,

$$4P = 40 + Q_S$$
$$P = \$10 + \$0.25Q_S$$

The competitive market demand curve for unlimited monthly long-distance telephone service is given by the equation

$$Q_D = 170 - 2P$$

or, solving for price,

$$2P = 170 - Q_D$$
$$P = \$85 - \$0.5Q_D$$

To find the market equilibrium levels for price and quantity, simply set the market supply and market demand curves equal to one another so that $Q_S = Q_D$. For example, to find the market equilibrium price, equate the market demand and market supply curves where quantity is expressed as a function of price:

$$\text{Supply} = \text{Demand}$$
$$-40 + 4P = 170 - 2P$$
$$6P = 210$$
$$P = \$35 \text{ per month}$$

To find the market equilibrium quantity, equate the market supply and market demand curves where price is expressed as a function of quantity, and $Q_S = Q_D$:

$$\text{Supply} = \text{Demand}$$
$$\$10 + \$0.25Q = \$85 - \$0.5Q$$
$$0.75Q = 75$$
$$Q = 100 \text{ (million)}$$

As shown in Figure 12.2, the equilibrium price–output combination for unlimited monthly long-distance telephone service is a market price of $35 with an equilibrium

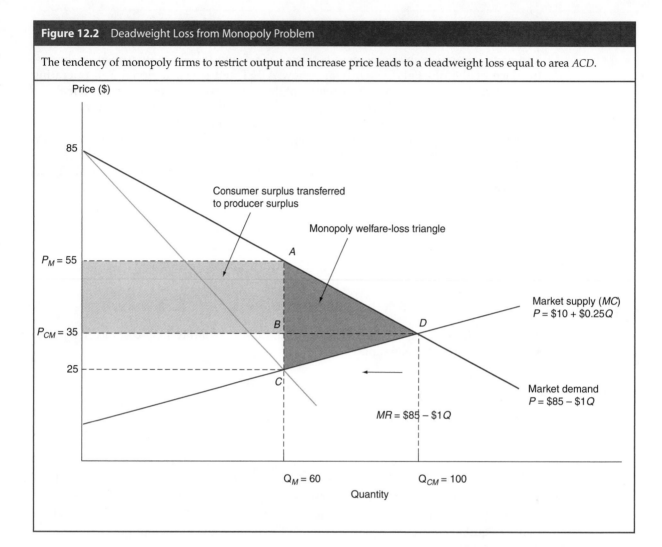

Figure 12.2 Deadweight Loss from Monopoly Problem

The tendency of monopoly firms to restrict output and increase price leads to a deadweight loss equal to area ACD.

output of 100 (million) customers. Also notice that the market demand curve $P = \$85 - \$0.5Q$ corresponds with the marginal revenue curve $MR = \$85 - Q$.

If the industry reverts to monopoly, the optimal price–output combination can be determined by setting marginal revenue equal to marginal cost and solving for Q:

$$MR = MC = \text{Market Supply}$$
$$\$85 - Q = \$10 + \$0.25Q$$
$$\$1.25Q = \$75$$
$$Q = 60 \text{ (million) customers}$$

At $Q = 60$,

$$P = \$85 - \$0.5Q$$
$$= \$85 - \$0.5(60)$$
$$= \$55 \text{ per month}$$

Under monopoly, the amount supplied falls to 60 (million) customers and the market price jumps to $55 per month. The amount of deadweight loss from monopoly suffered by consumers is given by the triangle bounded by ABD in Figure 12.2. Because the area of such a triangle is one-half the value of the base times the height, the value of lost consumer surplus equals

$$\text{Consumer Deadweight Loss} = \tfrac{1}{2}\,[(100-60)\times(\$55-\$35)]$$
$$= \$400 \text{ (million) per month}$$

The amount of deadweight loss from monopoly suffered by producers is given by the triangle bounded by BCD. Because the area of such a triangle is one-half the value of the base times the height, the value of lost producer surplus equals

$$\text{Producer Deadweight Loss} = \tfrac{1}{2}\,[(100-60)\times(\$35-\$25)]$$
$$= \$200 \text{ (million) per month}$$

The total amount of deadweight loss from monopoly suffered by consumers and producers is given by the triangle bounded by ACD. The area of such a triangle is simply the amount of consumer deadweight loss plus producer deadweight loss:

$$\text{Total Deadweight Loss} = \text{Consumer Loss} + \text{Producer Loss}$$
$$= \$400 \text{ (million)} + \$200 \text{ (million)}$$
$$= \$600 \text{ (million) per month}$$

Wealth Transfer Problem
An unwarranted transfer of wealth measured by the transformation of consumer surplus into producer surplus.

In addition to the deadweight loss from monopoly problem, there is a **wealth transfer problem** associated with monopoly. Notice in Figure 12.2 that the creation of a monopoly results in the transformation of a significant amount of consumer surplus into producer surplus. In a free market, the value of consumer surplus is equal to the region under the market demand curve that lies above the market equilibrium price, here $35 per month. Under monopoly, the value of consumer surplus is equal to the region under the market demand curve that lies above the monopoly price of $55 per month. In addition to the deadweight loss from monopoly suffered by consumers, there is a significant amount of consumer surplus that is transferred to producer surplus. This amount is shown as the area in the rectangle bordered by $P_{CM}P_{M}AB$:

$$\text{Transfer to Producer Surplus} = 60\times(\$55-\$35)$$
$$= \$1{,}200 \text{ (million) per month}$$

Therefore, from the viewpoint of consumers, the problem with monopoly is twofold. Monopoly results in both a significant deadweight loss in consumer surplus and a significant transfer of consumer surplus to producer surplus. In this example, the cost of monopoly to consumers is measured by a total loss in consumer surplus of $1,600 (million) per month. The wealth transfer problem associated with monopoly is seen as an issue of equity or fairness because it involves the distribution of income or wealth in the economy. Although economic profits serve the useful functions of providing incentives and helping allocate resources, it is difficult to justify monopoly profits that result from the raw exercise of market power rather than from exceptional performance.

SOCIAL BENEFITS OF MONOPOLY

Monopoly is not always harmful; it sometimes results from the superior efficiency or innovative capability of a dynamic leading firm.

Economies of Scale

Natural Monopoly
Market in which the market-clearing price occurs at a point at which the monopolist's long-run average costs are still declining.

Monopoly is sometimes the result of vigorous competition. A **natural monopoly** does not arise from government intervention or artificial barriers to entry, but can be a predictable result given the current state of technology and cost conditions in the industry. Monopoly naturally evolves in markets subject to overwhelming economies of scale in production created by extremely large capital requirements, scarce inputs, insufficient natural resources, and so on. In such instances, the market-dominant firm is called a natural monopoly because the market-clearing price, where $P = MC$, occurs at a point at which long-run average total costs are still declining. In such circumstances, market demand is insufficient to justify full utilization of even one minimum-efficient-scale plant. A single monopolist can produce the total market supply at a lower total cost than could any number of smaller firms, and vigorous competition naturally eliminates competitors that are too small, and hence inefficient, until only a single monopoly supplier remains. Water and sewer, natural gas pipelines, and electric utilities are classic examples of natural monopoly, because any duplication in production and distribution facilities would increase consumer costs.

From the standpoint of society in general, the creation of a natural monopoly is a positive development because it reflects the successful growth and development of a uniquely capable competitor. A natural monopoly is capable of producing the goods and services desired by customers at lower total cost than could a number of smaller competing firms. However, an established natural monopoly entails some risks, again from the standpoint of society in general. There is a chance that an established natural monopolist could use its dominance of the marketplace to unfairly restrict production and raise prices to further enhance economic profits. From a social standpoint, natural monopoly presents something of a dilemma. On the one hand, economic efficiency can sometimes be enhanced by allowing a single firm to dominate an industry. On the other hand, monopolies have an incentive to underproduce and can generate unwarranted economic profits.

In the public utility sector, government price and profit regulation has been justified on the basis that natural monopoly sometimes results from the public grant of valuable operating licenses or franchises. In return for such valuable operating rights, public utility regulation is seen as a means for making sure that reasonable prices and profits are maintained. Critics of such regulation argue that natural monopoly is extremely rare. Most real-world examples of monopoly do not naturally result from economies of scale in production. Many real-world monopolists owe their existence to government-created or government-maintained barriers to entry. Moreover, when natural monopoly does in fact evolve in industry, it is often a temporary phenomenon. Technical change and the onset of competition from new and established competitors is often a potent limit on the powers of natural monopoly.

Invention and Innovation

Patents
Explicit monopoly rights conferred by public policy.

To achieve the benefits flowing from dynamic, innovative, leading firms, public policy sometimes confers explicit monopoly rights. For example, **patents** grant an exclusive right to produce, use, or sell an invention or innovation for a limited period of time. For U.S.

patent applications filed on or after June 8, 1995, utility and plant patents can be granted for a term that begins with the date of the grant and usually ends 20 years from the date of the patent application. Utility patents may be granted to anyone who invents or discovers any new or improved process, machine, manufactured product, or composition of matter. Plant patents may be granted to anyone who invents or discovers and asexually reproduces any distinct and new variety of plant. Maintenance fees totaling a few thousand dollars must be paid over the life of such patents. Design patents may be granted to anyone who invents a new, original, and ornamental design for a manufactured product, and last 14 years from the grant date. Design patents do not involve maintenance fees.

Without patents, competitors could quickly develop identical substitutes for new products or processes, and inventing firms would fail to reap the full benefit of their technological breakthroughs. In granting patents, the public confers a limited opportunity for monopoly profits to stimulate research activity and economic growth. By limiting the patent monopoly, competition is encouraged to extend and develop the common body of knowledge. The patent monopoly is subject to other restrictions besides the time limit. Firms cannot use patents to monopolize or otherwise unfairly limit competition

It is important to recognize that monopoly is not always socially harmful. In the case of Microsoft Corp., for example, the genius of Bill Gates and a multitude of research associates have created a dynamic computer software juggernaut. Over the last three decades, computer software technology has helped transform work, play, and communication. Today, computer users can contact people and access information from around the world in an instant. Groundbreaking computer technologies have also opened the door to innovations in related fields of human endeavor, like biotechnology, delivering new opportunity, convenience, and value. Since its founding in 1975, Microsoft has been a leader in this transformation. The tremendous stockholder value created through these efforts, including billions of dollars in personal wealth for Gates and his associates, can be viewed only as a partial index of their contribution to society in general. Other similar examples include the DeKalb Corporation (hybrid seeds), Kellogg Company (ready-to-eat cereal), Lotus Corporation (spreadsheet software), and the Reserve Fund (money market mutual funds), among others. In instances such as these, monopoly profits are the just rewards flowing from truly important contributions of unique firms and individuals.

It is also important to recognize that monopoly profits are often fleeting. Early profits earned by each of the firms mentioned previously attracted a host of competitors. For example, note the tremendous growth in the money market mutual fund business since the November 1971 birth of the Reserve Fund. Today the Reserve Fund is only one of roughly 500 money market mutual funds available, and it accounts for only a small fraction of the roughly $1 trillion in industry assets. Similarly, Lotus Corporation is now a footnote in the computer software industry. The tremendous social value of invention and innovation often remains long after early monopoly profits have dissipated.

MONOPOLY REGULATION

Public utility regulation aims to enjoy the benefits of low-cost production by large firms while avoiding the social costs of unregulated monopoly.

Dilemma of Natural Monopoly

In the public utility sector, average costs sometimes decline as output expands, and a single large firm has the potential to produce total industry output more efficiently than any group of smaller producers. Demand equals supply at a point where the industry

Managerial Application 12.2

Is Ticketmaster a Monopoly?

In the 1980s, a small upstart named Ticketmaster decided to pay arenas millions of dollars for the right to sell their tickets and helped them develop effective marketing tactics. With Ticketmaster's help, selling tickets went from being a costly headache to a carefree and profit-maximizing endeavor. Ticketmaster covets exclusive marketing rights for initial ticket sales. Because on-site box offices open later, and only when tickets are left over, Ticketmaster often accounts for 85 percent to 90 percent of sales for hundreds of on-site facilities.

Ticketmaster provides valuable services for venue operators and their customers, but charges a hefty price. Ticketmaster levels enormous convenience fees, building facility charges, and order-handling charges. For example, on July 10, 2007, rock legend Sting played in Dolphin Stadium in Miami, Florida. A first-level seat cost $225. The Ticketmaster convenience and facility charge was $17.70, and the minimum order-handling

charge was $2.50 (see table). That's $242.70 for a ticket, provided standard mail delivery was okay; UPS delivery cost more. That's a price that might make anyone call The Police.

In defense of such high fees, Ticketmaster argues that venue promotion services do not come cheap. As the sole ticket vendor, Ticketmaster assures venue operators that tickets will be priced properly in light of booking alternatives. However, it is Ticketmaster's marketing savvy and choke-hold on information concerning the ticket-buying habits of the general public that has trustbusters worried about monopoly power in the computerized ticketing services industry.

Is it reasonable for society to limit the success of dominant, innovative companies like Ticketmaster?

See: Jessica E. Vascellaro and Ethan Smith, "Ticketmaster Halts Live Nation Talks," *The Wall Street Journal Online*, August 23, 2007, http://online.wsj.com.

The Cost of Being a Fan: Ticketmaster Ticket Charges				
Venue	Primary Act	Location	Ticket Prices ($)	Convenience, Building Facility, and Processing Charges ($)
AT&T Center	George Lopez	San Antonio, TX	58.40	11.50
Centre Bell Centre	Tool	Montreal, QC	65.50	13.50
Dolphin Stadium	The Police: VIP Package	Miami, FL	225.00	17.70
Giants Stadium	U.S. Women's Soccer Team vs. Brazil	East Rutherford, NJ	50.00	9.70
Lyric Opera House	Bruce Hornsby— Ricky Skaggs	Baltimore, MD	64.00	10.00
Shoreline Amphitheatre	Kenny Chesney	Mountain View, CA	77.75	15.80
Toledo Speedway	Monster Jam	Toledo, OH	16.00	5.25
Town Hall, New York, NY	Branford Marsalis	New York, NY	65.00	7.50
Tucson Arena	WWE Monday Night Raw	Tucson, AZ	50.00	9.85
Tweeter Center for the Performing Arts	Dave Matthews Band	Mansfield, MA	65.00	11.45

Author survey of costs for "best seat available," June 19, 2007. Additional delivery charges range from $2.50 to $25 per order depending upon delivery method.

long-run average cost curve is still declining. Natural monopoly describes this situation because monopoly is a natural result of the superior efficiency of a single large producer.

This situation is illustrated in Figure 12.3. Here the monopoly firm will produce Q units of output at an average cost of C per unit. Note that this cost level is above the minimum point on the long-run average cost curve, and average costs are still declining.

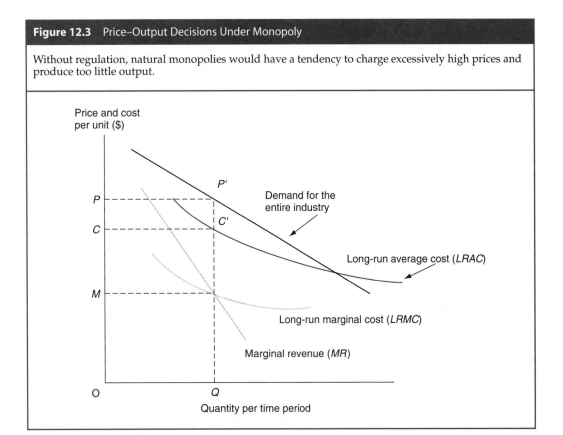

Figure 12.3 Price–Output Decisions Under Monopoly

Without regulation, natural monopolies would have a tendency to charge excessively high prices and produce too little output.

As a monopolist, the firm can earn an economic profit equal to the rectangle $PP'C'C$, or $Q(P-C)$. Underproduction occurs because the monopoly firm curtails production to a level at which the marginal value of resources needed to produce an additional unit of output (marginal cost) is less than the benefit derived from the additional unit. For example, at output levels just greater than Q in Figure 12.3, customers are willing to pay approximately P dollars per unit, so the value of additional units is P. However, the marginal cost of producing an additional unit is slightly less than M dollars and well below P, so marginal cost does not equal marginal value. Society would find an expansion of output desirable.

Thus, natural monopoly poses a dilemma because monopoly has the potential for greatest efficiency, but unregulated monopoly can lead to economic profits and underproduction. One possible solution is to allow natural monopoly to persist but to impose price and profit regulations.

Utility Price and Profit Regulation

The most common method of monopoly regulation is price and profit control. Such regulations result in larger output quantities and lower profits than would be the case with unrestricted monopoly. This situation is illustrated in Figure 12.4. A monopolist operating without regulation would produce Q_1 units of output and charge a price of P_1. If regulators set a ceiling on prices at P_2, the firm's effective demand curve becomes the kinked curve P_2AD. Because price is a constant from 0 to Q_2 units of output, marginal revenue equals

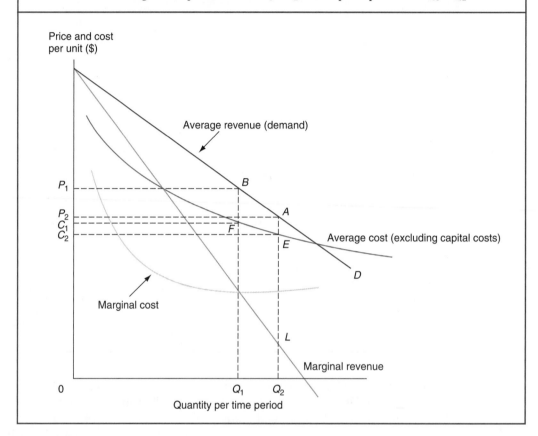

Figure 12.4   Monopoly Price Regulation: Optimal Price–Output Decision Making

Monopoly regulation imposes a price ceiling at P_2 just sufficient to provide a fair return (area P_2AEC_2) on investment. Under regulation, price falls from P_1 to P_2 and output expands from Q_1 to Q_2.

price in this range; that is, P_2A is the marginal revenue curve over the output range $0Q_2$. For output beyond Q_2, marginal revenue is given by the original marginal revenue function. The marginal revenue curve is now discontinuous at Q_2, with a gap between points A and L. This regulated firm maximizes profits by operating at Q_2 and charging the ceiling price, P_2. Marginal revenue is greater than marginal cost up to that output but is less than marginal cost from that point onward as more output is produced.

Profits are also reduced by this regulatory action. Without price regulation, price P_1 is charged, a cost of C_1 per unit is incurred, and Q_1 is produced. Profit is $(P_1-C_1)\times(Q_1)$, which equals the area P_1BFC_1. With price regulation, the price is P_2, the cost is C_2, Q_2 units are sold, and profits are represented by the smaller area P_2AEC_2.

To determine a fair price, a regulatory commission must estimate a fair, or normal, rate of return, given the risk inherent in the enterprise. The commission then approves prices that produce the target rate of return on the required level of investment. In the case illustrated by Figure 12.4, if the profit at price P_2, when divided by the investment required to produce Q_2, were to produce more than the target rate of return, price would be reduced until actual and target rates of return became equal. This assumes, of course, that cost curves in Figure 12.4 do not include equity capital costs. The profit that the regulator allows is business profit, not economic profit.

Utility Price and Profit Regulation Example

To further illustrate the concept of public utility regulation, consider the case of the Malibu Beach Telephone Company, a hypothetical telephone utility serving urban customers in southern California. At issue is the monthly rate for local telephone service. The monthly demand for service is given by the relation

$$P = \$22.50 - \$0.00004Q$$

where P is service price in dollars and Q is the number of customers served. Annual total cost and marginal cost curves, excluding a normal rate of return, are given by the following expressions:

$$TC = \$3,750,000 + \$70Q + 0.00002Q^2$$
$$MC = \partial TC / \partial Q = \$70 + \$0.00004Q$$

where cost is expressed in dollars.

To find the profit-maximizing level of output, demand and marginal revenue curves for annual service must be derived. This will give all revenue and cost relations a common annual basis. The demand curve for annual service is 12 times monthly demand:

$$P = 12(\$22.5 - \$0.00004Q)$$
$$= \$270 - \$0.00048Q$$

Total and marginal revenue curves for this annual demand curve are

$$TR = \$270Q - \$0.00048Q^2$$
$$MR = \partial TR / \partial Q = \$270 - \$0.00096Q$$

The profit-maximizing level of output is found by setting $MC = MR$ (where $M\pi = 0$) and solving for Q:

$$MC = MR,$$
$$\$70 + \$0.00004Q = \$270 - \$0.00096Q,$$
$$\$0.001Q = \$200,$$
$$Q = 200,000$$

The monthly service price is

$$P = \$22.50 - \$0.00004(200,000)$$
$$= \$14.50 \text{ per month (or } \$174 \text{ per year)}$$

This price–output combination generates annual total profits of

$$\pi = \$270Q - \$0.00048Q^2 - \$3,750,000 - \$70Q - \$0.00002Q^2$$
$$= -\$0.0005Q^2 + \$200Q - \$3,750,000$$
$$= -\$0.0005(200,000^2) + \$200(200,000) - \$3,750,000$$
$$= \$16,250,000$$

If the company has $125 million invested in plant and equipment, the annual rate of return on investment is

$$\text{Return on Investment} = \frac{\$16,250,000}{\$125,000,000} = 0.13, \text{ or } 13\%$$

Now assume that the State Public Utility Commission decides that a 12 percent rate of return is fair given the level of risk taken and conditions in the financial markets. With a 12 percent rate of return on total assets, Malibu Beach would earn business profits of

$$\pi = \text{Allowed Return} \times \text{Total Assets}$$
$$= 0.12 \times \$125,000,000$$
$$= \$15,000,000$$

To determine the level of output that would generate this level of total profits, total profit must be set equal to $15 million:

$$\pi = TR - TC$$
$$\$15,000,000 = -\$0.0005Q^2 + \$200Q - \$3,750,000$$

This implies that

$$-\$0.0005Q^2 + \$200Q - \$18,750,000 = 0$$

which is a function of the form $aQ^2 + bQ - c = 0$. Solving for the roots of this equation provides the target output level. We use the quadratic equation as follows:

$$Q = \frac{-b \pm \sqrt{b^2 - 4ac}}{2a}$$
$$= \frac{-200 \pm \sqrt{200^2 - 4(-0.0005)(-18,750,000)}}{2(-0.0005)}$$
$$= \frac{-200 \pm \sqrt{2,500}}{-0.001}$$
$$= 150,000 \text{ or } 250,000$$

Because public utility commissions generally want utilities to provide service to the greatest possible number of customers at the lowest possible price, the upper figure $Q = 250,000$ is the appropriate output level. To induce Malibu Beach Telephone to operate at this output level, the regulatory authorities would determine the maximum allowable price for monthly service as

$$P = \$22.50 - \$0.00004(250,000)$$
$$= \$12.50$$

This $12.50-per-month price provides service to the broadest customer base possible, given the need to provide Malibu Beach with the opportunity to earn a 12 percent return on investment.

Problems with Utility Price and Profit Regulation

Although the concept of utility price and profit regulation is simple, several practical problems arise in public utility regulation. In practice, it is impossible to exactly determine cost and demand schedules, or the minimum investment required to support a given level of output. Moreover, because utilities serve several classes of customers, many different rate schedules could produce the desired profit level. If profits for the local electric power company are too low, should rates be raised for summer (peak) or for winter (off-peak) users? Should industrial, commercial, or residential customers bear the burden of higher rates?

Regulators also make mistakes with regard to the optimal level and growth of service. For example, if a local telephone utility is permitted to charge excessive rates, the system will grow at a faster-than-optimal rate. Similarly, when the allowed rate of return exceeds the cost of capital, electric, gas, and water utilities have an incentive to overinvest in fixed assets and shift to overly capital-intensive methods of production. In contrast, if prices allowed to natural gas producers are too low, consumers will be encouraged to deplete scarce gas supplies, producers will limit exploration and development, and gas shortages can occur. If gas prices are too low and offer only a below-market rate of return on capital, necessary expansion will be thwarted.

Regulatory Lag
Delay between when a change in regulation is appropriate and the date it becomes effective.

A related problem is that of **regulatory lag,** or the delay between when a change in regulation is appropriate and the date it becomes effective. During the 1970s and 1980s, inflation exerted constant upward pressure on costs. At the same time, consumers and voters were able to reduce, delay, or deny reasonable rate increases. This caused severe financial hardship for a number of utilities and their stockholders. More recently, rapid changes in technology and competitive conditions have rendered obsolete many traditional forms of regulation in the electricity and telecommunications industries. When regulators are slow to react to such changes, both consumers and the industry suffer.

Traditional forms of regulation can also lead to inefficiency. If a utility is guaranteed a minimum return on investment, operating inefficiencies can be offset by higher prices. The process of utility regulation itself is also costly. Detailed demand and cost analyses are necessary to provide a reasonable basis for rate decisions. It is expensive to pay regulatory officials, full-time utility commission staffs, record-keeping costs, and the expense of processing rate cases. All of these expenses are ultimately borne by consumers. Although many economists can see no reasonable alternative to utility regulation for electric, gas, local telephone, and private water companies, the costs and inefficiency of such regulation are troubling.

Oligopsony
Market demand dominated by few buyers.

Monopsony
Market in which there is a single buyer of a desired product or input.

Monopsony Power
Ability to obtain prices below those that exist in a competitive market.

MONOPSONY

When buyer power exists, buyers have the ability to profitably affect the prices paid for products or inputs.

Buyer Power

If only a few buyers exist in a given market, there can be less competition than if there are many buyers. **Oligopsony** exists when there are only a handful of buyers present in a market. **Monopsony** exists when a market features a single buyer of a desired product or input. When a single buyer is confronted in a market with many sellers, **monopsony power** enables the buyer to obtain lower prices than those that would prevail in competitive markets. Monopsony power characterizes local labor markets with a single major employer and local agricultural markets with a single feed mill or grain buyer. The federal government is a monopsony buyer of military weapons and equipment. Major retailers such as Wal-Mart, Target, and Sears all enjoy monopsony power in the purchase of apparel, appliances, auto parts, and other consumer products. Such buyer power is especially strong in the purchase of "house brand" goods, where suppliers sell much if not all of their production to a single retailer. Monopsony is more common in factor input markets than in markets for final demand.

In terms of economic efficiency, monopsony is least harmful, and is sometimes beneficial; in those markets in which a monopsony buyer faces a monopoly seller, a situation called **bilateral monopoly** arises. For example, consider the case of the town in which one large manufacturer is the sole employer of unskilled labor. The manufacturer is a monopsony because it is a single buyer of labor, and it may be able to use its power to reduce wage rates below the competitive level. If workers organize a union to bargain collectively with their employer, a single monopoly seller of labor is created that could offset the employer's monopsony power and increase wages toward competitive market norms. Not only is monopsony accepted in such situations, it is sometimes encouraged by public policy.

Bilateral Monopoly
Markets in which a monopsony buyer faces a monopoly seller.

Bilateral Monopoly Illustration

Competitive market price–output solutions reflect perfect balance in buyer and seller power. In markets with varying amounts of seller and buyer power, some divergence from the competitive market equilibrium is to be expected. Effects of buyer power can be illustrated by considering the market price and supply effects of a large, well-known buyer with market power in the home improvement market. Home Depot, Inc., the nation's second-largest retailer, behind Wal-Mart Stores, Inc., was founded in 1978 in Atlanta, Georgia, and operates more than 1,500 stores across North America. The Home Depot caters to the do-it-yourself market and to professional installers who serve the home improvement, construction, and building maintenance markets.

Figure 12.5 illustrates the effects of bilateral monopoly that might occur when the Home Depot deals with Whirlpool Corporation, producer of Maytag brand appliances. Maytag appliances have a long-standing reputation for dependability and quality, and are a key offering in Home Depot stores. At the same time, the Home Depot is a major customer for Maytag. For illustration purposes, assume that competitive market demand and supply relations for Maytag's high-efficiency gas dryer are

$$P = \$1{,}080 - \$2Q \qquad \text{(Demand)}$$
$$P = \$180 + \$8Q \qquad \text{(Supply)}$$

where P is price and Q is output (in thousands). The competitive market price/output solution is found by setting the demand curve equal to the supply curve and solving for price and output:

$$\text{Demand} = \text{Supply}$$
$$\$1{,}080 - \$2Q = \$180 + \$8Q$$
$$10Q = 900$$
$$Q = 90 \ (000)$$

Figure 12.5 Bilateral Monopoly Illustration

Higher prices reflect monopoly power; lower prices reflect monopsony power.

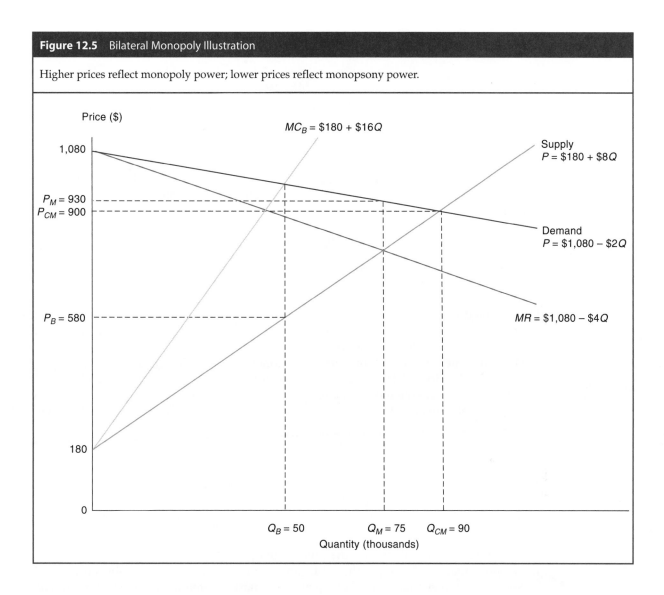

Solving for price gives

$$P = \$1,080 - \$2(90) = \$900 \text{ per unit} \qquad \text{(Demand)}$$
$$P = \$180 + \$8(90) = \$900 \text{ per unit} \qquad \text{(Supply)}$$

In competitive market equilibrium, there exists perfect balance between buyer and seller power. Neither has an upper hand. This result contrasts with both the unrestrained monopoly and unrestrained monopsony price–output solutions. Markets with unrestrained monopoly feature higher than competitive market prices. In markets with unrestrained monopsony, lower than competitive market prices are observed.

The outcome observed in unrestrained monopoly equilibrium is found by setting the seller's marginal revenue equal to marginal cost. In this case, Maytag's optimal price–

output combination can be determined by setting its marginal revenue equal to marginal cost (from the supply curve) and solving for Q:

$$MR = MC$$
$$\$1{,}080 - \$4Q = \$180 + \$8Q$$
$$12Q = 900$$
$$Q = 75$$

The monopoly seller's preferred price for this output level can be determined from the demand curve, which depicts the maximum price buyers are willing to pay for this level of output:

$$P_M = \$1{,}080 - \$2Q$$
$$= \$1{,}080 - \$2(75)$$
$$= \$930$$

Unrestrained monopoly results in higher than competitive market prices. As a result, buyers pay more than the marginal cost of production. Such high prices are inefficient in that they result in too little output being sold.

The outcome observed in unrestrained monopsony equilibrium is found by setting the buyer's (the Home Depot's) marginal cost curve equal to the demand curve. First, it is necessary to derive the buyer's marginal cost curve. This relationship is determined by taking the first derivative of the buyer's total cost derived from the market supply curve:

$$\text{Buyer's Total Cost} = P \times Q$$
$$= (\$180 + \$8Q)Q$$
$$= \$180Q + \$8Q^2$$
$$\text{Buyer's Marginal Cost} = \partial TC / \partial Q$$
$$= \$180 + \$16Q$$

Once this relationship depicting the buyer's marginal cost curve has been determined, the amount that would be purchased in unrestrained monopsony equilibrium is found by setting the buyer's marginal cost equal to the market demand curve, which represents the buyer's marginal revenue from purchases, and solving for quantity:

$$\text{Buyer's Marginal Cost} = \text{Buyer's Marginal Revenue}$$
$$\$180 + \$16Q = \$1{,}080 - \$2Q$$
$$18Q = 900$$
$$Q = 50 \text{ (000) units}$$

The monopsony buyer's preferred price for this output level can be determined from the supply curve, which depicts the minimum price required to attract this level of output:

$$P_B = \$180 + \$8Q$$
$$= \$180 + \$8(50)$$
$$= \$580$$

Unrestrained monopsony results in lower than competitive market prices. As a result, suppliers get paid less than the amount of economic value received by buyers. Such low prices are inefficient in that they result in too few workers being hired, and too little output being produced.

Bilateral monopoly moderates the price–output outcomes observed in unrestrained monopoly and unrestrained monopsony markets. Compromise achieved through bilateral monopoly has the beneficial effect of moving markets away from the inefficient unrestrained monopoly or monopsony solutions toward a more efficient competitive market equilibrium. However, only in the unlikely event of perfectly matched monopoly–monopsony protagonists will the competitive market outcome occur. Depending on the relative power of the seller and the buyer, either an above-market or a below-competitive market price will result. If a monopoly seller has the upper hand, higher than competitive market prices prevail. If a monopsony buyer has the upper hand, lower than competitive market prices will prevail. Typically, monopoly–monopsony bargaining produces a compromise price–output outcome that falls within the extremes of the unrestrained monopoly and unrestrained monopsony solutions. As such, bilateral monopoly often has the beneficial effect of improving economic efficiency by improving the situation faced under either unrestrained monopoly or unrestrained monopsony.

ANTITRUST POLICY

If unfair methods of competition emerge, antitrust policy is brought to bear.

Managerial Application 12.3

Is This Why They Call it "Hardball"?

Just prior to the last round of negotiations with the Major League Player's Association (MLPA), baseball commissioner Bud Selig argued that operating losses in the hundreds of millions of dollars per year are threatening to kill the game. According to Selig, congress and the players' union need to help reduce player salaries. Local governments also need to pony up for new and more elaborate stadiums.

Selig's ploy was nothing more than public posturing ahead of tough labor negotiations. Major league baseball (MLB) operates much like a corporation with 30 different regional offices (local franchises). Although individual clubs compete on the playing field, they aren't economic competitors. In a competitive market, one competitor's gain comes at the expense of others. In baseball, the success of one franchise brings increased prosperity for all. Through revenue sharing, all clubs prosper when Barry Bonds chases Hank Aaron's career home run record. When the Giants or the Yankees come to town, home team ticket sales soar. Ineptitude at one franchise weakens the profit picture for everyone.

MLB is clearly concerned about its poisoned collective bargaining environment. On the other side of the table is the MLPA. The players' association is a monopoly seller of baseball player talent, and the owners are a monopsony employer. The labor–market standoff in major league baseball is a classic confrontation between a powerful monopsony employer (the owners) and a powerful monopoly employee group (the players' association). Without a union, the owners would be able to drive player compensation down and earn monopsony rents. If owners were powerless, the players would be able to earn excessive salaries. Facing one another, they have to fight it out. It will be interesting to see who wins, and if Selig is successful in getting the general public to pay more of the tab for escalating player salaries and ever more elaborate stadiums.

See: Russell Adams, "Baseball Promotes from Within," *The Wall Street Journal Online*, October 12, 2007, http://interactive.wsj.com.

Overview of Antitrust Law

Antitrust Laws
Laws designed
to promote
competition.

Antitrust laws are designed to promote competition and prevent unwarranted monopoly. By itself, large firm size or market dominance is no offense; it is any unfairly gained competitive advantage that is against the law. The primary objection to monopolies, cartels, and other restraints of trade is that they injure consumers by increasing prices. High monopoly prices also curtail consumption and thereby reduce consumer welfare. A further objection to monopoly is that unrestrained economic power stifles innovation, and often fails to provide necessary incentives for operating efficiency. As British economist John Hicks once wrote, "The best of all monopoly profits is a quiet life." Thus, complacency on the part of monopolists can impede economic progress.

The choice between pure competition and monopoly is easy. Unfortunately, that is seldom the decision facing those charged with antitrust enforcement. Antitrust concerns tend to arise in industries where firms have some market power, but also face competition. In such instances, mergers and restrictive practices that may create or enhance market power may also promote efficiency and benefit consumers. Antitrust enforcement is made difficult by the need to identify corporate conduct whose primary effect is to lessen competition and harm consumers.

There is no single antitrust statute in the United States. Federal antitrust law is based on two important statutes—the Sherman Act and the Clayton Act—and their amendments. An important characteristic of these laws is that they broadly ban, but never define, "restraints of trade," "monopolization," "unfair competition," and so on. By never precisely defining such key terms, the statutes left the courts to decide the specific legality or illegality of various business practices. Because of this, many principles in antitrust law rest on judicial interpretation. Individual court decisions, called case law, and statutory standards, called statutory law, must be consulted to assess the legality of business behavior.

Sherman and Clayton Acts

The Sherman Act of 1890 was the first federal antitrust legislation. Section 1 forbids contracts, combinations, or conspiracies in restraint of trade. Section 2 forbids monopolizing behavior. Both sections can be enforced through the civil courts or by criminal proceedings. Even with landmark decisions against the tobacco, powder, and oil trusts, enforcement of the Sherman Act has been sporadic. On the one hand, businesspeople claim not to know what is legal; on the other, the Justice Department is sometimes criticized as being ignorant of monopoly-creating practices and failing to act in a timely fashion. Despite its shortcomings, the Sherman Act remains one of the government's main weapons against anticompetitive behavior. On conviction, corporate punishment can be in the form of fines not to exceed $10 million. Individuals face a felony conviction and may be fined up to $350,000, or imprisoned for up to 3 years. Violators of the Sherman Act also face the possibility of paying triple damages to injured parties who bring civil suits.

Congress passed two laws in 1914 to overcome weaknesses in the Sherman Act. The more important of these, the Clayton Act, addresses problems of mergers, interlocking directorates, price discrimination, and tying contracts. The Federal Trade Commission Act outlaws unfair methods of competition in commerce and establishes the Federal Trade Commission (FTC), an agency intended to enforce the Clayton Act.

Section 2 of the Clayton Act prohibits sellers from discriminating in price among business customers, unless cost differentials or competitive pressure justify the price differentials. At the time, it was feared that national firms would charge monopoly prices in certain markets and use resulting excess profits to subsidize cutthroat competition in other areas. The Robinson–Patman Act, passed in 1936, declares specific forms of price discrimination illegal, especially those related to chain-store purchasing practices. Section 3 of the Clayton Act forbids tying contracts that reduce competition. A firm, particularly one with a patent on a vital process, could use licensing or other arrangements to restrict competition. One such method is the tying contract, whereby a firm ties the acquisition of one item to the purchase of another. For example, IBM once leased its business machines to customers and then required them to buy IBM materials and maintenance service. This had the effect of reducing competition in these related industries. The IBM lease agreement was declared illegal under the Clayton Act, and the company was forced to offer machines for sale and to separate leasing arrangements from agreements to purchase other IBM products.

Finally, either the Antitrust Division of the Justice Department or the FTC can bring suit under Section 7 of the Clayton Act to prevent mergers that lessen competition. If mergers have been consummated prior to the suit, divestiture can be ordered. The Clayton Act also prevents individuals from serving on the boards of directors of competing companies. So-called competitors having common directors would obviously not compete very hard. Although the Clayton Act made it illegal for firms to merge through stock transactions in order to lessen competition, a firm could still purchase competing firm assets, through a loophole in the law, and thereby reduce competition. The Celler–Kefauver Act closed this loophole, making asset acquisitions illegal when the effect of such purchases is to reduce competition. It thus became clear that Congress intends to attack all mergers that threaten competition, whether vertical mergers between buyers and sellers, horizontal and market extension mergers between actual or potential competitors, or purely conglomerate mergers between unrelated firms.

Antitrust Enforcement

The Sherman Act is brought to bear—with both criminal and civil penalties—in cases involving monopolization, price-fixing agreements, and other unreasonable restraints on trade. The Clayton Act is used to address specific problems created by mergers and certain forms of price discrimination, exclusive dealing agreements, and tie-in sales conditioned on the purchase of related products.

The Justice Department and the FTC have overlapping enforcement responsibilities. The Justice Department may bring actions under the Sherman Act, and the FTC may initiate actions under the Federal Trade Commission Act. Both may initiate proceedings under the Clayton Act. In addition, major regulatory agencies, such as the Federal Communications Commission, the Federal Energy Regulatory Commission, and the Surface Transportation Board, all review mergers under their own statutory authority.

Generally speaking, the Justice Department concerns itself with flagrant offenses under the Sherman Act, as well as with mergers for monopoly covered by Section 7 of the Clayton Act. In most cases, the Justice Department brings charges under the Clayton Act only when broader Sherman Act violations are also involved. In addition to policing law violations, the Sherman Act assigns to the Justice Department the duty of restraining possible future violations. Firms found to be in violation of the law often receive detailed federal court injunctions that regulate future business activity. Injunctive relief in the form of dissolution or divestiture decrees is a much more typical outcome of Justice Department suits than are criminal penalties.

Although the Justice Department can institute civil and criminal proceedings, civil proceedings are typically the responsibility of the FTC. The FTC is an administrative agency of the executive branch that has quasi-judicial powers with which it enforces compliance with the Clayton Act. Because the substantive provisions of the Clayton Act do not create criminal offenses, the FTC has no criminal jurisdiction. The FTC holds hearings about suspected violations of the law and issues cease and desist orders if violations are found. Cease and desist orders under the Clayton Act are subject to review by appellate courts.

COMPETITIVE STRATEGY IN MONOPOLY MARKETS

In monopoly markets, development of an effective competitive strategy is vital to long-run success.

Market Niches

Above-normal returns tend to be fleeting in perfectly competitive industries but can be durable for efficient firms that benefit from monopoly advantages. As in any perfectly competitive industry, above-normal profit rates can be observed if monopoly firms temporarily benefit from some unanticipated increase in demand or decrease in costs. Similarly, monopolists can benefit from temporary affluence due to unexpected changes

Managerial Application 12.4

Price Fixing by the Insurance Cartel

In 2004, the nation's largest insurance companies were served with subpoenas from Eliot Spitzer, then New York attorney general, asking a simple but explosive question: Had they ever engaged in bid-rigging? Within weeks, tremors shook the $1 trillion dollar insurance industry as one leading insurance company after another admitted that they had in fact participated in a scheme to set prices and defraud insurance buyers. The conspiracy was apparently organized and worked through insurance brokers that companies use to negotiate and buy insurance coverage.

The way the system is supposed to work is for an insurance broker like Marsh & McLennan Cos. to use its clout to obtain favorable insurance rates. Marsh & McLennan is the world's largest insurance broker with about 20 percent of the market, and has long been a trusted source of insurance-pricing information. Apparently, Marsh & McLennan cheated corporate clients by rigging bids and collecting big fees from major insurance companies. Marsh & McLennan allocated business to various insurance companies based upon their willingness to pay "contingent commissions" or kickback fees tied to the amount of insurance purchased. Coverage costs were artificially inflated to provide the insurance companies and Marsh & McLennan with big profits. To mask this bid-rigging, Marsh & McLennan solicited phony bids from other insurance carriers, which were artificially inflated.

Wrongdoing was readily admitted to by officials at major insurance companies, including American International Group, Inc., Ace, Ltd., and Hartford Financial Services Group, Inc. Customers, industry observers, and investors are all left to wonder about the ultimate fallout from a continuing series of felony convictions, the dismissal of several top executives, and plummeting insurance company stock prices. One thing is for certain. The insurance business will be forever transformed, and for the better!

See: Ian McDonald and Liam Pleven, "Big Marsh & McLennan Unit Seeks CEO," *The Wall Street Journal Online*, September 15, 2007, http://online.wsj.com.

in industry demand or cost conditions or uniquely productive inputs. What is unique about monopoly is the potential for long-lasting above-normal profits.

With instant global communication and rapid technical advance, no monopoly is permanently secure from the threat of current or potential competitors. Product characteristics, the local or regional limits of the market, the time necessary for reactions by established or new competitors, the pace of innovation, unanticipated changes in government regulation and tax policy, and a host of additional considerations all play an important role in defining the scope and durability of monopoly power. Although attempting to describe monopoly advantages, it is always helpful to consider the number and size of potential competitors, degree of product differentiation, level of information available in the marketplace, and conditions of entry.

Market Niche

A segment of a market that can be successfully exploited through the special capabilities of a given firm or individual.

Only new and unique products or services have the potential to create monopoly profits. Imitation of such products may be protected by patents, copyrights, or other means. In many instances, above-normal profits reflect the successful exploitation of a market niche. A **market niche** is a segment of a market that can be successfully exploited through the special capabilities of a given firm or individual. Table 12.2 lists a variety of market niches where companies offer distinctive products and earn enviable profit rates. To be durable, above-normal profits derived from a market niche must not be vulnerable to imitation by competitors.

Purchase of a business that enjoys recognized monopoly power seldom leads to economic profits because anticipated abnormal returns on plant and equipment are reflected in purchase prices. Fertile land brings a price premium in the real estate market; monopoly franchises bring a premium price in the stock market. As a result, the purchase of a recognized monopoly leads to only a risk-adjusted normal rate of return for subsequent investors. Monopolists make money; investors in a fully appreciated monopoly do not.

Information Barriers to Competitive Strategy

Accounting profit data derived from a historical perspective give useful information for operating decisions and tax purposes. However, these data sometimes measure economic profits imperfectly. For example, advertising and research and development (R&D) expenditures are expensed for both reporting and tax purposes, even though each can give rise to long-term economic benefits. An expense-as-incurred treatment of advertising and R&D expenditures can lead to errors in profit measurement. Current net income is depressed when advertising and R&D are written off before the end of their useful lives; intangible assets can be understated when they fail to reflect the value of brand names and other innovative products. Depending on the true rate of economic amortization for advertising and R&D and the rate of growth in expenditures for each, business profit rates can be either understated or overstated. Reported business profit rates, such as ROE, can substantially misstate economic profits. At the same time, other imperfections in accrual accounting methods lead to imperfectly matched revenues and costs and, therefore, to some misstatement of economic profits over time.

Beyond these and other obvious limitations of accounting data, business practices are often expressly intended to limit the loss of valuable trade secret information. Why would anyone give competitors any more than the bare minimum of information? It is well-known that firms patent only what they cannot otherwise keep secret. Combined with the limitations of publicly available data on profitability, business practices create

Table 12.2 Corporate Profitability in 50 Industries with Niche Markets

Industry Group	Active Corporations	Profit Margin (% of sales)	Return on Equity (ROE)(%)
Accounting and auditing services	42,037	5.4	66.5
Air transportation	8,680	5.4	22.4
Aircraft, guided missiles, and parts	870	5.2	21.1
Alcoholic beverages	4,615	3.1	22.3
Apparel, piece goods, and notions	18,656	3.2	21.2
Bakery products	5,354	3.8	19.4
Bottled soft drinks and flavorings	653	9.8	21.2
Cement, hydraulic	226	14.3	23.9
Coating, engraving, and allied services	3,468	6.4	25.3
Commercial and other printing services	29,942	3.9	18.0
Commodity brokers and dealers	14,944	12.4	17.7
Computers and office machines	3,782	8.2	26.4
Concrete, gypsum, and plaster products	4,730	8.2	28.4
Construction and related machinery	2,457	7.9	24.4
Cutlery, hand tools, and hardware	3,059	13.4	24.0
Drugs	2,536	15.4	22.8
Electrical contractors	35,076	3.6	29.0
Electronic components and accessories	12,407	8.1	17.9
Fabricated structural metal products	9,448	5.8	21.2
Farm machinery	1,984	8.8	27.7
Furniture and home furnishings	9,978	3.3	28.6
General building contractors	180,935	1.9	22.1
General industrial machinery	4,385	8.1	19.6
Grocery stores	45,534	1.4	18.4
Insurance agents, brokers, and services	78,717	8.6	18.3
Legal services	72,848	4.8	101.5
Lessors of mining, oil, and similar property	1,636	121.9	20.2
Machinery, equipment, and supplies	55,650	3.4	20.5
Malt liquors and malt	35	10.1	19.5
Men's and boys' clothing	1,391	7.0	22.5
Metal forgings and stampings	4,916	5.1	22.7
Metalworking machinery	9,635	6.1	19.8
Miscellaneous fabricated metal products	23,529	6.4	25.5
Miscellaneous plastics products	10,363	4.8	19.1
Miscellaneous repair services	51,292	3.3	21.2
Mutual savings banks	206	222.7	17.5
Newspapers	5,936	14.9	25.2
Offices of dentists	47,344	3.6	77.1
Offices of other health practitioners	39,721	5.2	61.2
Offices of physicians	127,872	1.2	38.7
Ordnance and accessories	970	6.4	33.2
Paints and allied products	533	7.0	19.0
Personal services	95,807	5.4	17.9
Photographic equipment and supplies	186	9.2	21.8
Plumbing, heating, and air conditioning	50,435	2.6	24.3
Rubber products, hose, and belting	1,933	5.7	22.8
Security brokers and services	10,468	21.8	17.8
Soaps, cleaners, and toilet goods	3,056	11.5	33.7
Toys, sporting, and photographic goods	12,537	2.6	26.8
Water supply and other sanitary services	13,661	5.6	9.9
Averages		13.5	26.9
Median		6.0	22.4

Data Source: U.S. corporate federal income tax data, 2003, http://www.bizstats.com.

an information barrier that hides the true details about economic profit rates. Such obfuscation makes defining the scope of monopoly power difficult, as it hides the costs and benefits of entry into monopoly markets from both private and public decision makers.

SUMMARY

This chapter considers how monopoly firms come to dominate some markets, and the economic risks involved with government regulation.

- **Monopoly** exists when a firm is the sole producer of a distinctive good or service. The monopoly firm is the industry. Like competitive firms, the pricing discretion of monopoly firms is constrained by the customer's overall willingness to pay, as reflected by downward-sloping market demand curves. Still, the absence of close substitutes gives monopoly firms a significant amount of discretion when it comes to setting prices. Monopoly firms are **price makers** as opposed to competitive market firms who are price takers.

- Monopoly firms have incentives to restrict output so as to create scarcity and earn economic profits. **Monopoly underproduction** results when a monopoly curtails output to a level at which the marginal value of resources employed, as measured by the marginal cost of production, is less than the marginal social benefit derived, where marginal social benefit is measured by the price that customers are willing to pay for additional output. Under monopoly, marginal cost is less than price at the profit-maximizing output level.

- The tendency for monopoly firms to restrict output to increase prices and earn economic profits gives rise to a **deadweight loss from monopoly problem.** Like any restriction on supply, the reduced level of economic activity typical of monopoly markets creates a loss in social welfare due to the decline in mutually beneficial trade activity.

- In addition to the deadweight loss from monopoly problem, there is a **wealth transfer problem** associated with monopoly. The creation of monopoly results in the transformation of a significant amount of consumer surplus into producer surplus.

- A **natural monopoly** does not arise from government intervention or any artificial barriers

to entry, but can be a predictable result given the current state of technology and cost conditions in the industry. Monopoly naturally evolves in markets subject to overwhelming economies of scale in production created by extremely large capital requirements, scarce inputs, insufficient natural resources, and so on. In such instances, the market-dominant firm is called a natural monopoly, because the market-clearing price, where $P = MC$, occurs at a point at which long-run average total costs are still declining.

- To achieve the benefits flowing from dynamic, innovative, leading firms, public policy sometimes confers explicit monopoly rights. For example, **patents** grant an exclusive right to produce, use, or sell an invention or innovation for a limited period of time.

- Rapid changes in technology and competitive conditions have rendered obsolete many traditional forms of regulation in the electricity and telecommunications industries. When regulators are slow to react to such changes, both the consumers and the industry suffer due to **regulatory lag,** or the delay between when a change in regulation is appropriate and the date it becomes effective.

- If only a few buyers exist in a given market, there will tend to be less competition than if there are many buyers. **Oligopsony** exists when there are only a handful of buyers present in a market. **Monopsony** exists when a market features a single buyer of a desired product or input. When a single buyer is confronted in a market with many sellers, **monopsony power** enables the buyer to obtain lower prices than those that would prevail in a competitive market.

- In terms of economic efficiency, monopsony is least harmful, and is sometimes beneficial; in those markets in which a monopsony buyer faces a monopoly seller, a situation called **bilateral monopoly** arises.

- **Antitrust laws** are designed to promote competition and prevent unwarranted monopoly. By itself, large firm size or market dominance is no offense; it is any unfairly gained competitive advantage that is against the law.

- In many instances, above-normal profits reflect the successful exploitation of a **market niche.** A market niche is a segment of a market that can be successfully exploited through the special capabilities of a given firm or individual. To be durable, above-normal profits derived from a market niche must not be vulnerable to imitation by competitors.

Without superior capability or distinctive performance, the economic profits of pure monopoly are typically viewed as unwarranted. On the other hand, the above-normal returns of dynamic leading firms are often seen as a just reward for superior performance. Balancing the public desire for markets that are free and open social need for dynamic, innovative firms makes the study of monopoly a vital part of managerial economics.

QUESTIONS

Q12.1 Describe the monopoly market structure and provide some examples.

Q12.2 From a social standpoint, what is the problem with monopoly?

Q12.3 Why are both industry and firm demand curves downward sloping in monopoly markets?

Q12.4 Give an example of monopoly in the labor market. Discuss such a monopoly's effect on wage rates and on inflation.

Q12.5 Given the difficulties encountered with utility regulation, it has been suggested that nationalization might lead to a more socially optimal allocation of resources. Do you agree? Why or why not?

Q12.6 Antitrust statutes in the United States have been used to attack monopolization by big business. Does labor monopolization by giant unions have the same potential for the misallocation of economic resources?

Q12.7 When will an increase in the minimum wage increase employment income for unskilled laborers? When will it cause this income to fall? Based on your experience, which is more likely?

Q12.8 Explain why state tax rates on personal income vary more on a state-by-state basis than do corresponding tax rates on corporate income.

Q12.9 Do the U.S. antitrust statutes protect competition or competitors? What is the difference?

Q12.10 Describe the economic effects of countervailing power, and cite examples of markets in which countervailing power is observed.

SELF-TEST PROBLEMS AND SOLUTIONS

ST12.1 Capture Problem. It remains a widely held belief that regulation is in the public interest and influences firm behavior toward socially desirable ends. However, in the early 1970s, Nobel laureate George Stigler and his colleague Sam Peltzman at the University of Chicago introduced an alternative capture theory of economic regulation. According to Stigler and Peltzman, the machinery and power of the state are a potential resource to every industry. With its power to prohibit or compel, to take or give money, the state can and does selectively help or hurt a vast number of industries. Because of this, regulation may be actively sought by industry. They contended that regulation is typically acquired by industry and is designed and operated primarily for industry's benefit.

Types of state favors commonly sought by regulated industries include direct money subsidies, control over entry by new rivals, control over substitutes and complements, and price fixing. Domestic "air mail" subsidies, Federal Deposit Insurance Corporation (FDIC) regulation that reduces the rate of entry into commercial banking, suppression of margarine sales by butter producers, price fixing in motor carrier (trucking) regulation, and American Medical Association control of medical training and licensing can be interpreted as historical examples of control by regulated industries.

In summarizing their views on regulation, Stigler and Peltzman suggest that regulators should be criticized for pro-industry policies no more than politicians for seeking popular support. Current methods of enacting and carrying out regulations only make the pro-industry stance of regulatory bodies more likely. The only way to get different results from regulation is to change the political process of regulator selection and to provide economic rewards to regulators who serve the public interest effectively.

Capture theory is in stark contrast to more traditional public interest theory, which sees regulation as a government-imposed means of private-market control. Rather than viewing regulation as a "good" to be obtained, controlled, and manipulated, public interest theory views regulation as a method for improving economic performance by limiting the harmful effects of market failure. Public interest theory is silent on the need to provide regulators with economic incentives to improve regulatory performance. Unlike capture theory, a traditional view has been that the public can trust regulators to make a good-faith effort to establish regulatory policy in the public interest.

A. The aim of antitrust and regulatory policy is to protect competition, not to protect competitors. Explain the difference.

B. Starting in the 1970s, growing dissatisfaction with traditional approaches to government regulation led to a global deregulation movement that spurred competition, lowered prices, and resulted in more efficient production. Explain how this experience is consistent with the capture theory of regulation.

C. Discuss how regulatory efficiency could be improved by focusing on output objectives, like low prices for cable or telephone services, rather than production methods or rates of return.

ST12.1 SOLUTION

A. Entry and exit are common facts of life in competitive markets. Firms that efficiently produce goods and services that consumers crave are able to boost market share and enjoy growing revenues and profits. Firms that fail to measure up in the eyes of consumers will lose market share and suffer declining revenues and profits. The disciplining role of competitive markets can be swift and harsh, even for the largest and most formidable corporations. For example, in August 2000, Enron Corp. traded in the stock market at an all-time high and was ranked among the ten most valuable corporations in America. Nevertheless, Enron filed for bankruptcy just 16 months later as evidence emerged of a failed diversification strategy, misguided energy trading, and financial corruption. Similarly, once-powerful telecom giant WorldCom quickly stumbled into bankruptcy as evidence came to light concerning the company's abuse of accounting rules and regulations. In both cases, once-powerful corporations were brought to their knees by competitive capital and product markets that simply refused to tolerate inefficiency and corporate malfeasance.

In evaluating the effects of deregulation, and in gauging the competitive implications of market exit by previously regulated firms, it is important to remember that protecting competition is not the same as protecting competitors. Without regulation, it is inevitable that some competitors will fall by the wayside and that concentration will rise in some previously regulated markets. Although such trends must be watched closely for anticompetitive effects, they are characteristics of a vigorously competitive environment. Bankruptcy and exit are the regrettable costs of remedying economic dislocation in competitive markets. Though such costs are regrettable, experience shows that they are much less onerous than the costs of indefinitely maintaining inefficient production methods in a tightly regulated environment.

B. Although it is difficult to pinpoint a single catalyst for the deregulation movement, it is hard to overlook the role played by George Stigler, Sam Peltzman, Alfred E. Kahn, and other economists who documented how government regulation can sometimes harm consumer interests. A study by the Brookings Institution documented important benefits of deregulation in five major industries—natural gas, telecommunications, airlines, trucking, and railroads. It was found that prices fell from 4 percent to 15 percent within the first 2 years after deregulation; within 10 years, prices were 25 percent to 50 percent lower. Deregulation also leads to service quality improvements. Crucial social goals like airline safety, reliability of gas service, and reliability of the telecommunications network were maintained or improved by deregulation. Regulatory reform also tends to confer benefits on most consumers. Although it is possible to find narrowly defined groups of customers in special circumstances who paid somewhat higher prices after deregulation, the gains to the vast majority of consumers far outweighed negative effects on small groups. Finally, deregulation offers benefits in the sense of permitting greater customer choice.

Although many industries have felt the effects of changing state and local regulation, changing federal regulation has been most pronounced in the financial, telecommunications, and transportation sectors. Since 1975, for example, it has been illegal for securities dealers to fix commission rates. This broke a 182-year tradition under which the New York Stock Exchange (NYSE) set minimum rates for each 100-share ("round lot") purchase. Until 1975, everyone charged the minimum rate approved by the NYSE. Purchase of 1,000 shares cost a commission of ten times the minimum, even though the overhead and work involved are roughly the same for small and large stock transactions. Following deregulation, commission rates tumbled, and, predictably, some of the least efficient brokerage firms merged or otherwise went out of business. Today, commission rates have fallen by 90 percent or more, and the industry is noteworthy for increasing productivity and innovative new product introductions. It is also worth mentioning that since brokerage rates were deregulated, the number of sales offices in the industry, trading volume, employment, and profits have skyrocketed. This has led some observers to conclude that deregulation can benefit consumers without causing any lasting damage to industry. In fact, a leaner, more efficient industry may be one of the greatest benefits of deregulation.

In Canada, the deregulation movement led to privatization of government-owned Air Canada. Trucking, historically a regulated industry, also was deregulated. Specialized telecommunications services industries were deregulated and thrown open to competition. In other areas where the government considered continued regulation desirable and necessary, regulatory agencies were pressured to reform and improve the regulatory decision-making process to reduce inefficiencies, bureaucratic delays, and administrative red tape.

C. A significant problem with regulation is that regulators seldom have the information or expertise to specify, for example, the correct level of utility investment, minimum transportation costs, or the optimum method of pollution control. Because technology changes rapidly in most regulated industries, only industry personnel working at the frontier of current technology have such specialized knowledge. One method for dealing with this technical expertise problem is to have regulators focus on the preferred outcomes of regulatory processes, rather than on the technical means that industry adopts to achieve those ends. The FCC's decision to adopt downward-adjusting price caps for long-distance telephone service is an example of this developing trend toward incentive-based regulation. If providers of long-distance telephone service are able to reduce costs faster than the FCC-mandated decline in prices, they will enjoy an increase in profitability. By setting price caps that fall over time, the FCC ensures that consumers share in expected cost savings while companies enjoy a positive incentive to innovate. This approach to regulation focuses on the objectives of regulation while allowing industry to meet those goals in new and unique ways. Tying regulator rewards and regulated industry profits to objective, output-oriented performance criteria has the potential to create a desirable win/win situation for regulators, utilities, and the general public. For example, the public has a real interest in safe, reliable, and low-cost electric power. State and federal regulators who oversee the operations of utilities could develop objective standards for measuring utility safety, reliability, and cost efficiency. Tying firm profit rates to such performance-oriented criteria could stimulate real improvements in utility and regulator performance.

Although some think that there is simply a question of regulation versus deregulation, this is seldom the case. On grounds of economic and political feasibility, it is often most fruitful to consider approaches to improving existing methods of regulation. Competitive forces provide a persistent and socially desirable constraining influence on firm behavior. When vigorous competition is absent, government regulation can be justified through both efficiency and equity criteria. When regulation is warranted, business, government, and the public must work together to ensure that regulatory processes represent the public interest. The unnecessary costs of antiquated regulations dictate that regulatory reform is likely to remain a significant social concern.

ST12.2 Deadweight Loss from Monopoly.

The Las Vegas Valley Water District (LVVWD) is a not-for-profit agency that began providing water to the Las Vegas Valley in 1954. The District helped build the city's water delivery system and now provides water to more than 1 million people in Southern Nevada. District water rates are regulated by law and can cover only the costs of water delivery, maintenance, and facilities. District water rates are based on a four-tier system to encourage conservation. The first tier represents indoor usage for most residential customers. Rate for remaining tiers becomes increasingly higher with the amount of water usage.

To document the deadweight loss from monopoly problem, allow the monthly market supply and demand conditions for water in the Las Vegas Water District to be

$$Q_S = 10P \qquad \text{(Market Supply)}$$
$$Q_D = 120 - 40P \qquad \text{(Market Demand)}$$

where Q is water and P is the market price of water. Water is sold in units of 1,000 gallons, so a \$2 price implies a user cost of 0.2¢ per gallon. Water demand and supply relations are expressed in terms of millions of units.

A. Graph and calculate the equilibrium price–output solution. How much consumer surplus, producer surplus, and social welfare is produced at this activity level?

B. Use the graph to help you calculate the quantity demanded and quantity supplied if the market is run by a profit-maximizing monopolist. (Note: If monopoly market demand is $P = \$3 - \$0.025Q$, then the monopolist's $MR = \$3 - \$0.05Q$.)

C. Use the graph to help you determine the deadweight loss for consumers and the producer if LVVWD is run as an unregulated profit-maximizing monopoly.

D. Use the graph to help you ascertain the amount of consumer surplus transferred to producers following a change from a competitive market to a monopoly market. How much is the net gain in producer surplus?

ST12.2 SOLUTION

A. The market supply curve is given by the equation

$$Q_S = 10P$$

or, solving for price,

$$P = 0.1Q_S$$

The market demand curve is given by the equation

$$Q_D = 120 - 40P$$

or, solving for price,

$$40P = 120 - Q_D$$
$$P = \$3 - \$0.025Q_D$$

To find the competitive market equilibrium price, equate the market demand and market supply curves where quantity is expressed as a function of price:

$$\text{Supply} = \text{Demand}$$
$$10P = 120 - 40P$$
$$50P = 120$$
$$P = \$2.40$$

To find the competitive market equilibrium quantity, set equal the market supply and market demand curves where price is expressed as a function of quantity, and $Q_S = Q_D$:

$$\text{Supply} = \text{Demand}$$
$$\$0.1Q = \$3 - \$0.025Q$$
$$0.125Q = 3$$
$$Q = 24 \text{ (million) units per month}$$

Therefore, the competitive market equilibrium price–output combination is a market price of \$2.40 with an equilibrium output of 24 (million) units.

The value of consumer surplus is equal to the region under the market demand curve that lies above the market equilibrium price of \$2.40. Because the area of such a triangle is one-half the value of the base times the height, the value of consumer surplus equals

$$\text{Consumer Surplus} = \frac{1}{2}\,[24 \times (\$3 - \$2.40)]$$
$$= \$7.2 \text{ (million) per month}$$

In words, this means that at a unit price of \$2.40, the quantity demanded is 24 (million), resulting in total revenues of \$57.6 (million). The fact that consumer surplus equals \$7.2 (million) means that customers as a group would have been willing to pay an additional \$7.2 (million) for this level of market output. This is an amount above and beyond the \$57.6 (million) paid. Customers received a real bargain.

The value of producer surplus is equal to the region above the market supply curve at the market equilibrium price of \$2.40. Because the area of such a triangle is one-half the value of the base times the height, the value of producer surplus equals

$$\text{Producer Surplus} = \frac{1}{2}\,[24 \times (\$2.40 - \$0)]$$
$$= \$28.8 \text{ (million) per month}$$

At a water price of $2.40 per thousand gallons, producer surplus equals $28.8 (million). Producers as a group received $28.8 (million) more than the absolute minimum required for them to produce the market equilibrium output of 24 (million) units of output. Producers received a real bargain.

In competitive market equilibrium, social welfare is measured by the sum of net benefits derived by consumers and producers. Social welfare is the sum of consumer surplus and producer surplus:

$$\text{Social Welfare} = \text{Consumer Surplus} + \text{Producer Surplus}$$
$$= \$7.2\,(\text{million}) + \$28.8\,(\text{million})$$
$$= \$36\,(\text{million}) \text{ per month}$$

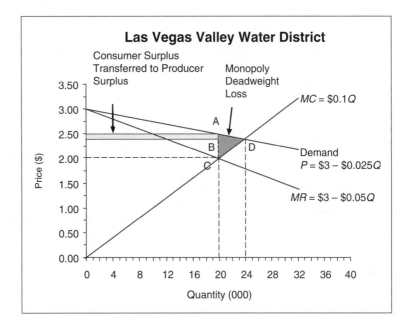

B. If the industry is run by a profit-maximizing monopolist, the optimal price–output combination can be determined by setting marginal revenue equal to marginal cost and solving for Q:

$$MR = MC = \text{Market Supply}$$
$$\$3 - \$0.05Q = \$0.1Q$$
$$\$0.15Q = \$3$$
$$Q = 20\,(\text{million}) \text{ units per month}$$

At $Q = 20$,

$$P = \$3 - \$0.025Q$$
$$= \$3 - \$0.025(20)$$
$$= \$2.50 \text{ per unit}$$

C. Under monopoly, the amount supplied falls to 20 (million) units and the market price jumps to $2.50 per thousand gallons of water. The amount of deadweight loss from monopoly suffered by consumers is given by the triangle bounded by *ABD* in the figure. Because the area of such a triangle is one-half the value of the base times the height, the value of lost consumer surplus due to monopoly equals

$$\text{Consumer Deadweight Loss} = \tfrac{1}{2}\,[(24 - 20) \times (\$2.50 - \$2.40)]$$
$$= \$0.2 \text{ (million) per month}$$

The amount of deadweight loss from monopoly suffered by producers is given by the triangle bounded by *BCD*. Because the area of such a triangle is one-half the value of the base times the height, the value of lost producer surplus equals

$$\text{Producer Deadweight Loss} = \tfrac{1}{2}\,[(24 - 20) \times (\$2.40 - \$2)]$$
$$= \$0.8 \text{ (million) per month}$$

The total amount of deadweight loss from monopoly suffered by consumers and producers is given by the triangle bounded by *ACD*. The area of such a triangle is simply the amount of consumer deadweight loss plus producer deadweight loss:

$$\text{Total Deadweight Loss} = \text{Consumer Loss} + \text{Producer Loss}$$
$$= \$0.2 \text{ (million)} + \$0.8 \text{ (million)}$$
$$= \$1 \text{ (million) per month}$$

D. In addition to the deadweight loss from monopoly problem, there is a wealth transfer problem associated with monopoly. The creation of a monopoly results in a significant transfer from consumer surplus to producer surplus. In the figure, this amount is shown as the area in the rectangle bordered by $2.40$2.50*AB*:

$$\text{Transfer to Producer Surplus} = 20 \times (\$2.50 - \$2.40)$$
$$= \$2 \text{ (million) per month}$$

Therefore, from the viewpoint of the producer, the change to monopoly results in a very favorable net increase in producer surplus:

$$\text{Net Change in Producer Surplus} = \text{Producer Deadweight Loss} + \text{Transfer}$$
$$= -\$0.8 \text{ (million)} + \$2 \text{ (million)}$$
$$= \$1.2 \text{ (million) per month}$$

From the viewpoint of consumers, the problem with monopoly is twofold. Monopoly results in both a significant deadweight loss in consumer surplus ($0.2 million per month), and a significant transfer of consumer surplus to producer surplus ($2 million per month). In this example, the cost of monopoly to consumers is measured by a total loss in consumer surplus of $2.2 million per month. The wealth transfer problem associated with monopoly is seen as an issue of equity, or fairness, because it involves the distribution of income or wealth in the economy. Although economic profits serve the useful functions of providing incentives and helping allocate resources, it is difficult to justify monopoly profits that result from the raw exercise of market power rather than from exceptional performance.

PROBLEMS

P12.1 Monopoly Concepts.   Indicate whether each of the following statements is true or false, and explain why.

A. The Justice Department generally concerns itself with significant or flagrant offenses under the Sherman Act, as well as with mergers for monopoly covered by Section 7 of the Clayton Act.

B. When a single seller is confronted in a market by many small buyers, monopsony power enables the buyers to obtain lower prices than those that would prevail in a competitive market.

C. A natural monopoly results when the profit-maximizing output level occurs at a point where long-run average costs are declining.

D. Downward-sloping industry demand curves characterize both perfectly competitive markets and monopoly markets.

E. A decrease in the price elasticity of demand would follow an increase in monopoly power.

P12.2 Natural Monopoly.   On May 12, 2000, the two daily newspapers in Denver, Colorado, filed an application with the U.S. Department of Justice for approval of a joint operating agreement. The application was filed by The E.W. Scripps Company, whose subsidiary, the Denver Publishing Company, published the *Rocky Mountain News,* and the MediaNews Group, Inc., whose subsidiary, the Denver Post Corporation, published the *Denver Post.* Under the proposed arrangement, printing and commercial operations of both newspapers were to be handled by a new entity, the "Denver Newspaper Agency", owned by the parties in equal shares. This type of joint operating agreement provides for the complete independence of the news and editorial departments of the two newspapers. The rationale for such an arrangement, as provided for under the Newspaper Preservation Act, is to preserve multiple independent editorial voices in towns and cities too small to support two or more newspapers. The Act requires joint operating arrangements, such as that proposed by the Denver newspapers, to obtain the prior written consent of the Attorney General of the United States in order to qualify for the antitrust exemption provided by the Act.

Scripps initiated discussions for a joint operating agreement after determining that the *News* would probably fail without such an arrangement. In their petition to the Justice department, the newspapers argued that the *News* had sustained $123 million in net operating losses while the financially stronger *Post* had reaped $200 million in profits during the 1990s. This was a crucial point in favor of the joint operating agreement application because the Attorney General must find that one of the publications is a failing newspaper and that approval of the arrangement is necessary to maintain the independent editorial content of both newspapers. Like any business, newspapers cannot survive without a respectable bottom line. In commenting on the joint operating agreement application, Attorney General Janet Reno noted that Denver was one of only five major American cities still served by competing daily newspapers. The other four are Boston, Chicago, New York, and Washington, DC. Of course these other four cities are not comparable in size to Denver; they're much bigger. None of those four cities can lay claim to two newspapers that are more or less equally matched and strive after the same audience.

A. Use the natural monopoly concept to explain why there is not a single city in the United States that still supports two independently owned and evenly matched, high-quality newspapers that vie for the same broad base of readership.

B. On Friday, January 5, 2001, Attorney General Reno gave the green light to a 50-year joint operating agreement between *News* and its longtime rival, the *Post*. Starting January 22, 2001, the publishing operations of the *News* and the *Post* were consolidated. At the time the joint operating agreement was formed, neither news organization would speculate on job losses or advertising and circulation rate increases from the deal. Based upon your knowledge of natural monopoly, would you predict an increase or decrease in prices following establishment of the joint operating agreement? Would you expect newspaper production (and employment) to rise or fall? Why?

P12.3   Price Fixing.   An antitrust case launched more than a decade ago sent tremors throughout the academic community. Over the 1989–1991 period, the U.S. Department of Justice (DOJ) investigated a number of highly selective private colleges for price fixing. The investigation focused on "overlap group" meetings comprised of about half of the most selective private colleges and universities in the United States. The group included 23 colleges, from small liberal arts schools like Colby, Vassar, and Middlebury to larger research universities like Princeton and MIT. DOJ found that when students applied to more than one of the 23 institutions, school officials met to coordinate the exact calculation of such students' financial need.

Although all of the overlap colleges attempted to use the same need formula, difficult-to-interpret information from students and parents introduced some variation into their actual need calculations. DOJ alleged that the meetings enabled the colleges to collude on higher tuition and to increase their tuition revenue. The colleges defended their meetings, saying that they needed coordination to fully cover the needs of students from low-income families. Although colleges want capable needy students to add diversity to their student body, no college can afford a disproportionate share of needy students simply because it makes relatively generous need calculations.

Although the colleges denied DOJ's price-fixing allegation, they discontinued their annual meetings in 1991.

A. How would you determine if the overlap college meetings resulted in price fixing?

B. If price fixing did indeed occur at these meetings, which laws might be violated?

P12.4   Tying Contracts.   In a celebrated case tried during 1998, The Department of Justice charged Microsoft Corporation with a wide range of anticompetitive behavior. Among the charges leveled by the DOJ was the allegation that Microsoft illegally "bundled" the sale of its Microsoft Explorer Internet browser software with its basic Windows operating system. DOJ alleged that by offering a free browser program, Microsoft was able to extend its operating system monopoly and "substantially lessen competition and tend to create a monopoly" in the browser market by undercutting rival Netscape Communications, Inc. Microsoft retorted that it had the right to innovate and broaden the capability of its operating system software over time. Moreover, Microsoft noted that Netscape distributed its rival Internet browser software Netscape Navigator free to customers, and that it was merely meeting the competition by offering its own free browser program.

A. Explain how Microsoft's bundling of free Internet browser software with its Windows operating system could violate U.S. antitrust laws, and be sure to mention which laws in particular might be violated.

B. Who was right in this case? In other words, did Microsoft's bundling of Microsoft Explorer with Windows extend its operating system monopoly and "substantially lessen competition and tend to create a monopoly" in the browser market?

P12.5   Monopoly Price–Output Decision. Calvin's Barber Shops, Inc., has a monopoly on barbershop services provided on the south side of Chicago because of restrictive licensing requirements, and not because of superior operating efficiency. As a monopoly, Calvin's provides all industry output. For simplicity, assume that Calvin's operates a chain of barbershops and that each shop has an average cost-minimizing activity level of 750 haircuts per week, with Marginal Cost = Average Total Cost = $20 per haircut.

Assume that demand and marginal revenue curves for haircuts in the south side of Chicago market are

$$P = \$80 - \$0.0008Q$$
$$MR = \$80 - \$0.0016Q$$

where P is price per unit, MR is marginal revenue, and Q is total firm output (haircuts).

A. Calculate the monopoly profit-maximizing price–output combination, and the competitive market long-run equilibrium activity level.

B. Calculate monopoly profits, and discusses the "monopoly problem" from a social perspective in this instance.

P12.6   Deadweight Loss from Monopoly. The Onondaga County Resource Recovery (OCRRA) system assumed responsibility for solid waste management on November 1, 1990, for 33 of the 35 municipalities in Onondaga County, New York. OCRRA is a nonprofit public benefit corporation similar to the New York State Thruway Authority. It is not an arm of county government. Its board of directors is comprised of volunteers who develop programs and policies for the management of solid waste. The OCRRA board is responsible for adopting a budget that ensures there will be sufficient revenues to cover expenditures. It does not rely on county taxes. OCRRA has implemented an aggressive series of programs promoting waste reduction and recycling where markets exist to create new products. While a number of communities struggle to surpass the 20 percent recycling mark, Onondaga County's households and commercial outlets currently recycle more than 67 percent of the waste that once was buried in landfills. Converting nonrecyclable waste into energy (electricity) is also a top priority.

To show the deadweight loss from monopoly problem, assume that monthly OCRRA's market supply and demand conditions are

$$Q_S = -2,000,000 + 10,000P \qquad \text{(Market Supply)}$$
$$Q_D = 1,750,000 - 5,000P \qquad \text{(Market Demand)}$$

where Q is the number of customers served, and P is the market price of annual trash hauling and recycling service.

A. Graph and calculate the equilibrium price–output solution. How much consumer surplus, producer surplus, and social welfare are produced at this activity level?

B. Use the graph to help you determine the deadweight loss for consumers and the producer if the market is run by unregulated profit-maximizing monopoly. (Note: If monopoly market demand is $P = \$350 - \$0.0002Q$, then the monopolist's $MR = \$350 - \$0.0004Q$.)

P12.7 Wealth Transfer Problem. The Organization of the Petroleum Exporting Countries (OPEC) was formed on September 14, 1960, in Baghdad, Iraq. The current membership is comprised of five founding members plus six others: Algeria, Indonesia, Iran, Iraq, Kuwait, Libya, Nigeria, Qatar, Saudi Arabia, the United Arab Emirates, and Venezuela. OPEC's stated mission is "to bring stability and harmony to the oil market by adjusting their oil output to help ensure a balance between supply and demand." At least twice a year, OPEC members meet to adjust OPEC's output level in light of anticipated oil market developments. OPEC's 11 members collectively supply about 40 percent of the world's oil output and possess more than three-quarters of the world's total proven crude oil reserves.

To demonstrate the deadweight loss from monopoly problem, imagine that market supply and demand conditions for crude oil are

$$Q_S = 2P \qquad\qquad \text{(Market Supply)}$$
$$Q_D = 180 - 4P \qquad\qquad \text{(Market Demand)}$$

where Q is barrels of oil per day (in millions) and P is the market price of oil.

A. Graph and calculate the equilibrium price–output solution. How much consumer surplus, producer surplus, and social welfare is produced at this activity level?

B. Use the graph to calculate the amount of consumer surplus transferred to the monopoly producer following a change from a competitive market to a monopoly market. How much is the net gain in producer surplus?

P12.8 Monopoly Profits. Portland Fluid Control, Inc., (PFC) is a major supplier of reverse osmosis and ultrafiltration equipment, which helps industrial and commercial customers achieve improved production processes and a cleaner work environment. The company has recently introduced a new line of ceramic filters that enjoy patent protection. Relevant cost and revenue relations for this product are as follows:

$$TR = \$300Q - \$0.001Q^2$$
$$MR = \partial TR/\partial Q = \$300 - \$0.002Q$$
$$TC = \$9,000,000 + \$20Q + \$0.0004Q^2$$
$$MC = \partial TC/\partial Q = \$20 + \$0.0008Q$$

where TR is total revenue, Q is output, MR is marginal revenue, TC is total cost, including a risk-adjusted normal rate of return on investment, and MC is marginal cost.

A. Compute PFC's optimal monopoly price–output combination.

B. Compute monopoly profits and the optimal profit margin at this profit-maximizing activity level.

P12.9 Monopoly Versus Competitive Market Equilibrium. During recent years, MicroChips Corp. has enjoyed substantial economic profits derived from patents covering a wide range of inventions and innovations for microprocessors used in high-performance desktop computers. A recent introduction, the Penultimate, has proven especially profitable. Market demand and marginal revenue relations for the product are as follows:

$$P = \$5,500 - \$0.005Q$$
$$MR = \partial TR/\partial Q = \$5,500 - \$0.01Q$$

Fixed costs are nil because research and development expenses have been fully amortized during previous periods. Average variable costs are constant at $4,500 per unit.

A. Calculate the profit-maximizing price–output combination and economic profits if MicroChips enjoys an effective monopoly because of patent protection.

B. Calculate the price–output combination and total economic profits that would result if competitors offer clones that make the market perfectly competitive.

P12.10 Monopoly–Monopsony Confrontation. Safecard Corporation offers a unique service. The company notifies credit card issuers after being informed that a subscriber's credit card has been lost or stolen. The Safecard service is sold to card issuers on an annual subscription basis. Relevant revenue and cost relations for the service are as follows:

$$TR = \$5Q - \$0.00001Q^2$$
$$MR = \partial TR/\partial Q = \$5 - \$0.00002Q$$
$$TC = \$50,000 + \$0.5Q + \$0.000005Q^2$$
$$MC = \partial TC/\partial Q = \$0.5 + \$0.00001Q$$

where TR is total revenue, Q is output measured in terms of the number of subscriptions in force, MR is marginal revenue, TC is total cost, including a risk-adjusted normal rate of return on investment, and MC is marginal cost.

A. If Safecard has a monopoly in this market, calculate the profit-maximizing price–output combination and optimal total profit.

B. Calculate Safecard's optimal price, output, and profits if credit card issuers effectively exert monopsony power and force a perfectly competitive equilibrium in this market.

CASE *Study*   Effect of R&D on Tobin's *q*

The idea of using the difference between the market value of the firm and accounting book values as an indicator of market power and/or valuable intangible assets stems from the pioneering work of Nobel laureate James Tobin. Tobin introduced the so-called *q* ratio, defined as the ratio of the market value of the firm divided by the replacement cost of tangible assets. For a competitive firm in a stable industry with no special capabilities, and no barriers to entry or exit, one would expect *q* to be close to one ($q \cong 1$). In a perfectly competitive industry, any momentary propensity for $q > 1$ due to an unanticipated rise in demand or decrease in costs would be quickly

erased by entry or established firm growth. In a perfectly competitive industry, any momentary propensity for $q < 1$ due to an unanticipated fall in demand or increase in costs would be quickly erased by exit or contraction among established firms. In the absence of barriers to entry and exit, the marginal value of *q* would trend toward unity ($q \rightarrow 1$) over time in perfectly competitive industries. Similarly, a firm that is regulated so as to earn no monopoly rents would also have a *q* close to one. Only in the case of firms with monopoly power protected by significant barriers to entry or exit, or firms with superior profit-making capabilities, will Tobin's *q* ratio rise above

continued

one, and stay there. In the limit, the theoretical maximum Tobin's q ratio is observed in the case of a highly efficient monopoly. If $q>1$ on a persistent basis, one can argue that the firm is in possession of market power or some hard-to-duplicate asset that typically escapes measurement using conventional accounting criteria.

Tobin's q ratio surged during the 1990s, and some made the simple conclusion that monopoly profits had soared during this period. In the early 1990s, however, the overall economy suffered a sharp recession that dramatically reduced corporate profits and stock prices. By the end of the 1990s, the economy had logged the longest peacetime expansion in history, and both corporate profits and stock prices soared to record levels. Corporate profits, stock, and Tobin's q ratios for major corporations took a sharp tumble over the 2000–2003 period as the country entered a mild recession. Therefore, much of the year-to-year variation in Tobin's q ratios for corporate giants can be explained by the business cycle. At any point in time, more fundamental changes are also at work. Leading firms today are characterized by growing reliance on what economists refer to as intangible assets, like advertising capital, brand names, customer goodwill, patents, and so on. Empirically, $q>1$ if valuable intangible assets derived from R&D and other such expenditures with the potential for long-lived benefits are systematically excluded from consideration by accounting methodology. The theoretical argument that $q \rightarrow 1$ over time only holds when the economic values of both tangible and intangible assets are precisely measured. If $q>1$ on a persistent basis, and Tobin's q is closely tied to the level of R&D intensity, one might argue successfully for the presence of intangible R&D capital.

In Table 12.3, q is approximated by the sum of the market value of common plus the book values of preferred stock and total liabilities, all divided by the book value of tangible assets, for a sample of corporate giants included in the Dow Jones Industrial Average (DJIA). To learn the role played by R&D intensity as a determinant of Tobin's q, the effects of other important factors must be constrained, including current profitability, growth, and risk. Current profitability is measured by the firm's net profit margin, or net income divided by sales. Positive stock-price effects of net profit margins can be anticipated because historical profit margins are often the best available indicator of a firm's ability to generate superior rates of return during future periods. Stock-price effects of profit margins include both the influences of superior efficiency and/or market power. Because effective R&D can be expected to enhance both current and future profitability, the marginal effect of R&D intensity on Tobin's q becomes a very conservative estimate of the total short-term plus long-term value of R&D when such impacts are considered in conjunction with the stock-price effects of current net profit margins. Revenue growth will have a positive effect on market values if future investments are expected to earn above-normal rates of return and if growth is an important determinant of these returns. While growth affects the magnitude of anticipated excess returns, a stock-price influence may also be associated with the degree of return stability. Influences of risk are estimated here using stock-price beta. With an increase in risk, the market value of expected returns is anticipated to fall.

A. Explain how any intangible capital effects of R&D intensity can reflect the effects of market power and/or superior efficiency.

B. A multiple regression analysis based upon the data contained in Table 12.3 revealed the following (t statistics in parentheses):

$q = 1.740 + 0.041$ Profit Margin $+ 0.018$ Growth $-$
   (2.33)   (1.74)   (0.31)

   0.421 Beta $+ 0.057$ R&D/S
   (-1.43) (2.15)

$R^2 = 41.1\%$, F statistic $= 4.36$

Are these results consistent with the idea that R&D gives rise to a type of intangible capital?

continued

Table 12.3 Economic Determinants of Tobin's *q* for the Dow Jones Industrial Average

Company Name	Industry Name	Tobin's *q* Ratio	Profit Margin (%)	5-Year Revenue Growth (%)	Beta	R&D Intensity (R&D/S, %)
Alcoa Inc.	Aluminum	1.479	5.18	5.63	1.68	0.88
Altria Group, Inc.	Cigarettes	1.787	10.93	1.48	0.33	0.90
American Express Company	Credit services	1.374	11.86	4.78	1.16	0.00
American International Group, Inc.	Property and casualty insurance	1.136	11.80	20.25	0.87	0.00
Boeing Company	Aerospace/defense	1.617	3.55	−2.10	0.71	3.23
Caterpillar Inc.	Farm and construction machinery	1.575	5.66	2.07	0.93	2.74
Citigroup Inc.	Money center banks	1.148	19.51	1.90	1.35	0.00
Coca-Cola Company	Beverages (soft drinks)	5.177	21.45	1.53	0.26	0.00
Disney (Walt) Company	Entertainment (diversified)	1.438	7.17	3.22	1.10	0.00
DuPont (E.I.) de Nemours	Chemicals (diversified)	1.840	3.94	−1.90	0.87	4.81
ExxonMobil Corporation	Major integrated oil and gas	2.162	9.11	10.25	0.36	0.28
General Electric Company	Conglomerate	1.346	11.51	4.80	1.09	1.55
General Motors Corporation	Auto manufacturer	1.001	1.97	3.01	1.18	3.10
Hewlett-Packard Company	Diversified computer systems	1.404	3.88	10.84	1.69	4.75
Home Depot, Inc.	Home improvement stores	2.610	6.68	14.23	1.43	0.00
Honeywell International	Conglomerate	1.640	5.72	4.15	1.34	3.14
Intel Corporation	Semiconductors (broad line)	4.305	20.51	0.06	2.05	13.87
International Business Machines Corp.	Diversified computer systems	2.212	8.54	0.23	1.46	5.56
J.P. MorganChase & Co.	Money center bank	1.073	16.28	5.02	1.78	0.00
Johnson & Johnson	Drug manufacturer	4.224	17.48	10.78	0.22	12.85
McDonald's Corporation	Restaurants	1.841	9.33	5.92	0.80	0.00
Merck & Co., Inc.	Drug manufacturer	3.102	22.24	−0.56	0.38	10.82
Microsoft Corporation	Application software	3.413	20.78	12.56	1.62	13.08
3M Company	Conglomerate	4.446	13.91	3.15	0.48	5.85
Pfizer Inc.	Drug manufacturer	3.526	3.21	23.87	0.44	24.79
Procter & Gamble Co.	Cleaning products	3.527	12.28	4.03	(0.17)	3.37
SBC Communications Inc.	Telecom services	1.401	13.45	1.57	0.80	0.00
United Technologies Corporation	Conglomerate	2.015	7.52	4.85	1.05	3.17
Verizon Communications	Telecom services	1.378	2.73	16.49	0.98	0.00
Wal-Mart Stores, Inc.	Discount variety stores	2.992	3.54	12.09	0.80	0.00
Averages		2.273	10.39	6.14	0.97	3.96

Data source: *MSN/Money* June, 11, 2004, http://moneycentral.msn.com/investor/finder/customstocks.asp. R&D data from *Compustat PC+*.

SELECTED REFERENCES

Deng, Yi. "The Effects of Patent Regime Changes: A Case Study of the European Patent Office." *International Journal of Industrial Organization* 25, no. 1 (February, 2007): 121–138.

Fafchamps, Marcel and Flore Gubert. "Risk Sharing and Network Formation." *American Economic Review* 97, no. 2 (May, 2007): 75–79.

Faleye, Olubunmi. "Classified Boards, Firm Value, and Managerial Entrenchment." *Journal of Financial Economics* 83, no. 2 (February, 2007): 501–529.

Fang, Hanming, Michael Keane, Ahm Khwaja, Martin Salm, and Dan Silverman. "Testing the Mechanisms of Structural Models: The Case of the Mickey Mantle Effect." *American Economic Review* 97, no. 2 (May, 2007): 53–59.

Gagnepain, Philippe and Pedro Pereira. "Entry, Costs Reduction, and Competition in the Portuguese Mobile Telephony Industry." *International Journal of Industrial Organization* 25, no. 3 (June, 2007): 461–481.

Gale, Douglas M. and Shachar Kariv. "Financial Networks." *American Economic Review* 97, no. 2 (May, 2007): 99–103.

Garcia del Barrio, Pedro and Francesc Pujol. "Hidden Monopsony Rents in Winner-Take-All Markets—Sport and Economic Contribution of Spanish Soccer Players." *Managerial and Decision Economics* 28, no. 1 (January, 2007): 57–70.

Gaspar, Jose Miguel and Massimo Massa. "Local Ownership as Private Information: Evidence on the Monitoring-Liquidity Trade-Off." *Journal of Financial Economics* 83, no. 3 (March, 2007): 751–792.

Gavazza, Alessandro and Alessandro Lizzeri. "The Perils of Transparency in Bureaucracies." *American Economic Review* 97, no. 2 (May, 2007): 300–305.

Gilbert, Richard J. and Michael H. Riordan. "Product Improvement and Technological Tying in a Winner-Take-All Market." *Journal of Industrial Economics* 55, no. 1 (March, 2007): 113–139.

Kang, Jun Koo and Wei Lin Liu. "Is Universal Banking Justified? Evidence from Bank Underwriting of Corporate Bonds in Japan." *Journal of Financial Economics* 84, no. 1 (April, 2007): 142–186.

Kuhn, Michael. "Minimum Quality Standards and Market Dominance in Vertically Differentiated Duopoly." *International Journal of Industrial Organization* 25, no. 2 (April, 2007): 275–290.

Marin, Pedro L. and Georges Siotis. "Innovation and Market Structure: An Empirical Evaluation of the 'Bounds Approach' in the Chemical Industry." *Journal of Industrial Economics* 55, no. 1 (March, 2007): 93–111.

Stuart, Harborne W., Jr. "Buyer Symmetry in Monopoly." *International Journal of Industrial Organization* 25, no. 3 (June, 2007): 615–630.

Wald, John K. and Michael S. Long. "The Effect of State Laws on Capital Structure." *Journal of Financial Economics* 83, no. 2 (February, 2007): 297–319.

Monopolistic Competition and Oligopoly

Named after the first mate in Herman Melville's classic novel Moby Dick, Seattle's Starbucks Coffee Company has become the premier purveyor of specialty coffee in the world. With more than 10,000 company-operated and licensed stores in the United States, Starbucks has a dominating presence in all 50 states plus the District of Columbia. More than 5,000 company-operated and licensed stores abroad make Starbucks highly visible in 38 foreign countries, including Australia, Canada, China, and the United Kingdom.

Keeping global coffee drinkers satisfied is an enormous and highly lucrative business. Starbucks has flourished because increasingly well-heeled coffee drinkers display a strong affinity for distinctive specialty blends offered in a convenient setting. Industry trade groups say that 15 percent of the U.S. adult population now enjoys a daily cup of specialty coffee. Starbucks aims to get a growing share of the specialty coffee business, and sell lots of baked pastries, sandwiches, and salads in the process. By 2012, analysts project that Starbucks will generate roughly $1.5 billion in annual profits on $20 billion per year in sales revenue.

The challenge facing Starbucks is to retain its reputation for excellence in the fresh delivery of coffee and related food items in the face of vigorous and growing competition. There are no patents in the coffee business, and Starbucks is widely imitated. This chapter gives perspective on how competition is affected by the number and size distribution of competitors, and illustrates the challenge faced by companies such as Starbucks.[1]

CONTRAST BETWEEN MONOPOLISTIC COMPETITION AND OLIGOPOLY

Economic theory offers differing perspectives on the nature of competition in imperfectly competitive markets.

Monopolistic Competition

The economic environment faced by many firms cannot be described as perfectly competitive. Likewise, few firms enjoy clear monopoly. Real-world markets commonly

---

1   See Janet Adamy, "Starbucks to Offer iTunes Access," *The Wall Street Journal Online*, September 5, 2007, http://online.wsj.com.

embody elements of both competitive markets and monopoly. Firms often introduce valuable new products or process innovations that give rise to above-normal rates of return in the short run. In the long run, however, entry and imitation by new rivals erode the dominant market share enjoyed by early innovators, and profits eventually return to normal. Still, in sharp contrast to perfectly competitive markets, the unique product characteristics of individual firms often remain valued by consumers. Consumers often continue to prefer Campbell's Soup, Nike, Oil of Olay, Rubbermaid, Tide, and other favorite brands long after comparable products have been introduced by rivals. The partly competitive, partly monopolistic market structure encountered by firms in the apparel, food, hotel, retailing, and consumer products industries is called monopolistic competition. Given the lack of perfect substitutes, monopolistically competitive firms exercise some discretion in setting prices—they are not price takers. However, given vigorous competition from imitators offering close but not identical substitutes, such firms enjoy only a normal risk-adjusted rate of return on investment in long-run equilibrium.

Monopolistic
Competition
A market structure
characterized by
a large number
of sellers of
differentiated
products

Monopolistic competition is similar to perfect competition in that it entails vigorous price competition among a large number of firms. The major difference between these two market structure models is that consumers perceive important differences among the products offered by monopolistically competitive firms, whereas the output of perfectly competitive firms is identical. This gives monopolistically competitive firms at least some discretion in setting prices. However, the availability of many close substitutes limits this price-setting ability and drives profits down to a normal risk-adjusted rate of return in the long run. As in the case of perfect competition, above-normal profits are possible only in the short run, before the monopolistically competitive firm's rivals can take effective countermeasures.

Oligopoly

Oligopoly
A market structure
characterized by
few sellers and
interdependent
price–output
decisions

Oligopoly markets comprise a handful of competitors sheltered by significant barriers to entry. Oligopoly firms might produce an identical product, such as aluminum, steel, or semiconductors; or differentiated products such as Cheerios, Coca-Cola, Marlboro, MTV, and Nintendo. Innovative leading firms in the ready-to-eat cereal, beverage, cigarette, entertainment, and computer software industries, among others, have the potential for economic profits even in the long run. With few competitors, economic incentives also exist for such firms to devise illegal agreements to limit competition, fix prices, or otherwise divide markets. The history of antitrust enforcement in the United States provides numerous examples of "competitors" who illegally entered into such agreements. Yet there are also examples of markets in which vigorous competition among a small number of firms generates obvious long-term benefits for consumers. It is therefore erroneous to draw a simple link between the number of competitors and the vigor of competition.

In an industry characterized by oligopoly, only a few large rivals are responsible for the bulk of industry output. As in the case of monopoly, high to very high barriers to entry are typical. Under oligopoly, the price-output decisions of firms are interrelated in the sense that direct reactions among rivals can be expected. As a result, decisions of individual firms anticipate the likely response of competitors. This competition among the few involves a wide variety of price and nonprice methods of rivalry, as determined by the institutional characteristics of each particular market. Even though limited numbers of competitors give rise to a potential for economic profits, above-normal rates of return are far from guaranteed. Competition among the few can be vigorous.

Dynamic Nature of Competition

In characterizing the descriptive relevance of the monopolistic competition and oligopoly models of seller behavior, it is important to recognize the dynamic nature of real-world markets. For example, as late as the mid-1980s it seemed appropriate to regard automobile and PC manufacturing as oligopoly markets. Today, it seems fairer to regard each industry as monopolistically competitive. In the automobile industry, GM, Ford, and Chrysler have found Toyota, Honda, Nissan, and a host of specialized competitors to be formidable foes. Aggressive competitors like Dell, Hewlett-Packard, Apple, and Gateway first weakened, and then obliterated, IBM's early lead in the PC business. Prices and profit margins for PCs continue to fall as improving technology continues to enhance product quality.

In many oligopoly markets, the market discipline provided by a competitive fringe of smaller domestic and foreign rivals is sufficient to limit the potential abuse of a few large competitors. In the long-distance telephone service market, for example, AT&T, Sprint, and Qwest dominate the traditional voice communications business. However, emerging competition from the RBOCs, VoIP service offered by cable operators, and the ongoing substitution of wireless and Internet instant messaging communications for traditional wire-line service cause long-distance phone service price and service quality competition to be spirited. Similarly, the competitive fringe in wireless communications and cable TV promises to force dramatic change throughout the telecommunications industry during the years ahead.

It is unfortunate, but public perceptions and government regulatory policy sometimes lag behind economic reality. It is essential that timely and accurate market structure information be available to form the basis for business investment decisions that relate to entry or exit from specific lines of business. Similarly, enlightened public policy requires timely information.

MONOPOLISTIC COMPETITION

Most firms face downward-sloping demand curves, signifying less-than-perfect competition.

Monopolistic Competition Characteristics

Monopolistic competition exists when individual producers have moderate influence over product prices, where each product enjoys a degree of uniqueness in the perception of customers. This market structure has some important similarities and dissimilarities with perfectly competitive markets. Monopolistic competition is characterized by

- *Large numbers of buyers and sellers.* Each firm produces a small portion of industry output, and each customer buys only a small part of the total.
- *Product heterogeneity.* The output of each firm is perceived to be essentially different from, though comparable with, the output of other firms in the industry.
- *Free entry and exit.* Firms are not restricted from entering or leaving the industry.
- *Perfect dissemination of information.* Cost, price, and product quality information is known by all buyers and all sellers.
- *Opportunity for normal profits in long-run equilibrium.* Distinctive products allow $P > MC$, but vigorous price and product-quality price competition keeps $P = AC$.

Managerial Application 13.1

Dell's Price War with Dell

Dell Computer Corp. is fighting a price war with itself. On any given business day, the company may offer different prices for the same personal computer (PC) sold to small businesses, large companies, or state and local governments. These price differences are no mistake. In the viciously price-competitive PC industry, the company must flexibly respond to the purchase plans of various customer groups. The company's salespeople constantly quiz customers on purchase plans, and on deals with Dell rivals. In a sense, Dell negotiates with its customers much like an auto dealer negotiates with car buyers to get the right price and financing package to close the deal.

To maintain profit margins, Dell demands flexible pricing in its contracts with suppliers. In fact, many suppliers continually update Dell on their own costs. This lets Dell adjust prices and incentives immediately in response to changes in its own costs. Dell's dynamic pricing policy lets prices adjust almost continuously. At times, Dell's PC price quote over the phone or on the company Web page can be up to $50 less than the price touted in print advertisements on the very same day!

Dell's "price war" strategy is aimed at aggressively collapsing profit margins throughout the PC market. With the lowest costs in the industry, constantly falling prices and razor-thin profit margins work to Dell's advantage. Rising sales volumes and increasing market share compensate for thinner margins and allow Dell to rapidly grow profits. Dell's "price war" policy is squarely aimed at forcing slower-moving and less efficient rivals to retrench or exit the business.

Dell's price war strategy is clearly paying off. Dell's shipments continue to grow much faster than the PC industry. In the United States, Dell accounts for more than a quarter of PC sales. As rivals cut back and retrench, Dell continues to power ahead in hand-to-hand combat with its toughest competitor—itself.

See: Christopher Lawton and Mei Fong, "Dell to Sell PCs Through China Retail Titan," *The Wall Street Journal Online*, September 24, 2007, http://online.wsj.com.

These basic conditions are not as restrictive as those for perfect competition and are fairly commonplace in actual markets. Vigorous monopolistic competition is evident in the banking, container and packaging, discount and fashion retail, electronics, food manufacturing, office equipment, paper and forest products, and most personal and professional service industries. Although individual firms are able to maintain some control over pricing policy, their pricing discretion is severely limited by competition from firms offering close but not identical substitutes.

Monopolistic competition is a realistic description of competition in a wide variety of industries. As in perfectly competitive markets, a large number of competitors make independent decisions in monopolistically competitive markets. A price change by any one firm does not cause other firms to change prices. If price reactions did occur, then an oligopoly market structure would be present. The most distinctive characteristic of monopolistic competition is that each competitor offers a unique product that is an imperfect substitute for those offered by rivals. Each firm is able to differentiate its product from those of its adversaries. Nevertheless, each firm's demand function is significantly affected by the presence of numerous competitors producing goods that consumers view as reasonably close substitutes. Exogenous changes in demand and cost conditions also tend to have a similar effect on all firms and frequently lead to comparable pricing influences.

Product differentiation takes many forms. Quality differentials, packaging, credit terms, or superior maintenance service can all differentiate products, as can advertising that leads to brand-name identification. Not only is a tube of Crest toothpaste different from Colgate toothpaste, but a tube of Crest at a nearby convenience store is also different from an identical tube available at a distant discount retailer. Because consumers evaluate products on the basis of their ability to satisfy specific wants, as well as when and where they have them, products involve not only quantity, quality, and price characteristics but time and place attributes as well. The important factor in all of these forms of product differentiation is that some consumers prefer the product of one seller to those of others.

The effect of product differentiation is to create downward-sloping firm demand curves in monopolistically competitive markets. Unlike a price taker facing a perfectly horizontal demand curve, the firm is able to independently determine an optimal price–output combination. The degree of price flexibility enjoyed depends on the strength of product differentiation. The more differentiated a firm's product, the lower the substitutability of other products for it. Strong product differentiation results in greater consumer loyalty, better control over price, and a steeper demand curve.

Monopolistic Competition Price–Output Decisions

As its name suggests, monopolistic competition embodies elements of both monopoly and perfect competition. The monopoly characteristic of these markets is typically observed in the short run. For example, consider Figure 13.1 which shows the demand curve D_1 for a highly differentiated product. With the demand curve, D_1, and its related marginal revenue curve, MR_1, the optimum output, Q_1, is found at the point where $MR_1 = MC$. Short-run monopoly profits equal to the area P_1LMAC_1 are earned. Such profits can be derived from the introduction of new and innovative products, process improvements, creative packaging and marketing, or other such factors.

Figure 13.1   Price–Output Combinations Under Monopolistic Competition

Long-run equilibrium under monopolistic competition occurs when $MR = MC$ and $P = AC$. This typically occurs between (P_2, Q_2) (the high-price/low-output equilibrium) and (P_3, Q_3) (the low-price/high-output equilibrium).

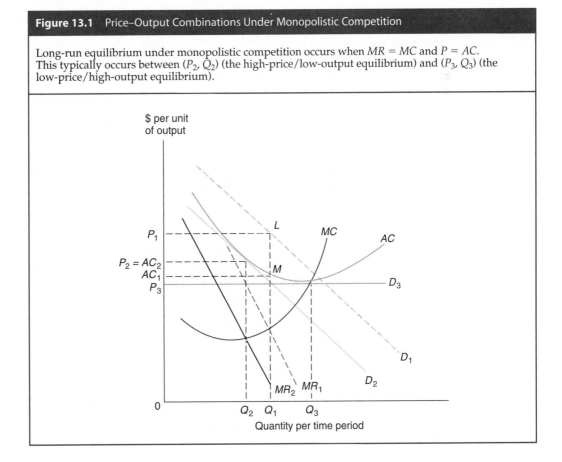

Over time, short-run monopoly profits attract competition, and other firms enter the industry. As competitors emerge to offer close but imperfect substitutes, the market share and profits of the initial innovating firm diminish. Firm demand and marginal revenue curves shift to the left as, for example, from D_1 to D_2 and from MR_1 to MR_2 in Figure 13.1. Optimal long-run output occurs at Q_2, the point where $MR_2 = MC$. Because the optimal price P_2 equals AC_2, where cost includes a normal profit just sufficient to maintain capital investment, economic profits are zero.

The price–output combination (P_2Q_2) describes a monopolistically competitive market equilibrium characterized by a high degree of product differentiation. If new entrants offered perfect rather than close substitutes, each firm's long-run demand curve would become more nearly horizontal, and the perfectly competitive equilibrium, D_3 with P_3 and Q_3, would be approached. Like the (P_2Q_2) high-differentiation equilibrium, the (P_3Q_3) no-differentiation equilibrium is something of an extreme case. In most instances, competitor entry reduces but does not eliminate product differentiation. An intermediate price–output solution, one between (P_2Q_2) and (P_3Q_3), is often achieved in long-run equilibrium. It is the retention of at least some degree of product differentiation that distinguishes the monopolistically competitive equilibrium from that achieved in perfectly competitive markets.

A firm will never operate at the minimum point on its average cost curve in monopolistically competitive equilibrium. Each firm's demand curve is downward sloping and is tangent to the AC curve at some point above minimum AC. However, this does not mean that a monopolistically competitive industry is inefficient. The very existence of a downward-sloping demand curve implies that consumers value an individual firm's products more highly than they do products of other producers. The higher prices and costs of monopolistically competitive industries, as opposed to perfectly competitive industries, reflect the economic cost of product variety. If consumers are willing to bear such costs, then such costs must not be excessive. The success of branded products in the face of generic competition, for example, is powerful evidence of consumer preferences for product variety.

Although perfect competition and monopoly are somewhat rare in real-world markets, monopolistic competition is frequently observed. For example, in 1960 a small ($37 million in sales) office-machine company, Haloid Xerox, Inc., revolutionized the copy industry with the introduction of the Xerox 914 copier. Xerography was a tremendous improvement over Electrofax and other coated-paper copiers. It permitted the use of untreated paper, which produced clearer and less expensive copies. Invention of the dry copier established Xerox Corporation at the forefront of a rapidly growing office-copier industry and propelled the firm to a position of virtual monopoly by 1970. Between 1970 and 1980, the industry's market structure changed dramatically because of an influx of competition as many of Xerox's original patents expired. IBM entered the copier market in April 1970 with its Copier I model and expanded its participation in November 1972 with Copier II. Eastman Kodak made its entry into the market in 1975 with its Ektaprint model. Minnesota Mining and Manufacturing (3M) had long been a factor in the Electrofax copier segment of the market. A more complete list of Xerox's recent domestic and international competitors would include at least 30 firms. The effect of this entry on Xerox's market share and profitability was dramatic. Between 1970 and 1978, for example, Xerox's share of the domestic copier market fell from 98 percent to 56 percent, and its return on stockholders' equity fell from 23.6 percent to 18.2 percent.

More recently, Xerox's leadership position has been squandered and its profitability has collapsed in the face of vicious price and product quality competition. Because Canon, Kodak, 3M, Panasonic, Ricoh, Savin, and Sharp copiers are only close rather than perfect substitutes for Xerox machines, the industry is commonly described as monopolistically competitive. Effective (but imperfect) competition for paper copies also comes from low-cost printers tied to PCs and from electronic communications, which obviate the need for paper copies. Make no mistake about it, monopolistic competition can be tough on industry leaders that fail to keep up—just ask Xerox.

MONOPOLISTIC COMPETITION PROCESS

The process of price-output adjustment and the concept of equilibrium in monopolistically competitive markets can be illustrated by the following example.

Short-Run Monopoly Equilibrium

The Skyhawk Trailer Company, located in Toronto, Ontario, has successfully introduced an ultralight camping trailer that can safely be towed by high-mileage subcompact cars. Skyhawk's reputation for high-quality products has given the company a head start in the regional market, but entry by large and highly capable national competitors can be expected within 3 years.

Assume Skyhawk's revenue and cost relations are as follows:

$$TR = \$20,000Q - \$15.6Q^2$$
$$MR = \partial TR/\partial Q = \$20,000 - \$31.2Q$$
$$TC = \$400,000 + \$4,640Q + \$10Q^2$$
$$MC = \partial TC/\partial Q = \$4,640 + \$20Q$$

Managerial Application 13.2

Intel: Running Fast to Stay in Place

Intel is the dominant and most profitable maker of integrated circuits, the microscopic pieces of silicon chips used to power electronic computers, calculators, video games, and a burgeoning array of other products. *intel inside*™ is a trademark that identifies products produced by a company whose microprocessors are the brains of more than five times as many personal computers as its nearest rival. So complete has been Intel's grip on the PC market that sales are expected to explode from $38 billion in 2005 to more than $50 billion in 2010, while profits surge from $10 billion to roughly $15 billion.

Despite its enviable record of success, and despite obvious strengths, Intel's core business is facing its biggest challenge in a decade. Led by Advanced Micro Devices, Inc., Cyrix, Inc., International Business Machines, Inc., Texas Instruments Inc., and a handful of foreign firms, competitors are rushing to produce alternatives to Intel chips. Imitators can quickly erode the profits of early innovators like Intel, a company that has come to count on giant-sized operating margins of over 40 percent. During recent years, investors

have both posed an important question: Is Intel's dominance of the integrated circuits market coming to an end?

Not without a fight, it won't. Intel is still inspired by visionary leader Andrew S. Grove, author of the best-seller *Only the Paranoid Survive*, and his handpicked successor current chairman Craig R. Barrett. Driven by paranoia, Intel is dragging competitors into court for patent infringement, slashing prices, and boldly promoting its products. The company is strengthening its close working relationship with manufacturers of end-user products to ensure compatibility and maximize the benefits of new microprocessor innovations. Most important, Intel has launched a campaign to speed product development and expand its potential market.

Intel's speedup of microprocessor technology will affect everyone who uses electronic products. Not the least of those affected will be Intel's competitors.

See: Faruq Ahmad, "Intel's Brilliant Culture Was Led by a Gentleman," *The Wall Street Journal Online*, October 19, 2007, http://online.wsj.com.

where TR is revenue (in dollars), Q is quantity (in units), MR is marginal revenue (in dollars), TC is total cost, including a risk-adjusted normal rate of return on investment (in dollars), and MC is marginal cost (in dollars).

To find the short-run profit-maximizing price-output combination, set Skyhawk's marginal revenue equal to marginal cost and solve for Q:

$$MR = MC$$
$$\$20{,}000 - \$31.2Q = \$4{,}640 + \$20Q$$
$$\$51.2Q = \$15{,}360$$
$$Q = 300 \text{ units}$$

and

$$P = \$20{,}000 - \$15.6(300)$$
$$= \$15{,}320$$
$$\pi = TR - TC$$
$$= -\$25.6(300^2) + \$15{,}360(300) - \$400{,}000$$
$$= \$1{,}904{,}000$$

To maximize short-run profits, Skyhawk should charge \$15,320 and produce 300 units per year. Such a planning decision results in roughly \$1.9 million in profits per year during the period prior to the onset of competition from large and highly capable national competitors.

Long-Run High-Price/Low-Output Equilibrium

Now assume that Skyhawk can maintain a high level of brand loyalty and product differentiation in the long run, despite competitor offerings of similar trailers, but that such competition eliminates any potential for economic profits. This is consistent with a market in monopolistically competitive equilibrium, where $P = AC$ at a point above minimum long-run average costs. Skyhawk's declining market share is reflected by a leftward shift in its demand curve to a point of tangency with its average cost curve. Although precise identification of the long-run price-output combination is very difficult, it is possible to identify the bounds within which this price-output combination can be expected to occur.

High-Price/Low-Output Equilibrium
In monopolistic competition, where differentiated products allow $P > MC$ but $P = AR = AC$

The **high-price/low-output equilibrium** is identified by the point of tangency between the firm's average cost curve and a new demand curve reflecting a parallel leftward shift in demand (D_2 in Figure 13.1). This parallel leftward shift assumes that the firm can maintain a high degree of product differentiation in the long run. The equilibrium high-price/low-output combination that follows a parallel leftward shift in Skyhawk's demand curve can be determined by equating the slopes of the firm's original demand curve to its long-run average cost curve. Because a parallel leftward shift in firm demand results in a new demand curve with an identical slope, equating the slopes of the firm's initial demand to average cost curves identifies the monopolistically competitive high-price/low-output equilibrium.

For simplicity, assume that the previous total cost curve for Skyhawk also holds in the long run. To determine the slope of this average cost curve, one must find out how average costs vary with respect to output.

$$AC = TC/Q = (\$400{,}000 + \$4{,}640Q + \$10Q^2)/Q$$

$$= \frac{\$400{,}000}{Q} + \$4{,}640 + \$10Q$$

$$= \$400{,}000Q^{-1} + \$4{,}640 + \$10Q$$

The slope of this average cost curve is given by the expression

$$\partial AC/\partial Q = -400{,}000Q^{-2} + 10$$

The slope of the new demand curve is given by

$$\partial P/\partial Q = -15.6 \text{ (same as the original demand curve)}$$

In equilibrium,

$$\text{Slope of } AC \text{ Curve} = \text{Slope of Demand Curve}$$
$$-400{,}000Q^{-2} + 10 = -15.6$$
$$Q^{-2} = 25.6/400{,}000$$
$$Q^2 = 400{,}000/25.6$$
$$Q = 125 \text{ units}$$
$$P = AC$$
$$= \frac{\$400{,}000}{125} + \$4{,}640 + \$10(125)$$
$$= \$9{,}090$$

and

$$\pi = P \times Q - TC$$
$$= \$9{,}090(125) - \$400{,}000 - \$4{,}640(125) - \$10(125^2)$$
$$= \$0$$

This high-price/low-output monopolistically competitive equilibrium results in a decrease in price from \$15,320 to \$9,090 and a fall in output from 300 to 125 units per year. Only a risk-adjusted normal rate of return will be earned, eliminating Skyhawk's economic profits. This long-run equilibrium assumes that Skyhawk would enjoy the same low price elasticity of demand that it experienced as a monopolist. This assumption may or may not be appropriate. New entrants often have the effect of both cutting a monopolist's market share and increasing the price elasticity of demand. It is often reasonable to expect entry to cause both a leftward shift of and some flattening in Skyhawk's demand curve. To see the extreme limit of the demand curve–flattening process, the case of a perfectly horizontal demand curve can be considered.

Long-Run Low-Price/High-Output Equilibrium

**Low-Price/
High-Output
Equilibrium**

In monopolistic
competition,
where entry of
identical products
drives prices
down to where
$P = MR = MC = AC$
(the competitive
market solution)

The **low-price/high-output equilibrium** combination assumes no residual product differentiation in the long run and it is identified by the point of tangency between the average cost curve and a new horizontal firm demand curve (D_3 in Figure 13.1). This is, of course, also the perfectly competitive equilibrium price–output combination.

The low-price/high-output (competitive market) equilibrium occurs at the point where $P = MR = MC = AC$. This reflects that the firm's demand curve is perfectly horizontal, and average costs are minimized. To find the output level of minimum average costs, set $MC = AC$ and solve for Q:

$$\$4{,}640 + \$20Q = \$400{,}000Q^{-1} + \$4{,}640 + \$10Q$$
$$\$10Q = \$400{,}000Q^{-1}$$
$$Q^2 = 40{,}000$$
$$Q = \sqrt{40{,}000}$$
$$= 200 \text{ units}$$
$$P = AC$$
$$= \frac{\$400{,}000}{200} + \$4{,}640 + \$10(200)$$
$$= \$8{,}640$$

and

$$\pi = P \times Q - TC$$
$$= \$8{,}640(200) - \$400{,}000 - \$4{,}640(200) - \$10(200^2)$$
$$= \$0$$

Under this low-price equilibrium scenario, Skyhawk's monopoly price falls in the long run from an original $15,320 to $8,640, and output falls from the monopoly level of 300 units to the competitive equilibrium level of 200 units per month. The company would earn only a risk-adjusted normal rate of return, and economic profits would equal zero. The monopolistic competition low-price/high-output equilibrium is the same result as the competitive market equilibrium.

Following the onset of competition from large and highly capable national competitors, competitor entry will reduce Skyhawk's volume from 300 units per month to a level between $Q = 125$ and $Q = 200$ units per month. The short-run profit-maximizing price of $15,320 will fall to a monopolistically competitive equilibrium price between $P = \$9{,}090$, the high-price/low-output equilibrium, and $P = \$8{,}640$, the low-price/high-output equilibrium. In deciding on an optimal short-run price–output strategy, Skyhawk must weigh the benefits of high near-term profitability against the long-run cost of lost market share resulting from competitor entry. Such a decision involves consideration of current interest rates, the speed of competitor imitation, and the future pace of innovation in the industry, among other factors.

OLIGOPOLY

When individual firm price–output decisions have predictable consequences for a handful of competitors, and those competitors can be expected to react, oligopoly exists.

Oligopoly Market Characteristics

In oligopoly markets, a large percentage of the overall market is taken up by a few leading firms. In some instances, a substantial competitive fringe may exist, like the microprocessor market dominated by Intel, or diamonds dominated by De Beers. In most cases, oligopoly firms produce distinctive, branded products and nonprice methods of competition, including advertising, are important. Some notable exceptions like aluminum exist where homogeneous products are produced in oligopoly markets. In all oligopoly markets, however, barriers to entry and/or exit exist and there is an obvious interdependence among competitors. This means that each firm must take into account the likely reactions of other firms when making pricing, output, and investment decisions.

Oligopoly firms have the ability to set pricing and production strategy, and enjoy the potential for economic profits in both the short run and the long run. Oligopoly markets can be characterized as follows:

- *Few sellers.* A handful of firms produce the bulk of industry output. Competing firms typically recognize their interdependence in price-output decisions.
- *Homogeneous or unique products.* Oligopoly output can be identical (e.g., aluminum) or distinctive (e.g., ready-to-eat breakfast cereal).
- *Blockaded entry and/or exit.* Firms are heavily restricted from entering or leaving the industry.
- *Imperfect dissemination of information.* Cost, price, and product quality information is withheld from uninformed buyers.
- *Opportunity for economic profits in long-run equilibrium.* Competitive advantages keep $P > MC$ and $P = AR > AC$ for efficient firms.

Some oligopoly markets are fairly static and appear similar in performance to monopoly markets. Other oligopoly markets are easy to characterize using traditional oligopoly theory. In many cases, however, oligopoly markets are dynamic and difficult to characterize. Rapid technical change, often vigorous competition from global competitors, and hard-to-predict changes in government regulation make it difficult to describe the competitive environment for oligopoly firms. As a result, a variety of models have developed to describe firm behavior in oligopoly markets.

Examples of Oligopoly

In the United States, aluminum, cigarettes, electrical equipment, filmed entertainment production and distribution, glass, long-distance telecommunications, and ready-to-eat cereals are all produced and sold under conditions of oligopoly. In each of these industries, a small number of firms produce a dominant percentage of all industry output. In the ready-to-eat breakfast cereal industry, for example, Kellogg, Ralcorp Holdings Inc. (*Post* cereals), General Mills, Nabisco, and Quaker Oats are responsible for almost all domestic production in the United States. Durable customer loyalty gives rise to fat profit margins and rates of return on assets that are two to three times food industry norms. Corn Flakes, Sugar Frosted Flakes, Cheerios, Raisin Bran, Wheaties, and a handful of other brands continue to dominate the industry year after year and make successful entry extremely difficult. Even multinational food giant Nestlé sought and obtained a joint venture agreement with General Mills rather than enter the potentially lucrative European breakfast cereal market by itself. Long-distance telephone service is also highly concentrated, with AT&T, Sprint, and Verizon providing the bulk of domestic wire-line long-distance service to residential customers.

Oligopoly is also present in a number of local markets. In many retail markets for gasoline and food, for example, only a few service stations and grocery stores compete within a small geographic area. Dry cleaning services are also sometimes provided by a relative handful of firms in small to medium-size cities and towns.

CARTELS AND COLLUSION

In some cases, oligopoly firms have informally or formally collaborated to charge monopoly prices and share monopoly profits.

Overt and Covert Agreements

Cartel
Firms operating with a formal agreement to fix prices and output

Collusion
A informal covert agreement among firms in an industry to fix prices and output levels

All firms in an oligopoly market could benefit if they formally or informally got together and set prices to maximize industry profits. A group of competitors operating under a formal overt agreement is called a **cartel.** If an informal covert agreement is reached, the firms are said to be operating in **collusion.** Both practices are illegal in the United States. However, cartels are legal in some parts of the world, and U.S. multinational corporations sometimes become involved with them in foreign markets. Several important domestic markets are also dominated by producer associations that operate like cartels and appear to flourish without interference from the government. Agricultural commodities such as milk are prime examples of products marketed under cartel-like arrangements.

A cartel that has absolute control over all firms in an industry can operate as a monopoly. To illustrate, consider the situation shown in Figure 13.2. The marginal cost curves of each firm are summed horizontally to arrive at an industry marginal cost curve. Equating the cartel's total marginal cost with the industry marginal revenue curve determines the profit-maximizing output and the price, P^*, to be charged. Once this profit-maximizing price-output level has been determined, each individual firm finds

Figure 13.2 Price–Output Determination for a Cartel

Horizontal summation of the MC curves for each firm gives the cartel's MC curve. Output for each firm is found by equating its own MC to the industry profit-maximizing MC level.

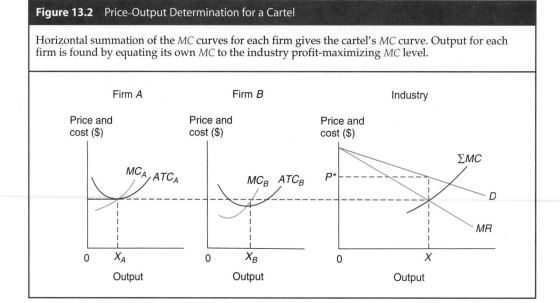

its optimal output by equating its own marginal cost curve to the previously determined profit-maximizing marginal cost level for the industry.

Enforcement Problems

Profits are often divided among firms on the basis of their individual level of production, but other allocation techniques can be employed. Market share, production capacity, and a bargained solution based on economic power have all been used in the past. For a number of reasons, cartels are typically rather short-lived. In addition to the long-run problems of changing products and of entry into the market by new producers, cartels are subject to disagreements among members. Although firms usually agree that maximizing joint profits is mutually beneficial, they seldom agree on the equity of various profit allocation schemes. This problem can lead to attempts to subvert the cartel agreement.

Cartel subversion can be extremely profitable. Consider a two-firm cartel in which each member serves 50 percent of the market. Cheating by either firm is very difficult, because any loss in profits or market share is readily detected. The offending party can also easily be identified and punished. Moreover, the potential profit and market share gain to successful cheating is exactly balanced by the potential profit and market share cost of detection and retribution. Conversely, a 20-member cartel promises substantial profits and market share gains to successful cheaters. At the same time, detecting the source of secret price concessions can be extremely difficult. History shows that cartels including more than a very few members have difficulty policing and maintaining member compliance. With respect to cartels, there is little honor among thieves.

OLIGOPOLY OUTPUT-SETTING MODELS

Oligopoly equilibrium depends upon whether firms choose to set output or prices.

Cournot Oligopoly

Cournot Model
Theory that firms in oligopoly markets make simultaneous and independent output decisions

Output–Reaction Curve
Relation between an oligopoly firm's profit-maximizing output and rival output

Duopoly
Market dominated by two firms.

The earliest model of oligopoly was developed in 1838 by Augustin Cournot, a French economist. The **Cournot model** posits that firms in oligopoly markets make simultaneous and independent output decisions. In other words, the Cournot model assumes that oligopoly demand curves are stable because each firm takes the output of its competitors as fixed, and then makes its own output decision. The relationship between an oligopoly firm's profit-maximizing output level and competitor output is called the oligopoly **output–reaction curve** because it shows how oligopoly firms react to competitor production decisions.

To illustrate the Cournot model and concept of Cournot equilibrium, consider a two-firm **duopoly** facing a linear demand curve

$$P = \$1,600 - Q$$

where P is price and Q is total output in the market. Thus $Q = Q_A + Q_B$. For simplicity, also assume that both firms have constant costs where $MC = MC = \$100$.

Total revenue for firm A is

$$TR_A = P \times Q_A$$
$$= (\$1{,}600 - Q)Q_A$$
$$= [\$1{,}600 - (Q_A + Q_B)]Q_A$$
$$= \$1{,}600Q_A - Q_A{}^2 - Q_AQ_B$$

Marginal revenue for firm A is

$$MR_A = \partial TR_A/\partial Q_A = \$1{,}600 - \$2Q_A - Q_B$$

Because $MC_A = \$100$, firm A's profit-maximizing output level is found by setting $MR_A = MC_A = \$100$:

$$MR_A = MC_A$$
$$\$1{,}600 - \$2Q_A - Q_B = \$100$$
$$\$2Q_A = \$1{,}500 - Q_B$$
$$Q_A = 750 - 0.5Q_B$$

Notice that the profit-maximizing level of output for firm A depends upon the level of output produced by itself and firm B. Similarly, the profit-maximizing level of output for firm B depends upon the level of output produced by itself and firm A. These relationships are each competitor's output–reaction curve

$$\text{Firm } A{:}\ Q_A = 750 - 0.5Q_B \qquad\qquad \textbf{13.1}$$

$$\text{Firm } B{:}\ Q_B = 750 - 0.5Q_A \qquad\qquad \textbf{13.2}$$

The Cournot market equilibrium level of output is found by simultaneously solving the output–reaction curves for both competitors. To find the amount of output produced by firm A, simply insert the amount of output produced by competitor firm B into firm A's output–reaction curve and solve for Q_A. To find the amount of output produced by firm B, simply insert the amount of output produced by competitor firm A into firm B's output–reaction curve and solve for Q_B. For example, from the firm A output–reaction curve

$$Q_A = 750 - 0.5Q_B$$
$$Q_A = 750 - 0.5(750 - 0.5Q_A)$$
$$Q_A = 750 - 375 + 0.25Q_A$$
$$0.75Q_A = 375$$
$$Q_A = 500 \text{ units}$$

Similarly, from the firm B output–reaction curve, the profit-maximizing level of output for firm B is $Q_B = 500$. With just two competitors, the market equilibrium level of output is

$$\text{Cournot Equilibrium Output} = Q_A + Q_B$$
$$= 500 + 500$$
$$= 1{,}000 \text{ units}$$

The Cournot market equilibrium price is

$$\text{Cournot Equilibrium Price} = \$1,600 - Q$$
$$= \$1,600 - \$1(1,000)$$
$$= \$600$$

With 500 units sold at a market price of $600, firm A and firm B will each generate revenues of $300,000 ($=600 \times \$500$). Using the simplifying assumption that each duopoly firm has no fixed costs and that $MC = AC = \$100$, each firm will generate profits of $250,000 [$=\$300,000 - \$100(500)$]. Given these underlying assumptions, Cournot equilibrium has resulted in a 50/50 sharing of this duopoly market. This stems from the fact that the duopoly firms face the same market demand curve and have the same cost curves.

Figure 13.3 illustrates this Cournot equilibrium price–output solution, and output–reaction curves for each competitor. Notice that Cournot equilibrium output is more than that achieved under monopoly. If this were a monopoly market, the monopoly firm total revenue and marginal revenue curves would be

$$TR = P \times Q$$
$$= (\$1,600 - Q)Q$$
$$= \$1,600Q - Q^2$$
$$MR = \partial TR/\partial Q = \$1,600 - 2Q$$

Because $MC = \$100$, the profit-maximizing output level for the monopoly firm is found by setting $MR = MC = \$100$:

$$MR = MC$$
$$\$1,600 - \$2Q = \$100$$
$$2Q = 1,500$$
$$Q = 750$$

The profit-maximizing monopoly price is

$$P = \$1,600 - Q$$
$$= \$1,600 - \$1(750)$$
$$= \$850$$

The monopoly curve illustrated in Figure 13.3 shows how the profit-maximizing level of output could be efficiently shared between the duopoly firms. With equally powerful duopoly firms and identical cost functions for each firm, an equal sharing of the market makes sense. In practice, the extent of market sharing depends upon the relative bargaining power and capability of each competitor.

Figure 13.3 also contrasts the Cournot equilibrium with the competitive market equilibrium. In this case, because $MC = \$100$, the intersection of market supply and demand occurs when the market price also equals $100. Given a market demand curve $P = \$1,600 - Q$, price would equal $100 when 1,500 units are produced and sold. With an equal sharing of the overall market, each firm would produce 750 units. Of course, in practice both marginal cost and price almost always exceed zero in competitive markets. Nevertheless, this simplified example documents that Cournot equilibrium output exceeds the amount produced under monopoly, but is less than the amount produced in a competitive market.

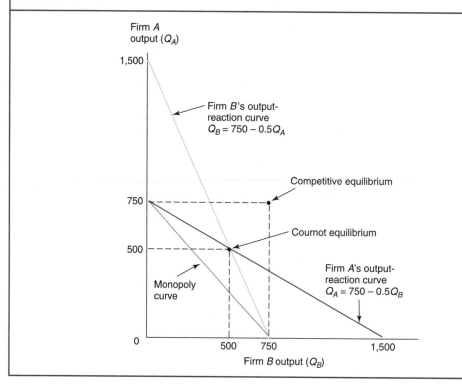

Figure 13.3   Cournot Equilibrium in a Two-Firm Duopoly

The Cournot model focuses upon output reactions. Cournot equilibrium results in less than monopoly profit.

Stackelberg Oligopoly

Stackelberg Model
Theory of sequential output decisions in oligopoly markets

First-Mover Advantage
Competitive advantage for the oligopoly firm that initiates the process of determining market output

The Cournot model is sometimes criticized because it fails to incorporate the fact that oligopoly markets often involve sequential versus simultaneous decision making. An alternative noncooperative **Stackelberg model,** developed by German economist Heinrich von Stackelberg in 1934, posits a **first-mover advantage** for the oligopoly firm that initiates the process of determining market output. Stackelberg modified the Cournot approach by assuming that the leading firm would take into account the expected output reaction of its following-firm rival in making its own output decision.

To illustrate Stackelberg first-mover advantages, reconsider the Cournot model but now assume that firm A, as a leading firm, correctly anticipates the output reaction of firm B, the following firm. With prior knowledge of firm B's output–reaction curve, $Q_B = 750 - 0.5Q_A$, firm A's total revenue curve becomes

$$TR_A = \$1{,}600Q_A - Q_A{}^2 - Q_A Q_B$$
$$= \$1{,}600Q_A - Q_A{}^2 - Q_A(750 - 0.5Q_A)$$
$$= \$850Q_A - 0.5Q_A{}^2$$

With prior knowledge of firm B's output–reaction curve, marginal revenue for firm A is

$$MR_A = \partial TR_A / \partial Q_A = \$850 - \$1Q_A$$

Because $MC_A = \$100$, firm A's profit-maximizing output level with prior knowledge of firm B's output–reaction curve is found by setting $MR_A = MC_A = \$100$:

$$MR_A = MC_A$$
$$\$850 - \$1Q_A = \$100$$
$$Q_A = 750$$

After firm A has determined its level of output, the amount produced by firm B is calculated from firm B's output–reaction curve

$$Q_B = 750 - 0.5Q_A$$
$$= 750 - 0.5(750)$$
$$= 375$$

With just two competitors, the Stackelberg market equilibrium level of output is

$$\text{Stackelberg Equilibrium Output} = Q_A + Q_B$$
$$= 750 + 375$$
$$= 1{,}125 \text{ units}$$

The Stackelberg market equilibrium price is

$$\text{Stackelberg Equilibrium Price} = \$1{,}600 - Q$$
$$= \$1{,}600 - \$1(1{,}125)$$
$$= \$475$$

Notice that market output is greater in Stackelberg equilibrium than in Cournot equilibrium because the first mover, firm A, produces more output while the follower, firm B, produces less output. Stackelberg equilibrium also results in a lower market price than that observed in Cournot equilibrium. In this example, firm A enjoys a significant first-mover advantage. Firm A will produce twice as much output and earn twice as much profit as firm B so long as firm B accepts the output decisions of firm A as given and does not initiate a price war. If firm A and firm B cannot agree on which firm is the leader and which firm is the follower, a price war can break out with the potential to severely undermine the profitability of both leading and following firms. If neither duopoly firm is willing to allow its competitor to exercise a market leadership position, vigorous price competition and a competitive market price–output solution can result. Obviously, participants in oligopoly markets have strong incentives to resolve the uncertainty surrounding the likely competitor response to leading-firm output decisions.

An informal but sometimes effective means for reducing uncertainty in oligopoly markets is through **price signaling. Price leadership** occurs when one firm establishes itself as the industry leader and other firms follow its pricing policy. This leadership may result from the size and strength of the leading firm, from cost efficiency, or as a result of the ability of the leader to establish prices that produce satisfactory profits throughout the industry.

A typical case is price leadership by a dominant firm, usually the largest firm in the industry. The leader faces a price–output problem similar to monopoly; other firms are price takers and face a competitive price–output problem. This is illustrated in Figure 13.4,

Price Signaling

Informal collusion by announcing pricing strategy in the hope that competitors will follow suit

Price Leadership

Situation in which one firm establishes itself as the industry trendsetter and all other firms in the industry accept its pricing policy

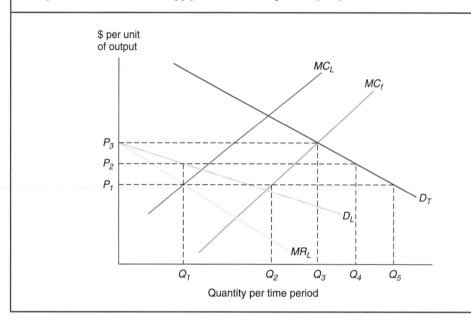

Figure 13.4   Oligopoly Pricing with Dominant-Firm Price Leadership

When the price leader has set an industry price of P_2, the price leader will maximize profits at Q_1 units of output. Price followers will supply a combined output of $Q_4 - Q_1$

where the total market demand curve is D_T, the marginal cost curve of the leader is MC_L, and the horizontal summation of the marginal cost curves for all of the price followers is labeled MC_f. Because price followers take prices as given, they choose to operate at the output level at which their individual marginal costs equal price, just as they would in a perfectly competitive market. Accordingly, the MC_f curve represents the supply curve for following firms. At price P_3, followers would supply the entire market, leaving nothing for the dominant firm. At all prices below P_3, the horizontal distance between the summed MC_f curve and the market demand curve represents the price leader's demand. At a price of P_1, for example, price followers provide Q_2 units of output, leaving demand of $Q_5 - Q_2$ for the price leader. Plotting all of the residual demand quantities for prices below P_3 produces the demand curve for the price leader, D_L in Figure 13.4, and the related marginal revenue curve, MR_L.

More generally, the leader faces a demand curve of the following form:

$$D_L = D_T - S_f \qquad\qquad \textbf{13.3}$$

where D_L is the leader's demand, D_T is total demand, and S_f is the followers' supply curve found by setting $P = MC_f$ and solving for Q_f, the quantity that will be supplied by the price followers. Because D_T and S_f are both functions of price, D_L is likewise determined by price.

Because the price leader faces the demand curve D_L as a monopolist, it maximizes profit by operating at the point where marginal revenue equals marginal cost, $MR_L = MC_L$. At this optimal output level for the leader, Q_1, market price is established at P_2. Price followers supply a combined output of $Q_4 - Q_1$ units. A stable short-run equilibrium is reached if no one challenges the price leader.

Barometric Price Leadership
Situation in which one firm in an industry announces a price change in response to what it perceives as a change in industry supply and demand conditions and other firms respond by following the price change

Another type of price signaling is **barometric price leadership.** In this case, one firm announces a price change in response to what it perceives as a change in industry supply and demand conditions. This change could stem from cost increases that result from a new industry labor agreement, higher energy or material costs, higher taxes, or a substantial shift in industry demand. With barometric price leadership, the price leader is not necessarily the largest or the dominant firm in the industry. The price-leader role might even pass from one firm to another over time. To be effective, the price leader must only be accurate in reading the prevailing industry view of the need for price adjustment. If the price leader makes a mistake, other firms may not follow its price move, and the price leader may have to rescind or modify the announced price change to retain its leadership position.

OLIGOPOLY PRICE-SETTING MODELS

The effects of price-setting behavior by oligopoly firms are very different in oligopoly markets that produce identical versus differentiated products.

Bertrand Oligopoly: Identical Products

Bertrand Model
Theory that firms in oligopoly markets make simultaneous and independent price decisions

In 1883, an early French economist by the name of Joseph Louis François Bertrand contended that oligopoly firms set prices, rather than quantities as maintained in the Cournot model. The **Bertrand model** focuses upon the price reactions, rather than the output reactions, of oligopoly firms. Bertrand equilibrium is reached when no firm can achieve higher profits by charging a different price.

According to Bertrand, when products and production costs are identical, all customers will purchase from the firm selling at the lowest possible price. For example, consider a duopoly where each firm has the same marginal costs of production. By slightly undercutting the price charged by a rival, the competing firm would capture the entire market. In response, the competing firm can be expected to slightly undercut the rival price, thus recapturing the entire market. Such a price war would only end when the price charged by each competitor converged on their identical marginal cost of production, $P_A = P_B = MC$, and economic profits of zero would result. The Bertrand model predicts cutthroat price competition and a competitive market price-output solution in oligopoly markets with identical products.

Critics regard as implausible Bertrand's prediction of a competitive market equilibrium in oligopoly markets that offer homogeneous products. Moreover, because the Bertrand equilibrium price depends only upon cost, it doesn't change with the number of competitors. In oligopoly markets with only a small number of firms, why wouldn't such competitors eventually recognize and act upon their mutual interest in higher prices? Some contend that the Cournot model appears more plausible because oligopoly market prices often change with demand conditions and the number of competitors, not just with changes in costs. Still others point out that some oligopoly markets, like airline passenger service, are vigorously price competitive and offer only meager profits for established incumbents.

Contestable Markets Theory
Hypothesis that oligopoly firms will behave much like perfectly competitive firms when sunk costs are minor

In 1982, American economists William Baumol, John Panzar, and Robert Willig suggested that oligopoly firms will sometimes behave much like perfectly competitive firms. According to **contestable markets theory,** there is no necessary link between the number of actual competitors and the vigor of competition. If potential entrants pose a credible threat, incumbent oligopoly firms are not free to charge high prices and earn economic profits. Potential entrants pose a serious threat when entry costs are largely fungible rather than sunk. For example, entry costs for the airline passenger service market are significant; even a small handful of commercial jets can cost upward of $500 million. However, aircraft can be easily rented or leased. Irretrievable or sunk costs represent only a small fraction of the expense associated with entering the airline passenger service market. As a result, potential entry is always a serious threat, and the established carriers like American, Delta, and UAL earn only meager profits. As predicted by Bertand, contestable markets theory suggests that oligopoly firms producing identical products will behave much like firms in perfectly competitive markets.

Bertrand Oligopoly: Differentiated Products

Many economists believe that price-setting models, including the Bertrand model, are more plausible than quantity-setting models, like the Cournot model, when products are differentiated. If oligopoly firms set prices for differentiated products, then consumers set market quantities by deciding how much to buy. On the other hand, if oligopoly firms merely set the quantity produced, it's not clear how market prices would be determined for differentiated products. In fact, price-setting behavior is common in oligopoly markets with differentiated products. Automobiles, beer and liquor, candy, cigarettes, and ready-to-eat breakfast cereals are all examples of oligopoly markets where firms set prices above marginal costs, and prices are sensitive to demand conditions.

Price–Reaction Curve
Relation between an oligopoly firm's profit-maximizing price and rival price

The Bertrand model demonstrates how price-setting oligopoly firms can profit by selling differentiated products. In the Bertrand model, the relationship between the profit-maximizing price level and competitor price is called the oligopoly **price–reaction curve** because it shows how the oligopoly firm reacts to competitor pricing decisions. To illustrate the Bertrand model and concept of Bertrand equilibrium, consider the effects of price competition under duopoly with differentiated products where

$$\text{Firm } A \text{ Demand: } Q_A = 60 - 2P_A + P_B$$
$$\text{Firm } B \text{ Demand: } Q_B = 60 - 2P_B + P_A$$

and firm A sells Q_A units of output at P_A, while firm B sells Q_B units of output at P_B. In each case, quantity is in thousands of units. Notice that each firm faces a downward-sloping demand curve with respect to the firm's own price. The quantity sold by firm A falls with an increase in P_A, but rises with an increase in P_B. Similarly, the quantity sold by firm B falls with an increase in P_B, but rises with an increase in P_A. For simplicity, assume that marginal cost is zero for each firm, $MC_A = MC_B = 0$.

Total revenue for firm A is

$$\begin{aligned} TR_A &= P_A \times Q_A \\ &= P_A(60 - 2P_A + P_B) \\ &= 60P_A - 2P_A^2 + P_A P_B \end{aligned}$$

When total and marginal costs are zero, total profit is

$$\begin{aligned} \pi_A &= TR_A - TC_A \\ &= 60P_A - 2P_A^2 + P_A P_B - 0 \\ &= 60P_A - 2P_A^2 + P_A P_B \end{aligned}$$

When price rather than output is taken as the decision variable, firm A's profit-maximizing price is found by setting

$$\partial \pi_A / \partial P_A = 0$$
$$\$60 - \$4P_A + P_B = 0$$
$$\$4P_A = \$60 + P_B$$
$$P_A = \$15 + \$0.25P_B$$

Notice that the profit-maximizing price for firm A depends upon the price charged by firm B. Similarly, the profit-maximizing price for firm B depends upon the price charged by firm A. These relationships are each competitor's price–reaction curve

Firm A: $P_A = \$15 + \$0.25P_B$ **13.4**

Firm B: $P_B = \$15 + \$0.25P_A$ **13.5**

The Bertrand market equilibrium price level is found by simultaneously solving the price–reaction curves for both competitors. To find the price charged by firm A, simply insert the amount charged by competitor firm B into firm A's price–reaction curve and solve for P_A. To find the price charged by firm B, insert the amount charged by competitor firm A into firm B's price–reaction curve and solve for P_B. For example, from the firm A price–reaction curve

$$P_A = \$15 + \$0.25P_B$$
$$P_A = \$15 + \$0.25(\$15 + \$0.25P_A)$$
$$P_A = \$15 + \$3.75 + \$0.0625P_A$$
$$0.9375P_A = \$18.75$$
$$P_A = \$20$$

Similarly, from the firm B price–reaction curve, the profit-maximizing price for firm B is $P_B = \$20$. Given an optimal market price of $P_A = P_B = \$20$, the optimal level of output for each firm is

Firm A Demand: $Q_A = 60 - 2P_A + P_B = 60 - 2(20) + 20 = 40$ (000) units
Firm B Demand: $Q_B = 60 - 2P_B + P_A = 60 - 2(20) + 20 = 40$ (000) units

With just two competitors, the Bertrand market equilibrium level of output is

$$\text{Bertrand Equilibrium Output} = Q_A + Q_B$$
$$= 40 + 40$$
$$= 80 \text{ (000) units}$$

With 40 units sold at a market price of $20, firm A and firm B will each generate revenues of $800(000). Using the simplifying assumptions of no fixed costs and $MC_A = MC_B = 0$, each firm will also generate profits of $800(000). This is a stable equilibrium because given the competitor price, neither firm has any incentive to change price.

Figure 13.5 illustrates this Bertrand market equilibrium price–output solution, and price–reaction curves for each competitor. Notice that Bertrand equilibrium price and profits are

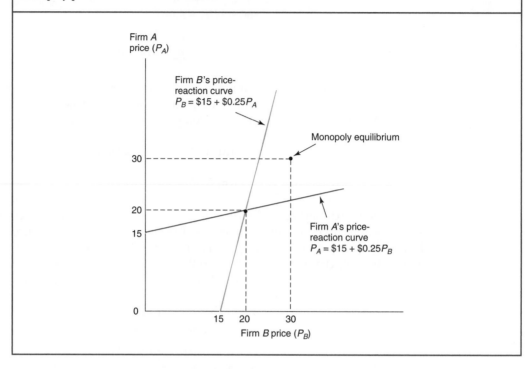

Figure 13.5   Bertrand Equilibrium in a Two-Firm Duopoly

The Bertrand model focuses upon oligopoly price reactions. Bertrand equilibrium results in less than monopoly profits.

less than that achieved under monopoly. If this were a monopoly market, $P_A = P_B$ and the monopoly firm total profit would be

$$\pi = P \times Q - TC$$
$$= P(60 - 2P + P) - 0$$
$$= \$60P - P^2$$

When price rather than output is taken as the decision variable, the monopoly profit-maximizing price is found by setting

$$\partial\pi / \partial P = 0$$
$$\$60 - \$2P = 0$$
$$\$2P = \$60$$
$$P = \$30$$

The profit-maximizing monopoly output is

$$Q = 60 - P$$
$$= 60 - 30$$
$$= 30\ (000)\ \text{units}$$

Monopoly profits are

$$\pi = \$60P - P^2$$
$$= \$60(30) - 30^2$$
$$= \$900 \ (000)$$

Through this simple example, the Bertrand model illustrates how price-setting oligopoly firms can profit by selling differentiated products. It also explains why firms such as Kellogg's and General Mills, Hershey's and Mar's, and Intel and Advanced Micro Devices go to great expense to maintain product differentiation in the eyes of consumers.

Sweezy Oligopoly

Sweezy Model

Theory that explains why an established price level tends to remain fixed for extended periods of time in some monopoly markets

Kinked Demand Curve

Firm demand curve that has different slopes for price increases as compared with price decreases

In 1939, Harvard economist Paul Sweezy developed a theory of oligopoly to explain "sticky prices," an often-noted characteristic of oligopoly markets. The **Sweezy model** hypothesizes that when making price decisions, oligopoly firms have a tendency to follow rival price decreases but ignore rival price increases.

Sweezy theory explains why an established price level tends to remain fixed for extended periods of time in some monopoly markets. Such rigid prices are explained as reflecting a **kinked demand curve.** A kinked demand curve is a firm demand curve that has different slopes for price increases as compared with price decreases. The kinked demand curve describes a behavior pattern in which rival firms follow any decrease in price to maintain their respective market shares but refrain from following price increases, allowing their market shares to grow at the expense of the competitor increasing its price. The demand curve facing individual firms is kinked at the established price/output combination, as illustrated in Figure 13.6. The firm is producing Q units of output and

Figure 13.6   Kinked Demand Curve

When price cuts are followed but price increases are not, a kink develops in the firm's demand curve. At the kink, the optimal price remains stable despite moderate changes in marginal costs.

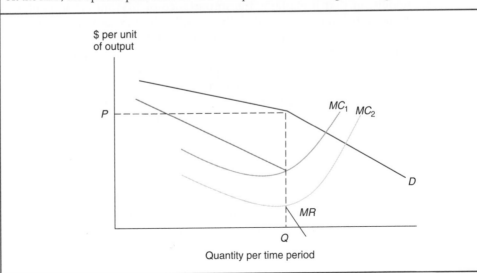

selling them at a price of P per unit. If the firm lowers its price, competitors retaliate by lowering their prices. The result of a price cut is a relatively small increase in sales. Price increases, on the other hand, result in significant reductions in the quantity demanded and in total revenue, because customers shift to competing firms that do not follow the price increase.

Associated with the kink in the demand curve is a point of discontinuity in the marginal revenue curve. As a result, the firm's marginal revenue curve has a gap at the current price-output level, which results in price rigidity. To see why, recall that profit-maximizing firms operate at the point where marginal cost equals marginal revenue. Typically, any change in marginal cost leads to a new point of equality between marginal costs and marginal revenues and to a new optimal price. However, with a gap in the marginal revenue curve, the price-output combination at the kink can remain optimal despite fluctuations in marginal costs. As illustrated in Figure 13.6, the firm's marginal cost curve can fluctuate between MC_1 and MC_2 without causing any change in the profit-maximizing price-output combination. Small changes in marginal costs have no effect; only large changes in marginal cost lead to price changes. In perfectly competitive grain markets, prices change every day. In the oligopoly ready-to-eat cereals market, prices change less frequently.

Oligopoly Model Comparison

Oligopoly Theory
Models that together help explain competition among the few

Oligopoly theory comprises a rich series of models that together help explain competition among the few. If oligopoly firms effectively collude or form a cartel, prices, profits, and output will mimic those found in monopoly markets. In many cases, however, theory and practice show that oligopoly prices and profits tend to lie between the competitive market and monopoly ends of the spectrum. The Cournot model predicts that quantity-setting oligopoly firms will produce somewhat more output and charge lower prices than monopoly firms. This approach is sometimes criticized as naive because the Cournot model assumes that rivals do not incorporate the expected output response of competitors in their own output decisions. Similarly, the Bertrand model is criticized because it assumes that rivals do not incorporate the expected price response of competitors in their own price decisions.

The Stackelberg model represents an improvement over the Cournot and Bertrand models, in that it explains the importance of first-mover advantages, and allows for strategic behavior by leading firms. Still, the Stackelberg model is limited in that it doesn't provide for strategic behavior by both leading and nonleading firms, and doesn't fully provide for differences in strategic moves and countermoves over time. Like the Sweezy model, the Stackelberg approach provides a useful but incomplete guide for the understanding of oligopoly firm behavior in "messy" real-world markets.

Modeling the behavior of firms in oligopoly markets is made difficult by the fact that assumptions about rival behavior are an important determinant of the firm's own decision-making process. Without accurate information about rival behavior, oligopoly firms must make their price-output decisions based upon reasonable assumptions concerning the expected behavior of interdependent rivals. Such interdependence creates uncertainty in oligopoly markets, and makes for a game-like atmosphere in which the competitors (players) must anticipate one another's competitive strategies (moves). Indeed, the theory of games provides a fertile framework for studying firm behavior and competitive strategy in oligopoly markets.

MARKET STRUCTURE MEASUREMENT

Data gathered by the federal government, market research firms, and trade associations are useful for describing competitive conditions.

Economic Census

Economic Census
A comprehensive statistical profile of the economy, from the national, to the state, and to the local level

The determination of distinct economic markets depends upon careful examination of cross-price elasticity of demand information. If different firms offer products for which the cross-price elasticity is large and positive, they produce substitutes and are competitors. If different firms offer products for which the cross-price elasticity is near zero, they make independent products and do not compete. This process for defining economic markets is the basis for extensive data collected, analyzed, and reported by the Bureau of the Census of the U.S. Department of Commerce. The **Economic Census** provides a comprehensive statistical profile of the economy, from the national, to the state, to the local level. The Economic Census gives vital input used to estimate gross domestic product, input–output measures, production and price indexes, and other statistical measures of short-term changes in economic conditions. Policymaking agencies of the federal government use the data to monitor economic activity and to assess the effectiveness of regulatory policies. State and local governments use the data to assess business activities and the tax bases within their jurisdictions and to develop programs to attract business. Trade associations use Economic Census information to study trends in their own and competing industries. Individual businesses use the data to locate

---

Managerial Application 13.3

Contestable Airline Passenger Service Markets

Southwest Airlines Co. builds air passenger service markets with frequent flights and low fares. Southwest's tight cost controls produce favorable margins and attractive profit growth. At the heart of Southwest's success is its point-to-point route system, which is far more efficient than the hub-and-spoke model used by the other major airlines. Southwest also uses second-tier airports where landing fees are lower and congestion is minimal, thereby minimizing costly delays. Southwest's average trip length is only about 500 miles, with an average duration of approximately 1.5 hours. Some of Southwest's biggest city-pair markets include Dallas to Houston, Phoenix to Las Vegas, and Los Angeles International to Oakland. Southwest is also a leading innovator in the use of the Internet for promotion and ticket sales. This reduces marketing costs and helps cut excess capacity.

Fares are cut in half and traffic doubles, triples, or even quadruples whenever Southwest enters a new market. Airport authorities rake in millions of extra dollars in landing fees, parking and concession fees soar, and added business

is attracted to the local area—all because Southwest has arrived! Could it be that Southwest has discovered what many airline passengers already know? Customers absolutely crave cut-rate prices that are combined with friendly service, plus arrival and departure times that are convenient and reliable. The once-little upstart airline from Texas is growing by leaps and bounds because nobody knows how to meet the demand for regional airline service like Southwest Airlines.

For example, in the early 1990s, Southwest saw an opportunity because airfares out of San Francisco were high and the nearby Oakland airport was underused. By offering cut-rate fares out of Oakland to Burbank, a similarly underused airport in Southern California, Southwest was able to spur dramatic traffic gains and revenue growth. During the first 12 months of operation, Southwest quadrupled traffic on the Oakland–Burbank following a 50 percent cut in air fares.

See: Susan Carey and Melanie Trottman, "Airlines Explore New Routes," *Wall Street Journal Online*, October 25, 2007, http://online.wsj.com.

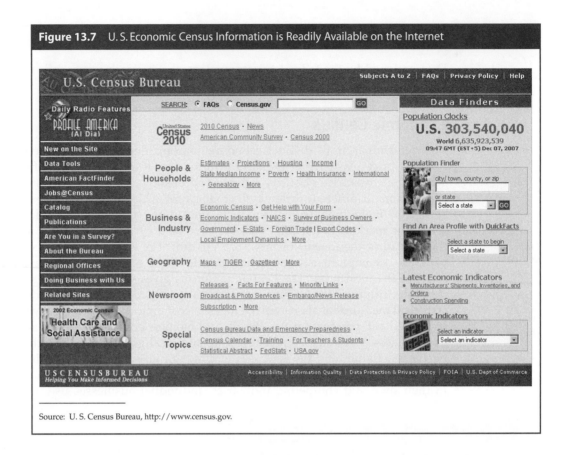

Figure 13.7 U. S. Economic Census Information is Readily Available on the Internet

Source: U. S. Census Bureau, http://www.census.gov.

potential markets and to analyze their own production and sales performance relative to industry or area averages. Economic Censuses are taken at 5-year intervals during years ending with the digits 2, 7, 12, and so on—for example, 2002, 2007, and 2012. Results are widely disseminated on the Internet at http://www.census.gov (Figure 13.7).

NAICS System

North American Industry Classification System (NAICS)
A method for categorizing establishments by the principal economic activity

Economic Census data are published using the **North American Industry Classification System (NAICS).** As shown in Table 13.1, the NAICS divides economic activity in 20 important sectors such as Manufacturing, Retail Trade, Finance and Insurance, and Professional, Scientific, and Technical Services. Not listed in Table 13.1 are the Agriculture, Forestry, Fishing, and Hunting sector (NAICS 11), partially covered by the Census of Agriculture conducted by the U.S. Department of Agriculture, and the Public Administration sector (NAICS 92), largely covered by the Census of Governments. The 20 NAICS sectors shown in Table 13.1 are subdivided into 100 subsectors using 3-digit codes, 317 industry groups using 4-digit codes, and 1,179 industries using 6-digit codes. Sectors covered account for roughly three-quarters of total economic activity originating in the private sector.

Economic Census statistics are collected and published primarily at the "establishment" level of aggregation. An establishment is a business or industrial unit at a single physical location that produces or distributes goods or performs services. Table 13.2 illustrates the makeup of a sample of NAICS industries taken from the 2-digit Information sector. Data are shown for the United States as a whole, the State of

Table 13.1 The Economic Census Covers 20 Major NAICS Sectors	
NAICS 2x-Digit Code	**Descripion**
21	Mining
22	Utilities
23	Construction
31–33	Manufacturing
42	Wholesale Trade
44–45	Retail Trade
48–49	Transportation and Warehousing
51	Information
52	Finance and Insurance
53	Real Estate and Rental and Leasing
54	Professional, Scientific, and Technical Services
55	Management of Companies and Enterprises
56	Administrative and Support and Waste Management and Remediation Services
61	Educational Services
62	Health Care and Social Assistance
71	Arts, Entertainment, and Recreation
72	Accommodation and Food Services
81	Other Services (except Public Administration)

Data source: *2002 Economic Census*, Issued May 2006, http://www.census.gov/.

Colorado, and the Denver–Aurora–Boulder Metropolitan Statistical Area (MSA). Notice the logical progression as one moves from the 2-digit Information (51) sector, to the 3-digit Publishing Industries (511) subsector, to the 4-digit Newspaper, Periodical, Book, and Directory Publishers industry group (5111), to the narrow 6-digit Newspaper Publishers (511110) industry. Economists generally agree that these 6-digit classifications correspond closely with the economic definition of a market. Establishments grouped at the 6-digit level produce products that are ready substitutes for one another and thus function as competitors. Managers who analyze census data to learn about the number and size distribution of actual and potential competitors focus their attention primarily on data provided at the 6-digit level.

CENSUS MEASURES OF MARKET CONCENTRATION

The U.S. census gives detailed information on the number and size distribution of competitors.

Concentration Ratios

In addition to those directly engaged in business, both government and the public share an interest in the number and size distribution of competitors. A small number of competitors can sometimes have direct implications for regulation and antitrust policy. Thus, considerable public resources are devoted to monitoring both the size distribution

Table 13.2 NAICS Data is Available at the U.S., State and Local Levels

The 20 two-digit North American Industry Classification System (NAICS) sectors are subdivided into 100 sub-sectors (three-digit codes), 317 industry groups (four-digit codes), and, as implemented in the United States, 1,179 industries (six-digit codes). This example shows the type of data avaible for various information service providers at the national, state and metropolitan statistical area (MSA) levels.

NAICS Code	Description	Establishments	Revenue ($1,000)	Annual Payroll ($1,000)	Paid Employees
Summary Statistics for United States					
51	Information	137,678	891,845,956	194,670,163	3,736,061
511	Publishing industries (except Internet)	32,287	242,216,369	65,680,724	1,089,585
5111	Newspaper, periodical, book, and directory publishers	22,334	138,710,521	30,745,775	732,877
511110	Newspaper publishers	8,603	46,179,063	13,734,533	401,170
511120	Periodical publishers	7,298	40,180,864	8,377,685	152,227
511130	Book publishers	3,526	27,928,786	4,966,519	97,080
511140	Directory and mailing list publishers	1,915	16,920,189	2,583,666	55,820
51119	Other publishers	992	7,501,619	1,083,372	26,580
Summary Statistics for Colorado					
51	Information	3,200	n.a.	5,090,490	102,169
511	Publishing industries (except Internet)	906	4,567,857	1,293,629	23,185
5111	Newspaper, periodical, book, and directory publishers	569	2,688,365	599,598	14,693
511110	Newspaper publishers	183	1,010,882	239,248	7,481
511120	Periodical publishers	190	368,495	96,899	2,250
511130	Book publishers	100	560,134	147,124	2,757
511140	Directory and mailing list publishers	59	650,703	92,571	1,638
51119	Other publishers	37	98,151	23,756	567
Summary Statistics for Denver-Aurora-Boulder Combined Statistical Area					
51	Information	2,095	n.a.	4,213,228	80,278
511	Publishing industries (except Internet)	578	3,535,313	961,189	249,303
5111	Newspaper, periodical, book, and directory publishers	327	2,086,447	454,140	10,095
511110	Newspaper publishers	89	767,179	158,733	4,515
511120	Periodical publishers	118	279,546	73,814	1,608
511130	Book publishers	60	n.a.	n.a.	n.a.
511140	Directory and mailing list publishers	35	n.a.	n.a.	n.a.
51119	Other publishers	25	n.a.	n.a.	n.a.

Note: n.a. means not available, and indicates data that witheld to avoid disclosing information for individual companies.

Data source: 2002 *Economic Census, Geographic Area Series,* Issued May 2006, http://www.census.gov/econ/census02/guide/geosumm.htm.

and economic performance of firms in several important sectors of the economy. Among those sectors covered by the economic census, manufacturing is the largest, accounting for approximately 20 percent of aggregate economic activity in the United States. Firm sizes in manufacturing are also much larger than in other major sectors such as retail and wholesale trade, construction, and legal and medical services. Among the more than 16 million business enterprises in the United States, manufacturing is the domain of the large corporation. Thus, the manufacturing sector provides an interesting basis for considering data that are available on the size distribution of firms.

Table 13.3 shows census information on the number of competitors, industry sales, and leading-firm market share data for a small sample of industries. Industries that contain a large number of firms of roughly equal sizes are generally regarded as vigorously competitive. Questions about the intensity of competition sometimes arise when only a limited number of competitors are present, or when only a handful of large firms dominate the industry.

Concentration Ratios

The percentage market share held by (concentrated in) a group of top firms

As shown in Table 13.3, the economic census uses two different methods to describe the degree of competitor size inequality within an industry. **Concentration ratios** measure the percentage market share concentrated in (or held by) an industry's top four (CR_4), eight (CR_8), twenty (CR_{20}), or fifty (CR_{50}) firms. The concentration ratio for a group of n leading firms is defined in percentage terms as

$$CR_n = \frac{\sum_{i=1}^{n} \text{Firm Sales}_i}{\text{Industry Sales}} \times 100 \qquad \textbf{13.6}$$

where i refers to an individual firm.

Concentration ratios can range between $CR_n = 0$ for an industry with a massive number of small competitors and $CR_n = 100$ for an industry represented by a single monopolist. In the manufacturing sector where concentration tends to be highest, four-firm concentration ratios tend to fall in a broad range between $CR_4 = 20$ and $CR_4 = 60$; eight-firm concentration ratios often lie in a range between $CR_8 = 30$ and $CR_8 = 70$. When concentration ratios are low, industries tend to include many firms, and competition tends to be vigorous. Industries in which the four leading firms are responsible for less than 20 percent of total industry sales (i.e., $CR_4 < 20$) are highly competitive and approximate the perfect competition model. On the other hand, when concentration ratios are high, leading firms dominate following firms in terms of size, and leading firms may have more potential for pricing flexibility and economic profits. Industries in which the four leading firms control more than 80 percent of total industry sales (i.e., $CR_4 > 80$) are often described as highly concentrated. Industries with a $CR_4 < 20$ or $CR_4 > 80$, however, are quite rare. Three-quarters of all manufacturing activity takes place in industries with concentration ratios falling in the range $20 \leq CR_4 \leq 80$.

Herfindahl–Hirschmann Index

Concentration ratios increase with greater competitor size inequality within a given industry, but are unaffected by the degree of size inequality within each respective group of leading firms. This can create problems because competition within industries featuring a handful of large competitors can be much more vigorous than in those where a single dominant firm faces no large adversaries. For example, although

Table 13.3 Number of Firms and Concentration Ratios for a Representative Sample of Manufacturing Industries from the U.S. Economic Census

The number of firms, concentration ratios, and the HHI give differing insight on the extent of competition as capured by the size distribution of competitors.

Industry	NACIS Code	Number of Firms	Industry Sales ($ millions)	Percentage of Sales Accounted for By:					Herfindahl Hirschmann Index (HHI) Top 50 Firms
				Top 4 Firms (CR_4)	Top 8 Firms (CR_8)	Top 20 Firms (CR_{20})	Top 50 Firms (CR_{50})		
Dog and cat food manufacturing	311111	176	10,624,932	64.2	81.3	93.2	98.0		1,845.4
Breakfast cereal manufacturing	311230	45	9,102,527	78.4	91.1	98.8	100.0		2,521.3
Confectionery manufacturing from purchased chocolate	311330	1,008	8,833,323	60.4	71.9	82.2	89.5		1,473.8
Fruit and vegetable canning	311421	632	18,869,098	23.7	37.9	59.7	78.5		256.7
Fluid milk manufacturing	311511	315	24,888,743	42.6	53.6	69.2	83.7		1,060.4
Tortilla manufacturing	311830	272	1,532,267	56.1	62.6	73.4	87.9		2,031.4
Cigarette manufacturing	312221	15	34,799,732	95.3	99.4	100.0	100.0		n.a.
Women's and girls' cut and sew dress manufacturing	315233	525	3,626,775	21.6	31.9	48.5	69.6		185.5
Manufactured home (mobile home) manufacturing	321991	241	6,726,900	44.6	63.7	81.1	92.5		685.3
Paper (except newsprint) mills	322121	174	42,190,901	53.1	69.5	84.5	95.6		810.2
Quick printing	323114	7,515	4,513,100	21.5	23.6	26.8	31.4		319.0
Petroleum refineries	324110	88	193,528,006	41.2	63.5	89.3	99.3		639.7
Plastics bottle manufacturing	326160	184	7,928,313	42.6	63.6	83.0	93.5		628.1
Tire manufacturing (except retreading)	326211	112	13,478,983	77.2	92.7	97.9	99.7		1,806.6
Ready mix concrete manufacturing	327320	2,614	21,619,989	11.1	17.1	28.2	42.2		63.1
Iron and steel mills	331111	285	47,035,279	44.4	58.5	77.7	93.0		656.7
Aluminum sheet, plate, and foil manufacturing	331315	79	12,009,684	70.8	86.8	97.3	99.7		1,856.1
Semiconductor machinery manufacturing	333295	262	12,234,067	59.9	68.9	81.5	92.2		2,023.9
Electronic computer manufacturing	334111	465	47,730,226	75.5	89.2	95.0	97.0		2,662.4
Semiconductor and related device manufacturing	334413	904	61,434,888	56.5	64.1	77.5	89.7		1,417.1
Automobile manufacturing	336111	164	88,127,061	75.5	94.2	99.3	99.8		1,910.9
Military armored vehicle, tank, and tank component manufacturing	336992	31	1,455,918	88.3	93.2	99.2	100.0		n.a.
Surgical appliance and supplies manufacturing	339113	1,617	23,853,321	27.3	38.0	56.4	73.2		279.1
Sporting and athletic goods manufacturing	339920	2,157	11,841,594	22.5	32.4	45.7	66.6		182.2
Burial casket manufacturing	339995	148	1,201,488	73.2	81.0	88.9	95.1		n.a.

Note: n.a. means not available, and indicates data that witheld to avoid disclosing information for individual companies.

Data source: *Concentration Ratios: 2002, 2002 Economic Census, Manufacturing, Subject Series,* Issued May 2006, http://www.census.gov/prod/ec02/ec0231sr1.pdf.

**Herfindahl–
Hirschmann
Index (HHI)**
The sum of
squared market
shares for all
n industry
competitors

$CR_4 = 100$ would signal monopoly in the case of a single dominant firm, it might describe a vigorously competitive industry if each of the leading four firms enjoys roughly equal market shares of 25 percent. The **Herfindahl–Hirschmann Index (HHI),** named after the economists who invented it, is a popular measure of competitor size inequality that reflects size differences among large and small firms. Calculated in percentage terms, the HHI is the sum of the squared market shares for all n industry competitors:

$$HHI = \sum_{i=1}^{n}\left(\frac{\text{Firm Sales}_i}{\text{Industry Sales}} \times 100\right)^2 \qquad \textbf{13.7}$$

For example, a monopoly industry with a single dominant firm is described by a $CR_4 = 100$ and an $HHI = 100^2 = 10{,}000$. A vigorously competitive industry where each of the leading four firms enjoys market shares of 25 percent is also described by a $CR_4 = 100$, but features an $HHI = 25^2 + 25^2 + 25^2 + 25^2 = 2{,}500$. Like concentration ratios, the HHI approaches zero for industries characterized by a large number of very small competitors. In general, markets are described as not concentrated if $HHI < 1{,}000$, moderately concentrated if $1{,}000 \leq HHI \leq 1{,}800$, and highly concentrated if $HHI > 1{,}800$.

Limitations of Census Information

A major drawback of concentration ratio and HHI information is that they take a long time to collect and publish. Economic Census forms were to be sent to 5 million businesses in December 2007, asking for information about business activity during calendar year 2007. The forms were due back by February 12, 2008, and results will be published during 2009 and 2010. In many fast-moving markets, these data are obsolete before they are published. Even in less dynamic markets, they provide only an imperfect guide to managerial decision making. As a result, many managers supplement Economic Census information with more current data available on the Internet (see Table 13.4).

A further weakness of census concentration ratio and HHI information is that they ignore domestic sales by foreign competitors (imports) as well as exports by domestic firms. Only data on domestic sales from domestic production, not total domestic sales, are reported. For example, that if foreign imports have a market share of 30 percent, the four leading domestic automobile manufacturers account for 52.9 percent (= 75.5 percent of 70 percent) of total U.S. foreign plus domestic car sales (NAICS 33611), rather than 75.5 percent, as Table 13.3 suggests. Concentration ratios and HHI information also overstate market power for industries in which foreign competition is vigorous. The impact of foreign competition is important in many industries, but it is particularly apparent in manufacturing industries such as apparel, steel, automobiles, cameras, copiers, motorcycles, and television sets.

Another limitation of concentration ratio data is that they are national totals. If high transportation costs or other product characteristics keep markets regional or local rather than national in scope, concentration ratios can significantly understate the relative importance of leading firms. For example, the leading firm in many metropolitan newspaper markets often approaches 80 percent to 90 percent of classified advertising and subscription revenues. Although national four-firm concentration ratios of less than 25 percent usually suggest a highly competitive market, a national CR_4 for newspapers significantly understates local market power in the industry. Other products with local or regional rather than national markets include milk, bread and bakery products, commercial

Table 13.4 Corporate Profitability in Monopolistically NAICS Data is Available at the U.S., State and Local Levels

Industry Group	Active Corporations	Profit Margin (% of sales)	Return on Equity (ROE %)
Construction			
General building contractors	180,935	1.9	22.1
Heavy construction contractors	23,071	3.2	11.1
Operative builders	1,843	4.0	14.7
Retail Trade			
Garden supplies	12,502	2.1	14.9
Eating and drinking places	215,393	2.5	15.0
Apparel and accessory stores	39,420	3.5	15.3
Building material dealers	20,171	3.4	15.6
Other automotive dealers	33,953	2.0	15.8
Grocery stores	45,534	1.4	18.4
Wholesale Trade			
Motor vehicles & automotive equipment	27,667	1.3	9.5
Chemicals and allied products	9,079	1.9	11.9
Other durable goods	53,381	1.7	13.6
Groceries and related products	29,201	1.0	15.5
Hardware, plumbing & heating equipment	14,301	2.7	15.6
Other non-durable goods	43,985	2.1	17.5

Industry Group	Active Corporations	Profit Margin (% of sales)	Return on Equity (ROE %)
Services			
Medical laboratories	6,567	-5.6	-12.9
Hospitals	1,493	1.5	1.4
Other medical services	45,299	0.5	2.3
Motion picture production & distribution	20,925	2.7	2.6
Nursing and personal care facilities	15,303	1.1	5.1
Membership organizations	14,971	3.1	6.7
Auto repair and services	98,333	1.3	9.4
Hotels and other lodging places	30,636	4.4	9.8
Educational services	23,810	1.7	11.6
Social services	21,400	1.9	13.0
Manufacturing			
Agriculture and other chemical products	3,159	5.0	11.3
Alcoholic beverages, except malt liquors	1,407	14.6	4.3
Books, greeting cards, and other publishing	11,890	5.9	5.2
Dairy products	1,180	2.3	14.3

Footwear, except rubber	191	4.0	14.2
Glass products	1,199	5.8	14.6
Industrial chemicals, plastics & synthetics	4,219	7.4	12.5
Motor vehicles and equipment	2,789	3.6	11.1
Optical, medical, and ophthalmic goods	5,028	6.3	10.7
Other electrical equipment	7,816	8.2	13.2
Periodicals	4,825	1.9	4.5
Petroleum refining	224	6.6	10.7
Preserved fruits and vegetables	730	5.9	13.0
Ship and boat building and repairing	2,066	3.8	10.5
Special industry machinery	3,481	4.5	12.8
Transportation and Public Utilities			
Air Transportation	8,680	5.4	22.4
Combination utility services	126	10.5	13.2
Electric services	963	11.7	10.9
Local and interurban passenger transit	18,155	2.0	10.8
Railroad transportation	780	3.1	2.1
Telephone & other communication services	17,302	7.3	9.2
Water supply and other sanitary services	13,661	5.6	9.9
Finance, Insurance & Real Estate			
Bank holding companies	5,225	78.4	8.8
Banks	3,820	21.9	11.2
Business credit institutions	2,387	18.3	9.3
Lessors of railroad & other real property	3,594	34.1	9.2
Life insurance companies	1,685	7.0	8.5
Mutual property & casualty insurance companies	1,723	7.6	8.1
Other credit agencies	25,845	26.2	12.3
Other holding and investment companies	54,088	68.7	6.7
Personal credit institutions	3,804	13.7	6.6
Small business investment companies	8,284	7.6	2.0
Stock property & casualty insurance companies	3,648	6.2	5.3
Monopolistically Competitive and Oligopoly Markets	**1,253,147**	**8.1**	**10.4**
All Corporations	**4,619,858**	**8.1**	**15.4**

Data source: U.S. corporate federal income tax data, May 8, 2007, http://www.bizstats.com/.

Managerial Application 13.4

Horizontal Merger Guidelines

The Federal Trade Commission (FTC) and the Department of Justice (DOJ) have issued quantitative standards used to guide their analysis of proposed mergers. The standards are as follows:

- *Unconcentrated Markets with Postmerger HHI Below 1,000.* Mergers resulting in relatively unconcentrated markets are ordinarily approved.
- *Moderately Concentrated Markets with Postmerger HHI Between 1,000 and 1,800.* Mergers producing an increase in the HHI of less than 100 points in moderately concentrated markets ordinarily will be approved. Mergers producing an increase in the HHI of more than 100 points in moderately concentrated markets have the potential to raise significant competitive concerns and would be scrutinized.
- *Highly Concentrated Markets with Postmerger HHI Above 1,800.* Mergers producing an increase in the HHI of less than 50 points, even in highly concentrated markets, are unlikely to have adverse competitive consequences and

ordinarily will be approved. Mergers producing an increase in the HHI of more than 50 points in highly concentrated markets have the potential to raise significant competitive concerns and would be scrutinized. Where the postmerger HHI exceeds 1,800, it will be presumed that mergers producing an increase in the HHI of more than 100 points are likely to create or enhance market power and would ordinarily not be approved.

From a public policy perspective, these guidelines make clear the public's interest in maintaining the benefits of competition while preserving the rights of individual companies to respond in an appropriate manner to dynamic competitive markets. From the perspective of merging firms, these guidelines also give a valuable framework for assessing the chances of merger approval.

See: Harry Wilson, "Europe's Merger Deals to Fall Short of Forecasts," *Wall Street Journal Online*, October 4, 2007, http://online.wsj.com.

printing, and ready-mix concrete. Census data also give an imperfect view of market structure by failing to reflect the influence of potential entrants. The mere presence of one or more potential entrants can constitute a sufficient threat to force competitive market behavior in industries with only a handful of established competitors. Major retailers such as Wal-Mart, Target, and Sears use their positions as potential entrants to obtain attractive prices on a wide range of private-label merchandise such as clothing, lawn mowers, and washing machines.

SUMMARY

Monopolistic competition and oligopoly models describe the behavior of competitors in imperfectly competitive markets in which price competition and a wide variety of methods of nonprice competition are observed.

- **Monopolistic competition** is characterized by vigorous price competition; a large numbers of buyers and sellers; differentiated, though comparable, products; free entry and exit; perfect information; and the opportunity for normal profits in long-run equilibrium. In some cases, distinctive

products allow $P > MC$, but vigorous price and product-quality price competition keeps $P = AC$.

- **Oligopoly** firms have the ability to set pricing and production strategy, and enjoy the potential for economic profits in both the short run and the long run. Oligopoly markets have few sellers, products that are identical or distinctive, blockaded entry and/or exit, imperfect information, and the opportunity for economic profits in long-run equilibrium. Competitive advantages keep $P > MC$ and $P = AR > AC$ for efficient firms.

- In the short run, firms in monopolistically competitive markets may enjoy monopoly profits. However, competition from firms offering similar products eliminates economic profits in long-run equilibrium. The monopolistic competition **high-price/low-output equilibrium** is identified by the point of tangency between the firm's average cost curve and a new demand curve reflecting a parallel leftward shift in firm demand. This parallel leftward shift assumes that the firm can maintain a high degree of product differentiation in the long run. While $P > MC$, because $P = AR = AC$, only a normal profit is earned by the firm in monopolistic competition high-price–low-output equilibrium. The monopolistic competition **low-price/high-output equilibrium** occurs when competitor entry eliminates product differentiation in the long run. This equilibrium is identified by the point of tangency between the average cost curve and a new horizontal firm demand curve, and is the perfectly competitive equilibrium price–output combination.

- A group of competitors operating under a formal overt agreement is called a **cartel.** If an informal covert agreement is reached, the firms are said to be operating in **collusion.** Both practices are generally illegal in the United States. However, cartels are legal in many parts of the world, and multinational corporations often become involved with them in foreign markets.

- The **Cournot model** posits that firms in oligopoly markets make simultaneous and independent output decisions. The relationship between an oligopoly firm's profit-maximizing output level and competitor output is called the oligopoly **output–reaction curve** because it shows how oligopoly firms react to competitor production decisions. The Cournot model is often illustrated using a two-firm, or **duopoly,** market.

- The Cournot model is sometimes criticized because it fails to incorporate the fact that oligopoly markets often involve sequential versus simultaneous decision making. An alternative noncooperative **Stackelberg model** posits a **first-mover advantage** for the oligopoly firm that initiates the process of determining market output.

- An informal but sometimes effective means for reducing uncertainty in oligopoly markets is through **price signaling. Price leadership** results when one firm establishes itself as the industry leader and all other firms accept its pricing policy. This leadership may result from the size and strength of the leading firm, from cost efficiency, or as a result of the recognized ability of the leader to forecast market conditions accurately and to establish prices that produce satisfactory profits for all firms in the industry. Under a second type of price leadership, **barometric price leadership,** the price leader is not necessarily the largest or dominant firm in the industry. The price leader must only be accurate in reading the prevailing industry view of the need for price adjustment.

- The **Bertrand model** focuses upon price reactions, rather than the output reactions, of oligopoly firms. Bertrand equilibrium is reached when no firm can achieve higher profits by charging a different price. In the Bertrand model, the relationship between the profit-maximizing price level and competitor price is called the oligopoly **price–reaction curve** because it shows how the oligopoly firm reacts to competitor pricing decisions.

- According to **contestable markets theory,** there is no necessary link between the number of actual competitors and the vigor of competition. If potential entrants pose a credible threat, incumbent oligopoly firms are not free to charge high prices and earn economic profits.

- The **Sweezy model** hypothesizes that when making price decisions, oligopoly firms have a tendency to follow rival price decreases but ignore rival price increases. Sweezy theory explains why an established price level tends to remain fixed for extended periods of time in some monopoly markets. Such rigid prices are explained as reflecting a **kinked demand curve.** A kinked demand curve is a firm demand curve that has different slopes for price increases as compared with price decreases.

- **Oligopoly theory** comprises a rich series of models that together help explain competition among the few. If oligopoly firms effectively collude or form a cartel, prices, profits, and output will mimic those found in monopoly markets. In many cases, however, theory and practice show that oligopoly prices and profits tend to lie between the competitive market and monopoly ends of the spectrum.

- The **Economic Census** provides a comprehensive statistical profile of the economy, from the national, to the state, to the local level. Censuses are taken at 5-year intervals during years ending with the digits 2, 7, 12, and so on—for example, 2002, 2007, and 2012. The **North American Industry Classification System (NAICS)** categorizes establishments by the principal economic activity in which they are engaged.

- **Concentration ratios** measure the percentage market share held by (concentrated in) a group of top firms. When concentration ratios are low, industries tend to be made up of many firms, and competition tends to be vigorous. When concentration ratios are high, leading firms dominate and sometimes have the potential for pricing flexibility and economic profits. The **Herfindahl–Hirschmann Index (HHI)** is a measure of competitor size inequality that reflects size differences among both large and small firms. Calculated in percentage terms, the HHI is the sum of the squared market shares for all n industry competitors.

The description of competition in imperfectly competitive markets is one of the most challenging and fascinating aspects of managerial economics. From a public policy perspective, competitive forces must be understood if the rules governing the competitive process are to maximize social benefits. From the firm's perspective, an appropriate characterization of competitive forces is a key ingredient in the development of successful competitive strategy.

QUESTIONS

Q13.1 Describe the monopolistically competitive market structure and give some examples.

Q13.2 Describe the oligopoly market structure and give some examples.

Q13.3 Explain the process by which economic profits are eliminated in a monopolistically competitive market as compared with a perfectly competitive market.

Q13.4 Would you expect the demand curve for a firm in a monopolistically competitive industry to be more or less elastic in the long run after competitor entry has eliminated economic profits?

Q13.5 "One might expect firms in a monopolistically competitive market to experience greater swings in the price of their products over the business cycle than those in an oligopoly market. However, fluctuations in profits do not necessarily follow the same pattern." Discuss this statement.

Q13.6 What is the essential difference between the Cournot and Stackelberg models?

Q13.7 Which oligopoly model(s) result(s) in long-run oligopoly market equilibrium that is identical to a competitive market price–output solution?

Q13.8 Why is the four-firm concentration ratio only an imperfect measure of market power?

Q13.9 The statement "You get what you pay for" reflects the common perception that high prices indicate high product quality and low prices indicate low quality. Irrespective of market structure considerations, is this statement always correct?

Q13.10 "Economic profits result whenever only a few large competitors are active in a given market." Discuss this statement.

SELF-TEST PROBLEMS AND SOLUTIONS

ST13.1   Price Leadership.   In the last century, The Boeing Co. has become the largest aerospace company in the world. Boeing's principal global competitor is Airbus, a company that has its roots in a European consortium of French, German, and, later, Spanish and U.K. companies. Though dominated by Boeing and Airbus, smaller firms have recently entered the commercial aircraft industry. Notable among these is Embraer, a Brazilian aircraft manufacturer. Embraer makes smaller commercial aircraft that offer excellent reliability and cost-effectiveness.

To illustrate the price leadership concept, assume that total and marginal cost functions for Airbus (A) and Embraer (E) aircraft are as follows:

$$TC_A = \$10,000,000 + \$35,000,000Q_A + \$250,000Q_A^2$$
$$MC_A = \$35,000,000 + \$500,000Q_A$$
$$TC_E = \$200,000,000 + \$20,000,000Q_E + \$500,000Q_E^2$$
$$MC_E = \$20,000,000 + \$1,000,000Q_E$$

Boeing's total and marginal cost relations are as follows:

$$TC_B = \$4,000,000,000 + \$5,000,000Q_B + \$62,500Q_B^2$$
$$MC_B = \partial TC_B/\partial Q_B = \$5,000,000 + \$125,000Q_B$$

The industry demand curve for this type of jet aircraft is

$$Q = 910 - 0.000017P$$

For simplicity, assume that Airbus and Embraer aircraft are perfect substitutes for Boeing aircraft, and that each total cost function includes a risk-adjusted normal rate of return on investment.

A. Determine the supply curves for Airbus and Embraer aircraft, assuming that the firms operate as price takers.

B. What is the demand curve faced by Boeing?

C. Calculate Boeing's profit-maximizing price and output levels. (Hint: Boeing's total and marginal revenue relations are $TR_B = \$50,000,000Q_B - \$50,000Q_B^2$ and $MR_B = TR_B/ \partial Q_B = \$50,000,000 - \$100,000Q_B$.)

D. Calculate profit-maximizing output levels for the Airbus and Embraer aircraft.

E. Is the market for aircraft from these three firms in short-run and in long-run equilibrium?

ST13.1 SOLUTION

A. Because price followers take prices as given, they operate where individual marginal cost equals price. Therefore, the supply curves for Airbus and Embraer aircraft are

Airbus

$$P_A = MC_A = \$35,000,000 + \$500,000Q_A$$
$$500,000Q_A = 35,000,000 + P_A$$
$$Q_A = -70 + 0.000002P_A$$

Embraer

$$P_E = MC_E = \$20,000,000 + \$1,000,000Q_E$$
$$1,000,000Q_E = -20,000,000 + P_E$$
$$Q_E = -20 + 0.000001P_E$$

B. As the industry price leader, Boeing's demand equals industry demand minus following firm supply. Remember that $P = P_B = P_M = P_E$ because Boeing is a price leader for the industry:

$$Q_B = Q - Q_A - Q_E$$
$$= 910 - 0.000017P + 70 - \$0.000002P$$
$$+ 20 - \$0.000001P$$
$$= 1{,}000 - 0.00002P_B$$
$$P_B = \$50{,}000{,}000 - \$50{,}000Q_B$$

C. To find Boeing's profit-maximizing price and output level, set $MR_B = MC_B$ and solve for Q:

$$MR_B = MC_B$$
$$\$50{,}000{,}000 - \$100{,}000Q_B = \$5{,}000{,}000 + \$125{,}000Q_B$$
$$45{,}000{,}000 = 225{,}000Q_B$$
$$Q_B = 200 \text{ units}$$
$$P_B = \$50{,}000{,}000 - \$50{,}000(200)$$
$$= \$40{,}000{,}000$$

D. Because Boeing is a price leader for the industry,

$$P = P_B = P_A = P_E = \$40{,}000{,}000$$

Optimal supply for Airbus and Embraer aircraft are

$$Q_A = -70 + 0.000002P_A$$
$$= -70 + 0.000002(40{,}000{,}000)$$
$$= 10$$

$$Q_E = -20 + 0.000001P_E$$
$$= -20 + 0.000001(40{,}000{,}000)$$
$$= 20$$

E. Yes. The industry is in short-run equilibrium if the total quantity demanded is equal to total supply. The total industry demand at a price of $40 million is

$$Q_D = 910 - 0.000017P$$
$$= 910 - 0.000017(40{,}000{,}000)$$
$$= 230 \text{ units}$$

The total industry supply is

$$Q_S = Q_B + Q_A + Q_E$$
$$= 200 + 10 + 20$$
$$= 230 \text{ units}$$

Thus, the industry is in short-run equilibrium. The industry is also in long-run equilibrium, provided that each manufacturer is making at least a risk-adjusted normal rate of return on investment. To check profit levels for each manufacturer, note that

$$\pi_A = TR_A - TC_A$$
$$= \$40,000,000(10) - \$10,000,000 - \$35,000,000(10) - \$250,000(10^2)$$
$$= \$15,000,000$$
$$\pi_E = TR_E - TC_E$$
$$= \$40,000,000(20) - \$200,000,000 - \$20,000,000(20) - \$500,000(20^2)$$
$$= \$0$$
$$\pi_B = TR_B - TC_B$$
$$= \$40,000,000(200) - \$4,000,000,000 - \$5,000,000(200) - \$62,500(200^2)$$
$$= \$500,000,000$$

Boeing and Airbus are both earning economic profits, whereas Embraer, the marginal entrant, is earning just a risk-adjusted normal rate of return. As such, the industry is in long-run equilibrium and there is no incentive to change.

ST13.2 Monopolistically Competitive Equilibrium. Soft Lens, Inc., has enjoyed rapid growth in sales and high operating profits on its innovative extended-wear soft contact lenses. However, the company faces potentially fierce competition from a host of new competitors as some important basic patents expire during the coming year. Unless the company is able to thwart such competition, severe downward pressure on prices and profit margins is anticipated.

A. Use Soft Lens's current price, output, and total cost data to complete the table:

Price ($)	Monthly Output (million)	Total Revenue ($ million)	Marginal Revenue ($ million)	Total Cost ($ million)	Marginal Cost ($ million)	Average Cost ($ million)	Total Profit ($ million)
20	0			0			
19	1			12			
18	2			27			
17	3			42			
16	4			58			
15	5			75			
14	6			84			
13	7			92			
12	8			96			
11	9			99			
10	10			105			

(Note: Total costs include a risk-adjusted normal rate of return.)

B. If cost conditions remain constant, what is the monopolistically competitive high-price/low-output long-run equilibrium in this industry? What are industry profits?

C. Under the same cost conditions, what is the monopolistically competitive low-price/high-output equilibrium in this industry? What are industry profits?

D. Now assume that Soft Lens is able to enter into restrictive licensing agreements with potential competitors and create an effective cartel in the industry. If demand and cost conditions remain constant, what is the cartel price–output and profit equilibrium?

ST13.2 SOLUTION

A.

Price ($)	Monthly Output (million)	Total Revenue ($ million)	Marginal Revenue ($ million)	Total Cost ($ million)	Marginal Cost ($ million)	Average Cost ($ million)	Total Profit ($ million)
20	0	0	—	0	—	—	0
19	1	19	19	12	12	12.00	7
18	2	36	17	27	15	13.50	9
17	3	51	15	42	15	14.00	9
16	4	64	13	58	16	14.50	6
15	5	75	11	75	17	15.00	0
14	6	84	9	84	9	14.00	0
13	7	91	7	92	8	13.14	−1
12	8	96	5	96	4	12.00	0
11	9	99	3	99	3	11.00	0
10	10	100	1	105	6	10.50	−5

B. The monopolistically competitive high-price/low-output equilibrium is $P = AC = \$14$, $Q = 6(000,000)$, and $\pi = TR - TC = \$0$. Only a risk-adjusted normal rate of return is being earned in the industry, and excess profits equal zero. Because $\pi = \$0$ and $MR = MC = \$9$, there is no incentive for either expansion or contraction. Such an equilibrium is typical of monopolistically competitive industries where each individual firm retains some pricing discretion in long-run equilibrium.

C. The monopolistically competitive low-price/high-output equilibrium is $P = AC = \$11$, $Q = 9(000,000)$, and $\pi = TR - TC = \$0$. Again, only a risk-adjusted normal rate of return is being earned in the industry, and excess profits equal zero. Because $\pi = \$0$ and $MR = MC = \$3$, there is no incentive for either expansion or contraction. This price–output combination is identical to the perfectly competitive equilibrium. (Note that average cost is rising and profits are falling for $Q > 9$.)

D. A monopoly price–output equilibrium results if Soft Lens is able to enter into restrictive licensing agreements with potential competitors and create an effective cartel in the industry. If demand and cost conditions remain constant, the cartel price–output and profit equilibrium is at $P = \$17$, $Q = 3(000,000)$, and $\pi = \$9(000,000)$. There is no incentive for the cartel to expand or contract production at this level of output because $MR = MC = \$15$.

PROBLEMS

P13.1 Market Structure Concepts. Indicate whether each of the following statements is true or false and explain why.

A. Equilibrium in monopolistically competitive markets requires that firms be operating at the minimum point on the long-run average cost curve.

B. A high ratio of distribution cost to total cost tends to increase competition by widening the geographic area over which any individual producer can compete.

C. The price elasticity of demand tends to fall as new competitors introduce substitute products.

D. An efficiently functioning cartel achieves a monopoly price–output combination.

E. An increase in product differentiation tends to increase the slope of firm demand curves.

P13.2 Monopolistically Competitive Demand. Would the following factors increase or decrease the ability of domestic auto manufacturers to raise prices and profit margins? Why?

A. Decreased import quotas

B. Elimination of uniform emission standards

C. Increased automobile price advertising

D. Increased import tariffs (taxes)

E. A rising value of the dollar, which has the effect of lowering import car prices

P13.3 Competitive Markets Versus Cartels. Suppose the City of Columbus, Ohio, is considering two proposals to privatize municipal garbage collection. First, a handful of leading waste disposal firms have offered to purchase the city's plant and equipment at an attractive price in return for exclusive franchises on residential service in various parts of the city. A second proposal would allow several individual workers and small companies to enter the business without any exclusive franchise agreements or competitive restrictions. Under this plan, individual companies would bid for the right to provide service in a given residential area. The City would then allocate business to the lowest bidder.

The City has conducted a survey of Columbus residents to estimate the amount that they would be willing to pay for various frequencies of service. The City has also estimated the total cost of service per resident. Service costs are expected to be the same whether or not an exclusive franchise is granted.

A. Complete the following table.

Trash Pickups Per Month	Price Per Pickup ($)	Total Revenue	Marginal Revenue	Total Cost ($)	Marginal Cost
0	5.00			0.00	
1	4.80			3.75	
2	4.60			7.45	
3	4.40			11.10	
4	4.20			14.70	
5	4.00			18.00	
6	3.80			20.90	
7	3.60			23.80	
8	3.40			27.20	
9	3.20			30.70	
10	3.00			35.00	

B. Determine price and service level if competitive bidding results in a perfectly competitive price–output combination.

C. Determine price and the level of service if local regulation results in a cartel.

P13.4 Monopolistic Competition.
Gray Computer, Inc., located in Colorado Springs, Colorado, is a privately held producer of high-speed electronic computers with immense storage capacity and computing capability. Although Gray's market is restricted to industrial users and a few large government agencies (e.g., Department of Health, NASA, and National Weather Service), the company has profitably exploited its market niche. Suppose a potential entrant into the market for supercomputers has asked you to evaluate the short- and long-run potential of this market. The following market demand and cost information has been developed:

$$P = \$54 - \$1.5Q$$
$$MR = \partial TR/\partial Q = \$54 - \$3Q$$
$$TC = \$200 + \$6Q + \$0.5Q^2$$
$$MC = \partial TC/\partial Q = \$6 + \$1Q$$

where P is price, Q is units measured by the number of supercomputers, MR is marginal revenue, TC is total costs including a normal rate of return, MC is marginal cost, and all figures are in millions of dollars.

A. Assume that these demand and cost data are descriptive of Gray's historical experience. Calculate output, price, and economic profits earned by Gray Computer as a monopolist. What is the point price elasticity of demand at this output level?

B. Calculate the range within which a long-run equilibrium price–output combination would be found for individual firms if entry eliminated Gray's economic profits. (Note: Assume that the cost function is unchanged and that the high-price/low-output solution results from a parallel shift in the demand curve while the low-price/high-output solution results from a competitive equilibrium.)

C. Assume that the point price elasticity of demand calculated in part A is a good estimate of the relevant arc price elasticity. What is the potential overall market size for supercomputers?

D. If no other near-term entrants are anticipated, should your company enter the market for supercomputers? Why or why not?

P13.5 Cartel Equilibrium.
Assume the Hand Tool Manufacturing Industry Trade Association recently published the following estimates of demand and supply relations for hammers:

$$Q_D = 60,000 - 10,000P \qquad \text{(Demand)}$$
$$Q_S = 20,000P \qquad \text{(Supply)}$$

A. Calculate the perfectly competitive industry equilibrium price–output combination.

B. Now assume that the industry output is organized into a cartel. Calculate the industry price–output combination that will maximize profits for cartel members. (Hint: As a cartel, industry $MR = \$6 - \$0.0002Q$.)

C. Compare your answers to parts A and B. Calculate the price/output effects of the cartel.

P13.6 Cournot Equilibrium. VisiCalc, the first computer spreadsheet program, was released to the public in 1979. A year later, introduction of the DIF format made spreadsheets much more popular because they could now be imported into word processing and other software programs. By 1983, Mitch Kapor used his previous programming experience with VisiCalc to found Lotus Corp. and introduce the wildly popular Lotus 1-2-3 spreadsheet program. Despite enormous initial success, Lotus 1-2-3 stumbled when Microsoft Corp. introduced Excel with a much more user-friendly graphical interface in 1987. Today, Excel dominates the market for spreadsheet applications software.

To illustrate the competitive process in markets dominated by few firms, assume that a two-firm duopoly dominates the market for spreadsheet application software, and that the firms face a linear market demand curve

$$P = \$1,250 - Q$$

where P is price and Q is total output in the market (in thousands). Thus $Q = Q_A + Q_B$. For simplicity, also assume that both firms produce an identical product and have no fixed costs and marginal cost $MC_A = MC_B = \$50$. In this circumstance, total revenue for firm A is

$$TR_A = \$1,250Q_A - Q_A{}^2 - Q_AQ_B$$

Marginal revenue for firm A is

$$MR_A = \partial TR_A / \partial Q_A = \$1,250 - \$2Q_A - Q_B$$

Similar total revenue and marginal revenue curves hold for firm B.

A. Derive the output–reaction curves for firms A and B.

B. Calculate the Cournot market equilibrium price–output solutions.

P13.7 Stackelberg Model. Imagine that a two-firm duopoly dominates the market for spreadsheet application software for PCs. Also assume that the firms face a linear market demand curve

$$P = \$1,250 - Q$$

where P is price and Q is total output in the market (in thousands). Thus $Q = Q_A + Q_B$. For simplicity, also assume that both firms produce an identical product and have no fixed costs and marginal cost $MC_A = MC_B = \$50$. In this circumstance, total revenue for firm A is

$$TR_A = \$1,250Q_A - Q_A{}^2 - Q_AQ_B$$

Marginal revenue for firm A is

$$MR_A = \partial TR_A / \partial Q_A = \$1{,}250 - \$2Q_A - Q_B$$

Similar total revenue and marginal revenue curves hold for firm B.

A. Calculate the Stackelberg market equilibrium price–output solutions.

B. How do the Stackelberg equilibrium price–output solutions differ from those suggested by the Cournot model? Why?

P13.8 Bertrand Equilibrium. Coke and Pepsi dominate the U.S. soft-drink market. Together, they account for about 75 percent of industry sales. Suppose the quantity of Coke demanded depends upon the price of Coke (P_C) and the price of Pepsi (P_P)

$$Q_C = 15 - 2.5P_C + 1.25P_P$$

where output (Q) is measured in millions of 24-packs per month, and price is the wholesale price of a 24-pack. For simplicity, assume average costs are constant and $AC = MC = X$ dollars per unit. In that case, the total profit and change in profit with respect to own price functions for Coke are

$$\pi_C = TR_C - TC_C = P_C Q_C - X Q_C = (P_C - X) Q_C$$
$$\partial \pi_C / \partial P_C = 15 - 5P_C + 1.25P_P + 2.5X$$

A. Set $\partial \pi_C / \partial P_C = 0$ to derive Coke's optimal price-response curve. Interpret your answer.

B. Calculate Coke's optimal price–output combination if Pepsi charges $5 and marginal costs are $2 per 24-pack.

P13.9 Kinked Demand Curves. Assume Safety Service Products (SSP) faces the following segmented demand and marginal revenue curves for its new infant safety seat:

1. Over the range from 0 to 10,000 units of output

$$P_1 = \$60 - Q$$
$$MR_1 = \partial TR_1 / \partial Q = \$60 - \$2Q$$

2. When output exceeds 10,000 units

$$P_2 = \$80 - \$3Q$$
$$MR_2 = \partial TR_2 / \partial Q = \$80 - \$6Q$$

The company's total and marginal cost functions are as follows:

$$TC = \$100 + \$20Q + \$0.5Q^2$$
$$MC = \partial TC / \partial Q = \$20 + \$1Q$$

where P is price (in dollars), Q is output (in thousands), MR is marginal revenue, TC is total cost, and MC is marginal cost, all in thousands of dollars.

A. Graph the demand, marginal revenue, and marginal cost curves.

B. How would you describe the market structure of the industry in which SSP operates? Explain why the demand curve takes the shape indicated previously.

C. Calculate price, output, and profits at the profit-maximizing activity level.

D. How much could marginal costs rise before the optimal price would increase? How much could they fall before the optimal price would decrease?

P13.10 Market Structure Measurement. In 2005, Federated Department Stores, Inc., proposed to acquire The May Department Stores Co., thereby combining the two largest chains in the United States of so-called traditional or conventional department stores. Conventional department stores typically anchor enclosed shopping malls, feature products in the midrange of price and quality, and sell a wide range of products. The proposed transaction would create high levels of concentration among conventional department stores in many metropolitan areas of the United States, and the merged firm would become the only conventional department store at certain of the 1,200 malls in the United States.

A. How is the cross-elasticity concept used to empirically define economic markets?

B. Explain how the government's finding that conventional department stores compete against specialty stores led them to approve the proposed merger.

CASE *Study*

Market Structure Analysis at Columbia Drugstores, Inc.

Demonstrating the tools and techniques of market structure analysis is made difficult by the fact that firm competitive strategy is largely based upon proprietary data. Firms jealously guard price, market share, and profit information for individual markets. Nobody should expect Target, for example, to disclose profit and loss statements for various regional markets or on a store-by-store basis. Competitors like Wal-Mart would love to have such information available; it would provide a ready guide for their own profitable market entry and store expansion decisions.

To see the process that might be undertaken to develop a better understanding of product demand conditions, consider the hypothetical example of Columbia Drugstores, Inc., based in Seattle, Washington. Assume Columbia operates a chain of 30 drugstores in the Pacific Northwest. During recent years, the company has become increasingly concerned with the long-run implications of competition from a new type of competitor, the so-called superstore.

To measure the effects of superstore competition on current profitability, Columbia asked management consultant Peter Parker to

continued

conduct a statistical analysis of the company's profitability in its various markets. To net out size-related influences, profitability was measured by Columbia's gross profit margin, or earnings before interest and taxes divided by sales. Columbia provided proprietary company profit, advertising, and sales data covering the last year for all 30 outlets, along with public trade association and Census Bureau data concerning the number and relative size distribution of competitors in each market, among other market characteristics.

As a first step in the study, Parker decided to conduct a regression-based analysis of the various factors thought to affect Columbia's profitability. The first is the relative size of leading competitors in the relevant market, measured at the Standard Metropolitan Statistical Area (SMSA) level. Given the pricing, marketing, and average-cost advantages that accompany large relative size, Columbia's market share, MS, in each area is expected to have a positive effect on profitability. The market concentration ratio, CR, measured as the combined market share of the four largest competitors in any given market, is expected to have a negative effect on Columbia's profitability given the stiff competition from large, well-financed rivals. Of course, the expected negative effect of high concentration on Columbia profitability contrasts with the positive influence of high concentration on industry profits that is sometimes observed.

Both capital intensity, K/S, measured by the ratio of the book value of assets to sales, and advertising intensity, A/S, measured by the advertising-to-sales ratio, are expected to exert positive influences on profitability. Given that profitability is measured by Columbia's gross profit margin, the coefficient on capital intensity measured Columbia's return on tangible investment. Similarly, the coefficient on the advertising variable measures the profit effects of advertising. Growth, GR, measured by the geometric mean rate of change in total disposable income in each market, is expected to have a positive influence on Columbia's profitability, because some disequilibrium in industry demand and supply conditions is often observed in rapidly growing areas. Columbia's proprietary information is shown in Table 13.5.

Finally, to gauge the profit implications of superstore competition, Parker used a "dummy" (or binary) variable where $S = 1$ in each market in which Columbia faced superstore competition and $S = 0$ otherwise. The coefficient on this variable measures the average profit rate effect of superstore competition. Given the vigorous nature of superstore price competition, Parker expects the superstore coefficient to be both negative and statistically significant, indicating a profit-limiting influence. The Columbia profit-margin data and related information used in Parker's statistical analysis are given in Table 13.5. Regression model estimates for the determinants of Columbia's profitability are shown in Table 13.6:

A. Describe the overall explanatory power of this regression model, as well as the relative importance of each continuous variable.

B. Based on the importance of the binary or dummy variable that indicates superstore competition, do superstores pose a serious threat to Columbia's profitability?

C. What factors might Columbia consider in developing an effective competitive strategy to combat the superstore influence?

continued

Table 13.5 Profit Margin and Market Structure Data for Columbia Drug Stores, Inc.

Store No.	Profit- Margin	Market Share	Concentration	Capital Intensity	Advertising Intensity	Growth	Superstor ($S = 1$ if present)
1	15	25	75	10.0	10.0	7.5	0
2	10	20	60	7.5	10.0	2.5	1
3	15	40	70	7.5	10.0	5.0	0
4	15	30	75	15.0	12.5	5.0	0
5	15	50	75	10.0	12.5	0.0	0
6	20	50	70	10.0	12.5	7.5	1
7	15	50	70	7.5	10.0	0.0	1
8	25	40	60	12.5	15.0	5.0	0
9	20	10	40	10.0	12.5	5.0	0
10	10	30	60	10.0	12.5	0.0	0
11	15	20	60	12.5	12.5	7.5	1
12	10	30	75	12.5	10.0	2.5	0
13	15	50	75	7.5	10.0	5.0	0
14	10	20	75	7.5	12.5	2.5	0
15	10	10	50	7.5	10.0	2.5	0
16	20	30	60	15.0	12.5	2.5	0
17	15	30	50	7.5	12.5	5.0	1
18	20	40	70	7.5	12.5	5.0	0
19	10	10	60	12.5	10.0	2.5	0
20	15	20	70	5.0	12.5	7.5	0
21	20	20	40	7.5	10.0	7.5	0
22	15	10	50	15.0	10.0	5.0	1
23	15	40	40	7.5	12.5	5.0	1
24	10	30	50	5.0	7.5	0.0	0
25	20	40	70	15.0	12.5	5.0	0
26	15	40	70	12.5	10.0	5.0	1
27	10	20	75	7.5	10.5	2.5	0
28	15	10	60	12.5	12.5	5.0	0
29	10	30	75	5.0	7.5	2.5	0
30	10	20	75	12.5	12.5	0.0	0
Average	14.7	28.8	63.5	9.8	11.3	3.9	0.3

continued

Table 13.6 Determinants of Profit Margins for Columbia Drug Stores, Inc. NAICS Data is Available at the U.S., State and Local Levels

Independent Variable (1)	Coefficient Estimate (2)	Standard error of Coefficient Estimate (3)	t Statistic (4) = (2)/(3)
Intercept	6.155	3.712	1.66
Market Share	0.189	0.037	5.06
Concentration	−0.156	0.041	−3.77
Capital Intensity	0.337	0.147	2.30
Advertising Intensity	0.619	0.276	2.24
Growth	0.854	0.178	4.81
Superstore	−2.460	1.010	−2.44

$R^2 = 77.7\%$

F statistic = 13.38

SEE = 2.1931%

SELECTED REFERENCES

Adams, Robert M., Kenneth P. Brevoort, and Elizabeth K. Kiser. "Who Competes with Whom? The Case of Depository Institutions." *Journal of Industrial Economics* 55, no. 1 (March, 2007): 141–167.

Aguirregabiria, Victor, Pedro Mira, and Hernan Roman. "An Estimable Dynamic Model of Entry, Exit, and Growth in Oligopoly Retail Markets." *American Economic Review* 97, no. 2 (May, 2007): 449–454.

Bertrand, Marianne, Antoinette Schoar, and David Thesmar. "Banking Deregulation and Industry Structure: Evidence from the French Banking Reforms of 1985." *Journal of Finance* 62, no. 2 (April, 2007): 597–628.

Cohen, Andrew M. and Michael J. Mazzeo. "Market Structure and Competition among Retail Depository Institutions." *Review of Economics and Statistics* 89, no. 1 (February, 2007): 60–74.

Duffie, Darrell, Leandro Saita, and Ke Wang. "Multi-Period Corporate Default Prediction with Stochastic Covariates." *Journal of Financial Economics* 83, no. 3 (March, 2007): 635–665.

Duflo, Esther and Rohini Pande. "Dams." *Quarterly Journal of Economics* 122, no. 2 (May, 2007): 601–646.

Duranton, Gilles. "Urban Evolutions: The Fast, the Slow, and the Still." *American Economic Review* 97, no. 1 (March, 2007): 197–221.

Ghironi, Fabio and Marc J. Melitz. "Trade Flow Dynamics with Heterogeneous Firms." *American Economic Review* 97, no. 2 (May, 2007): 356–361.

Giaccotto, Carmelo, Gerson M. Goldberg, and Shantaram P. Hegde. "The Value of Embedded Real Options: Evidence from Consumer Automobile Lease Contracts." *Journal of Finance* 62, no. 1 (February, 2007): 411–445.

Grossmann, Volker. "Firm Size and Diversification: Multiproduct Firms in Asymmetric Oligopoly." *International Journal of Industrial Organization* 25, no. 1 (February, 2007): 51–67.

Hendershott, Terrence and Mark S. Seasholes. "Market Maker Inventories and Stock Prices." *American Economic Review* 97, no. 2 (May, 2007): 210–214.

Hennessy, Christopher A., Amnon Levy, and Toni M. Whited. "Testing Q Theory with Financing Frictions." *Journal of Financial Economics* 83, no. 3 (March, 2007): 691–717.

Lichtenberg, Frank R. "The Impact of New Drugs on US Longevity and Medical Expenditure, 1990–2003: Evidence from Longitudinal, Disease-Level Data." *American Economic Review* 97, no. 2 (May, 2007): 438–443.

Spector, David. "Bundling, Tying, and Collusion." *International Journal of Industrial Organization* 25, no. 3 (June, 2007): 575–581.

Wang, X. Henry and Jingang Zhao. "Welfare Reductions from Small Cost Reductions in Differentiated Oligopoly." *International Journal of Industrial Organization* 25, no. 1 (February, 2007): 173–185.

Game Theory and Competitive Strategy

The most famous inference from Adam Smith's *Wealth of Nations* is that as each of us seeks our own personal gain we are led by an "invisible hand" to promote the overall good of society. Because this compelling idea is a cornerstone of economic theory, economists and mathematicians have long been fascinated by instances when the pursuit of rational self-interest does not lead to mutual well-being. Starting with the *Theory of Games and Economic Behavior*, a textbook published in 1944 by mathematician John von Neumann and economist Oskar Morgenstern, a new and exciting interdisciplinary field of game theory has evolved to study how independent rational self-interest can lead to sub-optimal group results. Many students are briefly familiar with game theory, if only through Russell Crowe playing the role of game theorist John Forbes Nash, Jr., in the film *A Beautiful Mind*. Nash made astonishing discoveries early in his career about the way people make decisions, and later received the Nobel Prize in economics. Today, the theory of games is used to set competitive strategy in business, settle civil litigation and arbitration disputes, and devise effective terrorist-fighting strategies that require cooperation among sovereign governments.

This chapter shows how game theory can be used to improve strategic decision making in competitive situations where the appropriate course of action depends upon the choices made by others. Determining the best course of action often requires thinking through an opponent's options, aims, and strategies.[1]

GAME THEORY BASICS

Game theory is a general framework to help decision making when payoffs depend on actions taken by others.

Types of Games

Game Theory
General framework to help decision making when payoffs depend on actions taken by others.

The theory of games, or **game theory** for short, is a method for the study of rational behavior by individuals and firms involved with interactive decision problems. In a game, several individual decision makers, called players or agents, strive to maximize their expected utility by choosing particular courses of action. Final payoffs depend on the player's own course of action and the courses of action chosen by other players. Game theory is applied during situations in which decision makers must take into account the reasoning of other decision makers. It has been used to determine the formation of business and political coalitions, the optimum price at which to sell products or services, the best site for a manufacturing plant, and even the behavior of certain species in the struggle for biological survival.

---

1   See Holman W. Jenkins, Jr., "You're Not Super Rich? You Lucked Out," *The Wall Street Journal Online*, October 17, 2007, http://online.wsj.com.

Zero-sum Game
One player's gain is another player's loss.

Positive-Sum Game
Game with the potential for mutual gain.

Negative-Sum Game
Game with the potential for mutual loss.

Cooperative Game
Game in which the strategies of the participants are coordinated.

In economics and business, game theory seeks to logically determine the strategies that individuals and firms should take to secure the best outcomes for themselves in a wide array of competitive circumstances. All economic and business games share the common feature of interdependence. In competitive games, the outcome for each firm depends upon the strategies conducted by all competitors. Many such interactions are **zero-sum games.** In a zero-sum game, one player's gain is another player's loss. In the options market, for example, any profit recorded by the buyer of an option is exactly matched by the loss suffered by the seller of that option. The only way for the seller of an option to gain is by having the buyer record a loss. In many other game-theory situations, there is the potential for mutual gain or mutual loss. If parties are engaged in a game that holds the potential for mutual gain, it is called a **positive-sum game.** When conflict holds the potential for mutual loss, it is called a **negative-sum game.** Early game theory research focused upon pure conflict and individual decisions in zero-sum games, or **cooperative games** where joint action is favored. More recently, game theory research has tended to focus on games that are neither zero-sum nor purely cooperative, but involve elements of both competition and cooperation.

Role of Interdependence

Sequential Game
Each player moves in succession.

Look Ahead and Extrapolate Back
General principle for players in a sequential game is to anticipate rational countermoves in initial decisions.

Simultaneous-Move Game
Players move without specific knowledge of countermoves by other players.

The essence of a game is the interdependence of player strategies. In a **sequential game,** each player moves in succession, and each player is aware of all prior moves. The general principle for players in a sequential game is to **look ahead and extrapolate back.** Each player in a sequential game makes moves based on the assumption that subsequent players will respond to any earlier move in a rational fashion. By anticipating how subsequent players will respond to earlier moves, players anticipate the resulting sequence of moves made by competing players. In business decision making, firms make their best strategic decision based on the premise that their initial decision will trigger a sequence of rational decision responses from competitors. In a **simultaneous-move game,** players act at the same point in time and must make their initial moves in isolation without any direct knowledge of moves made by other players.

Sequential games that end after a finite sequence of moves can be solved completely, at least in principle. Simple sequential games, like the children's game of tic-tac-toe, can be solved easily. Solving more complex sequential games, like chess, involve millions of calculations and becomes daunting, even with high-speed computers. In practice, when the solution to sequential games is overly complex, players form strategies for a limited number of future moves and try to evaluate resulting positions on the basis of experience. In contrast to the logical chain of reasoning that leads to a predictable conclusion for sequential games, the solution for simultaneous games depends upon a rational prediction of the best response by other players to prior moves.

Equilibrium Outcome
Payoff allocation that cannot be improved by unilateral action.

Game-Theory Strategy
Game theory plan of action designed to achieve a specific goal.

In any strategic game, various strategies result in different payoffs. Any given allocation of payoffs is called an outcome of the game. A given allocation of payoffs is called an **equilibrium outcome** if the payoff to no player can be improved by unilateral action. In other words, a given allocation of payoffs is an equilibrium outcome provided that no player can gain from unilaterally switching to another **game-theory strategy.** Only equilibrium outcomes are reasonable and stable outcomes for games because they represent the best possible outcome under a given set of conditions. Outside equilibrium, at least one player can improve its position by changing strategies. An implicit assumption of game theory is that rational players are able to anticipate the equilibrium calculations of any other player. As such, non-equilibrium outcomes are anticipated and thwarted by the look ahead and extrapolate back principle.

Strategic Considerations

Firms often use threats and promises to alter the expectations and actions of other firms. To succeed, threats and promises must be credible. Game theory shows that it can be in a firm's best interest to reduce its own freedom of future action. For example, Intel Corp. is a dominant firm in the rapidly growing market for microprocessors used in personal computers and a wide range of intelligent electronics. By building productive capacity ahead of the growth in market demand, Intel strongly signals to competitors its intention to fight aggressively to maintain market share. In favoring production facilities that feature large capital commitments and low production costs, Intel signals competitors that it will be a fierce competitor for new business. By vastly outspending its rivals, Intel has been able to continue and extend its near monopoly position.

To successfully implement game theory concepts, decision makers must understand the benefits to be obtained from concealing or revealing useful information. In card playing, each player knows something that others do not: the cards held in one's own playing hand. In business, firms know the strength of their own commitment to offer a market-beating price, superior service, or top-notch quality. Other firms can only guess. Because actions speak louder than words, card players and firms must know when to bluff and when to credibly signal their true intentions. Firms offer extended warranties and money-back guarantees as credible signals to the consumer that they are producing high-quality products. Recent advances in game theory have succeeded in describing and prescribing appropriate strategies in situations that involve conflict and cooperation.

Managerial Application 14.1

Asymmetric Information

A key assumption of perfectly competitive markets is that all buyers and sellers have free and complete access to product quality and price information. Markets become imperfectly competitive when this key assumption is violated. In economics, information asymmetry occurs when one party to a transaction has more or better information than the other party. In most instances, it is presumed that the seller knows more about the product than the buyer, but the buyer can sometimes know more than the seller.

Situations where the seller typically has better information than the buyer include used-car salespeople, stockbrokers, real estate brokers, and life insurance agents. During recent years, for example, predatory lending practices have been alleged in the U.S. sub-prime lending market due to asymmetric information between mortgage brokers and low-income homeowners. When financially unsophisticated individuals turn to greedy mortgage companies or con artists for financial assistance, abusive lending practices can result. In some instances, desperate homeowners were qualified using no documentation loans (sometimes called "liar loans")

that allowed them to qualify for adjustable-rate home mortgages on the basis of grossly overstated family income and financial resources. When mortgage rates adjusted upward, many unsophisticated homeowners lost their homes and the unscrupulous professionals who "helped them" end up profiting.

Examples of situations where the buyer can have better information than the seller include estate sales, rummage sales, flea markets, or the market for health insurance. Problems tied to adverse selection occur when missing information allows the informed party to take advantage of the uninformed party. For example, if an employer seeks to attract a talented and hard-working workforce by offering generous health insurance benefits, there can be the unintended consequence of attracting workers with significant hidden medical problems. In addition, people with health problems or preferences for high-risk lifestyles are attracted to companies with generous health benefits.

See: Michael Connolly, "Signs of More Subprime Pain Could Cool Markets," *The Wall Street Journal Online*, October 30, 2007, http://online.wsj.com.

PRISONER'S DILEMMA

The classic Prisoner's Dilemma game illustrates the difficulty of making decisions under uncertainty, and shows how interdependence among decision makers can breed conflict.

Classic Riddle

Payoff Matrix
Player rewards from selected strategies.

A game is described by listing the alternative choices or strategies available to each player. In the case of a simple two-player game, the strategies available to the first player form the first and second row in a two-row, two-column table. Strategies available to the second player form the first and second column. Because such a table describes the payoffs earned by both parties following their selection of various strategies, this table is commonly referred to as a **payoff matrix.** In a simple, two-player game, the first player's strategy is to select a given row based upon a rational assessment of which column strategy the opposing player will choose. The second player's strategy is to choose a given column of the table based upon a rational assessment of which row strategy the opposing player will choose. Each cell of the payoff matrix identifies two numbers representing the payoff to the first and second player, respectively. Neither player can unilaterally choose a given cell outcome from the payoff matrix. Cell outcomes result from the interdependent strategies chosen by both players.

One-Shot Game
One-time interaction.

Repeated Game
Ongoing interaction.

Prisoner's Dilemma
Famous simultaneous-move one-shot game showing that counterpart uncertainty leads to suboptimal outcome.

A game-theory strategy is a decision rule that describes the action taken by a decision maker at any point in time. In a **one-shot game,** the underlying interaction between competitors occurs only once; in a **repeated game,** there is ongoing interaction between competitors. A simple introduction to game-theory strategy is provided by the most famous of all simultaneous-move one-shot games: The so-called **Prisoner's Dilemma.** Suppose two suspects, Bonnie and Clyde, are jointly accused of committing a specific crime, say the falsification of accounting records at a major publicly traded company. Furthermore, assume that conviction of either suspect on the key charge cannot be secured without a confession by one or both suspects that admits their own guilt and implicates the other party. As shown in Table 14.1, Bonnie can choose to either "Don't Confess" ("Up") and *cooperate* with the other suspect or "Confess" ("Down") and *defect* by implicating Clyde. Clyde can choose to either "Don't Confess" ("Left") and *cooperate* with the other suspect or "Confess" ("Right") and *defect* by implicating the other suspect. In Table 14.1, Bonnie can choose a preferred row of outcomes, and Clyde can choose a preferred column of outcomes. While each suspect can control the range of sentencing outcomes, neither can choose an ultimate outcome.

If neither Bonnie nor Clyde confesses, the prosecutor will be able to obtain a conviction on lesser charges only, and both will receive modest 2-year prison terms. If only one suspect confesses, turns state's evidence, and implicates the other, then the one confessing will get 6 months in jail and the implicated party will receive the harsh sentence of 10 years in prison. If both suspects confess, then each will receive a stiff 5-year sentence. If both suspects are held in isolation, neither knows what the other will do, and a classic conflict-of-interest situation is created.

Dominant Strategy
Decision that gives the best result for either party regardless of the action taken by the other.

In this situation, the **dominant strategy** that creates the best result for either suspect regardless of the action taken by the other is to confess and implicate the other suspect. Both would be better off if they could be assured that the other would not confess, since if neither confesses both would receive relatively light sentences of 2 years in jail. However, in failing to confess, each would be exposed to the risk that the other will confess. By not confessing they could receive the harsh sentence of 10 years in prison. This uncertainty

Table 14.1 Classic Prisoner's Dilemma Payoff Matrix

		Suspect #2: "Clyde"	
	Confession Strategy	**Don't Confess ("Left")**	**Confess ("Right")**
Suspect #1 : "Bonnie"	**Don't Confess ("Up")**	Bonnie gets 2 years, Clyde gets 2 years	Bonnie gets 10 years, Clyde gets 6 months
	Confess ("Down")	Bonnie gets 6 months, Clyde gets 10 years	Bonnie gets 5 years, Clyde gets 5 years

creates the prisoner's dilemma. Confessing is a dominant strategy for both suspects because each suspect can reduce their expected sentence by confessing. Unfortunately for the suspects involved, this rational choice leads to a poor joint outcome whereby both confess and each receives the stiff 5-year sentence. This is the core of the prisoner's dilemma. Independent rational behavior leads to a sub-optimal outcome for all. Rational behavior converts them from suspects into prisoners!

Secure Strategy
Decision that guarantees the best possible outcome given the worst possible scenario.

A **secure strategy** sometimes called the maximin strategy, guarantees the best possible outcome given the worst possible scenario. In this case, the worst possible scenario for each suspect is that they remain quiet but the other suspect confesses and implicates them. Each suspect can avoid the worst possible outcome of receiving a harsh 10-year sentence only by choosing to confess. For each suspect, the secure strategy is to confess, thereby becoming a prisoner, because neither could solve the riddle posed by the prisoner's dilemma.

Business Application

Though the prisoner's dilemma is posed within the scope of a bargaining problem between two suspects, it has obvious practical applications in business. Competitors like Coca-Cola and Pepsi confront similar bargaining problems on a regular basis. Suppose each has to decide whether or not to offer discount prices.

In Table 14.2, Coca-Cola can choose a given row of profit outcomes by offering a discount price ("Up") or regular price ("Down"). Pepsi can choose a given column of profit outcomes by choosing to offer a discount price ("Left") or regular price ("Right"). Neither firm can choose a specific profit outcome; the profit outcome received by each firm depends upon the pricing strategies of both firms. While each company can control the range of profit outcomes, neither can unilaterally choose a profit outcome. Notice that Coca-Cola will earn more profit with a discount-price strategy regardless of whether Pepsi chooses a discount-price or regular-price strategy. Similarly, Pepsi will make more profit with a discount-price strategy irrespective of what Coca-Cola chooses to do. Therefore, the dominant strategy that creates the best result for either company regardless of the pricing action taken by the other is to adopt a discount-price strategy.

Both Coca-Cola and Pepsi would be better off if they charged regular prices and could be assured that their competitor would do the same. However, by charging regular prices each company is confronted with the possibility of earning substandard profits if its competitor decides on a discount-price strategy. This uncertainty creates a

Table 14.2 Prisoner's Dilemma Faced by *Coca-Cola* and *Pepsi*			
		Pepsi	
	Pricing Strategy	**Discount Price ("Left")**	**Regular Price ("Right")**
Coca-Cola	**Discount Price ("Up")**	*Coca-Cola* earns $4 billion, *Pepsi* earns $2 billion	*Coca-Cola* earns $8 billion, *Pepsi* earns $1 billion
	Regular Price ("Down")	*Coca-Cola* earns $2 billion, *Pepsi* earns $5 billion	*Coca-Cola* earns $6 billion, *Pepsi* earns $4 billion

prisoner's dilemma for Coca-Cola and Pepsi. Discount pricing is a dominant strategy for both companies because each company can increase expected profits by offering discount prices. Unfortunately for the companies involved, this rational choice leads to a poor joint outcome whereby both charge discount prices and earn less than optimal profits. The prisoner's dilemma in business is that independent rational behavior leads to a suboptimal profit outcome for competitors. Rational behavior prevents them from earning maximum profits.

In the case of Coca-Cola, the worst possible profit scenario of $2 billion results when it charges regular prices while Pepsi charges discount prices. The only secure means Coca-Cola has of avoiding the possibility of a meager $2 billion profit is to adopt a discount-price strategy. In the case of Pepsi, the worst possible profit scenario of $1 billion results when it charges regular prices while Coca-Cola charges discount prices. The only secure means Pepsi has of avoiding the possibility of meager profits of $1 billion is to also adopt a discount-price strategy. For both Coca-Cola and Pepsi, the secure strategy is to offer discount prices, thereby assuring consumers of bargain prices and themselves of modest profits of $4 billion and $2 billion, respectively. Each would be better off if both adopted a regular-price strategy, but the risk of low-profit outcomes precludes that possibility.

Broad Implications

The Prisoner's Dilemma game fascinates game theorists for a variety of reasons. First among these is the fact that it is a simple representation of a variety of important conflict situations. In public goods problems, Prisoner's Dilemma strategies might be labeled "contribute to the common good" or "behave selfishly." It might be best for the common good to build a bridge, but each individual is better off if someone else can be convinced to pay for it. The Prisoner's Dilemma is often used to describe decision problems involving positive and negative externalities. Similarly, the Prisoner's Dilemma describes a wide variety of business decisions made where the resulting payoff depends upon competitor responses. Entry/exit, high-price/low-price, high-quality/low-quality decisions can all be better understood within the context of the Prisoner's Dilemma.

Another significant feature of the Prisoner's Dilemma is that logical reasoning makes clear the best strategies for rational decision makers. No matter what an individual player believes about the behavior of the counterparty in a Prisoner's Dilemma game, the rational decision is to confess (or "defect") and thereby insure that both players bear significant costs. A dilemma is involved because rational behavior results in each player bearing much more in the way of prison time than would be true if neither party confessed. In a Prisoner's Dilemma game, the first-best solution of neither party confessing is thwarted by the risks involved with a "not confess" (or "cooperate") strategy. This conflict between the pursuit of individual goals and the common good is at the heart of many game-theory problems.

And finally, the Prisoner's Dilemma is important because it is clear that the way the game is played would change dramatically if the game were to be repeated, or if the players were allowed to collude and interact with each other. If neither suspect confesses and both receive light sentences, the probability of future cooperation is apt to increase. Similarly, if profits soar because neither Coca-Cola nor Pepsi offer discount prices, the possibility of tacit or overt price collusion is bound to rise. Repetition raises the possibility of future rewards or punishment for prior behavior. Theory and practice show that when games are repeated, the potential for cooperation or collusion increases.

NASH EQUILIBRIUM

Games result in stable outcomes if no player has an incentive to change their decision given the strategic choices made by other players.

Nash Equilibrium Concept

Nash Equilibrium
Set of decision strategies where no player can improve through a unilateral change in strategy.

In Table 14.2, each firm's secure strategy is to offer a discount price regardless of the other firm's actions. This outcome is called a **Nash equilibrium** because, given the strategy of its competitor, neither firm can improve its own payoff by unilaterally changing its own strategy. Given that Pepsi has chosen a discount-pricing strategy, Coca-Cola too would decide to offer discount prices. When Pepsi offers discount prices, Coca-Cola can earn profits of $4 billion rather than $2 billion by also offering discount prices as opposed to regular prices. Similarly, when Coca-Cola offers discount prices, Pepsi can earn maximum profits of $2 billion versus $1 billion per year, by also offering discount prices as opposed to regular prices. It is important to recognize that the discount-pricing Nash equilibrium for Pepsi and Coca-Cola also represents a dominant strategy equilibrium. Indeed, every dominant strategy equilibrium is a Nash equilibrium. However, the reverse does not hold. The Nash equilibrium concept is broader than the concept of dominant strategy equilibrium. Nash equilibrium can be present in game-theory situations in which there is no dominant strategy equilibrium.

It is worth emphasizing that the discount-pricing Nash equilibrium is inferior from the firms' viewpoint to a collusive outcome where both competitors agreed to charge regular prices. Nash equilibrium profits are clearly less than if they colluded and both charged regular prices. As seen in Table 14.2, Coca-Cola would earn $6 billion per year and Pepsi would earn $4 billion per year if both charged regular prices. Of course, if firms collude and agree to charge high prices, consumers are made worse off. This is why price collusion among competitors is illegal in the United States. Notice that if the firms agreed to collude and charge regular prices, joint profits of $10 billion per year would be maximized. However, this joint regular-price strategy is not a stable equilibrium. To see the instability of having both firms choose regular-price strategies, see how each firm has strong incentives to cheat on any covert or overt agreement to collude. If Pepsi chose a regular-price strategy, Coca-Cola could see profits jump from $6 billion to $8 billion per year by switching from a regular-price to a discount-price strategy. Similarly, if Coca-Cola chose a regular-price strategy, Pepsi could see profits jump from $4 billion to $5 billion per year by switching from a regular-price to a discount-price strategy. Both firms have strong incentives to cheat on any covert or overt agreement to charge high prices. Such situations are common and help explain the difficulty of maintaining cartel-like agreements.

In some instances, two-party games have no stable Nash equilibrium because a player's preferred strategy changes once the rival's strategy has been adopted. The classic case is where managers monitor worker performance. If a manager chooses to monitor worker performance, the worker will choose to perform as expected. However, given that a worker has chosen to perform as expected, there is no need for managerial monitoring. In such instances, both workers and managers have strong incentives to keep their planned moves secret. The lack of Nash equilibrium also provides incentives for **randomized strategies** whereby players flip a coin or otherwise randomly choose among available strategies in order to keep rivals from being able to predict strategic moves and countermoves.

Randomized Strategies
Haphazard actions to keep rivals from being able to predict strategic moves.

Nash Bargaining

Nash Bargaining
Where two competitors haggle over some item of value.

A **Nash bargaining** game is another application of the simultaneous-move, one-shot game. In Nash bargaining, two competitors or players "bargain" over some item of value. In a simultaneous-move, one-shot game, the players have only one chance to reach an agreement.

Suppose the board of directors specifies a $1 million profit-sharing pool provided that both management and workers can come to an agreement concerning how such profits are to be distributed. For simplicity, assume that this pool can be distributed only in amounts of $0, $500,000, and $1 million. If the sum of the amounts requested by each party total more than $1 million, neither party receives anything. If the sum of the amounts requested by each party total no more than $1 million, each party receives the amount requested.

Table 14.3 shows the nine possible outcomes from such a profit-sharing bargaining game. If the workers request $1 million, the only way that they would get any money at all is if management requests nothing. Similarly, if management requests $1 million, the only way they get money is if workers request nothing. If either party requests nothing, Nash equilibrium solutions are achieved when the other party requests the full $1 million. The ($1 million, $0) and ($0, $1 million) solutions are both Nash equilibriums.

Table 14.3 Nash Bargaining Over Profit-Pool Sharing

		Management		
	Request Strategy	$0 ("Left")	$500,000 ("Middle")	$1,000,000 ("Right")
Workers	$0 ("Top")	$0, $0	$0, $500,000	$0, $1,000,000
	$500,000 ("Middle")	$500,000, $0	$500,000, $500,000	$0, $0
	$1,000,000 ("Bottom")	$1,000,000, $0	$0, $0	$0, $0

However, suppose the workers request $500,000, then the Nash equilibrium response from management would be to also request $500,000. If management requests $500,000, then the Nash equilibrium response from workers would be to also request $500,000. The ($500,000, $500,000) payoff is also a Nash equilibrium. This game involves three Nash equilibriums out of nine possible solutions. In each Nash equilibrium, the entire profit-sharing pool is paid out. In the six remaining outcomes, some of the profit-sharing pool would not be distributed. In contemplating the bargaining process, workers are apt to note that a request for $0 is dominated by asking for either $500,000 or $1 million. If you do not ask for anything, you are sure to get nothing. Similarly, management will never do worse, and may do better, if it asks for something. As a result, the $0 request strategy is dominated for both parties and will tend not to be followed. Because a $0 request by either party is not likely, neither party is apt to request the full $1 million. In this case, the logical and rational request from each party is $500,000, or an equal 50/50 sharing of the profit pool.

INFINITELY REPEATED GAMES

Cooperation among competitors is possible if they interact on a continuous basis in a repeated game.

Role of Reputation

Infinitely Repeated Game
Game that is repeated over and over again without boundary or limit.

An **infinitely repeated game** is a competitive game that is repeated over and over again without boundary or limit. In an infinitely repeated game, firms receive sequential payoffs that shape current and future strategies. For example, in Table 14.2, both Coca-Cola and Pepsi might secretly agree to charge regular prices so long as the other party continues to do so. If neither firm cheats on such a collusive agreement, discounts will not be offered, and maximum profits will be earned. Although there is obvious risk involved with charging regular prices, there is also an obvious cost tied to charging discount prices. If each firm is convinced that the other will maintain regular prices, both will enjoy high profits. This resolve is increased if each firm is convinced that the other will quickly match any discount-pricing strategy. In fact, it is rational for colluding firms to quickly and severely punish colluding competitors who "cheat" by lowering prices.

While it is important to recognize that the repeat nature of competitor interactions can sometimes harm consumers, it is equally important to recognize that repetitive interactions in the marketplace can also be helpful to consumers. Repetitive interactions provide the necessary incentives for firms to produce high-quality goods. In any one-shot game, it would pay firms with high-quality reputations to produce low-cost or shoddy goods. In the real world, the ongoing interaction between firms and their customers provides incentives for firms to maintain product consistency. Both Coca-Cola and Pepsi have well-deserved reputations for providing uniformly high-quality soft drinks. They have invested millions of dollars in product development and quality control to ensure that consumers can depend upon the taste, smell, and feel of Coca-Cola and Pepsi products. Because the value of millions of dollars spent on brand-name advertising would be lost if product quality were to deteriorate, brand-name advertising is itself a type of quality assurance provided to customers of Coca-Cola and Pepsi. At Wal-Mart, *Satisfaction Guaranteed, or your money back,* is more than just a slogan. It is what separates

Wal-Mart from fly-by-night operators and low-quality discount stores. Customers of Mercedes-Benz depend upon that company's well-deserved reputation for producing high-quality cars and trucks. Like any written guarantee or insurance policy, repeat transactions in the marketplace give consumers the necessary confidence that they will get what they pay for.

Product Quality Games

There is an old saying in business: "If you fool me once, that's your fault. If you fool me twice, that's my fault." It stems from the fact that firms are involved in long-term relationships with customers, suppliers, and competitors. Consistency and reliability are cherished commodities. For example, Eddie Bauer opened his first retail store in Seattle, Washington, in 1920, and quickly established a reputation for delivering customer satisfaction. Eddie Bauer has become an enormously successful catalog retailer based on the slogan: *Every item we sell will give you complete satisfaction or you may return it for a full refund.* Like any honest company, Eddie Bauer makes mistakes. Despite its best efforts, poor-quality items sometimes make their way into the hands of disappointed customers. It is Eddie Bauer's response at such times that determines the sustainability of long-term customer relationships. In a one-shot game, Eddie Bauer would have an incentive to sell shoddy products, take the money, and run. The theory of infinitely repeated games can be used to show the desirability of maintaining a reputation for selling high-quality goods.

Consider the product-quality payoff matrix shown in Table 14.4. Assume these data pertain to a customer's catalog purchase. In a one-shot game, the Nash equilibrium is for the company to produce low-quality goods and for customers to shun these products ($0, $0). If the customer decided to order from the catalog, Eddie Bauer would choose to produce low-quality goods and earn $500 rather than the $150 derived from selling high-quality goods. Expecting low-quality goods, the customer will not choose to order because losing $0 is better than ordering low-quality goods and losing $500. In a one-shot game, Eddie Bauer is out of business.

In an infinitely repeated game, the situation changes dramatically for Eddie Bauer and other providers of high-quality goods. By establishing and maintaining a reputation for selling high-quality goods, customers will choose to buy because the $150 benefit obtained is greater than the $0 benefit associated with not buying. Although Eddie Bauer could cheat by offering low-quality goods and earn a one-time profit of $500 rather than the $150 associated with offering high-quality goods, this one-time benefit would come at the cost of losing all future profit-making opportunities. As a long-lived going concern, it doesn't pay to cheat customers. Even without government regulation or the threat of lawsuits, Eddie Bauer will adhere to its high-quality strategy.

Table 14.4 Product Quality Game

		Eddie Bauer	
	Quality Strategy	Low-Quality Goods ("Left")	High-Quality Goods ("Right")
Customer	Do Not Buy ("Up")	$0, $0	$0, −$500
	Buy ("Down")	−$500, $500	$150, $150

Managerial Application 14.2

The Market for Lemons

George Akerlof won the Nobel Prize in Economics based on research stemming from an oddly titled article, "The Market for Lemons: Quality Uncertainty and the Market Mechanism." Akerlof uses the used car market as a metaphor for the problem of quality uncertainty that can occur when sellers know more than buyers.

While there are high-quality used cars and defective used cars (or "lemons"), the prospective buyer of a given used car does not know beforehand whether it is of high quality or a lemon. Because the prospective buyer's best guess is that a typical used car is of average quality, the prospective buyer will only be willing to pay an amount equal to the price of a used car with average quality. As a result, owners of high-quality used cars will be unable to get a high enough price to make selling good used cars worthwhile, and they will not place high-quality vehicles on the used car market. The withdrawal of high-quality cars reduces the average quality of cars on the used car market, thereby causing prospective buyers to revise downward their expectations for any given used car. In turn, this motivates the owners of good-quality cars not to sell and so on. The ultimate result of such a process is that the used car market becomes a market for lemons, only vehicles of the lowest quality become available in the used car market.

Akerlof's research explains how low-quality goods can drive out high-quality goods in unregulated markets with asymmetric information. To combat the problem, the United States has a federal lemon law (the Magnuson-Moss Warranty Act) and state lemon laws provide remedies to consumers for automobiles that repeatedly fail to meet basic standards of quality and performance. Information freely available on the Internet helps buyers become better informed; buying from reputable dealers is also helpful. In all cases, the best advice is fairly simple: *Caveat emptor!* (*Buyer beware!*)

See: Jonathan Welch, "Getting the Best Price for Dad's Car," *The Wall Street Journal Online*, August 14, 2007, http://online.wsj.com.

FINITELY REPEATED GAMES

Some game-theory situations occur over a fixed period of time.

Uncertain Final Period

Finitely Repeated Game
Game that occurs only a limited number of times, or has limited duration in time.

Trigger Strategy
System of behavior that remains the same until another player takes some course of action that precipitates a different response.

A **finitely repeated game** takes place only a limited number of times, or has limited duration. If there is uncertainty about when a game will end, the conduct of a finitely repeated game mirrors an infinitely repeated game. To see this is the case, it is necessary to introduce the concept of a **trigger strategy.** A trigger strategy is a system of behavior that remains the same until another player takes some course of action that precipitates a different response.

Suppose Dell and Intel agree to a customer/supplier relationship strategy, as shown in Table 14.5. Dell computers are marketed with the logo "Intel Inside" signifying that Intel supplies Dell with microprocessors, a vital component. Assume that Dell agrees to use Intel microprocessors in its computers so long as Intel agrees not to market its own Intel brand of computers. If Intel breaks this supply agreement, it is understood that Dell will punish Intel by forever thereafter refusing to do business with Intel. If Intel breaks its supply agreement with Dell, such behavior triggers a "do not buy" response from Dell in every future period. So long as the supply agreement remains in place, Dell will earn $3 billion per year and Intel will earn $5 billion per year. If Intel breaks the supply agreement, Intel would earn $8 billion for one period while its new unsuspecting rival Dell would suffer a $3 billion loss. However, this one-time benefit for Intel is overwhelmed by the loss forever of the $5 billion per period benefit that would have been earned from maintaining the supply agreement with Dell.

Table 14.5 Supplier Strategy Game

Dell	Supplier Strategy	Intel	
		Intel Outside Strategy ("Left")	Intel Inside Strategy ("Right")
	Do Not Buy ("Up")	$1 billion, $1 billion	$2 billion, $3 billion
	Buy ("Down")	−$3 billion, $8 billion	$3 billion, $5 billion

In a finitely repeated game with an uncertain final period, and in infinitely repeated games, trigger strategies can be used to ensure that the costs of breaking agreements exceed any resulting benefits, where both costs and benefits are measured in present value terms.

End-of-Game Problem

What happens when participants know the end date of a game? To answer this question, remember that the general principle for players in any sequential game is to look ahead and extrapolate back to the decision point. By anticipating how subsequent players will respond to earlier moves, players anticipate resulting moves based on the premise that their initial decision will trigger a sequence of rational decision responses from other players. In business, how do you motivate managers and employees that are about to retire or quit?

End-of-Game Problem
Difficulty tied to inability to punish or reward final-period behavior.

Employers must be on guard against the **end-of-game problem.** The end-of-game problem stems from the fact that it becomes difficult to properly motivate managers and workers at the ends of their career. Young managers have lucrative future job opportunities both inside and outside the firm. These opportunities give younger workers powerful incentives for hard work and honest dealings with their current employer. Older managers enjoy no such future job opportunities and face correspondingly weaker incentives for hard work and honest dealings in their current employment. In the extreme, how do you motivate workers on their last day at work? This motivation problem is a classic example of a finitely repeated game. End date knowledge has a profound effect on the playing of the game. Finitely repeated games with a known end date become, in effect, one-shot games.

To illustrate, suppose a game is to be played on three successive days. After the second game, both players know that the game to be played on the third day will be the last game. After the third and final game, there is no subsequent opportunity to reward good final-game behavior, nor any means to punish bad final-game behavior. All players recognize that the third and final game is a one-shot game and use the look ahead and extrapolate back principle to adopt appropriate strategic behavior during prior games. In the third game, it is rational to expect one-shot game behavior. Because third-game behavior is known, the ability to discipline misbehavior in the second game is eliminated. Without the potential to discipline misbehavior, the second game also becomes a one-shot game. Similar reasoning results in the first-day game becoming a one-shot game as well. No matter how many games are involved, certain knowledge of the end date causes an unraveling of the potential to discipline misbehavior. Finitely repeated games with a known end date result in one-shot game behavior.

Savvy employers solve the end-of-game problem by using rewards or punishments that extend beyond the employment period. Employers are often asked to provide letters of recommendation to subsequent employers and can thereby punish workers who take advantage of the end-of-game problem. Police officers are modestly paid and often face strong temptation to accept bribes or give favors, especially late in their careers. To fight corruption, many cities require those convicted of corrupt behavior to forfeit all retirement pay and benefits. On Wall Street, firms typically require top managers to take a significant portion of total compensation in the form of pay tied to long-term stock-price appreciation. In some cases, managers cannot liquidate stock or employee stock options until several years after retirement. In these and other cases, employers have settled on simple means for solving the end-of-game problem: simply extend the game!

First-Mover Advantages

Multistage Games
Games where payoffs and strategy are shaped by the order in which various players make their moves.

First-Mover Advantage
Benefit earned by the player able to make the initial move in a sequential move or multistage game.

Payoffs and game strategy are often shaped by the order in which various players make their moves. Such games are called **multistage games** and involve special considerations. A **first-mover advantage** is a benefit earned by the player able to make the initial move in a sequential move or multistage game. In a multistage game, the timing of player moves becomes important.

For example, suppose a potential customer has identified a real bargain on a local used-car lot, and is willing to pay the full $7,500 asking price. Also suppose that this potential customer knows that this used-car dealer is commonly willing to discount the price of its cars by 10 percent for all-cash offers. This is a two-stage sequential bargaining game where the first mover is prone to make an all-or-none, take-it-or-leave-it offer. The second mover is able to accept or reject the offer. In such situations, the first mover earns a significant advantage.

This bargaining game is over the $750 amount of the hoped-for cash discount. If the potential customer gives the dealer a take-it-or-leave-it offer of $6,750, the dealer can decide to accept the offer and receive $6,750, or decline the offer and receive nothing. In such a situation, time is money because every day the car sits on the dealer's lot, bank financing charges increase costs and reduce the dealer's profit margin. If the dealer believes the potential customer's take-it-or-leave-it threat, the dealer will settle for $6,750. On the other hand, suppose the dealer tells the potential customer that another customer has plans to buy the car for $7,500, and the potential customer believes the dealer's threat to sell the car to someone else for $7,500. In this case, the dealer would enjoy a first-mover advantage, and the potential customer would be forced to pay the full asking price of $7,500.

In practice, multistage games and the assertion of first-mover advantages are complicated by the difficulty of making credible threats, especially between strangers. Without prior experience, how is the dealer or the potential customer able to judge the sincerity of any threats? If threats are not sincere, they simply represent the opening bid in an ongoing repeated game of uncertain duration.

GAME THEORY AND AUCTION STRATEGY

One of the most interesting uses of game theory is to analyze bidder strategy in auctions.

Auction Types

English Auction
Auction where the highest bidder wins.

The most familiar type of auction is an **English auction,** where an auctioneer keeps raising the price until a single highest bidder remains. The advantage of an English auction is that it is widely regarded as a fair and open process. It is an effective approach for obtaining high winning-bid prices. Because participants can see and hear what rivals are doing, bidders often act aggressively. In fact, winners sometimes overpay for their winning bids. The so-called **winner's curse** results when overly aggressive bidders pay more than the economic value of auctioned-off items. For example, participants in the bidding process for offshore oil properties in the Gulf of Mexico routinely seemed to overestimate the amount of oil to be found.

Winner's Curse
When overly aggressive bidders pay more than the economic value of auctioned-off items.

Another commonly employed auction method is a **sealed-bid auction,** where all bids are secret and the highest bid wins. Local and state governments, for example, employ the sealed-bid approach to build roads, to buy fuel for schools and government offices, and to procure equipment and general supplies. A compelling advantage of the sealed-bid approach is that it is relatively free from the threat of collusion because, at least ostensibly, no one knows what anyone else is doing. The downside to the approach is that it could yield less to the government when airwave space is auctioned off because the approach often encourages bidders to act cautiously.

Sealed-Bid Auction
All bids are secret and the highest bid wins.

A relatively rare sealed-bid auction method is a **Vickrey auction,** where the highest sealed bid wins, but the winner pays the price of the second highest bid. The reason for this design is that the technique tends to produce high bids because participants know beforehand that they will not be forced to pay the full amount of their winning bid. A disadvantage of the technique is that it creates the perception that the buyer is taking advantage of the seller by paying only the second highest price. Another uncommon auctioning method is the so-called reverse or **Dutch auction.** In a Dutch auction, the auctioneer keeps lowering a very high price until a winning bidder emerges. The winning bidder is the first participant willing to pay the auctioneer's price. A disadvantage of this approach is that bidders tend to act cautiously out of fear of overpaying for auctioned items.

Vickrey Auction
The highest sealed bid wins, but the winner pays the price of the second highest bid.

Dutch Auction
The winning bidder is the first participant willing to pay the auctioneer's price.

Public Policy Applications

Game theory and auction strategies are growing in popularity as effective tools for achieving public policy objectives. In 1993, for example, Congress gave the Federal Communications Commission (FCC) authority to use competitive bidding to allocate electromagnetic spectrum among multiple applicants. Electromagnetic spectrum covers a wide range of wavelengths used to transmit information by radio, television, cell phones, and other means. Prior to this legislation, the FCC relied upon hearings and lotteries to select a single licensee from a pool of applicants. The auction approach is intended to award licenses to those who will use them most effectively, reduce the average time from initial application to license grant, and give the general public a direct financial benefit from the award of licenses.

The FCC has conducted a host of auctions of licenses for electromagnetic spectrum. In the design of the auction process, the FCC has relied on advice from top game theorists at Stanford, Yale, and other leading universities. The agency has generally adopted a standard English auction in which the winner pays what it bids, and everyone can see all bids as they are made. Game theory research shows that open auctions stimulate bidding, whereas sealed auctions foster restraint for fear of needlessly paying too much.

Although the FCC initially favored auctioning off vital spectrum licenses all at once to make it easier for bidders to assemble efficient blocs of adjoining areas, this approach entails a nightmare of complexity. Bidders must be allowed some flexibility to withdraw bids when adjoining areas are sold to others, but if offers can be withdrawn easily the integrity of the process would suffer. A sequential auction, where areas are put up for bid one at a time, also denies participants the opportunity to bid more for economically efficient blocs of service areas.

Managerial Application 14.3

Wrigley's Success Formula

People have enjoyed chewing gum-like substances for a long time. From the Native Americans of New England, the early colonists learned to chew the gum-like resin that formed on spruce trees when the bark was cut. Lumps of spruce gum were sold in the eastern United States during the early 1800s, making it the first commercial chewing gum in the United States. Modern chewing gum began in the late 1860s when chicle was brought to this country and tried as a chewing gum ingredient. Chicle comes from the latex of the sapodilla tree, which grows in the tropical rain forests of Central America. It made possible a smooth, springy, satisfying chew and holds flavors longer and better. At the dawn of the twentieth century, modern chewing gum was well on its way to popularity.

This is when William Wrigley, Jr., came to Chicago from Philadelphia. His father sold Wrigley's Scouring Soap. As an extra incentive to merchants, Wrigley offered premiums. One of these premiums was baking powder. When baking powder proved to be more popular than soap, Wrigley switched to

the baking powder business. In 1892, Wrigley got the idea of offering two packages of chewing gum with each can of baking powder. Once again the premium—chewing gum—seemed more promising than the product it was supposed to promote. Wrigley began marketing chewing gum under his own name. His first two brands were Lotta and Vassar. Juicy Fruit and Spearmint came in 1893.

Wrigley built a loyal following with a simple motto: "Even in a little thing like a stick of gum, quality is important." Wrigley was also a pioneer in the use of advertising. He saw that consumer acceptance of Wrigley's gum could be built by telling people about the product through newspaper and magazine ads, outdoor posters, and other forms of advertising. For more than 100 years, quality products and relentless brand-name advertising has been Wrigley's success formula.

See: Home page information for Wrigley's can be found on the Internet, http://www.wrigley.com.

After considering a wide variety of options, the FCC has found that a modified sequential bidding approach assigns licenses more efficiently than either comparative hearings or lotteries. For additional information, see: http://wireless.fcc.gov/auctions/about/index.html.

COMPETITIVE STRATEGY

If competitor interactions are too complex to be modeled using game theory concepts, firms rely upon various competitive strategies to deal successfully with established and potential rivals.

Competitive Advantage

Competitive Advantage
Firm's unique or rare ability to create, distribute, or service products valued by customers.

Comparative Advantage
Nation's superior efficiency on a relative basis.

An effective competitive strategy in imperfectly competitive markets is based upon the firm's **competitive advantage,** a rare ability to create, distribute, or service products valued by customers. It is the business-world analog to the **comparative advantage** of nations that enjoy a relative advantage in the production of a given product. For example, when compared with the United States and Canada, Mexico enjoys a relative abundance of raw materials and cheap labor. Mexico is in a relatively good position to export agricultural products, oil, and finished goods that require unskilled labor to the United States and Canadian market. At the same time, the United States and Canada enjoy a relative abundance of highly educated people, capital goods, and investment resources.

The United States and Canada are in a relatively good position to export machine tools, computer equipment, education, and professional services to Mexico.

An effective competitive strategy in imperfectly competitive markets grows out of a sophisticated understanding of the rules of competition in a given line of business or industry. The ultimate aim of this strategy is to cope with or, better still, change those rules in the company's favor. To do so, managers must understand and contend with rivalry among existing competitors, entry of new rivals, threat of substitutes, bargaining power of suppliers, and the bargaining power of buyers. As shown in Figure 14.1, it is always helpful to consider the number and size distribution of competitors, degree of product differentiation, level of information available in the marketplace, and conditions of entry. In the business world, long-lasting above-normal rates of return require a sustainable competitive advantage that, by definition, cannot be easily duplicated.

Figure 14.1 Value Maximization Is a Complex Process

Value maximization is a complex process that involves an ongoing sequence of successful management decisions.

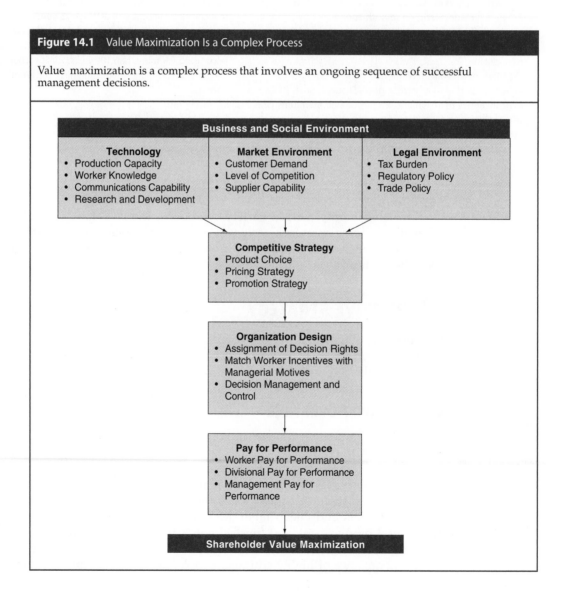

When Large Size Is a Disadvantage

Industries dominated by large firms tend to be those in which there are significant economies of scale, important advantages to vertical integration, and a prevalence of mass marketing. Huge organizations with sprawling plants emphasize large quantities of output at low production costs. Use of national media, especially TV advertising, is common. "Small is beautiful" in industries with diseconomies of scale, "just in time" assembly and manufacturing, and niche marketing that emphasizes the use of highly skilled individuals adept at personal selling. Small factories with flexible production schedules are common. Rather than emphasize long production runs, many smaller companies focus on product quality. Instead of the sometimes slow-to-respond hierarchical organizations of large companies, smaller companies feature "flat" organizations with quick, decentralized decision making and authority.

The villain sometimes encountered by large-scale firms is not any diseconomy of scale in the production process, but rather the burden that size places on effective management. Big means complex, and complexity often results in inefficiencies and bureaucratic snarls that can strangle effective communication. In the past, when foreign visitors wanted to experience firsthand the latest innovations in U.S. business and administrative practice, they found it mandatory to visit major corporations in Chicago, Detroit, New York, and Pittsburgh. Today, they are more apt to make stops along Boston's Route 128, in California's Silicon Valley, or within North Carolina's Research Triangle. In many industries, from electronics instrumentation to specialized steel, smaller companies have assumed positions of industry leadership. In fact, many large companies have found that better meeting customer needs requires a dramatic downsizing of the large-scale organization.

IBM, for example, has split into independent operating units that compete directly with each other to provide customers with the latest in computer equipment and software services. Mercedes-Benz, seeking to become more lean and agile like Japanese competitors, sold its Chrysler division. Exxon Mobil Corp. has divested domestic exploration and production operations to smaller independents that chop overhead and earn significant profits despite low volume. These examples suggest that some large corporations are going through a metamorphosis that will favor organizations especially adept at reallocating capital among nimble, entrepreneurial operating units.

PRICING STRATEGIES

In imperfectly competitive markets, firms define pricing strategies designed to reshape the competitive environment to their advantage.

Limit Pricing

Limit Pricing
Strategy to set less than monopoly prices in an effort to deter market entry by new and viable competitors.

Theory tells us that monopolists set profit-maximizing prices where $MR = MC$. Because the monopoly demand curve is downward sloping, the monopoly profit-maximizing price occurs at a point where $P > MR$, as shown in Figure 14.2. In monopoly equilibrium, stable above-normal profits are possible, and equal the area defined by the region $Q_M(P_M - AC_M)$. In practice, markets are dynamic and monopoly firms must remain sensitive to the possibility of entry by new and viable competitors. In some instances, it makes sense for monopoly firms to forego higher short-term profits if pricing moderation will forestall competitor entry and boost long-term profitability. **Limit pricing** is a competitive strategy to set less than maximum prices in an effort to deter market entry

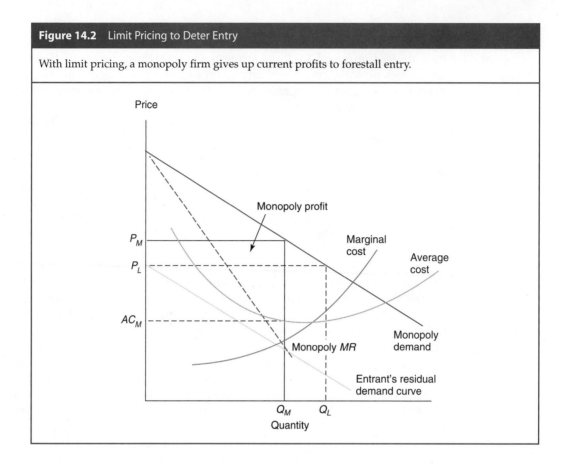

Figure 14.2 Limit Pricing to Deter Entry

With limit pricing, a monopoly firm gives up current profits to forestall entry.

by new and viable competitors. Limit pricing strategies are widely adopted by firms with pricing power as means for maintaining lead market positions, albeit with less than maximum short-term profits.

To illustrate, Figure 14.2 shows that the limit price P_L is lower than the monopoly price P_M and results in greater output, Q_L versus Q_M. If potential entrants believe that the incumbent monopolist will continue to sell Q_L during the post-entry period, then the potential entrant's residual demand curve is simply market demand minus the amount supplied by the monopoly incumbent. Notice that the entrant's residual demand curve begins at P_L because market demand minus the amount sold by the incumbent monopolist is zero at this point. In this case, the potential entrant's residual demand curve lies below the average cost curve at each and every point. Entry would bring economic losses and is precluded by the incumbent monopolist's limit pricing strategy. This assumes, of course, that the potential entrant has the same average cost capability as the incumbent monopolist. If the potential entrant had superior productive capability and lower average costs, profitable entry could still be possible despite the incumbent monopolist's limit pricing strategy. This is seldom the case, however. In most cases, monopolists have superior production capabilities and lower average costs. If potential entrants had superior production capability, how could one explain the creation of a monopoly in the first place?

Predatory Pricing
Pricing below marginal cost to knock out rivals and subsequently raising prices to obtain monopoly profits.

Predatory pricing is pricing below marginal cost in the hope of knocking out rival producers and subsequently raising prices to obtain monopoly profits. Like any limit pricing strategy, predatory pricing involves a trade-off between lower current prices and profits in return for higher subsequent prices and profits. Predatory pricing practices are illegal in the

United States under the Sherman Antitrust Act and rarely observed. Even if legal, successful predatory pricing would require that incumbent firms benefit from significant barriers to entry in order to permit higher monopoly prices and profits during subsequent periods. If aggressive predatory pricing strategies are necessary to limit competitor entry, it seems unlikely that incumbent firms would enjoy truly insurmountable barriers to entry.

Network Externalities

Customer Lock-In Effect
Benefit from establishing durable customer loyalty.

Network Externalities
Benefit in consumption of production tied to widespread adoption of a physical or economic standard.

Frequent flyer programs for the airlines and affinity programs for restaurant dining and other services reflect the fact that many successful firms are sometimes able to create a **customer lock-in effect** that yield important long-term benefits. Customer lock-in effects are tied to **network externalities** that lead to significant first-mover advantages. A network is a series of links among producers or customers that can be physical or economic in nature. In the railroad industry, customers are linked using railroad rights of way with a consistent size, or gauge, of track. The advantages of a consistent physical network are so significant that the trains could not run if different railroad companies required different sizes of track.

eBay, Inc., is an example of a company that takes big advantage of a network externality that is economic rather than physical in nature. eBay operates an electronic marketplace on the Internet in which anyone, anywhere, can buy or sell practically anything. Through its PayPal service, eBay also enables any business or consumer with an e-mail account to send and receive online payments securely and conveniently. eBay's auction platform is a fully automated and easy-to-use online service that is available 24 hours a day, 7 days a week. By being the first to offer such a service, eBay has built a large and growing customer base. eBay is also highly profitable.

Market Penetration Pricing

Market Penetration Pricing
Strategy of charging very low initial prices to create a new market or grab market share.

Market penetration pricing is a pricing strategy of charging very low initial prices to create a new market or grab market share in an established market. The objective is to gain a critical mass of customers, create strong network effects, and eventually establish a viable business. In the computer software business, Microsoft and other vendors are known to have sold initial versions of PC-based software programs at promotional prices in order to create a large base of enthusiastic customers. Once a large customer base is established, Microsoft and others increase prices and profit margins to take advantage of the fact that switching computer software becomes more difficult once use has become widespread throughout an organization or profession. On the Internet, several companies have taken the market penetration pricing concept to its logical extreme by actually giving away their services.

Yahoo! Finance is famous for its active and often rambunctious stock message boards. On the Yahoo! stock message boards, active investors trade insights, opinions, and barbs concerning the investment merits and demerits of literally hundreds of publicly traded securities. Many other companies have tried to establish active message board communities but failed given Yahoo!'s enormous head start and zero-price policy. Yahoo! doesn't charge for posting on its message boards in the hope that significant customer traffic can be built and maintained, thereby providing a platform for profitable advertising and for offering other profit-making services, like Internet search. So far, Yahoo!'s aggressive market penetration pricing strategy has built a large and loyal customer base, growing profits, and a significant stock market capitalization. It's working.

Managerial Application 14.4

Network Switching Costs

Americans are intimately familiar with networks for credit cards, telephone service, and computer systems. The value of all such networks grows as customer use becomes more widespread. New telephone subscribers increase the potential number of people that one can call; expanding use of the Internet increases the amount of information on the Web. When more retail outlets, department stores, and restaurants adopt a given credit card, the value of that credit card grows for all its holders. The added value that new users add to network goods and services is called a network externality.

Networks remain an important concern in antitrust policy because the Justice Department fears that if inferior networks got a decisive lead in "installed base" among consumers, switching costs might be sufficient to keep customers from switching to a superior standard. Switching costs might also constitute a barrier to entry in the industry and enable network monopolists to tie or bundle a second product in such a way as to foreclose competition in that secondary market.

Concern over competition and innovation among general-purpose credit cards prompted the Justice

Department to file a suit against the two largest networks, Visa and MasterCard. Although Visa and MasterCard began as separate and competing networks owned and governed by their card-issuing members, substantial overlap exists given the willingness of each network to accept new members. The Justice Department case focused on the potential innovation-reducing effects of this overlapping ownership and governance arrangement. In 2004, the Supreme Court let stand a ruling that the Visa and MasterCard credit card associations violated U.S. antitrust law by barring member banks from issuing credit and charge cards on rival networks owned by American Express Co. and Morgan Stanley. The ruling prevented the two dominant payment card networks from blocking competition.

The challenge for antitrust policy makers is to preserve competitive opportunities without punishing successful network competitors.

See: Robin Sidel, "More Merchants Complying with Visa's Security Rules," *The Wall Street Journal Online*, October 25, 2007, http://online.wsj.com.

NONPRICE COMPETITION

Firms compete for market share in a number of ways that do not directly involve pricing strategies.

Advantages of Nonprice Competition

Nonprice Competition

Competitive techniques tied to product quality, innovation, promotion, and so on.

"Meet it or beat it" is a pricing challenge that often results in quick competitor price reductions, and price wars always favor the deep pockets of established incumbents. As a result, many successful entrants find **nonprice competition** an effective means for growing market share and profitability in the face of entrenched rivals. Because rival firms are likely to retaliate against price cuts, many smaller firms often emphasize nonprice competition to boost demand. Nonprice competition takes a variety of forms: affinity and frequent user programs, home delivery systems, innovative use of technology, Internet shopping, media advertising, price incentives to shop at off-peak times, 24/7 shopping or service hours, and so on.

To illustrate, assume that a firm demand function is given by Equation (14.1):

$$Q_A = f(P_A, P_X, Ad_A, Ad_X, SQ_A, SQ_X, I, Pop, \ldots)$$
$$= a - bP_A + cP_X + dAd_A - eAd_X + fSQ_A$$
$$- gSQ_X + hI + iPop + \ldots$$

14.1

where Q_A is the quantity of output demanded from firm A, P_A is A's price, P_X is the average price charged by other firms in the industry, Ad is advertising expenditures, SQ denotes an index of styling and quality, I represents income, and Pop is population. The firm can control three variables in Equation (14.1): P_A, Ad_A, and SQ_A. If it reduces P_A in an effort to stimulate demand, it will probably cause a reduction in P_X, offsetting the hoped-for effects of the initial price cut. Rather than boosting sales, firm A may have simply started a price war.

Now consider the effects of changing Ad_A and SQ_A. Effective advertising shifts the firm's demand curve to the right, thus enabling the firm to increase sales at a given price or to sell the same quantity at a higher price. Any improvement in styling or quality would have a comparable effect, as would easier credit terms, better service, and more convenient retail locations. Although competitors react to nonprice competition, their reaction is often slower and less direct than that for price changes. Nonprice changes are generally less obvious to rivals, and the design of an effective response is often time-consuming and difficult. Advertising campaigns have to be designed; media time and space must be purchased. Styling and quality changes frequently require long lead times, as do fundamental improvements in customer service. Furthermore, nonprice competition can alter customer buying habits, and regaining lost customers can prove to be difficult. Although it may take longer to establish a reputation through nonprice competition, its advantageous effects are likely to be more persistent than the fleeting benefits of a price cut.

The optimal level of nonprice competition is defined by resulting marginal benefits and marginal costs. Any form of nonprice competition should be pursued as long as marginal benefits exceed marginal costs. For example, suppose that a product has a market price of $10 per unit and a variable cost per unit of $8. If sales can be increased at an additional cost of less than $2 per unit, these additional expenditures will increase profits and should be made.

Optimal Level of Advertising

Advertising is one of the most common methods of nonprice competition. Others include personal selling, improvements in product quality, expansions in customer service, research and development, and so on. The profit-maximizing amount of nonprice competition is found by setting the marginal cost of the activity involved equal to the marginal revenue or marginal benefit derived from it. For example, the optimal level of advertising occurs at that point where the marginal benefit derived from advertising just offset the marginal cost of advertising.

The marginal benefit derived from advertising is measured by the marginal profit contribution generated. This is the difference between marginal revenue, MR, and the marginal cost of production and distribution, MC_Q, *before* advertising costs:

$$\frac{\text{Marginal Revenue}}{\text{from Advertising}} = \frac{\text{Marginal}}{\text{Revenue}} - \frac{\text{Marginal Cost}}{\text{of Output}}$$

$$MR_A = MR - MC_Q \qquad \textbf{14.2}$$

The marginal cost of advertising expressed in terms of the marginal cost of selling one additional unit of output can be written as

$$\frac{\text{Marginal Cost}}{\text{of Advertising}} = \frac{\text{Change in Advertising Expenditures}}{\text{One Unit Change in Demand}}$$

$$MC_A = \frac{\partial \text{Advertising Expenditures}}{\partial \text{Demand}} = \frac{\partial Ad}{\partial Q}$$ **14.3**

The optimal level of advertising is found where

$$\frac{\text{Marginal Benefit}}{\text{Derived from Advertising}} = \text{Marginal Cost of Advertising}$$

$$MR - MC_Q = \frac{\partial Ad}{\partial Q}$$

$$MR_A = MC_A$$ **14.4**

In general, it will pay to expand advertising expenditures so long as $MR_A > MC_A$. Because the marginal profit derived from advertising is

$$M\pi_A = MR_A - MC_A$$ **14.5**

the optimal level of advertising occurs at the point where

$$M\pi_A = 0$$

This relation is illustrated in Figure 14.3. As long as $MR_A > MC_A$, $M\pi_A > 0$, and it will pay to expand the level of advertising. Conversely, if $MR_A < MC_A$, then $M\pi_A < 0$, and it will

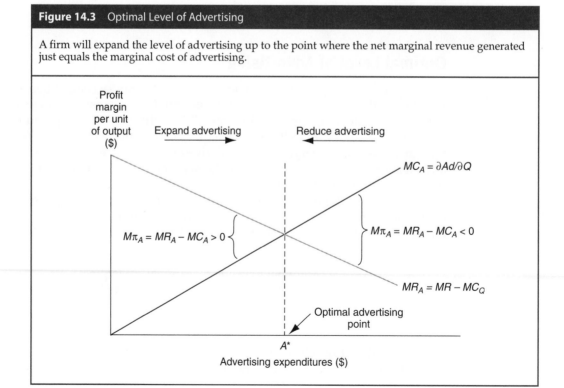

Figure 14.3   Optimal Level of Advertising

A firm will expand the level of advertising up to the point where the net marginal revenue generated just equals the marginal cost of advertising.

pay to reduce the level of advertising expenditures. The optimal level of advertising is achieved when $MR_A = MC_A$, and $M\pi_A = 0$.

Optimal Advertising Example

The effect of advertising on the optimal price–output combination can be illustrated with an example. Suppose that Consumer Products, Inc., has a new prescription ointment called Regain that can be used to restore hair loss due to male pattern baldness. Currently, Regain is marketed through doctors without any consumer advertising. Demand for Regain is expected to increase rapidly following the initiation of consumer advertising. Samantha Stevens, an ad executive with the McMann & Tate Advertising Agency, projects that demand would double following the start of a $500,000 per month advertising campaign. To illustrate the profit impact of the proposed advertising campaign, it is necessary to project the effect on demand and revenue relations.

Current monthly demand for the product is described by the following expressions:

$$Q = 25{,}000 - 100P$$

or

$$P = \$250 - \$0.01Q$$

This market demand implies total and marginal revenue functions of

$$TR = P \times Q = \$250Q - \$0.01Q^2$$
$$MR = \partial TR / \partial Q = \$250 - \$0.02Q$$

Total and marginal costs *before advertising expenses* are given by the expressions

$$TC = \$250{,}000 + \$50Q$$
$$MC = \partial TC / \partial Q = \$50$$

The optimal price–output combination is found by setting $MR = MC$ and solving for Q. Because marginal costs are constant at $50 per unit, the pre-advertising optimal activity level for Regain is

$$MR = MC$$
$$\$250 - \$0.02Q = \$50$$
$$0.02Q = 200$$
$$Q = 10{,}000$$

and,

$$P = \$250 - \$0.01Q$$
$$= \$250 - \$0.01(10{,}000)$$
$$= \$150$$
$$\pi = TR - TC$$
$$= \$250(10{,}000) - \$0.01(10{,}000^2) - \$250{,}000 - \$50(10{,}000)$$
$$= \$750{,}000 \text{ per month}$$

Following a 100 percent advertising-inspired increase in demand, the new monthly demand relations for Regain are

$$Q = 2 \times (25{,}000 - 100P)$$
$$= 50{,}000 - 200P$$

or

$$P = \$250 - \$0.005Q$$

This new advertising-induced market demand implies new total and marginal revenue functions of

$$TR = \$250Q - \$0.005Q^2$$
$$MR = \$250 - \$0.01Q$$

The new optimal price–output combination is found by setting the new $MR = MC$ and solving for Q. Because marginal costs remain constant at \$50 per unit, the new optimal activity level for Regain is

$$MR = MC$$
$$\$250 - \$0.01Q = \$50$$
$$0.01Q = 200$$
$$Q = 20{,}000$$

and,

$$P = \$250 - \$0.005Q$$
$$= \$250 - \$0.005(20{,}000)$$
$$= \$150$$
$$\pi = TR - TC$$
$$= \$250(20{,}000) - \$0.005(20{,}000^2) - \$250{,}000$$
$$= -\$50(20{,}000) - \$500{,}000$$
$$= \$1{,}250{,}000 \text{ per month}$$

Notice that sales have doubled from 10,000 to 20,000 at the \$150 price. The effect on profits is dramatic, rising from \$750,000 to \$1.25 million per month, even after accounting for the additional \$500,000 per month in media expenditures. Therefore, the new advertising campaign appears fully warranted. In fact, given the \$1.25 million in profits that are generated by a doubling in unit sales at a price of \$150, Consumer Products would be willing to pay up to that full amount to double sales. The \$500,000 price charge for the advertising campaign represents a bargain.

SUMMARY

Game theory is used to help improve decision making in situations where the best course of action depends upon the decisions made by others. It is a vital tool, and commonly employed to define effective competitive strategies in business.

- **Game theory** is used to study behavior by individuals and firms for interactive decision problems. In a **zero-sum game,** one player's gain is another player's loss. If parties are engaged in a game that holds the potential for mutual gain, it is called a **positive-sum game.** When conflict holds the potential for mutual loss, it is called a **negative-sum game.** Early game theory research focused upon pure conflict and individual decisions in zero-sum games, or **cooperative games** where joint action is favored.

- The essence of a game is the interdependence of player strategies. In a **sequential game,** each player moves in succession, and each player is aware of all prior moves. The general principle for players in a sequential game is to **look ahead and extrapolate back.** In a **simultaneous game,** players act at the same point in time and must make their initial moves in isolation without any direct knowledge of moves made by other players.

- A given allocation of payoffs is called an **equilibrium outcome** if the payoff to no player can be improved by unilaterally switching to another **game-theory strategy.** Cells in a table describing the payoffs earned by both parties following their selection of various strategies are commonly referred to as a **payoff matrix.**

- The most famous of all simultaneous-move one-shot games is the **Prisoner's Dilemma.** In a **one-shot game,** the underlying interaction between competitors occurs only once; in a **repeated game,** there is ongoing interaction between competitors. A **dominant strategy** creates the best result for either player regardless of the action taken by the other. A **secure strategy,** sometimes called the maximin strategy, guarantees the best possible outcome given the worst possible scenario.

- **Nash equilibrium** occurs when, given the strategy of the other players, no player can improve their own payoff through a unilateral change in strategy.

In the absence of Nash equilibrium, players often choose **randomized strategies** to keep rivals from being able to predict strategic moves. In **Nash bargaining,** two competitors bargain over some item of value. In a simultaneous-move, one-shot game, players have only one chance to reach an agreement. An **infinitely repeated game** is a competitive game that is repeated over and over again without boundary or limit. A **finitely repeated game** occurs a limited number of times, or has limited duration in time. If there is uncertainty about when a game will end, the conduct of a finitely repeated game mirrors an infinitely repeated game. A **trigger strategy** is a system of behavior that remains the same until another player takes an action that precipitates a different response.

- The **end-of-game problem** stems from the fact that it becomes difficult to properly motivate managers and workers at the ends of their career. Payoffs and game strategy are often shaped by the order in which various players make their moves. Such **multistage games** involve special considerations. In a multistage game, the timing of player moves becomes important. A **first-mover advantage** is a benefit earned by the player able to make the initial move in a sequential move or multistage game.

- The most familiar type of auction is an **English auction,** where the highest bidder wins. The so-called **winner's curse** results when overly aggressive bidders pay more than the economic value of auctioned-off items. Another commonly employed auction method is a **sealed-bid auction,** where all bids are secret and the highest bid wins. A relatively rare sealed-bid auction method is a **Vickrey auction,** where the highest sealed bid wins, but the winner pays the price of the second highest bid. Another uncommon auctioning method is the so-called reverse or **Dutch auction.** In a Dutch auction, the auctioneer keeps lowering a very high price until a winning bidder emerges. The winning bidder is the first participant willing to pay the auctioneer's price.

- A **competitive advantage** is a unique or rare ability to create, distribute, or service products. It is the business-world analog to what economists call **comparative advantage,** or when one nation or region of the country is better suited to the production of one product than to the production of some other product.

- **Limit pricing** is a competitive strategy to set less than monopoly prices in an effort to deter market entry by new and viable competitors. **Predatory pricing** is pricing below marginal cost in the hope of knocking out rival producers and subsequently raising prices to obtain monopoly profits. **Customer lock-in effects** are often tied to **network externalities** that lead to significant first-mover advantages. A network is a series of links among producers or customers that can be physical or economic in nature.

- **Market penetration pricing** is a strategy of charging very low prices to create a new market or grab market share in an established market. The objective is to gain a critical mass of customers, create strong network effects, and eventually establish a viable business.

- While competition often focuses on pricing schemes to increase the quantity demanded, **nonprice competition** focuses on a variety of other methods for increasing market share.

All of this information is useful to the process of business decision making and provides a useful starting point for the development and understanding of successful competitive strategy.

QUESTIONS

Q14.1 From a game-theory perspective, how would you characterize the bargaining between a customer and a used-car dealer?

Q14.2 Suppose Exxon Mobil Corp. independently reduced the price of gasoline, and that this price cut was quickly matched by competitors. Could these actions be described as reflective of a cooperative game?

Q14.3 Characterize the essential difference between a sequential game and a simultaneous-move game.

Q14.4 Explain how the Prisoner's Dilemma example shows that rational self-interested play does not always result in the best solution for all parties.

Q14.5 Does game theory offer a strategy appropriate for situations in which no strategy results in the highest payoff to a player regardless of the opposing player's decision?

Q14.6 Define the Nash equilibrium concept.

Q14.7 Instructors sometimes use quizzes to motivate students to adequately prepare for class. However, preparing and grading quizzes can become time-consuming and tedious. Moreover, if students prepare adequately for class, there is no need for quizzes. What does game theory prescribe for instructors facing the problem of needing to motivate class preparation among students?

Q14.8 The typical CEO of a major U.S. corporation is 56–58 years old and gets paid $3–5 million per year. From a game-theory perspective, explain why corporate governance experts advise that such executives be required to hold common stock worth 7–10 years of total compensation.

Q14.9 Describe the difference between limit pricing and predatory pricing strategies.

Q14.10 Explain why the establishment and exploitation of network effects are key elements in the competitive strategy of computer software provider Microsoft Corp.

SELF-TEST PROBLEMS AND SOLUTIONS

ST14.1 Game Theory Strategies. Suppose two local suppliers are seeking to win the right to upgrade the communications capability of the internal "intranets" that link a number of customers with their suppliers. The system quality decision facing each competitor and potential profit payoffs are illustrated in the table. The first number listed in each cell is the profit earned by U.S. Equipment Supply; the second number indicates the profit earned by Business Systems, Inc. For example, if both competitors, U.S. Equipment Supply and Business Systems, Inc., pursue a high-quality strategy, U.S. Equipment Supply will earn $25,000 and Business Systems, Inc., will earn $50,000. If U.S. Equipment Supply pursues a high-quality strategy while Business

Systems, Inc., offers low-quality goods and services, U.S. Equipment Supply will earn $40,000; Business Systems, Inc., will earn $22,000. If U.S. Equipment Supply offers low-quality goods while Business Systems, Inc., offers high-quality goods, U.S. Equipment Supply will suffer a net loss of $25,000, and Business Systems, Inc., will earn $20,000. Finally, if U.S. Equipment Supply and Business Systems, Inc., offer low-quality goods, both competitors will earn $25,000.

		Business Systems, Inc.	
	Quality Strategy	High Quality ("Left")	Low Quality ("Right")
U.S. Equipment Supply	High Quality ("Up")	$25,000, $50,000	$40,000, $22,000
	Low Quality ("Down")	−$25,000, $20,000	$25,000, $25,000

A. Does U.S. Equipment Supply and/or Business Systems, Inc., have a dominant strategy? If so, what is it?

B. Does U.S. Equipment Supply and/or Business Systems, Inc., have a secure strategy? If so, what is it?

C. What is the Nash equilibrium concept, and why is it useful? What is the Nash equilibrium for this problem?

ST14.1   SOLUTION

A. The dominant strategy for U.S. Equipment Supply is to provide high-quality goods. Irrespective of the quality strategy chosen by Business Systems, Inc., U.S. Equipment Supply can do no better than to choose a high-quality strategy. To see this, note that if Business Systems, Inc., chooses to produce high-quality goods, the best choice for U.S. Equipment Supply is to also provide high-quality goods because the $25,000 profit then earned is better than the $25,000 loss that would be incurred if U.S. Equipment Supply chose a low-quality strategy. If Business Systems, Inc., chose a low-quality strategy, the best choice by U.S. Equipment Supply would again be to produce high-quality goods. U.S. Equipment Supply's high-quality strategy profit of $40,000 dominates the low-quality payoff for U.S. Equipment Supply of $25,000.

Business Systems, Inc., does not have a dominant strategy. To see this, note that if U.S. Equipment Supply chooses to produce high-quality goods, the best choice for Business Systems, Inc., is to also provide high-quality goods because the $50,000 profit then earned is better than the $22,000 profit if Business Systems, Inc., chose a low-quality strategy. If U.S. Equipment Supply chose a low-quality strategy, the best choice by Business Systems, Inc., would be to produce low-quality goods and earn $25,000 versus $20,000.

B. The secure strategy for U.S. Equipment Supply is to provide high-quality goods. By choosing to provide high-quality goods, U.S. Equipment Supply can be guaranteed a profit payoff of at least $25,000. By pursuing a high-quality strategy, U.S. Equipment Supply can eliminate the chance of losing $25,000, as would happen if U.S. Equipment Supply chose a low-quality strategy while Business Systems, Inc., chose to produce high-quality goods.

The secure strategy for Business Systems, Inc., is to provide low-quality goods. By choosing to provide high-quality goods, Business Systems, Inc., can guarantee a profit payoff of only $20,000. Business Systems, Inc., can be assured of earning at least $22,000 with a low-quality strategy. Thus, the secure strategy for Business Systems, Inc. is to provide low-quality goods.

C. A set of strategies constitute a Nash equilibrium if, given the strategies of other players, no player can improve its payoff through a unilateral change in strategy. The concept of Nash equilibrium is very important because it represents a situation where every player is doing the best possible in light of what other players are doing.

Although useful, the notion of a secure strategy suffers from a serious shortcoming. In the present example, suppose Business Systems, Inc., reasoned as follows: "U.S. Equipment Supply will surely choose its high-quality dominant strategy. Therefore, I should not choose my secure low-quality strategy and earn $22,000. I should instead choose a high-quality strategy and earn $50,000." A natural way of formalizing the "end result" of such a thought process is captured in the definition of Nash equilibrium.

In the present example, if U.S. Equipment Supply chooses a high-quality strategy, the Nash equilibrium strategy is for Business Systems, Inc., to also choose a high-quality strategy. Similarly, if Business Systems, Inc., chooses a high-quality strategy, the Nash equilibrium strategy is for U.S. Equipment Supply to also choose a high-quality strategy. Thus, a Nash equilibrium is reached when both firms adopt high-quality strategies.

Although some problems have multiple Nash equilibriums, that is not true in this case. A combination of high-quality strategies for both firms is the only set of strategies where no player can improve its payoff through a unilateral change in strategy.

ST14.2   Nash Equilibrium.   Assume that Hewlett-Packard (H-P) and Dell Computer have a large inventory of personal computers that they would like to sell before a new generation of faster, cheaper machines is introduced. Assume that the question facing each competitor is whether or not they should widely advertise a "close out" sale on these discontinued items, or instead let excess inventory work itself off over the next few months. If both aggressively promote their products with a nationwide advertising campaign, each will earn profits of $5 million. If one advertises while the other does not, the firm that advertises will earn $20 million, while the one that does not advertise will earn $2 million. If neither advertises, both will earn $10 million. Assume this is a one-shot game, and both firms seek to maximize profits.

		Dell Computer	
	Promotion Strategy	**Advertise ("Left")**	**Don't Advertise ("Right")**
H-P	Advertise ("Up")	$5 million, $5 million	$20 million, $2 million
	Don't advertise ("Down")	$2 million, $20 million	$10 million, $10 million

A. What is the dominant strategy for each firm? Are these also secure strategies?

B. What is the Nash equilibrium?

C. Would collusion work in this case?

ST14.2   SOLUTION

A. The dominant strategy for both H-P and Dell is to advertise. Neither could earn higher profits with a "don't advertise" strategy, irrespective of what the other party chooses to do.

For example, if H-P chooses to advertise, Dell will also choose to advertise and earn $5 million rather than $2 million. If H-P chooses not to advertise, Dell will choose to advertise and earn $20 million rather than $10 million. No matter what H-P decides to do, Dell is better off by advertising. Similarly, if Dell chooses to advertise, H-P will also choose to advertise and earn $5 million rather than $2 million. If Dell chooses not to advertise, H-P will choose to advertise and earn $20 million rather than $10 million. No matter what Dell decides to do, H-P is better off by advertising.

These are also secure strategies for each firm because they ensure the elimination of worst outcome payoffs. With an advertising strategy, neither firm is exposed to the possibility of earning only $2 million.

B. A set of strategies constitute a Nash equilibrium if, given the strategies of other players, no player can improve its payoff through a unilateral change in strategy. The concept of Nash equilibrium is very important because it represents a situation where every player is doing the best possible in light of what other players are doing.

In this case, the Nash equilibrium is for each firm to advertise. Although some problems have multiple Nash equilibriums, that is not true in this case. An advertising strategy for both firms is the only set of strategies where no player can improve its payoff through a unilateral change in strategy.

C. Collusion will not work in this case because this is a "one shot" game where moves are taken simultaneously, rather than in sequence. Sequential rounds are necessary with enforcement penalties before successful collusion is possible. If H-P and Dell "agreed" not to advertise in the hope of making $10 million each, both would have an incentive to cheat on the agreement in the hope of making $20 million. Without the possibility for a second round, enforcement is precluded, and collusion isn't possible.

PROBLEMS

P14.1 Game Theory Concepts.   Recognize each of the following statements as being true or false and explain why.

A. A set of strategies constitutes a Nash equilibrium if no player can improve their position given the strategies chosen by other players.

B. A secure strategy is very conservative and should only be considered if the rival's optimal strategy is identical.

C. A dominant strategy is also a secure strategy, but every secure strategy is not necessarily a dominant strategy.

D. In a one-shot game, the Nash equilibrium is also the best outcome that can be achieved under collusion.

E. If a player has no dominant strategy, it pays to look at the game from the rival's perspective and anticipate the rival choosing its dominant strategy.

P14.2 Prisoner's Dilemma.   The classic Prisoner's Dilemma involves two suspects, *A* and *B*, who are arrested by the police. Because the police have insufficient evidence for conviction on a key charge, they place the prisoners in isolation and offer each of them the following deal: If one testifies for the prosecution against the other and the other remains silent, the betrayer goes free and the silent accomplice receives a 20-year sentence. If both stay silent, both prisoners are sentenced to only 6 months in jail on a minor charge. If each betrays the other, each receives a 5-year sentence. Each prisoner must make the choice of whether to betray the other or to remain silent. Neither prisoner knows for sure what choice the other prisoner will make. The dilemma is summarized as follows:

	Prisoner *B* Stays Silent	Prisoner *B* Betrays
Prisoner *A* Stays Silent	Each gets 6 months	Prisoner *A* gets 20 years Prisoner *B* goes free
Prisoner *A* Betrays	Prisoner *A* goes free Prisoner *B* gets 20 years	Each gets 5 years

A. Describe the best strategy for each prisoner if neither knows what the other will do.

B. What is the paradox of the situation?

P14.3 Dominant Strategies.

Conceive of two competitors facing important strategic decisions where the payoff to each decision depends upon the reactions of the competitor. Firm *A* can choose either row in the payoff matrix defined below, whereas firm *B* can choose either column. For firm *A* the choice is either "up" or "down;" for firm *B* the choice is either "left" or "right." Notice that neither firm can unilaterally choose a given cell in the profit payoff matrix. The ultimate result of this one-shot, simultaneous-move game depends upon the choices made by both competitors. In this payoff matrix, strategic decisions made by firm *A* or firm *B* could signify decisions to offer a money-back guarantee, lower prices, offer free shipping, and so on. The first number in each cell is the profit payoff to firm *A*; the second number is the profit payoff to firm *B*.

		Firm *B*	
	Competitive Strategy	**Left**	**Right**
Firm *A*	Up	$5 million, $10 million	$7.5 million, $4 million
	Down	$1 million, $3.5 million	$5 million, $5 million

A. Is there a dominant strategy for firm *A*? If so, what is it?

B. Is there a dominant strategy for firm *B*? If so, what is it?

P14.4 Secure Strategies.

The Home Depot, Inc., and the Lowes Companies are locked in a vicious struggle for market share in the home improvement market. Suppose each competitor is considering the advisability of offering 90-day free financing as a means for boosting sales during the important spring season. The Home Depot can choose either row in the payoff matrix defined below, whereas the Lowes Companies can choose either column. Neither firm can unilaterally choose a give cell in the payoff matrix. The ultimate result of this one-shot, simultaneous-move game depends upon the choices made by both competitors. The first number in each cell is the profit payoff to the Home Depot; the second number is the profit payoff to the Lowes Companies.

	Lowes Companies		
	Competitive Strategy	**90-day free financing ("Left")**	**No free financing ("Right")**
The Home Depot	90-day free financing ("Up")	$20 million, $20 million	$40 million, $10 million
	No free financing ("Down")	$15 million, $35 million	$25 million, $25 million

A. Is there a secure strategy for The Home Depot? If so, what is it?

B. Is there a secure strategy for The Lowes Companies? If so, what is it?

P14.5 Nash Equilibrium. The breakfast cereal industry is heavily concentrated. Kellogg, General Mills, General Foods (Post), and Ralcorp account for over 85 percent of industry sales. Advertising by individual firms does not convince more people to eat breakfast. Effective advertising simply steals sales from rivals. Big profit gains could be had if these rivals could simply agree to stop advertising. Assume Kellogg and General Mills are trying to set optimal advertising strategies. Kellogg can choose either row in the payoff matrix defined below, whereas General Mills can choose either column. The first number in each cell is Kellogg's payoff; the second number is the payoff to General Mills. This is a one-shot, simultaneous-move game and the first number in each cell is the profit payoff to Kellogg. The second number is the profit payoff to General Mills.

	General Mills		
	Competitive Strategy	**Advertise ("Left")**	**Don't Advertise ("Right")**
Kellogg	Advertise ("Up")	$800 million, $800 million	$1.5 billion, $600 million
	Don't Advertise ("Down")	$600 million, $1.5 billion	$1 billion, $1 billion

A. Briefly describe the Nash equilibrium concept.

B. Is there a Nash equilibrium strategy for each firm? If so, what is it?

P14.6 Collusion. In the United States any contract, combination, or conspiracy in restraint of trade is illegal. In practice, this means it is against the law to control or attempt to control the quantity, price, or exchange of goods and services. In addition to this legal prohibition, potential conspirators face practical problems in any overt or tacit attempt at collusion. To illustrate the problems encountered, consider the following profit payoff matrix faced by two potential conspirators in a one-shot, simultaneous-move game. The first number in each cell is firm A's profit payoff; the second number is the profit payoff to firm B.

	Firm B		
	Pricing Strategy	**Low Price ("Left")**	**High Price ("Right")**
Firm A	Low Price ("Up")	$5 million, $5 million	$40 million, −$20 million
	High Price ("Down")	−$20 million, $40 million	$25 million, $25 million

A. Is there a dominant strategy and a Nash equilibrium strategy for each firm? If so, what are they?

B. If the firms agreed to collude and charge high prices, both would earn $25 million and joint profits of $50 million would be maximized. However, the joint high-price strategy is not a stable equilibrium. Explain.

P14.7 Randomized Strategies.

Game theory can be used to analyze conflicts that arise between managers and workers. Managers can choose to monitor worker performance, or not monitor worker performance. For their part, workers can choose to perform the requested task within the time frame requested, or fail to perform as requested. The resulting payoff matrix for this one-shot, simultaneous move game shows the payoff to managers (first number) and workers (second number).

		Workers	
	Work Strategy	Perform ("Left")	Fail to Perform ("Right")
Managers	Monitor ("Up")	−$1,000, $1,000	$1,000, −$1,000
	Don't Monitor ("Down")	$1,000, −$1,000	−$1,000, $1,000

A. Document the fact that there is no Nash equilibrium strategy for each player.

B. Explain how each player will have a preference for secrecy in the absence of a Nash equilibrium and how randomized strategies might be favored in such circumstances.

P14.8 Predatory Pricing.

Prohibitions against predatory pricing stem from big business conspiracy theories popularized in the late nineteenth century by journalists such as Ida Tarbell, author of an influential book titled *History of the Standard Oil Company*. In that book, Tarbell condemned Standard Oil's allegedly predatory price-cutting. Business historians assert that Tarbell vilified John D. Rockefeller because of personal reasons, and not only because of an interest in reshaping public policy. Standard Oil's low prices had driven the employer of Tarbell's brother, the Pure Oil Company, out of the petroleum-refining business.

According to predatory pricing theory, the predatory firm sets price below marginal cost, the relevant cost of production. Competitors must then lower their price below marginal cost, thereby losing money on each unit sold. If competitors failed to match the predatory firm's price cuts, they would continue to lose market share until they were driven out of business. If competitors follow the lead of the predatory pricing firm and cut price below marginal cost, they will incur devastating losses, and eventually go bankrupt. Either way, the "deep pockets" of the predatory firm give it the financial muscle and staying power necessary to drive smaller, weaker competitors out of business. After competition has been eliminated from the market, the predatory firm raises prices to compensate for money lost during its price war against smaller competitors, and earns monopoly profits forever thereafter.

A. The ban against predatory pricing is one of the most controversial U.S. antitrust policies. Explain why this ban is risky from a public policy perspective, and why predatory pricing strategy can be criticized as irrational from a game-theory perspective.

B. Explain why the prohibition against predatory pricing might be politically popular even if predatory pricing is implausible from an economic perspective.

P14.9 Nonprice Competition. General Cereals, Inc. (GCI), produces and markets Sweeties!, a popular ready-to-eat breakfast cereal. In an effort to expand sales in the Secaucus, New Jersey, market, the company is considering a 1-month promotion whereby GCI would distribute a coupon for a free daily pass to a local amusement park in exchange for three box tops, as sent in by retail customers. A 25 percent boost in demand is anticipated, even though only 15 percent of all eligible customers are expected to redeem their coupons. Each redeemed coupon costs GCI $6, so the expected cost of this promotion is 30¢ ($= 0.15 \times \$6 \div 3$) per unit sold. Other marginal costs for cereal production and distribution are constant at $1 per unit.

Current demand and marginal revenue relations for Sweeties! are

$$Q = 16{,}000 - 2{,}000P$$
$$MR = \partial TR / \partial Q = \$8 - \$0.001Q$$

Demand and marginal revenue relations that reflect the expected 25 percent boost in demand for Sweeties! are the following:

$$Q = 20{,}000 - 2{,}500P$$
$$MR = \partial TR / \partial Q = \$8 - \$0.0008Q$$

A. Calculate the profit-maximizing price–output and profit levels for Sweeties! prior to the coupon promotion.

B. Calculate these same values subsequent to the Sweeties! coupon promotion and following the expected 25 percent boost in demand.

P14.10 Variability of Business Profits. Near the checkout stand, grocery stores and convenience stores prominently display low-price impulse items like candy, gum, and soda that customers crave. Despite low prices, such products generate enviable profit margins for retailers and for the companies that produce them. For example, Hershey Foods Corp. is the largest U.S. producer of chocolate and nonchocolate confectionary (sugared) products. Major brands include Hershey's, Reese's, Kit Kat, Almond Joy, and Milk Duds. While Hershey's faces increasing competition from other candy companies and snack-food producers of energy bars, the company is extremely profitable. Hershey's rate of return on stockholder's equity, or net income divided by book value per share, routinely exceeds 30 percent per year, or about three times the publicly traded company average. Profit margins, or net income per dollar of sales revenue, generally exceed 13 percent, and earnings grow in a predictable fashion by more than 10 percent per year.

A. Explain how the failure to reflect intangible assets, like the value of brand names, might cause Hershey's accounting profits to overstate Hershey's economic profits.

B. Explain why high economic profit rates are a necessary but not sufficient condition for the presence of monopoly profits.

CASE Study

Time Warner, Inc., Is Playing Games with Stockholders

Time Warner, Inc., the world's largest media and entertainment company, is best known as the publisher of magazines such as *Fortune, Time, People,* and *Sports Illustrated.* The Company is a media powerhouse comprised of Internet technologies and electronic commerce (America Online), cable television systems, filmed entertainment and television production, cable and broadcast television, recorded music and music publishing, magazine publishing, book publishing, and direct marketing. Time Warner has the potential to profit whether people go to theaters, buy or rent videos, watch cable or broadcast TV, or listen to records.

Just as impressive as Time Warner's commanding presence in the entertainment field is its potential for capitalizing on its recognized strengths during coming years. Time Warner is a leader in terms of embracing new entertainment-field technology. The company's state-of-the-art cable systems allow subscribers to rent movies, purchase a wide array of goods and services, and participate in game shows and consumer surveys—all within the privacy of their own homes. Wide channel flexibility also gives the company the opportunity to expand pay-per-view TV offerings to meet demand from specialized market niches. In areas where cable systems have sufficient capacity, HBO subscribers are now offered a choice of programming on different channels. Time Warner also has specialized networks, like TVKO, to offer special events on a regular pay-per-view basis.

Time Warner is also famous for introducing common stockholders to the practical use of game-theory concepts. In 1991, the company introduced a controversial plan to raise new equity capital through use of a complex "contingent" rights offering. After months of assuring Wall Street that it was close to raising new equity from other firms through strategic alliances, Time Warner instead asked its shareholders to ante up more cash.

Under the plan, the company granted holders of its 57.8 million shares of common stock the rights to 34.5 million shares of new common, or 0.6 rights per share. Each right enabled a shareholder to pay Time Warner $105 for an unspecified number of new common shares. Because the number of new shares that might be purchased for $105 was unspecified, so too was the price per share. Time Warner's Wall Street advisers structured the offer so that the new stock would be offered at cheaper prices if fewer shareholders chose to exercise their rights.

In an unusual arrangement, the rights from all participating shareholders were to be placed in a pool to determine their pro rata share of the 34.5 million shares to be distributed. If 100 percent of Time Warner shareholders chose to exercise their rights, the price per share would be $105, the number of shares owned by each shareholder would increase by 60 percent, and each shareholder would retain his or her same proportionate ownership in the company. In the event that less than 100 percent of the shareholders chose to participate, participating shareholders would receive a discount price and increase their proportionate interest in the company. If only 80 percent of Time Warner shareholders chose to exercise their rights, the price per share would be $84; if 60 percent chose to exercise their rights, the price per share would be $63. These lower prices reflect the fact that if only 80 percent of Time Warner shareholders chose to exer cise their rights, each $105 right would purchase 1.25 shares; if 60 percent chose to exercise their rights, each $105 right would purchase roughly 1.667 shares. Finally, to avoid the possibility of issuing equity at fire-sale prices, Time Warner reserved the privilege to cancel the equity offering entirely if fewer than 60 percent of holders chose to exercise their rights.

The terms of the offer were designed to make Time Warner shareholders feel compelled to

continued

exercise their rights in hopes of getting cheap stock and avoiding seeing their holdings diluted. Although such contingent rights offerings are a common capital-raising technique in Britain, prior to the Time Warner offering they had never been proposed on such a large scale in the United States. Wall Street traders and investment bankers lauded the Time Warner offer as a brilliant coercive device—a view that might have been colored by the huge fees they stood to make on the offering. Advisory fees for Merrill Lynch and Time Warner's seven other key advisers were projected at $41.5 million to $145 million, depending on the number of participating shareholders. An additional $20.7 million to $34.5 million was set aside to pay other investment bankers for soliciting shareholders to exercise their rights. Time Warner's advisers argued that their huge fees totaling 5.22 percent of the proceeds to the company were justified because the offering entered uncharted ground in terms of Wall Street experience. Disgruntled shareholders noted that a similar contingent rights offering by Bass PLC of Britain involved a fee of only 2.125 percent of the proceeds to the company, despite the fact that the lead underwriter Schroders PLC agreed to buy and resell any new stock that wasn't claimed by rights holders. This led to charges that Time Warner's advisers were charging underwriters' fees without risking any of their own capital.

Proceeds from the offering were earmarked to help pay down the $11.3 billion debt Time, Inc., took on to buy Warner Communications, Inc. Time Warner maintained that it was in intensive talks with potential strategic partners and that the rights offering would strengthen its hand in those negotiations by improving the company's balance sheet. Time Warner said that the rights offering would enhance its ability to enter into strategic alliances or joint ventures with partners overseas. Such alliances would help the company penetrate markets in Japan, Europe, and elsewhere. Critics of the plan argued that the benefits from strategic alliances come in small increments and that Time Warner had failed to strike any such deals previously because it wants both management control and a premium price from potential partners. These critics also maintained that meaningful revenue from any such projects is probably years away.

Stockholder reaction to the Time Warner offering was immediate and overwhelmingly negative. On the day the offering was announced, Time Warner shares closed at $99.50, down $11.25, in New York Stock Exchange composite trading. This is in addition to a decline of $6 suffered the previous day on the basis of a report in *The Wall Street Journal* that some form of equity offering was being considered. After trading above $120 per share in the days prior to the first reports of a pending offer, Time Warner shares plummeted by more than 25 percent to $88 per share within a matter of days. This was yet one more disappointment for the company's long-suffering common stockholders. During the summer of 1989, Time cited a wide range of synergistic benefits to be gained from a merger with Warner Communications and spurned a $200 per share buyout offer from Paramount Communications, Inc. This is despite the fact that the Paramount offer represented a fat 60 percent premium to the then prevailing market price of $125 for Time stock. During the succeeding 2-year period, Time Warner stock failed to rise above this $125 level and traded as low as $66 per share during the fall of 1990. Meanwhile, the hoped-for Time Warner synergy has yet to emerge.

A. Was Paramount's above-market offer for Time, Inc., consistent with the notion that the prevailing market price for common stock is an accurate reflection of the discounted net present value of future cash flows? Was management's rejection of Paramount's above-market offer for Time, Inc., consistent with the value-maximization concept?

continued

B. Assume that a Time Warner shareholder could buy additional shares at a market price of $90 or participate in the company's rights offering. Construct the payoff matrix that correspond to a $90 per share purchase decision versus a decision to participate in the rights offering with subsequent 100 percent, 80 percent, and 60 percent participation by all Time Warner shareholders.

C. Describe the secure game-theory strategy for Time Warner shareholders. Was there a dominant strategy?

D. Explain why the price of Time Warner common stock fell following the announcement of the company's controversial rights offering. Is such an offering in the best interests of shareholders?

SELECTED REFERENCES

Athey, Susan and Ilya Segal. "Designing Efficient Mechanisms for Dynamic Bilateral Trading Games." *American Economic Review* 97, no. 2 (May, 2007): 131–136.

Battigalli, Pierpaolo and Martin Dufwenberg. "Guilt in Games." *American Economic Review* 97, no. 2 (May, 2007): 170–176.

Bergemann, Dirk and Stephen Morris. "An Ascending Auctions for Independent Values: Uniqueness and Robustness to Strategic Uncertainty." *American Economic Review* 97, no. 2 (May, 2007): 125–130.

Brady, Malcolm P. "Firm Governance and Duopoly: In Weakness May Lie Strength." *Managerial and Decision Economics* 28, no. 2 (March, 2007): 145–155.

Chapman, James T. E., David McAdams, and Harry J. Paarsch. "Bounding Revenue Comparison Across Multi-Unit Auction Formats Under Epsilon-Best Response." *American Economic Review* 97, no. 2 (May, 2007): 455–458.

Hsu, Shih Hsun, Chen Ying Huang, and Cheng Tao Tang. "Minimax Play at Wimbledon: Comment." *American Economic Review* 97, no. 1 (March, 2007): 517–523.

Hortacsu, Ali and Chad Syverson. "Cementing Relationships: Vertical Integration, Foreclosure, Productivity, and Prices." *Journal of Political Economy* 115, no. 2 (April, 2007): 250–301.

Huang, Jennifer, Kelsey D. Wei, and Hong Yan. "Participation Costs and the Sensitivity of Fund Flows to Past Performance." *Journal of Finance* 62, no. 3 (June, 2007): 1273–1311.

Inderst, Roman and Holger M. Mueller. "A Lender-Based Theory of Collateral." *Journal of Financial Economics* 84, no. 3 (June, 2007): 826–859.

Jackson, Matthew O. and Leeat Yariv. "Diffusion of Behavior and Equilibrium Properties in Network Games." *American Economic Review* 97, no. 2 (May, 2007): 92–98.

Jansen, Thijs, Arie van Lier, and Arjen van Witteloostuijn. "A Note on Strategic Delegation: The Market Share Case." *International Journal of Industrial Organization* 25, no. 3 (June, 2007): 531–539.

Kalandrakis, Tasos. "On Participation Games with Complete Information." *International Journal of Game Theory* 35, no. 3 (2007): 337–352.

Kyle, Margaret K. "Pharmaceutical Price Controls and Entry Strategies." *Review of Economics and Statistics* 89, no. 1 (February, 2007): 88–99.

Lukach, R., P. M. Kort, and J. Plasmans. "Optimal R&D Investment Strategies Under the Threat of New Technology Entry." *International Journal of Industrial Organization* 25, no. 1 (February, 2007): 103–119.

Sorenson, Timothy L. "Credible Collusion in Multimarket Oligopoly." *Managerial and Decision Economics* 28, no. 2 (March, 2007): 115–128.

Pricing Practices

Millions use the Internet to book a last-minute travel deal for a visit home to see the folks, a spring break trip, or a vacation in Europe. If you are not one of them, just go to Google.com, type in "cheap travel," and you'll be amazed at the wonderful bargains that appear. Travelocity.com, expedia.com, and orbitz.com are a few of the most popular travel sites that offer a host of bargains. Regular price discounts of 40 percent, 50 percent, and more are common. What is going on here? Have the airlines, hotels, car rental companies—indeed, the whole travel industry—gone mad?

No, the travel bargains offered on the Internet are not crazy. Rather than a foolish scramble to build market share at any cost, travel bargains offered on the Internet represent a shrewd use of information technology. Any night that hotel rooms stand empty represents lost revenue, and because hotel costs are largely fixed, revenue losses translate directly into lost profits. A NYC luxury hotel room rate at 50 percent off regular prices does not begin to cover fixed construction, maintenance, and interest costs, but it makes a nice profit contribution when the alternative is weekend vacancy. By segmenting their markets, hotels are able to charge the maximum amount the market will bear on weekdays and on weekends.[1]

This chapter examines common pricing practices and shows their value as a practical means for achieving maximum profits under a wide variety of demand and cost conditions.

PRICING RULES-OF-THUMB

Economic theory and pricing practices suggest simple rules to make the determination of optimal prices quick and easy.

Competitive Markets

Competitive Market Pricing Rule-of-Thumb
In competitive markets, set $P = MR = MC$ for maximum profits.

Profit maximization always requires finding the price–output combination that will set $MR = MC$. In competitive markets, firms are price takers with a horizontal firm demand curve and price (average revenue) is always equal to marginal revenue, $P = MR$. For firms in competitive markets, the **competitive market pricing rule-of-thumb** for profit maximization is to set

$$P = MR = MC \qquad \textbf{15.1}$$

---

1 See Matt Phillips, "Pricing Power," *The Wall Street Journal Online*, October 29, 2007, http://online.wsj.com.

Given prevailing market prices, the competitive firm merely has to choose the output level that will set $P = MR = MC$. In competitive markets, price information is widely disseminated, so determining the appropriate market price is no problem. Because the marginal costs of production and distribution can be easily calculated for most goods and services, finding the profit-maximizing price–output combination where $P = MR = MC$ is a matter of simple calculation. Studies of pricing practices in competitive markets confirm that firms price their products in a manner consistent with profit maximization.

Imperfectly Competitive Markets

Products produced by firms in monopolistic competition, oligopoly, and monopoly markets all have elements of uniqueness that give rise to downward-sloping firm demand curves. When the firm demand curve is downward sloping, $P > MR$ and the competitive market pricing rule-of-thumb for profit maximization does not apply.

Firms facing monopolistic competition, oligopoly, and monopoly markets must find the price–output combination that will set $MR = MC$. In making this determination, such firms must take account of the fact that price is a function of output, $P = f(Q)$. If the demand curve is downward sloping, two effects on revenue follow a price reduction: (1) By selling an additional unit, total revenue goes up by P; (2) However, by charging a lower price, some revenue is lost on units sold previously at the higher price. This effect is captured by $Q \times \partial P/\partial Q$. Therefore, if price is a function of output, the total change in revenue following a change in output (marginal revenue) is given by the expression

$$MR = \mathrm{d}TR/\mathrm{d}Q = \mathrm{d}(P \times Q)/\mathrm{d}Q$$
$$= P + Q \times \partial P/\partial Q \qquad \textbf{15.2}$$

If Equation (15.2) is multiplied by P/P (a ratio equal to one), the numerical value on each side of this expression is unaffected and a simple relationship between marginal revenue and the point price elasticity of demand is suggested. By definition, the point price elasticity of demand is $\varepsilon_P = \partial Q/Q \div \partial P/P = \partial Q/\partial P \times P/Q$. Therefore, multiplying Equation (15.2) by P/P gives

$$MR = [P + Q \times \partial P/\partial Q] \times (P/P)$$
$$= P + P[Q/P \times \partial P/\partial Q]$$
$$= P + P(1/\varepsilon_P)$$
$$= P[1 + (1/\varepsilon_P)] \qquad \textbf{15.3}$$

Imperfectly Competitive Pricing Rule-of-Thumb
When $P = f(Q)$, set $P = MC/[1 + (1/\varepsilon_P)]$ for maximum profits.

Equation (15.3) suggests that when price is a function of output, the **imperfectly competitive market pricing rule-of-thumb** for profit maximization is to set price equal to marginal cost divided by the quantity 1 plus the inverse of the point price elasticity of demand

$$MR = MC$$
$$P[1 + (1/\varepsilon_P)] = MC$$
$$P = MC/[1 + (1/\varepsilon_P)] \qquad \textbf{15.4}$$

The practical usefulness of this rule-of-thumb for pricing is obvious. Just using information on marginal costs and the point price elasticity of demand, the calculation of profit-maximizing prices is quick and easy. Many firms derive an optimal pricing policy using easily calculated marginal costs and the price elasticity of demand estimated from point-of-sale information. Flexible pricing practices that reflect differences in marginal costs and the point price elasticity of demand can be an efficient method for ensuring that $MR = MC$ for each product sold.

MARKUP PRICING AND PROFIT MAXIMIZATION

Optimal markups are low when the underlying price elasticity of demand is low; optimal markups are high when the price elasticity of demand is high.

Optimal Markup on Cost

Markup on Cost
The difference between price and cost, measured relative to cost, expressed as a percentage.

Markup on cost is the **profit margin** for an individual product expressed as a percentage of marginal cost. The markup-on-cost formula is given by the expression

$$\text{Markup on Cost} = (P - MC)/MC \qquad \textbf{15.5}$$

The numerator on the right-hand-side of this expression is the difference between price and marginal cost. Notice from Equation (15.5) that

Profit Margin
The difference between the price and cost of a product.

$$P = MC(1 + \text{Markup on Cost}) \qquad \textbf{15.6}$$

Managerial Application 15.1

Markup Pricing Technology

The Wall Street Journal offers bargain rates to students because even at 50 percent off regular prices, student rates more than cover marginal costs and make a significant profit contribution. Similarly, senior citizens who eat at Holiday Inns enjoy a 10 percent to 15 percent discount and make a meaningful contribution to profits. Conversely, relatively high prices for popcorn at movie theaters, peanuts at the ballpark, and clothing at the height of the season reflect the fact that customers can be insensitive to price changes at different places and at different times of the year.

Markup pricing is a method for achieving optimal prices under a variety of demand and cost conditions. Firms estimate the average variable costs of producing and marketing a given product, add a charge for variable overhead, and then add a percentage markup, or profit margin. An item with a cost of $2.30, a 69¢ markup, and a price of $2.99 has a 30 percent markup on cost and a 23 percent markup on price. Successful firms that employ markup pricing use fully allocated costs

under normal conditions, but offer price discounts or accept lower margins during off-peak periods when excess capacity is available. "Early Bird" or afternoon matinee discounts at movie theaters are an interesting example.

Except for cleaning expenses, which vary according to the number of customers, most movie theater expenses are fixed. The revenue generated by adding customers during off-peak periods can significantly increase the theater's profit contribution. When off-peak customers buy regularly priced candy, popcorn, and soda, even lower afternoon ticket prices can be justified. Conversely, on Friday and Saturday nights when movie theaters operate at peak capacity, a small increase in the number of customers would require a costly expansion of facilities. Ticket prices during these peak periods reflect fully allocated costs.

See: Katherine Boehert, "Cinema Buffs Capture Hard-to-Find Films," *The Wall Street Journal Online*, September 5, 2007, http://online.wsj.com.

To derive the optimal markup-on-cost formula, simply substitute price from Equation (15.4) for price on the left-hand-side of Equation (15.6)

$$MC(1 + \text{Optimal Markup on Cost}) = MC/[1 + (1/\varepsilon_P)] \qquad \textbf{15.7}$$

Optimal Markup on Cost
When $P = f(Q)$, set $(P - MC)/MC = -1/(\varepsilon_P + 1)$ for maximum profits.

After simplifying Equation (15.7), the **optimal markup on cost,** or profit-maximizing markup on cost, formula can be written as

$$\text{Optimal Markup on Cost} = -1/(\varepsilon_P + 1) \qquad \textbf{15.8}$$

The optimal markup-on-cost formula can be illustrated through use of a simple example. Assume a catalog retailer pays a wholesale price of $25 per pair for Birkenstock sandals, and markets them at a regular price of $75 per pair. This typical $50 profit margin implies a standard markup on cost of 200 percent because

$$\begin{aligned} \text{Markup on Cost} &= (P - MC)/MC \\ &= (\$75 - \$25)/\$25 \\ &= 2 \text{ or } 200\% \end{aligned}$$

Suppose the catalog retailer offered a discounted "preseason" price of $70 and noted a moderate increase in weekly sales from 275 to 305 pairs per week. Using the arc price elasticity formula to evaluate the effect of this $5 discount from the regular price of $75, the implied arc price elasticity of demand on Birkenstock sandals is

$$\begin{aligned} E_P &= (Q_2 - Q_1)/(Q_2 + Q_1) \div (P_2 - P_1)/(P_2 + P_1) \\ &= (305 - 275)/(305 + 275) \div (\$70 - \$75)/(\$70 + \$75) \\ &= -1.5 \end{aligned}$$

In the absence of additional evidence, this arc price elasticity of demand $E_P = -1.5$ is the best available estimate of the current point price elasticity of demand. Using Equation (15.8), the $75 regular catalog price reflects an optimal markup on cost of 200 percent because

$$\text{Optimal Markup on Cost} = -1/(-1.5 + 1) = 2 \text{ or } 200\%$$

Optimal Markup on Price

Markup on Price
The difference between price and cost, measured relative to price, expressed as a percentage.

Profit margins, or markups, are sometimes calculated as a percentage of prices instead of costs. **Markup on price** is the profit margin for an individual product or product line expressed as a percentage of price, rather than unit cost as in the markup-on-cost formula. This alternative means of expressing profit margins can be illustrated by the markup-on-price formula

$$\text{Markup on Price} = (P - MC)/P \qquad \textbf{15.9}$$

The difference between price and marginal cost is the numerator of the markup-on-price formula, just as in the markup-on-cost formula. However, marginal cost has been replaced by price in the denominator.

The profit-maximizing markup on price is easily derived from Equation (15.4)

$$P[1 + (1/\varepsilon_P)] = MC$$
$$P + P/\varepsilon_P = MC$$
$$P - MC = -P/\varepsilon_P$$
$$(P - MC)/P = -1/\varepsilon_P \qquad \qquad \textbf{15.10}$$

Optimal Markup on Price
When $P = f(Q)$, set $(P - MC)/P = -1/\varepsilon_P$ for maximum profits.

Equation (15.10) shows the relation between the profit-maximizing markup on price and the point price elasticity of demand. Therefore, the **optimal markup on price,** or profit-maximizing markup on price, formula can be written as

$$\text{Optimal Markup on Price} = -1/\varepsilon_P \qquad \qquad \textbf{15.11}$$

The optimal markup-on-price formula can be illustrated by continuing with the previous example of a catalog retailer and its optimal pricing policy for Birkenstock sandals. The catalog retailer pays a wholesale price of $25 per pair, has a regular price of $75 per pair, and the arc price elasticity of demand $E_P = -1.5$ is the best available estimate of the current point price elasticity of demand. This typical $50 profit margin implies a standard markup on price of 66.7 percent because

$$\text{Markup on Price} = (P - MC)/P$$
$$= (\$75 - \$25)/\$75$$
$$= 0.667 \text{ or } 66.7\%$$

Using Equation (15.11), the $75 regular catalog price reflects an optimal markup on price because

$$\text{Optimal Markup on Price} = -1/(-1.5) = 0.667 \text{ or } 66.7\%$$

Table 15.1 shows optimal markups for products when the point price elasticity of demand varies from $\varepsilon_P = -2$ to $\varepsilon_P = -25$. The more elastic the demand for a product, the more price sensitive it is, and the smaller is the optimal margin. Products with less elastic demand have higher optimal markups.

Why Do Optimal Markups Vary?

Peak Periods
When facilities are fully utilized.

Off-Peak Periods
Periods of excess capacity.

Optimal prices can vary from one market to another, or among customers in a single market, because of differences in relevant marginal costs. For example, during **peak** periods, facilities are fully utilized and expenses tied to capacity utilization constitute relevant marginal costs. A firm has excess capacity during **off-peak** periods, and any fixed expenses tied to capacity utilization do not contribute to marginal costs. As a result, successful firms that employ markup pricing might base prices on fully allocated costs under normal conditions but offer price discounts or accept lower margins during off-peak periods when substantial excess capacity is available.

Optimal markups also vary between markets, or between customers in a single market depending upon differences in the price elasticity of demand. In a competitive market, $P = MC$, so the markup on price tends to converge toward zero as competitive pressures increase. Conversely, $P > MC$ in monopoly markets, so the markup on price can

	Table 15.1 Optimal Markups at Various Price Elasticity Levels			
Price Elasticity of Demand, ε_P	Grocery Items	Optimal Markup on Marginal Cost (%), $-1/(\varepsilon_P + 1)$	Optimal Markup on Price, $-1/\varepsilon_P$ (%)
−2.50	Nonprescription drugs, spices, greeting cards, seasonal items	66.7	40.0
−3.00	Fresh fruits and vegetables (in season), branded nongrocery items	50.0	33.3
−6.00	Fresh fruits and vegetables (out of season), candy bars, branded goods, pastries (cakes, pies, etc.)	20.0	16.7
−8.00	Cookies, cold cuts, ice cream, private-label goods	14.3	12.5
−12.00	Cake mixes, breakfast cereal, steak	9.1	8.3
−25.00	Milk, ground beef, bread, coffee, pop, laundry detergent, soup, tissue paper	4.2	4.0

be expected to rise as competitive pressures decrease. In 1934, American economist Abba Lerner proposed that the markup on price be used as an indicator of market power. The **Lerner Index of Monopoly Power** is defined as

Lerner Index of Monopoly Power
An interpretation of the optimal markup on price as an indicator of monopoly power.

$$\text{Lerner Index} = (P - MC)/P = -1/\varepsilon_P \qquad \textbf{15.12}$$

As suggested by Lerner, high markups on price suggest some pricing power. Nevertheless, superior economic efficiency can give rise to lower marginal costs and high profit margins despite an absence of monopoly power.

PRICE DISCRIMINATION

When the price elasticity of demand varies, profits can be enhanced by charging different markups to various customers and customer groups.

Profit-Making Criteria

Price Discrimination
A pricing practice that sets prices in different markets that are not related to differences in costs.

Price discrimination occurs whenever different customers are charged different markups for the same product. Price discrimination exists when diverse customers are charged the same price despite underlying cost differences, and when price differentials charged to separate groups fail to reflect cost discrepancies. The objective of price discrimination is to increase seller revenues by better matching the prices charged with the benefits derived from consumption. By charging higher prices to high-value customers, profits rise because revenues increase without affecting costs. As shown in Figure 15.1, the objective of price discrimination is to efficiently capture consumer surplus for sellers. Precise price discrimination would involve charging the maximum each customer or customer group is willing to pay. Price discrimination is charging what the market will bear.

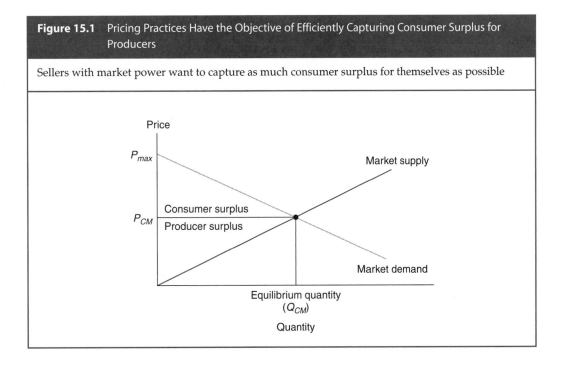

Figure 15.1   Pricing Practices Have the Objective of Efficiently Capturing Consumer Surplus for Producers

Sellers with market power want to capture as much consumer surplus for themselves as possible

Market Segment
A division or fragment of the overall market with essentially unique characteristics.

A **market segment** is a fragment of the overall market with unique demand or cost characteristics. For example, wholesale customers tend to buy in large quantities, are familiar with product costs and characteristics, and are well-informed about available alternatives. Wholesale buyers are highly price sensitive. Conversely, retail customers tend to buy in small quantities, are sometimes poorly informed about product costs and characteristics, and are often ignorant about available alternatives. As a group, retail customers are often not as price sensitive as wholesale buyers. Markups charged to retail customers usually exceed those charged to wholesale buyers.

Unless the price elasticity of demand differs among sub-markets, there is no point in segmenting the market. With identical price elasticities and identical marginal costs, a profit-maximizing pricing policy calls for the same price and markup to be charged in all market segments. For price discrimination to be profitable, the firm must also be able to efficiently identify relevant sub-markets and prevent reselling among affected customers. Highly profitable market segmentation between wholesale and retail customers can be effectively undermined if retail buyers are able to obtain discounts through willing wholesalers. Similarly, price discrimination among buyers in different parts of the country can be undermined if customers are able to resell in high-margin territories those products obtained in bargain locales.

Degrees of Price Discrimination

First-Degree Price Discrimination
Charging different prices to each customer.

Under **first-degree price discrimination,** the firm extracts the maximum amount each customer is willing to pay for its products. Each unit is priced separately at the price indicated along the demand curve in Figure 15.1. With first-degree price discrimination, the potential exists for sellers to capture all consumer surplus. Such pricing precision is rare because it requires that sellers know the maximum amount each buyer is willing to pay for each unit of output. Although first-degree price discrimination is uncommon, it has the potential to emerge in any market where discounts from posted prices are individually negotiated between buyers and sellers. When sellers possess a significant amount of market power, consumer purchases of big-ticket items such as appliances, automobiles, homes, and professional services all have the potential to involve first-degree price discrimination.

Second-Degree Price Discrimination
Charging different prices based on use rates or quantities purchased.

Second-degree price discrimination, a more commonly employed type of price discrimination, involves setting prices on the basis of the quantity purchased. Quantity discounts that lead to lower markups for large versus small customers are a common means of discriminating in price between retail and wholesale customers. Book publishers often charge full price for small purchases but offer 40 percent to 50 percent off list prices when 20 or more units are purchased. Public utilities, such as electric companies, gas companies, and water companies, also frequently charge block rates that are discriminatory. Consumers pay relatively high markups for residential service, whereas commercial and industrial customers pay relatively low markups. Office equipment such as copy machines and sophisticated mainframe computers (servers) are other examples of products for which second-degree price discrimination is practiced, especially when time sharing among customers is involved.

Third-Degree Price Discrimination
Charging different prices to each customer class.

Third-degree price discrimination, the most frequently observed form of price discrimination, results when a firm sets a different price for different groups of customers. Customer classifications can be based on for-profit or not-for-profit status, regional location, or customer age. For example, *Barron's, Forbes, The Wall Street Journal*, and other publishers routinely offer student discounts of as much as 80 percent off list prices. Publishers are eager to penetrate the classroom on the assumption that student users will become loyal future customers. Auto companies and personal computer manufacturers also offer educational discounts or first-time buyer discounts as part of their marketing strategy. Many hospitals offer price discounts to various patient groups. If unemployed and uninsured patients are routinely charged only what they can easily afford to pay for medical service, whereas employed and insured medical patients are charged maximum allowable rates, the hospital is price discriminating in favor of the unemployed and against the employed. Widespread price discounts for senior citizens represent a form of price discrimination in favor of older customers but against younger customers.

It is important to recognize that price discrimination does not necessarily carry any evil connotation in a moral sense. In some circumstances, price discrimination leads to wider availability of goods and services. For example, a municipal bus company might charge lower prices and thereby price discriminate in favor of elderly and handicapped riders and against other customers. This type of price discrimination provides elderly and handicapped customers a greater opportunity to ride the bus. Because of incremental revenues provided by elderly and handicapped riders, the bus company may also be able to offer routes that could not be supported by revenues from full-fare customers alone, or it may be able to operate with a lower taxpayer subsidy.

PRICE DISCRIMINATION EXAMPLE

Price discrimination is a fact of life in the airline, entertainment, hotel, medical, legal, and professional services industries.

Managerial Application 15.2

Do Colleges Price Discriminate?

Most college students receive financial aid. At many colleges, the average financial aid recipient comes from a family with annual income in excess of $50,000—and many come from families with incomes exceeding $100,000. As a result, some economists suggest that college financial aid is not about "needy students" but is instead a means of price discrimination designed to extract the largest net amount from students, their families, and the government.

Some economists argue that colleges levy a list price (tuition) set far above what most people can pay and then offer varying discounts (financial aid) so that each customer is charged what the traffic will bear. Financial aid is available when the cost of college exceeds the "expected family contribution," a measure based on family income, assets, the number of children, and so on. Even a small college could lose millions of dollars in federal aid if it kept tuition affordable. According to critics, federal subsidies and virtual exemption from antitrust laws have produced skyrocketing college costs and price discrimination. Economist Milton

Friedman estimates that colleges could operate at a profit by charging half of what the Ivy League schools charge.

School administrators point out that many would be unable to afford college without some cross-subsidization among students. Private schools also use endowment income to supplement student tuition and fees, whereas public colleges and universities enjoy substantial tax-revenue income. Even the premiums paid by out-of-state students at leading state universities fail to cover fully allocated costs per student. However, average costs may not be relevant for pricing purposes. The marginal cost per student is often nearly zero, and even very low net tuition-plus-fee income can often make a significant contribution to overhead. From an economic perspective, the pricing practices of colleges and universities may in fact be consistent with the theory of price discrimination.

See: Associated press, "Tuition Increases Outpace Financial Aid," *The Wall Street Journal Online*, October 23, 2007, http://online.wsj.com.

Price–Output Determination

Price discrimination is profitable because it allows sellers to enhance revenues without increasing costs. It is an effective means for increasing profits because it allows firms and other sellers to more closely match marginal revenues and marginal costs. A firm that can segment its market maximizes profits by operating at the point where marginal revenue equals marginal cost in each market segment.

For example, suppose that Midwest State University (MSU) wants to reduce the athletic department's operating deficit and increase student attendance at home football games. To achieve these objectives, a new two-tier pricing structure for season football tickets is being considered in light of the following demand and marginal revenue relations:

<table>
<tr><th>Public Demand</th><th>Student Demand</th></tr>
<tr><td>$P_P = \$850 - \$0.01Q_P$</td><td>$P_S = \$200 - \$0.0025Q_S$</td></tr>
<tr><td>$MR_P = \partial TR_P / \partial Q_P = \$850 - \$0.02Q_P$</td><td>$MR_S = \partial TR_S / \partial Q_S = \$200 - \$0.005Q_S$</td></tr>
</table>

From these market demand and marginal revenue curves, it is obvious that the general public is willing to pay higher prices than are students. The general public is willing to purchase season tickets up to a market price of $850, above which point market demand equals zero. Students are willing to enter the market only at season ticket prices below $200.

During recent years, the football program has run on an operating budget of $15 million per year. This budget covers fixed salary, recruiting, insurance, and facility-maintenance expenses. In addition to these fixed expenses, the university incurs variable ticket-handling, facility-cleaning, insurance, and security costs of $50 per season ticket holder. The resulting total cost and marginal cost functions are

$$TC = \$15{,}000{,}000 + \$50Q$$
$$MC = \partial TC / \partial Q = \$50$$

The athletic department's operating deficit is minimized by setting $MR = MC = \$50$ in each market segment and solving for Q. This is also the profit-maximizing strategy for the football program.

Public Demand

$$MR_P = MC$$
$$\$850 - \$0.02Q_P = \$50$$
$$\$0.02Q_P = \$800$$
$$Q_P = 40{,}000$$

and

$$P_P = \$850 - \$0.01(40{,}000)$$
$$= \$450$$

Student Demand

$$MR_S = MC$$
$$\$200 - \$0.005Q_S = \$50$$
$$\$0.005Q_S = \$150$$
$$Q_S = 30{,}000$$

and,

$$P_S = \$200 - \$0.0025(30{,}000)$$
$$= \$125$$

The football program's resulting total operating surplus (profit) is

$$\text{Operating Surplus (Profit)} = TR_P + TR_S - TC$$
$$= \$450(40{,}000) + \$125(30{,}000)$$
$$-\$15{,}000{,}000 - \$50(70{,}000)$$
$$= \$3.25 \text{ million}$$

Therefore, the optimal price–output combination with price discrimination is 40,000 in unit sales to the general public at a price of $450, and 30,000 in unit sales to students at a price of $125. This two-tier pricing practice results in an optimal operating surplus (profit) of $3.25 million.

One-Price Alternative

To gauge the implications of this new two-tier ticket pricing practice, it is interesting to contrast the resulting price–output and surplus levels with those that would result if MSU used a one-price ticket policy. If tickets are offered to students and the general public at the same price, the total amount of ticket demand equals the sum of student plus general public demand. The student and general public market demand curves are

$$Q_P = 85{,}000 - 100P_P \text{ and } Q_S = 80{,}000 - 400P_S$$

Under the assumption $P_P = P_S$, total demand (Q_T) equals

$$Q_T = Q_P + Q_S$$
$$= 165{,}000 - 500P$$

and,

$$P = \$330 - \$0.002Q$$

which implies that

$$MR = \partial TR / \partial Q = \$330 - \$0.004Q$$

These aggregate student-plus-general public market demand and marginal revenue curves hold only for prices below \$200, a level at which both the general public and students purchase tickets. For prices above \$200, students have been priced out of the market, and the public demand curve $P_P = \$850 - \$0.01Q_P$ represents total market demand as well. This causes the actual total demand curve to be kinked at a price of \$200, as shown in Figure 15.2.

Without price discrimination, set $MR = MC$ for the total market and solving for Q:

$$MR = MC$$
$$\$330 - \$0.004Q = \$50$$
$$\$0.004Q = \$280$$
$$Q = 70{,}000$$
$$P = \$330 - \$0.002(70{,}000)$$
$$= \$190$$

and

$$Q_P = 85{,}000 - 100(\$190) \qquad\qquad Q_S = 80{,}000 - 400(\$190)$$
$$= 66{,}000 \qquad\qquad\qquad\qquad\qquad = 4{,}000$$
$$\text{Operating deficit (loss)} = TR - TC$$
$$= \$190(70{,}000) - \$15{,}000{,}000$$
$$- \$50(70{,}000)$$
$$= -\$5.2 \text{ million (a loss)}$$

The total number of tickets sold equals 70,000 under both the two-tier and the single-price policies because the marginal cost of a ticket is the same under each scenario. Ticket-pricing policies featuring student discounts increase student attendance from 4,000 to 30,000 and maximize the football program's operating surplus at \$3.25 million (rather than suffer an operating deficit of \$5.2 million). It is the preferred pricing policy when viewed from MSU's perspective. However, such price discrimination creates both "winners" and "losers." Winners following adoption of student discounts include students and MSU. Losers include members of the general public, who pay higher football ticket prices or find themselves priced out of the market.

Figure 15.2 Price Discrimination for an Identical Product Sold in Two Markets

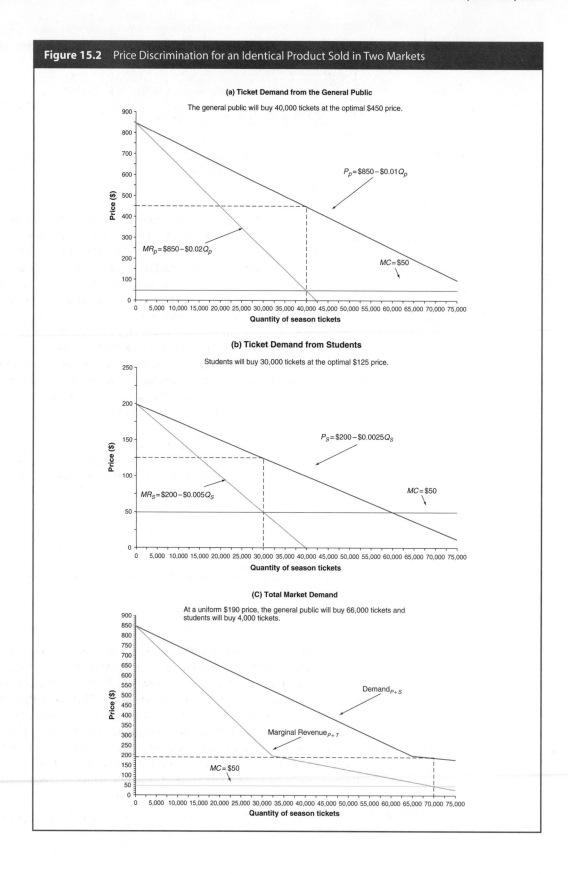

(a) Ticket Demand from the General Public

The general public will buy 40,000 tickets at the optimal $450 price.

$P_p = \$850 - \$0.01 Q_p$

$MR_p = \$850 - \$0.02 Q_p$

$MC = \$50$

(b) Ticket Demand from Students

Students will buy 30,000 tickets at the optimal $125 price.

$P_S = \$200 - \$0.0025 Q_S$

$MR_S = \$200 - \$0.005 Q_S$

$MC = \$50$

(C) Total Market Demand

At a uniform $190 price, the general public will buy 66,000 tickets and students will buy 4,000 tickets.

$Demand_{P+S}$

$Marginal\ Revenue_{P+T}$

$MC = \$50$

TWO-PART PRICING

Customers are sometimes charged a lump sum amount plus a usage fee to extract the maximum amount they are willing to pay for various goods and services.

One-Price Policy and Consumer Surplus

The total area under the demand curve, as shown in Figure 15.3, captures the value obtained from consumption. This area is comprised of two parts: the shaded triangle that reflects consumer surplus and the rectangle that represents total revenue. Recall that consumer

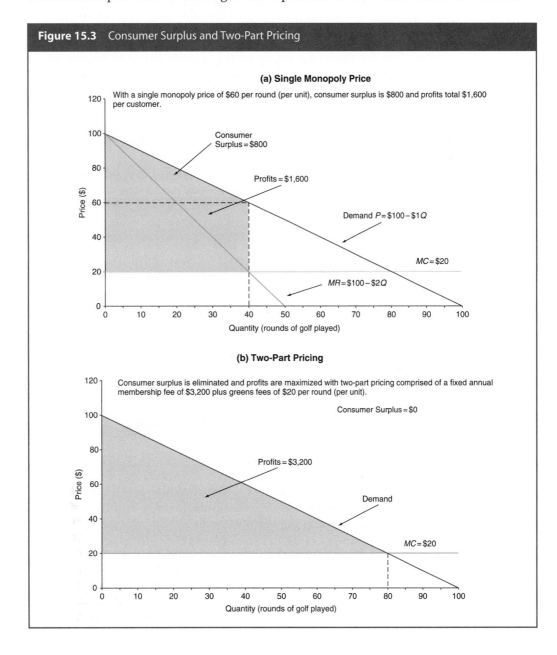

Figure 15.3 Consumer Surplus and Two-Part Pricing

(a) Single Monopoly Price

With a single monopoly price of $60 per round (per unit), consumer surplus is $800 and profits total $1,600 per customer.

Consumer Surplus = $800

Profits = $1,600

Demand $P = \$100 - \$1Q$

$MC = \$20$

$MR = \$100 - \$2Q$

Price ($)

Quantity (rounds of golf played)

(b) Two-Part Pricing

Consumer surplus is eliminated and profits are maximized with two-part pricing comprised of a fixed annual membership fee of $3,200 plus greens fees of $20 per round (per unit).

Consumer Surplus = $0

Profits = $3,200

Demand

$MC = \$20$

Price ($)

Quantity (rounds of golf played)

surplus arises because individual consumers place different values on goods and services. At high prices, only customers that place a relatively high value on the product are buyers; at low prices, both high-value and low-value customers are buyers. As one proceeds downward along the demand curve in Figure 15.3, customers that place a progressively lower marginal value on the product enter the market. Similarly, if the value placed upon consumption by given customer declines as usage increases, that customer also faces a downward-sloping demand curve.

To illustrate, assume that an avid golfer's demand and marginal revenue curves can be written as

$$P = \$100 - \$1Q$$
$$MR = \partial TR / \partial Q = \$100 - \$2Q$$

where P is the price of a single round of golf, and Q is the number of rounds played during a given year. For simplicity, also assume that the marginal cost of a round of golf is $20, and that fixed costs are nil. This gives the following total and marginal cost relations:

$$TC = \$20Q$$
$$MC = \partial TC / \partial Q = \$20$$

As shown in Figure 4.10(a), the profit-maximizing one-price policy is found by setting $MR = MC$, where

$$MR = MC$$
$$\$100 - \$2Q = \$20$$
$$2Q = 80$$
$$Q = 40$$

At the profit-maximizing quantity of 40, the optimal price is $60 and total profits equal $1,600 per customer because

$$P = \$100 - \$1(40)$$
$$= \$60$$
$$\pi = TR - TC$$
$$= \$60(40) - \$20(40)$$
$$= \$1,600$$

Notice from Figure 15.3(a) that the value of consumer surplus based upon the one-price policy is equal to the region under the demand curve that lies above the profit-maximizing price of $60. Because the area of such a triangle is one-half the value of the base times the height, the value of consumer surplus equals

$$\text{Consumer Surplus} = \tfrac{1}{2} [40 \times (\$100 - \$60)]$$
$$= \$800$$

Because consumer surplus equals $800, the avid golfer in question would have been willing to pay an additional $800 to play these 40 rounds of golf. This amount is above and beyond the $2,400 paid. The avid golfer received a real bargain at the single-unit price of $60 per round.

Capturing Consumer Surplus with Two-Part Pricing

Two-Part Pricing
A per unit fee equal to marginal cost, plus a fixed fee equal to the amount of consumer surplus generated at that per unit fee.

Athletic clubs, time-share vacation resorts, golf courses, and a wide variety of "membership organizations" offer goods and services using two-part pricing. A common **two-part pricing** technique is to charge all customers a fixed "membership" fee, plus a per unit usage charge. In general, a firm can enhance profits by charging each customer a per unit fee equal to marginal cost, plus a fixed fee equal to the amount of consumer surplus generated at that per unit fee.

In the case of golf course memberships, two-part pricing typically consists of a large annual membership fee plus "greens fees" charged for each round of golf played. As an alternative to charging a price of $60 per round, consider the profits that could be earned using a two-part pricing policy. To maximize profits, the golf course would charge a per unit price that equals marginal cost, plus a fixed fee equal to the amount of consumer surplus received by each consumer at this price. In Figure 15.3(a) the value of consumer surplus is equal to the region under the demand curve that lies above the per unit price. When the price per round is set equal to marginal cost, $P = \$20$, $Q = 80$ because

$$P = MC$$
$$\$100 - \$1Q = \$20$$
$$Q = 80$$

At the price of $20 per round and output level of 80, the value of consumer surplus equals

$$\text{Consumer Surplus} = \frac{1}{2}\,[80 \times (\$100 - \$20)]$$
$$= \$3,200$$

The consumer surplus of $3,200 is the maximum annual membership fee the golfer in question would pay to play 80 rounds of golf per year when additional greens fees of $20 per round are charged. The profit-maximizing two-part pricing practice is to charge such players an annual membership fee of $3,200 per year plus greens fees of $20 per round played. Golf course revenues of $4,800 represent the full value derived from playing 80 rounds of golf per year, cover marginal costs of $1,600 (= $20 × 80), and result in a $3,200 profit from each customer.

Sellers must enjoy market power in order to institute any such two-part pricing scheme. Otherwise, competitors would undercut annual membership fees, and per unit prices would converge on marginal costs. Therefore, it should not be surprising that high golf membership fees are most common in urban areas where conveniently located golf courses are in short supply. In outlying or rural areas, where restrictions on the location of new golf courses are less stringent, high membership fees are rare.

Bundle Pricing
When products are purchased together as a package of goods or services.

Consumer Surplus and Bundle Pricing

Another way firms with market power enhance profits is by a variant of two-part pricing called **bundle pricing.** If you've ever purchased a 12-pack of soft drinks, a year's supply of tax preparation services, or bought a "two-for-the-price-of-one" special, you have firsthand experience with the bundle-pricing concept. When significant consumer surplus exists, profits can be enhanced if products are purchased together as a single package or bundle of goods or services. Bundles can be of a single product, like soft drinks or legal services, or they can be comprised of closely related goods and services. For example, car manufacturers often bundle "luxury packages" comprised of new car options like power steering, power brakes, automatic transmissions, tinted glass, and so on. Similarly, car dealers often bundle services like oil changes, transmission fluid changes, radiator flushes, and tune-ups at a "special package price."

In the case of a single product sold in multiple-unit bundles, the optimal bundle price is derived in a manner similar to the optimal two-part price calculation described in Figure 4.10. As in the case of two-part pricing, setting price equal to marginal cost, and solving for quantity determines the optimal level of output. Then, the optimal bundle price is a single lump sum amount equal to the total area under the demand curve at that point. In Figure 15.3(b), for example, the optimal bundle price of $4,800 would include the total value of consumer surplus generated with a single per unit price (or $3,200), plus total cost (or $1,600).

Optimal pricing for bundles of related but not identical products is figured in an analogous manner. Again, the total amount charged equals the value of the total area under the demand curve at the optimal output level, where output is defined as a bundle of related goods or services. As in the case of two-part pricing, the optimal level of output is determined by setting price equal to marginal cost, and solving for quantity. The optimal bundle price is simply a lump sum amount equal to the total area under the demand curve at that activity level. In the case of related but not identical products, bundle pricing is sometimes used because firms are not able to precisely determine the amounts different consumers are willing to pay for different products. If exact information about the value of each individual product for each individual consumer was available, the firm could earn even higher profits by precisely tying the price charged to the value derived by each customer.

MULTIPLE-PRODUCT PRICING

Multiple-product pricing requires the same basic analysis as for a single product, but the analysis is complicated by demand and production interrelations.

Demand Interrelations

Demand interrelations arise because of substitute or complementary relations among various products or product lines. If products are interrelated, either as substitutes or as complements, a change in the price of one affects demand for the other. Multiple-product pricing decisions must reflect such influences. In the case of a two-product firm, the marginal revenue functions for each product can be written as

$$MR_A = \frac{\partial TR}{\partial Q_A} = \frac{\partial TR_A}{\partial Q_A} + \frac{\partial TR_B}{\partial Q_A} \qquad \textbf{15.13}$$

$$MR_B = \frac{\partial TR}{\partial Q_B} = \frac{\partial TR_B}{\partial Q_B} + \frac{\partial TR_A}{\partial Q_B} \qquad \textbf{15.14}$$

The first term on the right side of each equation represents the marginal revenue directly associated with each product. The second term depicts the indirect marginal revenue associated with each product and indicates the change in revenues due to a change in sales of the alternative product. For example, $\partial TR_B/\partial Q_A$ in Equation (15.13) shows the effect on product B revenues of an additional unit sold of product A. Likewise, $\partial TR_A/\partial Q_B$ in Equation (15.14) represents the change in revenues received from product A when an additional unit of product B is sold.

Cross-marginal revenue terms that reflect demand interrelations can be positive or negative. For complementary products, the net effect is positive because increased sales of one product lead to increased revenues from another. For substitute products, increased sales of one product reduce demand for another, and the cross-marginal revenue term is negative. Accurate price determination in the case of multiple products requires a complete analysis of pricing decision effects. This often means that optimal pricing requires an application of incremental analysis to ensure that the total implications of pricing decisions are reflected.

Production Interrelations

By-Product
Output that is customarily produced as a direct result of an increase in the production of some other output.

A **by-product** is any output that is customarily produced as a direct result of an increase in the production of some other output. Although it is common to think of by-products as resulting only from physical production processes, they are also generated in the process of providing services. One of the primary reasons why top tax accounting firms have become such a leading force in the financial planning business is that the information generated in preparing tax returns for corporations and high-income individuals gives valuable insight into investment strategies designed to maximize after-tax income. In this way, tax advice and financial planning services are joint products produced in variable proportions. Given the efficiencies of joint production, it is common for accounting firm tax clients to also become clients for a host of related financial services.

Multiple products are produced in variable proportions for a wide range of goods and services. In the refining process for crude oil, gasoline, diesel fuel, heating oil, and other products are produced in variable proportions. The cost and availability of any single by-product depends on the demand for others. By-products are also sometimes the unintended or unavoidable consequence of producing certain goods. When lumber is produced, scrap bark and sawdust are also created for use in gardening and paper production. When paper is produced, residual chemicals and polluted water are created that must be treated and recycled. Indeed, pollution can be thought of as the necessary by-product of many production processes. Because pollution is, by definition, a "bad" with harmful social consequences rather than a "good" with socially redeeming value, production processes must often be altered to minimize this type of negative joint product.

Production interrelations are sometimes so strong that the joint nature of production is relatively constant. For example, many agricultural products are jointly produced in a fixed ratio. Wheat and straw, beef and hides, milk and butter are all produced in relatively fixed proportions. In mining, gold and copper, silver and lead, and other precious metals and minerals are often produced jointly in fixed proportions. Appropriate pricing and production decisions are possible only when such interrelations are accurately reflected.

JOINT PRODUCTS

Optimal pricing practices depends upon whether joint products are produced in variable or fixed proportions.

Joint Products in Variable Proportions

The marginal costs of joint products produced in variable proportions equals the increase in total costs associated with a 1-unit increase in that product, holding constant the quantity of the other joint product produced. Optimal price–output determination for joint products in this case requires a simultaneous solution of marginal cost and marginal revenue relations. The firm maximizes profit by operating at the output level where the marginal cost of producing each joint product just equals the marginal revenue it generates. The profit-maximizing combination of joint products A and B, for example, occurs at the output level where $MR_A = MC_A$ and $MR_B = MC_B$.

Common Costs
Expenses that are necessary for manufacture of a joint product.

It is important to note, however, that although it is possible to determine the separate marginal costs of goods produced in variable proportions, it is impossible to determine their individual average costs. This is because **common costs** are expenses necessary for manufacture of a joint product. Common costs of production—raw material and equipment costs, management expenses, and other overhead—cannot be allocated to each individual by-product on any economically sound basis. Only costs that can be separately identified with a specific by-product can be allocated. For example, tanning costs for hides and refrigeration costs for beef are separate identifiable costs of each by-product. Feed costs are common and cannot be allocated between hide and beef production. Any allocation of common costs is wrong and arbitrary.

Joint Products in Fixed Proportions

When by-products are jointly produced in fixed proportions, all costs are common, and there is no economically sound method of cost allocation. Optimal price–output determination for output produced in fixed proportions requires analysis of the relation between marginal revenue and marginal cost for the combined output package. As long as the sum of marginal revenues obtained from all by-products is greater than the marginal cost of production, the firm gains by expanding output.

Figure 15.4 illustrates the pricing problem for two products produced in fixed proportions. Demand and marginal revenue curves for each by-product and the single marginal cost curve for production of the combined output package are shown. Vertical summation of the two marginal revenue curves indicates the total marginal revenue generated by both by-products. Marginal revenue curves are summed vertically because each unit of output provides revenues from the sale of both by-products. The intersection of the total marginal revenue curve MR_T with the marginal cost curve identifies the profit-maximizing output level.

The optimal price for each by-product is determined by the intersection of a vertical line at the profit-maximizing output level with each by-product's demand curve. Q_1 represents the optimal quantity of the output package to be produced, and P_A and P_B are the prices to be charged for each by-product.

Notice that the MR_T curve in Figure 15.4 coincides with the marginal revenue curve for product B at all output quantities greater than Q_2. This is because MR_A becomes negative at that point, and the firm would not sell more than the quantity of

Figure 15.4 Optimal Pricing for Joint Products Produced in Fixed Proportions

For joint products produced in fixed proportions, the optimal activity level occurs at the point where the marginal revenues derived from both products (MR_T) equal the marginal cost of production..

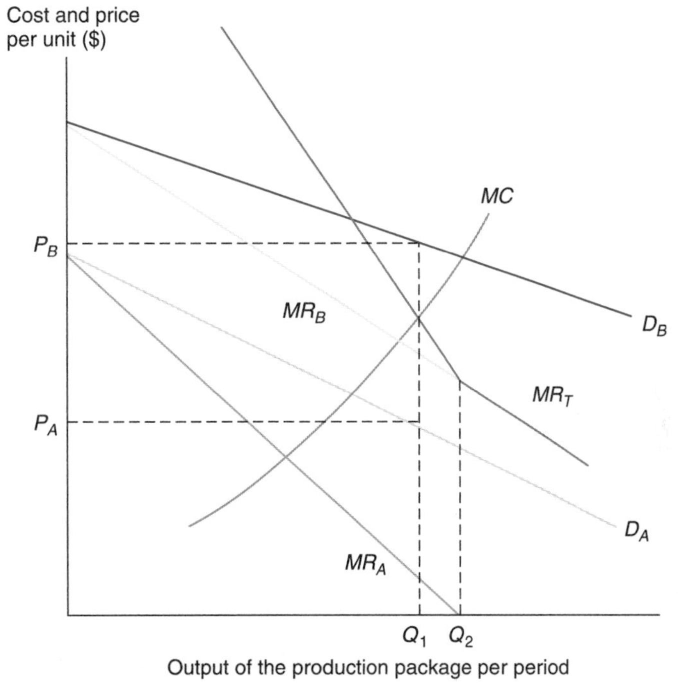

Output of the production package per period

product A represented by output package Q_2. The total revenue generated by product A is maximized at output Q_2; sales of any larger quantity of product A would reduce revenues and profits.

If the marginal cost curve for the output package intersects the total marginal revenue curve to the right of Q_2, profit maximization requires that the firm raise output up to this point of intersection. At that point, product B must be priced as indicated by its demand and marginal revenue curves. Because product B sales offer the sole motivation for production beyond the Q_2 level, the marginal revenue generated from product B sales must be sufficient to cover the marginal costs of producing the entire output package. In this instance, profit maximization requires that $MR_B = MC$. Beyond the Q_2 level, the marginal cost of product A is zero; product A is the unavoidable by-product of product B production. Beyond the Q_2 level, the price of product A is set in order to maximize profits in that $MR_A = MC_A = 0$. This pricing situation is illustrated in Figure 15.5, which shows the same demand and marginal revenue curves presented in Figure 15.4, along with a new marginal cost curve. The optimal output quantity is Q_3, determined by the intersection of the marginal cost curve and the total marginal revenue curve. Product B is sold in the amount indicated by output package Q_3 and is priced at P_B. The sales quantity of product A is limited to the amount in output Q_2 and is priced at P_A. The excess quantity of product A produced, shown as $Q_3 - Q_2$, must be destroyed or otherwise kept out of the market so that its price and total revenue is not lowered below that indicated at Q_2.

Figure 15.5 Optimal Pricing for Joint Products Produced in Fixed Proportions with Excess Production of One Product

When all of by-product A cannot be sold at a price that generates positive marginal revenue, its sales will be limited to the point where $MR_A = 0$. Excess production, shown as $Q_3 - Q_2$, will be destroyed or otherwise held off the market.

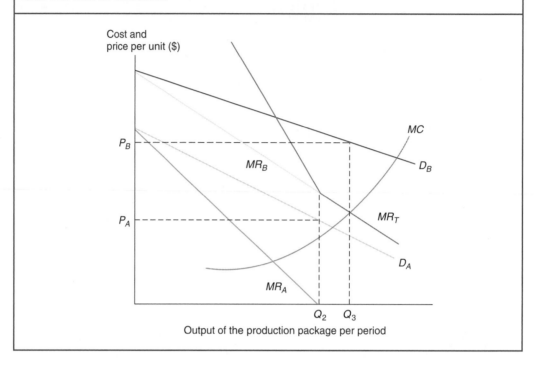

Output of the production package per period

An example of joint output that is sometimes destroyed or otherwise held off the market is provided by sliced pineapple and pineapple juice; juice is produced as a by-product as pineapples are peeled and sliced. Some years ago, an excessive amount of pineapple juice was produced, and rather than put it on the market and depress prices, the excess was destroyed. Seeing a profit-making opportunity, Dole, Del Monte, and other producers advertised heavily to shift the demand curve for pineapple juice outward. New products were also created, such as pineapple-grapefruit juice, to spur demand for the waste by-product. Canning machinery was also improved to reduce the amount of juice. Today, little if any pineapple excess juice by-product is produced. Similarly, firms in many other industries have discovered new and valuable uses for previously discarded by-products.

JOINT PRODUCT PRICING EXAMPLE

The solution of joint product pricing problems often requires detailed analysis.

Joint Products without Excess By-Product

Imagine that the Vancouver Paper Company, Ltd., produces newsprint and packaging materials in a fixed 1:1 ratio, or one ton of packaging materials per one ton of newsprint.

These two products, A (newsprint) and B (packaging materials), are produced in equal quantities because newsprint production leaves scrap by-product that is useful only in the production of lower-grade packaging materials. The total and marginal cost functions for Vancouver can be written as

$$TC = \$2,000,000 + \$50Q + \$0.01Q^2$$
$$MC = \partial TC/\partial Q = \$50 + \$0.02Q$$

where Q is a composite package or bundle of output consisting of one ton of product A and one ton of product B. Given current market conditions, demand and marginal revenue curves for each product are as follows:

Newsprint	Packaging Materials
$P_A = \$400 - \$0.01Q_A$	$P_B = \$350 - \$0.015Q_B$
$MR_A = \partial TR_A/\partial Q_A = \$400 - \$0.02Q_A$	$MR_B = \partial TR_B/\partial Q_B = \$350 - \$0.03Q_B$

For each unit of Q produced, the firm obtains 1 unit of product A and 1 unit of product B for sale to customers. The revenue derived from the production and sale of 1 unit of Q is composed of revenues from the sales of 1 unit of product A plus 1 unit of product B. Therefore, the total revenue function is merely a sum of the revenue functions for products A and B:

$$TR = TR_A + TR_B$$
$$= P_AQ_A + P_BQ_B$$

Managerial Application 15.3

10¢ for a Gallon of Gas in Dayton, Ohio

In every state, retail gasoline prices must be clearly visible to passing motorists. At the same time, octane content is regulated so that the gas available for sale meets minimum standards as a clean-burning fuel. With prominently displayed prices, and consistently high gas quality, the groundwork is in place for vicious price competition.

Price-conscious drivers commonly bypass high-price stations in the effort to save as little as 2¢ or 3¢ per gallon. As a result, profit margins on gasoline are notoriously low. Margins are typically so low that convenience stores see gasoline as a "loss leader" for other high-margin products. Although the typical driver will go out of the way to save no more than 50¢ on a tank of gas, that same driver will see nothing wrong with going inside the convenience store and paying $1.29 for a large cup of soda, 89¢ for a candy bar, or $3.49 for a pack of cigarettes. In no small way, convenience stores offer gasoline as a means of generating traffic for soda, candy, and cigarettes.

For example, in November 2001, Cincinnati-based Kroger Co., which has about 180 grocery stores with gas stations, opened a new store and gas station in Dayton, Ohio. During a three-day grand opening period, Kroger decided to price its gasoline 10¢ per gallon below local market norms as a means for generating favorable customer interest and publicity. Competitors took notice, too. Just down the street, the Meijer superstore/gas station, owned by closely held Meijer Inc. of Grand Rapids, Michigan, decided to cut its price. An all-out price war developed. Within hours, gasoline prices in Dayton fell from $1.08 (the Midwest market average) to 50¢ per gallon, and briefly all the way down to 10¢ per gallon! In commenting on the situation, Kroger officials said that such prices were not part of the company's "everyday price strategy," but "we intend to be competitive."

See: Maxwell Murphy, "Kroger Versus Meijer: Gasoline Price War Rages in Dayton," *The Wall Street Journal Online*, November 30, 2001, http://online.wsj.com.

Substituting for P_A and P_B results in the total revenue function:

$$TR = (\$400 - \$0.01Q_A)Q_A + (\$350 - \$0.015Q_B)Q_B$$
$$= \$400Q_A - \$0.01Q_A{}^2 + \$350Q_B - \$0.015Q_B{}^2$$

Because 1 unit of product A and 1 unit of product B are contained in each unit of Q, $Q_A = Q_B = Q$. This allows substitution of Q for Q_A and Q_B to develop a total revenue function in terms of Q, the unit of production:

$$TR = \$400Q - \$0.01Q^2 + \$350Q - \$0.015Q^2$$
$$= \$750Q - \$0.025Q^2$$

This total revenue function assumes that all quantities of product A and B produced are also sold. It assumes no dumping or withholding from the market for either product. It is the appropriate total revenue function if, as in Figure 15.4, the marginal revenues of both products are positive at the profit-maximizing output level. When this occurs, revenues from each product contribute toward covering marginal costs.

The profit-maximizing output level is found by setting $MR = MC$ and solving for Q:

$$MR = MC$$
$$\$750 - \$0.05Q = \$50 + \$0.02Q$$
$$0.07Q = 700$$
$$Q = 10{,}000 \text{ units}$$

At the activity level $Q = 10{,}000$ units, marginal revenues for each product are positive:

$$MR_A = \$400 - \$0.02Q_A \qquad\qquad MR_B = \$350 - \$0.03Q_B$$
$$= \$400 - \$0.02(10{,}000) \qquad\qquad = \$350 - \$0.03(10{,}000)$$
$$= \$200 \text{ (at 10,000 units)} \qquad\qquad = \$50 \text{ (at 10,000 units)}$$

Each product makes a positive contribution toward covering the marginal cost of production, where

$$MC = \$50 + \$0.02Q$$
$$= \$50 + \$0.02(10{,}000)$$
$$= \$250$$

There is no reason to expand or reduce production because $MR = MR_A + MR_B = MC = \$250$, and each product generates positive marginal revenues.

Prices for each product and total profits for Vancouver can be calculated from the demand and total profit functions:

$$P_A = \$400 - \$0.01Q_A \qquad\qquad P_B = \$350 - \$0.015Q_B$$
$$= \$400 - \$0.01(10{,}000) \qquad\qquad = \$350 - \$0.015(10{,}000)$$
$$= \$300 \qquad\qquad = \$200$$

and

$$\pi = P_A Q_A + P_B Q_B - TC$$
$$= \$300(10,000) + \$200(10,000) - \$2,000,000$$
$$- \$50(10,000) - \$0.01(10,000^2)$$
$$= \$1,500,000$$

Vancouver should produce 10,000 units of output and sell the resulting 10,000 units of product A at a price of \$300 per ton and 10,000 units of product B at a price of \$200 per ton. An optimum total profit of \$1.5 million is earned at this activity level.

Joint Production with Excess By-Product (Dumping)

The determination of a profit-maximizing activity level is only slightly more complex if a downturn in demand for either product A or B causes marginal revenue for one product to be negative when all output produced is sold to the marketplace.

Suppose that an economic recession causes the demand for product B (packaging materials) to fall dramatically, while the demand for product A (newsprint) and marginal cost conditions hold steady. Assume new demand and marginal revenue relations for product B of

$$P'_B = \$290 - \$0.02Q_B$$
$$MR'_B = \$290 - \$0.04Q_B$$

A dramatically lower price of \$90 per ton [= \$290 − \$0.02(10,000)] is now required to sell 10,000 units of product B. However, this price and activity level is suboptimal.

To see why, the profit-maximizing activity level must again be calculated, assuming that all output is sold. The new marginal revenue curve for Q is

$$MR = MR_A + MR'_B$$
$$= \$400 - \$0.02Q_A + \$290 - \$0.04Q_B$$
$$= \$690 - \$0.06Q$$

If all production is sold, the profit-maximizing level for output is found by setting $MR = MC$ and solving for Q:

$$MR = MC$$
$$\$690 - \$0.06Q = \$50 + \$0.02Q$$
$$0.08Q = 640$$
$$Q = 8,000$$

At $Q = 8,000$, the sum of marginal revenues derived from both by-products and the marginal cost of producing the combined output package each equal \$210, because

$$MR = \$690 - \$0.06Q \qquad\qquad MC = \$50 + \$0.02Q$$
$$= \$690 - \$0.06(8,000) \qquad\qquad = \$50 + \$0.02(8,000)$$
$$= \$210 \qquad\qquad\qquad\qquad = \$210$$

However, the marginal revenue of product B is no longer positive:

$$MR_A = \$400 - \$0.02Q_A \qquad\qquad MR'_B = \$290 - \$0.04Q_B$$
$$= \$400 - \$0.02(8{,}000) \qquad\qquad = \$290 - \$0.04(8{,}000)$$
$$= \$240 \qquad\qquad\qquad = -\$30$$

Even though $MR = MC = \$210$, the marginal revenue of product B is negative at the $Q = 8{,}000$ activity level. This means that the price reduction necessary to sell the last unit of product B causes Vancouver's total revenue to decline by \$30. Rather than selling product B at such unfavorable terms, Vancouver would prefer to withhold some from the marketplace. In contrast, Vancouver would like to produce and sell more than 8,000 units of product A because $MR_A > MC$ at the 8,000 unit activity level. It would be profitable for the company to expand production of Q just to increase sales of product A, even if it had to destroy or otherwise withhold from the market the unavoidable added production of product B.

Under these circumstances, set the marginal revenue of product A, the only product sold at the margin, equal to the marginal cost of production to find the profit-maximizing activity level:

$$MR_A = MC$$
$$\$400 - \$0.02Q = \$50 + \$0.02Q$$
$$\$0.04Q = \$350$$
$$Q = 8{,}750 \text{ units}$$

Under these circumstances, Vancouver should produce 8,750 units of $Q = Q_A = Q_B$. Because this activity level is based on the assumption that only product A is sold at the margin and that the marginal revenue of product A covers all marginal production costs, *the effective marginal cost of product B is zero*. As long as production is sufficient to provide 8,750 units of product A, 8,750 units of product B are also produced without any additional cost.

With an effective marginal cost of zero for product B, its contribution to firm profits is maximized by setting the marginal revenue of product B equal to zero (its effective marginal cost):

$$MR'_B = MC_B$$
$$\$290 - \$0.04Q_B = \$0$$
$$\$0.04Q_B = \$290$$
$$Q_B = 7{,}250$$

Whereas a total of 8,750 units of Q should be produced, only 7,250 units of product B will be sold. The remaining 1,500 units of Q_B must be destroyed or otherwise withheld from the market.

Optimal prices and the maximum total profit for Vancouver are as follows:

$$P_A = \$400 - \$0.01Q_A \qquad\qquad P_B = \$290 - \$0.02Q_B$$
$$= \$400 - \$0.01(8{,}750) \qquad\qquad = \$290 - \$0.02(7{,}250)$$
$$= \$312.50 \qquad\qquad\qquad = \$145$$

$$\pi = P_A Q_A + P'_B Q_B - TC$$
$$= \$312.50(8,750) + \$145(7,250) - \$2,000,000$$
$$- \$50(8,750) - \$0.01(8,750^2)$$
$$= \$582,500$$

No other price–output combination has the potential to generate as large a profit for Vancouver.

SUMMARY

This chapter examines a number of popular pricing practices. Methods commonly employed by successful firms reflect the use of marginal analysis to derive profit-maximizing prices.

- Profit maximization always requires finding the firm's price–output combination that will set $MR = MC$. The **competitive market pricing rule-of-thumb** for profit maximization is to set $P = MR = MC$. The **imperfectly competitive market pricing rule-of-thumb** for profit maximization is to set $P = MC/[1 + (1/\varepsilon_P)]$.

- **Markup on cost** is the profit margin for an individual product or product line expressed as a percentage of unit cost. The numerator of this expression, called the **profit margin**, is the difference between price and cost. The **optimal markup-on-cost** formula is $(P - MC)/MC = -1/(\varepsilon_P + 1)$.

- Profit margins, or markups, are sometimes calculated as a percentage of price instead of cost. **Markup on price** is the profit margin for an individual product or product line expressed as a percentage of price, rather than unit cost as in the markup-on-cost formula. The **optimal markup-on-price** formula is $(P - MC)/P = -1/\varepsilon_P$. Either optimal markup formula can be used to derive profit-maximizing prices solely on the basis of marginal cost and price elasticity of demand information.

- In competitive markets, $P = MC$, so the markup on price tends to converge toward zero as competitive pressures increase. Conversely, $P > MC$ in monopoly markets, so the markup on price can be expected to rise as competitive pressures decrease. Economist Abba Lerner proposed that the markup on price be used as an indicator of market power. The **Lerner Index of Monopoly Power** is defined as Lerner Index $= (P - MC)/P = -1/\varepsilon_P$, and is another interpretation of the optimal markup-on-price formula.

- During **peak** periods, facilities are fully utilized. A firm has excess capacity during **off-peak** periods. Successful firms that employ markup pricing typically base prices on fully allocated costs under normal conditions but offer price discounts or accept lower margins during off-peak periods when substantial excess capacity is available.

- **Price discrimination** occurs whenever different customers or customer groups are charged different price markups for the same product. A **market segment** is a fragment of the overall market with different demand or cost characteristics. Price discrimination exists whenever identical customers are charged different prices, or when price differences are not proportional to cost differences.

- Under **first-degree price discrimination**, the firm extracts the maximum amount each customer is willing to pay for its products. Each unit is priced separately at the price indicated along each product demand curve. **Second-degree price discrimination** involves setting prices on the basis of the quantity purchased. Quantity discounts that lead to lower markups for large versus small customers are a common means for second-degree price discrimination. **Third-degree price discrimination**, the most commonly observed form of price discrimination, results when a firm separates its customers into several classes and sets a different price for each customer class.

- A common **two-part pricing** technique is to charge each customer a per unit fee equal to marginal cost, plus a fixed fee equal to the amount of consumer surplus generated at that per unit fee. Another way firms with market power enhance profits is by a variant of two-part pricing called **bundle pricing**. When significant consumer surplus exists, profits can be enhanced if products are purchased together as a single bundle of goods or services.

- A **by-product** is any output that is customarily produced as a direct result of an increase in the production of some other output. Profit maximization requires that marginal revenue be set equal to marginal cost for each by-product. Although the marginal costs of by-products produced in variable proportions can be determined, it is impossible to do so for by-products produced in fixed proportions. **Common costs**, or expenses that are necessary for manufacture of a joint product, cannot be allocated on any economically sound basis.

Rule-of-thumb pricing practices employed by successful firms can be reconciled with profit-maximizing behavior when the costs and benefits of pricing information are properly understood.

QUESTIONS AND ANSWERS

Q15.1 Express the markup on cost formula in terms of the markup on price, and use this relation to explain why a 100 percent markup implies a 50 percent markup on price.

Q15.2 Explain why successful firms that employ markup pricing use fully allocated costs under normal conditions, but typically offer price discounts or accept lower margins during off-peak periods when excess capacity is available.

Q15.3 Discuss how seasonal factors influence supply and demand, and why markups on fresh fruits and vegetable are at their highest during the peak of season.

Q15.4 Why does *The Wall Street Journal* offer bargain rates to students but not to business executives?

Q15.5 "One of the least practical suggestions that economists have offered to managers is that they set marginal revenues equal to marginal costs." Discuss this statement.

Q15.6 "Marginal cost pricing, as well as the use of incremental analysis, is looked upon with favor by economists, especially those on the staffs of regulatory agencies. With this encouragement, regulated industries do indeed employ these rational techniques quite frequently. Unregulated firms, on the other hand, use marginal or incremental cost pricing much less frequently, sticking to cost-plus, or full-cost, pricing

except under unusual circumstances. In my opinion, this goes a long way toward explaining the problems of the regulated firms vis-à-vis unregulated industry." Discuss this statement.

Q15.7 What is price discrimination?

Q15.8 What conditions are necessary before price discrimination is both possible and profitable? Why does price discrimination result in higher profits?

Q15.9 Discuss the role of common costs in pricing practice.

Q15.10 Why is it possible to determine the marginal costs of joint products produced in variable proportions but not those of joint products produced in fixed proportions?

SELF-TEST PROBLEMS AND SOLUTIONS

ST15.1 George Constanza is a project coordinator at Kramer-Seinfeld & Associates, Ltd., a large Brooklyn-based painting contractor. Constanza has asked you to complete an analysis of profit margins earned on a number of recent projects. Unfortunately, your predecessor on this project got an abrupt transfer, and left you with only sketchy information on the firm's pricing practices.

A. Use the available data to complete the following table:

Price ($)	Marginal Cost ($)	Mark Upon Cost (%)	Mark Upon Price (%)
100	25	300.0	75.0
240	72		
680	272	150.0	60.0
750		100.0	
2,800			40.0
	2,700	33.3	
	3,360		20.0
5,800			10.0
6,250		5.3	
	10000		0.0

B. Calculate the missing data for each of the following proposed projects, based on the available estimates of the point price elasticity of demand, optimal markup on cost, and optimal markup on price:

Project	Price Elasticity	Optimal Mark Upon Cost (%)	Optimal Mark Upon Price (%)
1	−1.5	200.0	66.7
2	−2.0		
3		66.7	
4			25.0
5	−5.0	25.0	
6		11.1	10.0
7	−15.0		
8	−20.0		5.0
9			4.0
10	−50.0	2.0	

ST15.1 SOLUTION

A.

Price ($)	Marginal Cost ($)	Mark Upon Cost (%)	Mark Upon Price (%)
100	25	300.0	75.0
240	72	233.3	70.0
680	272	150.0	60.0
750	375	100.0	50.0
2,800	1,680	66.7	40.0
3,600	2,700	33.3	25.0
4,200	3,360	25.0	20.0
5,800	5,220	11.1	10.0
6,250	5,938	5.3	5.0
10,000	10,000	0.0	0.0

B.

Project	Price Elasticity	Optimal Mark Upon Cost (%)	Optimal Mark Upon Price (%)
1	−1.5	200.0	66.7
2	−2.0	100.0	50.0
3	−2.5	66.7	40.0
4	−4.0	33.3	25.0
5	−5.0	25.0	20.0
6	−10.0	11.1	10.0
7	−15.0	7.1	6.7
8	−20.0	5.3	5.0
9	−25.0	4.2	4.0
10	−50.0	2.0	2.0

ST15.2 Optimal Markup on Price. TLC Lawncare, Inc., provides fertilizer and weed control lawn services to residential customers. Its seasonal service package, regularly priced at $250, includes several chemical spray treatments. As part of an effort to expand its customer base, TLC offered $50 off its regular price to customers in the Dallas area. Response was enthusiastic, with sales rising to 5,750 units (packages) from the 3,250 units sold in the same period last year.

A. Calculate the arc price elasticity of demand for TLC service.

B. Assume that the arc price elasticity (from part A) is the best available estimate of the point price elasticity of demand. If marginal cost is $135 per unit for labor and materials, calculate TLC's optimal markup on price and its optimal price.

ST15.2 SOLUTION

A.

$$E_p = \frac{\Delta Q}{\Delta P} \times \frac{P_2 + P_1}{Q_2 + Q_1}$$

$$= \frac{5,750 - 3,250}{\$200 - \$250} \times \frac{\$200 + \$250}{5,750 + 3,250}$$

$$= -2.5$$

B. Given $\varepsilon_P = E_P = -2.5$, the optimal TLC markup on price is

$$\text{Optimal Markup on Price} = \frac{-1}{\varepsilon_p}$$

$$= \frac{-1}{-2.5}$$

$$= 0.4 \text{ or } 40\%$$

Given $MC = \$135$, the optimal price is

$$\text{Optimal Markup on Price} = \frac{P - MC}{P}$$

$$0.4 = \frac{P - \$135}{P}$$

$$0.4P = P - \$135$$

$$0.6P = \$135$$

$$P = \$225$$

PROBLEMS

P15.1 Markup Calculation. Controller Elliot Reid has asked you to review the pricing practices of Hollywood Medical, Inc. Use the following data to calculate the relevant markup on cost and markup on price for the following disposable items:

Product	Price ($)	Marginal Cost ($)	Mark upon Cost (%)	Mark upon Price (%)
A	2	0.20		
B	3	0.6		
C	4	1.2		
D	5	2		
E	6	3		

P15.2 Optimal Markup. Dr. John Dorian, the chief of staff at the Northern Medical Center, has asked you to propose an appropriate markup pricing policy for various medical procedures performed in the hospital's emergency room. To help in this regard, you consult a trade industry publication that provides data about the price elasticity of demand for medical procedures. Unfortunately, the abrasive Dr. Dorian failed to mention whether he wanted you to calculate the optimal markup as a percentage of price or as a percentage of cost. To be safe, calculate the optimal markup on price and optimal markup on cost for each of the following procedures:

Procedure	Price Elasticity	Optimal Mark upon Cost	Optimal Mark upon Price
A	−1		
B	−2		
C	−3		
D	−4		
E	−5		

P15.3 Markup on Cost. Brake-Checkup, Inc., offers automobile brake analysis and repair at a number of outlets in the Philadelphia area. The company recently initiated a policy of matching the lowest advertised competitor price. As a result, Brake-Checkup has been forced to reduce the average price for brake jobs by 3 percent, but it has enjoyed a 15 percent increase in customer traffic. Meanwhile, marginal costs have held steady at $120 per brake job.

A. Calculate the point price elasticity of demand for brake jobs.

B. Calculate Brake-Checkup's optimal price and markup on cost.

P15.4 Optimal Markup on Cost. The Bristol, Inc., is an elegant dining establishment that features French cuisine at dinner six nights per week, and brunch on weekends. In an effort to boost traffic from shoppers during the Christmas season, the Bristol offered Saturday customers $4 off its $16 regular price for brunch. The promotion proved successful, with brunch sales rising from 250 to 750 units per day.

A. Calculate the arc price elasticity of demand for brunch at the Bristol.

B. Assume that the arc price elasticity (from part A) is the best available estimate of the point price elasticity of demand. If marginal cost is $8.56 per unit for labor and materials, calculate the Bristol's optimal markup on cost and its optimal price.

P15.5 Markup Pricing Practice. Betty's Boutique is a small specialty retailer located in a suburban shopping mall. In setting the regular $36 price for a new spring line of blouses, Betty's added a 50 percent markup on cost. Costs were estimated at $24 each: the $12 purchase price of each blouse, plus $6 in allocated variable overhead costs, plus an allocated fixed overhead charge of $6. Customer response was so strong that when Betty's raised prices from $36 to $39 per blouse, sales fell only from 54 to 46 blouses per week.

At first blush, Betty's pricing policy seems clearly inappropriate. It is always improper to consider allocated fixed costs in setting prices for any good or service; only marginal or incremental costs should be included. However, by adjusting the amount of markup on cost employed, Betty's can implicitly compensate for the inappropriate use of fully allocated costs. It is necessary to carefully analyze both the cost categories included and the markup percentages chosen before judging the appropriateness of a given pricing practice.

A. Use the arc price elasticity formula to estimate the price elasticity of demand for Betty's blouses.

B. Determine Betty's optimal markup on cost using the arc price elasticity as an estimate of the point price elasticity of demand. Based upon relevant marginal costs, calculate Betty's optimal price. Explain.

P15.6 Peak/Off-Peak Pricing. Nash Bridges Construction Company is a building contractor serving the Gulf Coast region. The company recently bid on a Gulf-front causeway improvement in Biloxi, Mississippi. Nash Bridges has incurred bid development and job cost-out expenses of $25,000 prior to submission of the bid. The bid was based on the following projected costs:

Cost Category	Amount ($)
Bid development and job cost-out expenses	25,000
Materials	881,000
Labor (50,000 hours @ $26)	1,300,000
Variable overhead (40 percent of direct labor)	520,000
Allocated fixed overhead (6 percent of total costs)	174,000
Total costs	2,900,000

A. What is Nash Bridges' minimum acceptable (breakeven) contract price, assuming that the company is operating at peak capacity?

B. What is the Nash Bridges' minimum acceptable contract price if an economic downturn has left the company with substantial excess capacity?

P15.7 Incremental Pricing Analysis. The General Eclectic Company manufactures an electric toaster. Sales of the toaster have increased steadily during the previous 5 years, and, because of a recently completed expansion program, annual capacity is now 500,000 units. Production and sales during the upcoming year are forecast to be 400,000 units, and standard production costs are estimated as follows:

Materials	$6.00
Direct labor	4.00
Variable indirect labor	2.00
Fixed overhead	3.00
Allocated cost per unit	$15.00

In addition to production costs, GE incurs fixed selling expenses of $1.50 per unit and variable warranty repair expenses of $1.20 per unit. GE currently receives $20 per unit from its customers (primarily retail department stores), and it expects this price to hold during the coming year.

After making the preceding projections, GE received an inquiry about the purchase of a large number of toasters by a discount department store. The inquiry contained two purchase offers:

- Offer 1: The department store would purchase 80,000 units at $14.60 per unit. These units would bear the GE label and be covered by the GE warranty.
- Offer 2: The department store would purchase 120,000 units at $14.00 per unit. These units would be sold under the buyer's private label, and GE would not provide warranty service.

A. Evaluate the incremental net income potential of each offer.

B. What other factors should GE consider when deciding which offer to accept?

C. Which offer (if either) should GE accept? Why?

P15.8 Price Discrimination. Coach Industries, Inc., is a leading manufacturer of recreational vehicle products. Its products include travel trailers, fifth-wheel trailers (towed behind pick-up trucks), and van campers, as well as parts and accessories. Coach offers its fifth-wheel trailers to both dealers (wholesale and retail customers). Ernie Pantusso, Coach's controller, estimates that each fifth-wheel trailer costs the company $10,000 in variable labor and material expenses. Demand and marginal revenue relations for fifth-wheel trailers are

$$P_W = \$15{,}000 - \$5Q_W \quad \text{(wholesale)}$$
$$MR_W = \partial TR_W / \partial Q_W = \$15{,}000 - \$10Q_W$$
$$P_R = \$50{,}000 - \$20Q_R \quad \text{(retail)}$$
$$MR_R = \partial TR_R / \partial Q_R = \$50{,}000 - \$40Q_R$$

A. Assuming that the company can price discriminate between its two types of customers, calculate the profit-maximizing price, output, and profit contribution levels.

B. Calculate point price elasticity for each customer type at the activity levels identified in part A. Are the differences in these elasticity consistent with your recommended price differences in part A? Why or why not?

P15.9 Consumer Surplus. The Heritage Club at Harbor Town offers elegant accommodations for discriminating vacationers on Hilton Head Island, South Carolina. Like many vacation resorts, Heritage Club has discovered the advantages of offering its services on an annual membership or "time-sharing" basis. To illustrate, assume that an individual vacationer's weekly demand and marginal revenue curves can be written as

$$P = \$6{,}500 - \$1{,}250Q$$
$$MR = \partial TR / \partial Q = \$6{,}500 - \$2{,}500Q$$

where P is the price of a single week of vacation time, and Q is the number of weeks of vacation time purchased during a given year. For simplicity, assume that the resort's marginal cost for a week of vacation time is $1,500, and that fixed costs are nil. This gives the following total and marginal cost relations:

$$TC = \$1{,}500Q$$
$$MC = \partial TC / \partial Q = \$1{,}500$$

A. Calculate the profit-maximizing price, output, profit, and consumer surplus assuming a uniform per unit price is charged to each customer.

B. Calculate the profit-maximizing price, output, and profit assuming a two-part pricing strategy is adopted for each customer.

C. Now assume that fixed costs of $4 million per year are incurred, and that 500 time-share customers ("owners") are attracted when an optimal two-part pricing strategy is adopted. Calculate total annual profits.

P15.10 Joint Product Pricing. Each ton of ore mined from the Baby Doe Mine in Leadville, Colorado, produces one ounce of silver and one pound of lead in a fixed 1:1 ratio. Marginal costs are $10 per ton of ore mined.

The demand and marginal revenue curves for silver are

$$P_S = \$11 - \$0.00003Q_S$$
$$MR_S = \partial TR_S / \partial Q_S = \$11 - \$0.00006Q_S$$

and the demand and marginal revenue curve for lead are

$$P_L = \$0.4 - \$0.000005Q_L$$
$$MR_L = \partial TR_L / \partial Q_L = \$0.4 - \$0.00001Q_L$$

where Q_S is ounces of silver and Q_L is pounds of lead.

A. Calculate profit-maximizing sales quantities and prices for silver and lead.

B. Now assume that wild speculation in the silver market has created a fivefold (or 500 percent) increase in silver demand. Calculate optimal sales quantities and prices for both silver and lead under these conditions.

CASE *Study*

Pricing Practices in the Denver, Colorado, Newspaper Market

On May 12, 2000, the two daily newspapers in Denver, Colorado, filed an application with the U.S. Department of Justice for approval of a joint operating arrangement. The application was filed by The E.W. Scripps Company, whose subsidiary, the Denver Publishing Company, published the *Rocky Mountain News*, and the MediaNews Group, Inc., whose subsidiary, the Denver Post Corporation, published the *Denver Post*. Under the proposed joint operating agreement, printing and commercial operations of both newspapers were to be handled by a new entity, the "Denver Newspaper Agency," owned by the parties in equal shares. This type of joint operating agreement provides for the complete independence of the news and editorial departments of the two newspapers. The rationale for such an arrangement, as provided for under the Newspaper Preservation Act,

is to preserve multiple independent editorial voices in towns and cities too small to support two or more newspapers. The act requires joint operating arrangements, such as that proposed by the Denver newspapers, to obtain the prior written consent of the attorney general of the United States in order to qualify for the antitrust exemption provided by the act.

Scripps initiated discussions for a joint operating agreement after determining that the *News* would probably fail without such an arrangement. In their petition to the Justice Department, the newspapers argued that the *News* had sustained $123 million in net operating losses while the financially stronger *Post* had reaped $200 million in profits during the 1990s. This was a crucial point in favor of the joint operating agreement application because the attorney general must find that one of the

continued

publications is a failing newspaper and that approval of the arrangement is necessary to maintain the independent editorial content of both newspapers. Like any business, newspapers cannot survive without a respectable bottom line. In commenting on the joint operating agreement application, Attorney General Janet Reno noted that Denver was one of only five major American cities still served by competing daily newspapers. The other four are Boston, Chicago, New York, and Washington DC. Of course, these other four cities are not comparable in size to Denver; they are much bigger. None of those four cities can lay claim to two newspapers that are more or less equally matched and strive for the same audience. In fact, that there is not a single city in the United States that still supports two independently owned and evenly matched, high-quality newspapers that vie for the same broad base of readership.

Economies of scale in production explain why few cities can support more than one local newspaper. Almost all local newspaper production and distribution costs are fixed. Marginal production and distribution costs are almost nil. After the local news stories and local advertising copy are written, there is practically no additional cost involved with expanding production from, say, 200,000 to 300,000 newspapers per day. Once a daily edition is produced, marginal costs may be as little as 5¢ per newspaper. When marginal production costs are minimal, price competition turns vicious. Whichever competitor is out in front in terms of total circulation simply keeps prices down until the competition goes out of business or is forced into accepting a joint operating agreement. This is exactly what happened in Denver. Until recently, the cost of a daily newspaper in Denver was only 25¢ each weekday and 50¢ on Sunday at the newsstand, and even less when purchased on an annual subscription basis. The smaller *News* had much higher unit costs and simply could not afford to compete with the *Post* at such ruinously low prices. This is why the production of local newspapers is often described as a classic example of natural monopoly.

On Friday, January 5, 2001, the Justice Department gave the green light to a 50-year joint operating agreement between the *News* and its longtime rival, the *Post*. Starting January 22, 2001, the publishing operations of the *News* and the *Post* were consolidated. The Denver Newspaper Agency, owned 50/50 by the owners of the *News* and the *Post*, is now responsible for the advertising, circulation, production, and other business departments of the newspapers. Newsrooms and editorial functions remain independent. Therefore, the owners of the *News* and the *Post* are now working together to achieve financial success, but the newsroom operations remain competitors. Under terms of the agreement, E.W. Scripps Company, parent of the struggling *News*, agreed to pay owners of the *Post* $60 million. Both newspapers publish separately Monday through Friday. The *News* publishes the only Saturday paper and the *Post* the only Sunday paper.

A. Use your knowledge of monopoly pricing practices to explain why advertising rates and newspaper circulation prices were likely to increase and jobs were likely to be lost, following adoption of this joint operating agreement. Use company information to support your argument (see http://www.denverpost.com and http://www.rockymountainnews.com/).

B. Classified ads to sell real estate in a local newspaper can cost five to ten times as much as a similar ad used to announce a garage sale. Use your knowledge of price discrimination to explain how local newspaper monopolies generate enormous profits from selling classified advertising that varies in price according to the value of the item advertised.

C. Widely differing fares for business and vacation travelers on the same flight have led some to accuse the airlines of price discrimination. Do airline fare differences or local newspaper classified-ad rate differences provide stronger evidence of price discrimination?

SELECTED REFERENCES

Atkeson, Andrew and Ariel Burstein. "Pricing-to-Market in a Ricardian Model of International Trade." *American Economic Review* 97, no. 2 (May, 2007): 362–367.

Fort, Rodney. "Reply to 'the Paradox of Inelastic Sports Pricing'." *Managerial and Decision Economics* 28, no. 2 (March, 2007): 159–160.

Gabaix, Xavier, Arvind Krishnamurthy, and Olivier Vigneron. "Limits of Arbitrage: Theory and Evidence from the Mortgage-Backed Securities Market." *Journal of Finance* 62, no. 2 (April, 2007): 557–595.

Gans, Joshua S. and Stephen P. King. "Perfect Price Discrimination with Costless Arbitrage." *International Journal of Industrial Organization* 25, no. 3 (June, 2007): 431–440.

Leith, Campbell and Jim Malley. "A Sectoral Analysis of Price-Setting Behavior in U.S. Manufacturing Industries." *Review of Economics and Statistics* 89, no. 2 (May, 2007): 335–342.

Atkeson, Andrew and Ariel Burstein. "Pricing-to-Market in a Ricardian Model of International Trade." *American Economic Review* 97, no. 2 (May, 2007): 362–367.

Fort, Rodney. "Reply to 'the Paradox of Inelastic Sports Pricing'." *Managerial and Decision Economics* 28, no. 2 (March, 2007): 159–160.

Gabaix, Xavier, Arvind Krishnamurthy, and Olivier Vigneron. "Limits of Arbitrage: Theory and Evidence from the Mortgage-Backed Securities Market." *Journal of Finance* 62, no. 2 (April, 2007): 557–595.

Gans, Joshua S. and Stephen P. King. "Perfect Price Discrimination with Costless Arbitrage." *International Journal of Industrial Organization* 25, no. 3 (June, 2007): 431–440.

Leith, Campbell and Jim Malley. "A Sectoral Analysis of Price-Setting Behavior in U.S. Manufacturing Industries." *Review of Economics and Statistics* 89, no. 2 (May, 2007): 335–342.

Martimort, David and Salvatore Piccolo. "Resale Price Maintenance Under Asymmetric Information." *International Journal of Industrial Organization* 25, no. 2 (April, 2007): 315–339.

Massa, Massimo, Zahid Rehman, and Theo Vermaelen. "Mimicking Repurchases." *Journal of Financial Economics* 84, no. 3 (June, 2007): 624–666.

Matsuyama, Kiminori. "Credit Traps and Credit Cycles." *American Economic Review* 97, no. 1 (March, 2007): 503–516.

Noel, Michael D. "Edgeworth Price Cycles, Cost-Based Pricing, and Sticky Pricing in Retail Gasoline Markets." *Review of Economics and Statistics* 89, no. 2 (May, 2007): 324–334.

Noguera, Jose and Rowena A. Pecchecnino. "OPEC and the International Oil Market: Can a Cartel Fuel the Engine of Economic Development?" *International Journal of Industrial Organization* 25, no. 1 (February, 2007): 187–199.

Piazzesi, Monika, Martin Schneider, and Selale Tuzel. "Housing, Consumption and Asset Pricing." *Journal of Financial Economics* 83, no. 3 (March, 2007): 531–569.

Pierru, Axel. "Allocating the CO_2 Emissions of an Oil Refinery with Aumann-Shapley Prices." *Energy Economics* 29, no. 3 (May, 2007): 563–577.

Raskovich, Alexander. "Competition or Collusion? Negotiating Discounts Off Posted Prices." *International Journal of Industrial Organization* 25, no. 2 (April, 2007): 341–354.

Ravn, Morten O., Stephanie Schmitt Grohe, and Martin Uribe. "Pricing to Habits and the Law of One Price." *American Economic Review* 97, no. 2 (May, 2007): 232–238.

Uhlig, Harald. "Explaining Asset Prices with External Habits and Wage Rigidities in a DSGE Model." *American Economic Review* 97, no. 2 (May, 2007): 239–243.

Appendix 15A

Transfer Pricing

Sophisticated pricing practices have evolved to effectively deal with the transfer of goods and services within large organizations.

TRANSFER PRICING PROBLEM

Expanding markets brought about by improvements in communication and transportation, as well as falling trade barriers, have led to the development of large, multi-division firms that cut across national boundaries. They need to set appropriate prices for the transfer of goods and services among divisions.

Divisional Relationships

Vertical Relation
When the output of one division or company is the input to another.

Vertical Integration
When a single company controls various links in the production chain from basic inputs to final output.

Transfer Pricing
The pricing of products transferred among divisions of a firm.

The transfer pricing problem results from the difficulty of establishing profitable relationships among divisions of a single company when each separate business unit stands in **vertical relation** to the other. A vertical relation is one where the output of one division or company is the input to another. **Vertical integration** occurs when a single company controls various links in the production chain from basic inputs to final output. Media powerhouse Time Warner, Inc., is vertically integrated because it owns AOL, an Internet service provider (ISP) and cable TV systems, plus a number of programming properties in filmed entertainment (e.g., Warner Bros.) and television production (e.g., HBO, CNN), commonly referred to as content providers. Several vertically integrated companies in the entertainment field own and operate the distribution network and the programming that is sold over that network.

To combat the problems of coordinating large-scale enterprises that are vertically integrated, separate profit centers are typically established for each important product or product line. Despite obvious advantages, this decentralization has the potential to create problems. The most critical of these is the problem of **transfer pricing,** or the pricing of intermediate products transferred among divisions. To maximize profits for the vertically integrated firm, it is essential that a profit margin or markup only be charged at the final stage of production. All intermediate products transferred internally must be transferred at marginal cost.

Products Without External Markets

Consider the problem faced by a vertically integrated firm that has different divisions at distinct points along the various steps of the production process, and assume for the moment that no external market exists for transferred inputs. If each separate division is established as a profit center to provide employees with an efficiency incentive, a transfer pricing problem can occur. Suppose each selling division adds a markup over its marginal cost for inputs sold to other divisions. Each buying division would then set its marginal revenue from output equal to the division's marginal cost of input. This process would culminate in a marginal cost to the ultimate upstream user that exceeds the sum total of marginal costs for each transferring division. All of the markups charged by each transferring division drive a wedge between the firm's true marginal cost of production and the marginal cost to the last or ultimate upstream user. As a result, the ultimate upstream user buys less than the optimal amount of input and produces less than the profit-maximizing level of output.

For example, it would be inefficient if AOL, a major ISP, paid more than the marginal cost of programming produced by its own subsidiaries. If each subsidiary added a markup to the marginal cost of programming sold to the parent company, AOL would buy less than a profit-maximizing amount of its own programming. In fact, AOL would have an incentive to seek programming from other purveyors so long as the external market price was less than the internal transfer price. Such an incentive could create inefficiencies, especially when the external market price is less than the transfer price but greater than the marginal cost of programming produced by AOL's own subsidiaries.

Effective transfer pricing promotes activity in each division that is consistent with profit maximization for the overall enterprise. *When transferred products cannot be sold in external markets, the marginal cost of the transferring division is the optimal transfer price.* One practical means for insuring that an optimal amount of input is transferred at an optimal transfer price is to inform buying divisions that the marginal cost curve of supplying divisions is to be treated like a supply schedule. Alternatively, supplying divisions could be informed about the buying division's marginal revenue or demand curve and told to use this information in determining the quantity supplied. In either case, each division would voluntarily choose to transfer an optimal amount of input at the optimal transfer price.

Products with Competitive External Markets

The transfer pricing problem is only slightly more complicated when transferred inputs can be sold in external markets. When transferred inputs can be sold in a competitive external market, the external market price represents the firm's opportunity cost of employing such inputs internally. As such, it would never pay to use inputs internally unless their value to the firm is at least as great as their value to others in the external market. This observation leads to a second key rule for optimal transfer pricing: *when transferred products can be sold in perfectly competitive external markets, the external market price is the optimal transfer price.* If upstream suppliers wish to supply more than downstream users desire to employ at a perfectly competitive price, excess input can be sold in the external market. If downstream users wish to employ more than upstream suppliers seek to furnish at a perfectly competitive price, excess input demand can be met through purchases in the external market. In either event, an optimal amount of input is transferred internally.

Of course, it is hard to imagine why a firm would be vertically integrated in the first place if all inputs could be purchased in perfectly competitive markets. Neither Kellogg's nor McDonalds, for example, have extensive agricultural operations to ensure a steady supply of foodstuffs. Grains for cereal and beef for hamburgers can both be purchased at prices that closely approximate marginal cost in perfectly competitive input markets. On the other hand, if an input market is typically competitive but punctuated by periods of scarcity and shortage, it can pay to maintain some input producing capability. For example, Exxon Mobil Corp. has considerable production facilities that supply its extensive distribution network with gasoline, oil, and petroleum products. These production facilities offer Exxon Mobil some protection against the threat of supply stoppages. Similarly, Coca-Cola has long-term supply contracts with orange growers to ensure a steady supply of product for its Minute Maid juice operation. Both Exxon Mobil and Coca-Cola are examples of vertically integrated firms with inputs offered in markets that are usually, but not always, perfectly competitive.

Products with Imperfectly Competitive External Markets

The typical case of vertical integration involves firms with inputs that can be transferred internally or sold in external markets that are not perfectly competitive. Again, it never pays to use inputs internally unless their value to the firm is at least as great as their value to others in the external market. This observation leads to a third and final fundamental rule for optimal transfer pricing: *when transferred products can be sold in imperfectly competitive external markets, the optimal transfer price equates the marginal cost of the transferring division to the marginal revenue derived from the combined internal and external markets.* In other words, when inputs can be sold in imperfectly competitive external markets, internal input demand must reflect the opportunity to supply input to the external market at a price in excess of marginal cost. If upstream suppliers wish to offer more input than downstream users desire to employ when input $MC = MR$ from the combined market, excess supply can be sold in the external market. If downstream users want to employ more than upstream suppliers seek to furnish when $MC = MR$, excess internal demand can be met through added purchases in the external market. In both cases, an optimal amount of input is transferred internally.

GLOBAL TRANSFER PRICING EXAMPLE

Although the transfer pricing concept can be introduced conceptually through the use of graphic analysis, most real-world applications are complex and must be solved algebraically.

Profit Maximization for an Integrated Firm

Suppose Josiah Bartlet & Sons, Inc., is a small integrated domestic manufacturer of material handling equipment. Demand and marginal revenue curves for the firm are

$$P = \$100 - \$0.001Q$$
$$MR = \partial TR / \partial Q = \$100 - \$0.002Q$$

Relevant total cost, marginal cost, and profit functions are

$$TC = \$312,500 + \$25Q + \$0.0015Q^2$$
$$MC = \partial TC/\partial Q = \$25 + \$0.003Q$$
$$\pi = TR - TC$$
$$= \$100Q - \$0.001Q^2 - \$312,500 - \$25Q - \$0.0015Q^2$$
$$= -\$0.0025Q^2 + \$75Q - \$312,500$$

Profit maximization occurs at the point where $MR = MC$, so the optimal output level is

$$MR = MC$$
$$\$100 - \$0.002Q = \$25 + \$0.003Q$$
$$75 = 0.005Q$$
$$Q = 15,000$$

This implies that

$$P = \$100 - \$0.001(15,000)$$
$$= \$85$$
$$\pi = TR - TC$$
$$= -\$0.0025(15,000^2) + \$75(15,000) - \$312,500$$
$$= \$250,000$$

Therefore, the optimal price–output combination is $85 and 15,000 units for this integrated firm, and profits total $250,000. To be optimal, transfer prices must ensure operation at these levels.

Transfer Pricing with No External Market

Consider how the situation changes if the firm is reorganized into separate manufacturing and distribution division profit centers, and no external market exists for the transferred product. The demand curve facing the distribution division is precisely the same as the firm's output demand curve. Although the total cost function of the firm is unchanged, it can be broken down into the costs of manufacturing and distribution.

Assume that such a breakdown results in the following divisional cost functions:

$$TC_{Mfg} = \$250,000 + \$20Q + \$0.001Q^2$$
$$MC_{Mfg} = \partial TC_{Mfg}/\partial Q = \$20 + \$0.002Q$$

and

$$TC_{Distr} = \$62,500 + \$5Q + \$0.0005Q^2$$
$$MC_{Distr} = \partial TC_{Distr}/\partial Q = \$5 + \$0.001Q$$

With divisional operation, the total and marginal cost functions for the firm are

$$TC = TC_{Mfg} + TC_{Distr}$$
$$MC = MC_{Mfg} + MC_{Distr}$$

and precisely the same as before.

To demonstrate the derivation of an appropriate activity level, the net marginal revenue for the distribution division is set equal to the marginal cost of the manufacturing division:

$$MR - MC_{Distr} = MC_{Mfg}$$
$$\$100 - \$0.002Q - \$5 - \$0.001Q = \$20 + \$0.002Q$$
$$75 = 0.005Q$$
$$Q = 15,000$$

The 15,000-unit output level remains optimal for profit maximization. If the distribution division determines the quantity it will purchase by movement along its marginal revenue curve, and the manufacturing division supplies output along its marginal cost curve, then the market-clearing transfer price is the price that results when $MR - MC_{Distr} = MC_{Mfg}$. At 15,000 units of output, the optimal transfer price is

$$P_T = MC_{Mfg}$$
$$= \$20 + \$0.002(15,000)$$
$$= \$50$$

At a transfer price of $P_T = \$50$, the quantity supplied by the manufacturing division equals 15,000. This is the same quantity demanded by the distribution division at a $P_T = \$50$, because

$$MR - MC_{Distr} = P_T$$
$$\$100 - \$0.002 - \$5 - \$0.001Q = \$50$$
$$45 = 0.003Q$$
$$Q = 15,000$$

At a transfer price of $P_T > \$50$, the distribution division will accept fewer units of output than the manufacturing division wants to supply. If $P_T < \$50$, the distribution division will seek to purchase more units than the manufacturing division desires to produce. Only at a $50 transfer price are supply and demand in balance in the firm's internal market.

Competitive External Market with Excess Internal Demand

To consider the effects of an external market for the transferred product, assume that the company is able to *buy* an unlimited quantity of a comparable product from a foreign supplier at a price of $35. The product supplied by the foreign manufacturer meets the exact same specifications as that produced by Josiah Bartlet & Sons. Because an unlimited quantity can be purchased for $35, a perfectly competitive external market exists for the transferred product, and the optimal transfer price equals the external market price. For $P_T = \$35$, the quantity demanded by the distribution division is

$$MR - MC_{Distr} = P_T$$
$$\$100 - \$0.002Q - \$5 - \$0.001Q = \$35$$
$$60 = 0.003Q$$
$$Q = 20,000$$

whereas the quantity supplied by the manufacturing division is

$$P_T = MC_{Mfg}$$
$$\$35 = \$20 + \$0.002Q$$
$$15 = 0.002Q$$
$$Q = 7{,}500$$

In this case of excess internal demand, the distribution division will purchase all 7,500 units produced internally plus an additional 12,500 units from the foreign supplier. The price impact for customers and the profit impact for Josiah Bartlet & Sons are dramatic. Domestic customer prices and total profits are now calculated as

$$P = \$100 - \$0.001(20{,}000)$$
$$= \$80$$

and

$$\pi = TR - TC_{Mfg} - TC_{For} - TC_{Distr}$$
$$= \$100(20{,}000) - \$0.001(20{,}000^2) - \$250{,}000 - \$20(7{,}500)$$
$$-\$0.001(7{,}500^2) - \$35(12{,}500) - \$62{,}500 - \$5(20{,}000)$$
$$-\$0.0005(20{,}000^2)$$
$$= \$343{,}750$$

Josiah Bartlet & Sons' domestic customers benefit from the increased availability of goods, 20,000 versus 15,000 units, and lower prices, $80 versus $85 per unit. The opportunity to purchase goods at a price of $35 from a foreign supplier benefits the company because profits grow from $250,000 to $343,750. The firm now manufactures only 7,500 of the units sold to customers and has become much more of a distributor than an integrated manufacturer and distributor. Josiah Bartlet & Sons has been able to make its business and profits grow by focusing efforts on distribution, where it enjoys a comparative advantage.

Competitive External Market with Excess Internal Supply

It is interesting to contrast these results with those achieved under somewhat different circumstances. For example, assume that Josiah Bartlet & Sons is able to *sell* an unlimited quantity of its goods to a foreign distributor at a price of $80. For simplicity, also assume that sales to this new market have no impact on the firm's ability to sell to current domestic customers and that this market can be supplied under the same cost conditions as previously. If $P_T = \$80$, the quantity demanded by the distribution division is

$$MR - MC_{Distr} = P_T$$
$$\$100 - \$0.002Q - \$5 - \$0.001Q = \$80$$
$$15 = 0.003Q$$
$$Q = 5{,}000$$

whereas the quantity supplied by the manufacturing division is

$$P_T = MC_{Mfg}$$
$$\$80 = \$20 + \$0.002Q$$
$$60 = 0.002Q$$
$$Q = 30,000$$

In this instance of excess internal supply, the distribution division will purchase all 5,000 units desired internally, while the manufacturing division will offer an additional 25,000 units to the new foreign distributor. Again, the price impact for customers and the profit impact for Josiah Bartlet & Sons are dramatic. Domestic customer prices and total profits are now as follows:

$$P = \$100 - \$0.001(5,000)$$
$$= \$95$$

and

$$\pi = TR_{Dom} + TR_{For} - TC_{Mfg} - TC_{Distr}$$
$$= \$100(5,000) - \$0.001(5,000^2) + \$80(25,000) - \$250,000$$
$$- \$20(30,000) - \$0.001(30,000^2) - \$62,500 - \$5(5,000)$$
$$- \$0.0005(5,000^2)$$
$$= \$625,000$$

Under this scenario, the Josiah Bartlet & Sons domestic market shrinks from an initial 15,000 to 5,000 units, and prices rise somewhat from $85 to $95 per unit. At the same time, foreign customers benefit from the increased availability of goods, 25,000 versus none previously, and the attractive purchase price of $80 per unit. The opportunity to sell at a price of $80 to a foreign distributor has also benefitted the company, because profits grew from $250,000 to $625,000. The company now distributes only 5,000 of 30,000 units sold to customers and has become much more of a manufacturer than a distributor. By emphasizing manufacturing, Josiah Bartlet & Sons makes its business and profits grow by focusing efforts on what it does best.

PROBLEM

P15A.1 Transfer Pricing. Simpson Flanders, Inc., is a Motor City–based manufacturer and distributor of valves used in nuclear power plants. Currently, all output is sold to North American customers. Demand and marginal revenue curves for the firm are as follows:

$$P = \$1,000 - \$0.015Q$$
$$MR = \partial TR / \partial Q = \$1,000 - \$0.03Q$$

Relevant total cost, marginal cost, and profit functions are

$$TC = \$1,500,000 + \$600Q + \$0.005Q^2$$
$$MC = \partial TC / \partial Q = \$600 + \$0.01Q$$
$$\pi = TR - TC$$
$$= -\$0.02Q^2 + \$400Q - \$1,500,000$$

A. Calculate the profit-maximizing activity level for Simpson Flanders when the firm is operated as an integrated unit.

B. Assume that the company is reorganized into two independent profit centers with the following cost conditions:

$$TC_{Mfg} = \$1,250,000 + \$500Q + \$0.005Q^2$$
$$MC_{Mfg} = \partial TC_{Mfg} / \partial Q = 500 + \$0.01Q$$
$$TC_{Distr} = \$250,000 + \$100Q$$
$$MC_{Distr} = \partial TC_{Distr} / \partial Q = \$100.$$

Calculate the transfer price that ensures a profit-maximizing level of profit for the firm, with divisional operation based on the assumption that all output produced is to be transferred internally.

C. Now assume that a major distributor in the European market offers to buy as many valves as Simpson Flanders wishes to offer at a price of $645. No impact on demand from the company's North American customers is expected, and current facilities can be used to supply both markets. Calculate the company's optimal price(s), output(s), and profits in this situation.

Long-Term Investment Decisions

5

PART

Risk Analysis

At the dawn of the new millennium, stock market speculators scrambled to bet their hard-earned money on Amazon.com, Cisco Systems, Yahoo!, and others poised to take advantage of the Internet. Speculators piled into a handful of stock market favorites at unheard-of valuations, only to see a significant chunk of their portfolios vanish as the Internet bubble burst. Within 18 months, the S&P 500 crumbled by more than 30 percent and Nasdaq crashed by more than 70 percent. Many dot.com investors lost everything as *The Wall Street Journal* mused about "the madness of crowds."

Then, to make a bad situation worse, the terrorist attacks of September 11, 2001, on New York City and Washington, DC, sent a shiver through global financial markets that caused a plunge in both consumer confidence and retail sales. Add in a currency crisis emanating from Argentina and other emerging markets, and the essential elements fell into place for a sharp and lasting economic downturn in the United States, Europe, and Asia. It never happened. Rather than allowing the world economy to stumble along at less than full capacity, savvy risk management by public officials and business leaders helped bring quick economic recovery. Growing business activity, rising employment, and surging business profits all gave testimony to the importance of skillful risk management in both the public and private sectors.[1]

This chapter introduces practical methods for dealing with risk and uncertainty.

CONCEPTS OF RISK AND UNCERTAINTY

To make effective investment decisions managers must understand the many faces of risk.

Economic Risk and Uncertainty

Investors sometimes know with certainty the outcomes that each possible course of action will produce. A firm with $100,000 in cash that can be invested in a 30-day Treasury bill yielding 6 percent ($493 interest income for 30 days) or used to prepay a 10 percent bank loan ($822 interest expense for 30 days) can determine with certainty that prepayment of the bank loan provides a $329 higher 1-month return. A retailer can

---

1 Collin Levy, "Sam Zell: Professor Risk," *The Wall Street Journal Online*, October 20, 2007, http://online.wsj.com.

just as easily predict the cost savings earned by placing a given order directly with the manufacturer versus through an independent wholesaler; manufacturers can estimate the precise cost effect of meeting a rush order when overtime wages rather than standard labor rates are required. Order backlogs give a wide variety of consumer and producer goods manufacturers a clear indication of product demand conditions. Similarly, book, magazine, and trade journal publishers accurately judge product demand conditions on the basis of subscription revenues. Even when events cannot be predicted exactly, only a modest level of decision uncertainty is present in such situations.

Economic Risk
Chance of loss due to the fact that all possible outcomes and their probability of occurrence are unknown.

Many other important managerial decisions are made under conditions of risk or uncertainty. **Economic risk** is the chance of loss because all possible outcomes and their associated probabilities are unknown. Actions taken in such a decision environment are purely speculative, such as the buy and sell decisions made by speculators in commodity, futures, and options markets. All decision makers are equally likely to profit as well as to lose; luck is the sole determinant of success or failure. **Uncertainty** exists when the outcomes of managerial decisions cannot be predicted with absolute accuracy, but all possibilities and their associated probabilities are known. Under conditions of uncertainty, informed managerial decisions are possible. Experience, insight, and prudence allow investment managers to devise strategies for minimizing the chance of failing to meet business objectives.

Uncertainty
When the outcomes of managerial decisions cannot be predicted with absolute accuracy, but all possibilities and their associated probabilities of occurrence are known.

When the level of risk and the attitudes toward risk taking are known, the effects of uncertainty can be directly reflected in the basic valuation model of the firm. The certainty equivalent method converts expected risky profit streams to their certain sum equivalents to eliminate value differences that result from different risk levels. For risk-averse decision makers, the value of a risky stream of payments is less than the value of a certain stream, and the application of certainty equivalent adjustment factors results in a downward adjustment in the value of expected returns. For risk-seeking decision makers, the value of a risky stream of payments is greater than that of a certain stream, and application of certainty equivalent adjustment factors results in an upward adjustment in the value of expected returns. Another method used to reflect uncertainty in the basic valuation model is the risk-adjusted discount rate approach. In this technique, the interest rate used in the denominator of the basic valuation model depends on the level of risk. For highly risk-averse decision makers, higher discount rates are implemented; for less risk-averse decision makers, lower discount rates are employed. Using this technique, discounted expected profit streams reflect risk differences and become directly comparable.

Business Risk
Chance of loss associated with a given managerial decision.

Market Risk
Chance that a portfolio of investments can lose money because of swings in the financial markets as a whole.

Inflation Risk
Danger that a general increase in the price level will undermine the real economic value of any legal agreement that involves a fixed promise to pay over an extended period.

General Risk Categories

Business risk is the chance of loss associated with a given managerial decision. Such losses are a normal by-product of the unpredictable variation in product demand and cost conditions. For investors, a main worry is **market risk,** or the chance that a portfolio of investments can lose money because of overall swings in the financial markets. Managers also must be concerned about market risk because it influences the cost and timing of selling new debt and equity securities to investors. When a bear market ensues, investors are not the only ones to lose. If a company is unable to raise funds for new plant and equipment, it must forego profitable investment opportunities when the cost of financing escalates. **Inflation risk** is the danger that a general increase in the price level will undermine the real economic value of corporate agreements that involve a fixed promise to pay over an extended period. Leases, rental agreements, and corporate bonds are all examples of business contracts that can be susceptible to inflation risk. **Interest-rate risk** stems from the fact that a fall in interest rates will increase the value

Interest-Rate Risk
Market risk that stems from the fact that changing interest rates affect the value of any agreement that involves a fixed promise to pay over a specified period.

of any contract that involves a fixed promise to pay over an extended time frame. Conversely, a rise in interest rates will decrease the value of any agreement that involves fixed interest and principal payments.

Credit risk is the chance that another party will fail to abide by its contractual obligations. A number of companies have lost substantial sums because other parties were either unable or unwilling to provide raw commodities, rental space, or financing at agreed-upon prices. Like other investors, corporations must also consider the problem of **liquidity risk,** or the difficulty of selling corporate assets or investments that are not easily transferable at favorable prices under typical market conditions. Another type of risk is related to the rapidly expanding financial derivatives market. A financial derivative is a security that derives value from price movements in some other security. **Derivative risk** is the chance that volatile financial derivatives such as futures and options could create losses in underlying investments by increasing price volatility.

Credit Risk
Chance that another party will fail to abide by its contractual obligations.

Liquidity Risk
Difficulty of selling corporate assets or investments that have only a few willing buyers or are otherwise not easily transferable at favorable prices under typical market conditions.

Derivative Risk
Chance that volatile financial derivatives such as commodities futures and index options could create losses in underlying investments by increasing rather than decreasing price volatility.

Cultural Risk
Chance of loss because of product market differences due to distinctive social customs.

Currency Risk
Loss due to changes in the domestic-currency value of foreign profits.

Government Policy Risk
Chance of loss because foreign government grants of monopoly franchises, tax abatements, and favored trade status can be tenuous.

Expropriation Risk
Danger that business property located abroad might be seized by host governments.

Special Risks of Global Operations

Cultural risk is borne by companies that pursue a global investment strategy. Product market differences due to distinctive social customs make it difficult to predict which products might do well in foreign markets. For example, breakfast cereal is extremely popular and one of the most profitable industries in the United States, Canada, and the United Kingdom. In France, Germany, Italy, and many other foreign countries, breakfast cereal is much less popular and less profitable. Breakfast cereal doesn't "travel" as well as U.S.-made entertainment like movies and television programming.

Currency risk is another important danger facing global businesses because most companies wish to eventually repatriate foreign earnings back to the domestic parent. When the U.S. dollar rises in value against the Canadian dollar, for example, Canadian profits translate into fewer U.S. dollars. Conversely, when the U.S. dollar falls in value against the Canadian dollar, profits earned in Canada translate into more U.S. dollars. Because price swings in the relative value of currencies are unpredictable and can be significant, many multinational firms hedge against currency price swings using financial derivatives in the foreign currency market. This hedging is expensive and risky during volatile markets.

Global investors also experience **government policy risk** because foreign government grants of monopoly franchises, tax abatements, and favored trade status can be tenuous. In the "global friendly" 1990s, many corporate investors seem to have forgotten the widespread confiscations of private property owned by U.S. corporations in Mexico, Cuba, Libya, the former Soviet Union, and in a host of other countries. **Expropriation risk,** or the risk that business property located abroad might be seized by host governments, is a risk that global investors must not forget. During every decade of the twentieth century, U.S. and other multinational corporations have suffered from expropriation and probably will in the years ahead.

PROBABILITY CONCEPTS

A clear understanding of probability concepts provides a background for discussing various methods of effective risk analysis.

Managerial Application 16.1

Behavioral Finance

Finance is the part of economics that deals with the allocation of scarce capital resources. Because finance is such a large and vital part of economic analysis, it should not be surprising that a new branch of behavioral economics—called behavioral finance—has evolved. Behavioral finance applies scientific research on human and social psychology to the study of market prices, investor returns, and the allocation of scarce capital resources.

Techniques from cognitive psychology have been used to explain a number of financial anomalies. For example, "hyperbolic discounting" is an anomaly in which investors use extraordinarily high rates of discount between the present and the near future, but a much lower rate of discount for the near future versus the far future. Hyperbolic discounting is an irrational bias due to temporal myopia, a common shortsightedness that causes good or bad consequences that occur at a later point in time to have less bearing on choices the more distantly they fall into the future.

Other key observations from behavioral finance research include evidence about the lack of symmetry between decisions to acquire or keep resources, and strong loss

aversion attached to decisions involving emotionally important resources, like personal residences. Loss aversion explains investor unwillingness to sell investments at a loss, even when superior investment alternatives are present. Loss aversion also explains why housing market prices fail to adjust quickly during periods of falling demand. Behavioral researchers in finance also study episodes of apparent investor overreaction in the stock market, such as when stock market returns following a series of good news announcements is lower than the average rate of return observed following a series of bad news announcements. Bubbles in stock and real estate markets are a special focus of behavioral researchers.

One of the newest areas of research in behavioral finance, called neuroeconomics, uses insights from psychology, sociology, and anthropology to show how willpower, concern for other people, limits on calculating ability, and biology influence investment behavior.

See: For a fascinating video clip about Terry Burnham's *Mean Markets and Lizard Brains*, go to: http://www.pbs.org/newshour/bb/economy/jan-june05/brain_5-10.html.

Probability Distribution

Probability
Chance of occurrence.

Probability Distribution
List of possible events and probabilities.

The **probability** of an event is the chance, or odds, that the incident will occur. If all possible events or outcomes are listed, and if a probability is assigned to each event, the listing is called a **probability distribution.** For example, suppose a sales manager observes that there is a 70 percent chance that a given customer will place a specific order versus a 30 percent chance that the customer will not. This situation is described by the probability distribution shown in Table 16.1.

Both possible outcomes are listed in column 1, and the probabilities of each outcome, expressed as decimals and percentages, appear in column 2. Notice that the probabilities

Table 16.1 Simple Probability Distribution

Event (1)	Probability of Occurrence (2)
Receive order	0.7 = 70%
Do not receive order	0.3 = 30%
Total	1.0 = 100%

sum to 1.0, or 100 percent, as they must if the probability distribution is complete. In this simple example, risk can be read from the probability distribution as the 30 percent chance of the firm not receiving the order. For most managerial decisions, the relative desirability of alternative events or outcomes is not absolute. A more general measure of the relation between risk and the probability distribution is typically required to adequately incorporate risk considerations into the decision-making process.

Suppose a firm is able to choose only one of two investment projects, each calling for an outlay of $10,000. Also assume that profits earned from the two projects are related to the general level of economic activity during the coming year, as shown in Table 16.2. This table is known as a **payoff matrix** because it illustrates the dollar outcome associated with each possible state of nature. Both projects provide a $5,000 profit in a normal economy, higher profits in an economic boom, and lower profits if a recession occurs. However, project *B* profits vary far more according to the state of the economy than do profits from project *A*. In a normal economy, both projects return $5,000 in profit. Should the economy be in a recession next year, project *B* will produce nothing, whereas project *A* will still provide a $4,000 profit. If the economy is booming next year, project *B*'s profit will increase to $12,000, but profit for project *A* will increase only moderately, to $6,000.

Payoff Matrix
Table that shows outcomes associated with each possible state of nature.

Project *A* is clearly more desirable if the economy is in recession, whereas project *B* is superior in a boom. In a normal economy, the projects offer the same profit potential, and both are equally desirable. To choose the best project, one needs to know the likelihood of a boom, a recession, or normal economic conditions. If such probabilities can be estimated, the expected profits and variability of profits for each project can be determined. These measures make it possible to evaluate each project in terms of expected return and risk, where risk is measured by the deviation of profits from expected values.

Expected Value

Expected Value
Anticipated realization.

Expected value is the anticipated realization from a given payoff matrix and probability distribution. It is the *weighted-average* payoff, where the weights are defined by the probability distribution.

To continue with the previous example, assume that forecasts based on the current trend in economic indicators suggest a 2 in 10 chance of recession, a 6 in 10 chance of a normal economy, and a 2 in 10 chance of a boom. As probabilities, the probability of recession is 0.2, or 20 percent; the probability of normal economic activity is 0.6, or 60 percent; and the probability of a boom is 0.2, or 20 percent. These probabilities add up to 1.0 (0.2 + 0.6 + 0.2 = 1.0), or 100 percent, and thereby form a complete probability distribution, as shown in Table 16.3.

If each possible outcome is multiplied by its probability and then summed, the weighted average outcome is determined. In this calculation, the weights are the

Table 16.2 Payoff Matrix for Projects *A* and *B*

State of the Economy	Profits	
	Project *A*	Project *B*
Recession	$4,000	$0
Normal	5,000	5,000
Boom	6,000	12,000

Table 16.3   Calculation of Expected Values

	State of the Economy (1)	Probability of This State Occurring (2)	Profit Outcome if This State Occurs (3)	Expected Profit Outcome (4) = (2) × (3)
Project A	Recession	0.2	$4,000	$800
	Normal	0.6	5,000	3,000
	Boom	0.2	6,000	1,200
		1.0	Expected Profit A	$5,000
Project B	Recession	0.2	$0	$0
	Normal	0.6	5,000	3,000
	Boom	0.2	12,000	2,400
		1.0	Expected Profit B	$5,400

probabilities of occurrence, and the weighted average is called the expected outcome. Column 4 of Table 16.3 illustrates the calculation of expected profits for projects A and B. Each possible profit level in column 3 is multiplied by its probability of occurrence from column 2 to obtain weighted values of the possible profits. Summing column 4 of the table for each project gives a weighted average of profits under various states of the economy. This weighted average is the expected profit from the project.

The expected profit calculation is expressed by the equation

$$\text{Expected Profit} = E(\pi) = \sum_{i=1}^{n} \pi_i \times p_i \qquad \textbf{16.1}$$

Here, π_i is the profit level associated with the ith outcome, p_i is the probability that outcome i will occur, and N is the number of possible outcomes or states of nature. Thus, $E(\pi)$ is a weighted average of possible outcomes (the π_i values), with each outcome's weight equal to its probability of occurrence.

The expected profit for project A is obtained as follows:

$$E(\pi_A) = \sum_{i=1}^{3} \pi_i \times p_i$$
$$= \pi_1 \times p_1 + \pi_2 \times p_2 + \pi_3 \times p_3$$
$$= \$4,000(0.2) + \$5,000(0.6) + \$6,000(0.2)$$
$$= \$5,000$$

The results in Table 16.3 are shown as a bar chart in Figure 16.1. The height of each bar signifies the probability that a given outcome will occur. The probable outcomes for project A range from $4,000 to $6,000, with an average, or expected, value of $5,000. For project B, the expected value is $5,400, and the range of possible outcomes is from $0 to $12,000.

For simplicity, this example assumes that only three states of nature can exist in the economy: recession, normal, and boom. Actual states of the economy range from deep depression, as in the early 1930s, to tremendous booms, such as in the mid- to late 1990s, with an unlimited number of possibilities in between. Suppose sufficient information exists to assign a probability to each possible state of the economy and a monetary

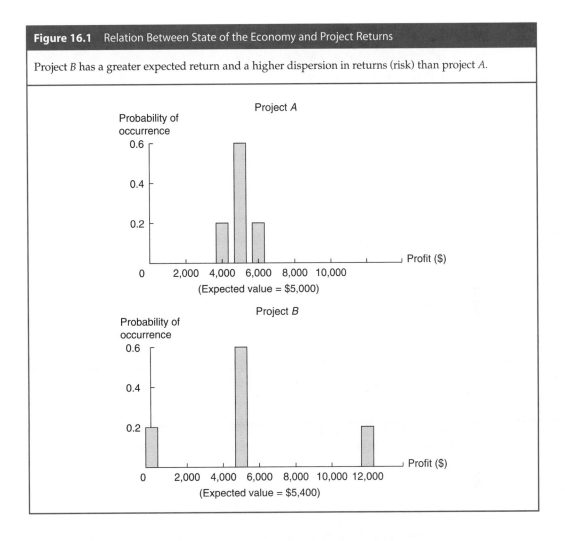

Figure 16.1   Relation Between State of the Economy and Project Returns

Project *B* has a greater expected return and a higher dispersion in returns (risk) than project *A*.

outcome in each circumstance for every project. A table similar to Table 16.3 could then be compiled that would include many more entries for columns 1, 2, and 3. This table could be used to calculate expected values as shown, and the probabilities and outcomes could be approximated by the continuous curves in Figure 16.2.

Figure 16.2 is a graph of the probability distribution of returns for projects *A* and *B*. In general, the tighter the probability distribution, the more likely it is that actual outcomes will be close to expected values. The more loose the probability distribution, the less likely it is that actual outcomes will be close to expected values. Because project *A* has a relatively tight probability distribution, its actual profit is more likely to be close to its expected value than is that of project *B*.

Absolute Risk Measurement

Common risk measures are based on the observation that tight probability distributions imply low risk because of the correspondingly small chance that actual outcomes will differ greatly from expected values. From this perspective, project *A* is less risky than project *B*.

Absolute Risk
Overall dispersion
of possible payoffs.

Standard deviation, shown as σ (sigma), is a popular and useful measure of absolute risk. **Absolute risk** is the overall dispersion of possible payoffs. The smaller the standard

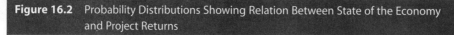

Figure 16.2 Probability Distributions Showing Relation Between State of the Economy and Project Returns

The actual return from project *A* is likely to be close to the expected value. It is less likely that the actual return from project *B* will be close to the expected value.

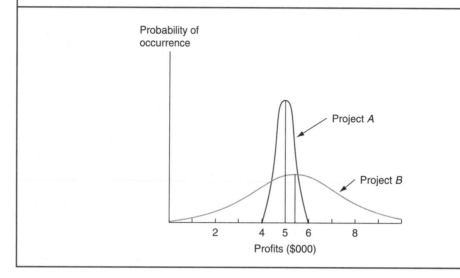

deviation, the tighter the probability distribution and the lower is risk in absolute terms. To calculate standard deviation using probability information, the expected value or mean of the return distribution must first be calculated as

$$\text{Expected Value} = E(\pi) = \sum_{i=1}^{n}(\pi_i\, p_i) \qquad \textbf{16.2}$$

In this calculation, π_i is the profit or return associated with the *i*th outcome; p_i is the probability that the *ith* outcome will occur; and $E(\pi)$, the expected value, is a weighted average of the various possible outcomes, each weighted by the probability of its occurrence.

The deviation of possible outcomes from the expected value must then be derived:

$$\text{Deviation}_i = \pi_i - E(\pi)$$

The squared value of each deviation is then multiplied by the relevant probability and summed. This arithmetic mean of the squared deviations is the variance of the probability distribution:

$$\text{Variance} = \sigma^2 = \sum_{i=1}^{n}[\pi_i - E(\pi)]^2 p_i \qquad \textbf{16.3}$$

The standard deviation is found by obtaining the square root of the variance:

$$\text{Standard Deviation} = \sigma = \sqrt{\sum_{i=1}^{n}[\pi_i - E(\pi)]^2 p_i} \qquad \textbf{16.4}$$

The standard deviation of profit for project A can be calculated to illustrate this procedure:

Deviation $[\pi_i - E(\pi)]$	Deviation^2 $[\pi_i - E(\pi)]^2$	Deviation^2 × Probability $[\pi_i - E(\pi)]^2 \times p_i$
$4,000 – $5,000 = –$1,000	$1,000,000	$1,000,000(0.2) = $200,000
$5,000 – $5,000 = 0	0	$0(0.6) = $0
$6,000 – $5,000 = $1,000	$1,000,000	$1,000,000(0.2) = $200,000
		Variance = σ^2 = $400,000

$$\text{Standard deviation} = \sigma = \sqrt{\sigma^2} = \sqrt{\$400,000} = \$632.46$$

Using the same procedure, the standard deviation of project B's profit is $3,826.23. Because project B has a larger standard deviation of profit, it is the riskier project.

Relative Risk Measurement

Problems sometimes arise when standard deviation is used to measure risk. If an investment project is relatively expensive and has large expected cash flows, it will have a large standard deviation of returns without being truly riskier than a smaller project. Suppose a project has an expected return of $1 million and a standard deviation of only $1,000. Some might reasonably argue that it is less risky than an alternative investment project with expected returns of $1,000 and a standard deviation of $900. The *absolute* risk of the first project is greater; the risk of the second project is much larger than the expected payoff. **Relative risk** is the variation in possible returns compared with the expected payoff amount.

Relative Risk
Variation in possible returns compared with the expected payoff amount.

A popular method for determining relative risk is to calculate the coefficient of variation. Using probability concepts, the coefficient of variation is

$$\text{Coefficient of Variation} = v = \frac{\sigma}{E(\pi)} \qquad \textbf{16.5}$$

In general, when comparing decision alternatives with costs and benefits that are not of approximately equal size, the coefficient of variation measures relative risk better than does the standard deviation.

Other Risk Measures

The standard deviation and coefficient of variation risk measures are based on the *total* variability of returns. In some situations, however, a project's total variability overstates its risk. This is because projects with returns that are less than perfectly correlated can be combined, and the variability of the resulting portfolio of investment projects is less than the sum of individual project risks. Much recent work in finance is based on the idea that project risk should be measured in terms of its contribution to total return variability for the firm's asset portfolio. The contribution of a single investment project to the overall variation of the firm's asset portfolio is measured by a concept known as **beta.** Beta is a measure of the systematic variability or covariance of one asset's returns with returns on other assets.

Beta
Measure of the systematic variability of one asset's returns with returns on other assets.

The concept of beta should be employed when the returns from potential investment projects are likely to greatly affect or be greatly affected by current projects. However, in most circumstances the standard deviation and coefficient of variation measures provide adequate assessments of risk.

STANDARD NORMAL CONCEPT

The standard normal concept is an intuitive and practical means for assessing the dispersion of possible outcomes in terms of expected value and standard deviation measures.

Normal Distribution

Normal Distribution
Symmetrical distribution about the mean or expected value.

The relation among risk, standard deviation, and the coefficient of variation can be clarified by examining the characteristics of a normal distribution, as shown in Figure 16.3. A **normal distribution** has a symmetrical dispersion about the mean or expected value. If a probability distribution is normal, the actual outcome will lie within ±1 standard deviation of the mean roughly 68 percent of the time; the probability that the actual outcome will be within ±2 standard deviations of the expected outcome is approximately 95 percent; and there is a greater than 99 percent probability that the actual outcome will occur within ±3 standard deviations of the mean. The smaller the standard deviation, the tighter the distribution about the expected value and the smaller the probability of an outcome that is very different from the expected value.

Probability distributions can be viewed as a series of *discrete values* represented by a bar chart, such as in Figure 16.1, or as a continuous function represented by a smooth curve, such as that in Figure 16.2. Probabilities associated with the outcomes in Figure 16.1 are given by the heights of the bars, whereas in Figure 16.2, the probabilities must be found by calculating the area under the curve between points of interest.

Figure 16.3   Probability Ranges for a Normal Distribution

When returns display a normal distribution, actual outcomes will lie within ±1 standard deviation of the mean 68.26 percent of the time, within ±2 standard deviations 95.46 percent of the time, and within ±3 standard deviations 99.74 percent of the time.

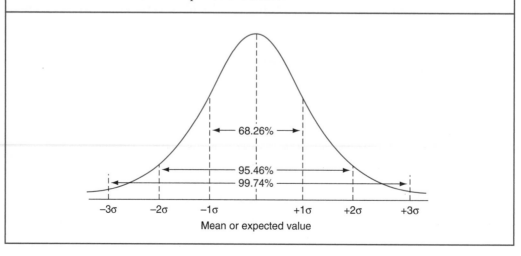

Mean or expected value

Standardized Variables

standardized variable
Variable with a mean of 0 and a standard deviation equal to 1.

Distribution of costs or revenues can be transformed or standardized. A **standardized variable** has a mean of 0 and a standard deviation of 1. Any distribution of revenue, cost, or profit data can be standardized with the following formula:

$$z = \frac{x - \mu}{\sigma}$$

16.6

where z is the standardized variable, x is the outcome of interest, and μ and σ are the mean and standard deviation of the distribution, respectively. If the point of interest is 1σ away from the mean, then $x - \mu = \sigma$, so $z = \sigma/\sigma = 1.0$. When $z = 1.0$, the point of interest is 1σ away from the mean; when $z = 2$, the value is 2σ away from the mean; and so on. Although the standard normal distribution theoretically runs from $-\infty$ to $+\infty$, the probability of occurrences beyond 3 standard deviations is very small.

Use of the Standard Normal Concept: An Example

Suppose that the Martha Stewart Realty is considering a boost in advertising to reduce a large inventory of unsold homes. Management plans to make its media decision using the data shown in Table 16.4 on the expected success of television versus newspaper promotions. For simplicity, assume that the returns from each promotion are normally distributed. If the television promotion costs $2,295 and the newspaper promotion costs $4,013, what is the probability that each will generate a profit?

To calculate the probability that each promotion will generate a profit, it is necessary to calculate the portion of the total area under the normal curve that is to the right of (greater than) each breakeven point (Figure 16.3). A breakeven point is where the profit contribution before advertising costs just equals the required advertising expenditure. Using methods described earlier, relevant expected values and standard deviations are $E(R_{TV}) = \$2,500$, $\sigma_{TV} = \$250$, $E(R_N) = \$5,000$, and $\sigma_N = \$600$. For the television promotion, the breakeven revenue level of $2,295 is 0.82 standard deviations less than (to the left of) the expected return level of $2,500 because

$$z = \frac{x_{TV} - E(R_{TV})}{\sigma_{TV}}$$

$$= \frac{\$2,295 - \$2,500}{\$250}$$

$$= -0.82$$

Table 16.4 Return Distributions for Television and Newspaper Promotions

	Market Response	Probability of Occurring (P_i)	Return (R_i) (profit contribution before ad costs)
Television	Poor	0.125	$2,000
	Good	0.750	2,500
	Very good	0.125	3,000
Newspaper	Poor	0.125	3,800
	Good	0.750	5,000
	Very good	0.125	6,200

Table B1 in Appendix C shows that the standard normal distribution function value for $z = -0.82$ is 0.2939. This means that 29.39 percent of the region under the normal curve lies between $2,295 ($z = -0.82$) and the expected revenue level of $2,500. Because 29.39 percent of the total area under the normal curve lies between x_{TV} and $E(R_{TV})$, the profit probability for the television promotion is $0.2939 + 0.5 = 0.7939$ or 79.39 percent. For the newspaper promotion, z is calculated as

$$z = \frac{x_{TV} - E(R_{TV})}{\sigma_{TV}}$$

$$= \frac{\$4,013 - \$5,000}{\$600}$$

$$= -1.645$$

After interpolating, the probability value for $z = -1.645$ is 0.45. This means that 0.45, or 45 percent, of the total area under the normal curve lies between x_N and $E(R_N)$, and it implies a profit probability for the newspaper promotion of $0.45 + 0.5 = 0.95$, or 95 percent. In terms of profit probability, the newspaper advertisement is the less risky alternative.

UTILITY THEORY AND RISK ANALYSIS

The assumption of risk aversion is basic to many decision models in managerial economics.

Managerial Application 16.2

Why Are Lotteries Popular?

The success of state-run lotteries is convincing evidence that many in our society display risk-seeking behavior, especially when small sums of money are involved. The popularity of lotteries stems from the fact that ticket buyers appear eager to pay $1 for a bet that has an expected return of less than $1. When only 50 percent of lottery-ticket revenues are paid out in the form of prizes, each $1 ticket has an expected return of only 50¢. In such circumstances, the "price" of $1 in expected return is $2 in certain dollars. The willingness to pay such a premium for the unlikely chance at a lottery payoff that might reach into the millions of dollars stems from the fact that such opportunities are rare and lottery-ticket buyers value them highly. Many of the poor, uneducated, or elderly have no opportunity for hitting the jackpot in their careers. The lottery is their only chance, however remote, at a substantial sum of money. It should therefore come as no surprise that lottery-ticket buyers tend to be poor, uneducated, and elderly.

The success of state-run lotteries is noteworthy because it reflects risk attitudes that are fairly unusual. Typically,

consumers and investors display risk-averse behavior, especially when substantial sums of money are involved. Still, the eagerness of consumers to take on enormous risks when small sums of money are involved has made gambling one of America's great growth industries. If legislative agendas are any indication, Americans can expect to see even more riverboat gambling, card clubs, offtrack betting parlors, and casinos in their own backyards. Indian-run casinos are also becoming increasingly popular. Americans are so eager to gamble that they are shifting long-established leisure-time expenditures. Today, U.S. consumers spend more on legal games of chance than on movie theaters, books, amusement attractions, and recorded music combined!

Pouring quarters into slot machines is easy and appealing to a growing number of Americans.

See: Jonathan Clements, "You're Not Super Rich? You Lucked Out," *The Wall Street Journal Online*, October 21, 2007, http://online.wsj.com.

Possible Risk Attitudes

Risk Aversion
Desire to avoid or minimize uncertainty.

Risk Neutrality
Focus on expected values, not return dispersion.

Risk Seeking
Preference for speculation.

Three possible attitudes toward risk are present: aversion to risk, indifference to risk, and preference for risk. **Risk aversion** characterizes individuals who seek to avoid or minimize risk. **Risk neutrality** characterizes decision makers who focus on expected returns and disregard the dispersion of returns (risk). **Risk seeking** characterizes decision makers who prefer risk. Given a choice between more risky and less risky investments with identical expected returns, a risk averter selects the less risky investment and a risk seeker selects the riskier investment. Faced with the same choice, the risk-neutral investor is indifferent between the two investment projects.

In practice, many individuals prefer high-risk projects and the corresponding potential for substantial returns, especially when relatively small sums of money are involved. Entrepreneurs, innovators, inventors, speculators, and lottery-ticket buyers are all examples of individuals who display some risk-seeking behavior. Risk-neutral behavior is exhibited in some business decision making. However, most managers and investors are predominantly risk averters, especially when substantial dollar amounts are involved.

Relation Between Money and Its Utility

Diminishing Marginal Utility
When additional increments of money bring ever smaller increments of added benefit.

At the heart of risk aversion is the notion of **diminishing marginal utility** for money. If someone with no money receives $50,000, it can satisfy his or her most immediate needs. If such a person then receives a second $50,000, it will obviously be useful, but the second $50,000 is not quite as necessary as the first $50,000. The marginal utility of the second $50,000 is less than the utility of the first $50,000. Diminishing marginal utility of money implies that the marginal utility of income diminishes for additional increments of money. Figure 16.4 graphs the relation between money and its utility, or value. In the figure, utility is measured in units of value or satisfaction, an index that is unique to each individual.

Figure 16.4 Example of a Money/Utility Relation

A risk seeker's marginal utility of money increases. A risk-indifferent individual has a constant marginal utility of money. A risk averter displays a diminishing marginal utility of money.

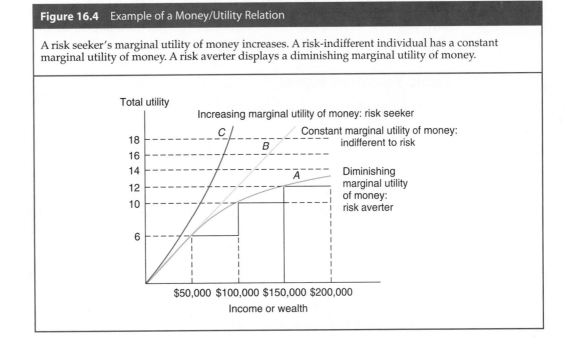

For risk averters, money has diminishing marginal utility. If such an individual's wealth were to double suddenly, he or she would experience an increase in material satisfaction, but the new level of well-being would not be twice the previous level. In cases of diminishing marginal utility, a less than proportional relation holds between total utility and money. Those who are indifferent to risk perceive a strictly proportional relationship between total utility and money. Such a relation implies a constant marginal utility of money, and the utility of a doubled quantity of money is exactly twice the utility of the original level. Risk seekers perceive a more than proportional relation between total utility and money. With increasing marginal utility of money, the utility of doubled wealth is more than twice the utility of the original amount. These relations are illustrated in Figure 16.4.

Because individuals with a diminishing marginal utility for money suffer more pain from a dollar lost than the pleasure derived from a dollar gained, they seek to avoid risk. Risk averters require a very high return on any investment that is subject to much risk. In Figure 16.4, for example, a gain of $50,000 from a base of $100,000 brings 2 units of additional satisfaction, but a $50,000 loss causes a 4-unit loss in satisfaction. A person with this utility function and $100,000 would be unwilling to make an investment with a 50/50 chance of winning or losing $50,000. The 9-unit expected utility of such a gamble $[E(u) = 0.5$ times the utility of $\$50,000 + 0.5$ times the utility of $\$150,000 = 0.5 \times 6 + 0.5 \times 12 = 9]$ is less than the 10 units of utility obtained by forgoing the gamble and keeping $100,000 in certain wealth.

Because an individual with a constant marginal utility for money values a dollar gained just as highly as a dollar lost, the expected utility from a fair gamble always exactly equals the utility of the expected outcome. An individual indifferent to risk makes decisions solely on the basis of expected outcomes and is not concerned with variation in the distribution of outcomes.

ADJUSTING THE VALUATION MODEL FOR RISK

Two primary methods are used to adjust the basic valuation model to account for decision making under conditions of uncertainty.

Basic Valuation Model

The basic valuation model developed in Chapter 1 is

$$V = \sum_{t=1}^{n} \frac{\pi_t}{(1 + i)^t}$$

16.7

This model states that the value of the firm is equal to the discounted present worth of future profits. Under conditions of certainty, the numerator is profit, and the denominator is a time-value adjustment using the risk-free rate of return i. After time-value adjustment, the profits to be earned from various projects are strictly comparable.

Under conditions of uncertainty, the profits shown in the numerator of the valuation model as π equal the expected value of profits during each future period. This expected value is the best available estimate of the amount to be earned during any given period. However, because profits cannot be predicted with absolute precision, some variability is to be anticipated. If the firm must choose between two alternative methods of operation,

Managerial Application 16.3

Stock Option Backdating Scandal

In a conventional employee stock-option plan, key employees are granted the right to buy a fixed number of shares for a predetermined period. The number of shares granted depends on the employee's level of responsibility and is commensurate with total compensation. According to current tax law, the exercise period for employee stock options cannot exceed 10 years. Because stock prices usually rise from 10 percent to 12 percent per year, on average, from the employee's perspective, the longer the exercise period, the better.

An employee can exercise the right to buy stock covered by a stock-option plan once the vesting period has been completed. The vesting period is an employment time frame after which granted options can be exercised. The length of the vesting period is designed by the employer to keep valued employees motivated. It is also designed to keep employees from bolting to the competition. Structured properly, an employee stock-option plan with appropriate vesting requirements can create "golden handcuffs" that benefit both valued employees and their employers. Once exercised, employee stock options create a taxable event for

the employee. The difference between the current market price and the original exercise price, multiplied by the number of shares covered, is used to calculate the amount of employee compensation derived from the option exercise. Recently, finance researchers made the stunning discovery that top executives at dozens of major U.S. corporations were retroactively manipulating option grant dates to enhance the value of their executive stock option. Hundreds of millions of dollars in excess compensation resulted. Dozens of top executives caught up in the scandal were fired; some faced criminal charges for income tax evasion. Scores of affected companies were forced to dramatically restate their financial performance; shareholders saw share prices tumble.

Therefore, while many still regard employee stock options as an attractive form of incentive-based pay, transparency and timely disclosure are needed to ensure fairness and accountability.

See: Randall A. Heron, Erik Lie, and Todd Perry, "On the Use (and Abuse) of Stock Option Grants," *Financial Analysts Journal*, vol. 63, no. 1 (May/June 2007), 17–27.

one with high expected profits and high risks and another with smaller expected profits and lower risks, an appropriate ranking of projects is possible only if each respective investment project can be adjusted for both the time value of money and risk. Two popular methods are employed to make such adjustments. In the first, expected profits are adjusted to account for risk. In the second, the interest rate used in the denominator of the valuation model is increased to reflect risk considerations. Either method can be used to ensure that value-maximizing decisions are made.

Certainty Equivalent Adjustments

The **certainty equivalent** method is an adjustment to the numerator of the basic valuation model to account for risk. Under the certainty equivalent approach, decision makers specify the certain sum that they regard comparable to the expected value of a risky investment alternative. The certainty equivalent of an expected risk amount typically differs in dollar terms but not in terms of the amount of utility provided. To illustrate, suppose that you face the following choices:

- Invest $100,000. From a successful project, you receive $1,000,000; if it fails, you receive nothing. If the probability of success is 0.5, or 50 percent, the investment's expected payoff is $500,000 ($= 0.5 \times \$1,000,000 + 0.5 \times \$0$).
- You do not make the investment; you keep the $100,000.

If you are indifferent between the two alternatives, $100,000 is your certainty equivalent for the risky expected return of $500,000. In other words, a certain amount of $100,000 provides exactly the same utility as the 50/50 chance to earn $1,000,000 or $0. You are indifferent between these two alternatives.

In this example, any certainty equivalent value of less than $500,000 indicates risk aversion. If the maximum amount that you are willing to invest in the project is only $100,000, you are exhibiting very risk-averse behavior. Each certain dollar is "worth" five times as much as each risky dollar of expected return. Alternatively, each risky dollar of expected return is worth only 20% in terms of certain dollars. Any risky investment with a certainty equivalent less than the expected dollar value indicates risk aversion; a certainty equivalent greater than the expected value of a risky investment indicates risk preference.

Certainty Equivalent
Assured sum that equals an expected risky amount in utility terms.

Any expected risky amount can be converted to an equivalent certain sum using the **certainty equivalent adjustment factor, α**, calculated as the ratio of a certain sum divided by an expected risky amount, where both dollar values provide the same level of utility:

Adjustment Factor, α
Ratio of a certain sum to an expected risky amount, where both dollar values provide the same level of utility.

$$\frac{\text{Certainty Equivalent}}{\text{Adjustment Factor}} = \alpha = \frac{\text{Equivalent Certain Sum}}{\text{Expected Risky Sum}} \qquad \textbf{16.8}$$

The certain sum numerator and expected return denominator may vary in dollar terms, but they provide the exact same reward in terms of utility. In the previous investment problem, in which a certain sum of $100,000 provides the same utility as an expected risky return of $500,000, the certainty equivalent adjustment factor $\alpha = 0.2 = \$100,000/\$500,000$. This means that the "price" of one dollar in risky expected return is 20¢ in certain dollar terms.

In general

If	Then	Implies
Equivalent certain sum $<$ Expected risky sum	$\alpha < 1$	Risk aversion
Equivalent certain sum $=$ Expected risky sum	$\alpha = 1$	Risk indifference
Equivalent certain sum $>$ Expected risky sum	$\alpha > 1$	Risk preference

The appropriate α value for a given managerial decision varies according to the level of risk and manager risk attitudes.

Risk-Adjusted Valuation Model
Valuation model that reflects time-value and risk considerations.

The basic valuation model [Equation (16.7)] can be converted into a **risk-adjusted valuation model**, one that explicitly accounts for risk:

$$V = \sum_{t=1}^{n} \frac{\sigma E(\pi_t)}{(1+i)^t} \qquad \textbf{16.9}$$

In this risk-adjusted valuation model, expected future profits, $E(\pi_t)$, are converted to their certainty equivalents, $\alpha E(\pi_t)$, and are discounted at a risk-free rate, i, to obtain the risk-adjusted present value of a firm or project. With the valuation model in this form, one can appraise the effects of different courses of action with different risks and expected returns.

To use Equation (16.9) for real-world decision making, managers must estimate appropriate αs for various investment opportunities. Deriving such estimates can prove difficult, because α varies according to the size and risk of investment projects and according to the risk attitudes of investors. In many instances, however, the record of past investment decisions offers a guide that can be used to determine appropriate certainty equivalent adjustment factors.

Certainty Equivalent Adjustment Example

Suppose that operations at Burns & Allen Industries have been disrupted by problems with a faulty boiler, and the company has retained the law firm of Dewey, Cheetum, & Howe to recover economic damages from the boiler manufacturer. The company has filed suit in state court for $250,000 in damages. Prior to filing suit, the attorney estimated legal, expert witness, and other litigation costs to be $10,000 for a fully litigated case, for which Burns & Allen had a 10 percent chance of receiving a favorable judgment. For simplicity, assume that a favorable judgment will award Burns & Allen 100 percent of the damages sought, whereas an unfavorable judgment will result in the firm receiving nothing. Also assume that $10,000 is the most Burns & Allen would be willing to pay to sue the boiler manufacturer.

In filing suit against the boiler manufacturer, Burns & Allen has made a risky investment decision. By its willingness to bear litigation costs of $10,000, the company has implicitly stated that it regards these out-of-pocket costs to be *at least* equivalent to the value of the risky expectation of receiving a favorable judgment against the boiler manufacturer. Burns & Allen is willing to pay $10,000 in certain litigation costs for the possibility of receiving a $250,000 judgment against the boiler manufacturer.

Burns & Allen's investment decision can be characterized using the certainty equivalent adjustment method. Realize that $10,000 in litigation costs is incurred irrespective of the outcome of a fully litigated case. $10,000 represents a certain sum that the company must value as highly as the expected risky outcome to be willing to file suit. The expected risky outcome, or expected return from filing suit, is

$$
\begin{aligned}
\text{Expected Return} &= \text{Favorable Judgment Payoff} \times \text{Probability} \\
&\quad + \text{Unfavorable Judgment Payoff} \times \text{Probability} \\
&= \$250,000(0.1) + \$0(0.9) \\
&= \$25,000
\end{aligned}
$$

To justify filing suit, Burns & Allen's certainty equivalent adjustment factor for investment projects of this risk class must be

$$
\begin{aligned}
\alpha &= \frac{\text{Certain Sum}}{\text{Expected Risky Sum}} \\
&= \frac{\text{Litigation Costs}}{\text{Expected Return}} \\
&= \frac{\$10,000}{\$25,000} \\
&= 0.4
\end{aligned}
$$

Each risky dollar of expected return from the litigation effort is worth, in terms of utility, *at least* 40¢ in certain dollars. Alternatively, $10,000 is the certain sum equivalent of the risky expected return of $25,000.

Assume that after Burns & Allen goes to court and incurs $5,000 in litigation costs especially damaging testimony by an expert witness dramatically changes the outlook of the case in Burns & Allen's favor. In response, the boiler manufacturer's attorney offers an out-of-court settlement in the amount of $30,000. However, Burns & Allen's attorney recommends that the company reject the offer, estimating that it now has a 50/50 chance of obtaining a favorable judgment. Should Burns & Allen follow the attorney's advice and reject the settlement offer?

In answering this question, one must keep in mind that having already spent ("sunk") $5,000 in litigation costs, Burns & Allen must consider as relevant litigation costs only the additional $5,000 necessary to complete litigation. These $5,000 litigation costs, plus the $30,000 out-of-court settlement offer, represent the relevant certain sum, because proceeding with the suit will require an "investment" of these additional opportunity costs. Given the revised outlook for a favorable judgment, the expected return to full litigation is

$$\text{Expected Return} = (\$250,000)(0.5) + (\$0)(0.5)$$
$$= \$125,000$$

In light of Burns & Allen's earlier decision to file suit on the basis that each dollar of expected risky return was "worth" 40¢ in certain dollars, this expected return would have a $50,000 (= $125,000 × 0.4) certainty equivalent value. Because this amount exceeds the settlement offer plus remaining litigation costs, the settlement offer is deficient and should be rejected. On the basis of Burns & Allen's revealed risk attitude, an out-of-court settlement offer has to be at least $45,000 to receive favorable consideration. At that point, the settlement plus saved litigation costs of $5,000 would equal the certainty equivalent value of the expected return from continuing litigation.

This simple example illustrates that historical decisions offer a useful guide to current decisions. If a potential project's required investment and risk levels are known, the α implied by a decision to accept the investment project can be calculated. This project-specific α can then be compared with αs for prior projects with similar risks. Risk-averse individuals should invest in projects if calculated αs are less than or equal to those for accepted projects in the same risk class. Given an estimate of expected return and risk, the maximum amount that the firm should be willing to invest in a given project can also be determined from the certainty equivalent adjustment factor. Risk-averse management will accept new projects if the level of required investment per dollar of expected return is less than or equal to that for historical projects of similar risk.

Risk-Adjusted Discount Rates

Risk-adjusted Discount Rate
Risk-free rate of return plus the required risk premium.

Risk Premium
Added expected return for a risky asset over that of a risk-free asset.

Another way to incorporate risk in managerial decision making is to adjust the discount rate or denominator of the basic valuation model [Equation (16.7)]. Like certainty equivalent factors, **risk-adjusted discount rates** are based on the trade-off between risk and return for individual investors. Suppose an investor is indifferent to a riskless asset with a sure 5 percent rate of return, a moderately risky asset with a 10 percent expected return, and a very risky asset with a 15 percent expected return. As risk increases, higher expected returns on investment are required to compensate for additional risk. In most cases, the required **risk premium** is directly related to the level of risk associated with a particular investment.

The basic valuation model shown in Equation (16.7) can be adapted to account for risk through adjustment of the discount rate, i, where

$$V = \sum_{i=1}^{N} \frac{E(\pi_t)}{(1+k)^t}$$ **16.10**

The risk-adjusted discount rate k is the sum of the risk-free rate of return, R_F, and the required risk premium, R_p:

$$k = R_F + R_p$$

In Equation (16.10), value is measured by the present worth of expected future income or profits, $E(\pi_t)$, discounted at a risk-adjusted rate.

Risk-Adjusted Discount Rate Example

Suppose the Property & Casualty Insurance Company (P&C) is contemplating the purchase of one of the two database and file management software systems offered by Rockford Files, Inc. System A is specifically designed for P&C's current computer software system and cannot be used with those of other providers; system B is compatible with a broad variety of computer software systems, including P&C's and those of other software providers. The expected investment outlay is $500,000 for each alternative. Expected annual cost savings (cash inflows) over 5 years are $175,000 per year for system A and $185,000 per year for system B. The standard deviation of expected annual returns from system A is $10,000, whereas that of system B is $15,000. In view of this risk differential, P&C management has decided to evaluate system A with a 10 percent cost of capital and system B with a 15 percent cost of capital.

The risk-adjusted value for each system is[2]

$$\text{Value}_A = \sum_{t=1}^{5} \frac{\$175,000}{(1.10)^t} - \$500,000$$

$$= \$175,000 \times \left(\sum_{t=1}^{5} \frac{1}{(1.10)^t} \right) - \$500,000$$

$$= \$175,000 \times 3.7908 - \$500,000$$

$$= \$163,390$$

$$\text{Value}_B = \sum_{t=1}^{5} \frac{\$185,000}{(1.15)^t} - \$500,000$$

$$= \$185,000 \times \left(\sum_{t=1}^{5} \frac{1}{(1.10)^t} \right) - \$500,000$$

$$= \$185,000 \times 3.3522 - \$500,000$$

$$= \$120,157$$

---

2   The terms

$$\sum_{t=1}^{5} \frac{1}{(1.10)^t} = 3.7908$$

and

$$\sum_{t=1}^{5} \frac{1}{(1.15)^t} = 3.3522$$

are present-value-of-an-annuity interest factors. Tables of interest factors for various interest rates and years (t values) appear in Appendix C.4.

Because the risk-adjusted value of system *A* is larger than that for system *B*, choice of system *A* will maximize the value of the firm.

DECISION TREES AND COMPUTER SIMULATION

Decision trees follow the sequential nature of the decision-making process and provide a logical framework for decision analysis under conditions of uncertainty.

Decision Trees

Decision Tree
Map of a sequential decision-making process.

Decision Points
Instances when management must select among choice alternatives.

Chance Events
Possible outcomes following each decision point.

A **decision tree** is a sequential decision-making process. Decision trees are designed for analyzing problems that involve a series of choice alternatives that are constrained by prior decisions. They illustrate the complete range of future possibilities and their associated probabilities in terms of a logical progression from an initial **decision point,** through each subsequent constrained decision alternative, to an ultimate outcome. Decision points are instances where management must select among several choice alternatives. **Chance events** are possible outcomes following each decision point.

Decision trees are widely employed because many important decisions are made in stages. For example, a pharmaceutical company considering expansion into the generic drug market might take the following steps:

- Spend $100,000 to survey supply and demand conditions in the generic drug industry.
- If survey results are favorable, spend $2 million on a pilot plant to investigate production methods.
- Depending on cost estimates and potential demand, abandon the project, build a large plant, or build a small one.

These decisions are made in stages; subsequent determinations depend on prior judgments. The sequence of events can be mapped out to visually resemble the branches of a tree—hence the term decision tree.

Figure 16.5 illustrates the decision-tree method for this decision problem. Assume that the company has completed its industry supply and demand analysis and determined that it should develop a full-scale production facility. Either a large plant or a small plant can be built. The probability is 50 percent for high demand, 30 percent for medium demand, and 20 percent for low demand. Depending on actual demand, the present value of net cash flows, defined as sales revenue minus operating costs, ranges from $8.8 million to $1.4 million for a large plant and from $2.6 million to $1.4 million for a small plant.

Because demand probabilities are known, expected cash flow can be determined, as in column 5 of Figure 16.5. Investment outlays are deducted from expected net cash flow to obtain the expected net present value for each decision. The expected net present value is $730,000 for the large plant and $300,000 for the small one. Notice the wide range of possible outcomes for the large plant. Actual net present values for the large plant investment equal the present value of cash flows (column 4) minus the large plant investment cost of $5 million. These values vary from $3.8 million to −$3.6 million. Actual net present values for the small plant investment range only from $600,000 to −$600,000. Clearly, the smaller plant appears less risky based on the width of the range of possible net present value outcomes. Because the investment requirement differs for each plant, the coefficient of variation for each plant's net present value can be examined to provide an alternate measure of relative risk. The coefficient of variation for the large plant's

Figure 16.5 Illustrative Decision Tree

The expected net present value of each investment alternative (column 5) is determined by linking possible outcomes (column 2), probabilities (column 3), and monetary values (column 4).

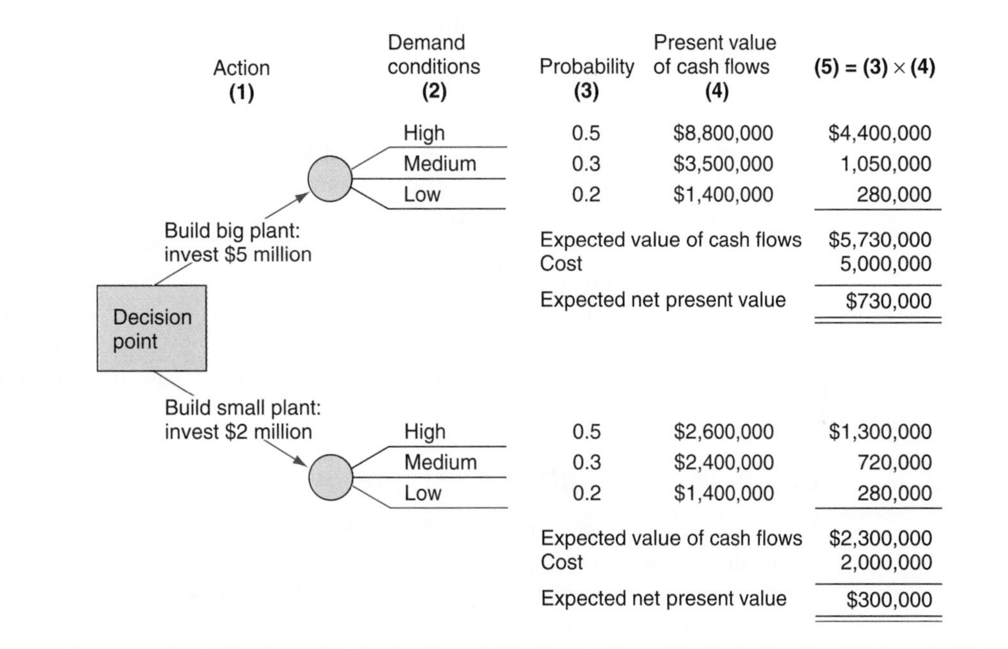

Action (1)	Demand conditions (2)	Probability (3)	Present value of cash flows (4)	(5) = (3) × (4)
	High	0.5	$8,800,000	$4,400,000
	Medium	0.3	$3,500,000	1,050,000
	Low	0.2	$1,400,000	280,000
Build big plant: invest $5 million			Expected value of cash flows	$5,730,000
			Cost	5,000,000
			Expected net present value	$730,000
Build small plant: invest $2 million	High	0.5	$2,600,000	$1,300,000
	Medium	0.3	$2,400,000	720,000
	Low	0.2	$1,400,000	280,000
			Expected value of cash flows	$2,300,000
			Cost	2,000,000
			Expected net present value	$300,000

Decision point

present value is 4.3, whereas that for the small plant is only 1.5.[3] Again, risk appears greater for the large plant alternative.

Risk and expected return differentials can be incorporated into the decision-making process in a variety of ways. Assigning utility values to the cash flows given in column 4 of Figure 16.5 would state column 5 in terms of expected utility. The company could then choose the plant size that provided the greatest expected utility. Alternatively, present values given in column 4 could be adjusted using the certainty equivalent or risk-adjusted discount rate method. The plant that offers the largest risk-adjusted net present value is the optimal choice.

Computer Simulation

Computer Simulation
Use of computer software and workstations or sophisticated desktop computers to create outcome scenarios.

Another technique designed to assist business decision makers in making decisions under uncertainty is **computer simulation.** Computer simulation involves the use of computer software and sophisticated desktop computers to create a wide variety of decision outcome scenarios. These simulations illustrate a broad range of possible outcomes to help managers assess the possible and probable consequences of decision alternatives. Using the computer simulation technique, a variety of hypothetical "What if?" questions can be asked and answered on the basis of measurable differences in underlying

3   Using Equation (16.6) and data on possible returns in Figure 16.5, the standard deviation for the big plant is $3.155 million and for the small plant it is $458,260. Dividing these standard deviations by the appropriate expected return for each respective plant size, as in Equation (16.5), gives the coefficient of variation.

assumptions. More than just informed conjecture, computer simulation allows managers to make precise judgments concerning the desirability of various choices on the basis of highly detailed probability information.

Computer simulations require probability distribution estimates for a number of variables, such as investment outlays, unit sales, product prices, input prices, and asset lives. In some instances, full-scale simulations are expensive and time-consuming and therefore restricted to projects such as major plant expansions or new-product decisions. When a firm is deciding whether to accept a major undertaking involving an outlay of millions of dollars, full-scale computer simulations provide valuable insights that are well worth their cost. Less expensive limited-scale simulations are used to project outcomes for projects or strategies. Instead of using complete probability distributions for each variable included in the problem, results are simulated based on best-guess estimates for each variable. Changes in the values of each variable are then considered to see the effects of such changes on project returns. Typically, returns are highly sensitive to some variables, less so to others. Attention is then focused on the variables to which profitability is most sensitive. This technique, known as **sensitivity analysis,** is less expensive and less time-consuming than full-scale computer simulation, but it still provides a valuable insight for decision-making purposes.

Sensitivity Analysis
Limited form of computer simulation that focuses on important decision variables.

Computer Simulation Example

To illustrate the computer simulation technique, consider the evaluation of a new minimill investment project by Remington Steel, Inc. The exact cost of the plant is not known, but it is expected to be about $150 million. If no difficulties arise in construction, this cost can be as low as $125 million. An unfortunate series of events such as strikes, greater-than-projected increases in material costs, and/or technical problems could drive the required investment outlay as high as $225 million. Revenues from the new facility depend on the growth of regional income and construction, competition, developments in the field of metallurgy, steel import quotas and tariffs, and so on. Operating costs depend on production efficiency, the cost of raw materials, and the trend in wage rates. Because sales revenues and operating costs are uncertain, annual profits are unpredictable.

Assuming that probability distributions can be developed for each major cost and revenue category, a computer program can be constructed to simulate the pattern of future events. Computer simulation randomly selects revenue and cost levels from each relevant distribution and uses this information to estimate future profits, net present values, or the rate of return on investment. This process is repeated a large number of times to identify the central tendency of projected returns and their expected values. When the computer simulation is completed, the frequency pattern and range of future returns can be plotted and analyzed. Although the expected value of future profits is of obvious interest, the range of possible outcomes is similarly important as a useful indicator of risk.

The computer simulation technique is illustrated in Figures 16.6 and 16.7. Figure 16.6 is a flowchart that shows the information flow pattern for the simulation procedure just described. Figure 16.7 illustrates the frequency distribution of rates of return generated by such a simulation for two alternative projects, X and Y, each with an expected cost of $20 million. The expected rate of return on investment X is 15 percent, and 20 percent on investment Y. However, these are only average rates of return derived by the computer simulation. The range of simulated returns is from −10 percent to 45 percent for investment Y, and from 5 percent to 25 percent for investment X. The standard deviation for X is only 4 percent; that for Y is 12 percent. Based on this information, the coefficient

Figure 16.6 Simulation for Investment Planning

Computer simulation allows detailed analysis of business problems involving complex cost and revenue relations.

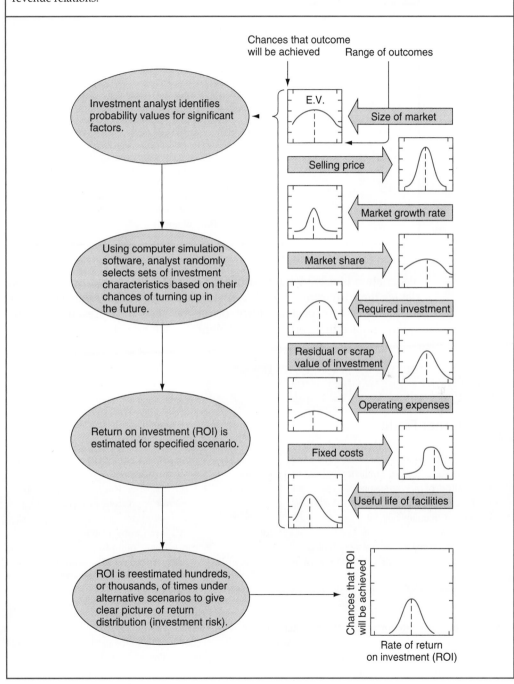

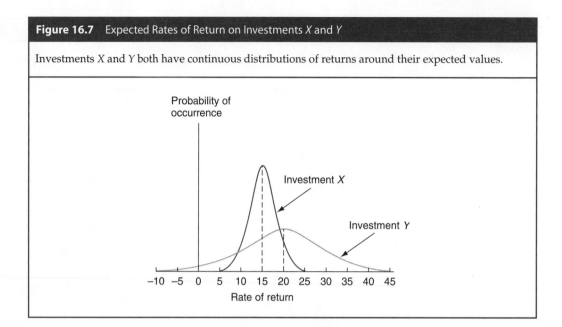

Figure 16.7   Expected Rates of Return on Investments *X* and *Y*

Investments *X* and *Y* both have continuous distributions of returns around their expected values.

of variation is 0.267 for investment *X* and 0.60 for investment *Y*. Investment *Y* is clearly riskier than investment *X*. A decision about which alternative to choose can be made on the basis of expected utility, or on the basis of a present value determination that incorporates either certainty equivalents or risk-adjusted discount rates.

Managerial Application 16.4

Internet Fraud

The Internet allows individuals or companies to communicate with a large audience without spending a lot of time, effort, or money. Anyone can reach tens of thousands of people by building an Internet Web site, posting a message on an online bulletin board, entering a discussion in a live "chat" room, or sending mass e-mails. It is easy for fraud perpetrators to make their messages look credible; it is nearly impossible for investors to tell the difference between fact and fiction.

Investment frauds seen online mirror frauds perpetrated over the phone or by mail:

- **The "pump and dump" scam.** Paid promoters sometimes accumulate stock and then leak imaginary favorable information to pump up the stock price. After the stock price has risen, fraudulent promoters dump their shares on an unsuspecting public.
- **The pyramid.** Many Internet frauds are merely electronic versions of the classic "pyramid" scheme in which

participants attempt to make money solely by recruiting new participants.

- **The "risk-free" fraud.** Be wary of opportunities that promise spectacular profits or "guaranteed" returns. If the deal sounds too good to be true, then it probably is.
- **Offshore frauds.** Watch out for offshore scams and investment "opportunities" in other countries. When you send your money abroad and something goes wrong, it is more difficult to find out what happened and to locate your money.

The Securities and Exchange Commission (SEC) is effectively tracking Internet investment fraud and has taken quick action to stop scams. With the cooperation of federal and state criminal authorities, the SEC has also helped put Internet fraudsters in jail.

See: If you believe any person or entity may have violated the federal securities laws, submit a complaint at http://www.sec.gov.

SUMMARY

Risk analysis plays an integral role in the decision process for most business problems. This chapter defines the concept of economic risk and illustrates how the concept can be dealt with in the managerial decision-making process.

- **Economic risk** is the chance of loss due to the fact that all possible outcomes and their probability of occurrence are unknown. **Uncertainty** exists when the outcomes of managerial decisions cannot be predicted with absolute accuracy, but all possibilities and their associated probabilities are known.

- **Business risk** is the chance of loss associated with a given managerial decision. Many different types of business risk are apparent in the globally competitive 1990s. **Market risk** is the chance that a portfolio of investments can lose money because of swings in the stock market as a whole. **Inflation risk** is the danger that a general increase in the price level will undermine real economic values. **Interest-rate risk** stems from the fact that a fall in interest rates will increase the value of any agreement that involves a fixed promise to pay interest and principal over a specified period. **Credit risk** is the chance that another party will fail to abide by its contractual obligations. Corporations must also consider the problem of **liquidity risk**, or the difficulty of selling corporate assets or investments that have only a few willing buyers or that are otherwise not easily transferable at favorable prices under typical market conditions. **Derivative risk** is the chance that volatile financial derivatives could create losses in underlying investments by increasing rather than decreasing price volatility.

- **Cultural risk** is borne by companies that pursue a global rather than a solely domestic investment strategy. Product market differences due to distinctive social customs make it difficult to predict which products might do well in foreign markets. **Currency risk** is another important danger facing global businesses because most companies wish to eventually repatriate foreign earnings back to the domestic parent. Finally, global investors also experience **government policy risk** because foreign government grants of monopoly franchises, tax abatements,

and favored trade status can be tenuous. **Expropriation risk**, or the risk that business property located abroad might be seized by host governments, is another type of risk that global investors must not forget.

- The **probability** of an event is the chance, or odds, that the incident will occur. If all possible events or outcomes are listed, and if a probability of occurrence is assigned to each event, the listing is called a **probability distribution**. A **payoff matrix** illustrates the outcome associated with each possible state of nature. The **expected value** is the anticipated realization from a given payoff matrix.

- **Absolute risk** is the overall dispersion of possible payoffs. The smaller the standard deviation, the tighter the probability distribution and the lower the risk in absolute terms. **Relative risk** is the variation in possible returns compared with the expected payoff amount. **Beta** is a measure of the systematic variability or covariance of one asset's returns with returns on other assets.

- A **normal distribution** has a symmetrical distribution about the mean or expected value. If a probability distribution is normal, the actual outcome will lie within ±1 standard deviation of the mean roughly 68 percent of the time. The probability that the actual outcome will be within ±2 standard deviations of the expected outcome is approximately 95 percent; and there is a greater than 99 percent probability that the actual outcome will occur within ±3 standard deviations of the mean. A **standardized variable** has a mean of 0 and a standard deviation equal to 1.

- **Risk aversion** characterizes individuals who seek to avoid or minimize risk. **Risk neutrality** characterizes decision makers who focus on expected returns and disregard the dispersion of returns (risk). **Risk seeking** characterizes decision makers who prefer risk. At the heart of risk aversion is the notion of **diminishing marginal utility**, where additional increments of money bring ever smaller increments of marginal utility.

- Under the **certainty equivalent** approach, decision makers specify the certain sum that they regard comparable to the expected value of a risky investment alternative. Any expected risky amount can be converted to an equivalent certain sum using the **certainty equivalent adjustment factor,** α, calculated as the ratio of a certain sum to an expected risky amount, where both dollar values provide the same level of utility. The **risk-adjusted valuation model** reflects both time-value and risk considerations.

- The **risk-adjusted discount rate** k is the sum of the risk-free rate of return, R_F, and the required risk premium, R_p. The difference between the expected rate of return on a risky asset and the rate of return on a riskless asset is the **risk premium** on the risky asset.

- A **decision tree** is a map of a sequential decision-making process. Decision trees are designed for analyzing decision problems that involve a series of choice alternatives that are constrained by previous decisions. **Decision points** represent instances when management must select among several choice alternatives. **Chance events** are possible outcomes following each decision point.

- **Computer simulation** involves the use of computer software and workstations or sophisticated desktop computers to create a wide variety of decision outcome scenarios. **Sensitivity analysis** focuses on those variables that most directly affect decision outcomes, and it is less expensive and less time-consuming than full-scale computer simulation.

Decision making under conditions of uncertainty is greatly facilitated by use of the tools and techniques discussed in this chapter. Although uncertainty can never be eliminated, its harmful consequences can be minimized.

QUESTIONS

Q16.1 In economic terms, what is the difference between risk and uncertainty?

Q16.2 Domestic investors sometimes miss out on better investment opportunities available to global investors. At the same time, global investors face special risks. Discuss some of the special risks faced by global investors.

Q16.3 The standard deviation measure of risk implicitly gives equal weight to variations on both sides of the expected value. Can you see any potential limitations of this treatment?

Q16.4 Confronted with a choice between $50 today or $100 1 year from now, economic experiments suggest that the vast majority of people will take the $50 today. At the same time, economic experiments show that most people will opt to take $100 in 10 years over $50 in 9 years. Is such behavior rational? Explain why or why not.

Q16.5 State-run lotteries commonly pay out 50 percent of total lottery-ticket sales in the form of jackpots and prizes. Use the certainty equivalent concept to quantify the minimum value placed on each risky dollar of expected return by lottery-ticket buyers. Why are such lotteries so popular?

Q16.6 Graph the relation between money and its utility for an individual who buys both household fire insurance and state-run lottery tickets.

Q16.7 When the basic valuation model is adjusted using the risk-free rate, i, what economic factor is being explicitly accounted for?

Q16.8 If the expected net present value of returns from an investment project is $50,000, what is the maximum price that a risk-neutral investor would pay for it? Explain.

Q16.9 "Market estimates of investors' reactions to risk cannot be measured precisely, so it is impossible to set risk-adjusted discount rates for various classes of investment with a high degree of precision." Discuss this statement.

Q16.10 What is the value of decision trees in managerial decision making?

SELF-TEST PROBLEMS AND SOLUTIONS

ST16.1 Certainty Equivalent Method. Courtney-Cox, Inc., is a Texas-based manufacturer and distributor of components and replacement parts for the auto, machinery, farm, and construction equipment industries. The company is presently funding a program of capital investment that is necessary to reduce production costs and thereby meet an onslaught of competition from low-cost suppliers located in Mexico and throughout Latin America. Courtney-Cox has a limited amount of capital available and must carefully weigh both the risks and potential rewards associated with alternative investments. In particular, the company seeks to weigh the advantages and disadvantages of a new investment project, project X, in light of two other recently adopted investment projects, project Y and project Z:

Expected Cash Flows After Tax (CFAT) Per Year ($)			
Year	Project X	Project Y	Project Z
2009	10,000	20,000	0
2010	10,000	18,000	2,500
2011	10,000	16,000	5,000
2012	10,000	14,000	7,500
2013	10,000	12,000	10,000
2014	10,000	10,000	12,500
2015	10,000	8,000	15,000
2016	10,000	6,000	17,500
2017	10,000	4,000	20,000
2018	10,000	2,000	22,500
PV of Cash Flow at 5 percent		91,131	79,130
Investment Outlay in 2000	60,000	60,000	50,000

A. Using a 5 percent risk-free rate, calculate the present value of expected cash flows after tax (CFAT) for the 10-year life of project X.

B. Calculate the minimum certainty equivalent adjustment factor for each project's CFAT that would justify investment in each project.

C. Assume that the management of Courtney-Cox is risk averse and uses the certainty equivalent method in decision making. Is project X as attractive as or more attractive than projects Y and Z?

D. If the company would not have been willing to invest more than $60,000 in project Y nor more than $50,000 in project Z, should project X be undertaken?

ST16.1 SOLUTION

A. Using a 5 percent risk-free rate, the present value of expected CFAT for the 10-year life of project X is $77,217, calculated as follows:

Expected Cash Flows After Tax (CFAT) Per Year ($)			
Year	Project X	PV of $1 at 5%	PV of CFAT at 5%
2009	10,000	0.9524	9,524
2010	10,000	0.9070	9,070
2011	10,000	0.8638	8,638
2012	10,000	0.8227	8,227
2013	10,000	0.7835	7,835
2014	10,000	0.7462	7,462
2015	10,000	0.7107	7,107
2016	10,000	0.6768	6,768
2017	10,000	0.6446	6,446
2018	10,000	0.6139	6,139
PV of Cash Flow at 5 percent			77,217

B. To justify each investment alternative, the company must have a certainty equivalent adjustment factor of at least $\alpha_X = 0.777$ for project X, $\alpha_Y = 0.658$ for project Y, and $\alpha_Z = 0.632$ for project Z, because

$$\alpha = \frac{\text{Certain Sum}}{\text{Expected Risky Sum}}$$

$$\alpha = \frac{\text{Investment Outlay (or opportunity cost)}}{\text{Present Value CFAT}}$$

Project X

$$\alpha_X = \frac{\$60,000}{\$77,217} = 0.777$$

Project Y

$$\alpha_Y = \frac{\$60,000}{\$91,131} = 0.658$$

Project Z

$$\alpha_Z = \frac{\$50,000}{\$79,130} = 0.632$$

In other words, each risky dollar of expected profit contribution from project X must be "worth" at least (valued as highly as) 77.7¢ in certain dollars to justify investment. For project Y, each risky dollar must be worth at least 65.8¢ in certain dollars; each risky dollar must be worth at least 63.2¢ to justify investment in project Z.

C. Given managerial risk aversion, project X is the least attractive investment because it has the highest "price" on each risky dollar of expected CFAT. In adopting projects Y and Z, Courtney-Cox implicitly asserted that it is willing to pay between 63.2¢ (project Z) and 65.8¢ (project Y) per expected dollar of CFAT.

D. No. If the prices described previously represent the maximum price the company is willing to pay for such risky returns, then project X should not be undertaken.

ST16.2 Project Valuation. The Central Perk Coffee House, Inc., is engaged in an aggressive store refurbishing program and is contemplating expansion of its in-store baking facilities. This investment project is to be evaluated using the certainty equivalent adjustment factor method and the risk-adjusted discount rate method. If the project has a positive value when both methods are employed, the project will be undertaken. The project will not be undertaken if either evaluation method suggests that the investment will fail to increase the value of the firm. Expected CFAT values over the 5-year life of the investment project and relevant certainty equivalent adjustment factor information are as follows:

In-Store Baking Facilities Investment Project		
Time Period (Years)	**Alpha**	**Project E(CFAT) ($)**
0	1.00	(75,000)
1	0.95	22,500
2	0.90	25,000
3	0.85	27,500
4	0.75	30,000
5	0.70	32,500
Total		62,500

At the present time, an 8 percent annual rate of return can be obtained on short-term U.S. government securities; the company uses this rate as an estimate of the risk-free rate of return.

A. Use the 8 percent risk-free rate to calculate the present value of the investment project.

B. Using this present value as a basis, use the certainty equivalent adjustment factor information given previously to determine the risk-adjusted present value of the project.

C. Use an alternative risk-adjusted discount rate method of project valuation on the assumption that a 15 percent rate of return is appropriate in light of the level of risk undertaken.

D. Compare and contrast your answers to parts B and C. Should the investment be made?

ST16.2 SOLUTION

A. The present value of this investment project can be calculated easily using a handheld calculator with typical financial function capabilities or by using the tables found in Appendix A. Using the appropriate discount factors corresponding to an 8 percent risk-free rate, the present value of the investment project is calculated as follows:

Hot Food Carryout Counterinvestment Project			
Time Period (Years)	Present Value of $1 at 8%	Project E(CFAT)	Present Value of E(CFAT) at 8%
0	1.0000	($75,000)	($75,000)
1	0.9259	22,500	20,833
2	0.8573	25,000	21,433
3	0.7938	27,500	21,830
4	0.7350	30,000	22,050
5	0.6806	32,500	22,120
Total		$62,500	$33,266

B. Using the present value given in part A as a basis, the certainty equivalent adjustment factor information given previously can be employed to determine the risk-adjusted present value of the project:

In-store Baking Facilities Investment Project					
Time Period (Years)	Present Value of $1 at 8%	Project E (CFAT) ($)	Present Value of E (CFAT) at 8%	Alpha	Risk-Adjusted Value ($)
0	1.0000	($75,000)	($75,000)	1.00	(75,000)
1	0.9259	22,500	20,833	0.95	19,791
2	0.8573	25,000	21,433	0.90	19,290
3	0.7938	27,500	21,830	0.85	18,556
4	0.7350	30,000	22,050	0.75	16,538
5	0.6806	32,500	22,120	0.70	15,484
Total		$62,500	$33,266		14,659

C. An alternative risk-adjusted discount rate method of project valuation based on a 15 percent rate of return gives the following project valuation:

In-store Baking Facilities Investment Project			
Time Period (Years)	Present Value of $1 at 15%	Project E(CFAT)	Present Value of E (CFAT) at 15%
0	1.0000	($75,000)	($75,000)
1	0.8696	22,500	19,566
2	0.7561	25,000	18,903
3	0.6575	27,500	18,081
4	0.5718	30,000	17,154
5	0.4972	32,500	16,159
Total		$62,500	$14,863

D. The answers to parts B and C are fully compatible; both suggest a positive risk-adjusted present value for the project. In part B, the certainty equivalent adjustment factor method reduces the present value of future receipts to account for risk differences. As is typical, the example assumes that money to be received in the more distant future has a greater risk, and hence, a lesser certainty equivalent value. In the risk-adjusted discount rate approach of part C, the discount rate of 15 percent entails a time-factor adjustment of 8 percent plus a risk adjustment of 7 percent. Like the certainty equivalent adjustment factor approach, the risk-adjusted discount rate method gives a risk-adjusted present value for the project. Because the risk-adjusted present value of the project is positive under either approach, the investment should be made.

PROBLEMS

P16.1 Risk Preferences. Identify each of the following as being consistent with risk-averse, risk-neutral, or risk-seeking behavior in investment project selection. Explain your answers.

A. Larger risk premiums for riskier projects

B. Preference for smaller, as opposed to larger, coefficients of variation

C. Valuing certain sums and expected risky sums of equal dollar amounts equally

D. Having an increasing marginal utility of money

E. Ignoring the risk levels of investment alternatives

P16.2 Certainty Equivalents. The certainty equivalent concept can be widely employed in the analysis of personal and business decision making. Indicate whether each of the following statements is true or false and explain why:

A. The appropriate certainty equivalent adjustment factor, α, indicates the minimum price in certain dollars that an individual should be willing to pay per risky dollar of expected return.

B. If $\alpha \neq 1$, a certain sum and a risky expected return of different dollar amounts provide equivalent utility to a given decision maker.

C. If previously accepted projects with similar risk have αs in a range from $\alpha = 0.4$ to $\alpha = 0.5$, an investment with an expected return of $150,000 is acceptable at a cost of $50,000.

D. A project for which NPV > 0 using an appropriate risk-adjusted discount rate has an implied α factor that is too large to allow project acceptance.

E. State-run lotteries that pay out 50 percent of the revenues that they generate require players who place at least a certain $2 value on each $1 of expected risky return.

P16.3 Expected Value. Perry Chandler, a broker with Caveat Emptor, Ltd., offers free investment seminars to local PTA groups. On average, Chandler expects 1 percent of seminar participants to purchase $25,000 in tax-sheltered investments and 5 percent to purchase $5,000 in stocks and bonds. Chandler earns a 4 percent net commission on tax shelters and a 1 percent commission on stocks and bonds. Calculate Chandler's expected net commissions per seminar if attendance averages 10 persons.

P16.4 Probability Concepts. Firefly Products, Inc., has just completed development of a new line of skin-care products. Preliminary market research indicate two feasible marketing strategies: (1) creating general consumer acceptance through media advertising or (2) creating distributor acceptance through intensive personal selling. Sales estimates for under each marketing alternative are as follows:

Media Advertising Strategy		Personal Selling Strategy	
Probability	**Sales ($)**	**Probability**	**Sales ($)**
0.1	500,000	0.3	1,000,000
0.4	1,500,000	0.4	1,500,000
0.4	2,500,000	0.3	2,000,000
0.1	3,500,000		

A. Assume that the company has a 50 percent profit margin on sales (i.e., profits equal one-half of sales revenue). Calculate expected profits for each plan.

B. Construct a simple bar graph of the possible profit outcomes for each plan. Which plan appears to be riskier?

C. Assume that management's utility function resembles the one illustrated in the following figure. Calculate expected utility for each strategy. Which strategy should the marketing manager recommend?

P16.5 Probability Concepts. Narcissism Records, Inc., has just completed an agreement to re-release a recording of "The Boss's Greatest Hits." The Boss had a number of hits on the rock-and-roll charts during the early 1980s. Preliminary market research indicates two feasible marketing strategies: (1) concentration on developing general consumer acceptance by advertising on late-night television or (2) concentration on developing distributor acceptance through intensive sales calls by company representatives. Estimates for sales under each alternative plan and payoff matrices according to an assessment of the likelihood of product acceptance under each plan are as follows:

Strategy 1 Consumer Television Promotion		Strategy 2 Distributor-Oriented Promotion	
Probability	**Outcome (Sales) ($)**	**Probability**	**Outcome (Sales) ($)**
0.32	250,000	0.125	250,000
0.36	1,000,000	0.750	750,000
0.32	1,750,000	0.125	1,250,000

A. Assuming that the company has a 50 percent profit margin on sales, calculate the expected profits for each plan.

B. Construct a simple bar graph of the possible profit outcomes for each plan. Which plan appears to be riskier?

C. Calculate the standard deviation and coefficient of variation of the profit distribution associated with each plan.

D. Assume that the management of Narcissism has a utility function like the one illustrated in the following figure. Which marketing strategy is best?

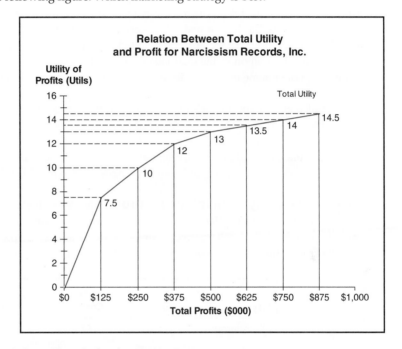

Relation Between Total Utility and Profit for Narcissism Records, Inc.

P16.6   Risk-Adjusted Discount Rates.   One-Hour Dryclean, Inc., is replacing an obsolete dry cleaning machine with one of two innovative pieces of equipment. Alternative 1 requires a current investment outlay of $25,373, whereas alternative 2 requires an outlay of $24,199. The following cash flows (cost savings) will be generated each year over the new machines' 4-year lives:

	Probability	Cash Flow
Alternative 1	0.18	$5,000
	0.64	10,000
	0.18	15,000
Alternative 2	0.125	$8,000
	0.75	10,000
	0.125	12,000

A. Calculate the expected cash flow for each investment alternative.

B. Calculate the standard deviation of cash flows (risk) for each investment alternative.

C. The firm will use a discount rate of 12 percent for the cash flows with a higher degree of dispersion and a 10 percent rate for the less risky cash flows. Calculate the expected net present value for each investment. Which alternative should be chosen?

P16.7 Certainty Equivalents. Recently, the housing market suffered the worst slump in nearly two decades. Hot housing markets like Boston, Ft. Lauderdale–Florida, and Washington DC cooled as rising interest rates and tightened lending standards eliminated lots of potential buyers. With job losses in the auto industry, the housing downturn was especially serious in Detroit and surrounding areas. Suppose a real estate speculator seeking to profit from the downturn bought a pool of home mortgages for $1 million on the expectation of quickly selling them to out-of-town investors for $1.5 million. If the deal falls through, the speculator would be able to just as quickly dump the pool of home mortgages in the secondary market for $800,000.

A. Calculate the speculator's expected payoff if there is a 50/50 chance of successfully selling the pool of home mortgages to out-of-town investors.

B. Calculate the certainty equivalent adjustment factor for this investment. Is the speculator's decision to buy the pool of home mortgages consistent with risk-averse behavior?

P16.8 Certainty Equivalent Method. Tex-Mex, Inc., is a rapidly growing chain of Mexican food restaurants. The company has a limited amount of capital for expansion and must carefully weigh available alternatives. Currently, the company is considering opening restaurants in Santa Fe or Albuquerque, New Mexico. Projections for the two potential outlets are as follows:

City	Outcome	Annual Profit Contribution	Probability
Albuquerque	Failure	$100,000	0.5
	Success	200,000	0.5
Santa Fe	Failure	$60,000	0.5
	Success	340,000	0.5

Each restaurant would require a capital expenditure of $1.4 million, plus land acquisition costs of $1million for Albuquerque and $2 million for Santa Fe. The company uses the 5 percent yield on risk-free U.S. Treasury bills to calculate the risk-free annual opportunity cost of investment capital.

A. Calculate the expected value, standard deviation, and coefficient of variation for each outlet's profit contribution.

B. Calculate the minimum certainty equivalent adjustment factor for each restaurant's cash flows that would justify investment in each outlet.

C. Assuming that the management of Tex-Mex is risk averse and uses the certainty equivalent method in decision making, which is the more attractive outlet? Why?

P16.9   Decision Trees.   Keystone Manufacturing, Inc., is analyzing a new bid to supply the company with electronic control systems. Alpha Corporation has been supplying the systems and Keystone is satisfied with its performance. However, a bid has just been received from Beta Controls, Ltd., a firm that is aggressively marketing its products. Beta has offered to supply systems for a price of $120,000. The price for the Alpha system is $160,000. In addition to an attractive price, Beta offers a money-back guarantee. That is, if Beta's systems do not match Alpha's quality, Keystone can reject and return them for a full refund. However, if it must reject the machines and return them to Beta, Keystone will suffer a delay costing the firm $60,000.

A. Construct a decision tree for this problem and determine the maximum probability that Keystone could assign to rejection of the Beta system before it would reject that firm's offer, assuming that it decides on the basis of minimizing expected costs.

B. Assume that Keystone assigns a 50 percent probability of rejection to Beta Controls. Would Keystone be willing to pay $15,000 for an assurance bond that would pay $60,000 in the event that Beta Controls fails the quality check? (Use the same objective as in part A.) Explain.

P16.10   Standard Normal Concept.   Speedy Business Cards, Inc., supplies customized business cards to commercial and individual customers. The company is preparing a bid to supply cards to the Nationwide Realty Company, a large association of independent real estate agents. Because paper, ink, and other costs cannot be determined precisely, Speedy anticipates that costs will be normally distributed around a mean of $20 per unit (each 500-card order) with a standard deviation of $2 per unit.

A. What is the probability that Speedy will make a profit at a price of $20 per unit?

B. Calculate the unit price necessary to give Speedy a 95 percent chance of making a profit on the order.

C. If Speedy submits a successful bid of $23 per unit, what is the probability that it will make a profit?

CASE *Study*   Stock-Price Beta Estimation for Google, Inc.

Statisticians use the Greek letter β to signify the slope coefficient in a linear relation. Financial economists use the same Greek letter β to signify stock-price risk because betas are the slope coefficients in a simple linear relation that links the return on an individual stock to the return on the overall market in the capital asset pricing model (CAPM). In the CAPM, the security characteristic line shows the simple linear relation between the return on individual securities and the overall market at every point in time:

$$R_{it} = \alpha_i + \beta_i R_{Mt} + \varepsilon_i,$$

where R_{it} is the rate of return on an individual security i during period t, the intercept term is described by the Greek letter α (alpha), the slope coefficient is the Greek letter β (beta) and

continued

signifies systematic risk (as before), and the random disturbance or error term is depicted by the Greek letter ε (epsilon). At any point in time, the random disturbance term ε has an expected value of zero, and the expected return on an individual stock is determined by α and β.

The slope coefficient β shows the anticipated effect on an individual security's rate of return following a 1 percent change in the market index. If $\beta = 1.5$, then a 1 percent rise in the market would lead to a 1.5 percent hike in the stock price, a 2 percent boost in the market would lead to a 3 percent jump in the stock price, and so on. If $\beta = 0$, then the rate of return on an individual stock is totally unrelated to the overall market. The intercept term α shows the anticipated rate of return when either $\beta = 0$ or $R_M = 0$. When $\alpha > 0$, investors enjoy positive abnormal returns. When $\alpha < 0$, investors suffer negative abnormal returns. Investors would celebrate a mutual fund manager whose portfolio consistently generated positive abnormal returns ($\alpha > 0$). They would fire portfolio managers that consistently suffered negative abnormal returns ($\alpha < 0$). In a perfectly efficient capital market, the CAPM asserts that investor rates of return would be solely determined by systematic risk and both alpha and epsilon would equal zero, $\alpha = \varepsilon = 0$.

As shown in Figure 16.8, managers and investors can estimate beta for individual stocks by using a simple ordinary least squares regression model. In this simple regression model, the dependent Y variable is the rate of return on an individual stock, and the independent X variable is the rate of return on an appropriate market index. Within this context, changes in the stock market rate of return are said to cause changes in the rate of return on an individual stock. In this example, beta is estimated for Google, Inc., (ticker symbol: GOOG), the Mountain View, California provider of free Internet search and targeted advertising services. The price data used to estimate beta for GOOG were downloaded from the Internet at the Yahoo! Finance Web site (http://finance.yahoo.com). Weekly returns for GOOG and for the Nasdaq stock market were analyzed over the 52-week trading period that ended on May 29, 2007, as shown in Table 16.5.

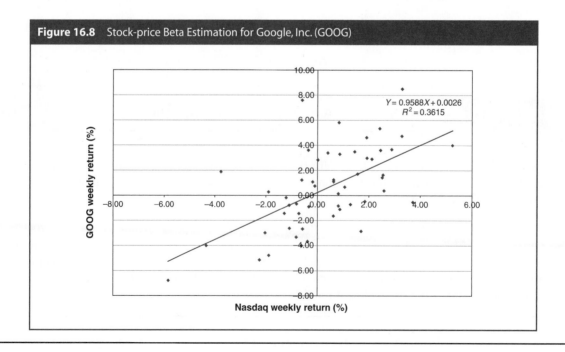

Figure 16.8 Stock-price Beta Estimation for Google, Inc. (GOOG)

continued

In this case, as predicted by the CAPM, $\alpha = 0.0026$ ($t = 0.70$). For a typical week when the Nasdaq market return was zero (essentially flat) during this initial 52-week trading period, the return for GOOG common stockholders was 0.26 percent. Because $\beta < 1$, GOOG was less volatile than the Nasdaq market during this period. During a week when the Nasdaq market rose by 1 percent, GOOG rose by 0.9588 percent; during a week when the Nasdaq market fell by 1 percent, GOOG fell by 0. 9588 percent. The slope coefficient $\beta = 0.9588$ is statistically significant ($t = 5.32$). This means that returns on GOOG stock had a statistically significant relationship to returns for the Nasdaq market during this period.

Table 16.5 Weekly Return Data for Google, Inc., (GOOG) and the Nasdaq Index

Date	GOOG Close	GOOG Weekly Return (%)	Nasdaq Close	Nasdaq Weekly Return (%)
29-May-07	497.91	2.98	2,604.52	1.85
21-May-07	483.52	2.81	2,557.19	−0.05
14-May-07	470.32	0.77	2,558.45	−0.15
7-May-07	466.74	−0.93	2,562.22	−0.39
30-Apr-07	471.12	−1.65	2,572.15	0.58
23-Apr-07	479.01	−0.72	2,557.21	1.22
16-Apr-07	482.48	3.47	2,526.39	1.38
9-Apr-07	466.29	−1.11	2,491.94	0.83
2-Apr-07	471.51	2.91	2,471.34	2.05
26-Mar-07	458.16	−0.79	2,421.64	−1.11
19-Mar-07	461.83	4.76	2,448.93	3.21
12-Mar-07	440.85	−2.67	2,372.66	−0.62
5-Mar-07	452.96	3.26	2,387.55	0.83
26-Feb-07	438.68	−6.79	2,368.00	−5.85
20-Feb-07	470.62	0.14	2,515.10	0.75
12-Feb-07	469.94	1.74	2,496.31	1.48
5-Feb-07	461.89	−4.07	2,459.82	−0.65
29-Jan-07	481.50	−2.89	2,475.88	1.66
22-Jan-07	495.84	1.24	2,435.49	−0.65
16-Jan-07	489.75	−3.02	2,451.31	−2.06
8-Jan-07	505.00	3.66	2,502.82	2.82
3-Jan-07	487.19	5.80	2,434.25	0.78
26-Dec-06	460.48	1.08	2,415.29	0.59
18-Dec-06	455.58	−5.15	2,401.18	−2.28
11-Dec-06	480.30	−0.79	2,457.20	0.81
4-Dec-06	484.11	0.69	2,437.36	1.00
27-Nov-06	480.80	−4.79	2,413.21	−1.91
20-Nov-06	505.00	1.25	2,460.26	0.59
13-Nov-06	498.79	5.33	2,445.86	2.35
6-Nov-06	473.55	0.37	2,389.72	2.53

continued

30-Oct-06	471.80	−0.72	2,330.79	−0.84
23-Oct-06	475.20	3.38	2,350.62	0.36
16-Oct-06	459.67	7.58	2,342.30	−0.64
9-Oct-06	427.30	1.62	2,357.29	2.49
2-Oct-06	420.50	4.63	2,299.99	1.84
25-Sep-06	401.90	−0.47	2,258.43	1.78
18-Sep-06	403.78	−1.49	2,218.93	−0.75
11-Sep-06	409.88	8.48	2,235.59	3.22
5-Sep-06	377.85	−0.20	2,165.79	−1.25
28-Aug-06	378.60	1.43	2,193.16	2.47
21-Aug-06	373.26	−2.63	2,140.29	−1.09
14-Aug-06	383.36	4.03	2,163.95	5.16
7-Aug-06	368.50	−1.43	2,057.71	−1.31
31-Jul-06	373.85	−3.68	2,085.05	−0.43
24-Jul-06	388.12	−0.51	2,094.14	3.65
17-Jul-06	390.11	−3.32	2,020.39	−0.83
10-Jul-06	403.50	−4.03	2,037.35	−4.35
3-Jul-06	420.45	0.27	2,130.06	−1.94
26-Jun-06	419.33	3.57	2,172.09	2.39
19-Jun-06	404.86	3.62	2,121.47	−0.40
12-Jun-06	390.70	1.07	2,129.95	−0.24
5-Jun-06	386.57	1.88	2,135.06	−3.80

Data source: Yahoo! Finance, June 15, 2007, http://finance.yahoo.com/.

In the case of GOOG, the usefulness of beta as risk measures is undermined by the fact that the simple linear model used to estimate stock-price beta fails to include other important systematic influences on stock market volatility. In the case of GOOG, for example, R^2 information shown in Figure 16.8 indicates that only 36.1 percent of the total variation in GOOG returns can be explained by variation in the Nasdaq market. This means that 63.9 percent of the variation in weekly returns for GOOG stock is unexplained by such a simple regression model.

A. Describe some of the attributes of an ideal risk indicator for stock market investors.
B. On the Internet, go to Yahoo! Finance (or MSN Money) and download weekly price information over the past year (52 observations) for GOOG and the Nasdaq market. Then, enter this information in a spreadsheet like Table 16.6 and use these data to estimate GOOG's beta. Describe any similarities or dissimilarities between your estimation results and the results depicted in Figure 16.8.
C. Estimates of stock-price beta are known to vary according to the time frame analyzed; length of the daily, weekly, monthly, or annual return period; choice of market index; bull or bear market environment; and other nonmarket risk factors. Explain how such influence can undermine the usefulness of beta as a risk indicator. Suggest practical solutions.

SELECTED REFERENCES

Alexander, Gordon J. and Mark A. Peterson. "An Analysis of Trade-Size Clustering and its Relation to Stealth Trading." *Journal of Financial Economics* 84, no. 2 (May, 2007): 435–471.

Alvarez, Luis H. R. and Rune Stenbacka. "Partial Outsourcing: A Real Options Perspective." *International Journal of Industrial Organization* 25, no. 1 (February, 2007): 91–102.

Ang, Andrew and Jun Liu. "Risk, Return, and Dividends." *Journal of Financial Economics* 85, no. 1 (July, 2007): 1–38.

Bramoulle, Yann and Rachel Kranton. "Risk Sharing Across Communities." *American Economic Review* 97, no. 2 (May, 2007): 70–74.

Bris, Arturo, William N. Goetzmann, and Ning Zhu. "Efficiency and the Bear: Short Sales and Markets Around the World." *Journal of Finance* 62, no. 3 (June, 2007): 1029–1079.

Brown, Gregory and Nishad Kapadia. "Firm-Specific Risk and Equity Market Development." *Journal of Financial Economics* 84, no. 2 (May, 2007): 358–388.

Chen, Long, David A. Lesmond, and Jason Wei. "Corporate Yield Spreads and Bond Liquidity." *Journal of Finance* 62, no. 1 (February, 2007): 119–149.

Chen, Nan and Paul Glasserman. "Additive and Multiplicative Duals for American Option Pricing." *Finance and Stochastics* 11, no. 2 (April, 2007): 153–179.

Cheridito, Patrick, Damir Filipovic, and Robert L. Kimmel. "Market Price of Risk Specifications for Affine Models: Theory and Evidence." *Journal of Financial Economics* 83, no. 1 (January, 2007): 123–170.

Chetty, Raj and Adam Szeidl. "Consumption Commitments and Risk Preferences." *Quarterly Journal of Economics* 122, no. 2 (May, 2007): 831–877.

MacKay, Peter and Sara B. Moeller. "The Value of Corporate Risk Management." *Journal of Finance* 62, no. 3 (June, 2007): 1379–1419.

Mahani, Reza and Dan Bernhardt. "Financial Speculators' Underperformance: Learning, Self-Selection, and Endogenous Liquidity." *Journal of Finance* 62, no. 3 (June, 2007): 1313–1340.

Pinar, Mustafa C. "Robust Scenario Optimization Based on Downside-Risk Measure for Multi-Period Portfolio Selection." *OR Spectrum* 29, no. 2 (April, 2007): 295–309.

Tularam, G. A. and A. S. Soomro. "Correction of Errors in Vetschera's (2004) Model of Behavioral Uncertainty and Investment." *Managerial and Decision Economics* 28, no. 1 (January, 2007): 71–76.

Wolpin, Kenneth I. "Ex Ante Policy Evaluation, Structural Estimation, and Model Selection." *American Economic Review* 97, no. 2 (May, 2007): 48–52.

Capital Budgeting

Berkshire Hathaway, General Electric, and Johnson & Johnson Inc. are standout performers in terms of the amount of wealth created for shareholders. What these diverse companies share is a common devotion to the capital budgeting process. They manage capital resources using two simple concepts: (1) Funds employed in the business have a cost that must be paid and (2) funds should be allocated where they generate the largest profit.

For example, careful asset redeployment within the General Electric empire allows GE to maintain rapid growth and an enviable rate of return on invested capital. At the cornerstone of GE's capital budgeting process is a "value added" concept that measures wealth created, or lost, for GE shareholders. To determine the value added from a given line of business or investment project, GE deducts the explicit or implicit cost of capital employed from the after-tax profit earned on operations. What's left over is the amount of value added for shareholders. GE then simply allocates its capital among those investment ideas that generate the most value added. If attractive investment opportunities are abundant, GE seeks additional debt or equity financing. If too few compelling investment projects are available, GE uses excess capital to buy back its stock or pay down debt. This simple philosophy has propelled GE, and companies like it, to stunning success.

This chapter describes the mechanics of capital budgeting as an application of marginal analysis.

CAPITAL BUDGETING PROCESS

Effective long-term planning and control is essential if the health and viability of the firm is to be assured.

What Is Capital Budgeting?

Capital budgeting is the process of planning expenditures that generate cash flows expected to extend beyond 1 year. The choice of one year is arbitrary, of course, but it is a convenient cutoff for distinguishing between classes of expenditures. Examples of capital outlays are expenditures for land, buildings, and equipment, and for additions to working capital (e.g., inventories and receivables) made necessary by expansion. New advertising campaigns or research and development programs have long-term impacts and represent important capital budgeting expenditures.

Although financial managers generally have administrative control of the capital budgeting process, the effectiveness of a firm's capital investments depends on input

---

1 See Yvonne Ball, "Buffett Rumors and Deal Talk Drive Home Depot, Dillard's," *The Wall Street Journal Online*, October 30, 2007, http://online.wsj.com.

from all major departments. The marketing department makes a key contribution by providing sales forecasts. Because operating costs must be estimated, the accounting, production, engineering, and purchasing departments are also involved. The initial outlay, or investment cost, must be estimated; again, engineering and purchasing typically provide input. Obtaining financing and estimating the cost of funds are major tasks of the financial manager. Finally, these various estimates must be drawn together in the form of a project evaluation. Although the finance department generally writes up the evaluation report, top management ultimately sets standards of acceptability.

Project Classification Types

Analyzing capital expenditure proposals is not a costless operation. For certain types of projects, a detailed analysis may be warranted; for others, simple procedures should be used. Firms generally classify projects into a number of categories and analyze those projects somewhat differently.

Replacement Projects
Maintenance of business investments.

    Replacement projects are expenditures necessary to replace worn-out or damaged equipment. These projects are necessary if the firm is to continue in its current businesses. Relevant issues are as follows: (a) Should the company continue to offer current products and services? and (b) Should existing plant and equipment be employed for this purpose? Usually, the answers to both questions are yes, so maintenance decisions are routine and made without an elaborate decision process.

Cost Reduction Projects
Expenditures to replace obsolete plant and equipment.

    Cost reduction projects include expenditures to replace serviceable but obsolete plant and equipment. The purpose of these investment projects is to lower production costs by reducing expenses for labor, raw materials, heat, or electricity. These decisions are often discretionary, so a detailed analysis is generally required. Decision-making authority usually rests at the manager or higher level in the organization. Capital expenditures made necessary by government regulation, collective bargaining agreements, or insurance policy requirements fall into a **safety and environmental projects** category. Such capital expenditures are sometimes called "mandatory" investments because they often are nonrevenue-producing in nature. How they are handled depends on their size and complexity; most often they are routine.

Safety and Environmental Projects
Mandatory nonrevenue-producing investments.

Expansion Projects
Expenditures to increase availability of existing products.

    Expansion projects involve expenditures to increase the availability of existing products and services. These investment decisions are relatively complex because they require an explicit forecast of the firm's future supply and demand conditions. Detailed analysis is required, and the final decision is made at a high level within the firm, perhaps by the controller or chief financial officer. Strategic decisions that could change the fundamental nature of the firm's business are also involved. Decisions concerning expenditures of large sums over extended investment horizons are made by the chief executive officer or board of directors.

STEPS IN CAPITAL BUDGETING

The more effective the firm's capital budgeting process, the higher its growth rate, and the greater its future value.

Sequence of Project Valuation

The capital budgeting process involves six logical steps. First, the cost of the project must be determined. Second, management must estimate the expected cash flows from the project, including the value of the asset at a specified terminal date. Third, the risk of projected cash flows must be estimated, so management needs information about the probability distributions of future cash flows. Fourth, given the risk of projected cash flows and the cost of funds under prevailing economic conditions, the firm must determine the appropriate discount rate, or cost of capital, at which the project's cash flows are to be discounted. Fifth, expected cash flows are converted into present values to obtain a clear estimate of the investment project's value to the firm. Finally, the present value of expected cash inflows is compared with the required outlay, or cost, of the project. If the present value of cash flows derived from a project exceeds the cost of the investment, the project should be accepted. Otherwise, the project should be rejected.

Cash Flow Estimation

It is difficult to make accurate forecasts of costs and revenues associated with large, complex projects, so forecast errors can be large. For example, when several major oil companies decided to build the Alaska pipeline, the original cost forecasts were about $700 million, but the final cost was closer to $7 billion, or 10 times larger. Miscalculations are common in forecasts of new product design costs. Initial plant and equipment costs are to hard to estimate; sales revenues and operating costs over the life of the project are generally even more uncertain.

In 2001, for example, a slowing economy and sluggish customer acceptance finally spelled the end to one of the most expensive Internet access projects in the nation. After 3½ years and $5 billion in expenses, Sprint Corporation pulled the plug on a project affectionately known as its integrated on-demand network, or ION. After attracting only 4,000 customers, ION proved to be an extravagant money pit. Sprint spent roughly $1.25 million per ION customer and staked ambitious growth plans on the prospect of marrying voice and data services. However, a sharp downturn in the telecom sector raised the risk of ION and other spending projects aimed at connecting local telecom customers to high-speed broadband communications networks.

The enormous burden imposed on shareholders and creditors by such capital budgeting mistakes makes clear the importance of sound forecasting in the capital budgeting process. For capital budgeting to be successful, the pattern of expected cash inflows and outflows must be established within a consistent and unbiased framework.

Incremental Cash Flow Evaluation

In capital budgeting, it is critical that decisions are based strictly on cash flows, the actual dollars that flow into and out of the company during each time period. The relevant cash flows for capital budgeting purposes are the incremental cash flows attributable to a project. **Incremental cash flows** are the period-by-period changes in net cash flows that are due to an investment project:

Incremental Cash Flows
Change in net cash flows due to an investment project.

$$\text{Project } CF_t = \frac{CF_t \text{ for Corporation}}{\text{with Project}} - \frac{CF_t \text{ for Corporation}}{\text{without Project}} \qquad \textbf{17.1}$$

It is possible to construct a firm's pro forma cash flow statements with and without a project for each year of the project's life and then measure annual project cash flows as the differences in cash flows between the two sets of statements. In practice, a number of problems must be addressed successfully if the incremental cash flows from a given investment project are to be estimated successfully.

Managerial Application 17.1

Market-Based Capital Budgeting

The real key to creating corporate wealth is to apply a market-based approach to capital budgeting. The power of the market-based capital budgeting concept stems from the fact that managers can't know if an operation is really creating value for the corporation until they calculate and apply the true cost of capital to all assets employed. To grow the company in a value-maximizing manner, the firm must weigh the answers to two important questions.

Question No. 1: What is the true cost of capital? The cost of borrowed capital is easy to estimate. It is the interest paid, adjusted to reflect the tax deductibility of interest payments. The cost of equity capital is more difficult to estimate. It is the return shareholders could get if they invested in a portfolio of companies about as risky as the company itself. From this perspective, the relevant cost of capital is its opportunity cost.

Question No. 2: How much capital is tied up in the operation? Capital traditionally consists of the current value of real estate, machines, vehicles, and the like, plus working

capital. Proponents of market-based capital budgeting say there is more. What about the money spent on R&D and on employee training? For decision-making purposes the return on all investments must be calculated over a reasonable life, say 3 to 5 years.

When both questions are answered, multiply the amount of capital from *Question No.* 2 by the rate of return from *Question No.* 1 to get the dollar cost of capital. The market value added by the capital budgeting process is operating earnings minus these capital costs, all on an after-tax basis. If the amount of market value added is positive, the operation is creating wealth. If market value added is negative, the operation is destroying capital.

The key is to ensure that the firm's investments generate a profit above and beyond the explicit and implicit cost of capital.

See: Julie Jargon, "Kellogg to Raise Ad Spending to Sell More Cereal," *The Wall Street Journal Online*, October 30, 2007, http://online.wsj.com.

CASH FLOW ESTIMATION EXAMPLE

A simple example of cash flow estimation and analysis can facilitate understanding of the capital budgeting process.

Project Description

Consider a hypothetical capital budgeting decision facing Silicon Valley Controls Corp. (SVCC), a California-based high-tech firm. SVCC's research and development department has been applying its expertise in microprocessor technology to develop a sophisticated computer system designed to control home appliances, heating, and air conditioning. SVCC's marketing department plans to target sales of the system to the owners of larger homes with 2,000 or more square feet of heated and air-conditioned space. Annual sales are projected at 25,000 units if the system is priced at $2,200 per unit. To manufacture the product, a new manufacturing facility could be built and made ready for production in 2 years once the "go ahead" decision is made. Such a plant would require a 25-acre site, and SVCC currently has an option to purchase a suitable tract of land for $1.2 million. If the decision is made to go ahead with the project, construction could begin immediately and would continue for 2 years. Because the project has an estimated economic life of 6 years, the overall planning period is 8 years: 2 years for plant construction (years 1 and 2) plus 6 years for operation (years 3 through 8). The building would cost $8 million and have a 31.5-year life for tax purposes. A $4 million payment would be due the building contractor at the end of each year of construction. Manufacturing equipment, with a cost of $10 million and a 7-year life for tax purposes, is to be installed and paid for at the end of the second year of construction, just prior to the beginning of operations.

The project also requires a working capital investment equal to 12 percent of estimated sales during the coming year. The initial working capital investment is to be made at the end of year 2 and is increased at the end of each subsequent period by 12 percent of the expected increase in the following year's sales. After completion of the project's 6-year operating period, the land is expected to have a market value of $1.7 million; the building, a value of $1 million; and the equipment, a value of $2 million. The production department has estimated that variable manufacturing costs would total 65 percent of dollar sales and that fixed overhead costs, excluding depreciation, would be $8 million for the first year of operations. Sales prices and fixed overhead costs, other than depreciation, are projected to increase with inflation, which is expected to average 6 percent per year over the 6-year production period.

SVCC's marginal federal-plus-state income tax rate is 40 percent, and its weighted-average cost of capital is 15 percent. For capital budgeting purposes, the company's policy is to assume that cash flows occur at the end of each year. Because the plant would begin operations at the start of year 3, the first operating cash flows would be realized at the end of year 3. A 15 percent corporate cost of capital is appropriate for the project.

Cash Flow Estimation and Analysis

A summary of investment outlays required for the project is shown in Table 17.1. Note that the land cannot be depreciated, and hence its depreciable basis is $0. Because the project will require an increase in net working capital during year 2, this is shown as an investment outlay for that year.

Once capital requirements have been identified, operating cash flows that will occur once production begins must be estimated; these are set forth in Table 17.2. Note that the sales price and fixed costs are projected to increase by 6 percent per year, and because variable costs are 65 percent of sales, they too will rise by 6 percent each year. Changes in net working capital (NWC) represent the additional investments required to support sales increases (12 percent of the next year's sales increase) during years 3 through 7, as well as the recovery of the cumulative net working capital investment in year 8. Amounts for depreciation were obtained by multiplying the depreciable basis by the depreciation allowance rates set forth in footnote c to Table 17.2.

Table 17.1 Investment Outlay Analysis for New Plant Investment Project

Fixed Assets	Year 0	Year 1	Year 2	Total Costs	Depreciable Basis
Land	$1,200,000	$0	$0	$1,200,000	$0
Building	0	4,000,000	4,000,000	8,000,000	8,000,000
Equipment	0	0	10,000,000	10,000,000	10,000,000
Total fixed assets	$1,200,000	$4,000,000	$14,000,000	$19,200,000	
Net working capital[a]	0	0	6,600,000	6,600,000	
Total investment	$1,200,000	$4,000,000	$20,600,000	$25,800,000	

a Twelve percent of first year's sales or 0.12 ($55,000,000) = $6,600,000.

Table 17.2 Net Cash Flows from Operations for New Plant Investment Project

	Year					
	3	4	5	6	7	8
Unit sales	25,000	25,000	25,000	25,000	25,000	25,000
Sale price[a]	$2,200	$2,332	$2,472	$2,620	$2,777	$2,944
Net sales[a]	$55,000,000	$58,300,000	$61,800,000	$65,500,000	$69,425,000	$73,600,000
Variable costs[b]	35,750,000	37,895,000	40,170,000	42,575,000	45,126,250	47,840,000
Fixed costs (overhead)[a]	8,000,000	8,480,000	8,988,800	9,528,128	10,099,816	10,705,805
Depreciation (building)[c]	120,000	240,000	240,000	240,000	240,000	240,000
Depreciation (equipment)[c]	2,000,000	3,200,000	1,900,000	1,200,000	1,100,000	600,000
Earnings before taxes	$9,130,000	$8,485,000	$10,501,200	$11,956,872	$12,858,934	$14,214,195
Taxes (40 percent)	3,652,000	3,394,000	4,200,480	4,782,749	5,143,574	5,685,678
Projected net operating income	5,478,000	5,091,000	6,300,720	7,174,123	7,715,361	8,528,517
Add back noncash expenses[d]	2,120,000	3,440,000	2,140,000	1,440,000	1,340,000	840,000
Cash flow from operations[e]	$7,598,000	$8,531,000	$8,440,720	$8,614,123	$9,055,361	$9,368,517
Investment in net working capital (NWC)[f]	(396,000)	(420,000)	(444,000)	(471,000)	(501,000)	8,832,000
New salvage value[g]						5,972,000
Total projected cash flows	$7,202,000	$8,111,000	$7,996,720	$8,143,123	$8,554,361	$24,172,517

a Year 3 estimate increased by the assumed 6 percent inflation rate.
b Sixty-five percent of net sales.
c MACRS depreciation rates were estimated as follows:

	Year					
	3	4	5	6	7	8
Building	1.5%	3%	3%	3%	3%	3%
Equipment	20	32	19	12	11	6

These percentages are multiplied by the depreciable basis to get the depreciation expense for each year. Note that the allowances have been rounded for ease of computation.
d In this case, depreciation on building and equipment.
e Net operating income plus noncash expenses.
f Twelve percent of next year's increase in sales. For example, year 4 sales are $3.3 million over year 3 sales, so the addition to NWC in year 3 required to support year 4 sales is (0.12)($3,300,000) = $396,000.
  The cumulative working capital investment is recovered when the project ends.
g See Table 17.3 for the net salvage value calculation.

Table 17.3 Net Salvage Value Calculation for New Plant Investment Project

	Land	Building	Equipment
Salvage (ending market value)	$1,700,000	$1,000,000	$2,000,000
Initial cost	1,200,000	8,000,000	10,000,000
Depreciable basis (year 2)	0	8,000,000	10,000,000
Book value (year 8)[a]	1,200,000	6,680,000	0
Capital gains income	$500,000	$0	$0
Ordinary income (loss)[b]	0	(5,680,000)	2,000,000
Taxes[c]	$200,000	$(2,272,000)	$800,000
Net salvage value (Salvage Value − Taxes)	$1,500,000	$3,272,000	$1,200,000

Total cash flow from salvage value = $1,500,000 + $3,272,000 + $1,200,000 = $5,972,000.

a Book value for the building in year 8 equals depreciable basis minus accumulated MACRS depreciation of $1,320,000. The accumulated depreciation on the equipment is $10,000,000. See Table 17.2.

b Building: $1,000,000 market value − $6,680,000 book value = $5,680,000 depreciation shortfall, which is treated as an operating expense in year 8.
   Equipment: $2,000,000 market value − $0 book value = $2,000,000 depreciation recapture, which is treated as ordinary income in year 8.

c All taxes are based on SVCC's 40 percent marginal federal-plus-state rate. The table is set up to differentiate ordinary income from captial gains because different tax rates often exist for these two income sources.

Cash flows generated by salvage values are summarized in Table 17.3. First is a comparison between projected market and book values for salvageable assets. Land cannot be depreciated and has an estimated salvage value greater than the initial purchase price. Thus, SVCC would have to pay taxes on the profit. The building has an estimated salvage value less than the book value; it will be sold at a loss for tax purposes. This loss will reduce taxable income and generate a tax savings. In effect, the company has been depreciating the building too slowly, so it will write off the loss against ordinary income. Equipment will be sold for more than book value, so the company will have to pay ordinary taxes on the $2 million profit. In all cases, the book value is the depreciable basis minus accumulated depreciation, and the total cash flow from salvage is merely the sum of the land, building, and equipment components.

As illustrated by this SVCC example, cash flow estimation involves a detailed analysis of demand, cost, and tax considerations. Even for fairly simple projects, such as that described here, the analysis can become complicated.

CAPITAL BUDGETING DECISION RULES

An economically sound capital budgeting decision rule must consistently lead to the acceptance of projects that will increase the value of the firm.

Net Present-Value Analysis

Net Present Value (NPV)
Current-dollar difference between marginal revenues and marginal costs.

The most commonly employed method for long-term investment project evaluation is **net present-value** (NPV) analysis. NPV is the difference between the marginal revenues and marginal costs for individual investment projects, when both revenues and costs are expressed in present-value terms. NPV analysis is based on the timing and magnitude of cash inflows and outflows. To see NPV analysis as a reflection of marginal analysis and the value maximization theory of the firm, consider the basic valuation model:

$$
\begin{aligned}
\text{Value} &= \sum_{t=1}^{n} \frac{\pi_t}{(1+k)^t} \\
&= \sum_{t=1}^{n} \frac{\text{Total Revenue}_t - \text{Total Cost}_t}{(1+k)^t} \\
&= \sum_{t=1}^{n} \frac{\text{Net Cash Flow}_t}{(1+k)^t}
\end{aligned}
$$ **17.2**

Net Cash Flow$_t$ represents the firm's total after-tax profit plus noncash expenses such as depreciation; k, which is based on an appraisal of the firm's overall risk, represents the average cost of capital to the firm. The value of the firm is simply the discounted present value of the difference between total cash inflows and total cash outflows. Any investment project is desirable if it increases the firm's net present value, and it is undesirable if accepting it causes the firm's net present value to decrease.

The use of net present-value analysis in capital budgeting involves the application of the present-value model described in Equation (17.2) to individual projects rather than to the firm as a whole. An important part of the analysis is the incorporation of an appropriate discount rate, or **cost of capital,** for the project. A high discount rate is used for high-risk projects, and a low discount rate is used for low-risk projects. After an appropriate cost of capital has been determined, the present value of expected cash outflows must be subtracted from the present value of expected cash inflows to determine the net present value of the project. If $NPV > 0$, the project should be accepted. If $NPV < 0$, the project should be rejected. In equation form, the net present value of an individual project is

Cost of Capital
Discount rate.

$$
NPV_i = \sum_{t=1}^{n} \frac{E(CF_{it})}{(1+k_i)^t} - \sum_{t=1}^{n} \frac{E(C_{it})}{(1+k_i)^t}
$$ **17.3**

where NPV_i is the NPV of the ith project, $E(CF_{it})$ represents the expected cash inflows of the ith project in the tth year, k_i is the risk-adjusted discount rate applicable to the ith project, and C_i is the project's investment cost or cash outflow.

To illustrate the NPV method, consider the SVCC capital investment project. Table 17.4 shows net cash flows per year over the entire 8-year planning period in nominal dollars, as well as in dollars discounted using the firm's 15 percent cost of capital. Overall, the net cash flow earned on the project expressed in nominal dollars is $38,379,720. This amount is the sum of column 2 and is equal to the last entry in column 3, which shows the culmination of net cash flows over the life of the project. Net nominal cash flow is a misleading measure of the attractiveness of the project because cash outlays necessary to fund the project must be made substantially before cash inflows are realized. A relevant measure of the attractiveness of this project is net cash flow expressed in present-value terms, where each dollar of cash outflow and inflow is converted on a common current-dollar basis. In column 5, net nominal cash flows from column 2 are multiplied by present-value interest factors from column 4 that reflect a 15 percent cost of capital assumption. These present-value interest factors are used to convert the nominal dollar outlays and returns from various periods on a common present-value basis.

Table 17.4 Consolidated End-of-Year Net Cash Flow Analysis for New Plant Investment Project Example

Year (1)	Net Nominal Cash Flows (2) ($)	Cumulative Net Nominal Cash Flows (3) ($)	Present-Value Interest Factor (PVIF) at 15% (4)	Net Discounted Cash Flows (5) = (2) × (4) ($)	Cumulative Net Discounted Cash Flows (6) ($)
0	(1,200,000)	(1,200,000)	1.0000	(1,200,000)	(1,200,000)
1	(4,000,000)	(5,200,000)	0.8696	(3,478,261)	(4,678,261)
2	(20,600,000)	(25,800,000)	0.7561	(15,576,560)	(20,254,820)
3	7,202,000	(18,598,000)	0.6575	4,735,432	(15,519,389)
4	8,111,000	(10,487,000)	0.5718	4,637,491	(10,881,898)
5	7,996,720	(2,490,280)	0.4972	3,975,783	(6,906,115)
6	8,143,123	5,652,843	0.4323	3,520,497	(3,385,618)
7	8,554,360	14,207,203	0.3759	3,215,901	(169,717)
8	24,172,517	38,379,720	0.3269	7,902,039	7,732,321
Sum	38,379,720			7,732,321	

Note: Negative net cash flows represent net cash outlays and are shown within parentheses.

The NPV for this investment project is given by the cumulative net discounted cash flow of $7,732,321 earned over the entire life of the project. This amount is given at the base of column 5 and is the sum of net discounted cash flows over the life of the project. Note also that this amount is given as the last entry in column 6, because it reflects the cumulative net discounted cash flow earned by the end of the project, year 8. Alternatively, NPV is simply the difference between the $27,987,141 present value of cash inflows from column 5, year 3 through year 8, and the $20,254,820 present value of cash outflows from column 5, year 0 through year 2. In equation form, the NPV for this project is calculated as follows:

$$NPV = PV \text{ of Cash Inflow} - PV \text{ of Cash Outflows}$$
$$= \$27,987,141 - \$20,254,820$$
$$= \$7,732,321$$

17.4

Because dollar inflows received in the future are worth less than necessary dollar outlays at the beginning of the project, the *NPV* for the project is much less than the $38,379,720 received in net nominal cash flows (see columns 2 and 3). This divergence between nominal and discounted cash flow figures reflects the time value of money. In present-value terms, the difference between the incremental costs and incremental revenues derived from this project is $7,732,321. This is a desirable project that if undertaken would increase the value of the firm by this amount.

Firms typically make investments in projects showing positive net present values, reject those with negative net present values, and choose between mutually exclusive investments on the basis of higher net present values. A complication arises when the size of the firm's capital budget is limited. Under these conditions, a variant of NPV analysis is used to select projects that maximize the value of the firm.

Profitability Index or Benefit/Cost Ratio Analysis

Profitability Index (PI)
Benefit/cost ratio.

A variant of *NPV* analysis often used in budgeting situations when capital is scarce is called the **profitability index** (PI), or the benefit/cost ratio method. The profitability index is calculated as follows:

$$PI = \frac{PV \text{ of Cash Inflows}}{PV \text{ of Cash Outflows}} = \frac{\sum\limits_{t=1}^{n} [E(CF_{it})/(1+k_i)^t]}{\sum\limits_{t=1}^{n} [C_{it}/(1+k_i)^t]}$$ **17.5**

The PI shows the *relative* profitability of a project, or the present value of benefits per dollar of cost.

In the SVCC example described in Table 17.4, *NPV* > 0 implies a desirable investment project and *PI* > 1. To see that this is indeed the case, we can use the profitability index formula, given in Equation (17.5), and the present value of cash inflows and outflows from the project, given in Equation (17.4). The profitability index for the SVCC project is

$$PI = \frac{PV \text{ of Cash Inflows}}{PV \text{ of Outflows}}$$

$$= \frac{\$27,987,141}{\$20,254,820}$$

$$= 1.38$$

This means that the SVCC capital investment project returns $1.38 in cash inflows for each dollar of cash outflow, when both figures are expressed in present-value terms.

In PI analysis, a project with *PI* > 1 should be accepted and a project with *PI* < 1 should be rejected. Projects will be accepted provided that they return more than a dollar of discounted benefits for each dollar of cost. Thus, the PI and NPV methods always indicate the same accept/reject decisions for independent projects, because *PI* > 1 implies *NPV* > 0 and *PI* < 1 implies *NPV* < 0. However, for alternative projects of unequal size, PI and NPV criteria can give different project rankings. This can sometimes cause problems when mutually exclusive projects are being evaluated. Before investigating the source of such conflicts, however, it is worthwhile to introduce two additional capital budgeting decision rules.

Internal Rate of Return Analysis

Internal Rate of Return (IRR)
Discount rate that equates present value of cash inflows and outflows.

The **internal rate of return** (IRR) is the interest or discount rate that equates the present value of the future receipts of a project to the initial cost or outlay. The equation for calculating the internal rate of return is simply the NPV formula set equal to zero:

$$NPV_i = 0 = \sum_{t=1}^{n} \frac{E(CF_{it})}{(1+k_i^*)^t} - \sum_{t=1}^{n} \frac{(C_{it})}{(1+k_i^*)^t}$$ **17.6**

Here the equation is solved for the discount rate, k_i^*, which produces a zero net present value or causes the sum of the discounted future receipts to equal the initial cost. That discount rate is the internal rate of return earned by the project.

It is often difficult to solve for the actual IRR on an investment without a computer spreadsheet or sophisticated calculator. For this reason, trial and error is sometimes employed. One begins by arbitrarily selecting a discount rate. If it yields a positive NPV, the internal rate of return must be greater than the discount rate used, and another higher rate is tried. If the chosen rate yields a negative NPV, the internal rate of return on the project is lower than the discount rate, and the NPV calculation must be repeated using a lower discount rate. This process of changing the discount rate and recalculating the net present value continues until the discounted present value of the future cash flows equals the initial cost. The interest rate that brings about this equality is the yield, or internal rate of return on the project.

Using trial and error, an electronic financial calculator, or a spreadsheet software program, the internal rate of return for the SVCC investment project is $IRR = 25.1$ percent. Because this IRR exceeds the 15 percent cost of capital, the project is attractive and should be undertaken. In general, internal rate of return analysis suggests that projects should be accepted when the $IRR > k$ and rejected when the $IRR < k$. When the $IRR > k$, the marginal rate of return earned on the project exceeds the marginal cost of capital. As in the case of projects with an $NPV > 0$ and $PI > 1$, the acceptance of all investment projects with $IRR > k$ will lead management to maximize the value of the firm. In instances in which capital is scarce and only a limited number of desirable projects can be undertaken at one point in time, the IRR can be used to derive a rank ordering of projects from most desirable to least desirable. Like a rank ordering of all $NPV > 0$ projects from highest to lowest PIs, a rank ordering of potential investment projects from highest to lowest IRRs allows managers to effectively employ scarce funds.

Payback Period Analysis

Payback Period
Number of years required to recover initial investment.

The **payback period** is the expected number of years of operation required to recover an initial investment. When project cash flows are discounted using an appropriate cost of capital, the discounted payback period is the expected number of years required to recover the initial investment from discounted net cash flows. Payback period calculation is quick and easy using actual or discounted net cash flows. In equation form, the payback period is

$$\text{Payback Period} = \text{Number of Years to Recover Investment} \qquad \textbf{17.7}$$

The payback period can be thought of as a breakeven time period. The shorter the payback period, the more desirable the investment project. The longer the payback period, the less desirable the investment project.

To illustrate, consider the SVCC capital investment project discussed earlier. Table 17.4 shows net cash flows per year over the entire 8-year planning period in nominal dollars, as well as in dollars discounted using the firm's 15 percent cost of capital. In nominal dollars, the total amount of investment is $25.8 million, which is the sum of the dollar outlays given in the first three rows of column 2. As shown in the third row of column 3, a negative $25.8 million is also the cumulative value of the nominal net cash flow as of the end of year 2, just prior to the beginning of plant operations. When the nominal cash outlay of $25.8 million is discounted using the firm's 15 percent cost of capital, the present value of the investment cash outlay is $20,254,820, the sum of discounted cash outlays given in the first three rows of column 5. As shown in the third row of column 6, a negative $20,254,820 is also the cumulative value of net discounted cash flow as of the end of year 2, just prior to the beginning of plant operations.

Based on nominal dollar cash outflows and inflows, the payback period is completed between the end of year 5, when the cumulative net nominal cash flow is a negative

$2,490,280, and the end of year 6, when the cumulative net nominal cash flow is a positive $5,652,843. Using nominal dollars, the payback period in years is calculated as

$$\text{Nominal Payback Period} = 5.00 + \$2{,}490{,}280/\$8{,}143{,}123$$
$$= 5.30 \text{ years}$$

Based on cash outflows and inflows discounted using the firm's 15 percent cost of capital, the payback period is completed between the end of year 7, when the cumulative net discounted cash flow is a negative $169,717, and the end of year 8, when the cumulative net discounted cash flow is a positive $7,732,321. Using discounted net cash flows, the payback period in years is calculated as

$$\text{Discounted Payback Period} = 7.00 + \$169{,}717/\$7{,}902{,}039$$
$$= 7.02 \text{ years}$$

Of course, these payback period calculations are based on the typical assumption that cash inflows are received continuously throughout the operating period. If cash inflows are received only at the end of the operating period, then the nominal payback period in this example would be 6 years and the discounted payback period would be 8 years. The exact length of the payback period depends on underlying assumptions concerning the pattern of cash inflows.

Payback methods have the serious deficiency of not taking into account any cash flows beyond the payback year. Other capital budgeting decision rules are more likely to lead to better project rankings and selections. The discounted payback period, however, does provide useful information about how long funds will be tied up in a project. The shorter the discounted payback period, the greater the project's liquidity. Because cash flows expected in the distant future are generally regarded riskier than near-term cash lows, the discounted payback period is a useful but rough measure of liquidity and project risk.

PROJECT SELECTION

An investment project should be pursued as long as the discounted net present value of cash inflows is greater than the discounted net present value of the net cash outlay.

Decision Rule Conflict Problem

High NPV projects are inherently more appealing and preferred to low NPV projects. Any investment project that is incapable of generating sufficient cash inflows to cover necessary cash outlays, when both are expressed on a present-value basis, should not be undertaken. If $NPV = 0$, project acceptance would neither increase nor decrease the value of the firm. Management would be indifferent to pursuing such a project. NPV analysis represents a practical application of the marginal concept, in which the marginal revenues and marginal costs of investment projects are considered on a present-value basis. Use of the NPV technique in the evaluation of alternative investment projects allows managers to apply the principles of marginal analysis in a simple and clear manner. Widespread practical use of the NPV technique lends support to the view that value maximization is the prime objective pursued by managers in the capital budgeting process.

Managerial Application 17.2

Is the Sun Setting on Japan's Vaunted MOF?

Long the power center of Japanese government, Japan's Ministry of Finance (MOF) is under attack for bungling economic policy and manipulating the Japanese stock market and real estate values. At risk is its bureaucratic authority and the whole concept of the managed Japanese economy. MOF officials argue that relinquishing control over the economy would imperil full employment and cause a stock-market crash in Japan. However, continued trade surpluses with Canada, the United States, and other trade partners have caused trade friction and stifled global economic growth.

The aura of infallibility that the MOF cultivated during Japan's postwar "economic miracle" has all but disappeared in the gloom of Japan's continuing economic malaise. No longer can supporters point to a continuing series of economic triumphs. Instead, the MOF has made a number of foolish public errors by failing to deal effectively with stock manipulation scandals and by botching privatization plans for government monopolies. It also alienated Japan's biggest

banks and brokerages throughout a series of embarrassing scandals. Politicians whom the MOF used to dominate now openly challenge the ministry's role in Japanese government.

It may be several years before fundamental economic reforms take hold in Japan. Many Japanese politicians and business leaders remain fervent nationalists who believe that Japan continues to work superbly as a society. It is a common view that the extent to which the country becomes less Japanese, or more integrated globally, it can no longer be Japan. In a real sense, the MOF sees itself as the guardian of Japan's conservative heritage. Although there is a clear move underway in Japan to make the MOF more accountable, any severe undermining of its authority seems years away, at best. Japanese bureaucracy, elected officials, and industry are strongly motivated to change, but they remain tightly bound to Japanese tradition and culture.

See: Akane Vallery Uchida, "Japan's Exports to Asia Fuel Record Trade Surplus," *The Wall Street Journal Online*, October 25, 2007, http://online.wsj.com.

Just as acceptance of $NPV > 0$ projects will enhance the value of the firm, so too will acceptance of projects for which the $PI > 1$ and the $IRR > k$. Acceptance of projects for which $NPV < 0$, $PI < 1$, or $IRR < k$ would be unwise and would reduce the value of the firm. Because each of these project evaluation techniques shares a common focus on the present value of net cash inflows and outflows, these techniques display a high degree of consistency in terms of the project accept/reject decision. This high degree of consistency might even lead one to question the usefulness of having these alternative ways of project evaluation when only one, the NPV method, seems sufficient for decision-making purposes.

However, even though alternative capital budgeting decision rules consistently lead to the same project accept/reject decision, they involve important differences in terms of project ranking. Projects ranked most favorably using the NPV method may appear less so when analyzed using the PI or IRR method. Projects ranked most favorably using the PI or IRR method may appear less so when analyzed using the NPV technique.

If the application of any capital budgeting decision rule is to consistently lead to correct investment decisions, it must consider the time value of money and rank projects according to their ultimate impact on the value of the firm. NPV, PI, and IRR methods satisfy both criteria, and each can be used to value and rank capital budgeting projects. The payback method should be used only as a complement to the other techniques. It is important to recognize that NPV, PI, and IRR methods incorporate assumptions that can affect project rankings. Understanding and dealing with such differences is an important part of knowing how to correctly evaluate investment projects.

Reasons for Decision Rule Conflict

NPV measures the relative attractiveness of alternative investment projects by the discounted dollar difference between revenues and costs. NPV is an absolute measure of project attractiveness. Conversely, PI reflects the difference between the marginal revenues and marginal costs in ratio form. The PI is the ratio of the discounted present value of cash inflows to the discounted present value of cash outflows. PI is a relative measure of project attractiveness. It follows that the NPV method leads to the highest ranking for large profitable projects. The PI method leads to the highest ranking for projects that return the greatest amount of cash inflow per dollar of outflow, regardless of project size. Application of the NPV method can create a bias for larger as opposed to smaller projects—a problem when all favorable $NPV > 0$ projects cannot be pursued. When capital is scarce, application of the PI method has the potential to create a better investment project mix.

Both NPV and PI methods differ from the IRR technique in terms of their underlying assumptions regarding the reinvestment of cash flows during the life of the project. In the NPV and PI methods, excess cash flows generated over the life of the project are "reinvested" at the firm's cost of capital. In the IRR method, excess cash flows are reinvested at the IRR. For especially attractive investment projects that generate an exceptionally high rate of return, the IRR can actually overstate project attractiveness because reinvestment of excess cash flows at a similarly high IRR is not possible. When reinvestment at the project-specific IRR is not possible, the IRR method must be adapted to take into account the lower rate of return that can actually be earned on excess cash flows generated over the life of individual projects. Otherwise, use of NPV or PI method is preferable.

Ranking Reversal Problem

When projects differ greatly in the magnitude and timing of cash flows, project's NPVs can react differently to changes in the discount rate. Changes in the appropriate discount rate can sometimes lead to reversals in project rankings. To illustrate the potential for ranking reversals, Table 17.5 shows a further consideration of the SVCC plant investment project example. Assume that the company is considering the original new plant investment project in light of an alternative proposal to buy and remodel an existing plant. Old plant and equipment can be purchased for an initial cash outlay of $11.5 million and can be remodeled at a cost of $2 million per year over the next 2 years. As before, a net working capital investment of $6.6 million will be required just prior to opening the remodeled production facility. For simplicity, assume that after year 2, all cash inflows and outflows are the same for the remodeled and new plant facilities.

Note that the new plant proposal involves an initial nominal cash outlay of $25.8 million, whereas the remodeled plant alternative involves a nominal cash outlay of $22.1 million. In addition to this difference in project size, the two investment alternatives differ in terms of the timing of cash flows. The new plant alternative involves a larger but later commitment of funds. To see the implications, notice how the "remodel old plant" alternative is preferred at and below the firm's 15 percent cost of capital using NPV and PI methods, even though the *IRR* of 25.06 percent for the new plant project exceeds the *IRR* of 23.57 percent for the "remodel old plant" alternative. Also troubling is the fact that the relative ranking of these projects according to NPV and PI methods is reversed at higher discount rates. Notice how the "build new plant"

Table 17.5 Comparison of the "Build New Plant" Versus "Remodel Old Plant" Investment Project Example Using Alternative Capital Budgeting Decision Rules

A. Investment Project Cash Flow Projections

Year	Build New Plan Project			Remodel Old Plant Project		
	Net Nominal Cash Flows ($)	15% ($)	25% ($)	Net Nominal Cash Flows ($)	15% ($)	25% ($)
0	(1,200,000)	(1,200,000)	(1,200,000)	(11,500,000)	(11,500,000)	(11,500,000)
1	(4,000,000)	(3,478,261)	(3,200,000)	(2,000,000)	(1,739,130)	(1,600,000)
2	(20,600,000)	(15,576,560)	(13,184,000)	(8,600,000)	(6,502,836)	(5,504,000)
3	7,202,000	4,735,432	3,687,424	7,202,000	4,735,432	3,687,424
4	8,111,000	4,637,491	3,322,266	8,111,000	4,637,491	3,322,266
5	7,996,720	3,975,783	2,620,365	7,996,720	3,975,783	2,620,365
6	8,143,123	3,520,497	2,134,671	8,143,123	3,520,497	2,134,671
7	8,554,360	3,215,901	1,793,979	8,554,360	3,215,901	1,793,979
8	24,172,517	7,902,039	4,055,475	24,172,517	7,902,039	4,055,475
Sum	38,379,720	7,732,321	30,180	42,079,720	8,245,176	(989,820)
IRR	25.06%			23.57%		

B. Evaluation Using Alternative Capital Budgeting Decision Rules

	Build New	Remodel Old
0% Discount Rate		
PV of cash inflows	$64,179,720	$64,179,720
PV of cash outflows	$25,800,000	$22,100,000
NPV	$38,379,720	$42,079,720
PI	2.49	2.90
Discounted payback period	5.30	4.85
15% Discount Rate		
PV of cash inflows	$27,987,142	$27,987,142
PV of cash outflows	$20,254,820	$19,741,966
NPV	$7,732,321	$8,245,176
PI	1.38	1.42
Discounted payback period	7.02	6.89
25% Discount Rate		
PV of cash inflows	$17,614,180	$17,614,180
PV of cash outflows	$17,584,000	$18,604,000
NPV	$30,180	($989,820)
PI	1.00	0.95
Discounted payback period	7.99	–

Note: Negative net cashflows represent net cash outlays and are shown within parentheses.

alternative is preferred using NPV and PI techniques when a 25 percent discount rate is employed.

Figure 17.1 displays the potential conflict between NPV, PI, and IRR project rankings at various interest rates by showing the effect of discount rate changes on the NPV of each alternative investment project. This **net present-value profile** relates the NPV for each project to the discount rate used in the NPV calculation. Using a $k = 0$ percent discount rate, the NPV for the "build new plant" investment project is $38.4 million, and it is $42.1 million for the "remodel old plant" alternative. These NPVs correspond to the difference between nominal dollar cash inflows and outflows for each project and also coincide with NPV line Y-axis intercepts of $38.4 million for the "build new plant" project and $42.1 million for the "remodel old plant" alternative. The X-axis intercept for each curve occurs at the discount rate where $NPV = 0$ for each project. Because $NPV = 0$ when the discount rate is set equal to the IRR, or when $IRR = k$, the X-axis intercept for the "build new plant" alternative is at the $IRR = 25.06$ percent level, and it is at the $IRR = 23.57$ percent level for the "remodel old plant" alternative.

Figure 17.1 illustrates how ranking reversals can occur at various NPV discount rates. Given higher nominal dollar returns and, therefore, a higher Y-axis intercept, the "remodel old plant" alternative is preferred when very low discount rates are used in the NPV calculation. Given a higher IRR and, therefore, a higher X-axis intercept, the "build new plant" alternative is preferred when very high discount rates are used in the calculation of NPV. Between very high and low discount rates is an interest rate where NPV is the same for both projects. A reversal of project rankings occurs at the **crossover discount rate,** where NPV is equal for two or more investment alternatives. In this example, the "remodel old plant" alternative is preferred when using the NPV criterion and a discount rate k that is less than the crossover discount rate. The "build new plant" alternative is preferred when using the NPV criterion and a discount rate k

Net Present-Value Profile
Graph relating NPV to the discount rate.

Crossover Discount Rate
Interest factor that equates NPV for two or more investments.

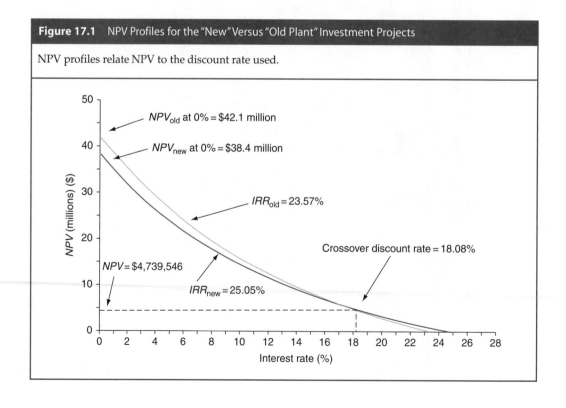

Figure 17.1   NPV Profiles for the "New" Versus "Old Plant" Investment Projects

NPV profiles relate NPV to the discount rate used.

that is greater than the crossover discount rate. This ranking reversal problem is typical of situations in which investment projects differ greatly in terms of their underlying NPV profiles. Hence, a potentially troubling conflict exists between NPV, PI, and IRR methods.

Making the Correct Investment Decision

Many comparisons between alternative investment projects involve neither crossing NPV profiles nor crossover discount rates as shown in Figure 17.1. As a result, there is often no meaningful conflict between NPV and IRR project rankings. When crossover discount rates are relevant, they can be calculated as the IRR of the cash flow difference between two investment alternatives. To see that this is indeed the case, consider how cash flows differ between each of the two plant investment alternatives considered previously. The "build new plant" alternative involves a smaller initial cash outflow of $1.2 million versus $11.5 million, but requires additional outlays of $2 million at the end of year 1 and an additional $12 million at the end of year 2. Except for these differences, the timing and magnitude of cash inflows and outflows from the two projects are identical. The IRR for the cash flow difference between two investment alternatives exactly balances the present-value cost of higher cash outflows with the present-value benefit of higher cash inflows. At this IRR, the cash flow difference between the two investment alternatives has an NPV equal to zero.

When k is less than this crossover IRR, the investment project with the greater nominal dollar return will have a larger NPV and will tend to be favored. In the current example, this is the "remodel old plant" alternative. When k is greater than the crossover IRR, the project with an earlier net cash flow pattern will have the larger NPV and be favored. In the current example, this is the "build new plant" alternative. When k equals the crossover IRR, the cash flow difference between projects has an $NPV = 0$, and each project has exactly the same NPV.

Once an economically relevant crossover discount rate has been determined, management must decide whether to rely on NPV or IRR decision rules in the resolution of the ranking reversal problem. NPV rankings typically dominate because that method will result in a value-maximizing selection of projects. In most situations, it is also more realistic to assume reinvestment of excess cash flows during the life of a project at the current cost of capital k. This again favors NPV over IRR rankings.

Given the size-based conflict between the NPV and PI methods, firms with substantial investment resources should use the NPV method. For firms with limited resources, the PI approach allocates scarce resources to the projects with the greatest relative effect on value.

COST OF CAPITAL

The correct discount rate for an investment project is the marginal cost of capital for the project.

Component Cost of Debt Financing

Component Cost of Debt
Interest rate investors require on debt, adjusted for taxes.

The **component cost of debt** is the interest rate that investors require on debt, adjusted for taxes. If a firm borrows $100,000 for 1 year at 10 percent interest, the before-tax cost is $10,000 and the before-tax interest rate is 10 percent. However, interest payments on debt are deductible for income tax purposes. It is necessary to account for tax deductibility by adjusting the cost of debt on an after-tax basis. The deductibility of interest payments

Managerial Application 17.3

Federal Government Support for R&D

The National Science Foundation (NSF) is an independent U.S. government agency responsible for promoting science and engineering in the United States. NSF programs invest over $5 billion per year in almost 20,000 research and education projects in science and engineering. NSF is also responsible for keeping track of research and development (R&D) spending and productivity in government agencies, firms, universities and colleges, or other nonprofit institutions.

At present, roughly $300 billion per year is spent in the United States on R&D. About 15 percent to 20 percent of this amount is spent on basic research that advances scientific knowledge but has no immediate commercial objective. Another 20 percent to 25 percent is spent on applied research that brings scientific knowledge closer to specific commercial application. The results of basic and applied research in science and engineering are ordinarily published and shared broadly within the scientific community. Such efforts can be distinguished from proprietary research and industrial development, the results of which are kept confidential for commercial reasons or for national security. Most R&D spending,

roughly 60 percent to 65 percent, is devoted to industrial development.

Federal government agencies provide about 30 percent of all R&D funding, but as much as 60 percent of basic research funding. The National Institutes of Health (NIH), for example, are a principal source of funding for biomedical research. NIH programs provide funds for such projects as AIDS/HIV treatment, cancer research, and the Human Genome Project. The government has also taken a direct role in scientific education through the NSF and other agencies such as the Department of Energy. Federally funded research has been directly responsible for major developments in space technology, defense systems, energy, medicine, and agriculture. Through grants, subsidies, and tax incentives, the federal government has supported basic research that underlies important applied advances in private industry. Partnerships with institutions such as universities have also proven to be an effective risk-sharing mechanism for R&D efforts that have the potential to create widespread social benefits.

See: Home page information for the National Science Foundations can be found on the Internet, http://www.nsf.gov/

means, in effect, that the government pays part of a firm's interest charges. This reduces the firm's cost of debt financing. The after-tax component cost of debt is given by the following expression:

$$k_d = \text{Interest Rate} \times (1 - \text{Tax Rate}) \qquad \textbf{17.8}$$

Assuming that the firm's marginal federal-plus-state tax rate is 40 percent, the after-tax cost of debt will be 60 percent ($=1.0 - 0.4$) of the nominal interest rate.

The relevant component cost of debt applies only to new debt, not to the interest on old or previously outstanding debt. In other words, the cost of new debt financing is what is relevant in terms of the marginal cost of debt. It is irrelevant that the firm borrowed at higher or lower rates in the past.

Component Cost of Equity
Rate of return stockholders require on common stock.

Risk-Free Rate of Return (R_F)
Investor reward for postponing consumption.

Risk Premium (R_P)
Investor reward for risk taking.

Component Cost of Equity Financing

The **component cost of equity** is the rate of return required by stockholders. This return includes compensation to investors for postponing their consumption, and a return to compensate for risk taking. Therefore, the component cost of equity consists of a **risk-free rate of return,** R_F, and a **risk premium,** R_P:

$$k_e = R_F + R_P \qquad \textbf{17.9}$$

The risk-free return is typically estimated by the interest rate on short-term U.S. Treasury bills. On a daily basis, these rates of return can be obtained from *The Wall Street Journal* and other sources. Various methods can be used to estimate R_P for different securities. Because dividends paid to stockholders are not deductible for income tax purposes, dividend payments must be made with after-tax dollars. There is no tax adjustment for the component cost of equity capital.

A first method for estimating k_e and R_P is based on the capital asset pricing model (CAPM). This method assumes that the risk of a stock depends on the sensitivity of its return to changes in the return on all securities. A stock that is twice as risky as the overall market would entail twice the market risk premium, a security that is one-half as risky as the overall market would earn one-half the market risk premium, and so on. In the CAPM approach, the risk of a given stock is measured by the variability of its return relative to the variability of the overall market, perhaps as measured by the Standard and Poor's 500 Index. A firm's **beta coefficient,** β, is a measure of this variability. In a simple regression model, the beta coefficient for an individual firm, β_i, is estimated as

Beta Coefficient
Measure of relative stock-price variability.

$$R_{it} = \alpha_i + \beta_i R_{Mt} + e_{it} \qquad \textbf{17.10}$$

where R_{it} is the weekly or monthly return on a given stock and R_{Mt} is a similar return on the market as a whole. A stock with average risk has a beta of 1.0. Low-risk stocks have betas less than 1.0; high-risk stocks have betas greater than 1.0. Although beta estimation is a relatively simple task, managers seldom need to actually run such regressions. Analysts at Merrill Lynch and other leading brokerage houses, as well as investment advisory services such as *The Value Line Investment Survey*, provide beta estimates that can be used for equity capital cost estimation for individual companies and/or operating divisions.

In addition to data on the R_F rate and β_i for a given company, the CAPM approach requires an estimate of the expected rate of return on the market as a whole. This return, k_M, is a relative benchmark for measuring the risk premium on the market. With these three inputs, R_F, β_i, and k_M, the CAPM estimate of the required rate of return on any given stock is

$$k_e = R_F + \beta_i(k_M - R_F) \qquad \textbf{17.11}$$

where the value $(k_M - R_F)$ is the market risk premium, or risk premium on an average stock. Multiplying this market risk premium by the index of risk for a particular stock, or β_i, gives the risk premium for that stock.

To illustrate, assume that $R_F = 4$ percent, $k_M = 10$ percent, and $\beta_i = 0.5$ for a given stock. Remember, $\beta_i = 0.5$ means that a given stock is only one-half as risky as the overall market. Under such circumstances, the stock's required return is

$$k_e = 4 + 0.5(10 - 4) = 4 + 3 = 7\%$$

If $\beta_i = 1.5$, indicating that a stock is 50 percent riskier than the average security, then k_e is

$$k_e = 4 + 1.5(10 - 4) = 4 + 9 = 13\%$$

A second common technique adds a premium of 4 percent or 5 percent onto the risk premium paid on a firm's long-term bonds. Using this approach, the total risk premium on equity equals the difference between the yield on the firm's debt and that on risk-free government bonds, plus 4 percent to 5 percent. For example, if risk-free government bonds yield 4 percent, and a firm's bonds are priced to yield 6 percent, the cost of equity, k_e, is

$$k_e = Risk\text{-}Free\ Rate + Bond\ Risk\ Premium + 4\%\ to\ 5\%\ Risk\ Premium$$
$$= 4\% + (6\% - 4\%) + (4\%\ to\ 5\%) = 10\%\ to\ 11\%$$

Given a 4 percent return on risk-free government bonds, this implies a total risk premium for equity of 6 percent to 7 percent, because

$$10\%\ to\ 11\% = 4\% + R_p$$
$$R_p = 6\%\ to\ 7\%$$

Managers that rely on this method often cite historical studies suggesting that the long-term annual risk premium on investments in common stocks is generally 6 percent to 7 percent over that earned on government bonds. The primary difficulty with estimating risk premiums from historical returns is that historical returns differ depending on the beginning and ending dates of the estimation period, and past differences in stock and bond returns may not precisely indicate future required risk premiums.

Yet another method for determining the cost of equity is to use a constant growth model. If earnings, dividends, and the stock price all grow at the same rate, then

$$Required\ Return\ on\ Equity = Dividend\ Yield + Capital\ Gains$$
$$= \frac{Expected\ Dividend}{Current\ Stock\ Price} + Expected\ Growth\ Rate$$
$$k_e = \frac{D_1}{P_0} + g \qquad\qquad \textbf{17.12}$$

The rationale for this equation is that stockholder returns are derived from dividends and capital gains. If past growth rates in earnings and dividends have been relatively stable, and if investors expect a continuation of past trends, then g may be based on the firm's historic growth rate. However, if the company's growth has been abnormally high or low, either because of its own unique situation or because of general economic conditions, investors cannot project historical growth rate into the future. Security analyst estimates of g must then be relied on. Earnings forecasts regularly found in *Barron's, The Value Line Investment Survey*, and other sources offer a useful proxy for the growth expectations of investors in general. When security analyst growth projections are combined with the dividend yield expected during the coming period, k_e can be estimated as

$$k_e = D_1/P_0 + Projected\ Growth\ Rate \qquad\qquad \textbf{17.13}$$

In practice, it is often best to use all of these methods to arrive at a consensus estimate of the component cost of equity financing.

Weighted-Average Cost of Capital

Weighted-Average Cost of Capital
Marginal cost of a composite dollar of debt and equity financing.

Optimal Capital Structure
Combination of debt and equity that minimizes the firm's weighted-average cost of capital.

The **weighted-average cost of capital** is the interest rate necessary to attract funds for new capital investment projects. It is the marginal cost of a composite dollar of debt and equity financing. The proper set of weights to employ in computing the weighted-average cost of capital is determined by the firm's optimal capital structure. The **optimal capital structure** is the combination of debt and equity financing that minimizes the firm's weighted-average cost of capital.

Investor risk is lower on debt and higher on common stock, so investor risk aversion makes equity the highest component-cost source of financing. Debt is the lowest component-cost source of funds. The firm's overall risk level increases as debt financing grows, because the higher the debt level, the greater the probability that under adverse conditions the firm will not make interest and principal payments. Because after-tax interest rates on debt are generally lower than the expected rate of return (dividends plus capital gains) on common stock, the weighted-average cost of capital can decline with modest amounts of debt financing. However, as more and more debt is added, default risk grows. As a result, the weighted-average cost of capital can first decline as a firm adds a modest amount of debt, hit a minimum, and then rise as default risk increases.

Figure 17.2 shows how the weighted-average cost of capital changes as the debt ratio increases. The weighted-average cost of capital figures shown in the graph are calculated in Table 17.6. In the figure, each dot represents one of the firms in the industry. The dot labeled "1" represents firm 1, a company with no debt. Because its projects are financed entirely with 10 percent equity, firm 1's average cost of capital is 10 percent. Firm 2

Figure 17.2 Industry Cost-of-Capital Schedule

A U-shaped weighted-average cost of capital reflects, first, lower capital costs because of the tax benefits of debt financing and, second, increasing capital costs due to bankruptcy risk for highly levered firms.

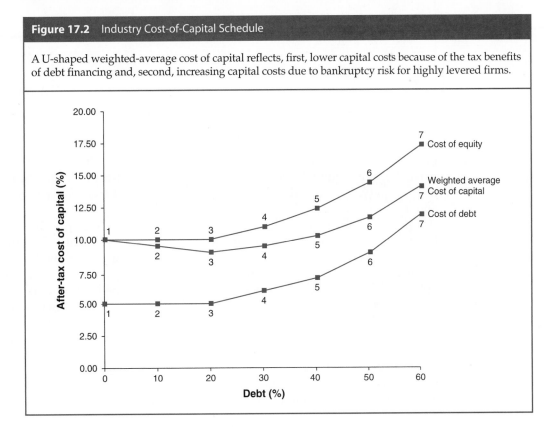

Table 17.6 Weighted-Average Cost of Capital for Firms with Different Debt Ratios

		Percentage of Total (1)	Component Cost (2)	Weighted Cost = [(1) × (2)]/100 (3)
Firm 1	Debt	0	5.0	0.00
	Equity	100	10.0	10.00
				Average cost 10.00%
Firm 2	Debt	10	5.0	0.50
	Equity	90	10.0	9.00
				Average cost 9.50%
Firm 3	Debt	20	5.0	1.00
	Equity	80	10.0	8.00
				Average cost 9.00%
Firm 4	Debt	30	6.0	1.80
	Equity	70	11.0	7.70
				Average cost 9.50%
Firm 5	Debt	40	7.0	2.80
	Equity	60	12.5	7.50
				Average cost 10.30%
Firm 6	Debt	50	9.0	4.50
	Equity	50	14.5	7.25
				Average cost 11.75%
Firm 7	Debt	60	12.0	7.20
	Equity	40	17.5	7.00
				Average cost 14.20%

raises 10 percent of its capital as debt, and has a 5 percent after-tax cost of debt and a 10 percent cost of equity. Firm 3 also has a 5 percent after-tax cost of debt and 10 percent cost of equity, even though it uses 20 percent debt. Firm 4 has an 11 percent cost of equity and a 6 percent after-tax cost of debt. Because it uses 30 percent debt, a before-tax debt risk premium of 1 percent and an equity risk premium of 1 percent have been added to account for the additional risk of financial leverage. Notice that the required return on both debt and equity rises with increasing leverage for firms 5, 6, and 7. In this particular industry, the threshold debt ratio that begins to worry creditors is about 20 percent. Below the 20 percent debt level, creditors are unconcerned about financial risk induced by debt; above 20 percent, they are aware of higher risks and require compensation in the form of higher expected rates of return.

In Table 17.6, debt and equity costs for the various firms are averaged on the basis of their respective proportions of the firm's total capital. Firm 1 has a weighted-average cost of capital equal to 10 percent, Firm 2 has a weighted-average cost of 9.5 percent, Firm 3 has a weighted-average cost of 9 percent, and Firm 4 has a weighted-average cost of 9.5 percent. These weighted costs, together with those of the other firms in the industry,

Managerial Application 17.4

Capital Allocation at Berkshire Hathaway, Inc.

Warren E. Buffett, the chairman and CEO of Berkshire Hathaway, Inc., has the uncommon ability to communicate management insights in a disarmingly modest and humorous fashion. Among his most important lessons are the following:

- *It is far better to buy a wonderful company at a fair price than a fair company at a wonderful price.* In a difficult business, no sooner is one problem solved than another surfaces. "There is never just one cockroach in the kitchen."

- *When a management with a reputation for brilliance tackles a business with a reputation for bad economics, it is the reputation of the business that remains intact.* According to Buffett, attractive economics include a 20 percent plus rate of return on capital without leverage or accounting gimmicks, high margins, high cash flow, low capital investment requirements, a lack of government regulation, and strong prospects for continuing growth. "Good jockeys do well on good horses," Buffett says, "but not on broken down old nags."

- *Management does better by avoiding dragons, not slaying them.* Buffett attributes his success to avoiding, rather than solving, tough business problems. As Buffett says, "We have been successful because we concentrated on identifying 1-foot hurdles that we could step over rather than because we acquired any ability to clear 7-footers."

- *It is not a sin to miss a business opportunity outside one's area of expertise.* By inference, it is a sin to miss opportunities that you are fully capable of understanding.

- *Do not join with managers who lack admirable qualities, no matter how attractive the prospects of their business.* When searching for businesses to buy, Buffett looks for first-class businesses accompanied by first-class management.

The approach seems to work. Buffett's personal stake in Berkshire is now worth more than $50 *billion!*

See: Take a look at Buffett's annual letters to shareholders. They're terrific, http://www.berkshirehathaway.com.

---

are plotted in Figure 17.2. Firms with approximately 20 percent debt in their capital structure have the lowest weighted-average after-tax cost of capital, equal to 9 percent. Accordingly, proper calculation of the cost of capital requires that the cost of equity for a firm in the industry be given a weight of 0.8 and the cost of debt be given a weight of 0.2—the firm's optimal capital structure.

OPTIMAL CAPITAL BUDGET

For the profit-maximizing firm, the marginal rate of return earned on the last acceptable investment project equals the firm's marginal cost of capital.

Optimal Capital Budget
Funding required to underwrite a value-maximizing level of new investment.

Investment Opportunity schedule (IOS)
Pattern of returns for all potential investment projects.

Investment Opportunity Schedule

The **optimal capital budget** is the funding level required to underwrite a value-maximizing level of new investment. The **investment opportunity schedule** (IOS) shows the pattern of returns for all of the firm's potential investment projects. Figure 17.3(a) shows an IOS for a hypothetical firm. The horizontal axis measures the dollar amount of investment commitments made during a given year. The vertical axis shows both the rate of return earned on each project and the percentage cost of capital. Each box denotes a given project. Project *A*, for example, calls for an outlay of $3 million and promises a 17 percent rate of return, project *B* requires an outlay of $1 million and

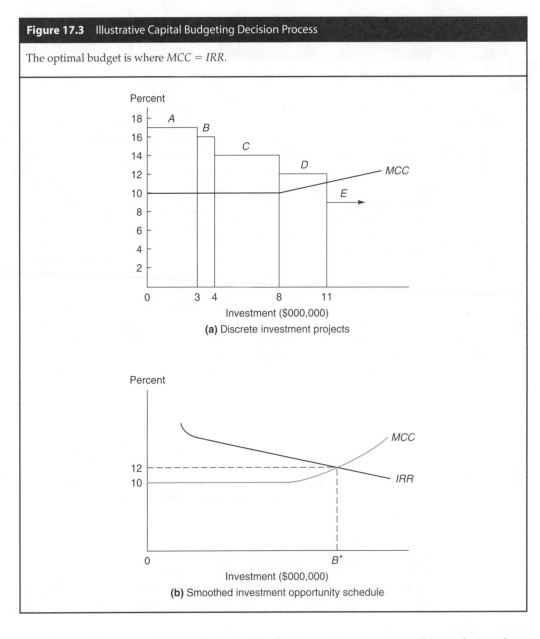

Figure 17.3   Illustrative Capital Budgeting Decision Process

The optimal budget is where $MCC = IRR$.

(a) Discrete investment projects

(b) Smoothed investment opportunity schedule

promises a 16 percent yield, and so on. The last investment, project E, simply involves buying 9 percent government bonds. By displaying this stepwise pattern of potential returns on a single graph, the firm's IOS is depicted. Figure 17.3(b) generalizes the IOS concept to show a smooth pattern of potential returns. The curve labeled IRR shows the internal rate of return potential for each project in the portfolio of investment projects available to the firm. It is important to remember that these projects are arrayed from left to right in terms of declining attractiveness as measured by the IRR criterion. Therefore, project A is more attractive than project E, and the IRR schedule is downward sloping from left to right.

Although the IOS provides important input into the capital budget decision-making process, by itself it is insufficient for determining the optimal capital budget. Both the returns *and* costs of potential projects must be considered. To define the optimal capital budget, a means for evaluating the marginal cost of funds must be incorporated into the process.

Marginal Cost of Capital

Marginal Cost of Capital
Financing cost of an additional investment project, expressed on a percentage basis.

The **marginal cost of capital** (MCC) is the extra financing cost necessary to fund an additional investment project, expressed on a percentage basis. When the firm is considering an entire portfolio of potential investment projects, the marginal cost of capital is the incremental financing cost of a relevant mix of debt and equity financing. Therefore, the MCC is typically given by the firm's weighted-average cost of capital. As drawn in Figure 17.3(b), the marginal cost of capital is constant at 10 percent up until the point where the firm has raised an additional $8 million. After this point, capital costs begin to rise. Given these IOS and MCC schedules, the firm should accept projects *A* through *D*, obtaining and investing $11 million. Project *E*, the government bond investment alternative, should be rejected. The smooth curves in Figure 17.3(b) indicate that the firm should invest *B** dollars, the optimal capital budget. At this investment level, the marginal cost of capital is 12 percent, exactly the same as the IRR on the marginal investment project.

Whenever the optimal capital budget *B** is determined, the IRR always equals the MCC for the last project undertaken. The condition that must be met for any budget to be optimal is that $IRR = MCC$. This means that the final project accepted for investment is a breakeven project, in that it provides an IRR that is just equal to the discount rate. For this project, $NPV = 0$, $P = 1$, and $IRR = k$. By accepting all earlier and more attractive projects, value maximization is assured because the firm has accepted all projects where $NPV > 0$, $PI > 1$, and $IRR > k$. This means that the area above the MCC schedule but below the *IRR* (or IOS schedule) represents the net profit earned on the firm's new investment projects. The $IRR = MCC$ optimal capital budget condition is completely analogous to the $MR = MC$ requirement for profit maximization. When $MR = MC$, all profitable units have been produced and sold. When $IRR = MCC$, all profitable investment projects have likewise been accepted.

Postaudit

Postaudit
Careful reconciliation of actual and predicted results.

To assure that an optimal capital budget has indeed been determined, the methods and data employed must be studied at the end of the capital budgeting process. The **postaudit** is a careful examination of actual and predicted results, coupled with a detailed reconciliation of any differences.

One of the most important advantages of the postaudit is that managerial forecasts of revenues and costs tend to improve when decision makers systematically compare projections to actual outcomes. Conscious or subconscious biases can be observed and eliminated, and new forecasting methods can be sought as their need becomes apparent. People simply tend to work better if they know that their actions are being monitored. It is important to remember that businesses are run by people, and people can perform at higher or lower levels of efficiency. When a divisional team has made a forecast in a capital budgeting proposal, it is putting its reputation on the line. Because of the postaudit, these managers have every incentive to make good on their projections. If costs rise above predicted levels or sales fall below expectations, managers in production, sales, and related areas have incentives to strive to bring results into line with earlier forecasts.

SUMMARY

Long-term investment decisions are important because substantial funds are often committed for extended periods. They are difficult because they entail forecasts of uncertain future events.

- **Capital budgeting** is the process of planning expenditures that generate cash flows expected to extend beyond 1 year. Several different types of investment projects may be involved, including **replacement projects,** or maintenance of business projects; **cost reduction projects** to replace obsolete plant and equipment; mandatory nonrevenue-producing **safety and environmental projects;** and **expansion projects** to increase the availability of existing products and services.

- In all cases, the focus is on **incremental cash flows,** or the period-by-period changes in net cash flows that are due to the investment project. The most common tool for project valuation is **net present-value** (NPV) analysis, where NPV is the difference between project marginal revenues and marginal costs, when both are expressed in present-value terms. The conversion to present-value terms involves use of an appropriate discount rate, or **cost of capital.**

- Alternative decision rules include the **profitability index** (PI), or benefit/cost ratio; **internal rate of return** (IRR), or discount rate that equates the present value of receipts and outlays; and the **payback period,** or number of years required to recover the initial investment.

- Managers must be aware of the **net present-value profile** for individual projects, a graph that relates the *NPV* for each project to the discount rate used in the NPV calculation. A reversal of project rankings occurs at the **crossover discount rate,**

where NPV is equal for two or more investment alternatives.

- The **component cost of debt** is the interest rate that investors require on debt, adjusted for taxes. The **component cost of equity** is the rate of return stockholders require on common stock. This includes a **risk-free rate of return** to compensate investors for postponing their consumption, and a **risk premium** to compensate them for risk taking. The risk of a given stock is measured in terms of the firm's **beta coefficient,** a measure of return variability.

- The **weighted-average cost of capital** is the marginal cost of a composite dollar of debt and equity financing. The proper set of weights to employ in computing the weighted-average cost of capital is determined by the firm's **optimal capital structure,** or combination of debt and equity financing that minimizes the firm's overall weighted-average cost of capital.

- The **optimal capital budget** is the funding level required to underwrite a value-maximizing level of new investment. Graphically, the optimal capital budget is determined by the intersection of the **investment opportunity schedule** (IOS), or pattern of returns for all of the firm's potential investment projects, and the **marginal cost of capital** (MCC), or IRR schedule.

- The **postaudit** is the final step in the capital budgeting process and consists of a careful examination of actual and predicted results, coupled with a detailed reconciliation of any differences.

Taken as a whole, the capital budgeting process is one in which the principles of marginal analysis are applied in a systematic way to long-term investment decision making.

QUESTIONS

Q17.1 "The decision to start your own firm and go into business can be thought of as a capital budgeting decision. You only go ahead if projected returns look attractive on a personal and financial basis." Discuss this statement.

Q17.2 What major steps are involved in the capital budgeting process?

Q17.3 OIBDA is an abbreviation for "operating income before depreciation and amortization." Like its predecessor EBITDA ("earnings before interest, taxes, depreciation, and amortization"), OIBDA is used to analyze profitability before noncash charges tied to plant and equipment investments. Can you see any advantages or disadvantages stemming from the use of OIBDA instead of net income as a measure of investment project attractiveness?

Q17.4 Toyota Motor Corp., like most major multinational corporations, enjoys easy access to world financial markets. Explain why the NPV approach is the most appropriate tool for Toyota's investment project selection process.

Q17.5 Level 3 Communications, Inc., like many emerging telecom carriers, has only limited and infrequent access to domestic debt and equity markets. Explain the attractiveness of a "benefit/cost ratio" approach in capital budgeting for Level 3, and illustrate why the NPV, PI, and IRR capital budgeting decision rules sometimes provide different rank orderings of investment project alternatives.

Q17.6 How is a crossover discount rate calculated, and how does it affect capital budgeting decisions?

Q17.7 An efficient firm employs inputs in such proportions that the marginal product/price ratios for all inputs are equal. In terms of capital budgeting, this implies that the marginal cost of debt should equal the marginal cost of equity in the optimal capital structure. In practice, firms often issue debt at interest rates substantially below the yield that investors require on the firm's equity shares. Does this mean that many firms are not operating with optimal capital structures? Explain.

Q17.8 Suppose that Black & Decker's interest rate on newly issued debt is 7.5 percent and the firm's marginal federal-plus-state income tax rate is 40 percent. This implies a 4.5 percent after-tax component cost of debt. Also assume that the firm has decided to finance next year's projects by selling debt. Does this mean that next year's investment projects have a 4.5 percent cost of capital?

Q17.9 Research in financial economics concludes that stockholders of target firms in takeover battles "win" (earn abnormal returns) and that stockholders of successful bidders do not lose subsequent to takeovers, even though takeovers usually occur at substantial premiums over pre-bid market prices. Is this observation consistent with capital market efficiency?

Q17.10 "Risky projects are accepted for investment on the basis of favorable expectations concerning profitability. In the postaudit process, they must not be unfairly criticized for failing to meet those expectations." Discuss this statement.

SELF-TEST PROBLEMS AND SOLUTIONS

ST17.1   NPV and Payback Period Analysis.   Suppose that your college roommate has approached you with an opportunity to lend $25,000 to her fledgling home healthcare business. The business, called Home Health Care, Inc., plans to offer home infusion therapy and monitored in-the-home healthcare services to surgery patients in the Birmingham, Alabama, area. Funds would be used to lease a delivery vehicle, purchase supplies, and provide working capital. Terms of the proposal are that you would receive $5,000 at the end of each year in interest with the full $25,000 to be repaid at the end of a 10-year period.

   A. Assuming a 10 percent required rate of return, calculate the present value of cash flows and the net present value of the proposed investment.

   B. Based on this same interest rate assumption, calculate the cumulative cash flow of the proposed investment for each period in both nominal and present-value terms.

   C. What is the payback period in both nominal and present-value terms?

   D. What is the difference between the nominal and present-value payback period? Can the present-value payback period ever be shorter than the nominal payback period?

ST17.1 SOLUTION

A. The present value of cash flows and the net present value of the proposed investment can be calculated as follows:

Year	Cash Flow ($)	Present-Value Interest Factor ($)	Present-Value Cash Flow ($)
0	(25,000)	1.0000	(25,000)
1	5,000	0.9091	4,545
2	5,000	0.8264	4,132
3	5,000	0.7513	3,757
4	5,000	0.6830	3,415
5	5,000	0.6209	3,105
6	5,000	0.5645	2,822
7	5,000	0.5132	2,566
8	5,000	0.4665	2,333
9	5,000	0.4241	2,120
10	5,000	0.3855	1,928
Cost of capital			10.0%
Present value of benefits			$30,723
Present value of cost			$25,000
Net present value			$5,723

B. The cumulative cash flow of the proposed investment for each period in both nominal and present-value terms is

Year	Cash Flow ($)	Present-Value Interest Factor	Present-Value Cash Flow ($)	Cumulative Cash Flow ($)	Cumulative PV Cash Flow ($)
0	(25,000)	1.0000	(25,000)	(25,000)	(25,000)
1	5,000	0.9091	4,545	(20,000)	(20,455)
2	5,000	0.8264	4,132	(15,000)	(16,322)
3	5,000	0.7513	3,757	(10,000)	(12,566)
4	5,000	0.6830	3,415	(5,000)	(9,151)
5	5,000	0.6209	3,105	0	(6,046)
6	5,000	0.5645	2,822	5,000	(3,224)
7	5,000	0.5132	2,566	10,000	(658)
8	5,000	0.4665	2,333	15,000	1,675
9	5,000	0.4241	2,120	20,000	3,795
10	5,000	0.3855	1,928	25,000	5,723
Payback period			5 years		
Present-value payback period			8.28 years (= 8 + $658/$2,333)		

C. Based on the information provided in part B, it is clear that the cumulative cash flow in nominal dollars reached $0 at the end of year 5. This means that the nominal payback period is 5 years. The cumulative cash flow in present-value dollars exceeds $0 when the year 8 interest payment is received. This means that the present-value payback period is roughly 8 years. If cash flows were received on a continuous basis, the present-value payback period would be 8.28 years ($= \$658/\$2,333$).

D. Assuming a positive rate of interest, the present-value payback period is always longer than the nominal payback period. This stems from the fact that present-value dollars are always less than nominal dollars, and it therefore takes longer to receive a fixed dollar amount back in terms of present-value dollars rather than in nominal terms.

ST17.2 Decision Rule Conflict. Bob Sponge has been retained to analyze two proposed capital investment projects, projects X and Y, by Square Pants, Inc., a local specialty retailer. Project X is a sophisticated working capital and inventory control system based upon a powerful personal computer, called a system server, and PC software specifically designed for inventory processing and control in the retailing business. Project Y is a similarly sophisticated working capital and inventory control system based upon a powerful personal computer and general-purpose PC software. Each project has a cost of $10,000, and the cost of capital for both projects is 12 percent. The projects' expected net cash flows are as follows:

	Expected Net Cash Flow ($)	
Year	Project X	Project Y
0	(10,000)	(10,000)
1	6,500	3,500
2	3,000	3,500
3	3,000	3,500
4	1,000	3,500

A. Calculate each project's nominal payback period, net present value (NPV), internal rate of return (IRR), and profitability index (PI).

B. Should both projects be accepted if they are interdependent?

C. Which project should be accepted if they are mutually exclusive?

D. How might a change in the cost of capital produce a conflict between the NPV and IRR rankings of these two projects? At what values of k would this conflict exist? (Hint: Plot the NPV profiles for each project to find the crossover discount rate k.)

E. Why does a conflict exist between NPV and IRR rankings?

ST17.2 SOLUTION

A. Payback:

To determine the nominal payback period, construct the cumulative cash flows for each project:

	Cumulative Cash Flow ($)	
Year	Project X	Project Y
0	($10,000)	($10,000)
1	(3,500)	(6,500)
2	(500)	(3,000)
3	2,500	500
4	3,500	4,000

$$\text{Payback}_X = 2 + \frac{\$500}{\$3,000} = 2.17 \text{ years}$$

$$\text{Payback}_Y = 2 + \frac{\$3,000}{\$3,500} = 2.86 \text{ years}$$

Net Present Value (*NPV*):

$$NPV_X = \$10,000 + \frac{\$6,500}{(1.12)^1} + \frac{\$3,000}{(1.12)^2} + \frac{\$3,000}{(1.12)^3} + \frac{\$1,000}{(1.12)^4}$$

$$= \$966.01$$

$$NPV_Y = \$10,000 + \frac{\$3,500}{(1.12)^1} + \frac{\$3,500}{(1.12)^2} + \frac{\$3,500}{(1.12)^3} + \frac{\$3,500}{(1.12)^4}$$

$$= \$636.72$$

Internal Rate of Return (*IRR*):

To solve for each project's *IRR*, find the discount rates that set *NPV* to zero:

$$IRR_X = 18\%$$

$$IRR_Y = 15\%$$

Profitability Index (*PI*):

$$PI_X = \frac{\text{PV Benefits}}{\text{PV Costs}} = \frac{\$10,966.01}{\$10,000} = 1.10$$

$$PI_Y = \frac{\$10,630.72}{\$10,000} = 1.06$$

B. Using all methods, project *X* is preferred to project *Y*. Because both projects are acceptable under the *NPV*, *IRR*, and *PI* criteria, both projects should be accepted if they are interdependent.

C. Choose the project with the higher *NPV* at $k = 12$ percent, or project *X*.

D. To determine the effects of changing the cost of capital, plot the *NPV* profiles of each project. The crossover rate occurs at about 6 percent to 7 percent. To find this rate exactly, create a project Δ, which is the difference in cash flows between projects *X* and *Y*:

Year	**Project X – Project Y** **= Project Δ Net Cash Flow ($)**
0	0
1	3,000
2	(500)
3	(500)
4	(2,500)

Then find the IRR of project Δ:

$$IRR_\Delta = \text{Crossover Rate} = 6.2 \text{ percent}$$

Thus, if the firm's cost of capital is less than 6.2 percent, a conflict exists, because $NPV_Y > NPV_X$ but $IRR_X > IRR_Y$.

Graphically, the crossover discount rate is illustrated as follows:

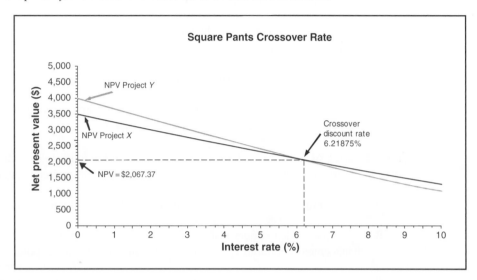

E. The basic cause of conflict is the differing reinvestment rate assumptions between NPV and IRR. The conflict occurs in this situation because the projects differ in their cash flow timing.

PROBLEMS

P17.1 Cost of Capital. Identify each of the following statements as true or false, and explain your answers.

A. Information costs both increase the marginal cost of capital and reduce the internal rate of return on investment projects.

B. Depreciation expenses involve no direct cash outlay and can be safely ignored in investment project evaluation.

C. The marginal cost of capital will be less elastic for larger firms than for smaller firms.

D. In practice, the component costs of debt and equity are jointly rather than independently determined.

E. Investments necessary to replace worn-out or damaged equipment tend to have low levels of risk.

P17.2 Decision Rule Criteria. The net present value (NPV), profitability index (PI), and internal rate of return (IRR) methods are often employed in project valuation. Identify each of the following statements as true or false, and explain your answers.

A. The IRR method can tend to understate the relative attractiveness of superior investment projects when the opportunity cost of cash flows is below the IRR.

B. A $PI = 1$ describes a project with an $NPV = 0$.

C. Selection solely according to the NPV criterion will tend to favor larger rather than smaller investment projects.

D. When $NPV = 0$, the IRR exceeds the cost of capital.

E. Use of the PI criterion is especially appropriate for larger firms with easy access to capital markets.

P17.3 Cost of Capital. Indicate whether each of the following would increase or decrease the cost of capital that should be used by the firm in investment project evaluation. Explain.

A. Interest rates rise because the Federal Reserve System tightens the money supply.

B. The stock market suffers a sharp decline, as does the company's stock price, without (in management's opinion) any decline in the company's earnings potential.

C. The company's home state eliminates the corporate income tax in an effort to keep or attract valued employers.

D. In an effort to reduce the federal deficit, Congress raises corporate income tax rates.

E. A merger with a leading competitor increases the company's stock price substantially.

P17.4 Present Value. New York City licenses taxicabs in two classes: (1) for operation by companies with fleets and (2) for operation by independent driver-owners having only one cab. Strict limits are imposed on the number of taxicabs by restricting the number of licenses, or medallions, that are issued to provide service on the streets of New York City. This medallion system dates from a Depression-era city law designed to address an overabundance of taxis that depressed driver earnings and congested city streets. In 1937, the city slapped a moratorium on the issuance of new taxicab licenses. The number of cabs, which peaked at 21,000 in 1931, fell from 13,500 in 1937 to 11,787 in May 1996, when the city broke a 59-year cap and issued an additional 400 licenses. However, because the city has failed to allow sufficient expansion, taxicab medallions have developed a trading value in the open market. After decades of often-explosive medallion price increases, fleet license prices rose to $600,000 in 2007.

A. Discuss the factors determining the value of a license. To make your answer concrete, estimate numerical values for the various components that together can be summarized in a medallion price of $600,000.

B. What factors would determine whether a change in the fare fixed by the city would raise or lower the value of a medallion?

C. Cab drivers, whether hired by companies or as owners of their own cabs, seem unanimous in opposing any increase in the number of cabs licensed. They argue that an increase in the number of cabs would increase competition for customers and drive down what they regard as an already unduly low return to drivers. Is their economic analysis correct? Who would gain and who would lose from an expansion in the number of licenses issued at a nominal fee?

P17.5   NPV and PI.   Suppose the Pacific Princess luxury cruise line is contemplating leasing an additional cruise ship to expand service from the Hawaiian Islands to Long Beach or San Diego. A financial analysis by staff personnel resulted in the following projections for a five-year planning horizon:

	Long Beach	San Diego
Cost ($)	2,000,000	3,000,00
PV of expected cash flow at $k = 15\%$	2,500,000	3,600,000

A. Calculate the net present value for each service. Which is more desirable according to the NPV criterion?

B. Calculate the profitability index for each service. Which is more desirable according to the PI criterion?

C. Under what conditions would either or both of the services be undertaken?

P17.6 NPV and PI.   Louisiana Drilling and Exploration, Inc., (LD&E) has the funds necessary to complete one of two risky oil and gas drilling projects. The first, Permian Basin 1, involves the recovery of a well that was plugged and abandoned five years ago but that may now be profitable, given improved recovery techniques. The second, Permian Basin 2, is a new onshore exploratory well that appears to be especially promising. Based on a detailed analysis by its technical staff, LD&E projects a 10-year life for each well with annual net cash flows as follows:

Project	Probability	Annual Cash Flow ($)
Permian Basin 1	0.08	500,000
	0.84	1,000,000
	0.08	1,500,000
Permian Basin 2	0.18	300,000
	0.64	900,000
	0.18	1,500,000

In the recovery project valuation, LD&E uses an 8 percent risk-fee rate and a standard 12 percent risk premium. For exploratory drilling projects, the company uses larger risk premiums proportionate to project risks as measured by the project coefficient of variation. For example, an exploratory project with a coefficient of variation 1½ times that for recovery projects would require a risk premium of 18 percent ($= 1.5 \times 12\%$). Both projects involve land acquisition as well as surface preparation and subsurface drilling costs of $3 million each.

A. Calculate the expected value, standard deviation, and coefficient of variation for annual net operating revenues from each well.

B. Calculate and evaluate the NPV for each project using the risk-adjusted discount rate method.

C. Calculate and evaluate the PI for each project.

P17.7 Investment Project Choice. Toby Amberville's Manhattan Café, Inc., is considering investment in two alternative capital budgeting projects. Project A is an investment of $75,000 to replace working but obsolete refrigeration equipment. Project B is an investment of $150,000 to expand dining room facilities. Relevant cash flow data for the two projects over their expected two-year lives are as follows:

Project A			
Year 1		**Year 2**	
Probability	**Cash Flow**	**Probability**	**Cash Flow**
0.18	$0	0.08	$0
0.64	50,000	0.84	50,000
0.18	100,000	0.08	100,000

Project B			
Year 1		**Year 2**	
Probability	**Cash Flow**	**Probability**	**Cash Flow**
0.50	$0	0.125	$0
0.50	200,000	0.75	100,000
		0.125	200,000

A. Calculate the expected value, standard deviation, and coefficient of variation for cash flows from each project.

B. Calculate the risk-adjusted NPV for each project using a 15 percent cost of capital for the riskier project and a 12 percent cost of capital for the less risky one. Which project is preferred using the NPV criterion?

C. Calculate the PI for each project, and rank the projects according to the PI criterion.

D. Calculate the IRR for each project, and rank the projects according to the IRR criterion.

E. Compare your answers to parts B, C, and D, and discuss any differences.

P17.8 Cash Flow Estimation. Cunningham's Drug Store, a medium-size drugstore located in Milwaukee, Wisconsin, is owned and operated by Richard Cunningham. Cunningham's sells pharmaceuticals, cosmetics, toiletries, magazines, and various novelties. Cunningham's most recent annual net income statement is as follows:

Sales revenue	$1,800,000
Total costs	
Cost of goods sold	$1,260,000
Wages and salaries	200,000
Rent	120,000
Depreciation	60,000
Utilities	40,000
Miscellaneous	30,000
Total	1,710,000
Net profit before tax	$90,000

Cunningham's sales and expenses have remained relatively constant over the past few years and are expected to continue unchanged in the near future. To increase sales, Cunningham is considering using some floor space for a small soda fountain. Cunningham would operate the soda fountain for an initial 3-year period and then would reevaluate its profitability. The soda fountain would require an incremental investment of $20,000 to lease furniture, equipment, utensils, and so on. This is the only capital investment required during the 3-year period. At the end of that time, additional capital would be required to continue operating the soda fountain, and no capital would be recovered if it were shut down. The soda fountain is expected to have annual sales of $100,000 and food and materials expenses of $20,000 per year. The soda fountain is also expected to increase wage and salary expenses by 8 percent and utility expenses by 5 percent. Because the soda fountain will reduce the floor space available for display of other merchandise, sales of other fountain items are expected to decline by 10 percent.

A. Calculate net incremental cash flows for the soda fountain.

B. Assume that Cunningham has the capital necessary to install the soda fountain and that he places a 12 percent opportunity cost on those funds. Should the soda fountain be installed? Why or why not?

P17.9 Cash Flow Analysis. Dunder-Mifflin, Inc., is analyzing the potential profitability of three printing jobs put up for bid by the State Department of Revenue:

	Job A	Job B	Job C
Projected winning bid (per unit) ($)	5.00	8.00	7.50
Direct cost per unit ($)	2.00	4.30	3.00
Annual unit sales volume	800,000	650,000	450,000
Annual distribution costs ($)	90,000	75,000	55,000
Investment required to produce annual volume ($)	5,000,000	5,200,000	4,000,000

Assume that (1) the company's marginal city-plus-state-plus-federal tax rate is 50 percent; (2) each job is expected to have a 6-year life; (3) the firm uses straight-line depreciation; (4) the average cost of capital is 14 percent; (5) the jobs have the same risk as the firm's other business; and (6) the company has already spent $60,000 on developing the preceding data. This $60,000 has been capitalized and will be amortized over the life of the project.

A. What is the expected net cash flow each year? (Hint: Cash flow equals net profit after taxes plus depreciation and amortization charges.)

B. What is the net present value of each project? On which project, if any, should the company bid?

C. Suppose that Dunder-Mifflin's primary business is quite cyclical, improving, and declining with the economy, but that job *A* is expected to be countercyclical. Might this have any bearing on your decision?

P17.10 Cost of Capital. Eureka Membership Warehouse, Inc., is a rapidly growing chain of retail outlets offering brand-name merchandise at discount prices. A security analyst's report issued by a national brokerage firm indicates that debt yielding 13 percent composes 25 percent of Eureka's overall capital structure. Furthermore, both earnings and dividends are expected to grow at a rate of 15 percent per year.

Currently, common stock in the company is priced at $30, and it should pay $1.50 per share in dividends during the coming year. This yield compares favorably with the 8 percent return currently available on risk-free securities and the 14 percent average for all common stocks, given the company's estimated beta of 2.

A. Calculate Eureka's component cost of equity using both the CAPM and the dividend yield plus expected growth model.

B. Assuming a 40 percent marginal federal-plus-state income tax rate, calculate Eureka's weighted-average cost of capital.

CASE *Study*

Sophisticated NPV Analysis at Level 3 Communications, Inc.

Level 3 Communications, LLC, provides integrated telecommunications services including voice, Internet access, and data transmission using rapidly improving optical and Internet protocol technologies (i.e., "broadband"). Level 3 is called a facilities-based provider because it owns a substantial portion of the fiber-optic plant, property, and equipment necessary to serve its customers.

The company traces its roots to Peter Kiewit Sons, Inc., which was incorporated in Delaware in 1941 to continue a construction business founded in Omaha, Nebraska, in 1884. In subsequent years, Kiewit invested a portion of the cash flow generated by its construction activities in a variety of other businesses. Kiewit entered the coal mining business in 1943, the telecommunications business [consisting of Metropolitan Fiber

continued

Systems (MFS) and related investments] in 1988, the information services business in 1990, and the alternative energy business in 1991. Kiewit has also made investments in several development-stage ventures.

In 1995, Kiewit distributed its MFS holdings to stockholders. In the 7 years from 1988 to 1995, the company had invested approximately $500 million in MFS. At the time of the distribution to stockholders in 1995, the company's holdings in MFS had grown to a market value of approximately $1.75 billion. In December 1996, MFS was purchased by WorldCom in a transaction valued at $14.3 billion, more than a 28:1 payout and a 52 percent annual rate of return over 8 years for investors. Following its enormously successful investment in MFS, Kiewit decided to sell unrelated assets and focus its energies on the telecommunications business. In December 1997, the company's stockholders ratified the decision of the Board to effect a split-off from the Kiewit Construction Group. As a result of the split-off, which was completed on March 31, 1998, the company no longer owns any interest in the Construction Group and adopted the name "Level 3 Communications, Inc." The Kiewit Construction Group changed its name to "Peter Kiewit Sons, Inc." The term Level 3 comes from the layered set of protocols, or standards that are often used in the industry to describe telecommunications networks. The company's strategy generally calls for services to be provided in the first three levels of these technical specifications.

During the first quarter of 2001, Level 3 completed construction activities relating to its North American intercity network. In 2003, the company added approximately 2,985 miles to its North America intercity network through acquisition of certain assets of Genuity Inc., a Massachusetts-based provider of communications services. Level 3 has also completed construction of an approximately 3,600-mile fiber-optic intercity network that connects many major European cities, including Amsterdam, Berlin, Copenhagen, Frankfurt, Geneva, London, Madrid, Milan, Munich, Paris, Stockholm, Vienna, and Zurich. Level 3's European network is linked to the North American intercity network by a transatlantic cable system that went into service during 2000.

In December 2000, the company signed an agreement to collaborate with FLAG Telecom on the development of the Northern Asia undersea cable system connecting Hong Kong, Japan, Korea, and Taiwan. During the fourth quarter of 2001, the company announced the disposition of its Asian operations in a sale transaction with Reach, Ltd. Although the company believed that Asia represented an attractive longer-term investment opportunity, given current volatile market and economic conditions the company determined that it was necessary to focus its resources, both capital and managerial, on the immediate opportunities provided by the company's operational assets in North America and Europe. This transaction closed on January 18, 2002. As part of the agreement, Reach and Level 3 agreed that Level 3 would provide capacity and services to Reach over Level 3's North American intercity network, and Level 3 would buy capacity and services from Reach in Asia. This arrangement allowed Level 3 to continue to service its customer base with capacity needs in Asia and provide Reach access to the Level 3 intercity networks in North America and Europe.

Today, Level 3 has grown to become an international communications and information services powerhouse headquartered in Broomfield, Colorado. Level 3 is one of the largest providers of wholesale dial-up service to Internet service providers (ISPs) in North America, and is the primary provider of Internet connectivity for millions of broadband subscribers through its cable and DSL partners. The company operates one of the largest

continued

communications and Internet backbones in the world. Level 3 provides services to the world's ten largest telecom carriers, the top largest ISPs in North America, and Europe's ten largest telecom carriers. A key contributor to the company's success is its highly sophisticated approach to capital budgeting.

To help investors, employees, customers, and the general public understand the economics of its business and the company's approach to capital budgeting, Level 3 has posted on the Internet what it calls a "Silicon Economics Model" (http://www.level3.com/about_us/company_history/index.html). Level 3 has developed this model in an effort to demonstrate in a simplified format the dynamic relationships that exist between pricing strategies, cost compression, demand growth, and capital budgeting in an optimized net present-value discounted cash flow model. In other words, the model represents an effort to demonstrate the effects of important economic relationships on capital budgeting decisions and the value of the firm. Because of its simplified nature, the Silicon Economics Model should not be interpreted as an attempt to predict Level 3's future operating performance or financial results. Level 3's internal optimization model contains tens of thousands of variables and relationships that for the sake of simplicity are not duplicated in this model.

In order to produce a model for public use that is not overly complex, several simplifying assumptions have been made in the Silicon Economics Model. The effects of market competition are not explicitly modeled, and only a single service offering is considered. In practice, Level 3 offers a wide variety of services in various geographic locations that have differing degrees of demand elasticity. The model places no limits on demand growth, such as would be imposed by limitations on Level 3's internal operating systems or external

supply chain requirements. Capital expenditures (CAPEX) are modeled using an initial (one-time) infrastructure cost plus an incremental cost per unit. Cost-saving improvements in technology are modeled as a reduction in unit cost, or annual cost compression rate. Operational expenses (OPEX) are modeled using a fixed annual infrastructure cost, variable cost represented as a percentage of revenue, per-incremental-unit cost (activation related), and per-total-unit cost (support related). Cost reductions over time in these latter two categories can be modeled by specifying an annual productivity improvement factor. Network expenses (NETEX) are modeled as a cost per incremental unit. This unit cost is reduced at the same rate as the activation and support-related operational expenses.

Users can see the effects of varying assumptions on operating and financial performance by choosing different input parameters on the "Data Entry" worksheet. All default input values can be changed. The model will produce the net present value of consolidated cash flow for any choice of input parameters. Details on the calculation of expected revenue, capital expenses, operational expenses, and cash flow that are graphed by the model can be reviewed and are displayed on the "Details" tab of the model. Five 3-dimensional charts are automatically produced to illustrate the sensitivity of net present value to four primary input parameters, including the annual price reduction rate, price elasticity of demand, annual CAPEX compression (cost-reduction) rate, and annual OPEX and NETEX compression (cost-reduction) rate. For simplicity, all other operating and financial parameters are held constant. The price and elasticity chart displays model sensitivity to the pace of price reduction and price elasticity; price and CAPEX illustrates effects of price reductions on capital spending. Price and OPEX and NETEX shows impacts of

continued

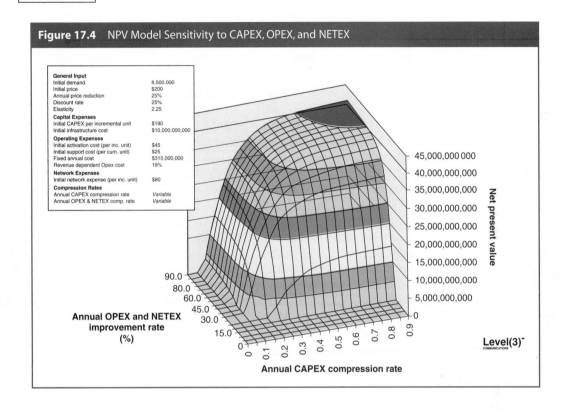

Figure 17.4 NPV Model Sensitivity to CAPEX, OPEX, and NETEX

the price reduction rate and operational and network expense compression rates; price and total cost shows sensitivity to the price reduction rate and total cost compression rate. CAPEX and OPEX and NETEX, shown in Figure 17.4, give the relationship between the capital expense compression rate and operational and network expense compression rates. For illustration purposes, input assumptions are an initial demand of 8.5 million units, an initial price of $200, annual price reductions of 25 percent, a discount rate of 25 percent, and a 2.25 price elasticity of demand.

Finally, Table 17.7 shows the net present-value implications of these model input assumptions for the discounted net present value of the enterprise. It is important to remember that these data are for illustration purposes only.

They are not predictions of actual operating and financial results for Level 3 or any other company.

A. Describe the essential components of Level 3's Silicon Economics Model.

B. Explain how Level 3's Silicon Economics Model differs from more standard and simplified approaches to capital budgeting. For comparison purposes, you may want to consider valuation spreadsheets compiled and maintained by various independent analysts and investors on the Internet, http://www.frontiernet.net/~codyklein/ LVLT/Level_3_Model.htm.

C. How would you judge the effectiveness and usefulness of the Silicon Economics Model?

continued

Table 17.7 Silicon Economics Model Details

Year	2001	2002	2003	2004	2005
Price	$200.00	$150.00	$112.50	$84.38	$63.28
Cumulative units	8,500,000	16,237,946	31,020,103	59,259,147	113,205,507
Incremental units	8,500,000	7,737,946	14,782,158	28,239,044	53,946,360
Revenue	$1,700,000,000	$2,435,691,845	$3,489,761,627	$4,999,990,552	$7,163,786,008
OPEX					
Activation cost	$(382,500,000)	$(174,103,777)	$(166,299,274)	$(158,844,622)	$(151,724,138)
Support cost	$(212,500,000)	$(202,974,320)	$(193,875,646)	$(185,184,835)	$(176,883,605)
Other (revenue based)	$(306,000,000)	$(438,424,532)	$(628,157,093)	$(899,998,299)	$(1,289,481,481)
Fixed	$(315,000,000)	$(315,000,000)	$(315,000,000)	$(315,000,000)	$(315,000,000)
OPEX – total	$(1,216,000,000)	$(1,130,502,629)	$(1,303,332,013)	$(1,559,027,757)	$(1,933,089,224)
NETEX	$(680,000,000)	$(309,517,825)	$(295,643,154)	$(282,390,439)	$(269,731,800)
EBITDA	$(196,000,000)	$995,671,391	$1,890,786,460	$3,158,572,356	$4,960,964,984
CAPEX	$(11,615,000,000)	$(735,104,835)	$(702,152,491)	$(670,677,293)	$(640,613,025)
Cash Flow	**$(11,811,000,000)**	**$260,566,555**	**$1,188,633,968**	**$2,487,895,062**	**$4,320,351,959**
OPEX per unit	$(143)	$(70)	$(42)	$(26)	$(17)
CAPEX per unit	$(1,366)	$(45)	$(23)	$(11)	$(6)
Cash flow per unit	$(1,390)	$16	$38	$42	$38

Discounted Cash Flow Analysis (with an 8x Terminal multiplier)

NPV of cash flows	$7,275,666,534
PV of Terminal Value	$29,786,628,288
NPV of Enterprise	**$37,062,294,822**

SELECTED REFERENCES

Albala Bertrand, J. M. "Relative Capital Shortage and Potential Output Constraint: A Gap Approach." *International Review of Applied Economics* 21, no. 2 (April, 2007): 189–205.

Aragon, George O. "Share Restrictions and Asset Pricing: Evidence from the Hedge Fund Industry." *Journal of Financial Economics* 83, no. 1 (January, 2007): 33–58.

Atanasova, Christina. "Access to Institutional Finance and the use of Trade Credit." *Financial Management* 36, no. 1 (Spring, 2007): 49–67.

Bacchetta, Philippe and Eric van Wincoop. "Random Walk Expectations and the Forward Discount Puzzle." *American Economic Review* 97, no. 2 (May, 2007): 346–350.

Baker, Malcolm, Joshua Coval, and Jeremy C. Stein. "Corporate Financing Decisions When Investors Take the Path of Least Resistance." *Journal of Financial Economics* 84, no. 2 (May, 2007): 266–298.

Becker, Bo. "Geographical Segmentation of US Capital Markets." *Journal of Financial Economics* 85, no. 1 (July, 2007): 151–178.

Bekaert, Geert, Campbell R. Harvey, Christian Lundblad, and Stephan Siegel. "Global Growth Opportunities and Market Integration." *Journal of Finance* 62, no. 3 (June, 2007): 1081–1137.

Boudoukh, Jacob, Roni Michaely, Matthew Richardson, and Michael R. Roberts. "On the Importance of Measuring

2006	2007	2008	2009	2010
$47.46	$35.60	$26.70	$20.02	$15.02
216,261,750	413,134,887	789,230,803	1,507,704,339	2,880,237,775
103,056,242	196,873,137	376,095,917	718,473,535	1,372,533,437
$10,263,985,390	$14,705,826,774	$21,069,919,032	$30,188,135,277	$43,252,349,956
$(144,922,841)	$(138,426,424)	$(132,221,221)	$(126,294,176)	$(120,632,822)
$(168,954,492)	$(161,380,815)	$(154,146,641)	$(147,236,752)	$(140,636,610)
$(1,847,517,370)	$(2,647,048,819)	$(3,792,585,426)	$(5,433,864,350)	$(7,785,422,992)
$(315,000,000)	$(315,000,000)	$(315,000,000)	$(315,000,000)	$(315,000,000)
$(2,476,394,703)	$(3,261,856,059)	$(4,393,953,288)	$(6,022,395,278)	$(8,361,692,424)
$(257,640,606)	$(246,091,421)	$(235,059,948)	$(224,522,980)	$(214,458,349)
$7,529,950,081	$11,197,879,294	$16,440,905,796	$23,941,217,020	$34,676,199,183
$(611,896,440)	$(584,467,125)	$(558,267,377)	$(533,242,077)	$(509,338,580)
$6,918,053,641	**$10,613,412,170**	**$15,882,638,420**	**$23,407,974,943**	**$34,166,860,603**
$(11)	$(8)	$(6)	$(4)	$(3)
$(3)	$(1)	$(1)	$(0)	$(0)
$32	$26	$20	$16	$12

Payout Yield: Implications for Empirical Asset Pricing." *Journal of Finance* 62, no. 2 (April, 2007): 877–915.

Broadie, Mark, Mikhail Chernov, and Michael Johannes. "Model Specification and Risk Premia: Evidence from Futures Options." *Journal of Finance* 62, no. 3 (June, 2007): 1453–1490.

Broadie, Mark, Mikhail Chernov, and Suresh Sundaresan. "Optimal Debt and Equity Values in the Presence of Chapter 7 and Chapter 11." *Journal of Finance* 62, no. 3 (June, 2007): 1341–1377.

Boudoukh, Jacob, Matthew Richardson, YuQing (Jeff) Shen, and Robert F. Whitelaw. "Do Asset Prices Reflect Fundamentals? Freshly Squeezed Evidence from the OJ Market." *Journal of Financial Economics* 83, no. 2 (February, 2007): 397–412.

Kayhan, Ayla and Sheridan Titman. "Firms' Histories and Their Capital Structures." *Journal of Financial Economics* 83, no. 1 (January, 2007): 1–32.

Rayo, Luis and Gary S. Becker. "Habits, Peers, and Happiness: An Evolutionary Perspective." *American Economic Review* 97, no. 2 (May, 2007): 487–491.

Sundaresan, Suresh and Neng Wang. "Investment Under Uncertainty with Strategic Debt Service." *American Economic Review* 97, no. 2 (May, 2007): 256–261.

Tamada, Yasunari and Tsung Sheng Tsai. "Optimal Organization in a Sequential Investment Problem with the Principal's Cancellation Option." *International Journal of Industrial Organization* 25, no. 3 (June, 2007): 631–641.

Organization Structure and Corporate Governance

Conventional wisdom has it that Dell Computer Corp. manufactures and services desktop computers, notebooks, and workstations. In fact, Dell "merely" oversees the quick assembly of parts supplied by Intel and other component manufacturers into customer-ordered configurations. Dell doesn't "make" computers in the sense of manufacturing them out of parts that Dell itself develops. Although Dell is justly praised for its deft use of the Internet for communicating efficiently with customers and suppliers, it is underappreciated the extent to which the company represents a newer type of "virtual" corporation.

Another virtual corporation is telecom-equipment maker Alcatel-Lucent, who recently launched Nonstop Laptop Guardian, a product that lets companies remotely clamp down on security breaches. Mobile security is a mounting concern for many companies as they try to keep track of ever-larger amounts of sensitive data stored on laptop computers spread across the globe. Because users need a wireless broadband subscription for the Nonstop Laptop Guardian to work, Alcatel-Lucent is teaming up with big telecom operators to market it. Verizon Wireless (jointly owned by Verizon Communications and Vodafone Group PLC) and Sprint Nextel Corp. offer the product to their corporate clients. More than a corporate strategy, virtual relationships are the essence of Alcatel's operating philosophy.

The days of companies trying to do everything in-house have given way to outsourcing deals, long-term contracts, strategic alliances, and joint ventures. As a result, issues of organization structure and corporate governance have reached a level of vital importance in "virtually" every corporation.[1]

ORGANIZATION STRUCTURE

What are the logical boundaries of the firm, and how do these boundaries evolve over time?

What Is Organization Structure?

Organization Structure
Institutional makeup

Vertical Relation
Business connection between companies at *different* points in the production-distribution chain

The optimal design of the firm is the organization type that most successfully meets customer demands. This **organization structure** is described by the vertical and horizontal relationships among the firm, its customers, and suppliers. A **vertical relation** is a business connection between companies at different points along the production-distribution chain

---

1 See Sally Beatty. "A New Way: The Chief Executive Of United Way Talks About The Challenges Facing The Organization." *The Wall Street Journal Online*, December 10, 2007, http://online.wsj.com.

from raw materials, to finished goods, to delivered products. An example of a vertical relation is the business linkage between Wal-Mart Stores, Inc., the giant discount retailer, and Rubbermaid, the leading manufacturer of rubberized food- and household-storage products. By way of contrast, a **horizontal relation** is a business affiliation between companies at the same point along the production-distribution chain. The commercial relationship between Wal-Mart Stores, Inc., and Target Corp., the parent company of Target discount stores, is an example of a horizontal relation.

Horizontal Relation
Business affiliation between companies at the *same* point along the production-distribution chain

If economics of scale are important, large corporations evolve to minimize production costs. If economies of scale are slight to nonexistent, small and nimble corporations evolve to exploit niche markets. When scope economies are relevant, it becomes attractive to offer bundles of related products and services. For example, there is an obvious complementary relationship between soda and pizza products. Pepsi-Cola goes great with pizza. Still, business success does not require that both products be owned and distributed by the same company simply because they are consumed together. Pepsico divested its Pizza Hut, KFC, and Taco Bell restaurant brands, now parts of YUM! Brands, Inc., because it failed to realize the expected synergy from jointly operating these soft drink and fast-food businesses. The fast-food business is mature in the United States and features both cutthroat pricing and razor-thin margins. This contrasts sharply with the soft drink industry. Coca-Cola and Pepsi-Cola dominate soft drinks, a business that features low capital investment requirements, generous profit margins, and above-average growth. Rather than extending its advantages in the soft drink industry by controlling an important segment of the fast-food business, Pepsico found itself at a disadvantage when McDonald's and other non-Pepsico chains refused to serve Pepsi products lest they help a prime competitor in the fast-food business. Coca-Cola's licensing agreements with fast-food franchises proved superior to Pepsico's joint ownership of fast-food and soft drink businesses. Thus, Coca-Cola solidified its lead as the dominant soft drink bottler in the world because its organization structure was superior to that featured by a prime competitor.

Optimal Design Is Dynamic

The optimal boundaries of the firm are not static; they are dynamic and responsive to the changing needs of the marketplace. Before the mid-nineteenth century, hierarchal organization structures were virtually nonexistent. Transportation and information technology had not yet progressed to the point where large-scale consolidation was possible. This changed radically when steamship and railroad transportation and the telegraph and telephone made for speedy transport and near-instantaneous communication. Suddenly, the means for coordination in large-scale enterprise became available. At the start of the twentieth century, company sizes grew rapidly to take advantage of economies of scale in production to better serve nations hungry for industrial and consumer products. This process of industrial consolidation flourished throughout the early post–World War II era.

The emerging information age of the twenty-first century promises to further refine corporate boundaries. The post–World War II corporate environment was designed for the efficient mass production of standardized industrial and consumer goods. Present-day customers are more interested in unique combinations of goods and services to meet specialized needs. The industrial revolution transformed the competitive landscape of the twentieth century; the information revolution is presently transforming corporate boundaries. Highly skilled managers no longer need to locate in New York, Chicago, or Los Angeles to find exciting career opportunities. Powerful desktop computers, the Internet, and low-cost satellite-based communications make it possible to work in Los Angeles while living on Catalina Island; in Sante Fe, New Mexico; or Durango, Colorado. Centralized authority supported by layers of managerial staff is being replaced by desktop computers and sophisticated software that make line personnel instantly accountable for bottom-line performance. Chief financial officers (CFOs) do not want detailed reports filed by cumbersome staffs of accounting and financial personnel; they want immediate access to the data with user-friendly software. Ramifications of the ongoing revolution in information technology should not be underestimated. Invention of the airplane did not make it important to become a faster walker; it changed the nature of travel. Similarly, invention of the Internet did not just increase the importance of computer literacy in the workplace; it fundamentally alters the size and scope of organizations throughout the economy.

TRANSACTION COST THEORY OF THE FIRM

The firm is a legal device that connects owners, managers, workers, suppliers, and customers.

Nature of Firms

Transaction Costs
Coordination expenses

Information Costs
Search outlays

Decision Costs
Bargaining expenditures

Enforcement Costs
Charges tied to contractual commitments

Nobel laureate Ronald Coase is famous for defining the firm as a collection of contractual agreements among owners, managers, workers, suppliers, and customers. The efficiency of firms depends upon their ability to minimize the **transaction costs** of coordinating productive activity. Important categories of transaction costs encountered within the firm include **information costs, decision costs,** and **enforcement costs.**

Information or search costs encompass expenses encountered in discovering the type and quality of goods and services demanded by consumers. Information costs also include expenses encountered in securing necessary raw materials, attracting and training a skilled workforce, developing brand-name recognition, and so on. Decision or bargaining costs include expenditures involved with successfully negotiating production agreements. For example, labor bargaining involves a continuously renegotiable agreement between management and labor. Even with a long-term union contract, the labor bargain is continuously renegotiable in the sense that the trade-off between pay and effort varies daily according to the level of effort expended. Reluctant workers do not work hard. Enforcement or policing costs include charges necessary to make sure that all parties live up to their contractual commitments. Supervisory costs are an example of enforcement costs. Some transaction costs involve cash outlays for insurance, legal fees, and so on. Many transaction costs involve implicit or opportunity costs. Necessary delays to facilitate consensus building, group meetings, and constant communication among team members are all manifestations of transaction costs.

In the early post–World War II period, notable transaction costs associated with coordinating large-scale production and distribution of industrial and consumer goods were more than offset by significant economies of scale in production. Top firms in the industrial world reached gigantic size in terms of assets, employment, sales revenues, and profits. More recently, consumers have tended to prefer distinctive goods and services tailored to specific needs. Economies of scale in production are less important when production needs are specialized and often nonexistent in the provision of services. At the same time, the costs of coordinating activity among increasingly specialized and highly educated professionals tend to be much higher than the costs of coordinating effort among less specialized workers. Therefore, it is not surprising to note the recent downsizing trend among giant corporations throughout the industrial world and the coincident growth in importance of entrepreneurship and small business.

Coase Theorem

According to Coase, firms exist because they are an effective means of minimizing transaction costs. It would be prohibitively expensive for each of us to organize production of all goods and services that we desire. For example, most consumers are unprepared to deal with the complexity of building a home. As a result, most consumers contract with real estate developers, who contract with builders who, in turn, contract with carpenters, electricians, plumbers, landscapers, and so on. If sufficient ongoing demand exists, builders employ their own staff of professionals; they form a firm. If demand is sporadic, contracting will ensue prior to the start of each independent home building project. In deciding whether or not to retain their own staff, builders compare the costs of negotiating for the completion of individual home projects with the costs of maintaining a less than fully utilized staff during slack periods. In the same way, law firms, medical practices, and professional consultants consider transaction costs in decisions concerning the scope and scale of professional enterprises.

Coase sees firms as well equipped to deal with traditional problems caused by negative externalities, such as pollution. Because individuals respond to economic incentives, they seek out mutually beneficial trades. Suppose a power plant reduced recreational opportunities by fouling a nearby river. Such a company might appease local residents by purchasing land for general recreation use upriver or by paying to reduce downriver pollution. The power plant might also pay some other local polluter, say, a municipal water treatment plant, to reduce its pollution, and hence the total amount of emissions, to an acceptable level. This latter alternative might prove especially attractive if the marginal cost of reducing pollution by the municipal water facility is less than the marginal cost of reducing power plant emissions. In fact, some local jurisdictions now award "pollution rights" that are traded among polluters who seek the lowest cost method for reducing total emissions. According to the **Coase Theorem,** resource allocation will be efficient so long as transaction costs remain low and property rights can be freely assigned and exchanged.

To understand the importance of organization structure in the ongoing success of firms, it is necessary to learn how organization structure is dictated by the nature of the firm's economic environment and competitive strategy.

Coase Theorem
Resource allocation is efficient if transaction costs are low and property rights are freely traded

THE FIRM'S AGENCY PROBLEM

There is natural conflict between owners and managers.

Sources of Conflict Within Firms

Agency Problem
Natural conflict between owners and managers

Agency Costs
Expenditures necessary to overcome owner–manager conflicts

Given their ownership position, stockholders are the principals of the firm. Managers and other employees without any ownership interest are hired hands, or agents of the stockholders. An **agency problem** is present to the extent that unresolved material conflict exists between the self-seeking goals of (agent) managers and the value maximization goal of (principal) stockholders. **Agency costs** are the explicit and implicit transaction

Managerial Application 18.1

Organization Design at GE

A home to over 320,000 employees, the General Electric Company (GE) is a diversified industrial giant producing a wide variety of products for the generation, transmission, distribution, control, and utilization of electricity. By 2012, GE sales revenue is expected to continue its steady climb to $225 billion, while profits grow to $30 to $35 billion. Expectations of rising profit margins due to ferocious cost-cutting have made GE a stock market darling. With a stock market capitalization in excess of $350 billion, the "Company that Jack Welch Built" is one of the most valuable and revered corporations in the world.

Although GE is a gigantic business, it has crafted an organization design that allows the company to take advantage of its large size and yet still function like a nimble organization. Like many large corporations, GE is divided into profit centers and operating units. Although each line of business is responsible for its own profit numbers, GE seeks synergy by having managers share management techniques that can work across functional areas. Stories of management success and failure are shared openly. Though GE has nine

layers of management, its legendary informality means that front-line managers and employees often "violate" the chain of command by communicating across layers of management. This is what many management theorists regard as being unique about GE. GE makes every executive, manager, and employee personally responsible for their own performance. Unexpected visits to plants and offices, surprise luncheons, and countless handwritten notes make everyone feel like an important part of a complex organization.

At GE, quality is an ongoing process of continuing improvement. With hundreds of specific projects, GE's quality initiative, dubbed Six Sigma, involves constant training of thousands of employees. In a real sense, GE is a learning and evolving organization. It is an organization designed to renew and reinvigorate itself. So far, it seems to be working for management employees, customers, and stockholders.

See: Kathryn Kranhold, "GE's Overseas Sales Boost Profit, but Investors Have Worries," *The Wall Street Journal Online*, October 13, 2007, http://online.wsj.com.

costs necessary to overcome the natural divergence of interest between agent managers and principal stockholders. Agency costs incurred by stockholders are reflected in expenses for managerial monitoring, the overconsumption of perquisites by managers, and lost opportunities due to excessive risk avoidance. This characterization of the conflict problem within firms has a long history in economics. Modern concern with the topic began in the 1930s when Adolf Berle and Gardiner Means predicted that managers with little direct ownership interest, and thus having "own" rather than stockholder interests in mind, would come to run the bulk of business enterprise by the latter part of the twentieth century. Before them, economists' concern with the "other people's money" problem dates from 1776 and the work of Adam Smith, who noted that people tend to look after their own affairs with more care than they use in looking after the affairs of others.

Agency problems exist because of conflicts between the incentives and rewards that face owners and managers. Such conflicts commonly arise given owner–manager differences in risk exposure, investment horizons, and familiarity with investment opportunities. Problems mount because differing economic incentives between owners and managers can cause predictable, but hard to correct, hurdles that must be overcome if the shareholder's value maximization objective is to be achieved.

Risk Management Problems

Excessive Risk-Taking Problem
Agent preference for value-reducing speculation

Significant differences in the risk exposure of managers and stockholders often lead to an **excessive risk-taking problem.** In 1995, for example, London's famous Barings Bank, a bank founded in 1762 that had helped fund Britain's war effort against Napoleon, was

---

Figure 18.1   The Goal of Incentive Compensation Is to Match Worker Incentives with Managerial Motives

Pay for performance must reward productive individual and group effort.

Individual pay for performance
* Reward productive effort
* Compensate general human capital
* Compensate specific human capital

Divisional pay for performance
* Reward productive teamwork
* Reward coordination among divisions
* Compensate beneficial spillover effects

---

brought to its knees given excessive risk taking by a single individual. A trader by the name of Nick Leeson in Barings' Singapore branch had been charged with the responsibility of overseeing the branch's risk-free arbitrage business. In risk-free arbitrage, banks and other financial institutions seek to profit by taking advantage of price discrepancies in different markets. By instantaneously buying and selling the same security in different markets, arbitrage by banks and other financial institutions can result in small but risk-free profits. Unfortunately, when imperfect hedging led to losses rather than profits, Leeson began to engage in the far riskier business of foreign currency market speculation. Leeson guessed wrong and lost $1.4 billion of the bank's money. Although Leeson ended up in jail, Barings was sold to ING, the large Dutch financial institution, for a mere £1.

Other People's Money Problem
Tendency by agents to be careless with principal's resources

The Barings Bank episode is an obvious manifestation of the **other people's money problem.** It stemmed from the fact that Leeson was not speculating with his own money; he was gambling with Barings Bank funds. Other related agency problems tied to differences between the investment horizons of stockholders and management can also emerge. Salary and bonus payments tied to short-term performance often constitute a large part of the annual total compensation package earned by management. Managers typically have huge personal incentives to report favorable year-to-year growth in revenues, profits, and earnings per share. This can sometimes have the unfortunate effect of focusing managerial attention on near-term accounting performance to the detriment of long-term value maximization. To combat such myopic behavior, companies increasingly insist that managerial compensation be directly tied to long-term performance. An efficient means for establishing this link is to demand that top management hold a significant stock position that cannot be sold until some time after retirement. When it was an independent entity, investment bank Salomon, Inc., established a compensation plan whereby managers were required to take a significant portion of total compensation in the form of common stock that could not be sold until 5 years after the employee left the bank. Over time, traders, managing directors, top management, and other employees at Salomon came to own roughly 35 percent of the company. Impressively, this significant employee ownership was achieved through direct stock purchases in the open market; no outright grants of employee or executive stock options were involved. At Salomon, a giant boost to employee stock ownership was accomplished in such a way as to preserve the ownership position of other stockholders. This contrasts with the common situation where generous stock option grants to top management are used to align managerial and shareholder interests, but at the significant cost of diluting the ownership interest of outside shareholders.

Investment Horizon Problems

The typical CEO of a giant U.S. corporation is 55 to 60 years old, has been with the company 20 to 25 years, and looks forward to a term in office of 8 to 10 years. With this demographic background, most top executives only expect to see the fruits of their actions if benefits accrue quickly. Similarly, many managers pin their hopes for promotion on the basis of results achieved during fairly short time frames. As a result, top corporate executives tend to have fairly short time horizons within which they evaluate investment and operating decisions. This short-term focus is reflected in and reinforced by compensation plans that rely on near-term corporate performance.

Managerial Myopia Problem
Inefficient preference for stable or short-term performance

To combat the potential for shortsighted operating and investment decisions, sometimes referred to as the **managerial myopia problem,** most corporations now tie a significant portion of total compensation for top executives and other managers to the company's long-term stock-price performance. Stock options and other payments tied to stock-price appreciation now account for a significant portion of top executive pay. Similarly, a wide variety of employee stock ownership plans give managers and other employees strong incentives to consider the long-term implications of present-day decisions. Such plans work best if they consider stock-price gains over extended periods, say 10 years. To reflect the *marginal* contribution of a given top executive or managerial team, the **board of directors** must only reward *above-average* stock-price appreciation.

Board of Directors
Group of people legally charged with the responsibility for governing a corporation

Finally, given the advanced age of most top executives and many senior managers, firms must be on guard against the **end-of-game problem.** The end-of-game problem is the most serious manifestation of inefficient risk avoidance and reflects the fact that it is difficult to discipline poorly performing managers at the end of their career. Young managers have lucrative future job opportunities both inside and outside the firm as an incentive for hard work and honest dealings with their current employer. Older managers enjoy no such future opportunities and face correspondingly weaker incentives for hard work and honest dealing. Most firms deal with the end-of-game problem by insisting that senior managers take a significant portion of total compensation in the form of pay tied to long-term stock-price appreciation.

End-of-Game Problem
Senior manager preference for value-reducing stable or short-term performance

Information Asymmetry Problem
Disadvantage created by management's inherently superior access to information inside the firm

Information Asymmetry Problems

Another potential source of agency problems is tied to management's inherently superior access to information inside the firm, or the **information asymmetry problem.** By definition, **insiders** know more than outsiders about the firm's performance, prospects, and opportunities. The problem is made more serious by the fact that most indicators of firm and top executive performance typically rely upon accounting measures that are collected and reported by management. Because managers are themselves responsible for the collection and processing of accounting information, they control the reporting mechanism designed to monitor managerial and firm performance. Incentive pay plans linked to accounting performance do more than provide incentives for efficient operating and financial decisions. They also give inducements for **accounting earnings manipulation** and bias.

Insiders
Members of top management and the board of directors

Accounting Earnings Manipulation
Accounting abuse to achieve better-than-actual earnings

Income Inflation
Accounting abuse to achieve higher earnings

Income Smoothing
Accounting abuse to achieve predictable earnings

Earnings manipulation and bias can occur when managers choose accounting methods that lead to **income inflation** and/or **income smoothing.** Managers have incentives for income inflation when higher reported earnings boost managerial compensation, provide greater job security, or both. Incentives exist for income smoothing to the extent that spectacular short-run performance creates expectations that are difficult or impossible to satisfy and, therefore, lead to stockholder disappointment and sanctions. Incentives for income smoothing are also present if stockholder risk aversion leads to an asymmetry of managerial rewards and penalties following short-term earnings success versus failure. Recent studies in managerial economics document the effects of executive incentive pay plans on the reporting strategy of top managers. Compensation schemes chosen by shareholders and/or boards of directors have a direct influence on the degree of earnings manipulation and bias.

ORGANIZATION DESIGN

Organization Design
Institutional framework

The value-maximizing **organization design** minimizes unproductive conflict within the firm.

Resolving Unproductive Conflict Within Firms

Successful firms get close to the customer, efficiently identify customer needs, and exceed customer expectations. Such firms are effective production and distribution systems. Similarly, they are effective means for collecting and processing sometimes conflicting information about customer demands, technology, input prices, raw material supplies, and so on. The information-processing function of firms is sometimes overlooked. Also neglected are the costs and benefits of effective information processing.

Useful information has a price. It must be identified, combined with complementary information, and effectively communicated within the organization. This is made difficult by the fact that bits of useful information are typically dispersed among several individuals at several levels up and down the organization. For example, research scientists may encounter problems communicating with engineering staff about problems with the commercial applications of a given discovery. Scientists share a common language, and it often conflicts with the common language of engineers. In turn, both scientists and engineers may confront obstacles in communicating with accounting staff, who share a language that is common to accountants, but foreign to many others. The problem is much more serious than just a failure to share a common vocabulary. Communication is made difficult by the fact that managers with valuable information within the firm have conflicting incentives to hide useful details.

Decision Authority
Control choice

Constructive communication within the firm is essential if customer needs are to be met effectively. The design of the organization is appropriate if it facilitates the firm's function as an information-processing mechanism. In considering the design of any organization, basic needs must be met to facilitate worthwhile activity. As shown in Figure 18.2, three prime considerations are the needs to allocate **decision authority,** monitor and evaluate performance, and reward productive behavior.

Authority is the ability to command, control, or influence. An effective organization design is one that allocates decision authority to that person or team of persons best able to perform a given task or influence a particular outcome. Decision authority allows individual employees to determine how and when to best deploy the productive resources and valuable information at their disposal.

Figure 18.2   Organization Design Must Facilitate Effective Decision Making and Efficient Performance

Constructive communication within the firm is essential.

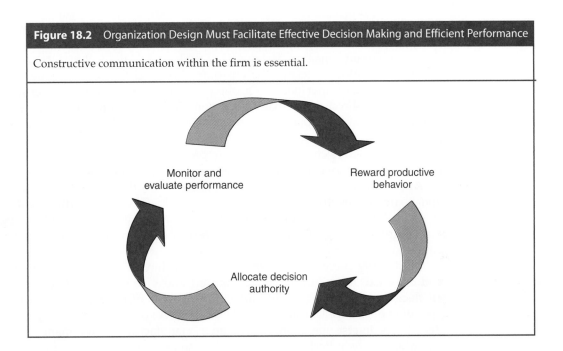

Decision authority involves responsibility. It thus becomes imperative to monitor and evaluate performance. Managers and all employees must be held accountable for outcomes tied to individual decisions. Accountability is assured by the tangible and intangible rewards derived from productive activity and the penalties or sanctions tied to unproductive behavior. To minimize the costs of unproductive conflict with the firm, it is essential that the design of the organization effectively allocate decision-making authority, monitor and evaluate performance, and reward productive behavior.

Centralization Versus Decentralization

Centralized Decision Authority
Top-down management style

Decentralized Decision Authority
Close-to-the-customer management style

Flat Organization
One or few levels of decision-making authority

With **centralized decision authority,** detailed judgments concerning how to best manage corporate resources, deal with suppliers and customers, and so on, are handled by top-line executives within the organization. Corporations with a centralized, or top-down, management style employ a significant central office staff. With **decentralized decision authority,** front-line employees, those in direct communication with customers, are empowered to make fundamental judgments concerning how to best serve customer needs. Companies that feature a decentralized, bottom-up, or **flat organization** structure employ minimal decision support staff in the central office. The decision to feature a centralized or decentralized management structure is often an evolutionary process. When the scale of operation grows, effective resource management often requires greater centralization of decision-making authority. However, even in large organizations, the need to remain nimble in responding to customers requires employee empowerment.

Decentralized decision authority works best when local employees working directly with customers have up-to-the-minute information about the needs and price sensitivity of customers. Decentralized decision-making authority and customer-specific knowledge can be a powerful combination when seeking to quickly satisfy local customers. Centralized decision making that requires local managers to seek permission to change prices or reconfigure products can result in costly delay. Of course, e-mail and related innovations in communications technology have greatly reduced the delay involved with telling customers "I'll get back to you with that information."

An important benefit of decentralized decision making is that it trains local managers and other employees to put the customer first and to accept personal responsibility for satisfying customer needs. On the other hand, decentralized decisions that fail to account for indirect or company-wide consequences can prove counterproductive. For example, a price cut in one region or for a single product line may divert sales from other regions or products. Local managers often ignore important interaction effects. Similarly, information about customer needs or product quality considerations may be more reliable and used more effectively when pooled from various local operations.

At most firms, strategic planning decisions are the responsibility of the chairman and board of directors, as supported by the chief executive officer and central office staff. At the same time, corporations that feature highly centralized strategic planning may emphasize significant decentralization and employee empowerment when it comes to operating decisions. Nowhere is this dichotomy more apparent than at extraordinarily successful Berkshire Hathaway, Inc. At $250 billion Berkshire, chairman and chief executive officer Warren Buffett and vice chairman Charles Munger make all decisions regarding capital allocation. Heads of operating subsidiaries make all operating decisions. Division heads have complete operating authority when it comes to Berkshire's diverse operations in insurance, manufacturing, and financial services. Buffett and Munger credit Berkshire's outstanding success to the fact that they are supported by an outstanding group of operating managers, but they alone are responsible for capital allocation decisions. Indeed, Berkshire's annual report to stockholders gives acquisition criteria for purchases in excess of $5 billion and emphasizes that the company is able to assess the level of its interest in a potential acquisition within 5 minutes!

DECISION MANAGEMENT AND CONTROL

The decision to centralize versus decentralize depends on defining the appropriate numbers of levels within the organization.

Assigning Decision Rights

Vertical Organization
Multiple levels of decision-making authority

A flat organization has few or a single level of decision-making authority; a **vertical organization** features multiple ascending levels of decision-making authority. Irrespective of which organizational form is appropriate, it becomes necessary to choose where in a given organization structure any given decision should be made. In all instances, the issue is one of making effective use of local or customer-specific knowledge, while at the same time maintaining an effective use of centralized information.

Tasks
Assignments

Jobs
Bundle of related tasks

At its most basic level, the production process encompasses a sequence of related **tasks,** or assignments necessary to effectively meet customer needs. Related tasks are bundled into **jobs** when such packaging facilitates cost savings and a more productive use of firm resources. Complex jobs involve the completion of a large number or wide variety of tasks. Simple jobs involve only one elementary chore or a few related responsibilities. Both simple and complex jobs can feature a mix of decision authority. Management trainees may be assigned fairly simple jobs with little or no decision authority; senior management routinely takes on complex jobs with complete decision authority. Thus, an appropriate organization design features a constructive mapping of individual skills with task assignments and a correct allotment of decision rights.

As in the case of deciding upon a centralized versus decentralized organization design, judgments regarding the correct bundling of tasks into jobs involve a trade-off between the costs and benefits of coordination and control. When the distribution of useful knowledge is broad and coordination costs are high, jobs tend to be complex and encompass significant authority to make important decisions about how to best serve customers. When the distribution of useful knowledge is narrow and coordination costs are modest, jobs tend to be simple and embody minimal decision authority. The recent explosion of small professional corporations implies rapid growth in the number of complex jobs with significant decision authority. The sophisticated types of goods and services offered by small professional corporations typically involve levels of complexity and customer-specific knowledge that make large-scale coordination uneconomic, even in the face of impressive recent advances in communications technology, like e-mail. This increasing complexity places a high premium on motivated individuals capable of independent, self-directed cognitive activity.

Team
Worker groups given shared responsibility

Many larger organizations facing the need to successfully deal with increasingly complex tasks have turned to **team** concepts. Production teams are often given responsibility for managing product flow, setting work schedules, maintaining quality control, and so on. Production teams are an effective means for empowering and motivating front-line employees. Teams are also adept at sharing local or customer-specific information that is sufficiently complex or far-reaching so as to be beyond the grasp of any individual. Teams are less effective in dealing with problems where the process of consensus building is slow or where monitoring and motivating an underperforming team member is prohibitively expensive. Because communication costs and shirking problems grow with team size, most effective teams involve just a handful of participants, often less than a dozen or so members. Optimal team size is defined by the trade-offs involved between the marginal costs and marginal benefits of adding additional team members.

Decision Process

Decision Management
Generating, choosing, and implementing management decisions

Decision management is the method of generating, choosing, and implementing management decisions. **Decision control** is the procedure of assessing how well the decision management process functions. As illustrated in Figure 18.3, it is useful to characterize the decision management and control process as consisting of four distinct parts. To be successful, this process must effectively generate attractive decision proposals, choose the best decision, implement the best decision, and accurately measure decision success.

Decision Control
Manner of assessing the decision management process

A recurring problem in decision management and control is that it is often difficult to generate a large number of attractive choice alternatives. Managers and other employees from a given work environment tend to have similar perspectives based upon a common work experience or educational background. This makes "groupthink" and the inability to take a fresh look at problems from new perspectives a common problem. To avoid this, successful management teams often look for input from different functional areas within the firm or from individuals who base their proposals on unconventional underlying assumptions. If the decision process is to represent a legitimate search among desirable alternatives, choices must represent valid options with the reasonable potential to offer an attractive trade-off between marginal costs and benefits. If the best decision alternative is to be chosen, the decision process must settle on the option that offers the best marginal net benefit after all direct and indirect costs and benefits to the firm have been considered.

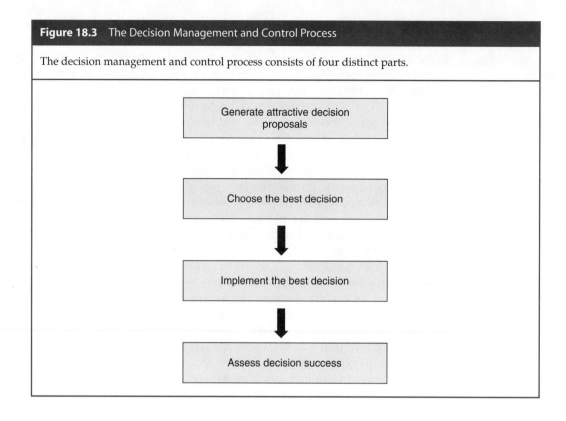

Figure 18.3   The Decision Management and Control Process

The decision management and control process consists of four distinct parts.

Finally, constructive management demands an ongoing assessment of the decision-making process and the success, or lack thereof, of past decisions. Correct investment and operating decisions are made on the basis of **economic expectations,** or a reasonable before-the-fact forecast of monetary implications. Judging the wisdom of past decisions involves much more than a simple after-the-fact analysis of **economic realizations,** or financial outcomes. For example, a decision to buy fire insurance is sound if the chance for material loss is present and insurance is obtained in a cost-effective manner. This is true whether or not a fire loss is actually incurred. Similarly, a given managerial decision is sound if expected profits yield a reasonable risk-adjusted return. Of course, if after-the-fact realizations consistently exceed or fall short of before-the-fact expectations, it becomes necessary to seek out and correct the biases or errors responsible for decision failures.

Economic Expectations
A reasonable before-the-fact forecast of monetary implications

Economic Realizations
Financial monetary outcomes

CORPORATE GOVERNANCE

Corporate governance is the system of controls that helps a corporation effectively manage, administer, and direct economic resources.

Corporate Governance
Control system that helps companies effectively manage, administer, and direct economic resources

Role Played by Boards of Directors

The most important and closely monitored corporate governance mechanism is the company board of directors. The board of directors is a group of people legally charged with the responsibility for governing a corporation. In a for-profit corporation, it is

Managerial Application 18.2

Company Information on the Internet

When looking for easy-to-use business data, news, or analysis, the best advice is to simply "Check the Internet." Company Web sites are a great place to start. The annual report to shareholders is where management tells about all of the good things they are doing for the company. Read financial statements carefully (especially the footnotes), but be skeptical about the commentary. Annual reports are notorious for overlooking shortcomings and glossing over problem areas. Quarterly 10Q and annual 10K reports to the Securities and Exchange Commission contain all necessary financial statements and include detailed information about competitive challenges and legal problems. In plain black and white, these SEC reports give the unvarnished truth about company performance at http://www.sec.gov. Don't miss the proxy statement, called the 14A report. The proxy statement is the annual meeting announcement and includes important information about legal matters brought up for shareholder vote. From an investor's standpoint, the proxy statement is also interesting because it gives detailed information about compensation and share ownership for members of the board of directors and top management. SEC reports are a good counterbalance to corporate annual report puffery and sometimes biased analyst research reports.

Any list of favorite Web sites for general business news and information on the Internet is long and getting longer. Here a few of the best places to start when looking for useful company information:

Name	Information	Internet Address
Bloomberg.com	Financial news and analysis	http://www.bloomberg.com/
The Wall Street Journal Online	Business News	http://online.wsj.com/home.html
Barron's Online	Business analysis	http://www.barrons.com/
msn Money Central	Company and industry data	http://www.msn.com/
Yahoo! Finance	Financial news, message boards	http://finance.yahoo.com/

See: Michael Neeley, "Will the Internet Be Good for What Ails Us?," *The Wall Street Journal Online*, October 17, 2007, http://online.wsj.com.

Corporate Stakeholders
Persons with an economic interest in the corporation

generally accepted that the board of directors is responsible to stockholders. Some adopt the broader perspective that the board is responsible to **corporate stakeholders**— that is, to everyone who has an economic interest in the corporation. Corporate stakeholders include stockholders, customers, employees, and the community at large. In a nonprofit corporation, the board generally reports to stakeholders, particularly the local communities in which the nonprofit serves. Boards of directors provide continuity for the organization by maintaining a legal existence. A primary responsibility is to select, appoint, and review the performance of a chief executive officer responsible for day-to-day decision making and administration of the organization.

Table 18.1 shows five important attributes of effective corporate boards of directors and corresponding limitations of ineffectual corporate boards. The National Center for Nonprofit Boards itemizes 10 responsibilities for nonprofit boards: determine the organization's mission and purpose, select the executive, support the executive and review his or her performance, ensure effective organizational planning, ensure adequate resources, manage resources effectively, determine and monitor the organization's programs and services, enhance the organization's public image, serve as a court of appeal, and assess its own performance. Though intended as a guide to nonprofit institutions, these responsibilities also apply to the boards of directors for profit-seeking corporations.

Table 18.1 Attributes of Effective and Ineffectual Boards of Directors

Attribute	Effective Board	Ineffectual Board
Integrity	Board members must take pains to ensure that words and actions are in the best long-term interests of large and small shareholders.	Board decisions and management compensation plans are sometimes structured to favor entrenched management at the expense of stockholders.
Competence	Training and business experience of board members must be up to the task of providing value-added oversight to managerial decisions.	Board members with little or no relevant training or business experience are too often encountered. Celebrities are great at cocktail parties, but make poor board members.
Independence	Through words and deeds, it must be clear that the board of directors effectively represents shareholder interests in its oversight of managerial decisions.	Cronies of top management, or cozy consulting arrangements between companies and board members, can compromise if not undermine board member independence.
Accountability	Clear lines of authority and responsibility must be drawn. Both the board and top management must be held accountable for corporate performance.	Some boards are too large by design. When the board of directors has more than a dozen members, it can quickly become impossible to wield effective decision-making power.
Transparency	Actions must be carefully and completely disclosed in timely shareholder reports and SEC filings.	Too many boards of directors allow management to hide subpar corporate performance through misleading corporate communications or endless restructuring.

Corporate Governance Inside the Firm

Corporate control mechanisms inside the firm are useful means for helping eliminate the potential divergence of interests between managers and stockholders. Organization design, including the degree of vertical integration and the horizontal scope of the corporation, is an example of essential corporate governance mechanisms inside the firm. When inputs can be reliably obtained from suppliers operating in perfectly competitive markets, it is seldom necessary to produce such components in-house. Market procurement works better. When important economies of scale in production are operative, it is preferable to obtain inputs from large specialized suppliers. A high degree of vertical integration only makes sense when input production is within the firm's core competency, supply is erratic, and/or suppliers charge excessive markups. In such instances, vertical integration can result in better coordination of the production process and protect the firm's tangible and intangible investments.

Vertical integration is sometimes seen as a useful means for deterring competitor entry into a company's primary market. Years ago, IBM made a huge strategic error in licensing Intel Corp. to manufacture key components for the personal computer. Intel started out as simply a microprocessor manufacturer supplying the "brains" to manufacturers of personal computers and other "smart" electronics. Today, Intel dominates that business with a market share approaching 90 percent, and enjoys sky-high margins and an enviable rate of return on investment. To spur future growth, Intel is now branching out into the production of other PC components like modems and network equipment. Soon, the famous trademark "Intel Inside" may have to be replaced with "Intel Inside *and* Outside." Meanwhile, IBM has exited the PC business. All manufacturers would do well to contemplate IBM's experience with Intel before licensing to others the production of key components.

Another useful means for controlling the flow of corporate resources is provided by internal markets established to better balance the supply and demand conditions for divisional goods and services. Incentive compensation is also an obvious corporate governance mechanism inside the firm. The proper design and implementation of a appropriate incentive pay plan is a fundamental determinant of whether or not corporate resources will be administered effectively and equitably. Like any effective corporate governance mechanism inside the firm, compensation plans must help minimize transaction costs by effectively joining decision authority with performance evaluation.

OWNERSHIP STRUCTURE AS A CORPORATE GOVERNANCE MECHANISM

Important corporate governance implications are tied to the complex variety of claims on the value of the firm.

Dimensions of Ownership Structure

Capital structure of the firm is traditionally described in terms of the share of total financing obtained from equity investors versus lenders (debt). Today, interest has

Managerial Application 18.3

Sarbanes–Oxley

For public companies, the Sarbanes–Oxley Act presents an all-encompassing to-do list that ranges from requiring outside auditors to be rotated every 5 years to hotlines that let employees become anonymous whistle-blowers.

While the law features a long list of mandates, a primary concern is the requirement that companies verify that their internal controls are effective. The more complex the company, the more internal controls are needed. Large global companies have hundreds of control mechanisms. An external auditor must also be paid to attest that the control check has been done adequately. The cost of the Act in total dollars falls heaviest on multinational giants, but falls disproportionately on smaller companies. Wal-Mart might spend $10 million per year to comply, but that represents a token percentage of Wal-Mart's huge sales and net income. Smaller companies are stumbling over the fact that minimum compliance costs often run in a range from $300,000 to $500,000 per year. That's a big burden for small companies. Some analysts predict that Sarbanes–Oxley compliance

costs are simply too high for companies with less than $100 million per year in annual revenues. As a result, many such companies will simply go private rather than struggle to pay prohibitive Sarbanes–Oxley compliance costs.

Unfortunately, nobody yet has a good handle on how to measure benefits from the Act. How do you estimate the value gained from increased financial transparency? What is the added value from greater investor confidence in the soundness of financial reports? How do you value more timely financial disclosure regarding sales of company stock by corporate insiders? Everyone seems to agree with the laudable aims of Sarbanes–Oxley; nobody seems able to value them precisely. Until useful estimates can be derived for the benefits gained through compliance with Sarbanes–Oxley, debate will continue concerning the law's effectiveness.

See: Deboroh Salomon, "Auditing the Auditors After Sarbanes-Oxley Audit Rules Likely to Ease," *The Wall Street Journal Online*, October 3, 2007, http://online.wsj.com.

Ownership Structure
Divergent claims on the value of the firm

Inside Equity
Common stock closely held by management and employees

Institutional Equity
Common stock held by mutual funds, pension plans, and other large investors

shifted from capital structure to **ownership structure,** as measured by **inside equity, institutional equity,** widely dispersed outside equity, bank debt, and widely dispersed outside debt. Among these, the percentage of inside equity receives the most attention. Inside equity is the share of stock closely held by the firm's CEO, other top managers, and members of the board of directors. Employees are another important source of inside equity financing, perhaps as part of an employee stock ownership plan, or ESOP. The balance of equity financing is obtained from large single-party outside shareholders, mutual funds, insurance companies, pension funds, and the general public.

When the share of insider holdings is "large," a similarly substantial self-interest in the ongoing performance of the firm can be presumed. Managers with a significant ownership interest have an obvious incentive to run the firm in a value-maximizing manner. Similarly, when ownership is concentrated among a small group of large and vocal institutional shareholders, called institutional equity, managers often have strong incentives to maximize corporate performance. When the amount of closely-held stock held is "small," and equity ownership is dispersed among a large number of small individual investors, top management can sometimes become insulated from the threat of stockholder sanctions following poor operating performance.

Table 18.2 shows insider and institutional stock ownership for a sample of large firms covered by the *Value Line Investment Survey*. These 1,300 large, publicly traded companies have an average market capitalization of $12.9 billion. The chief executive officer, other members of top management, and members of the board of directors together own an average 9.4 percent of the corporations they lead. Because insiders at the largest U.S. corporations typically own only a small percentage of the companies they lead, the median amount of inside ownership among large publicly traded companies is only 4.3 percent. In addition to inside ownership, institutions own an average 71.0 percent of these companies. The median amount of institutional ownership among such firms is 77.2 percent. Notice some double-counting in the insider and institutional holdings reported by very closely held firms because some insiders represent large institutional investors. Apart from these very closely held firms, insider holdings tend to be relatively large when institutional holdings are relatively small, and vice versa. The percentage of closely held shares, or insider plus institutional holdings, has a mean of 69.1 percent and a median of 80.2 percent. For a typical large, publicly traded company, only 20 to 30 percent of its common stock is widely dispersed among the general public.

Figure 18.4, panel *A*, depicts the percentage of insider and institutional holdings for large, publicly traded corporations. As illustrated in Figure 18.4, panel *A*, insider holdings are clearly skewed toward zero. The percentage of institutional holdings, shown in panel *B*, is more uniformly distributed. Together, concentrated insider and institutional ownership provide strong incentives for strong financial performance. Notice how the share of insider and institutional share ownership tends to vary according to firm size, even among corporate behemoths. Among true corporate giants like ExxonMobil, GE, and Citigroup, for example, insiders own little stock in their employer when insider ownership is measured on a percentage basis. For them, insider ownership is much smaller than institutional ownership. Still, insider holdings of roughly 1.0 percent at GE, for example, represent an equity commitment of $3.8 billion—more than enough to provide top management with strong incentives to operate efficiently. Thus, even though the percentage of common stock held by insiders is relatively low among corporate giants, the dollar values involved can be more than sufficient to provide necessary incentives for value maximization.

Table 18.2 Insider and Institutional Stock Ownership Among Large Companies

Company	Ticker	Market Capitalization ($ Millions)	Insider Holdings (%)	Institutional Holdings (%)	Total Concentrated Holdings (%)
A. High Market Capitalization Companies					
Exxon Mobil Corp.	XOM	461,703		53.2	53.2
Gen'l Electric	GE	378,193	1.0	60.8	61.8
Microsoft Corp.	MSFT	283,523	4.4	58.5	62.9
Citigroup Inc.	C	259,787	0.7	66.8	67.5
AT&T Inc.	T	244,431		64.9	64.9
Toyota Motor ADR	TM	222,250		3.8	3.8
Bank of America	BAC	221,021	1.0	61.1	62.1
BP PLC ADR	BP	215,201		12.4	12.4
WalMart Stores	WMT	205,559	41.0	37.9	78.9
Procter & Gamble	PG	196,241	0.5	60.1	60.6
Averages		268,791	8.1	47.9	52.8
B. High Inside Ownership Companies					
KSwiss, Inc.	KSWS	967	98.3	80.0	100.0
Telephone & Data	TDS	7,305	95.0	40.8	100.0
NIKE, Inc. 'B'	NKE	27,348	93.9	62.3	100.0
Interface Inc. 'A'	IFSIA	1,073	93.8	93.0	100.0
Genesee & Wyoming	GWR	1,231	93.2	86.8	100.0
Regeneron Pharmac.	REGN	1,196	89.2	73.7	100.0
Shaw Commun. 'B'	SJRB.TO	9,855	88.6	52.2	100.0
Skechers U.S.A.	SKX	1,389	88.4	69.2	100.0
Universal Health Sv. 'B'	UHS	3,321	85.0	89.3	100.0
Sinclair Broadcast	SBGI	1,289	85.0	51.7	100.0
Averages		5,497	91.0	69.9	100.0
C. High Institutional Ownership Companies					
Red Robin Gourmet	RRGB	675	2.8	99.5	100.0
Ambac Fin'l Group	ABK	9,288	1.6	99.9	100.0
LodgeNet Entertain.	LNET	613		99.9	99.9
CNA Fin'l	CNA	13,485		99.8	99.8
Amer. Tower 'A'	AMT	17,315	1.2	99.7	100.0
RegalBeloit	RBC	1,482	5.4	99.7	100.0
Warnaco Group	WRNC	1,597	5.2	99.7	100.0
TETRA Technologies	TTI	1,950	6.3	99.5	100.0
Valeant Pharmac.	VRX	1,554	4.6	99.5	100.0
PhillipsVan Heusen	PVH	3,289	1.9	99.5	100.0
Averages		5,125	3.6	99.7	100.0
Overall Sample Average		**12,914**	**9.4**	**71.0**	**69.1**
Overall Sample Median		**3,215**	**4.3**	**77.2**	**80.2**

Data source: *The Value Line Investment Survey for Windows*, June 17, 2007, http://www.valueline.com.

Figure 18.4 Insider and Institutional Stock Ownership Among Large U.S. Firms

Panel *A* shows that the percentage of insider holdings, or common stock held by persons or associated with the company, is strongly skewed toward zero. In panel *B*, the percentage of institutional holdings is seen as somewhat more evenly distributed than insider holdings, although moderate skewness toward zero is again evident. When the percentage of insider holdings shares and institutional holdings are added together, as in panel *C*, the distribution of ownership concentration becomes nearly normal. This suggests a substitute-type relationship between each source of ownership concentration.

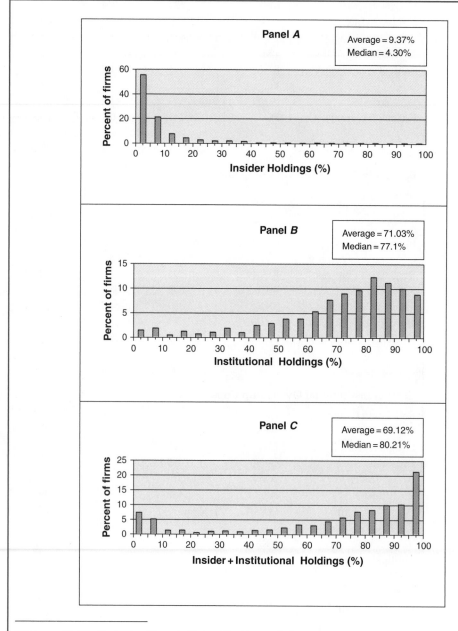

The level of independent monitoring by outside shareholders depends upon the costs and benefits such activity entails. Higher relative share ownership by institutional stockholders generally leads to greater monitoring incentives and monitoring activity. When a relatively large share of stock is held by the general public, relatively lower incentives for managerial monitoring can exist. Small investors have neither the incentive nor the resources to expend the substantial effort necessary for effective managerial monitoring. A positive relationship between ownership concentration and firm performance has been extensively documented for both the United States and abroad. Even in Japan, where corporate governance mechanisms are often thwarted by convention and government fiat, a positive relationship exists between ownership concentration and financial performance as predicted by **agency theory.**

Agency Theory
Hypothesis concerning the relationships between principals and agents, and means for resolving conflicts

Is Ownership Structure Endogenous?

Data described in Table 18.2 and in Figure 18.4 reflect a well-established trend in the United States toward replacement of small atomistic shareholders by large institutional investors. Because this trend towards institutional share ownership is relatively recent, the economic advantages it entails may be relatively unappreciated.

Clearly, the probability that outside investors will discover evidence of managerial inefficiency or malfeasance is increased when institutional ownership is substantial. Many institutional investors are forced to liquidate their holdings in the event of dividend omissions or bankruptcy filings. As a result, institutional investors are especially sensitive to such possibilities. Fiduciary responsibility also forces many institutional investors to tender their shares in the event of an above-market tender offer or takeover bid. At the same time, when institutional share ownership is high, the costs of proxy solicitations are reduced. Thus, managers of firms with high institutional ownership are relatively more susceptible to unfriendly takeover bids. Fiduciary responsibility and the dynamics of ownership concentration have the potential to make institutional stockholders especially effective in managerial monitoring.

Amenity Potential
Ownership value derived from the ability to control the type of output produced

Insider and institutional stock ownership represent alternative forms of ownership concentration that combine to form an effective method for monitoring managerial decisions. Remember, a relatively high concentration of insider *plus* institutional ownership is descriptive of the modern corporation. Economists have identified four general forces affecting corporate ownership structure, including **amenity potential, regulatory potential, quality control potential, and ownership control potential.**

Regulatory Potential
Limitation on ownership value due to government regulation or control

Amenity potential is derived from the ability to influence the type of goods produced. Such benefits can be derived from ownership of mass media and professional sports teams, for example, and explain why such endeavors tend to be tightly controlled by top management. The diffuse ownership structure of regulated utilities can be explained by extensive rate-of-return regulation, or regulatory potential, that limits the capacity of managers to influence firm performance. In the case of firms that produce easily identifiable products subject to economies of scale in production, a relatively diffuse ownership structure can be consistent with shareholder wealth maximization. In the case of firms that produce goods and services with the potential for high quality variation, or quality control potential, a more concentrated ownership structure may be required to give shareholders the control necessary to mollify suppliers and customers. Finally, the ownership control potential of the firm is the wealth gain achievable through more effective monitoring of managerial performance. Heavy advertisers and high-tech firms that depend on hard-to-monitor advertising or R&D activity for their success require

Quality Control Potential
Ownership value derived from the ability to control the quality of output

Ownership Control Potential
Ownership value achieved through more effective monitoring of managerial performance

more concentrated ownership structure. When the quality of output is hard to measure and production involves inputs with little collateral value, a high degree of ownership concentration gives outside investors, suppliers, and customers the confidence necessary for quality assurance. Taken as a whole, ownership structure appears to vary by firm size and industry in ways that are consistent with value maximization.

AGREEMENTS AND ALLIANCES AMONG FIRMS

Monitoring mechanisms outside the firm work together with mechanisms inside the firm to establish an optimal set of restrictions on corporate activity.

Franchising

Franchise Agreements
Contractual arrangements specifying a parent–subsidiary relationship

Franchise agreements are voluntary contractual arrangements outside the firm that can be viewed as corporate governance mechanisms. Franchise agreements give local companies the limited right to offer goods or services developed or advertised on a national basis. Franchise agreements are especially popular in instances where personalized customer service is crucial to success and when the performance of local managers is hard to measure over short periods of time.

Managerial Application 18.4

Institutional Investors Are Corporate Activists

Institutional investors have ready access to detailed financial information about corporate performance and are quick to sell underperforming companies. Rising dissatisfaction among institutional shareholders can lead to a rapidly falling stock price or prompt support for an unfriendly takeover bid. As a result, corporate management and boards of directors are responsive to suggestions by institutional shareholders that control a meaningful percentage of company stock. They are also listening carefully to detailed operating and strategic advice from institutional shareholders.

The Council of Institutional Investors announces an annual list of companies it says have significant performance problems. The Council's Focus List highlights 20 companies in the Standard & Poor's 500 that most underperform industry averages in 1-year, 3-year, and 5-year total shareholder returns. Separately, the California Public Employees Retirement System (CalPERS) gives companies letter grades on each board's performance in terms of corporate governance issues. As a means of applying pressure on individual members of boards of directors, CalPERS has gone so far as to publish lists naming those persons who have served most often on the boards of

underperforming companies. Such pressure tactics appear to work. Shareholder wealth tends to increase for responsive firms that adopt CalPERS suggestions; shareholder wealth decreases for unresponsive firms that reject CalPERS recommendations.

A growing role for institutional investors in corporate governance is a worldwide phenomenon. Institutional investors in Canada show an increased willingness to take on subpar management. In France, institutional investors have recently expressed their ire at bylaw changes that reduce the possibility for unfriendly takeovers. In most Italian companies, there is a major shareholder, or coalition of shareholders, who exercise majority control on the firm, and are thus able to choose and remove management. In New Zealand, Australia, and elsewhere, institutions are also becoming much more actively involved in corporate governance issues. All of this speaks well for the growing efficiency of corporate governance.

See: Craig Karmin and Shefali Anand, "Calpers Weighs a Fee Overhaul," *The Wall Street Journal Online*, June 5, 2007, http://online.wsj.com.

For example, McDonald's Corp. operates an extensive franchise system of fast-food restaurants throughout the world. Local franchise owners make a credible commitment to the company by paying for the construction of local restaurants and undergoing extensive training at "Hamburger University," as McDonald's likes to call its Oak Brook, Illinois, training facility. In turn, McDonald's makes a credible commitment by awarding local franchisees exclusive rights to market McDonald's food in a given trade area. In this way, McDonald's can be assured that local outlets will be run effectively, and local franchisees have the assurance that McDonald's will continue its aggressive advertising and franchise development programs. Both parties hold viable threats over the other. The valuable right to sell McDonald's food products can be taken away from local franchisees if food quality or store cleanliness falters. Local managers could choose to withhold their support for corporate marketing and pricing policies if they deem that insufficient support has been provided for local markets.

In addition to the fast-food business, franchise agreements are common in the automotive repair business. In automotive repair, performance is hard to measure because shoddy repair service shows up only over long periods of time. The quality assurance offered to repair service customers improves when local managers have an owner's incentive to stand behind work quality. Similarly, franchise agreements give local managers an owner's incentive to develop the economic potential of local markets. Like the local customers of gas and service stations, car buyers benefit from a network of new car dealers who promote and stand behind the quality of products produced by Ford, GM, Toyota, and other major automobile manufacturers. Without an owner's incentive to build and maintain customer loyalty, the new car business would suffer from many of the same problems that have dogged the used-car business for decades.

Strategic Alliances

Strategic Alliances
Operating agreements among independent companies

Strategic alliances are formal operating agreements between independent companies that can be viewed as corporate governance mechanisms. Such combinations are increasingly used to improve foreign marketing. Equity joint ventures are often preferred to contracts when cultural differences between partner firms are great, and when alliances involve upstream rather than downstream value chain activities. Contracts are preferred to equity joint ventures in cross-industry alliances and when technological intensity is high.

Cereal Partners Worldwide, a strategic alliance between General Mills, Inc., and Nestlè, is used to market breakfast cereal products. Snack Food Ventures Europe, a partnership between General Mills and Pepsico, markets snack foods in Belgium, France, Holland, Spain, Portugal, and Greece. A proposed alliance between British Airways and American Airlines was abandoned after serious antitrust concerns were raised because such an arrangement has the potential to allow the companies to squeeze out competition and dominate the lucrative U.S.–London travel market.

Cisco Systems, Inc., is one of the most aggressive proponents of corporate strategic alliances. At Cisco, strategic alliances are designed to help deliver a customer-centric, total solutions approach to solving problems. Cisco and its partners have found strategic alliances to be an effective means for exploiting business opportunities and creating sustainable competitive advantages for its customers. For example, IBM Global Services and Cisco Systems have a strategic alliance to deploy networking applications and jointly create e-business solutions. The IBM–Cisco strategic alliance is helping businesses successfully migrate to an Internet infrastructure and create higher levels of customer satisfaction. In another alliance, Hewlett-Packard and Cisco are collaborating to deliver network-enabled solutions that allow new and joint customers to optimize and reduce network complexity.

Strategic alliances also arise when participating companies enjoy complementary capabilities. For example, Oracle Corp. develops, manufactures, and distributes computer software that helps corporations manage and grow their businesses. Oracle systems software is used to deploy applications on the Internet and corporate intranets. In a collaborative alliance, Oracle and Cisco, a networking equipment supplier, have agreed to develop network-enhanced database technology and enterprise applications. Another longtime proponent of strategic alliances is TRW Inc., a global manufacturing and services company focused on supplying advanced technology. TRW strategic alliances produce automotive occupant safety systems, chassis systems, electronics, and engine components for spacecraft and space communications, defense systems, telecommunications products, information technology, public safety systems, and other complex integrated systems.

The growing popularity of strategic alliances follows recognition that competition is shifting from a "firm versus firm perspective" to a "supply chain versus supply chain perspective." Corporations are increasingly seeking competitive advantage through cooperative supply chain arrangements because such strategic alliances allow companies to quickly combine individual strengths and unique resources.

LEGAL AND ETHICAL ENVIRONMENT

Misdeeds by a handful of corporations have unleashed a torrent of economic sanctions from state and federal regulators.

Sarbanes–Oxley Act

Sarbanes–Oxley Act
Law that regulates governance and reporting obligations for public companies

Guarding against the exploitation of investors has long been at the heart of broad regulatory initiatives in the United States, such as establishment of the Securities and Exchange Commission (SEC) in 1934. Congress established the SEC to enforce newly passed securities laws, promote stability in the markets, and, most importantly, protect investors. In 2002, heightened public concerns with corporate wrongdoing led to passage of the **Sarbanes–Oxley Act,** the most dramatic change to U.S. securities laws in 70 years.

Sarbanes–Oxley radically redesigns federal regulation of corporate governance and corporate reporting obligations. It also significantly tightens accountability standards for directors and officers, auditors, securities analysts, and legal counsel. Corporate audit committees must now comply with a new list of requirements affecting auditor appointment, compensation, and oversight. Each company must disclose current information about the company's financial condition, and the audit committee appointed by the board of directors must consist solely of independent directors. CEOs and CFOs also must personally certify that corporate financial reports fully comply with SEC requirements and fairly represents the company's financial condition and operating results. Sarbanes–Oxley also tightens regulations concerning personal financial dealings between top managers and their companies. Now, public companies can only make personal loans to executive officers or directors under very limited circumstances, and insider trading in company securities must be reported within two business days. The Act creates several new crimes for securities violations: destroying, altering, or falsifying records with the intent to impede or influence any federal investigation or bankruptcy proceeding; willful failure by an accountant to maintain all audit or work papers for 5 years; and executing a scheme to defraud investors in connection with any security.

Calculated or inadvertent violations of securities laws have the potential to impose significant costs on investors, employees, and other corporate stakeholders. The pursuit of illegal short-term strategies is a form of self-dealing by managers who seek short-term personal gain while escaping detection. Actual or suspected violations of securities laws have the potential to result in significant costs measured in terms of investigation expenditures, litigation expenses, fines and seizures, and lost **reputation capital** for the firm—all of which can measurably reduce future cash flows and current market values. Within this context, securities laws can be seen as part of the institutional framework that contributes to the range of control mechanisms that originate outside the firm to comprise an effective system of corporate governance. Because short-term "hit and run" managers may possess incentives to "cut" legal and ethical corners, the design and administration of securities laws is a means of outside monitoring designed to ensure a coincidence of managerial incentives, stockholder interests, and broader social objectives.

Reputation Capital
Economic value derived from a good name and prominence

Business Ethics

Business Ethics
Moral standards in business

Economic theory and methodology offer an important insight into **business ethics** issues on at least three basic dimensions. First, economics provides a theory of how individuals make choices, including choices with ethical dimensions. Second, business ethics and the structure of the organization together establish an important context for corporate behavior. Third, a corporation's reputation for ethical behavior is part of the company's brand-name capital. As such, it is reflected in the value of company securities.

Some might argue that if a company's competitors adopt low ethical standards, it would be unprofitable for the firm to adopt high ethical standards. Economic theory and methodology document that this presumption is plainly incorrect. Potential customers reduce the prices they are willing to pay where there is significant uncertainty about the quality of the product to be supplied. By credibly promising to act in an ethical manner, a firm can differentiate its products and increase demand, possibly by a substantial amount. Similarly, bondholders and stockholders make their cost of capital calculations in light of the company's ongoing reputation for fair dealing. High-quality firms enjoy a relatively lower cost of capital as one of the many benefits tied to their reputation for fair dealing. Low-quality firms can expect a relatively higher cost of capital and higher supplier costs generally as typical disadvantages tied to their poor reputation.

Ethical considerations are one of the many important concerns that must be effectively addressed through the corporate governance process. Costly breakdowns in business ethics, like any costly breakdown in firm operations, reflect important failures of the firm's corporate governance system.

SUMMARY

Questions of what and how to produce become equally important as organizations strive to better serve demanding customers. The design and control of effective organizations have become an integral part of managerial economics.

- **Organization structure** is described by the vertical and horizontal relationships among the firm, its customers, and suppliers. A **vertical relation** is a

business connection between companies at *different* points along the production-distribution chain; a **horizontal relation** is a business affiliation between companies at the *same* point along the production-distribution chain.

- The efficiency of firms depends upon the ability of participants to find an effective means to minimize the **transaction costs** of coordinating productive activity. Search or **information costs** encompass expenses encountered in discovering the type and quality of goods and services demanded by consumers. Bargaining or **decision costs** include expenditures involved with successfully negotiating production agreements. Policing or **enforcement costs** include charges necessary to make sure that all parties live up to their contractual commitments.

- According to the **Coase Theorem**, resource allocation will be efficient so long as transaction costs remain low and property rights can be freely assigned and exchanged.

- The **agency problem** is the natural conflict between owners and managers. **Agency costs** are explicit and implicit transaction costs necessary to overcome any divergence of interest between agent managers and principal stockholders. Significant differences in the risk exposure of managers and stockholders lead to an **excessive risk-taking problem**. This and other examples of the **other people's money problem** arise when decision makers control resources that they do not own. To combat shortsighted operating and investment decisions, the **managerial myopia problem**, most corporations tie a significant portion of total compensation for top management to long-term performance. The **board of directors** is the group of people legally charged with the responsibility for governing a corporation. To guard against the **end-of-game problem**, corporations also set long-term goals for senior managers.

- The **information asymmetry problem** is tied to management's inherently superior access to information inside the firm. By definition, **insiders** know more than outsiders about the firm's performance, prospects, and opportunities. Incentive pay plans linked to accounting performance offer incentives for efficient operating and financial decisions, and inducements for **accounting earnings manipulation** and bias. Managers have incentives for **income inflation** when higher reported earnings boost compensation, provide greater job security, or both. Incentives exist for **income smoothing** to

the extent that spectacular short-run performance creates expectations that are difficult or impossible to satisfy and, therefore, lead to stockholder disappointment and sanctions.

- The value-maximizing **organization design** minimizes unproductive conflict within the firm. An effective organization design is one that allocates **decision authority** to that person or team best able to perform a given task. With **centralized decision authority**, detailed judgments are handled by top-line executives. With **decentralized decision authority**, front-line employees are empowered to make fundamental judgments concerning how to best serve customers. A **flat organization** has only one or very few levels of decision-making authority. A **vertical organization** features multiple ascending levels of decision-making authority.

- At its most basic level, the production process encompasses a sequence of related **tasks**, or assignments necessary to effectively meet customer needs. In turn, related tasks are bundled into **jobs**, when such packaging facilitates cost savings and a more productive use of firm resources. The word **team** refers to worker groups given shared responsibility for making and distributing products.

- **Decision management** is the vital process of generating, choosing, and implementing management decisions. **Decision control** is the essential process of assessing how well the decision management process functions. Decisions are made on the basis of **economic expectations**, or a reasonable before-the-fact forecast of monetary implications; judging past decisions involves more than a simple after-the-fact analysis of **economic realizations**, or financial outcomes.

- **Corporate governance** is the system of controls that helps a corporation effectively manage, administer, and direct economic resources. **Corporate stakeholders** include stockholders, customers, employees, the community at large, and everyone who has an economic interest in the corporation. **Ownership structure** is the array of divergent claims on the value of the firm. **Inside equity** is the share of stock closely held by the firm's managers, directors, and employees. When ownership is concentrated among insiders or a small group of large and vocal institutional shareholders, called **institutional equity**, managers often have strong incentives to maximize corporate performance. A number of studies show important advantages tied to high ownership concentration as predicted by **agency theory**.

- The ownership structure of corporations is sensitive to economic influences like **amenity potential**, or the ability to influence the type of products produced. Such benefits explain why mass media and professional sports teams tend to be tightly controlled by top management. Diffuse ownership structures are common for utilities because their **regulatory potential** limits the capacity of managers to influence firm performance. In the case of firms that produce goods and services with the potential for high quality variation, or **quality control potential**, a more concentrated ownership structure may be required to give shareholders the amount of control necessary to mollify other suppliers and customers. Finally, the **ownership control potential** of the firm is the wealth gain achievable through more effective monitoring of managerial performance.

- **Franchise agreements** are a prime example of voluntary contractual arrangements outside the firm that can be viewed as corporate governance mechanisms. **Strategic alliances** are formal operating agreements between independent companies that also can be viewed as corporate governance mechanisms.

- The **Sarbanes–Oxley Act** represents the most dramatic change to federal securities laws since the 1930s. Sarbanes–Oxley radically redesigns federal regulation of corporate governance and reporting obligations. Actual or suspected violations of securities laws have the potential to result in significant costs measured in terms of investigation expenditures, litigation expenses, fines and seizures, and lost **reputation capital** for the firm—all of which can measurably reduce future cash flows and the market value of the firm. Because short-term "hit and run" managers possess value-reducing incentives to "cut" legal and ethical corners, economic theory and methodology offer an important insight into **business ethics**.

QUESTIONS

Q18.1 Describe the difference between vertical and horizontal business relationships.

Q18.2 The personal computer has evolved from a tool for computation to an Internet-centered communications device. Is this likely to change corporate structures by increasing the efficiency of smaller, more nimble corporations?

Q18.3 Cite three important categories of transaction costs encountered within the firm, and give some examples.

Q18.4 What is the Coase Theorem, and why is it important in managerial economics?

Q18.5 In a typical corporation, who are the "principals" and who are the "agents"? What is the firm's agency problem?

Q18.6 Executive stock options are often seen as a simple and effective solution to the "other people's money" problem that can occur when managers with little ownership interest mismanage firm investment opportunities. Can you foresee any advantages and/or potential pitfalls to the use of executive stock options for this purpose?

Q18.7 What are agency costs? Describe some agency costs common among U.S. corporations.

Q18.8 Describe three basic needs that must be met in the design of any organization.

Q18.9 Discuss important differences between centralized and decentralized allocations of decision authority within an organization. Are these methods of decision authority allocation mutually exclusive?

Q18.10 Describe four essential components of an effective decision management and control system.

SELF-TEST PROBLEMS AND SOLUTIONS

ST18.1   Agency Problem.   In the 1930s, economists Adolf A. Berle and Gardiner C. Means expressed concern that managers with relatively little ownership interest might demonstrate a suboptimal focus on transitory short-term profits rather than on durable long-run value. Berle and Means also voiced concern for value-reducing risk avoidance on the part of management-controlled firms.

A. In general, describe the "agency problem" referred to by Berle and Means. Then, specifically describe how inefficient risk avoidance by top managers could be a problem.

B. What corporate governance mechanisms are commonly employed to combat the agency problems feared by Berle and Means?

ST18.1   SOLUTION

A. So-called agency problems stem from the natural conflict that exists between owners and managers. Given their ownership position, stockholders are the principals of the firm. Managers and other employees without any ownership interest can be thought of as hired hands, or agents of the stockholders. An agency problem is present to the extent that unresolved material conflicts exist between the self-seeking goals of (agent) managers and the value maximization goal of (principal) stockholders. Agency costs are the explicit and implicit transaction costs necessary to overcome the natural divergence of interest between agent managers and principal stockholders. Agency costs incurred by stockholders are reflected in expenses for managerial monitoring, the overconsumption of perquisites by managers, lost opportunities due to excessive risk avoidance, and so on.

   Managers have incentives for risk avoidance to the extent that spectacular short-run performance creates expectations that are difficult or impossible to satisfy and, therefore, lead to stockholder disappointment and sanctions. Incentives for managerial risk avoidance are also present if stockholder risk aversion leads to an asymmetry of managerial rewards and penalties following short-term "success" versus "failure."

B. Although the potential for such a managerial risk-avoidance problem clearly exists, long-term performance plans are employed on a widespread basis to force a convergence between managerial and stockholder interests. Some of these plans tie executive and employee pay to well-defined accounting performance measures, like the accounting return on equity or return on assets over extended periods. Others tie managerial rewards to long-term stock performance over, say, 5- to 10-year time intervals. Finally, executive stock option or stock ownership plans are an effective means of tying managerial incentives to the shareholder's preferred value maximization objective.

ST18.2   Ownership Structure.   Both General Electric and Microsoft Corp. feature charismatic and highly effective chief executive officers, display enviable records of serving growing markets with remarkable efficiency, and enjoy sterling accounting returns and stock market valuations. GE and Microsoft are also huge organizations that rank near the top in stock market valuation among U.S. companies. Interestingly, both feature significant institutional ownership, but are starkly different in terms of the amount of common stock held by insiders.

At GE, insider holding totals a mere 1 percent, about average among industrial giants. At Microsoft, insiders hold an astounding 4.4 percent of the company.

A. What economic differences in the products produced by GE and Microsoft could be used to explain such stark differences in ownership structure?

B. Legend has it that IBM turned down a chance to buy 50 percent of Microsoft for $50 million in the early 1980s. Was this a mistake on IBM's part?

ST18.2 SOLUTION

A. GE is a widely diversified manufacturer that produces a extensive variety of products in a broad array of industries. Many of GE's products are well known by long-satisfied customers and produced at standard production facilities in the United States. GE's operating facilities have good loan collateral value, and the company uses extensive financial leverage. Many outside investors find it easy to assess the financial performance and prospects of GE and have been eager to supply outside equity financing. As a result, it is easy to see why GE has been able to flourish despite having little of its huge capital needs supplied by insiders.

In contrast, Microsoft produces PC software and services that are hard to fathom for most customers, lenders, and outside suppliers of equity. Microsoft uses little in the way of traditional capital resources; most of the capital employed by Microsoft is human capital, not physical plant and equipment. When intangible assets such as patents, copyrights, and trademarks form the preponderance of firm resources, outside investors tend to be reluctant to supply the bulk of firm financing. Without clear loan collateral value, lenders back away from extending significant amounts of credit. Because the value of patents, copyrights, and trademarks is often closely tied to managerial efficiency, outside investors can also be reluctant to supply equity financing. Because Microsoft's success depends upon the efficiency with which its human capital is exploited, both lenders and outside suppliers of equity demand that the company feature a significant amount of inside equity financing so that insiders have a strong incentive to maximize the value of the firm.

B. With 20/20 hindsight, it is easy to say that IBM blew it by not purchasing 50 percent of Microsoft for $50 million in the early 1980s. After all, with a total market capitalization in excess of $275 billion for Microsoft today, IBM would have achieved an enormous windfall from such an investment. (We all made a mistake by not buying MSFT stock when it was first offered to the general public on March 13, 1986.)

However, it is not appropriate to evaluate this decision with the benefits of 20/20 hindsight. Back in the 1980s, it was not clear that bringing the graphical user interface of the Apple Computer to IBM-compatible PCs would be such an amazing success story. Before the fact, much of the unrealized value potential of Microsoft was tied up in the dreams and imagination of Bill Gates, Paul Allen, and a cadre of hardworking computer "geeks." If IBM had purchased 50 percent of Microsoft, would they all have worked as hard to make Microsoft a success? Maybe yes, maybe no. In the case of Microsoft, Coca-Cola, Intel, and other companies with significant intangible assets, investors and lenders require high levels of inside equity financing as a signal of the credible commitment by insiders to maximize the value of the firm.

PROBLEMS

P18.1 **Organization Structure.** Determine whether each of the following statements is true or false. Explain why.

A. A vertical relation is a business connection between companies at the same point along the production-distribution chain.

B. A work slowdown due to an unexpected strike by unionized workers is a type of decision cost.

C. A merger between rival retailers Wal-Mart and Target would be horizontal in nature.

D. When a corporation files for bankruptcy, it is an admission that the organization was unable to minimize transaction costs.

E. Because the Internet allows customers to lower information costs, it will have the obvious long-run effect of reducing costs and boosting corporate profits.

P18.2 **Agency Costs.** Indicate whether each of the following transaction costs is explicit or implicit, and describe how it is a manifestation of a particular type of agency problem.

A. A trader at an investment banking firm loses millions of corporate dollars through unsuccessful rank speculation.

B. A manager fails to achieve optimum efficiency by letting past-due accounts languish unpaid.

C. Senior executives decline value-increasing investment projects in order to make cash flow targets during the last year of employment.

D. Value-increasing product development projects are postponed in order to boost near-term accounting performance.

E. Executives manipulate accounting data to boost managerial compensation by placing dismal operating performance in a better light.

P18.3 **Ownership Structure.** Describe each of the following factors as being responsible for increasing, decreasing, or having no effect on the amount of concentrated inside equity. Explain why.

A. High research and development expenditure requirements

B. A corporate history of poor operating performance

C. High levels of brand-name recognition

D. Intense news coverage of corporate activities

E. Imposition of rate of return regulation

P18.4 Other People's Money Problem. In 2002, Congress held hearings to investigate the collapse of Houston-based energy giant Enron Corp., aiming to discover how to protect against similar disasters. The spectacular implosion of Enron led to the largest corporate bankruptcy in U.S. history and billions of dollars in losses for investors in the company's debt and equity securities. According to a 217-page report from a panel of Enron's independent directors, Enron's former CFO Andrew Fastow and former chief executive Jeffrey Skilling devised a complex scheme involving limited partnership arrangements that allowed some of the company's top executives to take millions of dollars "they should never have received." The document also revealed that Enron's former chief executive and chairman Kenneth Lay personally approved partnership arrangements that led to enormous liabilities being kept off of Enron's balance sheet, thereby misleading investors as to the company's financial soundness. Enron's collapse was not only scrutinized by more than a dozen Congressional committees, but it also became the subject of a criminal investigation by the U.S. Department of Justice.

A. Explain how the Enron fiasco can be seen as a manifestation of the other people's money problem.

B. How could it have been avoided?

P18.5 Coase Theorem. According to the Coase Theorem, resource allocation will be efficient so long as transaction costs remain low and property rights can be freely assigned and exchanged.

A. Does the Coase Theorem imply that government has little if any role to play in the market economy? Explain.

B. According to the Coase Theorem, are efficient and equitable economic outcomes assured? Explain.

P18.6 Decision Authority. At the end of World War II, goods production and services provision were each responsible for roughly one-half of economic activity and total employment in the United States. Today, the provision of services is responsible for roughly two-thirds of employment and three-quarters of total employment.

A. Can you explain the decline of centralized decision authority and the emergence of the "flat" organization style, as a natural result of these trends in aggregate economic activity and employment?

B. Is the emerging use of personal computers as Internet-centered communications devices likely to favor flat organization? Why or why not?

P18.7 Sarbanes–Oxley Act. The Sarbanes–Oxley Act, named for sponsors Sen. Paul Sarbanes, D-Md., and Rep. Michael Oxley, R-Ohio, is the most sweeping law affecting corporations since the 1930s. It is having a dramatic effect on the costs companies pay for independent audits of the financial numbers reported to the outside world. In many cases, companies now pay double historical auditing costs to get auditors to attest that all corporate internal controls have been checked and given their seal of approval. This is a big change for companies that have long accepted internal controls that are less than perfect, and for good reason. A company could eliminate padded travel expenses if it wanted to hire a small army in accounting to verify every taxicab receipt. However, such detailed oversight would often cost much more than direct savings. Critics of traditional failures in corporate governance point out that internal control has an importance beyond that of simply catching the occasional fraud. By going through the effort of complying with Sarbanes–Oxley, many companies are unearthing operating inefficiencies.

A. Critics of Sarbanes–Oxley contend that the act results in excessive compliance costs. Explain why risk-adverse corporate management may be overstating such costs.

B. Supporters of Sarbanes–Oxley argue that the act will produce significant net benefits as corporations improve both the transparency and accuracy of financial reporting. Describe some of the improvements in management efficiency that might be spurred by corporate compliance with Sarbanes–Oxley.

P18.8   Information Asymmetry Problem.   Shareholders face a daunting information asymmetry problem when it comes to measuring the performance of the CEO. As head of the corporation, the CEO is in charge of the firm's management information system. Accounting methods always leave room for managerial interpretation, and this flexibility can and has been used to understate expenses and inflate reported earnings. When CEO compensation is tied to various accounting performance targets, it is a bit like asking students to fill out their own final grade report. At a minimum, shareholders should not be surprised when accounting data place firm and managerial performance in a favorable light. Shareholders must take steps to guard against significant manipulation of accounting standards and/or accounting bias that results in a meaningful distortion of accounting performance.

A. What pitfalls are faced by independent auditors and boards of directors in their efforts to maintain the firm's accounting statements as independent and unbiased indicators of firm and managerial performance?

B. What corporate governance mechanisms might be used to guard against the manipulation of the firm's accounting statements?

P18.9   Executive Stock Options.   Warren Buffett, the chairman and CEO of Berkshire Hathaway, Inc., is an outspoken critic of executive stock option plans, at least as they are commonly employed. In a typical stock option plan, top executives are given the right to buy company stock at the current price for a period of up to 10 years in length. Such options have obvious economic value given the 10+percent long-run rate of return on common stocks. Nevertheless, the costs of executive stock option–based compensation are typically not reflected in the company's income statement.

A. Explain how the failure to include stock option–based compensation costs in the firm's income statement could lead to a type of information asymmetry problem.

B. How could the potential for such a problem be avoided? In other words, how would you design an effective executive stock option–based compensation plan?

P18.10   Institutional Stock Ownership.   During the amazing bull market of the 1990s, an investment strategy of simply mimicking the Standard & Poor's 500 Index became popular. The S&P 500 is a value-weighted market index of 500 common stocks thought to measure overall movement in the aggregate stock market. Under this investment strategy, the amount invested in each stock is proportionate to each component's share of the total market valuation of all 500 companies. If the largest component, ExxonMobil, accounts for roughly 3.4 percent of the index, and the second largest component, GE, accounts for roughly 2.8 percent, index followers simply invest 3.4 percent of their portfolio in ExxonMobil, 2.8 percent in GE, and so on.

A. Explain how the stock market's ability to discipline the managers of underperforming firms could be reduced if all investors simply purchased index funds that mimicked the S&P 500.

B. Explain how institutional investors, even those with index funds, actually discipline the managers of underperforming firms in practice.

CASE *Study*

Do Boards of Directors Make Good Corporate Watchdogs?

Is the large publicly traded corporation in eclipse? Some say yes. Harvard financial economist Michael Jensen, for example, argues that the experience of the past two decades indicates that corporate internal control systems have failed to deal effectively with economic changes, especially slow growth and the requirement for exit from declining industries. In some parts of the economy, new and smaller organizations are emerging to take the place of giant corporations. Although corporate in form, these agile organizations eschew public shareholders. Their major source of capital is public and private debt rather than publicly traded equity. In analyzing the late 1980s trend toward leveraged buyouts (LBOs), Jensen observed that LBOs differ from publicly held conglomerates in at least four important respects: management incentives are closely tied to performance, decentralization is common, a heavy reliance on leverage is typical, and obligations to creditors and residual claimants are clearly specified. In suggesting ways for public corporations to "heal" themselves, Jensen advised that public companies should become more like LBOs by decentralizing, borrowing to repurchase stock or pay large dividends, or increasing equity ownership among corporate directors, managers, and other employees.

Of course, given recent experience, it is quite valid to express concern with respect to the adaptive capability of some large corporations. Still, pronouncements on the "death" of the modern corporation may be premature. The corporate form has endured because it is a useful and effective means for gathering and deploying economic resources. Questions about corporate effectiveness are ultimately about what is referred to as "corporate governance." Corporate governance is the system of controls that helps the corporation effectively manage, administer, and direct economic resources.

Problems in corporate governance exist to the extent that unresolved material conflicts endure between the self-seeking goals of (agent) managers and the value maximization goal of (principal) stockholders. "Agency costs" incurred by stockholders are reflected in expenses for managerial monitoring, the overconsumption of perquisites by managers, and lost opportunities due to excessive risk avoidance. Although this agency cost characterization of the corporate governance issue is fairly recent, modern concern with the topic began more than 60 years ago when Berle and Means predicted that managers with little direct ownership interest, and thus having "own" rather than stockholder interests in mind would come to run the bulk

continued

of U.S. business enterprise. Interestingly, economists' concern with this "other people's money" problem dates from 1776 and the work of Adam Smith. One of the most important corporate governance mechanisms is a board of directors that is focused and motivated to further shareholder interests. Within this context, a relevant question is, "Do company boards of directors make good corporate watchdogs?" Perhaps the best way to answer this question is to look at some evidence.

Hiring the right chief executive officer is widely viewed as a board of director's most difficult task. However, firing a deficient CEO can be even more important because board negligence can leave a company permanently impaired. Dismissing an underperforming CEO is tough because it constitutes an implicit concession that the board failed to hire an executive that was up to the task. Indeed, researchers have found that turnover among directors after the dismissal of a CEO is higher than after a normal CEO succession. Still, faced with rapidly deteriorating corporate performance, boards sometime have no alternative but to seek new leadership.

Nowhere has the management turnstile been spinning faster than at high-tech giant Hewlett-Packard (H-P). When Hewlett-Packard merged with Compaq Computer in 2003, one of the many arguments for the deal was that the combination would benefit from a deeper pool of top managerial talent. However, top management from Compaq didn't last long on H-P CEO Carly Fiorina's team. Michael Capellas, who had been CEO of Compaq, quickly left H-P to try and salvage bankrupt telecom giant MCI. Jeff Clarke, who had been Compaq's CFO, also quit suddenly, apparently without another job lined up. Capellas' departure from H-P was understandable, if not predictable. There is seldom room for two supersized egos in any executive suite, and mergers are often followed by an exit for the acquired firm's CEO. The exit

of a highly regarded and effective CFO is more rare. Clarke stayed with H-P longer than his former boss Capellas, and is widely credited with helping his new boss Fiorina complete a critical integration of the computer maker's Compaq operations in Houston, Texas, with the H-P operation in Palo Alto, California. Clarke's financial and operating prowess was credited with helping achieve $3.5 billion in cost savings from the merger, and he was expected to play a significant role in the "new" H-P.

Within a year after leaving H-P, both Capellas and Clarke were working hard to overcome a history of accounting fraud at new and troubled employers. Capellas faced the herculean task of successfully dealing with creditors and customers to bring MCI out of bankruptcy, and Clarke was named chief operating officer of embattled software giant Computer Associates, which was being investigated by the SEC for cooking the books. Computer Associates CEO Sanjay Kumar stepped down under pressure in April 2004. As the Computer Associates board began its search for a new CEO, shareholder activists called for an outsider to come in and clean up the mess.

In many other instances, shareholder-led boardroom revolts have led to dramatically improved performance for trimmed down and refocused corporate giants. After such stunning success in improving management strategy and operating performance, stockholders and stockholder groups have finally gotten the attention they deserve from refocused and energized corporate boards of directors. As shown in Table 18.3, some of the best corporate boards have clearly gotten the message; some of the worst corporate boards still have much to learn.

A. Does incompetence by top management and corporate boards of directors invalidate the value maximization theory of the firm?

B. Many shareholder groups prefer to split the chairman and CEO posts, and install

continued

Table 18.3 10 of the Best and 10 of the Worst Boards of Directors

<u>10 Top Boards of Directors</u>

Company	Details
Campbell Soup	Board ties pay with performance for top management and the board itself.
Cisco Systems	Small and nimble board represents shareholder interests effectively in a rapidly changing industry.
General Electric Co.	Board reads like a business hall of fame; both inside and outside directors hold millions of dollars in GE stock.
Home Depot	Board members are required to get out and "kick the tires" as they visit the stores.
IBM	Blue chip board gets high marks for independence and accountability.
Intel	Business savvy and independent board boosts shareholder interests.
Johnson & Johnson	Board members are widely recognized for business expertise; company sets the standard for board independence and accountability.
Legg Mason, Inc.	Strong board has dealt decisively with mutual fund industry turmoil; supported value-enhancing merger policy.
Merck	Outsiders dominate this action-oriented board.
Texas Instruments	Industry smarts, mandated TI shareholding, and independence make for a shareholder-motivated board.

<u>**Worst Boards of Directors**</u>

Company	Details
Archer Daniels Midland	Company has the dubious distinction of consistently failing to heed shareholder interests; nepotism and cronyism run rampant.
Bally Total Fitness Holding Corp.	Board put this Chicago health-club operator (and bankruptcy candidate) deep into debt.
Bank of America	Big mergers have created a board that is too big and unwieldy to effectively look after shareholder interests.
Brocade Communications Systems Inc.	Paid $7 million SEC penalty for improper stock-option grants.
Dillards Department Stores	Dillard family rules the roost and has stood idly by while the fox ravaged the chicken coop.
El Paso Corp.	"Good ole boys" fiddled while management bungled mergers, overstated reserves, and wasted million on failed energy trading.
General Motors	The board has sat idly by while management focuses on financial engineering rather than on designing high-quality cars that customers like to drive.
The Walt Disney Co.	Board reads like a who's who of Hollywood celebrities; too bad so few have the business expertise to ensure shareholder-motivated decision making.
UnitedHealth Group, Inc.	Poster child for excessive CEO compensation, stock option abuse.
Waste Management	Insider trading questions hampered the company's "roll-up" merger strategy.

continued

an outsider as chairman of the board of directors. From the shareholder viewpoint, discuss some of the advantages and disadvantages of an "outside" chairman.

C. Shareholders often want change when corporate performance is poor, top executive pay is excessive, and/or management is unresponsive. However, removing corporate directors by shareholder vote remains almost impossible. In annual proxy contests, shareholders are generally offered only one slate of candidates, and they can express their dissatisfaction only by withholding votes from would-be board members. Does this mean that the current shareholder voting process is an ineffectual means of corporate control? How might this process be improved?

D. In addition to casting their vote in annual proxy contests, shareholders "vote with their feet" when they sell the stock of poorly performing companies. How is this likely to influence inferior performance by top management and the board of directors?

SELECTED REFERENCES

Alevy, Jonathan E., Michael S. Haigh, and John A. List. "Information Cascades: Evidence from a Field Experiment with Financial Market Professionals." *Journal of Finance* 62, no. 1 (February, 2007): 151–180.

Allcott, Hunt, Dean Karlan, Markus M. Mobius, Tanya S. Rosenblat, and Adam Szeidl. "Community Size and Network Closure." *American Economic Review* 97, no. 2 (May, 2007): 80–85.

Bennedsen, Morten, Kasper Meisner Nielsen, Francisco Perez Gonzalez, and Daniel Wolfenzon. "Inside the Family Firm: The Role of Families in Succession Decisions and Performance." *Quarterly Journal of Economics* 122, no. 2 (May, 2007): 647–691.

Benou, Georgina, Kimberly C. Gleason, and Jeff Madura. "Impact of Visibility and Investment Advisor Credibility on the Valuation Effects of High-Tech Cross-Border Acquisitions." *Financial Management* 36, no. 1 (Spring, 2007): 69–89.

Bergman, Nittai K. and Daniel Nicolaievsky. "Investor Protection and the Coasian View." *Journal of Financial Economics* 84, no. 3 (June, 2007): 738–771.

Bergstrom, Theodore C. "Some Evolutionary Economics of Family Partnerships." *American Economic Review* 97, no. 2 (May, 2007): 482–486.

Bernard, Andrew B. and J. Bradford Jensen. "Firm Structure, Multinationals, and Manufacturing Plant Deaths." *Review of Economics and Statistics* 89, no. 2 (May, 2007): 193–204.

Boone, Audra L. and J. Harold Mulherin. "How Are Firms Sold?" *Journal of Finance* 62, no. 2 (April, 2007): 847–875.

Calvo Armengol, Antoni and Joan de Marti. "Communication Networks: Knowledge and Decisions." *American Economic Review* 97, no. 2 (May, 2007): 86–91.

Cochet, Olivier and Thomas Ehrmann. "Preliminary Evidence on the Appointment of Institutional Solutions to Franchisor Moral Hazard—the Case of Franchisee Councils." *Managerial and Decision Economics* 28, no. 1 (January, 2007): 41–55.

Kale, Jayant R. and Husayn Shahrur. "Corporate Capital Structure and the Characteristics of Suppliers and Customers." *Journal of Financial Economics* 83, no. 2 (February, 2007): 321–365.

Leland, Hayne E. "Financial Synergies and the Optimal Scope of the Firm: Implications for Mergers, Spinoffs, and Structured Finance." *Journal of Finance* 62, no. 2 (April, 2007): 765–807.

Lerner, Josh, Antoinette Schoar, and Wan Wongsunwai. "Smart Institutions, Foolish Choices: The Limited Partner Performance Puzzle." *Journal of Finance* 62, no. 2 (April, 2007): 731–764.

Prendergast, Canice. "The Motivation and Bias of Bureaucrats." *American Economic Review* 97, no. 1 (March, 2007): 180–196.

Rajan, Raghuram and Arvind Subramanian. "Does Aid Affect Governance?" *American Economic Review* 97, no. 2 (May, 2007): 322–327.

Government in the Market Economy

In 1776, economist Adam Smith wrote that the "invisible hand" of the marketplace leads the self-interest of buyers and sellers to maximize the social benefits. More than 200 years of economic experience has proven the wisdom of Smith's invisible hand metaphor. In many cases, competitive markets provide a simple and useful mechanism for governing the production and allocation of economic resources. At the same time, economic experience documents that unregulated market activity can sometimes lead to inefficiency and waste.

In some instances, production or consumption activity leads to the production of significant ancillary products with negative consequences for third parties. These third parties are forced to bear some of the costs tied to products enjoyed by others. At the same time, production or consumption activity sometimes leads to positive consequences for third parties. In both cases, inefficiency and waste occur because some of the costs or benefits tied to production and consumption are not fully reflected in market prices. In such instances, economists have found that the careful "visible hand" of government policy can be used to improve upon the outcomes of unregulated competitive markets. Similarly, government policy can be used to improve economic efficiency when markets are faced with the problems of allocating supply and demand for goods with essentially public aspects of consumption and/or production.[1]

Wise government policies have the capacity to balance private and public interests and lay a better foundation for economic growth and a healthy environment.

EXTERNALITIES

An externality arises when economic activity among producers and consumers influences the well-being of a third-party who is neither compensated for damages nor pays for benefits.

Negative Externalities

Negative Externality
Uncompensated damage tied to production or consumption.

If economic activity among producers and consumers harms the well-being of a third party who is not compensated for any resulting damages, a **negative externality** exists. Air, noise, and water pollution are the most familiar types of negative externalities.

---

1   See Shane Romig, "In Grains, Argentina Doesn't Keep Distance: As Government Takes Firm Control Over Farming, Profits Drown Out the Protests," *The Wall Street Journal Online,* December 26, 2007, http://online.wsj.com.

Commuters enjoy the freedom and flexibility of driving their own car to work, but contribute to the smog that bedevils almost every major city in the world. Concert goers might enjoy an evening at an open-air music festival, but create havoc for nearby residents who crave a quiet and peaceful neighborhood.

Major employers are sometimes major polluters. For example, paper companies are important employers with thousands of high-paid jobs which give a vital boost to the local economy. At the same time, such companies generate significant negative externalities because paper making requires the use of poisonous solvents and chlorine compounds to bleach or lighten paper products. Paper companies also use toxins to prevent bacterial growth in pulp and finished paper products. As a result, the paper industry has been a major source of the toxic chemicals dumped into major rivers, streams, and the Great Lakes. In the past, toxic mercury compounds were used that contributed to mercury contamination problems in fish. Pulp and paper mills are also major sources of air pollutants, such as carbon dioxide, nitrous oxides, sulfur dioxides, carbon monoxide, and particulate matter. These pollutants contribute to ozone warnings, acid rain, global warming, and respiratory problems. Many paper mills are large enough to have their own coal-fired power plants, raising additional concerns about mercury, arsenic, and radioactive emissions. Paper making is an energy-intensive business; many mills draw large amounts of electricity from public utilities, and use a great deal of water. In the Green Bay, Wisconsin, area, the aquifer drawdown caused by high-capacity wells for the paper industry has been a major cause of municipal water woes that force local taxpayers to build expensive pipelines into Lake Michigan.

From a social welfare perspective, the problem created by negative externalities is shown in Figure 19.1(a). In a competitive market without externalities, the demand curve reflects the value to buyers, and the supply curve reflects the costs to sellers. In the absence of externalities, the competitive market equilibrium maximizes consumer surplus and is efficient. With negative externalities, such as pollution, the social cost of a good like paper exceeds the private cost of production. If the amount of social costs tied to pollution increase with production on a per unit basis, the social-cost curve will lie above the private-cost (supply) curve, as shown in Figure 19.1(a). In this case, the socially optimal amount of paper production falls from the competitive market equilibrium, Q_{CM}, to the socially optimal Q^*, as price rises from P_{CM} to P^*. Negative externalities give rise to an overproduction problem because sellers need not reflect the full social costs of production in the prices charged to buyers.

Positive Externalities

Positive Externality
Uncompensated benefit tied to production or consumption.

If economic activity among producers and consumers helps the well-being of a third party who does not pay for resulting benefits, a **positive externality** is created. Education generates the most famous type of positive externality. Like industrial training and research and development, education improves labor productivity and has broadly beneficial effects throughout the economy. Faster rates of productivity growth made possible by better education allow more output to be produced from a given amount of resources and helps improve living standards. Highly educated taxpayers also generate lots of income and income tax revenues that can be used to fund social programs. Similarly, R&D often results in chance or unintended discoveries that yield far-ranging benefits. Improved health care reduces worker absenteeism and the spread of infectious diseases, and creates a better quality of life for everyone. Flood protection and police and fire protection also yield important social benefits.

Figure 19.1   Externalities Can Create Inefficient Market Outcomes

In the absence of externalities, the competetive-market equilibrium is efficient. Negative externalities give rise to overproduction; positive externalities result in underproduction.

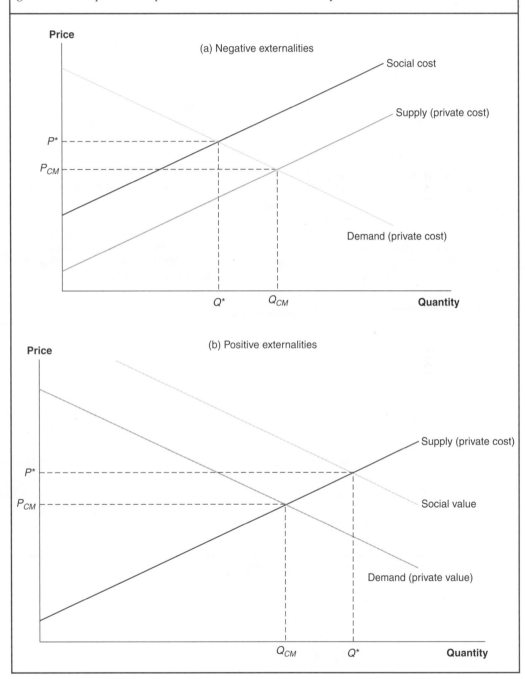

Managerial Application 19.1

"Tobacco" Ethics

The "tobacco" issue is charged with emotion. From the standpoint of a business manager or individual investor, there is the economic question of whether or not it is *possible* to earn above-normal returns by investing in a product known for killing its customers. From a philosophical standpoint, there is also the ethical question of whether or not it is *desirable* to earn such returns, if available.

Among the well-known *gloomy* particulars are

- Medical studies suggest that breaking the tobacco habit may be as difficult as curing heroin addiction. This fuels the fire of those who seek to restrict smoking opportunities among children and "addicted" consumers.
- With the declining popularity of smoking, there are fewer smokers among potential jurors. This may increase the potential for adverse jury decisions in civil litigation against the tobacco industry.
- Prospects for additional "sin" and "health care" taxes on smoking appear high.

Some underappreciated *positive* counterpoints to consider are

- While smoking is most common in the most price-sensitive sector of our society, profit margins remain sky-high.
- Tax revenues from smokers give the government an incentive to keep smoking legal.
- High excise taxes kill price competition in the tobacco industry. Huge changes in manufacturer prices barely budge retail prices.

While many suggest that above-average returns can be derived from investing in the tobacco business, a "greater fool" theory may be at work here. Tobacco companies and their investors only profit by finding "greater fools" to pay high prices for products that many would not buy for themselves. This is risky business, and a business plan that seldom works out in the long run.

See: Anna Wilde Mathewes, "FDA Head Questions Push to Regulate Tobacco," *The Wall Street Journal Online*, October 3, 2007, http://online.wsj.com.

To enhance social welfare in light of important positive externalities, society benefits when consumers are encouraged to increase their consumption of education, training, health care, and related services. From a social welfare perspective, the problem created by positive externalities is shown in Figure 19.1(b). With positive externalities, the social value of a service like education exceeds the private cost of production. If the amount of social value tied to education increases on a per unit basis, the social-value curve will lie above the private-value (demand) curve, as shown in Figure 19.1(b). In this case, the socially optimal amount of education lies above the competitive market equilibrium, Q_{CM}. At the socially optimal Q^*, price rises from P_{CM} to P^*. Positive externalities give rise to an underproduction problem because sellers cannot reflect the full social value of production in the prices charged to buyers.

SOLVING EXTERNALITIES

To solve economic problems posed by externalities, market and nonmarket solutions have arisen.

Internalize the Externality
Altering incentives so that externalities are considered in production and consumption decisions.

Government Solutions

In the face of negative or positive externalities, government uses a variety of means to **internalize the externality.** To successfully internalize an externality, producers and/or consumers must be provided with a set of incentives to take external costs and benefits into account when making production and consumption decisions. Taxes set to correct

Pigovian Taxes
Taxes set to correct the effects of negative externalities.

the effects of negative externalities are called **Pigovian taxes,** after economist Arthur Pigou who advocated their use. A Pigovian tax could be imposed on paper companies to reflect the social costs of air and water pollution tied to paper production. To be efficient, such taxes must be set in light of precise estimates of the amount of social costs involved, and the rate of taxation must be tied to the rate of pollution generated, for example, per ton of newsprint produced.

As an alternative to Pigovian taxes, or Pigovian subsidies in the event of positive externalities, government sometimes forbids or compels certain behavior. In the United States, the Environmental Protection Agency (EPA) has the task of developing and enforcing regulations aimed at protecting the environment. EPA regulations set air pollution controls for paper companies, and regulate the dumping of wastewater into public waterways. Such **command-and-control regulation** is consistent with the

Command-and-Control Regulation
Government rules to compel behavior.

principle that all persons are equal before the law. An important disadvantage is that such regulation often fails to provide efficient incentives for the reduction or elimination of harmful externalities, and is an imperfect tool for compelling the provision of goods and services with positive externalities.

Externalities pose a big challenge for public policy. Nobody is in favor of negative externalities, like global warming, but effectively dealing with such problems is seldom easy. In early 2004, for example, OPEC sought to deflect blame for historically high gasoline prices by blaming U.S. environmental policy. OPEC representatives said the lack of refining capacity in the United States was a key cause of high gasoline prices. There has not been a new oil refinery built in the United States for a generation, and it doesn't matter how much crude oil is produced if it cannot be refined into gasoline. Refiners have been stymied in their efforts to build new refining capacity by local NIMBY ("not in my back yard") opposition, and by uncertainty tied to rapidly changing fuel-mix requirements. It is also difficult for foreign oil companies and domestic suppliers to sell gasoline in the U.S. market because federal environmental regulations require dozens of different fuel blends to combat pollution. A refinery in Springfield, Illinois, for example, cannot sell gasoline in the Chicago market because of fuel-mix requirements. Improving the air quality in Chicago is an admirable objective, but such change doesn't come cheaply for gasoline buyers.

Market Solutions

The honey bee has long been at the center of discussions concerning the failure of unregulated markets to adequately support the production of goods and services with positive externalities. Of course, honey production results from the pollinating efforts of bees. As bees collect pollen to produce honey, they also create a positive externality by pollinating fruit trees. The more honey that is produced, the more fruit will be grown in the apple orchard or orange grove. It was once proposed that the pollinating virtues of honey bees were a pastoral example of how markets fail to reflect positive externalities. Without regulation, some suggested that producers would face insufficient incentives to produce honey and the beneficial positive externalities enjoyed by fruit growers. Alas, the situation is not so dire. It turns out that fruit growers have long been aware of the positive externalities tied to honey production. To ensure sufficient production of honey, and the beneficial externality of pollination, many fruit growers long ago went into the honey production business. As owners of both honey bees and fruit trees, fruit growers are able to ensure an optimal production of honey and fruit. In other instances, large fruit growers pay independent beekeepers to pollinate their orchards. In both cases, simple market solutions are capable of ensuring sufficient production of honey and fruit.

In general, a simple market solution is often capable of ensuring sufficient production of goods and services with significant externalities provided that information is freely available and transactions costs are moderate. A transaction cost is an expense that buyers and sellers incur in the process of arriving at and carrying through on a bargain. According to the Coase Theorem, if property rights are complete and private parties can bargain freely over the allocation of resources, then markets are capable of solving the problems posed by externalities and will operate efficiently. Tradable pollution permits are an example of how the Coase Theorem has been used to solve some pollution problems. Tradable pollution permits have been used to allow companies to trade the right to emit certain amounts of pollution. If some firms can easily limit their pollution, they will do so and sell their pollution rights to firms with high costs for pollution abatement. In this way, the maximum amount of air pollution abatement is achieved at minimum cost, and a market solution to the production of negative externalities is reached.

PUBLIC GOODS

An important function of government is to offer goods and services that cannot be provided and allocated in optimal quantities by the private sector.

Public Good
Goods that are neither excludable nor rival.

Nonrival Consumption
When use by certain individuals does not reduce availability for others.

Private Good
Goods that are both excludable and rival.

Rival Consumption
When one person's use diminishes another person's ability to use it.

Nonexclusion Concept
When it is impossible or prohibitively expensive to confine the benefits of consumption to paying customers.

Nonexclusionary
Goods or services subject to the nonexclusion concept.

Rivalry and Exclusion

If the consumption of a product by one individual does not reduce the amount available for others, and if nonpaying customers cannot be prevented from consumption, the product is a **public good.** Once public goods are provided for a single consumer, they become available to all consumers at no additional marginal cost. Classic examples of public goods include national defense and police and fire protection. Over-the-air radio and TV broadcasts are typical examples of public goods provided by the private sector in the United States, even though radio and TV programming is provided by the public sector in many foreign countries. A distinguishing characteristic of public goods is that they feature **nonrival consumption.** In the case of public goods, use by certain individuals does not reduce availability for others. For example, when an individual watches a network broadcast of a popular TV program such as *The Simpsons*, this does not interfere with the enjoyment of that same TV program by others. In contrast, if an individual consumes a 12-ounce can of Coke Zero, this same can of soda is not available for others to consume. A **private good** is one where consumption by one individual precludes or limits consumption by others. Food, clothing, and shelter are all private goods because the number of potential consumers of a fixed amount is strictly limited. All private goods share the characteristic of **rival consumption** because one person's use diminishes another person's ability to use it. Public goods that are nonrival in consumption would not be provided in the optimal amount by the private sector. Examples of such public goods are shown in Figure 19.2.

The idea of nonrival consumption can be distinguished from the **nonexclusion concept.** A good or service is **nonexclusionary** if it is impossible or prohibitively expensive to confine the benefits of consumption to paying customers. Nonrival consumption and nonexclusion often go hand-in-hand. Because national defense and network TV broadcasts can be enjoyed equally by more than one consumer at the same point in time, they are both public goods. National defense also exhibits the characteristic

Figure 19.2 Goods and Services Differ According to Exclusionary and Rivalry Aspects

	Exclusionary	Nonexclusionary
Rival	**Private Goods** Clothing Congested toll bridges Food Internet access Shelter	**Common Resources** Clean environment Fish in the ocean Open range for cattle grazing Public waterways Wild birds and animals
Nonrival	**Natural Monopolies** Air-traffic control Parks Police and fire protection Tunnels Uncongested toll bridges	**Public Goods** Concerts in the park Internet National Public Radio National defense Traffic lights

of nonexclusion because when it is provided for by taxpayers, nontax-paying citizens cannot be excluded from also enjoying the benefits of a strong national defense. On the other hand, the enjoyment of TV broadcasts can be made exclusive by restricting viewership, as is true with cable TV customers. A good or service is characterized by the **exclusion concept** if it is inexpensive to confine the benefits of consumption to paying customers. Public goods and services are neither rival nor exclusionary. Private goods and services are both rival and exclusionary.

Exclusion Concept
When it is inexpensive to confine the benefits of consumption to paying customers.

Rival goods and services that are nonexclusionary are **common resources.** For example, when fishermen over-harvest the world's ocean, it is because nobody owns the ocean and over-harvesting by others cannot be precluded. The tendency to overexploit common resources is the **tragedy of the commons.** It explains why the amount of fish and seafood found in world oceans is declining rapidly, and why the American bison disappeared from the Great Plains. One solution for the tragedy of the commons is to assign and enforce property rights. Interestingly, when individual ranchers were given ownership of the bison found on their property, bison were saved from extinction and are now making a comeback.

Common Resources
Goods and services that are rival but nonexclusionary.

Tragedy of the Commons
Tendency to overexploit and destroy common resources.

Some goods and services are exclusionary but nonrival. Such goods and services constitute a type of natural monopoly in that it is relatively easy to keep out nonpaying customers, but the marginal costs tied to serving an additional customer are negligible. A baseball stadium with a large amount of excess capacity is a typical example, as is an uncongested toll road. Many such natural monopolies tend to be provided by the public sector, or by private companies with exclusive franchises.

Free Riders and Hidden Preferences

Because public goods can be enjoyed by more than one consumer at the same point in time, aggregate demand for a public good is determined through the vertical summation of all individual demand curves. As shown in Figure 19.3, D_A is the demand curve of consumer A, and D_B is the demand curve of consumer B for public good Y. If consumers A and B are the only two individuals in the market, the aggregate demand curve for public good Y, D_T, is obtained by the vertical summation of D_A and D_B. This contrasts with the market demand curve for any private good, which is determined by the horizontal summation of individual demand curves. Given market supply curve S_Y for public good Y in Figure 19.3, the optimal amount of Y is Q_Y units per time period given by the intersection of D_T and S_Y at point T. At point T, the sum of marginal benefits enjoyed by both consumers equals the marginal social cost of producing Q_Y units of the public good. That is, $P_T = P_A + P_B = MSC_Y$.

Although the optimal quantity is Q_Y units in Figure 19.3, there are two related reasons why less than this amount is likely to be supplied by the private sector. Because individuals not paying for public good Y cannot be excluded from consumption, there is a tendency for consumers to avoid payment responsibility. A **free-rider problem** can emerge when several people share the cost of providing public goods, and consumers withhold payment because they believe that their failure to provide financial support has no effect on the provision of the good. When many individuals behave this way, less than the optimal amount of the public good is provided. This problem is generally overcome when the government initiates a tax on the general public to pay for the provision of important public goods, like national defense. In the private sector, free-rider problems are sometimes resolved through group consensus to support local zoning covenants, charitable associations, and so on.

A **hidden preferences problem** can emerge in the provision of public goods because individuals have no economic incentive to accurately reveal their true demand. Consumers

Free-Rider Problem
Tendency of consumers to avoid making any contribution toward covering the costs of public goods.

Hidden Preferences Problem
Difficulty of determining true desires for public goods.

Figure 19.3   Optimal Amount of a Public Good

Aggregate demand curve D_T for public good Y is obtained by the *vertical* summation of individual demand curves D_A and D_B. The reason for this is that each unit of public good Y can be consumed by both individuals at the same time. Given market supply curve S_Y, the optimal amount of Y is Q_Y units per time period (indicated by the intersection of D_T and S_Y). At Q_Y, the sum of the individual's marginal benefits equals the marginal social costs (i.e., $P_T = P_A + P_B = MSC_Y$).

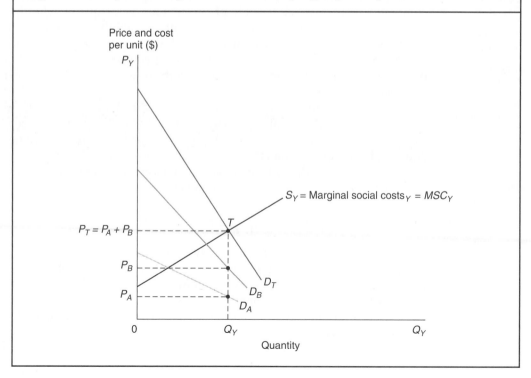

are reluctant to reveal high demand for public goods because they fear similarly high payment demands. With private goods, the price that consumers are willing to pay is a credible signal to producers regarding the quantity and quality that should be produced. No such pricing signals are available in the case of public goods and services. As a result, it is difficult to determine the optimal amount that should be provided.

Of course, many goods and services do not fit neatly within the categories of pure private goods or pure public goods. Examples include airports, basic research programs, day-care centers, highways, hospital facilities, immunization programs, the judicial system, parks, primary and secondary education, and trash collection. Given the many difficulties involved with accurately determining the demand for these and other quasi-public goods, it pays to be cautious when using the power of government to tax or otherwise compel popular support. Public policy must focus narrowly on the source of any perceived private-market imperfections and address these impediments directly.

For example, trash collection involves elements of a public good because it helps limit the propagation of insects and rodents and, therefore, the spread of infectious diseases. There are also economies of density in trash collection. It is far more efficient for a monopoly trash hauler to serve an entire neighborhood on a weekly basis than it is to have multiple competitors serve a single area. In recognition of the potential for problems with unregulated private-market trash collection, some local governments regulate private suppliers while others pay for this service out of general tax revenues. In theory, either approach has the potential to result in better trash collection services. In practice, regulation is seldom perfect, and local governments often find it difficult to maintain a high level of efficiency in the public provision of trash collection services.

Managerial Application 19.2

Political Corruption

Nobel Laureate Gary S. Becker believes that the best way to reduce undesirable business influence over the political process is to discard regulations that serve as tollgates for graft. Becker cites major scandals that involve corruption by prominent politicians and businessmen, and argues that corruption becomes a problem whenever big government infiltrates all facets of economic life.

Bribery and illegal favor-seeking do considerable damage. They always divert resources away from the production of useful goods and services. Such activities also promote policies that distort economic efficiency. Criminals are sometimes able to wrest monopoly prices through bribes and intimidation. Roads are sometimes badly built or diverted to less useful routes to reward builders and landowners with undue influence. Loans from government banks and agencies sometimes go to companies with political clout rather than where they can be invested most fruitfully.

In several countries, politicians caught with their hands in the till have been ousted. In the United States, evidence of

political corruption has been highlighted in investigations of Halliburton Co., a major U.S. government contractor in the oil well services and equipment businesses in Iraq and in Africa. Public corruption is often seen as rampant in Cameroon, Paraguay, Honduras, Iraq, Nigeria, and Tanzania. In these and other emerging markets, political corruption is a significant drag on economic growth. By contrast, Denmark, Finland, Sweden, New Zealand, and Canada benefit from having what are widely regarded as the cleanest political systems.

One way to discourage corruption is to vote out crooked politicians and punish people in business who illegally influence the political process. Becker argues that the only way to permanently reduce undesirable business influence over the political process is to simplify and standardize needed regulations. The temptation to bribe public officials is weakened considerably when they lack the power to "bend" the rules.

See: Glen R. Simpson, "Inside the Greed Zone," *The Wall Street Journal Online*, October 20, 2007, http://online.wsj.com.

OPTIMAL ALLOCATION OF SOCIAL RESOURCES

As the trustees of valuable public resources, public-sector managers must administer economic resources in a responsible manner.

Pareto Improvement

Pareto Satisfactory
Investment in public projects that make at least one individual better off and no one worse off.

Pareto Optimal
When all Pareto satisfactory programs and investment projects have been undertaken.

Potential Pareto Improvement
When an anticipated program or project involves positive net benefits.

Marginal Social Costs
Added private and public expenses.

Marginal External Costs
Expenses that are not directly borne by producers or their customers.

Marginal Private Costs
Production expenses borne by producers and their customers.

Marginal Social Benefits
Added private and public advantages.

Marginal Private Benefits
Value enjoyed by those who directly pay for any good or service.

Marginal External Benefits
Value enjoyed but not reflected in market prices.

If investment in a public project makes at least one individual better off and no one worse off, the project is described as **Pareto satisfactory,** after the noted Italian economist Vilfredo Pareto. When all such projects have been undertaken, the situation is deemed **Pareto optimal.** In practice, most public expenditures increase the welfare of some individuals while reducing the welfare of others. As a result, it is often regarded as too stringent to require that all public works fit the Pareto satisfactory criterion. Instead, it is often required that they meet the criteria of a **potential Pareto improvement,** where there are positive net benefits. A government program or project is deemed attractive under the potential Pareto improvement criterion when beneficiaries could fully compensate losers and still receive positive net benefit. Whether beneficiaries actually compensate losers is immaterial. The allocation of benefits and costs among various individuals is a separate equity issue. Much like the distribution of tax burdens, the allocation of costs and benefits from public programs and projects depends upon popular notions of fairness, rather than efficiency considerations.

The potential Pareto improvement criterion provides the rationale for benefit–cost analysis: Public programs and projects are desirable from a social standpoint so long as benefits exceed costs. Any public good or service should be supplied up to the amount that equates marginal social costs and marginal social benefits. This principle is similar to the profit-maximizing standard that output should increase to the point where marginal revenue equals marginal cost. For purposes of public-sector analysis, social benefits play the role of revenue and social costs play the role of production expenditures. Benefit–cost analysis presumes that all relevant pluses and minuses associated with public programs and projects can be measured in present-day dollar terms.

Marginal Social Costs and Benefits

The **marginal social costs** of any good or service equal the marginal cost of production plus any **marginal external costs,** such as air pollution, that are not directly borne by producers or their customers. Production costs borne by producers and their customers represent private economic costs; external costs include the value of foregone alternative goods and services. In the absence of marginal external costs, **marginal private costs** and marginal social costs are equal at all levels of output. **Marginal social benefits** are the sum of **marginal private benefits** plus **marginal external benefits.** Marginal private benefits are enjoyed by those who directly pay for any good or service; marginal external benefits are enjoyed by purchasers and nonpurchasers alike and are not reflected in market prices. When no externalities are present, marginal social benefits equal marginal private benefits.

The optimal allocation of social resources is shown in Figure 19.4 where the marginal social cost curve intersects the marginal social benefit curve at Q^*. Marginal social cost and marginal social benefit curves show that for all levels of output greater than Q^*, additional social costs exceed additional social benefits. For output levels less than Q^*, the marginal *net* benefit to society is positive. For output levels greater than Q^*, the marginal *net* benefit to society is negative.

Figure 19.4   Maximization of Social Benefits from Government Programs and Public-Sector Investments

Social benefits are maximized from government programs and public-sector investments when the marginal social cost equals marginal social benefits. Output level Q^* maximizes society's net benefits.

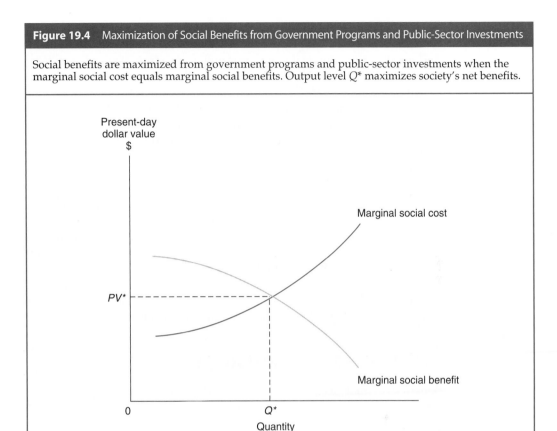

The optimal production of public-sector goods and services follows the same rules as optimal private-sector production. For example, consider the simplified case of two government programs or public-sector investment projects, project X and project Y. Optimal relative amounts of X and Y are made available to consumers so long as the ratio of marginal social benefits equals the ratio of marginal social costs for both projects:

$$\frac{\text{Marginal Social Benefit}_X}{\text{Marginal Social Benefit}_Y} = \frac{\text{Marginal Social Cost}_X}{\text{Marginal Social Cost}_Y} \qquad \textbf{19.1}$$

When the ratio of marginal social benefits is equal to the ratio of marginal social costs across all government programs and public-sector investment projects, each respective program and/or project represents an equally effective use of taxpayer funds in that it results in an identical payoff per dollar of marginal social cost.

Alternatively, optimal relative amounts of X and Y are made available to consumers so long as the marginal social benefit to marginal social cost ratio is equal for each respective program or public-sector investment project:

$$\frac{\text{Marginal Social Benefit}_X}{\text{Marginal Social Cost}_X} = \frac{\text{Marginal Social Benefit}_Y}{\text{Marginal Social Cost}_Y} \qquad \textbf{19.2}$$

Each side of Equation (19.2) shows the dollar amount of marginal social benefit relative to the dollar amount of marginal social cost for each project. When the MSB/MSC ratio is equal across all government programs and public-sector investment projects, each respective program and/or project represents an equally effective use of taxpayer funds and results in an identical payoff per dollar of marginal social cost. When the ratio $MSB/MSC > 1$, the value of marginal social benefits exceeds the value of marginal social costs. When the ratio $MSB/MSC < 1$, then the value of marginal social benefits is less than the value of marginal social costs. If the ratio $MSB/MSC = 1$, the value of marginal social benefits exactly equals the value of marginal social costs.

When $MSB/MSC = 1$, a dollar's worth of social benefit is received for each additional dollar spent on government programs and public-investment projects. This relationship implies an important decision rule, assuming that marginal social benefits fall and marginal social costs rise with an increase in the number of government programs and public-sector investment projects. If resources are fully employed throughout the economy, society's net benefit will be maximized when $MSB/MSC = 1$ for the last or *marginal* government program or public-sector investment project. Further net marginal benefits to society are possible through an expansion in the public sector when $MSB/MSC > 1$ for the marginal public-sector project; resources are being squandered in the public sector when $MSB/MSC < 1$ for the marginal public-sector project. Only when $MSB/MSC = 1$ for the marginal public-sector project and private-sector project are resources effectively allocated between the public and private sectors.

BENEFIT–COST METHODOLOGY

Benefit–cost analysis is often used when the economic consequences of a public project or a policy are apt to extend beyond 1 year.

Benefit–Cost Concepts

When compared to the capital budgeting process employed by a private firm, benefit–cost analysis is more complex because it seeks to measure both direct and indirect effects of government programs and public-sector investment projects. Although the activities of both private firms and public agencies produce externalities, private firms do not typically consider external effects because they are not able to charge for them. Because public agencies seek to maximize social benefits, they must measure both direct and indirect benefits and costs.

The guiding principle of benefit–cost analysis is economic efficiency in a global sense. Resources are allocated efficiently when they lead to the maximization of social benefits. The purpose of benefit–cost analysis is to determine if a given public expenditure would produce greater social benefits than if such funds were invested in an alternative public program, or if they were instead left in the private sector. The method has been used to determine whether a public-sector program should be undertaken or expanded and the funding level at which such programs should be supported. Although benefit–cost analysis was first applied in France in the 1840s, it was not until the early part of the twentieth century that it was used extensively in the United States to evaluate river and harbor projects. It has also been applied to projects involving defense, hydroelectric power, water supply availability, recreational facilities, transportation systems, urban renewal projects, educational systems, health, and job creation programs.

Benefit–cost analysis consists of five major elements: (1) statement of objectives, (2) discussion of alternatives, (3) quantification of related costs and benefits, (4) selection of a criterion for acceptable project determination, and (5) specification of an appropriate social discount rate. Benefit–cost analysis objectives clearly specify a target group, problem, or condition and the nature of the change expected as a result of implementing the program. For example, a clear objective for effective police department management would be to reduce burglaries by 20 percent and car thefts by 10 percent, following an increase in nighttime patrol hours by 15 percent. The discussion of project alternatives may consist of a choice between one project and no project, or among several public projects differing in purpose, scope, location, and size. If no public project is chosen, the implicit decision is to leave resources in the private sector. A common criticism of benefit–cost analysis is that sophisticated models are applied to poorly chosen alternatives. Because the goal of benefit–cost analysis is the efficient use of social resources, it is necessary to include all realistic alternatives.

Social Rate of Discount

Social Rate of Discount
Interest-rate cost of public funds.

Determining the appropriate **social rate of discount,** or interest-rate cost of public funds, is critical to the selection of appropriate alternatives. A low rate favors long-term investments with substantial future benefits; a higher rate favors short-term projects with benefits that accrue soon after the initial investment.

A common approach is to discount the benefits and costs associated with public projects based on the government's cost of borrowed funds. Because government loans are considered risk-free, the government's cost of borrowing is much lower than the private cost of borrowing. A disadvantage of low public-sector rates is that they fail to recognize the opportunity cost of funds transferred from the private sector to the public sector. Competition between public-sector and private-sector projects is essential to the efficient allocation of investment capital. Because private-sector resources are used to fund public-sector projects, the marginal private-sector opportunity cost of funds of roughly 10 percent is the appropriate social rate of discount. The opportunity cost of funds transferred from private investment to the public sector is computed from the average pretax rate of return on private corporate investments. This rate includes a risk premium for uncertainty about the returns accruing as a result of allocating funds for a given venture. The pretax rate of return for private investments must be used because returns from public-sector projects are not taxed.

The average pretax rate of return on government securities is a conservative estimate of the opportunity cost of private-sector consumption that is diverted to public use because it does not embody any default risk premium, as would be true of long-term corporate bonds. The average pretax rate of return on private-sector investment is another useful estimate of the opportunity cost of funds diverted from private investment. In both cases, the pretax rate of return is used because personal and corporate income taxes represent a redistribution of income from the private to the public sector. Because funds for public investments are likely to come from both private consumption and private investments, the weighted average of the opportunity cost of funds coming from these two components of the private sector should be used to compute the social rate of discount.

A typical pretax rate of return on long-term government bonds is 7.5 percent, a standard after-tax return on investment in the private sector is 10 percent, the marginal corporate and individual tax rate is roughly 40 percent, and consumption averages 94 percent of total income. Based on these assumptions, an appropriate social rate of discount of 8 percent is calculated as follows:

$$\begin{matrix} \text{Social Rate} \\ \text{of Discount} \end{matrix} = \begin{pmatrix} \text{Percentage of} \\ \text{Funds Diverted from} \\ \text{Private-Sector} \\ \text{Consumption} \end{pmatrix} \times \begin{pmatrix} \text{Before-Tax} \\ \text{Opportunity} \\ \text{Cost of} \\ \text{Private-Sector} \\ \text{Consumption} \\ \text{(Govt. Bond Rate)} \end{pmatrix}$$

$$+ \left| \begin{array}{c} \text{Percentage of} \\ \text{Funds Diverted from} \\ \text{Private-Sector} \\ \text{Investment} \end{array} \right| \times \left| \begin{array}{c} \text{After-Tax} \\ \text{Opportunity} \\ \text{Cost of} \\ \text{Private-Sector} \\ \text{Investment} \\ (1-\text{Tax Rate}) \end{array} \right|$$

$$= (94\%) \times (7.5\%) + (6\%) \times \left(\frac{10\%}{(1-40\%)} \right)$$

$$= 8\%$$

19.3

BENEFIT–COST CRITERIA

Appropriate benefit–cost decision rules rank-order alternatives so that net social benefits are maximized.

Social Net Present-Value

Social Net Present-Value
Present-value difference between marginal social benefits and marginal social costs.

Under the **social net present-value** (SNPV) criterion, marginal social benefits and marginal social costs are discounted back to the present using an appropriate social discount rate. Individual government programs and public-sector investment projects are acceptable if the present value of marginal social benefits is greater than or equal to the present value of marginal social costs. Public-sector projects are desirable when the difference between the present value of direct and indirect benefits and the present value of direct and indirect costs is greater than or equal to zero. Whereas all projects with $SNPV > 0$ represent a productive use of public-sector resources, the highest-value projects are those with the highest SNPV.

In equation form, the social net present-value of an individual government program or public-sector investment project is

$$SNPV_i = \sum_{t=1}^{N} \frac{\text{Marginal Social Benefits}_{it}}{(1+k_i)^t} - \sum_{t=1}^{N} \frac{\text{Marginal Social Costs}_{it}}{(1+k_i)^t}$$

19.4

where $SNPV_i$ is the social net present-value of the ith project, *Marginal Social Benefits*$_{it}$ represent the expected direct and indirect social benefits of the ith project in the tth year, k_i is the appropriate risk-adjusted social discount rate applicable to the ith public-sector project, and *Marginal Social Costs*$_{it}$ is the government program's or public-sector investment project's cost or initial cash outflow.

In the social net present-value approach, the appropriate interest-rate discount factor is the social rate of discount. This rate is comprised of a risk-free component to compensate taxpayers for the economic cost of waiting, plus a risk premium that reflects the amount of uncertainty surrounding the realization of program benefits. In equation form, the social rate of discount is

$$\text{Social Rate of Discount }(k_i) = \begin{array}{c} \text{Risk-Free Rate} \\ \text{of Return }(R_F) \end{array} + \begin{array}{c} \text{Risk Premium} \\ (R_P) \end{array}$$

19.5

To illustrate the SNPV method, consider the data contained in Table 19.1 for three hypothetical 20-year government programs. Dollar values of marginal social benefits

Table 19.1 Benefit-Cost Ratio Analysis for Three Government Programs

	Years	Annual Dollar Value of Marginal Social Benefit Arising		
		A	B	C
		($5,000,000)	($3,000,000)	($5,000,000)
	1	575,000	500,000	250,000
	2	560,000	500,000	350,000
	3	545,000	500,000	450,000
	4	530,000	500,000	550,000
	5	515,000	500,000	650,000
	6	500,000	500,000	750,000
	7	485,000	500,000	850,000
	8	470,000	500,000	950,000
	9	455,000	500,000	1,050,000
	10	440,000	500,000	1,150,000
	11	425,000	500,000	1,250,000
	12	410,000	500,000	1,350,000
	13	395,000	500,000	1,450,000
	14	380,000	500,000	1,550,000
	15	365,000	500,000	1,650,000
	16	350,000	500,000	1,750,000
	17	335,000	500,000	1,850,000
	18	320,000	500,000	1,950,000
	19	305,000	500,000	2,050,000
	20	290,000	500,000	2,150,000
Marginal social benefits (in nominal terms)		$8,650,000	$10,000,000	$24,000,000
Present value of marginal social cost (PV of MSC)		$5,000,000	$3,000,000	$5,000,000
Social rate of discount (interest rate)		8%	10%	12%
Present value of marginal social benefits (PV of MSB)		$4,609,087.90	$4,256,781.86	$6,364,117.84
Social net present value (= PV of MSB − PV of MSC)		−$390,912.10	$1,256,781.86	$1,364,117.84
Benefit-cost ratio [= (PV of MSB)/(PV of MSC)]		0.92	1.42	1.27

are shown for each year over the projected 20-year life of each program. Assume that these values are net of all ongoing costs for program administration; they can be thought of as net marginal social benefits per year. The present values of marginal social costs for each program are comprised of the initial cash outlay required. Notice that program *A* and program *C* have an identical investment requirement of $5 million, whereas program *B* has a somewhat smaller initial outlay of $3 million. Marginal social benefits in nominal terms, or before discounting, total $8.65 million for program *A*, $10 million for program *B*, and $24 million for program *C*. Marginal social benefits before discounting are a misleading measure of the attractiveness of each project because they do not reflect differences in the time frame over which program benefits and costs are generated.

A relevant measure of the attractiveness of each respective program is the social net present-value of each program, where each dollar of marginal social benefits and marginal social costs is converted to a current-dollar basis. The social rate of discount used to convert nominal dollar values into present-value terms is 8 percent for program A, 10 percent for program B, and 12 percent for program C. Each respective social discount rate plays the role of a present-value interest factor that can be used to convert nominal dollar costs and benefits to a common present-value basis. If a 5 percent yield to maturity on short-term Treasury bills is taken as a proxy for the risk-free rate, program A involves a 3 percent risk premium, program B entails a 5 percent risk premium, and program C employs a 7 percent risk premium.

Because social benefits received in the future are worth less than social costs incurred at the present, the SNPV for any public program tends to be much less than the nominal dollar amount of social benefits. Using a program-specific social rate of discount, the present value of marginal social benefits is \$4,609,087.90 for program A, \$4,256,781.86 for program B, and \$6,364,117.84 for program C. After considering the present value of marginal social cost for each program, the SNPV for program A is $SNPV_A = -\$390,912.10$, calculated as

$$
\begin{aligned}
SNPV_A &= PV \text{ of } MSB - PV \text{ of } MSC \\
&= \$4,609,087.9 - \$5,000,000 \\
&= -\$390,912.10
\end{aligned}
\qquad \textbf{19.6}
$$

The $SNPV = -\$390,912.10$ means that the present value of marginal social costs for this program exceeds the present value of marginal social benefits. Funding program A would represent an unwise use of public resources. Whenever $SNPV < 0$, program funding is unwise on an economic basis. A judicious use of social resources requires that $SNPV > 0$ for every public program or public investment project.

Using an appropriate program-specific social rate of discount, the present value of marginal social benefits is \$4,256,781.86 for program B and \$6,364,117.84 for program C. After considering the present value of marginal social cost for each program, the SNPV for program B is \$1,256,781.86 and for program C is \$1,364,117.84. Both programs B and C represent a wise use of public resources because $SNPV_B > 0$ and $SNPV_C > 0$. If public funding is sufficient to fund both projects at the same time, both should be underwritten. If public funding is scarce and both programs cannot be funded, program C is preferred to program B because $SNPV_C > SNPV_B$.

The SNPV can result in a bias toward larger projects because a large social net present-value typically requires the commitment of significant marginal social costs. This has the potential to result in a bias toward larger as opposed to smaller social programs and public-sector investment projects when the SNPV criterion is employed. To avoid such bias, it becomes necessary to introduce two additional public-sector capital budgeting decision rules.

Benefit–Cost Ratio

Benefit–Cost (B/C) Ratio Analysis
Present value of marginal social benefits per dollar of marginal social cost.

A variant of SNPV analysis used in complex capital budgeting situations is called **benefit–cost (B/C) ratio analysis.** The benefit–cost ratio is calculated as

$$
B/C \text{ ratio}_i = \frac{PV \text{ of } MSB_i}{PV \text{ of } MSC_i} = \frac{\sum_{t=1}^{N} [MSB_{it}/(1+k_i)^t]}{\sum_{t=1}^{N} [MSC_{it}/(1+k_i)^t]}
\qquad \textbf{19.7}
$$

The B/C ratio shows the relative attractiveness of any social program or public-sector investment project, or the present value of marginal social benefits per dollar of marginal social cost.

In Table 19.1, $SNPV > 0$ implies a desirable investment program and B/C $ratio > 1$. For example, the benefit–cost ratio for program B is

$$B/C \text{ ratio} = \frac{PV \text{ of } MSB}{PV \text{ of } MSC}$$
$$= \frac{\$4,256,781.86}{\$3,000,000}$$
$$= 1.42$$

This means that program B returns \$1.42 in marginal social benefits for each dollar of marginal social costs, when both figures are expressed in present-value terms. Program A returns only 92¢ in marginal social benefits for each dollar of marginal social costs, whereas program C returns \$1.27 in marginal social benefits for each dollar of marginal social cost.

In B/C ratio analysis, any social program with B/C $ratio > 1$ should be accepted; any program with B/C $ratio < 1$ should be rejected. Programs will be accepted provided that they return more than a dollar of discounted benefit for each dollar of cost. The B/C ratio and SNPV methods always indicate the same accept/reject decisions for independent programs, because B/C $ratio > 1$ implies $SNPV > 0$ and B/C $ratio < 1$ implies $SNPV < 0$. However, for alternative programs of unequal size, B/C ratio and SNPV criteria can give different program rankings.

Social Internal Rate of Return

Social Internal Rate of Return
Interest or discount rate that equates the present value of the future benefits to the initial cost or outlay.

The **social internal rate of return** (SIRR) is the interest or discount rate that equates the present value of future receipts to the initial cost or outlay. The equation for calculating the social internal rate of return is simply the SNPV formula set equal to zero:

$$SNPV_i = 0 = \sum_{t=1}^{N} \frac{MSB_{it}}{(1+k_i^*)^t} - \sum_{t=1}^{N} \frac{MSC_{it}}{(1+k_i^*)^t} \qquad \textbf{19.8}$$

This equation is solved for the discount rate, k_i^*, that produces a zero net present-value by setting discounted future marginal social benefits equal to marginal social costs. That discount rate is the social internal rate of return earned by the program, that is, $SIRR_i = k_i^*$.

Because the social net present-value equation is complex, it is difficult to solve for the actual social internal rate of return on an investment without a computer spreadsheet. For this reason, trial and error is sometimes employed. One begins by arbitrarily selecting a social discount rate, such as 10 percent. If it yields a positive SNPV, the social internal rate of return must be greater than the 10 percent interest or discount rate used, and another higher rate is tried. If the chosen rate yields a negative SNPV, the internal rate of return on the program is lower than the 10 percent social discount rate, and the SNPV calculation must be repeated using a lower social discount rate. This process of changing the social discount rate and recalculating the net present-value continues until the discounted present value of future marginal social benefits equals the present value of marginal social costs. The interest rate that brings about this equality is the yield, or social internal rate of return on the program.

Using trial and error, a financial calculator, or spreadsheet software, the internal rate of return for program A is $SIRR_A = 6.79$ percent. Similarly, $SIRR_B = 15.78$ percent and $SIRR_C = 14.81$ percent. Because $SIRR_B$ and $SIRR_C$ exceed the cost of capital, program B and program C are attractive and should be undertaken. Because $SIRR_A$ is less than the cost of capital, program A is unattractive and should not be undertaken. In general, social internal rate of return analysis suggests that programs should be accepted when the $SIRR > k$ and rejected when the $SIRR < k$. When the $SIRR > k$, the marginal rate of return exceeds the marginal cost of capital. As in the case of programs with an $SNPV > 0$ and B/C $ratio > 1$, the acceptance of all investment programs with $SIRR > k$ will lead public-sector managers to maximize net social benefits. In instances in which capital is scarce and only a limited number of desirable programs can be undertaken at one point in time, the SIRR can be used to derive a rank ordering of programs from most desirable to least desirable. Like a rank ordering of all $SNPV > 0$ programs from highest to lowest B/C ratios, a rank ordering of potential investment programs from highest to lowest SIRRs allows public-sector managers to effectively employ scarce public funds.

Limitations of Benefit–Cost Analysis

Benefit–cost analysis is conceptually appealing, but has limitations. Primary among these is the fact that existing measurement techniques are sometimes inadequate for comparing diverse public programs. Without competitive markets for public goods and services, it is difficult to ascertain the social value placed on public programs. How much is it worth to society to provide food stamps and other financial support to poor parents and their children? Is this value reduced when the poor refuse minimum-wage employment opportunities or when government funds are used for unintended purposes (e.g., to buy alcohol, cigarettes, or illegal drugs)? How do you measure the social value of sophisticated new defense weapons, and how do you compare this value to the value of other social programs? What is the social value of the milk-price support program?

Benefit–cost analysis requires public-sector managers to quantify all relevant factors in dollar terms. Where dollar-value estimation is not possible, qualitative factors must still be considered to prevent the omission of important indirect and intangible impacts. The inclusion of qualitative factors makes benefit–cost analysis more complex and its conclusions more ambiguous. At times, analytical results cannot be summarized in a single comparable ratio. Evaluation problems also occur when a conflicting objective, such as reducing the level of highway noise pollution around a schoolyard, must be considered alongside an efficiency objective, such as increasing business activity along a new highway corridor.

Despite these and other obvious problems, benefit–cost analysis enjoys well-documented success as a vital tool for public-sector decision making. At a minimum, benefit–cost analysis forces the itemization and computation of costs and benefits in a manner that is far more precise and useful than many other methods of public-sector decision making.

ADDITIONAL METHODS OF IMPROVING PUBLIC MANAGEMENT

Cost-Effectiveness Analysis
Method used to determine how to best employ resources in a given social program or public-sector investment project.

When all relevant factors cannot be measured in dollar terms, alternative means for assessing public-sector decision alternatives must be explored.

Cost-Effectiveness Analysis

The purpose of **cost-effectiveness analysis** is to determine how to best employ resources in a given social program or public-sector investment project. A common approach is to

Managerial Application 19.3

Free Trade Helps Everyone

In the early 1990s, backers of the North American Free Trade Agreement (NAFTA) argued that free trade would open Mexico's economy, causing a surge in exports from the United States and Canada. The case against NAFTA was most forcefully carried by the former head of Electronic Data Systems, ex-presidential candidate Ross Perot. Perot famously described "a giant sucking sound" that we all would hear as, in one great whoosh, the United States lost millions of jobs to low-wage Mexicans. Happily, the economic facts are far more positive than the doomsday political rhetoric.

When NAFTA went into effect on January 1, 1994, the United States and Canada already had a free trade agreement. NAFTA merely extended that agreement to include Mexico and permit duty-free and quota-free movement of goods across all of North America. The irony of the NAFTA debate is that the job opportunity loss feared by Perot and other critics failed to materialize. When productivity differences are considered, Mexican labor is no cheaper than higher-priced but more efficient labor from the United States and Canada. In fact, well-educated and highly paid U.S. workers compete effectively against low-wage competitors.

Free trade is enormously beneficial to all Americans, whether they be from Canada, Mexico, or the United States. Before NAFTA, the tariff imposed by the United States on Mexican goods averaged about 4 percent, while the tariff imposed by Mexico on U.S. goods averaged about 11 percent. With NAFTA, Mexican, U.S., and Canadian export industries, workers, and consumers benefit enormously from the increased access across national boundaries that follows from the abolition of all such tariffs. To extend the many benefits of free and open trade, Congress is now considering broad trade agreements that might encompass the southern hemisphere, and eventually America's European and Asian trade partners as well.

With free trade, economic activity flows to where business is most efficient in meeting consumer demand. That helps everyone.

See: Michele Tronconi, "Make Free Trade Fair, Too," *The Wall Street Journal Online*, October 31, 2007, http://online.wsj.com.

hold output or service levels constant and then evaluate cost differences resulting from alternative program strategies. For example, a local school board might be interested in evaluating alternative special education programs and their respective costs. The cost-effectiveness analysis approach might compare mainstreaming versus separate classrooms in terms of their effectiveness in meeting important special education goals. The most cost-effective method is the decision alternative that meets specific educational goals at minimum cost.

Cost-effectiveness analysis is useful for evaluating the effectiveness of social programs and public-sector investment projects where output can be identified and measured in qualitative terms but is difficult to express in monetary terms. For example, cost-effectiveness analysis can be used to evaluate the success of alternative transportation programs such as taxis or social service vehicles for the handicapped but cannot be used to determine if providing transportation for the handicapped is worthwhile from a resource allocation standpoint. Cost-effectiveness studies are also useful in situations where significant externalities or other intangibles exist that cannot be easily measured in dollar terms. In such cases, negative impacts of social programs can be dealt with by excluding all decision alternatives that generate negative impacts beyond a certain level. The selection of a preferred alternative is made on the basis of differences in tangible performance measures.

Privatization

Transfer of public-sector resources to the private sector.

Privatization

During the 1980s, a **privatization** movement began and accelerated in Europe, the former Soviet Union, and former Eastern Bloc countries. With privatization, public-sector resources are transferred to the private sector in the hope that the profit motive might spur higher product quality, better customer service, and lower costs. The privatization movement gained momentum during the 1990s in response to growing dissatisfaction with the low quality of some government services and increasing dissatisfaction with cost overruns at the federal, state, and local levels of government.

In the United States, privatization has failed to generate the type of enthusiasm seen abroad. Nevertheless, local municipalities across the United States are increasing the amount of private-sector contracting for snow removal, garbage collection, and transit services. Since the late 1980s, a majority of state and local governments have greatly increased the amount of public goods and services contracted out to private providers. At the federal level, the U.S. Postal Service, now a quasi-private monopoly, has long used private carriers for rural deliveries. The Department of Health and Human Services now uses private contractors to process Medicare claims. The privatization movement has clearly made dramatic inroads in countries throughout Europe and Latin America, where government control over the economy has traditionally been comprehensive. During the 1990s, European and Latin American governments greatly increased the pace by which previously nationalized companies have been returned to the private sector. Prominent examples include electrical utilities, railroads, telecommunications businesses, and steel companies.

The economic justification for privatization is that cheaper and better goods and services result when the profit motive entices firms to improve quality and cut costs. Public agencies and government employees that face competition from the private sector also display an encouraging tendency to improve performance and operating efficiency. In Chicago, for example, competitive bidding between private contractors and city cleanup and repair crews creates incentives for public employees and public managers to become more effective. In a similar situation, the Phoenix Public Works Department won back a number of garbage collection districts previously lost to private bidders after instituting innovations that lowered operating costs below that of private competitors. Several city and county administrators have reported similar cost savings as a result of privatizing public services. In Milwaukee, school vouchers are given to low-income children to select the private school of their choice. Although parental satisfaction with Milwaukee's school voucher program is high, it is too early to tell whether educational quality has risen for both private and public school children.

Opponents of privatization argue that the transfer of government programs to the private sector does not necessarily lead to smaller government and fewer budget deficits. Profit-seeking firms who become dependent on public financing lobby for an expansion of public-sector spending with as much vigor as public-sector employees. Evaluating the success of private firms in providing public goods is also made difficult by inadequate performance measures and lax performance monitoring. Another argument against privatization is that the goal of public services is not just to achieve a high level of efficiency but to provide benefits that private markets cannot or do not provide. A private firm may, for example, find it unprofitable to educate unruly children from single-parent homes with little commitment to education. For-profit hospitals may find it prohibitively expensive to offer emergency room care to violent teens from inner-city neighborhoods. Successful privatization requires specific goals and measurement criteria that clearly define the public interest, and a direct link between the achievement of recognized goals and the compensation of private-sector managers.

REGULATORY REFORM IN THE NEW MILLENNIUM

When vigorous competition is absent, government regulation can be justified through both efficiency and equity criteria.

Promoting Competition in Electric Power Generation

The electric power industry comprises three different components: the generation of electric power, the transmission of electric power from generators to local utilities, and the distribution of electricity by local utilities to commercial and residential customers. All three segments of the industry are currently subject to some state and federal regulation. Competition has generally been regarded as unlikely in the transmission and local distribution of electricity, given their natural monopoly characteristics. However, competition has emerged in the wholesale generation of electric power, and regulators now face the question of how to foster and encourage such competition.

While a mix of market forces and well-designed regulation can correct market failures, inappropriate regulation can worsen even imperfect market outcomes. For example, California's rolling blackouts in January 2001 appear to have stemmed at least in part from regulations that fixed retail electric rates during a period when wholesale rates skyrocketed. As a result, there was an insufficient supply of electricity during peak periods of demand. Fixed retail electric rates provided little incentive for consumers to reduce their consumption of electricity during high-usage periods. Such outmoded regulations can have the unintended effect of making the U.S. electricity supply less reliable and more expensive, and need to be reformed.

Fostering Competition in Telecommunications

The Federal Communications Commission (FCC) is charged with establishing regulatory policies that promote competition, innovation, and investment in broadband services in the United States. Universal and affordable access to broadband services is recognized as essential to economic growth. During recent years, the number of families and businesses with broadband access has increased sharply. In the United States, the U.S. online population exceeded 200 million people in 2006, and household broadband penetration approached 50 percent, or roughly 48 million households. The FCC has announced a goal of making broadband access universal throughout the United States.

The FCC struggles to prevent antiquated monopoly regulations from the analog era from hampering the progress of emerging telecommunications technologies. In many cases, new technologies like third generation wireless (3G), wireless networking (Wi-Fi), Voice over Internet Protocol (VoIP), and broadband over power lines (BPL) have evolved faster than the rules that govern their deployment. In drafting new rules, the FCC seeks to ensure a sound competitive framework for communications services provided by traditional phone companies, long-distance and wireless service providers, cable TV companies, satellite providers, power companies, and other new competitors. During a time of robust growth and dynamic change in telecommunications services, the FCC has worked to increase the number of competitive choices available to consumers. To facilitate competition, FCC rules were changed to allow consumers to keep their cell phone numbers when switching carriers. Benefits of growing competition can be seen in terms of increased usage and dramatically falling rates for domestic and international long-distance voice service.

During coming years, federal regulators face challenges in trying to moderate the burdens placed upon consumers by voice telemarketers and Internet spam providers. State and local regulators face similarly daunting challenges to make local phone companies and cable TV companies more price sensitive and responsive to consumer demands.

Reforming Environmental Regulation

By requiring firms and consumers to account for pollution costs, the Clean Air Act, the Clean Water Act, and the Resource Conservation and Recovery Act have all limited environmental waste. At the same time, each of these environmental regulations imposes significant costs on the private economy. Although the United States already spends more on pollution abatement than any other industrialized nation, this total is sure to rise sharply in the years ahead.

Significant uncertainties surround environmental issues and the costs and benefits of various means of environmental regulation. For example, in the case of acid rain, studies show that simple mitigation strategies can be much more cost-effective than the types of regulatory controls favored by Congress. Similarly, more efficient alternatives may exist for correcting externalities associated with gasoline consumption. A rise in gasoline consumption increases the nation's vulnerability to oil price shocks and pollution, and contributes to global warming. The most direct way of dealing with such problems would be to impose a user fee per gallon on gasoline consumption that is commensurate with resulting externalities.

The scope and importance of environmental concerns will become clearer as better information becomes available and more effective methods of regulation begin to yield results. It is obvious that economic incentives decrease compliance costs by allowing firms the flexibility to meet environmental regulations in the most efficient manner possible. With economic incentives tied to environmental objectives, rather than to the means used to achieve them, firms and society in general benefit through a practical approach to protecting the environment.

Improving Regulation of Health and Safety

Decisions to smoke, drink alcohol, go scuba diving in Baja, California, or ride a roller coaster at an amusement park involve risk. Decisions to take a job as a management consultant, as an ironworker in the construction trades, or as a commodities broker also involve a trade-off between the risks and perceived benefits of employment. In the United States, government seeks to control these risks by offering consumers and employees redress for wrongful injury through the tort system and by an extensive and growing policy of health and safety regulation.

Proponents of expanded government health and safety regulation assert that consumers and employees do not have sufficient information or are incapable of making appropriate decisions in these areas. If certain risks are extremely high or prohibitively expensive, society sometimes assumes the burden of paying for them out of equity considerations. Public concern over risk has also given rise to legislation that requires risk to be eliminated. For example, the Delaney Clause of the Food, Drug, and Cosmetics Act prohibits the use in food of substances shown to cause any cancer in animals or humans.

However, just as firms and individuals must balance risk and benefits when making decisions, so too must regulators. Although regulators often target catastrophic risks that have a small probability of occurring, they can overlook modest risks that occur frequently. It may be good politics to target products with a very small chance of leading to cancer, but it may be more economic to focus on methods for increasing consumer awareness on the dangers of obesity. In regulating health and safety, government must focus on regulations with benefits that outweigh unavoidable costs.

HEALTH CARE REFORM

Evolving plans for comprehensive health care reform seem to favor a managed competition approach.

Managed Competition

Americans are living longer, healthier lives. Since 1960, average life expectancy has increased by more than 5 years. American physicians have access to the best technology in the world, and more than one-half of the world's medical research is funded by private and public sources in the United States. At the same time, the share of national income devoted to health care has been growing rapidly from less than 6 percent of GDP in 1965 to more than 16 percent today, If present trends continue, U.S. spending on health care will reach more than 19 percent of GDP by 2014 (see Figure 19.5).

Table 19.2 summarizes general features of four well-known proposals for reining in U.S. health care spending. The most promising health care reform proposals involve market-based reforms designed to expand access to health insurance and to improve

Managerial Application 19.4

Price Controls for Pharmaceutical Drugs

In the United States, Medicare, Medicaid, and state-run health care cost reimbursement plans funnel federal and state dollars to help share the burden of exploding health care costs. What is not generally understood is that such programs in the United States and abroad can contribute to higher health care prices.

Consider the market for pharmaceuticals. If the market for prescription drugs were a typical free market, demand would be limited by the extent to which consumers are willing to pay for innovative therapies. However, if each dollar of consumer demand is matched by federal or state funds, the demand for prescription drugs skyrockets. Suppose a given prescription costs $15, but that 80 percent of this cost is borne by the government. Most consumers focus on the $3 cost that they must pay, rather than the overall cost of $15. As government health care benefits rise, it is the matching share paid by consumers that constrains industry demand. Rather than cut the cost to consumers of high-priced drugs, government matching schemes allow drug companies and other health care providers to raise prices. In the United States, the eruption in prescription

drug prices and other health care costs coincides with the growth of government-sponsored cost-sharing plans. It is perhaps ironic that government-sponsored plans designed to help consumers with sky-high drug prices actually contribute to higher drug prices.

Now, global governments are getting tightfisted. In the United States, cost containment measures are sure to pinch profit margins for prescription drugs. European governments go one step further and demand stiff discounts from drug prices prevalent in the United States. For example, French price controls set prices at roughly 40 percent of the U.S. average for prescription drugs. In Japan, allowed prices are based upon a weighted average of prices in other markets. Clearly, global governments are using their buying power to reduce the industry's pricing flexibility. It looks like price controls are ready to give the industry a headache. It remains to be seen how such cuts will affect the development of new and innovative drug therapies.

See: Sarah Lueck and John D. Mckinnon, "Health-Care Feud Intensifies," *The Wall Street Journal Online*, October 18, 2007, http://online.wsj.com.

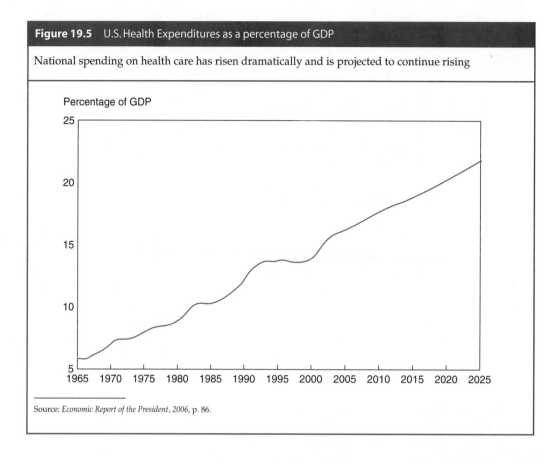

Figure 19.5 U.S. Health Expenditures as a percentage of GDP

National spending on health care has risen dramatically and is projected to continue rising

Source: *Economic Report of the President, 2006*, p. 86.

the private markets for health care services. Such market-based plans typically provide low-income Americans with tax credits for purchasing health insurance. Those who do not file tax returns would receive the credit in the form of a transferable health insurance certificate. Because low-income Americans would be able to purchase basic health insurance using tax credits, they would no longer have to rely on the public hospital safety net. At the same time, the fixed-dollar nature of the credit or deduction would discourage overconsumption of health care service.

Market-based plans would expand health insurance coverage by promoting the use of health insurance networks to act as group purchasing agents for smaller employers, thus obtaining more favorable premiums and reducing administrative costs. One such type of network is based upon so-called Association Health Plans (AHPs). The AHP proposal is designed to help small businesses and associations to purchase health insurance for employees and their families. These plans offer small businesses and self-employed individuals the potential for lower health insurance premiums resulting from decreased administrative costs and increased bargaining power with insurers and medical providers. This and similar plans would incorporate health risk pools that spread the cost of serious health problems among all those purchasing health insurance. Low- and middle-income people with chronic health problems would have greatly improved access to health care through this combination of tax credits and health risk pools. Under market-based plans, everyone would not be required to purchase health insurance. Those eligible for only a partial credit or deduction could decide not to purchase health insurance and continue to pay their own expenses or rely on the existing health care safety net.

Table 19.2   Side-by-Side Comparison of Health Care Reform Proposals

Issue	Market-Based Proposals	Managed Competition Proposals	Pay-or-Play	National Health Insurance
Moral hazard	Encourages managed care for public programs	Promotes use of basic benefit package	—	—
Cost containment	Increases competition in small group market and public programs Improves availability of health care quality information Simplifies record keeping and billing Reduces malpractice litigation costs	Increases competition in small group markets	Provider and hospital fee schedule	Global budgets Physician and hospital fee schedule
Access to poor	Provides low- and middle-income people with insurance certificate/ deduction	Mandates coverage through employers Provides subsidies to low-income people who are not employed and to part-time workers	Requires employers to offer insurance or pay into public plan	Universal coverage
Access for those in ill health	Implements health risk adjusters for high-risk people in individual and small group health insurance markets	Provides age-adjusted community-rated coverage in individual and small group health insurance markets	Covers employed persons in ill health	Universal coverage

Outlook for Health Care Reform

It is speculative to project that the U.S. health care system will evolve along any single market-based proposal, managed competition plans, or by more traditional "play-or-pay" or national health insurance proposals. Pay-or-play plans require firms to provide basic health insurance to employees and their dependents ("play") or pay a payroll tax to cover enrollment in a public health care plan ("pay"). Proposals for national health insurance envision replacing the private health insurance market with a single national health insurer. National health insurance would be funded through taxes and care would be free (as in Canada) or provided at a low cost-sharing level.

No plan for health care reform is without its pluses and minuses, costs and benefits. Although managed competition would encourage rivalry among health insurers providing a basic benefit package, the government would become responsible for defining the benefits that most Americans would receive. On the other hand, play-or pay proposals would improve access to insurance by mandating employer coverage, but they do not address the problem of rising medical costs and may cause firms to lay off low-wage workers. National health insurance proposals would provide insurance for all Americans but could lead to a cost explosion. Reforms that give appropriate incentives to consumers, insurers, and providers will be most effective in controlling costs, improving access, and giving consumers the quality of health care they want.

SUMMARY

Competing demands on public budgets force responsible public-policy makers to consider the marginal social benefits and marginal social costs of alternative programs and decision alternatives.

- If economic activity among producers and consumers harms the well-being of a third party who is not compensated for any resulting damages, a **negative externality** exists. If economic activity among producers and consumers helps the well-being of a third party who does not pay for benefits, a **positive externality** is created.

- Government has a variety of means used to make producers and/or consumers **internalize the externality.** Taxes that correct the effects of negative externalities are called **Pigovian taxes,** after economist Arthur Pigou, who advocated their use. Government sometimes uses **command-and-control regulation** to limit the effects of externalities.

- If the consumption of a product by one individual does not reduce the amount available for others, the product is a **public good.** The distinguishing characteristic of public goods is that they share the attribute of **nonrival consumption** because use by certain individuals does not reduce availability for others. A **private good** is one where consumption by one individual precludes or limits consumption by others. All private goods share the characteristic of **rival consumption** because one person's use diminishes another person's ability to use it. Nonrival consumption can be distinguished from the **nonexclusion concept.** A good or service is **nonexclusionary** if it is impossible or prohibitively expensive to confine the benefits of consumption to paying customers. A good or service is characterized by the **exclusion concept** if it is inexpensive to confine the benefits of consumption to paying customers. Public goods and services are neither rival nor exclusionary. Private goods and services are both rival and exclusionary. Goods and services that are rival but nonexclusionary are called **common resources.** The tendency to overexploit common resources is the **tragedy of the commons.**

- A **free-rider problem** often materializes in the case of public goods because each consumer believes that the public good will be provided irrespective of his or her contribution towards covering its costs. A **hidden preferences problem** also emerges in the provision of public goods because individuals have no economic incentive to accurately reveal their true demand.

- If investment in a public project makes at least one individual better off and no one worse off, then the project is **Pareto satisfactory.** When all such government programs and investment projects have been undertaken, the situation is **Pareto optimal.** In practice, it is often deemed adequate when public programs and projects meet the criteria of a **potential Pareto improvement,** in which there are positive net benefits.

- The **marginal social costs** of any good or service equal the marginal cost of production plus any **marginal external costs** that are not directly borne by producers or their customers. Production costs that are borne by producers and their customers represent private economic costs; external costs include the value of foregone alternative goods and services. In the absence of marginal external costs, **marginal private costs** and marginal social costs are equal at all levels of output. **Marginal social benefits** are the sum of **marginal private benefits** plus **marginal external benefits.** Marginal private benefits are enjoyed by those who directly pay for any good or service; marginal external benefits are enjoyed by customers and noncustomers alike and are not reflected in market prices. When no externalities are present, marginal social benefits equal marginal private benefits.

- The **social rate of discount** is the interest-rate cost of public funds. According to the **social net present-value** (SNPV) criterion, social programs and public-sector investment projects are acceptable if the present value of marginal social benefits is greater than or equal to the present value of marginal social costs. **Benefit–cost (*B/C*) ratio analysis** shows the present value of marginal social benefits per dollar of marginal social cost. The **social internal rate of return** (SIRR) is the interest or discount rate that

equates the present value of the future receipts of a program to the initial cost or outlay.

- **Cost-effectiveness analysis** seeks to determine how to best employ resources in a given social program or public-sector investment project. With **privatization,** public-sector resources are transferred to the private sector in the hope that the profit motive might spur higher product quality, better customer service, and lower costs.

Policies employed at all levels of government affect private-sector price–output decisions. This chapter demonstrates how the tools and techniques of microeconomics can improve decision making in the public sector and refine the management of scarce public resources.

QUESTIONS

Q19.1 Air pollution costs the United States billions of dollars per year in worker absenteeism, health care, pain and suffering, and loss of life. Discuss some of the costs and benefits of a Pigou tax on air pollution.

Q19.2 What role does the price elasticity of demand play in determining the short-run effects of regulations that increase fixed costs? What if they lead to increased variable costs?

Q19.3 What is the essential difference between public and private goods? Give some examples of each and some examples of goods and services that involve elements of both.

Q19.4 In the 1880s, cattlemen in the American West crowded more and more animals onto common grazing land to feed a growing nation. Cattlemen contended, "None of us knows anything about grass outside of the fact that there is lots of it, and we aim to get it while the getting is good." Explain this attitude as a manifestation of the tragedy of the commons, and discuss how to solve the problem. Does resolving the cattlemen's dilemma of the 1880s suggest how the world today can save the African elephant?

Q19.5 Does the fact that public decisions are sometimes made by self-interested politicians and bureaucrats undermine the efficiency of public-sector decision making?

Q19.6 A pipeline break reduced the supply of gasoline to the Phoenix, Arizona, area in August 2003. Press reports indicated that some stations ran out of gasoline, consumers waited in line for hours, and some drivers started following gasoline tankers as they made their deliveries. Explain the efficiency and equity considerations tied to a competitive-market allocation of supply versus government-controlled rationing in such circumstances.

Q19.7 In 1848, the idea of cost–benefit analysis originated with a French engineer by the name of Jules Dupuit. Economists argue that underlying calculations of costs and benefits must be based upon actual market behavior and not based upon consumer and producer surveys or "informed estimates." Why?

Q19.8 To measure public project desirability, positive and negative aspects of the project must be expressed in terms of a common monetary unit. Explain the importance of the present value concept in benefit/cost ratio calculations using a 5 percent interest rate assumption and a 5-year project life.

Q19.9 The former chairman of the Federal Communications Commission heralded Voice over Internet Protocol, or VoIP, as "the most important shift in the entire history of modern communications since the invention of the telephone." Using cheap computer software and the Internet, VoIP offers consumers bargain-priced voice and data communication services. In the process, VoIP threatens to make obsolete the regional Bell operating companies' (RBOCs) $125 billion investment in conventional telephone networks. Explain the risks involved with regulatory policies that encourage or discourage VoIP adoption. What should the government do?

Q19.10 "Regulation is often proposed on the basis of equity considerations and opposed on the basis of efficiency considerations. As a result, the regulation versus deregulation controversy is not easily resolved." Discuss this statement.

SELF-TEST PROBLEMS AND SOLUTIONS

ST19.1 Pollution Control Costs. Anthony Soprano is head of Satriale Pork Producers, Inc., a family-run pork producer with a hog-processing facility in Musconetcong, New Jersey. Each hog processed yields both pork and a render by-product in a fixed 1:1 ratio. Although the by-product is unfit for human consumption, some can be sold to a local pet food company for further processing. Relevant annual demand and cost relations are as follows:

$$P_P = \$110 - \$0.00005Q_P$$
(Demand for Pork)

$$MR_P = \partial TR_P/\partial Q_P = \$110 - \$0.0001Q_P$$
(Marginal Revenue from Pork)

$$P_B = \$10 - \$0.0001Q_B$$
(Demand for Render By-Product)

$$MR_B = \partial TR_B/\partial Q_B = \$10 - \$0.0002Q_B$$
(Marginal Revenue from Render By-Product)

$$TC = \$10,000,000 + \$60Q$$
(Total Cost)

$$MC = \partial TC/\partial Q = \$60$$
(Marginal Cost)

Here, P is price in dollars, Q is the number of hogs processed (with an average weight of 100 pounds), and Q_P and Q_B are pork and render by-product per hog, respectively; both total and marginal costs are in dollars. Total costs include a risk-adjusted normal return of 15 percent on a $50 million investment in plant and equipment.

Currently, the city allows the company to dump excess by-product into its sewage treatment facility at no charge, viewing the service as an attractive means of keeping a valued employer in the area. However, the sewage treatment facility is quickly approaching peak capacity and must be expanded at an expected operating cost of $3 million per year. This is an impossible burden on an already strained city budget.

A. Calculate the profit-maximizing price–output combination and optimal total profit level for Satriale.

B. How much by-product will the company dump into the Musconetcong sewage treatment facility at the profit-maximizing activity level?

C. Calculate output and total profits if the city imposes a $35 per unit charge on the amount of by-product Satriale dumps.

D. Calculate output and total profits if the city imposes a fixed $3 million per year tax on Satriale to pay for the sewage treatment facility expansion.

E. Will either tax alternative permit Satriale to survive in the long run? In your opinion, what should the city of Musconetcong do about its sewage treatment problem?

ST19.1   SOLUTION

A. Solution to this problem requires that one look at several production and sales options available to the firm. One option is to produce and sell equal quantities of pork (P) and by-product (B). In this case, the firm sets relevant $MC = MR$.

$$MC = MR_P + MR_B = MR$$
$$\$60 = \$110 - \$0.0001Q + \$10 - \$0.0002Q$$
$$0.0003Q = 60$$
$$Q = 200,000 \text{ hogs}$$

Thus, the profit-maximizing output level for production and sale of equal quantities of P and B would be 200,000 hogs. However, the marginal revenues of both products must be positive at this sales level for this to be an optimal activity level.

Evaluated at 200,000 hogs:

$$MR_P = \$110 - \$0.0001(200,000)$$
$$= \$90$$
$$MR_B = \$10 - 0.0002(200,000)$$
$$= -\$30$$

Because the marginal revenue for B is negative, and Satriale can costlessly dump excess production, the sale of 200,000 units of B is suboptimal. This invalidates the entire solution developed above because output of P is being held down by the negative marginal revenue associated with B. The problem must be set up to recognize that Satriale will stop selling B at the point where its marginal revenue becomes zero because, given production for P, the marginal cost of B is zero.

Set

$$MR_B = MC_B$$
$$\$10 - \$0.0002Q_B = \$0$$
$$0.0002Q_B = 10$$
$$Q_B = 50,000 \text{ units}$$

Thus, 50,000 units of B are the maximum that would be sold. Any excess units will be dumped into the city's sewage treatment facility. The price for B at 50,000 units is

$$P_B = \$10 - \$0.0001Q_B$$
$$= 10 - 0.0001(50,000)$$
$$= \$5$$

To determine the optimal production of P (pork), set the marginal revenue of P equal to the marginal cost of hog processing because pork production is the only motive for processing more than 50,000 units:

$$MR_P = MC_P = MC_Q$$
$$\$110 - \$0.0001Q_P = \$60$$
$$0.0001Q_P = 50$$
$$Q_P = 500{,}000 \text{ units}$$
$$[\text{Remember } (Q_P = Q)]$$

and

$$P_P = \$110 - \$0.00005Q_P$$
$$= 110 - 0.00005(500{,}000)$$
$$= \$85$$

Excess profits at the optimal activity level for Satriale are

$$\text{Excess profits} = \pi = TR_P + TR_B - TC$$
$$= P_P \times Q_P + P_B \times Q_B - TC_Q$$
$$= \$85(500{,}000) + \$5(50{,}000) - \$10{,}000{,}000 - \$60(500{,}000)$$
$$= \$2{,}750{,}000$$

Because total costs include a normal return of 15 percent on \$50 million in investment,

$$\text{Total Profits} = \text{Required Return} + \text{Excess Profits}$$
$$= 0.15(\$50{,}000{,}000) + \$2{,}750{,}000$$
$$= \$10{,}250{,}000$$

B. With 500,000 hogs being processed, but only 50,000 units of B sold, dumping of B is

$$\text{Units B Dumped} = \text{Units Produced} - \text{Units Sold}$$
$$= 500{,}000 - 50{,}000$$
$$= 450{,}000 \text{ units}$$

C. In part A, it is shown that if all P and B produced is sold, an activity level of $Q = 200{,}000$ results in $MR_B = -\$30$. A dumping charge of \$35 per unit of B will cause Satriale to prefer to sell the last unit of B produced (and lose \$30) rather than pay a \$35 fine. Therefore, this fine, as does any fine greater than \$30, will eliminate dumping and cause Satriale to reduce processing to 200,000 hogs per year. This fine structure would undoubtedly reduce or eliminate the need for a new sewage treatment facility.

Although eliminating dumping is obviously attractive in the sense of reducing sewage treatment costs, the \$35 fine has the unfortunate consequence of cutting output substantially. Pork prices rise to $P_P = \$110 - \$0.00005(200{,}000) = \$100$, and by-product prices fall to $P_B = \$10 - \$0.0001(200{,}000) = -\$10$. This means Satriale will pay the pet food company \$10 per unit to accept all of its by-product sludge. Employment will undoubtedly fall as well. In addition to these obvious short-run effects, long-run implications may be especially serious. At $Q = 200,000$, Satriale's excess profits are

$$\text{Excess profits} = TR_P + TR_B - TC$$
$$= \$110Q - \$0.00005Q^2 + \$10Q - \$0.0001Q^2 - \$10,000,000 - \$60Q$$
$$= \$110(200,000) - \$0.00005(200,000^2) + \$10(200,000) - \$0.0001(200,000^2) - \$10,000,000 - \$60(200,000)$$
$$= -\$4,000,000 \text{ (a loss)}$$

This means that total profits are

$$\text{Total profits} = \text{Required return} + \text{Excess profits}$$
$$= 0.15(\$50,000,000) + (-\$4,000,000)$$
$$= \$3,500,000$$

This level of profit is insufficient to maintain investment. Although a $35 dumping charge will eliminate dumping, it is likely to cause the firm to close down or move to some other location. The effect on employment in Musconetcong could be disastrous.

D. In the short run, a $3 million tax on Satriale has no effect on dumping, output, or employment. At the $Q = 500,000$ activity level, a $3 million tax would reduce Satriale's total profits to $7,250,000, or $250,000 below the required return on investment. However, following imposition of a $3 million tax, the firm's survival and total employment would be imperiled in the long run.

E. No. Satriale is not able to bear the burden of either tax alternative. Obviously, there is no single best alternative here. The highest fixed tax the company can bear in the long run is $2.75 million, the full amount of excess profits. If the city places an extremely high priority on maintaining employment, perhaps a $2.75 million tax on Satriale plus $250,000 in general city tax revenues could be used to pay for the new sewage system treatment facility.

ST19.2 Benefit–cost Analysis Methodology.

The benefit–cost approach first surfaced in France during 1844. In this century, benefit–cost analysis has been widely used in the evaluation of river and harbor projects since as early as 1902. In the United States, the 1936 Flood Control Act authorized federal assistance in developing flood-control programs "if the benefits to whomsoever they may accrue are in excess of the estimated costs." By 1950, federal agency practice required the consideration of both direct and indirect benefits and costs and that unmeasured intangible influences be listed. Despite this long history of widespread use, it has only been since 1970 that public-sector managers have sought to broadly apply the principles of benefit–cost analysis to the evaluation of agricultural programs, rapid transit projects, highway construction, urban renewal projects, recreation facility construction, job training programs, health care reform, education, research and development projects, and defense policies.

A. Briefly describe major similarities and differences between public-sector benefit–cost analysis and the private-sector capital budgeting process.

B. What major questions must be answered before meaningful benefit–cost analysis is possible?

C. Although the maximization of society's wealth is the primary objective of benefit–cost analysis, it is important to recognize that constraints often limit government's ability to achieve certain objectives. Enumerate some of the common economic, political, and social constraints faced in public-sector benefit–cost analysis.

D. In light of these constraints, discuss some of the pluses and minuses associated with the use of benefit–cost analysis as the foundation for a general approach to the allocation of government-entrusted resources.

ST19.2   SOLUTION

A. Benefit–cost analysis is a method for assessing the desirability of social programs and public-sector investment projects when it is necessary to take a long view of the public and private repercussions of such expenditures. As in the case of private-sector capital budgeting, benefit–cost analysis is frequently used in cases where the economic consequences of a program or project are likely to extend beyond 1 year in time. Unlike capital budgeting, however, benefit–cost analysis seeks to measure both direct private effects and indirect social implications of public-sector investment decisions and policy changes.

B. Before meaningful benefit–cost analysis is possible, a number of important policy questions must be answered. Among these policy questions are
- What is the social objective function that is to be maximized?
- What constraints are placed on the decision-making process?
- What marginal social benefits and marginal social costs are to be included, and how are they to be measured?
- What social investment criterion should be used?
- What is the appropriate social rate of discount?

C. A number of constraints impinge upon society's ability to maximize the social benefits derived from public expenditures. Among these constraints are
- Physical constraints. Program alternatives are limited by the available state of technology and by current production possibilities. For example, it is not yet possible to cure AIDS. Therefore, major emphasis for public policy in this area must be directed toward prevention, early detection and treatment, and research.
- Legal constraints. Domestic laws and international agreements place limits on property rights, the right of eminent domain, due process, constitutional limits on a particular agency's activities, and so on. These legal constraints often play an important role in shaping the realm of public policy.
- Administrative constraints. Effective programs require competent management and execution. Qualified individuals must be available to carry out social objectives. Even the best-conceived program is doomed to failure unless managers and workers with the proper mix of technical and administrative skill are available.
- Distributional constraints. Social programs and public-sector investment projects affect different groups in different ways. The "gainers" are seldom the same as "losers." When distributional impacts of public policy are of paramount concern, the objective of benefit–cost analysis might maximize subject to the constraint that equity considerations be met.
- Political constraints. That which is optimal may not be feasible because of slowness and inefficiency in the political process. Often what is best is tempered by what is possible, given the existence of strong competing special-interest groups.

- Budget constraints. Public agencies often work within the bounds of a predetermined budget. As a result, virtually all social programs and public-sector investment projects have some absolute financial ceiling above which the program cannot be expanded, irrespective of social benefits.
- Social or religious constraints. Social or religious constraints may limit the range of feasible program alternatives. It is futile to attempt to combat teen pregnancy with public support for family planning if religious constraints prohibit the use of modern birth control methods.

D. An important potential use of benefit–cost analysis is as the structure for a general philosophy of government resource allocation. As such, the results of benefit–cost studies have the potential to serve as a guide for resource-allocation decisions within and among government programs and investment projects in agriculture, defense, education, health care, welfare, and other areas. The objective of such a comprehensive benefit–cost approach to government would be to maximize the net present-value of the difference between the marginal social benefits and the marginal social costs derived from all social programs and public-sector investment projects.

Although a benefit–cost approach to evaluating all levels and forms of government is conceptually appealing on an efficiency basis, it suffers from a number of serious practical limitations. Perhaps most importantly, the measurement of marginal social benefits and marginal social costs for goods and services that are not or cannot be provided by the private sector is often primitive, at best. Measurement systems have not been sufficiently refined or standardized to permit meaningful comparisons among the social net present-value of "Star Wars" defense systems, the guaranteed student loan program for college students, funding for AIDS research, Medicare, and Medicaid. A further problem arises because benefit–cost analysis is largely restricted to a consideration of the efficiency objective; equity-related considerations are seldom accorded full treatment in benefit–cost analysis. In addition, as discussed previously, a number of important economic, political, and social constraints limit the effectiveness of benefit–cost analysis. As a result, significant problems arise when a given social program or public-sector investment project is designed to meet efficiency and equity-related objectives.

For these reasons, benefit–cost analysis is traditionally viewed within the narrow context of a decision technique that is helpful in focusing interest on the economic consequences of proposed social programs and public-sector investment projects. Its greatest use is in comparing programs and projects that are designed to achieve the same or similar objectives and as a tool for focusing resources on the best use of resources intended to meet a given social objective.

PROBLEMS

P19.1 Market Imperfections. Markets usually allocate resources in a manner that creates the greatest net benefit to society. An efficient allocation is one that maximizes the net benefits to society. Indicate whether each of the following statements is true or false, and explain your answer.

A. Markets sometimes fail to allocate resources efficiently. Under such circumstances, it always makes sense for the government to impose taxes in the case of negative externalities or subsidies in the case of positive externalities.

B. A negative externality exists when a voluntary market transaction between two parties imposes involuntary costs on a third party.

C. Efficiency mandates that the prices of goods and services reflect all incremental costs of production, including the cost of inputs, the value of producer time and effort, and any spillover effects.

D. With a Pigou tax, the costs that pollution imposes on the public will be considered when the firm decides where to locate a plant, which technologies to use, or how much to produce.

E. In all cases, the best remedy for externalities is to define property rights and allow the affected parties to transact privately to achieve mutually beneficial outcomes.

P19.2 Negative Externalities. Coal-fired electricity-generating plants emit substantial amounts of sulfur dioxide and particulate pollution into the atmosphere. Concerned citizens are appalled at the aesthetic and environmental implications of such pollution, as well as the potential health hazard to the local population.

In analyzing remedies to the current situation, three general methods used to control air pollution are generally considered:

- Regulations—licenses, permits, compulsory standards, and so on.
- Payments — various types of government aid to help companies install pollution-control equipment. Aid can take the form of forgiven local property taxes, income tax credits, special accelerated depreciation allowances for pollution-control equipment, low-cost government loans, and so on.
- Charges — excise taxes on polluting fuels (e.g., coal, oil, and so forth), pollution discharge taxes, and other taxes.

Answer the following questions in light of these alternative methods of pollution control.

A. Pollution is a negative externality and a major cause of market failure. Explain why markets fail.

B. What is the incentive provided to polluters under each method of pollution control?

C. Who pays for a clean environment under each form of control?

D. On the basis of both efficiency and equity considerations, which form of pollution control is most attractive?

P19.3 Costs of Regulation. Hathaway-Ross Instruments, Inc., manufactures an innovative piece of diagnostic equipment used in medical laboratories and hospitals. The Occupational Safety and Health Administration (OSHA) has determined that additional safety precautions are necessary to bring radioactive leakage occurring during use of this equipment down to acceptable levels. Total and marginal production costs, including a normal rate of return on investment but before additional safeguards are installed, are as follows:

$$TC = \$5,000,000 + \$5,000Q$$
$$MC = \partial TC / \partial Q = \$5,000$$

Market demand and marginal revenue relations are the following:

$$P_L = \$15,000 - \$12.5Q_L \qquad \text{(Medical Laboratory Demand)}$$
$$MR_L = \partial TR/\partial Q_L = \$15,000 - \$25Q_L$$
$$P_H = \$10,000 - \$1Q_H \qquad \text{(Hospital Demand)}$$
$$MR_H = \partial TR/\partial Q_H = \$10,000 - \$2Q_H$$

A. Assuming that the company faces two distinct markets, calculate the profit-maximizing price–output combination in each market and economic profits.

B. Describe the short- and long-run implications of meeting OSHA standards if doing so raises marginal cost by $1,000 per machine.

C. Calculate the point price elasticity at the initial (part A) profit-maximizing activity level in each market. Are the differential effects on sales in each market that were seen in part B typical or atypical?

P19.4   Incidence of Regulation Costs.   The Smokey Mountain Coal Company sells coal to electric utilities in the southeast. Unfortunately, Smokey's coal has a high particulate content, and, therefore, the company is adversely affected by state and local regulations governing smoke and dust emissions at its customers' electricity-generating plants. Smokey's total and marginal cost relations are

$$TC = \$1,000,000 + \$5Q + \$0.0001Q^2$$
$$MC = \partial TC/\partial Q = \$5 + \$0.0002Q$$

where Q is tons of coal produced per month and TC includes a risk-adjusted normal rate of return on investment.

A. Calculate Smokey's profit at the profit-maximizing activity level if prices in the industry are stable at $25 per ton and therefore $P = MR = \$25$.

B. Calculate Smokey's optimal price, output, and profit levels if a new state regulation results in a $5 per ton cost increase that can be fully passed on to customers.

C. Determine the effect on output and profit if Smokey must fully absorb the $5 per ton cost increase.

P19.5   Social Rate of Discount.   Because resources for social programs and public-sector investment projects come from private-sector consumption and/or investment, economists typically advocate the use of a social rate of discount that reflects this private-sector opportunity cost. A good estimate of the opportunity cost of funds diverted from private consumption is the rate of return on government securities that is available to individual investors. Similarly, the average rate of return on private investments can be taken as the opportunity cost of private-sector investment funds.

A. Should pretax or after-tax rates of return be used to estimate the opportunity cost of resources diverted from the private sector to fund social programs or public-sector investment projects? Why?

B. Assume that the rate of return on long-term government bonds is 8 percent, a typical after-tax return on investment in the private sector is 10 percent, the marginal corporate and individual tax rate is 30 percent, and consumption averages 95 percent of total income. Based on the information provided, calculate an economically appropriate social rate of discount.

P19.6 Equity Versus Efficiency in Benefit–Cost Analysis.

In benefit–cost analysis, public-sector managers seek to learn if society as a whole will be better off by the adoption of a specific social program or public-sector investment project. Rather than seeking to maximize profits or the value of the firm, public-sector managers use benefit–cost analysis to maximize, or at least move toward a maximization of, the excess of marginal social benefits over marginal social costs. With this goal in mind, from an efficiency perspective, the distribution of any social net present-value is of no importance. For example, when the city of Denver sponsors Denver International Airport at an initial cost of $3.5 billion, it makes no difference whether the city pays the entire cost or whether the city, the state of Colorado, and the federal government split these costs. Similarly, if the city of Denver is motivated by the desire to lure business and tourist traffic from Chicago or Los Angeles, the benefits of increased economic activity in Denver that has merely shifted from other transportation centers should not be counted. In both instances, the proper concern is the increase in aggregate social wealth, not aggregate local wealth.

A. Assume that the city of Denver and local airline customers must pay only 10 percent of the costs of Denver International Airport, with the federal government picking up the other 90 percent of the tab. Describe how a local benefit–cost analysis of the airport project might be distorted by this cost-sharing arrangement.

B. Under the federal revenue sharing program, the federal government collects tax revenues that are then returned to states and other local units of government to support a wide variety of social programs. Can you see any problems for an efficient allocation of public expenditures when the spending and taxing authority of government is divided in this manner?

C. Can the equity and efficiency implications of social programs and public-sector investment projects be completely separated?

P19.7 Benefit–Cost Analysis.

Highway crashes continue to claim the lives of thousands of Americans. Grim statistics underscore the need for better laws, stricter enforcement, and safer driving behavior. In 2006, approximately 43,300 persons died on the nation's highways. Alcohol-related fatalities accounted for 41.4 percent of the total. The majority of passenger vehicle occupants killed in crashes were not wearing safety belts.

As a practical matter, it is important to recognize that most highway fatalities are preventable. Using current technology, highway fatalities could be substantially reduced by draconian laws against drunk driving, mandatory seat belts, and strictly enforced speed limits. Needless to say, popular opposition would be intense. Speed limits as high as 75 mph on major highways are popular because consumers derive significant economic and social benefits from swift automobile transportation. However, by failing to sharply reduce or eliminate highway fatalities, speed limit policy places a finite and measurable value on human life.

A. From an economic standpoint, explain how public policy sets a dollar value on human life. Is it efficient to do so?

B. Are there equity considerations one must weigh in judging the fairness of dollar estimates of the value of human life?

P19.8   Privatization.   In Massachusetts, a state education law authorized the establishment of charter schools. Charter schools are public schools that receive state funding as well as some measure of autonomy from local school boards and the rules that govern conventional schools. As a result, students and educators in Boston face the ready prospect of classrooms with politicians as lecturers, academic instruction aided by yoga, school doors open from dawn to dusk, and public schools run on a for-profit basis.

Charter schools already are operating in Minnesota and California, and five other states promise to join the trend with recently enacted charter-school legislation. Advocates of such schools argue that they provide badly needed competition for existing public schools. Under the charter-school concept, anyone with a good education idea gets access to government funding, so long as they can attract and effectively train students.

A. Explain how breaking the public-school monopoly on access to public funding could help improve the quality of public- and private-school primary education.

B. Explain why primary-school privatization might not create such benefits.

P19.9   Economics of Health Care.   The United States spends more per person on health care than any other country in the world. Still, recent studies show that the United States ranks relatively low in the overall quality of health care provided. France is often described as providing its citizens with the globe's best health care. Japan wins the distinction as having the world's healthiest people. Although good at expensive care, like open-heart surgery, the U.S. health care delivery system is often described as poor at low-cost preventive care.

A. Explain the role of public and private insurance in making the demand for health care different from the demand for many other services.

B. Consumers buy health care to improve their health and well-being, but research suggests only a weak connection between health care spending and health. Explain why there might be only a weak link between health care expenditures and health.

C. Why is health care spending rising rapidly on a worldwide basis? Is robust growth in health care spending likely to continue?

P19.10   Health Care Reform.   Public support dropped for a Medicare prescription-drug law endorsed by President George W. Bush and passed by a Republican-controlled Congress following withering criticism from Democrats. Democrats were upset that the law prevented Medicare from negotiating lower prices from drug manufacturers and prohibited the purchase of cheaper medicines from Canada. The Congressional Budget Office projected the 10-year cost at $395 billion, but Medicare officials quickly raised that figure to $534 billion over 10 years. Meanwhile, conservatives argued that expensive drug benefits will encourage employers to drop existing coverage for retirees.

A. Explain how Medicare prescription-drug benefits might have the unintended effect of increasing drug prices.

B. Explain how Medicare prescription-drug benefits might affect the supply of new and innovative drugs.

CASE *Study*

Oh, Lord, Won't You Buy Me a Mercedes-Benz (Factory)?[2]

In 1993, Alabama emerged victorious as the site of Mercedes-Benz AG's first U.S. car plant. States like Alabama are vying more desperately than ever to lure new industrial jobs and hold on to those that they have. To start with, they give away millions of dollars in free land. After that come fat checks for site clearance, training, even employee salaries. Both foreign and domestic companies are finding ingenious ways to cash in.

Mercedes initially had so little interest in Alabama that Mercedes' site-selection team did not even plan to visit the state. Of more than 20 states that Mercedes looked at seriously, it initially leaned toward North Carolina, where Mercedes' parent, Daimler-Benz AG, already builds Freightliner trucks. North Carolina officials say that their governor pursued Mercedes harder than he ever had pursued any potential investor. Mercedes officials were reportedly surprised at the enthusiastic response to their request for tax and other subsidies, but they were quick to cash in. Mercedes would get offers for certain things from certain states, put it on their ideal contract proposal, and then come back to the other states and ask if they would be willing to do the same. For example, Mercedes persuaded all the main competitors to offer $5 million for a welcome center next to the factory, where customers could pick up cars, have them serviced, and visit an auto museum. It got commitments for free 18-month employee-training programs. It also got state governments and utilities to promise to buy large quantities of the four-wheel-drive recreational vehicles that the new factory would produce. Mercedes officials even asked the states to pick up the salaries of its 1,500 workers for their first year or so on the job, at a cost of $45 million. The workers would be in a training program and would not be producing anything, Mercedes explained. Although North Carolina

and other state officials said no, Alabama said yes, even to the salary request. Alabama economic development officials argued that the Mercedes project simply was worth more to Alabama than it was to any other state.

When Mercedes found North Carolina proposing to build a $35 million training center at the company's plant, the German automaker enticed Alabama to more than match the North Carolina offer. To outbid the competition, the Alabama governor hurriedly won legislative approval for lavish tax concessions—dubbed Alabama's Mercedes Law—and offered to spend tens of millions of dollars buying more than 2,500 Mercedes vehicles for state use. In the bargain, Mercedes says it agreed to limit itself to using just $42.6 million per year in income and payroll tax credits; Alabama officials say that was all Mercedes expected to be able to use, based on profit projections. It also will be allowed, however, to escape more than $9 million a year in property taxes and other fees, as permitted under existing law. Although South Carolina offered $80 million in tax credits over a period of 20 years, Alabama granted Mercedes a more attractive tax credit, available in advance in the form of an interest-free loan. Mercedes officials also say Alabama's promised education spending was double any other state's promise. Alabama officials even agreed to place Mercedes' distinctive emblem atop a local scoreboard in time for the big, televised Alabama–Tennessee football game. The price? Why, free, of course. In all, Alabama wound up promising Mercedes over $300 million in incentives, which economic development experts called a record package for a foreign company.

How has it worked out in the long run? Very well, say supporters of the Alabama program. In 2000, Mercedes announced it would invest another $600 million in a major expansion at its

---

2 For some interesting perspective on the "corporate welfare" issue, see the Cato Institute Web site at http://www.cato.org/pubs/pas/pa225.html. Also see E. S. Browning and Helene Cooper, "Ante Up: States' Bidding War over Mercedes Plant Made for Costly Chase; Alabama Won the Business, But Some Wonder if It Also Gave Away the Farm, Will Image Now Improve?" *The Wall Street Journal*, November 24, 1993, A1.

continued

Tuscaloosa, Alabama, site to double production for the next generation Mercedes-Benz M-class sport utility vehicle. The expansion doubled production capacity from 80,000 units to roughly 160,000 units at the Tuscaloosa facility and generated up to 2,000 new jobs. In announcing the expansion, company officials stressed that their success would not have been possible without the partnership they had formed with the state of Alabama and the strong workforce that they found there. With the new expansion, Mercedes is on target to become the fifth-largest employer in Alabama, with more than 7,000 employees between its Chrysler electronics plant in Huntsville, Alabama, and the Tuscaloosa Mercedes-Benz factory. The total capital investment made by the company in Alabama is expected to rise to more than $2.5 billion, once the expansion is complete.

Critics complain that Alabama subsidies used to land the Mercedes-Benz deal represent an egregious example of "corporate welfare." During recent years, as many as 44 of the 50 states have stepped up to offer economic incentives for corporations to relocate, rebuild, or remain in their jurisdictions. Detractors argue that handouts given corporations by local, state, and federal governments in the form of subsidies, grants, low-interest loans, or free government service amounts to $150 billion per year. Tax breaks and tax credits add to the bill. In the late1990s, when funding was cut for the federal Aid to Families with Dependent Children program, the action was justified as a means for breaking a "cycle of dependency" among the poor. Critics of government incentives for economic expansion argue that the same indictment applies to corporate welfare.

Moreover, instead of helping the poor, corporate welfare rewards the rich and powerful.

A. With $300 million in state aid to attract 1,500 new jobs, the initial marginal social cost to Alabama taxpayers of attracting the Mercedes plant was $200,000 per job. Estimate the minimum marginal social benefit required to make this a reasonable expenditure from the perspective of Alabama taxpayers. Do the facts of this case lead you to believe that it is more likely that Alabama underbid or overbid for this project? Explain.

B. Does the fact that the bidding process for the Mercedes plant took place at the state and local level of government have any implications for the amount of inducements offered? Would these numbers change dramatically if only the federal government could offer tax breaks for industrial development?

C. Explain how a benefit–cost analysis of the Alabama Mercedes project could account for any potential erosion of the local tax base at the state and local level.

D. Critics contend that taxpayers in Alabama were denied the opportunities provided by alternate privately directed capital investment projects because the state chose to redirect public and private investment toward the Mercedes plant project. Instead of enjoying an efficient increase in business activity among a number of smaller enterprises, employees, taxpayers, and consumers are left with a large and potentially inefficient state-directed investment in the auto plant. Do you agree? Why or why not?

SELECTED REFERENCES

Alesina, Alberto and Guido Tabellini. "Bureaucrats or Politicians? Part I: A Single Policy Task." *American Economic Review* 97, no. 1 (March, 2007): 169–179.

Asiedu, Elizabeth and James A. Freeman. "The Effect of Globalization on the Performance of Small- and Medium-Sized Enterprises in the United States: Does Owners' Race/Ethnicity Matter?" *American Economic Review* 97, no. 2 (May, 2007): 368–372.

Banal Estanol, Albert. "Information-Sharing Implications of Horizontal Mergers." *International Journal of Industrial Organization* 25, no. 1 (February, 2007): 31–49.

Battaglini, Marco and Stephen Coate. "Inefficiency in Legislative Policymaking: A Dynamic Analysis." *American Economic Review* 97, no. 1 (March, 2007): 118–149.

Baum Snow, Nathaniel. "Did Highways Cause Suburbanization?" *Quarterly Journal of Economics* 122, no. 2 (May, 2007): 775–805.

Beck, Thorsten, Asli Demirguc Kunt, and Maria Soledad Martinez Peria. "Reaching Out: Access to and Use of Banking Services Across Countries." *Journal of Financial Economics* 85, no. 1 (July, 2007): 234–266.

Blankenau, William F., Nicole B. Simpson, and Marc Tomljanovich. "Public Education Expenditures, Taxation, and Growth: Linking Data to Theory." *American Economic Review* 97, no. 2 (May, 2007): 393–397.

Card, David, Raj Chetty, and Andrea Weber. "The Spike at Benefit Exhaustion: Leaving the Unemployment System or Starting a New Job?" *American Economic Review* 97, no. 2 (May, 2007): 113–118.

Carroll, Anne, Hope Corman, Kelly Noonan, and Nancy E. Reichman. "Why Do Poor Children Lose Health Insurance in the SCHIP Era? The Role of Family Health." *American Economic Review* 97, no. 2 (May, 2007): 398–401.

Cunningham, Christopher R. "Growth Controls, Real Options, and Land Development." *Review of Economics and Statistics* 89, no. 2 (May, 2007): 343–358.

Mattozzi, Andrea and Antonio Merlo. "The Transparency of Politics and the Quality of Politicians." *American Economic Review* 97, no. 2 (May, 2007): 311–315.

McCrary, Justin. "The Effect of Court-Ordered Hiring Quotas on the Composition and Quality of Police." *American Economic Review* 97, no. 1 (March, 2007): 318–353.

Ong, Paul and Don Mar. "Differential Impacts of Immigrants on Native Black and White Workers." *American Economic Review* 97, no. 2 (May, 2007): 383–387.

Quinn, Stephen and William Roberds. "The Bank of Amsterdam and the Leap to Central Bank Money." *American Economic Review* 97, no. 2 (May, 2007): 262–265.

Rota Graziosi, Gregoire. "Secession and the Limits of Taxation: Toward a Theory of Internal Exit: Comment." *American Economic Review* 97, no. 1 (March, 2007): 534–537.

Appendix A

Compounding and the Time Value of Money

The concepts of compound growth and the time value of money are widely used in all aspects of business and economics. Compounding is the principle that underlies growth, whether it is growth in value, growth in sales, or growth in assets. The time value of money—the fact that a dollar received in the future is worth less than a dollar in hand today—also plays an important role in managerial economics. Cash flows occurring in different periods must be adjusted to their value at a common point in time to be analyzed and compared. Because of the importance of these concepts in economic analysis, thorough understanding of the material on future (compound) and present values in the appendix is important for the study of managerial economics.

FUTURE VALUE (OR COMPOUND VALUE)

Suppose that you deposit $100 in a bank savings account that pays 5 percent interest compounded annually. How much will you have at the end of 1 year? Let us define terms as follows:

PV = Present value of your account, or the beginning amount, $100;

i = Interest rate the bank pays you = 5 percent per year, or, expressed in decimal terms, 0.05;

I = Dollars of interest earned during the year;

FV_N = Future value, or ending amount, of your account at the end of N years. Whereas PV is the value now, at the present time, FV_N is the value N years into the future, after compound interest has been earned. Note also that FV_0 is the future value zero years into the future, which is the present, so $FV_0 = PV$.

In our example, $N = 1$, so $FV_N = FV_1$, and it is calculated as follows:

$$\begin{aligned} FV_1 &= PV + I \\ &= PV + PV \times i \\ &= PV(1 + i) \end{aligned}$$

A.1

We can now use Equation (A.1) to find how much the account is worth at the end of 1 year:

$$FV_1 = \$100(1 + 0.05) = \$100(1.05) = \$105$$

Your account earned $5 of interest ($I = \$5$), so you have $105 at the end of the year.

Now suppose that you leave your funds on deposit for 5 years; how much will you have at the end of the fifth year? The answer is $127.63; this value is worked out in Table A.1.

Notice that the Table A.1 value for FV_2, the value of the account at the end of year 2, is equal to

$$FV_2 = FV_1(1 + i) = PV(1 + i)(1 + i) = PV(1 + i)^2$$

FV_3, the balance after 3 years, is

$$FV_3 = FV_2(1 + i) = PV(1 + i)^3$$

In general, FV_n, the future value at the end of N years, is found as

$$FV_N = PV(1 + i)^N \qquad\qquad \textbf{A.2}$$

Applying Equation (A.2) in the case of a 5-year account that earns 5 percent per year gives

$$PV_5 = \$100(1.05)^5$$
$$= \$100(1.2763)$$
$$= \$127.63$$

which is the same as the value in Table A.1.

If an electronic calculator is handy, it is easy enough to calculate $(1 + i)^N$ directly.[1] However, tables have been constructed for values of $(1 + i)^N$ for wide ranges of i and N, as Table A.2 illustrates. Table B.1 in Appendix B contains a more complete set of compound value interest factors. Interest compounding can occur over periods of time different from 1 year. Thus, although compounding is often on an annual basis, it can be quarterly, semiannually, monthly, or for any other period.

The term *future value interest factor* ($FVIF_{i,N}$) equals $(1 + i)^N$. Therefore, Equation (A.2) may be written as $FV_N = PV(FVIF_{i,N})$. One needs only to go to an appropriate interest table to find the proper interest factor. For example, the correct interest factor for our

Table A.1 Compound Interest Calculations

Year	Beginning Amount, PV	×	$(1 + i)$	=	Ending Amount, FV_n
1	$100.00		1.05		$105.00
2	105.00		1.05		110.25
3	110.25		1.05		115.76
4	115.76		1.05		121.55
5	121.55		1.05		127.63

---

1   For example, to calculate $(1 + i)^N$ for $I = 5$ percent $= 0.05$ and $N = 5$ years, simply multiply $(1 + i) = (1.05)$ times (1.05); multiple this product by (1.05); and so on:

$$(1 + i)^N = (1.05)(1.05)(1.05)(1.05)(1.05) = (1.05)^5 = 1.2763$$

Table A.2 Future Value of \$1 at the End of n Periods: $FVIF_{i,n} = (1 + i)^n$

Period (n)	1%	2%	3%	4%	5%	6%	7%	8%	9%	10%
0	1.0000	1.0000	1.0000	1.0000	1.0000	1.0000	1.0000	1.0000	1.0000	1.0000
1	1.0100	1.0200	1.0300	1.0400	1.0500	1.0600	1.0700	1.0800	1.0900	1.1000
2	1.0201	1.0404	1.0609	1.0816	1.1025	1.1236	1.1449	1.1664	1.1881	1.2100
3	1.0303	1.0612	1.0927	1.1249	1.1576	1.1910	1.2250	1.2597	1.2950	1.3310
4	1.0406	1.0824	1.1255	1.1699	1.2155	1.2625	1.3108	1.3605	1.4116	1.4641
5	1.0510	1.1041	1.1593	1.2167	<u>1.2763</u>	1.3382	1.4026	1.4693	1.5386	1.6105
6	1.0615	1.1262	1.1941	1.2653	1.3401	1.4185	1.5007	1.5869	1.6771	1.7716
7	1.0721	1.1487	1.2299	1.3159	1.4071	1.5036	1.6058	1.7138	1.8280	1.9487
8	1.0829	1.1717	1.2668	1.3686	1.4775	1.5938	1.7182	1.8509	1.9926	2.1436
9	1.0937	1.1951	1.3048	1.4233	1.5513	1.6895	1.8385	1.9990	2.1719	2.3579
10	1.1046	1.2190	1.3439	1.4802	1.6289	1.7908	1.9672	2.1589	2.3674	2.5937
11	1.1157	1.2434	1.3842	1.5395	1.7103	1.8983	2.1049	2.3316	2.5804	2.8531
12	1.1268	1.2682	1.4258	1.6010	1.7959	2.0122	2.2522	2.5182	2.8127	3.1384
13	1.1381	1.2936	1.4685	1.6651	1.8856	2.1329	2.4098	2.7196	3.0658	3.4523
14	1.1495	1.3195	1.5126	1.7317	1.9799	2.2609	2.5785	2.9372	3.3417	3.7975
15	1.1610	1.3459	1.5580	1.8009	2.0789	2.3966	2.7590	3.1722	3.6425	4.1772

5-year, 5 percent illustration can be found in Table A.2. Simply look down the Period column to 5, then across this row to the 5 percent column to find the interest factor, 1.2763. Then, using this interest factor, we find the value of \$100 after 5 years as $FV_N = PV(FVIF_{i,N}) = \$100(1.2763) = \$127.63$, which is identical to the value obtained by the long method in Table A.1.

Graphic View of the Compounding Process: Growth

Figure A.1 shows how \$1 (or any other initial quantity) grows over time at various rates of interest. The higher the rate of interest, the faster the rate of growth. The interest rate is, in fact, the growth rate: If a sum is deposited and earns 5 percent, then the funds on deposit grow at the rate of 5 percent per period. Similarly, the sales of a firm or the gross domestic product (GDP) of a country might be expected to grow at a constant rate. Projections of future sales or GDP could be obtained using the compound value method.

Future value curves could be drawn for any interest rate, including fractional rates. In Figure A.1, we have plotted curves for 0 percent, 5 percent, and 10 percent, using the data from Table A.2.

PRESENT VALUE

Suppose that you are offered the alternative of receiving either \$127.63 at the end of 5 years or X dollars today. There is no question that the \$127.63 will be paid in full (perhaps the payer is the U.S. government). Having no current need for the money, you would deposit it in a bank account that pays 5 percent interest. (Five percent is your *opportunity cost*, or the rate of interest you could earn on alternative investments of equal risk.) What value of X will make you indifferent between X dollars today or the promise of \$127.63 5 years hence?

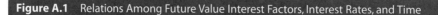

Figure A.1   Relations Among Future Value Interest Factors, Interest Rates, and Time

The future value interest factor rises with increases in the interest rate and in the number of periods for interest compounding.

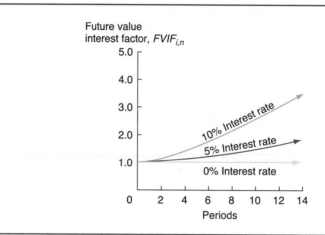

Table A.1 shows that the initial amount of $100 growing at 5 percent a year yields $127.63 at the end of 5 years. Thus, you should be indifferent in your choice between $100 today and $127.63 at the end of 5 years. The $100 is the present value, or *PV*, of $127.63 due in 5 years when the applicable interest rate is 5 percent. Therefore, if *X* is anything less than $100, you would prefer the promise of $127.63 in 5 years to *X* dollars today.

In general, the present value of a sum due *N* years in the future is the amount that, if it were invested today, would grow to equal the future sum over a period of *N* years. Because $100 would grow to $127.63 in 5 years at a 5 percent interest rate, $100 is the present value of $127.63 due 5 years in the future when the appropriate interest rate is 5 percent.

Finding present values (or *discounting,* as it is commonly called) is simply the reverse of compounding, and Equation (A.2) can readily be transformed into a present value formula:

$$FV_N = PV(1+i)^N$$

which, when solved for *PV*, gives

$$PV = \frac{FV_N}{(1+i)^N} = FV_N\left[\frac{1}{(1+i)^N}\right]$$

Tables have been constructed for the term in brackets for various values of *i* and *N*; Table A.3 is an example. For a more complete table, see Table B.2 in Appendix B. For the case being considered, look down the 5 percent column in Table A.3 to the fifth row. The figure shown there, 0.7835, is the *present value interest factor* (*PVIF*$_{i,N}$) used to determine the present value of $127.63 payable in 5 years, discounted at 5 percent

$$PV = FV_5(PVIF_{i,N})$$
$$= \$127.63(0.7835)$$
$$= \$100$$

Graphic View of the Discounting Process

Figure A.2 shows how the interest factors for discounting decrease as the discounting period increases. The curves in the figure were plotted with data taken from Table A.3; they show that the present value of a sum to be received at some future date decreases (1) as the payment date is extended further into the future and (2) as the discount rate increases. If relatively high discount rates apply, funds due in the future are worth very little today. Even at relatively low discount rates, the present values of funds due in the distant future are quite small. For example, $1 due in 10 years is worth about 61¢ today if the discount rate is 5 percent. It is worth only 25¢ today at a 15 percent discount rate. Similarly, $1 due in 5 years at 10 percent is worth 62¢ today, but at the same discount rate, $1 due in 10 years is worth only 39¢ today.

FUTURE VALUE VERSUS PRESENT VALUE

Notice that Equation (A.2), the basic equation for compounding, was developed from the logical sequence set forth in Table A.1; the equation merely presents in mathematical form the steps outlined in the table. The present value interest factor ($PVIF_{i,N}$) in Equation (A.3), the basic equation for discounting or finding present values, was found as the *reciprocal* of the future value interest factor ($FVIF_{i,N}$) for the same i, N combination:

$$PVIF_{i,N} = \frac{1}{FVIF_{i,N}}$$ **A.3**

For example, the future value interest factor for 5 percent over 5 years is seen in Table A.2 to be 1.2763. The present value interest factor for 5 percent over 5 years must be the reciprocal of 1.2763

$$PVIF_{5\%,5\ yrs} = \frac{1}{1.2763} = 0.7835$$

Table A.3 Present Values of $1 Due at the End of *n* Periods

$$PVIF_{i,n} = \frac{1}{(1+i)^n} = \left[\frac{1}{(1+i)}\right]^n$$

Period (n)	1%	2%	3%	4%	5%	6%	7%	8%	9%	10%	12%	14%	15%
1	.9901	.9804	.9709	.9615	.9524	.9434	.9346	.9259	.9174	.9091	.8929	.8772	.8696
2	.9803	.9612	.9426	.9246	.9070	.8900	.8734	.8573	.8417	.8264	.7972	.7695	.7561
3	.9706	.9423	.9151	.8890	.8638	.8396	.8163	.7938	.7722	.7513	.7118	.6750	.6575
4	.9610	.9238	.8885	.8548	.8227	.7921	.7629	.7350	.7084	.6830	.6355	.5921	.5718
5	.9515	.9057	.8626	.8219	.7835	.7473	.7130	.6806	.6499	.6209	.5674	.5194	.4972
6	.9420	.8880	.8375	.7903	.7462	.7050	.6663	.6302	.5963	.5645	.5066	.4556	.4323
7	.9327	.8706	.8131	.7599	.7107	.6651	.6227	.5835	.5470	.5132	.4523	.3996	.3759
8	.9235	.8535	.7894	.7307	.6768	.6274	.5820	.5403	.5019	.4665	.4039	.3506	.3269
9	.9143	.8368	.7664	.7026	.6446	.5919	.5439	.5002	.4604	.4241	.3606	.3075	.2843
10	.9053	.8203	.7441	.6756	.6139	.5584	.5083	.4632	.4224	.3855	.3220	.2697	.2472

Figure A.2   Relations Among Present Value Interest Factors, Interest Rates, and Time

The present value interest factor falls with increases in the interest rate and in the number of periods prior to payment.

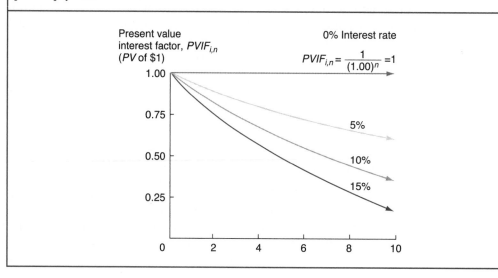

The $PVIF_{i,N}$ found in this manner does, of course, correspond with the $PVIF_{i,N}$ shown in Table A.3.

The reciprocal relation between present value and future value permits us to find present values in two ways—by multiplying or by dividing. Thus, the present value of $1,000 due in 5 years and discounted at 5 percent may be found as

$$PV = FV_N\left[\frac{1}{1+i}\right]^N = FV_N(PVIF_{i,N}) = \$1,000(0.7835) = \$783.50$$

or as

$$PV = \frac{FV_N}{(1+i)^N} = \frac{FV_N}{FVIF_{i,N}} = \frac{\$1,000}{1.2763} = \$783.50$$

To conclude this comparison of present and future values, compare Figures A.1 and A.2.[2]

FUTURE VALUE OF AN ANNUITY

An annuity is defined as a series of payments of a fixed amount for a specified number of periods. Each payment occurs at the end of the period.[3] For example, a promise to pay $1,000 a year for 3 years is a 3-year annuity. If you were to receive such an annuity and were to deposit each annual payment in a savings account paying 4 percent interest, how much

---

2   Notice that Figure A.2 is not a mirror image of Figure A.1. The curves in Figure A.1 approach 4 as n increases; in Figure A.2 the curves approach zero, not −4.

3   Had the payment been made at the beginning of the period, each receipt would simply have been shifted back 1 year. The annuity would have been called an *annuity due*; the one in the present discussion, with payments made at the end of each period, is called a *regular annuity* or, sometimes, a *deferred annuity*.

would you have at the end of 3 years? The answer is shown graphically as a *time line* in Figure A.3. The first payment is made at the end of year 1, the second at the end of year 2, and the third at the end of year 3. The last payment is not compounded at all, the second payment is compounded for 1 year, and the first is compounded for 2 years. When the future values of each of the payments are added, their total is the sum of the annuity. In the example, this total is $3,121.60.

Expressed algebraically, with S_N defined as the future value, R as the periodic receipt, N as the length of the annuity, and $FVIFA_{i,N}$ as the future value interest factor for an annuity, the formula for S_N is

$$S_N = R(1+i)^{N-1} + R(1+i)^{N-2} + \cdots + R(1+i)^1 + R(1+i)^0$$

$$= R[(1+i)^{N-1} + (1+i)^{N-2} + \cdots + (1+i)^1 + (1+i)^0]$$

$$= R\sum_{t=1}^{N}(1+i)^{N-t} \text{ or } = R\sum_{t=1}^{N}(1+i)^{t-1}$$

$$= R(FVIFA_{i,N}) \qquad\qquad\text{A.4}$$

The expression in parentheses, $FVIFA_{i,N}$, has been calculated for various combinations of i and N.[4] An illustrative set of these annuity interest factors is given in Table A.4.[5] To find the answer to the 3-year, $1,000 annuity problem, simply refer to Table A.4, look down the 4 percent column to the row of the third period, and multiply the factor 3.1216 by $1,000. The answer is the same as the one derived by the long method illustrated in Figure A.3:

$$S_N = R(FVIFA_{i,N})$$
$$S_3 = \$1,000(3.1216) = \$3,121.60$$

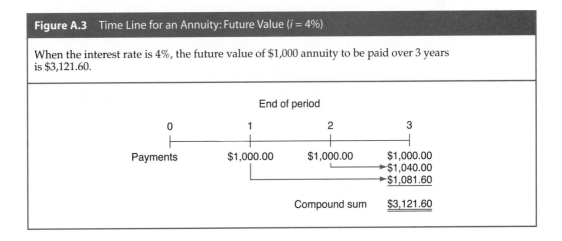

Figure A.3 Time Line for an Annuity: Future Value ($i = 4\%$)

When the interest rate is 4%, the future value of $1,000 annuity to be paid over 3 years is $3,121.60.

---

4   The third equation is simply a shorthand expression in which sigma (Σ) signifies *sum up* or add the values of N factors. The symbol $\sum_{t=1}^{N}$ simply says, "Go through the following process: Let $t = 1$ and find the first factor. Then let $t = 2$ and find the second factor. Continue until each individual factor has been found, and then add these individual factors to find the value of the annuity."

5   The equation given in Table A.4 recognizes that the *FVIFA* factor is the sum of a geometric progression. The proof of this equation is given in most algebra texts. Notice that it is easy to use the equation to develop annuity factors. This is especially useful if you need the *FVIFA* for some interest rate not given in the tables (for example, 6.5 percent).

Table A.4 Future Value of an Annuity of $1 per Period for n Periods

$$FVIFA_{i,n} = \sum_{t=1}^{n} (1+i)^{t-1}$$

$$= \frac{(1+i)^{n}-1}{i}$$

Number of Periods	1%	2%	3%	4%	5%	6%	7%	8%
1	1.0000	1.0000	1.0000	1.0000	1.0000	1.0000	1.0000	1.0000
2	2.0100	2.0200	2.0300	2.0400	2.0500	2.0600	2.0700	2.0800
3	3.0301	3.0604	3.0909	3.1216	3.1525	3.1836	3.2149	3.2464
4	4.0604	4.1216	4.1836	4.2465	4.3101	4.3746	4.4399	4.5061
5	5.1010	5.2040	5.3091	5.4163	5.5256	5.6371	5.7507	5.8666
6	6.1520	6.3081	6.4684	6.6330	6.8019	6.9753	7.1533	7.3359
7	7.2135	7.4343	7.6625	7.8983	8.1420	8.3938	8.6540	8.9228
8	8.2857	8.5830	8.8923	9.2142	9.5491	9.8975	10.2598	10.6366
9	9.3685	9.7546	10.1591	10.5828	11.0266	11.4913	11.9780	12.4876
10	10.4622	10.9497	11.4639	12.0061	12.5779	13.1808	13.8164	14.4866

Notice that for all positive interest rates, the $FVIFA_{i,N}$ for the sum of an annuity is always equal to or greater than the number of periods the annuity runs.[6]

PRESENT VALUE OF AN ANNUITY

Suppose that you were offered the following alternatives: a 3-year annuity of $1,000 per year or a lump-sum payment today. You have no need for the money during the next 3 years, so if you accept the annuity, you would simply deposit the receipts in a savings account paying 4 percent interest. How large must the lump-sum payment be to make it equivalent to the annuity? The time line shown in Figure A.4 will help explain the problem.

The present value of the first receipt is $R[1/(1+i)]$, the second is $R[1/(1+i)]^2$, and so on. Designating the present value of an annuity of N years as A_N and the present value interest factor for an annuity as $PVIFA_{i,N}$, we may write the following equation:

---

6   It is worth noting that the entry for each period t in Table A.4 equals the sum of the entries in Table A.2 up to the period $N-1$. For example, the entry for Period 3 under the 4 percent column in Table A.4 is equal to $1.000 + 1.0400 + 1.0816 = 3.1216$.

   Also, had the annuity been an *annuity due*, with payments received at the beginning rather than at the end of each period, the three payments would have occurred at $t = 0$, $t = 1$, and $t = 2$. To find the future value of an annuity due, look up the $FVIFA_{i,N}$ for $N+1$ years, then subtract 1.0 from the amount to get the $FVIFA_{i,N}$ for the annuity due. In the example, the annuity due $FVIFA_{i,N}$ is $4.2465 - 1.0 = 3.2465$ versus 3.1216 for a regular annuity. Because payments on an annuity due come earlier, it is a little more valuable than a regular annuity.

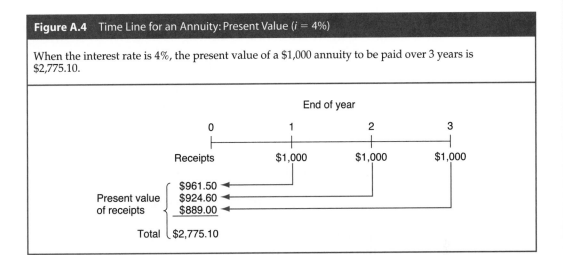

Figure A.4 Time Line for an Annuity: Present Value ($i = 4\%$)

When the interest rate is 4%, the present value of a $1,000 annuity to be paid over 3 years is $2,775.10.

$$A_N = R\left(\frac{1}{1+i}\right)^1 + R\left(\frac{1}{1+i}\right)^2 + \cdots + R\left(\frac{1}{1+i}\right)^N$$

$$= R\left(\frac{1}{(1+i)^1} + \frac{1}{(1+i)^2} + \cdots + \frac{1}{(1+i)^N}\right)$$

$$= R\sum_{t=1}^{N}\frac{1}{(1+i)^t}$$

$$= R(PVIFA_{i,N}) \qquad\qquad\qquad\qquad \textbf{A.5}$$

Again, tables have been worked out for $PVIFA_{i,N}$, the term in parentheses in Equation (A.5), as Table A.5 illustrates; a more complete listing is found in Table B.4 in Appendix B. From Table A.5, the $PVIFA_{i,N}$ for a 3-year, 4 percent annuity is found to be 2.7751.

Table A.5 Present Value of an Annuity of $1 per Period for n Periods

$$PVIFA_{i,n} = \sum_{t=1}^{n}\frac{1}{(1+i)^t} = \frac{1-\frac{1}{(1+i)^n}}{i}$$

Period	1%	2%	3%	4%	5%	6%	7%	8%	9%	10%
1	0.9901	0.9804	0.9709	0.9615	0.9524	0.9434	0.9346	0.9259	0.9174	0.9091
2	1.9704	1.9416	1.9135	1.8861	1.8594	1.8334	1.8080	1.7833	1.7591	1.7355
3	2.9410	2.8839	2.8286	2.7751	2.7232	2.6730	2.6243	2.5771	2.5313	2.4869
4	3.9020	3.8077	3.7171	3.6299	3.5460	3.4651	3.3872	3.3121	3.2397	3.1699
5	4.8534	4.7135	4.5797	4.4518	4.3295	4.2124	4.1002	3.9927	3.8897	3.7908
6	5.7955	5.6014	5.4172	5.2421	5.0757	4.9173	4.7665	4.6229	4.4859	4.3553
7	6.7282	6.4720	6.2303	6.0021	5.7864	5.5824	5.3893	5.2064	5.0330	4.8684
8	7.6517	7.3255	7.0197	6.7327	6.4632	6.2098	5.9713	5.7466	5.5348	5.3349
9	8.5660	8.1622	7.7861	7.4353	7.1078	6.8017	6.5152	6.2469	5.9952	5.7590
10	9.4713	8.9826	8.5302	8.1109	7.7217	7.3601	7.0236	6.7101	6.4177	6.1446

Multiplying this factor by the $1,000 annual receipt gives $2,775.10, the present value of the annuity. This figure is identical to the long-method answer shown in Figure A.4:

$$A_N = R(PVIFA_{i,N})$$
$$A_3 = \$1,000(2.7751)$$
$$= \$2,775.10$$

Notice that the entry for each period N in Table A.5 is equal to the sum of the entries in Table A.3 up to and including period N. For example, the $PVIFA$ for 4 percent, three periods as shown in Table A.5, could have been calculated by summing values from Table A.3:

$$0.9615 + 0.9246 + 0.8890 = 2.7751$$

Notice also that for all positive interest rates, $PVIFA_{i,N}$ for the *present value* of an annuity is always less than the number of periods.[7]

PRESENT VALUE OF AN UNEVEN SERIES OF RECEIPTS

The definition of an annuity includes the words *fixed amount*—in other words, annuities involve situations in which cash flows are *identical* in every period. Although many managerial decisions involve constant cash flows, some important decisions are concerned with uneven cash flows. Consequently, it is necessary to deal with varying payment streams.

The PV of an uneven stream of future income is found as the sum of the PVs of the individual components of the stream. For example, suppose that we are trying to find the PV of the stream of receipts shown in Table A.6, discounted at 6 percent. As shown in the table, we multiply each receipt by the appropriate $PVIF_{i,N}$, then sum these products to obtain the PV of the stream, $1,413.24. Figure A.5 gives a graphic view of the cash-flow stream.

Table A.6 Present Value of an Uneven Stream of Receipts ($i = 6\%$)

Year	Stream of Receipts	×	$PVIF_{i,n}$	=	PV of Individual Receipts
1	$100		0.9434		$94.34
2	200		0.8900		178.00
3	200		0.8396		167.92
4	200		0.7921		158.42
5	200		0.7473		149.46
6	0		0.7050		0
7	1,000		0.6651		665.10
					PV = Sum = $1,413.24

---

7   To find the $PVIFA_{i,N}$ for an *annuity due*, look up the $PVIFA_{i,N}$ for $N-1$ periods, then add 1.0 to this amount to obtain the $PVIFA_{i,N}$ for the annuity due. In the example, the $PVIFA_{i,N}$ for a 4 percent, 3-year annuity due is $1.8861 + 1.0 = 2.8861$.

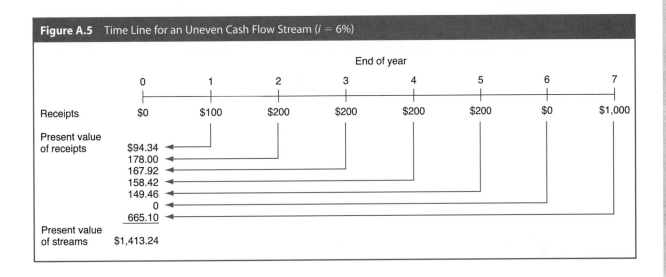

Figure A.5 Time Line for an Uneven Cash Flow Stream ($i = 6\%$)

The PV of the receipts shown in Table A.6 and Figure A.5 can also be found by using the annuity equation; the steps in this alternative solution process are as follows:

- *Step 1:* Find PV of $100 due in 1 year:

$$\$100(0.9434) = \$94.34$$

- *Step 2:* Recognize that a $200 annuity will be received during years 2 through 5. Thus, we can determine the value of a 5-year annuity, subtract from it the value of a 1-year annuity, and have the remaining value of a 4-year annuity whose first payment is due in 2 years. This result is achieved by subtracting the $PVIFA$ for a 1-year, 6 percent annuity from the $PVIFA$ for a 5-year annuity and then multiplying the difference by $200:

$$
\begin{aligned}
PV \text{ of the Annuity} &= (PVIFA_{6\%,5\ yrs} - PVIFA_{6\%,1\ yr})(\$200) \\
&= (4.2124 - 0.9434)(\$200) \\
&= \$653.80
\end{aligned}
$$

Thus, the present value of the annuity component of the uneven stream is $653.80.

- *Step 3:* Find the PV of the $1,000 due in year 7:

$$\$1,000(0.6651) = \$665.10$$

- *Step 4:* Sum the components:

$$\$94.34 + \$653.80 + \$665.10 = \$1,413.24$$

Either of the two methods can be used to solve problems of this type. However, the alternative (annuity) solution is easier if the annuity component runs for many years. For example, the alternative solution would be clearly superior for finding the PV of a stream consisting of $100 in year 1, $200 in years 2 through 29, and $1,000 in year 30.

ANNUAL PAYMENTS FOR ACCUMULATION OF A FUTURE SUM

Suppose that you want to know the amount of money that must be deposited at 5 percent for each of the next 5 years in order to have $10,000 available to pay off a debt at the end of the fifth year. Dividing both sides of Equation (A.4) by $FVIFA$ we obtain

$$R = \frac{S_N}{FVIFA_{i,N}}$$

Looking up the future value of an annuity interest factor for 5 years at 5 percent in Table A.4 and dividing this figure into $10,000 gives

$$R = \frac{\$10,000}{5.5256} = \$1,810$$

Thus, if $1,810 is deposited each year in an account paying 5 percent interest, at the end of 5 years the account will have accumulated to $10,000.

ANNUAL RECEIPTS FROM AN ANNUITY

Suppose that on September 1, 2007, you received an inheritance of $7,500. The money is to be used for your education and is to be spent during the academic years beginning September 2008, 2009, and 2010. If you place the money in a bank account paying 6 percent annual interest and make three equal withdrawals at each of the specified dates, how large can each withdrawal be so as to leave you with exactly a zero balance after the last one has been made?

The solution requires application of the present value of an annuity formula, Equation (A.5). Here, however, we know that the present value of the annuity is $7,500, and the problem is to find the three equal annual payments when the interest rate is 6 percent. This calls for dividing both sides

$$R = \frac{A_N}{PVIFA_{i,N}}$$

of Equation (A.5) by $PVIFA_{i,N}$ to derive Equation (A.7):

The interest factor is found in Table A.5 to be 2.6730, and substituting this value into Equation (A.7), the three annual withdrawals are calculated to be $2,806:

$$R = \frac{\$7,500}{2.6730} = \$2,806$$

This particular calculation is used frequently to set up insurance and pension-plan benefit schedules and to find the periodic payments necessary to retire a loan within a specified period. For example, if you want to retire in three equal annual payments a $7,500 bank loan accruing interest at 6 percent on the unpaid balance, each payment would be $2,806. In this case, the bank is acquiring an annuity with a present value of $7,500.

DETERMINING INTEREST RATES

We can use the basic equations developed earlier to determine the interest rates implicit in financial contracts.

Example 1. A bank offers to lend you $1,000 if you sign a note to repay $1,610.50 at the end of 5 years. What rate of interest are you paying? To solve the problem, recognize that

$1,000 is the *PV* of $1,610.50 due in 5 years, and solve Equation (A.3) for the present value interest factor ($PVIF_{i,N}$).

$$PV = FV_N \left[\frac{1}{(1+i)^N} \right] = FV_N(PVIF_{i,N})$$

$$\$1{,}000 = \$1{,}610.50(PVIF_{i,5\ yrs})$$

$$\$1{,}000/\$1{,}610.50 = 0.6209 = PVIF_{i,5\ yrs} \qquad \textbf{A.3}$$

Now, go to Table A.3 and look across the row for year 5 until you find 0.6209. It is in the 10 percent column, so you would be paying a 10 percent rate of interest.

Example 2. A bank offers to lend you $100,000 to buy a house. You must sign a mortgage calling for payments of $8,882.73 at the end of each of the next 30 years, equivalent to roughly $740.23 per month. What interest rate is the bank charging you?

1. Recognize that $100,000 is the *PV* of a 30-year, $8,882.73 annuity:

$$\$100{,}000 = PV = \sum_{t=1}^{30} \$8{,}882.73 \left[\frac{1}{(1+i)^t} \right] = \$8{,}882.73(PVIFA_{i,30\ yrs})$$

2. Solve for $PVIFA_{i,30\ yrs}$

$$PVIFA_{i,30\ yrs} = \$100{,}000/\$8{,}882.73 = 11.2578$$

3. Turn to Table B.4 in Appendix B, because Table A.5 does not cover a 30-year period. Looking across the row for 30 periods, find 11.2578 under the column for 8 percent. Therefore, the rate of interest on this mortgage is 8 percent.

SEMIANNUAL AND OTHER COMPOUNDING PERIODS

All of the examples thus far have assumed that returns were received once a year, or annually. Suppose, however, that you put your $1,000 in a bank that offers to pay 6 percent interest compounded *semiannually*. How much will you have at the end of 1 year? Semiannual compounding means that interest is actually paid every 6 months, a fact taken into account in the tabular calculations in Table A.7. Here the annual interest rate is divided by two, but twice as many compounding periods are used because interest is paid twice a year. Comparing the amount on hand at the end of the second 6-month period, $1,060.90, with what would have been on hand under annual compounding, $1,060, shows that semiannual compounding is better from the standpoint of the saver. This result occurs because you earn interest on interest more frequently.

Throughout the economy, different types of investments use different compounding periods. For example, bank and savings and loan accounts generally pay interest quarterly, some bonds pay interest semiannually, and other bonds pay interest annually. Thus, if we are to compare securities with different compounding periods, we need to put them on a common basis. This need has led to the development of the terms *nominal*, or *stated*, *interest rate* and *effective annual*, or *annual percentage rate* (APR). The stated, or nominal, rate is the quoted rate; thus, in our example the nominal rate is 6 percent. The annual percentage rate is the rate that would have produced the final compound value,

Table A.7 Compound Interest Calculations with Semiannual Compounding

	Beginning Amount (PV)	×	(1 + i/2)	=	Ending Amount, FV_n
Period 1	$1,000.00		(1.03)		$1,030.00
Period 2	$1,030.00		(1.03)		$1,060.00

$1,060.90, under annual rather than semiannual compounding. In this case, the effective annual rate is 6.09 percent:

$$\$1,000(1 + i) = \$1,060.90$$

$$i = \frac{\$1,060.90}{\$1,000} - 1 = 0.0609 = 6.09\%$$

Thus, if one bank offered 6 percent with semiannual compounding, whereas another offered 6.09 percent with annual compounding, they would both be paying the same effective rate of interest. In general, we can determine the effective annual rate of interest, given the nominal rate, as follows:

- *Step 1:* Find the *FV* of $1 at the end of 1 year, using the equation

$$FV = 1\left(1 + \frac{i_n}{M}\right)^M$$

Here i_n is the nominal rate, and *M* is the number of compounding periods per year.
- *Step 2:* Subtract 1.0 from the result in Step 1; then multiply by 100. The final result is the effective annual rate.

Example. Find the effective annual rate if the nominal rate is 6 percent, compounded semiannually:

$$\text{Effective Annual Rate} = \left(1 + \frac{0.06}{2}\right)^2 - 1.0$$
$$= (1.03)^2 - 1.0$$
$$= 1.0609 - 1.0$$
$$= 0.0609$$
$$= 6.09\%$$

The points made about semiannual compounding can be generalized as follows. When compounding periods are more frequent than once a year, use a modified version of Equation (A.2):

$$FV_N = PV(1 + i)^N$$
$$FV_N = PV\left(1 + \frac{i}{M}\right)^{MN} \qquad \textbf{A.2a}$$

Here *M* is the number of times per year compounding occurs. When banks compute daily interest, the value of *M* is set at 365, and Equation (A.2a) is applied.

The interest tables can be used when compounding occurs more than once a year. Simply divide the nominal, or stated, interest rate by the number of times compounding occurs, and multiply the years by the number of compounding periods per year. For example, to find the amount to which $1,000 will grow after 6 years with semiannual compounding and a stated 8 percent interest rate, divide 8 percent by 2 and multiply the 6 years by 2. Then look in Table A.2 under the 4 percent column and in the row for Period 12. You will find an interest factor of 1.6010. Multiplying this by the initial $1,000 gives a value of $1,601, the amount to which $1,000 will grow in 6 years at 8 percent compounded semiannually. This compares with $1,586.90 for annual compounding.

The same procedure applies in all of the cases covered—compounding, discounting, single payments, and annuities. To illustrate semiannual discounting in finding the present value of an annuity, consider the case described in the section "Present Value of an Annuity"—$1,000 a year for 3 years, discounted at 4 percent. With annual discounting, the interest factor is 2.7751, and the present value of the annuity is $2,775.10. For semiannual discounting, look under the 2 percent column and in the Period 6 row of Table A.5 to find an interest factor of 5.6014. This is now multiplied by half of $1,000, or the $500 received each 6 months, to get the present value of the annuity, $2,800.70. The payments come a little more rapidly—the first $500 is paid after only 6 months (similarly with other payments)—so the annuity is a little more valuable if payments are received semiannually rather than annually.

SUMMARY

Managerial decisions often require determining the present value of a stream of future cash flows. Also, we often need to know the amount to which an initial quantity will grow during a specified time period, and at other times we must calculate the interest rate built into a financial contract. The basic concepts involved in these processes are called compounding and the time value of money.

The key procedures covered in this appendix are summarized here

- *Future Value:* $FV_N = PV(1 + i)^N$, where FV_N is the future value of an initial amount, PV, compounded at the rate of i percent for N periods. The term $(1 + i)^N$ is the future value interest factor, $FVIF_{i, N}$. Values for $FVIF$ are contained in tables.

- *Present Value:* $PV = FV_N[1/(1 + i)^N]$. This equation is simply a transformation of the future value

equation. The term $[1/(1 + i)^N]$ is the present value interest factor, $PVIF_{i, N}$.

- *Future Value of an Annuity:* An annuity is defined as a series of constant or equal payments of R dollars per period. The sum, or future value of an annuity, is given the symbol S_N, and it is found as follows:

$$S_N = R\left[\sum_{t=1}^{N}(1 + i)^{t-1}\right].$$ The term $\left[\sum_{t=1}^{N}(1 + i)^{t-1}\right]$ is the future value interest factor for an annuity, $FVIFA_{i, N}$.

- *Present Value of an Annuity:* The present value of an annuity is identified by the symbol A_N, and it is found as follows: $A_N = R\left[\sum_{t=1}^{N}(1/1 + i)^t\right].$ The term $\left[\sum_{t=1}^{N}(1/1 + i)^t\right] = PVIFA_{i,N}$ is the present value interest factor for an annuity.

Appendix B

Interest Factor Tables

Table B.1 Future Value of \$1: $FVIF_{i,n} = (1 + i)^n$

Period	1%	2%	3%	4%	5%	6%	7%	8%	9%	10%
1	1.0100	1.0200	1.0300	1.0400	1.0500	1.0600	1.0700	1.0800	1.0900	1.1000
2	1.0201	1.0404	1.0609	1.0816	1.1025	1.1236	1.1449	1.1664	1.1881	1.2100
3	1.0303	1.0612	1.0927	1.1249	1.1576	1.1910	1.2250	1.2597	1.2950	1.3310
4	1.0406	1.0824	1.1255	1.1699	1.2155	1.2625	1.3108	1.3605	1.4116	1.4641
5	1.0510	1.1041	1.1593	1.2167	1.2763	1.3382	1.4026	1.4693	1.5386	1.6105
6	1.0615	1.1262	1.1941	1.2653	1.3401	1.4185	1.5007	1.5869	1.6771	1.7716
7	1.0721	1.1487	1.2299	1.3159	1.4071	1.5036	1.6058	1.7138	1.8280	1.9487
8	1.0829	1.1717	1.2668	1.3686	1.4775	1.5938	1.7182	1.8509	1.9926	2.1436
9	1.0937	1.1951	1.3048	1.4233	1.5513	1.6895	1.8385	1.9990	2.1719	2.3579
10	1.1046	1.2190	1.3439	1.4802	1.6289	1.7908	1.9672	2.1589	2.3674	2.5937
11	1.1157	1.2434	1.3842	1.5395	1.7103	1.8983	2.1049	2.3316	2.5804	2.8531
12	1.1268	1.2682	1.4258	1.6010	1.7959	2.1022	2.2522	2.5182	2.8127	3.1384
13	1.1381	1.2936	1.4685	1.6651	1.8856	2.1329	2.4098	2.7196	3.0658	3.4523
14	1.1495	1.3195	1.5126	1.7317	1.9799	2.2609	2.5785	2.9372	3.3417	3.7975
15	1.1610	1.3459	1.5580	1.8009	2.0789	2.3966	2.7590	3.1722	3.6425	4.1772
16	1.1726	1.3728	1.6047	1.8730	2.1829	2.5404	2.9522	3.4259	3.9703	4.5950
17	1.1843	1.4002	1.6528	1.9479	2.2920	2.6928	3.1588	3.7000	4.3276	5.0545
18	1.1961	1.4282	1.7024	2.0258	2.4066	2.8543	3.3799	3.9960	4.7171	5.5599
19	1.2081	1.4568	1.7535	2.1068	2.5270	3.0256	3.6165	4.3157	5.1417	6.1159
20	1.2202	1.4859	1.8061	2.1911	2.6533	3.2071	3.8697	4.6610	5.6044	6.7275
21	1.2324	1.5157	1.8603	2.2788	2.7860	3.3996	4.1406	5.0338	6.1088	7.4002
22	1.2447	1.5460	1.9161	2.3699	2.9253	3.6035	4.4304	5.4365	6.6586	8.1403
23	1.2572	1.5769	1.9736	2.4647	3.0715	3.8197	4.7405	5.8715	7.2579	8.9543
24	1.2697	1.6084	2.0328	2.5633	3.2251	4.0489	5.0724	6.3412	7.9111	9.8497
25	1.2824	1.6406	2.0938	2.6658	3.3864	4.2919	5.4274	6.8485	8.6231	10.834
26	1.2953	1.6734	2.1566	2.7725	3.5557	4.5494	5.8074	7.3964	9.3992	11.918
27	1.3082	1.7069	2.2213	2.8834	3.7335	4.8223	6.2139	7.9881	10.245	13.110
28	1.3213	1.7410	2.2879	2.9987	3.9201	5.1117	6.6488	8.6271	11.167	14.421
29	1.3345	1.7758	2.3566	3.1187	4.1161	5.4184	7.1143	9.3173	12.172	15.863
30	1.3478	1.8114	2.4273	3.2434	4.3219	5.7435	7.6123	10.062	13.267	17.449
40	1.4889	2.2080	3.2620	4.8010	7.0400	10.285	14.974	21.724	31.409	45.259
50	1.6446	2.6916	4.3839	7.1067	11.467	18.420	29.457	46.901	74.357	117.39
60	1.8167	3.2810	5.8916	10.519	18.679	32.987	57.946	101.25	176.03	304.48

Table B.1 Future Value of $1: $FVIF_{i,n} = (1 + i)^n$ (continued)

Period	12%	14%	15%	16%	18%	20%	24%	28%	32%	36%
1	1.1200	1.1400	1.1500	1.1600	1.1800	1.2000	1.2400	1.2800	1.3200	1.3600
2	1.2544	1.2996	1.3225	1.3456	1.3924	1.4400	1.5376	1.6384	1.7424	1.8496
3	1.4049	1.4815	1.5209	1.5609	1.6430	1.7280	1.9066	2.0972	2.3000	2.5155
4	1.5735	1.6890	1.7490	1.8106	1.9388	2.0736	2.3642	2.6844	3.0360	3.4210
5	1.7623	1.9254	2.0114	2.1003	2.2878	2.4883	2.9316	3.4360	4.0075	4.6526
6	1.9738	2.1950	2.3131	2.4364	2.6996	2.9860	3.6352	4.3980	5.2899	6.3275
7	2.2107	2.5023	2.6600	2.8262	3.1855	3.5832	4.5077	5.6295	6.9826	8.6054
8	2.4760	2.8526	3.0590	3.2784	3.7589	4.2998	5.5895	7.2058	9.2170	11.703
9	2.7731	3.2519	3.5179	3.8030	4.4355	5.1598	6.9310	9.2234	12.166	15.916
10	3.1058	3.7072	4.0456	4.4114	5.2338	6.1917	8.5944	11.805	16.059	21.646
11	3.4785	4.2262	4.6524	5.1173	6.1759	7.4301	10.657	15.111	21.198	29.439
12	3.8960	4.8179	5.3502	5.9360	7.2876	8.9161	13.214	19.342	27.982	40.037
13	4.3635	5.4924	6.1528	6.8858	8.5994	10.699	16.386	24.758	36.937	54.451
14	4.8871	6.2613	7.0757	7.9875	10.147	12.839	20.319	31.691	48.756	74.053
15	5.4736	7.1379	8.1371	9.2655	11.973	15.407	25.195	40.564	64.358	100.71
16	6.1304	8.1372	9.3576	10.748	14.129	18.488	31.242	51.923	84.953	136.96
17	6.8660	9.2765	10.761	12.467	16.672	22.186	38.740	66.461	112.13	186.27
18	7.6900	10.575	12.375	14.462	19.673	26.623	48.038	85.070	148.02	253.33
19	8.6128	12.055	14.231	16.776	23.214	31.948	59.567	108.89	195.39	344.53
20	9.6463	13.743	16.366	19.460	27.393	38.337	73.864	139.37	257.91	468.57
21	10.803	15.667	18.821	22.574	32.323	46.005	91.591	178.40	340.44	637.26
22	12.100	17.861	21.644	26.186	38.142	55.206	113.57	228.35	449.39	866.67
23	13.552	20.361	24.891	30.376	45.007	66.247	140.83	292.30	593.19	1178.6
24	15.178	23.212	28.625	35.236	53.108	79.496	174.63	374.14	783.02	1602.9
25	17.000	26.461	32.918	40.874	62.668	95.396	216.54	478.90	1033.5	2180.0
26	19.040	30.166	37.856	47.414	73.948	114.47	268.51	612.99	1364.3	2964.9
27	21.324	34.389	43.535	55.000	87.259	137.37	332.95	784.63	1800.9	4032.2
28	23.883	39.204	50.065	63.800	102.96	164.84	412.86	1004.3	2377.2	5483.8
29	26.749	44.693	57.575	74.008	121.50	197.81	511.95	1285.5	3137.9	7458.0
30	29.959	50.950	66.211	85.849	143.37	237.37	634.81	1645.5	4142.0	10143.
40	93.050	188.88	267.86	378.72	750.37	1469.7	5455.9	19426.	66520.	*
50	289.00	700.23	1083.6	1670.7	3927.3	9100.4	46890.	*	*	*
60	897.59	2595.9	4383.9	7370.1	20555.	56347.	*	*	*	*

*$FVIF > 99,999$.

Table B.2 Present Value of $1: $PVIF_{i,n} = 1/(1 + i)^n = 1/FVIF_{i,n}$

Period	1%	2%	3%	4%	5%	6%	7%	8%	9%	10%
1	.9901	.9804	.9709	.9615	.9524	.9434	.9346	.9259	.9174	.9091
2	.9803	.9612	.9426	.9246	.9070	.8900	.8734	.8573	.8417	.8264
3	.9706	.9423	.9151	.8890	.8638	.8396	.8163	.7938	.7722	.7513
4	.9610	.9238	.8885	.8548	.8227	.7921	.7629	.7350	.7084	.6830
5	.9515	.9057	.8626	.8219	.7835	.7473	.7130	.6806	.6499	.6209
6	.9420	.8880	.8375	.7903	.7462	.7050	.6663	.6302	.5963	.5645
7	.9327	.8706	.8131	.7599	.7107	.6651	.6227	.5835	.5470	.5132
8	.9235	.8535	.7894	.7307	.6768	.6274	.5820	.5403	.5019	.4665
9	.9143	.8368	.7664	.7026	.6446	.5919	.5439	.5002	.4604	.4241
10	.9053	.8203	.7441	.6756	.6139	.5584	.5083	.4632	.4224	.3855
11	.8963	.8043	.7224	.6496	.5847	.5268	.4751	.4289	.3875	.3505
12	.8874	.7885	.7014	.6246	.5568	.4970	.4440	.3971	.3555	.3186
13	.8787	.7730	.6810	.6006	.5303	.4688	.4150	.3677	.3262	.2897
14	.8700	.7579	.6611	.5775	.5051	.4423	.3878	.3405	.2992	.2633
15	.8613	.7430	.6419	.5553	.4810	.4173	.3624	.3152	.2745	.2394
16	.8528	.7284	.6232	.5339	.4581	.3936	.3387	.2919	.2519	.2176
17	.8444	.7142	.6050	.5134	.4363	.3714	.3166	.2703	.2311	.1978
18	.8360	.7002	.5874	.4936	.4155	.3503	.2959	.2502	.2120	.1799
19	.8277	.6854	.5703	.4746	.3957	.3305	.2765	.2317	.1945	.1635
20	.8195	.6730	.5537	.4564	.3769	.3118	.2584	.2145	.1784	.1486
21	.8114	.6598	.5375	.4388	.3589	.2942	.2415	.1987	.1637	.1351
22	.8034	.6468	.5219	.4220	.3418	.2775	.2257	.1839	.1502	.1228
23	.7954	.6342	.5067	.4057	.3256	.2618	.2109	.1703	.1378	.1117
24	.7876	.6217	.4919	.3901	.3101	.2470	.1971	.1577	.1264	.1015
25	.7798	.6095	.4776	.3751	.2953	.2330	.1842	.1460	.1160	.0923
26	.7720	.5976	.4637	.3607	.2812	.2198	.1722	.1352	.1064	.0839
27	.7644	.5859	.4502	.3468	.2678	.2074	.1609	.1252	.0976	.0763
28	.7568	.5744	.4371	.3335	.2551	.1956	.1504	.1159	.0895	.0693
29	.7493	.5631	.4243	.3207	.2429	.1846	.1406	.1073	.0822	.0630
30	.7419	.5521	.4120	.3083	.2314	.1741	.1314	.0994	.0754	.0573
35	.7059	.5000	.3554	.2534	.1813	.1301	.0937	.0676	.0490	.0356
40	.6717	.4529	.3066	.2083	.1420	.0972	.0668	.0460	.0318	.0221
45	.6391	.4102	.2644	.1712	.1113	.0727	.0476	.0313	.0207	.0137
50	.6080	.3715	.2281	.1407	.0872	.0543	.0339	.0213	.0134	.0085
55	.5785	.3365	.1968	.1157	.0683	.0406	.0242	.0145	.0087	.0053

Table B.2 Present Value of $1: $PVIF_{i,n} = 1/(1+i)^n = 1/FVIF_{i,n}$ (continued)

Period	12%	14%	15%	16%	18%	20%	24%	28%	32%	36%
1	.8929	.8772	.8969	.8621	.8475	.8333	.8065	.7813	.7576	.7353
2	.7972	.7695	.7561	.7432	.7182	.6944	.6504	.6104	.5739	.5407
3	.7118	.6750	.6575	.6407	.6086	.5787	.5245	.4768	.4348	.3975
4	.6355	.5921	.5718	.5523	.5158	.4823	.4230	.3725	.3294	.2923
5	.5674	.5194	.4972	.4761	.4371	.4091	.3411	.2910	.2495	.2149
6	.5066	.4556	.4323	.4104	.3704	.3349	.2751	.2274	.1890	.1580
7	.4523	.3996	.3759	.3538	.3139	.2791	.2218	.1776	.1432	.1162
8	.4039	.3506	.3269	.3050	.2660	.2326	.1789	.1388	.1085	.0854
9	.3606	.3075	.2843	.2630	.2255	.1938	.1443	.1084	.0822	.0628
10	.3220	.2697	.2472	.2267	.1911	.1615	.1164	.0847	.0623	.0462
11	.2875	.2366	.2149	.1954	.1619	.1346	.0938	.0662	.0472	.0340
12	.2567	.2076	.1869	.1685	.1372	.1122	.0757	.0517	.0357	.0250
13	.2292	.1821	.1625	.1452	.1163	.0935	.0610	.0404	.0271	.0184
14	.2046	.1597	.1413	.1252	.0985	.0779	.0492	.0316	.0205	.0135
15	.1827	.1401	.1229	.1079	.0835	.0649	.0397	.0247	.0155	.0099
16	.1631	.1229	.1069	.0930	.0708	.0541	.0320	.0193	.0118	.0073
17	.1456	.1078	.0929	.0802	.0600	.0451	.0258	.0150	.0089	.0054
18	.1300	.0946	.0808	.0691	.0508	.0376	.0208	.0118	.0068	.0039
19	.1161	.0829	.0703	.0596	.0431	.0313	.0168	.0092	.0051	.0029
20	.1037	.0728	.0611	.0514	.0365	.0261	.0135	.0072	.0039	.0021
21	.0926	.0638	.0531	.0443	.0309	.0217	.0109	.0056	.0029	.0016
22	.0826	.0560	.0462	.0382	.0262	.0181	.0088	.0044	.0022	.0012
23	.0738	.0491	.0402	.0329	.0222	.0151	.0071	.0034	.0017	.0008
24	.0659	.0431	.0349	.0284	.0188	.0126	.0057	.0027	.0013	.0006
25	.0588	.0378	.0304	.0245	.0160	.0105	.0046	.0021	.0010	.0005
26	.0525	.0331	.0264	.0211	.0135	.0087	.0037	.0016	.0007	.0003
27	.0469	.0291	.0230	.0182	.0115	.0073	.0030	.0013	.0006	.0002
28	.0419	.0255	.0200	.0157	.0097	.0061	.0024	.0010	.0004	.0002
29	.0374	.0224	.0174	.0135	.0082	.0051	.0020	.0008	.0003	.0001
30	.0334	.0196	.0151	.0116	.0070	.0042	.0016	.0006	.0002	.0001
35	.0189	.0102	.0075	.0055	.0030	.0017	.0005	.0002	.0001	*
40	.0107	.0053	.0037	.0026	.0013	.0007	.0002	.0001	*	*
45	.0061	.0027	.0019	.0013	.0006	.0003	.0001	*	*	*
50	.0035	.0014	.0009	.0006	.0003	.0001	*	*	*	*
55	.0020	.0007	.0005	.0003	.0001	*	*	*	*	*

*The factor is zero to four decimal places.

Table B.3 Future Value of an Annuity of $1 for *n* Periods

$$FVIFA_{i,n} = \sum_{t=1}^{n} (1 + i)^{t-1}$$

$$= \frac{(1 + i)^n - 1}{i}$$

Number of Periods	1%	2%	3%	4%	5%	6%	7%	8%	9%	10%
1	1.0000	1.0000	1.0000	1.0000	1.0000	1.0000	1.0000	1.0000	1.0000	1.0000
2	2.0100	2.0200	2.0300	2.0400	2.0500	2.0600	2.0700	2.0800	2.0900	2.1000
3	3.0301	3.0604	3.0909	3.1216	3.1525	3.1836	3.2149	3.2465	3.2781	3.3100
4	4.0604	4.1216	4.1836	4.2465	4.3101	4.3746	4.4399	4.5061	4.5731	4.6410
5	5.1010	5.2040	5.3091	5.4163	5.5256	5.6371	5.7507	5.8666	5.9847	6.1051
6	6.1520	6.3081	6.4684	6.6330	6.8019	6.9753	7.1533	7.3359	7.5233	7.7156
7	7.2135	7.4343	7.6625	7.8983	8.1420	8.3938	8.6540	8.9228	9.2004	9.4872
8	8.2857	8.5830	8.8923	9.2142	9.5491	9.8975	10.259	10.636	11.028	11.435
9	9.3685	9.7546	10.159	10.582	11.026	11.491	11.978	12.487	13.021	13.579
10	10.462	10.949	11.463	12.006	12.577	13.180	13.816	14.486	15.192	15.937
11	11.566	12.168	12.807	13.486	14.206	14.971	15.783	16.645	17.560	18.531
12	12.682	13.412	14.192	15.025	15.917	16.869	17.888	18.977	20.140	21.384
13	13.809	14.680	15.617	16.626	17.713	18.882	20.140	21.495	22.953	24.522
14	14.947	15.973	17.086	18.291	19.598	21.015	22.550	24.214	26.019	27.975
15	16.096	17.293	18.598	20.023	21.578	23.276	25.129	27.152	29.360	31.772
16	17.257	18.639	20.156	21.824	23.657	25.672	27.888	30.324	33.003	35.949
17	18.430	20.012	21.761	23.697	25.840	28.212	30.840	33.750	36.973	40.544
18	19.614	21.412	23.414	25.645	28.132	30.905	33.999	37.450	41.301	45.599
19	20.810	22.840	25.116	27.671	30.539	33.760	37.379	41.446	46.018	51.159
20	22.019	24.297	26.870	29.778	33.066	36.785	40.995	45.762	51.160	57.275
21	23.239	25.783	28.676	31.969	35.719	39.992	44.865	50.422	56.764	64.002
22	24.471	27.299	30.536	34.248	38.505	43.392	49.005	55.456	62.873	71.402
23	25.716	28.845	32.452	36.617	41.430	46.995	53.436	60.893	69.531	79.543
24	26.973	30.421	34.426	39.082	44.502	50.815	58.176	66.764	76.789	88.497
25	28.243	32.030	36.459	41.645	47.727	54.864	63.249	73.105	84.700	98.347
26	29.525	33.670	38.553	44.311	51.113	59.156	68.676	79.954	93.323	109.18
27	30.820	35.344	40.709	47.084	54.669	63.705	74.483	87.350	102.72	121.09
28	32.129	37.051	42.930	49.967	58.402	68.528	80.697	95.338	112.96	134.20
29	33.450	38.792	45.218	52.966	62.322	73.639	87.346	103.96	124.13	148.63
30	34.784	40.568	47.575	56.084	66.438	79.058	94.460	113.28	136.30	164.49
40	48.886	60.402	75.401	95.025	120.79	154.76	199.63	259.05	337.88	442.59
50	64.463	84.579	112.79	152.66	209.34	290.33	406.52	573.76	815.08	1163.9
60	81.669	114.05	163.05	237.99	353.58	533.12	813.52	1253.2	1944.7	3034.8

Table B.3 Future Value of an Annuity of $1 for *n* Periods (*continued*)

$$FVIFA_{i,n} = \sum_{t=1}^{n}(1+i)^{t-1}$$

$$= \frac{(1+i)^n - 1}{i}$$

Number of Periods	12%	14%	15%	16%	18%	20%	24%	28%	32%	36%
1	1.0000	1.0000	1.0000	1.0000	1.0000	1.0000	1.0000	1.0000	1.0000	1.0000
2	2.1200	2.1400	2.1500	2.1600	2.1800	2.2000	2.2400	2.2800	2.3200	2.3600
3	3.3744	3.4396	3.4725	3.5056	3.5724	3.6400	3.7776	3.9184	4.0624	4.2096
4	4.7793	4.9211	4.9934	5.0665	5.2154	5.3680	5.6842	6.0156	6.3624	6.7251
5	6.3528	6.6101	6.7424	6.8771	7.1542	7.4416	8.0484	8.6999	9.3983	10.146
6	8.1152	8.5355	8.7537	8.9775	9.4420	9.9299	10.980	12.135	13.405	14.798
7	10.089	10.730	11.066	11.413	12.141	12.915	14.615	16.533	18.695	21.126
8	12.299	13.232	13.726	14.240	15.327	16.499	19.122	22.163	25.678	29.731
9	14.775	16.085	16.785	17.518	19.085	20.798	24.712	29.369	34.895	41.435
10	17.548	19.337	20.303	21.321	23.521	25.958	31.643	38.592	47.061	57.351
11	20.654	23.044	24.349	25.732	28.755	32.150	40.237	50.398	63.121	78.998
12	24.133	27.270	29.001	30.850	34.931	39.580	50.894	65.510	84.320	108.43
13	28.029	32.088	34.351	36.786	42.218	48.496	64.109	84.852	112.30	148.47
14	32.392	37.581	40.504	43.672	50.818	59.195	80.496	109.61	149.23	202.92
15	37.279	43.842	47.580	51.659	60.965	72.035	100.81	141.30	197.99	276.97
16	42.753	50.980	55.717	60.925	72.939	87.442	126.01	181.86	262.35	377.69
17	48.883	59.117	65.075	71.673	87.068	105.93	157.25	233.79	347.30	514.66
18	55.749	68.394	75.836	84.140	103.74	128.11	195.99	300.25	459.44	700.93
19	63.439	78.969	88.211	98.603	123.41	154.74	244.03	385.32	607.47	954.27
20	72.052	91.024	102.44	115.37	146.62	186.68	303.60	494.21	802.86	1298.8
21	81.698	104.76	118.81	134.84	174.02	225.02	377.46	633.59	1060.7	1767.3
22	92.502	120.43	137.63	157.41	206.34	271.03	469.05	811.99	1401.2	2404.6
23	104.60	138.29	159.27	183.60	244.48	326.23	582.62	1040.3	1850.6	3271.3
24	118.15	158.65	184.16	213.97	289.49	392.48	723.46	1332.6	2443.8	4449.9
25	133.33	181.87	212.79	249.21	342.60	471.98	898.09	1706.8	3226.8	6052.9
26	150.33	208.33	245.71	290.08	405.27	567.37	1114.6	2185.7	4260.4	8233.0
27	169.37	238.49	283.56	337.50	479.22	681.85	1383.1	2798.7	5624.7	11197.9
28	190.69	272.88	327.10	392.50	566.48	819.22	1716.0	3583.3	7425.6	15230.2
29	214.58	312.09	377.16	456.30	669.44	984.06	2128.9	4587.6	9802.9	20714.1
30	241.33	356.78	434.74	530.31	790.94	1181.8	2640.9	5873.2	12940.	28172.2
40	767.09	1342.0	1779.0	2360.7	4163.2	7343.8	22728.	69377.	*	*
50	2400.0	4994.5	7217.7	10435.	21813.	45497.	*	*	*	*
60	7471.6	18535.	29219.	46057.	*	*	*	*	*	*

*FVIVA > 99,999.

Table B.4 Present Value of an Annuity of $1 for *n* Periods

$$PVIFA_{i,n} = \sum_{t=1}^{n} \frac{1}{(1+i)^t} = \frac{1 - \dfrac{1}{(1+i)^n}}{i}$$

Number of Payments	1%	2%	3%	4%	5%	6%	7%	8%	9%
1	0.9901	0.9804	0.9709	0.9615	0.9524	0.9434	0.9346	0.9259	0.9174
2	1.09704	1.9416	1.9135	1.8861	1.8594	1.8334	1.8080	1.7833	1.7591
3	2.9410	2.8839	2.8286	2.7751	2.7232	2.6730	2.6243	2.5771	2.5313
4	3.9020	3.8077	3.7171	3.6299	3.5460	3.4651	3.3872	3.3121	3.2397
5	4.8534	4.7135	4.5797	4.4518	4.3295	4.2124	4.1002	3.9927	3.8897
6	5.7955	5.6014	5.4172	5.2421	5.0757	4.9173	4.7665	4.6229	4.4859
7	6.7282	6.4720	6.2303	6.0021	5.7864	5.5824	5.3893	5.2064	5.0330
8	7.6517	7.3255	7.0197	6.7327	6.4632	6.2098	5.9713	5.7466	5.5348
9	8.5660	8.1622	7.7861	7.4353	7.1078	6.8017	6.5152	6.2469	5.9952
10	9.4713	8.9826	8.5302	8.1109	7.7217	7.3601	7.0236	6.7101	6.4177
11	10.3676	9.7868	9.2526	8.7605	8.3064	7.8869	7.4987	7.1390	6.8052
12	11.2551	10.5753	9.9540	9.3851	8.8633	8.3838	7.9427	7.5361	7.1607
13	12.1337	11.3484	10.6350	9.9856	9.3936	8.8527	8.3577	7.9038	7.4869
14	13.0037	12.1062	11.2961	10.5631	9.8986	9.2950	8.7455	8.2442	7.7862
15	13.8651	12.8493	11.9379	11.1184	10.3797	9.7122	9.1079	8.5595	8.0607
16	14.7179	13.5777	12.5611	11.6523	10.8378	10.1059	9.4466	8.8514	8.3126
17	15.5623	14.2919	13.1661	12.1657	11.2741	10.4773	9.7632	9.1216	8.5436
18	16.3983	14.9920	13.7535	12.6593	11.6896	10.8276	10.0591	9.3719	8.7556
19	17.2260	15.6785	14.3238	13.1339	12.0853	11.1581	10.3356	9.6036	8.9501
20	18.0456	16.3514	14.8775	13.5903	12.4622	11.4699	10.5940	9.8181	9.1285
21	18.8570	17.0112	15.4150	14.0292	12.8212	11.7641	10.8355	10.0168	9.2922
22	19.6604	17.6580	15.9369	14.4511	13.1630	12.0416	11.0612	10.2007	9.4424
23	20.4558	18.2922	16.4436	14.8568	13.4886	12.3034	11.2722	10.3711	9.5802
24	21.2434	18.9139	16.9355	15.2470	13.7986	12.5504	11.4693	10.5288	9.7066
25	22.0232	19.5235	17.4131	15.6221	14.0939	12.7834	11.6536	10.6748	9.8226
26	22.7952	20.1210	17.8768	15.9828	14.3752	13.0032	11.8258	10.8100	9.9290
27	23.5596	20.7069	18.3270	16.3296	14.6430	13.2105	11.9867	10.9352	10.0266
28	24.3164	21.2813	18.7641	16.6631	14.8981	13.4062	12.1371	11.0511	10.1161
29	25.0658	21.8444	19.1885	16.9837	15.1411	13.5907	12.2777	11.1584	10.1983
30	25.8077	22.3965	19.6004	17.2920	15.3725	13.7648	12.4090	11.2578	10.2737
35	29.4086	24.9986	21.4872	18.6646	16.3742	14.4982	12.9477	11.6546	10.5668
40	32.8347	27.3555	23.1148	19.7928	17.1591	15.0463	13.3317	11.9246	10.7574
45	36.0945	29.4902	24.5187	20.7200	17.7741	15.4558	13.6055	12.1084	10.8812
50	39.1961	31.4236	25.7298	21.4822	18.2559	15.7619	13.8007	12.2335	10.9617
55	42.1472	33.1748	26.7744	22.1086	18.6335	15.9905	13.9399	12.3186	11.0140

Table B.4 Present Value of an Annuity of \$1 for _n_ Periods (_continued_)

$$PVIFA_{i,n} = \sum_{t=1}^{n} \frac{1}{(1+i)^t} = \frac{1 - \dfrac{1}{(1+i)^n}}{i}$$

Number of Payments	10%	12%	14%	15%	16%	18%	20%	24%	28%	32%
1	0.9091	0.8929	0.8772	0.8696	0.8621	0.8475	0.8333	0.8065	0.7813	0.7576
2	1.7355	1.6901	1.6467	1.6257	1.6052	1.5656	1.5278	1.4568	1.3916	1.3315
3	2.4869	2.4018	2.3216	2.2832	2.2459	2.1743	2.1065	1.9813	1.8684	1.7663
4	3.1699	3.0373	2.9137	2.8550	2.7982	2.6901	2.5887	2.4043	2.2410	2.0957
5	3.7908	3.6048	3.4331	3.3522	3.2743	3.1272	2.9906	2.7454	2.5320	2.3452
6	4.3553	4.1114	3.8887	3.7845	3.6847	3.4976	3.3255	3.0205	2.7594	2.5342
7	4.8684	4.5638	4.2883	4.1604	4.0386	3.8115	3.6046	3.2423	2.9370	2.6775
8	5.3349	4.9676	4.6389	4.4873	4.3436	4.0776	3.8372	3.4212	3.0758	2.7860
9	5.7590	5.3282	4.9464	4.7716	4.6065	4.3030	4.0310	3.5655	3.1842	2.8681
10	6.1446	5.6502	5.2161	5.0188	4.8332	4.4941	4.1925	3.6819	3.2689	2.9304
11	6.4951	5.9377	5.4527	5.2337	5.0286	4.6560	4.3271	3.7757	3.3351	2.9776
12	6.8137	6.1944	5.6603	5.4206	5.1971	4.7932	4.4392	3.8514	3.3868	3.0133
13	7.1034	6.4235	5.8424	5.5831	5.3423	4.9095	4.5327	3.9124	3.4272	3.0404
14	7.3667	6.6282	6.0021	5.7245	5.4675	5.0081	4.6106	3.9616	3.4587	3.0609
15	7.6061	6.8109	6.1422	5.8474	5.5755	5.0916	4.6755	4.0013	3.4834	3.0764
16	7.8237	6.9740	6.2651	5.9542	5.6685	5.1624	4.7296	4.0333	3.5026	3.0882
17	8.0216	7.1196	6.3729	6.0472	5.7487	5.2223	4.7746	4.0591	3.5177	3.0971
18	8.2014	7.2497	6.4674	6.1280	5.8178	5.2732	4.8122	4.0799	3.5294	3.1039
19	8.3649	7.3658	6.5504	6.1982	5.8775	5.3162	4.8435	4.0967	3.5386	3.1090
20	8.5136	7.4694	6.6231	6.2593	5.9288	5.3527	4.8696	4.1103	3.5458	3.1129
21	8.6487	7.5620	6.6870	6.3125	5.9731	5.3837	4.8913	4.1212	3.5514	3.1158
22	8.7715	7.6446	6.7429	6.3587	6.0113	5.4099	4.9094	4.1300	3.5558	3.1180
23	8.8832	7.7184	6.7921	6.3988	6.0442	5.4321	4.9245	4.1371	3.5592	3.1197
24	8.9847	7.7843	6.8351	6.4338	6.0726	5.4510	4.9371	4.1428	3.5619	3.1210
25	9.0770	7.8431	6.8729	6.4642	6.0971	5.4669	4.9476	4.1474	3.5640	3.1220
26	9.1609	7.8957	6.9061	6.4906	6.1182	5.4804	4.9563	4.1511	3.5656	3.1227
27	9.2372	7.9426	6.9352	6.5135	6.1364	5.4919	4.9636	4.1542	3.5669	3.1233
28	9.3066	7.9844	6.9607	6.5335	6.1520	6.5016	4.9697	4.1566	3.5679	3.1237
29	9.3696	8.0218	6.9830	6.5509	6.1656	5.5098	4.9747	4.1585	3.5687	3.1240
30	9.4269	8.0552	7.0027	6.5660	6.1772	5.5168	4.9789	4.1601	3.5693	3.1242
35	9.6442	8.1755	7.0700	6.6166	6.2153	5.5386	4.9915	4.1644	3.5708	3.1248
40	9.7791	8.2438	7.1050	6.6418	6.2335	5.5482	4.9966	4.1659	3.5712	3.1250
45	9.8628	8.2825	7.1232	6.6543	6.2421	5.5523	4.9986	4.1664	3.5714	3.1250
50	9.9148	8.3045	7.1327	6.6605	6.2463	5.5541	4.9995	4.1666	3.5714	3.1250
55	9.9471	8.3170	7.1376	6.6636	6.2482	5.5549	4.9998	4.1666	3.5714	3.1250

Appendix C

Statistical Tables

Table C.1 Distribution of a Variable z (Percent of Total Area Under the Normal Curve Between x and μ)

z^1	0.00	0.01	0.02	0.03	0.04	0.05	0.06	0.07	0.08	0.09
0.0	.0000	.0040	.0080	.0120	.0160	.0199	.0239	.0279	.0319	.0359
0.1	.0398	.0438	.0478	.0517	.0557	.0596	.0636	.0675	.0714	.0753
0.2	.0793	.0832	.0871	.0910	.0948	.0987	.1026	.1064	.1103	.1141
0.3	.1179	.1217	.1255	.1293	.1331	.1368	.1406	.1443	.1480	.1517
0.4	.1554	.1591	.1628	.1664	.1700	.1736	.1772	.1808	.1844	.1879
0.5	.1915	.1950	.1985	.2019	.2054	.2088	.2123	.2157	.2190	.2224
0.6	.2257	.2291	.2324	.2357	.2389	.2422	.2454	.2486	.2517	.2549
0.7	.2580	.2611	.2642	.2673	.2704	.2734	.2764	.2794	.2823	.2852
0.8	.2881	.2910	.2939	.2967	.2995	.3023	.3051	.3078	.3106	.3133
0.9	.3159	.3186	.3212	.3238	.3264	.3289	.3315	.3340	.3365	.3389
1.0	.3413	.3438	.3461	.3485	.3508	.3531	.3554	.3577	.3599	.3621
1.1	.3643	.3665	.3686	.3708	.3729	.3749	.3770	.3790	.3810	.3830
1.2	.3849	.3869	.3888	.3907	.3925	.3944	.3962	.3980	.3997	.4015
1.3	.4032	.4049	.4066	.4082	.4099	.4115	.4131	.4147	.4162	.4177
1.4	.4192	.4207	.4222	.4236	.4251	.4265	.4279	.4292	.4306	.4319
1.5	.4332	.4345	.4357	.4370	.4382	.4394	.4406	.4418	.4429	.4441
1.6	.4452	.4463	.4474	.4484	.4495	.4505	.4515	.4525	.4535	.4545
1.7	.4554	.4564	.4573	.4582	.4591	.4599	.4608	.4616	.4625	.4633
1.8	.4641	.4649	.4656	.4664	.4671	.4678	.4686	.4693	.4699	.4706
1.9	.4713	.4719	.4726	.4732	.4738	.4744	.4750	.4756	.4761	.4767
2.0	.4773	.4778	.4783	.4788	.4793	.4798	.4803	.4808	.4812	.4817
2.1	.4821	.4826	.4830	.4834	.4838	.4842	.4846	.4850	.4854	.4857
2.2	.4861	.4864	.4868	.4871	.4875	.4878	.4881	.4884	.4887	.4890
2.3	.4893	.4896	.4898	.4901	.4904	.4906	.4909	.4911	.4913	.4916
2.4	.4918	.4920	.4922	.4925	.4927	.4929	.4931	.4932	.4934	.4936
2.5	.4938	.4940	.4941	.4943	.4945	.4946	.4948	.4949	.4951	.4952
2.6	.4953	.4955	.4956	.4957	.4959	.4960	.4961	.4962	.4963	.4964
2.7	.4965	.4966	.4967	.4968	.4969	.4970	.4971	.4972	.4973	.4974
2.8	.4974	.4975	.4976	.4977	.4977	.4978	.4979	.4979	.4980	.4981
2.9	.4981	.4982	.4982	.4982	.4894	.4984	.4985	.4985	.4986	.4986
3.0	.4987	.4987	.4987	.4988	.4988	.4989	.4989	.4989	.4990	.4990

1 z is the standardized variable, where $z = x - \mu/\sigma$ and x is the point of interest, μ is the mean, and s is the standard deviation of a distribution. Thus, z measures the number of standard deviations between a point of interest x and the mean of a given distribution. The table above indicates the percentage of the total area under the normal curve between x and μ. Thus, .3413 or 34.13% of the area under the normal curve lies between a point of interest and the mean when $z = 1.0$.

Table C.2 Critical F Values at the 90 Percent Confidence Level ($\alpha = .10$)[1]

Degrees of Freedom in the Numerator ($df = k - 1$)[1]

$df = n - k$	1	2	3	4	5	6	7	8	9	10	12	15	20	24	30	40	60	120	∞
1	39.86	49.50	53.59	55.83	57.24	58.20	58.91	59.44	59.86	60.19	60.71	61.22	61.74	62.00	62.26	62.53	62.79	63.06	63.33
2	8.53	9.00	9.16	9.24	9.29	9.33	9.35	9.37	9.38	9.39	9.41	9.42	9.44	9.45	9.46	9.47	9.47	9.48	9.49
3	8.54	5.46	5.39	5.34	5.31	5.28	5.27	5.25	5.24	5.23	5.22	5.20	5.18	5.18	5.17	5.16	5.15	5.14	5.13
4	4.54	4.32	4.19	4.11	4.05	4.01	3.98	3.95	3.94	3.92	3.90	3.87	3.84	3.83	3.82	3.80	3.79	3.78	3.76
5	4.06	3.78	3.62	3.52	3.45	3.40	3.37	3.34	3.32	3.30	3.27	3.24	3.21	3.19	3.17	3.16	3.14	3.12	3.10
6	3.78	3.46	3.29	3.18	3.11	3.05	3.01	2.98	2.96	2.94	2.90	2.87	2.84	2.82	2.80	2.78	2.76	2.74	2.72
7	3.59	3.26	3.07	2.96	2.88	2.83	2.78	2.75	2.72	2.70	2.67	2.63	2.59	2.58	2.56	2.54	2.51	2.49	2.47
8	3.46	3.11	2.92	2.81	2.73	2.67	2.62	2.59	2.56	2.54	2.50	2.46	2.42	2.40	2.38	2.36	2.34	2.32	2.29
9	3.36	3.01	2.81	2.69	2.61	2.55	2.51	2.47	2.44	2.42	2.38	2.34	2.30	2.28	2.25	2.23	2.21	2.18	2.16
10	3.29	2.92	2.73	2.61	2.52	2.46	2.41	2.38	2.35	2.32	2.28	2.24	2.20	2.18	2.16	2.13	2.11	2.08	2.06
11	3.23	2.86	2.66	2.54	2.45	2.39	2.34	2.30	2.27	2.25	2.21	2.17	2.12	2.10	2.08	2.05	2.03	2.00	1.97
12	3.18	2.81	2.61	2.48	2.39	2.33	2.28	2.24	2.21	2.19	2.15	2.10	2.06	2.04	2.01	1.99	1.96	1.93	1.90
13	3.14	2.76	2.56	2.43	2.35	2.28	2.23	2.20	2.16	2.14	2.10	2.05	2.01	1.98	1.96	1.93	1.90	1.88	1.85
14	3.10	2.73	2.52	2.39	2.31	2.24	2.19	2.15	2.12	2.10	2.05	2.01	1.96	1.94	1.91	1.89	1.86	1.83	1.80
15	3.07	2.70	2.49	2.36	2.27	2.21	2.16	2.12	2.09	2.06	2.02	1.97	1.92	1.90	1.87	1.85	1.82	1.79	1.76
16	3.05	2.67	2.46	2.33	2.24	2.18	2.13	2.09	2.06	2.03	1.99	1.94	1.89	1.87	1.84	1.81	1.78	1.75	1.72
17	3.03	2.64	2.44	2.31	2.22	2.15	2.10	2.06	2.03	2.00	1.96	1.91	1.86	1.84	1.81	1.78	1.75	1.72	1.69
18	3.01	2.62	2.42	2.29	2.20	2.13	2.08	2.04	2.00	1.98	1.93	1.89	1.84	1.81	1.78	1.75	1.72	1.69	1.66
19	2.99	2.61	2.40	2.27	2.18	2.11	2.06	2.02	1.98	1.96	1.91	1.86	1.81	1.79	1.76	1.73	1.70	1.67	1.63
20	2.97	2.59	2.38	2.25	2.16	2.09	2.04	2.00	1.96	1.94	1.89	1.84	1.79	1.77	1.74	1.71	1.68	1.64	1.61
21	2.96	2.57	2.36	2.23	2.14	2.08	2.02	1.98	1.95	1.92	1.87	1.83	1.78	1.75	1.72	1.69	1.66	1.62	1.59
22	2.95	2.56	2.35	2.22	2.13	2.06	2.01	1.97	1.93	1.90	1.86	1.81	1.76	1.73	1.70	1.67	1.64	1.60	1.57
23	2.94	2.55	2.34	2.21	2.11	2.05	1.99	1.95	1.92	1.89	1.84	1.80	1.74	1.72	1.69	1.66	1.62	1.59	1.55
24	2.93	2.54	2.33	2.19	2.10	2.04	1.98	1.94	1.91	1.88	1.83	1.78	1.73	1.70	1.67	1.64	1.61	1.57	1.53
25	2.92	2.53	2.32	2.18	2.09	2.02	1.97	1.93	1.89	1.87	1.82	1.77	1.72	1.69	1.66	1.63	1.59	1.56	1.52
26	2.91	2.52	2.31	2.17	2.08	2.01	1.96	1.92	1.88	1.86	1.81	1.76	1.71	1.68	1.65	1.61	1.58	1.54	1.50
27	2.90	2.51	2.30	2.17	2.07	2.00	1.95	1.91	1.87	1.85	1.80	1.75	1.70	1.67	1.64	1.60	1.57	1.53	1.49
28	2.89	2.50	2.29	2.16	2.06	2.00	1.94	1.90	1.87	1.84	1.79	1.74	1.69	1.66	1.63	1.59	1.56	1.52	1.48
29	2.89	2.50	2.28	2.15	2.06	1.99	1.93	1.89	1.86	1.83	1.78	1.73	1.68	1.65	1.62	1.58	1.55	1.51	1.47
30	2.88	2.49	2.28	2.14	2.05	1.98	1.93	1.88	1.85	1.82	1.77	1.72	1.67	1.64	1.61	1.57	1.54	1.50	1.46
40	2.84	2.44	2.23	2.09	2.00	1.93	1.87	1.83	1.79	1.76	1.71	1.66	1.61	1.57	1.54	1.51	1.47	1.42	1.38
60	2.79	2.39	2.18	2.04	1.95	1.87	1.82	1.77	1.74	1.71	1.66	1.60	1.54	1.51	1.48	1.44	1.40	1.35	1.29
120	2.75	2.35	2.13	1.99	1.90	1.82	1.77	1.72	1.68	1.65	1.60	1.55	1.48	1.45	1.41	1.37	1.32	1.26	1.19
∞	2.71	2.30	2.08	1.94	1.85	1.77	1.72	1.67	1.63	1.60	1.55	1.49	1.42	1.38	1.34	1.30	1.24	1.17	1.00

Degrees of Freedom in the Denominator ($df = n - k$)

1 The F statistic provides evidence on whether or not a statistically significant proportion of the total variation in the dependent variable Y has been explained. The F statistic can be calculated in terms of the coefficient of determination as: $F_{k-1,n-k} = R^2/(k-1) \div (1-R^2)/(n-k)$, where R^2 is the coefficient of determination, k is the number of estimated coefficients in the regression model (including the intercept), and n is the number of data observations. When the critical F value is exceeded, we can conclude with a given level of confidence (e.g., $\alpha = 0.01$ or 90 percent confidence) that the regression equation, taken as a whole, significantly explains the variation in Y.

Table C.2 Critical *F* Values at the 95 Percent Confidence Level ($\alpha = .05$) (continued)

Degrees of Freedom in the Numerator ($df = k - 1$)

Denominator $df = n - k$	1	2	3	4	5	6	7	8	9	10	12	15	20	24	30	40	60	120	∞
1	161.4	199.5	215.7	224.6	230.2	234.0	236.8	238.9	240.5	241.9	243.9	245.9	248.0	249.1	250.1	251.1	252.2	253.3	254.3
2	18.51	19.00	19.16	19.25	19.30	19.33	19.35	19.37	19.38	19.40	19.41	19.43	19.45	19.45	19.46	19.47	19.48	19.49	19.50
3	10.13	9.55	9.28	9.12	9.01	8.94	8.89	8.85	8.81	8.79	8.74	8.70	8.66	8.64	8.62	8.59	8.57	8.55	8.53
4	7.71	6.94	6.59	6.39	6.26	6.16	6.09	6.04	6.00	5.96	5.91	5.86	5.80	5.77	5.75	5.72	5.69	5.66	5.63
5	6.61	5.79	5.41	5.19	5.05	4.95	4.88	4.82	4.77	4.74	4.68	4.62	4.56	4.53	4.50	4.46	4.43	4.40	4.36
6	5.99	5.14	4.76	4.53	4.39	4.28	4.21	4.15	4.10	4.06	4.00	3.94	3.87	3.84	3.81	3.77	3.74	3.70	3.67
7	5.59	4.74	4.35	4.12	3.97	3.87	3.79	3.73	3.68	3.64	3.57	3.51	3.44	3.41	3.38	3.34	3.30	3.27	3.23
8	5.32	4.46	4.07	3.84	3.69	3.58	3.50	3.44	3.39	3.35	3.28	3.22	3.15	3.12	3.08	3.04	.301	2.97	2.93
9	5.12	4.26	3.86	3.63	3.48	3.37	3.29	3.23	3.18	3.14	3.07	3.01	2.94	2.90	2.86	2.83	2.79	2.75	2.71
10	4.96	4.10	3.71	3.48	3.33	3.22	3.14	3.07	3.02	2.98	2.91	2.85	2.77	2.74	2.70	2.66	2.62	2.58	2.54
11	4.84	3.98	3.59	3.36	3.20	3.09	3.01	2.95	2.90	2.85	2.79	2.72	2.65	2.61	2.57	2.53	2.49	2.45	2.40
12	4.75	3.89	3.49	3.26	3.11	3.00	2.91	2.85	2.80	2.75	2.69	2.62	2.54	2.51	2.47	2.43	2.38	2.34	2.30
13	4.67	3.81	3.41	3.18	3.03	2.92	2.83	2.77	2.71	2.67	2.60	2.53	2.46	2.42	2.38	2.34	2.30	2.25	2.21
14	4.60	3.74	3.34	3.11	2.96	2.85	2.76	2.70	2.65	2.60	2.53	2.46	2.39	2.35	2.31	2.27	2.22	2.18	2.13
15	4.54	3.68	3.29	3.06	2.90	2.79	2.71	2.64	2.59	2.54	2.48	2.40	2.33	2.29	2.25	2.20	2.16	2.11	2.07
16	4.49	3.63	3.24	3.01	2.85	2.74	2.66	2.59	2.54	2.49	2.42	2.35	2.28	2.24	2.19	2.15	2.11	2.06	2.01
17	4.45	3.59	3.20	2.96	2.81	2.70	2.61	2.55	2.49	2.45	2.38	2.31	2.23	2.19	2.15	2.10	2.06	2.01	1.96
18	4.41	3.55	3.16	2.93	2.77	2.66	2.58	2.51	2.46	2.41	2.34	2.27	2.19	2.15	2.11	2.06	2.02	1.97	1.92
19	4.38	3.52	3.13	2.90	2.74	2.63	2.54	2.48	2.42	2.38	2.31	2.23	2.16	2.11	2.07	2.03	1.98	1.93	1.88
20	4.35	3.49	3.10	2.87	2.71	2.60	2.51	2.45	2.39	2.35	2.28	2.20	2.12	2.08	2.04	1.99	1.95	1.90	1.84
21	4.32	3.47	3.07	2.84	2.68	2.57	2.49	2.42	2.37	2.32	2.25	2.18	2.10	2.05	2.01	1.96	1.92	1.87	1.81
22	4.30	3.44	3.05	2.82	2.66	2.55	2.46	2.40	2.34	2.30	2.23	2.15	2.07	2.03	1.98	1.94	1.89	1.84	1.78
23	4.28	3.42	3.03	2.80	2.64	2.53	2.44	2.37	2.32	2.27	2.20	2.13	2.05	2.01	1.96	1.91	1.86	1.81	1.76
24	4.26	3.40	3.01	2.78	2.62	2.51	2.42	2.36	2.30	2.25	2.18	2.11	2.03	1.98	1.94	1.89	1.84	1.79	1.73
25	4.24	3.39	2.99	2.76	2.60	2.49	2.40	2.34	2.28	2.24	2.16	2.09	2.01	1.96	1.92	1.87	1.82	1.77	1.71
26	4.23	3.37	2.98	2.74	2.59	2.47	2.39	2.32	2.27	2.22	2.15	2.07	1.99	1.95	1.90	1.85	1.80	1.75	1.69
27	4.21	3.35	2.96	2.73	2.57	2.46	2.37	2.31	2.25	2.20	2.13	2.06	1.97	1.93	1.88	1.84	1.79	1.73	1.67
28	4.20	3.34	2.95	2.71	2.56	2.45	2.36	2.29	2.24	2.19	2.12	2.04	1.96	1.91	1.87	1.82	1.77	1.71	1.65
29	4.18	3.33	2.93	2.70	2.55	2.43	2.35	2.28	2.22	2.18	2.10	2.03	1.94	1.90	1.85	1.81	1.75	1.70	1.64
30	4.17	3.32	2.92	2.69	2.53	2.42	2.33	2.27	2.21	2.16	2.09	2.01	1.93	1.89	1.84	1.79	1.74	1.68	1.62
40	4.08	3.23	2.84	2.61	2.45	2.34	2.25	2.18	2.12	2.08	2.00	1.92	1.84	1.79	1.74	1.69	1.64	1.58	1.51
60	4.00	3.15	2.76	2.53	2.37	2.25	2.17	2.10	2.04	1.99	1.92	1.84	1.75	1.70	1.65	1.59	1.53	1.47	1.39
120	3.92	3.07	2.68	2.45	2.29	2.17	2.09	2.02	1.96	1.91	1.83	1.75	1.66	1.61	1.55	1.50	1.43	1.35	1.25
∞	3.84	3.00	2.60	2.37	2.21	2.10	2.01	1.94	1.88	1.83	1.75	1.67	1.57	1.52	1.46	1.39	1.32	1.22	1.00

Degrees of Freedom in the Denominator ($df = n - k$)

Table C.2 Critical F Values at the 99 Percent Confidence Level (α = .01) (continued)

Degrees of Freedom in the Numerator ($df = k - 1$)

$df = n - k$	1	2	3	4	5	6	7	8	9	10	12	15	20	24	30	40	60	120	∞
1	4052	4999.5	5403	5625	5764	5859	5928	5982	6022	6056	6106	6157	6209	6235	6261	6287	6313	6339	6336
2	98.50	99.00	99.17	99.25	99.30	99.33	99.36	99.37	99.39	99.40	99.42	99.43	99.45	99.46	99.47	99.47	99.48	99.49	99.50
3	34.12	30.82	29.46	28.71	28.24	27.91	27.67	27.49	27.35	27.23	27.05	26.87	26.69	26.60	26.50	26.41	26.32	26.22	26.13
4	21.20	18.00	16.69	15.98	15.52	15.21	14.98	14.80	14.66	14.55	14.37	14.20	14.02	13.93	13.84	13.75	13.65	13.56	13.46
5	16.26	13.27	12.06	11.39	10.97	10.67	10.46	10.29	10.16	10.05	9.89	9.72	9.55	9.47	9.38	9.29	9.20	9.11	9.02
6	13.75	10.92	9.78	9.15	8.75	8.47	8.26	8.10	7.98	7.87	7.72	7.56	7.40	7.31	7.23	7.14	7.06	6.97	6.88
7	12.25	9.55	8.45	7.85	7.46	7.19	6.99	6.84	6.72	6.62	6.47	6.31	6.16	6.07	5.99	5.91	5.82	5.74	5.65
8	11.26	8.65	7.59	7.01	6.63	6.37	6.18	6.03	5.91	5.81	5.67	5.52	5.36	5.28	5.20	5.12	5.03	4.95	4.86
9	10.56	8.02	6.99	6.42	6.06	5.80	5.61	5.47	5.35	5.26	5.11	4.96	4.81	4.73	4.65	4.57	4.48	4.40	4.31
10	10.04	7.56	6.55	5.99	5.64	5.39	5.20	5.06	4.94	4.85	4.71	4.56	4.41	4.33	4.25	4.17	4.08	4.00	3.91
11	9.65	7.21	6.22	5.67	5.32	5.07	4.89	4.74	4.63	4.54	4.40	4.25	4.10	4.02	3.94	3.86	3.78	3.69	3.60
12	9.33	6.93	5.95	5.41	5.06	4.82	4.64	4.50	4.39	4.30	4.16	4.01	3.86	3.78	3.70	3.62	3.54	3.45	3.36
13	9.07	6.70	5.74	5.21	4.86	4.62	4.44	4.30	4.19	4.10	3.96	3.82	3.66	3.59	3.51	3.43	3.34	3.25	3.17
14	8.86	6.51	5.56	5.04	4.69	4.46	4.28	4.14	4.03	3.94	3.80	3.66	3.51	3.43	3.35	3.27	3.18	3.09	3.00
15	8.68	6.36	5.42	4.89	4.56	4.32	4.14	4.00	3.89	3.80	3.67	3.52	3.37	3.29	3.21	3.13	3.05	2.96	2.87
16	8.53	6.23	5.29	4.77	4.44	4.20	4.03	3.89	3.78	3.69	3.55	3.41	3.26	3.18	3.10	3.02	2.93	2.84	2.75
17	8.40	6.11	5.18	4.67	4.34	4.10	3.93	3.79	3.68	3.59	3.46	3.31	3.16	3.08	3.00	2.92	2.83	2.75	2.65
18	8.29	6.01	5.09	4.58	4.25	4.01	3.84	3.71	3.60	3.51	3.37	3.23	3.08	3.00	2.92	2.84	2.75	2.66	2.57
19	8.18	5.93	5.01	4.50	4.17	3.94	3.77	3.63	3.52	3.43	3.30	3.15	3.00	2.92	2.84	2.76	2.67	2.58	2.49
20	8.10	5.85	4.94	4.43	4.10	3.87	3.70	3.56	3.46	3.37	3.23	3.09	2.94	2.86	2.78	2.69	2.61	2.52	2.42
21	8.02	5.78	4.87	4.37	4.04	3.81	3.64	3.51	3.40	3.31	3.17	3.03	2.88	2.80	2.72	2.64	2.55	2.46	2.36
22	7.95	5.72	4.82	4.31	3.99	3.76	3.59	3.45	3.35	3.26	3.12	2.98	2.83	2.75	2.67	2.58	2.50	2.40	2.31
23	7.88	5.66	4.76	4.26	3.94	3.71	3.54	3.41	3.30	3.21	3.07	2.93	2.78	2.70	2.62	2.54	2.45	2.35	2.26
24	7.82	5.61	4.72	4.22	3.90	3.67	3.50	3.36	3.26	3.17	3.03	2.89	2.74	2.66	2.58	2.49	2.40	2.31	2.21
25	7.77	5.57	4.68	4.18	3.85	3.63	3.46	3.32	3.22	3.13	2.99	2.85	2.70	2.62	2.54	2.45	2.36	2.27	2.17
26	7.72	5.53	4.64	4.14	3.82	3.59	3.42	3.29	3.18	3.09	2.96	2.81	2.66	2.58	2.50	2.42	2.33	2.23	2.13
27	7.68	5.49	4.60	4.11	3.78	3.56	3.39	3.26	3.15	3.06	2.93	2.78	2.63	2.55	2.47	2.38	2.29	2.20	2.10
28	7.64	5.45	4.57	4.07	3.75	3.53	3.36	3.23	3.12	3.03	2.90	2.75	2.60	2.52	2.44	2.35	2.26	2.17	2.06
29	7.60	5.42	4.54	4.04	3.73	3.50	3.33	3.20	3.09	3.00	2.87	2.73	2.57	2.49	2.41	2.33	2.23	2.14	2.03
30	7.56	5.39	4.51	4.02	3.70	3.47	3.30	3.17	3.07	2.98	2.84	2.70	2.55	2.47	2.39	2.30	2.21	2.11	2.01
40	7.31	5.18	4.31	3.83	3.51	3.29	3.12	2.99	2.89	2.80	2.66	2.52	2.37	2.29	2.20	2.11	2.02	1.92	1.80
60	7.08	4.98	4.13	3.65	3.34	3.12	2.95	2.82	2.72	2.63	2.50	2.35	2.20	2.12	2.03	1.94	1.84	1.73	1.60
120	6.85	4.79	3.95	3.48	3.17	2.96	2.79	2.66	2.56	2.47	2.34	2.19	2.03	1.95	1.86	1.76	1.66	1.53	1.38
∞	6.63	4.61	3.78	3.32	3.02	2.80	2.64	2.51	2.41	2.32	2.18	2.04	1.88	1.79	1.70	1.59	1.47	1.32	1.00

Degrees of Freedom in the Denominator ($df = n - k$)

Table C.3 Students' *T* Distribution[1]

Degrees of Freedom	Area in the Rejection Region (Two-Tail Test)												
	0.9	0.8	0.7	0.6	0.5	0.4	0.3	0.2	0.1	0.05	0.02	0.01	0.001
1	0.158	0.325	0.510	0.727	1.000	1.376	1.963	3.078	**6.314**	**12.706**	31.821	**63.657**	636.619
2	0.142	0.289	0.445	0.617	0.816	1.061	1.386	1.886	**2.920**	**4.303**	6.965	**9.925**	31.598
3	0.137	0.277	0.424	0.584	0.765	0.978	1.250	1.638	**2.353**	**3.182**	4.541	**5.841**	12.924
4	0.134	0.271	0.414	0.569	0.741	0.941	1.190	1.533	**2.132**	**2.776**	3.747	**4.604**	8.610
5	0.132	0.267	0.408	0.559	0.727	0.920	1.156	1.476	**2.015**	**2.571**	3.365	**4.032**	6.869
6	0.131	0.265	0.404	0.553	0.718	0.906	1.134	1.440	**1.943**	**2.447**	3.143	**3.707**	5.959
7	0.130	0.263	0.402	0.549	0.711	0.896	1.119	1.415	**1.895**	**2.365**	2.998	**3.499**	5.408
8	0.130	0.262	0.399	0.546	0.706	0.889	1.108	1.397	**1.860**	**2.306**	2.896	**3.355**	5.041
9	0.129	0.261	0.398	0.543	0.703	0.883	1.100	1.383	**1.833**	**2.262**	2.821	**3.250**	4.781
10	0.129	0.260	0.397	0.542	0.700	0.879	1.093	1.372	**1.812**	**2.228**	2.764	**3.169**	4.587
11	0.129	0.260	0.396	0.540	0.697	0.876	1.088	1.363	**1.796**	**2.201**	2.718	**3.106**	4.437
12	0.128	0.259	0.395	0.539	0.695	0.873	1.083	1.356	**1.782**	**2.179**	2.681	**3.055**	4.318
13	0.128	0.259	0.394	0.538	0.694	0.870	1.079	1.350	**1.771**	**2.160**	2.650	**3.012**	4.221
14	0.128	0.258	0.393	0.537	0.692	0.868	1.076	1.345	**1.761**	**2.145**	2.624	**2.977**	4.140
15	0.128	0.258	0.393	0.536	0.691	0.866	1.074	1.341	**1.753**	**2.131**	2.602	**2.947**	4.073
16	0.128	0.258	0.392	0.535	0.690	0.865	1.071	1.337	**1.746**	**2.120**	2.583	**2.921**	4.015
17	0.128	0.257	0.392	0.534	0.689	0.863	1.069	1.333	**1.740**	**2.110**	2.567	**2.898**	3.965
18	0.127	0.257	0.392	0.534	0.688	0.862	1.067	1.330	**1.734**	**2.101**	2.552	**2.878**	3.922
19	0.127	0.257	0.391	0.533	0.688	0.861	1.066	1.328	**1.729**	**2.093**	2.539	**2.861**	3.883
20	0.127	0.257	0.391	0.533	0.687	0.860	1.064	1.325	**1.725**	**2.086**	2.528	**2.845**	3.850
21	0.127	0.257	0.391	0.532	0.686	0.859	1.063	1.323	**1.721**	**2.080**	2.518	**2.831**	3.819
22	0.127	0.256	0.390	0.532	0.686	0.858	1.061	1.321	**1.717**	**2.074**	2.508	**2.819**	3.792
23	0.127	0.256	0.390	0.532	0.685	0.858	1.060	1.319	**1.714**	**2.069**	2.500	**2.807**	3.767
24	0.127	0.256	0.390	0.531	0.685	0.857	1.059	1.318	**1.711**	**2.064**	2.492	**2.797**	3.745
25	0.127	0.256	0.390	0.531	0.684	0.856	1.058	1.316	**1.708**	**2.060**	2.485	**2.787**	3.725
26	0.127	0.256	0.390	0.531	0.684	0.856	1.058	1.315	**1.706**	**2.056**	2.479	**2.779**	3.707
27	0.127	0.256	0.389	0.531	0.684	0.855	1.057	1.314	**1.703**	**2.052**	2.473	**2.771**	3.690
28	0.127	0.256	0.389	0.530	0.683	0.855	1.056	1.313	**1.701**	**2.048**	2.467	**2.763**	3.674
29	0.127	0.256	0.389	0.530	0.683	0.854	1.055	1.311	**1.699**	**2.045**	2.462	**2.756**	3.659
30	0.127	0.256	0.389	0.530	0.683	0.854	1.055	1.310	**1.697**	**2.042**	2.457	**2.750**	3.646
40	0.126	0.255	0.388	0.529	0.681	0.851	1.050	1.303	**1.684**	**2.021**	2.423	**2.704**	3.551
60	0.126	0.254	0.387	0.527	0.679	0.848	1.046	1.296	**1.671**	**2.000**	2.390	**2.660**	3.460
120	0.126	0.254	0.386	0.526	0.677	0.845	1.041	1.289	**1.658**	**1.980**	2.358	**2.617**	3.373
∞	0.126	0.253	0.385	0.524	0.674	0.842	1.036	1.282	**1.645**	**1.960**	2.326	**2.576**	3.291

1 Columns in bold-face type indicate critical *t* values for popular levels of significance for two-tail hypothesis testing. Thus, critical *t* values for $\alpha = 0.1$ (90 percent confidence), $\alpha = 0.05$ (95 percent confidence), and $\alpha = 0.01$ (99 percent confidence) are highlighted. When the calculated *t* statistic $= b/\sigma_b$ exceeds the relevant critical *t* value, we can reject the hypothesis that there is no relationship between the dependent variable *Y* and a given independent variable *X*. For simple *t* tests, the relevant number of degrees of freedom (column row) is found as follows: $df = n - k$, where *n* is the number of data observations and *k* is the number of estimated coefficients (including the intercept).

Selected Check Figures for End-of-Chapter Problems

2.1
B. $Q = 5$

2.2
B. $Q = 5$
C. $Q = 8$

2.4
B. $WA = 5$, $OR = 3$, $ID = 2$
C. Commission Income = $8,000

2.5
B. $I = 3$
C. $I = 4$

2.6
B. $P = \$10$

2.7
A. $Q = 100,000$
B. $\pi = \$9$ million, $MGN = 6\%$

2.8
A. $Q = 4,000$, Surplus = $500,000
B. $Q = 3,800$, Surplus = $110,000
C. $Q = 4,000$, Surplus = $100,000

2.9
A. $Q = 55,000$, $MC = \$1,240$, $AC = \$1,240$, $P = \$1,470$, $\pi = \$12.65$ million
B. $Q = 50,000$, $MC = \$1,000$, $AC = \$1,242$, $P = \$1,500$, $\pi = \$12.9$ million

2.10
A. 6:00 am to 7:00 pm
B. $120,650 per year

3.2
A. $P = \$10$
B. $P = \$1$
C. $P = \$4$, $Q = 300,000$

3.5
A. $Q = 15,000$
B. $Q = 22,500$

3.6
B. $Q = 20,000$, $TR = \$2,000,000$

3.7
B. $P = \$50$, $Q = 0$
  $P = \$60$, $Q = 5,000,000$
  $P = \$70$, $Q = 10,000,000$
C. $Q = 4,000,000$, $P = \$58$
  $Q = 6,000,000$, $P = \$62$
  $Q = 8,000,000$, $P = \$66$

3.8
B. $P = \$325$, $Q_O = 0$, $Q_P = 875,000$
  $P = \$350$, $Q_O = 0$, $Q_P = 1,000,000$
  $P = \$375$, $Q_O = 500,000$, $Q_P = 1,125,000$

3.9
B. $P = \$8$, $Q_C = 0$, $Q_P = 0$
  $P = \$10$, $Q_C = 0$, $Q_P = 250$
  $P = \$12$, $Q_C = 500$, $Q_P = 500$

3.10
B. $P = \$1.50$, Shortage = 50
  $P = \$2$, Surplus = Shortage = 0
  $P = \$2.50$, Surplus = 50
C. $P = \$2$, $Q = 50$

4.6
A. $\varepsilon_P = -10$
B. $P = \$26,500$

4.7
A. $E_P = -2.75$
B. $E_{PX} = -3.67$

4.8
A. $E_I = 9.5$
B. $E_P = -8$

4.9
A. $E_{PX} = 1.5$
B. $E_P = -3$
C. $\Delta P = -\$20$

4.10
A. $E_P = -2$
B. $\Delta P = -\$2$
C. $E_A = 1$

5.3
A. $P = \$600$, $Q = 15,000$,
   $TR = \$9$ million per week,
   $\pi = -\$3$ million per week
B. $P = \$1,000$, $Q = 5,000$,
   $TR = \$5$ million per week,
   $\pi = \$1$ million per week

5.4
A. $P = \$35$, $Q = 35$,
   $TR = \$1,225$ per day,
   $\pi = \$175$ per day
B. $P = \$50$, $Q = 20$,
   $TR = \$1,000$ per day,
   $\pi = \$400$ per day

5.5
A. $P = \$2,000 - \$0.75P$
B. $Q = 900$, $P = \$1,325$

5.6
A. $P = \$1,900 - \$10Q$
B. $P = \$950$, $Q = 95$,
   $TR = \$90,250$ per month
C. Vacancy $= 5$

5.7
A. $P = \$60 - \$0.0004Q$
C. $Q = 50,000$, $P = \$40$, $\pi = \$250,000$.

5.8
A. Demand: $P = \$20 - \$0.005Q_D + \$10T$
   Supply: $P = \$10 + \$0.005Q_S$

5.9
C. $\varepsilon_A = 1$
D. $\Pr = 50\%$

6.1
A. $g = 3.1\%$
B. $g = 3.0\%$

6.3
A. $g = 10\%$
B. $S_5 = \$104,715,000$,
   $S_{10} = \$168,610,000$

6.4
A. $g = 7.4\%$
B. $t = 2$ years

6.5
B. $A_t = 80$

6.6
B. $S_{t+1} = \$295,000$

6.7
B. $D_{t+1} = 375$

6.8
B. $S_{t+1} = 12,500$

6.9
B. Regular Price: $TR = \$6,950$,
   Special Price: $TR = \$14,100$
C. Regular Price: $\pi = \$3,310$,
   Special Price: $\pi = \$7,905$

6.10
   $I = \$2,000$ billion
   $GDP = \$13,500$ billion
   $C = \$9,405$ billion
   $T = \$2,160$ billion
   $Y = \$11,340$ billion

7.1
C. $Y = 3$

7.5
A. Doyle $= 3.75\%$, Moon $= 4.5\%$,
   M. Crane $= 4\%$, N. Crane $= 3.33\%$
B. Doyle $= \$8,000$, Moon $= \$5,000$,
   M. Crane $= \$4,500$, N. Crane $= \$3,750$

7.6
B. Inquiries $= 4,000$

7.7
A. $MRP_L = \$75,000$

7.8
C. Advertising = 50

7.9
A. $MRP_P = \$156,250$, $MRP_A = \$87,500$

7.10
A. $\Delta Q/Q = -1.12\%$
B. $\Delta Q/Q = -2.88\%$

8.3
A. $\pi = \$175,000$

8.4
C. $Q_{BE} = 15,000$

8.5
A. $\Delta Q = 20,000$
B. $E_P = -3$.

8.6
A. $Q_{BE} = 12,500$
B. $Q_{BE} = 15,000$

8.7
A. $Q_{BE} = 1,000$
B. $\varepsilon_C = 0.82$

8.8
A. $Q_M = 60,000$, $Q_N = 55,000$, $Q_D = 47,500$
B. $\pi_S = \$87,500$, $\pi_M = \$75,000$
C. $\pi_S = \$262,500$, $\pi_M = \$275,000$

8.9
A. $TC = \$450,000$, $AC = \$112.50$
B. Learning $= -\$5.50$, or 5%

8.10
A. $\Delta Q_{BE} = 250,000$
B. $\Delta DOL = 0.4$
C. $\Delta\pi = \$1,000,000$

9.2
A. $L = 4$, $K = 400$, $Q = 1$
   $L = 16$, $K = 1,600$, $Q = 4$
B. $\Delta MP_L = -0.0625$, $\Delta MP_K = -0.000625$
C. $Q = 1,000$
D. $MP_L = 0.25$, $MP_K = 0$

9.3
C. $\pi = \$2,350$

9.4
B. $A = 1$, $B = 4$, $L_F = 4$, $L_R = 0$, $L_{FC} = 0$, $C = \$240,000$
C. $\Delta TC = -\$32,000$
D. $\Delta C_A > \$120,000$

9.5
B. $C = \$50$ million, $P = \$50$ million, $S_D = \$0$,
   $S_B = \$100$ million, $S_C = \$25$ million, $S_A = \$0$,
   $\pi = \$1,750,000$

9.6
B. $I = 0.75$, $J = 0.25$, $L_I = 0$, $L_J = 0.05$,
   $L_L = 0$, $i = 0.0975$
C. $\Delta R_J > -3\%$
D. Maximum Cash $= 20\%$

9.7
B. $E = 30$, $W = 40$, $S_H = 0$, $S_S = 0.15$, $S_P = 0$,
   $C = \$2,500$
C. $\Delta P_W = \$12.50$

9.8
B. $I = 120$, $C = 40$, $S_A = 0$, $S_B = 80$,
   $S_S = 0$, $\pi = \$18,000$
C. $\pi = \$1,900$
D. $\pi = \$5,500$
E. $L_I = L_C = 0$, $V_A = \$50$, $V_B = \$0$,
   $V_S = \$50$, $\pi^* = \$18,000$

9.9
B. $Q_1 = 5$, $Q_2 = 3$, $S_D = 0$, $S_A = 5$, $S_{AR} = 0$, $R = \$21,000$
   $L_1 = L_2 = 0$, $V_D = \$125$, $V_A = \$0$, $V_{AR} = \$250$,
   $R^* = \$21,000$

9.10
B. $Q_A = 0$, $Q_B = 2$, $Q_C = 2$, $S_L = S_P = 0$, $Q = 4$
   $L_A = 0.625$, $L_B = L_C = 0$, $V_L = 0.125$,
   $V_P = 0.375$, $Q^* = 4$

10.2
B. $P = MC = \$50$
C. $P = \$75$, $Q = 3$
   $P = \$100$, $Q = 6$

10.3
A. $Q = 500,000$
B. $AVC = \$0.14$

10.4
A. $Q = 800,000$
B. $ATC = \$1.77$

10.5
A. $Q = 5,000$, $P = \$400$
   $Q = 10,000$, $P = \$600$
   $Q = 15,000$, $P = \$800$
B. $P = \$200$, $Q = 0$
   $P = \$500$, $Q = 7,500$
   $P = \$1,000$, $Q = 20,000$

10.6

C. $Q_S = 31,250,000$

10.7

A. $Q = 750$

B. $\pi = \$0$

10.8

B. $P = \$4$, $Q_D = Q_S = 60$

10.9

A. $P = \$16.75$, $Q = 2,500(000)$, $\pi = \$26,750(000)$

B. $P = \$6$, $Q = 3,000(000)$, $\pi = \$0$

10.10

A. $Q = 200,000$, $\pi = \$3,000,000$

B. $Q = 50,000$, $\pi = -\$750,000$ (a loss)

C. $Q = 100,000$, $P = \$40$, $\pi = \$0$

11.3

A. $P = \$5$, $Q = 2,000$(million)

B. $CS = \$4,000$(million), $PS = \$2,500$(million), $SW = \$6,500$(million)

11.4

A. Before: $P = \$55$ and $Q = 100(000)$; After: $P = \$58$ and $Q = 88(000)$

B. $C_{Loss} = \$18(000)$, $P_{Loss} = \$36(000)$, $Total_{Loss} = \$54(000)$

11.5

A. $P = \$150$, $Q = 100,000(000)$, $PS = \$4,000,000(000)$

B. Maximum tax $= \$4,000,0000(000)$

11.6

A. Before: $P = \$10$ and $Q = 8,000(000)$; After: $P = \$12$ and $Q = 10,000(000)$

B. $P = \$8.75$ and $Q = 10,000(000)$

11.7

A. $P = \$2$ and $Q = 5,000$(million); Surplus $= 3,750$(million)

B. Producer Surplus$_{PS} = \$5,625$(million), Producer Surplus$_{FM} = \$2,500$(million), Gain $= \$3,125$(million)

11.8

A. Before: $P = \$60$ and $Q = 225$(million); After: $P = \$85$ and $Q = 162.5$(million)

B. $CS_{US+F} = \$10,125$(million), $CS_{US} = \$5,281.25$(million), $CS_{Loss} = \$4,843.75$(million), $PS_{Transfer} = \$4,062.5$(million), $CS_{DW} = \$781.25$(million)

11.9

A. $P = \$400$, $Q = 1,000(000)$, $\pi = \$0$

B. $P = \$520$, $Q = 1,400(000)$, $\pi = \$144,000(000)$

11.10

A. $P = \$6.25$, $Q = 400(000)$, $\pi = \$1,375(000)$

B. $P = \$2.75$, $Q = 500(000)$, $\pi = \$0$

12.5

A. Competitive: $P = \$20$ and $Q = 75,000$; Monopoly: $P = \$50$ and $Q = 37,500$

B. $\pi = \$22,500$ per shop per month, $\pi = \$1,125,000$ per month

12.6

A. $P = \$250$, $Q = 500,000$, $CS = \$25$ million, $PS = \$12.5$ million, $SW = \$37.5$ million

B. $P = \$290$, $Q = 300,000$, $CS_{Loss} = \$4$ million, $PS_{Loss} = \$2$ million, $Total_{Loss} = \$6$ million

12.7

A. $P = \$30$, $Q = 60$(million), $CS = \$450$ million, $PS = \$900$ million, $SW = \$1,350$ million

B. $PS_{Loss} = \$56.25$(million), $PS_{Transfer} = \$168.75$(million), $PS_{Net} = \$112.5$(million)

12.8

A. $P = \$200$, $Q = 100,000$

B. $\pi = \$5,000,000$, $MGN = 25\%$

12.9

A. $P = \$5,000$, $Q = 100,000$, $\pi = \$50,000,000$

B. $P = \$4,500$, $Q = 200,000$, $\pi = \$0$

12.10

A. $P = \$3.50$, $Q = 150,000$, $\pi = \$287,500$

B. $P = \$1.50$, $Q = 100,000$, $\pi = \$0$

13.3

B. $P = \$3.40$, $Q = 8$

C. $P = \$4.20$, $Q = 4$

13.4

A. $Q = 12$, $P = \$36$ million, $\pi = \$88$ million, $\varepsilon_P = -2$

B. High-price/low-output: $Q = 10$, $P = \$31$ million, $\pi = \$0$; Low-price/high-output: $Q = 20$, $P = \$26$ million, $\pi = 0$

C. $Q_2 = 16.2$, high-price/low-output; $Q_2 = 23.4$, low-price/high-output

13.5

A. $P = \$2$, $Q = 40,000$

B. $P = \$3.60$, $Q = 24,000$

13.6

B. $Q_A = Q_B = 400(000)$, $Q = 800$, $P = \$450$

13.7

A. $Q_A = 600$, $Q_B = 300$, $Q = 900$, $P = \$350$

13.8

B. $P_C = \$5.25$

13.9

C. $P = \$50$, $Q = 10(000)$, $\pi = \$150(000)$

D. $MC_{Min} = \$20$, $MC_{Max} = \$40$

14.2

A. Betray, Betray

14.3

A. Up

B. None

14.4

A. 90-day free financing

B. 90-day free financing

14.5

B. Advertise, Advertise

14.6

A. Low-price strategy, Low-price strategy

14.9

A. $P = \$4.50$, $Q = 7,000$

B. $P = \$4.65$, $Q = 8,375$

15.3

A. $\varepsilon_P = -5$

B. Optimal Markup on Cost = 25%, $P = \$150$

15.4

A. $E_P = -3.5$

B. Optimal Markup on Cost = 40%, $P = \$11.99$

15.5

A. $E_P = -2$

B. Optimal Markup on Cost = 100%, $P = \$36$

15.6

A. $P = \$2,875,000$

B. $P = \$2,701,000$

15.7

A. $\pi_1 = \$112,000$, $\pi_2 = \$104,000$

15.8

A. $Q_W = 500$, $P_W = \$12,500$, $Q_R = 1,000$,
    $P_R = \$30,000$, $\pi = \$21,250,000$

B. $\varepsilon_{WP} = -5$, $\varepsilon_{RP} = -1.5$

15.9

A. $Q = 2$, $P = \$4,000$, $\pi = \$5,000$ per customer,
    $CS = \$2,500$ per customer

B. $Q = 4$, $P = \$1,500$ per week plus $10,000 per year,
    $\pi = \$10,000$ per customer, $CS = \$0$ per customer

C. $1 million per year

15.10

A. $Q = 20,000$, $P_S = \$10.40$, $P_L = \$0.30$

B. $Q_L = 40,000$, $Dump_L = 110,000$, $Q_S = 150,000$,
    $P_L = \$0.20$, $P_S = \$32.50$

16.3

A. $E(NC_{TS}) = \$125$, $E(NC_{S\&B}) = \$25$, $E(NC) = \$125$

16.4

A. $E(\pi_{MA}) = \$1,000,000$, $E(\pi_{PS}) = \$750,000$

C. $E(U_{MA}) = 86$, $E(U_{PS}) = 81$

16.5

A. $E(\pi_1) = \$500,000$, $E(\pi_2) = \$375,000$

C. $\sigma_1 = \$300,000$, $CV_1 = 0.6$, $\sigma_2 = \$125,000$,
    $CV_2 = 0.33$

D. $E(u_1) = 1,172$, $E(u_2) = 1,162.5$

16.6

A. $E(CF_1) = \$10,000$, $E(CF_2) = \$10,000$

B. $\sigma_1 = \$3,000$, $\sigma_2 = \$1,000$

C. $NPV_1 = \$5,000$, $NPV_2 = \$7,500$

16.7

A. $E(R) = \$1,150,000$

B. $\alpha = 0.87$

16.8

A. $E(\pi_A) = \$150,000$, $\sigma_A = \$50,000$, $V_A = 0.33$,
    $E(\pi_{SF}) = \$200,000$, $\sigma_{SF} = \$140,000$, $V_{SF} = 0.7$

B. $\alpha_A = 0.8$, $\alpha_{SF} = 0.85$

16.9

A. $Pr = 40\%$

16.10

A. $Pr = 50\%$

B. $P = \$23.29$

C. $Pr = 93.32\%$

17.5

A. $NPV_{LB} = \$500,000$, $NPV_{SD} = \$600,000$

B. $PI_{LB} = 1.25$, $PI_{SD} = 1.2$

17.6

A. $E(CF_1) = \$1,000,000$, $\sigma_1 = \$200,000$, $V_1 = 0.2$;
    $E(CF_2) = \$900,000$, $\sigma_2 = \$360,000$, $V_2 = 0.4$

B. $NPV_1 = \$1,192,500$, $NPV_2 = -\$362,640$ (a loss)

C. $PI_1 = 1.40$, $PI_2 = 0.88$

17.7

A. $E(CF_{A1}) = \$50,000$, $\sigma_{A1} = \$30,000$, $V_{A1} = 0.6$
    $E(CF_{A2}) = \$50,000$, $\sigma_{A2} = \$20,000$, $V_{A2} = 0.4$
    $E(CF_{B1}) = \$100,000$, $\sigma_{B1} = \$100,000$, $V_{B1} = 1$
    $E(CF_{B2}) = \$100,000$, $\sigma_{B2} = \$50,000$, $V_{B2} = 0.5$
B. $NPV_A = \$9,505$, $NPV_B = \$12,570$
C. $PI_A = 1.13$, $PI_B = 1.08$
D. $IRR_A = IRR_B = 21.6\%$

17.8

A. $CF = \$8,000$

17.9

A. Net Cash Inflow:
    $A = \$1,576,667$, $B = \$1,603,333$, $C = \$1,323,333$
B. $NPV_A = \$1,131,185$, $NPV_B = \$1,034,881$,
    $NPV_C = \$1,146,045$

17.10

A. $k_e = 20\%$
B. $k = 16.95\%$

19.3

A. $P_L = \$10,000$, $Q_L = 400$, $P_H = \$7,500$,
    $Q_H = 2,500$, $\pi = \$3,250,000$
B. $P_L = \$10,500$, $Q_L = 360$, $P_H = \$8,000$,
    $Q_L = 360$, $\pi = \$620,000$
C. $\varepsilon_{PL} = -2$, $\varepsilon_{PH} = -3$

19.4

A. $Q = 100,000$, $\pi = \$0$
B. $Q = 100,000$, $\pi = \$0$
C. $Q = 75,000$, $\pi = -\$437,500$ (a loss)

19.5

B. Social Rate of Discount $= 8.3\%$

Index